OSTKRIEG

OSTKRIEG

Hitler's
War of Extermination
in the East

STEPHEN G. FRITZ

THE UNIVERSITY PRESS OF KENTUCKY

Scholarly publisher for the Commonwealth,
serving Bellarmine University, Berea College, Centre College of Kentucky,
Eastern Kentucky University, The Filson Historical Society, Georgetown
College, Kentucky Historical Society, Kentucky State University,
Morehead State University, Murray State University, Northern Kentucky
University, Transylvania University, University of Kentucky, University of
Louisville, and Western Kentucky University.
All rights reserved.

Editorial and Sales Offices: The University Press of Kentucky
663 South Limestone Street, Lexington, Kentucky 40508-4008
www.kentuckypress.com

15 14 13 12 11   5 4 3 2 1

Library of Congress Cataloging-in-Publication Data

Fritz, Stephen G., 1949-
    Ostkrieg : Hitler's war of extermination in the East / Stephen G. Fritz.
       p. cm.
    Includes bibliographical references and index.
    ISBN 978-0-8131-3416-1 (cloth : alk. paper) — ISBN 978-0-8131-3417-8 (ebook)
    1. World War, 1939-1945—Campaigns—Eastern Front. 2. World War, 1939-
1945—Campaigns—Soviet Union. 3. World War, 1939-1945—Atrocities—Europe,
Eastern. 4. Soviet Union—History—German occupation, 1941-1944.
5. Germany—Territorial expansion—History—20th century. 6. Germany—
Territorial expansion—Economic aspects. 7. Germany—Territorial expansion—
Social aspects. 8. Germany—Military policy. 9. Hitler, Adolf, 1889-1945—
Military leadership. I. Title.
    D764.F737 2011
    940.54'21—dc23   2011030914

This book is printed on acid-free paper meeting
the requirements of the American National Standard
for Permanence in Paper for Printed Library Materials.

Manufactured in the United States of America.

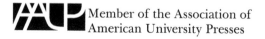 Member of the Association of
American University Presses

Contents

Maps   vii

Abbreviations and Foreign Terms   xv

Preface   xix

1. Dilemma   1

2. Decision   31

3. Onslaught   77

4. Whirlwind   135

5. Reckoning   199

6. All or Nothing   241

7. Total War   303

8. Scorched Earth   359

9. Disintegration   405

10. Death Throes   439

Conclusion   473

Acknowledgments   489

Appendix: Supplementary Data   491

Notes   499

Bibliography   555

Index   609

Photographs follow page 234

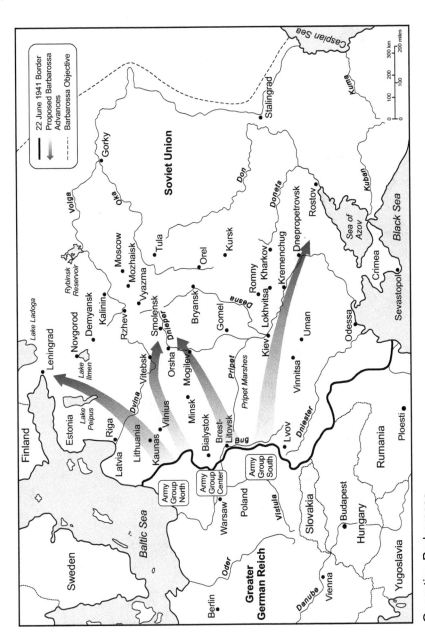

Operation Barbarossa

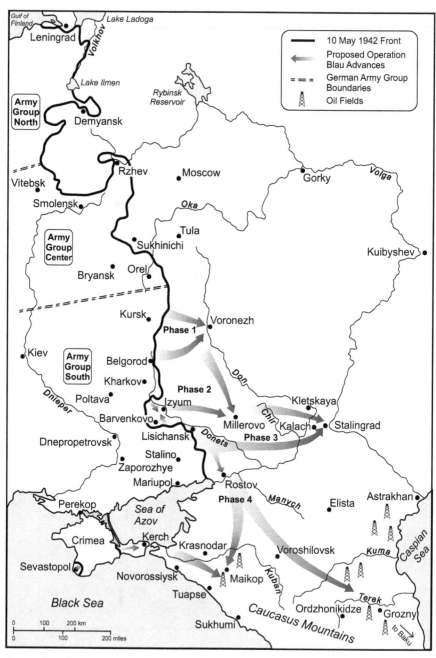

Operation Blau

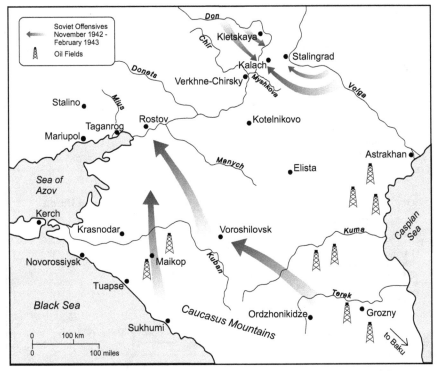

Stalingrad, September 1942–February 1943

Kursk and Ukraine, summer/fall 1943

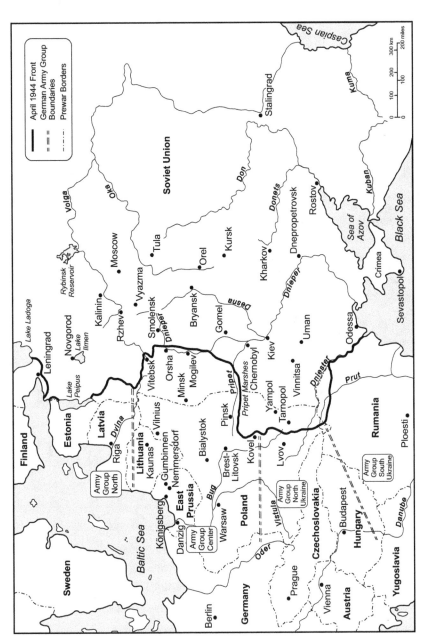

Destruction of Army Group Center, summer 1944

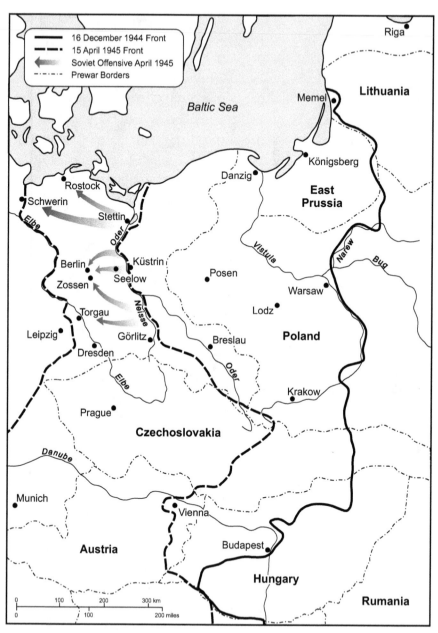

Riga

Lithuania

Baltic Sea

Memel

Königsberg

Rostock

Danzig

Schwerin

East
Prussia

Stettin

Elbe

Oder

Berlin

Küstrin

Vistula

Narew

Bug

Zossen

Seelow

Posen

Warsaw

Torgau

Neisse

Lodz

Leipzig

Görlitz

Poland

Dresden

Breslau

Oder

Elbe

Krakow

Prague

Czechoslovakia

Danube

Munich

Vienna

Budapest

Austria

Hungary

Rumania

0   100   200   300 km
0   100   200 miles

Vistula-Oder-Berlin Operations, 1945

Generalplan Ost

Abbreviations and Foreign Terms

AFV	armored fighting vehicle
AK	Armeekorps (army corps)
BA	Bundesarchiv (German Federal Archives)
Bagration	Soviet offensive in Belorussia, June–July 1944
Barbarossa	1941 invasion of the Soviet Union
Berghof	Hitler's Bavarian retreat (Obersalzberg)
Blau	Blue, 1942 summer offensive in the Soviet Union
blitzkrieg	lightning war
commissar	political officer attached to Red Army units
Commissar Order	"Guidelines for the Treatment of Political Commissars"; order of 6 June 1941 to shoot Red Army political officers
Edelweiss	advance into the Caucasus, July–November 1942
Einsatzgruppe	mobile killing squad
Einsatzkommando	subunit of an Einsatzgruppe
Fredericus	operation against the Izyum bulge, May 1942
Freikorps	German paramilitary groups
front	Soviet equivalent of an army group
Frühlingserwachen	Spring Awakening, German offensive toward Budapest, March 1945
Gauleiter	Nazi Party regional leader
Generalplan Ost	General Plan East
Gestapo	Geheime Staatspolizei (Secret State Police)
Hiwi	*Hilfswillige(r)*, Russian volunteers/auxiliaries who performed noncombat duties with the German army

Kampfgruppe	battle group (usually formed of units seriously reduced in strength)
Kessel	pocket; cauldron
Kesselschlacht	a battle of encirclement
Landser	German infantryman
Lebensraum	living space
Luftflotte	German air fleet
Luftwaffe	German air force
Mars	Soviet offensive against the Rzhev salient (Ninth Army), fall/winter 1942
NSV	Nationalsozialistische Volkswohlfahrt (National Socialist People's Welfare Organization)
OKH	Oberkommando des Heeres (Army High Command)
OKW	Oberkommando der Wehrmacht (Armed Forces High Command)
Ostfront	Eastern front
Ostheer	Eastern Army
Ostkrieg	Eastern war
panje	Russian horse-drawn wagon
Panther position	proposed German defensive position in the east
Panzerfaust	German one-shot anti-tank weapon
Pz III	German tank, from 1942 with 50 mm antitank gun
Pz IV	mainstay German tank with a long-barreled, high velocity 75 mm gun
Pz V	Panther tank (from 1943, with a long-barreled, high velocity 75 mm gun
Pz VI	Tiger tank (from 1942, with an 88 mm gun)
rasputitsa	lit., time without roads; spring and fall rainy season in the Soviet Union
Reichsführer-SS	Himmler's title
Reichsmarshall	Goering's title
Ring	final Soviet offensive against Stalingrad, January 1943
Rollbahn	main highway in the Soviet Union
RSHA	*Reichssicherheitshauptamt* (Reich Main Security Office)
SA	Sturmabteilung (Storm Troopers)
Saturn	proposed Soviet offensive west of Stalingrad aimed at Rostov, November 1942 ("Little Saturn" actually executed)

Schwerpunkt	focal point of an attack
SD	Sicherheitsdienst (Security Service, part of the RSHA)
Sonderkommando	smaller subunit of an Einsatzgruppe
SS	Schutzstaffel (elite Nazi troops)
Stavka	headquarters, Soviet Supreme Command
Stuka	Sturzkampfflugzeug (German dive bomber; JU-87)
T-34	Soviet mainstay tank (76 mm, then after 1944 an 85 mm gun)
Taifun	Typhoon, drive on Moscow, October–December 1941
Trappenjagd	Bustard Hunt, operation on the Kerch Peninsula, May 1942
trek	German refugee column
Uranus	Soviet counteroffensive at Stalingrad, November 1942
Vernichtungskrieg	war of annihilation
Viking	Fifth SS Division
Volk	people, nation
Volksdeutsche	ethnic German
Volksgemeinschaft	national community, people's community
Volkssturm	"People's Storm" (German national militia)
Waffen-SS	armed or combat SS
Wehrkraftzersetzung	undermining of the war effort
Wehrmacht	German armed forces, often used to refer specifically to the army
Wintergewitter	Winter Storm, operation to relieve Stalingrad, December 1942
Wolfsschanze	Wolf's Lair (Hitler's headquarters at Rastenburg, East Prussia)

Preface

For decades after the end of World War II, much of our understanding of the German-Soviet war came from the German perspective, for the very good reason that only German documents and archives were readily available. Equivalent Soviet sources were either unavailable, marred by ideology, or limited in their circulation because of language problems. Moreover, the various histories of the Ostfront, or eastern front, that emerged were skewed in other ways as well. Many of the earliest accounts were written by German generals who did not have access to original records but wrote from their own diaries or memories, the latter being, of course, both unreliable and easily distorted over time. In addition, German officers writing either on their own or under the auspices of the U.S. Army's historical project rather consciously sought to create an image of the Wehrmacht as professionally competent, technically proficient, and, above all, "clean." In this version of history, which largely confined itself to accounts of battles and military events, not only had the army suffered from Hitler's megalomania, constant interference, and poor strategic and operational judgments, but its leaders had neither known of nor condoned the massive crimes committed against the Soviet civilian population, especially the Jews. In the narrative the generals created after the fact, the military operations and the massive crimes perpetrated by German forces on the eastern front existed in two separate and parallel spheres, with little interaction between the two. This, of course, was later shown to be a self-serving cover-up, but for a variety of reasons—not least the growing impact of the Cold War—this initial version of events stuck in the Western mind. Thus, standard narratives of the Ostkrieg, the war in the east, available in English primarily focused very narrowly on the sweep of military events and ignored the intersection of the war and Hitler's overtly ideological, racial, and economic plans for the conquered eastern territories.

Two things have combined to change this view, at least among professional historians. The first was the collapse of the Soviet Union some twenty years ago, which gave historians unprecedented access to formerly unavailable archival material. As a result, over the past fifteen years there have been, and continue to be, a number of excellent new accounts in English of the eastern war from the Soviet perspective, ranging from the detailed studies of David Glantz to the narrative overview of Richard Overy to the integrative analysis of Evan Mawdsley. All these have deepened and enriched our understanding of the conflict by providing the badly needed Russian context. At the same time, the massive ten-volume "semiofficial" history of the war initiated some four decades ago by the Military History Research Office of the German Bundeswehr has not only exploded the myth of the clean Wehrmacht by showing its complicity in Nazi crimes in the east but has also integrated the separate "wars" on the eastern front into the *Vernichtungskrieg*, or war of annihilation, originally envisioned by Hitler. This history having finally been completed, the interested English-language reader faces a dual problem: not only have the English translations lagged behind the German originals, but the entire ten volumes (some with two parts) run to well over fifteen thousand pages. In addition, other German historians, in investigating specific issues, have produced outstanding works on a variety of topics ranging from the decision for and implementation of the Holocaust to the larger Nazi plans for a racial-demographic restructuring of the east to the question of the continuing support for the Nazi regime.

It is important, then, to note from the beginning what this book is not. It is not a work based on primary research; rather, it is intended as a synthesis, an integrated narrative based primarily on exhaustive research by German, British, and American historians over the past two or three decades. It is also clearly told from the German perspective, with no pretense of being a balanced account of the war. My aim is to provide a deeper understanding of the complexity and immensity of the Ostkrieg by anchoring the military events of the war within their larger ideological, racial, economic, and social context. There have been many military histories and numerous other works that have highlighted the atrocities committed on the eastern front but none that have attempted to integrate the military, ideological, and economic dimensions. Without a sense of the comprehensively murderous nature of Hitler's aims, the full scope of the eastern war cannot be grasped. The Holocaust, for example, cannot be adequately comprehended without reference either to German military success or to Nazi plans for a larger racial reordering of Europe. For all Hitler's anti-Semitism and verbal radicalism, the Final Solution neither was intended from the beginning, nor sprang out of the blue, but evolved as a result of specific time and spatial circumstances and largely as a result of the unprecedented scale and barbarity of the German war in the east. It was the Ostkrieg that radicalized and crystallized Nazi intentions regarding the Jews, while the process of annihilation was largely determined within the context of military events. By the same token, many of Hitler's seemingly irrational military decisions seem much more explicable when set within their larger economic or strategic context. A purely operational focus, such as has dominated narratives of the eastern front, is not merely incomplete but misleading.

Why is a book like this necessary? Despite the ongoing fascination with World War II in this country and the English-speaking world in general, there is surprisingly little on the German-Russian war and virtually nothing within the past thirty years that aims to cover the entire period 1941–1945—let alone a narrative that places the military events within a larger interpretive framework. In fact, it is not too much to say that a good bit of the genesis of this work was frustration, both with trying to find acceptable books for my World War II classes to read and with otherwise knowledgeable American readers who failed to understand the importance of the eastern front or acknowledge the inherent connection between military events and Nazi criminality. Contrary to the belief of many in the West, Hitler did not blunder into the war in the east. For him, the "right" war was always that against the Soviet Union, for to him Germany's destiny depended on attaining Lebensraum and solving the "Jewish question." Both of these, in turn, hinged on destroying the Soviet Union. Which of these aims was most important? Given Hitler's views, it would be artificial to attempt to prioritize or separate them. For him, the war against "Jewish-Bolshevism" and for Lebensraum was comprehensive and of whole cloth.

I have also attempted to infuse this account with irony, paradox, and complexity—all the things necessary for comprehending history but largely absent from the prevailing American view of World War II as the "good war" (which, again, is not so much wrong as incomplete). In addition, I have aimed to reestablish the eastern front as the pivotal theater of the war. The Second World War was not won or lost solely on the Ostfront, but it was the key—while the scale of fighting there dwarfed anything in the west. In retrospect, the disproportional nature of the Ostkrieg is striking: roughly eight of every ten German soldiers who died were killed in the east; from June 1941, in no single month of the war did more Germans die in the west than in the east, and the only month that came close was December 1944 (when during a "quiet" period over ten thousand more *Landsers* fell in the east than on all other fronts); the Red Army, at the cost of perhaps 12 million dead (or approximately thirty times the number of the Anglo-Americans), broke the back of the Wehr-macht; total German and Soviet deaths (military and civilian) numbered around 35 million, compared with less than 1 million for Great Britain and the United States. At times, indeed, the Ostkrieg often seemed more murder than war. That it took the most murderous regime in Europe's history to defeat its most genocidal certainly tarnishes Western notions of the good war. Nonetheless, Stalin's alleged observation—England pro-vided the time, America the money, and Russia the blood—contained a good deal of truth.

Why wars start, why they last so long, why they are so difficult to end, are all key questions that serious historians ask. In addition, a number of other themes infuse this work. Perhaps most important is the inter-section of impulses—military, ideological, economic, racial, and demo-graphic—that account for the violent, destructive nature of the eastern war. It was a war for hegemony, of conquest of Lebensraum, an ideo-logical war against Jewish-Bolshevism, a war for food and raw materials, a racial-demographic war to reshape the borderlands of East-Central Europe, perhaps even a sort of colonial war in its ultimate goal of creat-ing a vast "Greater Germany." Each of these points reflects a valid aspect of Hitler's war in the East and has elicited much recent research. Obtain-ing raw materials, for example, was regarded as vital by Hitler in his strategic goal of elevating Germany to a position of world power status. Without secure access to large quantities of key resources, a mid-sized power such as the Third Reich could never throw off its constraints and aspire to compete against the likes of Great Britain, the Soviet Union, and the United States. With it, however, a German-dominated Europe could aspire to maintain its world ascendancy. Indeed, in many respects, World War II can be seen above all as a war for oil, with those lack-ing it (Germany, Italy, Japan) seeking to defeat those who controlled it (Great Britain, America, and Russia). A war to secure Germany's eco-nomic future, however, could also serve to guarantee the Reich's racial future as well since the area targeted for expansion—European Russia—with its polyglot ethnic makeup seemed ripe for exploitation. Not for nothing did Hitler refer to it as "Germany's India" or note approvingly the opportunities for settlement similar to America's west. The "wild east" would be Germany's frontier, a space within which racial demog-raphers and economic planners could work from a blank slate—once x number of millions of native inhabitants had been resettled or killed. From the outset, the war against the Soviet Union was planned as a war of annihilation, with the full knowledge and complicity of the Wehr-macht leadership.

Related to this was Hitler's obsession with World War I as well as his realization of the looming potential of the United States. The first war colored all aspects of the second one for Hitler. The ruinous blockade that accentuated German deficiencies in food and raw materials, the searing memory of mass hunger and privation that sapped domestic morale, the actions by the so-called November criminals (Jews, Communists, socialists) that allegedly caused the collapse of the German war effort, the belief in an active "Jewish conspiracy" that had plunged an encircled Germany into war in the first place—all would have repercussions on the direction of "his" war, a war fought primarily to undo the results of the first. This second war could not be fought in a vacuum, however, because of the hulking presence of potential American power, which put significant time pressures on Hitler. The logic of many of his decisions, in fact, stemmed from his acute awareness of German deficiencies and the limited window of opportunity available to remedy the situation. To secure German hegemony in Europe, ironically, he first had to conquer the necessary resources and ruthlessly exploit them for his own purposes, a scenario fraught with vulnerability and danger.

A further theme, then, would be Germany's large-scale unpreparedness for war against the Soviet Union. While Stalin's hugely ambitious industrialization plans had turned the Soviet Union into the most gigantic military-industrial state in modern history, Hitler's rearmament had begun much more slowly than originally believed and by 1939 had brought Germany barely level with its western rivals, Britain and France. Although Hitler had blundered into a war for which his nation was ill-prepared, he had been saved by the twin good fortunes of Allied incompetence and the luck of a blitzkrieg attack that went largely according to plan. The latter, however, obscured the fact that Germany had enjoyed no material advantage over its western rivals, let alone vis-à-vis the Soviet Union. The myth of the Wehrmacht—that it was an invincible, mechanized juggernaut that had devised a war-winning strategy—was just that, a myth. The German army that assaulted the Red Army a year after its great triumph in France was barely stronger yet had to contend with a much larger foe in a vastly greater space. It could, in fact, project its power no farther than three hundred miles, a sobering fact when Moscow lay some seven hundred miles to the east, with the vital resources and oil of southern Russia even more distant. Nor was the German armaments industry, suffering from serious shortages of labor and raw materials, prepared for the rigors of a long campaign. With a few motorized divisions trailed by masses of men marching on foot and supported by a war industry that was hardly a model of rational efficiency, it was little wonder that everyone in the German leadership hoped for a quick victory. Operation Barbarossa was high-risk, high-cost warmaking, an all-or-nothing gamble on rapid success.

Paradoxically, although the Wehrmacht failed to deliver a swift knock-out blow, forcing Germany into an attritional war it likely could not win, its spectacular victories in 1941 and again in 1942 raised the prospect of just such a triumph, with the attendant planning and implementation of a whole host of murderous schemes, none more so than the Final Solution. By 1943, as a consequence of fierce Soviet resistance and the Germans' own mistakes and inadequacies, any sort of victory, even in the east, was unlikely. Total German defeat, however, resulted from the growing importance of the other fronts: in the Mediterranean, the Atlantic, the skies over Germany, and finally, Western Europe. In a coalition war, Hitler's Reich was at a decided disadvantage as his allies were no match for Stalin's. Why did German soldiers fight on in an increasingly hopeless situation? A complex set of motives was at work: ideology, the successful creation of a Nazified vision of the nation, a sense of duty, the material successes and rewards proffered by the regime, fear of communism, a strong sense of camaraderie, and the growing realization that the enormity of Nazi crimes left them no out. In any case, Hitler had long vowed that there would never again be another "November 1918," the ultimate symbol of disgrace in his mind. In keeping this vow, he plunged his nation into total ruin. He had insisted at the outset that Germany faced only two choices, world power or downfall; in failing at the former, he ensured the latter.

1

Dilemma

A small railway car stands in a clearing in the woods. Representatives of the defeated nation arrive after an arduous journey, dazed, weary, in despair and humiliation. They wait despondently for the armistice terms to be read to them by the victors, terms that will reduce their once-mighty nation to a position akin to vassalage. It is a somber scene, made more shocking by the seeming incomprehensibility of the military collapse that preceded it. A familiar image, but it is not November 1918, and the victors are not the French; it is, instead, a warm summer day, 21 June 1940, some twenty-two years after the German defeat in World War I.

Observing the scene, the American correspondent William L. Shirer watched as Adolf Hitler strode slowly toward the clearing in the woods. His face, Shirer noted, was "grave, solemn, yet brimming with revenge. . . . There was something else, difficult to describe, in his expression, a sort of scornful inner joy at being present at this great reversal of fate— a reversal he himself had wrought." Hitler and his delegation paused as they reached the great granite block erected to commemorate the earlier French triumph and read the inscription: "HERE ON THE ELEVENTH OF NOVEMBER 1918 SUCCUMBED THE CRIMINAL PRIDE OF THE GERMAN EMPIRE . . . VANQUISHED BY THE FREE PEOPLES WHICH IT TRIED TO ENSLAVE." Shirer, some fifty yards away, intently studied Hitler's face through binoculars. "I have seen that face many times at the great moments of his life," he remarked. "But today! It is afire with scorn, anger, hate, revenge, triumph. . . . He glances slowly around the clearing, and now, as his eyes meet ours, you grasp the depth of his hatred. . . . He swiftly snaps his hands on his hips, arches his shoulders, plants his feet wide apart. It is a magnificent gesture of defiance, of burning contempt for this place." Somewhat anticlimactically, Hitler proceeded to the rail carriage, where he received the French delegation in silence, then left, again without saying a word,

1

after ten minutes. The open wound, however, had been healed. "The humiliation is obliterated. One has a feeling of being reborn," Joseph Goebbels exulted, after Hitler had informed him of the proceedings in a late-night telephone call.[1]

Despite the relatively restrained performance by Hitler at Compiègne, these had been momentous weeks that marked an extraordinary personal triumph for the Führer. Twenty years earlier an obscure political agitator in Munich, and even a decade ago merely one of many aspirants to power in a Germany torn by political chaos and economic distress, Hitler stood at the pinnacle of his fame and popularity. He had undone the shame of November 1918, as he had vowed to do, had humiliated Germany's two tormentors from the Great War, had destroyed the hated Treaty of Versailles, and had made Germany master of a European bloc that in economic power compared favorably with the British Empire and the United States.

Although outwardly unmoved, Hitler appeared to be deeply affected by the events of May and June 1940. On 1 June, even as the battle for France was still raging, he made two visits of a deeply symbolic character. In the early afternoon he visited the German cemetery at Langemarck to pay homage to the young soldiers, now elevated to mythical status in Nazi lore, killed in the legendary "Children's Slaughter" (Kindermord) in November 1914, deaths that had now been redeemed by the victories of May 1940. Later that afternoon he made a more personal journey, one that took him back to the battlefields of World War I where he had experienced so much, including the temporary loss of his eyesight after a British gas attack in October 1918. Standing alone, absorbed in his thoughts, the impact of what had been and what had just happened must have been overwhelming. The Great War had shaped Hitler and many others of his generation, their personal traumas leaving deep wounds that never fully healed. Goebbels provided a glimpse of this deep emotion, noting in his diary, "The Führer himself was at the old battlefields, in his old trenches. He gave me a moving description of it." The sufferings of the past, however, would now be redeemed. "What great times!" Goebbels also exulted. "What happiness to be allowed to work in such times." Ominously, however, a few sentences later the means of that salvation became clearer, Goebbels threatening, "We will quickly finish with the Jews after the war," a comment, given Hitler's conviction of the nexus between the Jews and the earlier German defeat, that perhaps also revealed something of the thrust of Hitler's thoughts at the time.[2]

Having now redeemed the humiliation that had so seared his consciousness, Hitler returned to his military headquarters at Bruly-le-Péche.

Following the signing of a Franco-Italian armistice on 24 June, all fighting was to cease at 1:35 A.M. on the following morning. Shortly before the agreed time, Hitler, sitting in his field headquarters, gave orders to turn out the light and open the windows. "Silently," Albert Speer remembered, "we sat in the darkness, swept by the sense of experiencing a historic moment so close to the author of it. Outside, a bugler blew the traditional signal for the end of fighting. . . . Occasional flashes of heat lightning shimmered through the dark room. . . . Then Hitler's voice sounded, soft and unemphatic: 'This responsibility. . . .' And a few minutes later: 'Now switch the light on. . . .' For me it remained a rare event. I thought I had seen Hitler as a human being." Three days later, in the early morning hours of 28 June, Hitler and an entourage including Speer and the sculptor Arno Breker descended on Paris for a whirlwind visit. The Führer delighted in showing off his detailed knowledge of the Opéra, and appeared impressed by the Eiffel Tower and the tomb of Napoléon in the Invalides, but otherwise seemed disappointed in the famous city. During the course of the three-hour tour, the question arose of a German victory parade in the city, but Hitler eventually rejected the idea, saying, "I am not in the mood for a victory parade. We aren't at the end yet."[3]

What exactly Hitler meant by this cryptic remark is still open to interpretation. Some see in it only a reference to the expected impending victory over Great Britain, while others view the comment as evidence of Hitler's deeper ideological obsession with the Soviet Union. In any case, his assessment of the situation in late June was more accurate than perhaps even he realized at the time. Unbeknownst to Hitler, the British cabinet had made the key decision to continue to fight even before he began his historic tour of the old battlefields of Flanders. His gamble in September 1939 had now backfired, as he found himself entangled in a war in the wrong place, at the wrong time, and with the wrong enemy and one, moreover, from which he could not easily extricate himself.

In "Beim Propheten," a short story written in 1904, Thomas Mann described "strange places, strange minds, strange regions of the spirit . . . , on the peripheries of large cities where the street-lights grow fewer and the police go in pairs . . . , pale young geniuses, criminals of the dream, sit with folded arms and brood. . . . Here rules defiance, the most extreme consequences, the despairing, crowning 'I' . . . madness and death."[4] Written years before Adolf Hitler launched a career in politics, Mann's story cannot itself be seen as prophetic of a specific individual. Still, Hitler was almost the perfect incarnation of Mann's "criminal of the dream," a man who thought concretely and sought to shape the world according to his will. Hitler had little formal education, but he possessed a quick mind and an astonishing memory, and his weltanschauung (worldview) took shape and was nurtured in the hothouse atmosphere of post–World War I Munich. What emerged, cobbled together from rather standard ideas floating around Germany and Europe at the turn of the century, was a unique explanatory system with considerable inner logic: a curious combination of fear, anxiety, resentment, revenge, conspiratorial fantasies, and rational, pragmatic assessment. Above all, two things characterized his ideology: his all-encompassing hatreds and his belief in the importance of will and the power of ideas. Stunned by the sudden German collapse and defeat in World War I, Hitler, like most Germans, struggled to make sense of the seemingly inexplicable. His ideology— shaped by war, the trauma of German impotence and vulnerability in November 1918, the humiliation of the Treaty of Versailles, and the post- war political turmoil—not only pointed to those allegedly responsible for what had been done to Germany but explained why it had happened, promised revenge on the "November criminals," and outlined an ideal- istic vision of a new society.

Central to Hitler's ideology were an extreme social Darwinism that posited the struggle for survival as an all-or-nothing process that gov- erned the life of nations as well as individuals; a belief that racial conflict between peoples and nations of differing "value," and not class struggle, shaped the process of history; a radical anti-Semitism that viewed Jews as a conspiratorial, destructive force in world history; and the necessity of securing Lebensraum (living space) for the German nation as a means of ensuring its survival in this process of struggle for existence. By them- selves, none of these ideas was original; what was unique was the manner in which Hitler combined his pathological anti-Semitism with the notion of Lebensraum to imbue German expansion to the east with a sense of urgency and historic mission.[5]

In both *Mein Kampf* and his so-called *Second Book*, Hitler asserted that history unfolded as a result of the unceasing process of racial struggle, which provided "the key not only to world history but to all human cul- ture." This notion of culture was significant since he asserted that only people of a higher racial quality, so-called culture-creating races, could produce a sustainable civilization. What distinguished Hitler's racial- ist notions was his Manichaean belief that this was a struggle of good versus evil. Thus, to him, the alleged culture-destroying races—the Jews being the prime example—constantly sought to undermine the culture created by the superior racial entities. Lacking a nation of their own, the

Jews acted as a parasitic force, working from within to undermine and destroy the superior culture. For Hitler, the culmination of this process was unfolding before his very eyes in Russia, where the "blood Jew," ruling through Bolshevism, had "killed or starved about thirty million people with positively fanatical savagery, in part amid inhuman torture. . . . But the end is not only the end of the freedom of the peoples oppressed by the Jews, but also the end of this parasite upon the nations. After the death of his victim, the vampire sooner or later dies too."[6]

Moreover, Jewish-Bolshevism, as he now identified it, posed an imminent, existential threat to Germany that had to be confronted. From the beginning of his political activity, Hitler displayed an overriding, all-encompassing obsession with the danger posed by the Jews, on whom again and again he blamed the German collapse in 1918. In a famous passage in *Mein Kampf,* he made an explicit connection between the destructive workings of the Jews and the loss of the war: "If at the beginning of the war and during the war twelve or fifteen thousand of these Hebrew corrupters of the people had been held under poison gas . . . the sacrifice of millions at the front would not have been in vain. On the contrary: twelve thousand scoundrels eliminated in time might have saved the lives of a million real Germans." This passage should not be taken as evidence of a straight line from intention to later mass murder, but it does indicate, as Ian Kershaw has stressed, the connection in Hitler's mind between the loss of the war, the destruction of the Jews, and national salvation.[7]

Crucially, Hitler also viewed Jewry as an actual political entity, a hidden force that had started World War I, engineered the German defeat and humiliation, and ruined Russia and was now intent on exterminating Germany and the Germans. Unless the Jewish question was solved by a "bloody clash," he asserted in 1924, "the German people will end up just like the Armenians." As Saul Friedländer has stressed, Hitler's was a "redemptive anti-Semitism" that combined anxious, conspiratorial notions of an all-powerful, destructive Jewry with promises of redeeming Germany. For Hitler, the Jewish conspiracy constituted the primary obstacle to German renewal. "The Jew today is the great agitator for the complete destruction of Germany," Hitler insisted, while the ultimate goal of the Jewish conspiracy remained the "annihilation of Germany . . . , the next great war aim of Bolshevism." Once he made the link with Bolshevism, Hitler cemented in his own mind his mission of waging a racial struggle against a ruthless, implacable, and brutal foe for the very existence of German and Western culture. The mission of National Socialism became the destruction of Bolshevism and, with it, "our mortal enemy: the Jew." In this struggle, "A victory of the Marxist idea signifies the complete extermination of the opponents." To Hitler, there could be no middle ground: "There is no making pacts with Jews. There can only be the hard either-or." The outcome of the struggle, he stressed in a 1922 speech, would be "either victory for the Aryan side or else its annihilation and victory for the Jews."[8] Implicit in this was the notion of absolute destruction: either they would win and kill us, or we would win and eliminate them.

If this radical anti-Semitism gave Hitler's ideology its manic dynamism, it was Lebensraum that provided the vital link between dogma and a pragmatic program of territorial expansion. Notions of living space and expansion in the east were common currency in Germany both before and especially after World War I. Based on work by geopolitical theorists such as Friedrich Ratzel and Karl Haushofer, and popularized in the 1920s by Hans Grimm's best-selling novel *Volk ohne Raum* (People without space), Lebensraum stressed the necessity of a policy of expansion in order to achieve a positive ratio between population and resources. Ratzel emphasized that healthy states needed to expand and grow in order to survive, an idea hardly unique to Germany at the turn of the century. The British "hunger" blockade between 1914 and 1919, a plebeian form of killing that nonetheless had a profound impact on shaping Hitler's ideas, seemed to confirm the truth of these notions. Responsible for the death by starvation of perhaps 750,000 civilians, and regarded by many Germans as the main culprit in the collapse of the war effort, the blockade reinforced and gave legitimacy in the minds of millions of Germans to the urgency of securing living space. For Hitler, it provided proof of his contentions and justification for his actions: the decisive factor in the struggle for survival was obtaining the means by which the German nation could sustain itself. The Great War had clearly demonstrated that Germany, a resource-poor nation surrounded by hostile powers, possessed insufficient resources and was, thus, vulnerable to the murderous actions of its enemies. If Germany was to survive, it had to gain living space.[9]

Viewed from the perspective of the 1920s, Germany faced a series of stark choices: attempt to resurrect the liberal economic policy of free trade and export orientation that had characterized imperial Germany; promote a policy of colonial expansion to secure vital resources; or promote a policy of contiguous expansion to secure Lebensraum in Eastern Europe. As Hitler assessed the situation, the first two choices offered no realistic alternative, the first because Great Britain and the United States dominated the global trading system, German exports faced increasing trade barriers, and reliance on foreign trade did not solve Germany's ultimate problem. As World War I had demonstrated, its enemies, organized by the international Jewish conspiracy, could easily cut off imports and force Germany into defeat. The second option not only dispersed the German racial core but was also completely untenable in any case: no suitable land for colonization outside Europe existed, and Britain had in 1914 already shown its willingness to organize a coalition to quash German economic, naval, and colonial competition.[10]

As Adam Tooze has argued, from the vantage point of the early 1930s Germans looked back on a twenty-year period in which economic decline and insecurity dominated their experience. Despite their hard work, diligence, and technology, their country was poor, especially in comparison with the United States. Playing within the rules of the economic game as devised by the British and now dominated by the Americans clearly had not worked. Moreover, the Great Depression seemingly had made a mockery of the liberal doctrine of economic progress and only reinforced Hitler's notion that, in economics, as in race, life was an unceasing process of struggle for survival. As he stressed in 1928, the huge difference in living standards between the United States and Germany could be understood only in terms of the American advantages in resources and space. Now, in the midst of the Depression, his basic Darwinian outlook and economic understanding combined to point in one direction: the solution to the existential threats facing Germany, both economic and racial, lay in the conquest of Lebensraum in the east. "And so we National Socialists consciously draw a line beneath the foreign policy tendency of our pre-war period," Hitler emphasized in *Mein Kampf.* "We take up where we broke off six hundred years ago. We stop the endless German movement to the south and west, and turn our gaze toward the land in the east. At long last we break off the colonial and commercial policy of the pre-war period and shift to the soil policy of the future. If we speak of soil in Europe today, we can primarily have in mind only Russia and her vassal border states."[11]

Not only did expansion in the east accord with Hitler's ideology, but it also seemed to offer the fewest risks. Germany would conquer the necessary living space at the expense of the allegedly racially inferior Slavs, secure for Germany the resources needed to make it self-sufficient and powerful, and put it in position to wage a successful struggle against the Jewish-Bolshevik enemy. Moreover, expansion in the east seemed promising because Jewish-Bolshevik rule had, in Hitler's opinion, already ruined the Russian state and left it ripe for collapse. "The struggle for world hegemony," he claimed, betraying his constant obsession with

World War I, "will be decided for Europe by the possession of Russia's space: this will make Europe the most blockade-proof spot in the world." Finally, Hitler believed that such eastward expansion posed no fundamental threat to the British Empire. Thus, if Germany pursued a purely continental policy and avoided any challenge to Britain's colonial or commercial interests, which Hitler believed had been the key mistake of German governments before 1914, Britain might even aid in the destruction of Russia. Indeed, throughout the 1920s and 1930s, and even in the first years of World War II, he persisted in the belief that Britain would, ultimately, be an ally of German-dominated Europe in the eventual struggle with the United States for world domination.[12]

By the mid-1920s, then, Hitler had established in his own mind the key link between the destruction of Jewish-Bolshevism and the acquisition of Lebensraum in the east, both of which were necessary in order to secure Germany's existence. In the desperate period following World War I, this potent combination of nineteenth-century notions of social Darwinism, imperialism, racism, and anti-Semitism provided a seemingly plausible explanation for Germany's current quandary and a prescription for action to save and renew the nation. Once established, the quest for Lebensraum and the final reckoning with Jewish-Bolshevism remained the cornerstone of Hitler's life's work: only the conquest of living space could make good the mistakes of the past, preserve the racial value of the German *Volk*, and provide the resources to lift Germany out of its economic misery. Just a few days after becoming chancellor, Hitler announced unequivocally to his startled generals that his aim was "to conquer and ruthlessly Germanize new living space in the east." Everything, he stressed, had to be geared toward securing German predominance in Europe. From his first days in office, then, Hitler began preparing for war, for the struggle, as he saw it, for Germany's existence.[13]

Adolf Hitler was not one to appreciate paradox—he was far too humorless and self-absorbed for that. If he had been more detached, however, he might well have appreciated the great historical irony that confronted him in September 1939. Instead, his chief interpreter, Paul Schmidt, perfectly captured the Führer's mood on the early evening of 3 September 1939. Having been summoned to the Reich Chancellery to translate the British declaration of war, Schmidt described the funereal scene:

> After I finished there was total silence. . . . Hitler sat there as if petrified and stared straight ahead. He . . . did not rant and rave. . . . He sat in his seat completely quiet and motionless. After a

while, which seemed like an eternity . . . , he turned to Ribbentrop who kept standing at the window as if frozen. "What now?" Hitler asked his Foreign Minister with a furious gaze in his eyes as if he wanted to indicate that Ribbentrop had misinformed him about the reaction of the British. . . . Goering turned to me and said: "If we lose this war, may Heaven have mercy on us!"

Far from the arrogant, infallible, rigidly self-assured Führer of myth, Hitler had at that moment allowed Schmidt to glimpse the nearer reality: an uncertain figure whose guiding illusion had been crushed and who did not know how to proceed. His great gamble had failed, and what followed his invasion of Poland he neither wanted nor expected. His original intention had been to attack the Soviet Union with Polish help, but, when the Poles balked at playing their assigned role, he had hoped to neutralize Great Britain through the conclusion of the Nazi-Soviet Pact. This, he expected, would free his back in the west for a quick destruction of Poland followed by the showdown with Stalin's Russia. Rather than fight the British, Hitler desired an alliance with England based on a common anti-Bolshevik attitude and a complementary relationship between a maritime and a continental power. What he got instead was a war with an Anglo-French alliance supported by the latent power of the United States.[14]

The irony, then, was that the nation he had wooed for years had now become his implacable enemy while the country that he envisioned as his greatest adversary had emerged as his indispensable ally. Moreover, he had embroiled Germany in what looked to be, at minimum, a protracted war in the west against the two nations that had undone it in the Great War and with a woefully unprepared Wehrmacht in no way comparable to the powerful military force of 1914. Given Germany's position in the middle of Europe, the nightmare of its military planners had always been a two-front war, but Hitler had now conjured precisely this specter. Nor did his generals put faith in a supposed war-winning blitzkrieg strategy, for such a plan did not exist. In fact, they had absorbed all too well the lesson of World War I: they no longer believed that wars could be won quickly against opponents of superior strength. "The fixation upon a short war has been ruinous for us," asserted Colonel (later General) Georg Thomas, chief of the Wehrmacht Economic Staff in 1937. "We should therefore not be guided by the illusion of a short war in the age of air and Panzer squadrons." A 1938 study confirmed this opinion, stating categorically, "The possibilities of defeating an equivalent opponent by means of a Blitzkrieg are zero. . . . It is not military force that is strongest; instead, it is economic power that has become the most important." By plunging recklessly into war, Hitler had created a nearly insurmountable strategic dilemma for Germany: although his generals had worked out a plan of operations against Poland, no overall war-winning concept existed.[15]

This was certainly not what Hitler intended. Since the mid-1920s, he had consistently expressed his desire to have Great Britain as an ally in the struggle against Jewish-Bolshevism. Although there were tantalizing hints of an alignment, such as the Naval Agreement of 1935 or Chamberlain's policy of appeasement, by 1938 the hope of an alliance with Britain was illusory. If, in his ideologically blinkered world, the British did not act as Hitler wished, it meant that "world Jewry" had come to dominate in London and that "the Jew" had won over "the Briton."[16] This sense of a gathering worldwide Jewish conspiracy directed against Germany imparted a sense of urgency to Hitler's actions in 1938–1939, as did his recognition that Britain was beginning a rapid, if belated, rearmament. Beyond this lay the vast latent power of the United States, which was also beginning to rearm and which Hitler had already identified in the late 1920s as the long-term opponent with which a German-dominated Europe would have to fight a war for world supremacy. The problem was many-sided. In order to protect Germany in its existential struggle with the Jewish conspiracy, German military power had to be restored in order to wage a successful war for Lebensraum. This meant a policy of rearmament that violated the Treaty of Versailles and threatened to alarm Germany's neighbors. In addition, the provisions of the hated peace treaty had reduced German military strength so considerably that a crash program of rearmament would be necessary just to bring the military to adequate levels of self-defense. Moreover, all this was to be undertaken in a country only beginning to recover from the enormous economic and psychological trauma of the Great Depression. Just as the Nazis were beginning to reap the benefits of economic recovery, any overly ambitious rearmament program would imperil German economic recovery and Nazi popularity.

Hitler proved remarkably successful in striking a balance between these domestic and foreign policy demands between 1933 and 1936, but in August of that latter year, as he pondered Germany's economic and political situation at the Eagle's Nest on the Obersalzburg, he became more convinced than ever that Germany had to accelerate its preparations for war. His ideological fixation on struggle, along with his consciousness of Germany's shrinking lead in rearmament, made the time factor increasingly important. In turn, this self-imposed time pressure inhibited the rational strategic calculations that had largely governed the first phase of his foreign policy. The result of his deliberations was a memorandum that he showed to a small circle of advisers: the defense minister, Werner von Blomberg, the builder of the autobahns and the West Wall, Fritz Todt, and the head of the German air force and de facto second in command to the Führer, Hermann Goering. Characteristically, Hitler felt compelled to justify his actions and, as usual, returned to his central argument of the necessity of war against Jewish-Bolshevism. "The historical struggle of nations for life," he asserted, constituted the essence of politics; because of the growing military strength of the Soviet Union the world was moving "with ever-increasing speed towards a new conflict"; the present crisis rivaled that of the ancient world faced with the barbarian invasions or the long, violent struggle between Christianity and Islam; Germany could not "avoid or abstain from this historic conflict"; "the goal of Bolshevism [was] the elimination of those strata of mankind which have hitherto provided the leadership and their replacement by worldwide Jewry"; "a victory of Bolshevism over Germany would lead to the annihilation of the German people." Given this existential threat, against which "all other considerations must recede into the background," Hitler concluded that rearmament could not be "too large, nor its pace too swift."[17]

Germany's problems were also familiar, foremost among them overpopulation, lack of resources, and the need for living space. "I set the following tasks," Hitler concluded his memorandum. "I: The German Armed Forces must be operational within four years. II: The German economy must be fit for war within four years." With the announcement of the Four-Year Plan in October 1936, Hitler set Germany on a course of reckless rearmament with the express purpose of waging war in the near future. The primary function of economic activity was now to be preparation for war, so much so that by the spring of 1939 military production occupied one-quarter of the entire German labor force while German financial and economic stability had been imperiled by the breakneck speed of rearmament. The mandate given to Goering was clear: to make Germany ready for war, in terms of armaments and economic self-sufficiency in key raw materials, in four years. No specific war plan had yet been formulated, but implicit in this was Hitler's belief that a clash with Russia was unavoidable.[18]

Hitler also had a clear sense of the purpose of a war for Lebensraum: the hold of the so-called Jewish plutocrats over the world's economic resources and capital had to be broken in order to provide the German people with a living standard commensurate with their racial value.

World War I, the British blockade, starvation, German defeat, the Treaty of Versailles, debt and reparations, the ruinous inflation of 1923, and the calamity of the Great Depression served as proof to Hitler that the international economic system was stacked against Germany. The only way to gain national freedom, then, lay in unilateral action to smash the existing system and establish a German-dominated "New Order," a European economic bloc that could compete on an equal footing with the Anglo-American powers. This was, after all, a Darwinian world of struggle where the strong could do as they wished and the weak were compelled to do as they must. Ironically, Hitler proposed to free Germany from the shackles of this alleged Jewish-dominated system in much the same way he believed the two ascendant forces in the world economy, Great Britain and the United States, had achieved their predominance: through force.

The immediate dilemma for Hitler was that German rearmament could be achieved only through reckless financing that would imperil the domestic standard of living while also promising to so alarm Germany's potential adversaries that they, too, would begin rapid rearmament. The military constraints imposed by Versailles had left Germany so weakened that even the ambitious rearmament program of 1933–1935 had left it barely able to defend itself, with offensive operations out of the question. To make good his determination to resolve the vital issue of Lebensraum no later than 1943, which he revealed to his startled military and foreign policy leaders in November 1937, Hitler contemplated peacetime military expenditures unprecedented in a Western capitalist economy (only Stalin's actions in the Soviet Union after 1928 were comparable). In the event, this breakneck policy of rearmament did surprisingly little to increase the effective strength of the German military since it resulted in a series of production bottlenecks, raw material and foreign currency shortages, interservice feuds over allocation of scarce resources, and an inability to establish which weapons should be given priority in production. Furthermore, even if moves to absorb Austria and Czechoslovakia did not result in Western military action, aggressive German rearmament would almost certainly touch off a response by the other powers. Given its inferior economic and resource base relative to its rivals, this would inevitably touch off an economic competition that Germany ultimately could not win. Time was, thus, not on Germany's side, as any initial military advantage would not last. Hitler, however, believed that the only solution to Germany's dilemma lay in expansion, so the time factor merely dictated action sooner rather than later. Despite, or perhaps because of, its precarious financial, food, and raw material situation,

Germany, Hitler believed, had to escape the restrictions of Central Europe through force.[19]

Rearmament problems, awareness of German deficiencies in food, capital, and raw materials, irritation with the failure of Britain to act as he wanted, a growing fear of a renewed encirclement of Germany by hostile enemies: all acted to produce in Hitler a growing sense of frustration that exploded in late 1938. Since his racial obsessions infused all aspects of life and policymaking in the Third Reich, the racial-ideological dimension of policy represented the flip side of the military-strategic coin. From the beginning of his rule, Hitler faced a self-imposed "Jewish problem," for by definition Jews were considered aliens and, thus, could not be a part of the racial community, the *Volksgemeinschaft,* that Hitler promised as the cornerstone of his new Germany. From the outset, as well, the solution to this Jewish problem resulted in a myriad of difficulties, ranging from the failure of the economic boycott of April 1933, to troubles associated with the emigration of German Jews, to the international condemnation of Nazi anti-Jewish actions. In all this, Hitler saw his belief confirmed that a Jewish world conspiracy actually existed and that its mission was the destruction of Germany. Typically, the more radical and aggressive Nazi policies became both at home and abroad, the more Hitler imputed hostile intentions to this alleged Jewish conspiracy. In a virtually perfect self-reinforcing spiral of paranoia, stepped-up persecution of German Jews, followed by foreign condemnation and pressure, only further convinced Hitler of the truth of his great insight about the hostility of "international Jewry."[20]

In step with foreign policy, 1938 proved to be the key year in the radicalization of racial policy as well. From 1933, Nazi policy had aimed at the emigration of all German Jews, primarily to Palestine. By 1938, however, Nazi officials regarded these efforts as a failure: fully three-quarters of the 1933 Jewish population still lived in Germany, and other countries had mounted increasing obstacles to Jewish immigration. Moreover, top Nazis themselves, influenced by Foreign Office arguments, had become more sensitive to Arab opinion and alert to the perceived danger of creating a Jewish state that would threaten Germany in the future. New ideas were mooted, including one from Reinhard Heydrich's SD (Security Service) that the Jews be expelled to some inhospitable place such as Madagascar, an idea long circulating in European anti-Semitic circles. In any case, the final aim remained the removal of all Jews from Germany through some sort of emigration or expulsion, although Hitler, Heydrich, and others now assumed that such an action might take up to ten years. In the meantime, and characteristically, Hitler suggested to Goebbels that German Jews could be held as hostages.[21]

As perhaps the most radically anti-Semitic of all the top Nazis, Joseph Goebbels seethed with impatience at the lack of progress in "cleansing" Germany, and especially Berlin, of Jews. Typically, the Nazis blamed the Jews themselves for the emigration logjam and responded in characteristic fashion: they would simply increase the incentive for the Jews to leave, through a renewed wave of physical violence and terror. The way forward had already been shown in March in Vienna, where, following the annexation of Austria, a storm of violence and popular anti-Jewish rage had been unleashed. With the tacit approval of Hitler, Goebbels had already in the summer of 1938 launched a new round of discriminatory and propagandistic assaults against the Jews of Berlin, actions that were quickly taken up in other German cities. Significantly, this radicalization of Jewish policy accompanied a sharp increase in international tensions associated with the brewing Sudeten crisis: as Hitler's hopes for the realization of his long-anticipated alliance with Britain faded, his anger at international Jewry boiled over, for which the Jews of Germany would have to pay. Nor did the outcome of the Munich Conference at the end of September 1938 assuage the Führer. Hitler evidently had hoped to have a short war against Czechoslovakia that autumn, with the expectation that Britain and France, acquiescing once again in a fait accompli, would now grant him the desired free hand in the east. Instead, he had to be satisfied with the Sudetenland. Although foreign tensions had dissipated, the radical turn domestically had produced a menacing anti-Jewish atmosphere.[22]

This tension exploded in early November. On the morning of 7 November, a seventeen-year-old Polish Jew, Herschel Grynszpan, entered the German embassy in Paris and shot Ernst vom Rath, the third legation secretary, in an act of revenge for the recent deportation of his parents. As vom Rath lingered between life and death, Goebbels orchestrated wild attacks in the German press that, much to his satisfaction, resulted on the evening of 8 November in outbreaks of anti-Jewish violence organized by local party leaders. By chance, vom Rath died on the ninth, the same day that the Nazi old guard had gathered in Munich for the annual memorial of the failed 1923 putsch. From Goebbels's perspective, the time for action had come. That evening, following an animated conversation with the Führer, after which Hitler left the gathering unusually early, Goebbels gave a blistering anti-Jewish speech, during which he announced vom Rath's death, noted with approval the "retaliatory" actions of the day before, and made it clear that the party

should organize further anti-Jewish "demonstrations." He then enunci-
ated detailed instructions for what should be done as well as pressuring
and prodding occasionally reluctant officials into action. The result of
his efforts has come to be known as Reichskristallnacht (Night of broken
glass), a shocking outburst of physical violence, destruction of property,
burning of synagogues, and mass arrests of Jewish men that left the
world, and many Germans, stunned.[23]

Kristallnacht, and the conclusions Hitler drew from it, marked a significant turning point in Nazi policy and thinking. Although emotionally
satisfying for Goebbels and other party radicals, the pogrom was a political disaster both domestically and abroad. Harsh international condemnation of Nazi actions might have been expected, but the clear lack of
domestic approval for this outburst of public violence raised new obstacles to solving the Jewish question. The reaction to Kristallnacht, and its
meaning, clearly troubled Hitler. Not only did he see the international
response, especially that of the United States, as yet more evidence of the
hostility of world Jewry toward Germany, but the disappointing reaction
of the German public also seemed to reinforce once again his fear of the
power of the Jews to subvert even popular governments. In *Mein Kampf,*
Hitler had explicitly linked German defeat in war with the destructive
influence of the Jews; with the prospect of a new war ever present, the
threat of the Jews took center stage in his thoughts. A remark made on
12 November, at the conclusion of a high-level conference to deal with
the fallout from Kristallnacht, perhaps provided an indication of Hitler's thinking as well. "If the German Reich comes into foreign-political
conflict in the foreseeable future," Goering threatened, "it can be taken
for granted that we in Germany will think . . . of bringing about a great
showdown with the Jews."[24]

Over the next two months, in a variety of forums, Hitler and other
top Nazis expressed more or less the same sentiment. The use of German Jews as hostages in the event of a conflict was openly discussed
in the German press, while Goebbels unleashed a blistering anti-Jewish
and anti-American propaganda campaign that depicted New York as the
center of world Jewry and President Roosevelt as the stooge of the Jewish
conspiracy. The threat was clear: if a new conflict erupted in Europe, one
that could only result as a consequence of Jewish manipulation, German
Jews would be held responsible for the harm that world Jewry inflicted on
Germany. The SS organ, *Das schwarze Korps,* thundered in late November
1938: "We would therefore [in the event of war] be faced with the hard
necessity of eradicating the Jewish underworld. . . . The result would be
the actual and final end of Jewry in Germany, its complete annihilation."

Certainly, this should not be construed as evidence for an already existing plan for the Holocaust, but it does indicate the clear emergence of a murderous mentality. Hitler himself revealed such an attitude in a remarkably menacing comment to the Czech foreign minister in late January 1939: "The Jews here [in Germany] will be annihilated. The Jews had not brought about the 9 November 1918 for nothing. This day will be avenged."[25] Not for the first nor for the last time, Hitler vowed to gain retribution for the German defeat in World War I; indeed, the theme "never again another November 1918" ran as a leitmotif through his actions until the end of his life.

Anger, frustration, resentment, willingness to lash out violently at those perceived to be threatening Germany with destruction—these emotions formed the backdrop to Hitler's speech of 30 January 1939. Ostensibly given to mark the sixth anniversary of the Nazi ascension to power, it served primarily as a recitation of the alleged evils done to Germany by the Jewish conspiracy and a reply to the overt economic and military challenges that Hitler saw emanating from Britain and America. Denied access to vital economic resources, at a disadvantage in the global trading system, and held in debt bondage by the Jewish plutocrats, Hitler raised once again the familiar theme of Lebensraum as the only solution to Germany's existential dilemma. The Western democracies, however, blocked Germany's expansion to the east, meddling in an area "in which the English, or any other Western nation have no business at all." The Germans, Hitler asserted, "in the future will not accept the attempt of Western states to meddle at will in certain issues which are solely our business in order to prevent through their interference natural and rational solutions." He explicitly linked this obstructionism with the Jewish question, mocking ostensible Western concern but refusal to accept Jewish refugees, and then outlined a possible territorial solution: "I think that the sooner this problem is solved the better. For Europe cannot find rest until the Jewish Question is cleared up. It may well be possible that . . . an agreement on this problem may be reached in Europe. . . . The world has sufficient space for settlements."[26]

Hitler then turned to his obsession with Lebensraum. Significantly, he linked Western obstruction in solving this issue, the Jewish conspiracy, and his new fixation on Jews as hostages. If he were to be thwarted in achieving Lebensraum, he now outlined a radical alternative, one that eventually became a self-fulfilling prophecy:

And one more thing I would like to state on this day memorable perhaps not only for us Germans. I have often been a prophet in my life and was generally laughed at. During my struggle for power, the Jews primarily received with laughter my prophecies that I would someday assume the leadership of the state . . . and then, among other things, achieve a solution of the Jewish problem. I suppose that the laughter of Jewry in Germany is now choking in their throats.

Today I will be a prophet again: if the international finance Jewry within Europe and abroad should succeed once more in plunging the peoples into a world war, then the consequence will not be the Bolshevization of the world and a victory of Jewry, but on the contrary, the annihilation of the Jewish race in Europe.[27]

Again, this statement should be seen not as a blueprint for the Holocaust but as a warning, especially to America: stay out of European affairs, and refrain from interfering in matters important to German existence. To reinforce his threat, Hitler demonstrated his awareness of his options and his willingness to use them: the Jews under German control should be regarded as hostages. If the Jewish conspiracy plunged the world into another global war, he warned, he would not hesitate to deal harshly with the Jews under his control. The time for decisions was approaching. Hitler was going to gain living space for the German people; the choice for the Western powers was acceptance or opposition.

Nazism and war were inseparable. Born of a lost war, energized by the desire to gain redemption for the stain of defeat, determined to achieve Lebensraum in Europe as the key to survival in a world of enemies, preoccupied with solving a self-imposed Jewish problem, the National Socialist regime had, from the time it assumed power, set in motion a process of building a "new man and new society" in order to prepare for war. The key to this much-vaunted Volksgemeinschaft was, as Ian Kershaw has stressed, "an attempt at a perpetual re-creation of the 'spirit of 1914,'" a "true socialism" that would unite all racially valuable Germans and prepare them for the struggle ahead. Nor had Hitler left any doubt about the inevitability of conflict: the German future could be assured only by gaining living space, and it could be won only through force.[28]

Hitler's conception of Lebensraum had been informed and influenced not only by notions of social Darwinism but also by nineteenth-century European colonial and imperialistic practices. The European scramble for colonies in Africa and Asia had been justified not only by economic necessity but also by reference to the alleged racial inferiority of the "backward" and "uncivilized" peoples of those continents.

European domination thus seemed a natural and logical consequence, as did the brutalities inflicted on the native peoples. Since Hitler looked to Eastern Europe as the natural sphere of German expansion, and since he viewed the Slavic and Jewish inhabitants of the region as either inferior or threatening, his notion of Lebensraum harbored from the beginning murderous impulses. What had hitherto been done only to conquered populations overseas Hitler now stood ready to inflict on a European population.[29] In some respects, then, Lebensraum could be seen as merely a belated continuation of the nineteenth-century Western policy of imperialism, with Eastern Europeans substituting for Africans or Native Americans. At its heart, however, Hitler's program would prove far more radical and far-reaching, a racialist and exterminationist scheme of limitless aims and brutality.

Poland would be the first country to experience the full harshness of this policy, a sort of dress rehearsal for what would come later in the Soviet Union. From the beginning, Hitler had done little to hide his radical notions regarding the treatment of Poland from his top generals. A 31 July agreement between the army and the SS gave its killing units, the *Einsatzgruppen,* special tasks for combating anti-German activities behind the front lines, which in practice meant a license to murder. Meeting with his top commanders at the Berghof on 22 August, Hitler stressed, according to the notes of one present, the "destruction of Poland in the foreground. The aim is elimination of living forces, not the arrival at a certain line. . . . Have no pity. Brutal attitude. Eighty million people shall get what is their right. Their existence has to be secured. The strongest has the right. Greatest severity."[30] In part, army leaders raised no objections because they too longed for the destruction of Poland, that hated product of Versailles, and regarded Poles as racially and culturally inferior. Then, too, many likely regarded Hitler's rhetoric as mere hyperbole.

The terror unleashed on the Polish population from the first days of the invasion left no doubt, however, that Hitler's intentions matched his venomous words. Even as local militias composed of ethnic Germans (*Volksdeutsche*) began vigilante actions against Poles who had committed outrages against the German minority, Heydrich's units swept into action, armed with lists of perhaps thirty thousand people to be arrested or executed. On 9 September, Franz Halder confided to Major Helmuth Groscurth the chilling news that "it was the intention of the Führer and Goering to destroy and exterminate the Polish people." Apart from a few mild and scattered protests, however, the army leadership accommodated itself to the new reality. Rather than object in principle to this planned, wholesale murder, Brauchitsch, the army commander in chief, blandly informed his subordinates that the Einsatzgruppen had received orders from Hitler to carry out "certain ethnic tasks" that "lay outside the responsibility" of the army. Indeed, despite occasional mild protests about "excesses" committed by the Einsatzgruppen, most army commanders welcomed them as protection against presumed security threats. Although this campaign of ethnic cleansing had clearly been authorized by Hitler, it was Himmler and Heydrich, the ambitious leaders of the SS, as well as party radicals such as Hans Frank, Arthur Greiser, and Albert Forster, who grabbed the opportunity to expand their power. Hitler now made it clear that a "harsh racial struggle" would be carried out in Poland, the essence of which, as Groscurth succinctly noted, was to "exterminate." Within days of the outbreak of war, the initiative had passed to Nazi radicals who now sought, in the words of Hans Mommsen, the "realization of Utopia."[31]

Although Hitler's fixation on Lebensraum and intention to promote a "harsh racial struggle" in Poland had set the general direction of Nazi policy, surprisingly little practical consideration had been given to how to implement a comprehensive racial policy or to how best to "Germanize" this new Lebensraum. Such discussions began only in early September, with the resulting plans largely a consequence of two factors. The first was Hitler's characteristic method of ruling, in which he would set broad goals or the direction of policy and then allow his subordinates to compete among each other by submitting proposals for turning policy into reality, a process that quickly produced a manic dynamism as eager Nazis sought to prove themselves and gain a step up the career ladder. Moreover, these schemes tended to be highly ambitious, radical projects since no one was going to be punished for being too ruthless. The second key factor involved ongoing discussions with Soviet officials on a final delimitation of the spheres of interest in the Baltic region agreed on in the Nazi-Soviet Pact.[32]

As a result of the interplay of these two factors, by the end of September 1939 the Nazis had formulated a stunningly ambitious demographic scheme of racial reordering that involved millions of people. Though improvised at the time, these policies were fully consistent with Hitler's underlying ideological assumptions of the need to secure living space, life as a Darwinian struggle, the unequal racial value of ethnic populations, and a determination to solve the rapidly expanding Jewish problem. While, ultimately, the last of these obsessions came to dominate Nazi policy, in the autumn of 1939 securing and Germanizing the newly won living space clearly took precedence. Moreover, an agreement on 28 September between German and Soviet officials on a revision of their respective spheres of influence in the Baltic meant that Lithuania would now fall into the Soviet orbit. In exchange, however, the Germans secured the right to repatriate Volksdeutsche from the Soviet sphere. Nazi leaders now envisioned a comprehensive racial restructuring of Eastern Europe in which Germans would be consolidated in the newly annexed territories of formerly western Poland, Poles would be concentrated in a vassal state to the east, and Jews would be shoved to the outer reaches of the German domain. In order to make room for the resettlement of hundreds of thousands of ethnic Germans in West Prussia and the Wartheland, both former Polish provinces, the Nazis needed to clear the areas of their Polish and Jewish inhabitants. What had begun at the beginning of September as the intended liquidation of the Polish intelligentsia had now grown into a plan for the dispossession of millions of Poles. As Goebbels noted in his diary on 10 October, "The Führer's verdict on the Poles is devastating. More like animals than human beings."[33]

This question of living space was also inextricably connected with the search for a resolution to the Jewish question. Until 1939, the preferred Nazi solution for German Jews entailed emigration and occasional expulsion. The outbreak of war, however, changed the situation in fundamentally radical ways. Not only did the already diminishing avenues for emigration constrict even further, but the Nazis also now found themselves faced with an even greater problem. The spectacular military triumph in Poland left them with perhaps 2 million Jews under their control, a number that promised to overwhelm the already feeble strategy of emigration. Moreover, many Germans, especially young soldiers, for the first time encountered the seemingly alien eastern Jews, the *Ostjuden,* who had for years been the target of scurrilous Nazi propaganda. The reality, and staggering numbers, of these strange people seemed to confirm the Nazi message that they were the biological and spiritual antithesis of German culture. Finally, and of key significance, the outbreak of war both fueled party radicals and freed the Nazi leaders from various restraints in their handling of the Jewish problem. Hitler had long defined international Jewry as the enemy of Germany, and, now that the nation found itself in a war allegedly provoked by that same Jewish conspiracy, harsh measures against Jews under German control seemed necessary. Poland thus became, as Christopher Browning has put it, a "'laboratory' for Nazi experiments in racial imperialism, an area where [the Nazis] tried to turn into reality ideological slogans such as Lebensraum."[34] This process eventually involved much trial and error, and growing frustrations, before the Nazis settled on the Final Solution.

Even as the deportations of Poles and the resettlement of Volks-deutsche began in mid-October a host of problems ensued: Poles targeted for deportation were not provided the most basic necessities of life; German officials had not anticipated likely Polish resistance; Himmler's insistence on screening Poles for possible Germanization raised difficulties; and the whole operation threatened a serious disruption of economic life in the occupied territories. The latter objection, along with transportation shortages occasioned by the growing demands of army authorities for rolling stock to prepare the campaign in the west, resulted in a curbing of, if not a halt to, the deportations. Typical of the improvised nature of this demographic scheme, little thought had been given to what to do with the Jewish population of the affected areas. Nazi officials initially thought in terms of expelling them over the demarcation line between German- and Soviet-occupied Poland, then, after that idea failed, decided to place them in ghettos as a temporary measure until a final decision was made.[35]

While Poles could simply be dumped in the General Government, such a solution for Jews faced numerous obstacles, not least objections from Nazi occupation authorities such as Hans Frank. This oversight provided an opening for ambitious subordinates like Adolf Eichmann to find a more suitable long-term solution, which involved resettlement of Jews from the areas to be annexed into Germany to a reservation near Nisko in the Lublin district of southeast Poland. Concurrently with the resettlement actions under way elsewhere, Eichmann began organizing deportations of Jews. His plan foundered on many of the same difficulties as the other scheme, however, and by early 1940 the grand demographic projects had ground to a virtual standstill.[36] In characteristic fashion, the Nazis had tried to do everything at the same time, without assigning priorities, with the result that inadequate resources led to limited achievements. Along with their frustration, however, Nazi officials had gained valuable understanding of the problems involved in such a complicated scheme.

Events in Poland also demonstrated how Hitler's own radicalism could be reinforced through personal observations and contact with subordinates as well as how his prejudices could be exploited by officials pursuing ever more radical policies. Hitler's view of Jews as an active, predatory threat had certainly been intensified by his observations from Poland, but discussions with Goebbels that autumn fanned his anti-Jewish hatreds while allowing the latter an opportunity to regain the Führer's approval. Shortly after his humiliation in connection with Kristallnacht in November 1938, the propaganda minister had begun planning a series of films designed to instill and intensify anti-Jewish attitudes in the German public. Work had begun in 1939 on the notorious "documentary" film *Der ewige Jude* (The eternal Jew), which Goebbels intended as both a demonstration of the parasitical nature of the Jews and a justification for drastic measures against them.[37]

With the defeat of Poland, Goebbels seized the opportunity to have footage made of the detested Ostjuden in their habitat as well as to see the situation firsthand. His observations not only confirmed his own radical hatred of the Jews but exacerbated those of Hitler as well. In mid-October, Goebbels and Hitler viewed recent footage filmed in Warsaw, with the former's impression likely mirroring that of the latter: "Footage from the ghetto film. . . . Images so dreadful and brutal in their details that one's blood runs cold. . . . This Jewry must be destroyed." At the end of October, Goebbels once again viewed footage with Hitler, this time of ritual slaughter, scenes that left them "deeply shaken." A visit to Lodz a few days later only reinforced Goebbels's impressions while also emphasizing the connection in the Nazi mind between Lebensraum and the Jewish question: "Lodz itself is a hideous city. . . . Drive through the ghetto. We get out and inspect everything thoroughly. It is indescribable. They are no longer humans, they are animals. Therefore we no longer have a humanitarian but rather a surgical task. One must cut here, and indeed quite radically. Otherwise Europe will perish from the Jewish disease. . . . This is Asia already. We will have much to do to Germanize this area."[38]

Goebbels took pains to keep Hitler informed of the film's progress and of his own escalating radicalism, both of which the Führer approved. On 2 November, Goebbels exulted, "My explanation of the Jewish problem finds his complete agreement. The Jew is a waste product." On 19 November, he noted in his diary, "I inform the Führer about our Jew film. He gives some ideas for it. . . . The film is a very valuable propaganda medium for us just now." Finally, on 5 December, he reported more extensively to Hitler on his trip to Poland, recording with satisfaction, "He listens to everything very carefully and totally shares my opinion on the Jewish and Polish question. We must exorcize the Jewish danger."[39] If, in Ian Kershaw's famous formulation, Hitler's subordinates were clearly "working toward the Führer" in implementing racial policy, their own radicalism could, as the example of Goebbels showed, in turn inform and affect Hitler's views, reinforcing his radical ideological predispositions.

Despite this growing determination and enormous effort to engineer a New Order through vast demographic reorganization, Nazi policymakers faced an impasse by the spring of 1940. Hitler's frustration was evident by mid-March 1940. According to Walther Hewel, the Foreign Office liaison to Führer Headquarters: "The Jewish question really was a space question which was difficult to solve, particularly . . . since he had no space at his disposal." After dismissing the Lublin project as unsuitable, Hitler intimated that he "would welcome a positive solution to the Jewish question, if only he could indicate a solution. This, however, was not possible under present conditions when he had not even sufficient space for his own people."[40] Conditions were about to change, however, and in the stunning military triumph over France beckoned a possible "final solution" to the Jewish question. Ironically, however, just as the earlier victory over Poland had promised more, in demographic terms, than it delivered, similar frustrations were to follow the even more glorious victory over France.

In the event, however, beginning to realize the magnitude of their developing triumph, and intoxicated with success, top Nazis once again engaged in wild flights of imagination. The first to act was Himmler, always alert for possibilities to please his master and expand his own power. In mid-May 1940, he produced a manuscript, "Reflections on the Treatment of Peoples of Alien Races in the East," that again illustrated the connections in Nazi thinking between living space for Germans and a solution to the Jewish problem. Although much of his memo was a rehashing of Nazi plans for reclaiming and racially reordering Eastern Europe, in turning to the Jews Himmler expressed his "hope that the concept of Jews will be completely extinguished through the possibility of a large emigration of all Jews to Africa or some other colony." He then concluded that, however "cruel and tragic each individual case may be, this method is still the mildest and best one if, out of inner conviction, one rejects as un-German and impossible the Bolshevik method of physical extermination of a people." Having penned his statement of intent, Himmler waited for the proper moment to approach the Führer. This he did on 25 May, as the magnitude of German success in the western campaign was just sinking in, recording with great satisfaction, "The Führer read the six pages and considered them very good and correct."[41]

This document and this episode are instructive not only because they reveal something of the way racial policy was made: Hitler simply approved an initiative from Himmler, informed him with whom he should make contact, and then left the details of implementation to his subordinates. It is significant as well because it confirms that top Nazis such as Himmler were aware of the brutal methods of Stalin in the Soviet Union but that they themselves had not yet crossed the threshold to outright mass murder. The Nazis were grappling for a solution to their growing Jewish problem, but Himmler at least could not yet envisage one that entailed physical extermination. Still, his knowledge of these as yet unacceptable Bolshevik methods left open the possibility that, if other options failed, there remained the ultimate Final Solution.

With the triumph over France in sight, in early June 1940 Nazi planners in both the SS and the Foreign Office busied themselves with working out the details of what came to be known as the Madagascar Plan. As early as 3 June, an ambitious young official in the Foreign Office, Franz Rademacher, sought to clarify the key question, "Whereto with the Jews?" Rademacher essentially answered his own question by pointing to the island of Madagascar as a possible destination for a Jewish reservation. Since Nazi racial demographic plans in Poland had been stymied, Madagascar now loomed as a *Verlegenheitslösung,* a makeshift way out of a dilemma. When on 20 June Hitler indicated his intention to resettle European Jews in Madagascar, planning took on a furious intensity. The seriousness with which the operation was regarded can be seen in the swift move that Heydrich made to assert control of it for the SS. On 24 June, he wrote Foreign Minister Ribbentrop to remind him in no uncertain terms that in January 1939 Goering had placed him in charge of Jewish emigration from all German territory, a mandate that the head of the Reichssicherheitshauptamt (RSHA) meant to preserve. As word spread of the latest solution to their self-imposed Jewish problem, planners and bureaucrats throughout the Nazi Empire set to work sorting out the implications and details of the plan.[42]

Nor was this merely an empty planning exercise. Goebbels recorded in his diary on 26 July 1940, "[A] great plan for the evacuation of the Jews from Berlin has been approved. For the rest, all remaining Jews of Europe are to be deported after the war to Madagascar." As late as 17 August, Goebbels still believed this solution to be operative, first noting harsh measures to be taken against enemies of the state, then remarking, "Later we will ship the Jews off to Madagascar. There they can build their own state."[43] For all the Nazis' hopes and expectations, however, by the late summer it had become clear that the Madagascar Plan had foundered on an insurmountable hurdle: as long as Great Britain remained in the war, the Germans had neither the means nor the opportunity to deport millions of Jews to the distant island. Once again, military triumphs had compounded the Jewish problem by adding more Jews to the German Empire and raised the possibility of a territorial solution, only to result in a frustrating dead end.

In the year since the beginning of the war, Nazi planners had sought to engineer a demographic reorganization of the German sphere based on racial principles, only to be stymied by circumstances. The connection between the war and developing racial policy was clear, if frustrating: military triumphs brought the possibility of Lebensraum along with the nightmare of millions of "alien peoples" under German occupation. Moreover, the Jewish problem had mushroomed in scale. Where his original intent had been to free Germany from the alleged Jewish yoke, Hitler now perceived the need for a European-wide solution. The Nazis, however, increasingly came to understand that they could not effect a final solution to the Jewish problem because they could not end the war, and every effort at a suitable interim solution ended in frustration. These false starts with possible interim solutions, however, provided valuable practical experience in matters such as transportation, logistics, and deception that would later be applied in a more sinister environment. The clear trend in Nazi racial policy was in the direction of a steady radicalization. While Hitler provided the general direction and aims, his subordinates scrambled in a frantic example of "institutional Darwinism" to win his favor, with each impasse prompting the consideration of ever more radical schemes. The Nazis were clearly feeling their way in a process of trial and error, but each successive stage resulted in more ruthless and expansive racial plans than the one before. As summer 1940 gave way to autumn, Rademacher's earlier question, "Whereto with the Jews?" remained as vexing as ever.

"What now?" That had been Hitler's comment on hearing the news of the British declaration of war on 3 September. The German-Soviet Non-aggression Pact of 23 August—that pact "with Satan in order to drive the devil out"—had failed in its central purpose of preventing an Anglo-French intervention, but it had provided Hitler the protection and resources he needed to make quick work of Poland. After a desultory peace offer to Britain and France on 6 October, which he likely never expected to succeed, Hitler answered his own question with an insistence on an attack in the west as soon as possible since Germany could proceed in the east only when its borders in the west had been secured. "Time," Hitler asserted in late September, "will in general work against us when we do not use it effectively. The economic means of the other side are stronger. . . . Time does not work for us in the military sense either." In making this judgment, Hitler looked to the east as well as the west, for he now found himself in the uncomfortable position of economic and strategic dependence on the one state whose destruction was key to his ideology. Russia, he remarked to his top commanders a few weeks later, would remain "dangerous in the future." While "shocking reports" of Soviet actions in Poland confirmed Hitler's belief in the destructiveness of Jewish-Bolshevism, the manifest deficiencies of the Red Army in the autumn of 1939 seemed to make apparent the "catastrophic condition" of this "gigantic colossus." Germany, therefore, had a brief window of opportunity that had to be exploited. What Hitler had in mind in October 1939, however, in no way resembled what eventually resulted: a rapid and brilliant blitzkrieg rout of his Western enemies. Instead, he envisioned simply a limited operation to push the western armies out of the Low Countries and northeastern France, seize the Channel ports, and make Germany less vulnerable to Allied counterattack.[44] This would then allow him to turn his attention back to the east.

Even that limited scenario, however, horrified his generals. Acutely aware of Germany's economic difficulties, raw materials shortages, and military deficiencies, they had risked everything in throwing virtually all German military force against Poland. That gamble had succeeded thanks to French inaction, but the French certainly would not remain passive in the face of a direct German assault. Having witnessed first-hand in World War I the tough fighting qualities of the French soldier, virtually all German commanders agreed that Hitler's ideas were a recipe for disaster. The army would need months of refitting and retraining before it was again ready for action, almost half of its soldiers were over the age of forty, and a desperate shortage of equipment limited its striking power. To take just one example, motor vehicles were in such short supply that Halder suggested a "demotorization program" that entailed a "drastic and ruthless restriction of motor vehicles in existing and newly activated units." Amazingly, with the spectacular blitzkrieg success looming, the chief of staff of the German army proposed that the horse take the place of the engine. Nor could the shortages be made good quickly since the German armament and economic mobilization plans had been based on the assumption that the war in the west would be a repeat of the attrition struggle of World War I. Only in October 1940 would a significant increase in production be achieved, with maximum levels of output not projected until the autumn of 1941. Nowhere in these economic plans can one detect a clear tactical or strategic blitzkrieg concept.[45]

From the German perspective, the situation appeared gloomy in the extreme. One leading expert, in fact, has likened the Wehrmacht in the autumn of 1939 to a "lance whose point consisted of hard steel, but [whose] wooden shaft looked . . . ever more brittle." Hitler's generals, aware of their inferiority in both quantity and quality of weapons, numbers of soldiers, and economic preparation, were virtually unanimous in their rejection of an immediate attack in the west, which they considered tantamount to suicide. Colonel-General Walter von Reichenau, widely considered to be a "Nazi general," called an attack in the autumn of 1939 "just about criminal," while the head of the Oberkommando der Wehrmacht (OKW), the otherwise obsequious Wilhelm Keitel, regarded the idea as so crazy that he offered his resignation. An autumn attack on France so distressed Halder that he, not for the first time, sounded out like-minded individuals about the possibility of a coup d'état. Following a stormy meeting on 5 November with Brauchitsch, the head of the OKH (Oberkommando des Heeres, or Army High Command), at which Hitler berated the defeatism of his generals and raged against the sabotage emanating from the army command, Halder panicked and had all incriminating plans destroyed. Still, the situation seemed so desperate that he toyed with the idea of assassinating the Führer. "Amid tears," a close associate noted later in his diary, "Halder said that he had for weeks had a pistol in his pocket every time he went to Emil [the plotters' code name for Hitler] in order possibly to gun him down."[46] In the end, however, Halder lost his nerve and could not bring himself to violate his soldier's oath of personal loyalty.

In the event, a combination of bad weather and Hitler's own doubts about the original plan of attack led to a postponement of the assault on France until the following spring. During the course of the long winter, the so-called Phony War, or *Sitzkrieg*, German plans changed substantially. Despite considerable opposition among top commanders, the audacious idea of General Erich von Manstein, chief of staff of Army Group A, to send motorized units in a surprise attack through the Ardennes in order to cut off the enemy's main body of troops began to gain converts. First General Heinz Guderian, the leading German tank expert, and then Halder himself embraced Manstein's plan. Since Hitler had been thinking, albeit in vague tactical terms, along similar lines, he also proved an enthusiastic supporter of the conception.

The brilliance with which Operation Sichelschnitt (Sickle Cut) unfolded in May and June 1940 has obscured several key points that accounted for its success. The decisive German victory resulted not from a premeditated strategy of blitzkrieg eagerly embraced by Wehrmacht leaders, but in spite of their doubts, hesitations, and obstructions. Indeed, the plan worked largely as a result of the calculated insubordination of the leading panzer general, Guderian, and the willingness of Halder to take enormous risks. In operational terms, Sickle Cut depended for success on the all-or-nothing gamble of concentrating all available German forces at the key *Schwerpunkt* (focal point of an attack) for a decisive knockout blow and counting on the enemy cooperating by doing as he should. In strategic terms, it represented the ultimate risk: the German nightmare of being strangled in a slow war of attrition would be resolved with a single throw of the dice. Win, and Germany would break free of the specter of encirclement and blockade; lose, and the result would be catastrophe. Far from being the result of a rational plan of blitzkrieg strategy that would enable Germany to achieve Lebensraum in a series of small wars, Sickle Cut was an act of operational expediency designed to extract Germany from an economically and strategically desperate situation. The country had gone to war in 1939 seriously short of raw materials and unprepared economically to sustain a long war; success in the west had bought needed time.[47]

Although initially planned or projected not as a blitzkrieg operation but as a conventional conflict similar to the Great War, the unexpected victory over France had significant consequences for German thinking. The new Greater Germany now constituted a formidable economic bloc, but, once the initial elation wore off, German economic planners realized that the area under their control suffered from serious deficiencies and was not the self-sufficient Lebensraum that Hitler desired. Foremost among these deficiencies, and almost perversely designed to rekindle nightmares of blockade and crippling shortages, were shortfalls in foodstuffs and energy. Despite their conquest of an area rich in skilled labor, technology, and sophisticated industrial plant, the Germans found themselves starved of food, coal, and oil. The food requirements of some 25 million people had to be imported, and that was just the peacetime deficit: the British blockade was bound to aggravate the situation, especially since food supplies were already running short in 1940. One bad harvest, the Nazis feared, could again trigger unrest and defeatism on the order of 1917–1918. Far from being blockade proof, Nazi war economists realized, Western Europe lacked a "spare feeding capacity."[48]

While their short-term gains had been immense, particularly in terms of war booty seized from the French, Nazi authorities found themselves faced with the task of supplying not only the needs of Germany but also those of the allied and occupied areas. Ironically, rather than immediately reaping the economic benefits of conquest, the Nazis were forced to export oil, coal, and foodstuffs from outside Germany. The most persistent and troubling shortage continued to be in oil, although the dire food situation in the fall and winter of 1940–1941 raised fears of unrest in the occupied urban centers. In economic terms, the Wehrmacht's great victory in 1940 had not released it from dependence on deliveries from the Soviet Union, nor had it given the Greater German Reich resources comparable to those of the British Empire or the United States.[49]

Strategically and operationally, however, the situation looked rather different. After the triumph in the west, a blitzkrieg myth emerged; once again, as in the days before World War I, German military thinkers began to believe that quick, operational victories could solve the nation's strategic dilemma. Perhaps Lebensraum could be achieved without fighting bloody wars of attrition after all. Only one problem remained: for all the celebration surrounding the defeat of France, the other enemy, Great Britain, stubbornly refused to come to terms. This obstinacy, moreover, now threatened a fundamental alteration in the balance of power in Europe, a change Hitler began to perceive during the summer of 1940. The fall of France, far from ensuring German hegemony on the Continent, turned a European conflict into a potential world war as both the United States and the Soviet Union emerged as key factors. For Britain, survival as a great power required continuing in the war. Doing so, however, meant enlisting the support of the United States and perhaps eventually that of the Soviet Union as well. In any case, Stalin had already moved quickly to take advantage of his leverage vis-à-vis Germany in Eastern Europe. Such a scenario clearly posed a problem for the Third Reich.[50] Despite its spectacular military triumph of the spring, Nazi Germany still faced a strategic, economic, and racial impasse. Hitler, in Paris, had been correct: the war was not yet ended.

2

Decision

At 3:00 P.M. on 6 July 1940, under a glittering early summer sun, an unadorned train pulled slowly into the Anhalter Bahnhof in Berlin amid scenes of jubilation and pure joy unequaled in German history. People had been gathering in the flower-strewn streets of the capital since early morning, many waiting over six hours for a chance to glimpse the Führer. "An unimaginable excitement filled the city," exulted Joseph Goebbels in his diary, overcome by the festive mood of the "sea of humanity" that thronged the avenues. After a short discussion with Goering, who feared a British air attack on the city, Goebbels exclaimed, "Then the Führer arrived. A wild enthusiasm filled the train station. The Führer is deeply moved. Tears come to his eyes. . . . The storm of jubilation of a completely joyous people is indescribable. The Führer drove [to the Reich Chancellery] completely over flowers." Once there, as Field Marshal Keitel lauded him as "the greatest military commander of all time," Hitler soaked in the adulation of the wildly cheering throng below. For perhaps the only time during the Third Reich, Germans evinced a genuine enthusiasm for the war, sensing as they did that final victory was at hand.[1]

Even at this moment of ultimate triumph, however, disquieting notes of uneasiness intruded, as evidenced by Goering's fears. Goebbels also betrayed a host of concerns nestled amid the triumphalism. "Even in Germany we have rather too much as too little optimism," he wrote on 9 June. "One takes the victory too lightly." Throughout this period of historic triumph, in fact, the propaganda minister kept an anxious eye on the two peripheral powers of great concern, noting both American attitudes and Russian actions. Above all, he took note of the inflammatory reports of the "Jewish press" in America designed to create, in his opinion, an atmosphere of hate toward Germany that would force President

Roosevelt, whom he regarded as a stooge of the alleged Jewish conspiracy, to intervene in European affairs. The rapid German triumph, however, eased his fears of direct American action against Germany, at least until after the November presidential election.[2]

Stalin was another matter. Although Goebbels conceded that the Soviet dictator had remained faithful to the spirit of the Nazi-Soviet Pact by rejecting British overtures in late May, he still brooded over his further actions in the Baltic and the Balkans. Goebbels noted anxiously on 16 June, "Lithuania has received a Russian ultimatum. . . . The Lithuanian answer did not satisfy Moscow. Russian troops marching into Lithuania." Although Goebbels accepted with seeming equanimity Soviet demands on Latvia and Estonia and the growing pressure on Rumania to cede the provinces of Bessarabia and Bukovina, his tone changed in July as he realized just how thoroughly Stalin meant to benefit from German success in the west. "Slavism is spreading across the entire Balkans. Stalin is utilizing the moment," he recorded on 5 July. He then added ominously, "Perhaps later we will once again have to take action against the Soviets." In late July, on receiving news of the Soviet absorption of the Baltic states, Goebbels conceded grudgingly, "That is our price for Russia's neutrality," a price that seemed too costly. Add to these concerns growing irritations over persistent food and fuel shortages, the increasingly pesky nightly British air raids, and frustrations at the inability to solve the Jewish problem, and Goebbels's diary presented a surprisingly gloomy view of the situation in the summer of 1940.[3]

The German victory in the west had unquestioningly unleashed a wave of optimism, a feeling, as Goebbels put it, that "a new Europe is in being." Despite this and his own newly confirmed opinion of his own genius, Hitler himself appeared uncertain and unsure how to proceed, especially since Great Britain continued to display a determination to fight on. "From all that he says it is clear that he wants to act quickly to end it," noted Count Ciano, the Italian foreign minister, in his diary, adding astutely, "Hitler is now the gambler who has made a big scoop and would like to get up from the table risking nothing more." The problem, however, was how to exit the game while ahead. Indeed, Goebbels admitted warily, "With England we still have a tough nut to crack." On 29 June, the propaganda minister declared that "the decision whether war or peace must come soon" but conceded, "The Führer is not yet clear . . . whether he should develop a constructive peace program." Goebbels again recorded Hitler's doubts on 2 July: "He wants to speak to the Reichstag and give England one last chance. Would it then be accepted? Churchill probably not. . . . But perhaps other understanding elements."

Goebbels then noted, "But the Führer does not want to destroy the empire, for all that would be lost would in all probability not fall to us but to other foreign powers. . . . Therefore the Führer must make the effort and give England a last chance. . . . Where it might lead, no one knows."[4]

Hitler seemed genuinely disconcerted by British defiance, both ambivalent and frustrated at the course of events. Even though he had lost his gamble in 1939 on Great Britain staying out of the war, he refused to believe that his earlier assessment of the British could be so wrong and, thus, clung stubbornly to the conviction that they would soon "see reason" and agree to peace. On any number of occasions, and to a host of associates, he expressed his preference for peace with the English instead of a continuation of the war. Churchill's actions, however, especially the British attack on the French fleet at Mers-el-Kebir on 3 July, forced Hitler to delay his speech, which he had just about finished, and reconsider his options. His uncertainty was reflected in a long talk with Goebbels five days later. Even as Hitler detailed postwar plans for the Germanization of Europe, the harsh treatment of France, and a new colonial policy, he vacillated with regard to Great Britain. "Despite everything the Führer still has a very positive attitude toward England," remarked Goebbels. "He is not yet ready for the final blow. He wants to think over his speech again in peace so will go to the Obersalzberg. . . . If London rejects our last offer, then it will immediately be dealt a destructive blow." Despite this outburst of bravado, however, Hitler continued to procrastinate and characteristically shrank from making a decision, much to Goebbels's growing frustration. Not until 16 July did Hitler inform Goebbels that he intended to deliver his long-awaited speech to the Reichstag on Friday, 19 July.[5]

In the meantime, Hitler summoned his military leaders to the Berghof for talks about the possibility of an invasion of Great Britain should his peace offer be rejected. On the eleventh, Admiral Raeder insisted that a landing could be attempted only if the Luftwaffe secured aerial superiority over southern England, while, the next day, Jodl laid out operational planning for any such invasion. The following day, Franz Halder, chief of the Army General Staff, journeyed to the mountaintop to brief the Führer, where he too discovered that Hitler regarded a landing as a last resort. "The Führer is greatly puzzled by Britain's persistent unwillingness to make peace," he noted in his diary on 13 July. "He sees the answer as we do in Britain's hope on Russia, and therefore counts on having to compel her by main force to agree to peace. Actually that is much against his grain . . . [since] a military defeat of Britain will bring about the disintegration of the British Empire. This would not be of any benefit to Germany. German blood would be shed to accomplish something that would benefit only Japan, the United States, and others."[6]

This halfheartedness revealed itself again on the sixteenth when Hitler issued Directive No. 16, "Preparations for a Landing Operation against England," a document that contained so many qualifications that it convinced many of his top commanders that he never seriously intended an invasion. Indeed, Hitler told Goering in confidence that he never meant to carry out the operation. In order to launch an invasion of Britain, Germany needed control of the Channel both by air and by sea. To those around him, it seemed clear that, given the strength of the British navy and the crippling of the already weak German navy by the Norwegian operation in April, Hitler regarded the risk of an invasion as unacceptably high. Instead, he would put his hopes in his peace proposal.[7]

Perhaps Hitler never really expected the British to accept his offer, vague and imprecise as it was. The greatest part of a very long speech, over two hours, was, in fact, devoted to boasting about German military triumphs and praising the accomplishments of German commanders, a number of whom gained promotions. This latter was just as disingenuous as his peace proposal since Hitler believed that the army leadership had been found seriously wanting and that his own judgment had once more been proved correct. Only at the end did he make his brief appeal to common sense, declaring that his conscience forced him to offer the British one last chance to end a war that had no purpose. William Shirer, observing Hitler, thought it one of his best speeches:

> The Hitler we saw in the Reichstag tonight was the conqueror, and conscious of it. . . . [H]e mixed superbly the full confidence of the conqueror with the humbleness which always goes down so well with the masses. . . . His voice was lower tonight; he rarely shouted as he usually does. . . . I've often admired the way he uses his hands. . . . Tonight he used those hands beautifully, seemed to express himself almost as much with his hands . . . as he did with his words. . . . I noticed too his gift for using his face and eyes . . . and the turn of his head for irony, of which there was considerable in tonight's speech.

The great irony, which Shirer understood very well, was that Hitler offered peace not in the expectation that Churchill would accept, but to justify to the German people, who longed for it, the continuation of the war. He had given the British the choice; if they now rejected his offer, the war would go on, and it would be England's fault.[8]

The British rejection came swiftly, within the hour, although even now Hitler seemed puzzled by the English attitude and could not quite bring himself to accept it. Although the British had acquiesced in German expansion in 1938, the situation in 1940 differed markedly: making peace on Hitler's terms now meant recognition of German hegemony on the Continent and the likely end of Britain as a major power. Still, as Goebbels noted, "At the moment the Führer cannot bring himself to accept the British answer."[9] Once again, a British decision had confounded Hitler and confronted him with a dilemma. After he had blundered into war in 1939, the brilliant German military victories had seemed to offer a way out of his strategic, economic, and political impasse. The Germans, however, had only conquered their way into a strategic cul-de-sac, as their victories in 1940 had not secured hegemony in Europe. Now, faced with mounting time pressures from the Anglo-American powers in the west and growing concerns over German dependence on the Soviet Union in the east, Hitler had once more to make a decision.

The key question to be answered regarding Hitler's decision for war with the Soviet Union is not so much why he chose to attack the Soviet Union—Lebensraum in the east, after all, formed the linchpin of his ideology—as why he chose to attack when he did. Why risk a two-front war at a time when the pact with the Soviet Union had essentially made Germany blockade proof? Why not dispose of Great Britain first, leaving his rear secured for any future action against Russia? And why the seeming urgency in the last week of July, after the failure of his peace overture, to come to a decision? Certainly, his underlying motivation, as it had been since the mid-1920s, was ideological. His entire program depended on securing living space in the east and dealing a death blow to the Jewish-Bolshevik conspiracy allegedly threatening Germany's existence. A successful attack on the Soviet Union would not only destroy the power of the Jews but also procure for Germany the resources necessary ultimately to challenge the United States for world supremacy. Additionally, a Nazi-dominated Europe would allow Hitler the utopian opportunity to create a racially purified empire and solve the Jewish question for all time.

Originally, Hitler had expected to accomplish this task with Britain as an ally, but, even though British obstinacy forced him to make a detour through Western Europe, he retained a consistent focus on the east. As numerous conversations with Goebbels illustrated, Soviet actions in Poland and in the Winter War against Finland confirmed his racist hatreds, contempt, and determination to prevent the spread of the "Jewish virus" into Western Europe. When in a January 1940 letter Mussolini chastised him for losing sight of his anti-Bolshevik mission, Hitler replied that "only a bitter compulsion" had caused him to cooperate "with this country." The pact with Russia, Hitler reminded the *duce,* was merely a tactical and economic necessity until he had safeguarded his rear in the west. For the rest, "Germany and Russia were two [alien] worlds." Indeed, since late October 1939, Hitler had made no secret of his intention to turn German forces eastward. Above all, he was preoccupied with his two great tasks: achieving space for the German nation and the final confrontation with Bolshevism. Within days of the armistice with France, Hitler told his Wehrmacht adjutant, Colonel Schmundt, and Foreign Minister Ribbentrop that he was playing "with the idea of leading a war against Russia."[10]

The ten days from the failure of his peace offer to the end of July 1940 appear to have been the crucial period during which Hitler conceived the idea of an actual attack on the Soviet Union, with a number of nonideological considerations influencing him. Interestingly, it was not Hitler but Halder who apparently first began to think in concrete terms of action against the Soviet Union. At the end of June, the army chief of staff had been briefed by State Secretary Ernst von Weizsäcker on the political situation and Hitler's increasing focus on the east. Halder was a close disciple of his predecessor, General Ludwig Beck, and shared his mentor's staunch anti-Bolshevism and fear that the Nazi-Soviet Pact had opened the way for increased Soviet influence in Eastern Europe and the Balkans. Soviet troop movements and pressure on the Baltic states and Rumania evidently caused alarm in army leaders, even as Hitler momentarily regarded them as nothing more than irritations. The ink was barely dry on the armistice with France when, on 30 June, without direct instructions from Hitler, Halder ordered his staff to study the possibility of a campaign against Russia. Increasingly, too, he saw a connection between British obstinacy and the problem of Russia, with the latter being the key to the attitude of the former.[11]

In view of the Red Army's assertiveness in Eastern Europe, Halder saw the need for "striking power in the east" and, thus, ordered German units transferred to new staging areas in Poland. On 3 July, he requested an examination of the "requirements of a military intervention which will compel Russia to recognize Germany's dominant position in Europe." At this point, he envisaged a limited preventive strike that would reduce the Soviet Union to a second-rate power and secure for Germany much of the same territory conquered in World War I: the Baltic states, Ukraine, and White Russia. Halder's actions sprang not only from his own anti-Bolshevism and fear that Stalin meant to exploit German preoccupation in the west but also from his assessment that London's attitude rested on hopes in Russia. British obstinacy raised the distinct possibility of a protracted war of attrition and the alarming threat of a repetition of the enemy coalition of 1917. A blow against the Soviet Union would presumably end London's hopes of continuing the war and alleviate German concerns.[12]

Hitler evidently had not yet come to such definitive conclusions. In June, he still expected to reap the fruits of his great military victory over France, including a peace that would leave Germany dominant on the Continent. His anticipation of a global settlement with the British can be seen in his decision in mid-June to disband thirty-nine divisions and reduce the army to its peacetime strength, which would release some 500,000 men for the armaments industry. He also accorded both the Luftwaffe and the navy priority in armaments production, which hardly indicated any intention to launch an immediate war against Russia. Once again, it was Halder who seemed to have his eyes turned to the east. Given the reduced role for the army in the west, on 25 June Halder ordered his staff to study the restructuring of the army with the goal of creating highly mobile "special defense groups" to counter any possible Soviet moves in the Balkans or threats to the important Rumanian oil fields. As thoughts turned to a preventive strike, these mobile forces became the spearheads for a German offensive operation. Ironically, on the same day Halder ordered his study, Hitler had remarked optimistically, "The war in the west has ended . . . and I shall come, in the shortest possible time, to an understanding with England. There still remains the conflict with the east. That, however, is a task which throws up worldwide problems. . . . One might perhaps tackle it in ten years' time. . . . Now we have our hands full digesting and consolidating what we have obtained in Europe."[13] At the end of June, then, Hitler seems not yet to have turned his eyes firmly toward the east.

What changed the Führer's mind? Clearly, the failure of the peace offer played a role, as did growing concerns about Russian and American actions. On 21 July, apparently clinging to the illusory hope that a peace party in Britain would even now alter Churchill's course, Hitler still wavered on what to do, according to notes in Halder's diary: "No clear picture on what is happening in Britain. Preparations for a decision by arms must be completed as quickly as possible. The Führer will not let the military-political initiative go out of his hand. As soon as situation becomes clear, political and diplomatic procedures will take its place." Hitler, however, understood that the situation was not likely to clear anytime soon. A cross-Channel attack seemed "very hazardous to the Führer. On that account invasion is to be undertaken only if no other way is left to bring terms with Britain." Why, however, did England hold out? To Hitler, the answer seemed obvious: "Hope for a change in America. . . . Puts hope in Russia. . . . Create trouble in the Balkans through Russia, to cut us off from our fuel source." Nor did he doubt that the Soviet dictator hoped for a prolonged war in the west: "Stalin is flirting with Britain to keep her in the war and tie us down, with a view to gain time and take what he wants. . . . He has an interest in not letting Germany get too strong."[14]

But what could be done, especially since Hitler had declared the prerequisites for Operation Sea Lion, the invasion of Great Britain, to be absolute command of the air and sea, both of which had to be achieved by the beginning of September? Since this appeared doubtful at best, how was Britain to be subdued? Frankly, Hitler had no good answer. He pondered forming "a solid political front, Spain, Italy, Russia," against it, then seemed to put his hopes once again on the Luftwaffe and the navy: "air assaults and submarine warfare . . . smash enemy fighter strength . . . combined with intensified submarine warfare." He also speculated on promoting opposition to Churchill by encouraging an English peace party thought to be forming around David Lloyd George and the Duke of Windsor. Only lastly was mention made of the possibility of "tackling the Russian problem" in the autumn, as Brauchitsch outlined for Hitler the hastily conceived army plan:

Object: To crush Russian army or at least take as much Russian territory as is necessary to bar enemy air raids on Berlin and Silesian industries. . . .

Political aims: Ukrainian state; federation of Baltic states; White Russia. . . .

Strength required: Eighty to one hundred divisions. Russia has fifty to seventy-five good divisions. If we attack Russia this fall, pressure of air war on Britain will be relieved. United States could supply both Britain and Russia.

Operations: What operational objective could be attained. . . ?

Protect Berlin and Silesian industrial area. Protection of Rumanian oil fields.

Clearly, the main theme at this conference was how to proceed against
Great Britain, with discussion only belatedly turning to military action
against Russia. Significantly, however, the earlier notion of a spoiling
action seemed to have expanded; even if what was presented to Hitler
was not the blueprint for a war of extermination, it was hardly a "limited
war," given territorial aims reminiscent of those obtained by the Treaty
of Brest-Litovsk that would both secure vital raw materials for the Reich
and force Russia to acknowledge German hegemony.[15]

At this 21 July conference, then, the alternatives available at the
moment—the invasion of Britain or an attack on the Soviet Union—were
both raised and discussed. Hitler, however, doubted that either operation could succeed. He pointed out the great risk of failure of a cross-
Channel assault, noting that it was "not just a river crossing, but the
crossing of a sea dominated by the enemy," and responded to the proposal of an autumn attack on Russia with skeptical questions. Shortly
after the conference, in fact, Jodl and Keitel had to admit that time,
space, and weather factors rendered an autumn attack "totally imprac-
ticable." Ironically, Halder, too, had succumbed to doubts. The latest
estimates of Soviet strength proved far higher than expected, while Italian difficulties in North Africa signaled a possible drain on German
resources. As a result, Halder now put greater emphasis on knocking
Britain out of the war before plunging ahead in the east. Indeed, on 30
July, he and Brauchitsch agreed that it would be better to remain "on
terms of friendship with Russia" and concentrate instead on attacking
British positions in the Mediterranean and the Middle East.[16]

In reality, Hitler faced an impasse, unable to end the war against
England, and fretting as the military-political initiative slipped away.
Moreover, considerations of possible Russian and American actions, and
the threat they posed to Germany, increasingly preoccupied the Führer: Great Britain had to be gotten out of the war in order to prevent
the United States and Russia from entering. The intensifying American
support for England, and its surging military potential, introduced a
crucial time factor into Hitler's calculations: if he was to realize his goal
of Lebensraum in the east, he needed to do so quickly. In mid-May, even
as German panzers raced to the sea, President Roosevelt had put before
Congress a proposal, swiftly approved, for an enormous expansion of
American military power; the result would be that by 1941 the United
States, while still neutral, produced virtually as much war materiel

as either Great Britain or Germany. Nor were the Germans unaware against whom this military might was ultimately to be directed. From the summer of 1940, Goebbels stepped up anti-American propaganda, with a sharp focus on the alleged Jewish dominance in Washington and the determination of the Jewish conspiracy to exterminate the German nation. Significantly, on the same day that Hitler delivered his peace offer, Roosevelt was nominated for a third term at the Democratic Party's convention in Chicago. This was "a blow to Hitler," William Shirer noted, "which the Wilhelmstrasse scarcely hid. . . . Hitler fears Roosevelt. He is just beginning to comprehend that Roosevelt's support of Great Britain is one of the prime reasons why the British decline to accept his kind of peace. . . . [To the Germans] Roosevelt is the father of English illusions about the war."[17]

To Hitler, however, it was no illusion; Britain would go on as long as Roosevelt provided it with massive material aid. Measures such as the destroyers-for-bases deal in September 1940, which seemed to confirm the creation of an Anglo-American coalition, and Lend-Lease in March 1941, which the German leadership regarded as a virtual declaration of war, simply confirmed Hitler in his determination to solve his strategic problem before American power irretrievably tipped the scales against Germany.[18] Hitler now faced a decision. The United States would not be ready for active military intervention until 1942; Germany thus had a brief window of opportunity that had to be seized if it was to secure the resources necessary for the looming confrontation with America. In 1940, Germany stood at the height of its military strength vis-à-vis its enemies and for the near term possessed virtual freedom from the reality of a two-front war, so, if Hitler meant to realize his goal of Lebensraum in the east, the time for action was at hand.

Economic pressures also contributed to Hitler's sense of urgency, in addition to reinforcing his notions of the absolute necessity of securing living space in Eastern Europe. The situation in the summer of 1940, in fact, resembled that of 1914–1918, when Germany was defeated because of deficiencies in raw materials and foodstuffs. Starvation as yet was not a problem, but, by the fall of 1940, grain stockpiles would be exhausted. Although Germany had derived short-term economic advantages from the alliance with the Soviet Union, the occupation of Western Europe and the threat of a drawn-out war meant that Russia's willingness to supply food and raw materials was crucial. Increasingly, too, the Germans expected that Moscow would exact a high price for such deliveries, certainly highly valued industrial and military goods, perhaps even hegemony in Eastern and Southeastern Europe. For his part, Stalin, in line with his notion that a protracted war of attrition between the capitalist powers would benefit the Soviet Union, had always intended to derive the greater advantage from the economic relationship with Germany, both to promote Soviet expansive aims and to force the Germans to provide vital goods and technology. The Germans got a first glimpse of Stalin's willingness to use his new leverage six weeks before the start of the offensive in the west, when the Soviet Union temporarily suspended vital oil and grain deliveries. Although the situation had been quickly resolved, Germany now found itself in a far greater measure of economic dependence on the Soviet Union than anticipated, a dependence that was likely to increase the longer the war continued.[19]

German reliance on Soviet grain supplies, which could only rekindle anxious memories of the hunger blockade of 1914–1918, proved especially stressful. Hitler's economic experts also made him aware that, in any protracted war against Great Britain and the United States, which seemed increasingly likely, Germany would need vastly greater deliveries of food and raw materials from the Soviet Union, a prospect that seemed to invite an inexorably deeper dependence. This Hitler simply could not tolerate. The Führer agreed with his economics minister, Walter Funk, that the "greater German economic sphere [Großraumwirtschaft]" could not "become dependent on forces or powers over which we have no influence." Equally troublesome was the German inability to force Russia into the role originally assigned it, that of a supply source for the Reich economy. Both the massive buildup of Soviet armaments and the autarkic direction of the Russian economy represented a long-term threat to Germany. By the summer of 1940, in fact, it had become doubtful whether, given the increasing consumption of raw materials and foodstuffs within the Soviet Union, Stalin could or would make large quantities available to Germany. Ironically, besieged Great Britain had largely secured the economic resources it needed to continue the war; for Hitler, the question remained to be answered.[20]

Fearful of Soviet blackmail, and sensitive to threats to their vital supplies of oil and other key raw materials, German officials increasingly viewed Soviet actions in Eastern Europe with alarm. Since Germany absorbed most of the agricultural exports of the Baltic countries and Rumanian oil was absolutely vital to the German war economy, Soviet moves in these areas were at best inconvenient and at worst, as the German Foreign Office noted, "a serious danger for us in so far as these essential supplies are concerned." With Western Europe insufficient as a source of Lebensraum and serious fuel and food shortages looming in the occupied areas, German officials realized anew that only the Soviet

Union possessed the raw materials needed to sustain the war economy. The economic arguments for action in the east were made explicit in a 28 July memorandum by Rear Admiral Fricke, "Observations on Russia." In it, he stressed that Germany's security required "the most self-sufficient economy possible, especially with regard to commodities vital in war." These materials were to be found in sufficient quantities only in Russia. For Fricke, moreover, "the strong economic pressure" emanating from Germany's giant neighbor, its threatening economic position in the Baltic and Southeastern Europe, and "the spirit of Bolshevism" compelled Germany to liquidate "this chronic danger."[21]

Whether Hitler ever saw Fricke's memo is uncertain, although Raeder likely outlined its main ideas for him. In any case, he had long believed in the necessity of territorial expansion in the east. By late July 1940, then, the logic of the strategic, military, economic, and political situation seemed to be pointing in one direction: an attack on the Soviet Union. The increasing frustration at the stalemate with Great Britain, concern over growing American power, and fear of losing the military-political initiative resulted in a self-imposed time pressure in Hitler's mind: time was not on his side, as the enemies of Germany were growing stronger daily, so a decision one way or another had to be made. To the Führer, a strike eastward offered the tantalizing possibility of solving all Germany's problems simultaneously. Economically, the dream of Lebensraum would be fulfilled; politically, a fatal blow would be struck at Jewish-Bolshevism; and, strategically, Britain's last two hopes would be eliminated. Not only would Russia be annihilated, but the resultant increase in Japanese power in the Pacific would also force the United States to turn its attention away from Europe. Deprived of its twin swords, Britain would have no choice but to make peace. Less than a week after the inconclusive conference on 21 July, Hitler informed Jodl of his decision to launch a surprise attack on the Soviet Union at the earliest possible moment, May 1941, in order "once and for all" to eliminate the Bolshevik danger from the world. War with the Soviet Union was unavoidable, Hitler remarked, so it was better to have it now, at the height of German power, than to wait. The next day, economic officials briefed Hitler on the mounting problems facing Germany, which merely confirmed the Führer in his decision.[22]

When Hitler called Field Marshal Brauchitsch, General Halder, Admiral Raeder, Field Marshal Keitel, and General Jodl to a gathering at the Berghof on the last day in July, then, he intended not to ask their advice but to inform them of the decision he had made. Ironically, much of the conference was devoted to an intense discussion of Operation Sea

Lion. While army leaders pressed for action against Britain directly or through operations in the Mediterranean, Raeder expressed serious reservations about any cross-Channel invasion in September, proposing instead a postponement until the spring. Hitler, too, appeared mindful not only of the enormous risks of an invasion but also of the dangers in delaying the operation, since the British position could only improve with the passage of time. Nonetheless, he reassured Raeder that a landing would be attempted only if the air campaign against Britain proved successful. When Brauchitsch pressed for action in the Mediterranean in support of the Italians, Hitler dismissed the suggestion as a diversionary maneuver, one that depended on the problematic staying power of the Italians.[23]

What, however, would be done if an invasion did not take place? In that event, Hitler asserted, "our action must be directed to eliminate all factors that let England hope for a change in the situation." He now revealed his preference for a swift decision in the east to a war of attrition against the British Empire. "*Britain's hope lies in Russia and the United States,*" Halder noted, retaining the Führer's emphasis in his diary:

If Russia drops out of the picture, America, too, is lost for Britain, because elimination of Russia would tremendously increase *Japan's power* in the Far East. *Russia is the factor on which Britain is relying the most. . . . With Russia smashed, Britain's last hope would be shattered.* Germany will then be master of Europe and the Balkans. *Decision: Russia's destruction must therefore be made a part of this struggle. Spring 1941. The sooner Russia is crushed the better.* Attack serves its purpose only if Russian state can be shattered to its roots with one blow. . . . Resolute determination to eliminate Russia. . . . *Object* is destruction of Russian manpower.

Although Hitler justified his decision with reference to strategic arguments, this was, as Barry Leach has noted, a weak charade: a German attack was the most certain way to bring about the alliance he professed to fear. The key to Hitler's thinking lay instead in his emphasis on the absolute destruction of the Soviet Union, a necessity if Germany was to be able to fight and win a protracted war of attrition against the Western democracies.[24]

War against the Soviet Union, which had formed the core of Hitler's ideological-racial conceptions for years, now assumed the key role in his comprehensive military-strategic-economic outlook: victory in the east would cut the Gordian knot and allow Germany at last to break free of its external constraints. Ideological obsessions had now come to the fore. As Goebbels noted after a conversation with Hitler on 9 August, "Bolshevism is world enemy number one. . . . The Führer thinks so too." Noteworthy as well was the absence of any opposition to Hitler's plans from the army leadership, in distinct contrast to the mood of autumn 1939, when he had faced an incipient revolt with his determination to attack France. Traditional disdain for the Slav, fear and contempt of Bolshevism, agreement on the necessity of securing the economic resources of the east, the long-term threat of Russia to German hegemony, the temporary weakness of the Red Army owing to Stalin's purges, belief in German military superiority: the Army High Command shared all these attitudes with Hitler and, thus, saw no reason to object to his momentous decision. Time was also a factor. If Hitler was to retain the strategic initiative and realize his goal of living space in the east, he had to act now, before the United States mobilized its extraordinary potential might. Strategic, economic, and time factors thus reinforced Hitler's fundamental inclination: the struggle for Germany's existence would be won or lost in the east. In this case, calculation and ideology, rational thought and dogma, proved complementary, a fact that must have convinced Hitler of the correctness of his decision.[25]

Hitler's 31 July decision to attack the Soviet Union was not confirmed in a military directive until 18 December. In the interim, the Germans muddled through a period of strategic confusion during which they squandered the momentum of their earlier triumphs and struggled to regain the initiative. Having decided to strike at Russia in the spring of 1941, they now found it desirable to force Britain to make peace in order to eliminate the threat of a two-front war. None of the options at hand offered the prospect of a quick victory, a fact that Hitler both understood and had difficulty accepting. Over the next four months, the Germans pursued a variety of means by which to compel Britain to surrender, even as Hitler, at the height of his power, again lapsed into typically vacillating behavior, preferring to choose not to choose. Military planning, Halder complained in exasperation on 27 August, went in all directions: "Spain is to be brought into war, but the economic consequences . . . are ignored. North Africa is viewed as a theater of operations against Britain. . . . Rumania is to be drawn into our orbit. . . . We are going to be ready in the north when Russia attacks Finland. The army is supposed to have everything nice and ready without ever getting any straightforward instructions." Strategically, only two realistic alternatives emerged: the creation of a Eurasian continental bloc and a peripheral war in the Mediterranean.[26] Although both these ideas were complementary in that they were directed against the Anglo-American powers, they differed crucially in their attitude toward the Soviet Union.

Typical of the chaotic style of rule in the Third Reich, differing factions championed each initiative, while Hitler chose to keep his options open as long as possible. The idea of a Eurasian bloc was the brainchild of Foreign Minister Ribbentrop, who for years had sought to build a global anti-British coalition. The Nazi-Soviet Pact of August 1939 had been his crowning achievement since, despite the ideological differences, it seemed to wed the Soviet Union to the anti–Comintern Pact members, Germany, Italy, and Japan. The alliance with Stalin, however, had stunned the Japanese, which resulted in a reorientation of their policy. In the summer of 1940, Ribbentrop now tried to revive and extend his old plan: with the inclusion of the Soviet Union, he hoped to create a bloc that would be anti-British as well as prevent the United States from intervening in European affairs. Japanese policy, influenced by the German defeat of the European colonial powers, which opened unexpected avenues of expansion in Southeast Asia, had changed as well.[27]

Ironically, that same German triumph had cooled Hitler to the idea of a military alliance with Japan since he expected an early end to the war. Only with the realization by the late summer that Britain would not accept his peace offer and the conclusion of the destroyers-for-bases deal that signaled American intention to support England did Hitler again warm to a deal with Japan as a way to deter the United States. Renewed negotiations culminated on 27 September 1940 with the conclusion of the Tripartite Pact, under which Germany, Italy, and Japan agreed to assist each other in the event one of the signatories was attacked by an external power not involved in the European or Sino-Japanese conflict. This, of course, was clearly meant to warn the United States against either opposing Japanese expansion or intervening on behalf of Great Britain. The result, however, was the exact opposite as American pressure on Japan increased while the Roosevelt administration deepened its economic and political support for Great Britain.[28] Still, despite the American reaction, Hitler did not categorically shelve the idea of a continental bloc, preferring instead to see how the other option developed.

The Mediterranean strategy, advocated primarily by Admiral Raeder and the Naval Staff, as well as Jodl at the OKW, also aimed at pressuring Great Britain into leaving the war and preventing the Americans from entering. Its supporters argued that the best way to strike a decisive blow at Great Britain was to weaken its empire through war in the Mediterranean. By seizing Gibraltar in cooperation with the Spanish and the Suez Canal in a joint operation with the Italians, the Germans would strengthen the Axis position enormously: Vichy French colonies in Africa would be safeguarded, vital raw materials from the Balkans would be secured, Turkey would tilt toward the Germans, oil from the Middle East would be readily available, British possessions in the Indian Ocean would be threatened, and Axis control of the Iberian Peninsula and Atlantic islands would push its power well to the west, thus menacing American supplies to England. The unspoken assumption, of course, was that Churchill's government could not survive such a succession of blows and, thus, would either collapse, opening the way for a more sympathetic government, be forced to make peace itself, or at the very least be rendered incapable of action while Germany disposed of Russia. In addition, the realization of such a program would put the "Russian problem" in a completely different light as numerous avenues of invasion would open up.[29]

This last was an important consideration for Hitler since he quickly grasped that, in contrast to the continental bloc, the Mediterranean strategy did not necessarily rule out an attack on the Soviet Union but could be seen as a complement to it. When Raeder briefed Hitler on 26 September, the Mediterranean strategy had gained new urgency since a few days earlier the Free French Forces had attacked Dakar, in West Africa, which also put in question Vichy control of Morocco, Algeria, and Tunisia. Hitler indicated both agreement with Raeder's arguments and willingness to implement the basic strategy but pointed to two key failings: the inadequate size of the German fleet and the necessity of gaining the cooperation of Spain, Italy, and Vichy France. Both, in turn, highlighted the deeper German dilemma: in order for the Mediterranean strategy to work, Germany had to depend on the support of what Hitler suspected were unreliable allies. Since Germany lacked the requisite military strength in the Mediterranean to achieve its aims on its own, it was now hostage to Hitler's ability to come to satisfactory agreements with leaders whose aims were mutually antagonistic.[30]

Perhaps sensing the impossibility of his mission—satisfying all the conflicting demands, he remarked, would require a gigantic fraud—in his diplomatic offensive in October 1940 Hitler seemed hesitant and halfhearted. In July, such a mission might have succeeded: France was reeling from defeat, Franco and Mussolini eager for easy gains. By the autumn, however, the failure of Germany to subdue Great Britain had changed the situation dramatically. French and Spanish leaders were markedly more wary of any commitment to fight, while Mussolini seethed at his reduction to an afterthought in the alliance. In addition, the price each demanded for aiding Germany had risen enormously, while their territorial claims still collided. Hitler's meeting with Mussolini at the Brenner Pass on 4 October went well, with both expressing support for a Mediterranean strategy, which pleased the Italians since it promised to raise their status. Eight days later, however, the cordiality faded when Mussolini heard, without warning, of Hitler's decision to act unilaterally to protect the Rumanian oil fields, seemingly excluding Italy from an area it regarded as within its own sphere of influence. The *duce's* retaliation was to present Hitler with a fait accompli at the end of the month, the invasion of Greece, which Hitler had repeatedly warned against and which resulted in a near disaster for the Axis.[31]

A meeting with French foreign minister Pierre Laval on 20 October went well enough, with Laval hoping through cooperation with Germany to secure French colonial possessions and release from heavy reparations. Hitler did not make any commitments but did request a meeting with Marshal Petain, which Laval agreed to arrange. Hitler's train then traveled on to Hendaye, on the Spanish border, where he met with Franco on the twenty-third. This meeting lacked all promise from the beginning. Hitler knew that Spanish entry into the war would put a serious economic strain on Germany, and he was also aware that he could not offer Spain any territorial concessions from France since he was attempting to get the latter to enter the war against Britain. He thus had little to offer the Spanish *caudillo*, even as Franco intended to extract maximum gains for Spanish entry into the war. From this unpromising beginning, negotiations floundered almost immediately. Franco's train arrived late, and Hitler took an almost instant dislike to the short, garrulous dictator. After a long monologue on Spanish economic difficulties, Franco offered to join the war against Britain in January 1941, but only if Spain acquired extensive French territories in Africa and received exorbitant quantities of food, raw materials, and armaments from Germany. Further irritated by Franco's observation that Britain would likely continue the conflict indefinitely, given American support, Hitler at one point got up and seemed ready to walk out of the talks. Although they continued, nothing was accomplished. Hitler, still seething at Franco, remarked to Mussolini a few days later in Florence that he "would prefer to have three or four teeth taken out" than have another discussion with the Spanish dictator.[32]

Nor were the talks the next day in Montoire with Petain and Laval any more profitable, even if they were more pleasant. Despite Hitler's bluster about the strength of the German position, both Petain and Laval remained noncommittal, hinting that French cooperation hinged on generous treatment by Germany and the acquisition of British colonies after a peace settlement. Although Hitler professed himself satisfied with the talks and impressed by Petain, in reality discussions with these potential allies had revealed not German strength but German weakness. Hitler had nothing substantive to offer either Spain or France since he could not satisfy one without antagonizing the other, nor could he move closer to France without alienating Italy. Moreover, any long-term benefits of Spanish and French participation in the war against England had to be weighed against the enormous short-term drain on the already hard-pressed German economy.[33] Finally, Germany lacked the requisite naval and air strength to go it alone in the Mediterranean, a fact that hardly escaped the notice of the other leaders. Despite Hitler's assurances that the British were practically out of the war, the view from Madrid and Vichy looked decidedly different; to them, waiting to see which way the wind blew appeared at the moment to be a far safer bet.

As Hitler, discouraged by his failure to make any headway with the Spanish and French, traveled by train back to Italy for another meeting with the *duce,* the conviction grew that his initial instincts were correct: the solution to Germany's dilemma lay in action in the east. He once again emphasized to Keitel and Jodl his intention to attack and defeat the Soviet Union in the spring, after the threat to the German flank in the Balkans had been removed. Still, in late October and early November, he had not definitively decided on a course of action. He retained some hope that Franco might yet be pressured into cooperating in seizing Gibraltar, but the goal now had faded from forcing Britain out of the war merely to protecting the German rear as decisive victory was sought in the east. During his talks with Mussolini, Hitler mentioned the upcoming visit to Berlin of Soviet foreign minister Molotov and his hope of directing Russian expansive energies against Great Britain in the Persian Gulf and India. In early November, however, the Führer observed to his military leaders that Russia remained "the great problem of Europe" and that everything had to be done "to prepare for when the showdown comes." At the meeting, Hitler had seemed to his army adjutant, Major Engel, "visibly depressed," as if "at the moment he [did] not know how things should proceed."[34]

The discussions with Molotov had, in fact, come at the behest of Ribbentrop, who hoped to realize his plan for a continental bloc by incorporating Russia into the Tripartite Pact. Although the spheres of interest of the four powers would touch, Ribbentrop hoped that they need not clash. For his part, Stalin seemed genuinely interested in the prospect since it would prolong the "capitalist war," provide time for the further growth of the Soviet war economy, and add to the booty he had acquired from the 1939 pact with Germany, which had also allowed him to push the Soviet security zone to the west. The Germans, however, were much less sanguine. The Soviet acquisition of Bessarabia and northern Bukovina had prompted direct German involvement in Rumania in order to protect its oil supplies. This not only raised protests from Moscow that Berlin had violated the 1939 agreement but also strained German relations with Italy while exacerbating a Hungarian-Rumanian territorial dispute. All this threatened unrest in the one region that Hitler most needed calm. German intervention stabilized the situation, but Mussolini's pique had also been one of the motives behind the invasion of Greece, which now threatened to destabilize the region anew. The increasing German dependence on deliveries of vital food and raw materials from Russia also drove fears that the long-term interests of Germany and the Soviet Union were incompatible.[35]

Although skeptical of any agreement, Hitler nonetheless bowed to Ribbentrop's argument that Soviet inclusion in the Tripartite Pact would prove decisive in the struggle against Great Britain. Still, on 12 November, the very day Molotov arrived in Berlin, Hitler signed Directive No. 18, which, after laying out the various combat possibilities inherent in the Mediterranean strategy, finally declared, "Political discussions for the purpose of clarifying Russia's attitude in the immediate future have been initiated. Regardless of the outcome of these discussions, all preparations for the east for which verbal orders have already been given [i.e., military operations against the Soviet Union] will be continued." Though no military options had been closed in this directive, the implication seemed to be that Hitler had grown very doubtful of the possibilities offered by alternative schemes and increasingly viewed the strategy he had always favored, attack on the Soviet Union, as the only realistic way to achieve a swift victory.[36]

In any case, the meetings with Molotov did not go at all well, merely confirming Hitler's assessment of the incompatibility of their positions. While Hitler and Ribbentrop delivered rambling monologues, the cold, steely-eyed Molotov sat impassively. When it came his turn to speak, he shot a series of specific questions at the visibly discomfited Führer about German intentions in the Baltic and Balkans, the proposed spheres of interest, and the aims of the Tripartite Pact. The Soviet foreign minister pointedly ignored Hitler's suggestion that Russia expand toward the Persian Gulf and India, making demands instead on Finland, Rumania, and Bulgaria, expressing Soviet interest in control of the Dardanelles and the Bosporus, and demanding as well a secure exit from the

Baltic Sea. Molotov further suggested, perhaps not so innocently, that Germany should seek its gains in the remains of the British Empire. He also pressed Hitler on German actions in Rumania and Finland, which Moscow viewed as clear violations of the 1939 agreement. Even when the Soviet foreign minister mentioned the mutual benefits of the German-Soviet relationship, without which German victories would have been impossible, it served merely to reinforce in Hitler's mind German dependence and exposure to Russian blackmail. By the end of the second day of talks, despite Molotov's indication of Russia's willingness to cooperate with the Tripartite Pact, Hitler recognized that the aims of the two sides remained irreconcilable. All in all, the talks proved a fiasco, best symbolized by the British air raid during the closing banquet that forced the dignitaries into a bomb shelter.[37]

Although Molotov's demands in Berlin were almost certainly intended as a tactical maneuver, the opening proposals in an ongoing negotiation that would result in Soviet accession to the Tripartite Pact, Hitler viewed them as extortionist and confirmation of the long-term Russian threat to Germany. Neither Hitler nor the German Foreign Office even bothered to reply to Molotov's further note of 25 November, in which he moderated the Soviet demands. Even before Molotov's visit, according to his army adjutant, Major Engel, Hitler had viewed the talks as a test of Moscow's intentions, of whether Germany and the Soviet Union would stand "back to back or chest to chest." The Führer now had his answer. The talks had clearly shown the incompatibility of Soviet and German territorial aims. "Molotov had let the cat out of the bag," Engel recorded Hitler as saying. "He [the Führer] was really relieved. It would not even remain a marriage of convenience." The day after Molotov's departure, Admiral Raeder observed that Hitler believed the Mediterranean strategy posed greater risks than an attack in the east and, thus, was "still inclined toward a confrontation with Russia," while, on the seventeenth, Weizsäcker noted the talk in Hitler's circle, "It would be impossible to create order in Europe without the liquidation of Russia." Hitler's conviction, formed in the summer and shaped by the failure of the alternative strategies, had been reinforced: the way out of Germany's dilemma lay in the east.[38]

On 5 December, Hitler ordered Brauchitsch and Halder to prepare the army for an attack on the Soviet Union in the spring. Soviet ambitions in the Balkans, he declared, threatened Germany. He then added, "The decision concerning hegemony in Europe will come in the battle against Russia." The aim of the operation, he stressed, echoing his arguments of 31 July, was the annihilation of "Russia's manpower."

Bock noted the Führer's emphasis once again on the importance of Russia and America for Britain: "If the Russians were eliminated England would have no hope of defeating us on the continent, especially since an effective intervention by America would be complicated by Japan, which would keep our rear free." Three days later, the last attempt to convince Franco to join the war failed, and the Germans suspended preparations for the proposed attack on Gibraltar. The failure of the Mediterranean and continental bloc strategies now prompted Hitler to concentrate his energies on the defeat of the Soviet Union. On 17 December, after a briefing by Jodl, the Führer summarized his estimate of the global situation. "All continental European problems," he stressed, would have to be solved in 1941 "since the United States would be in a position to intervene from 1942 onwards."[39]

Hitler's great goal since the 1920s had now become the sole means of extricating Germany from its deadlock. The alternative was no longer, if it had ever been, either a Mediterranean or a continental bloc strategy; the choice now was between destruction of the Soviet Union and Germany's ruin. With time running against him and the Mediterranean strategy dependent on the cooperation of unwilling or unable allies, Hitler decided to go it alone. The attack on the Soviet Union was the only practical alternative left—and one, moreover, that not only accorded with his long-term goals but also seemed the less risky option. On 18 December 1940, therefore, he signed Directive No. 21 (Operation Barbarossa), which demanded that the Wehrmacht should "crush the Soviet Union in a rapid campaign." On 9 January 1941, he told his generals, "The enormous Russian space holds immeasurable riches. Germany must control it economically and politically. . . . In that way it would have at its disposal the means by which in the future to fight a war of continents: it could no longer be beaten by anyone." This operation, he boasted, would "make the world hold its breath."[40]

In a bitter irony, the victories of 1940 had not brought Germany relief from its strategic and economic problems, nor had they resulted in a swift end to the war. As a result, Hitler saw the way out of the German dilemma not through negotiation but by expanding the war. He most likely decided for war against Russia in late July 1940 but in characteristic fashion proved willing to keep his options open and explore alternatives. If they served to knock Great Britain out of the war and cleared Germany's rear for the showdown in the east, fine; if not, he could do nothing in the east until spring 1941 anyway. None of the alternatives proved successful, which simply reinforced his conviction that he had been correct in opting to invade Russia. Germany could not afford to wait since from 1942 on the German position was bound to deteriorate while a successful operation promised to remove the Soviet threat, drive Britain from the war, forestall any American intervention, and win living space necessary for German security. In the end, Hitler believed that the only way to get out of his dilemma and to retain the initiative was to expand the violence. Given the geographic and economic constraints on Germany, the success of blitzkrieg in 1940 offered the means by which to escape this straitjacket. From Hitler's perspective, then, a compelling logic—a combination of strategic, economic, political, ideological, and time pressures—had driven him in the direction he wanted to go in any case. The logic of escalatory violence, however, also meant that the resulting war in the Soviet Union would be pitiless and harsh.[41]

With his decision for war with the Soviet Union, Hitler had closed off other strategic options. The Soviet Union, he stressed, posed a long-term threat to Germany that had to be eliminated, and, in any case, the time was right as at the moment the Red Army was poorly trained, inadequately led, and badly equipped. Besides, as Halder recorded his revealing admission, "Once England is finished, he would not be able to rouse the German people to a fight against Russia; consequently, Russia would have to be disposed of first." The Wehrmacht would launch a mighty blow that would catch the Red Army by surprise and force it to fight as far to the west as possible, thus exposing it to annihilating encirclement battles. After this initial sledgehammer blow, Hitler simply expected the Soviet state, a colossus of clay, to collapse. The resulting operation would merely be to follow up and destroy the broken remnants of the Red Army, a "railroad advance" reminiscent of 1918.[42]

Between July and December 1940, the OKH, and principally General Erich Marcks, had developed a series of ideas on how to conduct a campaign against the Soviet Union. Marcks assumed that the Red Army would have to stand and fight west of the rivers Prut, Dniester, Dnieper, and Dvina in order to defend their main economic and industrial areas as well as the key cities of the western Soviet Union. Since the capture of Moscow, which was seen as the political, economic, and spiritual heart of the Soviet Union, would eliminate a major part of the armaments industry as well as shatter the Soviet command and control system, Marcks made it his main operational goal. The sheer size of the front, however, and the presence of the Pripet Marshes in the middle dictated a second offensive directed toward Kiev, which would then link up with the right flank of the northern force east of the marshes for a joint thrust on Moscow. While agreeing in principle with the Marcks Plan, Hitler also stressed the economic importance of seizing the Baltic states. General Friedrich Paulus, the newly appointed deputy chief of the General Staff, resolved the conflicting visions by distributing much of the army's reserve units among three army groups, North, Center, and South, each of which would now fight its own separate envelopment battle. What had begun as a single main thrust with a central focus had, by the autumn of 1940, evolved into a three-pronged attack with no clear Schwerpunkt and insufficient forces for any of the three army groups to accomplish their tasks.[43]

During this period, in fact, German planning reflected an odd combination of hubris and wishful thinking as the hope that the enemy would act in the desired manner replaced rational assessment of relevant factors. OKH planners, for example, simply assumed that the Red Army would stand and fight in order to safeguard the principal Soviet economic and industrial centers, thus allowing the Wehrmacht to encircle and destroy it. The General Staff was also aware that the Soviets had built new industrial centers in the Urals that could be strengthened and reinforced by an evacuation of machines and equipment from the western borderlands but never pursued this consideration further. The German military leadership, in fact, displayed a woeful lack of understanding of economic factors. By training and tradition focused almost exclusively on the operational-tactical aspects of planning, the OKH designed a plan based on the lessons of the 1940 French campaign that emphasized a swift, decisive, concentric thrust toward the enemy capital, unconcerned by the fact that the economically vital regions lay in the south.[44]

They thus chose to launch a blitzkrieg not over ground favorable for mobile tank warfare, the rolling countryside of Ukraine, and toward the vital oil supplies of the Caucasus, but through the endless expanse of forest and marsh in central Russia, an area of few roads and unsuitable for motorized warfare. The OKH also defined an operational plan that ignored the fact that it would be impossible to supply the army with the necessary rations, munitions, spare parts, and material for an extended period over long distances and the fact that there was insufficient manpower to safeguard these long, exposed supply lines. Shortages of oil, gasoline, and vehicles, German planners realized, would of necessity reduce German striking power in Russia while demands elsewhere would drain troop strength even as, virtually all the prime manpower having already been conscripted, no large available reserves remained. As a result, the relative punch of German formations available for the Russian campaign would in some respects be lesser than the previous year in the west, even though the army had embarked on a crash program to increase offensive firepower. Moreover, because of production bottlenecks, a large percentage of the troops assembling in the east suffered from noticeable deficiencies in armaments and equipment. Only about a fifth of the available forces possessed capabilities suitable for the envisioned rapid, wide-ranging war of movement. Because of the lack of vehicles, over half the units entered Russia the way Napoléon's Grand Army did, on foot with horse-drawn supply wagons. The traditional German bias against the intelligence function, as well as the generally poor quality of information coming out of the Soviet Union, also posed a problem. German planners consistently underestimated Soviet strength, Stalin's ability to maintain control after the initial German blows, the problems of space, terrain, and climate, the difficulties of supply and logistics, and the problems of waging a blitzkrieg in a vast area with few good roads.[45]

More critically, the OKH suffered from a lack of imagination. By and large, operational planners simply took the lessons learned from the successful French campaign and applied them to the completely different context of the Soviet Union. This resulted in a clever tactical scheme but not a clear strategy for achieving a war-winning victory. Significantly, the German approach to Barbarossa overlooked or ignored a number of key factors that contributed to the success of the Sickle Cut plan. The French had been routed because Manstein had delineated a clear focal point for the German attack and advance, one that, if successful, would pin enemy forces against a natural obstacle and give them no possibility other than surrender. It depended for success on daring thrusts deep into the enemy flanks, a risk that could be taken because of the stationary nature of French forces on the Maginot Line. The distances to be covered in the decisive, initial thrust were manageable, while supply posed no insurmountable problems given the excellent road and rail network of Western Europe. In addition, the Germans enjoyed the great advantages of speed and surprise against an enemy that had never encountered the methods of mechanized warfare. Nor were the German forces markedly inferior to those of the enemy in terms of either quality or quantity. Vitally, with no threat to its rear and small distances, the Luftwaffe had been able to concentrate all its forces to provide a decisive edge. Moreover, the French system of command and control faltered almost immediately, while political leaders failed to maintain their nerve or to mobilize the full resources of the French state. Crucially, none of these factors would apply in the Soviet context. Most importantly, perhaps, Sickle Cut had been designed as a war-winning operation, an all-or-nothing gamble in which the outcome rested on German ability to gather all available strength for a stunning knockout blow at the beginning of the campaign. Failure meant not just the loss of a battle but outright disaster, a stark fact that the planners of Barbarossa chose to ignore.[46]

Although these various plans agreed on two broad notions—that Soviet forces needed to be encircled and destroyed as quickly as possible and that the ultimate goal was a line running roughly from Archangel on the Arctic Sea to Astrakhan on the Caspian Sea—the main direction of the attack had been left unresolved, a lapse that reflected fundamental disagreement over the purpose of the operation. To Hitler, the key objective of the campaign, despite his justification of it on strategic grounds, remained the winning of Lebensraum, especially food, oil, and industrial resources, so he gave priority to economic objectives. For Halder, crushing the Soviet state with a single blow in a short campaign took precedence, which meant seizing Moscow. A powerful thrust toward Moscow—the economic, political, ideological, and communications center of a tightly controlled totalitarian regime—would force the Soviets to concentrate their forces, thus assuring their destruction. Hitler, however, dismissed Moscow as "not very important." He agreed with the aim of rapidly enveloping Soviet forces but suggested that this could best be accomplished by diverting troops from the center to the north and south, rather than merely driving Russian forces back toward Moscow. This would achieve the additional purpose of opening the Baltic coast as a supply route and securing economic and industrial resources in Ukraine but would result in a dispersal of forces.[47]

Typically, given their strained relationship, Hitler and Halder neither discussed nor clarified the points of conflict in their differing operational conceptions. Instead, Hitler assumed that his army chief would simply follow his guideline, while Halder believed that the development of the operation would confirm the correctness of his ideas. Army planners, in fact, seemed to have succumbed to the blitzkrieg myth, fully expecting the campaign to be decided after the first few weeks, and, thus, elected not to choose between the two conflicting views. Instead, they simply assumed that a quick military decision would deny the Soviets the ability to mobilize their resources, that the Wehrmacht could be fed off the land, and that the rapid collapse of the Soviet Union would allow for the easy conquest of the foodstuffs and raw materials vital to the German war economy.[48]

Despite their apparent confidence and resolve, however, both Hitler and his army leaders harbored persistent doubts about the strength of the Soviet Union and the ability of the Wehrmacht to carry off a successful offensive. Goering, too, appeared ambivalent, dreading the extension of the war, the enormous size of Russia, and the probable entry of the United States, but hungering for the economic spoils to be gained. The period between January and March 1941, then, as operational plans were prepared and approved by Hitler, was a time of disturbing uncertainties. As preparations intensified, German planners became aware of numerous problems. The presence of the Pripet Marshes dictated that the Ostheer (the Eastern Army) had to be deployed in two largely uncoordinated groups, making a single decisive encirclement battle, such as achieved in France, virtually impossible. The terrain and primitive road network of Russia argued against any rapid thrusts into the interior, while the increasing breadth of the front as the Germans advanced eastward and diverging locations of key targets such as Leningrad, Moscow, and Ukraine threatened a dispersal of forces. The enormous size of Russia put in question the Luftwaffe's ability to accomplish its tasks. Nor had a clear decision been made as to the Schwerpunkt of the attack: Halder still favored a concerted strike directly at Moscow, while Hitler gave priority to economic targets in the Baltic and Ukraine. Supply and logistic problems also arose, even as the Germans became uncomfortably aware that Soviet strength was considerably greater than expected. In the end, the generals began to suspect that, as in 1914, they did not have sufficient forces to achieve their goals.[49]

As in 1914 and 1940, everything would depend on deciding the battle in the first weeks of the campaign through a rapid thrust and encirclement operation that would trap the Red Army west of the Dvina-Dnieper River line. Unlike Manstein's encircling blow in 1940, which had not exceeded 150 miles in depth, the Germans would now have to advance some 300 miles in order to bag the Russians. This would tax their rather small and rudimentary supply system to the limit. Organizationally, the German army had always accorded priority to combat formations rather than the administrative tail, but this left a supply system suited only to limited campaigns of short distance and duration. Unlike the French campaign, which had already strained the Germans to the limit, in this campaign supplies could not simply be shuttled to the front by trucks from depots in Germany. The deeper the advance, moreover, the larger amounts of gasoline the trucks would use themselves just to deliver decreasing amounts of supplies. As a result of these greater distances, the German quartermaster corps thus decided to split its motor pool into two segments: one set of trucks would accompany the panzer units and shuttle fuel and supplies from intermediate dumps that themselves would be resupplied by the remainder of the fleet. Since the gauge of the

Russian railways differed from the German, little could be expected initially from use of rail transport, and everything depended on the use of trucks. This, however, was a system of diminishing efficiency, as between two-thirds and three-fourths of the truck space would be filled with fuel and rations and the rest with ammunition.[50]

To compound the problem, despite images of a motorized blitzkrieg force, the German army lacked adequate motor vehicle capacity. Halder, in fact, had toyed with the idea of demotorizing the army after the Polish campaign because of a serious lack of vehicles and fuel. Amazingly, the German army used almost twice as many horses in World War II as it had in the previous war, 2.7 million as compared to 1.4 million. The Wehrmacht that attacked Russia was essentially composed of a steel tip mounted on a brittle wooden shaft as only a quarter of the invading force consisted of motorized units. The great mass of German soldiers advanced into Russia in June 1941 as soldiers had done for centuries, on foot and supported by horse-drawn transportation; indeed, the Germans employed some 650,000 horses in their blitzkrieg into Russia. The Wehrmacht, as Adam Tooze has stressed, was essentially a "poor army," as the Versailles restrictions and years of economic hardship in the 1920s and early 1930s had stifled the development of a large motor vehicle industry.[51]

In order to make good their shortages, the Germans had come to rely on booty from their earlier successes. As a result, they possessed a bewildering variety of vehicles, some two thousand in all, which meant that for their repair a single army group had to stockpile a million different spare parts. Since the Germans could not assume that they would capture large stocks intact, the entire supply system depended crucially on trucks, a fact that preoccupied Halder. "Space—no pause; that alone guarantees victory," he noted in late January. "Continuous movement is a supply issue. . . . Complications through differing equipment types. . . . Since the railroad . . . cannot be counted on for the desired tempo, the continuous operation depends on motor transport. . . . We must destroy the Russian army without pause over the Dnieper-Dvina line."[52] If serious fighting extended beyond this initial period, the problems would only multiply as the Wehrmacht would then be dependent on the inadequate Soviet rail system, the speed with which it could be converted and maintained, and the increasingly primitive road network.

Just as worrisome was the growing realization of the serious materiel deficiencies facing the German armed forces. Following the defeat of France, Hitler had ordered a redirection in armaments production to favor the navy and air force, but with the decision for Barbarossa the priority had to shift, at least somewhat, back to the army. To compound problems, in expectation of a quick victory in Russia only part of German war production was targeted at the needs of the Russian campaign, with the remainder continuing to produce for the anticipated confrontation with Britain and America. Since German industry could not quickly or easily convert from one type of production to another, delays were inevitable, with one result being a serious deficiency in ammunition. Between July and December 1941, that is, the first six months of Barbarossa, the production of army weapons actually fell by an average of 38 percent. The German war economy also suffered from a lack of skilled labor. To free workers for a return to industry, an elaborate system had been worked out in the winter of 1940–1941 whereby experienced soldiers were given an "armaments holiday" while new recruits were trained for the army. In this way, soldiers would manufacture the weapons they and their comrades would later use in the Soviet Union. Once these worker-soldiers returned in large numbers to the army, however, production would suffer, a potential for disaster that could be averted only if the campaign in Russia was short and did not involve above-average losses in men and materiel. Further compounding the problem, armaments industries attempted to delay the release of soldiers back to the army as long as possible, which cut into the time available for the training of the new divisions.[53]

Nor were production problems the only concern. In late December, General Friedrich Fromm, head of the Reserve Army, informed Halder of existing shortages in key raw materials and warned that food requirements could be met only by "swindling ourselves through 1941." A month later, OKW economic staffers reinforced this message, pointing out that an invasion of the Soviet Union would interrupt deliveries of key raw materials and accelerate the depletion of already inadequate stocks of fuel and rubber. At a conference on 28 January called by Halder to address the economic situation, General Georg Thomas, the economic expert in the OKW, presented a devastating picture: tire requirements were deficient by some 50 percent, while sufficient fuel existed for only about two months of combat. Halder observed soberly in his diary, "Purpose [of Barbarossa] not clear. We do not hit the British that way. Our economic potential will not be substantially improved. Risk in the west must not be underestimated. It is possible that Italy might collapse. . . . If we are then tied up in Russia, a bad situation will be made worse." Halder's spirits certainly did not improve three days later when he met with his army group commanders, all of whom voiced misgivings about the operation. In a meeting with Hitler on 1 February, Field Marshal von Bock gave voice to these anxieties, agreeing that "we would defeat the Russians if they stood and fought," but worrying that it might not be possible to force them to make peace. Hitler, visibly upset, replied, "If the occupation of the Ukraine, and the fall of Leningrad and Moscow did not bring about peace, then we would just have to carry on . . . and advance to Yekaterinburg." In any case, Hitler insisted angrily, "I will fight. . . . Our attack will sweep over them like a hailstorm."[54]

Despite Hitler's protestations, the key dilemma had been voiced by Halder—that a conquest of Russia would not improve German economic potential—for it called into question Hitler's fundamental assumptions about the gains to be realized from military conquest. As early as 10 August 1940, a study completed by the Military Geography Branch of the General Staff warned that the capture of Moscow, Leningrad, and Ukraine would not necessarily compel Russia to make peace as, beyond the German reach in the Urals, the Soviets had built a significant armament industry along with a solid industrial and agricultural base. In October, Gebhardt von Walther, a staffer at the German embassy in Moscow, sent an even more pessimistic assessment to Halder, warning against the expectation of Soviet collapse or any immediate economic benefits from Ukraine, especially foodstuffs. The German occupation in 1918 had yielded meager results, Walther argued, and the area was now even more overpopulated and impoverished. Furthermore, Thomas pointed out, maintaining or increasing agricultural production in Ukraine depended on using a huge fleet of tractors and trucks. This would be impossible without simultaneously seizing the oil fields of the Caucasus, which were beyond the initial German reach. Reich minister of finance von Krosigk also noted that the Russians would likely burn their fields and storage facilities, with the result that less grain would actually be collected through an invasion.[55] Since the mid-1920s, Hitler had justified an inevitable showdown with Russia on economic and racial grounds; now, the former assumption seemed to be put in serious doubt.

Despite this gloomy prognosis, Halder and the army leaders, perhaps remembering their falsely pessimistic assessments in spring 1940, could not bring themselves to confront Hitler. At a conference on 3 February, Halder mentioned supply and economic difficulties only briefly, preferring instead to stress the means by which these could be overcome as well as the poor quality of Russian troops and equipment. Still, on 5 February, Hitler called for a study of the various Soviet industrial areas to gauge their ability to sustain centers of resistance. The War Economy and Armaments Office under Thomas had already prepared such a study, one that again pointed to serious economic deficiencies. Keitel, however, informed Thomas that Hitler would not be influenced by such arguments, so Thomas began to modify his conclusions to better suit the Führer. On 13 February, Thomas issued a larger report, "The Effects of an Operation in the East on the War Economy," that now predicted Germany's food and raw material situation would be markedly improved if a rapid conquest should succeed in capturing large stocks intact. In the event of a longer war, Germany would have to solve a number of problems, among them transportation, securing oil supplies, and guaranteeing delivery of food and raw materials. The collapse of the Soviet Union, moreover, could be expected only by the loss or destruction of the industrial areas of the Urals. Still, Thomas predicted that the campaign would overrun 75 percent of the Soviet war industry, a conclusion that would hardly discourage Hitler. Indeed, if anything, the urgent economic needs outlined in Thomas's report served to justify an invasion as a solution for Germany's problems, a point Hitler could hardly miss.[56]

What transpired now was indicative both of the amorphous decision-making process in the Third Reich and of the incremental way in which Barbarossa took on the dimension of an ideological and racial war of destruction. Nazi occupation policy in Poland and the various proposals for solving the Jewish question already assumed, in a rather inchoate fashion, the deaths of large numbers of people. In thinking through the economic imperatives of the invasion, economic planners, ministerial officials, and others now adopted a merciless pragmatism, independent of direct orders from the Führer, that helped set in motion a process of escalating radicalization and mass murder. As it became clear that Hitler was determined to achieve Lebensraum in Russia, that for him the question was not whether to proceed but how to achieve maximum profit, Thomas began to collaborate more closely with the one economic official, State Secretary Herbert Backe in the Agriculture Ministry, who had long been an advocate of expansion in the east on economic grounds. Given Germany's experience in World War I, Backe's main priority was securing the food situation of the Greater Reich. By the end of 1940, this necessity loomed even larger since occupied Western Europe also faced substantial net grain deficits. Furthermore, the massive Ostheer, numbering some 3 million men, would also have to be fed. Since the British blockade precluded the importation of additional foodstuffs from outside Europe, Germany faced the bitter prospect, as in 1917–1918, of food shortages, hunger, and political upheaval. Worryingly, Belgian miners had already gone on strike in the winter of 1940–1941 to protest the meager food supplies, while on 1 May 1941 German civilians had to face a drastic reduction in their own rations. Nazi leaders, obsessed by the example of World War I, would not again allow domestic convulsions to undermine a war effort, so Ukraine had to be exploited as a source of grain. Backe, however, knew full well that Ukraine was not the limitless granary of myth, that, as a result of backward Soviet agricultural methods and rapid population growth, it barely produced a surplus of grain. The problem, then, was that even a successful German invasion would result in little immediate benefit.[57]

For Hitler, the conquest and immediate exploitation of food supplies and raw materials was the key priority, so a solution had to be found. Steps in that direction came in February 1941, when Thomas's office broached the idea that not the entire occupied territory, but only its economically important parts, should be sustained. Territories that were of "no economic importance for the conduct of operations, or for the greater German war economy" were to be "economically neglected after the most extensive exploitation." Special importance was attached to attaining surpluses in foodstuffs and oil. Even the experts in Backe's office, however, had to admit that any invasion would disrupt normal harvests for at least two years: "These losses can only be made good over several years. . . . For that reason, no surpluses should be expected . . . for several years." His agricultural experts, however, had calculated that Germany and occupied Europe needed 8–10 million tons of grain, which had to be collected from Russia. Backe had promised Hitler that possession of Ukraine would end all economic worries, so a way out of the conundrum had to be found. The solution worked out by Backe's staff was breathtakingly radical: a deliberate strategy of hunger and starvation. The agricultural surpluses of southern Russia would be diverted to Central Europe, while the areas of deficiency in central and northern Russia, especially the big industrial cities, would be cut off from their food sources. A double burden, in fact, would be imposed on these "deficit areas," for the army's supply plan was based on the assumption that the troops would live off the land for the duration of the campaign. Not only would the local population of these areas receive no incoming foodstuffs, but their own inadequate supplies would also first be used to feed the German forces.[58]

At a 2 May conference of state secretaries representing the ministries involved in the occupation, Thomas and Backe spelled out with remarkable clarity what this "hunger policy" meant:

1. The war can be continued only if the entire armed forces are fed from Russia in the third year of the war.

2. Tens of millions of people will undoubtedly starve to death if that which we require is taken out of the country.
3. Of greatest importance is the securing and removal of oil crops . . . , with grain occupying a lower priority. Available fat and meat will presumably be consumed by the troops.

Amazingly, with no evidence of protest or disagreement, key representatives of the German state agreed with a proposal that sentenced millions to death as an acceptable price to pay for the acquisition of maximum food "surpluses." In order to serve the needs of the German Großraumwirtschaft, the Soviet Union was to be exploited as a colonial possession, with the only question being, "How does this help Germany?" The consequences for the affected areas were inescapable and discussed in detail. "The gradual death both of the industry and of a large portion of the population in the former deficit areas" was indispensable, concluded one report: "Many tens of millions will become superfluous in those areas and will have to die or emigrate to Siberia. Any attempts to save the local population from death by starvation through the importation of surpluses . . . can only be at the expense of the food supplies for Europe. They would undermine Germany's and Europe's immunity to blockade."[59]

How many "tens of millions" would be affected? Backe himself put the figure for the "surplus population" at between 20 and 30 million. Practical implementation, not concern for their fate, dominated discussions, as Goering dismissed their starvation as essential to the German war effort. Indeed, to top Nazis a beneficial side effect of the hunger policy would be the elimination of precisely those elements of the population that were considered racially unworthy or politically threatening. Their starvation would then create a colonial land open to settlement by racially valuable German colonizers. Himmler certainly understood this, remarking, "It is a question of existence . . . , a racial struggle of pitiless severity in the course of which twenty to thirty million Slavs and Jews will perish through military actions and crisis of food supply." In his instructions to agricultural administrators, Backe stated dismissively, "Poverty, hunger, and frugality have been borne by the Russian individual for centuries. His stomach is elastic—therefore, no false pity." Alfred Rosenberg on 20 June put it more brutally, saying, "The feeding of the German people undoubtedly holds the top place now on the list of German demands in the east. . . . We certainly do not see that we have any duty to feed the Russian people." For Rosenberg, in fact, both economic policy and racial policy justified the starvation of millions. German rule was to be ensured, and vast lands opened for German settlement, by the annihilation of millions of racially inferior peoples. "The Russians," he conceded, "will have some very hard years ahead of them."[60]

Not as well understood but no less significant, the material gains secured by the seizure of Lebensraum in the east would profit not only the state and heavy industry but everyone in Germany as well. Nazi propaganda had long promoted the notion that the key to increasing the German standard of living was securing resources commensurate with the racial value of the Volk. The war for Lebensraum was, thus, not one for "throne and altar," as Goebbels put it dismissively, but one

> for grain and bread, for a well-rounded breakfast, lunch, and dinner, a war for the achievement of the material prerequisites for the solution of the social question, the question of housing and street construction, the construction of a military, commercial, and cruise fleet, the construction of automobiles and tractors, of theaters and cinemas for the people even in the tiniest village, a war for raw materials, for rubber, for iron, and ores. . . . We want finally, just once, to cash in. . . . In the immense fields of the east sways the golden grain, enough and more than enough, to nourish our people and all of Europe. . . . That is our war aim.

Goebbels expressed well the feeling, as Adam Tooze has put it, of "beleaguered poverty" that afflicted Germans in the interwar period, a fierce resentment at economic inequality and the stranglehold the "Anglo-Saxons" had on the resources of the world. Hitler had long insisted that the German people deserved better, that the principal domestic goal of National Socialism was to raise the individual's living standard. Ultimately, however, this could be accomplished, Hitler believed, only through conquest of the vast resources of European Russia. That had been the lesson of World War I. Only by securing Lebensraum within the "area of our own weapons" could Germany become economically secure and prosperous.[61]

At the height of his power, and in order to celebrate the eighth anniversary of his appointment as chancellor, Hitler on 30 January 1941 delivered a rousing speech in the Berlin Sportpalast, one that left him in a radiant mood. And why not? He mocked the hypocrisy of the British, noting gleefully that their empire had, in fact, been acquired and maintained through force, that Britain and not Germany controlled vast areas of the globe, and that Britain had used its power to the detriment of

Germany. The latter had been the lesson of 1918, he fumed, when Germany had been deceived and undone by both the British and the internal November criminals. That this centuries-old swindle was changing, that Germany was breaking free of the tyranny of the old order, the Führer boasted, resulted from the liberating energy and dynamism of National Socialism. The capitalist plutocrats, however, motivated by Jewish hatred, were ruthless. Not only had they intervened unnecessarily in the war, but they now also prolonged the conflict in the futile hope that Germany would somehow collapse, as in 1918. This, however, would not happen, Hitler promised, and then reminded the audience of his earlier prophecy:

> And I do not want to forget the warning that I gave on 1 September 1939 [*sic*] in the German Reichstag, that if Jewry were to plunge the world into war, the role of Jewry would be finished in Europe. They may laugh about it today, as they laughed before about my prophecies. The coming months and years will prove that I prophesied rightly in this case too. . . . [Other nations] . . . will one day recognize the greater inner enemy, and they too will then enter with us into a great common front . . . against Jewish-International exploitation and destruction of nations.[62]

What exactly Hitler meant by this scarcely veiled threat—expulsion from Europe, confinement in ghettos, deportation across the Urals to Asia, or extermination—cannot now be determined. Perhaps he himself had no clear idea what he intended to do. Significantly, however, although unsure how the role of Jewry would be finished, he was certain that his prophesy would prove correct. Characteristically, as well, and highly revealing for a man with a photographic memory, Hitler on this and subsequent occasions recalled his original prophesy being made not on 30 January 1939 but on the day that war in Europe began, as if in his mind international Jewry had, indeed, perpetrated the conflict.

Most likely Hitler intended this as yet another warning to the United States to stay out of the struggle since Roosevelt had just introduced his Lend-Lease bill into Congress. Still, the Jewish question was never far from Hitler's mind, and it would have been reinforced through regular contact with radical anti-Semites in the leadership such as Joseph Goebbels as well as anti-Jewish films such as the "documentary" *Der ewige Jude*, a scurrilous hate film that had premiered in Berlin just two months earlier. Thus, even as military and civilian planners, on the basis of concerns about the insufficient food supply, began to envisage the impending war in Russia as one of annihilation, a similar radicalizing process was occurring among those responsible for solving the Jewish problem. With the Madagascar Plan a nonstarter, Hitler now authorized Heydrich to come up with a new plan for removing the Jews from German-dominated Europe. Theodore Dannecker of Eichmann's office noted on 21 January 1941, "According to the will of the Führer, after the war a final solution of the Jewish question within the parts of Europe under German rule or control will be implemented." To this end, Dannecker wrote, Heydrich had received orders to "submit a proposal for the final solution . . . the success of which can only be guaranteed through the most careful of preparations. This preparation must include the preliminary work necessary for a general deportation of all Jews, as well as detailed plans for resettlement measures in a territory yet to be determined." Heydrich evidently envisioned placing the Jews in the General Government area of Poland but, according to Eichmann, met fierce resistance from Hans Frank. Nonetheless, Heydrich instructed top officials in the RSHA in January 1941 to prepare for a large police action in the east. Shortly after his late January 1941 speech, Hitler also discussed the Jewish question with a group of close associates, remarking that he was thinking of new, "not exactly more friendly" schemes to replace the Madagascar project.[63]

With Hitler pressured both by Nazi leaders in Germany to deport Jews from the Reich and by administrators in Poland who struggled to cope with the horribly overcrowded ghettos, the glimmer of a truly radical solution to the Jewish problem began to emerge. The rapid defeat of the Soviet Union would open myriad new prospects, not least the deportation of the Jews of Europe to the harsh, inhospitable outer extremes of European Russia or even across the Ural Mountains. Such a territorial solution certainly would result in the deaths of millions of people, but Nazi planners already assumed vast numbers of "superfluous eaters" would be eliminated in any case.[64] The twin wars of Hitler's ideological obsessions—for Lebensraum and to solve the Jewish question—began in spring 1941 to converge in German planning. Final victory would make possible the grand demographic projects envisioned by Hitler and to be implemented by Himmler and Heydrich, both eager in any case to expand their empire. Earlier, Hitler had thought only of solving the Jewish problem in Germany; now, once the war had been won, it could be a European-wide solution.

Although no decision had yet been made regarding the Final Solution, the extermination of the Jews of Europe, Hitler was clearly thinking in terms of a destructive racial war. The prerequisite for achieving his goals, the successful defeat of the Soviet Union, necessarily involved the army in this war of annihilation. On 26 February, General Thomas, the Wehrmacht's economic expert, had learned from Goering that one of the first objectives of a German occupation would be "to finish off the Bolshevik leaders as soon as possible." Less than a week later, on 3 March, Jodl, the chief of staff of the OKW, met with Hitler to discuss the guidelines for occupation policy. The Führer stressed that this was a showdown "between two world views. . . . The Jewish-Bolshevik intelligentsia, up to now the oppressor of the people, must be eliminated. . . . These tasks are so difficult that one can not burden the army with them. . . . The necessity of immediately rendering harmless all Bolshevik leaders and commissars [justified these measures]." Accordingly, on 13 March the OKW issued "Guidelines for Special Areas concerning Directive No. 21 (Operation Barbarossa)," which created a very shallow zone of army operations behind which "the Reichsführer SS [Himmler] is entrusted on behalf of the Führer with special tasks . . . that result from the necessity of finally resolving the conflict between two opposing political systems. Within the framework of these tasks, the Reichsführer SS will act independently and on his own responsibility."[65]

Nor could army leaders harbor any illusion as to the nature of these tasks. At a conference on 17 March, Hitler again revealed his murderous intentions. "The intelligentsia put in by Stalin," he emphasized, "must be exterminated. The controlling machinery of the Russian empire must be smashed. . . . Force must be used in its most brutal form. . . . The nation will break up once the functionaries are eliminated." On 26 March, Heydrich presented Goering his proposal regarding the solution of the Jewish question, noted the Reichsmarshall's request for a manual instructing the troops on the threat posed by the political commissars and Jews, and received Goering's assurances that the army would not interfere in operations behind the front. That same day the army negotiator, Quartermaster-General Wagner, and Heydrich also agreed on a draft, issued as an order by Brauchitsch on 28 April, pertaining to the responsibilities of the Einsatzgruppen, the special commandos of the Security Police. While the murder squads were to carry out their tasks on their own responsibility, the army would furnish logistic support and also coordinate its activities with an army liaison officer. This agreement made the army command complicit in mass murder since, given their prior experience with SS killing squads in Poland, they could hardly have had any illusions about SS intentions. The day after initial agreement had been reached with the SS, in fact, Brauchitsch told senior commanders that the troops "have to realize that this struggle is being waged by one race against another, and proceed with the necessary harshness."[66]

By March at the latest, then, Heydrich, with the agreement of army leaders, had begun preparing for a territorial solution of the Jewish problem that envisioned the rapid deaths of very large numbers of people.

If some in the army leadership still failed to get the message, Hitler made it crystal clear on 30 March when he addressed a gathering of some two hundred officers for over two hours. Halder's notes indicated that no one in attendance could doubt the Führer's aims or what was expected of the army. After beginning with the familiar strategic justification of the invasion and stressing the economic importance of securing the resources of Russia, Hitler then bluntly laid out the ideological aims of the war:

> *Clash of two ideologies.* Crushing denunciation of Bolshevism, identified with a social criminality. Communism is an enormous danger for our future. We must forget the concept of comradeship between soldiers. . . . This is a war of extermination. . . . We do not wage war to preserve the enemy. . . .
>
> *War against Russia:* Extermination of the Bolshevist commissars and of the Communist intelligentsia. . . . This is no job for military courts. The individual troop commanders must know the issues at stake. They must be leaders in this fight. The troops must fight back with the methods with which they are attacked. Commissars and GPU [secret police] men are criminals and must be dealt with as such. . . .
>
> This war will be different from the war in the west. In the east, harshness today means lenience in the future. Commanders must make the sacrifice of overcoming their personal scruples.

Although some generals later claimed that they expressed shock and outrage at the lunch that followed, General Warlimont admitted after the war that, far from protesting to Hitler, no one even mentioned his demands during the meal.[67]

So little shocked were the generals, in fact, that the next day preparation began on guidelines, in accordance with Hitler's demands, for the treatment of political functionaries and commissars. Over the next two months, Hitler's intentions for the conduct of the war in the east were given shape in a series of orders that formalized the army's acceptance of mass murder. In late April, a draft order authorized troops to combat guerrilla activity through "all means at their disposal," while commanders were freed from any obligation to prosecute troops for criminal actions against civilians, except when necessary to maintain order. "In judging such deeds," the draft noted, "it had to be taken into consideration that the collapse of 1918, the later suffering of the German people, and the struggle against National Socialism with the countless blood sacrifices of the movement were clearly traced back to the influence of Bolshevism." This draft, modified on 6 May and signed by Keitel on 13 May, explicitly granted German troops the right to use any and all measures against Soviet citizens, including collective reprisals, while prohibiting the prosecution of soldiers for offenses committed "out of bitterness over the atrocities . . . of the carriers of the Jewish-Bolshevik system."[68] Murderous actions against Russian civilians, then, were to be seen as just retribution for earlier misdeeds allegedly committed against Germans or understandable outrage at the excesses of a criminal element.

At the same time, another draft circulated that sought to define the army's role in the treatment of political leaders and commissars. The OKW issued a first draft, "Guidelines for the Behavior of the Troops in Russia," on 19 May that again emphasized, "Bolshevism is the deadly enemy of the National Socialist German people. Germany's struggle is directed against this subversive ideology and its functionaries . . . [and] requires ruthless and energetic action against Bolshevik agitators, guerrillas, saboteurs, and Jews, and the total elimination of all active or passive resistance." Keitel then signed the final version of the notorious "Commissar Order" on 6 June. Typically, it began with a justificatory statement: "In the struggle against Bolshevism, we cannot count on the enemy acting according to the principles of humanity or international law. In particular the political commissars at all levels, as the real leaders of resistance, can be expected to treat prisoners of war in a hate-filled, cruel, and inhuman manner." Having attributed to the enemy the very treatment the Germans themselves planned to inflict, the directive went on:

The troops must be made aware:

1. In this struggle to show consideration and apply principles of international law to these elements is wrong. They are a danger for our own security and the rapid pacification of the conquered areas.

2. Political commissars are the originators of barbaric, Asiatic methods of fighting. Thus, they have to be dealt with immediately and . . . with the utmost severity. As a matter of principle, therefore, they will be shot at once.

Significantly, only commissars apprehended in rear areas were required to be turned over to the Einsatzgruppen for disposal; otherwise, they were to be shot immediately by the army units that had captured them. During the Polish campaign, some army commanders had been repelled by the executions carried out by the SS murder squads. On the eve of Barbarossa, they had now, despite a few protests, become accomplices to premeditated murder.[69]

How had this come to pass? In part, it was but the latest in a process of accommodation to Nazi criminality dating to the June 1934 Röhm purge. Once again, as in the past, army leaders made acquiescence tolerable, this time through several supplementary decrees issued by Brauchitsch that seemed to give commanders some autonomy in carrying out these orders: according to circumstances, officers could choose to impose lesser penalties on commissars; soldiers would not be allowed to do as they pleased; officers were to maintain discipline and avoid arbitrary outrages. Then, too, the army leadership was anxious not to lose any more power and influence to the SS, as had happened following the Polish campaign. Poland proved significant in another way as well. Eighteen months of brutal occupation and subjugation of the Poles had seemingly hardened the attitudes of many in the officer corps, who had come to regard the Poles as racially inferior colonial subjects.[70]

The Commissar Order also struck a raw nerve in the officer corps, whose attitudes had been shaped by both tradition and two haunting World War I experiences: the blockade that had slowly strangled Germany's ability to wage war and caused the starvation deaths of hundreds of thousands of civilians and the traumatic collapse of 1918, when the "stab in the back" by the November criminals (Communists, socialists, and Jews) had destroyed their world. In addition to a traditional contempt for the Slavic peoples of Eastern Europe, then, most senior army officers supported Hitler in his contention that political commissars were criminal and had to be dealt with accordingly. At various gatherings, officers expressed opinions hardly at variance with those of the Führer. Germany had to secure its food supply, Colonel-General Georg von Küchler, head of the Eighteenth Army, emphasized to his divisional commanders, and the only means was by the conquest of European Russia. In any case, he stressed, "A deep chasm separates us ideologically and racially from Russia. . . . The aim has to be to annihilate European Russia. . . . The political commissars and GPU people are criminals." Colonel-General Erich Hoepner, the commander of Panzergruppe 4, who would be executed three years later for his part in the plot to kill Hitler, expressed his sentiments even more bluntly: "The war against the Soviet Union is an important part of the struggle for existence of the German people. It is the old battle of Germans against the Slavs, the defense of European culture against Muscovite-Asiatic inundation, the repulse of Jewish-Bolshevism. This struggle . . . has to be conducted with unprecedented severity. Every military encounter . . . must be directed . . . toward the merciless and complete annihilation of the enemy. In particular, there is to be no mercy for the supporters of the current Russian-Bolshevik system." The mentality of Germany's military elite, then, hardly varied from that of the Führer. Both saw the world in social Darwinist terms, accepted the need for Lebensraum, regarded the Slavs as inferior and fitting subjects for German domination, and viewed communism as a malignancy that had to be eliminated. Crucially, both also accepted the need for a war of annihilation, within which the destruction of the Jews played a key role.[71]

Even as the army leadership fell into line ideologically, the SS had been busy preparing for its role. Heydrich not only supervised the negotiations that granted his special units broad authority as well as logistic support from the army but also initiated the process of selecting and training suitable leaders. Four Einsatzgruppen composed of between six hundred and one thousand men each, further subdivided into *Einsatzkommandos* and *Sonderkommandos,* would accompany the army into Russia. For the most part, the commanders of these various units came from educated backgrounds, with academics, lawyers, economists, civil servants, an opera singer, and even a Protestant minister among them; three of the four Einsatzgruppen commanders, in fact, totaled four doctorates among them. Heydrich drew the top leadership almost exclusively from the ranks of the Security Police and the SD, men who were ambitious, energetic, ruthless, prone to take the initiative, ideologically reliable, and staunchly anti-Semitic. In the second half of May, the roughly three thousand men selected for these killing squads received training at a police school near Leipzig. Heydrich visited the school on a number of occasions to remind the men of the necessity of their special tasks, to reinforce the life-and-death nature of the upcoming struggle, and to stress the special danger posed by the Jews.[72]

Despite the later prominence and notoriety of the Einsatzgruppen, they constituted only one part, and the smallest at that, of the forces to be deployed in this ideological war. In addition, numerous battalions of the Order Police and the Reserve Police, together numbering perhaps twenty thousand men, were made available for participation in these special tasks, as were the First SS Brigade and the SS Cavalry Brigade, with another eleven thousand men. The Order Police units, in particular, three-quarters of whose officers were party members, had been educated for toughness and inculcated with a spirit of "soldierly warriors" and, thus, could be expected to carry out their murderous duties with brutal efficiency. Throughout the Order Police units, a process of institutional socialization had instilled an ethos focused on ruthlessness, German racial superiority, the need for Lebensraum, and hatred of Communists and Jews. By the time of the invasion of Russia, then, Hitler, leading party officials, the army command, the heads of the SS, and top bureaucrats had crossed the threshold to planned, deliberate murder. For Hitler, military operations against the Soviet Union designed to gain Lebensraum and political-police measures aimed at the extermination of ideological and racial enemies were simply different facets of the same war. As Ian Kershaw aptly observed, "The genocidal whirlwind was ready to blow."[73]

Unlike the Phony War, this second interregnum, between the summer of 1940 and June 1941, did not benefit the Germans but instead illuminated the weaknesses of their position. Great Britain had used the respite to strengthen itself substantially, most vitally by gaining assurance of material aid from the United States, which itself increasingly geared up for war. Despite the logic of the Mediterranean strategy, Hitler had to concede that Germany had neither the strength to bring it off on its own nor the ability to coerce its reluctant allies into action and, thus, had no way to force England to make peace. The economic situation also remained precarious as, far from solving their food and raw material problems, the Germans' conquests had added the burden of feeding the occupied populations of Western Europe without the benefit of imports, which were cut off by the British blockade. The twin Italian fiascos in Greece and North Africa struck at the prestige of the Axis and promised to drain limited German resources, nor could the Japanese be persuaded to strike at Singapore in order to distract and weaken the British.

Operations in the Balkans now proved necessary in order to protect key supplies of raw materials and the southern flank of the intended invasion of Russia. German triumphs over Yugoslavia and Greece and the daring airborne conquest of Crete certainly reinforced the image of the invincible Wehrmacht but came at a considerable price. They strained the German logistic system on the eve of Barbarossa, added considerable wear and tear to vital mechanized units, and persuaded Hitler and the army command of the uselessness of airborne operations just as the Germans had the most need for mobile assault forces that could seize key river crossings or block enemy retreats. Ironically, despite later claims to the contrary, the one thing they did not do was significantly affect the timing of Barbarossa, which would have been delayed in any case by German economic and transportation difficulties as well as the flooded condition of most of western Russia in the spring of 1941.

As the confident expectation of an imminent end to the war faded, the mood in Germany grew cloudy. During the autumn of 1940, Goebbels anxiously tracked the deterioration in popular opinion, which resulted not only from the prolongation of the war but also from the persistent British air attacks on the civilian populations of German cities, which necessitated the unpopular evacuation of children from many urban areas. Although Goebbels undertook a propaganda blitz that stabilized the situation, the popular attitude remained a concern: average Germans wanted an end to the war. Instead, rumors swirled of worsening relations with Russia, of troop concentrations in the east, of further cuts in food rations. Nor could there be much reassurance when they heard Hitler speak of "a hard year ahead of us" and of providing better weapons for German soldiers for use in the "next year."[74]

In the last weeks before Barbarossa, Hitler became characteristically jittery and irritable. Although a gambler willing to play for the highest stakes, before every major coup the Führer would lapse into a state of hesitancy, vacillation, nervousness, and anxiety. In a conference with Mussolini on 2 June, he kept his Italian ally in the dark about his plans, although rumors circulated as to the reason behind the German buildup in the east. The Japanese ambassador better understood the broad hints but remained noncommittal about possible cooperation. On 14 June, Hitler held his last military conference before the start of Barbarossa, where once again confidence was expressed that, although the Russians possessed a numerical advantage, German qualitative superiority would prove decisive. He reemphasized the reasons for attacking the Soviet Union, stressing that every soldier had to know what was at stake. The Russians would fight tenaciously, he observed, but had to be crushed in order to save Europe from Bolshevization. Was he having second thoughts? A few days before Barbarossa, Goering sought to flatter him that his greatest triumph was at hand. Hitler sternly rebuked the Reichsmarshall. "It will be our toughest struggle yet—by far the toughest. Why? Because for the first time we shall be fighting an ideological enemy, and an ideological enemy of fanatical persistence at that."[75]

On the afternoon of 16 June, Hitler summoned Goebbels to the Reich Chancellery—he entered through a back door in order to avoid detection—to discuss the situation and, perhaps, to gain a bit of reassurance. The Führer looked superb, Goebbels thought, despite "living in a state of tension that is not to be described." Clearly in a state of nervous excitement, with words pouring out seemingly at random, Hitler laid before his propaganda minister his thoughts and justifications for the impending invasion. The Greek campaign had taken a toll on German equipment, but it should be ready for Barbarossa. The weather had delayed the wheat harvest in Ukraine, which gave hope that most of it could be seized. The attack would be the largest in history and would avoid the mistakes of Napoléon, a remark that perhaps revealed his innermost fear. The Russians had massed their troops on the border, a perfect situation to ensure their destruction. "The Führer estimates the action at around four months," Goebbels noted. "I estimate much less. Bolshevism will collapse like a house of cards. We stand before a victory march without comparison."[76]

"We must act," Hitler insisted, then sketched a surprisingly accurate assessment of Stalin's intentions. "Moscow will remain out of the war until Europe is exhausted and bled white. Then Stalin would act to Bolshevize Europe." The coming struggle would not be geographically limited, he noted, but would continue until Russian military power no longer existed. In addition to his usual strategic arguments, Hitler now added a new one: Tokyo would not move against the United States as long as Russia loomed intact in its rear. This was, he claimed in rather inverted logic, "a preventive war" designed to avoid a two-front war since "Russia would attack us when we are weak." He also stressed the economic advantages to be gained from the invasion, from raw materials and foodstuffs to the freeing of large numbers of German soldiers to return to the factories. In any case, "The Bolshevist poison had to be driven from Europe. . . . That which we have fought against our entire lives will now be annihilated. . . . Whether right or wrong, we must triumph. . . . Once we have won, who will ask us about the methods?" Despite his nervous ramblings, virtually all the key components of his ideology were on display, from Lebensraum and anti-Bolshevism to the conspiratorial notion that Germany was surrounded by rapacious enemies. The other crucial element, anti-Semitism, emerged clearly four days later when Goebbels met again with Hitler, along with Hans Frank, the governor-general of Poland. Frank talked of the situation in the General Government and his joy that the Jews would soon be "pushed out." Then Goebbels noted, "The Jews are bit by bit falling to ruin in Poland. A just punishment for their incitement of the peoples and instigation of the war. The Führer had also prophesied that about the Jews."[77]

The next day, the twenty-first, in oppressive, muggy heat, Hitler appeared completely worn out, pacing for hours in his apartment in nervous agitation, dictating his proclamation to the German people, and discussing minutiae such as the fanfare to be played on the radio when the attack was announced. Hitler clearly still wrestled with his momentous decision. Himmler conveyed to Heydrich his impression that "the Führer is not so optimistic as his military advisors." As the time for the attack approached, Goebbels noticed that Hitler became calmer: "The Führer is freed from a nightmare, the closer the decision comes. It is always that way with him. . . . All the fatigue appears to have gone from him." Indeed, Hitler seemed once more to have resolved in his own mind the correctness of his decision: "There is nothing else for us to do but attack. This cancerous growth has to be burned out." As Goebbels remarked, "He has worked since last July [on preparations for the invasion], and now the time is at hand. Everything has been done that could have been done. Now the fortunes of war must decide." At 2:30 A.M. on the twenty-second, Hitler absented himself to get a bit of sleep. Goebbels, too agitated to rest, went in pitch blackness to his office. There he received the first news of the attack at 3:30 A.M., then two hours later read Hitler's proclamation to the German people. It was, Halder noted with scorn, a "long-winded manifesto . . . in a predominant political tenor," a thin justification of German action based on the claim that the Jewish-Bolshevik conspiracy sought to destroy Germany. "The hour has now therefore arrived," Hitler declared, "to counter this conspiracy of the Jewish-Anglo-Saxon warmongers and the equally Jewish rulers of the Bolshevik headquarters in Moscow." To Goebbels, "The burden of the last weeks and months fell away." Months later, however, Hitler admitted to his own doubts. "At the moment of our attack, we were entering upon a totally unknown world. . . . On June 22 a door opened before us and we did not know what was behind it. . . . The heavy uncertainty took me by the throat."[78]

In 1941, as in 1914, Germany was essentially a European continental power striving to become a world power, in both instances firm in the belief that a daring operational plan would accomplish the goal. The failure of the Schlieffen Plan in 1914 had sobered a generation of officers, until the brilliant success of May and June 1940 raised the notion of blitzkrieg from a tactical idea to a war-winning doctrine. Seduced by the myth of blitzkrieg into again believing that they could conquer the resources necessary for the breakthrough to world power, German leaders hoped to solve their conundrum through another gamble. Just one more triumph, they sensed, would provide the nation the means, still lacking despite the previous success, to conduct war at the next level. In this, they resembled a gambler hoping that one more successful throw of the dice would enable him to cover his past debts and finance future operations and harboring the false belief that he has figured out a foolproof scheme to beat the odds and break the bank.

The war that began on 22 June 1941, however, was more than just a gamble. It was, in a very real sense, Hitler's war, the showdown with Jewish-Bolshevism he had sought since the 1920s. His failure to subdue Great Britain meant that it had not come about under the conditions he preferred, but he decided to take advantage of the favorable circumstances of the moment both to secure living space for Germany and to free it from the strategic impasse into which his policy had plunged the nation. Hitler had long accepted the risks involved in his attempt to overturn the global balance of power and break the bonds he saw shackling Germany. Once committed to this policy, he had no choice but to strike fast and hard in an attempt to seize and retain the initiative. The risk of a new war, which he and his military advisers expected to be short, appeared more tolerable than doing nothing and allowing the Anglo-American powers to build up their resources for another contest of attrition. In any case, as Hitler well understood, the areas already conquered by Germany were unsuitable to sustain a material war, so conquest of European Russia was necessary to provide a decisive way out of the Reich's economic dilemma. Moreover, for Hitler, military-political strategy was inseparably intertwined with racial ideology. The realization of Lebensraum in the east and the final confrontation with the ideological and racial enemies of Germany had formed the core of Hitler's program for two decades, so the Führer was being pushed by circumstances in the direction he always intended to go. The threat posed by the emerging Anglo-American alliance only made this aim more necessary and urgent.[79]

The decision for war against the Soviet Union thus came, as Jürgen Förster has emphasized, not as a result of England's intransigence, but despite it. Even if Great Britain had made peace, Hitler would still have pursued war in Russia, for his ideology made no sense otherwise. As early as February 1939, he had stressed to his army commanders that the next war "would be a pure war of ideologies, that is, consciously a national and racial war." Brauchitsch, conveying Hitler's ideas to his top commanders, declared in November 1939, "Racial war has broken out [that] will decide who will rule in Europe and the world." In Hitler's eyes, the final goal, the racial restructuring of Europe, determined from the beginning the methods, with the result that, in the war against the Jewish-Bolshevik deadly enemy, means and ends were identical. The purpose of Operation Barbarossa was not merely the winning of territory for Germany but the final reckoning with Jewish-Bolshevism. As such, victory was more important than morality. When, after the German assault, Stalin responded in kind on 3 July 1941, declaring the struggle against Germany to be a merciless, life-and-death people's war, Hitler now had what he had long dreamed of, "the chance to exterminate that which is opposed to us."[80]

From the beginning, the concept of annihilation constituted an integral part of Operation Barbarossa, as the planning for occupation policy and the formation of the Einsatzgruppen demonstrated. In Hitler's view, military operations and SS actions would fuse into a unique dynamic of destruction. Despite a few rumblings, the belief in an unbridgeable racial and ideological chasm between Nazi Germany and Bolshevik Russia was accepted by virtually all in the army command. The lack both of opposition to the planned measures of the SS and of any outcry at the hunger policy demonstrated their integration into the National Socialist worldview. The special character of the war in the east was self-evident. Hitler had once boasted, "We have only to kick in the front door and the whole rotten structure will come crashing down," a statement that expressed well his destructive vision. With the commencement of Operation Barbarossa, he now more accurately predicted, "The world will hold its breath."[81]

3

Onslaught

The night of 21–22 June, Goebbels noted in his diary, was oppressively hot and humid, and he worried, with no hint of irony, that "our troops will not have it easy in battle." At the front, it was not the heat but rather the nervous anticipation that burdened many—most—of the men. Those in the first wave studied maps, surveyed the terrain in front of them, prepared their weapons, reviewed their tasks, and looked anxiously for any sign of enemy activity. Some expected quick victory; a few pondered the example of Napoléon; most were unenthusiastic but determined to do their duty. An unnatural silence hung over the front; movements had halted, vehicles were quiet, and men spoke in hushed tones. With muted voices officers read the Führer's rather pedestrian appeal to small groups of troops, ending with the portentous words: "Soldiers of the eastern front, you are about to enter a difficult and all important struggle. The fate of Europe, the future of the German Reich, the existence of our people henceforth lie in your hands." The troops stood silently and seriously. For some dawn would bring their baptism of fire, for others their last passage. Then, again in silence, with no talking and no clanking of equipment to betray their movement, the men entered their jumping-off positions. The silence, now an inward muteness, was stifling. Then, at 3:15 A.M. on the morning of 22 June, exactly 129 years after Napoléon had launched his invasion of Russia, the entire thousand-mile front from the Baltic to the Black Sea erupted: a thunderous cascade of artillery fire, tank engines roaring as they jolted into action, waves of droning aircraft filling the sky, the clatter of machine-gun fire, the sharp burst of mortars and hand grenades, and the earth rumbling and shaking amid the shrill shouts of racing men released from an almost unbearable nervous tension.[1]

Deploying over 3 million men, 3,600 tanks, 600,000 motorized vehicles (as well as 625,000 horses), 7,000 artillery pieces, and 2,500 aircraft (a number that was actually smaller than that employed during the invasion of France), the Germans had launched the largest military operation in history. Just as Friedrich Barbarossa over seven hundred years earlier had taken up a crusade against the Muslim presence in the Holy Land, so Hitler now launched his own crusade against the Jewish-Bolshevik menace. Astonishingly, the Wehrmacht found itself opposed by an even larger force: the Red Army possessed well over 5 million men, 24,000 tanks (of which almost 2,000 were new type T-34 and KV models), over 91,000 artillery pieces of all types, and over 19,000 aircraft (of which over 7,000 were based in the western districts). Given the willingness of Stalin to mobilize ruthlessly all elements of his population, the Red Army could also exploit an enormous pool of manpower to make good its losses. By contrast, the Wehrmacht could draw on a population less than half the size of its adversary and one from which the prime manpower had already been conscripted.[2]

As in France, the Germans again gambled on assembling all their available resources in hopes of deciding the outcome of the battle in the first few weeks. Ironically, while in 1914 the German military had overestimated the Russians and underestimated the French, in 1940–1941 it would prove to be the other way around. If France, the great foe of the First World War, had been defeated easily, the reasoning now went, the Soviet Union, weakened by communism and Stalin's irrational purges, must surely collapse at the first blow. If, however, the Red Army did not disintegrate and survived the first weeks of combat, the Wehrmacht would not have the resources to pursue and destroy it. Barring the expected Soviet collapse, the German forces were simply too small, too poorly equipped, and too badly supplied to accomplish their task of defeating the Red Army before the onset of winter.

The initial assault, however, matched German expectations of a rapid campaign. "Tactical surprise of the enemy has apparently been achieved along the entire line," Halder noted drily in his diary. "As a result of this tactical surprise, enemy resistance directly on the border was weak and disorganized, and we succeeded everywhere." That the Soviets had been caught unawares despite numerous warnings to Stalin throughout 1941 has long been recognized by historians, who have struggled to shed light on his seemingly erratic and illogical behavior. Most have dismissed the Soviet dictator's actions as a futile attempt at appeasement of Hitler, while a few have argued that he actually intended a preventive strike against Germany but that the Führer simply beat him to the punch. In reality, a complex mix of factors influenced Stalin's assessment of the situation, with the relative significance assigned to them largely depending on the perspective of the observer. The most common interpretation, that Stalin simply could not bring himself to believe the warnings or believed them to be an attempt by the British to draw the Soviet Union into the war, have focused on Russian weaknesses. The purge of the Red Army in the late 1930s that resulted in a decimation of the officer corps, the poor performance against Finland that seemed to confirm Soviet military haplessness, the seeming constant reorganization that left the Red Army in a state of disarray, the prompt delivery of food and raw materials to Germany: all these indicated to many observers a policy of abject appeasement.[3]

Stalin's actions and decisions can be considered from another perspective, however, one that, if not absolving the Soviet dictator, both better illuminates his view of the situation and sheds significant light on the scale of the task facing the Germans. Although still guilty of miscalculations, Stalin, in this view, acted largely from a sense of strength rather than weakness. Thus, he almost certainly understood that Germany would attack; the key questions in his mind were when and where. On numerous occasions, he had dismissed notions that Hitler would launch an attack on the Soviet Union with the (not incorrect) observation that Germany did not have the resources to win a two-front war and, thus, would not risk starting one. He expected that Germany would end the war in the west before entering any conflict with Russia. In the spring of 1941, he most feared being drawn into the war through British duplicity or being the victim of a sudden peace between Germany and England. The flight of Rudolf Hess to England, which most historians dismiss as merely a bizarre episode, appeared to him to raise the prospect of just such a peace. As late as 1944, Stalin still maintained to Churchill that Hess had been involved in a plot to organize a joint Anglo-German crusade against Russia. "All believed," recalled Maxim Litvinov, "that the British fleet was steaming up the North Sea for a joint attack, with Hitler, on Leningrad and Kronstadt."[4]

Given previous German behavior toward its intended victims, Stalin also thought that any military action would be preceded by an ultimatum, which would provide time for a Soviet military response. This assumption was important since from the mid-1930s Soviet military doctrine had stressed the notion of quickly transferring a war to the enemy's territory. The task of defense, then, involved absorbing the attacker's initial blow on the frontier while establishing the preconditions necessary to wrest the initiative away through a counteroffensive. Unknown to Stalin, however, Hitler intended to act differently this time, as Goebbels noted in his diary on 16 June: "We will take a completely different approach than usual . . . : we will not polemicize in the press, we will wrap everything in deepest silence and simply attack on X-day." Still, in anticipation of a possible German attack at some point, and in accordance with Red Army doctrine, Stalin had ordered large numbers of Soviet troops to the border areas.[5]

This concentration of force was also intended as a deterrent to any German attack. In early April, when Soviet intelligence had identified only seventy-two German divisions on the border facing over three hundred Red Army divisions, Stalin's brash reply to rumors of a German attack, "Let them try it," seemed appropriate. Similarly, Stalin rejected a mid-May proposal by Timoshenko and Zhukov to launch a preemptive strike against Germany, arguing that mobilization for such an action might provoke the very attack he thought he could avoid. Since the Wehrmacht deliberately brought units in at the last moment so as to avoid detection, Stalin's exchange with Timoshenko and Zhukov on the night of 13–14 June also revealed confidence rather than weakness. When Timoshenko requested that more units be moved into the border areas, Stalin refused, then asked how many divisions were in place already. When told 149, he replied, "Well, isn't that enough? . . . According to our information the Germans do not have so many troops." At roughly the same time, Molotov expressed similar confidence in Russian strength, telling an associate, "Only a fool would attack us."[6]

From these and other such statements, the conclusion can be only that, although Stalin and the Soviet High Command were aware of the German military buildup, they thought that they had more than matched it and were, thus, acting from a position of strength, not weakness. Stalin's miscalculation, then, was believing that the Germans would be deterred by these massive Russian forces. His angry remark to Churchill in late 1943—"I did not need any warnings. I knew war would come, but I thought I might gain another six months or so"—was in line with his expectations that Hitler could not wrap up the war with England before 1942 and would not dare launch an assault on Russia in late June. Undone by an odd combination of intense suspicion and rational calculation, Stalin feared stumbling into war through outside provocations but at the same time could not bring himself to believe that Hitler would disregard the evidence of Soviet strength and risk a two-front war. The mood of confusion and anxiety noted by Zhukov on 21 June reflected a man struggling to make sense of the inexplicable.[7]

As the Germans were soon to discover, Stalin's assumption of Soviet power had a great deal to recommend it. From the outset, the Wehrmacht confronted an adversary with a remarkably high level of equipment that could draw on eight times the number of tanks, with the newest models superior in armament, speed, and fighting power. Most Soviet tanks were obsolete, to be sure, but they had to be destroyed nonetheless, a process that cost the Germans time, effort, and staggering quantities of munitions. Moreover, in the second Five-Year Plan (1933–1938), the Soviets had significantly increased the size of their armaments industry, with the result that by 1941 the Soviet Union had come to resemble an armed camp. This militarization had produced a "warfare state" whose goal was to be in a position "to wage war from a running start." The Soviet Union possessed not only the largest military-industrial complex in the world but also one with a trained cadre of administrators already experienced in managing a war economy. As a result, despite its serious flaws, the Soviet system and the Stalinist apparatus of control proved far more resilient than the Germans anticipated. This enormous expansion of the industrial potential of the Soviet Union, both in size and in geographic distribution, was decisive in 1941, as the Soviets absorbed extraordinary losses but kept fighting. The Germans did, indeed, kick in the front door, but, contrary to Hitler's expectations, the structure wobbled but did not collapse. The Wehrmacht's qualitative edge in terms of training, leadership, and equipment provided it an advantage in a short struggle, but, if the initial onslaught failed, the Soviets had the capability of overwhelming Germany in the long term.[8]

In addition, German political and military leaders had fallen prey to the illusion of a quick victory, which clouded all their assessments of Russia. After all, they reasoned, they had finished off the apparently much stronger czarist empire in World War I and, thus, made sweeping generalizations based on previous experience. Since their entire plan rested on the assumption that the Red Army would disintegrate immediately under a series of sharp blows, as the French had a year earlier, they ignored unpleasant realities. That it was three hundred miles to the Dvina-Dnieper River line and another seven hundred miles to the Volga in a country with roads that were muddy and nearly impassable for much of the year did not seem to matter. That even the European part of Russia was vastly larger than British India, with which Hitler liked to make comparisons; that it dwarfed the German conquests in Western Europe; that it was a region of rough terrain, harsh climate, and poor infrastructure; that large areas of dense woods and swampy marshlands were perfect for partisan warfare; that the Russian railway system would have to be rebuilt to the narrow-gauge European standard, which required manpower the Germans lacked: all of this seemed not to register. That the

Soviet Union possessed enormous resources and a growing industrial base while Germany suffered a serious lack of key materials, especially oil, was put aside. The French campaign remained the prototype, and the myth of blitzkrieg convinced the skeptics: the campaign would be decided in a few weeks by quick operational victories on the frontier.[9]

Skepticism, however, did occasionally seep through. In the seven-week campaign against France, the depth of the longest drive was 250 miles, while the active operational area extended only about 150 miles across. In the Soviet Union, by contrast, the "frontier" area in which the battle of annihilation was to take place extended anywhere from 200 to 350 miles to the rear and covered some 750 miles in breadth, with the attacking armies diverging rather than converging. Even if the attack was successful, a diminishing number of German divisions would face the prospect of conquering an area that was doubling in width. More-over, a Soviet defeat in the western borderlands would not put Moscow in the immediate danger that the German drive to the Channel had with Paris as the Soviet capital was another 350 miles to the east of the Dvina-Dnieper line. As a result, there would be less likelihood of the same panic affecting Soviet leaders as that which overwhelmed their French counterparts in May 1940. At the end of January 1941, Bock and Halder had already expressed doubts concerning the vast distances and German ability to destroy the Red Army, an unease that was not lessened when initial German operational plans had to be modified on a number of occasions as it became clear that the Wehrmacht did not possess sufficient strength to accomplish its task.[10]

In this creeping recognition of inherent German weakness lay the larger problem facing Hitler. War always involves a complex mixture of political, economic, and military factors. Although the first two might have priority in timing or goals, success in war ultimately depends on the proper application of military force. Thus, the planners of Barbarossa proceeded in accordance with Clausewitz's fundamental rule that the aim of any campaign is to defeat the enemy's military forces in the field, from which the seizure of economic and political objectives would follow. To be sure, Clausewitz had also noted the need to destroy the enemy's will to fight, for, if the popular will remained intact, a new military force could be formed, but the assumption remained that destroying the ability would also eliminate the will to resist.[11]

At the heart of Barbarossa, however, was a dilemma, which Hitler well expressed in his insistence on securing as quickly as possible the economic and industrial resources of the Soviet Union. Lebensraum, of course, whether referring to economic resources or a utopian idea of racial resettlement, had always been the ultimate goal, but in this instance it meant something very specific to Hitler. The outbreak of war in 1939 had left Germany in a precarious position with regard to many key raw materials—none more critically than oil as overseas imports were cut off by the British blockade. By 1940, an astonishing 94 percent of German oil imports came from Rumania. This dependence proved a source of constant worry for Hitler, especially that the Rumanian oil fields might be crippled by Soviet or British bombers. Although the rapid conquests of 1940 had temporarily augmented the stocks of oil available, these increases had been outweighed by a greater liability as the Third Reich was now responsible for supplying the oil needs of both the occupied countries and its oil-poor allies. The stark reality facing the German war machine was inescapable, and, as early as March 1941, General Georg Thomas of the War Economy and Armaments Office had warned that existing stocks of oil would be exhausted by October. The only possibility of alleviating this desperate shortage would be "to seize quickly and exploit the Caucasus oilfields, at least the areas around Maikop and Grozny. . . . If this is not successful, we must expect the most serious repercussions, with unpredictable consequences for military operations after [September 1941] and for the survival of the economy."[12]

Barbarossa, however, promised the consumption of an enormous amount of oil, which Germany might be able to sustain in the short term, but with which it would be hard-pressed to cope if the campaign lasted longer than a few months. In addition, the Third Reich needed large quantities of oil and other raw materials in order to conduct the anticipated war of attrition against Great Britain and the United States. Winning quickly in the Soviet Union, and securing these vital resources, was, thus, an absolute necessity. In order to achieve this, Hitler ordered the creation of more mechanized units, but the problem of insufficient supplies of oil and gasoline with which to run and maintain these vehicles remained. As a result, the Wehrmacht was forced to rely extensively on horse-drawn transport, which led to further problems: the tremendous differences in the pace of march between the motorized and other units raised the issue of when and how to close pockets; horse-drawn columns were vulnerable to attacks that aggravated logistic problems; and the lack of fodder and replacement animals put a strain on civilian supplies.[13]

All the while, the larger questions of the main focus of the attack and how to win a quick victory remained unresolved. Hitler's ideas certainly violated Clausewitz's principles, but they were based not merely on an ideological agenda but on a clear understanding of German economic needs. In view of the later criticism of his meddling, it is worth mentioning that, in this instance, he had a far keener appreciation of the economic weaknesses faced by Germany than did his military advisers. Ironically, he had not initially insisted on his ideas but left planning for Barbarossa to the OKH, which stressed the classic military dictum of destroying the enemy army. His suggestions had eventually been incorporated in the overall plan, but not in such a way as to settle the question of the Schwerpunkt of the attack. Typically, Hitler and Halder did not discuss this obvious dichotomy in their views: Hitler simply assumed that the General Staff would accept his ideas, while Halder believed that operational developments would prove his emphasis on the capture of Moscow correct. As a result, no single objective dominated planning; three primary goals were identified, with an army group detailed to each, but with little regard for an eventual concentration of force. Subsequent attempts by army leaders to shape the operations in accordance with their plan led to a dispersal of effort and crippling delays while the key issues that should have been resolved in the beginning were now debated. Would it have been better to have focused the attack in the south? Stalin and Soviet military leaders certainly thought so and had placed the larger part of the Red Army in that area. They believed, given Hitler's obsession with the Balkans and especially Rumanian oil, that any German attack would target Ukraine and the Caucasus, with the aim of quickly acquiring the industrial, economic, and oil resources of southern Russia.[14]

The German operational plan thus failed to achieve clarity in how to destroy the Soviet will and ability to fight on: by crushing the main Soviet forces and seizing the capital or by conquering the key military-industrial areas of the country. In order to win, Germany had to capture the oil fields of the Caucasus as quickly as possible but launched its main effort against Moscow, far to the north. Even here, however, compromise and vacillation ruled as, in the final plan, significant forces had been peeled away from the central front and dispersed both to the north and to the south. In trying to do everything at once, German planners had largely assured that none of the three army groups had the means by which to achieve success. Nonetheless, even though it had military forces and economic resources clearly inadequate to accomplish its goals, Hitler once again hurled the Wehrmacht against a powerful opponent in an all-or-nothing gamble on short-term victory. Given the Wehrmacht's limited quantities of oil and gasoline, along with serious deficiencies in logistic preparation and supply capabilities, Barbarossa was from the outset a dangerous undertaking. Success meant that Germany would have the resources to fight a war of attrition against the Anglo-Saxon powers; failure would convert the temporary risk of a two-front war into strategic disaster. Although Goebbels recorded gleefully the initial frightful Russian losses and predicted, "We will soon have pulled it off," he also noted, with surprising candor: "We have to pull it off. There's a somewhat depressed mood among the people. . . . Each newly opened theater of war causes concern and worry."[15]

Despite the enormous quantitative strength of the Soviet defenders, the opening phase of Barbarossa seemed to vindicate German assumptions of a quick destruction of the Red Army. Along the entire front, German infantry and armored forces caught the startled Soviet defenders by surprise and advanced quickly against initially weak and patchy resistance. Intercepts of Soviet radio traffic confirmed the impression of surprise as up and down the line the common question was posed, "What should we do?" In some local areas, Russian troops fought stubbornly to the last man and delayed the German advance for a few hours, but this failed to alter the larger picture: the invaders had completely shattered Soviet border defenses. In the skies above the onrushing German forces, the Luftwaffe launched more than twelve hundred aircraft in an assault on Soviet airfields that destroyed over a thousand enemy planes, most on the ground, on the first day alone. In addition, the Luftwaffe sought to destroy Soviet command and control centers in an effort to turn the Red Army into a disorganized and chaotic mob. The Germans had seized the tactical initiative and now aimed to develop such momentum that the Soviets would be unable to organize an effective resistance, an urgency based on the realization that the campaign would have to be won in the first two weeks.[16]

In the first few hours, the shattering impact of the German ground and air onslaught destroyed the operational cohesion of the Red Army and paralyzed its ability to react, a calamity intensified by Stalin's initial unwillingness to order Soviet countermeasures. Fearing that the German attack was a provocation, the Soviet dictator seemed at first not to comprehend the magnitude of the disaster, thinking even that German generals had launched an attack without Hitler's knowledge. Then, when he did authorize Soviet resistance, he and the Red Army command had difficulty imposing control over the utter chaos at the front and comprehending the speed of the German advance, which confounded all their expectations of initial probing attacks on the border. With communications disrupted and little information about the situation at the front, Stalin moved in a dream world where orders such as the one issued on the evening of 22 June to launch an immediate counteroffensive were passed on by subordinate officers, even though they knew the reality, simply because they feared retribution for refusing to obey. Not for a few days, in fact, would Stalin truly comprehend the magnitude of the looming catastrophe facing the Soviet Union, and, when he finally did, on 27 June, his subsequent actions revealed a man on the verge of a nervous breakdown.[17]

Nowhere was the magnitude of the initial German triumph more evident than in Belorussia, the sector of Army Group Center, which, under the command of Field Marshal Fedor von Bock, had been assigned the main area of operations. Bock was an experienced officer who had led armies in both Poland and Holland, a man in whom Hitler had great confidence. Given the task of penetrating Soviet defenses north and south of the Bialystok salient, advancing eastward along the Minsk-Smolensk axis, then encircling and destroying enemy forces west of the Dnieper River, Bock's army group contained the bulk of German armor and aircraft. His two mechanized formations, Panzergruppe 2 under General Heinz Guderian and Panzergruppe 3 under General Hermann Hoth, were to strike rapidly to the east on either side of the sector and envelop enemy forces, which would then be destroyed by the infantry armies under Field Marshal Günther von Kluge. Although several major rivers would have to be crossed, this area of rolling land was generally favorable to mobile warfare.[18]

On the southern sector, the German attackers in Panzergruppe 2 caught the Soviet defenders by surprise, quickly crossed the Bug, bypassed the fortress of Brest-Litovsk (which held out until 12 July), ignored enemy units on their flanks, and advanced rapidly to the east. On the northern wing, Panzergruppe 3 captured three bridges over the Neman intact and, by 24 June, had captured Vilnius, the capital of Lithuania. Two days later, elements of Guderian's force took Slutsk, sixty miles south of Minsk, while Hoth's troops were only eighteen miles to the north of the city. That same day, Guderian, who aimed to thrust farther to the east, received orders to turn the bulk of his forces northward and close the pocket by linking up with Hoth. Although both panzer generals preferred to continue the advance to Smolensk, some two hundred miles to the east, before closing the pincers, they reluctantly obeyed the order, closing the outer ring and seizing Minsk on 28 June. A weak inner ring had also been closed around Bialystok by Kluge's infantry, although they had trouble keeping pace with the advancing armor. As a result, numerous Red Army soldiers escaped eastward, where their presence as partisans and roaming groups caused continuing difficulties in

German rear areas, tying down mobile units, and delaying their advance eastward. They also fed Hitler's anxiety about deep penetrations and the fear that encircled Soviet forces might simply escape through the overextended panzer forces, a fear not without justification.[19]

The inadequacy of German power, in fact, now sparked the first signs of disagreement among Hitler and his generals. Bock and his panzer commanders had always favored a deep envelopment, such as achieved in France, while Hitler preferred the certain destruction of enemy forces in small, tighter, tactical envelopments, fearing that, otherwise, the encircled area would be so large that German forces would be insufficient to destroy the trapped Russians. Halder vacillated, at first accepting Hitler's argument, then, when he became convinced that Soviet forces were not attempting a strategic withdrawal, expressing the hope that the field commanders would on their own initiative "do the right thing [i.e., advance toward Smolensk] even without express orders." As Halder struggled to this conclusion, however, Bock fumed, "We are unnecessarily throwing away a major success." The battles at Bialystok-Minsk tied down roughly half the strength of Army Group Center in the effort to destroy enemy forces that refused to surrender. Previous experience with blitzkrieg, when an enemy maneuvered into a trap lost the will to fight, was turned upside-down as Soviet troops fought on even in hopeless conditions. The German attack was, thus, constrained by the new reality on the ground. Tactics that had proved successful in France failed against the much less compliant adversary in the east. By themselves, the panzer units had insufficient forces with which to seal off an encirclement totally, and, since poor roads, lack of motorization, and the fierce fighting delayed the Landsers, the gap between the slogging infantry and the driving panzers widened. The result was that, in the trackless spaces of Russia, large numbers of Soviet troops slipped through encirclements.[20]

The problem, then, stemmed not so much from Hitler's meddling as from the unexpectedly strong Russian resistance. After the chaotic first days of the invasion, the Soviets succeeded in regaining a measure of control over their units and in bringing up reinforcements. In some areas, they even launched vigorous counterattacks using reserve divisions equipped with armor. The encircled Soviet units also fought with a disconcerting fury while inflicting heavy losses on the attacking German infantry. From the outset, the Germans encountered sharp, fierce fighting that unnerved even veterans of the previous campaigns, accustomed as they were to an enemy who would give up when surrounded, not one who put up a stubborn defense, refusing to surrender while inflicting not inconsiderable casualties. Goebbels admitted with some amazement that Soviet troops fought courageously while worrying about growing illusions of a quick, easy victory among the German people. This continuing Russian resistance, despite the sledgehammer blows of the first days, faced the Germans with a dilemma. To accomplish the main task of the first phase of the campaign, the destruction of Soviet forces west of the Dnieper, the armored formations needed to race eastward toward Smolensk in order to maintain the momentum of the attack, but the presence of large numbers of Red Army soldiers continuing to resist tied down precisely these mobile forces until the slower advancing infantry units arrived. As would become increasingly apparent, the Germans lacked sufficient strength, a weakness that operational skill could mask only so long. Still, on 30 June, Goebbels noted exultantly the fall of Minsk, the enemy loss of over 2,000 tanks and 4,000 aircraft, the enormous booty, and lines of prisoners without end. Nor did he exaggerate as the double envelopment of Bialystok-Minsk, within which the fighting concluded only on 9 July, resulted in 324,000 Red Army prisoners, 3,300 tanks, and 1,800 artillery pieces captured or destroyed.[21]

In the north, the forces of Army Group North under Field Marshal Wilhelm Ritter von Leeb had achieved similar success. Attacking northeastward from East Prussia, his three armies aimed at a rapid movement through the Baltic states, an area in which the population to be freed from recent Soviet rule was assumed to be friendly, in order to seize the Dvina River crossings before large numbers of Red Army troops could escape. Colonel-General Erich Hoepner's Fourth Panzergruppe, consisting of Colonel-Generals Hans Reinhardt's and Erich von Manstein's Forty-first and Fifty-sixth Motorized Corps, ripped apart the Soviet frontier defenses in a rapid and violent assault, quickly building momentum that the Russians could not stop. Although Soviet resistance stiffened steadily, by 1 July the Germans had crushed Soviet defense lines, were across the Dvina, had seized Riga, and had begun advancing into Estonia and the Leningrad region. With shorter supply lines, better railroads, and the quick capture of Baltic seaports, Army Group North also enjoyed better logistic support. The fact that German forces captured large quantities of Soviet supplies and that numerous bridges and rail lines were seized intact also aided the German invaders. In the opening battles, the Soviets had lost almost 100,000 soldiers, more than 1,000 tanks, 4,000 guns, and over 1,000 aircraft and still had not been able to slow the German advance, let alone establish a credible defensive line. As in the center, Russian troops had begun to fight stoutly, but the initial defeats threatened Leningrad with disaster.[22]

Only in the south had the Germans experienced less initial success. Halder's original plan for a large envelopment operation from Rumania and southern Poland had been abandoned for lack of reliable allied forces. Army Group South under the command of Field Marshal Gerd von Rundstedt thus faced the task of destroying Soviet forces in Galicia and western Ukraine in a single thrust from Lublin to Kiev, then driving down the Dnieper River to the southeast to prevent Red Army troops in the west from escaping. Rundstedt's undertaking was made difficult by a number of factors, of which two were most critical. First, the terrain, and especially the vast tract of the Pripet Marshes, impeded his initial assault and provided the Soviets valuable time to react. Second, since Stalin and his military advisers assumed that the goal of any German attack would be to seize the economic riches of Ukraine, Soviet forces in the area were not only more numerous but also better trained, equipped, led, and prepared for the German onslaught. Although the German attack achieved a relative degree of tactical surprise, therefore, enemy resistance stiffened almost immediately as their actions indicated clearly that the Soviets meant to fight stubbornly along the borders. Counterattacks with large forces slowed the German advance, as did heavy rains that turned the primitive road system into muddy quagmires and impeded supply efforts. Fierce fighting at Lvov as well as furious Soviet counterattacks to the northeast at Rovno and Dubno, along the main axis toward Kiev, slowed the German advance for a week while creating a crisis on his southern flank that, ultimately, tempted Hitler to redirect forces from Army Group Center away from Moscow in order to secure Ukraine. Significantly, this energetic and stubborn Soviet defense came in the area that held the most important objectives of Operation Barbarossa, the raw materials and industrial centers of Ukraine and the oil fields of the Caucasus. The border battles in Ukraine also clearly demonstrated that, given time and leadership, Red Army soldiers were capable of effective resistance, but the price paid was dear. The Soviets lost 242,000 soldiers, over 4,300 tanks, 5,800 guns, and 1,200 combat aircraft.[23]

Hitler's crusade in Russia had, thus, begun spectacularly. Displaying operational skill, superb training and leadership, excellent coordination between ground and air forces, and high morale, German forces had in the first three weeks of the war thrust some three hundred miles into the Soviet Union, swallowing up Belorussia and the Baltic states, seizing large swaths of Ukraine, and advancing to the Dnieper River along the road to Moscow. The Wehrmacht had demolished the Red Army's border defenses and ripped apart numerous frontline Soviet formations. Red Army losses had been staggering: by mid-July over 1 million men killed, wounded, missing, or captured and roughly 10,000 tanks and 4,000 aircraft destroyed. The Soviet mechanized forces that had initially engaged the Germans had been reduced to perhaps 10 percent of their original strength. Although not inconsiderable, German losses from 22 June to 16 July totaled a little over 100,000 men killed, wounded, and missing, a figure one-third lower than that for a comparable period in the French campaign a year earlier. By any measure, the German victory appeared both astounding and complete.[24]

Despite the slow progress in the southern sector, senior German political and military leaders exulted in their triumph. "On the whole, then," Halder recorded in his diary on 3 July, "it may be said even now that the objective to shatter the bulk of the Russian army this side of the Dvina and Dnieper has been accomplished. . . . East of the Dvina and Dnieper we [will] encounter nothing more than partial forces, not strong enough to hinder realization of German operational plans." The army chief of staff then declared, "*It is thus probably no overstatement to say that the Russian campaign has been won in the space of two weeks*" (emphasis added). He went on to add a note of caution: "Of course, this does not yet mean that it is closed. The sheer geographical vastness of the country and the stubbornness of the resistance, which is carried on with all means, will claim our efforts for many more weeks to come." Still, Halder seemed confident: "Once we are across the Dvina and Dnieper, it will be less a question of smashing enemy armies than of denying the enemy possession of his production centers and so prevent his raising a new army with the aid of his gigantic industrial potential and his inexhaustible manpower resources." The next day, Hitler put the matter more succinctly: "I constantly try to put myself in the situation of the enemy. He [Stalin] has practically lost the war already. It is good that we have destroyed the Russian tank and air forces at the outset. The Russians can no longer replace them."[25]

Although these evaluations were based on incorrect assumptions, as would soon become evident, they nonetheless resulted in a series of far-reaching decisions whose significance for the shape and outcome of the war cannot be overstated. Even before the invasion, on 11 June, Hitler had issued Directive No. 32, "Preparations for the Period after Barbarossa," which anticipated only a relatively small force in Russia in the winter of 1941–1942. Then, on 14 July, he ordered a reorientation in armaments production to favor the Luftwaffe and navy, a clear indication that he expected the imminent end of the war in the east and, unlike the year before, aimed to be prepared for the next showdown, that with the Anglo-American powers. The immense surface and air fleets envisioned by the Führer, fueled by the oil from the Caucasus, would enable Germany to fight the anticipated war for world supremacy against America. In conversations with the Japanese ambassador, Hitler even talked grandiosely of a common war with Japan against the United States. In the present, however, this decision meant that, while the Soviets made good their staggering tank losses and with better models, German tank production declined throughout the remainder of 1941.[26]

Similar optimism, with ominous implications for the people of the newly occupied eastern territories, pervaded the Führer's seemingly endless monologues. In early July, he talked of the beauty of the Crimea, of spreading the prosperity to be created through this conquest of Lebensraum to the German masses, of spreading the area of German settlement eastward even beyond the Urals. He related his hatred of the Bolsheviks, his plans to eradicate Leningrad and Moscow, his contempt for the Slavic peoples, who would simply be put to hard work under German control, and his admiration for Stalin's brutality. His model for domination and exploitation, he mentioned on numerous occasions, was British India. To Hitler, the raj represented not just an example of how a small country could control a large area, but power and prosperity, the means by which Great Britain had become a world power. Through ruthless economic exploitation and harsh rule, the vast expanse of European Russia would be the key to a large, integrated economic area that would provide prosperity and economic security for the Greater German Reich. "The struggle for hegemony in the world will be decided in favor of Europe by the possession of the Russian space," he declared to his entourage. "It will make Europe into an impregnable fortress, the most blockade-proof place on Earth." The United States could then "get lost, as far as we are concerned."[27]

His consistent social Darwinism, in fact, provided all the justification Hitler needed for his actions. In order to secure the existence of the Volk, all measures were acceptable: might made right. Indeed, a culturally superior people denied adequate living space had an obligation to take what it needed; that was, after all, the law of nature. Nor would the struggle ever end; for Hitler, only two options existed: fight and win or die. Shaped profoundly by his own experience of war, Hitler saw in it the essence of human activity. "What meeting a man means for a girl," Jochmann recalled him revealing, "war meant for him." Living meant killing: "Coming into being, existing, and passing away, there's always a killing. Everything that is born must later die."[28]

Less well-known but no less important to Hitler were his ideas on a new social order, which perhaps could be termed *racialist modernism*. The other formative experience of his life, his resentment that his "talents" had been left unrecognized by a class-bound society, smoldered constantly. Much of the appeal of National Socialism in the 1930s, in fact, was based on Hitler's promise to build a new society that would reward talent. He thus advocated free education for all talented young people, regardless of social or class origin, the improvement of working conditions in factories, the provision of holidays for workers, the creation of a cheap automobile the average worker could afford, and the construction of suitable housing for working families. He was fascinated as well with modern technology and the way in which it could improve the quality of life of a people. In a sense, Hitler sought to create a modern, classless, mobile society that rewarded talent and provided security, but one that substituted racial for class distinctions. The fault line in the National Socialist Volksgemeinschaft was clear: those classified as Aryans would enjoy the benefits of the new social order and prosperity to be created out of exploitation of the east; those outside the community, depending on their racial status, could expect victimization, enslavement, or death.[29]

Barbarossa, as Adam Tooze has stressed, thus marked a significant departure: it was not only the most massive military campaign in history, but it also unleashed an unprecedented campaign of genocidal violence, of which the Holocaust remains the best-known example. This Judeocide, however, was not an isolated act of murder; rather, it formed part of a deliberate, comprehensive plan of exploitation, a utopian scheme of racial reorganization and demographic engineering of vast proportions. The Nazis had attempted, and failed, in 1939–1940 amid appalling brutality to carry off a smaller resettlement scheme in Poland and had seen the inflated hopes of the Madagascar Plan come to naught because of the intransigence of the British, but, if anything, these failures only intensified their enthusiasm for population transfer and resettlement. Why not? The presumed quick victory in the east would bring millions more Jews under Nazi control, and it conjured visions not only of solving the Jewish question but also of reordering the racial composition of Eastern Europe. At the same time, vast areas would be opened to German colonization. Best of all, it could be accomplished entirely under German control. In the short term, German administrators of the conquered eastern territories would ruthlessly exploit the food resources of the area to ensure, as Hitler emphasized repeatedly, that in this war it would not be Germans who starved. Complementing this would be the long-term project of racial engineering that would open the eastern

lands to German colonization and development, as the ethnic boundary of Germany was to be pushed to the Ural Mountains. In the process,
tens of millions of Slavic inhabitants (and Jews) would be killed, either
through deliberate starvation or as a result of forcible emigration.[30]

If in execution the German plans for the occupied east resembled the
last act in the bloody history of European colonialism, in inspiration Nazi
ideas actually had more in common with American Manifest Destiny. Hitler had little interest in colonies, preferring, along the lines of the American frontier myth, millions of farmers who would settle and develop the
area, modernize it, and make it a realm of new beginnings. "Our Mississippi must be the Volga, not the Niger," Hitler declared in the autumn of
1941, while emphasizing that the bloody conquest of the American West
provided both historical precedent and justification. "Here in the east a
similar process will repeat itself for the second time as in the conquest
of America," he exulted, whereby an allegedly superior settler population had displaced a supposedly inferior native population, thus opening unlimited economic possibilities. "Europe—and not America—will be
the land of unlimited possibilities." This was a modernizing vision, one
closely tied to the Nazi promise of the 1930s that the Germans should
finally achieve a quality of life commensurate with their racial value. The
abundant resources of the east, combined with German expertise and
capital investment, would propel a dramatic increase in the standard of
living, made possible at the expense of the eastern peoples.[31]

The concrete expression of this program of racial reorganization, the
blueprint for the social order to be erected in the east, was *Generalplan
Ost* (General plan for the east), developed by Professor Konrad Meyer of
Himmler's Reich Commissariat for the Strengthening of the German
People (RKFDV). Officially charged by Himmler just one day before the
launch of Barbarossa with drawing up a blueprint for the colonization
and restructuring of the eastern territories, Meyer presented a first draft
of the plan just three weeks later, on 15 July, that clearly indicated that
he had been working on the matter for some time. A project that envisioned extensive German settlement and exploitation of the east as well
as the forced Germanization, displacement, and expulsion of millions of
people, it necessitated the creation of slave labor camps whose inmates
would be set to work on the enormous construction projects. Meyer himself foresaw the "resettlement" of 65–85 percent of the Baltic, Polish,
Ukrainian, and Belorussian populations, with numbers thrown around
ranging from 31 to 51 million people. Since the ultimate destination
of those displaced remained unclear, "natural wastage" on a vast scale
must have been assumed, so genocide was implicit in Generalplan Ost

from the beginning. In its assumption of mass death through slave labor and the physical destruction of certain groups (Bolsheviks, Communist bureaucrats, Jews, the urban population of Russia), the plan anticipated and was directly linked to the so-called Final Solution.[32]

By the time German forces invaded the Soviet Union, then, a considerable murderous momentum had already been built up. Large numbers of Jews were already dying of "natural causes" in the wretchedly overcrowded ghettos of Poland, while the brutal treatment of the local population in occupied Poland as well as Hitler's firm intention to fight a war of annihilation in Russia both lowered the threshold of genocidal violence. If the purpose of the war was threefold—to destroy the threat of Jewish-Bolshevism, to find a solution to the Jewish question, and to secure living space for Germany's elevation to great power status—the ends would determine the means. The SS and Einsatzgruppen would implement the first two goals, while the Ostheer, in feeding itself off the land, would reduce the strain on the German home front while ensuring that malnutrition would claim the lives of millions of Soviet citizens.

Given the set of criminal orders issued to the army and the creation of the SS murder squads, it should be no surprise that killings of civilians began almost immediately after German forces crossed the Soviet frontier and quickly escalated in scope and intensity. Although Heydrich had briefed Einsatzgruppen leaders on their tasks, his early instructions had been relatively restrictive, even if imprecise. The initial killings were to target those groups listed in the Commissar Order: political officers in the army, Communist Party officials and functionaries, the Jewish-Bolshevik intelligentsia, and young male Jews (as the likely source of any partisan resistance). Still, Heydrich granted wide discretionary powers to squad leaders to interpret their instructions in a suitably radical fashion. Not atypically, then, zealous local commanders often interpreted the vague guidelines in more radical fashion in order, for example, to kill all male Jews in a village or rural area. The first killings, in fact, were perpetrated by a local Gestapo official in Tilsit, in East Prussia along the Lithuanian border, who on his own initiative but in accordance with directives issued by the leader of Einsatzgruppe A, Franz Walter Stahlecker, on 24 June ordered the shooting of two hundred male Jews in Garsden. A few days later, a police battalion slaughtered two thousand Jews in Bialystok, including women and children, many of them burned alive in a synagogue that had been set on fire. German police officials also encouraged the local population, especially in Lithuania, to foment pogroms against the Jewish population. Some, such as that in Kaunas, the Lithuanian capital, on the night of 25–26 June involved appalling brutality, with more than fifteen hundred Jews "eliminated" and several synagogues burned in a chaos of horror. In one frightful scene, a young Lithuanian with a club beat fifteen to twenty Jews to death amid a chorus of enthusiastic cheers and laughter from the onlooking crowd, which burst into the national anthem at the end. Invariably, these destructive precedents established on the local level were sanctioned by Himmler or Heydrich, thus setting new levels of acceptable violence.[33]

Einsatzgruppen units had also swung into deadly action by early July. On the third, the head of an Einsatzkommando in eastern Poland had 1,160 Jewish men shot. In Kaunas, Lithuania, units of Einsatzgruppe A shot almost 500 Jews on 4 July, while two days later they killed 2,514. In Bialystok, almost 1,000 Jews were murdered in the first half of the month. The other Einsatzgruppen were active as well, with shootings widespread in Belorussia and Ukraine, although the various murder squad leaders in these areas interpreted their orders differently. While Einsatzgruppe A seemed virtually unconstrained in its murderous activities, Einsatzgruppe B in Belorussia initially targeted Jewish intellectuals, while its counterpart in Ukraine, Einsatzgruppe C, indicated its intention of working Jews to death in labor projects. Himmler and Heydrich also fomented the killing process through their frequent visits to the field, appealing to their subordinates' sense of initiative, and exhorting police and SS officials to greater efforts in killing Jews. In this initial phase of the killing process, a complex dynamic developed. Instructions issued from the center both encouraged radical action and protected individuals from any legal consequences, but, in the absence of a specific killing order, top Nazi leaders left considerable room for local initiative. As commanders on the ground began to act in an increasingly murderous fashion, encouraged by SS officials to interpret their orders liberally, news of their actions spread to other commanders, who, anxious to be seen as diligent in such an important matter, also stepped up the pace of killings. This furthered the radicalizing process while at the same time encouraging the top leadership to amend policy in a more deadly direction since little resistance to the killing had emerged. As orders and encouragement from the top mingled with murderous initiatives from below, a tornadic spiral of violence resulted, one that quickly accelerated the pace of radicalization.[34]

Although local inhabitants had been encouraged to instigate pogroms, with the exception of a few areas, mostly in Lithuania, this proved much more difficult than anticipated. As a result, the Einsatzgruppen developed a more or less typical routine in which a murder squad would enter a town, assemble the intended victims, march them to a relatively remote area nearby, and shoot them. A killing operation in Lithuania in early July was characteristic of such actions across the breadth of the Soviet Union. According to an onlooker, a soldier with a motorized infantry unit, hundreds of Jews from the local village had been marched to a gravel pit, where they were sent in groups to be shot. "The firing squad," the eyewitness recalled,

> which was made up of ten men, positioned itself . . . about six to eight meters in front of the group [to be killed]. . . . The group was shot by the firing squad after the order was given. The shots were fired simultaneously so that the men fell into the pit behind them at the same time. The 400 Jews were shot in exactly the same way over a period of about an hour. . . . They were covered with a thin sprinkling of sand. . . . Parts of their bodies protruded out of the sand. . . . The mass shootings in Paneriai were quite horrific.

Similar scenes took place throughout the newly conquered areas. Often, little direction from above was needed. An SS officer recorded in his diary the scene in Drohobycz, in Galicia, where at the fortress "soldiers stood with fist thick clubs" and struck down the Jews, who lay about "whimpering like pigs." When asked who led the squad, the reply was, "Nobody. . . . Out of rage and hatred the Jews were being struck down." Inevitably, the killing process developed a bloody momentum, one that could be seen in the meticulously recorded figures of the reports of the various murder squads. Daily numbers in the scores rapidly escalated to the hundreds, then to the thousands, as local commanders, on their own initiative and in response to encouragement from above, broadened the scope of the killing operations. This first killing sweep, in fact, proved to be crucially important for later developments, for it illustrated that few logistic, political, or moral impediments stood in the way of mass murder. A new threshold had been crossed.[35]

In all this, the Wehrmacht leadership took an active role. In prewar briefings, Einsatzgruppen commanders and police leaders had been urged to observe scrupulously the agreement between the SS and the army, which suggests that Heydrich was unsure of the extent of Wehrmacht cooperation. Given the negative reaction of some army commanders in Poland in 1939, he could not be sure that they would tolerate mass executions. Despite these concerns, reports from commanders of the murder squads indicated both surprise and relief that from the beginning the army had raised no problems and that cooperation was proceeding "extremely satisfactorily and without friction."

Despite instances of hesitant implementation of the criminal orders, the army attitude was described as "generally good," "excellent, almost cordial," "extraordinary," and "especially successful." The Einsatzgruppe B leader, Arthur Nebe, in fact, praised the "excellent" cooperation with Army Group Center that had made possible the successful killing actions in Bialystok and Minsk. Similarly, Stahlecker hailed the spirit of cooperation between Einsatzgruppe A and Army Group North, even though Field Marshal Leeb had expressed initial reservations about their activities. So extensive was the collaboration that in many sectors the Einsatzgruppen, although limited by the prewar agreement only to the rear areas, were allowed to follow immediately behind the advancing troops. Sections of some commandos often advanced with the tank spearheads. Nor was there much doubt about what these special units were doing; one frontline officer noted in early December that the combat officer corps was fully informed about the execution of Jews.[36]

Important in these early days was the blurring of the distinction between ideologically inspired murder and the pacification operations of the rear-area security units of the army. The Army High Command consistently encouraged a harsh response to "anti-German" elements as an effective preventive measure, while the OKW had already in mid-May issued guidelines demanding "ruthless and energetic action against Bolshevik agitators, guerrillas, saboteurs, and Jews." Some commanders had, on their personal initiative, gone even further. Colonel-General Hoepner, the commander of Panzergruppe A, asserted that the war against the Soviet Union touched on the very existence of Germany and, thus, demanded the "complete destruction of the enemy," especially the "exponents of the present Russian-Bolshevik system." To many officers, the political commissars, the "exponents of the Jewish-Bolshevik world outlook," had introduced "Asiatic methods" of barbarity into the war. These "Asiatic methods," Hitler had stressed in an earlier order, "could not be countered with western European means." As one staff officer concluded in a mid-July report: "We have all come to know these Asiatic methods, every town, every village in the Ukraine harbors its unfortunate victims. . . . Our duty and our right to free the world from the Red plague are all the greater."[37]

In addition, top German commanders had a visceral hatred of communism based on their traumatic experiences of the revolutionary chaos and political collapse of November 1918, for which they held the Jews primarily responsible, an attitude reinforced by the growing brutality of the war in the east. In early October, Field Marshal von Reichenau, commander of the Sixth Army, stressed to his men that the goal of the campaign was the complete destruction of the Jewish-Bolshevik system, reminding his troops, "The soldier in the east is not just a fighter according to the rules of war, but also the bearer of an implacable national idea, and the avenger of all the bestialities inflicted on the German[s]. . . . For that reason, the soldier must have full understanding of the need for a harsh but just punishment of Jewish subhumanity." Nor was Reichenau's attitude unique. Colonel-General Hoth also understood the war as an ideological struggle to the death, urging his troops to recognize, "This struggle can only end with the annihilation of one or the other; there can be no settlement." Hoth justified this harsh attitude, and the executions being carried out by Einsatzgruppe C, by pointing to the alleged guilt of the Jews for German sufferings after World War I. Manstein, too, picked up on this theme of justified revenge, stressing to his men, "The Jewish-Bolshevik system must be wiped out once and for all. . . . [The German soldier must be] the bearer of a national idea, and avenger of all the atrocities inflicted on him and the German people." The Jews, as the supporters of the partisans and the intellectual carriers of "Bolshevik terror," Manstein stressed, had to be harshly punished. Terror had to be legitimized; mass executions were to be seen not as murder but as justifiable reprisals for atrocities against the German people as well as a preventive measure to provide security in the present.[38]

Nor were non-Nazi generals unaffected by the poisoned ideological climate. When General Franz von Roques, the commander of Rear Army North, complained to the commander in chief, Field Marshal Ritter von Leeb, about mass executions of Lithuanian Jews in Kaunas, Leeb, a deeply religious man, noted in his diary, "We have no influence over these measures. The only thing to do is keep clear of them. Roques is no doubt correct that the Jewish question will probably not be solved in this manner. The surest way to solve it would be through sterilization of all Jewish men." If even Leeb, surely no friend of the Nazis, saw mass sterilization as a humane alternative to mass murder, it could surely be no surprise, then, that army personnel shot large numbers of political commissars, regarded as Jews and easily recognizable by their special uniform insignia, in the first weeks of the war.[39]

Although Hitler had intended just such an overlapping of motivations, two other factors also encouraged a radicalization of operations: the shootings and mutilation of German prisoners of war by Soviet troops and Stalin's call on 3 July for unleashing partisan war against the invaders and killing them everywhere. Hitler positively welcomed the latter measure, remarking in mid-July that the partisan war "gives us the possibility of exterminating anyone who opposes us." As for the former, within the first two weeks of the war, numerous incidents of shootings of German prisoners had been reported as well as instances of inhuman treatment. Both were played up by Goebbels's propaganda machine as typical examples of the perfidy of Jewish-Bolshevism, the propaganda minister boasting that Soviet atrocities had demonstrated to the Landsers the justice and necessity of the German attack while assuring that "our soldiers will return from the Soviet Union as radical anti-Bolsheviks."[40]

Nor did German troops, increasingly concerned for their own survival, find it difficult to dehumanize an enemy who chose to resist fanatically. "It's not people we're fighting against here, but simply animals," concluded one Landser in early July after witnessing the mutilated remains of comrades recently taken prisoner by the Russians. Karl Fuchs, a committed Nazi ideologue, remarked of Russian prisoners of war in a letter to his wife, "Hardly ever do you see the face of a person who seems rational and intelligent. . . . The wild, half crazy look in their eyes makes them appear like imbeciles." The tendency of Soviet troops to respond in kind to German atrocities led one soldier to conclude, "Bestiality breeds bestiality." Nazi propaganda had demonized and dehumanized the Soviet population even before the campaign, but specific actions, such as the early July massacre and mutilation of 153 German prisoners, found with eyes gouged out and limbs and genitals hacked off, seemed to confirm this judgment while instilling an elemental fear of the enemy in many Landsers.[41]

One Landser in early July expressed well this intersection of the political and personal, noting graphically in a letter to his parents what he and his fellow soldiers had done after discovering the bound and mutilated bodies of German Landsers, as well as some two thousand Ukrainians and ethnic Germans, left behind by the retreating Soviets:

> Revenge was quick to follow. Yesterday we and the SS were merciful, for every Jew we found was shot immediately. Today things have changed, for we again found 60 fellow soldiers mutilated. Now the Jews must carry the dead out of the basement, lay them out nicely, and then they are shown the atrocities. After they have seen the victims, they are killed with clubs and spades.
>
> So far, we have sent about 1,000 Jews into the hereafter, but that is far too few for what they have done. The Ukrainians have said that the Jews had all the leadership positions and, together with the Soviets, had a regular public festival while executing the Germans and Ukrainians. I ask you, dear parents, to make this

known. . . . If there should be doubts, we will bring photos with us. Then there will be no more doubts.[42]

The presence of SS personnel was also revealing, confirming as it did the reports of excellent cooperation between the army and the death squads. This cooperation, at a minimum, involved providing the Einsatzgruppen with equipment, supplies, ammunition, transport, and housing. Without the logistic and administrative support provided by the Wehrmacht, murder on such a large scale would hardly have been possible. At times, army units played a more active role, helping set up ghettos, identifying and guarding the victims, and participating in the shootings themselves. An early July diary entry of Robert Neumann, a corporal in the Sixty-second Infantry Division, illustrated well the de facto nature of the cooperation of army units in the killing process: "We arrived in Minsk. Our battalion got the task of guarding six-thousand prisoners and shooting all the Jews in the city. Many prisoners fled in the night and we had to make use of our weapons. We killed five-hundred Jews alone." A few months later, evidently hardened to such tasks, Neumann reported on a mass execution near Orsha. "Yesterday our lieutenant sought fifteen men with strong nerves," he noted.

> Naturally I volunteered. . . . The lieutenant explained to us what we had to do. There were about a thousand Jews in the village of Krupka and they were all supposed to be shot today . . . Punctually at 7:00 A.M. all the Jews reported to the assembly point—men, women, and children. . . . The whole formation then marched off in the direction of the nearest swamp. The execution squad, to which I belonged, marched in front. . . . The Jews had been told that they were all going to be sent to Germany to work there. But as we went straight over the tracks . . . and further in the direction of the swamp, the light went on for most of them. A panic broke out and the guard detail had their hands full to keep the bunch together. As we reached the swamp . . . fifteen yards ahead was a deep ditch full of water. The first ten had to stand next to this ditch and undress to the waist, then wade into the water, and the firing squad, that is us, stood over them. . . . Ten shots, ten Jews bumped off. It went on like that until we had disposed of all of them. . . . It was a spectacle that one will not quickly forget.

Two days later, Neumann was at it again, this time, since there was no nearby swamp, "depositing" Jews in the sand.[43]

The assumption of an implicit link between Jews and Communists, as well as the notion that Jews instigated atrocities and acts of resistance, was widespread among officers and in the ranks. The major concern of officers, in fact, seemed to be the often overenthusiastic participation of Wehrmacht soldiers in the shootings as well as the chronic problem of "execution tourism" as soldiers would often flock to scenes of executions and snap photographs. Although some officers urged a different approach, favoring a policy of winning the cooperation of the local population and decrying the large-scale shooting of hostages, the OKH insisted that the security of the German soldier and the rapid pacification of such a vast area required hard and merciless action. Any leniency, it was believed, would be misinterpreted as weakness that would only encourage partisan resistance. By the autumn, in fact, just such an upsurge in the partisan war fed a growing sense of vulnerability among average soldiers as they realized the inadequacy of German security forces in the immensity of Russia. Those assigned to security units, generally older and less trained, often felt beleaguered and isolated in a hostile and alien landscape. Atrocity fed atrocity, as one soldier explained: "We . . . may be ruthless, but the partisans also wage an inhuman war and show no mercy." War brutalizes, with some dehumanization of the enemy to be expected, but the vicious cycle of atrocities and revenge unleashed by partisan war increased the pressure to participate in or ignore excesses. In this battle for naked existence, as Christian Hartmann has emphasized, many men, seemingly unlikely candidates to commit such crimes because of their age or previous socialization, "began to orient themselves much more strongly around social Darwinistic principles." Fear of partisans contributed mightily to the Landsers' readiness to cooperate with the Einsatzgruppen and security forces. By the autumn, both army units and, more frequently, rear security units routinely shot Jews as a "retaliatory measure" aimed at quashing the increasingly effective partisan movement.[44]

By late summer, Wehrmacht, SS, and police officials agreed on the inseparable link between Jews and partisans, which both increased the need for interagency cooperation and meant that intensified pacification measures fell most harshly on Jews. Racial and security concerns thus trumped the economic considerations of using Jews as a labor force; that autumn, Himmler repeatedly assured his men in the field of the need to liquidate Jews in order to crush Bolshevism and secure territory for German settlement. In mid-September, Keitel demanded "relentless and energetic measures, above all against the Jews, the main supporters of Bolshevism," while, a month later, Brauchitsch echoed this with his own call for "ruthless and merciless" action. Jews, the commander of one security division emphasized, were "the sole supporters that the partisans can find" and, thus, should be remorselessly destroyed. Throughout Belorussia and Ukraine in late September and early October, as a result, SS and police units, supported by Wehrmacht security divisions, employed a task-oriented, flexible approach, mimicking the famed *Auftragstaktik* (mission-oriented tactics) in the military arena, in order to promote an efficient "de-Jewification" of the region.[45]

The best known of these ubiquitous mass executions by the murder squads, that of over thirty-three thousand men, women, and children at Babi Yar in late September 1941, illustrated well the intersection of security and ideological motives as well as the ample cooperation between army and SS. Beyond the obvious fact that it was German military success that created the conditions for the murder of the Jews of Kiev, relations between Reichenau, the commander of the Sixth Army, whose units seized the city on 19 September, and the head of Sonderkommando 4a of Einsatzgruppe C, SS Colonel Paul Blobel, were excellent. The two had already worked closely on coordinating the murder of Jews during the preceding months, with Blobel in personal contact with Reichenau during this period. The two also shared similar racial and ideological views that made the killing of Jews imperative. Just over a month earlier, in fact, Reichenau had personally intervened to order the Jewish children of Belaya Tserkov, temporarily spared when their parents had been murdered, to be shot as well. The head of Einsatzgruppe C, Otto Rasch, also valued Reichenau's cooperation highly, while the latter often praised the valuable work of the special murder commandos. From the outset, a harmonious working relationship had been created between the army and the Einsatzgruppe, with the latter repeatedly encouraged to operate as far forward as possible.[46]

The capture of Kiev took place against a backdrop of continued frantic Soviet resistance and unexpected difficulties in occupying the city. Numerous buildings and facilities had been booby-trapped, putting German soldiers and authorities on edge. Between 24 and 26 September, powerful explosions rocked the city center, destroying a number of buildings in which the Wehrmacht had set up headquarters, and killing several hundred occupation troops. Obsessed with security, and determined to punish the guilty party, army and SS officials met on 26 September to discuss the situation and settle on appropriate "retaliatory measures." Not surprisingly, the decision was taken to kill a large number of Jews. Einsatzgruppe representatives were informed, "You have to do the shooting," even though army leaders had no objections to such a massacre and were, in fact, promoting it. In this instance, security concerns and ideology blended seamlessly; the excuse of retaliatory measures could be used to justify what would have happened in any case. As an SS report to Berlin confirmed, "The Wehrmacht welcomes the measures and requests a radical approach."[47]

Implementation of this "security" decision was entrusted to the reliably murderous men of Blobel's Sonderkommando 4a, composed of members of the Security Police and the SD, as well as Waffen-SS men on special assignment and two detachments of Police Regiment South (along with Ukrainian auxiliary police). As with other such actions in larger cities, the operation began with the posting of orders in Russian, Ukrainian, and German ordering the Jewish population to assemble at a designated location at 8:00 A.M. on 29 September, with failure to comply punishable by death. That morning a far larger number of Jews appeared at the *Umschlagplatz* (assembly point) than anticipated, with most, amazingly in retrospect, believing the German promise that they were to be resettled. German officials on the spot then ordered the Jews to begin walking toward the area of the city where the Jewish cemetery and a section of the Babi Yar ravine were located. Photographs taken at the time show long columns of well-dressed people moving calmly, despite the presence of occasional bloody corpses. The route itself was guarded by army soldiers, with the killing site manned by men of the murder squad.[48]

Once at the ravine, the Jews had to strip and hand over their clothes and luggage, then were sent by the Ukrainian helpers in groups through a narrow opening into the ravine. Then, as a participant remembered,

> The Jews had to lie face down on the earth by the ravine walls. There were three groups of marksmen down at the bottom of the ravine, each made up of about twelve men. . . . Each successive group of Jews had to lie down on top of the bodies of those that had already been shot. The marksmen stood behind the Jews [i.e., walked on the bodies] and killed them with a shot in the neck. I still recall today the complete terror of the Jews. . . . It's almost impossible to imagine what nerves of steel it took to carry out that dirty work. . . . I had to spend the whole morning down in the ravine. For some of the time I had to shoot continuously. . . . The shooting that day must have lasted until . . . 5:00 or 6:00 P.M. Afterwards we were taken back to our quarters . . . [and] given alcohol again.

Although another participant remembered the chaos, shouting, and tumult at the scene, official SS reports regarded the two-day shooting as quite successful: "The operation went smoothly, with no unforeseen incidents. The measures to 'relocate' Jews were definitely regarded favorably by the population. Hardly anyone is aware that the Jews were in fact liquidated. . . . The Wehrmacht also expressed its approval of the measures carried out." The local army commanders had, in fact, done more than merely condone the killings; not only had they helped plan and organize the massacre, but the political unit of the Sixth Army also produced two thousand wall posters in its printing shop directing the Jews to their fate, and after the shootings a pioneer unit concealed the action by blowing up the area.[49] In alleged retaliation for the bombings in Kiev, 33,771 Jews were executed on 29–30 September 1941.

Killings had escalated into mass butchery. Security was now to be achieved through the ruthless pursuit and annihilation of partisans and their accomplices, especially the Jews. Reports from the summer and fall of 1941 show the grisly result: a vast discrepancy between the number of partisans killed and casualties suffered by German soldiers and only slight differences between the number of people arrested and those shot. One unit, unusual only in its murderous efficiency and not in the trend, killed over ten thousand people in a single month, with the loss of only two dead and five wounded. To promote this policy of pacification, army officials even inaugurated an exchange of ideas and experiences between army and SS officers. "It's good when the horror precedes us that we are exterminating Jewry," Hitler remarked to Himmler and Heydrich in late October 1941, significantly enough, after he had blamed the Jews for the dead of the First World War and reminded them of his 1939 prophecy. As events on the ground demonstrated, criminal orders from above and vengeful impulses from below created a climate of violence that would remove any inhibitions about murder. The four Einsatzgruppen and their helpers killed well over 500,000 Soviet Jews in the first six months of Barbarossa in addition to tens of thousands of partisans and Soviet prisoners of war, none of which would have been possible without the willing and active cooperation of the Wehrmacht.[50] Hitler had long considered military operations against the Soviet Union to win Lebensraum and political-police measures aimed at securing the newly won territory and exterminating racial-ideological enemies as simply different facets of the same war. As events in the field demonstrated, those involved in the killing process fully understood this complementarity.

On 15 July, Himmler returned to the Führer headquarters at Rastenburg in East Prussia after a quick trip to Berlin. As always, it seemed, when these two huddled in these days, bloody consequences followed. In mid-July, in the euphoria of apparent victory, Hitler now set in motion steps to accelerate the translation of his vision of a National Socialist New Order into horrible reality. With the military situation evidently going even better than expected—"No one doubts anymore our victory in Russia," Goebbels confided to his diary on 8 July—Hitler in the first half of July was in a self-congratulatory mood, proclaiming himself the Robert Koch of politics, the man who had exposed the "Jewish bacillus" of social decomposition. For the Führer, the connection between the Jews and war was inescapable, a mentality shaped by the personal and national humiliation of defeat in World War I, for which Hitler held the Jews responsible as fomenters of internal unrest and revolution. From his very first public statement, in September 1919, in which he advocated a complete removal of the Jews from Germany, through the notorious passage in *Mein Kampf* in which he expressed the wish that the imperial government had killed thousands of Jews at the beginning of the war, to his political testament at the very end of a second war, Hitler displayed a recurring obsession with the theme of Jews and war. Indeed, he regarded himself as nothing less than the architect and executor of a historic will: a second war had to be fought to undo the disaster of the first. This meant not only achieving Germany's historic destiny of great power status but also rewriting history on a racial basis, gaining revenge on those held responsible for the nation's misfortunes, the Jews. For Germany to win, Jewry had to lose.[51]

From the late 1930s, as war loomed closer, Hitler and other top Nazi leaders displayed, more than a mere conspiratorial outlook, a vengeful mentality that demanded retribution against the Jews as the cause of wars in general and of Germany's suffering in particular. The key to the Nazi outlook was not that the Jews were inferior but that the Jewish conspiracy represented nothing less than the supreme existential danger, the ultimate threat to Germany's existence. The racial community that Hitler sought to build could never be secure until Jewish power, values, and corruption were eliminated forever. Germany's salvation, as Saul Friedländer has stressed, thus required a "redemptive anti-Semitism" that would remove not just Jewish influence but, one way or another, the Jews themselves.[52]

In this mood of expectant victory, Hitler met for five hours on 16 July with Goering, Bormann, Rosenberg, Lammers, and Keitel to discuss and establish fundamental guidelines for the administration and exploitation of the occupied areas. After vowing that Germany would never leave these lands, he proclaimed his intention of creating a "Garden of Eden" for the benefit of all Germans, "our India." The Crimea, the Baltic states, the oil area around Baku, and former Austrian Galicia would be annexed, with the rest to be treated as a "colonial land" to be ruled and exploited by a handful of administrators. He dismissed the Slavs as by nature a "slave mass crying out for a master." The goals of German occupation policy would be brutally simple: "First, rule; second, administer; third, exploit." To accomplish these goals, "all necessary measures—shootings, resettlements, etc."—would be used. "This vast area must naturally be pacified as quickly as possible," Hitler emphasized. "This will best be done by shooting anyone who even looks sideways at us."[53]

Although Himmler was noticeably absent from this meeting, it was his response that was arguably most critical to the future course of events. In outlining his program, Hitler regarded himself as an architect reconstructing history on a racial basis, but he still needed someone to execute his will. The Führer had sketched a vision of a future utopia for Germans, but realizing this vision would necessitate destruction on a vast scale. That was to be Himmler's task. Nor could he harbor any doubts about what it would entail. The minutes of the meeting, which he received on 17 July, clearly expressed Hitler's will—exterminate anyone who opposes us—a task that would require a large-scale increase in available police forces. On both 19 and 22 July, he designated units from his own *Kommandostab* (command staff), the SS Cavalry Brigade and the First SS Brigade, totaling eleven thousand men, for use in antipartisan sweeps in the central and southern sectors of the front. He also reassigned a number of police battalions, over five thousand men in all, for use in the killing operations, which were now to be expanded, according to an evident Himmler edict on 21 July, to include all Soviet Jews. Searching for new sources of manpower, Himmler on 25 July ordered his police officials to form auxiliary police units from the Baltic, Ukrainian, and Belorussian populations since "the task of the police in the occupied eastern territories cannot be accomplished with the manpower of the police and SS now deployed or yet to be deployed." Within a few days in late July 1941, then, Himmler, responding to his Führer's wishes, initiated a swift buildup of precisely those units necessary for a rapid escalation of murder. The number of men involved in the killing activities rose from barely three thousand to over sixteen thousand, a figure that would rise to some thirty-three thousand by the end of the year, an elevenfold increase. Himmler then culminated this whirlwind of activity on 31 July by issuing an explicit order to top police officials: "All Jews must be shot. Drive female Jews into the swamp [i.e., Pripet Marshes]." In issuing orders for a radical escalation of the killing operations, Himmler surely felt confident that, in Ian Kershaw's phrase, he was "working towards the Führer."[54]

In late July, as if the Nazi leaders needed another reason to justify their anti-Semitic crusade, a curious and otherwise unimportant episode in the United States provided further "proof" of the destructive conspiracy they had warned against. On 24 July, a bloodcurdling headline, "The War Aim of Roosevelt and the Jews: Complete Extermination of the German People," with the subtitle "A Monstrous Jewish Extermination Plan according to the Guidelines of Roosevelt," adorned the front page of the *Völkischer Beobachter*, the main Nazi newspaper. From the beginning of the war in the east, the Nazi press had hammered home the importance of the Jewish dimension of the enemy, that Jews pulled the strings behind the scenes. In both public and private, Goebbels had thundered against the Jewish conspiracy of plutocrats and Bolsheviks that was determined to destroy Germany. Now, he evidently had his proof. In early 1941, Theodore Kaufman, a thirty-one-year-old Jewish businessman from New Jersey angry at the harsh treatment of Jews in Nazi-occupied Europe, self-published a small book he had written entitled *Germany Must Perish!* In it, he advocated the sterilization of all German men and the division of the country into five parts. The book caused a minor stir in the early spring of 1941; then Kaufman faded back into obscurity.[55]

By late July, the book, "a clear prophesy of what threatens us if we lose our will and thereby throw away our victory . . . , the extermination or sterilization of the entire German people," had come to Goebbels's attention. He saw in it confirmation of Nazi claims of the existence of a bloodthirsty conspiracy of plutocracy and Bolshevism and further justification for harsh measures in the east. Over the next few months, the German press and radio promoted the Kaufman story in endless variations, most notably to present the war, in a perverse inversion of reality, as a Jewish attempt to exterminate Germans. "Who should die, the Germans or the Jews?" was the stark question posed as Goebbels worked tirelessly to expose the "true goals" of the nation's enemies. "One has to imagine what the Jews would do with us if they had the power," he noted in his diary on 20 August, "in order to know what one should do with them when we have the power." The propaganda minister also issued a short brochure designed to create a more determined German attitude toward the war and allow "even the stupidest idiot . . . [to] figure out what threatens us" and that the only choice was victory or death. In fact, Kaufman's book paid instant dividends, an SD report of 31 July on the German mood noting, "The situation in the United States was being followed with the greatest attention. Increasingly the view spreads that

. . . this war is really a life-and-death struggle. The Kaufman plans have deeply impressed even the most obdurate skeptics." By October, with the "book . . . devoured by all sectors of society," Goebbels concluded, "It has been extraordinarily useful for us domestically. It is impossible to imagine a better illustration of the desires and goals of the other side."[56]

Even as the SD noted a hardening of the German public mood, on that same 31 July, Heydrich received a written authorization (actually drafted by Adolf Eichmann on instructions from Heydrich) from Goering to make "all necessary preparations with regard to organizational, technical, and material matters for bringing about a complete solution of the Jewish question within the German sphere of influence in Europe": "I request you further to send me, in the near future, an overall plan covering the organizational, technical, and material measures necessary for the accomplishment of the final solution of the Jewish question which we desire." Controversy still surrounds the question of whether Heydrich viewed this authorization to mean merely an extension of his earlier mandate of 24 January 1939 to organize a solution to the Jewish question based on emigration or whether he understood it as marking a significant new departure. The Führer himself, in a conversation with the Croatian field marshal Kvaternik on 22 July, indicated that he was still thinking along lines of mass deportation to an inhospitable region. Once again referring to the Jews as a bacillus of decomposition that had to be destroyed, he then remarked, "Wherever one sends the Jews, to Siberia or Madagascar, is all the same." The key, Hitler emphasized, was to "annihilate them," to "do away with them." If Hitler was openly talking of annihilating the Jews in front of a Croatian field marshal, however, Christopher Browning is surely correct in arguing that Heydrich must have sensed that something radically different was brewing since he had not sought a new authorization when the earlier emigration schemes evolved into plans for mass resettlement and expulsion. At the least, he believed it necessary, at this key juncture, to have a new authorization in order to have decisive influence over the heads of rival agencies and administrations. In any case, and whatever solution emerged, Heydrich certainly understood that he was to draw up a feasibility study that would result in the mass death, one way or another, of European Jews.[57]

In retrospect, then, the meeting of 16 July can be seen as a key point at which the mass killing of Soviet Jews, partisans, and anyone else deemed a threat to German rule became the foundation for future policy. The consequences were immediate. Most Einsatzgruppen commanders understood very well what was expected of them and set about implementing the new policy, although one SS officer complained in an

11 August report, "Driving women and children into the swamps did not have the success it was supposed to have as the swamps were not deep enough [to drown them]." Still, sufficient actions were being taken that, on that same day, Goebbels gloated, "Vengeance was being wreaked on the Jews. . . . What the Führer prophesied is taking place: that if the Jews succeeded in provoking another war, [they] would therefore lose [their] existence."[58]

Pressure, in fact, was mounting among Nazi officials to take a more radical approach to the Jews. SD reports in early August mentioned increasing hostility to Jews on the streets of western German cities subjected to British air raids, while Goebbels complained that the continued presence of "parasitical Jews" in Berlin undermined morale and outraged soldiers home on leave. In mid-August, in fact, one of his close advisers had proposed that the Berlin Jews, some seventy-six thousand, simply be "carted off to Russia. . . . Best of all actually would be to kill them." Determined to do something about this intolerable situation, Goebbels flew to the Führer Headquarters on 18 August for discussions with Hitler. Although the Führer was ill and under acute nervous strain, Goebbels related his complaints about Jews damaging morale, a claim that fell on fertile ground. Venting his hatred for the Jews seemed to act as a tonic, in fact, as Goebbels noted,

> The Führer is convinced that his past prophecy in the Reichstag, that if the Jews succeeded in provoking a world war, it would end with the annihilation of the Jews, is being confirmed. It is coming true in these weeks and months with an almost eerie certainty. In the east the Jews must pay the bill; in Germany they have in part already paid and will in the future pay still more. . . . Jewry is an alien body among civilized nations, and their activity in the last three decades has been so devastating that the reaction of the peoples is absolutely understandable, necessary . . . , [and] urgent.

Evidently warming to the subject, Hitler noted ominously, "In this matter a man like [the Rumanian dictator] Antonescu proceeds much more radically than we have done. But I will not rest or be idle until we too have drawn the final consequences with regard to the Jews."[59]

Hitler's reference to his prophecy, the fact that he was ill and irritable, and the mid-August crisis in military affairs have tempted some historians, most notably Tobias Jersak, to make a connection with another key mid-August event: the issuance on 14 August of the Atlantic Charter. To Jersak, the Atlantic Charter, which indicated certain American entry into the war and pledged both the United States and Great Britain to the destruction of Nazism, along with a joint letter two days later by Roosevelt and Churchill offering support to Stalin, must have been seen by Hitler as confirmation of his worst nightmare: a global war of the Jewish conspiracy to annihilate Germany. After all, as Hitler remarked at the time to the Spanish ambassador, "The main guilty parties in this war . . . are the Americans, Roosevelt . . . , Jews and the entirety of Jewish Bolshevism. . . . The Americans are the greatest scoundrels. . . . America will pay a bitter price." In consequence, with the Jews no longer possessing any preventive value as hostages, and with hopes of a blitzkrieg victory dashed, Hitler now made the decision to kill all the Jews of Europe during the war, not after it, as originally intended. Only the timing and method of killing remained to be determined.[60]

Tidy though this argument may be—and it has the great value of locating the Final Solution firmly within the context of the war—available evidence fails to offer much support. Both Goebbels and Hitler dismissed the Atlantic Charter at the time as a bluff, typical Wilsonian bluster that had little impact on the war, Hitler concluding that it "can do us no harm at all." Only years later did he claim to have seen in it a Jewish threat to exterminate Germany. Further, when Goebbels and Heydrich tried to push the pace of radical anti-Jewish measures, they met with only partial success. Hitler gave the go-ahead to Goebbels's suggestion that German Jews be required to wear an identifying mark but rebuffed the two on a more radical idea, the immediate deportation of German Jews, promising Goebbels only that evacuations would take place once transportation problems had been resolved. Since the transportation situation could not possibly improve before the end of the eastern campaign, however, Hitler in effect had postponed any action until after the war. Heydrich was allowed to prepare plans for a partial evacuation of the larger German cities, but, here again, Hitler "rejected evacuations during the war." If Hitler had decided in mid-August to kill all the Jews of Europe, his immediate actions certainly gave no indications of it.[61]

Murder, however, was clearly in the air as the destructive dynamism on the ground had gained momentum. Perhaps the best known of the carefully compiled statistical reports of an individual murder unit, that of Karl Jäger of Einsatzkommando 3 of Einsatzgruppe A, showed a sharp increase in early August, not just in the total numbers of Jews killed, but especially in the numbers of women and children.[62] The verbal transmission of orders, varying interpretations of these orders, and differences in logistic and manpower capabilities meant that the timing and the escalation of the murder operations were not uniform. By mid-August, however, it seemed to be generally known among SS officials that all Soviet Jews were to be murdered.

On 15 August, Himmler witnessed just such an execution of partisans and Jews near Minsk, at which he became nauseated. The Reichsführer-SS also found himself pressed to find an alternate method of execution. Afterward, Himmler gave a speech to SS officers that legitimized such killings as necessary for security and, according to some present, ordered the liquidation of all Jews in the east on the basis of a directive from Hitler. That afternoon he visited a hospital with mental patients and discussed the possibility of killing through methods other than shooting, such as gas vans. At roughly the same time, Himmler was pressured by several top subordinates, among them Franz Walter Stahlecker, the commander of Einsatzgruppe A, to adopt "a radical treatment of the Jewish question now possible for the first time in the east." By late August, then, while a decision had not been taken to kill all the Jews of Europe, the factors were in place to ensure the murder of the Jews of the Soviet Union.[63] Spectacular military success had created, at least temporarily in early July, a mood of unlimited possibilities, the consequences of which reverberated throughout the Soviet Union. By late summer, even as military operations slowed and showed signs of an impending crisis, the racial war increased in tempo. Barbarossa had always assumed a war of annihilation on a number of levels, so, despite the very real problems facing the fighting forces, no slowdown was apparent in the ideological war.

Despite the impressive triumphs won by the hard-charging Wehrmacht and the sanguine assertions of top Nazi leaders, in mid-July the assured expectations of imminent success had begun to mingle with an undercurrent of doubt, not yet enough to undermine overall confidence in victory, but a nagging concern that things were not as they seemed. Both Halder and Bock, often in stunned amazement, routinely noted in their diaries instances of stubborn enemy resistance and refusal to surrender. Goebbels, too, registered the desperate Soviet resistance but hastened to emphasize that it was more "a courage of dullness than of heroism." From the first days of the invasion, Hitler worried, as he had during the French campaign, that the deep armored thrusts had left the German flanks exposed to attack from both the north and the south. Although Halder dismissed these concerns as the "old refrain," persistent Soviet counterattacks had, indeed, set nerves on edge and not just in the High Command.[64]

One Landser, surely speaking for many, noted his shock and dismay at his first experience of a Soviet attack:

I can never forget the first mass attack by Russian infantry. . . . The Soviet assaults . . . were carried out by masses of men who made no real attempt at concealment but trusted in sheer weight of numbers to overwhelm us. . . . The whole mass of Russian troops came tramping solidly and relentlessly forward. It was an unbelievable sight, a machine gunner's dream. . . . At 600 meters we opened fire and whole sections of the first wave just vanished leaving here and there an odd survivor still walking stolidly forward. It was uncanny, unbelievable, inhuman. . . . Then, as if on a signal, the lines of men began running forward . . . [with] a low, rumbling "Hoooooraaay." . . . The rush by the fourth wave came on more slowly for the men had to pick their way through a great carpet of bodies. . . .

About an hour later a further five lines of men came on in a second attack. We smashed this and then crushed a third and fourth assault. The numbers of the enemy seemed endless and new waves of men advanced across their own dead without hesitation. . . . The number, duration, and fury of those attacks had exhausted and numbed us completely. Not to hide the truth, they had frightened us. Our advance had been no great strategic drive but an ordinary move . . . and yet they had contested it for day after day and with masses of men. If the Soviets could waste men on our small move . . . , how often, we asked ourselves, would they attack and in what numbers if the objective was really a supremely important one? . . . Some of us began to realize for the first time that the war against the Soviet Union was going to be bigger than we had thought it would be and a sense of depression, brought about by a fear of the unknown, settled upon us. That we would win, we had no doubt, but what we were now engaged in would be a long, bitter and hard fought war.[65]

In truth, despite Halder's frustration at Hitler's worries, both the Führer and the anonymous Landser had valid grounds for concern and for the same reason: it had become increasingly clear that, despite the rosy projections of the Barbarossa planners, the German army lacked the ability to accomplish all the objectives set for it. The assumption had been that the Red Army would collapse at the initial blow; if it survived, as it now showed signs of having done, the Wehrmacht had insufficient strength to finish the task. The growing tension between Hitler and the OKH reflected this problem. Hitler's operational directive of December 1940 had stressed the importance, after the initial victories on the central front, of shifting forces to the north to seize Leningrad and the Baltic coast as well as to the south to secure the economic resources of Ukraine. Although Halder and the Army General Staff acknowledged the significance of capturing these regions, they had always favored a direct thrust on Moscow, itself an important industrial and communications center, as the best way to lure the Red Army into a destructive trap. In agreeing to the Barbarossa plan, Halder had intended from the beginning to develop an attack in the center with such momentum that Hitler would be forced to concede to OKH wishes. In the first two weeks of the campaign, then, even as Hitler expressed concern that Bock's units were overreaching themselves and allowing the formation of loose pockets from which the enemy might escape, Halder issued orders and guidelines that ignored or undermined the Führer's instructions. Halder's obstructionism, however, only angered Hitler and intensified his suspicions, dating to the French campaign, of the Army General Staff.[66]

Since the Wehrmacht lacked the necessary resources to execute both operational conceptions, a decision had to be made, and soon, as to whether to sustain the drive of Army Group Center toward Moscow or to adhere to the original plan and turn forces to the flanks. "Turn to the north or south?" Hitler puzzled on 4 July. "It will perhaps be the most difficult decision of this war." The next day, Hitler again grappled with the issue of the future direction of operations, recognizing not only that the moment had come to make a choice but also that it might be the most decisive of the war, indeed, "perhaps in general the only critical decision in this war." Still, the Führer hesitated three more days, on 8 July finally picking the strategy favored by Halder: Army Group Center would press ahead toward Smolensk with the aim of destroying Red Army forces west of Moscow, while Army Group North would continue the operation toward Leningrad with its own forces. Significantly, what Hitler termed his *ideal solution* also entailed leveling Moscow and Leningrad to the ground and making them uninhabitable, thus relieving the Germans of the necessity of feeding the civilian populations through the winter. In this instance, the perfect military solution dovetailed nicely with the requirements of the hunger policy: "useless eaters" would be left to starve. More importantly, Hitler had, at least temporarily, also abandoned the Barbarossa plan, an implicit admission that it had failed to accomplish its original goals. Nor had he really made a decisive choice, for, in the following weeks, he and the OKH would continually reopen the festering dispute over the focal point of operations.[67]

Was Hitler engaging in hyperbole in claiming that this was the most important decision of the war? Not necessarily. Although virtually all his top military leaders believed that Germany would win, they also recognized the need to set priorities and make the best use of their increasingly limited resources. Moreover, there was a gnawing sense that the initial gamble had failed, that, despite the impressive victories, the Red Army remained an intact fighting force and, thus, that the Wehrmacht now needed to make use of all its considerable operational skills in order to resolve the situation satisfactorily. Thus, the ongoing assessments of the comparative strength of the Red Army and the Wehrmacht played a key role in influencing these deliberations over the sequence and timing of future operations. To the Germans, the summit seemed tantalizingly close; the problem was how to attain it. Hitler and the Army High Command were not sure how to proceed, an uncertainty reflected in the protracted discussions, confusion, vacillation, and contradictory orders that characterized the period from mid-July through August.

Although Halder was clearly aware that the initial objective, the destruction of the enemy's strength west of the Dnieper line, had not been accomplished, he nonetheless assumed that the serious losses suffered by the Red Army had nearly exhausted its ability to continue fighting. On 8 July, he estimated that 89 of the 164 known enemy infantry divisions, and 20 of the 29 armored units, could be considered destroyed or largely eliminated, with only 46 Russian combat divisions left to contest the Germans. By his reckoning, the Soviets were no longer in a position to organize a continuous front, nor would the activation of new units offer much help since they would lack officers, equipment, and training. To Halder, the Soviet goal seemed simply to drain German strength through ceaseless counterattacks. These attacks, in which the Russians fought "with wild ferocity and enormous human sacrifice," were admittedly worrisome, but the very scale of the enemy losses encouraged his belief that the resistance must soon slacken. Using the rough formula that 1 million civilians could provide soldiers for two divisions, German experts assumed that the limits of Soviet manpower had been reached.[68] Despite the continual appearance of new enemy divisions, the Germans were slow to draw the proper conclusions; when they finally did, it was too late.

Not only the profligate manner of Red Army counterattacks, but also the size and quality of the Soviet tank force, came as an unpleasant surprise. In early July, enemy tank strength had been reestimated at fifteen thousand, but the total was likely closer to twenty-four thousand. The armament and thickness of armor on the new T34 and KV model tanks, which had come into service a few months earlier, also came as a shock, as German antitank crews often saw their shells bounce harmlessly off the Soviet tanks. "Each shot seems to be a direct hit," one antitank gunner remarked in astonishment, "[but] the shells bounce off. . . . The fire doesn't bother the tanks in the least." German tactical ingenuity and experience soon began to level the odds, but the appearance of the heavier and obviously superior Soviet tanks chipped away at German confidence and assurance of victory. Even the mammoth destruction of Russian aircraft at the outset of the fighting proved a mixed blessing. Since most of the planes had been destroyed on the ground, Russian losses in crew had not been so severe, allowing the Soviets to rebuild their formations with new planes from factories beyond the range of German bombers.[69]

The Soviets had also made a considerable effort to evacuate factories to the east, especially those engaged in aircraft manufacture and the production of arms and ammunition, tractor works, metallurgical installations, and chemical plants. In this regard, the stubborn Red Army resistance in Ukraine proved particularly important, for it allowed time to disassemble and remove entire factories from a key industrial region. Estimates of the total number of factories relocated to the Urals, western Siberia, and Kazakhstan vary from fifteen to twenty-five hundred, with the overwhelming majority related to the armaments industry. Although there were numerous problems with the evacuation—industrial equipment arriving damaged, at the wrong destination, or not at all—the action nonetheless secured roughly 8–10 percent of prewar Soviet productive capacity. Even more remarkably, despite the loss of highly important industrial regions, the Soviets managed to increase their output of key military equipment in 1941. In the first half of the year, Soviet factories had produced 1,800 tanks, 3,950 aircraft, 15,600 artillery pieces and mortars, 11,000 machine guns (and submachine guns), 792,000 rifles, and 18.8 million shells. In the final six months of 1941, however, the Soviets churned out 4,700 tanks, 8,000 aircraft, 55,500 artillery pieces and mortars, 143,000 machine and submachine guns, 1.5 million rifles, and an astounding 40.2 million shells. Stalin, using draconian tactics, far more effectively mobilized the Soviet population for the war effort than did Hitler. Even allowing for problems raised by the relocation, including a sharp slump in production in the winter of 1941–1942, the evacuation of industry was an impressive economic and organizational achievement.[70]

At the same time Soviet military production was increasing, Halder understood that the fighting power of the frontline German combat units was eroding. The Wehrmacht had entered Russia with forces only marginally larger than those engaged in France the year before.

As in France, it had gambled on hitting the Soviets with virtually all its available strength and, thus, had practically nothing left in reserve. Everything had been front-loaded, aimed at a knockout blow in the first round, with nothing held back in the event of a prolonged match. The 3,050,000 men who had invaded the Soviet Union on 22 June had been backed by only 385,000 men in the Replacement Army, a figure for trained reserves that the army estimated would be exhausted by the beginning of October. Army leaders had been willing to accept this risk, largely because they had been misled by the surprisingly low losses—fewer than 100,000 killed—in the first two years of war. Now, after three weeks of hard fighting, and with the size of the front expanding both in width and in depth, the Germans were hard-pressed to satisfy even the minimal replacement requirements of the individual army groups. On 6 July, Halder estimated that almost 12,000 Germans had been killed in the fighting to date, a number too low by at least half since in June alone 25,000 had died on the eastern front. A month later, his figures indicated that the Eastern Army had suffered a total of 180,000 casualties but had received only 47,000 replacements. Once again, the casualty figure was too small since in July more than 63,000 Landsers were killed, making the two-month death toll some 88,000. OKW figures from early January 1942 listed a total of 213,301 casualties from 22 June through the end of July 1941, with another 197,000 in August, for a two-month total of roughly 410,000, a figure larger than the total Replacement Army.[71] The numbers were indisputable; the fierce Soviet resistance in July had begun seriously to erode the fighting strength of the German Eastern Army. Although the winter fighting in front of Moscow has received the bulk of attention, in terms of hollowing the Wehrmacht July 1941 remained for the Ostheer the single worst month, at least for deaths, until December 1942, when the savage struggle in Stalingrad finally surpassed it in deadly intensity.

Not only were casualties rising and replacements lacking, but the materiel strength of the armored units, the key to success, had also declined significantly. Although the Germans had invaded with some 3,600 tanks, nearly 1,000 of those were obsolete Pz I and II models, while the panzer armies possessed only 444 of the modern Pz IV tank. Not only were these numbers wholly inadequate, but the war in Russia also quickly revealed deficiencies in performance, armor, armament, and tactical mobility. Most German tanks, it seemed, were suited only for fair weather and good roads. In early July, Halder estimated that the army had only 431 tanks in reserve. Nor were replacements at hand since earlier production estimates of 900 panzers a month gave way to 650, although even this lower figure could not be attained. By mid-July, the combat strength of the panzer and motorized divisions in Army Group Center had declined to 60 percent of normal, while in some units of Army Group South it had been reduced to 40 percent. Two months later, the four armored divisions of Guderian's Second Panzer Army had been reduced to 20–30 percent of their combat strength.[72]

To make matters worse, Hitler, still expecting a quick victory, ordered that new tanks being produced should remain in Germany in order to equip fresh panzer divisions for use in 1942 in offensives planned for the Middle East. Only under pressure from army leaders was he persuaded to release all captured Czech tanks, some new model Pz III and IV tanks, and some 350 tank engines, but this meager allocation did not suffice to maintain the strength of even depleted panzer units. Hitler implicitly acknowledged this, in late July ordering that panzer divisions suffering heavy losses should simply be disbanded and their personnel and equipment used to reinforce the remainder. With only minor exceptions, he clung to this policy through the end of 1941. By the end of August, the Eastern Army had lost almost 1,500 armored fighting vehicles (AFVs) and had been allocated only 96 replacements out of a total new production from June to August of 815. The Germans often had more tanks out of service owing to lack of spare parts than to enemy action. By the end of October, for example, the Eighteenth Panzer Division had lost 59 tanks to enemy action, but 103 were out of operation because of a lack of spare parts. Troops even resorted to obtaining spare parts directly from Germany rather than attempting to get them through army supply services. To compound problems further, the army groups lacked sufficient repair workshops, with the result that tanks knocked out of action but salvageable had to be sent back to Germany to be repaired. Since tank losses were greater than expected, this centralized system of panzer repair could not cope, especially since it added a further burden to the already overtaxed railway system. Many tanks needing repair were thus away from the front for long periods of time.[73] As a result, operational successes could not be fully exploited. Even though German armored units had achieved astounding victories with inferior resources, Hitler failed to reinforce this success with the means by which to achieve a strategic triumph.

The original operational plan had taken into account the need for rest and replenishment of units after the Dnieper line had been reached. This pause, following the assumed destruction of most of the enemy's fighting strength, would be used for rehabilitation and stocking fresh supplies necessary for the next phase of the operation. Certainly, the

German formations needed such a rest. Despite the fact that the infantry divisions still averaged about 80 percent of their normal establishment, the men were exhausted after marching three hundred miles in hot weather over dusty roads and engaging in constant, and often severe, fighting. For many men, the most vivid impression of the first weeks of the campaign, in addition to the sharp fighting, was the endless marching that "puff[ed] dust into the air so that it rose and clung to [them]": "The loose sand was nearly as tiring . . . as deep mud. . . . The men marched in silence, coated with dust, with dry throats and lips." As another Landser put it, "Each man's war at this stage was circumscribed by the next few steps he would take, the hardness of the road, the soreness of his feet, the dryness of his tongue, and the weight of his equipment." The stiff limbs, the blisters, the numbing fatigue, the sheer monotony produced by marching endlessly into the vast sameness, meant that skirmishes were often seen as a welcome respite. "We wished the Russians would make a stand," said one soldier, "anything, a battle even, to relieve the painful monotony of this ceaseless, timeless tramping." Closing with the enemy, however, added a psychological burden to the already enormous physical ordeal endured by the troops. After the outpouring of fear, nervous energy, and adrenaline produced by combat had subsided, many troops sank into a lethargy that was increasingly difficult to overcome.[74]

In addition, with over 2,000 different types of vehicles, 170 kinds of guns, 73 different tanks, and 52 models of antiaircraft guns, the Germans faced a logistic nightmare in spare parts and maintenance in the best of circumstances. Yet the relentless Soviet resistance did not allow the necessary time for replenishment of the mechanized formations. Driving ahead constantly, fighting a seemingly endless series of engagements and encirclement battles, often isolated and alone deep in hostile territory, confronted by the enemy on all sides, and with little time for rest, the motorized troops were subjected to an enormous physical and psychological burden. Even as the advance continued, apparently successfully, the nearly constant fighting resulted in a steady casualty toll obvious to all. But, because of the dogged opposition of Soviet troops and their continual counterattacks, German units could not be withdrawn from the line for rest, nor, because of the dismal state of the logistic system, could large stocks be accumulated for decisive future operations.[75]

Despite the prodigious efforts of the supply organization to maintain the momentum of the German advance, by mid-July the system was showing signs of collapsing. Because of anticipated railway problems, specifically the need to convert the differing gauges between the German and the Soviet lines, German planners had committed to a motorized, road-bound movement of supplies in the crucial first phase of the campaign. The materiel and infrastructure basis for such a system, however, was alarmingly slender. Despite Hitler's attempt in the 1930s to motorize Germany, it lacked both the absolute numbers of vehicles and the requisite motor industry to supply the vast numbers of vehicles needed in Russia. In order to achieve the planners' goal, the German motorized transport capacity would have had to be increased ten times, a task clearly beyond their ability. The severe fuel shortage as well as a lack of tires also complicated matters, as did the enormous need for replacement parts for an army that had a myriad of different types of vehicles in use. Moreover, the majority of roads in Russia were unpaved, which meant that they were choked with clouds of dust during dry weather while heavy rains, as in early July, turned them into rutted, impassable, muddy quagmires. The few surfaced roads proved incapable of bearing heavy truck traffic and were often ruined after a few days. The battering taken by the trucks resulted in breakdowns that led to a reduction of 25–30 percent in haulage capacity, while most repair facilities were sited far to the rear. These notoriously bad roads also led to an unexpected rise in fuel consumption, with the result that fuel sufficient for sixty miles in normal conditions sufficed for only forty miles in Russia. Even the occasional capture of enemy fuel stocks offered little relief since Soviet fuel had a lower octane rating and could be used in German vehicles only after adaptation. The Germans quickly turned to horse-drawn vehicles as a substitute, but they suffered problems as well. Not only were the rubber tires on the larger German wagons quickly torn to shreds, but German horses, perhaps in a fitting metaphor, were not up to the demands placed on them. The Germans soon found it better to replace them with the small Russian *panje* wagons pulled by lighter, more agile Russian horses.[76]

Nor could the declining motor transport capacity be made good by the rail system. The Germans failed to capture large quantities of Soviet locomotives and rolling stock and, thus, faced the time-consuming, labor-intensive task of relaying rail network to German gauge. Even this proved more difficult than expected, however, since the Soviet rail beds were normally so weak and the rails so lacking in load-carrying capacity that only light model German engines could be used to pull freight cars. In addition, because of inadequate investment in the railroad between the wars, German locomotives and rolling stock were limited in number and already considerably overstrained. Increased wear and tear and inevitable breakdowns thus further reduced the efficiency of the Reichs-bahn. Because of time pressures as well as constraints on personnel and materials for a thorough reconstruction of the railway network, neces-sary repair work was limited to a few main lines. Inevitably, bottlenecks resulted as the transportation system often became hopelessly jammed. As a consequence, adequate supply of the three army groups became impossible. By late July, Army Group Center needed twenty-five trains a day to meet its needs but often received as few as eight and never more than fifteen, while Army Group South secured on average only fourteen of the necessary twenty-four trains daily. Army Group North enjoyed a relatively better situation as it had shorter distances to cover, the rail net-work in the Baltic states was better, and the capture of Baltic ports eased the strain on land transport. Even here, however, the attack on Lenin-grad in July had to be postponed for supply reasons on seven occasions. By the time the supply difficulties were resolved and the attack resumed in early August, the Soviets had gained valuable time to build defenses.[77]

The constraints on the transportation system also forced difficult choices. The incessant Soviet counterattacks had caused German troops to consume huge quantities of ammunition. When priority was given to ammunition trains, however, drastic reductions in the supply of fuel and rations were necessary, which limited the mobility of German units and forced troops to live off the land. By mid-July, the unprecedented problems of supplying a rapidly advancing army over great distances in a country with poor infrastructure with the necessary equipment, ammu-nition, fuel, and supplies to maintain a simultaneous offensive on three fronts had nearly broken the German supply organization. The original assumption—that the Eastern Army could be adequately supplied only to the Dnieper line—had proven accurate. In the absence of the antici-pated Soviet collapse, the Germans now faced the prospect of creating a new supply chain that reflected the changed situation. Failing this, they had hardly any likelihood of being able to provide the troops with the supplies they needed for large-scale operations beyond the Dnieper. In the summer of 1941, time, distance, and the very primitive nature of its transportation system was helping ensure the Soviet Union's survival as a state.[78]

Barely a month into the war, then, the German army leadership was forced to recognize that the Red Army had survived the best the Wehr-macht could throw at it and that, not only had it not been beaten, but its resistance was also growing in intensity. This realization took hold during the Battle of Smolensk, which had originally been intended as the culmination of the initial phase of Barbarossa but now took place within the context of deliberations among Hitler and the OKH about the future axis of German advance. If Soviet actions at Smolensk did not cause a full reappraisal of German policy, they certainly contributed to a palpable sense of crisis in the second half of July. More importantly, they confronted the OKH, once the initial assumptions of Barbarossa had proved false, with the necessity of improvising its way to victory. However, each gamble on encirclement, however successful it might be in defeating Soviet forces in its sector, also promoted the exhaustion of German forces before they could accomplish the general defeat of the Red Army, a vicious cycle that was eroding the strength of the Wehrmacht.

Hitler himself expressed the dilemma well, complaining to Halder on 26 July, "You cannot beat the Russians with operational successes . . . because they simply do not know when they are defeated." Although Halder admitted that Hitler's observation had some merit, he noted, presciently as it turned out, that the Führer's prescription, to destroy them bit by bit in small encircling actions, would simply let the enemy dictate German actions as well as reduce the tempo of operations to a pace that would not allow success. Beginning at Smolensk, the Ostheer found itself drawn increasingly into a series of operations that ended in victories but that taxed its already strained logistics system to the limit, eroded irreplaceable combat strength, and gave the Soviets time both to call up new levies of manpower and to organize their remaining economic potential. The dogged Soviet resistance, moreover, had begun to have a noticeable effect on German civilian morale, always a crucial concern to the Nazi leadership. Already by 24 July Goebbels had noted his surprise at the failure of the Soviet state to collapse and concerns about the progress of the war. "Without a doubt our situation at the moment is tense," he admitted. He then complained, "In the eastern campaign we have not had so many symbolic victories to record, as in the previous year in the western campaign, that can ignite the . . . excitement of the people. . . . The mood in Germany has grown more serious. One is gradually becoming aware that the eastern campaign is no stroll to Moscow. . . . Maintaining domestic morale is made noticeably more difficult by the lack of special reports [announcing victories]. In the western campaign we had something new almost every day. . . . Now people must wait and wait. . . . That results in a certain weariness." "It is clear," the propaganda minister acknowledged on the last day of July, "that we have underestimated Bolshevism." At Smolensk, the Red Army in fact forced German plans for a *Blitzfeldzug* (lightning campaign) of rapid annihilation to give way to a recognition that the war, if not yet one of attrition, would likely require a second campaign in 1942.[79]

Even as many German infantry units were still engaged in fierce fighting to reduce pockets of encircled Soviet troops at Minsk and others lacked the motorized transport to keep pace with the panzer divisions, Hoth's and Guderian's Panzergruppen struck along both sides of the Minsk-Smolensk highway in early July with the intent of converging east of Smolensk to spring yet another giant trap. Presumably, following this success, the way to Moscow would be clear. The Germans largely ignored any difficulties raised by the potential gap between the infantry and the armored formations since they assumed that the Soviets no longer possessed sufficient forces to form a coherent defense. By 5 July, however, it was clear that the enemy was deploying new armies, and, by 7 July, vigorous Soviet counterattacks had stalled both armored groups. While Hitler's 8 July order seemed to give precedence to the drive toward Moscow, it also subtly undermined the momentum of the central thrust since, after reaching the areas assigned them northeast and southeast of Smolensk, the two armored groups were to be kept available for deployment either to the north or to the south. Although this prevented Hoth and Guderian from closing the trap, for the moment Halder seemed unconcerned as he assumed that Soviet forces were finished. On 9 July, in fact, he noted the favorable situation at Kiev and the possibility of seizing the city in a surprise thrust, while three days later he commented, remarkably in view of his later bitter argument with Hitler, "I am by no means advocating an eastward race of the two armored groups. It is quite clear to me that Hoth might have to swing northward with a considerable body of his group . . . and that Guderian might have to swing southward to encircle the new enemy appearing on his southern wing."[80]

What Halder thought would largely be a mopping-up operation, however, was turning into something else entirely as the Soviets scrambled furiously to bring new forces into play. Clinging to the doctrine of an active defense in order to blunt the enemy attack and regain the initiative, the Stavka in early July ordered a series of counterattacks near Smolensk in order to slow German momentum, gain time to mobilize Soviet resources and build defenses, and ensnare the enemy in a series of costly tactical engagements. In the race to assemble forces, the Soviets enjoyed the advantage. While the Germans neared the limits of their logistic abilities, Smolensk, as a key rail and transportation hub, enabled the Soviet High Command to feed fresh forces into the area in a timely manner. Thus, although Hoth had, despite stiff resistance, seized Vitebsk on 9 July and Guderian the next day threw units across the Dnieper both north and south of Mogilev, the supply system to Army Group Center was already beginning to display an advanced case of sclerosis. In addition, a serious gap had opened between the German infantry and the mechanized divisions, while large Soviet forces in the Pripet Marshes posed an increasing danger both for the stretched German supply lines and for the flanks of Army Groups Center and South. These exposed flanks were a persistent cause of concern, especially to Hitler, influencing both decisionmaking and subsequent actions.[81]

By 10 July, the Soviet leadership had also begun to recover from the initial paralyzing shock of the German invasion and had regained control over its battlefield units. The Stavka, in fact, now planned an ambitious series of coordinated counterattacks that would not only halt the German advance but also allow them to encircle exposed enemy forces. Furious attacks on Hoth, to the north, on 6 July had succeeded in blunting his assault and forcing him to divert units in a northeasterly direction. On 13 July, it was the turn of Guderian's forces to absorb the Soviet blow as they were the target of a fierce attack from the area around Gomel. Forays from the enemy bridgeheads at Orsha and Mogilev accompanied this assault, and, although the Germans successfully fought off the Soviets, Guderian was forced to change the direction of advance of some of his units. As ferocious Soviet attacks continued over the next few days, the Germans began to realize that, because of the diversion of panzer units to the north and south, they lacked the combat power to close the pocket east of Smolensk. They also recognized that the Soviets had now consciously begun to use encircled forces as a means to tie down German units, inhibit their freedom of action, and disrupt the pace of the enemy advance.[82]

With their infantry units trailing far behind, the Germans had little choice but to throw the armored divisions into a furious attempt to close the Smolensk pocket. In ten days of savage fighting between 10 and 20 July, however, the Germans failed to close the hole east of Smolensk or prevent the timely withdrawal of strong enemy forces. The struggle was, marveled one Landser, "madness, total madness. They fought like wild animals—and died as such." Bock simply noted in his diary, "Hell was let loose." The fierce Russian attacks of 13–16 July, dubbed the "Timoshenko Offensive" by Guderian, also led the Germans to rethink their assumptions about the second phase of the campaign. Substantial Soviet combat power still confronted Army Group Center, a recognition that sparked a crisis mood in the OKH. After noting the difficulties and slow pace of progress of Army Group South, Halder on 20 July admitted of the central front: "The costly battles involving some groups of our armored forces, in which the infantry divisions arriving from the west can take a hand only slowly, together with loss of time due to bad roads which restrict movement and the weariness of the troops marching and fighting without a break, have put a damper on all higher HQ. Its most visible expression is the severe depression into which [Brauchitsch] has been plunged." The next day, Bock grudgingly acknowledged the effect of the Soviet pressure on the Germans, "a quite remarkable success for such a badly battered opponent!" Two days later, as large numbers of Soviet troops fought their way out, he complained, "We have still not succeeded in closing the hole at the east end of the Smolensk pocket."[83]

After ten days of fighting, the Germans desperately needed to regroup, reorient, and concentrate their scattered armored formations in order to continue the advance against an enemy that clearly had not been destroyed. The Soviets, however, refused to grant a respite. Instead, on 20 July, Stalin telephoned Marshal Timoshenko to inform him that the time had come for a Soviet counteroffensive that would regain the initiative. The plan, as envisioned by the Stavka, entailed three simultaneous blows from the south directed at Smolensk, with the aim of cutting off both German pincers east of the city and transforming the would-be encirclers into the encircled. Although the Soviets hoped with this attack to orchestrate a major turnabout in the war, because of command and control problems the counteroffensive that began on 21 July unfolded in a piecemeal fashion. Nonetheless, over the next few days, the Soviets did achieve some successes, most notably in delaying the closing of the Smolensk pocket until 27 July. The relentless Soviet counterstrokes—"astonishing for an opponent who is so beaten," Bock admitted on 26 July; "they must have unbelievable masses of materiel"—also put intense pressure on the seriously overextended German panzer units. Even though these attacks ultimately failed owing to poor coordination, the Russians continued to resist through August in intense fighting that resulted in frightful casualties to both sides. The Battle of Smolensk thus came to a close with neither side having achieved a decisive result. Despite their repeated, fierce assaults, the Soviets failed to destroy the main forces of Army Group Center, which crossed the Dnieper on a broad front and advanced some 100–150 miles to the east. However, having had to repel these vigorous enemy attacks, it had been so weakened that a direct thrust on Moscow was out of the question until the precarious supply situation had been remedied. As one Landser noted perceptively, "The faces of the youngsters exude the same image as First World War veterans. . . . Despite the pleasure at sudden Russian withdrawals, one notes this change in the faces of the soldiers."[84]

The Germans netted well over 300,000 prisoners and destroyed over 3,000 tanks at the Battle of Smolensk and had by early August in Army Group Center's sector alone taken over 600,000 prisoners and destroyed or captured over 6,000 tanks. Still, despite losses of over 2 million men, the Red Army showed no sign of slackening their stubborn resistance or that their vital strength had been broken. The way to Moscow was still not open, while the deterioration of the Germans' combat power, especially among the armored units, was causing mounting anxieties and gradually curtailing their available options. By late July, the OKH estimated the combat power of the panzer and motorized infantry divisions to be only about half of what it had been at the start of the campaign. The deficiencies were so serious, in fact, that, even after a ten-day pause to resupply and reequip, the goal was merely to bring the armored divisions up to 60–70 percent of their former strength. Both Hoth's and Guderian's Panzergruppen were badly overextended, with their thinly stretched front lines covered by few strategic reserves. Halder himself on 26 July noted the danger that German forces were being drawn into a series of minor successes that would lead only to positional warfare, while on 5 August he fretted that present developments were leading to a solidification of the fronts like World War I. Bock, too, lamented the Führer's suggestion, as a result of Smolensk, that "for the moment we should encircle the Russians tactically wherever we meet them . . . and then destroy them in small pockets," an idea Bock thought would reduce grand blitzkrieg sweeps to mere tactical actions.[85] Although the Soviets had not reclaimed the strategic initiative, they had broken the momentum of the German offensive. Once again, as in the border battles, the Germans failed to concentrate their forces and gain a swift, crushing victory, a pattern that would continue with regularity through 1942. Major disputes about the Schwerpunkt of the attack, which had receded in the earlier glow of success, now erupted with a fury in late July and August as the Germans struggled to prevent their Blitzfeldzug from deteriorating into a war of attrition.

On 19 July, at the height of the fighting at Smolensk, the OKW issued Führer Directive No. 33, which reflected Hitler's recognition that the large-scale encirclement operations had not achieved decisive success and that such success was not likely to be expected soon. Both Army Group Center and Army Group South had been slowed by the creation of pockets and by the continuing presence in the rear areas (the Pripet Marshes) of substantial Soviet forces. The aim over the next few weeks would be simply to prevent enemy units still within reach from withdrawing further into the vast spaces of this enormous land and to destroy them. As many German commanders realized, this policy would slow their exploitation of any offensive successes and allow the enemy time to construct new defenses. Since the Germans had largely outrun their fragile supply system, the poor roads made it difficult for infantry to keep pace with the tanks (whose number was dwindling rapidly), and the frontline units had received only scanty replacements, there seemed little alternative to such a decision. The order thus took account of the fact that significant time would still be required to eliminate the remnants of Soviet forces in the Smolensk area, a task that was to be left to the infantry. The bulk of the two Panzergruppen would then be shifted to the north and south, to support the drive on Leningrad and to clear the Soviet Fifth Army from the Pripet Marshes. As was becoming uncomfortably apparent, the Wehrmacht bested the Red Army in individual battles time and again but found itself lacking the strength to accomplish all that it needed to do to secure victory.[86]

Given the dogged resistance on the central axis, the continuing attacks from the Pripet area that delayed the advance of the Sixth Army to the south and threatened to sever its supply lines, rainy weather that further hobbled the Germans, and the possibilities raised by the situation at Kiev noted by Halder on 9 July, Hitler's order appeared neither unrealistic nor unreasonable. In fact, however, Halder protested immediately and sought to have it canceled, worrying that it presaged a disastrous abandonment of a concentrated attack on Moscow. In response, on 23 July Hitler issued the Supplement to Directive No. 33, which could hardly have calmed Halder's anxieties. Although the transfer of armored units was made dependent on the operational and supply situation, this addendum nonetheless clearly intended that significant units from Guderian's Second Panzergruppe would be turned south to clear enemy forces west of the Dnieper, then strike to the east, capture the key industrial areas of Kharkov and the Donets Basin, and proceed on toward the Caucasus oil region. At the same time, Hoth's Third Panzergruppe would temporarily be assigned to Army Group North to aid in its attack on Leningrad. Army Group Center would be left with only "sufficiently powerful infantry formations" to advance "as far as possible to the east." Only at the beginning of September, and then only if the armored units temporarily stripped from it were returned, could Army Group Center expect to resume its offensive toward Moscow. As the OKW conceded, the Soviets had forced this delay and deflected the immediate threat to Moscow, which represented a significant political victory. In addition, the pause would give the enemy a month to strengthen its defenses west of the capital as well as have use of the considerable armaments industries of

the Moscow region. Although the directive noted that Moscow should
be brought under attack by the Luftwaffe and that rapid progress could
be expected once the offensive resumed, its sober tone left little doubt
that the German High Command recognized that it faced serious
difficulties.[87]

Halder understood immediately the implications of this directive,
which meant a fundamental shift in the operational-strategic objective
from the destruction of enemy combat power in front of Moscow to the
occupation of vital economic regions. That evening, he and Brauchitsch
met with Hitler to express their deep concern and persuade the Führer
to concentrate available German forces against Moscow. In part, their
arguments followed familiar lines: since most of the remaining enemy
forces would be concentrated in front of Moscow, that offered the best
chance of decisive victory. The capture of the city and its communications and "leadership apparatus" as well as its significant armaments
industry, the two argued, would split Russia in half and make further
organized resistance "extraordinarily difficult." As with France a year
earlier, Halder (and Bock) expected the capture of the Soviet capital to
induce such political shockwaves that the entire system would collapse.
Halder also raised a new and disquieting concern: the Germans lacked
sufficient time and strength to complete the Barbarossa plan before winter. The Russians, he noted, were desperately trying to delay the German
advance until the onset of winter. If reduced to "positional warfare,"
Halder warned, the enemy would be able to organize its defenses and
mobilize its industries so that next spring the Wehrmacht would face
newly raised and equipped Soviet formations. As a result, "the military
goal of the war against Russia, the rapid elimination of one opponent
in a two-front war in order to turn full strength against the other [En-
gland], could not be achieved." Halder concluded that the enemy had
been "decisively weakened" but not yet "completely defeated" and, thus,
that the aim of future operations had to be the destruction of the enemy
ability to resist.[88]

Hitler, however, was not impressed by Halder's arguments, not least
because he considered the capture of Soviet economic and oil resources
of far greater importance in undermining the enemy ability to resist.
Moreover, in the absence of an inescapable position into which to push
Russian forces, such as the English Channel, he believed that a frontal assault on Moscow would simply allow Soviet troops once again to
withdraw, an argument seemingly confirmed by the operations at Minsk
and Smolensk. His advice—that the army should concentrate on "tactical battles of destruction over smaller areas in which the enemy could

be pinned down and completely destroyed"—must have come as a stinging rebuke to Halder and his conduct of operations. Over the next few
days, indeed, the chief of the OKH fumed that the campaign was becoming little more than static warfare while sarcastically noting the impossibility of avoiding all risks. On 26 July, he bluntly told Hitler that he
was playing into Russian hands by resorting to "tactical envelopments"
while trying to rally the top army leaders, including Jodl, his rival in
the OKW, to his position. Both corps commanders of panzer forces in
the north, Manstein and Hoepner, reported that the area facing them
between Lakes Peipus and Ilmen was unsuitable for mobile warfare, as
did Paulus, who was dispatched to the region on a fact-finding mission.[89]

In the event, it was less Halder's arguments and more the reality
of growing Soviet strength and increasing German supply difficulties
that caused Hitler first to suspend and then to cancel the Supplement
to Directive No. 33. Although on hearing the news Halder exclaimed,
"This decision frees every thinking soldier of the horrible vision obsess-
ing us these last few days, since the Führer's obstinacy made the final
bogging down of the campaign appear imminent," the reality of Directive No. 34 was a bit less cheering. In it, Hitler still called for operations
to envelop Leningrad and destroy Soviet forces at Kiev and in Ukraine
west of the Dnieper while ordering Army Group Center to go on the
defensive while it was refitted and reequipped. Halder clearly expected
that the developments on the front would strengthen his position and
that, after the enforced supply halt, the central front would again become
the main axis of advance.[90]

Amid much vacillation, the "July Crisis" of the German military leadership had thus ended, at least temporarily, although it was clear that,
after the replenishment period, a decision would still have to be taken.
The crucial decision—for or against Moscow—had merely been postponed. Nor, in retrospect, is it clear that Halder's arguments were markedly better than Hitler's. In view of the logistic situation, any further
advance on the central axis was for the time being out of the question.
The quartermaster-general's staff had already concluded that a major
attack on the central front was unfeasible since an adequate rate of supply to sustain an offensive could not be provided. At the same time, Hitler's decision corresponded with continued fighting still raging in the
Smolensk pocket, so the stable situation necessary for replenishment of
the front units did not exist. Because of the early capture of the Baltic
ports, an action Hitler had urged from the outset, Army Group North
had accumulated sufficient supplies to sustain its operations, although
terrain difficulties would hamper its movement. Moreover, the strong

Soviet forces in the Pripet Marshes did represent a significant threat to the flanks of both Army Group Center and Army Group South as well as a menace to the already strained supply lines to the Sixth Army. In addition, large numbers of German troops, some six divisions, were tied down in combating enemy forays from the swamps. Even Bock admitted that "a precondition for any further operation is the defeat of the enemy on the army group's flanks, both of which are lagging far behind." As a result, by the late summer of 1941, the envelopment of Kiev was probably the only major operation feasible. Although supply difficulties still dogged a move to the south, the supply organizations of Army Groups Center and South could at least share the burden, while the terrain was largely favorable to mobile operations.[91]

Strong Soviet resistance, a failure to resolve supply problems, and rainy weather that hampered the German advance all ensured that the mood of crisis would continue into August. The bitter fighting at Smolensk had sobered the German commanders and impelled them to alter their original strategy. The fear that the blitzkrieg momentum had slipped away was palpable, with little agreement on a course of action to regain the strategic initiative. By early August, the Barbarossa campaign had already exceeded in length that in the west the previous summer, with no clear way to end it in evidence. Victories had been won, yet a terrible price had been paid. "We are at the end of our tether," Bock admitted on 2 August. "The nerves of those burdened with great responsibility are starting to waver." Landsers, too, sensed that the fighting might be as endless as Russia itself. "We shouldn't be allowed to continue much longer, otherwise the burden will be really heavy," complained one on 10 August, while another noted on the same day, "Our losses are immense, more than in France." A third wrote simply, "I have never seen such vicious dogs as these Russians. . . . They have an inexhaustible supply of tanks and material."[92] Underpinning the gloom was the gnawing anxiety that the war could not be won in 1941. In early August, the Führer remained wedded to the position that a decisive weakening of the Soviet ability to wage war meant the seizure of Leningrad in the north and the key economic, oil, and industrial regions of Ukraine and the Caucasus in the south, an implicit recognition that Moscow could probably not be taken by the onset of winter.

The ruthless Soviet mobilization of resources and unrelenting counterattacks had both surprised and unnerved German generals. "The situation is extremely tense," Bock worried on 7 August. "I don't exactly know how a new operation is to take place . . . with the slowly sinking fighting strength of our . . . forces." Still, he consoled himself with the thought that "things are undoubtedly even worse for the Russians!" A few days later, however, he confessed: "In spite of his terrific losses in men and materiel the enemy attacks at several places daily, so that any regrouping, any withdrawal of reserves . . . has so far been impossible." He then added, in a revealing concession, "If the Russians don't soon collapse somewhere, the objective of defeating them so badly that they are eliminated will be difficult to achieve before the winter."[93]

At the same time, Halder, too, succumbed to gloom, noting on 4 August, "We could not expect to reach the Caucasus before onset of this winter," a virtual admission that Barbarossa had failed. Nor did his mood improve substantially in the next week. "On the fronts . . . reigns the quiet of exhaustion," he admitted pessimistically in his diary on 11 August:

> What we are now doing is the last desperate attempt to prevent our front line from becoming frozen in position warfare. . . . Our last reserves have been committed. . . . The whole situation makes it increasingly plain that we have underestimated the Russian colossus, who consistently prepared for war with that utterly ruthless determination so characteristic of totalitarian states. . . . At the outset of the war we reckoned with about 200 enemy divisions. Now we have already counted 360. These divisions indeed are not armed and equipped according to our standards, and their tactical leadership is often poor. But there they are, and if we smash a dozen of them, the Russians simply put up another dozen. The time factor favors them, as they are near their own resources, while we are moving farther and farther away from ours. And so our troops, sprawled over an immense front line, without any depth, are subjected to the incessant attacks of the enemy.[94]

As the invading armies were swallowed in the immensity of the Soviet Union, as every triumph brought German forces deeper into the quagmire, a bitter irony became clear: the Wehrmacht was winning itself to death in the vast expanses of Russia. Despite the failures of the encirclement battles at Minsk and Smolensk to destroy the Soviet will and ability to resist, however, Halder could think of nothing else but to try again. If the remnant of the Red Army was to be destroyed, it would have to be done in front of Moscow.

Hitler, on the other hand, drew an entirely opposite conclusion. If the Soviets were, indeed, massing their last forces in front of the capital, that surely meant easier pickings in the north and south, precisely where his primary objectives lay. During the first two weeks of August, then, Hitler and his army chief of staff wrestled with the key issue of the main axis of German operations. Halder achieved a certain success on 12 August when the Führer conceded, in the Supplement to Directive No. 34, that the aim was "the removal from the enemy before the winter of the entire state, armaments, and communications center around Moscow." The army chief's triumph, however, was limited by the further stipulation that the attack on Moscow would go ahead only once the threat to the flanks of Army Group Center had been eliminated. Three days later, in fact, strong Soviet counterattacks again disrupted Halder's intentions as Hitler ordered panzer units away from Army Group Center to the north to counter the danger and directed that Bock's forces should refrain from any further attacks toward Moscow.[95]

Faced once more with a dissipation of forces, Halder believed that the decisive moment had arrived to settle the matter conclusively. Enlisting the support of Brauchitsch, Halder on 18 August sent Hitler a proposal justifying a concentration of strength against Moscow. In addition to the familiar argument of destroying the last enemy forces, Halder asserted that, though important, successes on the flanks in winning resources could never be decisive in themselves. Halder, however, had picked the wrong time for a showdown. Hitler almost certainly believed that in the Supplement to Directive No. 34 he had already made a major compromise. In addition, the strain of the past month had clearly taken a toll on the Führer both physically and psychologically. Although a chronic hypochondriac, in mid-August he suffered an attack of dysentery, accompanied by evidence of rapidly progressing coronary sclerosis. When Goebbels visited the Führer's headquarters on 18 August, he was taken aback by Hitler's physical and mental exhaustion. Signs of extreme nervous strain abounded: he was obsessed with the gross underestimation of Soviet strength given him before the war by German intelligence, so much so that he implied that he might have hesitated to launch the attack had he known the truth. He also shocked Goebbels with the suggestion that he might accept a negotiated peace with Stalin. Churchill, the Führer rambled on, was grasping at straws, such as the recently announced Atlantic Charter; indeed, his government might well collapse and the war end suddenly, just as the Nazis had been unexpectedly swept into power in 1933. The Führer's nerves were clearly frayed, while Goebbels was sobered by the realization that the eastern campaign would not be over in 1941 and that the best that could be hoped for were good winter positions.[96]

Hitler's moment of strategic realism had immediate operational implications. If Germany could not destroy enemy forces, economic considerations became paramount. His detailed reply to Halder came quickly and was a terse rejection of the army chief's proposals. On 21 August, Hitler issued an order through the OKW reaffirming that the principal objectives to be attained before the onset of winter continued to be the capture of the economic and industrial areas of Ukraine as well as the oil region of the Caucasus. Conquest of the Crimea was also a priority in order to secure the Rumanian oil supply, while the encirclement of Leningrad still took precedence over the capture of Moscow. The next day, in a detailed study, Hitler justified his operational priorities not only with the usual political and economic arguments but with military considerations as well. It was, he stressed, as Bock had already conceded, necessary to eliminate the enemy threat on the flanks before launching any attack on Moscow, so the operation into Ukraine to secure economic resources would at the same time serve the aim of securing the southern flank of Army Group Center. In any case, Hitler noted caustically, the original operational plan anticipated movements to the north and south, so, not he, but the Army High Command, had altered the script. Moreover, in a stinging rebuke to the army leadership, he noted that not only had they deviated from the plan, but they had also then failed to achieve a decisive victory. In the ultimate insult, the Führer then contrasted their shaky performance with Goering's firm leadership of the Luftwaffe. Although Hitler ended with some conciliatory words affirming his acceptance of the thrust on Moscow, he nonetheless emphasized that this would be undertaken only after the other operations had concluded.[97]

Beside himself with anger, and perhaps also a bit embarrassed that Hitler had seen through his obstructionism, Halder raged in his diary against the Führer, blaming him for the vacillation and indecision of the past weeks, and furious at the humiliating treatment of Brauchitsch. Halder even urged that he and Brauchitsch tender their resignations together, but the latter rejected the proposal. Deeply upset, Halder flew to Army Group Center headquarters the next day to rally support for his preference for resuming the offensive on Moscow. He arranged for Guderian, one of Hitler's favorite generals and particularly vocal in his opposition to a move south, to accompany him to Führer Headquarters in an attempt to dissuade the dictator from his course of action. Rather amazingly to those present, on the evening of 24 August, Hitler allowed Guderian, in the absence of Halder, to make the case for an attack on Moscow. The Soviet capital, Guderian asserted, was not just the political, transportation, and communications center of Russia but, in a telling analogy that illuminated the military mind-set, "the nerve center of Russia . . . like Paris is to France." Hitler then argued the alternative. The raw materials and agricultural resources of Ukraine, he noted, were absolutely vital to a continuation of the war, as was securing the German oil supply. "My generals," he remarked in a biting comment, "know nothing of the economic aspects of war." Although the day before he had asserted that an attack to the south by his armored group was impossible, Guderian now reversed himself and affirmed his ability to launch just such a drive. When they heard the news of Guderian's volte-face, both Halder and Bock were furious, but, in truth, there had been little the panzer commander could do to alter the situation. Hitler's mind was made up: the battle for Ukraine would go ahead.[98]

Nor, despite the later self-serving contentions of the generals, were Hitler's criticisms without merit. The bulk of the Red Army had not been destroyed, Soviet leaders had managed to organize an effective defense in spite of catastrophic losses, and the steadily declining German strength and the vastness of the area to be conquered posed almost insuperable difficulties. In addition, the German logistic system had neared the point of collapse: railroads had not been repaired quickly enough, and the dire state of Soviet roads overwhelmed German motorized transport. The number of trains arriving at Army Group Center could barely sustain daily operations, let alone allow a buildup sufficient to support an advance on Moscow. Although it needed at least twenty-four trains a day to supply its needs, at times in August it received only half that number. Clearly, the basic prerequisite for an attack on Moscow was lacking. Moreover, even holding the ground already taken proved difficult since the Soviets launched unrelenting attacks around Smolensk. By early September, in fact, the Red Army had forced the Germans to withdraw from Yelnya, important both as a psychological victory for the Soviets and as the loss by the Germans of a springboard for later operations. The continuing attacks at Smolensk further convinced Hitler of the need to eliminate the southern threat to any advance on Moscow.[99]

With the failure to win a quick victory on the frontier, the stark reality facing the Wehrmacht High Command was that, in late August, no one seemed able to produce a war-winning strategy that would finish off a reeling foe. Halder and Jodl both expected operations to continue into the following year, a conclusion arrived at independently in an OKW study and a point also made by Hitler in his study. Given the facts of the situation, Hitler likely had a more realistic view than did Halder. Despite the failure of his key assumption, the latter produced no new plan for victory. Where Halder, despite the evidence of increasing enemy resistance and eroding German strength, clung to the hope that one last blow would lead to the collapse of Soviet defenses, Hitler drew the conclusion dictated by his recognition that the war would not end in 1941: securing economic resources had a higher priority than achieving another operational triumph. At the same time, the advance to the south, and the promise of another vast encirclement operation, might at last break the Red Army. The deeper problem, of course, was the one that had festered since the beginning. Hitler and Halder had never agreed on the fundamental aims of Barbarossa; with no clarity on the overall goals of the campaign, it had from the start been a muddled gamble on luck and good fortune. With his late August decision to strike south, Hitler implicitly acknowledged that the luck had run out and the gamble had failed.[100]

4

Whirlwind

As the turbulent events on the eastern front and at Führer Headquarters unfolded, domestically the summer of 1941 proved difficult as well. Always sensitive to the popular mood, and with memories of 1918 constantly at the forefront, Nazi officials anxiously studied the weekly SD reports on the state of public opinion. Although the outbreak of war in September 1939 had been accepted unenthusiastically, the brilliant military triumphs in Poland and France had led to unprecedented popularity for Hitler. These victories, however, had not resulted in an end to the war. Instead, the German people faced first the uncertainty of a long war and then the shock of the attack on the Soviet Union. Although the assault on Jewish-Bolshevism was popular with party loyalists, news of Barbarossa had been received by the populace with muted skepticism. As in France a year earlier, initial successes had led Germans to expect another quick and relatively painless victory, but, as the campaign dragged on into the summer with no end in sight, the mood grew resigned and weary.

Initial announcements of spectacular triumphs that had done so much to raise hopes, in fact, now backfired, as Goebbels recognized. As the summer wore on and it became obvious that the Soviets continued to resist ferociously with seemingly endless manpower reserves, hopes of an early peace gave way to rising concerns. Whatever the scale of victories, propaganda announcements of "Bolshevik atrocities," bestialities committed by "Jewish criminals," and the "inhumane way of fighting" of the Bolsheviks did little to reassure the friends and relatives of those at the front. Moreover, the Soviet success in destroying significant grain stocks before they could be seized by the onrushing Wehrmacht forced German authorities to reduce the food ration in late July. Since the weekly meat ration for normal consumers had already been cut in early June, this second reduction was a disturbing blow for a population with long memories of the lean times of 1914–1918 and a leadership sensitive to the link between hunger and revolution.[1]

For most Germans, the summer of 1941 meant the end of the good times of the 1930s, when the Nazis had provided jobs and economic security, promoted social programs, and restored a sense of national pride. Daily concerns over food shortages, rising prices, and the fate of loved ones now dominated the popular mood. Already in late June Goebbels worried, "Food situation in Berlin is very bad. No potatoes, few vegetables." Although the situation improved temporarily, by mid-July he noted that the "extraordinarily precarious" food situation was producing "worries and also some nervousness," while at the end of the month he fretted that of "a whole series of explosive items in popular opinion" the most troubling was "now the question of food." By mid-August, fears of a repetition of the "Jewish subversion" of the Great War crept in, SD reports noting that, with an increase in black market activity, "once again an old problem" had become acute. "Unstable prices," Goebbels noted with concern, "had made people surly and nervous." In southwest Germany, the SD reported people grumbling that "in this war the little people are the losers once more. . . . Can one still speak of a Volksgemeinschaft?" For a movement intent on creating a society strong enough to withstand the rigors of war, such statements raised alarms. When anxiety over food persisted, the popular mood having grown "somewhat critical in August," Goering ordered that food rations be maintained at all costs since the enemy's "only hope is to wear down the morale of the home front."[2]

Goebbels ultimately concluded that, despite the grumbling, morale in Germany remained stable, but he did take note of two potentially explosive problems: signs of panic and nervous strain among the urban population of some of the western German cities exposed to repeated British bombing raids and a growing unease among German Catholics over Nazi actions against religion and the handicapped. Nor were the two concerns unrelated. Although virtually all top Nazis believed that Christianity and National Socialism were incompatible, Hitler, for pragmatic reasons, desired that the "church question" be left until after the war. Nonetheless, by mid-1941, party activists at the local and regional levels had inflamed passions by seeking to break the irksome power of the churches. In part, military success fueled this antireligion campaign as the imminent end of the war made a final reckoning with Christianity possible; in part, the campaign reflected party anger that wartime anxieties had strengthened church ties with the populace.

Party actions in the first half of 1941 aimed specifically at reining in the power of the Catholic Church, first by banning Catholic publications, and then by having charity work taken over by the National Socialist People's Welfare Organization (NSV). The closure of some monasteries raised fears of a renewed state assault on Catholicism, while the action of Adolf Wagner, the *Gauleiter* of Bavaria, in ordering all crucifixes removed from schoolrooms touched off a storm of protest. Some complained that, while their sons were fighting Bolshevism in the east, Nazi officials were attacking religion at home, while women wrote their husbands in Russia that they had better "come home to fight Bolshevism here."[3]

This disquiet with attacks on the church also merged with anxieties caused by bombing raids in the cities of the heavily Catholic Ruhr industrial area and growing unease over the Nazi policy of euthanasia to create a serious internal crisis. "The heavy night attack on Münster had some regrettable psychological consequences," Goebbels conceded on 10 July. "These continuing bombardments on a city that in its clerical attitude is also delicate has had an unpleasant effect." The bishop of Münster, Clemens August Graf von Galen, was responsible for much of the Nazi discomfort. A deeply conservative and anti-Communist individual, he had initially welcomed the assault on the Soviet Union. Nazi actions against the Catholic Church and the persistent British bombing raids, however, caused him to deliver a series of sermons in July denouncing the Gestapo's suppression of religion. He also protested the closing of monasteries as an affront at a time when "the unity of the Volk needed to be preserved" and people needed special spiritual care. In late July, he wrote a letter to the Reich Chancellery that was a scarcely veiled attack on Hitler himself. His most confrontational action came on 3 August, however, when in a sermon he again condemned the attack on religion, then raised the explosive issue of euthanasia. "There is a general suspicion verging on certainty," Galen asserted, "that these numerous deaths of mentally ill people do not occur of themselves but are deliberately brought about, that the doctrine is being followed according to which one may destroy so-called 'worthless life,' that is to kill innocent people if one considers their lives of no further value for the nation and state." He then pointed to the obvious implications: people who became invalids, soldiers with severe wounds, anyone who in the opinion of Nazi officials had become unproductive, could be put on the list to be murdered. Who, then, he asked, would protect us? Who could average Germans trust? Who would give the murderer the punishment he deserved?[4]

"An outrageous and provocative speech," thundered Goebbels. "He even had the impudence to assert that our euthanasia efforts will go so far that wounded soldiers, if they are no longer needed for practical work, will be murdered by us." To Nazi officials, Galen's speech, in which he implicitly tied the war to murder and none too subtly suggested that the bombing raids were God's punishment on an unjust government, connected too many dots, for there was, indeed, a connection between war and euthanasia. The pseudoscientific eugenics movement that materialized in the late nineteenth century out of social Darwinism postulated a belief that human inequality was based on genetics and that, by limiting or encouraging the procreation of certain people, the general level of humankind could be improved. Although the eugenics movement had emerged most strongly in Great Britain and the United States, in Germany after World War I it took on a more sinister tone. Eugenics advocates, in a climate poisoned by the recent large loss of life and the economic burdens of a lost war, went beyond customary calls for sterilization of the "unfit" and suggested the right of the state to kill those judged "unworthy of life." Since the "fit" had given disproportionately of their lives in the war, the state needed to intervene to avoid a demographic disaster. In an idea promoted by the Nazis and embraced by many proponents of "racial hygiene," the Volk had to be cleansed of the unfit in order again to be healthy. By eliminating the "socially burdensome," moreover, the state could use its limited resources in a more "socially productive" fashion.[5]

Hitler had been an early and enthusiastic advocate of eugenics, and, once in power, the Nazis moved swiftly to implement eugenics measures such as compulsory sterilizations and abortions. These actions resulted in the predictable opposition of the Catholic Church, but Hitler could count on not inconsiderable support from the German medical community. In 1935, he revealed his intention to implement a program of involuntary euthanasia in case of war. In the event, the Nazis had already in the summer of 1939 begun to kill handicapped infants. This "children's euthanasia" was soon followed by a full-blown program of "adult euthanasia" under the direction of two young, ambitious, and ideologically fanatic officials in the Führer Chancellery, Philipp Bouhler and Viktor Brack. That same summer, Hitler again advocated euthanasia in the context of war, reiterating his belief that mental patients should be killed as hospitals and medical personnel could be better employed caring for wounded soldiers.[6]

The link between war and euthanasia was hardened with the German invasion of Poland. Within weeks of the attack, special units began killing mental patients, both Polish and German, in Polish institutions, some by shooting, and some, significantly, through the use of a sealed gas van. In October, Hitler signed an authorization typed on his own letterhead stationery—backdated to 1 September, the day the war began—that stated: "Reichsleiter [Reich Leader] Bouhler and Dr. Med. Brandt are commissioned with the responsibility of extending the authority of specified doctors so that, after critical assessment of their condition, those judged incurably ill can be granted mercy-death." With that death sentence, the only time he was to affix his signature on such an order, Hitler had sealed the connection between war and euthanasia. The program for adult euthanasia, called T-4 after its headquarters in Berlin (Tiergartenstrasse 4), quickly recruited a pool of doctors to process the necessary forms and began work on six special killing centers. Those to be killed, primarily the German adult handicapped, were transported to the killing centers by special buses, then sent to gas chambers where they were murdered by carbon monoxide gas. By the spring of 1941, in cooperation with the SS, the program was extended into the concentration camps. By the time of Bishop Galen's speech, over 70,000 and perhaps as many as 100,000 people had already been murdered in the euthanasia killing centers. Public protests unleashed by the bishop's speech, and the fact that the Nazis felt constrained in moving against Galen in wartime, led Hitler to order an end to the adult euthanasia program on 24 August. Both the children's and the concentration camp programs were continued, however, with more victims dying after the stop order was issued than before. The stop order also meant that a large staff of professional killers experienced in the methods and techniques of murder by gassing were suddenly available for other assignments.[7]

If the euthanasia program was not the direct precursor of the Holocaust, certainly there existed key conceptual, technological, and organizational connections between the two. Moreover, both were vital aspects of the Nazis' larger project of creating a racial utopia. This demographic vision, subsumed in the larger concept of Lebensraum, encompassed the cleansing of the German Volk, the ethnic restructuring of Central and Eastern Europe, and the destruction of the ultimate enemy, the Jews. Just as importantly, the implementation of this abhorrent scheme could not have been undertaken without war. Hitler's prophecy, the euthanasia program, the resettlement measures in Poland, the early notions of expelling the Jews from Europe, plans for a vast Jewish reservation in the east—all depended for realization on the stunning successes of the Wehrmacht. At each stage, however, expectations of the imminent realization of this racial utopia gave way to frustration as various obstacles thwarted Nazi planners. Time and again, however, military triumphs opened new avenues for ever more radical ventures. The mid-July burst of euphoria had resulted in the expansion of killing operations to include all Soviet Jews. Similarly, despite the official halt to the euthanasia program, a new round of combat successes in September and October would remove the last barriers to the full-blown implementation of the Final Solution. By the autumn of 1941, the various strands of the Nazi war of annihilation were to merge into one enormously deadly enterprise.

If domestic protest had stymied Hitler's euthanasia plans, that same month opposition from the military had paralyzed army operations. Ironically, when the Wehrmacht resumed large-scale offensive action after the August pause, the bitter debate between Hitler and his generals seemed to work to German advantage since it had convinced Stalin of the Germans' intention to replenish their forces and strike directly at Moscow. Hitler, however, had other plans. Throughout July, even as the fighting raged on the central axis at Smolensk, German forces had continued a steady if unspectacular advance in the south in hopes of seizing the important agricultural and industrial areas of Ukraine before winter. Operations here had been difficult from the outset. Not only did Rundstedt face the largest concentration of the Red Army, but geography favored the defenders as well. Soviet troops could anchor their line on the Carpathian Mountains in the south, while the Pripet Marshes in the north posed an impenetrable obstacle. At the same time, the Ukrainian front was larger in depth and breadth than the other two. Kiev lay some 350 miles from the border, compared to the 200 miles Bock's forces had to cover to Minsk, while, south of the Ukrainian capital, German forces would have to advance into the wide expanse of the great bend of the Dnieper River. Even if the Soviets collapsed as expected, just occupying this huge swath of territory would have taxed the Germans. Supply was a constant problem, with the usual absence of good roads compounded by incessant rain in early July. Pulling off encirclement battles as in Belorussia would be difficult, especially since the Red Army had a decided advantage in tanks and aircraft. Added to the mix was better Soviet leadership, so the progress of Army Group South lagged significantly behind that of its neighbor to the north.[8]

Nonetheless, by mid-July, the Sixth Army had advanced to within ten miles of Kiev, even as ferocious Soviet resistance, attacks from the Pripet area, and worsening supply problems meant that Reichenau had insufficient force to take the city. Still, Rundstedt planned to press ahead to the south, hoping to cross the Dnieper at Cherkassy, Dnepropetrovsk, or Zaporozhye in order to capture the key Donets industrial area in a vast encirclement operation. Because of stout Soviet resistance along the Rumanian frontier west of the Bug River, which accentuated Hitler's ever-present worries about the security of his oil supply, both he and Halder favored a tighter envelopment. They insisted that Rundstedt turn forces south from Zhitomir along the Bug River in the direction of Odessa on the Black Sea in order to trap Soviet forces in that area. The ensuing encirclement at Uman resulted in the first great German victory in the south as, after weeks of grinding battles, Rundstedt's forces destroyed some twenty Soviet divisions and bagged over 100,000 prisoners as well as large quantities of equipment and supplies. Nonetheless, the skillful Soviet defense, poor roads, and rain that hindered German movement enabled large enemy forces to escape to the east. Thus, even though Stalin regarded the battle at Uman to be little short of a disaster and, in response, issued his notorious Order No. 270 that declared surrender a form of treason and allowed the arrest of the families of commanders who capitulated or retreated, the Germans had not accomplished their goal.[9]

For the Soviets, however, something far worse than Uman was brewing. By 20 August, having reached Kremenchug, 180 miles to the southeast of Kiev, the Germans controlled virtually all the territory west of the Dnieper. Over 300 miles straight north, the leading spearheads of Army Group Center had occupied Yelnya. In between these two powerful pincers, whose apex was roughly 300 miles to the west at Kiev, lay the entire Soviet Southwest Front, comprising six armies with well over fifty divisions. Intense Soviet attacks from the Pripet Marshes against the northern wing of the Sixth Army had prompted increasing German concern for the viability of any further advance east and southeast into the vital Ukrainian industrial areas as well as stretching Hitler's patience to its limit. His directive on the twenty-first for Army Groups Center and South to cooperate sprang as much from his frustration at continued enemy resistance in the Pripet area, which also made any further move on Moscow impossible, as it did from any larger strategic consideration. Guderian's Second Panzergruppe would have to be diverted to the south despite his reservations about the road and fuel situation as well as the need for his units to be replenished. With many of his divisions reduced to little more than reinforced regiments, with barely 30–50 percent of the normal complement of tanks, and seriously low on gasoline and oil, supply officers estimated that it would take eight to ten days just to bring his forces up to 60 percent of normal strength. Halder, concerned as ever about the need to conserve resources for the attack on Moscow, also undermined Hitler's directive by limiting the number of units of the Second Panzergruppe assigned to this new operation.[10] At the outset, then, even though the conditions existed for a great encirclement battle, neither the Germans nor the Soviets seem fully to have recognized the possibilities (and dangers) in the situation. Stalin, in fact, rejected Zhukov's suggestions that Soviet troops be withdrawn to more defensible positions, transferring the troublesome general to the Leningrad front.

Despite his doubts about the operation, Guderian received orders to begin a southerly push on 25 August. At 5:00 A.M. on what would prove to be a blisteringly hot day, General Leo Geyr von Schweppenburg's Twenty-fourth Corps, with only about one-third of its tank strength operational, set off for the Desna River. Initially, it made rapid gains, even capturing a key bridge at Novgorod-Seversk intact. The primitive, sandy roads that limited progress to forty miles before the columns had to be refueled as well as the habitual ferocious Soviet resistance quickly slowed the advance. By the twenty-seventh, the Third Panzer and the Tenth Motorized Divisions had been so weakened that they had to go on the defensive, with only the Fourth Panzer capable of offensive operation. At that point, Army Group Center relented and released another two and a half mobile divisions to Guderian, but it took another four days for resupply sufficient to allow the resumption of the offensive. Bock admitted on the thirty-first that, with both his flanks under attack, Guderian was "in a difficult situation." On 1 September, the Twenty-fourth Corps continued its advance, but strong enemy resistance, poor roads, rainy weather, damaged bridges, and inadequate provisions slowed the German advance to a crawl. The next day, following the loss of a bridgehead south of the Desna, a sense of crisis pervaded the German High Command. "Guderian's description of the situation was so pessimistic," Bock noted, "that I had to decide if I should propose . . . that the armored group be pulled back across the Desna." On the fourth, an anxious and dissatisfied Hitler intervened, demanding that Guderian concentrate his forces for the drive south. The latter requested still more reinforcements, a demand that led Bock seriously to consider dismissing him. On the sixth, torrential rains turned the roads into a muddy quagmire that ground all movement to a halt.[11] Despite later images of a swift encirclement operation, by the end of the first week of September the Second Panzergruppe struggled to maintain any momentum at all.

At roughly the same time, to the south, units of the Seventeenth Army and the First Panzergruppe of Army Group South had reached their assembly areas for the crossing of the Dnieper. In a series of engagements between 30 August and 2 September, the Seventeenth Army seized river crossings at Kremenchug. Although the original intention had been for these forces to continue to advance eastward once the river had been breached, the stiffening of enemy resistance and the realization that the Soviets were throwing units from other areas into the battle for Kiev caused a fundamental German reassessment. As it became clear that Stalin had ordered the Dnieper line to be held at all costs, the OKW now saw a chance to inflict a disastrous defeat on the Soviets. Already on 1 September, the chief of staff of Army Group South, General Sodenstern, had contacted his counterpart at the Second Army to the north in order to discuss the possibility of an encirclement of Soviet forces east of Kiev that would clear the way for the Moscow operation. On the sixth, the OKW ordered the Seventeenth Army and the First Panzergruppe to turn north and, in conjunction with the Second Army and the Second Panzergruppe, trap the bulk of Soviet forces gathering to the east of Kiev, while the next day Halder and Rundstedt conferred to hammer out the details of the destruction of all enemy forces in the Kiev-Dnieper-Desna bend. Although this meant that the mobile units of Panzergruppe 1 would be tied down in protracted operations in closing and holding the ring and, thus, would be unable to exploit a breakthrough to the east, the lure of a giant envelopment that would free the danger to the southern flank of the Moscow attack proved alluring. In the north, Guderian's forces were to drive on Sumy, and the Second Army was to aim for Romny, while the southern wing would advance on Lubny.[12]

While the Germans acted quickly to exploit the emerging opportunity, the Soviets obliged their enemy by putting their head further into the noose. Although Zhukov and others had from mid-August tried in vain to warn Stalin of the looming danger at Kiev, the Soviet dictator stubbornly insisted that the city, the ancient center of medieval Russia, the capital of Ukraine, and the third largest city in the Soviet Union, be defended. Stalin had more than historical or sentimental reasons for his seemingly irrational decision. He feared that the loss of the city, the political center of an area that had borne the brunt of his calamitous policy of collectivization of agriculture in the 1930s, might touch off a process of internal disintegration of the Soviet system. Signs of decomposition, which even the notorious blocking units could not stem, had, indeed, become evident by early September in some Soviet units. The

Soviet dictator also wanted to inspire the defenders of Leningrad and Odessa and was anxious as well to reassure nervous American and British leaders that the Soviet Union could survive the German onslaught. Stalin, too, regarded a German move on Moscow, given the importance of the city, as self-evident. He thus initially perceived Guderian's attack as simply part of a typical German maneuver to encircle the capital rather than drive straight at it.[13]

For Soviet commanders, unwilling to challenge Stalin's orders and risk execution by ordering a withdrawal, events now unfolded as in a script they had seen but were powerless to alter. On 9 September, Guderian's forces, fighting through stubborn resistance "in every village" in driving rain, crossed the Sejm and the next day reached Romny, where over the next two days they beat back violent Soviet counterattacks. After laboriously receiving fuel from trucks that had to be towed through the nearly impassable mud, Guderian's forces, aided by the clearing weather on the twelfth, were able to drive on toward Lokhvitsa and a possible linkup with elements of the First Panzergruppe. The southern wing had been delayed in fierce fighting, but on 13 September its armored spearheads met those of the Second Panzergruppe at Lubny. Two days later, the 120-mile-deep trap, with sides 300 miles long, snapped shut at Lokhvitsa, snaring elements of five Soviet armies inside. Euphoric German newsreels, seeking to give their viewers a sense of the magnitude of the achievement, boasted that the pocket would encompass most of Germany, extending from Stettin in the north to Cologne in the west and Munich in the south. "The 'Battle at Kiev,'" Bock exulted, "has thus become a dazzling success."[14]

Even now, however, the Germans were under no illusions: if they were to achieve a decisive victory, the Soviet forces had to be annihilated, a task, given previous experience, every Landser knew meant bitter fighting and heavy casualties. Having already marched hundreds of miles and engaged the Russians in seemingly unending battles, nearing the limits of their physical and psychological endurance, most men were left cold by the prospect of further wild combat with a trapped enemy desperate to break out. "Probably," noted one such veteran, Günter von Scheven, "we will have to annihilate everything before this war is going to end." Stalin's actions reinforced this gloomy prediction: the Stavka forbade a breakout attempt and ordered Timoshenko, who had replaced the hapless Budenny, to hold Kiev. Not until the night of 17–18 September did a written order allowing the abandonment of Kiev arrive, but, by then, an orderly withdrawal proved impossible. The city fell to the Germans on the nineteenth, even as frantic fighting continued over the next few days as Soviet troops, often in desperate human-wave attacks, sought to break free. As German troops drove into the pocket, subpockets were created, which resulted in chaotic and frantic combat. Fearful losses on both sides resulted, with roadsides strewn with corpses and piles of bodies stacked before German positions. German soldiers, hungry, thirsty, fatigued, and stunned by the hand-to-hand fighting, were worn down by the remorselessly bloody process of reducing the Kiev pocket. In some German companies, losses ran to 75 percent, yet no end appeared in sight. "I have strong reservations," one Landser despaired, "whether we will see an end to the war in Russia this year. . . . The land is too big and the Russians are not thinking of surrender."[15]

As in previous encirclements, this one was not airtight, and for days small groups of Red Army troops, including Budenny, Timoshenko, and Khrushchev, managed to escape the cauldron. Despite this, the Kiev encirclement was an unprecedented catastrophe for the Red Army, which had certainly experienced its share of disasters in the first three months of war. When the fighting ended on 25 September, the Germans had bagged some 665,000 prisoners, a very high proportion of whom had simply chosen to surrender rather than continue to fight. Four Soviet field armies, consisting of forty-three divisions, had ceased to exist, while the Soviet defeat cleared the way for Rundstedt's forces to seize the important industrial city of Kharkov and advance into the rich economic areas of the Donets Basin and the Caucasus. Since Soviet replacements had to be sent from the center to cover the gap to the south, little protected Moscow from the southwest.[16]

Guderian and his Second Panzergruppe now had the chance, supply permitting, to seize the capital in a concentrated thrust. The enormous losses suffered by the Red Army at Kiev and in the first three months of the war seemed to justify the German assumption that the attack on Moscow, Operation Taifun (Typhoon), could still succeed despite the lateness of the season. Guderian's already exhausted and depleted forces, however, had been further worn down in the *Kesselschlacht* (battle of encirclement) at Kiev. Their casualties had been high, while, by late September, the Second Panzergruppe had only 33 percent of its armored vehicles in service. The gasoline situation remained precarious, while the redeployment of the Second Army and the Second Panzergruppe from the Kiev area, hampered by incessant rain and muddy roads, took much longer than anticipated. Army Group South's pursuit to the east was hindered by the fact that it now had to give up significant forces to Army Group Center for use in Operation Typhoon. The great economic goals still lay up to three hundred miles away as the Germans were left to ponder once again the principal bugaboo of the campaign to date: the lack of sufficient forces to capture all the targets temporarily open to them. As with the other envelopments, the Battle of Kiev had been a great tactical triumph but had not resulted in decisive victory. Even as Bock conceded the success at Kiev, he noted ruefully in his diary, "But the main Russian force stands unbroken before my front and . . . the question is open as to whether we can smash it quickly and so exploit this victory before winter comes."[17]

The same dilemma, providing the necessary combat strength to achieve decisive success in an expanding theater of operations, played out to the north as Leeb's forces lurched toward Leningrad. Hitler attached considerable importance to the capture of the city, not merely because it was the birthplace of Bolshevism, but more practically because control of the Baltic would ease the German supply situation and free up troops to be used elsewhere. Although Army Group North had achieved great operational success, Leeb was forced to the realization by late July that he simply did not have adequate forces to seize Leningrad. On 15 August, units of the Third Panzergruppe, including the Twelfth Panzer and the Eighteenth and Twentieth Motorized Divisions, were diverted from the center to the north. By throwing in all his available units, including his last reserves, Leeb was able to push through Novgorod and on the twentieth captured Chudovo, thus cutting the main rail line between Moscow and Leningrad. On the twenty-eighth, Tallinn, the capital of Estonia, fell, while, on the thirtieth, the Twelfth Panzer Division reached the Neva River, further isolating Leningrad. The city, however, was well situated for defense as the western approaches were protected by the Gulf of Finland, the northern by the narrow Karelian Isthmus, the eastern by Lake Ladoga, and the southern by swampy ground difficult to traverse. By early September, steady rains and stubborn Soviet resistance ground the German advance to a crawl. On 8 September, the Germans managed to seize Shlisselburg, where the waters of Lake Ladoga enter the Neva, and Demyansk to the southeast, but persistent enemy counterattacks forced Leeb continually to regroup his forces.[18]

The loss of Shlisselburg, however, meant that Leningrad could be supplied only via Lake Ladoga, which encouraged the German belief that the city was ripe for the taking. Three days earlier, in fact, Halder had remarked in his diary, "Leningrad: Our object has been achieved. Will now become a subsidiary theater of operations," followed by the hope that the drive on Moscow could begin in eight to ten days. Since Hitler had no intention of taking the city in any case, preferring to subdue it through hunger and terror bombing, on 5 September he ordered the transfer of a number of mobile and air units from Army Group North to Army Group Center, to take effect on the fifteenth. The next day, reflecting his optimism that successes on the flanks had opened the way to Moscow as well as illustrating his awareness of the crucial time factor, Hitler issued Directive No. 35. "Within the limited time available before the onset of winter," it stated, the enemy before Moscow should be wiped out by concentrating all forces, including those that could be freed from the flanks, for one last encirclement battle. Leeb immediately protested the loss of these units, and, since Halder realized that the attack on Moscow could not commence before the end of the month, he reluctantly allowed Leeb to keep them temporarily.[19]

Over the next few days, Leeb won a number of local successes, but fighting in the north did not abate as Soviet counterattacks increased in intensity. Although the Fourth Panzergruppe began shifting units to Army Group Center on 15 September, Leeb managed to retain the three divisions of Schmidt's Thirty-ninth Motorized Corps of the Third Panzergruppe. Leeb now faced the task of tightening the ring around Leningrad against stiffening enemy resistance with a significantly reduced combat force insufficient to fulfill the objectives assigned it. On 22 September, the Soviets launched a series of strong attacks against both the northern and the southern wings of the army group that inflicted such high losses on German forces that Leeb feared he would not be able to hold his positions. Schmidt's forces had been so ground down that the Twelfth Panzer had only fifty-four tanks left, about a quarter of its normal strength, while the Eighteenth and Twentieth Motorized Divisions had been reduced to roughly 46 and 65 percent of their respective troop complements. Two days later, in fact, Leeb admitted to the OKH that the situation had worsened considerably and that he could no longer continue offensive operations toward Leningrad.[20]

By the end of the month, stalemate had settled on the northern front. Leningrad was besieged, but the Germans had not closed the ring tight enough to allow effective artillery bombardment of the city or to cut it off completely from its hinterland. As a result, even the possibility of starving the city into submission—which at least had the advantage, Leeb noted coldly, that large numbers of people would die, "but at least not before our eyes"—seemed remote.[21] Even though the city remained in mortal danger, the Germans had not been able to end the fighting in the north, which meant that large numbers of troops would not be available for operations elsewhere. September thus proved a frustrating month for the Germans. As at Kiev, an apparently great triumph had resulted in actual gains much less than those anticipated. Worse, the struggle would continue as the Wehrmacht sought the elusive decisive battle that would finally end Soviet resistance.

Hitler intended that "final battle" to be the much-delayed assault on Moscow that Bock and Halder had advocated in August. Even as German forces completed the encirclement of Leningrad and pulled off the spectacular envelopment operation east of Kiev, the two fretted that time to force the decisive showdown was slipping away. The bitter arguments of July and August between Hitler and the OKH, the persistence with which Hitler promoted his ideas against the advice of the army leadership, and the flurry of often contradictory directives led to charges at the time, and ever since, that Hitler's dilettantism and diversion of forces from the center caused the German defeat. Hitler's views, however, were not as odd as they have been made to seem, nor were those of his advisers necessarily more incisive. Not only did Hitler's ideas correspond more closely to the original Barbarossa plan, but the growing realization that Halder had subverted his wishes from the beginning, combined with the indecision of the hopelessly ineffective Brauchitsch, undermined his trust in both. Nor, given the economic and supply problems facing Germany, was his strategy of seizing the Baltic and the vital resources of Ukraine before launching an attack on Moscow without merit. Moreover, far from pursuing a defeated foe, as advocates of the thrust to Moscow imply, German commanders readily acknowledged that Soviet resistance was stiffening rather than slackening.

Therein lay the cause of the mounting problems facing the Germans. The assumption that the Red Army could be defeated quickly and that the Soviet system would collapse like a house of cards had proved horribly wrong. The Germans had signally failed to destroy Soviet forces in the first weeks of the war, an omission Halder now sought to remedy by the capture of Moscow. Stalin, however, fully expected such a move and, thus, had prepared strong defenses to meet it. At the same time, Soviet forces in Ukraine posed an intolerable danger for the long, exposed southern flank of a thrust on Moscow and had to be eliminated before any attack on the capital. Nor did most in the German leadership really expect the capture of Moscow to trigger a collapse of the enemy's will to resist, as had happened in France, hoping instead merely to gain favorable starting positions for the next year's campaign. Stalin had long since mastered the crisis of the early weeks of the war and regained control of his system. Given the Soviets' furious mobilization of their enormous resources as well as the promise of massive Western aid, the war would have continued even with the loss of Moscow. In any case, regardless of these other factors, a rapid drive toward the Soviet capital could not have taken place since German resources were already stretched to the breaking point. Without substantial reinforcements and resupply, Army Group Center was in September incapable of launching an offensive.[22]

The continuous fighting since late June had taken an enormous toll on the Eastern Army. Since the Germans had assumed that the destruction of Soviet forces on the border would allow them to leap the three hundred miles to the Dnieper, then pause for a rest, they had gambled that a logistic system dependent on truck columns would suffice to provide the necessary supplies. In the event, however, Russian resistance, the absence of paved roads, persistent rains that turned even good roads into muddy tracks, the wear and tear on machinery, constant congestion and traffic jams, and the higher-than-expected fuel expenditure produced a logistic nightmare. In the best of times, driving conditions were harsh, but the long distances to be covered meant that German truck columns had to snake slowly across decrepit roads day and night, their long lines vulnerable to attack by partisans. By the time the fighting at Smolensk had ended, Guderian's Second Panzergruppe was 450 miles from its original base, barely within reach of motorized supply. The relentless Soviet counterattacks throughout July and August, moreover, not only denied Landsers the opportunity to rest but also resulted in a serious ammunition crisis. German transport capacity was so limited that a switch in priorities to munitions, however, necessitated a drastic cut in the supply of fuel and food rations. Expedients such as giving precedence in supply to the motorized units also backfired since this served only to increase the gap between them and the marching infantry. The supply situation with regard to tanks, motor vehicles, and fuel was so precarious, in fact, that on 11 September the quartermaster-general's office warned that the strength of the Ostheer might be "insufficient to bring the eastern campaign to a conclusion in the autumn." "A great reduction in the fighting power and mobility of the army, perhaps at the crucial moment," might result unless drastic measures were adopted.[23]

Although the supply and transportation services worked round the clock to remedy the situation, the inadequacies of motorized transport could not be easily overcome. By the end of September, the shortfall in motor vehicles was estimated at 22 percent, a situation that would only worsen given the deteriorating weather, the lack of spare parts, and the rugged road conditions. The result was a shortage of supplies in nearly every category, a fact that significantly reduced the army's mobility and fighting power. Nor could increased use of the railroads plug the gap.

In preparation for Barbarossa, the railroad net in Poland had been expanded, which in a terrible irony would serve to assist in the Final Solution, but Russian railroads did not conform to the German gauge. Relatively few railway troops had been assigned the task of converting the Russian tracks, however, so their progress lagged behind demands. As a result, bottlenecks occurred at the exchange points between German and Russian rail lines, with waits of up to three days to unload some trains, while others were simply lost. Even converted track proved problematic as Russian rail beds were lighter, which prevented the use of heavy locomotives. In addition, German engines needed additives in order to burn Russian coal efficiently. Finally, deportations of German Jews began on 15 October, which meant that the Reichsbahn was able to furnish only half the required boxcars for supplying the Ostheer, while much of the remaining rolling stock was engaged in transporting food, cereals, and meat back to the Reich.[24]

To stockpile sufficient supplies of fuel for Operation Typhoon, the Eastern Army needed twenty-seven fuel trains daily throughout the month of September and twenty-nine in October, but the OKW promised delivery of twenty-seven trains only for the first half of September. It agreed to twenty-two daily through October, while in November the number fell to three. In practice, however, even these figures could not be achieved, with the result that, at the beginning of the offensive, Army Group Center had barely enough fuel to reach Moscow and stocks of ammunition sufficient for only two weeks. Nor were other supplies getting through. Army Group Center in August needed at least twenty-four supply trains daily to meet its requirements and twenty-six in September, but at times only half this number arrived and seldom more than eighteen trains a day. Supplying winter equipment to the troops, which had not yet begun, would put further demands on the system. The offensive, as a result, would have to be decided quickly. A report from Forty-first Panzer Corps admitted that "the supply stations cannot cope with even modest demands on account of their lack of supplies from the outset." Once available stocks were consumed, the sclerotic German supply system could not cope.[25] The initial German assumption that the army could be adequately supplied to the Dnieper had been correct; beyond that line, serious logistic difficulties now put sharp limits on the further conduct of operations.

Just as worrisome, the combat power of the armored divisions that were to spearhead the attack on Moscow had declined precipitously as a result of the continuous fighting and lack of rehabilitation. By the end of August, the Ostheer had lost 1,488 armored vehicles and, since Hitler was hoarding tanks for "the time after Barbarossa," had received only 96 replacements. Even though 125 tanks were in the supply pipeline and Halder had requested the release of a further 181, these numbers were still astonishingly low when the decisive battle of the campaign was being planned. In early September, Halder noted that 30 percent of the Eastern Army's tanks were completely out of action and that another 23 percent were back in Germany being overhauled. In Army Group Center, the situation was worse, with only a third of tanks ready for action, while in some individual units the figure hovered around 20 percent. Moreover, because of bad weather, muddy roads, and the inadequacy of the railways, the redeployment of forces back to Bock was taking longer than expected. In a dreary reprise, the Germans again faced the reality that they could not concentrate sufficient strength for a knockout blow. The Second Panzergruppe in late September had only 33 percent of its armored vehicles in operation and faced a parlous fuel situation yet was expected to play a major role in the attack on Moscow. Similarly, to the north, Panzergruppe 3 had been forced to leave three motorized divisions in the Leningrad area, while combat and the strain of moving some four hundred miles exacted a considerable toll on the men and equipment of those units returned to Army Group Center.[26]

In another key measure, as well, it proved impossible to bring Army Group Center back up to strength. While the "beaten" Red Army continued to form reserves, the operational strength of the OKH had been exhausted, as Halder was well aware. At five weeks, roughly the same amount of time as it had taken to defeat the French, total German casualties were almost 17 percent higher, while, by the end of September, the Germans had three times the casualties as in the previous year. Even before the start of Operation Typhoon, the Wehrmacht had lost 185,000 men killed, a figure larger than the total casualties of the entire French campaign. By the end of August, virtually all available forces in the Replacement Army had been brought to the front, with the result that casualties sustained after mid-September could not be replaced. Bock's forces, which through September had suffered almost 220,000 casualties, had received only 151,000 replacements. Moreover, officer and NCO casualties had been extremely high. These were men, normally the experienced elite of the combat spear, who could not easily be replaced. They were the ones who were schooled in initiative and independent action that gave the Wehrmacht its qualitative edge, whose skills allowed tactical and operational flexibility, who maintained the steadiness, motivation, and morale of their troops in spite of the fanatic enemy resistance. By the end of August, nearly thirty division equivalents of officers and noncommissioned officers (NCOs) had been killed or wounded, a staggering figure that had a profound impact on the effectiveness of the Eastern Army. Combined with the constant hardships of daily existence—the filth, mud, lice, fatigue, hunger, and diseases—the sight of trusted officers and NCOs, on whose ability one's own survival often depended, being struck down in droves was profoundly discouraging. Inevitably, men began to question the extent and duration of their sacrifices or whether the objective could ever be attained, especially since the Russians did not seem beaten. Thus, although Army Group Center had roughly 1.9 million men, it did not possess the fighting power these figures would suggest since veteran soldiers were exhausted and the replacements were not comparable in training or experience to those whose places they were taking. Such losses could not continue, one divisional commander warned, "if we do not want to win ourselves to death."[27]

By the end of September, just such a prospect seemed at hand as German leaders could look back at a series of spectacular triumphs—grabbing an enormous swath of territory; taking some 2 million prisoners; destroying entire Soviet army groups in impressive encirclement operations; seizing Kiev and isolating Leningrad—yet enemy resistance had still not been broken. German operations, bedeviled all summer by frequent changes of emphasis, a dispersal of effort, and the resultant failure to concentrate sufficient forces for a final knockout blow, continued in typical fashion as the decisive battle of the campaign loomed, struggling to assemble the strength necessary for Army Group Center to accomplish its task.

Nonetheless, by the end of September, the Germans had assembled a force of 1.9 million men and over one thousand tanks for Operation Typhoon, which the Führer assumed would be the last great battle of the eastern war. Mindful of the experiences of large numbers of the enemy escaping loose pockets, he stipulated in his directive a close-knit, tight encirclement east of Smolensk in the area of Vyazma before the attack on Moscow itself would proceed. Since both Halder and Bock considered such a move too limited to accomplish the destruction of remaining Soviet forces, the former, as he had done consistently, did his best to undermine Hitler's intentions by indicating to the latter that he need not take his orders too seriously. Although Bock initially planned to use the Third and Fourth Panzergruppen to encircle Soviet forces in the Vyazma region, thus seizing a vital railway junction and tearing a gap in the enemy's defenses that could be exploited quickly, discussions during September, influenced by the magnitude of the triumph at Kiev, led to a broadening of the offensive. Guderian's Second Panzergruppe, to be hastily reassembled after its action in Ukraine, would form a third concentration in the south, with the objective of crushing Soviet forces near the equally vital rail center of Bryansk. If successful, the three armored groups would collapse the Soviet front and leave Moscow utterly defenseless.[28]

Moscow had always been the prime target for Halder, so, despite the lateness of the season and the diminished fighting power of his units, he pushed the offensive forward. Although it was not the moment he had originally envisioned for the showdown, he proceeded in the hope that the presumed superiority of the German soldier would allow one last triumph. Although Hitler, clearly aware of the time factor, had hoped that the offensive could begin as soon as mid-September, the heavy fighting at Leningrad and in Ukraine meant that some units were delayed in reassembling while others did not return at all. From the outset, then, the Germans had difficulty concentrating their forces as well as ensuring adequate supply. Tellingly, at the last planning conference on 24 September, the decision was taken that Guderian's forces would launch their attack on 30 September, two days before the general offensive, in order to reach the surfaced road between Orel and Bryansk, vital for logistic purposes, as soon as possible. This meant that many of his formations would enter the attack after three months of nearly constant fighting with no rest or replenishment.[29]

The relative lull in the central sector of the front had also given the Soviets time to build deeply echeloned defenses on the main routes to the capital. The forwardmost line extended from Vyazma to Bryansk, with successive belts to the east, the most important of which was centered on Mozhaisk, just to the west of Moscow. Special efforts had also been made to beef up the Red Air Force in the Moscow area. Although the Red Army had manned this defense system with 1.25 million troops, German pressure in the north and south meant that the great majority of them were new, poorly trained and equipped formations sprinkled with veteran units worn down in earlier battles. With a lack of vehicles and poor communications, Soviet units were, thus, not fully adequate to conduct a skillful defense. Nor did the Stavka, despite intelligence reports warning of a German attack, fully appreciate the significance of this information. Soviet officials had expected an attack earlier but now, with the impending onset of the autumn muddy season, seem not to have anticipated that the Germans would launch another large offensive so late in the year. Not until 27 September did the Stavka issue a warning to expect a possible German attack, and even then the warning failed to reach Russian troops in the forwardmost positions.[30]

When, on 30 September, a clear, sunny autumn day, Guderian's Second Panzergruppe struck between the Sejm and the Desna Rivers in the direction of Orel and Bryansk, it initially profited from Soviet communication and intelligence shortcomings. By the end of the day, spearheads from the Forty-seventh and Twenty-fourth Motorized Corps had driven a twelve-mile wedge into the defending Soviets, whose commander, Eremenko, assumed that this was only a local offensive. The next day, the Soviets launched piecemeal counterattacks without adequate air or armored support to close the gap, but Guderian's forces brushed them aside and continued the advance. By day's end, Geyr's Twenty-fourth Motorized Corps had penetrated nearly fifty miles in the direction of Orel. Since the rest of the front was quiet, Eremenko still did not see the situation as critical and, thus, allowed counterattacks to continue. Early on the morning of 2 October, however, following a short artillery bombardment, Bock's main force sprang into action to the north. Hoth's Third Panzergruppe shattered the Soviet defenses facing it, while, by day's end, units of Hoepner's Fourth Panzergruppe had advanced nearly twenty-five miles to the rear. The Stavka, however, preoccupied by the threat in the south, failed to realize that a disaster greater than Kiev was looming in the north. On the fifth, in fact, nobody would believe reports from a Soviet reconnaissance pilot who spotted a German armored column some fourteen miles long advancing unopposed toward Yukhnov, to the west of Moscow. Even as second and third flights confirmed the initial report, the Stavka had difficulty accepting that German spearheads were only one hundred miles from the capital. Only belatedly were ad hoc forces assembled and sent to block the German advance.[31]

The Germans, however, faced problems of their own that prevented them from taking full advantage of their initial successes. Over the first few days, spearheads from the Third and Fourth Panzergruppen drove deep into Soviet positions, captured the city of Kholm, and pushed across the Dnieper in hopes of encircling strong enemy forces near Vyazma. On the fourth, however, with its supply columns stuck on unpaved roads, the Third Panzergruppe ran out of fuel, and its rapid advance came to a sudden halt. Twenty-four hours were lost while the Luftwaffe transported supplies to the front, time that the Soviets used to good advantage to withdraw troops from the threatening encirclement. Not until the seventh did the Germans manage to close the pocket east of Vyazma, but, by that time, aerial reconnaissance indicated that large numbers of the enemy had already escaped eastward. To the south, Guderian's panzers pushed through heavy resistance and seized Orel, a key road and rail junction 120 miles to the east, on 3 October. "Our seizure of the town took the enemy so completely by surprise," Guderian noted, "that the electric trams were still running as our tanks drove in." The Soviets, however, reacted swiftly and launched furious counterattacks with a tank brigade equipped with new T-34s, trapping the Fourth Panzer Division as it approached Mtsensk. Unable to break out of the ambush with its undergunned and underarmored Pz IVs, the Fourth Panzer saw many of its tanks reduced to smoking hulks. These rapid countermeasures forced the Germans to abandon their advance on Tula for a week. The "vast superiority" of the Soviet tanks caused such shock and "grievous casualties" that Guderian admitted, "The exhaustion that was now noticeable was less physical than spiritual. It was indeed startling to see how deeply our best officers had been affected by the latest battles."[32]

Nonetheless, German success was such that Army Group Center concluded on the seventh, after the capture of Bryansk, that the destruction of the bulk of the enemy forces was imminent. Halder thought that with "moderately good weather" the encirclement of Moscow was certain to succeed. Bock, usually more cautious, also brimmed with optimism. As opposed to earlier encirclements, where the enemy had succeeded in tying down large German forces and delaying their advance, this time, he believed, he had sufficient force simultaneously to clear the pockets and to push on to Moscow. The Stavka, too, was thunderstruck by the rapid encirclement and imminent destruction of its forward forces. Zhukov, hastily recalled from Leningrad, recognized the danger immediately: virtually all routes to Moscow lay open, while available reserves had been sent south to deal with the consequences of the Kiev disaster.[33]

In Berlin, Goebbels, who had grown increasingly concerned about sinking morale in Germany and had been pressing Hitler for some time to address the German public, now took the opportunity to orchestrate a speech by the Führer at the Sportpalast. On 3 October, before a wildly cheering crowd, Hitler launched a thundering denunciation of the Jews, stressed the enormity of the alleged danger to Germany that had been averted, and declared that the Soviets had been "broken and will not rise up again." Nor was this mere public bravado. In private talks with Goebbels, Hitler stressed that the advance was going better than expected and conveyed his confidence that "if the weather stays moderately favorable the Soviet army will essentially be smashed within fourteen days." Significantly, however, he deemed it unlikely that Stalin would capitulate, nor did he expect the Soviet state to collapse. Although the worst of the war in the east was over, Hitler opined, he still expected the British to put up tough resistance. Control of Russian agricultural and industrial areas, however, positioned Germany well for the final showdown with the "London plutocracy."[34]

At headquarters, the generals were just as ecstatic. Halder and Jodl believed the victory at Vyazma to be the most decisive of the eastern campaign, while Quartermaster-General Wagner thought that the collapse of the Soviet system was imminent. On the eighth, to Goebbels's chagrin, the Reich press chief, Otto Dietrich, announced to the startled foreign press that the defeat of the Soviet Union was at hand. Even as the German leadership celebrated, however, events began to slip out of control. Impressed by the scale and magnitude of the victory, the German High Command now altered its plans by expanding the offensive; instead of concentrating forces for the final drive on Moscow, the OKH dispersed its strength in an attempt to attain a variety of objectives simultaneously. On the seventh, on the basis of a Führer directive, it ordered the Third Panzergruppe to advance north to Kalinin to assist Army Group North in seizing the Moscow-Leningrad railroad, thus further isolating Leningrad. At the same time, the Second Panzergruppe (now renamed the Second Panzer Army) was to send one wing northeast through Tula, then around Moscow to the south, while another arm was to take Kursk, nearly one hundred miles to the southeast. Moreover, all these moves were to begin even as German troops were struggling to reduce Soviet forces at Vyazma and Bryansk. Thus, only part of the Second Panzer Army, the Fourth Army, and the Fourth Panzergruppe were now to envelop the capital. Fearing a dispersal of forces that would weaken his attack, Bock vigorously protested these nonconcentric moves, but to no avail. While Halder believed that Bock had adequate forces to accomplish his task, Hitler thought that the more important goal was to weaken the enemy decisively, achieve favorable winter positions, and prepare to resume the campaign in 1942, an implicit admission that a defeat of the Soviet Union in 1941 was unlikely. As a result, however, Bock lacked sufficient forces at perhaps the decisive moment in the campaign, when the new Russian defense lines had not been fortified and reserve troops had not yet been brought up.[35]

As German units crept closer to Moscow, on the thirteenth seizing Kaluga and breaching the Mozhaisk defense line while the next day occupying Kalinin, a key city on the Volga about one hundred miles north of the capital, nascent panic began to spread in the city. Fearing the imminent loss of the capital, the Communist Party Central Committee and State Defense Committee made plans to destroy key installations and evacuate government agencies from the city, even as frantic efforts began to prepare defenses and recall reserve units. Evacuations began during the night of 15–16 October amid scenes of hysteria at rail stations. Signs of collective panic abounded as people looted shops and rushed to escape the city. Offices and factories stopped working amid proliferating rumors of an imminent surrender. Stalin seems even to have tried, via the Bulgarian ambassador in Moscow, to initiate discussions for a negotiated peace with Germany, offering the cession of extensive territories in the western Soviet Union, but nothing came of the effort. Churchill and Roosevelt, fearing the danger of a Soviet collapse, both sent urgent messages to Stalin pledging support.[36]

On the eighteenth, the Soviet dictator prepared to leave the capital but at the last moment was persuaded to stay by his military advisers. The next day, the State Defense Committee declared a state of siege in the Moscow region and decreed that any disturbances of public order would be punished by military tribunals. NKVD (Soviet Security Police) troops were also told to "shoot provocateurs, spies, and other agents of the enemy . . . on the spot." At the same time, Zhukov ordered that extensive defenses be constructed in depth to slow the attacking Germans by forcing them continuously to break through new positions. Within weeks, 100,000 laborers—women, children, and factory workers—had constructed over two hundred miles of tank ditches and erected numerous tank obstacles. Zhukov also pioneered new methods of defensive fighting, emphasizing smaller units and the concentration of anti-tank guns and artillery at key points. By the twentieth, the crisis was surmounted; in retrospect, those few days in mid-October, which coincided with the faltering of the German offensive, were likely the most dangerous period for the Soviet regime. Stalin, however, quickly recovered his resolve, while German weakness limited any attempt to exploit the crisis. Still, the giant encirclements at Vyazma and Bryansk had been catastrophic. In two weeks of fighting, the Germans had ripped through the Soviet defense lines, encircled or killed roughly a million men, and left the enemy, at least temporarily, with no strategic reserves to plug a gap three hundred miles wide.[37]

Despite the Germans' intention to move relentlessly in the direction of the Soviet capital, two factors—the beginning of the muddy season and fierce enemy resistance—hobbled their advance. A key qualifier in the optimistic German assessments of the situation had been that the sunny, dry late autumn weather continue. Beginning on 6 October in the southern sector, however, and on the seventh and eighth in other areas, the fall rains began, steady downpours that turned the roads into bottomless quagmires, stymied all movement, and prevented supply columns from reaching the front. Having expected the campaign to be over by mid-October, the OKH seems not to have taken the effects of the *rasputitsa* (lit., the time without roads), the wet period during the spring and fall when much of western Russia dissolves in water, into consideration. Ironically, despite efforts at the time, and ever since, to portray the weather as unusually bad, rainfall totals from mid-October through November were actually less than average. The Russian saying "in the autumn a spoonful of water makes a bucketful of mud" nonetheless proved devastatingly accurate. "The roads, so far as there were any in the western sense of the word, disappeared in mud," remarked one officer, "knee-deep mud . . . in which vehicles stuck fast." Ill versed in how to negotiate the unpaved tracks, German columns continued to drive through the same ruts, which only made the already poor roads worse. At the same time, the strain of grinding through the endless mud sent fuel consumption soaring and led to an alarming rate of vehicle breakdowns. Motorized divisions, mired in the mud and stretched over many miles, were unable to concentrate and vulnerable to attack.[38] The Germans discovered, to their distress, that pursuit was impossible over muddy tracks without supplies, equipment, and fuel.

Advance units had not outrun their supply lines; instead, provisions simply could not be moved forward. Any systematic delivery of supplies was impossible, both because of the rains and because the few paved highways were repeatedly broken on a daily basis by time-delay explosive charges that ripped holes ten yards deep and thirty yards wide. The Minsk-Moscow highway was so badly damaged that an entire infantry division had to be employed to make it serviceable again. "We can't go on," wrote one disgusted Landser. "There is no more gasoline and nothing is coming up behind us. . . . Rations still do not arrive and we sit in filth the entire day." Complained another, "The so-called *Rollbahn* upon which we are marching is a sea of knee-deep mud. Vehicles sink up to the axle and in many places the morass is up to the bellies of the horses." Thousands of trucks were stranded, while moving even five miles might take a day or two. In the Second Panzer Army, progress was reduced to a half mile per hour. The terrible roads and abysmal weather, moreover, led to fuel consumption three times that of normal, but the dismal state of the railways made it impossible to deliver extra quantities of fuel. Taxed to the limit, emaciated horses collapsed in the mire. "In some cases," Bock observed, "twenty-four horses are required to move a single artillery piece." Motorized supply, which was inadequate in any case, could no longer be maintained, nor, given the huge losses of horses, could the Ostheer move even by traditional means. The operational mobility of the troops had been reduced to the next laborious step.[39]

At times in mid-October, temperatures dropped, and snow mingled with the rain. "We watched it uneasily," admitted one Landser of the snow, for it meant the impending onset of winter. Bock, too, worried about the effect on morale since the question, "What will become of us in the winter?" was on everyone's mind. Without heavy coats, soldiers stuffed "newspapers in the boots . . . between vest and shirt . . . round the belly . . . in the trousers . . . round the legs," anything to preserve warmth. Constantly soaked, covered in mud, unable to dry their clothing or boots, susceptible to trench foot and other maladies in the near-freezing temperatures, covered in lice, exhausted, and with limited rations, the infantry endured wretched conditions as they struggled to advance. Many were so tired that they no longer bothered to seek protection when enemy shelling began. Others struggled in the wet, cold weather with hands frozen stiff. "My gloves were so wet I could not bear the ache any longer," wrote Harald Henry. "My contorted face was streaked with tears, but I was in a trance-like state. I plodded forward, babbling incoherently. . . . All the others were in the same state."[40]

Some noticed a strange, and troubling, phenomenon: the foot soldiers were beginning to overtake the "fast" motorized divisions. As the arrival of supplies faltered, the pursuit of the Russians failed to deliver the expected results. "The beaten Russians seemed unaware that as a military force they had almost ceased to exist," noted one officer sarcastically. "During these weeks . . . the fighting became more bitter with each day." With this realization, morale dropped alarmingly. "After four months," concluded another officer, "one has had enough." Confirmed Harald Henry, "We can't take much more." By late October, Army Group Center worried about the morale of soldiers "exhausted from marching in mud, rain and cold, and very much aware of the lack of an effective weapon to defend themselves against the heavy Russian tanks. In places the troops are not always capable of meeting the demands of battle." Few at the front or at home now expected the war to conclude by the end of the year. Once again, German triumphs, as Bock admitted, were only partial successes that "mean[t] nothing": "The splitting apart of the army group together with the frightful weather has caused us being bogged down. As a result, the Russians are gaining time to bring their shattered divisions back up to strength and bolster their defense." The Ostheer was nearing the limits of its endurance; for many men, the most important thing was no longer a strategic objective but simply finding shelter.[41]

In a hauntingly familiar refrain, Bock's hope that this time the cauldrons could be reduced quickly was dashed as well, for the Kesselschlachten at Vyazma and Bryansk proved, if anything, even more intense than in previous pockets, perhaps the hardest fighting of the entire eastern campaign. Once again, maneuver alone, which had induced the French to capitulate a year earlier, failed to produce a similar response from the Soviets, who doggedly fought on regardless of cost. The Germans trapped, then blasted Red Army units into splintered groups, but fighting raged for nearly two weeks, tying down some 70 percent of the army group's divisions. In the process, blitzkrieg once more ground to a standstill amid irrecoverable losses. The Sixth Panzer Division, for example, which on 10 October still had over 200 tanks, was left with only 60 less than a week later. At the same time, the fighting at Mtsensk left the Fourth Panzer with 38 tanks, while on 16 October the Second Panzer Army as a whole had only 271 panzers. By early November, the Ostheer had lost over 2,000 of its original 3,580 armored vehicles but received only 601 replacements. The fighting power of a panzer division in Army Group Center had declined to just 35 percent of its normal strength. Vehicle losses had also assumed catastrophic dimensions. By now, most supply trucks had ground thousands of miles over dusty, then muddy, roads that caused numerous breakdowns. Reliance on low-grade motor oil led to numerous engine failures, while a chronic shortage of spare parts resulted in junking and cannibalizing of otherwise repairable vehicles. By mid-November, only 15 percent of vehicles in the Ostheer were still in good working order, a further 15 percent needed minor repair, while fully 40 percent required complete overhaul and had to be sent back to Germany. Raids by partisans added to losses, which often totaled a quarter or a third of trucks in supply columns. On 4 November, the Second Panzer Army noted, "There is not a single road . . . on which larger units can continue moving unhindered or that permits delivery of supplies to the fighting troops. . . . Operations have come to a standstill." Less than a week later, it lamented, "Normal provisioning can no longer be guaranteed."[42]

Nor was it just the armored divisions that suffered heavy losses; the infantry, too, paid a very high price for success. In just a little over two weeks, Army Group Center lost roughly 50,000 men in savage fighting that unnerved even veteran troops, while, by mid-October, total losses stood at 277,000. German infantry withstood frantic enemy attempts to break out as, day after day, Soviet troops, amid nerve-shattering cries of "Hurrah," launched desperate human-wave assaults against under-manned German positions. A confusing melee of savage one-on-one combat ensued as Landsers fought with anything available—pistols, spades, and grenades—to check the onslaught. As the infantry fought to the limit of its endurance, the commander of the Fourth Army, Kluge, believed that "the psychologically most critical moment of the campaign in the east" had arrived. German troops, lacking suitable clothing, struggling through impassable terrain, facing the prospect of surviving in winter with inadequate shelter, and confronting an enemy that showed no sign of capitulating, began to realize that an end to operations was unlikely. For many, expectations of victory turned into hopes for survival. The intense fighting and awful road conditions had caused the German advance to falter. "A success for the Russians," Bock conceded, "whose stubbornness paid off."[43]

As Bock had feared, the Soviets also incorporated the effects of the *rasputitsa* in their defense plans. Zhukov, aware that the German advance could continue only on the paved main roads, concentrated his sparse forces on the key approaches to Moscow as well as using the rail lines that converged on the city to bring in a steady stream of reinforcements. By mid-October, then, the Russians resumed their customary ferocious counterattacks against a German advance weakened by the transfer of troops and the precarious supply situation. On the southern wing, when the Second Panzer Army resumed its offensive to the northeast on the seventeenth, it discovered in the vicinity of Mtsensk an "enemy as strong as ever . . . [that] put up unusually tough resistance." Both the Second and the Fourth Armies, meanwhile, suffered from supply difficulties and steady enemy counterattacks that exhausted the troops and forced them to take sporadic defensive action. The Russian air force, operating from bases near Moscow, also became increasingly active, to the dismay of the advancing Germans. In the north, Reinhardt's Third Panzergruppe (Hoth had in the meantime been appointed commander of the Seventeenth Army) faced fierce and unremitting enemy assaults that stalled its further progress, forcing Bock on the twenty-third to shelve all plans for an attack beyond Kalinin. On its left, the Ninth Army had taken Rzhev and sought to move north but, on the eighteenth, warned that it would not be able to continue the advance without extensive resupply, while, to its right, the Fourth Army faced similar problems after advancing through Mozhaisk. With the roads worsening in the wet conditions, with vehicles and horses stuck fast in the muck, and with the failure of the railways, the fighting units simply had insufficient supplies to advance. The OKH's apparent fear that large numbers of Soviets were pulling back and insistence on forming special pursuit detachments to cut them off thus bordered on the fantastic. "The enemy," Bock admitted, "has moved in new forces from Siberia and the Caucasus and has launched counterattacks." The Germans were dealing not with a defeated enemy but with a determined opponent bent on defending the capital with all means at his disposal.[44]

Faced with an advance on Moscow that had slowed to a crawl, Hitler sought a solution on the flanks, further dispersing German strength. On 28 October, he ordered the deployment of units from the Third and Fourth Panzergruppen in an effort to eliminate Soviet forces between the Volga and Lake Ladoga to the north, effectively writing off the bulk of the Fourth Panzergruppe from the attack on Moscow. At the same time, the Second Panzer Army was ordered not to advance eastward beyond Tula but to strike toward Voronezh on the Don, some two hundred miles to the southeast, in order to cut off strong enemy forces. Although Hitler believed that the right wing of the Fourth Army was strong enough to assume the tasks of the Second Panzer Army, on 28 October Kluge had to use his last remaining reserves and go over to the defensive in order to cover the growing gap in the German front. Although strategic fantasy reigned at the OKH, the hard fact was that, by the end of October, the Germans had run out of troops. The supply situation, the sheer exhaustion of the Landsers, and the miserable weather all made it impossible to continue the advance. His units out of fuel, doubtful that Hitler had read his reports on the bleak situation at the front, reduced to the absurd proposal that detachments equipped with machine guns mounted on horse-drawn *panje* wagons be employed as mobile combat teams, and driven "to despair," on 1 November Bock ordered that "further advances should be temporarily suspended" until supply problems could be overcome. "Our losses," he admitted in his diary, "have become quite considerable. In the army group's area more than twenty battalions are under the command of lieutenants." The attempt to smash the remainder of the Red Army in a quick battle, he acknowledged, had failed. If the enemy was to be beaten, a new, full-scale offensive would have to be launched, although the army group could not replace the heavy casualties it had already suffered, nor could the decrepit German supply system provide the necessary material help.[45]

In his 21 August directive to the OKW, Hitler had stressed that the most important aim to be achieved before the onset of winter was not capturing Moscow but seizing the industrially and economically vital regions of southern Russia and the Caucasus. Even as the German troops creeping toward Moscow captured the world's attention, then, he kept his eyes firmly fixed on developments to the south. Although the Kiev encirclement had ripped a hole in Soviet defenses, Army Group South anticipated problems and heavy fighting as it moved to the southeast to occupy the Crimea and establish positions for advancing into the Caucasus. The Eleventh Army, under Manstein, ran into stubborn Soviet resistance and suffered heavy losses in its late September attempt to seize the strongly fortified Crimean Peninsula. At roughly the same time, the First Panzergruppe, attacking from Dnepropetrovsk, made disappointingly slow progress, although it did take Zaporozhye on 1 October and by the eleventh had reached the Mius River north of Taganrog. To the north, the attack on the key industrial city of Kharkov further dissipated the strength of the offensive as once again the Germans sought to gain all their objectives simultaneously. Heavy rain, the onset of cold weather, exhaustion, vehicle breakdowns, and supply difficulties slowed all movements, causing Hitler to give priority to the attack on the Donets Basin. By 12 October, however, this drive too had stalled as a result of the now familiar combination of mud, inadequate supply, exhaustion, and stiff opposition.[46]

With the southern sector of the army group almost immobilized, Hitler intervened on 14 October. Fearing that Soviet forces would escape across the Donets, he ordered the Seventeenth Army to send two divisions northward to cooperate with the Sixth Army in a new attempt to seize Kharkov. Since this would imperil the drive southeast into the Donets Basin and beyond into the Caucasus, opposition arose from Rundstedt, the army group commander, and the OKH. Following three days of wrangling, and after aerial reconnaissance revealed Soviet forces withdrawing from Kharkov, Hitler relented: Manstein would now renew his attack on the Crimea, and the First Panzer Army (formerly the First Panzergruppe) would drive on Rostov, while the Sixth and Seventeenth Armies would strike straight east to occupy all the territory up to the Don River, then establish bridgeheads across it in the direction of Stalingrad.[47]

Manstein launched his attack on the Crimea on the eighteenth, but his forces, which lacked armored support, suffered heavy losses in the attempt to batter through strong Soviet defenses. The fall of Odessa two days earlier also contributed to German difficulties since many of the units evacuated from that city were now used in defense of the peninsula. With his attacking units exhausted, Manstein demanded the transfer of a mobile division, but, in view of the fuel situation and the priority of seizing Rostov, Hitler refused. Manstein did, however, receive Luft-waffe reinforcements on 24 October, which enabled his troops to break through Soviet positions and occupy most of the Crimea, except for the fortress city of Sevastopol. This triumph, however, could not offset the increasing supply problems caused by the incessant rain, muddy roads, lack of vehicles and horses, and absence of converted rail lines. Hal-der, however, demanded the crossing of the Don in order to secure a base for future operations. Despite grumbling from his commanders about the unreliable supply situation, on 25 October Rundstedt ordered Reichenau, whose Sixth Army had finally captured Kharkov, to advance as far as Belgorad, Stülpnagel (the Seventeenth Army) to force a bridge-head over the Don at Izyum, and Kleist (the First Panzer Army) to move on Rostov. A pause would then follow, during which the troops would lay in supplies and wait for the ground to freeze before resuming the advance. Fearing that the momentum of the offensive would be lost, Hal-der pressured Rundstedt not to halt but to make every effort to meet his long-range strategic objectives. German commanders, lacking vehicles and fuel, responded to Halder's urging by forming pursuit detachments consisting of infantry and peasant carts. Although Rundstedt noted the link between supplies and the ability of his troops to attack and could have pointed to a morale report signaling a growing apathy among his troops, the OKH persisted in its impossible order for Army Group South to seize Maikop and Stalingrad. Even Hitler possessed a more realistic view, telling Brauchitsch in early November that the Ostheer could no longer hope to achieve its furthest objectives in 1941. Instead, the goal would be to weaken the Soviets and secure positions from which to com-plete operations in 1942.[48]

Despite a critical shortage of fuel and supplies, Kleist's First Pan-zer Army began its attack on Rostov on 5 November and achieved good initial success, advancing eighteen miles to the east. Two days later, however, torrential rains paralyzed all movement and gave the Soviets time to regroup and prepare their defenses. Kleist could resume the attack only on 17 November, after the rains had given way to tempera-tures as low as $-8°F$. Rostov fell three days later, but an enemy counter-attack was already in the works. Soviet armies moved to reclaim Rostov on the twenty-second, putting such heavy pressure on Kleist that he was forced to abandon the city on the twenty-eighth. The psychologi-cal impact was marked on both sides: this was the first time the Ger-mans had been forced out of a key city by a well-orchestrated Soviet counterattack.[49]

Since neither troops, supplies, nor operational assistance was available, a withdrawal of the armored army from the hard-won Don crossing was inevitable, a proposition unthinkable to the OKH, whose directives were now so completely unrealistic as to border on the ludicrous. Hitler agreed that Army Group South no longer had the mobility or the strength to mount any further attacks but considered the location of a winter defensive line to be of the utmost importance. He objected to Rundstedt's proposed withdrawal to a position running from Taganrog along the Mius to the mouth of the Bakhmut and demanded that the retreat from Rostov be halted farther to the east. Although both Rundstedt and Kleist regarded Hitler's intermediate position as completely untenable—the army group commander remarking that the order could not be carried out—through a series of miscommunications Hitler received the impression that Rundstedt was openly defying his wishes. At 2:00 A.M. on 1 December, therefore, the Führer relieved the field marshal of his command and replaced him with Reichenau, ironically the army commander most vocally critical of any offensive operations. Later that day, Reichenau telephoned with the news that the Russians had broken through and requested permission to withdraw to the line originally proposed by Rundstedt. Hitler granted Reichenau's request. On the second, Hitler flew to Kleist's headquarters to see the situation for himself. There, not only did he realize that Rundstedt had been correct in his assessments, but he also learned of the full sequence of events. He exonerated both Rundstedt and Kleist of any blame but did not reinstate the former; such an action would have been an admission of his own error. Reichenau's earlier assessment had been correct: an attack with exhausted troops who could not be supplied was irresponsible.[50]

Even had the logistic organization been a model of efficiency, however, German forces would have faced dire straits that autumn. A study by General Thomas's War Economy and Armaments Office concluded in early October that deliveries from the United States and Great Britain would to a great extent offset the lost industrial production of western Russia while the Germans could do little to interrupt the flow of such goods. At the same time, Thomas also made it clear that only the capture of the oil regions of the Caucasus along with the industrial areas of the Urals and Donets, targets hundreds of miles distant, would lead to a considerable weakening, but not necessarily a collapse, of the Soviet war economy. Thomas thus shattered Hitler's key assumption, that a seizure of western Russia would necessarily cripple the Soviet economy, although the Führer refused to believe this analysis. The Soviets had lost so much material, he asserted, that it would take the democracies five years to replace it all; in any case, the Russians were beaten, and the campaign in the east had "essentially finally been decided."[51]

If this sobering assessment of Soviet capabilities was not depressing enough, by October it had also become obvious that the German armaments industry could not satisfy the most pressing needs of the front. The German war economy suffered from two serious deficiencies, both of which had been aggravated by the failure to win a quick victory: a shortage of manpower and a lack of vital raw materials. Because of the extensive losses on the eastern front, in the autumn more young men had to be drafted for the army, while many skilled laborers in reserved occupations were also sent to the front. This resulted in a serious shortage of workers in the armaments industry that the Germans attempted to remedy by employing more women and older men. The only really effective solution, however, was to use Russian prisoners of war. Not until the very end of October, however, did Hitler drop his racial and ideological objections to the employment of Russian labor within Germany. On 31 October, he ordered the greatest possible exploitation of Russian labor, but, for most prisoners of war, this change of policy came too late. Amazingly, even as economic officials hoped that the serious labor problems could be overcome by deploying a large number of the 3 million Soviet prisoners, they seemed unaware of the fact that most of these men were either dead or physically unable to work. By German estimates, only 200,000 could be used immediately, as most of the others were "unfit for employment owing to typhus and malnutrition." Goering, as head of the Four-Year Plan, should have had more than a passing interest in providing suitable workers for the German armaments industry. Instead, he joked about the plight of Russian prisoners of war, telling Ciano in November, "Hunger among Russian prisoners had reached such an extreme that . . . it was no longer necessary to send them under armed guard [to the rear]. It is enough to put at the head of a column of prisoners a camp kitchen . . . ; thousands and thousands of prisoners trail along like a herd of famished animals." The situation did not begin to improve until the spring of 1942, when Hitler ordered that Russian prisoners be given enough to eat.[52]

Soviet prisoners of war were, in fact, among the first to feel the full brunt of Nazi racial policy; of those taken in 1941, few survived. In the first six months of the war, the Germans captured some 3.3 million Red Army soldiers, of whom barely a million were still alive by the end of 1941, with less than half of those in sufficiently good physical condition eventually to be employed as workers. Given the assumption of the Nazi leadership that success in the larger struggle against the Anglo-Saxon powers depended on maintenance of solid morale at home, which in turn hinged on the provision of near-peacetime levels of nutrition, the food supply of the east had to be ruthlessly exploited. The logic of the hunger policy meant that countless millions of people in the east had to starve: the first to do so were Soviet prisoners of war. From the start, preparations for handling prisoners had been inadequate, deliberately so. Since the Soviet Union had signed neither the Hague nor the Geneva conventions on the treatment of prisoners, German authorities issued orders even before the invasion to disregard these standards of treatment. Reports from the summer of 1941 indicated that Red Army prisoners of war received daily rations as low as "20 grams of millet and 100 grams of bread without meat" or "100 grams of millet without bread."[53]

By August, the consequences of this systematic neglect had become obvious. "News from the east is terrible again," wrote Helmuth James von Moltke, later one of the leading figures in the German resistance to Hitler, in an August 1941 letter to his wife. "Again and again one hears reports that in transports of prisoners or Jews only 20 percent arrive, that there is starvation in the prisoner-of-war camps, that typhoid and all the other deficiency epidemics have broken out." In the autumn, the military leadership launched a propaganda campaign opposing the humane treatment of Soviet prisoners of war. German troops were urged to avoid "false" sympathy for the starving and were reminded that "every item of food that is granted to the prisoners . . . must be taken from relatives at home or from German soldiers." Since many Russians were already undernourished when they were captured, it was not surprising that thousands perished during the forced marches from the front. Some camps reported that only a fifth of prisoners arrived alive on transports; many desperate prisoners tried to survive by eating bark, leaves, and grass. In Minsk, where over 140,000 prisoners were kept in an extremely small area, men killed each other for a piece of bread or a drop of water.[54]

Conditions, and the mortality rate, became catastrophic in the autumn. The great encirclement battles netted the Germans hundreds of thousands of malnourished captives, most of whom were immediately sent off in columns on long marches lasting days or weeks. Those who dropped out along the way were simply shot, while the unlucky ones who survived found themselves confined in appalling conditions behind barbed wire in huge open-air camps that lacked even the most rudimentary accommodations. Already in a state of extreme exhaustion, the prisoners lived in the most primitive manner, with only holes dug into the ground or rude sod houses as shelter. In a rear-area camp near Rzhev supporting the Ninth Army, 450 people were shoved into one-story barracks measuring thirty-six by seventy-two feet. Death was endemic since there were only two latrines for eleven thousand men. Prisoners subsisted on bark, leaves, grass, and nettles, with occasional instances of cannibalism reported. One German soldier noted with shock that many Soviet prisoners carried human body parts with them in order to have something to eat, not surprising since watchdogs received fifty times the rations of a Soviet prisoner of war. Mortality rates soared as men suffering from malnutrition succumbed to infectious diseases and hunger-induced epidemics.[55]

Despite this, in late October General Wagner, the army quartermaster-general, ordered a reduction in rations for those prisoners unable to work. This, coupled with the onset of severe winter weather, resulted in skyrocketing death rates, sometimes as much as 1 percent per day. Since army officials forbade the transporting of prisoners in anything but open railcars, large numbers, perhaps 20 percent of the total, now froze to death en route to camps. Even when the army relented and allowed them to be transported in closed but unheated cars, the effect, in the brutal Russian cold, was little different. Since these catastrophic conditions also existed in camps in the Reich, the mass deaths of Soviet prisoners of war was not due to ignorance or incompetence. To the Nazi leadership, it was axiomatic that Germans and Russians could not both be fed; the former would, thus, be supplied at the expense of the latter, regardless of the consequences. In a particularly macabre episode, beginning in December 1941 wounded Soviet prisoners were simply released into the civilian population because they had become "an unnecessary burden on the supply situation." The result was that, during the extraordinarily harsh winter of 1941–1942, thousands of former prisoners, "who appeared to be almost emaciated, living skeletons, with festering, stinking wounds," wandered among the local population.[56]

An earlier, mid-July decision meant a more immediate death for untold thousands of Soviet prisoners. That month, representatives of the OKW and the RSHA agreed that politically and racially "unacceptable elements" among the prisoners should be separated out of prisoner-of-war camps by special SS units and murdered. Over the course of the next few years, this action resulted in the deaths of tens of thousands of Soviet prisoners. All these actions, of course, were from the outset stamped by Nazi racial and political ideology and fit seamlessly into the war of annihilation. On the eve of the invasion, Hitler had demanded that German troops be prepared to take extraordinary measures to exterminate the enemy mercilessly and totally. As events illustrated, many officers and men of the Wehrmacht possessed the necessary qualities to carry out their Führer's wishes. It was, however, a Pyrrhic victory since Russian soldiers quickly came to realize that they had no alternative but to fight on, thus strengthening their resolve to resist.[57]

Even if Russian labor had been readily available, the second key problem facing the German armaments industry, a critical shortage of raw materials, could not easily be remedied. With the desperately needed materiel from the Soviet Union unavailable, German industry was unable to meet the requirements of even the most important production programs. Even though the severe shortage of fuel and rubber had forced the OKW in mid-September to curtail considerably the use of motor vehicles, not until the beginning of November did the implications of the military failure in Russia affect German industry as a whole. The lack of skilled workers and the scarcity of key raw materials and machine tools prevented any immediate, substantial increase in production. An acute shortage of aluminum, for example, meant that, from November, Luftwaffe losses in the east could no longer be replaced. A lack of steel and vital alloys made it impossible for industry to reach production goals for key army weapons programs such as panzers and antitank guns, although ammunition levels would just about suffice to meet needs. The OKH estimated in early November that the output of tanks and antitank guns would reach only 68–73 percent of the production targets and that the situation would not improve in 1942. That same month, however, a drastic shortfall in coal production led to power reductions and the closure of some factories, further burdening armaments production.[58]

Moreover, the length of the eastern campaign resulted in such a shortage of oil that it was impossible to provide the required quantities of fuel to the Wehrmacht and industry. Even before the invasion, German officials understood that, if the war persisted beyond early September, there would be severe repercussions. At the end of October, therefore, the civilian and nonarmament sectors of the economy experienced sharp reductions in allocations of oil. Despite this, the quartermaster-general, Eduard Wagner, warned that, by January 1942, supplies would be exhausted and new oil fields would need to be captured. Confronted with the "unexpected urgency" of the oil situation, Goering sought, to no avail, to persuade the Rumanians to increase their oil production, even insisting that their wells should be pumped dry. The only alternative was a severe restriction on the operational mobility of the troops. Nor could Goering's demand on 8 November that "the eastern territories . . . be exploited economically as colonies and using colonial methods" rectify the situation in the short term, owing to widespread destruction by the Russians. Even in the absence of such sabotage, the

German transportation system still could not have coped: the Reichsbahn lacked sufficient locomotives and, in any case, could provide only 142,000 of a daily requirement of 240,000 freight cars. By late autumn, the bitter fighting, difficult terrain, appalling weather, and worn-out engines had combined to cause the Germans to use three times the quantity of fuel originally supplied.[59] Little wonder, then, that Hitler kept insisting on distant economic objectives or that Bock and Rundstedt had been driven to despair, given the utopian objectives set for them by the OKH.

Notions of racial struggle constituted an unalterable part of Nazi ideology; from the beginning of the war in the east, as we have seen, a war of annihilation had been waged against certain segments of the population. German actions thus reinforced Nazi ideological tenets. On a daily basis, Landsers witnessed the evident worthlessness of Soviet lives as the awful brutality of the war strengthened Nazi propaganda concepts of the Slavic "subhuman." Apart from the Nazis' treatment of the Jews, nothing demonstrated their contempt for the peoples of the Soviet Union as well as their moves to implement the hunger policy, which took a devastating toll on Soviet prisoners of war and the civilian population. Nazi authorities had intended from the beginning to strip the eastern lands of foodstuffs, but the unexpected prolongation of the war now intensified the food problems facing the German government. Determined to avoid placing any burdens on the German population, however, they chose instead to exploit the newly conquered eastern territories even more ruthlessly. The certain consequence of this radical starvation policy, Goebbels noted with a homicidal coldness tinged with the dire memories of the World War I experience, "would be the outbreak of a famine in Russia in the coming winter that would leave all previous ones in history far in its shadow. But that is not our concern. . . . If Europe should go hungry, then we Germans will be the last to starve." To the authorities in Berlin, feeding the native population in the east was merely an incidental concern. As Goering noted in mid-September, after listing the priorities in food distribution, with the troops first and the occupied peoples a distant third, "Even if one wished to feed all the rest of the inhabitants, one could not do so in the newly occupied eastern territory. As for issuing food to Bolshevik prisoners, we are . . . not bound by any international obligations."[60]

Large parts of the Soviet population had, thus, been deliberately condemned to death by starvation. Since feeding much of the Soviet population could come only at the expense of ensuring adequate foodstuffs for German consumers, this was never an option, especially given Hitler's constant association of hunger with revolutionary domestic unrest during World War I. Backe's hunger policy intended the murder of millions of people simply by denying food to certain segments of the civilian population, most notably urban dwellers and those in the agriculturally deficient areas. This attitude was clearly genocidal and not coincidentally linked to the murder of Jews, considered, as they were, to be useless eaters. In areas swept over by the Einsatzgruppen, those Jews not killed immediately were to be denied access to food markets or the opportunity to buy directly from farmers, thus condemning them to a slow death by starvation. Jewish inhabitants of many cities, for example, received no more than 420 calories per day. A mid-July memorandum to Eichmann from the head of the SD in Posen specifically made the connection with ethnic cleansing. "There is the danger this winter," the official noted, "that the Jews can no longer all be fed. It is to be seriously considered whether the most humane solution might not be to finish off those Jews not capable of labor by some sort of fast-working preparation."[61]

This vision of mass death through malign neglect turned out to be extremely naive. With the failure to achieve a quick victory, the Germans lacked the security forces to seal off the targeted areas effectively. As a result, the Soviet urban population managed stubbornly to hang on by returning to the countryside or using the black market. Landsers, it appeared, also showed more humanity than their superiors and, contrary to regulations, fed civilians from their own field kitchens. German soldiers, the quartermaster-general complained to Halder, were often "very considerate" toward the population. From late 1941, as well, some military administrators attempted to ensure at least minimal levels of foodstuffs for Soviet civilians, not for humane reasons but as a matter of practical self-interest. "If the Russian campaign had been a Blitzkrieg, then we would not have had to take the civil population into consideration," attested one army official. "But an end is not in sight. . . . Under these circumstances it is irrational to follow a course that turns the civilian population 100% against us." Observed another, in a harsh criticism of the illogic of Nazi policy: "If we shoot the Jews, let the prisoners of war die, deliver a large part of the urban population to death by hunger, in the coming year lose a part of the rural population to hunger, the question remains unanswered: Who then will actually produce anything of economic value?" By the autumn, civilians doing "useful work," whether as laborers, agricultural workers, or security forces, received 1,200 calories a day, a starvation diet to be sure, but better than the 850 calories accorded those not working for the Germans or the 420 for children under the age of fourteen and Jews.[62]

The Wehrmacht nonetheless did its best to feed itself from the land, with the inevitable consequences for the civilian population. Within weeks of the invasion, not insignificant parts of the invading force were redirected to the requisitioning of food. At the same time, given the inadequacies of the supply system, German troops plundered huge quantities of livestock, grain, and dairy produce for their own use. The army, however, failed to seize large quantities of grain reserves as the Soviets succeeded in destroying much of the existing stocks. In reprisal, Hitler ordered mass starvation. "The Führer is for a somewhat more radical course in the occupied areas," Goebbels noted laconically on 19 August. In Belorussia, where supplies were already inadequate, Army Group Center adopted a ruthless policy of "eating the country bare." In the Baltic and Ukraine, enough food was seized to feed the army tolerably well and to create a substantial Reich reserve, but, because of transportation difficulties, it proved impossible to send much of it back to Germany. Much of the reserve stockpiled in the east, in fact, spoiled during the winter of 1941–1942. As a result, virtually nothing was left to feed the Soviet population, which, in Goering's words, faced "the greatest mortality since the Thirty Years War."[63]

Lest Landsers take pity on Soviet civilians and offer them food from their own resources, the OKH issued a directive on 1 November: "In the fight against Bolshevism we are concerned with the survival or destruction of our people. . . . German soldiers will be tempted to share their provisions with the people. They must, however, say to themselves: 'Every gram of bread or other food that I may give out of generosity to the population in the occupied territories I am withholding from the German people and thus my own family. . . .' In the face of starving women and children German soldiers must remain steadfast. If they refuse to do so they are endangering the nutrition of our own people." Although the Germans failed to implement the hunger policy in its full horror, in many cities famine still raged during the winter of 1941–1942, most notably in Leningrad, Kiev, and Kharkov. In the areas most seriously affected, the starving inhabitants could not be dissuaded by even the most draconian threats from roaming the front lines in search of food. Even horses that had died and been buried were dug up and eaten. If fewer Soviet citizens starved to death in the first year of German occupation than expected or desired, a situation that clearly mystified German officials, it was certainly not for a lack of effort.[64]

This reprieve, if such it could be called, did not extend to the Jews. By mid-August, as we have seen, the question had turned from why the Jews in the Soviet Union should be killed to why they should not be killed. As any perceived economic value they might have as laborers was trumped by ideological or security concerns, their status as useless eaters or the "bearers of Bolshevism" marked them for annihilation. Two months of continual killings had created a reliable body of executioners, while the steady drumbeat of Nazi propaganda had convinced many of the necessity of eliminating "this scum that tossed all of Europe into the war." Both local authorities and officials at the center in Berlin now began to perceive the possibility for a large-scale solution of the Jewish question. If in mid-August the onslaught against Soviet Jews and a final solution of the Jewish question in Europe were still separate entities, time, space, and opportunity intersected in the autumn of 1941 to transform regional murder into European-wide genocide. "The occupied Soviet areas," Alfred Rosenberg announced in a mid-November speech, "should become the scene of the biological elimination of all European Jews." Thus, although in mid-August Hitler had rejected proposals for the deportation of German Jews during the war, by December a training journal of the Order Police could proclaim openly,

> The word of the Führer [in his January 1939 speech] that a new war, instigated by Jewry, will not bring about the destruction of . . . Germany but rather the end of Jewry, is now being carried out. The gigantic spaces of the east, which Germany and Europe have now at their disposition for colonization, also facilitate the definitive solution of the Jewish problem in the near future. This means not only removing the race from power, but its elimination. . . . What seemed impossible only two years ago, now step-by-step is becoming a reality: the end of the war will see a Europe free of Jews.[65]

Clearly, then, the autumn of 1941 marked a watershed at which the threshold to mass murder, not just of Soviet Jews but of all the Jews of Europe, was crossed. In this complex process of decisionmaking and evolving policy formulation, pressures from the periphery, events at the center, and seemingly decisive military triumphs resulted in key decisions being made in mid-September, when it looked as if the war in the east would soon be over and Germany left as the master of the Continent. Preparations and plans for implementation of mass murder, set in motion before the drive on Moscow lagged in late October, continued apace despite the increasing military difficulties—and, in some cases, such as transportation, deportations took place that even aggravated shortages at the front.

As with the earlier decision to expand the killing of Jews in the Soviet Union, perceptions of the ongoing war effort proved pivotal. With the slowing of the Germans' advance in the face of stout Russian resistance and growing doubts about their ability to win the war in 1941, Hitler's mid-August decision reflected the recognition that it was impractical at that juncture to deport Jews from the Reich into the Soviet Union. Perhaps, too, in the wake of the recent meeting between Churchill and Roosevelt, the old notion of using Jews as hostages to warn America against entering the war played a role in Hitler's thinking. His decision, however, did not stifle mounting pressures from local and regional officials in Germany and the occupied east for a clearer definition of Jewish policy. As pressure for deportation and other anti-Jewish measures mounted in Germany, in the east ambitious administrators pressed for approval from Berlin of more comprehensively radical measures. Military officials, too, voiced concerns over the partisan war and the deteriorating security situation. At the same time, given the severe food shortages, local administrators stressed the untenable conditions within the Polish ghettos. If the ghettos were to support themselves financially, productive jobs had to be created. That, however, would require significant investment that would likely pay off only in the long term. By the autumn, however, Nazi authorities had begun to see the solution to their labor problem in the exploitation of Soviet prisoners of war and civilians. Murdering the Jews thus appeared to many the most utilitarian solution to a burdensome problem. Amid growing frustration and impatience, then, those at the periphery clamored for some basic policy direction.[66]

By mid-September, the military situation had changed substantially for the better. German forces had cut off Leningrad early in the month, while the encirclement east of Kiev, completed on the fifteenth, promised a spectacular triumph. That same day, following an aerial bombing, the Gauleiter of Hamburg, Karl Kaufmann, urged Hitler to allow the evacuation of Jews from the city in order that their dwellings be distributed to victims of the raid. This suggestion followed by a day a proposal from Rosenberg that all Jews from Central Europe be deported to the east in retaliation for Stalin's deportation of the Volga Germans to Siberia. Although noncommittal, the Führer expressed interest in Rosenberg's "very important and urgent matter." At the same time, Hitler was pressured by officials in France to evacuate a number of Jews to the east as part of a reprisal policy. All the while, of course, Heydrich and Goebbels had continued to push for the removal of German Jews. On 16 and 17 September, Hitler had a cluster of meetings with top officials in which he discussed the Jewish question, talked of turning the conquered eastern territories into Germany's India, and stressed the importance of resettling ethnic Germans. He also gave approval to Kaufmann on the seventeenth for the removal of Jews from Hamburg.[67]

The next day, clearly searching for a place to put more than a few thousand Hamburg Jews, Himmler informed Arthur Greiser in the Warthegau that he would have to accept sixty thousand Jews into the Lodz ghetto since "the Führer wishes that the Old Reich and Protectorate be emptied and freed of Jews from west to east as quickly as possible." Hitler had, thus, not only permitted the evacuation of Hamburg's Jews, but now, in light of new military successes, also sanctioned what he had prohibited just a month before, the removal of all German Jews during the war. "The spell is broken," Hitler told Goebbels in late September, in meetings also attended by Himmler and Heydrich. "In the next three to four weeks we must once again expect great victories." The serious fighting, Hitler thought, would last until 15 October, after which Bolshevism would be beaten. Heydrich even delighted in pointing to the irony of his suggestion that the Jews should be "transported into camps that have been erected by the Bolsheviks. These camps were erected by the Jews, so what should be more fitting than that they now also be populated by Jews." With this seemingly offhand mid-September decision to permit the deportation of German Jews, Hitler set in motion a process that would culminate in genocide.[68]

By early October, with Operation Typhoon enjoying great success, Hitler remained optimistic about the deportations, his only reservation being a possible shortage of trains. On the tenth, however, Heydrich held a conference in Prague at which he removed any further obstacles. "Because the Führer wishes that by the end of this year as many Jews as possible be removed from the German sphere," he stressed, "all pending questions must be solved. . . . Even the transportation question must not present any problems." Symbolically, the first deportation train left Vienna on 15 October, the date Hitler expected the defeat of Russia to be sealed and the same day panic broke out in Moscow. Although local authorities had prepared the evacuations from Vienna, Prague, and Berlin with remarkable speed, the problem of reception areas in the east remained. Greiser succeeded in getting the figure dispatched to Lodz reduced to twenty thousand, but that simply meant that larger numbers were sent further east to Kaunas, Riga, and Minsk. In those cities, in the absence of clear guidelines for what to do with the deportees, local officials, reflective of a process of cumulative radicalization that rewarded personal initiative, largely acted as they saw fit and took whatever measures they deemed necessary.[69]

In practice, this meant that the Jews arriving from the old Reich were treated differently in the various reception areas. In Lodz and Minsk, German Jews were crammed into the ghettos, with the twist that, in the latter city, over eleven thousand Belorussian Jews were shot to make room for the new arrivals. The situation in Kaunas, in Lithuania, was different, however. There, the men of Karl Jäger's murderously efficient Einsatzkommando 3 were waiting as the deportation trains arrived, shooting nearly five thousand German Jews within a few days in late November. In Riga, Latvia, all the deportees on a train from Berlin were murdered on 30 November, a situation that aroused quite a stir since many of the victims were *Mischlinge* (part Jews), war veterans, or married to Aryans. Shooting Ostjuden was one thing; executing German Jews, "from our cultural sphere . . . [and not] the native bestial hordes," as Wilhelm Kube put it, clearly presented a problem. Himmler, in fact, had telephoned that afternoon in an attempt to halt the execution but was too late. After this incident, German Jews arriving in Riga were no longer executed immediately. Instead, they were confined in temporary camps outside the city, where the atrocious conditions meant that many died within a short time. By mid-December, after some twenty-five thousand local Jews were executed, deportees from Germany were allowed into the Riga ghetto, where large numbers died of "natural causes." Others were shot in small groups in a nearby forest, while the deportees on several trains that arrived in late December, January, and February were liquidated on arrival.[70]

These gruesome activities confirmed a pattern of confused local reactions but also a sinister long-term trend. Local objections forced a reduction in the number of deportation trains leaving Germany in the late autumn, but the transports themselves could not be stopped entirely, despite the fact that they contributed to a severe shortage of railcars and bottlenecks in the transportation system crippling the German advance toward Moscow. Bock protested the continuing presence of "Jew trains," fearing that the "arrival of these trains must result in the loss of an equal number of trains vital to supplying the attack," but to little avail. Once the Jewish deportations had begun, Himmler and Heydrich refused to halt them. Clearly, no blueprint for systematic mass murder had been devised and no general order issued when the deportations began to execute German Jews on arrival in the east, but chaotic conditions in the ghettos in Poland, the public nature of mass shootings, the drain on German manpower, and the psychological burden on the perpetrators all demanded a more discrete, efficient, and orderly process of killing the Jews. Bolstered by his authorization of 31 July to prepare some sort of final solution for European Jewry for implementation after the Russian campaign, which now seemed to be in its concluding stages, Heydrich began to bring together elements from three existing programs: the concentration camp, the euthanasia program, and the resettlement program. Out of this fluid process of experimentation would come perhaps the most sinister invention of the twentieth century: the extermination camp (*Vernichtungslager*).[71]

In July and August, even before the euthanasia killings had spread to the concentration camps, Nazi authorities had been searching for a more humane way—more humane for the killers, not the victims—to dispose of large numbers of people. As Walter Rauff, an official of the Criminal Technical Institute of the RSHA, explained to an aide, a "more humane method of execution" was needed for the Einsatzgruppen since members of the firing squads suffered from frequent nervous breakdowns. Out of this necessity came a number of proposals, some disastrous, such as a test using explosives on mental patients that left body parts strewn about, and others more promising. By mid-September, a number of officials were exploring the possibilities of using poison gas. Hitler had suspended the adult euthanasia program on 24 August, which meant that trained killing experts were available to lend their expertise. Rauff himself charged his technicians with constructing a gas van that would channel engine exhaust into a sealed compartment, thus killing the victims by carbon monoxide poisoning. In September and October, experiments using Zyklon-B, a common agent used in the pest extermination business in Germany, were undertaken at the concentration and prisoner-of-war camp at Auschwitz. Although many of these trials were clearly associated with the expansion of the euthanasia program into the concentration camps, Nazi officials were quick to see the broader implications. That fall, for example, a gassing facility at Chelmno, originally conceived by local officials for the Wartheland, was accelerated to completion since it now fit well with broader goals at the center. By early October, plans had been made for the construction of a second large camp at Birkenau, adjacent to Auschwitz, complete with underground cellar rooms with large forced air ventilation systems attached to crematories. At roughly the same time, near Lublin, under the supervision of Christian Wirth, a leading functionary of the euthanasia program, construction began on a facility at Belzec that would use exhaust gas from engines channeled into sealed rooms to kill Jews. The Nazis also began preliminary work on another camp near Lublin, at Sobibor, that autumn.[72]

Significantly, Adolf Eichmann, the Nazi deportation expert who later claimed that Heydrich had told him in the fall of 1941, "The Führer has ordered the physical destruction of the Jews," also met with Wirth at Belzec. Although Eichmann's postwar testimony was admittedly somewhat contradictory, the fact that Hitler had authorized the deportation of German Jews and the dispatch of euthanasia personnel to the east adds credence to his recollections. So does the fact that, on 17 October, Heydrich intervened to prevent the evacuation of Spanish Jews interned in France to Morocco, on the grounds that "these Jews would be . . . out of direct reach of the measures for a basic solution to the Jewish question to be enacted after the war." The next day Himmler noted to Heydrich, "No emigration by Jews to overseas," while on the twenty-third the emigration gates were sealed. That day, Gestapo chief Heinrich Müller circulated a Himmler order to the various police and SD agencies announcing that all Jewish emigration was to be stopped. A fateful divide had been passed; what had formerly been official Nazi policy, a *Judenfrei* Europe through expulsion, had been definitively altered. The Jews of Europe would now be deported to the east.[73]

Nor would their eventual fate be in doubt. Talking with Fritz Sauckel and Fritz Todt on 17 October, Hitler, in an expansive mood, sketched his vision of the Germanization of the eastern territories. The Slavs, he mused, would be treated "as Indians," with some elements "sifted." For the rest, "We are getting rid of the destructive Jews entirely. . . . I proceed with these matters ice-cold. I feel myself to be only the executor of a will of history." Four days later, meeting with Bormann, Hitler clearly sketched his sense of mission: "When we exterminate this plague, then we perform a deed for humanity, the significance of which our men out there can still not at all imagine." On the night of the twenty-fifth, Hitler recalled to Himmler and Heydrich his Reichstag prophecy, then boasted, "We are writing history anew from the racial standpoint." By that time, not only was the extermination camp at Chelmno, near Lodz, nearly completed, but plans were also set in motion to construct two other such facilities, at Mogilev (in Belorussia) and Riga. In mid-November the Topf company had been commissioned to construct a huge crematorium at Mogilev, with the first oven actually delivered in December. By then, however, military events had interceded, and the camp and gas chambers were never constructed; instead, the crematory units were sent to Auschwitz.[74]

To all appearances, a fundamental decision had been taken in the early autumn to kill the Jews of Europe, a decision that even the deteriorating military situation would not reverse. In early November, a time resonant in Hitler's mind with the shameful capitulation of 1918, events at the front seemed to harden his determination to destroy the Jews. At lunch with Himmler on 5 November, Hitler vowed that he would not allow "criminals" to stay alive while "the best men" were dying at the front. "We experienced that in 1918," he added, with little need to expand on what he meant, given the notorious passage in *Mein Kampf* in which he rued the Kaiser's failure to kill "Hebrew polluters" at the beginning of World War I. That evening, he launched a diatribe against the Jews, vowing that the war would bring their ruin. In Munich three days later to address the old comrades on the anniversary of the failed putsch, the Führer once again blamed the Jews for the war, noting that it was merely the continuation of the struggle that had not ended in 1918. Germany had been cheated of victory then, he remarked bitterly, "But that was only the beginning, the first act of this drama. The second and the finale will now be written. And this time we will make good what we were then cheated of." Finally, at his field headquarters in the early hours of 2 December, just days before the Soviet counterattack in front of Moscow, he remarked bitingly of the Jews, "He who destroys life, exposes himself to death. And nothing other than this is happening to them." Just a few days later, the first extermination center, at Chelmno, went into operation. The day before, however, the Japanese bombed the American naval base at Pearl Harbor. The European war was now part of a world war. On the twelfth, meeting with party leaders the day after having declared war on the United States, Hitler again referred to his prophecy, drawing the logical, if murderous, conclusion. As Goebbels noted, "He warned the Jews that if they were to cause another world war, it would lead to their own destruction. Those were not empty words. Now the world war has come. The destruction of the Jews must be the necessary consequence. We cannot be sentimental about it." With his insistence that his prophecy be taken literally, Hitler had finally resolved any remaining ambiguity about the timing of the Final Solution: the destruction of Europe's Jews would take place immediately and not be delayed until after the war.[75]

In a strict sense, no plan yet existed for the coordinated murder of Europe's Jews, although, since October, Heydrich had been sending reports to various ministries in the Berlin bureaucracy both to acquaint them with the ongoing annihilation of Soviet Jewry and to prepare the ground for their eventual cooperation. To that end, Heydrich had on 29 November sent out invitations to those in the civilian bureaucracies most concerned with Jewish policy for a conference to be held on 9 December to clarify matters. The worsening military situation forced a postponement of the meeting, and not until 20 January did Heydrich convene the conference, with lunch included, at a confiscated Jewish villa on the Wannsee, a large lake on the outskirts of Berlin. In the meantime, Hitler and other top Nazis had not been idle. In the two days following his speech to party leaders, Hitler and Himmler had a flurry of meetings with Philipp Bouhler and Viktor Brack, the key figures in the euthanasia organization, securing the extensive use of euthanasia personnel in the solution to the Jewish question. Himmler also expressed a new sense of urgency, stressing to Brack, "One must work as quickly as possible." Then, in a meeting with Alfred Rosenberg on the sixteenth, Hitler remarked that the Jews "had brought the war down on us, they had started all the destruction, so it should come as no surprise if they became its first victims." Time and again in these momentous mid-December days, Hitler referred to the retribution that would be visited on world Jewry for its alleged anti-German activities and responsibility for the war. The Jews having lost their role as hostages who might deter American entry into the war, nothing now stood in the way of their mass annihilation.[76]

Back from Berlin, Hans Frank on 16 December conveyed to his subordinates in the General Government the attitude at the top: "The Jews will disappear. . . . We must destroy the Jews wherever we find them. . . . But what is going to happen to these Jews? Do you imagine there will be settlement villages for them. . . ? In Berlin we were told . . . : Liquidate them yourselves!" As if to confirm Frank's assessment, in a reply on 18 December to an official inquiry from Reichskommissariat Ostland asking whether all Jews were to be liquidated, Berlin indicated: "Clarity on the Jewish question has been achieved through oral discussion: economic interests are to be disregarded . . . in the settlement of this problem." That same day, Himmler, following a meeting with Hitler, expressed clearly in his appointment book what that meant: "Jewish question/to be exterminated as partisans."[77]

By the time of the Wannsee Conference, then, none of the participants harbored any doubts about the fate of the Jews: what they were to organize and prepare was not a resettlement operation but the deportation and systematic destruction of Europe's Jews. Although Heydrich referred to using Jewish labor to build roads in the east, during which project a large number would die from overwork and starvation (which, in fact, was already occurring in Polish Galicia), the idea of annihilating Jews through forced labor after a victorious war had given way to the recognition that the Jews would be destroyed during the war, and not in the Soviet Union but in the newly created death camps in Poland. "Practical experiences," Heydrich mentioned cryptically, were being gathered that would be of great significance for the "imminent" Final Solution. Heydrich had been quite pleased at the outcome of the meeting. He had anticipated difficulties, but, instead, his authority had been recognized, no objections had been raised to the extermination of the Jews, the state secretaries of the relevant bureaucracies were enthusiastic about doing their part, and the basic outline for the practical implementation of the Final Solution had been agreed on. Not all the details had been settled, and the methods and techniques being experimented with were still untried on a large scale, but no one at the conference could doubt the ultimate goal: every Jew in Europe was to be killed.[78]

The gas chambers at Belzec, Sobibor, Treblinka, and Auschwitz did not begin operation until March 1942, and not until July would large-scale deportations from Western Europe begin, but the key decision about the fate of the Jews had been taken. Until the summer of 1941, the Nazi leadership had envisioned the solution to its self-imposed Jewish problem through emigration, expulsion, and resettlement, only to be frustrated at every turn. With the magnitude of the problem increased through territorial conquest in Russia, military success itself led to a further radicalization: the Jews of the Soviet Union would be shot where they were found, with the fate of the remainder of the European Jews left hanging. By mid-October, the expectation of imminent victory led to the ultimate radicalization: no European Jews were to be allowed to escape what would now not be a slow death through hunger, disease, and harsh labor. Instead, the goal would be the immediate physical destruction of the Jews even as the war continued, as the regional killing operations were merged into a comprehensive program of systematic mass murder. The decision was not made all at once but instead reflected a process of incremental radicalization within which Hitler often responded to, and approved, the initiatives of his subordinates. But, for the ultimate step to mass murder, both Hitler's authorization and the context of the war were vital. On 30 January 1942, just ten days after the Wannsee Conference, Hitler spoke before a packed house at the Sportpalast, where he once again referred to his prophecy. The war, he declared, "can only end either with the extermination of the Aryan peoples or the disappearance of Jewry from Europe." He thought, however, that the war would not end as the Jews imagined: "The result of this war will be the annihilation of Jewry. For the first time the old Jewish law will now be applied: an eye for an eye, a tooth for a tooth. . . . And the hour will come when the most evil world-enemy of all time will have played out its role."[79] The Wehrmacht had invaded the Soviet Union as the vanguard of a regime with murderous intentions; Barbarossa had now become a war of annihilation in the fullest sense.

The genocidal process now set in motion came, ironically, just at the moment the German attack passed the culmination point, the crucial stage at which an offensive degenerates into nothing more than a dangerous gamble vulnerable to enemy counterattack. In late October, the OKW estimated the actual fighting power of the 136 divisions in the Ostheer to be the equivalent of only 83 divisions; moreover, the morale and combat strength of individual soldiers and units had also declined perceptibly. Having already conceded that the war against the Soviet Union would continue into 1942, the Germans now sought primarily to weaken the enemy to such an extent that he could not recover and to gain favorable jumping-off positions for the spring offensive. In order to weaken the enemy decisively, however, the Germans had to capture key railway lines and armament centers, which meant that even the minimum goals—reaching Voroshilovgrad, Ivanov, Yaroslavl, and Rybinsk—were ambitious, if not completely unattainable given the parlous state of the Ostheer. The maximum goals set by Halder—advancing to Maikop, Stalingrad, Gorky, and Vologda in order to seize the oil fields of the Caucasus and the armaments centers of the interior while cutting the transport routes for Lend-Lease supplies—were so utterly unrealistic that they bordered on the delusional.[80]

Bock, in fact, vigorously opposed Halder's aims, telling the latter, "The objectives . . . surely cannot be reached before winter, because we no longer have the required forces and because it is impossible to supply those forces." To Bock, the only realistic remaining operational goal was a line along the Moskva River and the Moscow-Volga Canal (i.e., the western outskirts of Moscow) since the reduced strength of the army group made any encirclement of the city unlikely. Moreover, the supply situation necessitated a staggered advance of individual armies rather than a unified strike against the capital, even though Bock knew that the only chance for success lay in a concentrated thrust. More worrisome, if anything went amiss, Bock did not believe that the front as it then stood could be defended. His doubts, in fact, highlighted the key question of how to proceed: whether it was best to stop early, conserve strength, and rebuild for the following spring or press ahead in an attempt to achieve the maximum disruptive effect in the time left for campaigning.[81]

In order to discuss these options, Halder convened a conference of chiefs of staff of the army groups and armies at Orsha on 13 November. Desperately hoping for six more weeks of suitable weather that would allow major operations to be carried out, he posed the question of the extent to which the next year's offensive could be prepared through further winter advances. Like Hitler, he clearly intended one last great effort to achieve the maximum possible effect. He found himself opposed virtually across the board by staff officers who, concerned about the sheer survival of the Ostheer, stressed that the serious deficiencies in manpower and supplies, the imminent physical and psychological collapse of the troops, and the lack of winter clothing and equipment ruled out any further large-scale offensives. Even the limited attack on Moscow proposed by Bock's chief of staff, a direct thrust without any broad envelopment of the city, involved major risks that made success highly unlikely. Despite this uniformly bleak picture, however, Halder demanded that the attack on Moscow proceed and that all the army groups push on until mid-December. When pressed a few days later by a member of the quartermaster-general's office who pointed out that it would be impossible to supply Army Group Center even as far as the Moskva River, Halder replied, "Your calculations are certainly correct, but we should not like to stand in Bock's way if he thinks he can succeed; you also need a little bit of luck in war."[82] Amazingly, German operational assessments had been reduced to the hope for a streak of gambler's good fortune, hardly an adequate response at such a critical moment, especially in view of the condition of German forces.

Having from the outset of planning argued for the key importance of Moscow, and having done everything he could operationally to force a decision there, Halder now seemed compelled to push on, despite all available information indicating that the attack would miscarry. In spite of the failure of earlier encirclement battles to cripple the Red Army, he still sought to destroy its vital fighting strength at Moscow. Perhaps one more tactical success, the capture of the enemy's capital, would produce a Soviet collapse, just as a little over a year earlier the fall of Paris had achieved just such decisive results. The conviction was general, after all, that the Soviets were making a last effort and that the stronger will would prevail. "We are not doing too well," Halder summed up the situation, "but the Russians are doing far worse!" This attitude meant that the OKH did not attach much importance to reports indicating the transfer of fresh Soviet units from the Far East to Moscow. Instead, it simply placed its hopes in the superiority of its own soldiers. This inaccurate assessment of Soviet strength fueled a further consideration, one replete with historical significance. The Army High Command feared a repeat of the battle at the Marne in September 1914, when the fight was prematurely abandoned and an imminent strategic victory thrown away. A final effort seemed mandatory in view of the proximity of the enemy's capital and the presumed weakness of his forces; having squandered possible victory in an earlier war through a failure of will, army commanders would not now repeat the same mistake. After all, aid from the Anglo-Americans might enable Stalin to recoup his losses, just as France had recovered in 1914. A final effort thus seemed mandatory, even though Bock was ambivalent (as were others) and displayed little optimism about a possible triumph.[83]

Political calculations also played a role, for the mood in Germany had darkened considerably since the heady days of early October when Hitler had confidently predicted imminent victory. By November, people had begun to wonder whether it would be possible to end the war at all; a peace with Stalin seemed hardly possible, nor could Germany, in view of its limited manpower, reasonably expect to occupy all of the Soviet Union. Moreover, the lack of official announcements was disturbing. After hearing that the bulk of the Red Army had been destroyed and that German troops had advanced to within forty miles of Moscow, the German people found that reports suddenly stopped. Goebbels, in fact, had already begun shifting German propaganda from an emphasis on when Germany would win to the more important topic of how the war would end: "If we win, then we have won everything. . . . If we lose . . . we have lost all." A triumph at Moscow was necessary to restore optimism at home and the old conviction that the Wehrmacht was invincible. As a result, the OKH ignored warnings from the front such as that from General Sodenstern, the chief of staff of Army Group South, who cautioned at the end of October: "It is no longer possible to mitigate the situation by saying: 'It will be all right, it has always been all right up to now despite frequent reports that the troops cannot go on any longer.' There comes a time when—physically—they really cannot go on any longer. . . . I believe that this point has now . . . been reached."[84]

With time short, and facing the imminent transfer on 18 November of part of Luftflotte 2 to the Mediterranean, Army Group Center hastened preparations to resume the offensive. As it was considered virtually impossible to envelop Moscow, the plan now called for the Ninth Army and the Third Panzergruppe in the north to advance to the Volga reservoir and the Moscow-Volga Canal, then turn south toward the capital. In the center, the Fourth Panzergruppe and elements of the left wing of the Fourth Army would strike toward the northwest suburbs of Moscow, although Kluge opposed the idea of attacking with his right wing. To the south, the Second Panzer Army was to swing north through Tula and Kolomna. The pitifully weak Second Army was to protect the southern flank of the army group while also thrusting to the Don and capturing Voronezh, even though it could expect no help from the Sixth Army of Army Group South. Even this limited attack, which Bock dismissed as "no great strategic masterpiece," had little chance of success since the mobile forces on the wings were too weak to meet at Moscow and the troops to be used in the frontal assault were no longer considered capable of attack. Moreover, to succeed, the operation would have to be launched simultaneously in every sector to prevent the Russians from shifting forces to imperiled areas. The Fourth Army's inability to attack with most of its units, however, meant that it would be incapable of tying down enemy troops. Moreover, the attacking units faced crippling shortages of men and materiel, with infantry companies down to fifty to sixty men. Since the start of Operation Typhoon, Army Group Center had suffered 87,000 casualties, which brought its total to nearly 317,000 men, or almost half of all the casualties in the Ostheer to date. Despite this, the army group had received no replacements since the beginning of October and had been forced to transfer four divisions. In literally throwing his last battalion into the battle in hopes of tipping the balance, Bock had to remind his commanders at the outset that they were on their own since the army group had only a single division in reserve.[85]

Serious logistic problems that went from bad to worse compounded the critical manpower shortage. Trucks moving supplies from the railheads had long since gotten stuck to their axles in the deep mud. When the weather froze in mid-November, the trucks were hauled out, but many suffered severe damage in the process: the Fourth Army had been reduced to barely a tenth of its original complement of trucks, while 50 percent of Army Group Center's truck fleet was out of action. Even those vehicles that remained were frequently immobilized by a lack of antifreeze. "What stupidity is this," exclaimed one soldier, "starting an attack with units whose trucks will not move?" Resupply by rail, now vital to sustain any further advance, continued to deteriorate as well in the freezing conditions. As the temperatures plummeted, some 70–80 percent of German steam locomotives, whose water pipes, unlike those of Russian engines, were outside their boilers, froze and burst, contributing to a supply crisis that reached epic proportions. Only five fuel trains reached the Ninth Army between 23 October and 23 November, but this dwarfed the number arriving at the Second Army, which received only one fuel train and virtually no supply trains from the end of October. Often, the contents of even those trains that did arrive could not be distributed since many trucks lacked fuel. Little wonder, then, that, when the chief of staff of the Second Panzer Army saw that it had been assigned the task of seizing Gorky, some three hundred miles east of Moscow, he burst out in frustration, "This is not May again and we are not fighting in France." He succeeded in altering the immediate objective to Venev, just thirty miles beyond Tula, but doubted that even that could be reached. In a moment of rare strategic reality, even Halder admitted privately, "The time for spectacular operational feats is past. . . . The only course lies in purposeful exploitation of tactical opportunities."[86]

The Wehrmacht had also sacrificed the element of surprise since Moscow was the only objective left of any merit. Once Typhoon had come to a standstill in late October, the Soviets had busied themselves with extensive reinforcements to their field positions, constructing defenses in depth, laying a sizable number of mines, creating hundreds of kilometers of antitank ditches, and preparing bunkers, strongpoints, dugouts, and artillery positions. Workers' battalions, the civilian population of Moscow, and even the fighting troops toiled away at the defenses around the city, all designed to delay a German attack by forcing it to continue breaking through new positions until, ultimately, it exhausted itself. The hilly and wooded terrain also aided the defenders, as did the proximity of the Moscow supply base and the extensive system of intact railways, which allowed rapid delivery of troops and supplies to any sector of the front. Additionally, while German air support had noticeably slackened, the Red Army benefited from the large number of well-placed airfields around the city. A steady stream of reinforcements also arrived during November, divisions from Siberia, Central Asia, and the Far East as well as hastily raised and trained units. On top of this, the Soviet command hustled wounded soldiers back to the front in order to reemploy battle-experienced men. While German numbers were seriously depleted, therefore, the Stavka now managed to array eighty-four divisions and twenty brigades against the seventy-three divisions left to Army Group Center. The Soviets had made it clear that they intended to fight for Moscow. "Russia is big," went Zhukov's exhortation to the defenders, "but there is no room to retreat. Moscow is behind us."[87]

When the Ninth Army opened the final phase of Operation Typhoon on 15 November, followed the next day by attacks by the Third Panzergruppe and elements of the Fourth Panzergruppe to the north of Moscow, progress was surprisingly good. Despite tough initial resistance, the Germans had by the eighteenth broken though Soviet lines south of the Volga reservoir and moved on Klin. Almost by chance they had struck at a vulnerable spot in the Russian defenses created by Stalin's insistence on the thirteenth that Zhukov launch a series of spoiling attacks.

The Soviet forces had sustained heavy casualties, which contributed to a weakness in the Soviet defenses that the Third Panzergruppe now exploited. Although, for a time, it appeared that Zhukov's entire right flank might collapse, the Russian attacks had not been entirely a failure since they had convinced Kluge, commanding the Fourth Army, to halt his attack and go over to the defensive, thus creating a pocket in the center between the two enveloping panzer prongs. To the south, the Second Panzer Army, with only 150 tanks remaining of the 400 it had in September, on the eighteenth pushed around Tula, where it had been tied down for weeks, in the direction of Kolomna. Guderian's forces broke through Soviet defenses in the face of stout resistance, but the failure of the Fourth Army to advance caused a salient to form based on Tula that immediately threatened the inner flank of the Second Panzer Army's left wing. Since the Second Army, on the army group's southern flank, was heading east toward Kursk and Voronezh, it could offer little support to Guderian. Despite these early gains, a shortage of fuel that halted operations in some areas as early as the eighteenth meant that the German attack increasingly resembled a feeble thumb and finger unlikely ever to meet at Moscow.[88]

By now, the sputtering offensive had assumed a distinctly surreal quality since it was apparent to commanders at the front, if not to the OKH, that they lacked strength to go on—and in persisting only put their troops, and perhaps the entire Ostheer, at risk. Seemingly in his own fantasy world where wishful thinking clouded hard realism, Halder dismissed reports about the poor condition of the troops, writing on the twenty-first, "It is true, they did have to fight hard and a very long way; and still they have come through victoriously. . . . So we may hope that they will be able to fight on, even against the repeatedly reinforced enemy until a favorable closing line is reached." This last task, however, was clearly beyond their abilities. By the twentieth, the German offensive in the south had largely run its course. That day, Guderian informed the army group that his attack northeastward would have to be suspended because of the serious threat to his flank, continuing fuel shortages, heavy casualties, and the exhaustion of his troops. The next day, Bock noted gloomily, "Many second lieutenants are leading battalions, one first lieutenant leads a regiment, regimental combat strengths of 250 men, also the cold and inadequate shelter . . . , the overexertion of units. . . . It is doubtful if we can go any further." Nonetheless, Bock urged Guderian on; his forces did make further gains over the next two days, but on the twenty-third he met with Bock to impress on him the reality of the situation. His troops could seize a few more objectives, Guderian stressed, but none would have any decisive impact, while his army, bled to death, would be left "hanging in the air" with open flanks on both sides. Bock, sobered by this pessimistic assessment from the usually optimistic Guderian, now realized the full gravity of the situation: "the eleventh hour" was approaching, and troop strength had been reduced to such a degree that his troops would be unlikely to mount any resistance in case of Soviet attack.[89]

The consequences of the massively costly victories were all too apparent at the front, where the symbols that the OKH pushed around on a map had little relation to the actual combat value of individual units. Without significant resupply, the provision of winter clothing and equipment, and meaningful reinforcements, the fighting power of most German divisions had been reduced to little more than raiding parties. Nor could the dispatch of specialized troops to the front remedy the situation since most had not been trained for infantry combat. As one general admitted, "We wound up with valuable tank crews fighting . . . in the snow as infantrymen—and being totally wasted." As these men discovered, living in foxholes and fighting in ice and snow were not comparable to life in a tank; some 70 percent of losses were from frostbite. Employment of Luftwaffe crews and maintenance personnel at the front also proved catastrophic: not only were they ineffective in combat, but they were also then lost for the tasks for which they had been trained. Moreover, with the high rate of losses suffered by officers, the very structure of the Wehrmacht was disintegrating. In the absence of experienced veterans, both morale and operational effectiveness declined as German tactical expertise could no longer compensate for inferior numbers or tanks. In the icy cold and snow that reduced German mobility, a sense of vulnerability began to take hold as Landsers realized that their only effective defense against the T-34, the fearsome eighty-eight-millimeter antiaircraft gun, was often too cumbersome to bring into action in the Russian winter. As temperatures plunged, machine guns, rifles, artillery, and vehicles froze, further contributing to a sense of helplessness, especially as spare parts were lacking to make them operable.[90]

Nor could men keep warm since winter clothing failed to arrive; on average, only one man in five had a greatcoat. The bottlenecks in the German transportation system meant that trains loaded with winter gear had to be shunted aside in favor of higher-priority ammunition and fuel trains. To make do, German soldiers looted Russian homes of coats, boots, blankets, white sheets—anything that would provide protection from the numbing cold. Simply struggling through the deep snow burned considerable energy that could not be made good by the inadequate rations reaching the front. Daily life was a constant struggle. "Bread had to be chopped with hatchets," noted one soldier, "gasoline froze . . . , and the skin from hands remained frozen to rifles. The wounded froze to death within minutes." Infantry companies down to thirty men found it taxing to post sentries since men had to be relieved every thirty minutes or so in the biting cold, making it nearly impossible to get any rest. "Our people are kaputt," admitted Wilhelm Prüller. "One hour outside, one hour in the hut, watch, alarm sentry duty, listening duty, observer duty, occupy the MG [machine gun] posts. . . . For weeks and weeks one hour of sleep, then one hour of duty." Even going to the toilet was a chore, as one Landser remembered: "You try coming out and dropping your trousers when it's 40° below zero!" Behind this sardonic comment was a troubling reality, however, as frostbite claimed many men suffering from dysentery. Drugged by the cold, poorly nourished, numbed by fatigue, Landsers succumbed to lethargy as morale plummeted. "Our best strength was murdered here on these snow fields," Harald Henry wrote bitterly in early December while lying in front of Moscow, then added, "A tremendously deep hatred, a resounding 'No' collected in our breasts." Another Landser conceded that many a man, "when it came to the decisive moment, opted not to stick his head out as far as he might have done otherwise." Brutalized, demoralized, and overwhelmed by the savage winter conditions, Landsers had reached the limits of their endurance. "We are all so tired of Russia," lamented Klaus Hansmann, "tired of the war."[91]

Hitler, too, was noticeably uneasy about the offensive, remarking to Halder on 19 November that he expected a negotiated peace since "the two belligerents cannot annihilate each other." On the twenty-fourth, General Fromm, the head of the Replacement Army and chief of Military Armaments, warned that the "catastrophic worsening" of the situation in the armaments economy made an imminent peace a "necessity." The next day, according to his adjutant, Major Gerhard Engel, Hitler expressed great concern about the Russian winter, fearing, "We started too late." Time, he mused, was "his greatest nightmare." Two days later, on the twenty-seventh, Quartermaster-General Wagner told Hitler, "We are at the end of our personnel and material strength." As if sobered by this, Hitler let slip that same day a revealing remark to the Danish foreign minister: "If the German people are no longer strong enough and ready to sacrifice their own blood for their existence, they should perish." Two days later, Hitler received yet another jolt of bad news, this time from one of his most trusted and able advisers, the ardent Nazi and minister for armaments and munitions Fritz Todt. Along with Walter Rohland, the head of the tank production program, Todt met with Hitler on the twenty-ninth and painted a disturbing picture of supply problems, materiel deficiencies on the eastern front, and the superiority of Soviet tank production, then observed: "This war can no longer be won by military means." Hitler listened without interruption, then asked calmly, "How, then, should I end this war?" Todt replied that it could be concluded only politically, a path already pondered by Hitler in August, to which the Führer responded simply, "I can scarcely see a way of coming politically to an end." Although that same day, in separate discussions with Goebbels and Ciano, the Italian foreign minister, he projected an optimistic facade, Hitler surely realized that his plans for Russia could no longer be realized.[92] With no clear way out of his dilemma, however, he had little recourse but to pursue some sort of military solution, even if it would not result in the complete triumph he had originally expected.

As a result, the Führer did not intervene when both Brauchitsch and Halder insisted that the Second Panzer Army keep attacking to inflict as much damage as possible on the enemy, despite the obvious fact that the Germans, too, would suffer heavy casualties for which they had no replacements. Halder conceded in a meeting on the twenty-third that the means for continuing the war were limited, that Germany would never again have an army like it had in June 1941, and that the main effort had now shifted to sustaining morale and holding out economically. Amazingly blind to reality, however, he still hoped to reach the Caucasus oil fields by the end of the year as well as sustain pressure on the enemy everywhere else on the vast front line. Moreover, his injunction to accomplish this without proper winter quarters or supplies, all the while maintaining "frugality in the employment of our forces and arms and ammunition," must have seemed a mockery to front officers, as did his assurance that Soviet forces were cracking under the German attack. "We are in a situation like the battle of the Marne," he claimed, once more invoking the historic memories that had such deep significance for German leaders. Despite Halder's exhortations, the gap between rhetoric and reality was now unbridgeable. Guderian had to halt his advance toward Kolomna on the twenty-fifth because of fierce enemy counterattacks, while the attempt to seize the key city of Tula failed. By 5 December, with temperatures plummeting to –30° F, virtually no fuel, vehicles and weapons inoperable in the bitter cold, and fewer than forty tanks in the entire army, Guderian suspended the offensive. It was, he emphasized to the army group, more important to preserve his remaining fighting strength than to continue the attempt to seize Tula.[93]

To the north, Landsers struggled forward, not so much out of belief that Soviet forces were near collapse as out of the hope that the capture of Moscow would bring some respite. For the troops, the campaign had become a search for shelter, a fight for self-preservation. Panzer thrusts were little more than probing raids, and the offensive as a whole had degenerated into a series of confused, hotly contested engagements conducted with pitiless ferocity. As they inched nearer to Moscow, German troops were stunned to find, if anything, that Russian resistance grew more fanatic. By 27 November, the Third Panzergruppe had taken Klin, while spearheads of the Fourth Panzergruppe had pushed to within twenty miles of the Kremlin, but, in the absence of an attack in the center by the Fourth Army to prevent the Soviets transferring troops to the wings, they stood little chance of reaching the city. In the early morning hours of the twenty-eighth, a battle group of the Seventh Panzer Division of the Third Panzergruppe seized an intact bridge spanning the Moscow-Volga Canal at Yakhroma, a mere eighteen miles to the north of the capital, an action that raised German hopes and Soviet fears that the entire Soviet northwestern front might collapse. The Germans, however, lacked fuel to rush troops to the bridgehead, while the Soviets immediately dispatched units of the First Shock Army, which had assembled in secret behind the front, to the threatened area. Under pressure from fierce Soviet counterattacks, "Kampfgruppe Manteuffel" had to abandon the bridgehead after midnight on the twenty-ninth, an action that shattered the belief, which had sustained the German forces, that the capture of Moscow was imminent.[94]

Twenty miles to the south, at Krassnaya Polyana, the Second Panzer Division also came to a standstill on the twenty-eighth, as did units from the Fourth Panzergruppe—the Fifth, Tenth, and Eleventh Panzer Divisions and the Second SS Division Das Reich—as they battered futilely against the minefields and fiercely defended earthworks of the Soviet defense line, with the spires of the Kremlin visible some twelve miles in the distance. Two incidents were telling. On the twenty-eighth, German troops knocked out both British- and American-made tanks, a clear indication of the material aid arriving from the West, while, on 1 December, a detachment of motorcyclists from the Second Panzer Division conducting a reconnaissance got within five miles of Moscow. Having no way to exploit this gap in Soviet defenses, however, all the frustrated motorcyclists could do was turn and drive back to German lines. By now, Bock doubted that his forces could go any further, especially in view of the enemy's ability to draw on seemingly inexhaustible reserves of men. "If we do not succeed in bringing about a collapse of Moscow's northwestern front in a few days," he noted on 29 November, "the attack will have to be called off; it would only lead to a soulless head-on clash with an opponent who apparently commands very large reserves of men and material; but I don't want to provoke a second Verdun." Significantly, in a matter of weeks, the Great War analogy invoked had changed from the Marne, where the Germans threw away a chance at victory through a failure of will, to Verdun, where the spectacle of relentless material attrition highlighted fatal German weakness.[95]

Although Kluge now belatedly launched an attack with his depleted forces, an action urged by the OKH despite Bock's reservations, the state of his troops ensured that it would sputter to a halt almost immediately. The lack of realism at the OKH once again convinced Bock that no one at headquarters had actually read his reports on the true condition of the troops, prompting him on 1 December to issue another stark warning. "I lack the strength for large-scale encirclement movements," he stressed, then outlined with precision the dire consequences:

> The attack will, after further bloody combat, result in modest gains . . . but it will scarcely have a strategic effect. The fighting of the past fourteen days has shown that the notion that the enemy in front of the army group had "collapsed" was a fantasy. . . . The attack thus appears to be without sense or purpose, especially since the time is approaching when the strength of the units will be exhausted. . . . In this state, with the heavy losses in officers and the reduced combat strengths, it could not withstand even a relatively well-organized attack. In view of the failure of the railroads there is also no possibility of preparing this extended front for a defensive battle or supplying it during such a battle.

The Ostheer had now clearly passed the culmination point. On 3 December, both the Fourth Army and the Fourth Panzergruppe reached the end of their strength and broke off the attack. Physically and psychologically, the troops had reached the limit of their endurance, with half the units unable to resist an assault. Most of the divisions of Army Group Center had fallen below 50 percent of their strength, while the army group itself had now suffered a total of 350,000 casualties.[96]

Signs of apathy abounded: on two days in early December, the Sixth Panzer Division reported a total of "eighty cases of fainting owing to exhaustion." Just as worrisome, the steady erosion of German strength had serious psychological repercussions and effects on morale. One report noted signs of panic among the troops, who could no longer be completely relied on. Another stressed the demoralizing effect of facing day after day new enemy forces that not only were superior in number and equipment but had also learned German tactics. As his qualitative superiority slipped away, "the German frontline soldier also realizes . . . that he is alone in the Far East with thinned ranks; he is suffering in the cold Russian winter . . . constantly aware of the heavy casualties . . . [and] that no replacements arrive. . . . The frontline soldier today quite openly states that this campaign still has a long way to go." Noted another, in stark terms, "The troops are exhausted and kaputt; they are completely indifferent." Letters home complained of the dismal situation at the front and the lack of winter clothing and equipment, with unflattering comparisons with the enemy, who was "much better . . . equipped for the winter." With three-quarters of German supply trains put out of action by the cold and partisan raids, any regular provision of supplies was impossible. The extreme cold, now dropping to as low as –30°F, inadequate clothing and shelter, lack of food, losses of weapons and equipment—in addition to the impact of combat—all sapped German morale.[97] Even before the Soviet counterattack, then, the German offensive had ground to a halt. In the absence of an enemy attack, the Germans would have been hard-pressed to maintain their positions since the lines reached by 5 December had long, unprotected flanks. Now, they would face an even bigger challenge: preventing the disintegration of the Ostheer itself.

"We must solve all continental European problems in 1941," Hitler had told Jodl on 17 December 1940, "since from 1942 on the United States would be in the position to intervene." Now, as the turn of events in front of Moscow cast a gloomy mood over the Führer Headquarters, came the news on 7 December of the Japanese attack on Pearl Harbor, which might have been expected to deepen the sense of apprehension even more. After all, as a German officer in Warsaw noted in his diary, "What probably every German has feared has come true." Even Goebbels worried that Germany could "probably not avoid a declaration of war on the United States." For Hitler, however, the news produced a "euphoric mood," as if he "had been freed from a nightmare." To him, in fact, it was nothing less than "a deliverance": "We now have an ally that has never been conquered in 3,000 years."[98] With the Japanese attack on Pearl Harbor and Hitler's subsequent declaration of war on the United States on 11 December, a European war, Hitler's war, had become a global war, one, moreover, that Hitler knew had come too soon and for which Germany was unprepared. Why, then, did he see this turn of events as hopeful for Germany?

Hitler had been aware of the potential power of the United States ever since his *Second Book*, written in 1928 but never published, and increasingly from the late 1930s America entered into his strategic calculations. In common with many German nationalists, his extremely negative view of the United States had been shaped by two events: American entry into World War I, which was, he thought, the result of the manipulation of Jewish finance capital, and President Wilson's "betrayal" of Germany in both the armistice and the Treaty of Versailles. This had resulted in revolution, chaos, and national humiliation, which could never be forgiven. By the late 1930s, as Roosevelt moved in a more outspoken anti-German direction, Hitler once again detected the hand of Jewish finance directing American actions in a warlike manner, the consequences of which he had laid out in his infamous 30 January 1939 speech. Despite his realization that the United States could do little in the short term to disturb his plans, he was aware of the rapid American rearmament and the likelihood of its support for Britain and France in the event of war. At the beginning of hostilities, he expressed confidence that Germany would solve all its problems in Europe before the Americans could intervene, but he also registered deep concern "if we're not finished by then," for all assessments indicated that the United States would be ready for war by 1942. The western war, Hitler clearly understood, had to be won quickly and decisively. The failure to do so, as we have seen, put him under a considerable time pressure and greatly influenced the timing of his move against the Soviet Union. The war he had always planned to fight on ideological grounds now had an urgent strategic goal: establish German continental dominance by the end of 1941 and remove any British hope of holding on before American intervention became a reality.[99]

To Hitler, doing nothing in the spring of 1941 raised the specter of a possible two-front war against Germany engineered by the Jews acting from both Russia and the United States. If he needed any confirmation of America's hostile intentions, the Lend-Lease Act, enacted in March 1941, and Roosevelt's actions in deliberately escalating the naval conflict in the Atlantic were regarded in Berlin as a virtual declaration of war on Germany. Hitler, however, did not want to give the American president an incident he could use to justify intervention, as had happened in World War I, so he ordered his naval leaders, chomping at the bit for a confrontation with the United States, to avoid any provocations. At the same time, the Führer began to see his erstwhile ally, Japan, in a new light. If Japanese expansion could be encouraged in the Pacific, he believed, that would not only strike a blow against British power but also distract U.S. attention from Europe. The key to enticing a more aggressive Japanese posture, in turn, would be the rapid defeat of the Soviet Union. That would eliminate the threat to both Germany and Japan and allow each to proceed unhindered against their remaining adversary. The Germans thus set about trying to encourage a more belligerent attitude in Tokyo.[100]

By the autumn, with the defeat of the Soviet Union in 1941 increasingly unlikely, and with concern growing in Berlin over a possible Japanese-American rapprochement, Japan now assumed a key role in Hitler's thinking. In order to buy time for a 1942 campaign that would secure its material base in Europe, if not destroy the Soviet Union outright, it was urgently necessary that Berlin coax Tokyo into taking action in the Pacific. Much to German relief, a mid-October change of government had set Tokyo on a more confrontational path with the United States. By early November, in fact, it was the Japanese who were seeking assurances of support from Germany in the event of a Japanese-American conflict, guarantees that Berlin was happy to provide. Ribbentrop not only assured the Japanese ambassador on 28 November that Germany would aid Japan in the event of war but also reaffirmed its commitment not to make a separate peace with the United States.[101]

By now, German leaders sensed that Japanese action was imminent, but they were taken completely by surprise—"a bolt from the blue," Goebbels admitted—by the bold attack on the key American naval base in the Pacific. Hitler now took a step that some historians have seen as "the most puzzling" of his decisions, indeed, as a "suicidal" impulse without any strategic purpose: declaring war on the United States. After all, Germany was under no treaty obligation to enter the conflict against the United States since Japan had not been attacked, and he had what he wanted at no apparent cost, a war in the Pacific that would preoccupy the Americans. The Führer's action, however, was not as irrational as it seemed. At the beginning of December, he certainly understood that his original concept of the war had failed, that the Soviet Union would not be defeated in 1941, that Germany did not yet possess the economic or armaments ability to fight a sustained war, that the intervention of the United States was only a matter of time, and that Germany could not win a two-front war against the United States and the Soviet Union. The Japanese action, however, gave Germany a last opportunity to defeat the unexpectedly resilient Soviets or at least produce some sort of satisfactory result, such as a deal with Stalin. For this to succeed, for Germany to have the time to accomplish its aims, Japan would have to tie down the Americans as long and as completely as possible in the Pacific.[102]

Germany's role, in turn, would be to prevent the Americans from concentrating all their considerable resources on the Japanese and, thus, win a quick victory before turning on Germany. The United States, through German action, would be compelled to divert resources to the Atlantic, thus forcing it into a war across two broad oceans. The tables, neatly enough, would be turned: this time, the Americans, not the Germans, would have to disperse their strength. Not surprisingly, then, on the eighth, even before the declaration of war three days later, Hitler removed the shackles from his U-boats and now ordered them to attack American shipping, a move that certainly would have resulted in an American declaration of war. He not only hoped thereby to disrupt American supplies to the British, and, thus, weaken their position, but also aimed to send a signal to the Japanese that Germany would support them fully. In retrospect, he grossly overestimated Japanese military abilities and underestimated those of the United States, but his decision, given his assessment of the situation, was certainly not irrational. Faced with a two-front war, he believed that the only way out of his dilemma was to help the Japanese preoccupy American power long enough to allow him to win the resources necessary to continue what was now a war of attrition from a solid material base. Nor, given Roosevelt's actions in the past year, did he assume that he was taking some sort of fateful step; after all, given its undeclared war in the Atlantic, the United States could be expected to declare war on Germany.[103]

Prestige and propaganda, as always, were also important for Hitler, who sought to use the declaration of war as a means by which to regain the initiative. In his speech to the Reichstag on 11 December, he stressed the endless series of provocations by the United States, until now unanswered, behind which he saw the "Satanic insidiousness" of the Jews, set on the destruction of Germany. He had at last, his patience exhausted, been forced to act. Now, however, with the support of the Japanese, he could take the gloves off and boost Germany's prospects in the Atlantic. The next day, in a speech to his Gauleiter, he stressed the inevitability of the confrontation with the United States but also revealed something of his strategic thinking. He indicated his firm intention of finishing off Russia in the coming year or at least its European portion. "Then it would perhaps be possible to reach a point of stabilization in Europe through a sort of half-peace" by which this German-dominated continent could exist as a self-sufficient fortress. Problems had arisen that had delayed the German timetable, he acknowledged, but once again he emphasized his vision of the east as Germany's India. He also stressed, as we have seen, his determination to solve the Jewish problem. "If the German people has again sacrificed 160,000 dead in the eastern campaign," he vowed, "the originators of this bloody conflict will have to pay for it with their own lives." To Hitler, the Jews had begun the war in Europe and had succeeded, despite his warnings, in making it a world war. They would now pay the price; indeed, from Hitler's point of view, they had to be eliminated to ensure that Germany was not again "stabbed in the back." On several occasions in 1943 and 1944, both Hitler and Himmler voiced their belief that only the timely "removal" of the Jews had enabled the Nazi regime to survive military reverses and the aerial bombardment of German cities. This time, unlike 1918, there would be no revolutionary unrest. The matter, Hitler said, could not "have been handled more humanely" since Germany was "in a fight to the death."[104]

Given his assumptions, then, Hitler's decision to declare war on the United States was not all that baffling, nor was it fraught with the deep significance claimed by many historians. It was not the decisive moment in taking Germany down the path of catastrophe: that had already happened. Hitler himself had acknowledged, if only fleetingly, German failure in grasping at world power status in his late November remark to the Danish foreign minister quoted above. Certainly, American entry into the war sealed Germany's fate, but not before it was able to recover, remarkably well, from the winter crisis that threatened to destroy the Ostheer and achieve amazing victories in 1942. Nor was Hitler's analysis fundamentally incorrect, for the United States was forced to commit significant resources in the Pacific in 1942, despite Roosevelt's "Europe first" approach, and not until 1944 was it able to bring to bear substantial ground forces in Europe. Germany had gained a year to win the Lebensraum necessary to compete with the United States and came amazingly close to achieving some sort of triumph over the Soviet Union. Not until the end of 1942, with the Battle of Stalingrad and the Anglo-American invasion of North Africa, did Hitler's gamble finally, definitively, fail. Even then, as Churchill remarked, it was not the beginning of the end, but only the end of the beginning. The war had a long way to go, and, despite his admission that he had no idea how to defeat the United States, Hitler hoped that some sort of victory over the Soviet Union in 1942, combined with a Japanese stalemating of the Americans in the Pacific, might yet retrieve the situation. Unlike the year before, however, Germany had clearly lost its freedom of action and could no longer depend on its own resources for victory. Hitler's worst fear had proved correct: time was against him.[105]

The six months between June and December 1941 had proved crucial in determining the fate of the Third Reich. In attacking the Soviet Union, in seeking to realize his ideological vision, Hitler gambled that

Germany could remedy its strategic dilemma in a quick campaign that would elevate it to world power status and leave it in control of a continental imperium. In so doing, he also set in motion all the aspects of his war of annihilation: the extermination of the Jews, the starvation and murder of the Soviet civilian population, the homicidal treatment of prisoners of war and partisans, and the colonial exploitation of the conquered territories. Military reverses at the end of the year meant that it was likely that he could not now win the war in the way he originally envisioned, but the change of fortune was not so great that he had to abandon the murderous projects already begun. Although his gamble would ultimately fail, the number of his victims would also soar over the next few years.

5

Reckoning

When the Soviet counteroffensive came on the night of 5–6 December, it could not have been better timed. German troops, having passed the culmination point, were overextended, mentally and physically exhausted, without supplies or winter equipment, and with dangerously vulnerable supply lines. No preparations for the defense had been made, nor could any positions now be built, for both manpower and construction materials were lacking. The Wehrmacht had thrown the last available men into the attack, struggling on largely out of fear of the alternative. As Bock stressed in a telephone call to Jodl on 3 December, "If the attack is called off then going over to the defensive will be very difficult. This thought and the possible consequences of going over to the defensive with our weak forces have . . . contributed to my sticking with this attack so far." Two days later, however, Bock admitted that the offensive strength of his forces was shot. The unbearable cold (temperatures had plunged to –36°F on 5 December) not only exhausted his troops but also left German tanks inoperable. Assessing the reasons for the German failure, Bock cited the autumn muddy period that paralyzed movement and robbed him of the ability to exploit the victory at Vyazma as well as the failure of the railroad system. Significantly, he also acknowledged that the Germans had underestimated Soviet reserves of manpower and materiel. The enemy, he marveled, had ruthlessly mobilized so that the Red Army actually had twenty-four more divisions now than in mid-November. The headlong pursuit of the Russians had been justified as long as the OKH believed that the enemy was fighting with the last of his forces; now, Bock noted accusingly, this had proved a grave mistake that placed his army group in serious danger. In this serious situation, however, the Germans comforted themselves with the belief that the Russians could not launch a major attack.[1]

German intelligence had, in fact, noted at the end of November a buildup of strong, new Russian forces behind the front but believed that they could not mount an immediate, serious counteroffensive. By then, however, Soviet counterattacks designed to achieve local success as well as hold German troops in place had already begun at the far ends of the front, at Tikhvin in the north and Rostov in the south. At the same time, preparations for a far more ambitious attack near Moscow had been completed. The Soviets had begun raising new divisions as early as October, while, in November, troops from Siberia, the Far East, the Volga area, and the Caucasus had been moved into the Moscow region. The true extent of Soviet manpower reserves would have shocked Bock, had he known, for, instead of the twenty-four new divisions he thought he faced, the Russians had formed thirty-three rifle divisions, seven cavalry divisions, thirty rifle brigades, and two tank brigades. These troops were admittedly badly trained, poorly equipped, inexperienced in combat, and led by officers with little training or experience, but they were there, at a time when just the appearance of new enemy formations had been enough to panic the depleted German forces. Despite their astounding losses, the Soviets managed to assemble slightly more than a million men, with more than seven hundred tanks and thirteen hundred aircraft for the operation; actual Soviet combat strength opposite Army Group Center was now greater than it had been when Operation Typhoon began in October. The time was right, Zhukov stressed to Stalin on 29 November, for German strength was sapped. The Soviet dictator agreed and sanctioned the attack. Ironically, in the first two days of December, it appeared as if the Soviet action might have come too late. To the surprise of the Germans as much as the Soviets, units of the Fourth Army broke through the Russian defense line south of the Smolensk-Moscow highway, while elements of Guderian's Second Panzer Army made headway around Tula. By the third, however, declining strength, stiffening resistance, and the cold forced Bock to call off the attack.[2]

The Soviets having brought the Germans to a standstill, the time had come for them to go over to the counteroffensive, an action that resulted, over the next few months, in a vicious dogfight as both sides struggled in the shadow of the events of 1812. The initial Soviet intent was modest: to force the enemy away from Moscow in order to eliminate the immediate threat to the capital. The Soviet plan originally aimed not at the large-scale encirclement and destruction of German forces but merely at biting off the Third and Fourth Panzergruppen as well as the Second Panzer Army to the south. The point of main effort was in the north, where German forces had penetrated closest to the city, with the objective of relieving pressure on the Moscow-Volga Canal and driving toward Klin. While the central sector was supposed to contain German troops and prevent their deployment elsewhere, a stronger southern wing was to rupture the link between the Second Panzer Army and the Second Army and thrust deep into the rear of the former, threatening it with encirclement. Still, the Soviets hoped merely to push the Germans back some thirty miles in the north and sixty miles in the south. Armed with good intelligence indicating a lack of supplies and instances of panic among German troops, Zhukov believed the enemy to be exhausted and likely to be caught off balance, but he was unwilling to risk anything more ambitious in view of the enfeebled state of his own men.[3]

Although most of the Soviet troops were untried in battle, they were at least fresh and warmly dressed as they launched their attack in bitter cold on the morning of 5 December. That night the temperature had again plunged, so, when reports of enemy action came in, the Germans discovered, to their distress, that tanks failed to start, machine guns and artillery would not fire because lubricants and oil had congealed in their recoil mechanisms, and many men suffered from frostbite. The assault, led by shock armies heavy in armor, motorized vehicles, and automatic weapons, succeeded in breaking through German lines, but both it and attacks over the next two days in the center and south failed to meet Soviet expectations. The pace of the advance was disappointingly slow as Red Army commanders still lacked experience in executing offensive operations. As a result, time and again they would attack German positions frontally rather than bypassing points of resistance to drive deep into the enemy flank and rear. Still, Russian successes raised immediate concerns since German efforts to shift troops to stem the tide were hampered by lack of fuel, equipment breakdowns, icy roads, massive snowdrifts that blocked rail lines, and the general exhaustion of the troops. Gradually, the many local penetrations and the serious damage done to some German divisions had a cumulative impact that allowed Soviet forces to advance deep into the rear and threaten supply lines.[4]

Although front commanders sent increasingly panicked messages, Hitler and the OKH were slow to recognize the brewing disaster. In a detailed discussion of the military situation with Halder on the sixth, Hitler dismissed German and enemy casualty figures as not reflective of the true fighting strength of the two armies. Nor did the Führer entertain any notion of abandoning territory to shorten the line and, thus, free up troops. Instead, his thoughts had turned already to planning for the spring offensive. Brauchitsch, amazingly enough, even issued orders to Army Group Center that, "after the conclusion of the operation against Moscow," it was to organize itself so as to turn away the Russian attacks directed at its center and flanks. Halder was only slightly less deluded; he took note of Soviet actions but regarded them as merely of limited tactical importance.[5]

By the eighth, however, enemy pressure on the left flank of Army Group Center had built to such an extent that Bock felt compelled to shake the OKH out of its illusions. Not least, he was influenced by dire warnings from the Third Panzergruppe that its forces were no longer operational as well as a bleak telephone call from the usually confident Guderian, who warned of a growing "crisis of confidence." Bock now presented his quandary to Halder in stark terms. If he was to have any chance of holding the line, he needed immediate replacements and supplies, which were not likely to arrive in time. If, on the other hand, he attempted a withdrawal, the deep snow, shortage of fuel, and lack of tractors to pull the heavy weapons meant that an enormous loss of equipment and supplies was unavoidable. His troops would, thus, arrive at unprepared defensive positions with no heavy weapons with which to halt the Russian advance. Bock had posed a devil's dilemma: German troops could fight where they were, and likely be destroyed, or carry out a large-scale withdrawal, with the threat that any retreat might turn into a rout. Halder attempted to reassure him by dismissing the attacking Russian units as only rear elements and untrained recruits, adding, "I presume that [the Russian counterattacks] will continue until the middle or end of the month and then things will quiet down." To that Bock replied bitterly, "By then, the Army Group will be kaputt." Aghast, Halder tersely rejoined, "The German soldier does not go kaputt."[6]

Despite Halder's bravado, things looked rather different at the front. Even as Bock snatched all available men from logistics, signals, and headquarters units and transferred rear security divisions to the front, the Germans proved unable either to halt the breakthroughs or to eliminate the growing gaps in their lines. By the tenth, a near-complete breakdown of the transportation system led to a rations crisis, with virtually no supplies getting through to the troops. On the thirteenth, the Sixth Panzer Division reported that it had only 350 riflemen and no tanks, while, three days later, the Seventh Panzer was left with only 200 men, ten fighting vehicles, and no heavy tanks: the last one had broken down and been blown up. Continuous fighting had brought the Landsers to the brink of physical and mental collapse. Morale suffered as confidence in the higher command faltered, a private complaining on 6 December, "My God, what is this Russia going to do to us all? Our superiors must

. . . listen to us, otherwise, in this state, we are going to go under." Sacrifices were not unexpected, noted another, "but when nothing of use" resulted, "then that is something to think about." Discipline and order mingled with panic and unalloyed fear at the prospect of being captured by the Russians. A Third Panzergruppe report illuminated well the dramatic state of impending collapse: "Discipline is breaking down. More and more soldiers are heading west on foot without weapons, leading a calf on a rope or pulling a sled loaded with potatoes. The road is under constant air attack. Those killed by bombs are no longer being buried. All the hangers on . . . are pouring back to the rear in full flight." A system of strongpoints slowed the Russian advance but left individual Landsers with a sense of isolation and abandonment. As Harald Henry despaired, "I seem to be the last single survivor from the whole company."[7]

Although in the north the Ninth Army and the Fourth Panzergruppe had managed, at the cost of very high casualties, to slow the Russian advance, to the south the enemy attack launched on 6 December had been more successful. By the seventh, the Soviets had taken Mikhailov, where panic erupted among German troops, and the next day punched through German lines. With his army under attack from three sides, Guderian began to pull his units back from Tula in order to prevent encirclement and with hopes of forming a coherent defense. Attempts to close the widening gap in his lines failed for lack of troops, vehicle breakdowns, the numbing cold, and deep snow that hindered all movement. By the tenth, the gap stretched to twelve miles; in desperation, Bock ordered the First SS Brigade, the 221st Security Division, and two police battalions withdrawn from the rear area and sent to the front. Guderian, with no more than forty panzers in his whole army, pleaded with Bock for more troops, but the latter had none to give. Hitler had forbidden the dispatch of any intact divisions to the front; only men returning from leave and convalescent battalions could be expected. After all, he told Schmundt, his military adjutant, he "could not send everything out into the winter just because Army Group Center had a few gaps in its front." At the same time, a serious crisis faced the Second Army as Soviet forces broke through and drove in the direction of Livny. The Germans' attempt to seal the breach by attacking the Russian flanks failed, raising the worrisome possibility of a deep operational breakthrough toward Kursk and Orel that would cut their supply and retreat routes as well as those of the Second Panzer Army to the north. As a last resort, the divisional headquarters and two reinforced regiments from two infantry divisions in Army Group South were sent to the Second Army, but they would not arrive before the thirteenth or fourteenth.[8]

Only on the twelfth, with the entire front in danger of disintegrating, did Halder begin to realize the seriousness of the situation. When, in reply to yet another of Bock's reports about the untenable situation at the front, he persisted in doubting that the enemy could build on his success, he was shocked by Bock's response: "Of course they can! We cannot stop our troops running away as soon as they see a Russian tank!" Finally shaken to reality, Halder admitted that Germany faced "the most serious situation of the two [world] wars." It was, he conceded, a question of the very existence of the Ostheer. With little hope that the army group could hold out, Bock emphasized the next day to Brauchitsch that key decisions had to be made that went beyond the military and that only the Führer could make.[9]

Despite the alarming reports from the front, Hitler had steadfastly resisted making a decision. In part, this resulted from his reluctance to give up his offensive plans for 1942; in part, it reflected the limits he faced since he could hardly afford a large-scale call-up of workers owing to the precarious situation of the labor market. He was also notoriously mistrustful of army reports and in any case evidently had not seen Bock's evaluation of the situation. Not until the fourteenth, when Schmundt confirmed Brauchitsch's report on the catastrophic state of affairs at the front, that, indeed, he saw no way of "getting the army out of this difficult situation," did Hitler realize that he had to act immediately if Army Group Center was to be saved. He agreed to a straightening of the front at Klin and Kalinin and the withdrawal of Guderian's forces in the south, but no other retreats were to be made until rear defense lines had been prepared. After all, he stressed, only in a few places had there been deep penetrations. That same night, he ordered General Fromm, the commander of the Replacement Army, to mobilize what units he could— barely four divisions—and dispatch them to the front. The next day, he ordered that five divisions be sent from Western Europe, although, in order to expedite their movement, only "rifle bearers" were to be gathered and sent, while an additional four divisions would be made available from forces in the Balkans. At the same time, the home front was to be scoured for men who could be sent east for construction tasks. Since these transfers would take time, however, Hitler could see no alternative at the present but to hold the line and not retreat.[10]

With the German command system at odds—the generals continued to advocate retreat, while Hitler insisted that such a move made no sense if, at the end of it, the troops found themselves in the same situation but without heavy weapons and artillery—the Führer on 16 December asserted control. Having heard that day from both Bock and Guderian that their forces faced destruction without the speedy arrival of replacements and supplies, Hitler that night made a decision based largely on Bock's earlier arguments, which, to the Führer, justified the "great gamble" of risking the loss of the army group: without prepared positions, and having abandoned most of their equipment, any withdrawal might well turn into a panicked rout. Hitler, who prided himself on his ability both to master and to profit from a crisis, now set out to resolve this one. That night, he issued his controversial *Haltebefehl* (order to hold out), which allowed Army Group North to withdraw to the Volkhov but then ordered "the front to be defended down to the last man." He thus hoped to overcome the danger with an iron will and by seeing to the rapid transfer of all available units to the east. In a step toward the further Nazification of the army, he also demanded: "The commanders-in-chief, commanders, and officers are to take personal charge of forcing the troops into their positions to put up fanatical resistance. . . . Only with this style of leadership can the time required to bring up the reinforcements . . . be gained." Since Hitler would now take all decisions personally, any withdrawal would require his approval, which meant a near-complete loss of autonomy for front commanders. In effect, he assumed direct command of the army itself. His stand-and-fight order, which at least provided clarity and removed the uncertainties of the situation, also stripped his generals of the flexibility and command initiative that had been the key to German operational success.[11]

Although, in retrospect, this decision has been much criticized by historians, at the time it likely seemed the only possible course of action. Withdrawal meant losing the heavy weapons and would not have halted the Russians in any case, while Bock himself worried about the very real possibility that, once begun, a retreat would turn into a disaster of Napoleonic proportions. Nor was a mobile defense a serious alternative, given the lack of vehicles, tanks, fuel, supplies, and the difficulty of movement on the snow-covered roads. As Bock and his army commanders had repeatedly pointed out, the only feasible solution lay in holding their positions and rushing reserves to fill the gaps. Hitler, then, was largely acceding to the advice of his generals, but with a new twist: not only had he taken command initiative away from them, but the order to stand fast would now be carried out in a rigid and uncompromising manner that meant the needless death of many Landsers. In the event, Hitler's intent to hold out up front until reinforcements arrived failed, not because it was inherently unreasonable, but as a result of the deficient German transportation system.[12]

The immediate result of the stand-and-fight decision was the removal of both Brauchitsch and Bock, neither of whom appeared to Hitler fit to deal with the crisis. More consequential, since virtually all regarded Brauchitsch as irrelevant and no more than a messenger boy, was the fact of Hitler's assumption on the nineteenth of formal command of the army. Although Halder initially believed that he might profit from the new situation, he was quickly left in no doubt that the OKH would be little more than a transmission service for Hitler's wishes. On the twentieth, the Führer gave orders to Halder on how the war in the east should be conducted, emphasizing again that "a fanatical will to fight" had to be instilled in the troops by "all, even the most severe, means." Every soldier, even those in support services, was to "defend himself where he is." Otherwise, he noted, "a crisis of confidence in the leadership threatens to develop from every retreat." Significantly, in order to retain a sense of assertive will and deny the enemy anything of value, the most brutal scorched earth policy was to accompany any evacuation of territory: "All abandoned farms were to be burned to the ground; prisoners and inhabitants were to be ruthlessly stripped of their winter clothing." "There was," he declared, "no reason that the troops should lose their sense of superiority . . . over this enemy."[13]

That same day, in a remarkable five-hour meeting, Hitler rebuffed efforts by Guderian, who had flown to Führer Headquarters to get him to rescind the rigid Haltebefehl, dismissing his commander's concerns as exaggerated since he, too, had endured enemy break-ins in World War I. When Guderian indicated his intention to retreat, Hitler said that the troops should dig in where they stood. When the panzer commander pointed out that the earth was frozen to a depth of five feet, the Führer retorted that they would have to blast holes with howitzers, as was done in Flanders during the earlier war. To Guderian's observation that the loss of life would be enormous, Hitler pointed to the sacrifices made by Frederick the Great's soldiers. None wanted to die, Hitler noted, but like the great king, he stressed, he had the right to demand sacrifices from his troops. Guderian, he thought, was too close to the suffering of his men. "You are seeing events at too close a range," he told the panzer commander. "You should stand back more. Believe me, things appear clearer when examined at longer range." If Guderian had hoped to convince the Führer of the reality of the situation at the front, he failed dismally, for, in a strongly worded directive to Army Group Center, Hitler merely reaffirmed his order forbidding withdrawals.[14]

While Hitler and the German commanders were debating what to do in response to the crisis facing them, the Soviets, too, were pondering the situation. Zhukov's original idea had been to gain space in front of Moscow by driving back the German armored spearheads, something that the Soviets had clearly accomplished. Although they had failed to destroy the bulk of the panzer forces, the near-total collapse of Army Group Center raised the possibility of an envelopment, but, since the Russians had planned for only a shallow operation, their initial momentum was petering out even as Hitler was making the decision to stand and fight. For the second phase of the counteroffensive, Zhukov still thought conservatively, hoping to drive the Germans back some 150 miles to the line just east of Smolensk from which Operation Typhoon had begun. Stalin and the Stavka, however, now filled with militant enthusiasm, were beginning to think in more ambitious terms—the complete encirclement of Army Group Center—but allowed Zhukov to proceed with his new round of attacks, which resumed on 18 December.[15]

By now, the appearance of a seemingly endless supply of enemy troops able to endure the harsh cold and supplied with clearly superior weapons began to frighten the German troops, as if they were fighting a superhuman force. Halder tried to contain what he termed "a numbers psychosis" by urging German intelligence to stress the often low quality of the new Soviet troops rather than their absolute number, but, to Landsers on the sharp end, this was scant comfort. With little winter clothing, short of food, fuel, and ammunition, bedeviled by equipment breakdowns and malfunctions in the awful cold, confronted with a warmly dressed opponent whose tanks, with their compressed-air starters and wide tracks, could not only run but also traverse the deep snow, many German soldiers were, little wonder, spooked by even the appearance of Russian troops. Nothing so demoralized the Landsers as the sight of their antitank shells bouncing off the thick armor of the Russian T-34s, but, in a bitter irony, even the antidote to this superiority was denied them. In the fall, the Germans had tested a new, vastly more effective hollow-charge shell (*Rotkopf*) that could penetrate Soviet armor, but Hitler had them recalled in November for fear that they would fall into enemy hands, be imitated, and then used against German tanks. Not until 22 December, after much pleading by his army commanders, did he release the Rotkopf ammunition. By that time, a report of Army Group Center indicated, a mood of fear, a feeling of defenselessness, and a general unwillingness to attack had so undermined fighting efficiency that even the admittedly poor-quality Soviet troops could not be repulsed.[16]

The renewed Soviet attacks had, by the twentieth, forced the entire Second Panzer Army to retreat again, a move strenuously opposed by Bock's replacement, Kluge, who ordered Guderian to hold his line at all costs. Guderian, with the connivance of Bock, had grown accustomed to ignoring or evading orders with which he disagreed. But, with Kluge, that was to change. Even as he reported his suspicions to Halder that Guderian had lost his nerve and intended to retreat to the Oka, Kluge was confronted the next day with a Russian breakthrough of the Second Army in the area of Tim, which forced a withdrawal of the Forty-third Army Corps to the Oka. Although the withdrawal was approved by Hitler, Halder vehemently opposed the idea of disengagement, once again insisting, "If we hold out everywhere, everything will be over in fourteen days. The enemy cannot pursue these frontal attacks forever." By the twenty-second, however, the breakthrough at Tim had spread further westward, and, by the twenty-fourth, the commander of the Second Army, Schmidt, had been forced to withdraw from Livny, even though such an action had been forbidden by Hitler. At the same time, the Second Panzer Army argued that these withdrawals forced it to pull back as well and asked permission to retreat to the Oka. Although Halder tentatively agreed to this, the mood between Kluge and Guderian, already hostile, intensified when the latter refused the former's order to send the Fourth Panzer Division to Sukhinichi to hold this vital rail and road juncture against a Russian advance. Guderian, in fact, had given further orders for his units to withdraw, and, when, on Christmas Day, Kluge learned of this, he took Guderian to task, then demanded his ouster. Hitler complied, removing Guderian from his post and replacing him with General Schmidt.[17]

The removal of Guderian, however, did nothing to improve Kluge's position, for Russian advances so threatened the Second, Fourth, and Ninth Armies with envelopment that he informed Halder on 26 December of the necessity of withdrawing the entire army group. Halder countered with Hitler's warning that it would be impossible to hold out once the front started to move, but Kluge, surprisingly forceful, insisted that, with nothing to eat and no ammunition, his men could hardly be expected to fight, adding: "Whether the Führer likes it or not he will have to order a retreat. If supplies cannot be delivered, things will soon collapse. . . . The Führer will have to come down from cloud-cuckoo-land and . . . set his feet firmly on the ground." Hitler, however, refused to accede to Kluge's demand, telling him that "one day the Russians will no longer have the strength to attack," an assurance that did little to assuage Kluge since the number of German troops freezing to death exceeded the number of replacements. When, on the thirtieth, Kluge tried to make a case for retreat, Hitler accused him of wanting to "go right back to the Polish border." Unlike his front commanders, Hitler stressed, he had to see things with "cool reason." After all, he had experienced days of extended artillery fire in World War I and had continued to hold on. When, in exasperation, Kluge replied that this was a winter war in Russia, with physically and mentally exhausted troops facing temperatures far below zero, Hitler ended the discussion by saying, "If that is the case, then it means the end of the German Army."[18]

At dawn on New Year's Day, with temperatures hovering at –25°F and blanketed by waist-deep snow, with equipment inoperable, with tank and truck engines left idling so that vehicles that did not move still continued to consume precious fuel, and with the fate of Army Group Center hanging precariously on a few roads that could drift shut within hours, it was apparent to front commanders that, despite Hitler's latest ban on withdrawals, the lines could not be held much longer. By this time, according to OKH calculations, the Ostheer had lost over 830,000 men, or over 25 percent of its original strength, and, even if replacements could be found, weapons of all types were lacking. Even as Hitler stressed the need to hold out at all costs in order to buy time for the units being sent from the west, he seemed at last to have realized that he was dangerously close to losing his grip on the army group. The pullback of the Ninth Army against his will occasioned a wild outburst at OKH headquarters that the army command had been "parliamentarized" and that front commanders no longer had the courage "to make hard decisions." Still, as the Germans began to discern that the Soviets now intended to encircle Army Group Center, a certain clarity descended on their defensive measures. Efforts at holding out everywhere in order to buy time now gradually gave way to a priority on holding key road and rail junctions and protecting vital supply lines.[19]

The precipitating event seemed to be a breakthrough in the Fourth Panzer Army's front that threatened the Twentieth Army Corps with encirclement. Hoepner in vain requested permission on 6 January for these units to be withdrawn since the OKH still believed that the Russians were at the end of their strength and the situation would soon ease. By the eighth, with the supply route to the corps cut, Hoepner once again demanded that Kluge allow him to pull these units out of the developing trap. Kluge did not dare make a decision on his own and, thus, referred the request to Halder, who indicated that he would have to get a decision from Hitler. Frustrated, and tired of waiting, just after noon on the eighth Hoepner ordered the army corps to break out. That same night, Hitler relieved Hoepner of his command and ordered that he be dishonorably discharged from the army. This, however, did nothing to improve the situation at the front, for the Fourth Army now faced similar pressure and that same day demanded permission to withdraw in order to protect its main supply route. As one commander summarized the situation succinctly, "I cannot put a policeman behind every soldier." Faced with the inevitable, Hitler now relented and granted the request.[20]

To the south, both the Second Army and the Second Panzer Army had managed unexpectedly to stabilize their sectors, although a bulge of some fifty miles between Sukhinichi (encircled since 29 December) and Yukhnov separated the latter and the Fourth Army. While forces from the Second Panzer Army were to attack the Soviet flank near Sukhinichi, the task of the Fourth Army remained keeping the supply route from Roslavl to Medyn open. To the north, the Ninth Army was to cut off the enemy penetration west of Rzhev. Significantly, none of these orders any longer contained a demand that the front be held unconditionally and inflexibly. Hitler's effort to maintain the stand-fast doctrine was now hopelessly at odds with reality. Since the reserves from Germany that he had counted on had not arrived in sufficient strength, permission for a withdrawal of Army Group Center could no longer be avoided.[21]

The growing pressure on the German front that forced it to retire resulted from a change in Soviet plans that, ironically, ensured German survival. Stalin, emboldened by success in front of Moscow and in line with Soviet military doctrine, now judged the time right for a general offensive by the Red Army to crush the entire German eastern front, despite the fact that the Russians had paid dearly for their limited victory. Repeating Hitler's mistake of overestimating his own striking power, and underestimating enemy resistance, Stalin failed to listen to his front commanders, who warned that the Germans, desperate and fighting for their lives, were increasingly difficult to expel and that their own strength was rapidly waning. Nor did he heed Zhukov's advice that the Red Army lacked the forces to carry out such a broad offensive and would be better served by concentrating all available means at the point where the enemy was already withdrawing in order to achieve a complete success in that sector. Zhukov also failed to convince Stalin that the Germans had recovered from their initial crisis and were no longer "demoralized." Nonetheless, phase 3 of the counteroffensive opened on 7 January, when Stalin ordered the Red Army not only to encircle Army Group Center and cut off its supply and retreat routes, but also to raise the siege of Leningrad, clear the Crimea, and launch attacks in the south. These goals proved overly ambitious, given that Russian troops had been attacking continuously for a month and had not received sufficient replacements and supplies. Stalin, lured by the prospect of a grand counterstroke, thus dispersed his forces over too many objectives and frittered away a chance at a decisive triumph in much the same way the Germans had earlier. In the event, German armies not only would be spared encirclement but also would be able to isolate and destroy over-extended Soviet units.[22]

In the central sector, forces of the Kalinin, West, and Bryansk Fronts, attacking from Rzhev in the north and Sukhinichi in the south, hoped to trap German armies in an envelopment that would close on the main Moscow highway at Vyazma. The deep Russian breakthrough at Rzhev and heavy attacks on the Third and Fourth Panzer Armies opened a gap that the Germans found impossible to close—and that finally impressed on Hitler that it was only a matter of time before the entire army group front collapsed. Under pressure from events, therefore, on 15 January, Hitler rescinded his Haltebefehl and ordered Army Group Center to withdraw the Fourth Army and the two northern armies to a line east of Yukhnov, Gzhatsk, and Zubtsov and north of Rzhev that approximated the original Typhoon starting point the previous October. He insisted that this line be held at all costs while demanding that the gap west of Rzhev be closed, that the Fourth Army and the Second Panzer Army close the gap north of Medyn, that the Fourth Army keep the vital supply route between Roslavl and Yukhnov open, and that the Second Panzer Army relieve Sukhinichi. Aware of the possible ramifications of his first order to "pull back a major sector of the front," Hitler insisted it be implemented in such a way that "the troops' feeling of superiority over the enemy and their fanatic will to do him the greatest possible damage must prevail." Although Halder, too, worried about the psychological ramifications of the withdrawal on the troops, shortening the front freed units for counterattacks that sealed the worst gaps.[23]

In heavy fighting over the next two weeks, German troops managed to stabilize the situation in Army Group Center. By late January, the Ninth Army, now commanded by the energetic and able General Walter Model, had managed not only to close the gap at Rzhev but also to cut off elements of the Soviet Twenty-ninth Army that had broken through to the south as well as part of the Thirty-third Army near Vyazma. On the northernmost sector of the central front, attacks by the Fourth Shock Army south of Toropets, conducted through dense forests over trackless terrain with no flank support, in cold that reached –40°F, with few supplies and little intelligence on the enemy, posed no threat and dwindled to little more than localized fighting. To its right, on the Volkhov River in the sector of Army Group North, the Second Shock Army under General A. A. Vlasov penetrated the rear of the German Eighteenth Army but had its supply line cut and became isolated in the forest and marsh. It eventually capitulated in June. On the southern end of the army group's sector, the Twenty-fourth Panzer Corps, given the task of breaking the enemy encirclement at Sukhinichi, caught the Soviets by surprise with its attack on 18 January and by the twenty-first had seized the town, giving Hitler hope that it could advance further to the east and cut off enemy forces along the supply route between Roslavl and Yukhnov. Because of heavy losses, temperatures that had now fallen to −44°F, and strong Soviet counterattacks on their flanks, the Germans abandoned the town on the twenty-eighth, but their action had forced Stalin to dispatch troops from the north, further dissipating his strength. The ragtag German forces, as the Soviets discovered to their dismay, could still strike back savagely.[24]

Even though the situation of the Fourth Army remained tenuous and Soviet partisans continued to threaten German supply lines, by the end of January both sides were spent. In some Soviet units, as few as ten men remained in companies and seventy in battalions, while artillery shells were being rationed to one or two shots per day per gun. As had the earlier German offensive, the Russian counterattack had ground to a standstill because of a shortage of men and materiel. The situation had so improved, in fact, that in mid-February Hitler could assure his army group commanders that the threat of a repeat of 1812 had been eliminated. Unfinished business remained, however, since in February German front maps showed a crazy quilt of German units (in blue) intermingled with Soviet forces (in red) in wild contortions, especially in the center, where German and Soviet salients jutted crazily to the east and west. In some sectors, front lines could not be drawn at all, while, in others, the Germans simply marked large areas *partisans*. Eyeing this convoluted front, with the need to shorten the line to conserve men as well as eliminate the peril to their supply routes, the Germans took action to repair the front that was self-evident.[25]

Soviet forces, too, were as dangerously snarled as the Germans, with some units trapped behind enemy lines, although Stalin did not view the situation pessimistically, instead seeing in it the possibility of inflicting further damaging blows on a reeling foe. Both sides were aware, moreover, that the spring *rasputitsa*, a much more elemental force than that in the autumn, would begin in late March. The bitter cold of the Russian winter, having frozen the earth to a depth of six or seven feet, would lock in much of the previous fall's rain. Several feet of snow and ice would then accumulate on top of the frozen surface. The spring thaw, however, worked from the top down, so that the melting of the winter snowfall resulted in large lakes of water sitting on top of the still-frozen ground. As the subsoil began gradually to thaw, the ground became sodden to a depth of several feet, creating a progressively deepening layer of watery mud. In the generally flat terrain, the water had no place to drain until the ground completely thawed. The entire process might last as long as two months, and, for several weeks, the mud would be so deep that any movement on unpaved roads, except by Russian *panje* wagons, with their high wheels and light weight, would be impossible.[26]

As a result, both sides, locked in a deadly embrace, hammered away with increasingly ineffective body blows that served only to exhaust their remaining strength. The Stavka sought to mount offensives on either side of the central sector, with the hope of relieving the siege of Leningrad, further threatening German lines of communication, and disrupting any enemy buildup to the southwest of Moscow, which the Russians had incorrectly identified as the likely area for the main German advance in the summer. The Soviets achieved most success in the north, where they encircled considerable German forces around Kholm and Demyansk. Unlike the earlier pocket at Sukhinichi, the Germans refused to abandon Kholm and Demyansk; instead, the Luftwaffe mounted a major operation to supply the pockets by air. By holding on to these areas, not only did the Germans retain key strategic positions, but, if their forces at Demyansk and Rzhev could join hands, they would also trap many Soviet divisions in the Toropets salient. In the event, however, the Germans lacked sufficient force to unite the two pockets. Instead, they mounted a major effort to relieve Demyansk, driving a thin corridor to the pocket in early March. Ironically, the relief column was commanded by General Walter von Seydlitz, who would later be captured at Stalingrad and emerge as a key figure in a Soviet-sponsored anti-Nazi movement. Indeed, the relief of Demyansk and Kholm (achieved on 1 May) had a direct impact on the later disaster on the Volga since the successful resupply of the smaller pockets encouraged Hitler in the belief that the operation could be repeated on a much larger scale at Stalingrad.[27]

To the northwest of Demyansk, the Russians planned an ambitious operation in conjunction with the Volkhov Front that aimed at nothing less than cutting the lines of communication of Army Group North and raising the siege of Leningrad. Despite some success in recapturing mostly swamps and forests of little military value, the Soviets never seriously threatened the position of the army group, despite their numerical superiority. As elsewhere across the front, after an initial advance, the fighting along the Volkhov degenerated into a confusing series of battles with isolated forces of exhausted men, literally bogged down in the woods and swamps, trying to encircle each other. Eventually, as noted above, the Second Shock Army under Vlasov found itself encircled following sharp German counterattacks and was forced to surrender in late

June. Despite the urgency attached by Moscow to the Leningrad operation, it failed to achieve anything of significance, a failure that meant a starvation death for hundreds of thousands of Leningraders, for the worst period of the nine-hundred-day siege was the three months from January to March 1942. Subjected to constant artillery bombardment, and cut off from fuel and food supplies, with rations that guaranteed only death by famine, an estimated 1 million civilians starved to death in the city during the course of the war, the great majority in the first months of 1942. The Soviets having failed, for a variety of reasons, to evacuate enough of the civilian inhabitants of the city, the result was the worst single demographic disaster of the war. But, as we have seen from his orders, even the surrender of Leningrad would not have averted a catastrophe, for Hitler had no intention of feeding the inhabitants in any case. The logic of a racial war of annihilation precluded such action.[28]

Although Hitler's blitzkrieg failed in front of Moscow, Stalin's effort to force a decisive result before the spring *rasputitsa* miscarried as well. Zhukov, in his memoirs, put it best when he observed bitterly, "If you consider our losses and what results were achieved, it will be clear that it was a Pyrrhic victory." The most optimistic aim, the destruction of Army Group Center, had not been achieved, nor had the more pragmatic goal of Zhukov, to drive the line back to the starting point of Operation Typhoon been satisfactorily attained. Red Army losses had been staggering, the central Rzhev-Vyazma operation alone costing the Soviets some 272,000 lives. Overall, in the roughly four months of fighting between December and March, Zhukov's West Front lost 250,000 men and Konev's Kalinin Front some 150,000, while the battles around Demyansk cost the Soviets another 89,000 men. Red Army losses across the entire eastern front totaled 620,000 from January to March, compared with roughly 136,000 German deaths in the same period. Soviet mobility and operational effectiveness, too, were limited by the deep snow, bitter cold, and difficulties in moving supplies. Nor did the Red Army possess enough mechanized forces to block roads and railways permanently or take the villages that the Germans had fortified, Zhukov complaining that it was impossible to encircle without tanks. The Stavka had made the same mistakes as the Germans; not only had it assumed that the enemy was exhausted and shattered, but it had also attacked everywhere and, thus, dispersed its own limited forces. The Germans had mounted a remarkably successful defense, which the quality of the Landser had made possible, but the Soviets' failure to concentrate their resources had, ultimately, allowed the Wehrmacht to escape a disaster.

Stalin's strategy of wearing down the Germans did not work; in return for huge losses, the Soviets regained little territory and now faced the task of again rebuilding their weakened forces.[29]

The Germans, however, were powerless to take advantage of the Russian predicament, for, even though Hitler grasped the seed of a victory in the overextended enemy positions, he had nothing left to employ. Despite the Führer's promises, in December and January Army Group Center received a total of only 60,000 replacements but in the same two months suffered nearly 250,000 casualties. For the December–March period, the army group received 180,000 troops but suffered almost 437,000 casualties. Thus, even though the monthly death totals that resulted from Hitler's Haltebefehl and subsequent operations were not out of line with preceding months, relatively they were far worse since they came from ranks already depleted by the earlier bloodletting and could not be offset with replacements, there being no more reserves. By the end of January, there had been over 900,000 casualties in the Ostheer as a whole, a figure that the Germans could not remotely make good. The consequences were readily apparent to anyone in the ranks: Heinrici reported that, in the Ninth Army, each battalion was down to about seventy men, five light machine guns, and two heavy machine guns. In December 1941, an additional 282,300 conscripts entered the army, but they needed training before they could be employed, and, in any case, two-thirds had come from the armaments industry. These vital war workers proved impossible to replace in the short term with Russian prisoners of war since German policy had depleted their ranks through mass starvation and epidemic diseases. The shortage of labor was made even more acute because of the need now to step up armaments production considerably.[30]

Nor, had replacements been available, could they have been equipped with weapons. German materiel losses in Operation Barbarossa had been staggering, with the bulk of armaments produced in 1941 lost on the battlefields of the east. In many areas, the Wehrmacht was reduced to the level of armaments of 1940 or even September 1939. In the first three weeks of December alone, 424 tanks had been lost, while, in the first ten days of January, another 242 were destroyed. In just two months, December and January, the Ostheer lost a total of 974 tanks and armored assault vehicles, with the result that total losses on the eastern front to the end of January rose to 4,241. During the same period, only 873 tanks had been delivered to the Ostfront; indeed, between June 1941 and January 1942, only 2,842 tanks and assault guns had been manufactured in Germany. By the end of March 1942, the sixteen panzer divisions had only 140 operational tanks. In late February, the Second Panzer Army counted only forty-five combat-ready tanks, with another forty-four undergoing repair. Enormous losses in motorcycles, trucks, and motor vehicles, some 25 percent of the original strength, as well as horses severely restricted the mobility of the Ostheer, a bloodletting from which the most mobile forces never recovered. In addition, fuel and ammunition supplies were virtually exhausted. Accentuating the problem, the units of Army Group South, which would conduct the main German attack in 1942, could be brought up to 85 percent of their authorized equipment levels only by stripping Army Groups Center and North, further reducing their limited operational abilities.[31]

Losses in artillery and mortars were also severe, with the lost guns not replaced. In December, for example, although 452 light field howitzers and 200 heavy field howitzers were lost, only 21 and 10 new models, respectively, were produced. In January, production of light howitzers stopped altogether. In all this, of course, lay a deeper problem: German industry could not produce enough to offset the material losses, nor could much of what was produced be supplied to the troops because of transportation deficiencies. By the end of March 1942, of the 162 divisions employed on the eastern front, only eight were fully operational, three needed only minor rest and resupply, and forty-seven were limited in their ability to attack, while the bulk of the units could be used only in defense. Arguably, in the early spring of 1942, the military strength of the Wehrmacht was not only lower than a year previously but also lower than when the war had begun. Only in mid-December 1941 had Hitler ordered an increase in war production and a reorientation in favor of the army. He also directed that armaments production be rationalized on mass production principles while, in a blow to the military, putting civilian industrialists in charge of the war economy. Still, these changes would take time, so he faced the very real prospect that his objectives could no longer be attained by a Wehrmacht torn apart by the savage fighting in Russia, especially since his opponent could rely on a steady stream of Lend-Lease supplies from his allies.[32]

Although Hitler could claim, and some of his generals would reluctantly concede, that his iron will and ruthless determination had prevented Germany from suffering the fate of Napoléon, his tactic had worked as much because of Soviet mistakes as because of German strengths. When attempted again the following winter, it would fail disastrously. Further, despite the gloating over his genius, Hitler had no idea how or even whether Germany could still win the war. Jodl, in fact, asserted after the war that as early as spring 1942 the Führer realized that the war was lost and there could be no victory. The crisis had taken a toll on him mentally and physically. Goebbels was shocked by his appearance in late March and especially by his admission that at times he doubted whether it was possible to win the war. Still, as relative calm returned to the front during the period of *rasputitsa*, Hitler's confidence began to return. The Japanese entry into the war, he insisted, had been a key turning point, although he lamented that the Japanese advance meant a loss for the "white race." The fall of Singapore affirmed his belief that the Japanese would play their assigned strategic role, but his pleasure was tinged with regret that the British had not thrown in their lot with a German-dominated Europe against the United States. Despite the massive losses of the Barbarossa campaign and the near disaster of the winter, he looked expectantly to the approaching summer offensive. Having survived the onslaught of the "Bolshevik hordes" as well as the worst winter in a century and a half, Hitler was speaking again of ultimate victory. After all, as Goebbels exulted, "Troops who can cope with such a winter are unbeatable." The winter crisis overcome, Hitler spent little time reassessing his strategy, which had been flawed from the beginning, or seeking alternative ways to end the war. The Russians, too, had suffered grievously during the winter: it was imperative that this wounded but still dangerous enemy be destroyed as soon as possible. For a man obsessed with the problem of time, it was, he knew, Germany's last chance to secure its hegemony on the Continent before America's massive resources tipped the balance irretrievably against the Reich.[33]

As a project of national and social renovation based on war, the invasion of the Soviet Union had from the beginning posed the existential question of survival or annihilation. The characteristic dynamism of Nazi policy, its sense of urgency, was based as much on a notion of must do as on one of can do. This insistent desire to prevent the destruction they imagined their enemies were about to visit on them produced in the Nazis a feeling of liberation from conventional morality and a willingness to use maximum violence. Not surprisingly, then, despite, or perhaps because of, the military crisis in the winter of 1941–1942, the process of radicalization of Nazi racial policy accelerated. With the growing recognition that Germany now faced a long war, top Nazi leaders drew certain conclusions: the labor problem had to be solved and armaments production increased; the food situation had to be stabilized; any unrest at home had to be stemmed by moving against "privilege"; and, above all, the underlying source of all such discontent, the Jews, had to be eliminated immediately. "It must be done quickly," Hitler told

Himmler in late January 1942. "The Jew must be ousted from Europe. . . . He incites everywhere. . . . I see only one thing: total extermination. . . . Why should I look at a Jew any differently from a Russian prisoner. . . ? Why did the Jews start this war?" In mid-February, Goebbels, always sensitive to the Führer's mood, recorded Hitler's mounting fury and decision "to do away ruthlessly with the Jews in Europe": "The Jews have deserved the catastrophe that they are now experiencing. We must accelerate this process with cold determination." This "clear-cut anti-Jewish position" was also conveyed, Goebbels gloated, to a number of top army officers.[34]

Nor did Hitler's apocalyptic vision wane as the situation at the front stabilized. In a late February gathering of the "Old Fighters" in Munich, Hitler promised "the elimination of these [Jewish] parasites," a vow that was hardly meant to be kept secret since the next day many German newspapers headlined the speech, "The Jew will be exterminated." That this threat had now materialized as a comprehensive process of destruction was evident to Goebbels in late March when he recorded with some trepidation in his diary:

> Starting with Lublin [the first ghetto to be liquidated], the Jews are now being deported from the General Government to the East. The procedure used is quite barbaric and should not be described in any further detail. Not much remains of the Jews themselves. . . . The Jews are being subjected to a sentence that is barbaric, but they have fully deserved it. The prophecy that the Führer made . . . starts to come true in the most terrible way. In these things no sentimentality should be allowed. If we didn't defend ourselves, the Jews would exterminate us. . . . Thank God, during the war we now have a range of possibilities that we couldn't use in peacetime.

This thundering crescendo of anti-Jewish threats and abuse culminated in a late April speech to the Reichstag in which Hitler set out the "historical context" of Nazi policy. The Jews, he claimed, had played an evil role and done great harm to Germany in World War I. Now they were trying to complete the second act of their destructive process but would fail since Germany had declared war on "this Jewish infection." Victor Klemperer, an acute observer of the anti-Semitic mood in Germany, noted worriedly of this speech, "The concentration of hatred has this time turned into utter madness. Not England or the USA or Russia—*only*, in everything, nothing but *the Jew*."[35]

Even at the height of the danger on the eastern front, then, when it appeared as if Army Group Center, if not the entire Ostheer, might collapse, Nazi killers on the ground kept at their murderous task while top officials continued to refine procedures for a more efficient destruction of the Jews. In the east, the men of Einsatzgruppe B spent the winter in the vicinity of Smolensk, Mogilev, and Bryansk, but, even as they recoiled from the Russian counteroffensive, their advanced commandos systematically killed the surviving Jews in the rear area of Army Group Center. To the south, during the early months of 1942, Einsatzgruppen C and D engaged in more extensive operations, murdering perhaps 75,000 people in all between the beginning of the Soviet attack and the end of March. In one particularly gruesome incident, 4,000–5,000 Jews were placed in stables that were then doused with the gasoline in such scarce supply to the army and set afire. In Transnistria, 43,000 Jews, in groups of 300–400, were shot while kneeling naked in the icy weather on the rim of a precipice; the shootings continued for days, interrupted only by the celebration of Christmas. Almost 30,000 Jews were deported to the makeshift camp of Berezovka, some sixty miles northeast of Odessa, where most perished from the abysmal conditions or being shot. The shootings had been conducted so haphazardly that some of the corpses had been left on the main road or thrown into a local lake, raising fears of epidemics in the spring. To the north, in the Baltic, Einsatzgruppe A also continued its operations, with the murderously reliable Karl Jäger and his Einsatzkommando 3 alone accounting for over 138,000 victims between the start of operations and early February 1942.[36]

Even as the Einsatzgruppen worked nonstop during the winter months to kill as many Jews as possible, officials in Berlin discussed ways in which to extend the reach of the Final Solution. In the wake of the Wannsee Conference, a number of smaller meetings, involving lower-ranking officials, were held to work out the details of the complicated process. News about the decisions made at Wannsee spread quickly throughout the bureaucracy, where there was no lack of willingness to participate. In Heydrich's original scheme, Europe was to be "combed from west to east," but, in practice, because transportation problems were less acute in Poland, the systematic extermination of the Jews at death camps began in the General Government. Already on 26 January 1942, Albert Speer had informed Rosenberg that, owing to the rail crisis, any additional Jewish transports from the west would have to be postponed until April. Even the deportations of Reich Jews to concentration camps approved by Himmler on the same day had to be delayed for a time.[37]

These difficulties, however, merely caused Nazi officials to shift their focus, rather than postpone their plans. In early December 1941, the Germans had begun killing Jews in gas vans at the extermination camp at Chelmno. As the killers gained experience in and skill at their deadly craft, the pace and scope of their operations expanded accordingly, and increasing numbers of Jews from the Warthegau and the Lodz ghetto, deemed unsuitable for work and, therefore, useless eaters, were sent to their fate. Beginning in early February 1942, selections also began to be made in Riga: Jews deemed incapable of work were shot or murdered in gas vans. In Minsk, too, executions became a regular feature. That same February, 150 Jews were killed in the first test of the gas chambers at the newly constructed camp of Belzec, near Lublin. Similarly, construction of a new camp to accommodate large numbers of Soviet prisoners of war had begun at Auschwitz-Birkenau in October 1941. But, by early 1942, with it increasingly evident that large numbers of Soviet prisoners would never reach the camp, the site's mission began to change: Birkenau would now assume the same role, killing nonworking Jews, as Chelmno and Belzec. Systematic mass murder was clearly in the air as winter gave way to early spring, but the process initially used to kill euthanasia victims in Germany had to be shown to be feasible on a large scale in the east. The first transports of Jews from Galicia and Lublin arrived in mid-March at Belzec, where they were successfully gassed to death in one large operation. The technical hurdle to assembly-line murder had been overcome. In April, when the Reichsbahn again supplied special trains for Jewish deportations, so had the transportation obstacle. The will was never in doubt. Late that month, in a detailed discussion of the Jewish question, Goebbels found that Hitler's attitude remained "unrelenting": the Jews had to disappear from Europe.[38]

The end of March witnessed another important event, one that also had an impact on the pace of the developing Final Solution: on the twenty-first, Hitler appointed Fritz Sauckel, the Gauleiter of Thuringia, as Plenipotentiary for Labor Development. An old-line Nazi from the "socialist" wing of the party, Sauckel was given the task of solving the crippling manpower problem. Nothing exposed the gulf between ideology and economic reality more than the question of labor. Bringing foreign workers into Germany, especially from Eastern Europe, challenged the very goal of a racially pure state, but the dictates of the war economy were forcing a radical revision of Nazi ideas since it was now clear that the war could not be won without foreign labor. German losses on the eastern front had been staggering in the first nine months of the war, while there remained in Germany virtually no young men who had not already been conscripted or sent into the labor force. At the height of the winter crisis, the Wehrmacht had taken at least 200,000 men from the armaments factories, a short-term expedient that could not last since

Germany desperately needed to expand its war production and, thus, needed more workers. In addition, men had to be found to fill out the depleted ranks of the Ostheer. By March, the Wehrmacht was short some 700,000 men, while the armaments industry lacked a million workers. In addition, even at the start of the war, foreigners made up almost half the agricultural workforce, a figure that had risen to 60 percent by 1940. Ironically, given Hitler's obsession with food security, the Reich depended more and more on primarily Polish labor to feed itself.[39]

A greater use of women could take up some of the slack, but even a rigorous mobilization would not have produced much more than 700,000 additional workers. In 1939, German women were already more heavily engaged in the labor force than British women would be at the end of the war, while Germany's level of female mobilization during the war was considerably higher than that of Britain or the United States. By late 1944, women made up two-thirds of the native workforce in agriculture and over 51 percent of the native civilian workforce. Even if Nazi authorities had used, as one put it, Stalinist methods to force all available women into the workforce, there still would have remained a shortage of several million workers. The only way to satisfy the insatiable demand for labor was ruthlessly to exploit the occupied areas. From a racial standpoint, the war had produced an absurd situation. "We no sooner get rid of 500 Jews from the area of the Reich," complained an analyst in the winter of 1941–1942, "than we immediately bring in ten times the number of racially undesired foreign races."[40]

Charged by Hitler with solving this urgent problem, Sauckel responded with a staggering ruthlessness. The invasion of the Soviet Union had touched off multiple programs of mass murder, of which the forced recruitment of foreign labor was to be one. In the spring of 1941, Germany already employed over 1.2 million prisoners of war (mainly from France) and 1.3 million civilian laborers, mainly Poles, and, during the course of the year, this number swelled by a further million foreign workers, again primarily from Poland. These workers, however, were employed mainly in agricultural occupations; not until the end of the year and the debacle at Moscow did the needs of industry begin driving the importation of foreign workers. Over the next year and a half, Sauckel mobilized millions of workers from all over occupied Europe, although the great majority came from Poland and the conquered Soviet territories. Through wild and ruthless manhunts in which people were seized off the streets, in churches and theaters, and from villages that were then burned to the ground, Sauckel's men engaged in a brutal hunt for slave labor. These so-called *Ostarbeiter* (eastern workers), overwhelmingly young men and women, often just teenagers (their average age was twenty), were put to work, normally in deplorable conditions, in the Reich's factories, mines, and fields. By the end of July, over 5 million foreign workers were employed in Germany, while, by the summer of 1943, the total foreign workforce had risen to 6.5 million, a figure that would increase by the end of 1944 to 7.9 million. By that time, foreign workers accounted for over 20 percent of the total German workforce, although, in the armaments sector, the figure topped 33 percent. In some specific factories and production lines, foreign workers routinely exceeded 40 percent of the total; indeed, by the summer of 1943, the Stuka dive bomber was, as Erhard Milch boasted, being "80% manufactured by Russians."[41]

Given its existential dilemma, then, the Reich had responded in the winter crisis of 1941–1942 with a brutal logic: if Germany suffered from a shortage of workers, replacements would simply be brought, often through coercion, to Germany. Once in the Reich, however, the Nazis faced a basic contradiction between their genocidal racial policy and the pragmatic need to use this labor wisely to raise production. This contradiction had first surfaced in the fall of 1941 when the employment of Soviet prisoners as workers failed to achieve adequate results. Not only had the great majority already been killed, but even those shipped to Germany continued to be so ill-treated that they died in large numbers. Even before Sauckel's appointment, military officials had pointed to the absurdity of importing these men only to starve them to death before they could do any work. Although efforts were belatedly made to raise the food rations of forced laborers, in the summer of 1942 the thousands of civilians arriving daily in the Reich's cities from the east still faced horrendous living and working conditions, with long hours, starvation rations, and the most primitive accommodations. As a result, by the autumn, thousands of half-dead Ostarbeiter, emaciated, starving, many suffering from tuberculosis, were shipped back eastward under nightmarish conditions. Adam Tooze has calculated that, during the course of the war, some 2.4 million foreign workers, overwhelmingly Ostarbeiter, died as a result of their treatment by the Nazi regime, a figure that could be increased by several million if Soviet prisoners of war were included. At a time when a crucial impediment to the German war effort was a lack of labor, then, the Nazi inability to resolve the contradiction between ideology and practicality resulted in an enormous wastage of labor power.[42]

Tooze has noted that this seemingly irrational squandering of a vital war resource also extended to Jewish labor, another 2.4 million potential workers, by his estimate, falling victim to the Nazi racial madness. Here, however, as he emphasizes, the picture is, perhaps, less illogical than it seems. Sauckel's very success in recruiting foreign workers had, as one further murderous consequence, the result that the labor crisis could largely be solved without resorting to the full-scale mobilization of Jewish labor. In the most brutal sense, the Jews had now become, to the Nazis, useless eaters. Thus, even though some Jewish workers continued to be kept alive for war production in the dwindling ghettos of Poland and the factories built near Auschwitz, Sauckel's successful mobilization of non-Jewish labor allowed the racial ideologues to gain the upper hand: the genocidal imperative triumphed over that of the more pragmatic, although still deadly, idea of *Vernichtung durch Arbeit* (destruction through labor). Although some Jews arriving at Auschwitz received a temporary stay of execution through the *Selektion* process, the great majority, perhaps 90 percent, were killed immediately. Thus, the apparent paradox that the destruction of the Jews—set in motion in June 1941, accelerated in 1942, and largely completed, except for Hungarian Jews, in 1943—took place against the backdrop of a desperate German need for labor can be resolved in large part by the simultaneous successful Nazi effort to import large numbers of Ostarbeiter. By the end of 1943, with three-quarters of the eventual Jewish victims of the Holocaust dead, the most counterproductive mistreatment of the foreign workers had also ended. In the instance of foreign workers, the contradictions in Nazi racial policy had been resolved in favor of the priority of the war effort; for Jews, there would be no such respite.[43]

The military reverses of the winter of 1941–1942 also meant a setback for the policy of immediate economic exploitation of the conquered eastern territories in order to sustain the war effort. Not only would German industry be unable to obtain and utilize important Soviet raw materials, but also, and just as crucially, it left Germany facing once again the nightmare of 1914–1918: a severe food crisis. Frustrated in their attempt to obtain sufficient quantities of foodstuffs from the Soviet Union, Nazi officials now faced the bleak prospect of an expansion of the war into the indefinite future. With the outbreak of war in 1939, the Nazi regime had imposed strict rationing on the population, but this Spartan regimen had been tempered by the promise of a secure, if monotonous, diet. The German and European grain harvest in both 1940 and 1941 had been disappointing, however, which meant that Nazi officials had been unable to import enough food to cover domestic deficits. Meat rations had already been cut in June 1941, and the bread ration had been sustained only by drawing on reserve stocks of grain. By the end of the year, these had largely been exhausted, and now food officials faced the task of feeding the additional hundreds of thousands of foreign workers to be sent into Germany. When Herbert Backe protested to Goering, the latter suggested cynically that the Ostarbeiter could be fed on cats and horse meat. Backe, however, checked the statistics and reported back to Goering that there were not enough cats to provide a ration and that horse meat was already being used to supplement the rations of the German population.[44]

Although German authorities initially attempted to stretch scarce food resources simply by providing the Ostarbeiter with starvation rations, this was clearly a counterproductive strategy. It served no purpose to import workers into the country only to starve them so that they could perform little useful labor. Nor, given the "crushing impact" and "deterioration in morale" among Germans at the regime's ration cuts in the spring of 1942, could Nazi officials seriously countenance further deep reductions in consumption. As early as mid-February, on learning of the need for ration cuts, Goebbels worried that the situation was resembling that of World War I. Given Hitler's near-pathological anxieties about a food crisis triggering domestic unrest, the propaganda minister had little difficulty persuading his Führer to act in a radical manner against privilege so that the hardships of war would be seen to fall equally on all. Indeed, as early as April, the Nazi state proclaimed the death sentence for anyone engaged in black market activity. That same month, Hitler was granted special new powers by the Reichstag to take action against anyone harming the Volksgemeinschaft, which, given the powers he already possessed, had to be seen as a populist warning.[45]

Nazi officials also drew the logical, if radical, conclusion from the brewing food crisis: if not enough food was available to sustain everyone, the optimal solution would be to concentrate rations on those who did productive labor while reducing the population of those who did not. The Führer, after all, had long made it clear that it was unacceptable for anyone to starve in Germany while the Wehrmacht controlled Ukraine; German authorities would simply have to find better ways to utilize the meat and grain of the occupied areas. Although the hunger policy had not produced the desired results in 1941, Backe, put in charge of the Ministry of Food and Agriculture in April, in essence returned to its basic principles in 1942: food had to be distributed from east to west on a massive scale; the Wehrmacht would have to feed itself completely from the eastern territories as all food shipments from the Reich would cease; and entire groups, most notably the Jews, were to be excluded completely from the food supply. Backe, who combined in his person the ice-cold technocrat and the ideologue with close ties to Himmler and Heydrich, recognized the intersection of ideology and opportunism. The hunger policy was now to be directly coupled to the strategy of racial genocide; if the decision to accelerate the killing of the Jews had been taken for other reasons, the food crisis now supplied a powerful additional incentive. The German food supply would be secured at any price.[46]

By early summer, Backe made the connection between food policy and genocide specific. There were, he indicated in response to protests from administrators in Poland about the reduction in rations, "in the General Government . . . still 3.5 million Jews. Poland is to be sanitized within the coming year." In mid-July, Himmler communicated orders that all Jews in Poland not needed for work were to be killed by the end of the year; the food crisis had helped accelerate the Final Solution. Indeed, the hunt for grain was to be pursued with utter ruthlessness whether the victims were Jews or Slavs. After a tense meeting on 5 August with the Gauleiter, who gave vent to the growing resentment of the German population at the uncertain food situation, Goering the next day, in a meeting of the *Reichskommissars* and military commanders of the occupied areas, gave full scope to Backe's plan, authorizing a fundamental rearrangement of the food supply in Europe. To Goering, it was inconceivable that the Third Reich controlled "regions . . . such as we never had during the last world war, and yet I have to give a bread ration to the German people. . . . The Führer repeatedly said . . . if anyone has to go hungry, it shall not be the Germans, but other peoples." It was time, Goering emphasized, to reassert basic priorities:

> God knows, you are not sent out there [to the east] to work for the welfare of the people in your charge, but to get the utmost out of them so that the German people can live. . . . It makes no difference to me in this connection if you say that your people will starve. Let them do so, as long as no German faints from hunger. . . . We conquered such enormous territories through the valor of our troops, and yet our people have almost been forced down to the miserable rations of the First World War. . . . I am interested only in those people in the occupied regions who work in armaments and food production.

In former times, Goering noted, the matter had been simpler: "Then one called it plundering." Perhaps unnecessarily, Gauleiter Koch, the Reichskommissar for Ukraine, assured Goering that the grain from his area would be obtained at any price.[47]

The radical demands formulated by Backe and Goering meant that anyone not working for the German war effort would be cut off from the food supply. The first group to disappear, as always, was the Jews. By the autumn of 1942, the gas chambers at Treblinka, Chelmno, Belzec, and Auschwitz were operating full bore, and a palpable sense of relief descended on Berlin. Not only had the food crisis been averted, but rations for both Germans and foreign workers had also been increased substantially. Total European deliveries of grain more than doubled, while there was a huge increase in deliveries of potatoes, meats, and fats, especially from France, Poland, and the occupied Soviet territories. Nor, despite expectations, had the food ration been completely cut in the General Government, where there had been an unexpectedly good harvest. By year's end, however, virtually all the 3 million Jews residing there had been killed; if the harvest had not been so good, millions of Poles would have joined them. The desperate German effort to improve the dismal food situation had created a functional connection between the accelerated extermination of the Jews and the improvement in the food rations that would sustain the Nazi labor force. Sauckel's mobilizations had provided Germany vital labor, while the synthesis of racial and food policies had resolved the food crisis; in both cases, those left on the outside were the Jews of Europe.[48]

As labor and food problems were being resolved in the most inhumane ways, another obstacle loomed. If the slim thread of German hopes rested on completing the defeat of the Red Army in 1942 and seizing the oil, food, and raw materials of European Russia vital to the confrontation with the Anglo-American powers, the offensive capacity of the Ostheer, or at least Army Group South, had to be rebuilt as quickly as possible. This, in turn, required a drastic increase in weapons production from the armaments industry, a sector of the economy that was sputtering badly as a result of a variety of overlapping problems. Just six months after his mid-July decision to reorganize the armaments industry in favor of the Luftwaffe and the navy, Hitler now had to reverse course and give priority to the army, but production lines could not simply be switched overnight. This constant shifting in weapons priorities also made the rational allocation of scarce resources difficult, especially in the absence of any clear central direction of the war economy. The welter of agencies clamoring for dominance over the war economy made things worse as it led to a confusion of responsibility and stifling bureaucratic interference. In addition, the catastrophic state of the transport system slowed the delivery of vital raw materials, especially coal, which resulted in crippling power shortages and the shutdown of numerous factories. The shortage of labor and lack of key raw materials further hampered production, especially given the reluctance to make severe cuts in the civilian sector. Even the celebrated Nazi effort of the 1930s to win the support of workers through appeals to quality German craftsmanship backfired, as antiquated modes of production resulted in the waste of scarce materials and left many firms resistant to rationalization and mass production methods. Despite having access to the resources of much of Europe, the German war economy was badly underperforming. As Fritz Todt noted in January 1942, with obvious understatement, Germany "should have been more prepared to fight a total war."[49]

Reeling from the crisis in front of Moscow, German economic leaders now scrambled to put just such a system in place. On 15 January, Goering demanded a rigorous conversion to a war economy, emphasizing that the civilian sector could no longer be maintained at existing levels and that all production capacity should be concentrated on the needs of the Wehrmacht. On the twenty-first, General Thomas echoed Goering's opinion and took the further step of calling for the German war economy to be centrally controlled. Thomas obviously expected that he would be the person given extensive powers to manage the armaments sector, but, in a blow to the military, he was outmaneuvered by Todt, who, as minister for armaments and munitions, had already taken vital steps to rationalize arms production. An advocate of doing away with the "inertia of the old," Todt had earlier pioneered a system of industrial autonomy that left the development and production of weapons and equipment to industry. In December 1941, he sought even greater efficiencies of production by replacing what had been a cost-plus system of letting contracts, in which firms were reimbursed the full production costs as well as a profit based on a percentage of the costs, in favor of a system of fixed prices. In the former, firms had little incentive to cut costs since, the greater the expenditure, the larger the profits. With the fixed-price system, Todt introduced greater competition, forcing firms to rationalize production, reduce costs, and work more efficiently. The firm that had the lowest production costs for the same performance was now the yardstick for all others. Those firms that chose the lowest price calculated by Todt's ministry for a particular product did not have to pay any taxes on its manufacture, while those choosing the middle price category had to pay taxes. Those electing the highest price had to prove special difficulties. Under the new system, a manufacturer who did not cut costs quickly, which, in practice, meant increasing productivity, was soon eliminated from the supply chain.[50]

Despite the improvements promised by his system, Todt understood that, for production levels to rise significantly, the entire German economy had to be mobilized fully for war. By the end of January, he presented Hitler, who greatly admired his talented minister, with plans for the centralization of the German armaments industry. Hitler, now aware of the gross inefficiencies of weapons production and eager to increase the output of weapons, backed the changes. On 6 February, Todt chaired the first joint meeting of all the committee chairmen in the Ministry for Armaments and Munitions, at which time he revealed that the focal point for the reorganization of production had been switched from the army to his ministry. His triumph, however, proved short-lived. Two days later, after a contentious private meeting with Hitler at Rastenburg, Todt's plane burst into flames shortly after takeoff and crashed, killing all aboard. The nature of his death and the fact that Hitler rejected the findings of the crash investigation and personally dictated the official version led to speculation at the time and since that Todt had been murdered, although by whom remained unclear. Suspicion naturally fell on the Führer, but, even though Todt expressed doubts about the war to Hitler, he nonetheless remained a loyal and dedicated supporter who had just taken energetic efforts to reorganize war production. Speculation has also centered on the SS, but the most likely culprit was Goering, a man rapidly losing his influence and control over the economy to his ambitious rival. Goering, in fact, hurried to the Führer immediately on learning of Todt's death in order to declare himself ready to take over the latter's tasks, only to find Hitler already meeting with Todt's successor, Albert Speer. The unaccustomed speed with which Hitler had named Speer the new minister of armaments only confirmed his intention to maintain the changes Todt had introduced and to avoid a relapse into the tired intrigues and rivalries that had plagued war production until now. In March, he made this clear when he finally approved the subordination of the entire economy to the needs of the war.[51]

Whatever the reality of Todt's death, it now launched the meteoric rise of Albert Speer, who proceeded both to expand on and to benefit from the changes already introduced by Todt. The so-called production miracle launched by Speer in 1942 was, in fact, largely the result of a continuation of the reforms already set in motion by Todt. Key to Speer's success was both tighter administration and central control of important physical resources such as raw materials, factory equipment, and labor as well as the standardization of production practices. Speer also introduced a system of industrial committees, a fundamental change in regulatory practice that aimed at mobilizing industry through a process of self-regulation, by which industrialists would be allowed input into the allocation of raw materials and the awarding of contracts. In April, he established the Zentrale Planung, a central planning agency that permitted the coordination of all armaments plans that came under his jurisdiction. Although the Luftwaffe and the navy retained their independence, in practice Speer cooperated closely with Erhard Milch, the head of Luftwaffe armaments programs, thus extending his influence. Speer also staffed his new offices and committees with younger men from an engineering and business background, bringing needed expertise into the design, development, and organization of weapons programs as well as allowing him to circumvent army obstruction.[52]

With the new administrative structure in place, which for the first time allowed for the coordination of much of the German armaments industry, Speer was able fairly quickly to raise production levels simply by utilizing industrial capacity more fully and rationally. By August 1942, production of weapons had risen 27 percent from its February low, that of tanks by 25 percent, and that of ammunition by 97 percent. Although vital to the continuance of the war, Speer's ability to increase production was hardly miraculous. In most cases, his ministry better exploited factory space by encouraging more shift work, rationalized the supply chain, reduced the number of firms engaged in the manufacture of weapons and equipment, and concentrated output in the largest or most efficient firms. At the same time, Speer established a new set of organizations, known as *rings*, to manage the supply of raw materials, semifinished products, and components. Based on the principle of self-responsibility, the rings essentially amounted to an Auftragstaktik policy for industry, in which the Reich Armaments Ministry would set targets, leaving responsibility for meeting them to industry. Finally, Speer also attempted to get the army to reduce the number of modifications to weapons in the pipeline as well as to accept both a reduction in the number of weapons types and a standardization of parts and components. Through such simplification and standardization, not only would a more rational use of labor resources and higher levels of automation be possible, but the need for highly skilled labor would also be reduced. The result of this de-skilling and increased use of machine tools was a sharp rise in labor productivity in the armaments industries, while more effective allocation of raw materials and the massive labor mobilization campaign provided an additional boost to production.[53]

Speer's success thus rested on the radical mobilization of labor and raw materials as well as the beneficial effects of rationalization, although persistent problems in coal and steel production always threatened to unravel his tightly wound system. Nonetheless, his "armaments miracle," and the underlying promise that more could be done with less, provided an important political and mythical function for Hitler's regime. Goebbels's propaganda manipulated the dramatic increases in production in 1942 and into the following years to dispel any lingering defeatism and to demonstrate to the German people that the winter crisis of 1941–1942 had been overcome and the war could still be won. The remarkable performance of German industry not only fortified morale on the home front; it also reassured Germans that success was still possible, that, as Goebbels's slogan had it, "the best weapons bring victory." The increase in arms production was certainly real enough, but its mythical dimension was just as vital to the continuing German effort as its physical manifestation: as long as Germany could continue to produce weapons at an ever-increasing rate, there would not be another November 1918.[54]

Goebbels's propaganda, however, was self-deceiving. Even as German armaments production increased and new investments were made that would result in a substantial jump in output by 1944, Germany, as we have seen, had already been outproduced in 1941 by the Soviet Union. Nor was this a one-year aberration. Despite resource losses and a disruption to production that resulted in a 25 percent fall in total national product, in 1942 the Soviet Union alone, even without the contributions of Great Britain and the United States, would once again outproduce the Reich in virtually every weapons category. In the key areas of small arms and artillery, the advantage was three to one, while, in tanks, it was a staggering four to one, accentuated by the higher quality of the Soviet T-34. As Adam Tooze has noted, the real productive miracle in 1942 took place in the Urals, not in the Ruhr. Buoyed by the flow of vital goods and raw materials through Lend-Lease, the Soviets could concentrate production on a limited number of weapons while at the same time employing the full range of Stalinist methods of oppression to exact enormous sacrifices from the Russian home front, where millions of civilians died for the sake of the "Great Patriotic War." This effort was not sustainable, and by 1944 German production roughly equaled Soviet, but by then it was too late. The key year was 1942, the last time that Hitler could dictate the course of events to his enemies. If the Third Reich was going to survive, German forces would have to win some sort of decisive victory before the awesome power of the United States was fully mobilized.[55]

"Will this winter never end? Is a new glacial age in the offing?" mused Joseph Goebbels in late March 1942 as he paid a visit to Führer Headquarters. There he found morale to be "extraordinarily good, although the endless winter has a somewhat depressing effect." At first glance, the propaganda minister thought the Führer looked to be in good health, although "he has gone through exceedingly difficult days, and his whole bearing shows it. . . . He must take the entire burden of the war upon his shoulders, and nobody can relieve him of the responsibility for all the decisions that must be made." Despite the successes in stabilizing the military situation and the promise of increased armaments production, the anxieties touched off by the winter crisis were not far from the surface. On closer look, Goebbels found Hitler to be psychologically shaken by the recent reverses. The Führer had been wracked with doubts during this "cruel winter" as to whether the Eastern Army could be saved. Goebbels referred openly to a "crisis in the regime, of dancing on a razor," while Hitler himself railed at the incompetence and cowardice of his generals. He had wanted to seize the Caucasus and strike a mortal blow at the Soviet regime, but *they* knew better, had, in fact, consistently interfered with and undermined his plans. Then, confronted with military reverses and a collapsing supply system, they lost their nerve. Only his iron will and determination had surmounted the crisis and avoided a "Napoleonic disaster." Indeed, the crisis of the past months only intensified his belief that he had to struggle not only against external enemies but also against those within his own ranks who were either inadequate or disloyal. "Stalin's brutal hand," he remarked with approval, "had saved the Russian front. . . . We shall have to apply similar methods." Not surprisingly, his first target was to be the Jews, toward whom Goebbels found the Führer's attitude "as uncompromising as ever. The Jews must be got out of Europe . . . by applying the most brutal methods."[56]

Hitler also revealed to Goebbels the outline of a plan that, if not exactly designed to end the Ostkrieg—he talked of a "hundred years' war in the east"—would by the end of October leave Germany in a very formidable position to wage a global war over an extended period. This plan, submitted to Hitler on 28 March under the code name Fall Blau (Case Blue), sketched the goals for the German summer offensive. After reworking by the OKH and Hitler, it received concrete expression in Directive No. 41, which Hitler signed on 5 April 1942. Declaring that it was vital to seize the strategic initiative and "force our will on the enemy," Hitler directed that all available forces would be concentrated in the southern sector, "with the aim of definitively destroying the remaining vital enemy forces and, as much as possible, depriving him of the most important military-economic sources of strength." The ultimate goal, however, was "to secure the Caucasian oil fields and the passes through the mountains themselves."[57]

Faced with the dilemma of what to do in Russia now that blitzkrieg had failed, German planners came to the only conclusion possible given their history, training, and assumptions: launch another blitzkrieg campaign. In the operational plan for 1942, however, they departed from tradition and past practices in two key areas: first, it was to be an exceedingly complex operation based on a series of sequential actions directed from the top, and, second, little decisionmaking freedom was to be accorded field commanders. Moreover, success would be assured only if the enemy cooperated once again in his destruction. Since the distances involved were so great, the supply situation so tenuous, and the necessary manpower insufficient, in order to achieve a maximum concentration of force at crucial points the campaign was planned as a series of mutually supplementary partial attacks, staggered from north to south. The aim, in short encirclements modeled on Vyazma and Bryansk, would be to seize Voronezh, then destroy enemy forces west of the Don to prepare the way for an advance to Stalingrad. Having neutralized, although not necessarily seized, this industrial and communications center and cut the Volga supply line, only then would German forces move into the Caucasus. At the conclusion of this operation, which Hitler expected by the end of October, German troops would immediately go into winter quarters; haunted by the frightful death toll of the previous winter, the Führer was determined that strong defensive positions be prepared. All plans for after the operation in the Caucasus, he told Mussolini at the time, would have to be shelved since all would depend on the outcome of that battle. As with the blitzkrieg of the previous summer, it was an all-or-nothing gamble on a short campaign, but, in the spring of 1942, the discrepancy between his aims and his military power was even greater than the year earlier.[58]

With Directive No. 41, Hitler indicated both his intention to make the eastern front the decisive theater of operations—"The war will be decided in the east," Halder noted in late March—and the fact that, even with a victory in the summer offensive, he had no clear idea how to extract Germany from the war. The first point, given the altered circumstances in the spring of 1942, was not self-evident since a German victory in the east would not necessarily be decisive. With the failure of Barbarossa and the entry of the United States into the war, Hitler's freedom of action was seriously constrained. Still, he had several conceivable options at his disposal, although none offered much certainty. He might, theoretically, have gone over to the strategic defensive and used the time fully to mobilize the German war economy and develop new weapons. Goebbels, in fact, referred in late March to a report he received indicating that German research "in the realm of atomic destruction has now proceeded to a point where its results may possibly be made use of in the conduct of this war. . . . It is essential that we be ahead of everybody, for whoever introduces a revolutionary novelty into this war has the greater chance of winning it." Or Hitler might have ordered an increase in weapons such as U-boats or antiaircraft guns that might have significantly affected the outcome of the war in the Atlantic or over the skies of Germany. He might also have built on Japanese successes and revived the Mediterranean strategy rejected the previous year, in hopes of striking east through Egypt to acquire the oil fields of the Middle East and link up with Japanese forces in India. The naval leadership did propose a plan, which Halder sarcastically dismissed, to redirect German efforts against the British Empire and the oil of the Middle East, but, although Hitler found it intriguing, it was ultimately rejected, not least because of force limitations and its failure to offer a quick solution to the problem of economic constraints.[59]

Although senior military leaders complained privately of "utopian plans for an offensive," the striking fact was that none could offer a convincing alternative strategy, especially since the Germans possessed neither the manpower, the materiel, nor the economic resources to conduct a strategic defense. Nor, given the psychological impact of the events of the recent winter, was a resumption of the assault on Moscow a viable option, especially since that operation had largely been Halder's idea and disaster had evidently been averted only by Hitler's resolve. Both at the OKH and among field commanders, concerns were expressed that Army Group South lacked the resources to occupy the enormous area between the Black and the Caspian Seas, while Fromm regarded the proposed operation as a "luxury" inappropriate to a "poor man." General Thomas warned of "the disproportion between war requirements and the capacity to meet them" and demanded that German military operations in the summer of 1942 take account of the fuel situation, but he could offer nothing beyond that. Speer merely observed that, if Germany had to fight another winter in Russia, then it would have lost the war. None, however, could offer a convincing alternative, nor did any have any impact on Hitler, who observed with asperity in late May, "Again and again so-called experts . . . declared: that is not possible, that can't be done. . . . There are problems that absolutely have to be solved. Where real leaders are present, they have always been solved and will always be solved."[60]

This operational problem, however, concealed a larger dilemma. If the goal of the war in the Soviet Union was Lebensraum, how was this to be achieved? The Germans no longer had the resources to conquer

European Russia, if they ever had. If the Red Army could avoid being drawn into encirclement battles, the destruction of the enemy forces would prove to be beyond German capabilities. At best, then, Hitler might hope to destroy sufficient numbers of Soviet units to hold the remnants of Stalin's regime at bay. At the same time, the Soviet Union's Western allies were steadily assembling their massive economic and military resources to use against Germany. For their part, the Germans found themselves increasingly dependent on their allies, Italy, Rumania, and Hungary, nations that could marshal far fewer resources than those of the enemy coalition. Once again, the Germans confronted their basic dilemma, how to do more with less. Even as they won on the operational level, they failed to find a way to translate these triumphs into a strategic victory, a conundrum that grew the more the Germans achieved success on the battlefield as they had to disperse their scarce resources over a wider area.

Realistically, the only two alternatives left to Germany in early 1942 were to end the war politically, an option Hitler refused to countenance, or to create as rapidly as possible the preconditions for fighting a long war. Operation Blau, which aimed to acquire the oil and raw materials necessary for German survival and deny these equally vital resources to the Soviets, was, thus, an operational attempt to pass through the danger zone before the Western allies could intervene on the Continent. As Hitler understood, perhaps the most serious consequence of the altered strategic situation was to put Germany under an extraordinary time pressure. With the American entry into the war, a concrete threat of a second front had now materialized, and, in order to avoid the strategic encirclement of Germany, as in World War I, a victory in the east was needed "to clear the tables." Halder, despite his misgivings and fear that losses in 1942 would be greater than the entire cohort of young men to be drafted into the army, recognized the bloody logic of the Ostkrieg: the Caucasus operation, he concluded, was "an inescapable necessity." That spring, Goebbels began alerting the German public to the meaning of the coming summer offensive. In an article in *Das Reich,* the propaganda minister stressed the importance of ideals but underscored that this was also "a war for raw materials."[61]

One thing above all obsessed Hitler and gave credence to his strategic arguments: the absolute necessity of acquiring oil supplies, a fact that had not escaped Soviet military leaders. "The only thing that matters is oil," Marshal Timoshenko asserted at the end of 1941. "We have to do all we can to make Germany increase her oil consumption and to keep German armies out of the Caucasus." As if confirming this observation,

German troops in Russia, summer 1941. NARA 242-GAP-286B-4.

German assault gun on the move over dusty roads, June–July 1941. Note the juxta-
position of mechanized and horse-drawn transport. BA Bild 101I-136-0882-13.

German infantry marching through a village in the Baltic, June 1941. BA Bild 101I-208-0027-04A.

German infantryman before a dead Red Army soldier and burning Soviet BT-7 tank, Ukraine, June 1941. BA Bild 101I-020-1268-36.

German soldiers watch a burning synagogue in a small Lithuanian village, June 1941. BA Bild 183-L19427.

The intensification of anti-Jewish policy began simultaneously with the invasion of the Soviet Union. Here, Jewish men and women are shoveling their own graves under the watchful gaze of SS men, Storov, Ukraine, 4 July 1941. BA Bild 183-A0706-0018-029.

Red Army prisoners were not spared the impact of the hunger policy. Distribution of bread to Soviet prisoners of war, Vinnitsa, Ukraine, 28 July 1941. BA Bild 146-1979-113-04.

Himmler visiting a camp for Soviet prisoners of war, Minsk, Belorussia, August 1941. At roughly the same time as this visit, Himmler, acting on an order from Hitler, vastly expanded the killing operations in the east. NARA 242-HB-47721-306.

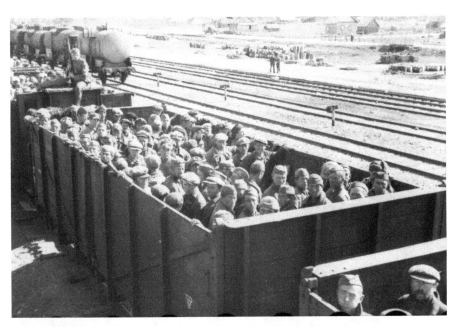

Vitebsk: Transport of Soviet prisoners of war in an open rail car, 21 September 1941. In the winter of 1941–1942, this policy often resulted in large numbers of the prisoners freezing to death before arrival at the prison camps. BA Bild 101I-267-0124-20A.

Two German soldiers before a burning building and a billowing cloud of flames, October 1941. BA Bild 101I-268-0154-11.

The impact of weather and primitive Russian roads is clearly visible as a German vehicle attempts to negotiate a muddy road in a small village in the Moscow region, November 1941. BA Bild 183-B15500.

The fierce snowstorms of Russia burdened both humans and animals, making movement virtually impossible. A German soldier urges on a horse pulling a *panje* wagon through deep snow, winter 1941–1942. BA Bild 101I-215-0366-03A.

Hunger! Russian women carve a dead horse for food, February 1942. BA Bild 183-B15171.

The fierce fighting of the winter is clearly evident from this photograph of the Kholm pocket, where Germans have stacked dead Red Army soldiers to form a protective wall, early 1942. BA Bild 101I-004-3633-30A.

The spring *rasputitsa* turned western Russia into a sea of mud. A horse-drawn wagon struggles through deep mud near Kursk, March–April 1942. BA Bild 101I-289-1091-26.

The lack of a quick victory and the need for workers forced the Germans to resort to foreign workers. Here we see the deportation of forced laborers for the German armaments industry, Artemovsk, Ukraine, May 1942. BA Bild 183-B19867.

The decision to use Ostarbeiter in German industry doomed Jews to a different fate. Deportation of Jews to an extermination camp (probably summer 1942). BA Bild 183-68431-0005.1942.

The second attempt at a blitzkrieg triumph. A panzer commander on the Don-Stalingrad front surveys the situation as his forces seem swallowed by the vastness of the steppe, July 1942. BA Bild 101I-218-0510-22.

German infantry on the march in southern Russia, August–September 1942. BA Bild 101I-217-0465-36.

Stalingrad: A German captain takes cover in the debris of the Barrikady artillery factory, October 1942. BA Bild 116-168-618.

Stalingrad: The nerve-wracking nature of house-to-house fighting is illustrated as German soldiers with an MG 34 machine gun and rifles anxiously peer out the window of a building, autumn 1942. BA Bild 101I-617-2571-04.

Stalingrad: German soldiers patrol in a destroyed industrial area, autumn 1942. BA Bild 116-1974-107-66.

Stalingrad: The swastika flies bravely from the ruins of the department store in whose cellar Paulus had his headquarters, October 1942. BA Bild 183-B22531.

Stalingrad: The face of an exhausted Landser after storming the Barrikady artillery factory, November 1942. BA Bild 183-R1222-501.

Executed Soviet partisans, 20 January 1943. The sign at the top says, "We are bandits; we have not only murdered and plundered German soldiers but also Russian citizens." The sign at the bottom reads, "Photography prohibited!" BA Bild 101I-031-2436-05A.

The cruelty of the partisan war: Soldiers of the Ordnungspolizei (Order Police) throw grenades at a burning building in an antipartisan operation somewhere in the Soviet Union, probably spring 1943. BA Bild 146-1993-025-03.

"Victory or Bolshevism," February 1943. A poster designed to promote Goebbels's total war effort. BA Plak 003-029-043.

The German need for foreign workers was insatiable. Forced laborers being marched to a train station for transport to Germany, Jankovo, Soviet Union, March 1943. BA Bild 183-J22099.

Hitler visits a tank factory to urge increased production, 5 April 1943. BA Bild 146-2007-0122.

Kursk, Operation Citadel: Pz. VI Tiger tank of the Waffen-SS in action, July 1943. BA Bild 101III-Groenert-019-23A.

Scorched earth: A burning village in Russia, 10 January 1944. BA Bild 146-1971-059-20.

Grinding defensive war: Three men of a tank destruction unit anxiously await a Soviet tank near Nevel, November–December 1943. BA Bild 146-1977-041-01.

Retreat: German soldiers struggle along a muddy, snowy road in the southern Ukraine, early 1944. BA Bild 101I-711-0438-05A.

Retreat: The Leningrad front between Lake Ilmen and Lake Peipus, February 1944. BA Bild 101I-725-0190-15.

A lone German soldier with a hand grenade mans the front just before the start of Operation Bagration, 21 June 1944. BA Bild 101I-696-0442-29.

Soldiers of the Grossdeutschland Division mount a counterattack from woods and a cornfield, mid-August 1944. BA Bild 183-J27512.

Young men of the Reich Labor Service construct a protective wall in East Prussia, August 1944. BA Bild 183-J30355.

The ravages of defeat: A refugee trek in East Prussia with a dead horse in the foreground, early 1945. BA Bild 146-1990-001-30.

The last defense, Frankfurt (Oder): A Volkssturm unit occupies a defensive position on the Oder River, February 1945. BA Bild 183-J28787.

The last gasp, Berlin: A woman being instructed in the use of a Panzerfaust antitank weapon, March 1945. BA Bild 146-1973-001-30.

Nordhausen concentration camp (Mittelbau-Dora): Some of the hundreds of slave laborers who died building the V-2 rockets, 12 April 1945. NARA 111-SC-203456.

The wages of total war, Berlin: Destruction at the Brandenburg Gate, early June 1945. BA Bild B145-P054320.

Keitel admitted to General Thomas in late May that "the operations of 1942 must get us to the oil"; otherwise, the army's operational freedom would be lost. A few days later, Hitler confessed to his assembled generals, "If I do not get the oil of Maikop and Grozny, then I must end the war." Oil, to Hitler, was the key. In late May, he voiced confidence that the war could still be won once this "business in the east" was finished, but, by August, the Führer again stunned an audience by remarking that, if the oil wells of the Caucasus could not be taken by the end of 1942, it would mean the end of the war. Much, in fact, supported this contention, for as late as 1938 the Soviet Union obtained some 90 percent of its oil supplies from the Caucasus. If his forces could seize these vital fields, Hitler reasoned, this, along with the other mineral, agricultural, and industrial resources gained along the way, would not only boost the German war effort but also throw the Soviet war economy into an existential crisis.[62]

Hitler's urgency was also fueled by the realization that the only chance of successfully opposing the establishment of a second front in Western Europe, given the growing threat from the United States, lay in German control of the economic resources of the southern Soviet Union. Although aware of the enormous potential of American industry, the Führer nonetheless believed that the Japanese entry into the war and its string of victories in early 1942 would sufficiently preoccupy the Americans, allowing him the precious time to secure the oil needed for the consolidation of Europe. If, for him, the original impetus for the eastern war had been the destruction of Bolshevism and the conquest of Lebensraum, in the spring of 1942 the goal had become even more far-reaching: the acquisition of resources that would allow the Reich to wage global war. Once that was accomplished, Hitler asserted, "then the war is practically won for us" since the Anglo-Saxon powers could not seriously challenge a German-dominated Europe. It was, however, a situation of "triumph or destruction."[63]

If, in retrospect, the Third Reich in 1942 had little chance of triumphing over the coalition of its enemies, at the time a narrow window of opportunity seemed open. America's entry into the war might not prove fatal if Germany could strike a shattering blow against the Soviet Union in the coming year, the last time the bulk of the Wehrmacht could be employed largely undisturbed on a single front. The America factor had significantly altered the strategic equation and had drastically reduced Germany's freedom of action, but, if the Ostheer could secure the resources vital to its survival, the Third Reich might yet successfully traverse this danger zone. All possibilities remained open, at least in the minds of Nazi leaders: 1942 was to be the watershed year. Thus, even as Nazi planners worked furiously to realize the original economic and racial goals associated with Lebensraum—1942 was, after all, the year of the Wannsee Conference and the attempt to realize Generalplan Ost—the operational war plans for 1942 revolved around the necessity of securing oil resources, without which the grand Nazi schemes would be mere chimeras. Expectations that the new campaign would finally secure German conquests in the east fueled a surge in planning for various colonial schemes, while the mass murder of the Jews accelerated with breathtaking speed. Still, without the resources of southern Russia with which to continue the war, all these assorted racial and imperial schemes would come to naught.[64]

Operation Barbarossa had been launched on the gamble of a quick knockout and had failed because of unrelenting Soviet resistance; in 1942, Hitler now placed his hopes on a similar throw of the dice, but with even less chance of success. From the start of the invasion to March 1942, the Ostheer had suffered losses in excess of 1.1 million men, or 35 percent of its average strength. An influx of 450,000 men, virtually the entire 1922 cohort, still left the army so short of troops that the infantry divisions of Army Groups North and Center experienced a shortfall of no fewer than 4,800 and 6,900 men, respectively, per division. In late April, Halder estimated that infantry units in Army Group South were 50 percent of their original strength, with those of the other two army groups at only 35 percent. Nor could any more trained reservists be pulled out of the armaments factories, which left only those recovering from wounds as a ready pool of trained personnel. By 1942, the Germans had run out of manpower. The general fatigue of the men, the great losses of experienced officers and NCOs, the shortage of specialists, and the limited combat experience of the newly raised formations all seriously impaired the fighting efficiency of the Eastern Army. Nothing reflected the stark reality of the woeful scarcity of German manpower more than the decision in the spring to increase the size of the Italian, Rumanian, and Hungarian contingents fighting in the east, under the slogan of a "European defensive war against Bolshevism." Of the forty-one new divisions arriving in the south for Fall Blau, fully twenty-one were non-German, certainly not an auspicious indicator of success. Although poorly motivated, deficient in training, and lacking experience, they were necessary to plug gaps in the overstretched front.[65]

In addition, the massive losses of tanks, vehicles, and artillery could not be made good by current production, nor could German factories supply enough ammunition to compensate for the unexpectedly high rate of consumption, thus sharply reducing the firepower of German units. Fuel, too, was in such short supply that the Wehrmacht High Command cut the fuel ration to the Ostheer considerably, a blow to its mobility accentuated by the serious loss of horses. The extension of the operations that had made the railroads the principal means of supply, as well as the poor state of the roads that undermined truck transportation, also hampered German operational mobility. Since the key to the entire operation lay in the swift encirclement and destruction of remaining Soviet forces in the south, thus allowing the timely occupation of the vital economic resources, the impediments to German mobility at the outset of the campaign were nearly catastrophic. An OKW report in June warned prophetically that, given the army's deficiencies, "a measure of de-motorization" that would seriously affect the army's mobility was inevitable. Tellingly, at a time when the Soviets were rapidly rebuilding and mechanizing their forces, the Wehrmacht was in the process of reequipping its reconnaissance units with bicycles. This demodernization of the Ostheer did not bode well given that the success of the campaign depended on seizing objectives more than eight hundred miles from the German start line, an operational and logistic challenge greater even than that of the previous summer.[66]

Although the rail system had recovered somewhat from its near-catastrophic collapse in January 1942, the lack of locomotives and rolling stock, the demands of providing supplies for the new offensive, and the increasing frequency of transports of Jews to the newly opening extermination camps in Poland all contributed to a continuing gulf between the demands of the military and the ability of the Reich railways to deliver. Even the funnel-shaped widening of the area of operations raised the danger of a serious overextension of the already greatly overstretched supply lines. The conclusion of all who looked objectively at the figures was inescapable: the Ostheer in the spring of 1942 was a pale shadow of the imposing force that had launched Operation Barbarossa just a year earlier. In June 1941, 134 of 209 divisions, 64 percent, had been classified as "capable of any offensive action." Just nine months later, at the end of March 1942, the number of formations "suitable for any task" had shrunk to 8 of 162 divisions, a mere 5 percent. As one report noted sarcastically, "Armored divisions with their 9–15 battle-worthy tanks do not at present deserve that name."[67]

Ironically, Hitler's optimism regarding the impending summer offensive stemmed not so much from his belief in German strength as from his assessment of Soviet weakness. His operational thinking in 1942 was based on the assumption that the Red Army was at the end of its strength and had only limited powers of regeneration. This assessment, in turn, resulted not only from the compulsory optimism afflicting those at Führer Headquarters but also from incorrect information. That spring, Hitler had received reports detailing a severe lack of food and widespread cannibalism among both Soviet civilians and Soviet soldiers, while the state of equipment in the Red Army was said to be abysmal. In a reprise of its costly tendency to miscalculate the strength of the Russian enemy, Foreign Armies East also reckoned in April that Soviet manpower reserves were "by no means inexhaustible" and, if subjected to losses such as those suffered in 1941, would run out by the onset of the muddy season. In the event, this assessment suffered from two key flaws: Soviet manpower reserves were larger than assumed, and German forces would be unable to inflict devastating losses on the Red Army. In 1942, the Soviets would not cooperate in their own destruction, largely evading encirclement.[68]

Economically, as well, the plan was flawed. German analysts had misjudged the extent of Soviet industrial production in the eastern part of European Russia, the magnitude of the factory evacuation program, and the speed with which production could be resumed in the Urals area. Even during the second half of 1941, despite the enormous losses inflicted on its key economic areas and the strain of industrial evacuation, the Soviet Union had nearly equaled the entire German yearly production of tanks, aircraft, artillery, mortars, machine and submachine guns, and rifles. Moreover, since the Soviets could count on Lend-Lease aid from the United States, a fact the Germans realized would result in a "substantial strengthening of the Soviet Union's power of resistance," a key goal of the summer offensive was to cut the Allied supply line via Persia and the Volga River. By the spring of 1942, however, the bulk of shipments were already reaching the Soviet Union through Murmansk and Archangel. Even if the Ostheer had succeeded in reaching the Volga and seizing the oil fields of the Caucasus, then, a fatal weakening of the Soviet ability to continue fighting would not likely have resulted. Even the Führer seemed dimly to recognize this dilemma, remarking to Goebbels, despite his assertion that the Soviet Union was on its last legs, that it would be necessary to build a stronger defensive line this coming winter. Seared by the savage winter fighting, Hitler also revealed to Goebbels that he no longer wished to see snow; it had become physically repulsive to him.[69]

Germany thus faced the same ticking time bomb as in World War I: inferiority in resources and economic production would eventually prove decisive on the battlefield. German economic and manpower resources were overburdened, while the production, transportation, and supply problems that shackled German efforts in the last months of 1941 could not possibly be resolved in time to bring German units anywhere near the combat strength of the previous year. Speer's efforts would, ultimately, pull German production back to Soviet levels by 1944, but, by then, it was too late: 1942 was the pivotal year. Hitler clearly understood the risks involved in the new operation but believed that he had no choice. His window of opportunity had been reduced to a few months; if he had any hope of a successful outcome of the war, he had to cripple the Soviet Union by the end of autumn. "If it proved impossible in 1942 to defeat Russia definitively, or at least get as far as the Caucasus and the Urals," General Thomas noted anxiously in May, "Germany's war situation must be judged as extremely unfavorable, if not hopeless."[70] The Red Army had suffered staggering casualties in 1941; perhaps, the Führer thought, it could not now resist another German onslaught. Having concentrated his forces in the south and phased even that operation into staggered assaults, he had made, he believed, sufficient allowance for the Ostheer's loss of strength. His grand strategic vision reduced to little more than an operational advance on a distant target that might, in any case, not provide the necessary oil to continue fighting, Hitler risked everything on yet another calamitous miscalculation.

6

All or Nothing

If in early 1942, as opposed to the previous spring, Hitler and the German military leadership had the comfort of operational clarity, they also faced a number of vexing problems, an unwelcome reminder of the winter's desperate fighting, that had to be resolved before Operation Blue could commence. Foremost among them was control of the Crimea, important both as a springboard to the Caucasus and, if left in Soviet hands, as a persistent threat to the vital Rumanian oil fields. The Soviet Black Sea Fleet's naval air arm had already bombed the oil production facilities and refineries on numerous occasions, and, while the raids were generally ineffectual, a few had caused significant damage and disruption. From Hitler's perspective, concern over the safety of his sole source of oil, coupled with his belief that Soviet long-range bombers posed a constant threat, justified an operation to seize the Caucasus. Moreover, the Führer had repeatedly expressed interest in the Crimea, which was to be cleansed of its native population and resettled by "pure Germans," as a key area of colonization that would secure German Lebensraum as far as the Urals. Complete control of the peninsula, including the fortress of Sevastopol, would also limit the effectiveness of the pesky Soviet Black Sea Fleet as well as possibly influence the neutrality of Turkey. Finally, army planners saw strong Soviet formations in the Crimea as a persistent threat to communications and supply lines along their long, exposed southern flank.[1]

In bitter autumn fighting that resulted in staggering casualties, Manstein's Eleventh Army had seized the Kerch Peninsula, the gateway to the Caucasus, and all of the Crimea except for Sevastopol, only to be thrown back by fierce Soviet counterattacks. By the time the fighting had stopped in April 1942, the Germans still controlled the bulk of the Crimea, excluding Sevastopol, but were blocked from the Kerch

Peninsula by stout Soviet fortifications along the Parpach line. Retaking Kerch, Manstein realized, would be a formidable undertaking. Not only did the Soviets outnumber his forces in terms of both men and materiel, but they had also erected what seemed a nearly impregnable series of defenses. Although the narrow isthmus was only about ten miles across, at Parpach the Red Army had massed some 210,000 well-equipped troops behind three extensive defense lines. The first, the Parpach line, was protected by two wide antitank ditches, behind which lay thick mine-fields, barriers of barbed wire, iron hedgehogs made of welded railway tracks, concrete emplacements, and disabled tanks that served as pro-tected machine-gun nests. Five miles to the rear lay the second position, the Nasyr line, while beyond it the Sultanovka line, the so-called Turkish Wall, cut across the Kerch Peninsula at its widest point. Because the sea on either side of the Parpach line excluded the possibility of flanking attacks, the only option looked to be a frontal assault. The port of Kerch, forty miles to the east, seemed a world away.[2]

Given the forces at Manstein's disposal—five German infantry divi-sions, the Twenty-second Panzer Division, and two Rumanian divisions—which the Russians outnumbered three to one, a frontal assault against the Parpach line would have been suicidal. Manstein decided, however, to take advantage of recent events and poor Soviet judgment. In a series of local attacks in the northern sector, the Russians had pushed the Ger-mans back roughly four miles. Not only did the Russian front now pro-trude in the north, making it vulnerable to German counterattack, but the Soviet command had also compounded the problem by massing two-thirds of its troops in this zone. Manstein now saw the possibility, in con-junction with strong Luftwaffe support, of launching a holding attack in the north while bursting through the Parpach line in the southern sector. After a three- or four-mile advance, these units would then turn sharply north and drive into the rear of the concentrated Soviet forces, cutting them off and, eventually, destroying them. At the same time, mobile units would race toward Kerch to seize the port and prevent any effective enemy counterattack.[3]

Although it was a bold and risky plan, especially considering the dis-crepancy in forces, Hitler provided the operation a good chance at suc-cess by ordering a substantial increase in German air power in the region. General Wolfram von Richthofen, the cousin of the famous World War I ace, was ordered to support the offensive with his powerful Fliegerkorps 8 (the Eighth Air Corps), which packed a lethal combination of fight-ers, ground support aircraft, and bombers. Having come to appreciate the value of effective air support during the crisis months of the winter,

Hitler demanded "massed air power" as a precondition for success in the Crimea. Only then, he emphasized, could Soviet defenses be breached and enemy forces be cut off from their supplies. Manstein himself conceived of the attack as a ground operation that had its Schwerpunkt in the air, where the planes would "pull the infantry forward." The Führer also put great faith in the employment of deadly SD2 fragmentation bombs, developed for use specifically in the east. Dubbed *devil's eggs* by the air crews, these small five-pound bombs fragmented into deadly pieces of shrapnel that sprayed out over a fifteen-foot radius. They were, he explained, "best used against living targets. A satisfactory result can only be achieved when the bombs are used against crowds." Vital as this concentration of air power was, however, it could be accomplished only at the expense of denuding other fronts of air support, again demonstrating the serious reduction in German strength. Although Hitler took obvious murderous glee in new German antipersonnel weapons, Goering got closer to the heart of the matter when he ruefully admitted that the operational strength of the Luftwaffe was "no longer sufficient for the great tasks."[4]

Since the operation, now dubbed Trappenjagd (Bustard Hunt), depended on everything going perfectly—including a bungling response on the part of the Soviet commander, Kozlov, and his political commissar, the brutally incompetent Lev Mekhlis—German commanders remained uneasy. Although Bock, now commanding Army Group South, was impressed by the "careful preparation," he nonetheless expressed anxiety at the "enormous risk" entailed, while Manstein, who rarely underestimated himself, still worried about the weakness of German forces. Nor did the mood improve when the operation, originally slated for 5 May, had to be postponed for three days because Richthofen still had to assemble his aircraft. Surprise seemed out of the question in any case since Soviet troops had already put up placards along the front reading, "Come on. We're waiting." Manstein, realizing that the enemy knew that an attack was coming but not where or when, decided to give them a dose of the unexpected: German combat engineers and infantry would be sent in small assault boats to circumvent the southern Soviet defenses, aiming to seize and demolish the largest of the antitank ditches in the Parpach line.[5]

In the event, the operation came off virtually as planned. At 3:15 in the morning of 8 May, German artillery, accompanied by antiaircraft guns and waves of Stukas and bombers, unleashed a thunderous barrage that shattered enemy bunkers and gun emplacements on the front line. As ground support aircraft struck crushing blows at Soviet airfields, communication facilities, and logistic targets, the infantry surged forward into the barbed-wire emplacements protecting the Soviet line. Within an hour, and at roughly the same time leading elements of the infantry reached it, the assault boats carrying the combat engineers, under the protective cover of German fighters, stormed from the sea straight into the antitank ditch itself. Before the startled Russian defenders could react, German troops leaped from the boats and began spraying machine-gun fire into their positions. Even as the Landsers continued to struggle forward through seemingly endless minefields, engineers began blasting away the steep walls of the antitank ditch but were unable to bridge it sufficiently to allow heavy tanks across. Over the next two days, however, the Soviet defenses began to crumble before the skillful German attack. The Twenty-second Panzer finally crossed the Parpach ditch late in the afternoon of the ninth, drove eastward a few miles, fought off a Soviet counterattack, then swung to the north to close the trap. At the same time, a swiftly moving force of motorized infantry, the "Grodeck Brigade," drove eastward toward Kerch and, by the tenth, exploiting a gap in Soviet defenses, had burst across both the Nasyr and the Sultanovka lines; only friendly fire from German Stukas seemed to impede their progress. The Soviet command, its communications shattered by the initial bombardment, was paralyzed and incapable of responding to the swift enemy advance.[6]

Early on the eleventh, the Twenty-second Panzer finally closed the gap in the north, trapping ten panic-stricken Soviet divisions, while those who escaped had devil's eggs rained on them in what Richthofen called "a wonderful scene": "We are inflicting the highest losses of blood and materiel." Over the next two days, 12–13 May, as disorganized Soviet units streamed to the east in disarray, perfect targets for the Luftwaffe, the limits of German power became painfully apparent. Near disaster had struck to the north, where Timoshenko had launched an armored offensive out of the Izyum bulge toward Kharkov. As a result, Hitler ordered Richthofen to transfer many of his best units northward, which caused a perceptible slackening of air activity in the Kerch Peninsula. Goering's assessment had been correct: the Luftwaffe could no longer manage the great tasks. Although Manstein feared that the Soviets would be able to pull off a Dunkirk-style evacuation across the narrow Kerch Straits, this was not Stalin's intent. By the time the bulk of Manstein's units closed on Kerch, they found masses of Soviet troops on the exposed shore below the cliffs, perfect targets for German artillery. Although Kerch fell on 15 May, sporadic resistance, some fanatic, continued for the next week. Still, on 19 May, Manstein declared Trappenjagd completed.

It had been an astounding success: over 170,000 prisoners, 1,133 guns, and 258 tanks had been taken. A much smaller German-Rumanian force had smashed through a formidable defensive system and destroyed two full armies and remnants of a third. German skill had certainly been on full display, rekindling confidence in the troops, but the Soviet conduct of the battle illustrated once more the disastrous consequences of the rigidly centralized, ideological method of command that had so often produced fatal results the year before—and that the Germans, to their ultimate regret, fully expected to continue in the summer offensive.[7]

The stunningly swift victory at Kerch now opened the road for a renewed attempt to seize Sevastopol, a goal that had eluded Manstein in the autumn. In retrospect, wasting further precious time, manpower, and resources on taking the fortress seemed pointless, especially since the threat to the Rumanian oil fields from the "permanent aircraft career" of the Crimea had been eliminated and access to the Caucasus secured. At the time, however, and despite the Soviet penetrations near Kharkov, there appeared to be little discussion of the issue between Hitler and the OKH. The Führer, in fact, seemed eager to keep the victorious momentum going, if only to restore the confidence and reputation of his shaken troops. The fighting here, however, would be entirely different than that on the Kerch Peninsula; instead of dealing a swift surprise blow in open terrain, Manstein's limited forces would have to blast through an entrenched enemy, who had done everything possible to strengthen his positions, in a series of elaborate fortifications. Although Sevastopol was protected by two defensive belts, its defenders had added a formidable array of concrete bunkers, gun positions, tank traps, antitank ditches, and minefields, all tied together by a labyrinth of underground tunnels, even as the battle for Kerch raged.[8]

To seize the fortress, then, Manstein would need to blast it open with annihilating firepower, especially since the weak German Black Sea Fleet allowed an attack solely from land. To that end, the Germans had assembled the largest artillery pieces in their arsenal: 305-, 350-, and 420-millimeter howitzers as well as two 615-millimeter guns ("Thor" and "Odin") that fired nearly five-thousand-pound shells specially designed for use against concrete fortifications. The largest gun, "Dora," was an 800-millimeter monster that was the world's largest artillery piece. With a barrel over a hundred feet long and a bore almost three feet wide, Dora required a crew of two thousand, a sixty-car train, and six weeks to assemble. Although it could fire a shell weighing five tons forty-eight miles or seven-ton armor-piercing shells the height of a two-story building that could penetrate twenty-four feet of concrete, it demanded constant protection from two flak battalions. Although impressive, these weapons remained of limited value because of their slow rate of fire and inaccuracy.[9]

Arguably just as important as this unprecedented concentration of superheavy guns was the accumulation of some six hundred ground support aircraft to pinpoint strikes against enemy communications, artillery, and key defensive strongpoints as well as the use of eighty-eight-millimeter flak guns to penetrate armored strongpoints. The attack itself began on 2 June with a massive air assault that increased in intensity over the next four days as both aircraft and heavy artillery pounded incessantly at Soviet positions. When infantry attacks began on the seventh, it quickly became apparent that the softening up of the enemy's defensive front had not achieved the desired result: Soviet resistance was stronger than expected, and German troops could achieve no decisive breakthrough. Over the next few days, as German infantry struggled to make headway against tenacious Russian defenders who were clearly not demoralized or broken, Hitler for a time seriously considered abandoning the entire offensive. Time pressure was now an issue as the Sevastopol operation had to be brought to a conclusion soon so that the vital air units could be made available for Operation Blue. Over the next few days, in a precursor to Stalingrad, small groups of soldiers on both sides fought bitter hand-to-hand struggles for control of ruined buildings. The German attackers, using flamethrowers, satchel charges, and hand grenades, inflicted appalling carnage, yet the Red Army defenders fought on stubbornly. On 13 June, German forces, in savage fighting that resulted in the death or wounding of every officer in two battalions, finally began to crack the outer ring of Soviet defenses in the north. The decisive breakthrough came on the seventeenth, although again at the cost of disturbingly high casualties, when the Fifty-fourth Corps captured six key fortifications. Over the next six days, against a backdrop of continuing high losses, German forces seized the entire northern shore of Severnaya Bay. To the south, the Thirtieth Corps also pushed relentlessly forward, with the result that, by 26 June, Axis forces had succeeded in breaching the outer defense line.[10]

Faced now with a lengthy regrouping of his forces for an assault on the inner belt of defenses, time that the Germans did not have and that would have given the hard-pressed Soviet defenders the chance to reorganize as well, Manstein decided on an unorthodox and risky operation. During the night of 28–29 June, as the Thirtieth Corps assailed the Sapun Heights to the south, elements of the Fifty-fourth Corps crossed Severnaya Bay in one hundred assault boats and took the steep, heavily fortified shore in a wild rush before the stunned defenders could respond. By the evening of the twenty-ninth, with the Fiftieth Infantry Division pressing through the breach in the north toward Sevastopol itself and other Axis forces rolling up the front in the south, the battle was effectively won. Deeply impressed by the courage and fanatic spirit of the Russian defenders, however, and having already paid a terrible price in German lives for his triumph, Manstein resolved to avoid costly house-to-house fighting by having his artillery and air units pulverize the city. As a result, the occupation of the city and port on 1 July took place against only slight resistance, although some Russian units fought fiercely on the Khersones Peninsula until the fifth. Soviet troops had, in fact, fought so heroically and so impressed many German observers that Goebbels forbade any mention of such courage in press reports—it undermined the propaganda image of the Soviet opponent as being subhuman.[11]

Manstein had again directed a brilliant battle of annihilation (for which Hitler promoted him to field marshal), one that cost the Soviets tens of thousands killed and 95,000 prisoners. German losses, too, had been heavy, estimates ranging from 75,000 to 100,000 total casualties, with perhaps 25,000 dead. The key question, however, as Manstein himself put it in his memoirs, was whether the success attained at Sevastopol had justified tying down the entire Eleventh Army or simply encircling and besieging the fortress would have been sufficient. A good jumping-off point for the summer offensive had already been secured with the triumph in the Kerch operation, while seizing Sevastopol cost the Germans dearly in lives, materiel, and, what they perhaps had in shortest supply, time. Although Hitler was jubilant at the spring triumphs in the Crimea and North Africa, where Rommel had stormed Tobruk, the benefits gained from seizing Sevastopol, despite the humiliation to Stalin, seem far less than the costs.[12]

If victory in the Crimea had done much to reinstall confidence in the Wehrmacht, the larger tank action to the north at Kharkov did even more to send German spirits soaring. As a result of the confused and desperate winter fighting, the front line in the south, as elsewhere in Russia, was a tangled web of protrusions and salients that planners on both sides regarded as both a threat and an opportunity. For the Germans, who began thinking of regaining the initiative even before the late winter fighting had abated, these bulges had to be eliminated in order to secure favorable jumping-off positions for their planned summer offensive. Nowhere was this more apparent than in the Izyum bridgehead, a protrusion some sixty miles in depth and breadth into the German line on the west bank of the Donets River. Not only did it tie down numerous German formations, but Soviet forces jammed into the salient also posed a constant danger to the key industrial city of Kharkov, less than forty miles to the northwest, as well as threatening to roll up the entire southern front.

The menacing Soviet position, however, also posed an opportunity. To planners envisioning a summer campaign based on the rapid encirclement and destruction of enemy forces, the Izyum bulge, where the Red Army had already stuck its head in the noose, cried out to be snapped shut. As with the Crimean operation, elimination of the Izyum bridgehead would serve to create an advantageous starting point for Operation Blue as well as provide a morale boost for German troops left shaky by the rigors of the winter. To that end, Bock designed a cautious plan in which the Sixth Army, to the north, would strike along the Donets River, using the spring flood to protect its exposed left flank, while troops from the Seventeenth Army under Ewald von Kleist would attack from the south, with the intention of annihilating the enemy near Barvenkovo. Code-named Fredericus I, this operation aimed for a late April start date, when the spring flood would be at its height, but logistic problems caused its postponement. Both Hitler and Halder, moreover, raised objections to Bock's plan, favoring a much bolder operation that would have the Sixth Army first driving east across the Donets, then turning south. Although risking a Soviet counterthrust against the German flank, a deeper strike also promised a greater haul of prisoners once the trap sprang shut. Bock, perhaps remembering the nightmare in front of Moscow, was reluctant to accept the revision. He asked Halder whether the Führer was not worried about the prospect of a Russian attack at Kharkov, to which Halder replied, "No, such strong German forces are assembling near Kharkov that the enemy . . . will take care not to attack us there." Not happy, but recognizing the inevitable, Bock bowed to Hitler's will and drew up plans for Fredericus II, with a start date of 18 May.[13]

The Soviets, too, saw temptation and opportunity at Izyum, for, just as the Germans, they underestimated their opponent. Stalin, like Hitler, drew the lesson from the winter fighting that the enemy was on his last legs and, thus, favored aggressive offensive operations aimed at delivering the fatal blow. To senior leaders on the Stavka—both the chief of staff, Shaposhnikov, and his deputy, Vasilevsky, as well as Zhukov—the most sensible approach in 1942 was to remain on the strategic defensive, continue to build Soviet strength, absorb the anticipated German blow (which was expected to be aimed at Moscow), and only then, when the Germans were exhausted, go over to the offensive. For an army whose doctrine was based on "deep battle," however, and ruled by a dictator they were loathe to cross who favored aggressive action, it was hardly surprising that many Soviet generals proposed plans for local offensives within the overall defensive context. To Stalin, a limited offensive out of the Izyum bulge seemed especially appealing, not only because the commanding general, Timoshenko, was an old ally from Civil War days, but also because, if circumstances fell right, even a short breakthrough might have a strategic impact. Although the stated intent of Timoshenko's operation was simply to encircle and destroy German forces at Kharkov, by implication success here might well allow the entire southern front to be rolled up. Although both Shaposhnikov and Vasilevsky were horrified at Timoshenko's plan, which meant stuffing even more forces into a constricted space, the old warhorse convinced Stalin to approve it. Although the operation was originally scheduled to start on 5 May, difficulties in assembling his forces caused Timoshenko to postpone it until 12 May. Amazingly, then, the focus of both armies along the entire length of the Russian front had fallen on a small protrusion to the west of the Donets River.[14]

Despite repeated warnings by Foreign Armies East of the likelihood of an enemy attack out of the Izyum bulge and the fear expressed by Bock to Halder on 5 May that "the Russians might beat us to it and attack on both sides of Kharkov," the Soviet offensive caught the Germans unprepared. As Bock anticipated, Timoshenko's operation was designed as a dual pincer movement: a lesser attack to the northeast of Kharkov from the Volchansk bridgehead across the Donets would tie down German forces, while the major operation would be launched from the Izyum bulge to the southeast of Kharkov. The aim of the southern pincer was not merely to envelop Kharkov but to send forces to the west to seize Krasnograd and possibly threaten even Poltava, where Army Group South had its headquarters. Moreover, the Soviet command had learned the hard lessons of 1941 and reorganized the Red Army along German lines. Rather than rely on masses of poorly trained men, the Soviets now employed a smaller infantry component supported by massively expanded tank, artillery, and air formations. Although these new tank corps performed poorly in the spring and summer of 1942, primarily for lack of motorized infantry and antitank units, they nonetheless presaged a new style of waging war that aimed to match the Germans in shock, mobility, and coordination of the supporting arms. Significantly, as well, in planning the attack, the Soviets carefully aimed their initial blow in the north at the weak Hungarian 108th Light Infantry Division, and in the south at the poorly equipped German 454th Security Division.[15]

Thus, although Timoshenko severely underestimated the size and skill of his opponents, almost entirely neglecting the presence of Kleist's forces to the south of Barvenkovo, for example, his attack achieved considerable tactical surprise. Early in the morning of 12 May, following massive artillery and air bombardments, Soviet forces struck a powerful blow against the Germans that resulted, in some sectors, in profound shock and even panic. Although the inexperienced troops of the Soviet Twenty-eighth Army struggled to make headway against the prepared German defenses, the Thirty-eighth Army ripped through the Hungarian lines. To the south, the lightly armed German security division was no match for heavy armor and quickly gave way, enabling the Soviets over the next two days to open a breach in German lines over thirty miles in depth and breadth. General Paulus, in his first action as commander of the Sixth Army, reacted hesitantly and cautiously to the Soviet breakthroughs, intending, much as the Germans had done in front of Moscow, to conduct a defense based on using bypassed units as strongpoints. Paulus also demanded from Bock reinforcements, which could come only from the units designated for Fredericus. Reproached by Halder for worrying about every little "blemish" in the line, Bock exploded in anger that it was "no blemish, rather our very existence is at stake."[16]

Still, although the Soviet attack had struck hard, rapid German reaction, swift movement of troops and air units, and local counterattacks had checked the enemy advance in the north twelve miles from Kharkov, even as the situation in the south remained threatening. Both sides now had to make key decisions, and, in the event, it was the Germans who acted more decisively. Having saved his armored reserves for use at the right moment, Timoshenko now, on the fifteenth, hesitated to insert them into the battle. In part, this reflected his unease at strong local German counterattacks in the north. In part, it also resulted from inexperience: Soviet forces in the south had advanced so rapidly that getting reserves to the front proved far more difficult and time-consuming than anticipated. For the Germans, the situation appeared to offer much promise: with the northern sector stabilized, substantial numbers of Richthofen's squadrons heading north, and extensive Soviet forces to the west of the Izyum salient, a successful attack by Kleist's tanks from the south would nab an immense haul of infantry and armor. The Soviets had thrust their head deep into the noose, practically inviting the Germans to act.[17]

Although it was in retrospect a brilliant tactical maneuver, at the time Bock voiced pessimism as to whether Fredericus would succeed. An operation conceived as a dual envelopment would now have to proceed with only the southern pincer and no operational reserves, so he found it "difficult to see how the attack by . . . Kleist . . . will be sustained." Hitler nevertheless decided in favor of the thrust out of the Izyum pocket. This offensive, supported by a massive array of air power and a furious artillery barrage, kicked off on 17 May, just as Timoshenko compounded his dilemma by belatedly committing his Twenty-first and Twenty-third Tank Corps to exploiting the breakthrough in the south. The German attack, spearheaded by General Eberhard von Mackensen's Third Panzer Corps, struck northward through totally surprised troops of the Soviet Ninth and Seventeenth Armies, seizing Barvenkovo by the end of the first day, and by the evening of the eighteenth completely caving in the southern flank of the salient.[18]

Despite the stunning German success, senior Soviet leaders reacted remarkably slowly. A huge Soviet force faced the imminent danger of being trapped, but Timoshenko and his staff officers, including his political commissar, Nikita Khrushchev, failed to appreciate that the offensive had gone wrong. Instead, they continued to hammer away wildly in the mistaken belief that the German counteroffensive could be contained. Nor could Vasilevsky convince Stalin, who had gloated in the initial success of the Kharkov operation, to recall the tank spearheads and redirect them against Kleist's forces. Not until the evening of the nineteenth did Timoshenko awaken to the full gravity of the situation, but, by then, only immediate retreat could save any of the Soviet forces. Timoshenko, however, had made no contingency plans for such a withdrawal, nor did his forces have sufficient quantities of fuel and ammunition. Even attempting to supply the troops trapped in the shrinking pocket proved suicidal since the Luftwaffe ruled the sky and, one by one, German troops seized the vital bridges over the Donets on which Soviet survival depended. In addition, by the twentieth, Soviet command and control had largely broken down. The confusion was so great that German reconnaissance aircraft reported two large columns of Soviet troops and tanks: one was moving westward toward the front, while the other, the original attacking force, was desperately streaming toward the east.[19]

By 23 May, the Germans had snapped the trap shut and, amid terrible carnage, on the twenty-fifth turned away a desperate Soviet attempt to break out. Bock, watching events unfold from a hilltop observation post, was stunned by the "overwhelming scene." Ferocious fighting continued for the next three days, but, on the twenty-eighth, resistance collapsed. In addition to 267,000 casualties, the Red Army lost 240,000 men taken prisoner, 1,200 tanks, and 2,600 guns. In a brilliant display of skill and aggressiveness, the Germans had not only fought off a Soviet offensive but also encircled the would-be encirclers. Despite vast supplies of new weapons and an organizational restructuring, the Red Army remained plagued by command weaknesses, poor planning, supply difficulties, and inadequate control of the battlefield. Although elated at their success, thoughtful German observers remained troubled by the other constants in their Soviet enemy: his seemingly bottomless resources and the continued ferocity of his resistance. Kleist, surveying the battlefield, was startled by "the harshness of the struggle": "In places of the heaviest fighting, as far as one can see, the ground is so thickly covered with the bodies of men and horses that it is difficult to find a passage through for one's command car." Mackensen, too, observed soberly that, if anything, the Russians had been "more fanatical, more ruthless" than the year before and had displayed "incredible courage and determination." This was an annihilating battle, but one won "only by an all-out effort."[20]

Victory, moreover, had demanded deployment of virtually the entire Luftwaffe on a limited area of the front, while the supply and logistic system was as dismal as ever. The panzer units on which the success of the summer campaign depended had suffered significant losses in men and materiel, while time was slipping away as schedules were constantly revised. Finally, the Germans were fortunate that the Soviets had attacked first and in an area where they had built up forces for the summer campaign: the enemy could not always be expected to be so cooperative in his own destruction. Indeed, the defeat at Kharkov convinced many Soviet leaders that it might, after all, be better to stay on the strategic defensive for the time being and as much as possible avoid encirclement battles. All these were sobering thoughts considering the main German operation was still to come.

Such gloomy assessments seemed not to trouble Hitler. The failed Kharkov offensive had seriously weakened the Soviets precisely at the Schwerpunkt for Fall Blau, and the Führer intended to exploit German successes by annihilating as many enemy units as possible as quickly as possible. As early as 27 May, he ordered that the remaining Soviet penetrations near Volchansk and Izyum be cleared up. The Volchansk bulge, to the north, was to be tackled first since Blau was to unfold from north to south. The operation, code-named Wilhelm, was set to begin on 7 June, but heavy rain postponed the attack for three days. Once again, the Germans caught the Soviets by surprise and finished the operation by 15 June; although Wilhelm was successful in gaining territory, the hoped-for bag of prisoners never materialized as the Soviets, in a significant new trend, managed to pull out the bulk of their forces in time.[21]

The quick success at Volchansk raised the issue of whether the Izyum operation should be undertaken at all since the Wehrmacht now had a good launching pad for Blau and any action at Izyum would simply delay the main campaign even more. Bock argued that every day Blau was postponed meant a loss, but, on 14 June, Hitler nonetheless decided in favor of Fredericus II, a pincer operation whose goal was to seize the key transportation junction of Izyum as well as destroy enemy forces. After repeated delays caused by continuous thunderstorms, Kleist finally attacked on 22 June, the first anniversary of Barbarossa. As with Wilhelm, the German advance was swift but not entirely successful owing to continued rain that hampered mobility and the evasive maneuvers of the enemy. Although completed by the twenty-sixth and resulting in a more favorable jumping-off position for Blau, the operation had signally failed to annihilate the enemy. Bock, moreover, worried that the Soviet reaction showed that "he intends to avoid any major defeats now in order to gain time for the Americans to intervene." Foreign Armies East also shared this assessment, predicting that the Red Army would turn away from an extravagant wastage of its forces and would seek instead to "withdraw most of its forces from German surprise thrusts and attempts at encirclement." Now, more than ever, the Germans needed deep thrusts into the enemy rear, but fuel and supply limitations as well as Hitler's insistence on short encirclements raised the very real possibility that the summer campaign would simply punch into air. Even worse, Foreign Armies East now forecast that the expected material and manpower losses to be inflicted on the enemy would not appreciably affect his ability to continue the war, a grim conclusion that called into question basic German assumptions for the summer campaign. Halder might have shared these doubts but seemed not to have passed them on to Hitler. After all, the Führer was at the height of his self-assurance and once again basking in the glow of German triumphs. The warning from Foreign Armies East was accurate but too late—and, in any case, Hitler believed that he had no other option but to attack. "The crisis," Bock had already realized in late January, "was to be solved by offensive means."[22]

At the end of May, just as victories in the Crimea and Kharkov once again set Hitler's optimism rising that a victory could yet be obtained, Professor Konrad Meyer put the final version of his Generalplan Ost on Himmler's desk. By that time, too, the gassing of Jews at Chelmno, Belzec, and Sobibor was proceeding smoothly, with operations just beginning at Auschwitz, soon to be joined by Treblinka. Along with these "industrial" killings, the murder squads had swung back into action in occupied eastern Poland, Belorussia, and Ukraine. The Nazi regime had clearly embarked on something more than mere exploitation of conquered territory. Hitler had long emphasized that the war in the east was a matter of triumph or destruction; it was, in fact, nothing less than an opportunity to remake the racial map of Europe. Through huge population transfers, colonial resettlement schemes, and wholesale murder, the Nazis would not just reclaim territory Germany had lost following the First World War, but create a vast racial empire that would dominate Europe, eliminating for all time the alleged threat to the German Volk from Jews, Slavs, and Bolsheviks. That, to Hitler, was the meaning of the war—the enormous sacrifice of German blood could be justified only if a new society would be created out of the victory. Deeply committed to racial science—not for nothing had Rudolf Hess once termed National Socialism *applied biology*—the Nazi regime had already begun the process of "filtering" the domestic German population. With its spectacular military victories, it could now set about transforming the east, applying its characteristic mix of racial mysticism, science, modern planning techniques, and brutality. Generalplan Ost envisioned nothing less than a transformation of the vast resource-rich east through superior expertise and planning. The result would be a solution to the German economic dilemma highlighted by World War I and the Weimar years and an elevation of the nation's standard of living. Then, Hitler boasted, "Europe, and not America, would be the land of unlimited possibilities." Germany would also, he promised, become the most self-sufficient state in the world.[23]

As we have seen, the process of Germanization had already begun in the areas of western Poland to be incorporated in the Reich, where ruthless methods had been used not merely to expel Poles from their homes and farms to make way for the repatriation of Volksdeutsche, but to "denationalize" the Poles as well. Through a process of selective murder of the Polish national intelligentsia, rigorous repression, and the "reclaiming" of young people who looked German, Nazi agencies, led by the newly formed RKFDV, had set out to make the land German. Initially, however, this project was limited not only in its scope but also in its murderous intentions. As Himmler indicated in a famous May 1940 memorandum, Jews were not yet to be murdered, but deported to Africa. "Cruel and tragic as every individual case may be," he concluded, "this method is still the mildest and best one if . . . one rejects as un-German and impossible the Bolshevist method of physical extermination of a people." Although large numbers of people still would have died in such a project, in the spring of 1940 the Nazis had not yet crossed the threshold to mass murder.[24]

As with the onset of the Final Solution, which was still more than a year away, Nazi plans for the east also evolved, with the catalyst for radicalization in both cases being the invasion of the Soviet Union. Preliminary planning by Meyer had resulted in rough drafts of a general plan for the east being submitted to Himmler just before and after the start of Operation Barbarossa. As Nazi victories grew during the summer and fall of 1941, so did the ambitions of those involved in the project. Working under Meyer's direction, a small group of bright young SS-affiliated academic researchers expert in agriculture, racial science, urban planning, and economic geography had by the spring of 1942 altered the plan from one to secure food and other vital economic resources from the conquered areas of the east into a scheme that envisioned nothing less than the region's complete transformation into an area of German settlement, complete with model towns, villages, and farmsteads, all linked by a system of superhighways. The key to this new conception was the creation of three major zones of German colonization, from "Ingermanland" (Leningrad region) in the north through the Baltic region to "Gothengau" in the Crimea and southern Ukraine. These settlement areas would be connected by a series of strongpoints, German towns and villages at key rail and road junctions strung across Galicia and Ukraine. The land in the envisioned settlement area, a territory larger than the Reich in 1938, would be owned by the state and farmed out on long-term leases to Volksdeutsche, settlers from the old Reich, and SS/Wehrmacht veterans. Eventually, the Germanic peoples would be gathered in an empire that would stretch all the way to the Urals, where a *Wehrgrenze* (defense wall) would stand as a barrier protecting Europe from Asia's hordes. Germany would, thus, be freed from one of Hitler's most persistent racial nightmares: being overwhelmed by the sheer weight of numbers of alien peoples.[25]

Even as the scheme expanded in scope, however, officials within the SS and from other ministries voiced critical objections. On 3 September 1941, for example, Rolf-Heinz Hoeppner, the head of the Central Resettlement Office in Posen (West Prussia), a man experienced in the practical difficulties of translating grand visions into reality, sent a memo to Adolf Eichmann that raised a crucial question that needed to be resolved. "Is the goal," he asked, "to permanently secure [the non-German peoples] some sort of existence, or should they be totally eradicated?" He might have been the first to raise the issue, but Hoeppner was hardly the only bureaucrat vexed by the demographic complexity of the proposal. Dr. Erhard Wetzel, a race expert in Rosenberg's employ and, thus, a rival to Himmler's SS, pointedly criticized Generalplan Ost in April 1942 for its faulty population calculations. Not only had Meyer's experts engaged in highly wishful thinking in projecting the German birthrate, but they had also grossly underestimated the size of the Slavic populations to be dealt with. If more than 80 percent of the population of Poland, 64 percent of the population of Belorussia, and 75 percent of the population of Ukraine were to be expelled from the proposed colonization area as racially undesirable, the total number of people involved would be, not the 31–45 million estimated by Meyer, but closer to 60–65 million, of whom at least 46–51 million would have to be deported. Resettling them in western Siberia—especially the Poles, whom Wetzel considered particularly troublesome—would be dangerous since they would create "a source of continual unrest against German rule." The alternative, however, was both problematic and revealing. "It should be obvious," he stressed, "that one cannot solve the Polish problem by liquidating the Poles in the same way as the Jews." Wetzel, it should be stressed, fully shared the goal of the Germanization of Eastern Europe; he was simply confounded by its implementation. Finally, Helmut Schubert, an economist in Himmler's own RKFDV, raised practical objections. The entire plan, he noted, depended on reversing the historic German trend toward urbanization and industrialization and, thus, posed a basic dilemma: industrialization and prosperity or racial homogeneity and stagnation?[26]

None of these objections troubled Himmler, however. Amazingly, despite the sweeping scope and murderous implications of Meyer's proposal, he ordered its architects to be even more ambitious: the Baltic states and the General Government should all be included in the Germanization project, while the time frame should be shortened from thirty years to twenty. In fact, Himmler stressed, Meyer and his team should think of expanding their proposal for the east into a general settlement plan that would link the eastern project with plans for Alsace-Lorraine, the Czech lands, and Slovenia. As to any difficulties in implementation, Himmler simply reminded his subordinates of what he had insisted since the *Kampfzeit* (struggle for power) of the 1920s: "that the so-called social question can only be solved by killing the other in order to get his land." Himmler's murderous dreams received a decisive boost on 16 July when he presented Hitler with the final version of the Generalplan, complete with architectural drawings and maps of the proposed German settlements. Again convinced that the war in the east would be won, the Führer, according to Himmler, "not only listened to me, he even refrained from constant interruptions, as is his usual habit. . . . Today he went so far as to approve of my proposals." It was, the Reichsführer confessed, "the happiest day of my life. Everything I have been considering and planning . . . can now be realized. I shall set to it at once."[27]

Not surprisingly, his first decision concerned the Jews, for in mid-July there was yet another of those convergences of factors that spelled their doom under Nazi rule. Hitler's optimism about the military situation and Sauckel's success in resolving the labor shortages in Germany through his brutal "recruitment drives" meant that Jewish labor was no longer regarded as necessary even for war-related projects. The domestic food crisis, meanwhile, added to the murderous "logic" that they be eliminated as useless eaters. Moreover, in all discussions surrounding Generalplan Ost, one thing had been assumed by all: the Jews would have no place. The day after Hitler's approval of Generalplan Ost, Himmler visited the newly expanded camp at Auschwitz, where he and his entourage viewed a "selection" and murder of Dutch Jews at nearby Birkenau. On 18–19 July, he issued three key orders to Globocnik and his boss in Lublin, Higher SS and Police Leader Friedrich Krueger, that illustrated the pattern in his thinking. The first explicitly instructed them to complete "the resettlement [i.e., murder] of the entire Jewish population of the General Government" unfit for work by the end of the year, while the second aimed at beginning the settlement program of Generalplan Ost. The third, finally, ordered draconian measures used to ensure the success of the fall harvest; the hunt for grain was to be pursued with complete ruthlessness. Three days later, on 22 July, deportations from the Warsaw ghetto to Treblinka commenced; by the end of the year, only 300,000 Jews, by German reckoning, remained alive in the General Government. In all, prewar Poland's Jewish population of 3.25 million had been reduced to barely half a million. If the Nazis were intent on a New Order in the east, the first step in creating it would be the Final Solution of the Jewish problem.[28]

In anticipation of imminent victory, and eager to realize his utopian blueprint, Himmler hurriedly pushed ahead with his pilot schemes. Thus, even though Nazi authorities had already begun work in the spring of 1942 on a limited plan for building a "Germanic bridge" between Lithuania and the Czech lands by resettling Volksdeutsche, Himmler promoted a much more ambitious project. The focal point for the immediate implementation of his plans was to be the provincial town of Zamosc, southeast of Lublin. In the Generalplan, Lublin lay in a key region, situated at the junction of two main axes of settlement, so the project at Zamosc was seen as a key test of the entire colonization policy. The SS experts responsible for carrying out the scheme planned to "bottle up" the Polish population living in the region and "suppress their economic and biological development." In blunter terms, Himmler meant to tear down the entire town, deport the Poles living in the region, and replace them with German settlers. The Nazi governor-general, Hans Frank, worried about opposition by the Poles and the possible disruption of their contribution to the war economy, wanted to wait until the end of the war for implementation of the project, but Himmler saw no reason for delay.[29]

Put under the direction of the thuggish and odious Odilo Globocnik, this trial run to sort out the problems involved in the implementation of population policy proved disastrous, as Globocnik's violent and harsh methods provoked exactly the sort of backlash that Frank had feared. In order to make room for German colonists, in November 1942 Globocnik's men began uprooting over 100,000 people from some three hundred villages in the Zamosc region who were then sent for "selection" to camps at Maidanek and Auschwitz. There, they were racially screened: some of the adults and children were to be Germanized and "won back to the German nation"; the remaining children and the elderly were sent to "retirement villages," where they would starve to death; other adults were to replace Jewish forced laborers, who would then be killed; the rest would be sent to the gas chambers at Auschwitz.[30]

From mid-December on, transports with the first Zamosc deportees began arriving at Auschwitz, while other trains arrived in Berlin with Poles bound for work in the armaments industry. There, they were exchanged with the so-called arms factory Jews, who had stayed alive working in the armaments industry but were now superfluous. Trains from Berlin would then carry the Jews to Auschwitz; after unloading their "cargo," they would then transport Volksdeutsche, primarily from Southeastern Europe, to the Zamosc region. Here, the incoming German colonists would be met by SS resettlement agents, relocated in the surrounding area, and given land that had been seized from the Poles. From Zamosc, the trains would return to Auschwitz with those Poles deemed "undesirable." This "population exchange" was, thus, part of a pilot demographic project in which highly productive German agricultural settlements would be created in the east, with the Poles displaced either Germanized, put in forced labor, or killed and the Jews murdered immediately.[31]

In the Zamosc area, things did not go as smoothly as in Berlin or Auschwitz. Within weeks of the first "evacuation" drive, the region was in revolt: the new settlers were attacked and some killed; farmers fled to join partisan bands; and partisan warfare flared in an area that up to that point had been quiet. Himmler ordered vicious reprisals against the Poles, but this failed to quell the unrest, which continued into the spring of the following year. Frank was furious; because of Himmler's impatience and Globocnik's brutality, the Poles in the General Government were in an uproar, fearful that, as an SS leader put it, "after the Jews are annihilated [the Germans] will try to use the same methods to drive the Poles out of this area and liquidate them just like the Jews." In May 1943, Frank complained that "a state of open rebellion" existed in the Zamosc area, with SS actions having caused an "indescribable panic." Entire districts were being depopulated, both by the resettlement action and by Poles fleeing the land, with resulting disruption of both the economic and the security situation.[32]

Himmler, however, doggedly pursued his utopian dreams. In mid-September 1942, he stressed to his associates that the chief task in the first two decades after the war would be to gather the Germanic peoples and finish construction of the great German empire that would stretch to the Urals. Amazingly, on 23 November, the very day that the Soviet ring closed around Stalingrad, he could assert in a speech that the east "would be colonies today, settlement area tomorrow, and German territory the day after tomorrow." In practice, however, the turnabout in the military situation at Stalingrad largely caused his schemes to grind to a halt in the winter of 1942–1943. His pilot project at Zamosc, and similar smaller ones in Ukraine, had failed miserably and brought only turmoil and economic disruption. The Nazis had amply demonstrated their willingness and ability to uproot and destroy entire groups of people, but the very war that had made these radical measures possible now forced a halt to their utopian ventures. Generalplan Ost had envisioned a vast racial restructuring of Eastern Europe. One component was to be the extermination of the local Jewish population as well as the deportation and annihilation of perhaps 30–40 million Slavs. A second aspect was the resettlement of millions of Volksdeutsche, Germans, or others of Germanic origins in the evacuated areas, while the final component was the employment of millions of Slavs in forced labor. By the end of 1942, the destruction of the Polish Jews under German control was largely complete, while military setbacks halted the vast resettlement schemes. Those same military reverses, however, now brought the third aspect of the plan to the forefront as the Germans desperately needed foreign labor for their war economy.[33]

While, as noted above, Sauckel proved adept in his *Menschenjagd* (slave labor hunts), Himmler, with a nose for power, sensed a way for the

SS to profit as well. With the demands of the war economy paramount, and with labor a key commodity within that economy, he realized that control of the flow of workers would confer great power. Although ideological imperatives were always predominant in Himmler's mind, the Reichsführer-SS also understood that huge pools of labor would be required for the vast construction projects of Generalplan Ost. "If we do not fill our camps with slaves," he emphasized in June 1942, "with worker slaves who will build our cities, our villages, our farms . . . , then even after years of war we will not have enough money to be able to equip the settlements in such a manner that real Germanic people can live there." In conjunction with implementation of Generalplan Ost, then, Himmler expanded the WVHA (Economic and Administrative Main Office) of the SS to take full advantage of the forced labor potential in the concentration camp system. Under the leadership of the energetic Oswald Pohl, the population of the camp system skyrocketed, growing from roughly 20,000 in September 1939, to 75,000 in April 1942, and 224,000 in August 1943. By January 1945, the camp system held an astonishing 714,000 people, the great majority non-Jewish (political prisoners, Soviet prisoners of war, and Ostarbeiter), and had effectively been transformed into a Soviet-style labor gulag. Although Himmler wanted to extract maximum economic benefit from these prisoners, he could not quite suspend his racial principles, so a sort of murderous compromise between ideology and pragmatism evolved: Vernichtung durch Arbeit. Thus, although Pohl urged his camp commandants to act as managers and make their enterprises economically productive, he still reminded them that the work must be "in the true meaning of the word, exhaustive."[34]

Pohl also held out the lure of cheap labor in order to attract industrial investment as a means to expand the scope of the WVHA from construction projects to armament work. The result was a dramatic expansion of its network of labor camps adjacent to the larger concentration and extermination facilities. Auschwitz, for example, not only rented out its inmates to the nearby I. G. Farben facilities at Monowitz, but also sent prisoners to industrial sites throughout Silesia. Eventually, when Himmler's opposition to such workers within the Reich receded, the SS supplied forced labor to Heinkel (Oranienburg), Siemens (Ravensbrück), BMW (Dachau), and Daimler-Benz (Sachsenhausen and Mauthausen). Opposition from Speer to Himmler's power grab, however, prevented a large penetration of the SS into armaments production in 1942. Not only were such enterprises grossly inefficient, but camp managers also tended to take Vernichtung durch Arbeit far too seriously. Mortality rates in 1942 soared so high that the WVHA could not meet its own targets for the slave labor population. If Himmler was going to be able to leverage the labor reservoir of the concentration camps to increase the power of his SS empire, these staggeringly high rates of attrition would have to be brought down. Only after the military debacle at Stalingrad in the winter of 1942–1943, however, did the SS set about making changes, but by then it would be too late. The key period was 1942, the last opportunity the Reich had to win the war in the east before it faced the full power of the enemies stacked against it. The tension between racial impulses and economic pragmatism, as well as the use of brutal colonial methods against other European peoples, resulted in an astonishing misuse of labor. Although the Nazis modified their policies in 1943, the damage could not be undone: in the crucial phase of the war, they had not been able to convert the resources under their control into weapons as effectively as their opponents. Nazi officials had begun to realize their conundrum: they could have racial purity or an effective war economy, but not both.[35]

In late June, the operation that Hitler expected finally to end this "business in the east" began to unfold—two weeks late, beset by supply and transportation problems that hampered the assembly and deployment of the attacking force, and bedeviled by poor weather that worsened the already primitive road system. As originally conceived, Blue was an exceedingly complex operation designed to unfold in four successive stages, with success in each phase creating the condition for triumph in the next—with the intended result the destruction of Soviet forces west of the Don and cascading momentum that would propel German forces into the Caucasus. The operation would begin in the north, where Blue I aimed at seizing crossings over the Don River and the important transportation city of Voronezh, all the while trapping enemy forces and providing flank protection against Soviet counterattack. In the next phase, Blue II, German mobile forces would strike south from Voronezh along the Don while the Sixth Army launched an offensive from the area around Kharkov, with the spearheads to meet near the city of Millerovo. Again, if all went correctly, Soviet units would be herded together in another *Kessel* (pocket). At this point, Blue III dictated that Army Group South split in two, with Bock's Army Group B advancing across the great bend of the Don River toward Stalingrad. Seizing the city itself was regarded as largely inconsequential; the important thing was simply to neutralize it as a center for armaments production and transportation. Only then, after a solid defensive line had been established, would Army Group A under List unleash the final stage of the operation, with Blue IV the key drive into the Caucasus to seize the vital oil fields and the passes over the mountains. Everything depended on the organization, coordination, and timely movement of forces across distances even greater than those covered by the central thrust the year before—and, above all, on speed since Hitler hoped to make up for the time lost in the preliminary operations by advancing the second and third phases of the operation.[36]

Beneath its complexity, Fall Blau betrayed a number of assumptions that should have given German generals pause to reflect on the prospect of success. In order to avoid the problems with large-scale encirclement operations experienced in the previous year, Directive No. 41 specified small, tight Kessels. Deep encirclements looked good on maps but had too often resulted in the mobile formations thrusting far ahead of the infantry, with panzer units being tied down, often for weeks, in fierce cauldron battles while large numbers of enemy troops managed to slip through the porous pockets. Smaller encirclements, both Hitler and many in the OKH believed, would allow the infantry to close faster, thus destroying a higher percentage of those trapped while allowing the panzers to move on. Certainly, much tactically spoke for this argument, but, at bottom, it meant a shift away from the flexibility and operational freedom that German commanders had traditionally enjoyed and from which much of their success had sprung. Instead, their actions would be monitored from Führer Headquarters, with Hitler increasingly micromanaging troop movements. Success now depended, to a great degree, on the Führer's willingness not to attempt to seize everything at once, never a good bet. In addition, the stress on small pockets was an implicit recognition of German deficiencies in mobile formations, fuel, and supply capabilities. From mid-July 1941, German logistic problems had limited advances to about ten days and no more than a hundred miles, after which the attacking forces had to pause for up to a week to replenish their depleted fuel and ammunition stocks. In terms of logistics, little had changed in 1942. In effect, Hitler and the OKH were trying to make a virtue of necessity since the Ostheer increasingly lacked the vital strength to conduct "deep war." Finally, as Hitler recognized, the ranks of the newly constituted units of the Eastern Army were rife with young, hastily trained draftees for whom it was crucial that the initial battles go well. "The operation must begin with success," Hitler emphasized in late March; "young troops must not suffer any setbacks." Success in short encirclements, however, depended not just on German skill but on Soviet cooperation as well.[37]

As intended, victories in the Crimea and Kharkov had done much to restore German confidence and morale, while the shaky Soviet performance rekindled inflated notions of easy triumphs leading to a quick seizure of the Caucasian oil fields. Still, a curious episode on the eve of Blau threatened the entire German operation and revealed deep suspicions between Hitler and the Army High Command that would lead to a permanent schism with profound consequences. On 19 June, Major Joachim Reichel, the chief of staff of the Twenty-third Panzer Division, had set out to reconnoiter the proposed route of march of his division, but his plane went off course and crashed behind Soviet lines. The pilot was killed immediately, and the major was shot trying to escape. Reichel carried with him a copy of a memorandum summarizing Blau I as well as a map showing corps and army objectives. A German combat patrol reached the wrecked plane two days later and found the bodies but not the documents, so the OKH had to assume, correctly, that they had fallen into enemy hands. Given the magnitude of this security breach, some in the High Command believed that the operation now had to be called off or significantly altered. Others, however, including Bock and Halder, argued that, given the time it would take for the information to work its way up the Soviet chain of command and the fact that deployment preparations were largely complete, the attack should go ahead as soon as possible.[38]

For the army command, then, the "Reichel Affair" was largely inconsequential and merely another reason to launch Blau I immediately. To Hitler, however, the matter ran deeper: it was yet another sign that the generals were flouting security, disobeying his orders, and undermining his leadership. The reason for this was not hard to see since this case closely resembled an incident in January 1940 in which plans for the invasion of France were similarly lost. Hitler thereafter had insisted on tight security controls over all operational plans. Only major headquarters were to receive copies, and plans were never to be taken by air near the front lines, restrictions specifically mentioned in Directive No. 41. These precautions, sensible though they were, directly contradicted a key aspect of the German tradition of command autonomy: staff officers had long shared the plans of adjacent or higher units in order to better coordinate and execute operations. This flow of information, and the flexibility it entailed, was regarded as vital for success in battle. Hitler, however, was furious at this obvious violation of both the spirit and the letter of his orders and demanded that the officers responsible be punished. In addition, on the twenty-fifth, he summoned Bock personally to the Wolfsschanze (Wolf's Lair) to report on the affair. Although the latter managed to persuade Hitler that there was no disobedience other than that of the dead Reichel, the matter hardly ended there. For days afterward, the OKW used the issue to conduct a campaign against the OKH, while the Führer continued to seethe and see conspiracies against his dictates; indeed, the issue festered in his mind all during the summer, exploding finally in the fall into a major command crisis.[39]

For their part, neither Stalin nor the Stavka seemed inclined to regard the lost plans as anything but part of a deception operation. Although Stalin was aware of German oil problems, he nonetheless insisted, as did Vasilevsky, that Moscow would again be the main objective of the anticipated German summer offensive. In the ultimate irony, Stalin, steeped in Communist ideology that regarded economic interests as paramount, ignored the obvious significance of oil for his enemy and, instead, focused on defending the political heart of the regime. Although the Germans had pushed elaborate deception measures designed to encourage this notion, Stalin needed little persuading. Indeed, as late as November, he still insisted that isolating Moscow from the hinterland was the main German objective and that the advance in the south was merely secondary. Despite his mistaken evaluation of the overall situation, however, he hedged his bets; since the Kursk-Voronezh area was regarded as a logical place for a German flanking attack on Moscow, on 23 and 24 June he ordered considerable reinforcements, including powerful tank formations, into the area.[40]

Two weeks late, while fighting still raged at Sevastopol and against a backdrop of simmering tension among the German leadership, Blau I finally opened on 28 June. Remarkably, the attack achieved almost complete surprise; accompanied by overwhelming air support, German units broke through Soviet lines and began racing eastward. Hoth's Fourth Panzer Army advanced up to thirty miles in the direction of Voronezh on the first day, while, on the extreme left flank, Weichs's Second Army also made good progress. With the Soviet defenders stunned by the speed and ferocity of the assault, about the only thing that slowed the Germans in the first few days was heavy rain. Even then, by 4 July, lead units of the Fourth Panzer Army had reached the Don in numerous places, over one hundred miles from the start line, and advanced to the outskirts of Voronezh. To its left, the Second Army had also kept pace, although, alarmed at the rapid German advance and fearful that this important armaments and transportation center would fall to the enemy, Stalin ordered strong Soviet forces into position for counterattacks from the north. On the right, heavy rain delayed the Sixth Army's attack until 30 June, but it, too, after overcoming initial resistance, met only relatively light opposition as it set out for the Don. Soviet forces seemed in disarray and, in places, to have dissolved. With German forces in the north already across the Don, Paulus's troops in the south lunging eastward, and most of the Red Army defenders still west of the river, the Germans seemed poised once again to pull off a spectacular encirclement operation reminiscent of 1941. Doubts remained, however. "The actual picture of the enemy situation is not yet clear to me," Halder admitted on 6 July. "There are two possibilities: either we have overestimated the enemy's strength and the offensive has smashed him, or the enemy is conducting a planned disengagement . . . to forestall being irretrievably beaten in 1942." In the event, the second assessment proved more accurate than the first as strong Soviet counterattacks at Voronezh delayed subsequent German advances and provoked a command crisis.[41]

To Hitler and Halder, reports that the enemy "was gone" evinced alarm since the goal of Blau I was the destruction of Soviet forces west of the Don. To their minds, the key now was speed—German mobile formations in the north had to be turned as swiftly as possible to the south to trap the Red Army before it could escape. Neither could understand what appeared to be Bock's obsession with taking the city. The latter, however, faced an increasing danger: Soviet attacks on his left flank had grown steadily, while reconnaissance indicated enemy troops massing across the Don to the north. Bock was surprised to learn on the second that Hitler and Halder now placed no importance on the capture of the city and, instead, urged him to wheel his mobile units to the south. He was reluctant to do this as long as his left flank was unsecured and hung in the air, and, in any case, he thought that the bulk of the enemy facing the Sixth Army had already escaped. Fearful that the vital mobile formations would get bogged down in pointless positional fighting, Hitler flew to Army Group South headquarters at Poltava on 3 July to order Bock to leave the city alone. If anything, however, the meeting only further confused the issue. Confronted with the aloof and aristocratic field marshal, the Führer evidently lost his nerve and left the decision to Bock, who himself was confused. "Am I right in understanding you as follows?" Bock queried. "I am to capture Voronezh if it can be done easily. . . . But I am not to get involved in heavy fighting for the city?" Hitler confirmed this with a nod. Ironically, although Bock believed that his command autonomy had been confirmed, the Führer thought that he had made plain his preference for a move south.[42]

Since Hoth's panzers reached the outskirts of Voronezh the next day and, despite erroneous reports that Soviet reinforcements had flooded the city, took it largely unopposed on the sixth, Bock likely felt confirmed in his actions. The damage, however, had been done. Reacting to the false reports, Hitler on the fifth exploded in rage at the field marshal's incompetent leadership. Insisting that he had made it "emphatically clear" on the third that he placed no value on Voronezh, Hitler now ordered Bock to detach the Twenty-fourth Panzer and Grossdeutschland Divisions and send them to the south. On the morning of the sixth, however, the attacks on Bock's left flank demanded by Stalin, but never anticipated in the plan for Blau I, began in earnest and continued with increasing intensity for the next week. Only with some difficulty, and primarily because of air supremacy, did the Second Army manage to sta-bilize the situation, although the northern flank of Blau would remain a source of concern since Hungarian divisions would eventually be responsible for its security. These onslaughts, combined with a shortage of fuel, meant that, much to Hitler's fury, Bock's mobile divisions were now tied down in the fighting around Voronezh. This not only threat-ened a crippling delay in German plans but also exacerbated the time pressure under which the Germans labored.[43]

The Führer's anger at Bock's allegedly poor handling of the situa-tion merely obscured the deeper problems confronting the Wehrmacht. Soviet actions had again demonstrated that the Germans lacked the mobile forces necessary simultaneously to defend their flanks against determined assaults and to press an offensive, especially one plunging into the limitless realm of southern Russia. More troubling, not only did the Soviets already outnumber the Germans in men and tanks, but in the first days of July Stalin also finally accepted reality and ordered a flexible defense and strategic withdrawals in order to conserve strength. Although these evasive maneuvers often turned into headlong flight in which Soviet officers lost control of their units, the result was largely the same. Success in encirclement operations depended as much on Soviet as on German actions, a fact understood by Bock but unappreciated by those above him. "The Army High Command," he noted bitterly on the seventh, "would like to encircle an enemy who is no longer there." The next day, he underscored the consequences of Soviet withdrawal. The attempted envelopment, he judged, would "probably hit nothing": "Operation Blue II is dead."[44]

This latter judgment remained to be confirmed, but, clearly, Hitler and Halder were worried that Soviet forces were evaporating. On the sev-enth, Army Group South was, over the vigorous protests of Bock, split into two forces, while, on the ninth, Kleist's First Panzer Army, now part of List's Army Group A, launched Blue II two weeks earlier than antici-pated. At a time when the situation called for the Germans to concentrate their power and act boldly, they now began the fatal dissipation of force that would characterize their summer operations. A major reason for this development was undoubtedly the continuing large-scale pullback by the Red Army, which rendered German plans obsolete. Kleist had no sooner sent his forces hurtling from Lisichansk, southeast of Izyum, across the Donets to the northeast than his orders were altered and then revised again. Soviet withdrawals clearly confounded German plans. On the evening of the eleventh, for example, the OKH ordered an inner encirclement centered on Millerovo involving forces from the First and Fourth Panzer Armies as well as the Sixth Army. Bock immediately protested this order, warning Halder early on the morning of 13 July that "annihilation of substantial enemy forces can no longer be achieved" at Millerovo. Instead, he argued that the main thrust should be sent farther east through the Morozovsk area and in the direction of Stalingrad. Given the often chaotic nature of Russian withdrawals, deep thrusts to the east, reminiscent of those the year before, might well have succeeded in trapping large numbers of the enemy. Given the catastrophic logistic system, any hopes for a dash to the east depended on a concentration of effort; already, a number of German units had been immobilized for lack of fuel. Despite Hitler's criticism, the Fourth Panzer Army's move to the south had been hindered more by a lack of fuel, for which the OKH was responsible, than by the field marshal's intransigence.[45]

Nonetheless, the reaction to Bock's proposal was swift and final: the OKH curtly informed him that his mission lay in the south, not the east, while Hitler, after fuming for days that Bock's decisions at Voronezh had caused avoidable delays in sending mobile units south, on the thirteenth relieved the strong-willed field marshal of his command. That same day, the Führer issued an order that demanded that "a thrust be made as quickly as possible from the north" to seize "the crossings of the Don at Konstantinovka and Zymlyanskaya [east of Rostov] in order to prevent the enemy from pulling out into the region south of the lower Don." In firing Bock and further marginalizing Halder, Hitler assumed increasing control over the day-to-day conduct of military operations, a quest for absolute authority that would have calamitous consequences. At the same time, and equally disastrously, he had abandoned the overall concept of Blue as a sequential operation in which each stage was vital for the success of the whole and, in its place, left only strategic confusion, with German columns apparently advancing aimlessly, often across each other's line of march. Although these twin dictates are often regarded simply as examples of Hitler's impulsive behavior, when combined with other decisions at roughly the same time, they reveal a pattern that shows the way in which time pressures had begun to affect his decisions.[46]

Although Hitler had undertaken operations in 1942 convinced that he had a year in which to wrap up the eastern war, Molotov's visit to London and Washington in May and June and the Western allies' apparently solid commitment to a second front in 1942 profoundly disturbed him. The Anglo-Americans, he believed, would not tolerate a collapse of the Soviet Union; ironically, then, the likelihood of an early Allied landing in Norway or Northwest Europe increased with German success in the east. His window of opportunity apparently narrowing rapidly, Hitler decided to forestall any Allied intervention on the Continent. "The rapid and great successes in the east," Hitler explained in an order of 9 July, "could face Britain with the alternative of either executing a major landing at once to establish a second front or losing Soviet Russia." Nervous about just such a possibility, the Führer directed that the powerful First and Second SS Panzer Divisions (Leibstandarte Adolf Hitler and Das Reich), which should have spearheaded the First Panzer Army's drive into the Caucasus, be transferred to the west. Two weeks later, he further ordered that the elite Grossdeutschland Motorized Division be prepared for transportation to the west. Finally, he also decreed, despite the drain on the Wehrmacht's meager fuel supplies, that the Channel and Atlantic coasts be developed into an "unassailable fortress" in order "to avoid the establishment of a second front." There could, he declared to Speer and Keitel, be "only one fighting front." A more accurate explication of the German dilemma was hard to imagine: by building up his defenses in the west, Hitler hoped to deter the Allies from launching a second front in 1942, but at a cost to what was most important, seizing the oil fields in the Caucasus.[47]

Fear of an early second front, in turn, made a rapid seizure of the oil of the Caucasus even more imperative. On 11 July, Hitler thus issued orders for Manstein's Eleventh Army, fresh off its triumph at Sevastopol, to prepare a crossing of the Kerch Straits, with the aim of facilitating the rapid seizure of the Maikop region and its vital oil fields. The target date of the operation, early August, in itself suggested that Hitler was already thinking of launching the push into the Caucasus before the Stalingrad operation was finished, reflecting the new time pressure under which he was acting. Just six days later, however, he suddenly reversed his decision and, instead, ordered the bulk of the Eleventh Army transferred north to the Leningrad front. Certainly, the fall of the northern city would have had a deleterious impact on the Soviets' ability to continue in the war, but Hitler's decision also reflected his belief that events in the Don area were proceeding so favorably that he could now launch simultaneous rather than staggered operations against the Volga and the Caucasus. This characteristic Hitlerian tendency to try to do everything at once stretched already thin German resources to the breaking point and largely ensured that none of the key objectives would be reached.[48]

Even as on the sixteenth the Germans closed the pocket at Millerovo, which was, as Bock had predicted, "a blow into thin air," they plunged ahead in the futile search for an annihilating battle, with the focus now clearly in the south on Rostov. As Landsers marched in suffocating mid-July heat, their progress easily charted by great clouds of dust thrown into the air, the combination of an overtaxed logistic system, terrain problems, and evasive actions by the enemy resulted in the capture of much territory but few prisoners. Although the Thirteenth and Twenty-second Panzer Divisions, supported by the Fifth SS Viking Division, reached Rostov on 23 July, furious resistance by NKVD security troops not only led to a four-day house-to-house struggle that presaged the later fighting at Stalingrad, but also enabled the bulk of Soviet formations in the area to escape across the Don. To the chagrin of both Hitler and List, the German thrust south had merely confirmed Bock's prediction: the pincer operation had bagged only 83,000 prisoners. Taken together, Blau I and II had resulted in perhaps 220,000 Soviet deaths and 150,000 taken prisoner, certainly a damaging blow to the Russians, but nothing on the order of the previous year. Nor, given the change in Soviet tactics, had the Germans been able to annihilate the remaining vital strength of the enemy; the key story in 1942 was the survival, not the destruction, of the Red Army. Moreover, by committing the bulk of Wehrmacht forces to List, Hitler and the OKH had starved the Sixth Army of the resources it needed to advance quickly to the east. Bock had in mid-July correctly observed that Stalingrad was ripe for the taking, but only if adequate armored forces were available to do so. Valuable days had been lost in the planned thrust to Stalingrad, giving the Soviets time to strengthen the city. Although a victory, Blau I and II seemed to keen observers rather ordinary; despite impressive territorial gains, a lack of fuel and mobile units had allowed the Soviets to evaporate into the vastness of southern Russia. Time and space, as well as the Red Army, had become very real enemies.[49]

Halder, in fact, had grown increasingly alarmed at the rapid reinforcement of both the Stalingrad and the Southern Fronts, which could mean only that the Soviets were determined to hold both the city on the Volga and the Caucasus. Upset by what he saw as the "meaningless" concentration of forces around Rostov, which merely "crammed" the area "with armor which has nothing to do," and anxious about having to embark on the "battle of Stalingrad" even while fighting continued in the south, Halder attempted without success to convince Hitler of the need for a concentrated thrust to the Volga. Only then, with a free rear, secure flank, and adequate logistics, would the Caucasus operation be executed. Hitler, however, saw things differently. "The Russian is finished," he told Halder breezily on 20 July, the next day expressing his conviction that the Germans, on the verge of seizing the Donets industrial region, severing the Volga supply line, and taking control of 90 percent of Soviet oil production, had dealt the enemy a fatal blow. This, along with an outburst three days later of "insane rage and . . . gravest reproaches against the General Staff" for its alleged negativity, pessimism, and caution, caused the head of the OKH to explode. "The chronic tendency to underrate enemy capabilities is gradually assuming grotesque proportions," he wrote angrily in his diary on 23 July, "and develops into a positive danger. . . . This so-called leadership is characterized by a pathological reacting to the impressions of the moment and a total lack of any understanding." Halder's objections, however, served only to rekindle the poisonous atmosphere of the previous winter. Convinced that the Soviets were fleeing for their lives and not, as Halder argued, conducting a planned withdrawal, Hitler saw in the swift seizure of Rostov proof that the enemy was incapable of mounting an effective defense west of the Volga or preventing a German occupation of the Caucasus.[50]

Operation Blue had begun to fall apart almost immediately, a consequence of both German and Soviet actions. The experience of 1941 had proved significant for both sides. Determined to avoid the operational chaos of the latter stages of the 1941 campaign, and faced with insufficient economic and military resources, German planners disdained deep battles of encirclement, instead relying on Soviet forces to stay in place in order to conduct a rolling series of shallow encirclements. In the event, whether from sheer panic, a Soviet decision to withdraw into the vast expanse of southern Russia, or a combination of both, the initial German thrusts in the summer of 1942 netted few prisoners despite conquering much territory. The Wehrmacht found itself punching air. Moreover, when the Soviets did resist, as with their relentless counterattacks at Voronezh, the result was to upset the ambitious German timetable and delay sending vital mobile formations to the south. Rather than striking in depth to the east and trapping large Soviet formations against the natural line of the Volga, the Germans found themselves sliding ineffectually to the south in an operation that stretched their hopelessly overburdened supply lines to the breaking point. Almost from the beginning, then, the Soviet retreat rendered the operational plan for 1942 pointless.

Hitler now, in late July, further compounded this increasingly unfavorable situation with his impatience and impetuosity. On the basis of his overly optimistic assessment, he attempted to do too much, too fast, in too many areas: he split the already overstretched German forces, dictated that they conduct operations simultaneously that had been planned sequentially, and ignored the threatening situation on the exposed German flanks. On 23 July, the same day that Rostov fell, Hitler issued Directive No. 45, which irrevocably severed the campaign into two partial offensives, to be conducted at the same time but in divergent directions. The main effort of the new operation lay with Army Group A, whose task was to destroy enemy formations that had escaped south across the Don, occupy the eastern coastline of the Black Sea, seize the oil facilities in the Maikop and Grozny areas, and penetrate to Baku. As a sign of Hitler's overweening ambition, occupation of the passes across the Caucasus Mountains would create the prerequisite for a subsequent thrust into Persia and Iraq. Breathtaking as this vision was, it was to be accomplished even as Army Group B smashed enemy forces at Stalingrad, blocked the Volga supply line, and sent mobile formations down the river to its mouth at Astrakhan, all the while providing cover for the southern operation.[51]

Ambitious can hardly describe the scope of this new operation; in addition to a war for oil, German forces were to establish as well the preconditions for waging a global conflict against the Anglo-American powers. If Hitler had asked the Wehrmacht to do too much with too few resources in 1941, he now compounded his strategic error by demanding that an even smaller force achieve truly grandiose aims. Although prone to ridiculing "the layman" (Hitler) for his clumsy direction of operations, Halder exploded in anger at his order not least because in Directive No. 45 he noted something more ominous than mere ineptitude. Already insufficient German combat forces were to be split, sent off in different directions, advance into territory that widened like a funnel, and rely for flank protection on undependable Axis troops—all while being supplied by a logistic system incapable of meeting the demands of even one operation. Serious deficiencies in fuel, in fact, meant that Army Group A, which had clear priority, could be supplied only at the expense of Army Group B. Entire convoys of trucks that had supplied the latter would now be shifted to the former, with the inevitable result that, in its advance toward Stalingrad, the Sixth Army would be seriously impaired in its mobility and striking power. At one point, in fact, fuel shortages left it immobile for over a week, even as the Soviets worked furiously to build defenses in the city. Just as worrisome, as both army groups drove to the east, they would advance further away from the railheads, with the result that precious gasoline supplies would have to be brought over increasingly long distances by trucks that themselves consumed much of the gas they were hauling. At the height of their success, German forces in the Caucasus would be receiving only a trickle of fuel.[52]

Such obstacles might have been overcome if the Germans possessed a preponderance of force, but the opposite was the case. Army Group B faced an overall five-to-one disadvantage in tanks, but, since the bulk of its combat power lay in the Sixth Army, this left the Axis divisions on its flanks extremely vulnerable to a Soviet counterattack. Even Paulus, with fewer than three hundred tanks as against an enemy force of over twelve hundred tanks, lacked any clear superiority in his attempt to seize Stalingrad. Army Group A had sufficient force to carry out its initial advance into the Caucasus, but it, too, would eventually have to dilute its strength in moving into the vast area between the Black and the Caspian Seas. Baku, accessible by only two roads over the passes suitable for motor vehicles, lay some seven hundred miles from Rostov, which was itself roughly the same distance from Warsaw. This meant that a logistic apparatus initially designed for distances of around three hundred miles and straining to supply just one army group at twice that distance would have to keep two such forces equipped at distances of over one thousand miles in a region with few highways and a virtually nonexistent rail system. Finally, since the two army groups were on diverging axes, neither would be able to help the other as the campaign developed. Rather than concentrate their already insufficient forces on a single objective, Hitler's order resulted in two armies acting independently of, and moving away from, each other, with each starved of the resources needed to accomplish its task.[53]

With neither of their prerequisites achieved (the destruction of Soviet forces and the capture of Stalingrad), German forces nonetheless on 26 July thrust into the Caucasus (Operation Edelweiss). In the west, one arm of Army Group A struck south from Rostov with the goal of destroying the enemy south of the Don, rolling up Soviet defenses along the Black Sea coast, and seizing the city of Batum. This would not only aid a crossing of the Kerch Straits by German forces but also open the Black Sea ports to shipments of oil directly to Rumanian refineries as well as enable German supply to arrive by sea, a crucial factor in a mountainous area devoid of roads. In the middle, and on the left, German forces would seize the fertile Kuban region and the first (and least important) oil area around Maikop while driving across the Terek River and the key passes over the Caucasus to reach the vital oil fields at Grozny and Baku. Having accomplished this, they would then be in a position to spearhead a further assault into Persia and the Middle East.[54]

The decisive stage of the war had been reached. For both sides it seemed to be all or nothing: German occupation of the critical oil fields would be as much of a blow to the Soviet ability to continue in the war effectively as it would be a significant boost to the Germans. The loss of the Donets Basin, an area that accounted for 40 percent of the Soviet population and a third of its gross industrial output, had plunged the country into another grave crisis. Although, as the year before, much of the industrial plant had been dismantled and sent east, the organizational and transport effort involved as well as the loss of numerous crucial raw materials temporarily sent economic production into a tailspin. Moreover, although the Soviets' flexible defense had prevented a complete annihilation of their forces, recent withdrawals, with disorderly, panic-stricken troops throwing away their weapons, abandoning their equipment, and running for their lives, raised the nightmarish prospect of complete disintegration of the southern armies.[55]

In response, on 28 July, Stalin issued Order No. 227, his famous "Not one step back" decree. In frank language, the dictator set out the reasons why withdrawal was no longer an option and what would happen to those who fled. The enormous demographic and economic losses, Stalin admitted, compelled utmost resistance: "From now on we are not superior to the Germans either in reserves of manpower or in stocks of grain. Further retreat means our end and that of our motherland. Every inch of ground which we yield henceforward strengthens the enemy and weakens our defense and country. . . . Unless our retreat is halted, we shall remain without bread and fuel, without metals and raw materials, without factories and railways. It follows, therefore, that it is high time to arrest our retreat. 'Not one step back' must henceforth be our most important slogan." To fight such uncompromising warfare, the decree continued, the "strictest order and iron discipline" would be maintained: "Defeatists and cowards must be liquidated on the spot." To give teeth to his words, Stalin authorized draconian punishments, such as penal battalions as well as the establishment of "blocking units," whose task would be, "in the event of panics or unauthorized retreats, to shoot spreaders of panic or cowards." In addition to abandoning the principle of flexible defense and restating his willingness to use the utmost brutality against his own troops, Stalin's Order No. 227 was significant in that it appealed to the troops' loyalty in unabashedly patriotic tones. Soviet patriotism was now merged with Russian nationalism; the heroes and legends of Russian history would be invoked to raise the morale of the troops and to save Stalin's regime.[56]

Soviet propaganda at the time also sought to stiffen resolve by invoking one other emotion: hatred of the invader. On 19 July, the army news-paper *Red Star* had published Konstantin Simonov's poem "Kill Him," which conjured images of German marauders murdering mothers, pil-laging farms, and burning homes, then demanded:

> If you do not want to give away all that you call your country,
> then kill a German . . .
> Kill a German so that he, and not you, should lie in the ground,
> Kill him so that the tears should flow in his home, not yours . . . ;
> Let his mother weep, and not yours . . . ;
> Kill him, kill him every time you see him.

Simonov's theme was taken up by Ilya Ehrenburg, whose article in *Red Star* on 13 August, "Kill the Germans," dripped with hatred:

> Russia's heart is bleeding. The enemy is trampling underfoot the rich fields of the Kuban. He can already smell the oil of the Cauca-sus. . . . The map seems drenched in blood. The country is crying in its agony: 'Cleanse me of the Germans. . . .' One cannot bear these fish-eyed oafs contemptuously snorting at everything Rus-sian. . . . We cannot live as long as these grey-green slugs are alive. . . . Today there is only one thought: Kill the Germans. Kill them all and dig them into the earth. . . . Then we can think again of life. . . . But now we must fight like madmen, live like fanatics. . . . The German is the screen standing between us and life. We want to live. And, in order to live, we must kill Germans. . . . But we must do it quickly, or they will desecrate the whole of Russia and torture to death millions more people.

This was followed by his even more famous injunction:

> The Germans are not human beings. Henceforth the word Ger-man means to us the most terrible curse. . . . If you have not killed at least one German a day, you have wasted that day. . . . If you do not kill the German, he will kill you. If you cannot kill your German with a bullet, kill him with your bayonet. . . . If you kill one German, kill another—there is nothing more amus-ing for us than a heap of German corpses. Do not count days; do not count miles. Count only the number of Germans you have killed. Kill the German—this is your old mother's prayer. Kill the German—this is what your children beseech you to do. Kill the

German—this is the cry of your Russian earth. Do not waver. Do not let up. Kill.[57]

Hitler had, from the beginning, intended a war of annihilation against the Soviet system and its people; they were now responding in kind.

Little evidence of any immediate stiffening of Russian resolve was apparent as German forces pushed southward across the Don and easily broke through the thin crust of Soviet defenses. All across the front, the main obstacle to a rapid advance appeared to be more the blazing heat, fuel shortages, and vehicle breakdowns than enemy resistance. Within a few days, the Germans had crossed the Manych River and seized the towns of Salsk and Proletarskaya, in the process cutting the main railway line to Stalingrad. On 1 August, the Fifty-second Corps, on the extreme left flank, captured the city of Elista in the broiling, desolate Kalmyk Steppe, nearly 200 miles on the way to the fabled city of Astrakhan. By 9 August, the Fifth Corps had sped over 150 miles and seized the strategic rail junction at Krasnodar, the principal city of the Kuban. That same day, Kleist's Fifty-seventh Panzer, Third Panzer, and Forty-fourth Corps converged on the oil city of Maikop. The next day, having raced 300 miles across the steppe, the Fortieth Panzer Corps reached Piatigorsk, little more than 30 miles from the Terek River, the last major obstacle in front of the oil region around Grozny. Despite these rapid advances, however, the enemy again evaded encirclement, a problem that Halder realized was not likely to be solved given increasing terrain difficulties and fuel shortages. At a conference at Führer Headquarters on 30 July, the head of the OKH reacted to a proposal for further attempts to intercept the enemy with outraged disbelief. "That is rankest nonsense," he recorded in his diary. "This enemy is running for dear life and will be in the northern foothills of the Caucasus well ahead of our armor." The OKH, indeed, quickly dropped the idea of encirclements, opting instead to drive forward as fast as possible.[58]

These spectacular advances, which seemed evidence of the collapse of enemy resistance, now induced Hitler once again to intervene in the course of operations. Halder had for days unsuccessfully been trying to convince Hitler of the importance of the Stalingrad axis: a drive to the Volga would be over more favorable terrain, would be easier to supply, and would create the defensive shoulder needed to cover the advance into the Caucasus. Halder, then, was greatly annoyed when, at the situation conference on 30 July, Jodl announced "pompously that the fate of the Caucasus will be decided at Stalingrad and that . . . it would be necessary to divert forces from Army Group A to Army Group B. This is a dressed up version of my own proposal . . . [though] no one in the illustrious company of the OKW seemed to be able to grasp its significance." In the face of a large Soviet buildup at Stalingrad, Hitler now acquiesced and the next day ordered a reinforcement of Army Group B, for the first time making Stalingrad a priority. Less than a week after the start of Edelweiss, then, Hitler's impetuosity, albeit abetted by Jodl and Halder, resulted in yet another redistribution of forces. List's Army Group A found itself stripped not only of Manstein's Eleventh Army, which was on its way to Leningrad, but also now of Hoth's Fourth Panzer Army (and, soon, the Rumanians, as well). His powerful force of five armies reduced to just two, List was left to struggle on with the Seventeenth Army in the west and the First Panzer Army in the east, separated by three hundred miles and now with secondary priority for fuel, ammunition, and replacements. Just as crucially, Edelweiss lost much of its air support. The Schwerpunkt of the summer campaign, if one even remained, had switched once again, this time to Army Group B, even though Hitler demanded that List's reduced force seize the key objectives set for it. Although List argued that sending a "relatively weak force" deep into the Caucasus would be a "great gamble," his only consolation was Halder's sarcastic comment that the diversion of troops would at least ease his supply problems.[59]

The consequences of the Führer's decision were quick and profound. Although Foreign Armies East reported that enemy formations in the Caucasus were "not top-quality troops" and were "increasingly heading for disintegration," even predicting that the Soviets would likely now turn the burden of the war over to the British and defend the region only on a "slight scale," Stalin had no such intention, instead using the respite to organize an effective defense along the Terek River line. The swift German advance of the first weeks suddenly stalled in the face of growing enemy reinforcements and increasingly fierce resistance. In many respects, the seizure of Maikop was representative of the new dynamic of the fighting, being both the culmination of German success and the harbinger of tough times ahead. Kleist's forces took the city, to Hitler's great glee, on 9 August, but only after hard street fighting and heavy losses. Euphoria at the first of the oil complexes to fall into German hands soon turned to gloom, however, when it was found that the vital oil installations had been destroyed by the Soviets: derricks toppled, power plants wrecked, refineries demolished, and the wells themselves filled with stones and iron parts or sealed with concrete. It was such a thorough and irreparable job of demolition, in fact, that the technical experts sent to rebuild the facilities recommended that the drilling equipment earmarked for the Caucasus would be better employed in Rumania or in the Vienna region than at Maikop. Not only would it have required six months to a year before any significant extraction of oil could begin again, but oil exports to the Reich would have to be sent via the Black Sea, control of which was far from assured. At Maikop in early August, the illusions underpinning the summer campaign began to give way to harsh reality.[60]

By mid-August, German forces had left the fertile valleys of the Kuban and reached the foothills of the imposing Caucasus mountain range, over 600 miles long, up to 120 miles deep, and with peaks soaring to heights of more than 16,000 feet. As German troops advanced south, they seemed to be leaving civilization, swallowed up by vast, trackless primeval forests. Supplying even the most basic items in such a primitive area became unimaginably difficult: field kitchens could not keep up, so food had to be brought to the troops by long, grueling marches; ammunition, artillery, and mortar shells were brought forward on horses; the lack of villages meant that most frontline soldiers spent the night in the open even in rain and snow. Not least, the Germans also faced increasing resistance from the Russians, who found the terrain ideal for the defense. Finally, Army Group A fell victim to Paulus's insatiable demand for troops. The elite Italian Alpine Corps, the Twenty-second Panzer Division, and much of the available air support departed for the Stalingrad region in mid-August, while the Grossdeutschland Division left at the same time for the west, victim of Hitler's persistent fear of a second front. By the end of the month, Hitler, worried by an enemy buildup near Astrakhan, ordered the Sixteenth Motorized Division to Elista in the Kalmyk Steppe. Over the next few months, supported by Cossack auxiliaries, it patrolled another 150 miles to the southeast to the outskirts of Astrakhan, although the very fact that one division was left to control such vast distances reflected all too clearly the inadequacy of German strength. With forces barely sufficient for one operation, List faced the challenge of simultaneously trying to clear the Black Sea coast, breach the Terek River line and seize Grozny, and capture the high passes through the Caucasus before snow blocked the way. Little wonder, then, that the German momentum slowed perceptibly in late August and bogged down completely in September.[61]

By 18 August, the tempo of operations had changed completely, with the thirty-mile advances of the first weeks giving way to daily struggles to advance a mile or two. List had hoped a surprise attack launched on the twelfth from Krasnodar and Maikop through the western Caucasus toward the port city of Tuapse, which aimed at pinning Soviet forces against the Black Sea, might finally break enemy resistance. In what was to become an all-too-familiar refrain, however, the twin German thrusts had, after some initial success, by the eighteenth bogged down in the mountains in the face of impenetrable terrain and fierce Soviet counterattacks. Although List still hoped that the opposition was merely that of strong enemy rearguards aiming to delay the German advance, Kleist at the First Panzer Army knew better. Following a mid-August trip to view conditions in the area, Major Engel, Hitler's adjutant, summarized the mood: "Troops more or less finished. . . . Caucasus south of Krasnodar and Maikop crossable only by four mule-tracks by mountain troops with mules. Creation of a point of main effort in no way possible. . . . Away from roads and paths operation totally impossible because of jungle-like thicket and no visibility. Armored divisions totally inappropriate. Tough Russian resistance in the mountains, heavy losses." Informed of the difficulties, Hitler's reaction was typical: "Engel will swallow anything he is told."[62]

Nor were more southerly attempts to push through mountain passes in the direction of the port of Sukhumi any more successful. By the second half of the month, German mountain troops had forced their way to, and in some instances across, the key passes, but a swift enemy response, in the form of small, mobile detachments of combat engineers who blocked the few roads and mountain paths, effectively stymied their movement further. Although German and Rumanian forces crossed the Kerch Straits on 2 September, cleared the Taman Peninsula, and on the sixth reached the key port and naval base of Novorossiysk, thus threatening to roll up the entire Soviet coastal defenses, they could go no further. After five days of heavy fighting, the invaders had by the eleventh managed to push only as far as the southern industrial suburbs, but there the front line remained until early December, when the Germans began abandoning the Kuban. With Soviet reinforcements arriving by sea and determined to defend the area at all costs, German hopes for a swift advance south evaporated into a grim stalemate.[63]

Pressed by an increasingly impatient Hitler to break through to the coast, List remained skeptical, recommending, given his shrinking manpower and critical fuel situation, shortening the line and concentrating his mountain troops on a single thrust toward Tuapse. Even this limited move gave the field marshal nightmares as he worried that an isolated thrust by a single formation across the passes would be both impossible to supply and vulnerable to enemy counterattack. Hitler, however, would have none of it, instead demanding that List pursue simultaneous attacks on both Tuapse and Sukhumi, roughly one hundred miles to the south. With tensions rising and time running out before snow closed the passes, Hitler ordered List to come to his headquarters at Vinnitsa on 31 August. There, he confronted the field marshal with, of all things, the accusation that he had failed in his attacks because he had dissipated his strength. Unable to put his misgivings effectively to the Führer, List left the meeting with the promise that he would renew his attacks toward the coast. Once back at his headquarters at Stalino, however, all his doubts resurfaced. On 7 September, he requested that Jodl, as Hitler's closest operational adviser, visit the army group's headquarters in order to discuss the situation. That same day, Jodl flew to Stalino, discussed the situation with List for several hours, then flew back that evening to Vinnitsa. By the time of his return to Führer Headquarters, Jodl had come to share List's concerns, a stance that would unwittingly bring to a head the tension of the last weeks and touch off a serious command crisis.[64]

Tempers had been strained at the Werwolf complex at Vinnitsa ever since the Führer had arrived in mid-July, to be confronted with stifling heat (often surpassing 100°F) and mosquito-infested surroundings. Clearly uncomfortable in the heat, impatient with the slow progress of operations, and increasingly paranoid about his food, water, and even oxygen, Hitler was already in a feverish state. When Jodl, who seldom stood up to his domineering boss, gathered his courage and reported that List had faithfully followed all directives given to him and had not engaged in insubordinate behavior, the Führer exploded in an "indescribable outburst of fury." By siding with List, Jodl had implicitly criticized Hitler's own conduct of operations and placed the blame for any failures squarely on the Führer. This alone would have been enough to set Hitler off, but the deeper problem lay in the calendar: time was running out. For weeks, Hitler had been subject to alternating moods of euphoria and frustration. On 19 August, for example, he had boasted privately to Goebbels that operations in the Caucasus were going extremely well, that he still expected to seize the oil regions of Grozny and Baku and, once these had been taken, to burst through to the Middle East. Just three days later, however, he flew into a rage at news that mountain troops had planted a German flag on Mount Elbrus, the highest peak in Europe. Speer claimed that he had seldom seen Hitler so enraged, and for days afterward he fumed at the pointless stunt of "these mad mountaineers" who had wasted valuable time and resources when he was concentrating everything on taking Sukhumi. It was, Speer said, as if Hitler believed these few men had ruined his entire operational plan.[65]

With that observation, Speer hit the crux of the matter. By early September, Hitler had evidently come to the realization that the goals for

1942, especially reaching the vital Caucasus oil regions, were not likely to be achieved. For the second time a throw of the dice had failed and with it any reasonable chance of a favorable outcome to the war. Believing that his generals had again failed him and deliberately sabotaged his orders, he now demonstratively separated himself as much as possible from their presence. After past contretemps, Hitler had always made small conciliatory gestures to those around him, but this blowup seemed to mark a psychological watershed. Warlimont was shocked by the intense hatred on Hitler's face, as if he realized that his last gamble had been lost. He now reduced contact with his closest entourage to an absolute minimum: he ate alone, withdrew to his windowless hut, where the two daily military briefings were held "in an icy atmosphere" and which he would leave only at dusk, refused to shake hands with his generals, demanded to see all the directives he had given to Army Group A, and ordered a verbatim record kept of all situation conferences to eliminate further malicious distortions of his words. Although he quietly dropped any further plans for an offensive in the western Caucasus Mountains, he nonetheless dismissed List on 9 September, with hints that other changes were to follow. These seem to have involved a reorganization of the OKW, where, following the capture of Stalingrad, Jodl and Keitel were to be replaced, respectively, by Paulus and Kesselring.[66]

In the event, however, the fallout from Hitler's displeasure settled on the OKH, where Halder's situation had become increasingly untenable. Relations between the two had hit rock bottom on 24 August when Halder, in a criticism that Hitler could not have missed, complained that soldiers were being sacrificed because their commanders lacked the authority to make even the most basic decisions to deploy them more sensibly. At that, Hitler exploded in withering ridicule of his army chief. "What can you tell me about troops, Herr Halder," he mocked, "you who even in the First World War only sat in the same swivel chair, you, who don't even wear the black wound badge." Deeply humiliated, the chief of staff must have known that his days were numbered, but the final break did not come until a month later, on 24 September, when Hitler finally sacked him. Halder's nerves, the Führer said, were used up, and his too had suffered from their confrontations. With that, Halder's long service to Hitler ended, and with his departure came a downgrading of the position of chief of the General Staff. Halder's successor, Kurt Zeitzler, was an outsider, a young and energetic officer with the reputation of being a Nazi who could be expected to be compliant to the Führer's wishes. The process of turning the army into Hitler's tool had been completed. But his desire to have as his new OKH chief a man who was more than just professionally competent, who was, instead, fired with a "fanatical faith in the idea" and the "fervor of a National Socialist credo," was itself an implicit admission of impending defeat.[67]

At the beginning of August, Hitler had prophesied that the next six weeks "would be decisive for the outcome of the war." By mid-September, the balance sheet, as even the normally optimistic Halder could see, was clearly unfavorable: the Red Army, far from being destroyed, was increasing its strength while the Germans could not make good their losses; the Caucasus operation had stalled; heavy fighting had erupted in Stalingrad; Soviet forces were threatening German positions in the north; and, in North Africa, Rommel's offensive had petered out at El Alamein. The second culmination point of the war had been reached, and Germany's time had run out. Hitler's late July decision to split the offensive, which Halder had been unable to prevent, had been crucial. Until now, German tactical superiority had been able to offset Hitler's poor operational decisions, but the overall strategic implications of this blunder could not be remedied: given the time factor and the powerful coalition being arrayed against it, the Wehrmacht could not now hope to overcome the disaster on the Volga that would likely result from the Führer's decision.[68]

Indeed, other actions by Hitler at the time suggest as much. On 8 September, he issued a Führer order on "fundamental tasks of defense" that, in its stress on holding the line "under all circumstances," mirrored Stalin's "Not one step back" decree. A few days later, he ordered an east-west exchange of battle-weary divisions for the purpose of their rehabilitation, another implicit signal that the war in the east would not be over by winter. On 14 October, finally, he directed all forces, except those battling inside Stalingrad and pushing toward Grozny, to prepare winter lines of defense, an explicit admission of failure. "This year's summer and fall campaigns," he announced, "excepting those operations underway . . . , have been concluded." Once the Soviets decided to withdraw their forces rather than squander them in encirclement battles, there had been little the Germans could do, given their deficiencies in manpower, mobility, and fuel. Hitler, according to his army adjutant, Schmundt, saw no end to the war in Russia and was "at the very end of his tether": "He hates everything that is field gray . . . and is longing for the day when he could cast off his tunic." The great operational victories of the spring and summer had yet to be converted into a strategic triumph; whether such could be achieved in the Caucasus or along the Volga remained to be seen.[69]

Deadlocked in the western Caucasus, List's operations now shifted their center of gravity east to the Terek River region, where German forces once more raised hopes of the decisive breakthrough to the oil fields beyond. The Terek, a swiftly flowing river 100–250 yards wide with steep, rocky banks, protected the key targets: Grozny, Ordzhonikidze, and the Ossetian and Georgian Military Roads. These latter, the only two routes through the mountains capable of carrying heavy military traffic, were especially important since their capture would raise the possibility of a swift thrust through the mountains to the great prize: the rich oil fields of Baku. Kleist's mobile divisions had reached the Terek at Mozdok in late August, and in the first week of September managed to punch out bridgeheads across the river in a few spots, but fierce enemy resistance, the transfer of units elsewhere, and a lack of fuel forced them to halt attacks.[70]

By October, Kleist concentrated all available units of the First Panzer Army along the Terek in the hope of waging one last breakthrough battle. Leading off the attack on 25 October, the Third Panzer Corps forced its way across the river, punched a hole in Soviet defenses, and cut off enemy forces at Nalchik. The panzer divisions now wheeled to the southeast and over the next few days crossed numerous swiftly flowing rivers as they skirted the edge of the Caucasus Mountains. By the twenty-ninth, they had reached the Ardon River, at the head of the Ossetian Military Road. The Twenty-third Panzer Division seized Alagir, thus closing the road, on 1 November, while that evening spearheads of the Thirteenth Panzer were only ten miles from Ordzhonikidze on the Georgian Military Road. With the tantalizing prospect of opening the route to Baku, the Germans redoubled their efforts, while, equally frantic at the threat facing them, the Soviets put up increasingly stiff opposition. Facing ferocious resistance every inch of the way, battling the cold and swirling snowstorms over treacherous roads that did not suffice for resupply, let alone movement, and easy prey for enemy air attacks, Kleist's forces struggled forward. By the third, a handful of German battalions had battled to less than two miles from the city, but now gains were being measured in yards rather than miles. On the sixth, little more than a mile from the city, the Germans had their hopes crushed by a Soviet counterattack that forced a retreat. Transport difficulties and partisan attacks had now forced almost half of all supply trains to the Caucasus temporarily to a halt: too weak to pursue any further offensive operations, the Germans had lost the initiative, which now passed over to the enemy. A crossing of the eastern Caucasus was no longer in the offing, a reality Hitler had implicitly accepted in early October when he ordered the refineries and oil storage facilities at Grozny, Saratov, Kamyshin, Baku, and Astrahkan, once the key objective of the campaign, to be bombed. Over a thousand miles from the German border, with just a few company-strength battalions sputtering forward, and a mere mile from the objective, the drive to the oil fields had finally failed and with it the Caucasus campaign.[71]

The propaganda images became familiar to Germans in the summer of 1942: scenes of tramping soldiers, their deeply bronzed faces and arms caked in dust, marching into the never-ending horizon of the Russian steppe against an apparently nonexistent foe; tanks raising enormous clouds of dust as they fanned out over the trackless expanse, commanders erect in their turrets, urging their compatriots on; German troops entering Cossack villages being greeted as liberators. While these images were not completely inaccurate, they failed to tell the whole story. While they had recovered much of their morale and spirit in the victories of the spring and early summer, these Landsers also knew that sooner or later the Russians would resist furiously, that the endless daily marches brought them no closer to trapping their elusive foe, that the blazing heat, lack of water, and insufficient supplies sapped their strength and left them vulnerable to dysentery, typhus, and typhoid fever, and that the enemy had largely destroyed anything of value in this sparse region.[72]

The Germans very likely could have seized Stalingrad in late July if they had possessed the ability to do so. That they did not. At the time, the two German panzer corps under Paulus's command had a total of perhaps 200 tanks, against a Russian figure of 1,289. Moreover, while a large Soviet buildup around Voronezh threatened the German left flank, the bulk of its panzer units were, just as Halder had complained, tangled in a great armored knot around Rostov. In addition, Hitler's decision to split the offensive on 23 July meant that the bulk of available fuel and supplies had been redirected to Army Group A, effectively paralyzing the Sixth Army for days. Its mobility impaired, unable to concentrate its scattered units, and suffering a perilous shortage of ammunition and fuel, the Sixth Army had to wait in frustration as the enemy made good use of the respite. Not only did the Soviets strengthen their defenses west of the Don, but, beginning on the twenty-fifth and continuing for the next few days, they also launched a series of counterblows. Although these were hasty and uncoordinated, the very frenzy with which they were undertaken halted the German forward progress and inflicted not insignificant losses in men and material. On the twenty-seventh, Halder noted in his diary that "the battle of Sixth Army west of the Don is still raging with unabated fury," while the next day he worried, "Due to lack of fuel and ammunition, Sixth Army was unable to attack." By the thirtieth, the note of concern had risen visibly in Halder's entries, the OKH chief now writing anxiously, "A wild battle is raging in Sixth Army sector inside the Don bend west of Stalingrad. . . . Sixth Army's striking power is paralyzed by ammunition and fuel supply difficulties." Although Weichs, the commander of Army Group B, succeeded in a late July telephone call to Hitler in getting priorities rearranged in his favor, valuable time had been lost. Stopgap logistic measures such as using JU-52 transport planes to bring fuel and ammunition to forward units helped restore some mobility but were hardly feasible in the long run.[73]

Just a week after the issuance of Directive No. 45 (which might well be subtitled "Too much, too few, too far"), its great fault became clear: in demanding that German forces do everything at once, it effectively stripped each army group of the ability to achieve its objectives. Having now decided that taking Stalingrad was vital, in contrast to the original view that it was a secondary goal that need only be neutralized, Hitler found to his great frustration that his forces could not seize it in a rapid thrust. Both Weichs and Paulus, in fact, doubted that the Sixth Army had the strength to attack the city at all, a point seemingly confirmed by the unrelenting Soviet counterattacks. On 29 July, they communicated their concerns to Major Engel, Hitler's adjutant, stressing that "for the battle of Stalingrad not enough infantry is available," that their "forces [were] too weak in relation to their tasks and that . . . counterattacks could no longer be mastered with the forces available." Hitler now realized that, if the Sixth Army's stalled advance was to be got going again, it would have to be reinforced, inevitably at the expense of Army Group A. On 31 July, then, he put Hoth's Fourth Panzer Army, then striking into the Caucasus, under the control of Army Group B in order to support the Sixth Army's attack from the south while also redeploying the Italian Eighth Army to the Don River as flank protection, thus freeing German divisions for the attack to the Volga. The commitment to taking Stalingrad having been made, there could now be no turning back. Hitler had denuded the Caucasus operation of the forces it needed to succeed, so, for military, political, and psychological reasons, conquering the city on the Volga was an absolute necessity.[74]

Doing so meant reactivating the Sixth Army, which sat largely motionless, crippled by a lack of fuel, for the first week of August as well as clearing the stubborn Soviet defenders west of the Don. By 4 August, even as the crisis triggered by the enemy counterattacks abated and the supply situation improved somewhat, the Sixth Army's motorized units could still move only within a radius of twenty-five to thirty miles, while the infantry divisions were limited to a mere five to ten miles. Nonetheless, the reinforcements he had received as well as the arrival of German units from the northern Don flank allowed Paulus to plan a Cannae-style envelopment of the enemy: the Fourteenth Panzer Corps, with its left wing brushing the Don, was to attack southward, while the Twenty-fourth Panzer Corps, similarly sweeping along the Don, was to spearhead an attack to the north, with both pincers meeting at Kalach. Although Paulus preferred to wait until 8 August, Hitler and Halder, fearful of a possible Soviet withdrawal, pushed for the assault to begin on the seventh. That morning, supported by massive Luftwaffe air strikes that destroyed practically every bridge over the Don, the German armored spearheads smashed through Soviet defenses and raced toward the key transportation center of Kalach. By dawn on the eighth, the two armored thrusts met just southwest of the city, trapping some 100,000 Soviet defenders. By the tenth, Soviet forces were crowded into a pocket less than four miles in diameter where, after frenzied resistance, they were annihilated the next day.[75]

The swift destruction of the Soviet Sixty-second and First Tank Armies in the tight Kalach Kessel raised hopes at Hitler's headquarters for a similarly swift seizure of Stalingrad, roughly forty miles to the east. Even as the pocket at Kalach tightened, Paulus had spun forces off to prepare for the further advance to the Volga, but he faced a dilemma. On his northern flank, the Soviets still held a number of bridgeheads across the Don that had to be eliminated, notably at Kremenskaya and Serafimovich, but Paulus's hasty mid-August efforts to clear them amounted to little. At the cost of considerable losses, the enemy stubbornly clung to his foothold south of the Don, which tied down substantial portions of the Fourteenth Panzer Corps and the Eleventh Corps for a prolonged period. Lacking both the time and the resources needed to reduce the remaining enemy pockets, Paulus turned his attention to pushing across the Don and making for the northern suburbs of Stalingrad. Not for the last time, German failure to reduce a Soviet bridgehead would have dire consequences. Nor was German success west of the Don as complete as it might have seemed. As a result of persistent fuel and ammunition shortages as well as stiff Soviet resistance, it had taken Paulus a month to clear the bulk of enemy forces from the Great Bend of the Don and then only at the cost of time and considerable losses in men and materiel. By mid-August, even before the plunge to the Volga, his armored forces had lost half their strength. Given the slow pace of advance to the Don and the disconcertingly high numbers of Red Army soldiers who had escaped the German trap, it was foolish to believe that Stalingrad could be seized quickly with forces sapped of strength and fighting power by the stubborn fighting along the Don.[76]

Significantly, the Sixth Army's offensive strength had been reduced to such an extent that initially all it had available for the push across the Don was a single armored division, two motorized divisions, and four infantry divisions. Suspecting that the Russians had strongly fortified the direct route east from Kalach, which in any case was crisscrossed with deep gullies that offered splendid defensive opportunities, Paulus ordered his forces to cross the Don to the north at Vertyachiy. His mobile units were then to move quickly along a high ridge of ground to reach the Volga, thirty-five miles to the east, in the northern suburbs of Stalingrad. At the same time, the trailing infantry divisions would offer flank support, with some wheeling to the southeast to occupy the city itself while others turned to the south to link up with the forces of Hoth's Fourth Panzer Army. Neither an attempt to destroy enemy forces west of the city nor a gamble on a swift drive into the heart of Stalingrad, this move of Paulus's seemed primarily intent on occupying the land bridge between the Don and the Volga and protecting his flanks. With such a limited force, it was perhaps no surprise that he struck a cautious, almost defensive note. Russian troops, he stressed, could be expected to defend Stalingrad stubbornly and to launch heavy counterattacks, although he added the almost wistful hope that perhaps, after all, the fighting in the Don bend had finally destroyed the enemy's ability to resist.[77]

In order to secure a lodgment area for the main attack, Paulus's spearhead groups pushed across the Don against strong resistance on 21 and 22 August. Despite Soviet counterattacks on the northern flank and efforts to destroy the two floating bridges across the Don, the German attack went off as planned on the twenty-third. Supported by massed aircraft, and with utter disregard for its flanks, at dawn the Fourteenth Panzer Corps burst out of the bridgehead and raced for the Volga. Encountering virtually no resistance from the surprised Soviet defenders, German tanks raised enormous clouds of dust on the arid grasslands of the steppe as they rolled eastward. By midafternoon, spearheads of Hans Hube's Sixteenth Panzer Division had leaped the thirty-five miles and reached Rynok, to the north of Stalingrad, where they brushed aside fire from antiaircraft and antitank guns operated by local women who had been given only rudimentary training and established defensive positions along the Volga. They also seized American Lend-Lease jeeps, which proved very popular with German officers. Late that evening, the Sixteenth Panzer reported its achievement to the Fourteenth Panzer Corps. Within a half hour, Hube received a terse order from Hitler: "16th Panzer Division will hold its positions under all circumstances."[78]

That same evening, the Luftwaffe struck Stalingrad in a massive terror attack, the largest air assault it had mounted since the opening day of Barbarossa. Arguing that "we must tell the army and the people that there is nowhere left to retreat," Stalin had forbidden the evacuation of the city, so its population was swollen by masses of peasant refugees, with livestock in tow, desperately seeking to cross the Volga. The extensive use of incendiaries caused the city, already broiling under the summer heat, to blaze "like a gigantic torch," visible for forty miles. Over the next two days, the Luftwaffe completed its destructive work. Richthofen noted with dry satisfaction in his diary that the city was "destroyed, and without any further worthwhile targets." Another, less sober German observer was overcome by the spectacle of Stalingrad ablaze. It was, he recorded, "a fantastic picture in the moonlight." The three-day attack left Stalingrad in ruins, with tens of thousands of people killed, utilities disrupted, and communications with the outside world severed. For a time, in fact, the cessation of news left Moscow with the impression that the city had already fallen.[79]

The speed of the Germans' advance and the savagery of their aerial assault had clearly stunned the Soviet defenders, so much so that Richthofen, disgusted up to now by what he saw as the army's lack of fighting spirit, believed that the city could be taken in an all-out assault, albeit with high casualties. Stalin, too, feared that his namesake city might fall at any time but in his usual fashion averted a nascent crisis by quick and firm action. On the twenty-fourth, he demanded absolute defense of the city and ordered Eremenko, the commander of the Stalingrad Front, to launch a series of counterattacks. These latter posed a serious dilemma for the Germans since, despite their impressive dash to the Volga, Hube's forces had carved out only a narrow corridor a few miles wide. Paulus's original intention of exploiting this breakthrough by a swift move into the city quickly faded as Soviet assaults left the Fourteenth Panzer Corps the hunted rather than the hunter. Unable to penetrate into Stalingrad, with its communications and supply lines cut, and with its strength severely reduced, the Fourteenth Panzer Corps had no choice but to assume a hedgehog position on the twenty-sixth and go on the defensive. That same day, General Wietersheim, commanding the Fourteenth Panzer Corps, called for the immediate withdrawal of his units, a request that Paulus tersely rejected. Although Hube was able to hold on to the narrow corridor, his victory was costly. The incessant Soviet counterattacks against both the northern corridor and the

German Fifty-first Corps moving toward the city from the northwest did not achieve all that Stalin had hoped, but they nonetheless strained Paulus's resources to the limit. By the end of the month, the Sixth Army had been largely confined to holding and consolidating its gains while awaiting the arrival of the Fourth Panzer Army from the south. In a bad sign, the German leap into Stalingrad from the north had turned into a limp because of insufficient force.[80]

Even as Paulus's troops pushed ahead to Stalingrad from the northwest, Hoth's weak Fourth Panzer Army launched its drive on the city from the southwest, but, since it ranked only third on the priority list for fuel, its ability to move quickly was greatly diminished. In addition, as it moved north in scorching heat across the arid steppe, it had to drop formations off for flank protection, units that were desperately needed at the sharp end. Nonetheless, Hoth had devised an ambitious plan of attack. The Forty-eighth Panzer Corps was to push across the lower Don on 1 August, wheel eastward, then, with the Rumanian Sixth Army Corps protecting its left flank, strike swiftly to the north in the hope of seizing the southern part of the city in a surprise attack. All went as planned for most of the first week, with his forces advancing up to thirty miles a day, but Stalin and the Stavka responded with great urgency. On the sixth, Soviet forces not only delayed the German advance along the Aksai River, some forty miles to the southwest of Stalingrad, but also succeeded in throwing the Rumanians back across it. Over the next two weeks, Soviet forces under General Chuikov thwarted the Germans and forced Hoth to probe further to the east to find a way through enemy defenses. In grinding fighting, Hoth's forces wrestled forward through heavily mined Soviet defense lines and against repeated counterattacks, pushing slowly through to the Abganerovo area by the seventeenth, where the attack stalled.[81]

After pausing for a few days because of fuel shortages and to reorganize his forces, Hoth resumed the onslaught on the twentieth, this time attacking on his right flank. Once again, stout resistance forced slow going as over the next week Hoth struggled to gain the decisive breakthrough, hoping to push through first at Tundutovo Station, then at Tinguta Station, both south of Stalingrad. By the twenty-seventh, with his forces seriously depleted, Hoth again paused to concentrate and redeploy his armored units, this time to the west. Renewing the assault on the twenty-ninth to the west of Abganerovo Station, Hoth finally found the weak spot in the enemy defenses. His forces pressed forward through Zety and Gavrilovka, with his spearheads on 31 August reaching the Kalach-Stalingrad railroad just east of Basargino Station, only twelve miles west of the city's center and in position to link up with the Sixth Army. On 1 September, however, the Twenty-fourth Panzer Division thrust straight east in an attempt, foiled by Soviet defenders, to seize the center of the city. Nor, fearing continued attacks on his vulnerable northern corridor to the Volga, was the cautious Paulus willing to risk turning sizable forces to the south. Not until the morning of the third, then, did spearheads of the Sixth Army and the Fourth Panzer Army meet in the Pitomnik-Gonchara-Gumrak Station area less than fifteen miles from the center of Stalingrad. Any brief hopes that the city might yet be captured on the fly quickly evaporated as probing attacks over the next two days revealed that the Soviets had every intention of defending it.[82] German forces, seriously weakened by the bitter two-week struggle just to reach Stalingrad, now faced the daunting task of bitter urban fighting in order to secure it.

Moreover, although a series of stubborn Soviet counterattacks across the Don against Italian forces holding the northern shoulder of Army Group B had been contained, these short and violent bridgehead actions had serious implications. Unable, as Halder admitted, to set the situation right and throw the Russians back across the river, the flank battles of the last week of August underscored the fatal weakness of the overstretched Axis defenses along the Don. Even Hitler had come to suspect that "the crucial danger" lurked in the area of the Italian Eighth Army, but he could reinforce the Italians only by stripping German divisions from the fighting front. The Stavka, too, took note of the poor performance and exposed position of the Italians. Once again, exaggerated hopes for a swift victory by an inadequate force had proved illusory as the Germans lacked sufficient power to achieve the objectives set them by the Führer. Once the Fourteenth Panzer Corps had reached the Volga, it not only lacked the strength to penetrate into Stalingrad but had to fight hard just to ward off its own annihilation. While the rest of Paulus's troops were engaged in a stalemate, Hoth's panzer army, with only around 150 tanks, was itself too weak to carry out its assigned task in one sweep, let alone provide much relief to the Sixth Army. Having left Italian, Hungarian, and Rumanian units guarding their exposed and vulnerable flanks, the Sixth Army and the Fourth Panzer Army had struggled to the city on the Volga but faced a sobering question: What now?[83]

On 3 September, both Hitler and Stalin thought the fall of Stalingrad imminent, a belief that caused the one to avoid reflection and the other to redouble his frenzied efforts to save the city. With its huge steel mills, tractor factories, and ordnance works, Stalingrad was one of the key armaments production centers, especially for tanks, in the Soviet

Union. At the same time, with much of European Russia now under German occupation, the Volga, navigable all the way to Moscow, had become the vital transport artery of the Soviet war economy. Stalingrad, as the major port, rail junction, and communications center along the lower Volga, had, thus, assumed even greater significance. Finally, the city had a certain symbolic importance, the successful defense during the civil war of Tsaritsin, as it was then known, being attributed to the young chairman of the regional war council, Josef Stalin. Not surprisingly, then, the dictator was frantic in his efforts to defend "his" city, in late August ordering his favorite troubleshooter, Zhukov, to take charge of its overall defense. Ironically, with German troops perched on the Volga and the city wrecked by the massive late August bombing raids, the goal set for the Sixth Army—to neutralize the city of Stalingrad—had seemingly been accomplished. Hitler himself had throughout the summer regarded the seizure of Stalingrad as of secondary importance. But, with it evidently ripe for the taking, he now failed to weigh the prospect of halting the attack. Indeed, his order on 2 September to annihilate all the men and deport all the women because the entire population was Communist and therefore "particularly dangerous" already hinted that seizing Stalingrad for ideological and prestige reasons was assuming decisive importance in his mind.[84]

Before that murderous action could be imposed, however, the city had to be taken. The problem was how since the Germans would be unable to use their favorite tactic of the Kesselschlacht. Stretching for some thirty to forty miles along the west bank of the Volga but rarely more than five miles in depth, Stalingrad was less a city than an urbanized, industrialized bridgehead. In the south lay the old town, which bordered the main rail station and the main river docks, while the central section was a modern city center with wide boulevards, government buildings, and department stores. The northern part of the city was dominated by four huge industrial complexes that had been converted to armaments production: the Dzerzhinsky tractor works, which now made tanks; the Barrikady ordnance factory; the Lazur chemical works; and the Krasny Oktyabr (Red October) metal plant. The Tsaritsa River bisected the southern sector, the center was dominated by the three-hundred-foot-high Mamayev Kurgan, an ancient burial ground, while high bluffs along the west bank of the river afforded defensive shelter. Such a city would be difficult to envelop, especially by German forces who were already at the end of overextended supply lines and threatened by strong enemy opposition from their flanks, while its very narrowness seemingly invited frontal assaults to seize control of the riverbank. In either case, however, German commanders were aware of the danger of getting drawn into prolonged and bloody urban fighting, such as that at Sevastopol just a few months earlier, which had cost them seventy-five thousand casualties. The original plan of Blau, in fact, had been designed to avoid just such a confrontation, yet here they were. With winter rapidly approaching and the Sixth Army at the end of a long and very tenuous supply chain, the Germans had to do something. Characteristically, they chose to attack.[85]

With defenses around the city incomplete and the bulk of Soviet formations consisting of battle-weary or poorly trained rifle units, hastily assembled and thrown together with shortages of every type of weapons, this was precisely what Stalin feared. On 3 September, he frantically implored Zhukov to mount an offensive against the vulnerable German northern corridor. "Situation in Stalingrad worsened," he telegraphed. "Enemy about three kilometers [two miles] from Stalingrad. City can be taken today or tomorrow. . . . Attack enemy immediately. . . . No delay permissible. Delay would be criminal." Although Zhukov was able to persuade a skeptical Stalin that an attack could not be mounted before the fifth, when it came, it was too uncoordinated and disjointed to have the desired impact. Not least, German air superiority and near constant Stuka attacks did much to blunt the Soviet assault. The Soviet attack did, however, manage to tie down scarce German forces that might have been better employed elsewhere. On that same day, in fact, Hoth's Forty-eighth Panzer Corps had launched a thrust into the city that, after five days of intense fighting and heavy losses by both sides, finally reached the Volga at Kuporosnye. Hoth's forces had not only split the city in two, with the center and industrial areas to the north, but also separated the Soviet Sixty-second and Sixty-fourth Armies, leaving the former isolated in its defense of the city. Already, however, things were slipping out of German control. The savage combat clearly indicated that the Sixth Army had squandered its chance to encircle Soviet defenders before they could retreat into the rubble of Stalingrad. To root them out now was going to take a great deal of time and cost many lives. That realization, along with his frustration at the slow pace of operations in the Caucasus, had occasioned Hitler's bitter outburst on 7 September.[86]

What to do in light of this reality was the subject of two conferences on 12 September, one in Moscow, and the other in Vinnitsa. Zhukov had flown to Moscow to discuss the looming disaster at Stalingrad as well as to seek ways to turn the situation around. With Vasilevsky's support, he persuaded Stalin that repeated attacks on the northern corridor were futile since the Soviets lacked the strength to punch through, and that in any case it was pointless to waste their forces in local defensive fighting. A permanent solution to the crisis, he and Vasilevsky argued, required not just an active defense but a large-scale counteroffensive that would transform the strategic situation. With an eye on the weak German flanks, Zhukov and Vasilevsky proposed that Soviet forces be built up for a counterattack against the vulnerable Rumanian and Italian forces. Both estimated that it would be the middle of November before the necessary units could be assembled and the counterblow struck. Significantly, however, they also assumed that the Germans now lacked the strength to realize their strategic goals for 1942, with the result that the bulk of Red Army reserves could be committed to Uranus, the code name for the planned counteroffensive.[87]

That same day, Weichs and Paulus discussed similar concerns at Hitler's headquarters in Vinnitsa. Although Paulus later claimed that the Führer had disregarded their warnings about the exposed flanks, insisting instead that the Russians had exhausted their resources, this seems unlikely. As early as 16 August, concerned that Stalin would repeat Bolshevik tactics from the Civil War and thrust powerful forces across the Don in the direction of Rostov, he had ordered the Twenty-second Panzer Division into the area behind the Italian Eighth Army to bolster its defenses. Similarly, on 9 September, he ordered that the Don sector be mined and strengthened as much as possible since "strong enemy attacks" aiming at Rostov had to be expected against the Italians. Just four days after the conference with Paulus, in fact, Halder specifically noted that "Hitler was still greatly worried about the Don front." The persistent overextension of the army, of course, made it impossible to deal effectively with the weakness on the flanks until the situation in Stalingrad had been resolved. Only the quick capture of the city would permit the necessary redirection of forces to alleviate the growing threat on the flanks. A race of sorts had, thus, begun, with the Soviets hoping to cling to the city long enough to scrape forces together for a counterattack and the Germans desperately hoping to avoid just such a stalemate.[88]

At first glance, the odds seemed to favor the Germans since, with the addition of two corps from Hoth's Fourth Panzer Army, the Sixth Army was the strongest formation in the Ostheer. Of the twenty-one largely understrength divisions in his army, however, Paulus could commit only eight to the fighting in the city, with most of the remainder manning the nearly 130 miles of front to the north and south of the city; only one division was left in reserve. Moreover, this was no longer an operational battle of movement that required skill, coordination, and effective cooperation of all arms, something at which the Germans excelled. This had become, as the Landsers termed it, a *Rattenkrieg* (rat's war), fought by small squads from street to street and house to house, in ruined buildings, in piles of rubble, in factories with twisted metal frames and shattered machines, in grain silos and cellars, through sewers from one house to the next to pop up behind the enemy in a sudden spray of submachine-gun fire and a blast of grenades. Here, in the words of General Hans Doerr, the chief of staff of the Fifty-second Corps, "the kilometer as a unit of measurement gave way to the meter, the staff map to the city plan." This was fighting reminiscent of the trench warfare of World War I; the Germans had lost their great blitzkrieg advantage. Nor did Paulus, although a competent commander, have the imagination or verve to wage such a battle.[89]

Insofar as Chuikov, the tough, determined, inspirational commander of the Soviet Sixty-second Army, had a plan, it was to "hug" the enemy—to hold positions as close as possible to the Germans so that they would be reluctant to call in artillery and air strikes, thus negating their superior firepower. Since Chuikov had noted that the Germans disliked fighting at night, he also ordered small combat squads to infiltrate enemy positions in the darkness, to rattle the Germans psychologically as well as exhaust them physically. "If only you could understand what terror is," wrote one Landser from Stalingrad. "At the slightest rustle, I pull the trigger and fire off . . . bursts from the machine gun." Constant ambushes, the presence of deadly snipers, and continual nightly air raids by Soviet planes were all part of the wearing-down process to exhaust the Germans and shatter their nerves. To blunt the carefully prepared German attacks, Chuikov established a system of fortified strongpoints, "breakwaters," manned by infantry with antitank rifles and machine guns designed to fragment and deflect the attackers into channels where camouflaged tanks and antitank guns waited. Trench mortars and grenades would be used against the advancing infantry while Katyusha rocket launchers, normally protected within the steep bluffs of the Volga, would be backed out to launch their deadly arsenal, then just as hurriedly returned to safety. All the while, heavy artillery removed to the east bank of the river would pound German positions. All this was designed to force the German infantry into a style of fighting that it loathed and for which it was not prepared: close-quarter combat. In fighting such a savage war of attrition, the Russians aimed not only to erode the Germans' strength but also to destroy their morale. Little wonder, then, that even at the time Stalingrad became known as "Verdun on the Volga."[90]

In retrospect, the battle for Stalingrad can be divided into four main phases, with the Germans in each aiming to break Soviet defenses and reach the west bank of the Volga. The first phase, accompanied by a thunderous artillery bombardment and savage air assault, began in the early morning of 13 September, with the goal of taking the old town south of the Tsaritsa River, occupying the main river docks and landing area, and splitting the Soviet Sixty-second Army. North of the Tsaritsa, the Germans aimed at seizing the heights of Mamayev Kurgan, which would allow their artillery to dominate the entire city. Although the attack achieved some initial success—in the south, troops from Hoth's Forty-eighth Corps took the major part of the old city and penetrated into the harbor, while, in the north, Paulus's Fifty-first Corps gained the railway station and reached the Volga in a narrow corridor—it soon bogged down in the rubble of the inner city. The key point in the battle, both symbolically and in actuality, came early on the fourteenth, when German troops reached the crest of the Mamayev Kurgan and seemed poised to surge to the Volga, the central landing site, and Chuikov's headquarters, not more than eight hundred yards away. It might as well have been eight hundred miles, however, as troops from Alexander Rodimtsev's elite Thirteenth Guards Rifle Division were hurriedly ferried across the Volga, leaped from their boats, and, with the Germans less than a hundred yards away, charged up the steep banks and straight into the melee. Nearly a third of his men were lost in the first day, but Rodimtsev's fierce counterattack saved the riverbank and swept the Germans back off the Mamayev Kurgan. Chuikov later claimed that, without Rodimtsev's determined intervention, Stalingrad would likely have fallen in mid-September.[91]

Although certainly inspiring from the Soviet perspective, the incident pointed to two persistent problems confronting the Germans: their inability to stop the flow of enemy reinforcements across the river into the city and Paulus's uninspiring direction of the battle. Despite the massive and effective employment of his Stuka dive bombers, for example, Richthofen was exasperated by what he saw as Paulus's bland and timid leadership, his failure to exploit opportunities by driving his units on, and the lack of fighting spirit in the troops. The absence of bold, reckless leadership seemed especially obvious when compared with the fanatic actions of the Soviet commanders. To Richthofen, not merely motivation but a recognition that audacious action now would save lives in the future was lacking. The cautious clearing of the city block by block, which Paulus preferred, simply gave the enemy time to recover and would lead to a slow strangulation of German forces.[92]

Nothing illustrated Richthofen's point more than the ferocious battle that raged for days for control of an enormous concrete grain elevator in the south of the city near the river. With only two old machine guns and a few antitank rifles, the fifty-odd defenders of the silo, with the grain on fire and in choking smoke and dust, without water, and with no chance of relief, turned away at least ten German assaults on the eighteenth alone. "Our battalion, plus tanks, is attacking the elevator, from which smoke is pouring," noted Wilhelm Hoffman in his diary. "Barbarism. . . . The elevator is occupied not by men, but by devils that no flames or bullets can destroy." Although the attacks continued, not until the twentieth were German tanks able to finish the place off. Even then, the fighting hardly abated, as Hoffmann despaired a few days later: "Our regiment is involved in constant heavy fighting. After the elevator was taken the Russians continued to defend themselves just as stubbornly. You don't see them at all; they have established themselves in houses and cellars and are firing on all sides, including from our rear. . . . Barbarians, they use gangster methods. . . . Stalingrad is hell." The wearing, consuming fighting, of an intensity the men had never experienced, not only accelerated the "approaching exhaustion" of the battle-weary troops, but also sapped their morale. Despite German successes—by the twenty-sixth Paulus had declared the south and the center of the city won, with the swastika flying over the Stalingrad party building—the mid-September action clearly showed what an enormous expenditure of time and forces a systematic mopping up of the city would entail when every block, every key feature of the cityscape—a grain silo, the main railway station, Mamayev Hill, the various factory complexes in the north—had to be fought over for days. Yet that was precisely what Paulus had in mind—and was the type of unimaginative leadership that drove Richthofen to despair.[93]

With winter fast approaching and German combat strength wasting away at an alarming rate, the Sixth Army headquarters knew that there was no time to waste and, thus, even before the southern and central sectors of the city had fallen prepared for the knockout blow in the industrial areas of the north. Although the struggle for Mamayev Kurgan continued, the focal point of the second phase of fighting would be the mammoth industrial complexes of the north: the Lazur chemical works, the Krasny Oktyabr metal plant, the Barrikady gun factory, and the Dzerzhinsky tractor works. Once more, a massive aerial barrage on the morning of 27 September preceded the infantry assault, with the fighting repeating that of the first phase as well. After some initial success, Soviet counterattacks again threw the enemy off the summit of Mamayev Hill, while German assault forces slowly ground their way through the tangle of ruined buildings and wrecked machinery of the factory complexes. On the thirtieth, hoping to speed the attack, Paulus threw two divisions from the southern sector into the battle, which raged amid appalling destruction for the next week. As German troops smashed through one building after another, the hard-pressed Chuikov's position hung by a thread.[94]

Evidently buoyed by this progress, Hitler returned to Berlin to give a speech on 30 September at the Sportpalast for the beginning of the annual Winter Relief campaign. Whether unaware of the extent of German losses or, as his adjutant, Below, believed, now a prisoner of self-deception, he surprised the skeptical Goebbels with his upbeat assessment of the situation at Stalingrad. The propaganda minister, worried by growing public anxiety and impatience about the battle on the Volga, which was coming to be regarded by many as the key turning point of the war, had sought to keep reckless predictions of imminent victory out of the German media. He had been greatly annoyed when Dietrich, the Reich press chief, had announced in mid-September that the battle was nearing "its successful conclusion," not least because of his fear that any extended fighting would cause home-front morale to plummet.[95]

That night, however, the Führer treated his audience to a splendid performance, at once promising, threatening, mocking, and boastful. The worst hardships and perils of the war, he assured his listeners, were behind them as the imminent victory in the east would soon allow economic benefits to flow to the German people, thus elevating their living standards. But the speech was most noticeable for two predictions. For the third time in a speech that year, and in the most menacing and open language to date, the Führer again referred to the Jews. "The Jews used to laugh . . . about my prophecies," he noted. "I don't know if they're still laughing today, or whether the laughter has already gone out of them. But I, too, can now only offer the assurance: the laughter will go out of them everywhere. And I will also be right in my prophecies." In references to Stalingrad, Hitler also assumed a triumphal posture. In mocking, sarcastic tones, the Führer ridiculed the British for their string of failures, including the recent Dieppe raid. "Obviously we cannot even begin to compare our own modest successes with them!" he jeered to the approving crowd. "If we advance to the Don, finally reach the Volga, overrun Stalingrad, and capture it . . . in their eyes this is all nothing." "You can be sure," he added in a boast that was soon to ring hollow, "that nobody will get us away from this place again!"[96]

The next afternoon, in a speech to the Gauleiter, his most faithful party comrades, Hitler, according to Goebbels, assumed that the capture of Stalingrad was an accomplished fact and that, with it, the oil of the Caucasus would soon be secured for Germany. He even expressed the belief that "the war was practically lost for the opposing side." Such outlandish optimism, however, hardly corresponded to the situation on the ground. By this time, virtually all his top military advisers favored a withdrawal from the city, which by now had been thoroughly destroyed as an armaments and communications center. Any further sacrifice of lives could no longer be justified on those grounds. Nor could holding on to the city as winter quarters be warranted; living off the land was out of the question in the sparse steppe, while the German logistic system could not possibly supply the stocks of food, fuel, coal, wood, and ammunition that the Sixth Army would need to survive. Not only was the Stalingrad area serviced by only three single-track rail lines, but even these were now being regularly interrupted by Soviet air attacks and sabotage by partisans. Already in October (i.e., before the onset of winter), the Sixth Army was on average receiving less than half its required daily trainloads of supplies, a situation that would only worsen as the weather deteriorated. Motor transport offered little promise of relieving the logistic bottleneck since roads were limited, trucks worn out, and fuel scarce. Moreover, not even horse transport could fill the gap since most of the surviving horses had been herded to the rear for winter quarters. Given the enormous pressures on the troops and the tremendous expenditure of ammunition in the bitter house-to-house fighting, the Sixth Army could not satisfy the day-to-day needs of the forces, let alone engage in any long-term stocking of supplies. Little wonder that German commanders were worried. The growing discrepancy between the demands made on the troops and the nutrition they received resulted in a noticeable reduction in the physical strength of the combat forces as well as in their morale. The final shock was an October report that showed that, although the ration strength of the Sixth Army was roughly 334,000 men, only 66,569 were combat troops. Even if the Sixth Army had managed to seize all of the city, German logistic failures meant that Paulus's troops faced a hunger catastrophe and likely could not have held on to Stalingrad in any case.[97]

When the second phase of the fighting broke off in early October, then, army leaders pleaded for a withdrawal of the Sixth Army to defensible winter lines. Hitler, however, would have none of it, for the first time stressing that the capture of the city was necessary to deliver a crushing blow, not just militarily, but psychologically as well. Ever sensitive to internal upheavals on the home front, Hitler the politician now seemed to be reacting to a perceived decline of the Führer myth, itself vital to the stability of the regime. Moreover, he needed a spectacular victory of German arms, not only to boost domestic morale, but also for the sake of his allies and "the world public," especially important neutrals such as Sweden and Turkey. Ever more contemptuous of his fainthearted generals and military advisers, and convinced more than ever of the value of will over resources, he refused to entertain any suggestions of retreat. Although his stand-fast order of the previous winter had possessed some tactical merit, this time his decision flew in the face of all military reason. "Will Stalingrad turn into a second Verdun?" Helmuth Groscurth had written anxiously to his brother on 4 October, just days after the Sportpalast speech. With his decision two days later, the Führer ensured that it would. Hitler the politician was now holding Hitler the military leader hostage; for prestige considerations, he had to take the city.[98]

Paulus, too, felt the tremendous pressure to finish the job. Dismayed by the appalling losses suffered by his troops, he had developed an increasingly noticeable facial tic that betrayed his anxieties. Although pressed by Führer Headquarters to continue the battle, on 6 October he had to suspend offensive operations. As he put it to Weichs, his units were so depleted that "even breaking out of individual blocks of houses can only be accomplished after lengthy regroupings to bring together the few combat-worthy assault elements that can still be found." The Führer, however, insisted that Stalingrad be taken even though it was now broken well beyond the point that it could be of any use to the Soviets. Accordingly, after assembling all available forces of the Fifty-first Corps and the Fourteenth Armored Corps, Paulus resumed the attack on 14 October, aiming finally to subdue Soviet resistance in the northern industrial district.[99]

Focused on a narrow front, using every available Stuka, and with all artillery and flak guns roaring, the fighting, in the words of one of Chuikov's officers, "assumed monstrous proportions." Amid appalling conditions and terrible fighting "in ruins, cellars, and factory sewers," as an officer in the Fourteenth Panzer Division recorded, the Germans slowly pushed the stubborn Russians back through mounds of rubble, wrecked machinery, and shattered tanks. The nervous strain of the close-quarter fighting threatened to shatter the remaining strength of the Germans. "Fighting has been going on continuously for four days, with unprecedented ferocity," noted Wilhelm Hoffmann on 17 October of the merciless struggle for the Barrikady gun factory. "The Russian firing is causing us heavy losses. Men and officers alike have become bitter and silent." Five days later, he wrote bitingly, "Our regiment has failed to break into the factory. We have lost many men; every time you move you have to jump over bodies. . . . [Our] soldiers are calling Stalingrad the mass grave of the Wehrmacht." On the twenty-seventh, Hoffmann noted the capture of all of the Barrikady factory, but there was more fear than jubilation in his words: "The Russians are not men, but some kind of cast-iron creatures; they never get tired and are not afraid of fire." The next day he admitted, "Every soldier sees himself as a condemned man. The only hope is to be wounded and taken back to the rear." Two days later, the inner destruction was complete: "Stalingrad has turned us into beings without feelings—we are tired, exhausted, bitter." By the end of October, the Germans had taken most of the factory area and had squeezed the Russians into a narrow strip along the Volga, yet still they refused to give up. "It is," wrote a Stuka pilot in his diary, "incomprehensible to me how people can continue to live in that hell, but the Russians are firmly established in the wreckage, in ravines, cellars, and in a chaos of twisted steel skeletons of the factories." By the end of the month, the German offensive had petered out, a victim of exhaustion—of both men and ammunition.[100]

At the beginning of October, Richthofen had grumbled, "We simply can't go on fumbling around everywhere at once with . . . weak forces." By the end of the month, his worst fears had been realized: the time-consuming mopping up of the factories, the hemorrhaging of strength in the endless scenario of attack-counterattack, the diminished penetrating power as the rubble battle negated German strengths, the shortage of infantry and ammunition, and the inability to keep the Russians from bringing nightly reinforcements across the Volga all pointed to looming disaster. Even the impossibility of letting Paulus have a few more regiments to finish his task pointed to the disastrous state in which the Germans now found themselves. With growing evidence of a menacing enemy buildup on their flanks, the time had come to pull out of the ruined city.[101]

But, as Bernd Wegner has put it, Hitler the politician now robbed Hitler the military leader of his last option. En route from Berlin to Munich in order to give his traditional address marking the anniversary of the 1923 putsch attempt, the Führer found his special train halted early on 8 November so that he could receive a dramatic message from the Foreign Office: Allied troops were landing in North Africa. Already reeling from Rommel's precipitous retreat at El Alamein on 2 November, he was caught off guard by this first commitment of American ground troops in Europe. Although he immediately ordered the defense of Tunis, he had to have realized that his time had run out; Axis forces in North Africa could be reinforced only at the expense of German troops in Russia. Even a limited second front would strain German resources to the breaking point. But, when Foreign Minister Ribbentrop, who had joined the train at Bamberg, pleaded with him to be allowed to put out peace feelers to Stalin via the Soviet embassy in Stockholm, the Führer brusquely rejected the suggestion. "A moment of weakness," he said, "[was] not the right time for negotiations with the enemy."[102]

Hitler arrived in Munich, then, in a highly charged atmosphere of military crisis: the landing in North Africa raised serious concerns, while the situation in the east had not yet been resolved. According to Goebbels, the Old Fighters in attendance at Hitler's evening speech at the Löwenbräukeller fully understood that Germany stood "at a turning point of the war." The Führer had little to offer, however, other than uncompromising determination to fight on and unyielding hatred of his enemies; any notion of how to achieve even a limited victory was conspicuously absent. He specifically ruled out any prospect of a negotiated peace with his foreign adversaries. In a war for the very existence of Germany, there could be no compromise: "From now on there will be no more offers of peace." As to the Jews, the "eternal enemy," Hitler claimed that they had wanted destruction and now had it. For the fourth and final time that year, he invoked his murderous prophecy, again noting how the Jews had mocked him, then sneered, "Of those who laughed then, countless ones are no longer laughing today. And those who are still laughing will also perhaps not be doing so before long." On the issue of most pressing concern to Germans, however, he could hold out only the promise of imminent victory. "I wanted to reach the Volga, at a particular spot, at a particular city," he boasted. "By coincidence, it is blessed with the name of Stalin himself, but don't think we marched there for that reason. . . . There you can cut off thirty million tons of river transport, including almost nine million tons of oil. . . . That is why I wanted to take it and, you know, we are modest: we have it. There are only a few more tiny pockets. Now some may say: 'Then why don't you fight faster?' Because I don't want a second Verdun. . . . Time is of no importance. Not a single ship comes up the Volga any more, and that's the main thing." If Hitler had hoped to reassure his wider audience with this speech, he failed dismally. The gap between boastful rhetoric and painful reality had become too large. Invoking Verdun before a public weary of a never-ending war, of soaring death tolls, and of increasingly destructive air raids and against the backdrop of the Allied landing in North Africa could only intensify concern that the regime had lost control of events.[103] Moreover, in emphasizing economic goals and admitting the slow pace of the battle, Hitler had implicitly criticized his own handling of the operation. Taking the city itself was irrelevant, and time, as he was about to discover, was important.

Already in mid-September, the nights on the steppe had turned bitingly cold, but it was not until early November that the real winter arrived, with temperatures plunging to near zero. Ironically, this provided the Germans one last chance; as ice floes began to make the Volga unnavigable, it would be impossible, as Chuikov knew, to bring reinforcements across the river. On 11 November, Paulus launched his final offensive, a carefully prepared assault by specially trained pioneer battalions; not infantry as such, these were men expert in the art of demolition and the use of explosives. Their task was to blaze a trail that would be exploited by any able-bodied infantry that could be scrounged. With ruthless efficiency, the pioneers blasted and demolished buildings in their path and managed to carve a small corridor into the Lazur chemical works, but the Germans lacked the infantry to pass into the breach and exploit this last opportunity. On the night of 15 November, a Soviet counterattack forced the commander of the Fifty-first Corps, Seydlitz, to use his last reserves. Once again, the Germans had achieved meager gains at the cost of enormous casualties.[104]

On the seventeenth, even Hitler seemed to have recognized the futility of it all. "I am aware of the difficulties of the fighting in Stalingrad," he acknowledged in his order of the day, to be read to all the troops, "and of the decline in combat strengths." All he could offer, however, was the hollow assertion that "the difficulties of the Russians are even worse" while urging his troops to make one last effort to secure the factory district and break through to the Volga. Time was up, however; the Sixth Army now judged that almost half its battalions, with company strengths under fifty men, were "fought out," while all available units in the east were being dispatched to North Africa to deal with that crisis. The Sixth Army had taken virtually all of Stalingrad but had largely destroyed itself in the process; two days later, the Russians would seal its fate. In truth, even as the Germans limped into Stalingrad, they had reached their limits. Not only had the stubborn Soviet resistance in the peripheral battles of the summer as well as Hitler's ill-judged splitting of the German offensive eroded the strength of the Wehrmacht and ensured that the campaign goals of 1942 could not be attained; they had even inverted those aims. Lost in Hitler's belated determination to seize Stalingrad, for reasons of prestige and to stabilize his regime, was the original target of the summer offensive, the oil fields of the Caucasus. The second, and final, culmination point had been passed; once again, Hitler had lost his race against time. But, as Robert Citino has soberly reminded us, "the most shocking aspect of 1942 . . . is how absurdly close the Wehrmacht came to taking not one but all of its objectives."[105]

7

Total War

Despite repeated Soviet efforts in 1942 to relieve Leningrad and eliminate the German salient at Rzhev, the northern and central sectors of the front had remained stable, so German victories in the south had produced a huge bulge, which seemed to invite an enemy counterattack in the direction of Rostov. When it came at dawn on 19 November, it was as if the whole weight of the front came pushing down on the weak Don sector, threatening to cave in the entire overextended edifice. As some in the German command had feared and Hitler had predicted, the Soviets aimed not just to cut off the Sixth Army in Stalingrad but to seize Rostov in order to trap both Army Group A and Army Group B, with the ultimate goal nothing less than the destruction of the entire southern sector of the front.

Even as the fate of Stalingrad hung in the balance, the Soviets in mid-September had begun tentative planning for a possible counteroffensive. Although in his memoirs Zhukov outlined a dramatic scene at Stalin's headquarters, where he and Vasilevsky on 12–13 September—at the same time Rodimtsev's Thirteenth Guards were about to be sent across the Volga to prevent the fall of Stalingrad—allegedly outlined plans for a bold, war-turning attack, the truth seems both more pedestrian and more ambitious. Almost certainly, initial ideas of a counterstrike at Stalingrad revolved around merely saving the beleaguered city itself from falling to the Germans. When it became obvious that the forces were lacking for any immediate relief action, thoughts turned to the possibility of building the necessary strength for a more decisive counterstroke. Any chance of success, in turn, depended on a rapid buildup of Soviet forces as well as the continued pinning down of enemy troops in Stalingrad. Although Zhukov claimed later that the plan all along was to feed just enough Soviet troops into the Stalingrad meat grinder to keep the battle going, this is likely an overstatement of the Stavka's control of events. At least as important as the stubborn resistance put up by Chuikov's men was the fact of insufficient German strength as well as Paulus's uninspired direction of the battle. Without the Germans' failure to take advantage of their early September opportunities, Zhukov would have had no chance to reverse the situation.[1]

In the event, however, and to Stalin's surprise, the Red Army held at Stalingrad, even as troops were ruthlessly stripped from the front lines and sent into the reserve, to be rebuilt and reequipped for the coming offensive. By mid-October, too, Soviet plans had grown in scale and ambition. Operation Uranus, the plan to encircle the Sixth Army, had a companion, Operation Mars, that was, in fact, regarded as at least its equal in importance, not least because the Stavka allocated it forces equal to the southern operation and Zhukov was personally involved in its planning. Directed at the encirclement of German forces in the Rzhev salient, Mars was, if successful, to be followed up by an even more ambitious operation, Jupiter, which aimed at nothing less than the destruction of Army Group Center. By the same token, Uranus was to set the stage for Saturn, an operation aimed at recapturing Rostov and trapping Army Group A in the Caucasus. Where Uranus seemed a high-risk venture that depended for its success not only on Stalingrad holding out until it could be launched, but also on the Germans not then breaking out of the encirclement, Mars appeared a more certain proposition. Soviet troop dispositions certainly pointed to the initially greater importance of Mars. The Stavka deployed 1.9 million men, nearly 3,500 tanks, 25,000 artillery pieces, and more than 1,000 aircraft against Army Group Center, the target of Mars, while it massed 1.1 million troops, 1,500 tanks, 15,500 artillery pieces, and fewer than 1,000 aircraft in the south. The only problem with Operation Mars, as Geoffrey Roberts has noted, was that it failed, at a loss of some 350,000 total casualties, because the Germans expected the major counteroffensive to come in the center. What they had not expected, however, was that the Soviets could simultaneously launch another large offensive in the south. In any case, in both these offensives, relatively small assaults (Mars, Uranus) were to be followed by large encirclement operations (Jupiter, Saturn) that, if successful, would have shattered the entire German eastern front. In effect, the Soviets intended nothing less than to win the war in 1943.[2]

Anyone at Hitler's headquarters who could read a map, including the Führer, understood the potential threat along the understaffed Don front. Still, despite Hitler's fears and increasing indications of Soviet preparations, Uranus caught the Germans by surprise. Although Foreign

Armies East had been warning since late August of an enemy ability to launch an offensive, it had consistently pinpointed the sector of Army Group Center as the most likely area of Russian activity. This failure resulted not only from a chronic underestimation of enemy capabilities but also from elaborate Soviet concealment and deception measures. Learning from earlier German actions, the Soviets kept knowledge of the upcoming attack on a strictly need-to-know basis, troop and supply movements took place at night, and the assault forces were brought forward only at the last moment. They also employed false signals to convince the Germans that they were preparing defenses in the south, thus reinforcing the German belief that any enemy offensive would be on the central sector. They also effectively fed the Germans' illusion that Soviet strength was just as exhausted as their own. On the eve of the offensive, General Zeitzler stated categorically, "The Russians no longer have any resources worth mentioning and are not capable of launching a large scale offensive."[3]

Zeitzler's assurances might have comforted some, but they hardly corresponded to reality. Their ambitious plans for a dual offensive, in fact, revealed just how successfully the Soviets had again absorbed the German blows while continuing to expand their economic output. By November 1942, half of European Russia, an area of some 80 million people that contained nearly half the cultivated land and the bulk of the industrial resources of the Soviet Union, had been lost. In addition, the Red Army had suffered frightful casualties, with the dead, wounded, and missing totaling well over 8 million, with millions more Soviet civilians perishing under German occupation. Losses in weapons, tanks, and artillery had been equally calamitous. Yet, by the end of 1942, the Soviets vastly outproduced the Germans in every category of weapons. Already a highly militarized society with a centrally directed economy, the Soviets managed through ruthless mobilization measures to better convert their remaining resources into the weapons of war than did the Germans. Nor did it hurt that they had increasing access to Lend-Lease supplies. Although the bulk of the considerable American contribution to the Soviet war effort arrived after Stalingrad, the fact remained, as Mark Harrison has emphasized, that a Soviet economy always on the edge of collapse benefited even from the limited quantities of Western aid made available to it in 1942. As it turned out, Zeitzler was only half right: the Germans had exhausted their immediately available resources, while the Soviets were soon to deploy a combined attack force of 3 million men on the central and southern sectors.[4]

Despite Hitler's flash of insight and mid-August prediction that

Stalin would repeat the "Russian attack of 1920" with a thrust across the Don aimed at Rostov, not until late October, amid increasing signs of an enemy buildup, did the focus of German attention shift to the Don front. Despite his concern over the steadfastness of his Rumanian and Italian allies, however, there was little Hitler could do other than urge the rapid seizure of Stalingrad, which would free German troops for defensive operations. The Führer also directed that the Don front be "fortified as strongly as possible and mined," but this was of little value given the paucity of construction materials and the near-complete absence of antitank weapons on the part of the Rumanians. In the event, some Luftwaffe field divisions were shifted into defensive positions, even though the army command had grave doubts about their battleworthiness. Despite his public assertions to the contrary, then, Hitler's attitude and actions betrayed a deep fear at the prospect of powerful Soviet attacks directed at the weakest part of the Axis line.[5]

On 2 November, alarmed by growing signs of a Soviet buildup along the vulnerable Don front, Hitler ordered the bombing of bridges erected by the Soviets to funnel troops into bridgeheads south of the river, while, the next day, he directed the transfer from the west of the Sixth Panzer Division and two infantry divisions. With the situation growing more threatening by the moment, Army Group B on the ninth shifted the Forty-eighth Panzer Corps into the Don bend as a mobile reserve in order to brace the Rumanian position. On paper a formidable force, in reality it had been badly depleted by the fighting at Stalingrad, with the Twenty-second Panzer Division possessing only forty-two operational tanks, the Fourteenth Panzer Division lacking its infantry regiments, and the Rumanian First Armored Division barely combat ready. At the same time, anticipating the possibility of deep enemy penetrations, the army group command directed that the cities of Karpovka and Kalach be made into "fortified areas" and ordered that a number of "alarm battalions" be created for rapid deployment in the rear. Far from being overconfident, both Hitler and much of the German command appeared to be profoundly disquieted by the prospect of an imminent enemy attack and fully aware of the limited German ability to respond.[6]

Yet neither the Führer nor the OKH could summon the courage to do anything really decisive, such as suspend the fighting in Stalingrad, pull the Sixth Army out to defensive positions, or shorten other sectors of the front. In reality, given the exhaustion of German reserves, there was little the Führer could do. He could hardly denude the central sector of troops in the face of strong indications of a major enemy operation, while giving up the Caucasus would negate the whole purpose of the summer campaign. At the same time, he so misjudged the urgency of the situation that he left his military headquarters to give his traditional speech in Munich marking the anniversary of the failed putsch, at which he assured the Old Fighters that Stalingrad would soon fall, then decamped to the Berghof, where he planned a long holiday. Instead, events in North Africa demanded his immediate attention. Preoccupied with the need to secure the Mediterranean flank, and troubled by the necessity of dispersing his already inadequate forces, Hitler could only hope for "no new surprises" in the east. The Führer's fabled luck, however, was about to run out. Ironically, during a roughly two-week span while he was away from the military nerve centers of the Reich, the most dramatic events of the year, and perhaps of the war, unfolded: Rommel's retreat from El Alamein, followed by the Allied invasion of North Africa and the Soviet counterattack at Stalingrad.[7]

The offensive that Zeitzler believed the Russians incapable of launching began just before dawn on 19 November in thick fog and driving snow following an eighty-minute artillery barrage. Although facing an equal number of Axis troops, which admittedly were supported by far fewer tanks and artillery, the Soviets, again emulating the Germans, had skillfully massed their forces, creating points of main effort at which they enjoyed a marked superiority in strength. Moreover, they had carefully aimed their assault at the poorly trained, equipped, and motivated Rumanian divisions, rather than tangle with frontline German units. Attacking out of the Kletskaya and Bolshaya bridgeheads, the Soviets planned for troops from the Don front to strike southeast toward Kalach, while the next day Red Army forces from the Stalingrad Front would attack south of the city and advance northwest toward the same objective. At the same time, an outer defense line would be established along the Chir and Krivaya Rivers so that, if all went as planned, the double encirclement would net not only the Sixth Army in Stalingrad but also Axis forces in the Don bend as well.[8]

Advancing in white camouflage suits and in a thick mist "as white as milk," Soviet units soon overwhelmed the outmatched Rumanian defenders. Although in many areas the Rumanians put up stout resistance against the waves of Soviet infantry, their complete lack of tanks and deficiencies in heavy antitank guns doomed their efforts. By midday, Soviet armored formations had pushed through the inadequate defense line, with increasing numbers of Rumanian units giving way to "tank fright." General Ferdinand Heim's Forty-eighth Panzer Corps swung into action almost immediately in an attempt to stem the Red tide, but a series of misadventures robbed it of any chance to make a decisive impact on the battle. The crews of the Twenty-second Panzer Division, for example, which formed the nucleus of Heim's forces, had dug their tanks into pits and covered them with straw in an attempt to protect them from the cold. When they hurriedly moved to aid the Rumanians, however, they found, much to their distress, that mice had eaten through the electrical wiring, with the result that only 42 of the division's 102 tanks could be sent forward to meet the enemy. This problem was compounded by disagreement in the German command as to the key Soviet threat. While Army Group B ordered General Heim's forces to seal off the enemy breakthrough at Kletskaya, Zeitzler, after consulting with Hitler, redirected the corps to the northwest to blunt the Soviet thrust at Bolshaya. With fewer than a hundred serviceable tanks, and so short of fuel that they had to borrow it from the Rumanians, Heim's units were sent from sector to sector "on a wild goose chase" that merely dissipated their already insufficient strength. When they did engage the Soviets, they performed well, destroying large numbers of enemy T-34s, but, with any hope of a concentrated counterthrust lost in the confusing welter of orders, the Forty-eighth Panzer Corps was itself soon forced on the defensive.[9]

As it became apparent during the course of the day that the usual German strengths of tactical skill, coordination of forces, mobility, and air power were all negated by fuel shortages and poor weather, the command of Army Group B began to consider seriously the possibility that the Soviet penetrations could not be halted and that German forces in Stalingrad might be in danger of encirclement. By nightfall, Soviet armored spearheads had ripped a hole nearly fifty miles wide in the Rumanian front and were halfway to Kalach. Amazingly, the Sixth Army command itself seemed unaware of the full import of events to the west, continuing its attacks in the city. Although word had been sent from Army Group B at 6:00 P.M. that some units might need to be shifted from Stalingrad, not until 10:00 that evening did Weichs make the seriousness of the situation clear, ordering the Sixth Army to suspend offensive operations in the city and send strong mobile forces westward for the protection of its left flank as quickly as possible. Paulus immediately complied, pulling three armored units, the Fourteenth, Sixteenth, and Twenty-fourth Panzer Divisions, and an infantry division from the line to form the relief force. Since there was a lack of fuel in Stalingrad and some of the units had first to extricate themselves from heavy fighting in the city, they could not be employed en masse on the west bank of the Don for several days, making any immediate halt to the Soviet attack unlikely.[10]

Even as Paulus's Fourteenth Panzer Corps and other assorted units managed on the twentieth to form a thin defensive line and slow the Soviet advance in the north, disaster struck to the south. At 10:00 that morning, artillery and Katyusha rockets along the Stalingrad front south of the city had launched a thunderous barrage. Forty-five minutes later, when "masses of Soviet tanks and waves of infantry" assaulted Axis lines, the ill-equipped Rumanians, despite fighting bravely in many places, had no chance of resisting for long. As Rumanian troops again succumbed to tank fright and began fleeing to the rear, the only reserve of the Fourth Panzer Army, the Twenty-ninth Motorized Infantry Division, quickly moved to stanch the Red tide. Even though it inflicted a sharp reverse on advancing Soviet columns, it alone had insufficient strength to master the situation. By the end of the day, the Fourth Panzer Army had been split in two. As along the Don front, in the south, too, the Germans were now paying the price for having sent all available units into Stalingrad. Had they possessed a mobile reserve, as the success of the Twenty-ninth Motorized Infantry indicated, the Soviet attack in the south might well have been blunted. No such reserve existed, however, and, with the smashing of the Axis line in the south, the situation now assumed alarming proportions. Back in Berchtesgaden, Hitler reacted with two decisions that revealed his full understanding of the danger that the Sixth Army might be, at least temporarily, encircled: he ordered Field Marshal Manstein to assume command of the new Army Group Don, with the task of stabilizing the situation and recovering the lost position, and at the same time he directed that preparations be made for supplying the Sixth Army by air.[11]

Until the twenty-first, Paulus's staff at Sixth Army headquarters, just twelve miles north of Kalach at Golubinsky, had remained cautiously optimistic that the Soviet advance might yet be checked, early that morning sending "a not unfavorable description of the situation" to Army Group B. During the course of the day, however, the realization ripened that the southern breakthrough also had Kalach as its goal and that a double envelopment now loomed as a possibility. Paulus ordered the Fourteenth Panzer Corps to attack to the southwest in an attempt to safeguard the rail line from Kalach to Stalingrad, the vital artery for maintaining the operational capability of the Sixth Army, but a lack of fuel that hampered operational mobility forced a growing recognition that the Soviets would likely win the race to Kalach and that, at the least, a temporary encirclement was probable. Shortly after noon, in fact, Soviet tanks on the way to Kalach appeared on the steppe to the west, forcing a precipitate evacuation of Sixth Army headquarters that quickly turned into panicked flight. As German command cars, trucks, and motorcycles raced away, they collided with each other, overturned, and blocked the road, while men on foot, rushing to save themselves, threw away weapons and abandoned ammunition carts, field kitchens, and supply vehicles. In their hurried departure, they also missed a midafternoon Führer directive that acknowledged the danger of encirclement but ordered that the rail line be held as long as possible. By that time, however, any hope of stopping the Soviet advance had evaporated. The defenses at Kalach were badly prepared and inadequately manned, with a few Luftwaffe flak emplacements supported by mainly supply troops and some units of the field police. Early on the twenty-second, against virtually no opposition, an advanced detachment of the Soviet Twenty-sixth Tank Corps seized the key rail bridge across the Don at Kalach. Lacking the fuel and troops for a counterattack to retake the bridge, the Germans were now reduced, despite the grave doubts of virtually all commanders on the spot about its feasibility, to dependence on an air bridge as the only way to maintain the Sixth Army's fighting power. When the pincers finally slammed the pocket shut on the twenty-third, the Soviets had trapped, not the 85,000–95,000 men they had thought, but well over 250,000 Axis troops.[12]

Decisions had to be made and quickly. Hitler's order on the afternoon of the twenty-first that the Sixth Army hold its fronts "despite the danger of temporary encirclement" as well as another similar directive the next morning clearly indicated his intention to hold on to Stalingrad. With this in mind, and in view of the steadily worsening situation, on the morning of 22 November, Paulus and his staff took a fateful decision: the army would form a hedgehog position in order to prepare for a later breakout to the southwest. In view of the number of transport aircraft available and the unpredictable weather conditions, virtually none of the top frontline commanders put any hope in the supply of the army from the air, but, given their tactical position and lack of sufficient fuel reserves to allow an immediate breakout attempt, there was little other choice. The result on the ground was a chaos of uncertainty and confusion as German troops, often separated from their command and transport, had to fight a desperate defensive battle in the open on all sides. With hard, dry, fine snow lashing their faces, Landsers now withdrew along roads littered with discarded weapons, helmets, and equipment. At bridges across the numerous rivers, long traffic jams formed, while periodic panic broke out at reports of Russian tanks. Villages in the area were packed with frightened, exhausted German soldiers seeking food and shelter from the terrible cold. Supply depots were plundered in a wild fashion, then set afire, with vital food supplies often destroyed unnecessarily. Lacking fuel, tanks had to be blown up and artillery abandoned. The worst scenes were in the field hospitals, however, where the wounded, unable to be evacuated, were often simply abandoned to their fate.[13]

Even as, amid the swirling chaos, Paulus initiated preparatory steps for the intended breakout, Hitler's actions revealed a rather different set of ideas. Although Paulus envisioned a breakout for 25–26 November and repeatedly emphasized both the deteriorating state of affairs and the impossibility of adequate supply from the air, his request for "freedom of action" in case the hedgehog did not succeed was brusquely rejected by the Führer. With the seriousness of the situation growing by the hour, Hitler on the evening of the twenty-second decided to leave the Obersalzberg and return to his headquarters at the Wolf's Lair in East Prussia. A few hours before his departure, however, he had discussed the possibility of air supply with General Hans Jeschonnek, the chief of the Luftwaffe General Staff. Although aware of the doubts of Richthofen, among others, Jeschonnek, evidently believing that the encirclement would last for only a few days, indicated that, in principle, such an operation was feasible. After all, he noted, the previous winter the Luftwaffe had supplied 100,000 troops in the Demyansk pocket for several months. The comparison with Demyansk was specious, as Jeschonnek, much to his regret, quickly realized. Not only were three times as many men trapped at Stalingrad, but also, because many of the Ju-52s necessary for an airlift had been transferred to the Mediterranean, the Luftwaffe had nowhere near the requisite transport capacity.[14]

After all Hitler's boasts and promises to take and hold the city, however, Jeschonnek's spontaneous assurance was exactly what the Führer wanted to hear. His attitude was shaped not only by considerations of political prestige and, since the near debacle of the previous winter, the belief that holding on in a crisis was always preferable, but also by a fundamental misjudgment of the changed power relationship between German and Soviet forces. Hitler certainly conceded the dangers in the situation but, given past Wehrmacht superiority, placed unrealistic hopes in the likelihood of a successful relief operation as well as on the feasibility of aerial provisioning. The Sixth Army, after all, had regularly been receiving some of its supplies by air even before the encirclement, so to Hitler air supply did not mark anything fundamentally new, but merely an intensification of the existing state of affairs. Moreover, the trapped forces could not break out without fuel, which would have to be flown in to them in any case. The deeper problem, of course, lay in Hitler's inability to acknowledge the decisive Soviet superiority. Even then, his decision was not made in a vacuum. Jodl, for example, argued with seeming logic that a breakout should not be attempted and the gains of the summer abandoned without first attempting a relief operation. Although on the twenty-third Zeitzler mistakenly thought that he had secured Hitler's consent for a breakout, Goering's assurance that over a limited period the Luftwaffe could fly in the necessary supplies sealed Hitler's decision. Zeitzler, likely on the twenty-seventh and not on the twenty-fourth, tried one final time to convince Hitler that supply by air was an impossibility, going so far as to accuse Goering to his face of being a liar for his assurances regarding aerial provisioning, but the Führer would have none of it. Manstein would get his attempt at a relief operation, while the Luftwaffe was to keep the Sixth Army supplied.[15]

Although on the night of 23–24 November Seydlitz, the commander of the Fifty-first Corps, tried to force Paulus into attempting a breakout by withdrawing his troops on the northern flank farther than ordered, the latter, despite his equally grim assessment of the situation, could not bring himself to act on his own responsibility. Beyond the instinctive caution of a staff officer who could not countenance a risky operation without its first being properly prepared and supplied, Paulus was also deferring to Manstein, a man of towering reputation who seemed the one person with the skill and ability to reverse the situation. Having been appointed commander of the newly created Army Group Don, the field marshal arrived on 24 November at Army Group B headquarters, where Weichs pressed the urgency of an immediate breakout. Despite the fact that the Red Army was hourly consolidating its position and that the weather was steadily worsening, Manstein nonetheless considered a breakout only "a last resort." Confident that the army could be supplied by air—and, admittedly, he was little interested in logistics—Manstein thought the best option to be a relief operation that would open a corridor to the beleaguered Sixth Army and allow supplies to be funneled into Stalingrad. Only in the event that such an operation failed would he urge a breakout of the Sixth Army. Whatever the basis of his decision, Manstein's assessment came as a devastating blow to the generals advocating a breakout and as an equally large boost to Hitler. With his decision seemingly given the imprimatur of the general of the hour, the Führer now became even more intolerant of dissenting opinions, reducing the OKH, in Richthofen's devastating phrase, to the status of "highly paid NCOs."[16]

Although Manstein was forced to revise his initially optimistic assessment after a talk with Richthofen on the twenty-seventh, at which he was informed that the Luftwaffe could not supply even the minimum of three hundred tons a day, the brief window of opportunity for a breakout had already closed. In truth, while higher commanders had favored a breakout, such an operation seemed far less palatable to regimental and battalion commanders in the infantry. After all, most of their troops were already exhausted, fought out, and nearly immobile because of the lack of fuel. None relished the prospect of abandoning their positions and equipment to march out into the desolate, snowy steppe, where they would be exposed to Russian attack in the open. Moreover, most believed the slogan coined by General Schmidt, the chief of staff of the Sixth Army, "Just hold out, the Führer will get us out," a testament to the power of the Führer myth. Hitler, however, never intended to get them out; the relief operation was to enable them to stay. As Richthofen noted in his diary on the twenty-fifth, "The Führer heard everything we had to say, but decides against [withdrawal] because he believes the army can hold on and he does not think we could reach Stalingrad again." Within a few weeks, this sentiment had hardened to a firm conviction. At a conference with Zeitzler on 12 December, Hitler emphasized:

> We must not give it up now under any circumstances. We won't win it back again. . . . Things would have been quicker if we hadn't hung about Voronezh so long. . . . But to imagine that one can do it a second time . . . , that's ridiculous. . . . We can't possibly replace the stuff we have inside. If we give that up, we surrender the whole meaning of this campaign. To imagine that I shall come here another time is madness. . . . We are not coming back here a second time. That is why we must not leave here. Besides, too much blood has been shed for that.[17]

The original purpose of the campaign, however, had been to seize the oil of the Caucasus, not take Stalingrad. Although his decision to stay in Stalingrad was not self-evidently wrong, Hitler's observation had the ring of desperation, of a man who knew the game was up but hoped for one last winner that might retrieve the situation.

This time, however, the Wehrmacht lacked the means to pull victory from defeat. The success of the planned relief operation, Wintergewitter (Winter Storm), depended on the rapid assembly of a powerful striking force, but precisely this was now beyond its abilities. Strapped by commitments elsewhere, both on the eastern front and in North Africa, the army could not possibly gather in time the forces necessary for the attack originally envisioned by Manstein. That operation, aimed at restoring the German position, projected a dual advance, with one force striking northeast toward Kalach and Karpovka from the bridgehead at Verkhne-Chirsky, only thirty miles from the Sixth Army's western front, and the Fifty-seventh Panzer Corps moving from the Kotelnikovo area northeast toward Stalingrad. Citing the nature of the terrain and insufficient German forces, however, Hoth, commanding the Fourth Panzer Army, objected to the offensive from the Don-Chir bridgehead, even though it was the shortest distance to Stalingrad. Instead, he pleaded for a single thrust from Kotelnikovo, over twice the distance to the city. Despite his misgivings that such an operation could crack the enemy formations facing the Sixth Army's southwestern front, Manstein yielded to Hoth's entreaties. Himself beset by increasing doubts that this operation could restore the situation, Manstein cautiously suggested the necessity of an attack by the Sixth Army to the southwest to link up with Hoth's approaching forces, with the likelihood that the Stalingrad area would be abandoned. On 3 December, however, Hitler once again rejected any suggestion of leaving Stalingrad: the attack was to allow supplies to be sent in to the Sixth Army, not to allow it to be funneled out.[18]

Despite Hitler's optimism about the success of the looming relief operation, Manstein's and Hoth's fears about the inadequacy of German forces proved accurate. In the event, the basic prerequisites of a successful operation—the maintenance of the Sixth Army's fighting power, the assembly of a powerful German strike force, and the wearing down of enemy forces—all were lacking. Even as the Luftwaffe struggled to get its air bridge functioning, the Soviet command, anticipating just such a German ground operation, moved both to increase its forces in the area and to launch a series of spoiling attacks, principally in the Don-Chir triangle. Not only did these problems force the Germans to delay the attack beyond its original date of 8 December, but also, when it finally came on the twelfth, Hoth could strike the "decisive" blow with only two armored units, the Sixth and the Twenty-third Panzer Divisions. While the Sixth, newly transferred from France and superbly equipped with 160 long-barreled Pz IVs, was fully battleworthy, the battered Twenty-third was considered only "conditionally suitable" for offensive action. It could muster only 101 largely obsolete Pz IIIs and 32 Pz IVs, although a battalion of the new Tiger tanks with their eighty-eight-millimeter guns had been sent to the Fifty-seventh Panzer Corps. Of the rest of the twenty divisions originally promised, two barely battleworthy Rumanian divisions took part in the attack, while the others either were in transit, were tied down by the fighting in the Don-Chir sector, or had been withdrawn to fight elsewhere. The anticipated air support also failed to materialize, with demands on other sectors forcing the withdrawal of air units; when the attack came, only two-thirds of the originally envisioned air units were available. In the Kessel, meanwhile, the Sixth Army could muster for its part of the operation only some eight battalions and eighty tanks, with only enough fuel for twenty to twenty-five miles. Amazingly, only 25,000 of the over 250,000 troops trapped in the Stalingrad pocket were infantry. Little wonder, then, that Paulus regarded any breakout attempt as a "catastrophic solution." From the outset, Winter Storm was doomed to failure, "more like a demonstration that all had been done" to help the trapped Sixth Army than an operation with a realistic chance to succeed.[19]

During the first three days, however, the attack went more or less according to plan. By the fifteenth, both the Sixth and the Twenty-third Panzer Divisions were north of the Aksay River, over twenty miles from the start line, but their progress had slowed considerably in the face of a substantially reinforced enemy. On that day, in fact, Manstein stressed to the OKH that he saw no realistic chance of the operation succeeding unless he received further reinforcements. Although Hitler had agreed a few days earlier to release the Seventeenth Panzer Division, its arrival on 17 December failed to have any decisive impact, its entry into the battle more than offset by the withdrawal a day earlier of additional air units. Moreover, any further ground reinforcements were out of the question for fear that the Rumanian front would collapse. Thus unable to concentrate their forces, the Germans' piecemeal attack to relieve an encircled army proved just as ineffective as similar Soviet ones had a year earlier. Even as Hoth's forces continued to struggle forward, reaching the Myshkova River, thirty miles short of the pocket on the nineteenth, it had become clear that, without a breakout attempt by the Sixth Army, any linkup was impossible. Hitler on the eighteenth and again the next evening rejected just such an attempt, arguing that, if, as the army reported, it had sufficient fuel for only some twenty miles, it could not break out anyway. Although a successful relief action had been improbable from the outset, this decision confirmed, as Richthofen had remarked bitterly in his diary a few days earlier, "the writing off of the 6th Army and its murder."[20]

Although Hitler firmly resisted any withdrawal of German troops from Stalingrad, by 19 December he was no longer a free actor. Three days earlier, on the sixteenth, the Soviets responded to the anticipated German relief attack with Little Saturn, an offensive designed to smash through the Italian Eighth Army into the rear of Army Group Don. Originally intended to seize Rostov and trap Army Group A in the Caucasus

(Saturn), this lesser plan, Zhukov and Vasilevsky had convinced Stalin, offered the best means by which to blunt the German drive to relieve Stalingrad. Although the Soviet attack initially got off to a bad start, with units blundering into minefields and meeting unexpectedly strong resistance, by the nineteenth the Italians were in full flight, the front had been torn open over a length of one hundred miles, and the Germans had no reserve ready to counterattack. The problem for Manstein now was not how to relieve the Sixth Army but how to prevent his Army Group Don from suffering the same fate. Compelled to protect its crumbling left flank, with his tank force on the Myshkova receiving a heavy battering, and with the fate of the entire southern wing of the eastern front hanging in the balance, on the evening of 23 December Hoth's forces received the order to pull back. Saving Army Group Don had now taken priority over rescuing the Sixth Army, which itself now had a new function: tie down as many enemy formations as possible for as long as possible.[21]

On Christmas Eve 1942, then, any remaining illusions about saving the Sixth Army had evaporated. Three days later, Zeitzler arrived unannounced at the Führer's private headquarters, informing him in stark terms that, if German forces were not withdrawn from the Caucasus, not only would they be trapped in an even worse Stalingrad, but Manstein's efforts to rebuild the southern flank would also be doomed. Struck by the force of his OKH chief's arguments, Hitler quietly told Zeitzler, "Go ahead and issue the orders." The latter, correctly worried that Hitler would change his mind, used the phone in the anteroom to pass on the order immediately. As soon as he arrived back at his quarters, Zeitzler was informed that the Führer had rung; when he called back, Hitler told Zeitzler to cancel the withdrawal, to which the chief of staff replied, "It is too late. I dispatched the order from your headquarters . . . and the withdrawal has begun." Although clearly annoyed, Hitler grudgingly acquiesced. The next day, 28 December, he issued Operational Order No. 2 formally authorizing the withdrawal of Army Group A from the Caucasus and the combination of both army groups under Manstein's command. By the beginning of the new year, the Germans would be back at roughly the same positions they had occupied before the start of the ill-fated summer campaign.[22]

The men trapped at Stalingrad were the victims of an odd sort of historical vengeance, although few at the time would have appreciated it. From the beginning, as we have seen, the National Socialist leadership envisioned the war in the east as a war for Lebensraum, for the foodstuffs that would guarantee that the German Volk would not starve, as they had in World War I. To ensure that the German masses would literally enjoy the fruits of the victory, and to enable the Ostheer to feed itself off the land, Nazi planners devised a deliberate hunger policy, whereby countless millions of Soviet citizens were to perish as useless eaters. At the same time, in order to accelerate the process of the Germanization of the east, SS planners further designed a grandiose scheme, Generalplan Ost, that, if fully implemented, would have resulted in the deaths of well over 30 million people. The instrument, the enabler, of this economic and racial war of annihilation was the Wehrmacht, and, as one of its spearheads, the men of the Sixth Army had both participated in and witnessed the consequences of this war for Lebensraum: the death marches of hundreds of thousands of prisoners of war; the starvation, decreed by the German leadership, of citizens of cities such as Kiev and Kharkov; the forcible seizure of people for compulsory labor in the Reich; the murder of those incapable of work. Nor were the inhabitants of Stalingrad to be treated any differently. In anticipation of the capture of the city, Hitler had in September considered shooting all male civilians who fell into German hands. Dissuaded from this idea, he instead ordered that all those captured, whether civilians or Red Army soldiers, were to be brought out of the city to a camp on the Don at Belaja Kalitva, where, in a macabre imitation of the process at Auschwitz, those suitable for work would be selected and dispatched to Germany and the rest sent off into the steppe to die of hunger.[23]

Perhaps as a sort of retribution, however, the deeper into the desolate steppe they marched, the more the men of the Sixth Army themselves experienced hunger. As the possibility of feeding themselves or their horses off the land was rapidly reduced, they became increasingly reliant on supplies brought in from the outside, whether by rail or by large cattle drives reminiscent of the American West. By the beginning of October, Landsers were living hand to mouth, dependent on supplies brought over a thousand miles on three single-track rail lines increasingly cut by partisan attacks. "Winter stands threatening before the door," wrote the chief of staff of the Eleventh Corps at the end of the month, "and fills us with the greatest concern." Nor was this hyperbole. Because of the vicious fighting in the city, munitions and other war material had been given preference over food in the supply chain. Moreover, so long as the intense combat in Stalingrad continued, the provision of winter clothing or the stockpiling of adequate food supplies was impossible. The conclusion was inescapable: without a retreat to winter quarters, which Hitler forbade, the Sixth Army faced a hunger catastrophe in the coming winter. Even without the Soviet counterattack, then, the troops in Stalingrad had been sentenced by their Führer to starvation. As Rolf-Dieter Müller has noted, once the Soviets had severed the supply artery, the 250,000 "inhabitants"' of Stalingrad resembled those similarly trapped almost a thousand miles to the west in the Warsaw ghetto—and, just as the Jews perished at the will of Hitler, so, too, were German troops going to be sacrificed by the same man.[24]

Despite Goering's boastful promises, from the start those involved in the effort to bring supplies in by air doubted that even the minimum daily requirements of ammunition, fuel, and food—some three hundred tons—could be achieved. Even before the encirclement, as we have seen, the Sixth Army was living a hand-to-mouth existence, with barely a week's worth of supplies laid up, so the loss of a large part of its outlying stores plunged it immediately into a serious crisis. In anticipation of an immediate breakout attempt, munitions and fuel rather than food supplies took initial priority in the airlift. As a result, within a week of its encirclement, food rations were cut in half, and then on 1 December they were cut again. Nor, given the shortage of wood on the steppe, could defensive positions or shelter be constructed, with men left to sleep open in the snow in plunging temperatures. "Mornings and evenings two thin slices of bread," complained a Landser in a letter on 9 December, "at noon a thin soup, no potatoes. And with that the men day and night have to lie on the naked steppe in snow and storms. . . . Today we get horsemeat—an absolutely great day." With the failure of the relief offensive, the focus of the airlift shifted, and for four days between 18 and 22 December it looked as if the Luftwaffe might be able to supply the army with sufficient quantities of foodstuffs. Indeed, given the difficulties of assembling transport and other aircraft, the horrendous weather conditions, and the fearsome Soviet antiaircraft fire on the approaches to the airports in the pocket, the fact that from 24 December to 12 January the Luftwaffe managed to deliver a daily average of one hundred tons of supplies was astonishing. Still, preserving the strength of the troops could be achieved only at the expense of reduced supplies of ammunition and fuel, which meant that the forces fighting within the pocket were virtually immobile and could not respond to Soviet attacks. The Luftwaffe, in effect, provided just enough to allow the trapped men to hold on but not enough to assure their survival.[25]

On 21 December, the Sixth Army reported its first official death from starvation, and with it the sense of being "betrayed and sold out" grew among many soldiers. By Christmas, even horsemeat had become rare, and, as one soldier groused, "You can't eat it raw, and there is no firewood in the middle of this tree-less steppe." The result was a further physical weakening, more deaths from "exhaustion," and a general lethargy occasioned by hunger, cold, lice, and hopelessness. "We survivors," noted a corporal on New Year's Eve, "can barely still walk from hunger and weakness." A week later, on 6 January 1943, the chief army doctor characterized the previous month as a "large-scale experiment in hunger." Three days later, rations were cut again, and on 13 January the Sixth Army quartermaster radioed from the Kessel, "We have no more bread, munitions, and fuel." Nearly mad with hunger, men were seen hacking away at dead horses, smashing open the heads and eating the brains raw. Rumors abounded of cannibalism among German soldiers driven mad with hunger, of cadavers with flesh cut off the thigh, calf, and buttocks. Epidemic diseases such as typhus also added to the "organized mass death" that General Hube complained of in a telephone conversation with Zeitzler. By mid-January, almost a thousand men were dying daily of hunger, anonymous and uncounted, while thousands more, exhausted, with bloodstained bandages about their heads or stomachs, with untreated wounds, with frostbite, sought shelter in ruined cellars. Even as Hitler belatedly authorized Field Marshal Milch to reorganize the airlift it was too late. If the Russians had done nothing, the Sixth Army would have perished of starvation at the latest by the end of February; for Hitler, its soldiers too had become useless eaters. "Supplies all gone," radioed Paulus from the Kessel on 22 January, adding in a biting tone, "What orders should I give to troops that have no more ammunition?"[26]

The Soviets had hoped to reduce the pocket quickly in order to free forces to trap Army Group A and, from the outset, had launched persistent assaults on the enemy in the Kessel. Despite their hardships and misery, however, the morale and fighting spirit of the trapped Germans remained remarkably high. Their fierce resistance, in fact, both amazed and frustrated the Soviets. Not until 10 January, following Paulus's rejection of a surrender offer and accompanied by an unparalleled artillery barrage, did 280,000 men, supported by 250 tanks and 10,000 artillery pieces, of Rokossovsky's Don Front launch Operation Ring, the long-awaited final assault on the Kessel. Although Paulus had cobbled together battle groups out of fought-out units, he had barely 25,000 functioning frontline troops, with only 95 operational tanks, 33 assault guns, and 310 heavy and medium antitank guns at their disposal, most of which because of lack of fuel could not be moved or maneuvered. Once again, given their physical and material weakness, the Germans put up astonishing resistance. During the first three days of the attack, the Don Front lost over half its tank force and suffered 26,000 casualties. Still, the final result was never in doubt, especially when the Soviets seized Pitomnik, the principal German airfield in the pocket, on the morning of 16 January. From this point, Luftwaffe air crews were forced either to land at Gumrak, which was clearly inadequate for an airlift, or simply to throw supplies out of their planes. In the latter case, German troops were usually unable, because of exhaustion, to reach the supply canisters, or, if they did get to them, lack of fuel prevented their retrieval.[27]

The final act of the Sixth Army's agony began on 22 January, with Hitler brusquely rejecting Paulus's suggestion that he should enter negotiations with the Soviet commander. The next day, the Red Army ripped the German defensive front to shreds and, on the twenty-sixth, effectively split the Sixth Army in half. Even though the Luftwaffe was frantically dropping supplies, on a few days even reaching one hundred tons, its effort was now completely irrelevant to the outcome of the battle. From the twenty-eighth, amid appalling conditions, with food no longer being handed out, and with Dantesque scenes of horror in the cellars—where starving, freezing, wounded, sick, and unarmed men sought shelter—the fighting dissolved into individual actions. The next day, on the eve of the tenth anniversary of Hitler's accession to power, Paulus sent a signal of congratulation: "To the Führer! The 6th Army greet their Führer on the anniversary of your taking power. May our struggle be an example to present and future generations never to surrender in hopeless situations so that Germany will be victorious in the end."[28]

In a speech on the thirtieth marking the tenth anniversary of the Nazi assumption of power, one broadcast by radio to the beleaguered city, Goering attempted to stylize Stalingrad as a German Thermopylae, a sacrifice that would ensure its place in history. The trapped men, however, were hardly cheered by their role as the sacrificial victims. Nor was Paulus much comforted by the news on the thirty-first that he had been promoted to the rank of field marshal—Hitler's none-too-subtle invitation for him to commit suicide since no German field marshal had ever surrendered. At 6:15 that same morning, the Sixth Army radioed from its headquarters in the basement of the Univermag department store, "Russians at the entrance. We are preparing to destroy [the radio equipment]." An hour later came the final message, "We are destroying [the equipment]," a sign that the end was near. Paulus, his faith in Hitler shattered, refused to play his assigned role in the Führer's tragedy, but neither could he bring himself to surrender. Like many of his colleagues, he had so internalized the anti-Bolshevik nature of the struggle that formal capitulation was unthinkable, so he simply let himself be taken prisoner. Even that was too much for Hitler, who received the news with a mixture of disgust, outrage, and puzzlement. By his action, Paulus had tarnished the myth of Stalingrad before it could even be created. "This hurts me because the heroism of so many soldiers is nullified by one single characterless weakling," Hitler complained the next day. "What is Life? Life is the Nation. The individual must die anyway." For days he kept coming back to it. "How can he give himself up to the Bolsheviks?" he asked, enraged by what he saw as Paulus's betrayal. "How easy it is to do something like that [shoot oneself]. The pistol—that's simple. What sort of cowardice does it take to pull back from it?" While Hitler fumed, the thirty-three thousand men under General Strecker fought on amid the wreckage of the tractor works in the northern part of the city, not surrendering until 2 February. At 8:30 that morning, Army Group Don received the last message from Strecker, which concluded defiantly, "Long live the Führer." A Luftwaffe reconnaissance plane flying over the city at noon sent back the message, "No more sign of fighting in Stalingrad."[29]

Paulus, deeply depressed and suffering from dysentery, was one of the 24 generals, 2,500 officers, and over 90,000 German troops marched off to captivity by the Soviets. He, however, was among the fortunate. By May 1943, barely 15,000 of the 90,000 prisoners were still alive, a staggering rate of attrition occasioned not only by Soviet mistreatment but also by the condition of the Landsers when they were captured. While some 90 percent of ordinary soldiers died in captivity, the death rate among junior officers dropped to 50 percent, while that of senior officers was only 5 percent. Of those 15,000 survivors, only 5,000 eventually made it back to Germany, the last in the late summer of 1955. Little certainty exists on the total number of Germans killed at Stalingrad. Soviet accounts claim 147,000 German dead at the time and 91,000 prisoners, of whom 86,000 died in captivity, making a total of 233,000. While Rüdiger Overmans suggests that somewhat fewer than 200,000 Germans had been trapped, Manfred Kehrig estimates a total closer to 232,000, with perhaps 12,000 Rumanians and anywhere from 20,000 to 50,000 "Hiwis," or Hilfswilligers, Russian auxiliaries pressed into service by the Germans, also in the pocket. Both are agreed that some 25,000 wounded and specialists were flown out of the Kessel and that close to 60,000 had been killed between 22 November and the surrender, leaving between 115,000 and 147,000 German troops, of whom, again, only 5,000 survived captivity. With perhaps 50,000 killed in the fighting for the city before encirclement, the total German dead in the Stalingrad campaign was likely anywhere between 220,000 and 250,000. While the exact figures on deaths will never be known, it was by any reckoning a disaster. For the Germans, who at the beginning had feared a Verdun on the Volga, the words of Soviet propaganda rang true: Stalingrad really was a *Massengrab* (mass grave). Soviet losses, too, had been staggering, with "permanent losses," that is, killed, missing, and taken prisoner, for the entire Stalingrad campaign estimated at almost 500,000 men.[30]

For both sides, the unthinkable had occurred. Not only had Hitler insisted on the capture of Stalingrad, in itself unnecessary, and then reacted to both the threatening situation on the flanks of the Sixth Army and the Soviet offensive in an equivocal manner, but also in all of this he never seemed seriously to consider the possibility that the Soviets might actually win the decisive battle he sought. Now faced with the delicate task of explaining to the German people the truth of a catastrophe when they had been led to expect a definitive triumph, Goebbels proclaimed on 3 February that, despite being overwhelmed by the Bolshevik hordes, the "sacrifice of the 6th Army was not in vain. As the bulwark of our historic European mission, it has held out against the onslaught of six Soviet armies. . . . They died so that Germany might live." The disaster at Stalingrad had altered the mission in the east significantly. No longer was it an expansive one of attaining living space for the German people; now it was framed as protecting Germany, and Europe, from the Bolshevik threat. In the Soviet Union, meanwhile, morale soared as many people for the first time genuinely believed that it might be possible to defeat the Nazis, an unthinkable, unimaginable notion just a few months earlier.[31]

Such a triumph, however, was still a long way distant, as events in the first months of 1943 demonstrated. Although the dying Sixth Army had at least performed the valuable service of tying down several hundred thousand Soviet troops, allowing Army Group A to escape possible entrapment in the Caucasus, Hitler's original hope of forming a front to the east of Rostov proved unrealistic. From the outset of the retreat, in fact, Manstein and other commanders pushed for the withdrawal of as many forces as possible beyond Rostov to the Mius in order to stabilize the position of Army Group Don. Still, having lost the Caucasus and any hope of attaining the oil fields that his economic advisers had considered vital to a continuation of the war, Hitler insisted that Manstein hold on to the Donets industrial basin. Without its coal and steel production, he feared that the ambitious armaments program just launched, especially that aimed at increasing tank production, would not be realizable and that, without that program, any chance of a satisfactory conclusion of the war in the east would be lost.[32]

Despite these real economic arguments, however, the weight of renewed Soviet attacks, begun at the end of January, forced Manstein's hand. By early February, in fact, the Russians appeared well on the way not merely to regaining lost territory but to collapsing the entire southern sector of the eastern front. In pursuit of a "super-Stalingrad," the Soviet leadership even envisioned a plan, similar to Manstein's 1940 Sichelschnitt operation, in which Soviet armored units would penetrate to the Sea of Azov, thus trapping Army Group South in a vast pocket. Huge gaps in the line allowed the Soviet attackers, who in the meantime had learned from the enemy to flow around the islandlike German strongpoints, to stream to the west, recapturing Voronezh, Kursk, and Belgorod, and threatening to retake the key industrial city of Kharkov. Although, for both economic and prestige reasons, Hitler categorically forbade its loss, the SS Armored Corps attempting to hold it found itself in a helpless position and on 16 February abandoned the city. The fall of Kharkov, the most shattering German defeat since Stalingrad, appeared to confirm the German collapse and embolden Soviet hopes to "entomb an estimated seventy-five German divisions in the Ukraine." Stalin's goal, as a year earlier, was not just an operational victory but a decisive, war-winning strategic success.[33]

The Russian position, however, was not as grand as it seemed since the Red Army was, after a long advance, approaching its logistic and combat limits and Stalin once again seriously underestimated the Wehrmacht's ability to recover. German forces, reorganized by Manstein, were poised for an ambitious counterstrike. Although at a meeting with Manstein at the latter's headquarters near Zaporozhye from 17 to 19 February Hitler clung to a linear notion of defense, a breakthrough by Soviet spearheads that forced an abrupt end to the gathering occasioned an uncommon concession from him. Granted a rare freedom of action by the Führer, and with SS armored formations recently arrived from France to augment those of Hoth's Fourth Panzer Army, Manstein aimed to strike against the exposed southern flank of the enemy, whose offensive had now passed the culmination point, not so much to retake Kharkov as to destroy the formations of the Soviet Southwestern Front. Compounding the problem for the Soviets was the fact that they completely misread German intentions, interpreting troop movements as an impending sign of further withdrawals rather than preparations for a counterattack. When it came on 20 February, the German assault caught the Soviets off guard, with SS units making swift progress over the next week against an increasingly disintegrating enemy. The success of the attack so revived Hitler's spirits, in fact, that he now demanded that the advance be continued beyond Kharkov to the southern wing of Army Group Center.[34]

Faced with deteriorating conditions owing to the imminent start of the *rasputitsa,* however, Manstein abandoned his original bold plan of crossing the Don downstream of Kharkov in order to wheel and take the city from the east. Instead, he opted to strike past the Ukrainian metropolis on the west, thus threatening the enemy's southern flank and forcing him to abandon the city. Favored by a renewed drop in temperatures that aided German mobility, Hoth ordered Hausser's SS Panzer Corps (with the powerful Leibstandarte Adolf Hitler and Das Reich Divisions, along with parts of Totenkopf and Grossdeutschland) to seize Kharkov from the north, then advance on Belgorod. The former was reconquered on 14 March, with the latter falling a few days later. With that, the Soviet offensives begun at Stalingrad had run their course, while the front line at the end of March 1943, when the onset of the *rasputitsa* gave the Germans a much-needed respite, roughly resembled that at the beginning of the 1942 summer campaign.[35]

The stabilization of the front not only demonstrated that the Wehrmacht remained a formidable fighting force but also illustrated misjudgments by Stalin and the Stavka, who had pushed ahead on a broad front without a point of main effort. Although impressive as an operational achievement, Manstein's remarkable success could neither disguise nor alter the true state of affairs: although the Ostheer was able to inflict serious losses in a fighting retreat, it was no longer a force capable of winning the war. The significance of Manstein's achievement, in fact, lay less in what he had won and more in what he prevented: an early spring attack by the Red Army that might well have shattered the eastern front. Having lost the Caucasus and a good bit of the Donets industrial area, and now faced with a multifront war, Hitler saw any lingering hopes he might have had of bringing the Ostkrieg to a satisfactory conclusion largely evaporate. Stalin, too, had been sobered, now finally realizing that his dream of a single decisive offensive that would reverse the strategic situation was illusory. The war in the east would have to be won gradually and incrementally rather than by a Soviet blitzkrieg, despite the judgments of a mid-February 1943 American intelligence report that termed Germany's defeat in the east *irreversible,* suggesting even that "organized German resistance in Russia might collapse."[36]

Certainly, the Germans had suffered casualties and equipment losses that they could not easily make good, while the Soviets could count not only on their own resources but on a significantly increased delivery of Lend-Lease goods as well. Still, not losing the war was a far cry from winning it, and, as Manstein's successful defensive battles had shown, the way west was likely to be long and bloody. The reality facing Stalin of a protracted, costly struggle, as well as his habitual morbid suspicion of his Western allies, led to a renewed Soviet attempt to explore new ways out of the war through a separate peace. Perhaps it was merely to apply pressure to the Anglo-Americans to spur them to greater activity in building a second front that Stalin explored contacts with the Germans that were hardly secretive. In any case, in the months after Stalingrad the Soviet leader did not act like a man certain of triumph. Significantly, it was Hitler who continually rejected Soviet offers. The enforced inactivity of the *rasputitsa*, then, found both sides pondering their next move.[37]

Was Stalingrad the turning point of the war? Certainly, many contemporary observers, both inside and outside Germany, perceived it as such. Already in late August, SD reports noted that Germans displayed "overwhelming" interest in the fighting around Stalingrad, assuming that the "capture of this important cornerstone would bring a militarily decisive turning-point" and an end to the war in the east. By early November, the "blood sacrifice" at Stalingrad had become a "nightmare" that even Hitler's effort to downplay the comparison with Verdun could not dispel. In late January 1943, the SD reported that the imminent destruction of the Sixth Army occasioned "deep worries about the further development of the war," adding that the "entire population was shaken to its depths." "Universally," another report stressed in early February, "there is a conviction that Stalingrad represents a turning-point in the war." Not only had the popular mood reached a low point, but anxious questions were raised: "How will it all end?" "How long can we hang on?" Significantly, in their desire to get an accurate picture of the situation, Germans increasingly began to listen to foreign radio. Even the person of the Führer was no longer spared criticism. By March, images of Hitler were often found defaced with the slogan "The Stalingrad Murderer." Events in North Africa—termed a *second Stalingrad* or *Tunisgrad*—also contributed to a "growing war weariness." In Vienna, the numbers *1918* were scrawled on walls, while, in Berlin, people were reminded of that fateful year in leaflets. As in 1918, people whispered, "The United States had not yet really begun to fight, even as Germany was already drained." Not only had it become an idée fixe among many Germans that "a third winter of fighting in the east meant a loss of the war," but Germany's fate had also become an object of speculation: some argued that, following a defeat, southern Germany would be "given over to the Anglo-American sphere of interest," while others asserted that eastern Germany would be "delivered to the Soviets."[38]

Rather than thinking in terms of *the* turning point in the war, especially since modern wars were no longer winnable in a single, decisive battle, it might instead be worth recasting the issue. In order to win, or at least stalemate, the global war in which they were now engaged, the Germans would have had both to cripple their Soviet enemy and to capture the oil and other resources of the Caucasus necessary for a prolonged struggle with the Anglo-American powers. Seen in this light, the Battle of Stalingrad was, perhaps, not the turning point, but rather the breaking point for the German effort, "the final conclusion," as Bernd Wegner has put it, "of a process of diminishing options of victory in the east." In this view, Stalingrad was not the turning point in the larger conflict, in the sense that a still-winnable war had suddenly turned into a losing one, for the Battle of Smolensk, the failure in front of Moscow, American entry into the war, and the lopsided distribution of human and economic resources all meant that, from December 1941, Germany had little chance of victory in the global struggle. Some sort of victory *in the east,* however, had been possible, where German triumphs had brought the Soviet Union to the point of collapse. The battle at Stalingrad would tip the balance one way or another, but Hitler's mid-July decision to split the German forces ensured that the balance tipped against Germany. At Stalingrad, the failure of all Hitler's assumptions over the previous year had become clear: the Soviets had not been smashed in a single blow; the British had not sued for peace; the United States had not been deterred from entering the war; the resources necessary to prevail in a global conflict had not been secured; the Wehrmacht would no longer be able to concentrate its resources on a single front. Rather than a turning point, then, Stalingrad marked a "point of no return," as the Germans plunged over the abyss. Still, even as, by his own admission, Hitler now "muddled through from one month to the next," the realization that any hope of victory was gone served to occasion not a softening in German war policy but its radicalization.[39]

It was a dramatic moment, as all in attendance and those listening on the radio were well aware. After two weeks of mourning the catastrophe at Stalingrad, Joseph Goebbels on the evening of 18 February 1943 addressed a handpicked audience of the party faithful in Berlin's Sportpalast, itself emblazoned with rousing slogans ("Hail, Victory!" "Führer command, we'll follow!" "Total War, Shortest War!"). After praising the spirit of the defenders of Stalingrad, Goebbels promised "an unvarnished picture of the situation." The events in the east, he admitted, had been a serious blow, and Germans had to be made aware of the possibility of defeat, of the threat from the "Bolshevist-capitalist tyranny" of the Jews. Describing precisely what the Germans had already done to the Poles, Jews, and Russians, Goebbels raised the specter of "the liquidation of our educated and political elite," "forced labor battalions in the Siberian tundra," and "Jewish liquidation commandos." "We must act quickly and radically," he stressed, then, adroitly exploiting class antagonisms with effective populist rhetoric, outlined a series of measures designed to root out luxury and complacency among the German population. Making it clear that worker outrage was the driving force behind these actions, he blasted privileged elites, those who persisted in a frivolous lifestyle, and those who indulged in comfortable entertainments. Invoking a "community of fate," Goebbels demanded that radical methods be employed to achieve results. Having stoked the populist resentments of his listeners, the propaganda minister then posed a series of ten provocative questions, at the end of each of which he asked, "Do you want total war?" At each question, fourteen thousand frenzied voices rang out in unison to affirm loyalty to Hitler and the war effort. As his speech, which had been interrupted more than two hundred times with shouts of approval and thunderous applause, moved to its climax, Goebbels screamed, amid a wild tumult and choruses of approval, "Do you want total war? Do you want it . . . more total and more radical than we can even imagine it today?" As the crowd erupted once more in hysteria, Goebbels closed by invoking the words used by the nationalist poet Theodor Körner in the struggle against Napoléon, "Now people, arise—and let the storm burst forth!"[40]

Although generally well received at the time, especially by the working class, which understood and approved the element of egalitarian social revolution implicit in it, the speech marked the culmination, not the beginning, of a process to reorient the German war economy and society—a process itself that was only indifferently successful. Long convinced that only "the total commitment of all of our resources and reserves" could produce victory, Goebbels had argued at least since the first winter crisis in December 1941 for radical measures to mobilize the German population. Although some steps had been taken in early 1942 to reorganize the war economy, the stabilization of the front, the success of Sauckel's labor roundups, the opposition of the Gauleiter, and the military triumphs of the summer all undermined the effort at a comprehensive mobilization of the Reich's resources. Even as Goebbels attempted to dampen the "illusionary mood" at home and Hitler, chastened by the September crisis, issued orders for a fundamental reorganization of the war effort, resistance persisted. Goebbels's proposals in

December 1942 to use sixteen- and seventeen-year-old boys and girls as flak helpers and to require labor service for all men and women aroused howls of opposition. Ever conscious of the collapse of morale on the home front during World War I that had allegedly undermined the war effort and led to revolution, and convinced of the reality of a Jewish conspiracy, top Nazis, including Hitler and Goering, instinctively recoiled from imposing any increased hardships and material sacrifices on the home front. Others such as Sauckel, who claimed that labor deployment was his responsibility alone, sought to guard their own jurisdictions.[41]

Goebbels persisted nonetheless, arguing forcefully that "too much has been expected of the front, too little of the homeland." The massive losses suffered by the Ostheer, combined with the need drastically to increase arms production, meant that superfluous personnel had to be redirected from the bureaucracy and civilian economy to the war effort. His own nervous exhaustion—on Christmas Day he admitted that the dire situation demanded "the complete mobilization of the entire German people in this decisive struggle for existence"—and a palpable mood of panic among the top leadership persuaded the Führer that the regime could gain a breathing space only through a total effort in both the Reich and the occupied territories. The result was a competition among leading government figures to translate the Führer's will into reality. While Bormann demanded that the party return to "the spirit and methods of the period of struggle for power [the Kampfzeit]," army officials quickly prepared a new personnel plan for raising troops for the Wehrmacht. Armed with a special authorization from Hitler—"Tanks must be produced, no matter the cost"—Speer rushed to put into place a new program that would drastically escalate tank production but that would also require millions of additional workers. As a first step to secure that labor, by the end of January measures had been put in place that required all women between the ages of seventeen and fifty (with the upper limit quickly reduced to forty-five) to register for work and young men and women to be used as Luftwaffe spotters and flak helpers.[42]

Goebbels, however, had hoped not only to speed this process of total mobilization but also to gain decisive control over it. In addition, troubled by what he saw as a fracturing of the Volksgemeinschaft, he intended to use patriotic themes and a radicalization of the war itself to promote a revolutionary restructuring of German society. In this scenario, Hitler would use Stalingrad in much the same way that Churchill had used Dunkirk, as a means by which to rally the nation to unity and sacrifice. For all his efforts, however, and despite the Führer's accord with the spirit he was trying to invoke, Goebbels largely failed in his personal efforts. His control over the total war effort remained confined to psychological mobilization, although the resolve and defiance he provoked, along with ever-intensifying measures of oppression, assured that there would be no collapse of the German home front.[43]

The move to total war also unleashed a contest for dominance in the new power spheres that were opening up, a burst of feverish activity that, in the absence of any consistent leadership from Hitler, lacked the coherent, coordinated planning that might have made a difference in the German war effort. Amid the jumbled jurisdictions and institutional Darwinism characteristic of Hitler's preferred style of rule, a half-hearted effort was initially made to achieve some overall coordination of policy. In mid-January 1943, Hitler authorized Keitel, Bormann, and Lammers, the heads of the three main branches of the Führer's authority (the Wehrmacht, the party, and the Reich Chancellery)—and men not likely to challenge him—to oversee the total mobilization of the German population for the war effort. Predictably, however, from the outset this triumvirate found its efforts undermined by opposition from men such as Speer, Goebbels, and Goering as well as by the fact that Hitler reserved for himself the right to make the final decision on anything of importance. Within a week of his total war speech, in fact, Goebbels had defined the problem precisely. "We have not only a 'leadership crisis,'" he mentioned privately to Speer, among others, "but strictly speaking a 'leader crisis.'"[44]

Still, despite the inevitable chaos and inefficiencies that resulted from this shapeless system of rule, it often resulted in impressive short-term successes. Such seemed to be the case in the first part of 1943. By the end of May, the output of aircraft, artillery, ammunition, and infantry weapons was nearly 120 percent higher than the year before, while the total production of armaments more than doubled from the beginning of 1942 to the end of 1943. For Hitler and Speer, however, the key to victory was not so much a general increase in output as a decisive rise in the production of tanks, the weapon deemed critical for success in the east. Announced to much propaganda fanfare at the end of January 1943, the Adolf Hitler Panzer Program, with its promise to double and triple the production of tanks, including the much heralded Panther and Tiger models, was as important symbolically as it was materially. If total war demanded total exertion, there had to be the prospect of some payoff for such efforts: the tank program was that reward. Certainly, the Ostheer badly needed tanks since it had fewer than five hundred at the end of January 1943. Nor can the success of the Adolf Hitler Panzer Program be denied: tank production in May was more than double that of the autumn, while, in all of

1943, 41 percent more tanks were built than the year before, with fully 40 percent of them the Panther and Tiger models.[45]

The ultimate problem, however, was twofold: for all its success, German armaments output in 1943, including tank production, was being swamped by that of its enemies. In that year alone, the Allies produced just about six times more aircraft, nearly five times the number of artillery pieces, and almost four times more tanks. In each of these categories, the United States alone doubled and tripled German output. More vitally, in the spring of 1943, the German war economy itself was drawn directly into the fighting as the Anglo-American bomber offensive began to achieve significant results. Tank production required massive amounts of steel, which Hitler had now reallocated to the army rather than the navy or Luftwaffe. Pursing ruthless efficiency, German steel mills had in March 1943 managed an impressive jump in output, a feat that, combined with the stabilization of the front in April, left Speer and Hitler optimistic that further large gains in steel production would follow. Instead, beginning hesitantly in March, then increasing in frequency and intensity from April through July, British Bomber Command began the Battle of the Ruhr. Intended both to cripple output in this vital industrial area and to destroy the fabric of urban life, the bombers not only killed thousands of people but also disrupted steel production just as the Nazis anticipated an armaments surge. Where a significant increase had been expected, steel output now fell. Not only did that lead to an immediate cutback in tank and ammunition production, but the disruption in the Ruhr also resulted in a supplier crisis as all manner of parts, castings, forgings, and components vital for continued production in plants outside the Ruhr were now in short supply. The result was sobering: in the second half of 1943, armaments output stagnated. As Speer acknowledged, Allied bombing negated the plans for a substantial increase in production. Not until spring 1944 would the armaments index again show a significant increase, one that would last through September, but by then it was too late.[46]

The Allied bomber offensive also provoked a crisis of morale among the German civilian population best illustrated by the three-day assault on Hamburg in late July. It created a firestorm so intense that bodies mummified, glass melted, and asphalt ran in the streets; 40,000 people suffocated or were burned alive, and another 500,000 were left homeless. Large parts of the great port city had been reduced to mountains of rubble, while thousands fled in sheer terror, spreading panic and disorder throughout the surrounding area. As the news from Hamburg leaked out, the Gestapo reported shock and dismay across the country, while the SD noted that hardly any senior industrial leaders believed any longer that victory was possible. In mid-August, in despair at the destruction of German cities, Hans Jeschonnek, the chief of staff of the Luftwaffe, shot himself. Among average Germans, anger at the failure of the regime to protect them from enemy air raids was widespread. Speer feared that a few more such raids might lead to a total collapse of German morale and a complete halt to arms production. The disaster was put off for another year, however, as the Allies mistakenly chose not to keep hammering at the Ruhr choke point, while the Germans initiated effective new defensive measures. At the same time, the regime responded to the crisis, in typical fashion, by imposing greater discipline on the home front. At the end of July, Speer had agreed to allow the SS to oversee security operations in the armaments industry, while, in early October, he authorized the SD to check on civilian production in industry. Moreover, any hint of defeatism was met with harsh punishment, including the death penalty. As Hitler repeatedly emphasized, there would not be another November 1918.[47]

Even as the Germans struggled to maintain output under the onslaught of Allied bombers, a shortage of the other key resource necessary to step up production—labor—loomed as a major obstacle. Although German industrialists had long been pressing for an increased use of women, Hitler had consistently rejected their conscription into war industries, whether from ideological objections (the birth rate would fall, undermining the nation's racial essence) or fears of domestic unrest such as occurred in 1918. When the war began, Germany actually experienced a fall in female employment as consumer goods production was cut back. Over the next few years, the number working in war production gradually rose, but generous government allowances to wives and widows of soldiers offset any inducements to work. By early 1943, however, the worsening labor situation compelled Hitler to concede that a greater use of female workers could no longer be avoided. The problem, however, was that any dramatic increase in female employment in industry was unlikely. Despite claims to the contrary, German women participated in the labor force to a much higher degree than in either Great Britain or the United States, with the great majority engaged in agriculture. In 1943, millions of women labored on the small farms so characteristic of much of Germany, an obstacle both to efficient production and to the employment of women in industry. Most experts conceded that even the most vigorous measures to mobilize women would result in little more than a million new workers, a fraction of the number needed if output was to be increased significantly.[48]

A brutal logic now emerged: if larger numbers of German women could not be brought into the workforce, Sauckel's legions would simply have to procure more workers from the east. After all, foreign workers could be forced to do tough physical labor for longer hours at low pay, could not take holidays, and were docile and compliant. Despite the fact that Sauckel's roundups continued to foment unrest and contributed to a surge in partisan resistance, the needs of the Reich came first. The urgency, after Stalingrad, of securing foreign labor was reflected in the numbers: almost half the nearly 8.5 million forced laborers in Germany at the end of the war had arrived since 1943. Although the living and working conditions for foreign workers continued to be atrocious, noticeable improvements were made after the declaration of total war, when Nazi officials recognized the necessity of increasing the output of Ostarbeiter. From mid-1943, almost all sectors reported a rise in productivity and output, and, by mid-1944, foreign labor had become the backbone of the German war economy. Any improvement in the working conditions of the eastern workers, however, was more than offset by the harsh racial attitudes with which they were confronted. The racial inferiority of the Ostarbeiter was constantly emphasized to both German civilians and the workers themselves through leaflets and posters, with pointed reminders to Germans to act as racial masters. Reich authorities worried incessantly about sexual contact between the eastern workers and German women and, thus, imposed draconian punishments for any sort of fraternization of a sexual nature. Moreover, Ostarbeiter were frequently warned that they risked being sent to a concentration camp if they slacked off at work or upset production. They were paid minimal wages, worked long hours, kept under strict control, subjected to harsh discipline, and regarded with utter contempt. When Allied bombers rumbled overhead, foreign workers were kept out of the municipal air raid shelters, with the result that disproportionate numbers died in the bombing attacks. Little wonder, then, that most felt they were "no better off than pigs."[49]

The same economic requirements that led to the brutal Menschenjagd also contributed to an intensification of the partisan war in the occupied areas of the Soviet Union. Although Hitler had initially welcomed Stalin's call to action in July 1941 as a cover for the deadly operations of the Einsatzgruppen, the Wehrmacht had from the outset struggled to control the vast regions it had conquered. The harsh measures directed at the local population, the often contemptuous behavior of German troops, the brutal treatment of Soviet prisoners of war, and the mass shootings of the murder squads all contributed to a growing embitterment that aided the spread of the partisan movement. German security divisions, with their overage, badly trained, ill-equipped, and overstretched troops, struggled against a ruthless foe who used a mix of inducements and terror to tighten his hold over ever-larger areas. By early summer 1942, economic exploitation, harsh pacification policies, and increasing impoverishment of the rural population had created a cruel dynamic that fed the growth of the partisan forces. As they became increasingly bold and began to assume operational importance in some rear areas, German forces responded with large-scale search-and-destroy operations that resulted in very high civilian body counts but little diminution of partisan activities.[50]

In the first year of the war, German security troops killed some 80,000 alleged partisans, at a loss of a little over a thousand of their own men, only to find that their brutality had simply fueled an increase in guerrilla numbers. In Belorussia alone, German figures indicated a kill ratio of seventy-three to one, and, during the entire war, German *casualties* in the central sector of roughly 34,000 were dwarfed by some 300,000 partisan *deaths*, yet partisan numbers tripled during 1942. Although many German officers on the ground understood the necessity of better treatment of the rural population as a prerequisite for regaining their support, Hitler responded by entrusting the SS with sole authority for combating the partisans. Thus empowered, Himmler in August 1942 appointed the ruthless SS police leader and Obergruppenführer Erich von dem Bach-Zelewski to lead the fight against "bandits," charging him with the pacification of central Russia. If von dem Bach was not already aware of what pacification meant, an addendum by Hitler to his own October directive that all partisans were to be killed spelled it out with brutal clarity: the partisan war in the east, he stressed, was "a struggle for the total extirpation of one side or the other."[51]

Although the partisans enjoyed some sporadic success in disrupting rail traffic and supply movements, the partisan war itself was hardly, in 1942, the great "people's struggle" of later Soviet myth. Despite often brutal measures directed against the peasantry, the partisans largely failed to break their wait-and-see attitude—that resulted primarily from the military setbacks of 1942–1943, which made a German victory less likely, and the Reich's escalating economic demands, which inherently contradicted any attempt at real pacification. Faced with the pitiless logic of total war, German officials combined economic considerations with existing ideological predispositions and security concerns to unleash devastation on great swaths of occupied territory. The large-scale combing sweeps, the *Großunternehmen*, now aimed not so much at rooting out guerrillas as at plundering anything of value in the so-called bandit areas. German economic officials directed the seizure of crops and live-stock, the destruction of villages, the wholesale evacuation of the inhab-itants for forced labor, and the liquidation of those deemed unfit for work. The sheer ruthlessness and brutality of this policy have led the historian Christian Gerlach to speak of the emergence of a *Tote Zonen* (dead zones) policy that envisioned the cultivation of select parts of the rear area and the complete evacuation and utter destruction of others. By the end of the year, the explosion of brutality associated with the Tote Zonen policy had resulted in tens of thousands of civilian deaths as well as the emergence of a full-blown partisan movement capable of extensive disruption of rear-area operations. This counted for little with Nazi officials, however, obsessed as they were with avoiding a repetition of 1918.[52]

By mid-1943, growing coercion on the home front, the need to mobi-lize all resources for war, and the increasing demand for labor had cre-ated a logic of escalating terror. Determined to root out defeatism and mobilize fully for war, Speer now moved into an ever-closer alliance with Himmler as both made use of the full repressive apparatus of the Nazi state. Forced by military reverses on the eastern front to abandon Gener-alplan Ost, for which the SS had begun creating slave labor camps under the catchphrase Vernichtung durch Arbeit, Himmler from spring 1943 sought to gain advantage from the crisis by emphasizing the economic utility of turning concentration camps into work facilities for arms pro-duction. Speer was also eager to use these labor resources to aid the war effort, as was German industry, which, in its search for cheap and docile labor, looked eagerly at concentration camp inmates. As a wide range of businesses made use of prisoner labor, a vast network of sub-camps sprang up throughout Germany, with the result that by late 1943, as Richard Evans has noted, "there was scarcely a town in the Reich that did not have concentration camp prisoners working in or near it."[53]

As with the Ostarbeiter, living and working conditions were deplor-able, even though the need for labor somewhat reduced the ideological pressure for annihilation. Mortality rates were appallingly high, partic-ularly when the supply of such prisoners seemed unending. Although conditions improved somewhat through 1943, Himmler conceding that "the food issued should be like that provided . . . to Egyptian slaves, which contained all the vitamins and was simple and cheap," the hope of sur-vival of most individual inmates depended on special skills or training that could not be easily replaced. By August 1943, SS-run labor camps held 224,000 prisoners, a number that would double and then triple over the next year and a half; in January 1945, nearly 715,000 inmates toiled in the system. The Nazi attitude toward this slave labor was, perhaps, best epitomized by the August 1943 decision to use thousands of prisoners to blast tunnels out of the Harz Mountains for the production of V-2 rockets. Urged on by the head of the SS Building Directorate, Hans Kammler, a "cold, ruthless schemer, a fanatic . . . [and] unscrupulous," the men toiled in inhuman conditions. Determined to finish the project as quickly as possible, and, thus, unwilling to waste time and money to build barracks off site, Kammler instead forced the workers to sleep in wooden bunks four levels high within the cold, damp confines of the tunnels, with no proper sanitary facilities or adequate water supplies. They were allowed outside only once a week during weekly roll call. Each morning, SS guards punched workers in the face: those who did not fall were considered fit for work. "Pay no attention to the human cost," Kammler declared in response to the rising death toll from dysentery and sheer exhaustion. "The work must go ahead, and in the shortest possible time." Eventually, one in every three of the men forced to work on the V-2 production facility would die of disease, starvation, or maltreatment, some 20,000 in all. Speer, however, was ecstatic, in mid-December congratulating Kammler on his success in setting up the production center in only two months, an accomplishment "that far exceeds anything ever done in Europe, and is unsurpassed even by American standards."[54]

Speer's cooperation with Himmler was sealed in early October at a joint appearance at the annual gathering of Gauleiter in Posen. In his address to the regional party leaders, Speer bluntly accented the critical military situation, noting the damage done to armaments production by Allied bombing and the stark fact that the enemy now dictated what Germany had to do. Only the "sharpest measures," he stressed, could improve the state of affairs. As if to stiffen the resolve of the Gauleiter for the "necessary brutality" in mobilizing all Germany's resources, Himmler then made them openly complicit in the ongoing Judeocide: "You all accept happily the obvious fact that there are no more Jews in your province. All Germans, with very few exceptions, realize perfectly well that we could not have lasted through the bombs and stresses of the . . . war, if this destructive pestilence were still present within our body politic. . . . The hard decision had to be taken to have this people disappear from the face of the earth. . . . About the matter of the Jews . . . you are now informed." Aside from revealing his belief in the existence of a Jewish conspiracy and reminding his audience that they had no choice but to fight on since, with the murder of the Jews, the Nazi bridges were burned behind them, Himmler's speech was notable for one other aspect: he pointedly threatened the Gauleiter that methods similar to those used against the Jews would now be employed against Germans who refused to accept the sacrifices necessary for radical mobilization of the economy and society.[55]

Despite these exertions and the deaths of tens of thousands of slave laborers, Speer was never able to boost German war production sufficiently to challenge that of Germany's enemies. In the end, no amount of rationalization, labor mobilization, threats, or intimidation would have worked once the war became one of attrition. Given Hitler's unwillingness to squeeze civilian living standards as harshly as Stalin had done, Speer and Himmler responded with a brutal exploitation of foreign labor. The crisis unleashed by the stunning defeat at Stalingrad thus fed a process of intensifying violence and radicalism that allowed the Reich to continue the war beyond 1943, but with no hope of actually winning. When, in January 1944, the realization finally sank in that all his efforts would, ultimately, be fruitless, Speer suffered a physical breakdown that incapacitated him for nearly four months. The forces that he had helped set in motion, however harsh and irrational, nonetheless ensured that the regime would not crumble—a collapse of war production in 1943 had been averted. Although the British Joint Intelligence Subcommittee expressed the hope that autumn that "the German people [would] no longer be willing to endure useless bloodshed and destruction" and, consequently, that "some sudden change of regime to prepare the way for . . . an armistice" might result, these experts were to be terribly disappointed. November 1943 also marked the twenty-fifth anniversary of the armistice of 1918, a humiliation that Hitler had repeatedly vowed would never happen again. In this, he was true to his word, but the struggle over the next year and a half would cost the Wehrmacht more than twice as many soldiers as the first four years of war combined.[56]

As 1942 gave way to 1943, an air of unreality hung over German military planning. The reflections of the OKW, set down in a memorandum of 10 December, revealed not so much a sense of strategic helplessness as a complete absence of realistic thinking. Not only must North Africa be held and the Balkans secured against a possible Allied invasion, but the Ostheer was also to launch another summer offensive in the east. Even more bizarre was the operational goal: the OKW staff not only proposed taking Leningrad but also envisioned a large offensive that would "finally separate the Soviets from their economic sources of strength in the Caucasus," with the ultimate goal of advancing into the Middle East. In view of the relation of forces between Germany and its enemies in early 1943, this was not merely utopian but delusional.[57]

Hitler himself was under no such illusions, recognizing clearly in March 1943 that the "question of personnel is our greatest worry and by far the most serious problem," one for which no ready solution was at hand. Although Foreign Armies East calculated total Red Army losses to the end of 1942 at between 11.7 and 11.9 million men, a figure that was, if anything, low, and despite the fact that the Soviets had in 1942 lost another 1.5 million as prisoners (or over ten times the number of Germans taken at Stalingrad), its conclusion was sobering. Through ruthless mobilization measures, Gehlen's office stressed, the Soviets would have in 1943 an available reserve of 3.4 million men as opposed to a Wehrmacht total of only 500,000. Moreover, this seven-to-one inferiority would be even greater in practice since the Red Army could concentrate all its forces against the Ostheer, while German reserves had to be stretched across all possible fronts. Nor did materiel production offer any hope of relief, for, despite the fact that German output soared—at least until the Battle of the Ruhr commenced—Soviet production was higher still and, once again, could be used entirely against the Germans. In addition, American and British production had to be weighed in the balance, as did the possibility of the opening of a second front in Europe.[58]

For the second key problem facing Hitler, and one no less urgent than that of personnel and production, was the growing interconnectedness of the various fighting fronts. The question of the defense of Fortress Europe not only demanded more attention from the German leadership but also eroded the dominant role of the eastern front as the great bulk of German resources could no longer be concentrated in one area. Prevention of a second front in the west was now the command of the hour: "no front," Hitler declared in mid-May, could be allowed "to come into being on the borders of the Reich." Just the threat of a second front, in fact, compelled the Germans, over a year before the Normandy invasion, to transfer forces from the east to other threatened areas, from Norway to France to Italy and the Balkans, while the Soviets could mass virtually all their strength against the Germans. The consequence of this was alarming; if in 1917 and 1918 a German division on the western front defended a sector of roughly two and a half miles, in the summer of 1943 on the eastern front that same division, likely with fewer men, would be covering four times the area. Sectors that in the First World War were held by a division were now being defended by a battalion. This inferiority in numbers and the German need to prepare for a possible defense against Allied attack somewhere in the west meant not only that the Soviets would be in a position to launch several offensives simultaneously in the summer of 1943, but also that any German response would of necessity be limited. Little wonder, then, that so many in the German leadership put their faith in "the higher leadership abilities and the greater worth of the individual German soldier."[59]

Although Hitler was clearly aware of the difficulties facing Germany, remarking on 18 February 1943 that he could "undertake no great operations in this year . . . but only small strikes," he nonetheless refused, largely for economic reasons, to countenance a large-scale withdrawal in order to free up manpower. Giving up the Donets Basin, with its steel production and vital raw materials, Hitler emphasized, would not only strengthen the Soviet opponent but also cripple German production. He raised similar objections to Manstein's proposal for a flexible defense based on the "backhand blow," which would invite the enemy, much as at Kharkov, to advance beyond his limits, only to be dealt a devastating defeat by a timely counterstrike. Although he certainly understood the merits of this strategy, he could not accept its prerequisite: giving up the Donets Basin. Nor, given the precarious situation facing Germany over the entirety of the eastern front, could he allow a concentration of forces in the south, which would imperil the other sectors, on the chance that the Soviets would attack precisely where the Germans wished. The counterstrike at Kharkov had worked because of a failure of intelligence, a mistake the Soviets were not likely to repeat given the exact information they possessed in the spring of 1943 about German intentions. Moreover, the Soviets themselves were preparing a backhand stroke against the Germans in the areas around Orel and Kharkov. Hitler, in fact, far from being an incompetent strategist, recognized that Germany no longer had freedom of action. The vast power differential between the two sides, the absolute importance of armaments production, and the looming threat of a second front all demanded his attention and seemed more pressing than a disagreement over an active or passive defense in the east.[60]

Despite the enduring fascination and exaggerated claims made about the battle at Kursk—the greatest tank battle, the turning point of the war—Operation Citadel can in no way be compared with its predecessors. Where Barbarossa and Blue both aimed at decisive strategic victories that would have defeated, or at least crippled, the Soviet Union, Citadel was little more than a grandiose spoiling attack, "only a limited offensive," as Hitler put it, designed not to allow the initiative to slip completely from Germany's hands. Its most important goal, as Goebbels noted, was to shorten the front and "strike a couple of blows on the Bolsheviks that will cost them a few armies, not to mention an army group." Still, even this limited aim, as framed in Operational Order No. 5, issued on 13 March 1943, had much to offer. Planned as a pincer operation, a successful attack at the Kursk salient would shorten German lines appreciably, knock Soviet plans for an offensive off balance, and destroy large numbers of enemy forces. Victory at Kursk might even allow the Germans to focus on events in the west in 1943; after all, if the Battle of the Atlantic and the bomber war over Germany could at least be stalemated (and German failure in both would not be apparent for some months), then the threat of a second front might be greatly reduced. Aware of the obvious advantages of such an action, Manstein quickly dropped his alternative plans and pleaded for an immediate attack at Kursk. Having just bloodied the Russians at Kharkov, "Army Group Center could," he believed, "now take Kursk without any great difficulty." Worried about an enemy attack in the Donets area, however, Hitler rejected an immediate strike, instead ordering preparations for two smaller actions south of Kharkov as an alternative to Citadel. Thus began a period of interminable delay that, according to some, cost the Germans any possibility of even an operational success.[61]

The reality, however, was considerably different, for, in truth, the Germans had no chance of launching an attack in late March or April, even if the other operations had not been considered. In order to triumph at Kursk, they needed to act quickly and to achieve surprise, neither of which was within their power. After the difficult winter battles, German forces were exhausted and desperately needed to be replenished and reinforced. Colonel-General Hoth, the commander of the Fourth Panzer Army within Army Group South, which would spearhead the southern pincer, was under no illusions. "The troops," he warned on 21 March, "having been in battle day and night without rest for months, are used up. . . . Some are apathetic and have reached their goal—the Donets—only under strongest pressure from their officers. The truck situation was bad even at the beginning of the counteroffensive, while the equipment levels have sunken noticeably." Without a significant pause for rest, resupply, rebuilding of stocks, and distribution of heavy weapons, any attack had little chance of success. Furthermore, any German prospect for a quick strike was dependent on the notoriously unpredictable *rasputitsa;* without a drying up of the roads, virtually all movement was impossible. The Soviet General Staff, in fact, assumed that any German offensive would be impossible until the second half of May. More optimistically, the OKW, in Operational Order No. 6, issued on 15 April, set 3 May as the earliest possible date for an attack at Kursk.[62]

Even this proved impossibly early, given the dreadful transportation situation in the area of Army Group Center. Model's Ninth Army needed some 300,000 soldiers and roughly 1,000 tanks brought in as quickly as possible and under the greatest secrecy, conditions that the Ostbahn could not possibly meet. Not only were rail transport and off-loading facilities in the Orel area insufficient to meet the needs of a rapid buildup of troops and equipment, but also Soviet partisans had so disrupted the rail network that the Ninth Army was compelled to launch a series of large antipartisan operations to clear the area. For the biggest of these, "Gypsy Baron," a panzer corps had even been dispatched to vanquish the partisans, with the consequence that additional time would be needed to collect and refit the relevant units for the Kursk operation. Moreover, German intelligence had detected large Soviet troop movements into the area, with the result that, even in mid-April, the enemy enjoyed a nearly two-to-one advantage in troop strength.[63]

Clearly troubled by the growing problems confronting Citadel, Hitler on 18 April proposed an alternative. Instead of a pincer attack that looked likely to need a long preparatory period, he now suggested a frontal assault into the Kursk salient with the aim of splitting the assembled Soviet forces. Manstein, concerned by the uninspired nature of the proposed pincer attack, had developed a similar plan, one that sought to achieve surprise by striking at the Soviets' positions in the center, where their fortifications were weakest, then, after a relatively easy breakthrough, wheeling to the left and right to drive Soviet troops into their own minefields. Although Zeitzler later claimed that he dissuaded Hitler from this "odd variant," in reality it seemed to have been dropped out of concern that there was too little time to redeploy the units. A further proposal by Manstein to launch a deep envelopment movement that would include a strike at Soviet reserve forces was also rejected, for reasons that remain unclear. With his top generals riven by doubts and personal animosities as well as a growing lack of confidence in him, the Führer on 3 May convened a conference in Munich with Zeitzler, Kluge, Manstein, Jeschonnek, and Guderian at which he decided to postpone the offensive until early June. While Zeitzler and Kluge argued vehemently against any delay and Manstein waffled, Guderian expressed his utter skepticism about the entire operation, dependent as it was on new tank models that had not yet been battle tested, preferring instead to stand on the defensive in 1943 and build German tank strength.[64]

Ironically, in part because of Guderian's promise of stepped-up tank production, Hitler postponed the attack on numerous occasions in June as technical and production problems delayed the arrival of the much-anticipated new Panther and Tiger models. Still, it would be a mistake to make too much of the Führer's alleged "technology mania" as the primary reason for putting off the operation. Hitler certainly had high hopes for these new weapons, but more important, in addition to tactical and logistic problems, were strategic considerations. Above all, developments in the Mediterranean area—the final defeat of German and Italian forces in North Africa, the fear that Italy might leave the war, and anxiety over a possible Allied landing in the Balkans—shook Hitler and convinced him of the need to keep sizable reserves available for any contingency. In early May, in fact, he had already speculated with Goebbels that it might be better "under the circumstances to wait to see whether the Bolsheviks want to beat us to it [an attack]. That might give us an even more favorable opportunity than if we seized the initiative." Only when he was convinced that Italy would continue in the war and that sufficient defensive forces were available in the Mediterranean, according to Warlimont, did Hitler finally order that Citadel proceed. Significantly, however, as early as 15 May he had decided to transfer strong forces from the eastern front in the event of any danger in Italy, an action that would bring an immediate stop to Citadel. Strategic concerns and not an obsession with tank numbers played the key role in delaying the Kursk operation; more time to deliver additional Panther tanks to the front likely only influenced the last postponement, from the end of June to early July.[65]

In any case, the largely enforced delay had little bearing on the other major difficulty—catching the enemy by surprise was out of the question since the Kursk salient offered such obvious rewards for an attack. Already in mid-April, the Soviet leadership knew the direction of the German offensive, and, moreover, the Germans knew that the Soviets knew. Not only had the Russians obtained information from their own spy rings and from British intelligence, which was decoding German radio transmissions, but more conventional intelligence methods (aerial reconnaissance, interrogation of prisoners, and agents in the occupied areas) had given the Red Army leadership a rather exact picture of German intentions. The Germans, in fact, seemingly made little effort to keep the target of the attack a secret, evidently hoping to entice the Soviets to concentrate more troops into the salient, where they could then be destroyed. Such a tactic was highly risky, however, for it invited disaster if the enemy became too strong to defeat. This, in fact, was precisely what the Soviets intended, for they had decided on their own version of a backhand stroke: they would allow the enemy to strike first in order to destroy his exhausted and depleted forces in a savage counteroffensive. This was precisely what Gehlen feared since Foreign Armies East had established by mid-June that the Soviets had shoved so many troops, tanks, and artillery into the salient that the operation was rendered unfeasible. "The Russians have anticipated our attack," he wrote in a memo the day before the assault began. "[The enemy] has built many positions . . . and has done everything he can to absorb our blow early on. It is therefore hardly likely that the German attack will break through. Given the sum total of ready reserves at the disposal of the Russians it is not to be expected that Citadel will lead to such a high level of losses for him that his intention to choose the proper moment [for an attack] will be unrealizable because of insufficient strength. . . . I hold the intended operation to be a totally decisive mistake."[66]

Although Hitler probably never saw Gehlen's memo, its content was not likely to upset him any more than he already was—in mid-May, he admitted to Guderian, who had attempted to persuade him not to proceed with the operation, "Whenever I think of this attack my stomach turns over." Despite their own misgivings, neither Manstein nor Kluge attempted to dissuade Hitler from going forward with Citadel, at a time when he clearly was uncertain as to how to proceed. For its part, the OKW expressed serious reservations about the attack, urging in mid-June that it be abandoned in favor of building reserves for the anticipated Allied invasion in the Mediterranean. Jodl bluntly told Hitler that it was dangerous to commit troops to an offensive that, at best, would achieve limited results while the chief danger lay elsewhere. These warnings, however, fell victim to the rivalry between the OKW and the OKH, with Zeitzler now intervening decisively in favor of the attack. Although Hitler informed the OKW on 18 June that he was definitely going ahead with Citadel, just a week later his ambivalence was again on display. On 25 June, he underscored to Goebbels the necessity, in view of a likely Anglo-American invasion, of "holding our reserves in hand" yet in the same conversation reiterated his belief that the east remained "the decisive front." Not until 1 July did he finally decide to go ahead with the operation, telling Manstein, "We cannot wait until the enemy, perhaps in the winter or after the establishment of a second front, begins an attack." The offensive, he informed German troops on the morning of 5 July, "must be of decisive significance and bring a turning-point in the war." No one knew better than Hitler that this was not likely to happen, even under the most favorable circumstances, but, by this time, the Kursk operation seemed to have taken on a life of its own.[67]

Its purpose, however, seemed less than clear. Neither Hitler nor the OKH conceived of Kursk as a decisive battle of annihilation, let alone the prelude to a return to the Caucasus. They saw it primarily as a spoiling attack that would knock the anticipated Soviet summer offensive off balance. If successful, it would also allow the transfer of troops to the west to confront the expected Allied invasion. From the outset, however, the unfavorable ratio of forces made the attack in the Kursk salient highly risky even for a gambler like Hitler, with much to lose and little to gain. Although an old military rule of thumb has it that an attacker needs a 3-to-1 superiority in force, the Germans in early July confronted a staggering numerical inferiority. In the entire Kursk-Orel double salient, including reserves, the Germans had scraped together 625,271 combat troops, supported by 2,699 armored vehicles, 9,467 artillery pieces of all types, and 1,372 aircraft. These figures, however, were dwarfed by corresponding Soviet tallies: 1,987,463 combat troops, 8,200 armored vehicles, 47,416 barrels, and 5,965 aircraft. Across the board, the Germans faced disadvantages ranging from 3.2 to 1 to 5 to 1, ratios that remained largely unchanged even if comparing only those forces engaged directly at Kursk.[68]

Nor, despite all the talk of the Tiger and Panther tanks, could the Germans counter quantitative inferiority with decisive qualitative superiority. Of the 2,465 combat vehicles the Germans threw into action at the Kursk salient on 5 July, only 328 were modern battle tanks: 128 Tigers and 200 Panthers. As an example of the semimodern condition of the Ostheer, the Ninth Army, which was to spearhead the attack in the north, had only 26 Tiger tanks but some 85,000 horses. This lack of mobility against an opponent whose forces had been substantially mechanized and motorized through Lend-Lease deliveries negated the Germans' one remaining advantage—their skill at deep, mobile operations. Moreover, the interminable delays in launching the attack gave the Soviets precious time to construct the most formidable system of fortifications in the world, an elaborate labyrinth of eight separate defensive lines consisting of antitank ditches, tank traps, minefields, barbed-wire obstacles, antitank guns, flamethrowers, and machine-gun nests that stretched 180 miles to the rear.[69]

In addition, relying on their accurate intelligence information, the Soviets had placed the deepest system of minefields precisely at the points of the German main effort. Instead of the fast, freewheeling, mobile operations in which the Wehrmacht specialized, then, the Germans now faced a static "biting-through" operation reminiscent of the trench struggles of World War I, a battle of attrition that they could not win. It was, as a German tank commander later admitted, "unbelievable": "The Soviets had prepared a defensive system whose depth was inconceivable to us. Every time we broke though a position in bitter fighting, we found ourselves before another new one." As at Stalingrad, the

German leadership allowed itself to be drawn into a test of strength in a confined area against a numerically superior enemy, one that negated the Germans' own strengths and accentuated Soviet advantages. Worse, even had the Germans managed a breakthrough, it likely would have been a Pyrrhic victory so costly that it would have been indistinguishable from defeat.[70]

Paradoxically, the last German offensive in the east, planned for 3:30 A.M. on 5 July as a simultaneous strike from both sides of the Kursk salient, actually began with a preventive attack by Red artillery and air forces. Supplied with incorrect information by a German soldier captured while clearing minefields, Soviet commanders sought to catch the Germans off guard and inflict enormous losses on their assembled troops. At 2:00 that morning, therefore, Russian artillery opened a thunderous barrage in both north and south, while the Soviets hurled a fleet of bombers at German airfields crammed with aircraft. Luftwaffe radar, however, spotted the hundreds of attacking Soviet bombers, giving the Germans precious minutes to send their own fighter planes aloft. The element of surprise now worked against the Soviets; instead of catching the Germans off guard, Luftwaffe fighters dove into the unprotected enemy bombers with a vengeance. In the early morning hours of 5 July, one of the most lopsided aerial battles of World War II ended with a Soviet rout: 425 Russian planes were shot down with a loss of only thirty-six German machines. Nor had the artillery barrage had any impact, for German troops for the most part were still in their trenches or dugouts. It was, both literally and figuratively, a shot in the dark.[71]

The German assault thus started on time, although the attackers immediately encountered fierce resistance. In the northern sector, under the operational control of Kluge's Army Group Center, Model's Ninth Army spearheaded the attack. Although Model, a particular favorite of Hitler's, was regarded as a fighting general, his plan of attack was uncharacteristically cautious. Violating the key rule of Schwerpunkt, he chose to preserve his tank forces, keeping some in reserve, and having others follow the infantry rather than punch holes in the enemy defenses. Not only did this slow the advance, but, as the attacking infantry inevitably got hung up on the extensive Soviet defenses, Model was forced to throw tanks into the battle, where they were blown up by mines. The reasons for Model's prudence were not hard to find. From the outset of planning, he had been unconvinced of any chance of success at Kursk and had tried to scuttle the operation by raising endless objections, which served only to delay it. In addition, he was ever mindful of the weak Second Panzer Army (a tank army in name only since, until the eve of the battle, it had no battle tanks), which was to protect his left flank. Given the double-S nature of the Kursk-Orel salient and the large Soviet reserves to his north, Model knew that any enemy counterstrike would not only easily slice through the German defenses but also immediately threaten his own army with encirclement and destruction. It was fear of just such an attack, which the Soviets had, in fact, prepared, that led him to keep mobile tank forces in deep reserve.[72]

On the first day, in fighting of "unimaginable toughness," Model's troops ground forward almost five miles, but at high cost. Buoyed by the effect of the dense defenses on the German attacker, the Soviet commander of the Central Front, Rokossovsky, the next day prematurely threw his considerable reserves into a counterattack. This foray ended with a rude shock, as the burning hulks of Soviet T-34s, in their first encounter with the Tiger tank, were left strewn about. Once the kings of the battlefield, T-34 crews watched in amazement as their shells bounced off the thickly armored Tiger, itself largely invulnerable to any but a close shot from the side or rear but able to knock out a T-34 over a mile away. Rokossovsky now ordered his tanks to bury themselves in defensive positions so that only the turrets were visible, an order that he admitted was dictated by their complete inferiority to the Tigers. Amazingly, the Ninth Army had only twenty-six Tigers when the battle began, with eighteen knocked out of action by mines in the first two days. Nevertheless, the Ninth Army made steady, if laborious, progress and, by the seventh, had advanced over ten miles and reached the main Soviet defenses at Ponyri, a key town on the Orel-Kursk railway, as well as the decisive heights of Olkovatka, which commanded the terrain all the way to Kursk.[73]

Here, however, the enemy had massed such extensive defensives that the Germans later referred to it as a "second Verdun" and the "Stalingrad of the Kursk salient." In bitter house-to-house fighting on both the seventh and the eighth, German and Soviet forces traded control of Ponyri, with the Germans, their strength exhausted, finally securing most of it by the evening of the eighth. Supported by Ferdinand tank destroyers, German troops that day also stormed the heights at Olkovatka. Dismayed at finding so formidable an obstacle miles behind the front, however, Model was forced to suspend operations for a day while he regrouped his forces. Even these successes, he gloomily predicted, would not open the way to Kursk, terming the offensive a "rolling battle of attrition." On the tenth, he resumed the attack, supported by air units from Army Group South, but Rokossovsky, who had also regrouped his forces, threw his last reserves into the battle. Once again, Model was forced to suspend the offensive in order to reform his units, but he also took the opportunity to rethink his options. Aware that he was not likely to prevail with the forces available if he clung to his present direction of attack, he resolved to continue the assault on the twelfth with his reserve units, among them the Fifth, Eighth, and Twelfth Panzer Divisions, but with the main effort now planned for the right flank, which was to move south around the fortified heights. Amazingly, this was to be the first time in the operation that his tank units were to be used as a combined force; just as astonishing was the fact that, to date, the Ninth Army had suffered only 63 total losses of tanks, assault guns, and tank destroyers (for all of Citadel, the Ninth Army lost 77 battle tanks, compared with 526 Soviet tanks destroyed).[74]

At the culmination point of his attack, however, as he was introducing his last reserves, the Soviet Bryansk Front and the left wing of West Front launched, as Model had feared, a powerful offensive aimed at Orel. Although the initial probing assaults on the eleventh had been contained, the next day powerful Soviet forces broke through on a wide front in quick, deep penetrations that the Second Panzer Army was unable to check. If Orel fell, not only would Model's main supply line be broken, but his army would also be threatened with encirclement. With the Second Panzer Army unable to close the gaps on its own, Kluge at Army Group Center thus had no choice on the twelfth but to order numerous armored and infantry divisions of the Ninth Army to break off the attack and hurry to the aid of the neighboring army. With that, Model realized, any continuation of the attack became pointless; for the Ninth Army, the Battle of Kursk had ended.[75]

To the south, Manstein's initial blow achieved considerably better results than Model's. Not only did his leading units, Hoth's Fourth Panzer Army and Army Detachment Kempf, possess more tanks overall (1,377 to 988), but they also had far larger numbers of the Tigers (102 to 26) and Panthers (200 to 0). Just as significant, Manstein, in contrast to Model, deployed his tanks at the tip of the spear in the classic blitzkrieg manner. Although slowed by the onerous Soviet minefields, the Germans found their major problem in the first few days to be the mechanical failure of the new tanks. During the march to the assembly areas on the night of 4–5 July, forty-five of the Panthers, almost a quarter of the total force, had broken down, some bursting into flames because of faulty fuel pumps, seeming confirmation of Guderian's protests against the premature use of a weapon that had not been fully tested. Very quickly, however, the Panther and the Tiger began to assert their superiority over the

Soviet T-34s. By the second day, not only had Jakovlevo, an important transportation center fifteen miles from the start line, fallen, but the Soviet leadership had also begun to show signs of great anxiety. Reports of the initial tank battles indicated that, overwhelmed by a sense of powerlessness, the Soviet crews were now succumbing to the same panic that had afflicted the Germans when first encountering the T-34s.[76]

On 6 July, just the second day of the battle, the Soviets made two key decisions. First, at a surprisingly early point, they decided to throw their strategic reserve, originally intended for use as part of the counteroffensive after the Germans had been halted, into action at Kursk. Second, General Vatutin, the commander of the Voronezh Front, ordered his tanks buried to the turret in order to form a compact antitank defense. Although bitterly criticized by Zhukov, who wanted instead to launch an energetic counterattack that, under the circumstances, would have been disastrous for the Soviets, Vatutin's order, although made out of desperation, was clearly correct. German tanks now had to creep extremely close to the buried enemy tanks in order to destroy them, which negated their great advantage of range. The well-camouflaged Russians typically let the Tigers and Panthers pass by before opening fire from the side or the rear, a tactic that was effective but required enormous courage, for it amounted to a virtual death sentence for the Soviet tank crews. Nonetheless, Vatutin's order to bury his tanks, along with the transfer on 7 July of considerable portions of Manstein's air support to the north to support Model, contributed to a noticeable slowing of the tempo of the German advance.[77]

Still, the superiority of the new German tanks was striking. In one extraordinary incident on 8 July, a single German Tiger tank, in a workshop and not fully repaired, engaged a force of some fifty to sixty Soviet tanks, destroying twenty-two T-34s before the remainder fled in panic. By 11 July, Army Group South had already destroyed some seven hundred tanks and assault guns of the Voronezh Front while suffering only 116 total losses. The Psel River, the last natural obstacle before Kursk, was reached on the ninth, while, on the eleventh, Army Detachment Kempf, on Manstein's right flank, finally broke through stiff Soviet defenses on the Donets, driving to within ten miles of the southern edge of Prokhorovka, and effectively trapping large parts of the Soviet Sixty-ninth Army. That same day, units of the Second SS Panzer Corps seized Hill 252.2, a key height just one and a half miles southeast of the city. Believing that the last defenses had been breached and the way to Kursk was now open, Manstein's headquarters radiated a mood of euphoria. The Soviet command, however, planned a surprise of its own for the next day, a battle of annihilation. The stage was set for one of the most famous—and mythical—battles of World War II.[78]

As part of the preparations for its planned summer offensive, the Soviet High Command had succeeded in creating, and hiding from German intelligence, a large strategic reserve (the Steppe Front) whose strongest element was the Fifth Guards Tank Army under General Pavel Rotmistrov. Sensing that the Germans had passed the culmination point of their offensive, the Soviets now proposed a three-pronged counterattack for 12 July that intended, not merely to stop, but to encircle and destroy German forces. In the north, the Bryansk Front was to strike toward Orel, while, in the south, the Seventh Guards Army was to drive into the flank of Army Detachment Kempf. The Fifth Guards Tank Army, an elite unit with almost one thousand tanks and assault guns, was to play the key role. Striking directly at the Second SS Panzer Corps at Prokhorovka, its task was to annihilate the German force as the first step in a grand counteroffensive that, gathering momentum like an avalanche, would sweep away everything in its path. The Battle of Prokhorovka, according to Soviet and Western historians, thus was the turning point in the Kursk offensive, a legendary battle in which over fifteen hundred tanks slugged it out at close range, with some four hundred German tanks destroyed, a decisive defeat that, according to Marshal Konev, marked "the swan song of the German tank troops."[79]

The reality, however, was considerably different. The Germans, for example, could not possibly have lost 400 tanks on 12 July because on that day the entire Second SS Panzer Corps had only 211 battle tanks, 58 assault guns, and 43 tank destroyers; the units directly involved in the battle, the Leibstandarte Adolf Hitler and Das Reich, possessed a total of only 186 armored vehicles (117 tanks, 37 assault guns, and 32 tank destroyers). Nor did all of Rotmistrov's considerable force go into action on the twelfth; of his roughly 950 armored vehicles, fewer than 700 seem actually to have been engaged at Prokhorovka, with perhaps only 500 in the first attack wave. Finally, despite Konev's claim of vast German losses, it was, in fact, the Soviets who suffered a catastrophe. Ironically, the immense discrepancy between German and Soviet losses seems to have occasioned the legend in the first place. Confronted by an angry Stalin, who demanded to know what he had done with his "magnificent tank army," Rotmistrov, in league with Vatutin and his political commissar, Nikita Khrushchev, protected themselves from his wrath by concocting the story of equally massive German losses to balance the Soviet disaster. Since the attack at Prokhorovka had been Stalin's idea in the first place, the mythical outcome of the battle suited the dictator's purposes as well. Spread through the memoirs of various Soviet gener-als, the legend took on a new life when it was adopted uncritically by Western historians.[80]

In fact, as Karl-Heinz Frieser has shown, what actually transpired at Prokhorovka can be readily reconstructed from German war diaries. Hav-ing on the eleventh seized Hill 252.2, along with a hastily constructed anti-tank ditch in front of the heights to the southwest built as part of the Soviet defenses, the men of the Leibstandarte Adolf Hitler, exhausted from seven days of hard fighting, collapsed into deep sleep. Eager to catch the Germans by surprise, Rotmistrov, under orders from Vasilevsky, rushed to attack without proper reconnaissance, preparation, coordination of com-bined units, or basic intelligence gathering. Amazingly, the Soviets seemed unaware of the existence of the antitank ditch that they themselves had dug. Under the mistaken impression that the enemy possessed far larger numbers of Tigers than he did in actuality (the silhouette of the new model Pz IVs resembled that of the Tiger, leading to the error), Soviet tank crews, perhaps inspired as well by liberal doses of vodka, launched their attack at 7:30 A.M. on 12 July at high speed in order to close the dis-tance and nullify German advantages as quickly as possible.[81]

What followed was an inferno of smoke and fire in which both sides lost control and the battle deteriorated into a chaos of close-quarter combat. The battle-weary Germans, taken completely by surprise by this seeming kamikaze-type attack and overwhelmed by the tempo of the Soviet onslaught, were swept off the crest of Hill 252.2 and down the back slope. As the first wave of Soviet T-34s raced down the hill, how-ever, they failed to notice the roughly fourteen-foot-deep antitank ditch and plunged headlong into it. When those following spotted the danger, they veered wildly in all directions, crashing into each other and burst-ing into flame as German tanks went into action. By the middle of the day, when the Soviet attack was largely spent, the area in front of the antitank ditch resembled a tank graveyard, with perhaps 100 burning Soviet wrecks, while the Germans claimed another 190 abandoned Rus-sian tanks as the spoils of war. Although the reported numbers seemed so high that the commander of the Second SS Panzer Corps, Obergrup-penführer Paul Hausser, came to the battlefield to see the scene for him-self, the most recent Russian figures indicate that, on the twelfth, the Soviet Twenty-ninth Tank Corps alone lost 172 tanks, 118 as total losses.[82]

In all, the magnitude of the Soviet debacle at Prokhorovka was breath-taking: one Russian tally, admittedly incomplete, put the total losses at 235, while the chief of staff of the Fifth Guards Tank Army reported the loss between 12 and 16 July of 334 tanks, virtually all on 12–13 July.

A preliminary count by the Second SS Panzer Corps on the evening of the twelfth showed 244 enemy tanks put out of action, with another 249 counted the next day, for an astounding total of 493 losses. Rotmistrov himself admitted that 420 tanks had been put out of action, although 112 of those had been reparable. Even if we settle on the smallest figure, 235, it dwarfs the German losses, which were not the 400 of legend but only 3. Far from being decimated, the Leibstandarte Adolf Hitler and Das Reich actually gained tank strength. On 11 July, the two units reported a total of 186 operational armored vehicles, while, on the thirteenth, after the Battle of Prokhorovka, the number was 190. For all of Citadel, in fact, the Second SS Panzer Corps suffered only 33 total losses of tanks and assault guns, while it lost no Panthers for the simple reason that it had none. Nor did the Russians destroy 70 Tigers; on 12 July, the corps had only 15 operational Tigers, of which only 5 fought at Prokhorovka. The losses of men were equally lopsided, the Soviets suffering fifteen hundred dead and missing to the Germans' ninety-seven. At the end of the day, the Germans controlled the battlefield, which accounted for their astonishingly low total losses since they were able to tow disabled tanks to repair shops. They had not only repulsed the fanatic Soviet attack but also regained all their lost ground. Despite the immense sacrifice of men and tanks and the fanatic spirit of the Russians that shook even many SS troopers, the Soviet attack at Prokhorovka had been a complete disaster. The mood was clearly triumphant at Army Group South headquarters as Manstein prepared to resume the offensive the next day.[83]

The climax to Manstein's efforts, however, never materialized. His victory at Prokhorovka took place against a backdrop of a rapidly deteriorating situation elsewhere. The Soviet breakthrough at Orel threatened not only the encirclement of the Ninth Army but also, if left unchecked, the destruction of Army Group Center. More importantly, Hitler's worst fear, and the key reason he had delayed the Citadel offensive, had now come true: on 10 July, Anglo-American forces had invaded Sicily, and the two-front war had become a reality. Both Hitler and the OKW had worried from the start about throwing away the valuable German tank reserves for limited gains at Kursk, with the Führer, fearful of a front near the German border, determined to take immediate action in case of a threat in the Mediterranean. By the twelfth, it had become apparent that neither Sicily nor Italy could be held without significant German aid, triggering his reflexive decision to transfer strong panzer forces to Southern Europe. For the first time since the invasion of the Soviet Union, strategic concerns in the west superseded the war in the east. On the thirteenth, Hitler called Manstein and Kluge to his headquarters to inform them of his decision to break off Citadel and transfer the Second SS Panzer Corps to Sicily. Kluge, having already halted his portion of the attack, received the news with relief. Manstein, believing his forces to be on the edge of victory, protested vigorously that to give up the battle at the decisive moment was like "throwing victory away." The enemy in front of him was defeated, had already lost some 1,800 tanks, and had squandered a great part of its operational reserve, he stressed, yet he still had his trump card: the Twenty-fourth Panzer Corps, with 181 armored vehicles in the SS Panzergrenadier Division Viking and the Seventeenth and Twenty-third Panzer Divisions, had not yet gone into action.[84]

Hitler not only rejected Manstein's demand to continue the attack but effectively gutted his forces, not only ordering the transfer of tank units to Italy but also dispatching a further third of his air units to Army Group Center. Manstein, in view of the massive enemy tank losses, believed it still possible to pull a partial success out of the Kursk operation and, thus, proposed a plan (Operation Roland) that would allow him to destroy some Soviet forces while putting space between him and the enemy. Instead of continuing his attack north, the field marshal now aimed at turning his units abruptly to the west along the Psel River in a one-armed pincer movement in order to encircle Soviet troops in the southwest corner of the Kursk salient. Hitler halfheartedly approved Manstein's plan, but with the proviso that he use only forces presently engaged and not deploy his reserves. Although the OKH conspired to limit the impact of Hitler's order, Zeitzler hoping that Manstein could achieve a partial operational victory, the Führer intervened again on the sixteenth, ordering the Fourth Panzer Army to break off the battle the next day and reassemble to the west near Belgorod. Although Manstein, with his eyes firmly glued on his own situation, rightly claimed that he had been forced prematurely to give up yet another victory, Hitler, viewing the overall state of affairs, was also correct in his worries about the Soviet breakthrough at Orel. In addition, an expected enemy offensive on the southern flank of Army Group South threatened the loss of the vital Donets industrial area, while the opening of the Mediterranean front meant that limited German resources would have to be split even further. Ironically, in the event, only the Leibstandarte Adolf Hitler was actually sent to Italy; the withdrawal of the panzer corps, as Karl-Heinz Frieser has noted, was, thus, too late to be of help in Sicily but too early for any successful conclusion of the Kursk operation.[85]

For the first time, a German summer offensive had failed in its tracks and the attacking units been almost immediately forced onto the defensive, a situation, Goebbels noted laconically, to which the Germans "were not accustomed." Material and manpower deficiencies, the delay in launching the attack, the absence of the element of surprise, the decision to attack the enemy's strongest positions rather than seek the mobile operations that played to the Germans' tactical strength, and, not least, the realization of their nightmare of a two-front war all contributed to the result. Still, Citadel can hardly be seen as any sort of turning point. Far from being the swan song of the German tank corps or the graveyard of the German army, as it is sometimes described, it resulted in astonishingly light German losses. For the entire operation, the Wehrmacht lost only 252 armored vehicles, as opposed to 1,956 for the Soviets, an astonishing 8-to-1 kill ratio; of those 252, only 10 were Tigers. Similarly, German aircraft losses totaled 159 to 1,961 for the Red Air Force, a 12-to-1 ratio. For the Luftwaffe, the invasion of Sicily meant the opening of a third front, which, combined with the costly defensive battles over Germany and occupied Western Europe, proved insurmountable. In July and August, for example, it lost 702 aircraft on the eastern front but 3,504 in the west and on the home front. In manpower terms, the Germans lost 54,182 casualties (11,023 dead and missing; 43,159 wounded) to 319,000 for the Red Army, a 6-to-1 ratio, amazing for an inferior force attacking into the heart of well-prepared and formidable defenses. If personnel losses are broadened to include dead, wounded, prisoners, and the sick, the Red Army lost, according to figures from Boris Sokolov, 1.68 million men as against 203,000 for the Wehrmacht, an 8.25-to-1 ratio. Nor were the materiel losses unsustainable. In July, German industry produced 817 new armored vehicles, three times more than lost at Kursk, with an increasing proportion the new Tigers and Panthers that enjoyed a considerable technical superiority over the T-34. While German casualties were costly, especially among the infantry, they were balanced by 89,480 replacements.[86]

The reasons for these enormous discrepancies in losses are not hard to find. Certainly, the introduction of the Panther and Tiger tanks, as well as the improved Pz IVs, produced a genuine "tank shock," a devastating qualitative advantage the Germans would enjoy for at least the next year. While the German tanks could penetrate the T-34's armor at some considerable range, the Soviets were more likely merely to cause temporary damage that could be repaired. For all its undeniable improvement, the Red Army still lagged behind the Wehrmacht in training of tank crews, tactical efficiency, emphasis on Auftragstaktik, coordination of combined arms, and communication. The interaction of these factors could be quite lethal. Since in the Red Army, for example, only company commanders typically had a radio in their tanks, the German tactic of targeting that tank for initial destruction had cascading consequences. Soviet crews, trained only in rigid *Befehlstaktik* (command tactics) and, thus, lacking flexibility in decisionmaking and action, were left without direction as combat descended into chaos. As masses of Soviet tanks often simply maneuvered in a directionless manner, they became easy targets. In addition, too many Soviet commanders continued to throw their troops into battle with little concern for casualties and with inadequate preparation and planning, expecting the sheer weight of numbers to overwhelm the enemy. This was often the result, but at a horrendous cost borne by average Soviet soldiers. Still, Citadel had only two modest goals—to shorten the front to conserve forces and to weaken the Red Army sufficiently to forestall its summer offensive—yet had failed utterly at both. Even if it had been successful, it would have remained a largely meaningless tactical triumph, for the Germans could no more prevail in a material war now than they could in the war of attrition between 1914 and 1918. As in the Great War, they now also faced the grim reality of a two-front war.[87]

If further proof were needed of this iron law of attrition, the Soviets supplied it on 12 July 1943. With the German offensive still in progress, the Red Army launched its long-awaited counterstroke against Orel, to be followed by offensives on the Donets-Mius and at Belgorod-Kharkov. More than a million fresh troops surged into battle, supported by 3,200 tanks and 4,000 aircraft, two to three times the number of the Stalingrad counteroffensive. Moreover, the numerical and material superiority of the Red Army was now so great that it could launch simultaneous offensives up and down the front, supported by partisan operations in the German rear. Smashing into the Second Panzer Army, which, until it received reinforcements (the Fifth and Eighth Panzer Divisions, with 234 armored vehicles), had no actual tanks of its own (and barely 100,000 troops), Operation Kutuzov spotlighted the German dilemma. Having pressed all available forces into the attack at Kursk, not only were other sectors thinly held (at the point of attack, the Russians had ten- to fifteen-to-one advantages in men and tanks), but the OKH also had no operational reserve and, thus, was forced to plug the holes opened by the enemy attack by pulling troops from other areas of the front. This, in turn, simply opened new holes, with the result that the panzer divisions found themselves being sent hither and yon as fire brigades to stamp out any conflagration that erupted. In this case, since the majority of units dispatched to aid the beleaguered Second Panzer Army came from the Ninth Army, Model on the thirteenth was given operational control of both. Regarded as a master of defense, the field marshal immediately halted the Kursk offensive and sent a number of units to the north to plug the dangerous gaps blasted open by the Soviets.[88]

The worst was in the northwest. Having punctured German defenses at Ulianovo, Soviet units, if left unchecked, threatened to cave in the entire Orel salient, trapping considerable German forces. Despite their initial success, however, the Soviets proved unable to translate their break-in into an operational breakthrough. The Germans had constructed an extensive defense in depth in the salient, with the result that, in many areas, Soviet attacks breached a thinly held position only to lurch forward into a strongpoint, where their offensive momentum was shattered. The decisive role here was played by the German panzer units; within the first two weeks, the Soviet attackers had lost well over half their tanks. These local triumphs allowed the Germans to slow, if not stop, the enemy advance, a circumstance that forced Hitler to relent on his customary stand-firm orders. Model, on his own initiative, took steps to conduct an elastic defense, justifying his actions by claiming that they corresponded to the spirit of the Führer's orders. Confronted with a series of faits accomplis, Hitler on 22 July validated Model's actions. At the same time, work had begun on the Hagen position, a line of field fortifications at the base of the Orel salient designed to stabilize the situation and, by shortening the front, free troops both to form a reserve and to be transferred to Italy, which had assumed an "absolute priority" for the Führer.[89]

On 1 August, then, Model's elastic defense gave way to a skillful withdrawal executed under extraordinarily adverse circumstances, not least because German troops had been ordered to destroy infrastructure as they pulled back. The Russians not only kept up steady pressure on Model's forces but also increased their activities elsewhere. Soviet partisans had already been active in the Orel area, in the last two weeks of July blowing up numerous rail lines in support of the offensive, but, on 3 August, over 100,000 partisans launched an extensive, coordinated operation aimed at nothing less than crippling supply into all of Army Group Center. The damage done to the rail network was so extensive that, from the fourth to the sixth, rail traffic was effectively halted. To restore order, already scarce German units had to be sent to the rear to fight the partisans. Then, on the seventh, the Soviets launched an attack to the north of the Orel salient against the Fourth Army that, although generally unsuccessful, forced Model to transfer units to his neighbor. Nonetheless, by 16 August, Model had completed his retreat to the Hagen position, where all Soviet attempts to break through were repulsed at such heavy cost that the Stavka had no choice but to end its assaults. Soviet casualties had been staggering. In little more than a month of fighting, the Red Army lost, according to official figures, almost 430,000 men (112,259 dead and missing) and nearly 2,600 armored vehicles, numbers that are almost certainly too low. German losses totaled a little over 86,000 casualties (25,515 dead and missing) and perhaps 343 armored vehicles. Even taking the official figures, the Soviets' losses ran at a ratio five to one and eight to one, respectively, against which their failure to achieve a decisive operational breakthrough, let alone the destruction of German forces in the Orel salient, must have been a bitter disappointment. For the Germans, the withdrawal to the Hagen position meant the freeing up of some nineteen divisions (eleven infantry, five panzer, and three panzergrenadier) for use elsewhere on the front.[90]

That these divisions would be needed had been apparent since 3 August, when the Red Army opened its first summer offensive in the Belgorod-Kharkov area. Once again, the main goal was not just the destruction of German armies (in this case, the Fourth Panzer Army and Army Detachment Kempf as well as the First Panzer Army and the Sixth Army, to be trapped against the Black Sea coast) but the shattering of the entire German position in southern Russia. As at Orel, the Soviets had assembled an overwhelming force of over 1 million men and 2,400 tanks supported by 1,311 aircraft. Ominously for the defenders, the Fourth Panzer Army and Army Detachment Kempf were mere shadows of the units they had been in July, forced to transfer most of their tank strength to Model in the north. Together, they could muster between them only 237 operational armored vehicles, fewer than 800 aircraft (for all of Army Group South), and perhaps 175,000 men to fend off an enemy that seemed again to have arisen from the dead. With a ten-to-one advantage across the board, the Soviets opened the offensive in the early morning hours of the third with a massive three-hour aerial and artillery bombardment, followed by an assault of massed tanks that swept away the German defenders. On the first day, Soviet spearheads advanced fifteen miles, while, on the evening of the fifth, the Germans were forced to abandon Belgorod, a key pillar of their defense. By the seventh, the enemy had opened a thirty-mile gap between Hoth and Kempf and seemed, for the first time, in a position to exploit a real operational breakthrough.[91]

The German leadership reacted with skill and alacrity to this new crisis. Not only were units transferred back to Manstein (the Fourth Panzer Army received the Twenty-fourth Panzer Corps, the Seventh Panzer, the Tenth Panzergrenadier, and Grossdeutschland Divisions, while Kempf was strengthened by the addition of the Third Panzer Division as well as the Third Panzer Corps with Das Reich, Totenkopf, and SS Panzergrenadier Division Viking), but plans made to pinch off the Soviet breakthrough. On 12 August, the Third Panzer Corps launched a counterattack and cut off and destroyed a number of Soviet units in a series of engagements in which the enemy again suffered appalling tank losses. In order to close the gap between them, the Twenty-fourth Panzer Corps, attacking from the north, and the Third Panzer Corps, moving from the south, struck simultaneously on 18 August and, by the evening of the twentieth, closed a weak ring around a large part of the Sixth Guards Army and the Twenty-seventh Army. Although the shocked Soviet units suffered considerable losses, the Germans proved unable to prevent many of the trapped forces escaping to the east.[92]

Nor were they able to prevent the loss of Kharkov in the fourth and final battle for the key Ukrainian industrial city. The German forces defending the city were so weak—the two infantry regiments of the 168th Infantry Division, for example, had only 260 men between them, while the Sixth Panzer Division could boast of only six tanks—that Kempf had already warned that the city could not be held. For his crime of pointing to reality, Kempf was sacked on 16 August, with his unit renamed the Eighth Army. Still, without reinforcements, the new designation meant nothing, and Kempf's replacement, General Otto Wöhler, quickly demanded that the city be evacuated. Hitler, fearing the loss of this prestige object, nonetheless ordered Kharkov "to be held under all circumstances," prompting Manstein, pondering the loss of six divisions for vague political reasons, to comment, "I would rather lose a city than an army." In the event, the field marshal got his wish, for, on the eighteenth, even the Führer bowed to reality and gave permission for the city to be abandoned, if necessary, although he urged that it be held for a few more days. On the twenty-second, faced with a catastrophic situation, Manstein finally gave approval to evacuate Kharkov during the night. The next day, enemy troops streamed into the ruined city as the prize of the offensive, but, with its seizure, their drive to the west largely ended.[93]

The capture of Kharkov clearly demonstrated that the Soviets now held the initiative on the eastern front, but, as at Orel, the victory had been achieved at a savage cost, one that was even more painful when the meager results were tallied. The Red Army not only failed to crush a numerically far inferior German foe but also had not even come close to achieving the real goal of the offensive: the destruction of Army Group South. Stalin had expected to reach the German border by year's end, something first accomplished a year later. The results were especially sobering considering the price paid: in twenty days, the Red Army had lost at least 255,000 (and perhaps as many as 500,000) casualties, among them 72,000 men killed, and almost 2,000 tanks against German totals of 10,000 killed and missing, 30,000 casualties, and some 230 armored vehicles, figures that left even Stalin fuming at the inexcusably large Soviet losses. Nor could a look at the totals for the entire Kursk salient operations of July and August have improved the dictator's foul mood. In roughly fifty days of fighting, the Red Army lost, by its own admission, 863,000 men, of whom 254,000 were killed or missing, numbers that are almost certainly too low since a recent estimate by a Russian historian puts the figure at 1,677,000 casualties. In addition, the Soviets lost over 6,000 tanks—the Fifth Guards Tank Army alone was destroyed twice within two months—and 4,200 aircraft. The Germans' losses seemed almost a pittance by comparison (170,000–200,000 total casualties; 46,000 dead; roughly 760 tanks and 524 aircraft destroyed), except that they could not afford even these numbers.[94]

Although they had inflicted astonishing losses on the Soviets, the Germans were afforded scant comfort since they could not as easily make theirs good. The savage fighting in the Kursk salient had reduced some German units to virtual nonexistence. On 2 September, for example, the Thirty-ninth Infantry Division had a total of six officers and three hundred men. Tellingly, the great majority of Panthers and Tigers lost resulted not from actual combat but from mechanical failures and subsequent abandonment. The Soviets now controlled the battlefield; the Germans had lost the initiative on the Ostfront and never regained it. Still, Kursk did not destroy the German tank force; it was the long and bloody defensive battles, the unrelenting pressure of overwhelming numbers, following on Citadel that inexorably ground it down. At Kursk, Soviet leaders had hoped to absorb the initial German blow, wear the enemy down, then springboard into a counteroffensive that would sweep enemy forces away like an avalanche. Instead, the defender had suffered far more losses than the attacker; then, when the roles were reversed, the onrushing Red Army again sustained appalling casualties. Not just Stalin's, but the entire Soviet system's utter disregard for its own people was breathtaking. As long as troops remained to be sacrificed, the Germans would be ground down in senseless, frontal assaults to the bitter end. As Karl-Heinz Frieser has noted, in April 1945 the daily loss of tanks by the Soviets was higher even than at Kursk, a truly staggering indictment of the Stalinist system. Confrontation with the Moloch, however, induced a sense of despair in many Landsers. It was, confessed one, more than a feeling of hopelessness; rather, it was a sense that a world was going under, of "collective metaphysical despair." Citadel meant a final reversal of roles: no longer the hammer, Germany had now become the anvil.[95]

8

Scorched Earth

All through July and August, the continual hammer blows by the numerically superior enemy had put the German army on the defensive and threatened a breakthrough along the entire front. By late September, it had become clear that the hopes of the spring had been dashed: the great offensive had been shattered; the U-boats proved unable to block the flow of American troops and materiel to Europe; the resource discrepancy between the warring sides continued to grow; the defection of its alliance partners left Germany isolated; and both troop and civilian morale had plummeted. Faced with such realities, the German leadership was forced to concede that "ultimate defeat was now likely unavoidable." "With the fate of the German people at stake," the only option left was to seek an armistice and immediate peace negotiations. The leader who voiced that sentiment, as Bernd Wegner has noted, was not Adolf Hitler in 1943 but Erich Ludendorff in 1918. Now, precisely twenty-five years later, thoughts turned back to the events of that fateful autumn. Although British intelligence analysts optimistically expected a repeat of the 1918 scenario, American assessments were more skeptical, seeing a German collapse as highly unlikely. In contrast to 1918, the Americans argued, the Nazi regime had at its disposal better material and agricultural reserves, suffered no debilitating morale crisis, and faced an Allied demand of unconditional surrender.[1]

In Germany, too, thoughts of 1918 were not far from the surface. Although SD reports indicated that some circles in Germany yearned for just such a compromise peace, the obstacles were formidable. In practice, the unconditional surrender doctrine meant an end to his regime and, thus, gave Hitler an incentive to fight on, especially since, in conscious rejection of 1918, the Western allies explicitly refused any negotiations. Moreover, although Germany could no longer win the war, it might be able to stalemate it long enough to split the brittle Allied coalition. In any case, Hitler had long vowed, and continued to insist, that another November 1918 would never again happen. Finally, and perhaps of decisive importance, the realistic American report also stressed a key, but often overlooked, point: Germany had much more reason to fear Allied retribution than in 1918. Genocide now loomed as the ultimate barrier to any negotiated peace.[2]

The Führer had long proclaimed that this was an ideological war, a "life and death struggle," a view confirmed as more than mere bombast by his merciless war of annihilation against Jewish-Bolshevism. "On the Jewish question, especially," Goebbels had noted already in early March 1943, "we are in it so deeply that there is no getting out any longer. And that is a good thing. Experience teaches that a movement and a people who have burned their bridges fight with much greater determination and fewer constraints than those that still have a chance of retreat." The Nazis had, indeed, burned their bridges. As Christopher Browning has noted, the great majority of the Jews who perished in the Holocaust, some 75–80 percent, were murdered in an extraordinary spasm of killing lasting roughly from spring 1942 to the early summer of 1943. Moreover, if the victims of Einsatzgruppen shootings in 1941 are included, the percentages move even higher. By the time military events turned decisively against them, then, the Nazis were well on their way to accomplishing their murderous goal. Given such facts, Hitler understood that the logic of events in 1943 pointed in only one direction: further radicalization of the war.[3]

Nor was the principal target of this radicalization in doubt. After all, in his total war speech, Goebbels had already raised the specter of "Jewish liquidation squads" overrunning Germany in the event of defeat. All Jews under Nazi control, without exception, thus had to be killed, a point made explicitly by Hitler in an early February 1943 speech to *Reichsleiter* (Reich leaders) and Gauleiter. All through the spring of 1943, in fact, Hitler seemed even more than usually obsessed with the Jews. On the German Memorial Day, 21 March, he again raised his extermination prophecy and demanded its fulfillment, while, in mid-April, Goebbels noted, "The Führer issues instructions to set the Jewish question once more at the forefront of our propaganda, in the strongest possible way." Central to this renewed emphasis was the discovery in the Katyn Forest near Smolensk of a mass grave containing the remains of thousands of Polish army officers murdered by the Soviet Security Police in 1940. The Nazi press claimed that "Jewish commissars" had carried out the murders, further proof, it alleged, that "the extermination of the peoples of Europe" was a "Jewish war aim."[4]

Back in Berlin for the early May funeral of SA chief Viktor Lutze, Hitler exhorted the assembled faithful to "set anti-Semitism again at the core of the ideological struggle," while, in mid-May, Goebbels recorded the Führer's extensive musings on the Jewish threat. The Jews, Hitler asserted, were the same all over the world and simply followed a basic racial instinct for destruction. They had unleashed the war, with all its devastation, but were now on the verge of a catastrophe, their own annihilation: "That is our historic mission, which cannot be held up, but only accelerated by the war." On 16 May, just a few days after this conversation, Hitler received the news of the eradication of the Warsaw ghetto following a month of fierce fighting. His satisfaction at this triumph was mingled with anger at Jewish resistance and a fear of Jewish subversive activity; just a month later, he told Himmler that the destruction of the Jews had to be carried through to its radical conclusion.[5]

Needing little prompting, the Reichsführer-SS worked strenuously to complete the destruction of the Jews of Poland. By the autumn, with the conclusion of "Aktion Reinhard," some 1.5 million Jews had been killed at Treblinka, Belzec, and Sobibor, while the remaining Jews in the Lublin district had been murdered as part of Operation Harvest Festival (Erntefest). In all, 3–3.5 million Jews had perished in the six death camps, with roughly 750,000 killed by various murder squads. Speaking frankly to SS leaders on 4 October at Posen, Himmler boasted that "the Jewish evacuation program, the extermination of the Jews," was "a glorious page in our history," although one that "can never be written." Then, connecting the alleged Jewish threat to the war, both present and previous, he asserted: "For we know how difficult we would have made it for ourselves if, on top of the bombing raids, the burdens and deprivations of the war, we still had Jews in every town as secret saboteurs, agitators, and troublemakers. We would now probably have reached the 1916–1917 stage." "We had the moral right . . . , the duty to our people," he insisted, "to destroy this people which wanted to destroy us." Two days later, Himmler pushed the same theme in the same hall in an address before the Reichsleiter and Gauleiter, stressing that all Jews, including women and children, had to be killed in order to prevent a generation of "avengers" from growing up. In both addresses, and in a further series of speeches before Wehrmacht officers from December 1943 through June 1944, the Reichsführer not only justified the Final Solution with reference to self-defense but also emphasized the joint responsibility of all in attendance. They were all complicit in genocide and, thus, had no choice but to fight to the end. As the official communiqué put it, "The entire German people know that it is a matter of whether they exist or do not exist.

The bridges have been destroyed behind them. Only the way forward remains."[6]

Through the winter of 1943 and into the spring of 1944, SS leaders turned their attention to the acceleration of the Final Solution in all areas of the Nazi Empire, pressing for the evacuation of Danish, Slovak, Greek, Italian, Rumanian, and, especially, Hungarian Jews. Although long allied with Nazi Germany, Hungary had under the leadership of Admiral Horthy effectively become a sanctuary for the Jews, with nearly a million in the country by early 1944. This situation was increasingly intolerable to Hitler, sensitive as he was to alleged Jewish subversion. His fears were seemingly confirmed when German intelligence supplied evidence that Horthy was negotiating with the Allies to take his country out of the war, which would endanger the German position in the Balkans. Faced with such open treachery, Hitler resolved in mid-March on a German occupation of the country. Initially unable in a tempestuous meeting on 18 March to browbeat the aged admiral into acquiescing in this action, the Führer simply stepped up the pressure until Horthy agreed to install a puppet regime. The next day, 19 March, German troops occupied the country.[7]

At one stroke, not only had Hitler secured vital raw materials and labor for the German war effort, but also, as he told Goebbels two weeks later, the Jewish question could now be solved in Hungary. Eichmann's men entered the country with the German troops and within days began organizing the roundup, ghettoization, and deportation of Jews. At the end of April, the first train left for Auschwitz, with full-scale deportations from the Hungarian provinces, at a rate of 12,000–14,000 deportees a day, commencing on 14 May. The crush of victims was so great that the gas chambers and crematoria at Auschwitz worked around the clock; one crematorium even broke down under the strain. Urged by the new Hungarian prime minister in early June to stop the deportations, Hitler responded with a tirade. The Jews, he screamed, were responsible for the death of tens of thousands of German civilians in Allied bombing raids. As a result, "nobody could demand of him that he should have the least pity for this global plague," for he was only applying "the old Jewish saying, 'An eye for an eye, a tooth for a tooth.'" By the time the deportations stopped on 9 July, almost 438,000 Jews had been sent to the death camps, with roughly 394,000 exterminated immediately. Of those selected for work, few would survive the war. In Budapest, perhaps 250,000 Jews clung tenuously to life, still awaiting their fate. Though the military events of 1943 had put the Germans on the defensive, Harvest Festival and the closing of the Operation Reinhard camps showed that

Hitler had gone a long way toward winning his other war, that against the Jews. The stubborn prosecution of what had become an unwinnable war—both Goebbels and Ribbentrop suggested in September 1943 that peace feelers be put out to Stalin and the British—thus offered the Führer the chance to complete his "historic task." To Hitler, the trauma of 1918 had been the work of the Jews; by destroying this threat once and for all, he would ensure that this "shame" would not recur.[8]

That the Reich could continue the war at all was largely due to an unexpected upward turn in military production in late 1943. Despite the setback to armaments output caused by the Allied bombing raids of the summer, by the autumn the gloom had lifted a bit. Instead of remaining focused on industrial targets in western Germany, RAF Bomber Command shifted to an ultimately fruitless effort to create another "Hamburg" in Berlin. For its part, the U.S. Eighth Air Force continued to hammer at industrial facilities, but improvements in German technology and defense tactics resulted in such a heavy toll of bombers that, in October, the Americans were forced temporarily to halt operations. By the end of the year, the sense of crisis had passed as the Allied bombers had clearly not crippled German production. After months of stagnation, in fact, all indices of armaments production began to shoot upward in February 1944, with spectacular increases in the output of aircraft, ammunition, and weapons.[9]

Nor had the feared collapse of morale occurred, even though Fortress Europe seemed to many Germans a fortress without a roof. In 1943, the Allies dropped on Germany more than double the tonnage of bombs as had fallen in the previous three years combined, a figure that would be dwarfed by the 1944 and 1945 numbers, yet the German civilian population stubbornly adapted. Despite Speer's concerns about the difficulties posed by bombed-out workers and Goebbels's frustration at Hitler's unwillingness to visit the afflicted cities, the "terror bombing," as the propaganda minister astutely realized, brought the Volksgemeinschaft closer together. The bombed out, the "proletarians of the aerial war," Goebbels thought, received valuable lessons in National Socialism through the activities of the NSV and other agencies that provided aid. In addition, the experiences of "terror from the air," he believed, made average Germans tougher and more unyielding.[10]

Further increases in production, however, depended not only on the morale of the civilian population but also on larger numbers of workers and an enhanced work rate. The size of the German labor force, however, had actually shrunk because of conscription of men into the military, with much of the shortfall made up by foreign workers. As part of planned withdrawal actions in the east in the autumn of 1943, German authorities once again envisioned the forced conscription of civilian labor to the Reich. As German troops abandoned their often long-held positions, they took as many as 1.5 million men and women capable of work with them, leaving the remainder—the sick, elderly, and young—to an uncertain fate. Although this brutal evacuation of civilians aimed at a substantial increase in workers for the German war effort, the local demand for labor to construct defensive fortifications (an estimated 500,000 workers, e.g., were needed to construct the Ostwall) as well as to perform support duties often meant that relatively few of these people were sent back to Germany, thus forcing officials to search elsewhere for workers.[11]

Already in the summer of 1942, as we have seen, Himmler had sought to build his SS empire through the use of slave labor; by 1944, almost 500,000 concentration camp prisoners were regarded as fit to work, although Jews, considered the arch racial threat, had been explicitly excluded from such labor. The frantic search for new workers now took an ironic twist, one that offered some Jews a glimmer of hope of survival. Within weeks of the German occupation of Hungary, the possibility of using Hungarian Jews in the aircraft industry was being openly discussed at the Führer's headquarters, with Hitler deciding, in early April, that he would "personally contact the Reichsführer SS [Himmler] and ask him to supply . . . 100,000 men . . . by making available contingents of Jews." Himmler himself acknowledged in late May 1944 the paradoxical nature of the situation, remarking to a group of generals: "At this time—it is one of those things peculiar to this war—we are taking 100,000 male Jews from Hungary to the concentration camps to build underground factories, and will later take another 100,000." Amazingly, then, just eighteen months after his decision to make Germany *Judenrein* (free [lit., cleansed] of Jews), Hitler now decided to bring Jewish workers back to Germany, albeit under draconian circumstances. The working and living conditions of the workers varied substantially according to the type of job, the attitude of the management, foremen, and guards at the individual firms, and the reaction of the local population, many of whom regarded the Jews with fear, suspicion, and hostility, often urging that harsh measures be taken against them. Still, perhaps 120,000 Jews survived the war as forced laborers, although those engaged in armaments production had a far better chance of survival than those forced to carve the tunnels for rocket production.[12]

The period on the eastern front from the autumn of 1943 to the summer of 1944 has, with considerable justification, been termed *the forgotten year* of the war, a time of debilitating German retreats and equally inglorious Soviet victories bought at horrendous cost. Despite his stubborn determination to hold the line in the east, Hitler found his hand forced by events as now began what seemed an endless series of grinding defensive battles, punctuated by brief pauses, that continued until the end of the war. The summer fighting had left the Wehrmacht an organization clearly in decline. Its panzer and air fleets had been greatly reduced, while its infantry was in desperately poor condition, with few troops, inadequate antitank defenses, and declining mobility. This latter, in turn, constantly left the choice of two evils: either stand and fight, and face destruction, or withdraw prematurely in order to save heavy equipment and artillery. Army Groups North and Center, forced to transfer units to Army Group South, were in an especially acute situation, dangerously undermanned, with many of their divisions reduced to regimental strength, and with virtually no tanks or air support. Even the spurt in industrial production at the end of the year could do little but patch a broken machine. Moreover, constant Soviet pressure meant that the Germans had to throw their newly raised infantry and tank units into battle before they were fully prepared, resulting in abnormally large casualties among the inexperienced troops. These losses then forced commanders to call in the next wave of reinforcements prematurely, thus starting a vicious cycle. For its part, the Soviet leadership, with a decisive numerical and material superiority, made ambitious plans for offensive actions and breakthrough operations. In the event, these tended to be poorly executed, with the Red Army, unable to pull off decisive encirclement operations, reverting primarily to bloody frontal assaults with masses of men and tanks. The Germans were able (barely) to fend off these assaults with nimble tactics, but the sheer weight of the enemy onslaught forced them inexorably back.[13]

Despite Hitler's outward show of optimism and repeated vow to hold out with an iron will, the defeats of the summer on all fronts meant that Germany had finally, definitively, lost any freedom of action. The surest indication of this was Hitler's newfound willingness to sanction the construction of the so-called Ostwall, a line of fortifications running from Melitopol on the Sea of Azov along the Dnieper and Desna Rivers to Chernigov, then almost due north to Narva on the Baltic. Although he had categorically rejected the idea earlier in the year, on 12 August he issued Führer Order No. 10, which belatedly ordered work to begin on this defense system. There was less to this decision, however, than met the eye, for Hitler still struggled with the implications of building a defensive barrier. Not only did he fear that the construction of the

Ostwall would encourage a "withdrawal psychosis" among his troops, which perhaps explains why the system was quickly renamed the Panther position (or the Wotan position in the extreme south). More importantly, he continued to insist that German forces could not evacuate the Donets Basin for strategic-economic reasons, a position supported by other powerful voices in the regime. Luftwaffe officials stressed the loss of key airfields that would hinder the German ability to strike at Soviet industrial areas while putting eastern German war production within range of Soviet bombers. At the same time, some segments of the armaments industry feared the consequences of the loss of foodstuffs and the coal resources of Ukraine. This, they argued, would have an immediate negative impact on food supplies for the troops, the operation of the railroads, and iron and steel production, which, in turn, would undermine armaments output. Although Speer evidently had already discounted the resources of the Donets Basin in his calculations, Hitler certainly regarded them as of key economic importance, a point he used to chide his military advisers. "My generals," he remarked with open contempt to Zeitzler that summer, "think only of military matters and withdrawals. They never think of economic matters. They therefore have absolutely no understanding. If we give up the Donets area, then we lack coal. We need it for our armaments industry."[14]

Compounding the tension in the German leadership was the fact that, although he still proclaimed the east to be the "decisive front," after the defeat at Kursk Hitler was clearly losing interest in the Ostkrieg as his concern grew about an Anglo-American invasion in the west. At best, in strategic terms, he could aim to defeat the second front in France and, perhaps, prolong the war in the hope that their divergent interests would lead to a falling out among his opponents (although, curiously, he did little to exploit these tensions). In any case, the need to build a Fortress Europe in the west meant that the Führer had little choice but to transfer units from east to west, thus further thinning the already dangerously overstretched German lines. This was confirmed by Führer Directive No. 51, issued on 3 November 1943, which, for the first time since the invasion of the Soviet Union, gave precedence to the war in the west. Despite the continued significance of the struggle against Bolshevism in the east, Hitler now declared that a greater immediate danger had arisen in the west: the threat of an Anglo-American invasion. "In the most extreme instance," he said, Germany could still sacrifice territory in the east, but in the west any breakthrough would have ruinous consequences "in a short time."[15]

In issuing this directive, Hitler clearly sided with the OKW against the OKH, which had hoped to retain the resources necessary to at least stabilize the Ostfront. Although faced with a *potential* threat in the west, Hitler's directive left the OKH to deal with an *actual* danger in the east with only limited resources, which had catastrophic consequences for the Ostheer. Although it continued to suffer the great majority of the Wehrmacht's casualties (some 90 percent to the eve of the Normandy invasion), it now disposed of only 57 percent of German forces. With barely 2.6 million troops to defend against almost three times that number in the Red Army, each division of the Ostheer now defended a ten-mile stretch of front. On the western front twenty-five years earlier, by contrast, each German division covered only two miles; moreover, on a front four times longer, the Ostheer had fewer artillery. Nor did the material situation offer much comfort, for, despite the undeniable German gains in output, Soviet production, combined with Lend-Lease deliveries, added up to an overwhelming Russian superiority in tanks, artillery, aircraft, and motor vehicles. The constant wearing-away process on the eastern front, as well as the new demands in the west, also meant that the Ostheer could not maintain its strength despite increased armaments output. Moreover, in spite of his intimation that he would trade space for time in the east, in the event Hitler was not prepared to make the strategic withdrawals that would have significantly shortened the front and freed up precious manpower. Nor had Guderian been able to convince him, in view of the poor state of the infantry, to use the qualitative superiority of the new German tanks to build a mobile panzer reserve to backstop the infantry. In any case, given the vast preponderance of enemy strength, Guderian's remedy of an operational reserve consisting of only eight panzer or panzergrenadier divisions supported by a few infantry divisions with tank sections, whose place in the line would be taken by security units or Rumanian and Latvian divisions of dubious quality, seems in retrospect naive at best.[16]

Although there was a certain truth to Hitler's complaint that his generals lacked faith in him, which left Goebbels to ponder Stalin's solution—the shooting of his generals—with a greater appreciation, military contingencies had a way of simplifying the great strategic problems with which the Führer grappled, as he was rather unceremoniously reminded by Manstein. Although himself favoring a mobile defense, in a meeting with Hitler at Vinnitsa on 27 August, the field marshal pointed out that his troops had suffered 133,000 casualties but received only 33,000 replacements and that, without reinforcements, he could not possibly hold on to the Donets Basin. Perhaps most significantly from Hitler's point of view, Manstein, with Kluge present and in support, proposed a unified command in the east under his, Manstein's, direction, for the purpose of conducting an effective fighting retreat. The idea of ending the rivalry between the OKH and the OKW and instituting a single command structure certainly was sound but, as the two field marshals must have known, had little chance of approval. This step would not only deprive Hitler of day-to-day command in the east but also undermine his ability to play the OKH and the OKW off against each other, thus enhancing his authority. In the end, Hitler merely used the challenge to reinforce his control, ordering that, henceforth, all troop transfers between OKH and OKW areas be subject to his personal approval. Manstein's effrontery, however, would not go unremarked as the field marshal's suggestion was seen by the Führer not as a valid operational proposal but as a sign of defeatism and opposition. His star now began rapidly to wane.[17]

At a meeting a week later at the Führer Headquarters, Manstein was even blunter in his implicit criticism of Hitler's conduct of operations. "Mein Führer," he told Hitler pointedly on 3 September, "you no longer have the decision as to whether the Donets area can be held or not. You only have the decision as to whether or not you will lose it along with an army group." On the eighth, with a crisis brewing on the eastern front, and the same day Anglo-American forces invaded Italy, Hitler flew to Manstein's headquarters at Zaporozhye, the last time he was to set foot on occupied Soviet territory. Although he once again forbade Manstein's request for a speedy withdrawal of his threatened forces, events soon outpaced his will. On the fourteenth, in the face of Soviet breakthroughs, Manstein acted to avert catastrophe, summarily informing the OKH that, in order to avoid destruction, the next day his armies would begin retreating to the Panther position. Disturbed by this independent assertion of authority, Hitler on the fifteenth summoned both Manstein and Kluge to his headquarters. He was, however, again unable to counter Manstein's blunt observation that it was no longer a matter of holding an economically important region but a question of "the fate of the eastern front." With that, Hitler reluctantly approved a withdrawal behind the Dnieper but insisted that it be as gradual as possible.[18]

Kluge, for his part, was not unsupportive of this decision since Army Group Center had been able since late August to hold its front largely intact while conducting a dogged fighting retreat. The basic problem, however, the law of numbers, was insoluble: the Germans were trying to stem the tide against an overwhelmingly superior enemy force. In hammering operations from Smolensk in the north to Chernigov in the southern sector of the front, the Soviets, although able to achieve breakthroughs along the line, proved unable to pull off a decisive success. In the process, moreover, the Red Army suffered striking losses. The three simultaneous offensives against Smolensk, Bryansk, and Chernigov cost the Soviets almost 225,000 permanent losses (dead, missing, and prisoners) and well over 2,000 tanks and assault guns. Although the corresponding German figures were a fraction of these losses, even these were unsustainable. On 10 September, for example, the Second Army reported that all its infantry divisions combined could muster fewer than 7,000 combat troops. The response of the OKH was to order it to attack to close a gap in its line.[19]

From mid-September, however, the situation deteriorated rapidly as Kluge struggled to avert a catastrophe with only sixteen fully combat-ready divisions (eleven infantry, one panzer, and four Luftwaffe field divisions of dubious value). Soviet pressure forced him to evacuate Bryansk on the seventeenth, while Smolensk, the scene of such bitter fighting two years earlier, was lost virtually without a fight on the twenty-fifth after a series of Soviet penetrations. More worrisome, the inability of most of his units, equipped only with horse-drawn transport, to withdraw quickly meant that any race to the Dnieper was bound to be lost, especially since they had to herd over 500,000 civilians and 600,000 head of cattle to the rear. The extraordinary mobility of the Wehrmacht, which had proved so decisive in earlier triumphs, had vanished; most Landsers simply walked without stopping back to the Dnieper. Hitler's faith in his panzer divisions to close gaps in the front through swift counterattacks also proved misplaced since they could not be moved from place to place quickly enough to plug the gaps. Not surprisingly, the Soviets won the race to the Dnieper, achieving the key breakthrough on 22 September when they pushed spearheads across the river at Chernobyl, north of Kiev. By 1 October, they had managed to seize the city and widen their bridgehead. Although a counterattack regained the city three days later, the Germans were unable to reduce the bridgehead itself, an "open wound" that stretched thirty-six miles along the Dnieper to a depth of eighteen miles, a sad testament to Hitler's failure to authorize a timely withdrawal.[20]

For all the drama in Army Group Center's sector, the focus of the enemy offensive lay in the south as the Soviets sought to liberate, and Hitler desperately to retain, the valuable economic area of the Donets Basin and Ukraine. For the Battle of the Dnieper, the Soviets had massed 2.6 million troops, more than twenty-four hundred armored vehicles, and almost twenty-nine hundred aircraft, figures that represented 50 percent of the troops and aircraft and 70 percent of the tanks available to the

Red Army. With such numerical superiority and the far greater mobility afforded by their stock of Lend-Lease trucks, the Soviets might have been expected to strike to the south to trap large numbers of the enemy east of the Dnieper. Instead, perhaps wary of previous German lessons in the art of counterattack, Stalin insisted on driving the Germans out of eastern Ukraine in a frontal push. The irony, as Karl-Heinz Frieser has noted, was that, early in the war, the Red Army engaged in all manner of risky adventures that overtaxed its operational abilities; now, with many German units barely capable of putting up resistance, the Soviet High Command had grown cautious.[21]

On Army Group South's southern flank, the initial Soviet attempt to cross the Donets River at Izyum had been successfully repulsed by the First Panzer Army in late July. Renewed enemy efforts beginning on 16 August also achieved little, despite concentrations of artillery fire described by the Germans as the heaviest yet seen in the war, but enemy breakthroughs to the south undermined the First Panzer Army's efforts. On the eighteenth, the Red Army repeated its pattern of intense artillery bombardment on a narrow front, this time pushing through the depleted Sixth Army defenses on the Mius. Without a single tank, the Sixth Army stood little chance of resisting the onslaught of over eight hundred Soviet armored vehicles and could only watch helplessly as on the twenty-seventh enemy spearheads turned south to the Sea of Azov, temporarily trapping the Twenty-ninth Army Corps. Nor was the situation any better in the First Panzer Army's sector. By 23 August, its strength at Izyum reduced to fewer than six thousand combat troops, the First could not even maintain a continuous line. Forced to give ground by the retreat of its neighbor to the south, it still put up a stubborn defense until 6 September, when an enemy breakthrough at Konstantinovka opened a gap between the two armies and resulted in the loss on 10 September of the key railroad junction at Sinelnikovo, just east of Dnepropetrovsk. Once more, however, the Red Army was forced to absorb a harsh lesson as German counterattacks at Sinelnikovo on 12 September pinched off and drubbed Soviet forward units.[22]

Despite enemy progress in the south, the army group's brittle northern flank posed the most serious concerns. The Eighth Army reported in early September that it could no longer hold a continuous line, opting instead to establish a system of strongpoints supported by patrols. One of its divisions reported a strength of only six officers and three hundred men, while among all the troops exhaustion and apathy had taken hold, with the "most severe measures" unable any longer to stiffen their resistance. If anything, the Fourth Panzer Army to the north was in even worse shape; the infantrymen, it reported at the end of August, were "completely exhausted and physically and psychologically at the end of their strength." Although confronted with a yawning gap to its north as the Second Army retreated, it could create only a few islands of resistance in its open left flank, primarily around the key juncture of Nezhin, to the east of Kiev. Its loss on the fifteenth touched off a near panic at Führer Headquarters as Soviet units pushed toward the Dnieper at Chernobyl. By the middle of September, faced with the possibility that its entire front could be rolled up from the north, and with a defense east of the Dnieper clearly impossible, Army Group South also began a withdrawal to the Panther position. Still, the Soviet frontal assaults had proved as costly as they were inelegant, the Red Army losing in roughly four weeks of fighting nearly 170,000 dead and missing, along with 2,000 armored vehicles and 600 aircraft.[23]

Welcome as it was, the decision to go behind the Dnieper posed enormous problems for Army Group South that tested its organizational skills and fighting abilities to the limit. Its three armies occupied a four-hundred-mile-wide front stretching from Chernobyl to Zaporozhye yet had only five major crossings of the Dnieper, itself at places over a mile wide. In practice, this meant that the armies not only had to disengage in the face of enemy forces pressing hard on their fronts but also then had to be funneled to the few major bridges over the river. Once across, the troops then had to fan out quickly behind the river before the Russians could get bridgeheads of their own on the undefended west bank. In addition, very little had been done to improve the crossings or to make available engineers and additional bridging equipment. As part of the withdrawal, moreover, some 200,000 wounded, along with medical personnel and field hospitals, over 500,000 civilians (technical specialists, forced laborers, Ukrainians fearful of the return of Soviet authorities, and ethnic Germans, with their motley possessions), along with thousands of head of cattle, embarked on a trek westward. Large quantities of goods were also sent west, causing even further congestion at the crossing points. Further complicating matters, Hitler insisted at the last moment that the First Panzer Army should defend a bridgehead east of the river at Zaporozhye in order to protect the nearby manganese mines at Nikopol, a decision that forced Manstein to move precious reserves that could have been better used plugging the numerous gaps in his front into a tactically worthless position. Finally, all this was accompanied by the systematic destruction of Soviet infrastructure, villages, and anything of economic value to a depth of twenty miles along the east bank of the river.[24]

By the end of the month, Army Group South had withdrawn the last of its troops across the Dnieper, an action that marked the end of a two-month period in which Army Groups Center and South had been forced back an average of 150 miles along a roughly 650-mile front. In the process, they had lost the economically most valuable territory they had conquered. In an effort to deny the enemy any advantage from the reconquest of this area, Hitler ordered a scorched-earth policy to destroy anything of potential economic value. Using as a precedent the similar Soviet action in the summer of 1941, the Germans, in a characteristic mix of professional ability, military necessity, individual rage, and an ideological will to destruction, proceeded to lay waste to large areas. The troops were instructed not only to evacuate or destroy potentially useful industrial equipment but also to blow up or burn buildings, villages, individual dwellings, bridges, wells—anything that could be of use to the enemy. In addition, all men between the ages of fifteen and sixty-five were to be taken along by the troops as labor for the construction of field fortifications, while able-bodied women were to be sent back to Germany as forced labor.[25]

What followed, in many areas, was an orgy of destruction, as the Germans left behind only smoking ruins and heaps of rubble. "Orel," wrote a Landser to his fiancée in mid-August, had been "leveled to the ground," its inhabitants "driven to the rear areas." Six weeks later, the same soldier noted, "The Russians will find only the rubble from blown up buildings and bridges. . . . People and animals from an enormous area . . . are streaming to the west. The Russians will find only an empty, barren land." "Everything has been burning fiercely for days," confirmed another Landser to his wife from the Dnieper, "for . . . all the towns and villages in the areas that we are now evacuating are being set ablaze, even the smallest house in the village must go. All the large buildings are being blown up. The Russians are to find nothing but a field of rubble. . . . It is a terribly beautiful picture." In a similar vein, Helmut Pabst enthused during the retreat toward Kiev, "The villages burned. They burned with raging power. . . . Long before evening the sun was already red, as it hung sick and thirsty over the march of destruction. . . . It unfurled war in all its terrible splendor." More prosaically, but perhaps more honestly, another Landser stressed the spontaneous, personal nature of scorched earth: "In the event we just go into the houses and simply take what is there." Agreed another, "Better that we have it [food] in our bellies than the Russians."[26]

Although justified by Hitler on military grounds, this extraordinary effort at scorched earth in fact raised a number of problems. From a purely tactical viewpoint, burning buildings and blowing up installations signaled only too clearly to the enemy the German intention to withdraw, thus complicating the effort to disengage in good order. Moreover, the work of destruction, combined with the effort to evacuate civilians and goods, wasted considerable time and energy, further burdening troops already exhausted by nightly retreats, the hasty construction of trenches in the mornings, and daily skirmishes with the hard-pressing enemy. Under this strain, some troops chose simply to retreat on their own, without waiting for orders, when the situation began to look critical. Nor, for all the effort, did the Germans accomplish anything decisive. At the end of September, Army Group Center reported that it had succeeded in evacuating only 20–30 percent of the economic goods in its areas, while Army Group South almost certainly did worse. Many power plants, factories, railroads, and bridges had, in fact, been destroyed, but many had never been fully restored following the Soviet retreat of 1941. By the same token, the lack of personnel meant that the Germans never came close to stripping the evacuated areas bare of grain and livestock; in the event, they were forced to leave behind far larger quantities than they were able to carry off. As a result, the Soviets quickly exploited the newly liberated areas both for grain resources and for replacements for the Red Army.[27]

Caught in the middle, as always, was the long-suffering civilian population of the affected areas. The exploitation, plundering, evacuation, and conscription of the local peoples formed an integral part of scorched earth, for human as well as material resources had to be denied the enemy. Combined, the four German army groups forced over 2 million civilians out of the territory east of the Panther line; at the same time, tens of thousands of superfluous eaters—the elderly, the sick, mothers with young children—were either left behind amid the vast desolation or driven into "bandit areas." Those capable of work—men between fifteen and sixty-five and women from fifteen to forty-five—were then divided, with the women often sent to Germany for compulsory labor service and the men dispatched to work camps to build field fortifications and perform support duties. Those caught in the roundup were treated as prisoners of war, which meant that anyone attempting to resist or escape was liable to be shot. In most areas, as well, the luckless civilians became part of a larger tug-of-war as local commanders often ignored orders to send them back to Germany in order to put them to work—twelve hours a day, seven days a week—at backbreaking construction tasks at the front.[28]

For the troops, scorched earth contributed to a further radicalizing process, resulting in growing indiscipline, brutalization, and a sharp increase in violence and the will to destruction. For many Landsers, the initial actions came as a rude shock; after all, fighting an armed enemy was one thing, but driving the sick, elderly, and young children into the wild was something else again. In addition, while the troops were exhorted (and ordered) to destroy anything of value as they retreated, there was a very thin line between denying the enemy valuable resources and plundering, burning, and murdering out of a destructive lust. As the retreat, in places, threatened to become a rout, company and battalion commanders struggled to retain discipline over their men, reminding them constantly that only things of military or economic value were to be destroyed. In practice, however, this meant virtually everything, with many Landsers falling victim to the temptation. "We also moved through the villages and shot pistol flares in the dry straw roofs," admitted one participant after the war. "In this way we were able in a very short time to burn down entire villages." The similarity between the methods used in combating the partisan war and scorched earth often enabled soldiers to rationalize their actions, although that hardly helped officers in restraining the destructive rage. Even as many tried to preserve discipline, however, they were instructed that "the complete removal of the labor resources [of these areas] is essential to the conduct of this war. How much more cruel and brutal would be the mayhem directed at the German people by the Soviets if they entered our country because we had neglected, out of a cheap humanitarian sentiment, to organize all labor resources to enforce the final victory." Whoever failed to carry out these measures, it was warned, would be regarded, and treated, as a "traitor to the German people." Littler wonder, then, that the average Landser came to believe that the scorched-earth policy gave him a "free zone" in which anything could be justified by considerations of military expediency.[29]

This desperate retreat behind the Dnieper, during which the Germans had fended off repeated, reckless Soviet frontal assaults that invariably cost the Red Army many times the losses of the Germans—but losses that were made good within a dishearteningly short time—inevitably raised doubts about the possibility of victory in the minds of many Landsers. What, then, kept German soldiers doggedly fighting, not only in the autumn of 1943, but to the end of the war? This is not an easy question to answer, for, as in any large organization, there was a complex mix of motives among the men and often within individual soldiers as well. Loyalty to Germany, support for Hitler or National Socialism, racist and anti-Semitic attitudes, primary group attachments, patriotism, fear of Bolshevik revenge, brutalization, and the embrace of a destructive passion—all these and more played a role. The very cheapness with which the enemy evidently regarded his own life seemed to confirm Nazi racialist arguments. Political education and indoctrination also played a role, as one Landser revealed in March 1942: "This is a matter of two great world views. Either us or the Jews." "The Jews," wrote another in May 1943, "must actually be behind all those that want to destroy us," then a few weeks later noted incredulously, "It surely cannot be that the Jews will win and rule." "We will win because we must win," Jodl put it with a characteristic mixture of pathos, credulity, and ideology in November 1943, "for otherwise world history has lost its meaning." As the front moved closer to Germany, a note of fear also crept in, infusing racialist beliefs with a sense of desperation to defend the homeland from the Jewish-Bolshevik Asiatic hordes. If Germany was defeated, warned one Landser in August 1944, "the Jews will then fall on us and exterminate everything that is German, there will be a cruel and terrible slaughter."[30]

The fighting spirit of the younger soldiers, those in their mid- to late twenties who made up the bulk of frontline combat troops, seems to have been sustained primarily through an intermingling of Nazi ideas with traditional nationalism, leavened by a good dose of primary group loyalty. As Christoph Rass has shown for the 253rd Infantry Division, findings that can be applied across the army, the institutional setting in which ordinary soldiers found themselves was surprisingly stable for most of the war. By forming divisions from common geographic regions, raising replacements from these same areas, returning convalescents to their old units, and mixing experienced troops with young recruits, the German army created a relatively cohesive and stable setting within which primary group loyalties and a strong sense of camaraderie could develop. The savage fighting and high losses of the war in Russia certainly damaged these bonds of loyalty, but Rass has shown convincingly that these disruptive effects were mitigated by a number of factors. Until late in the war, for example, units were rotated out of combat regularly and, thus, managed to retain a core group of comrades. While units were in reserve, recruits from the same region arrived and mingled with convalescents sent back to their old units, a fact that contributed to relatively homogenous regiments in which the men quickly bonded. Finally, the insistence, again until late in the war, that replacements be trained thoroughly before being thrown into battle, ensured a high level of combat effectiveness.[31]

To this essentially primary group argument, however, Rass has added an intriguing mixture of ideology and nationalism. While most of the soldiers would likely have seen themselves as fighting for Germany, their conception of the nation had often been decisively altered by Nazi ideology and indoctrination. Depending on year of birth, anywhere from 60 to 85 percent of the men in combat units would have spent time in one or another (and some in all) of various Nazi organizations ranging from the Hitler Youth to the Reich Labor Service to the prewar army. In addition to the general dose of propaganda supplied by Goebbels's mass media, the men would have been trained not just to be soldiers but more subtly (and effectively) to see themselves as a new kind of man, a racial comrade who fought to protect and, if necessary, was willing to sacrifice himself for the racial community. This emphasis on the Volksgemeinschaft, the racial and organic national community the Nazis had promoted with such emotion and fanfare in the 1930s, now appeared to many Landsers as not merely a superior new society in creation but an everyday reality affirmed by their staunch camaraderie and mutual support in adversity. In this sense, as Richard Evans has argued, it was not the destruction of such primary groups but their very persistence that led to the brutalization of war in the east as these tough cells, sustained by experienced veterans and Nazified young men, turned their aggressive sense of community outward against a Soviet population seen as racially inferior, indeed, as barely human.[32]

To stiffen German morale even further, Keitel had, from the autumn of 1943, urged the intensification of National Socialist education for all German troops. They must understand, emphasized the head of the OKW, that in this ongoing "struggle of ideologies" the only option was "victory or ruin," meaning that every soldier had to become "a political-ideological fighter" with a "fanatical devotion to the National Socialist idea." Responding to Keitel's initiative, Hitler in late December 1943 ordered the establishment of the National Socialist Leadership Corps, a Nazi equivalent of the political commissars in the Red Army. Through lectures, special courses, and the distribution of ideological leaflets, the men at the front were to be strengthened in their resolve by belief in the Nazi idea. In response, officers' orders and actions became more overtly National Socialist in an attempt to infuse their men with an urgent will to resist. Although it is difficult to determine with any precision how many men were inspired to fanatic resistance, certainly a good many were fortified by this bracing mixture of ideology and sense of beleaguered front community.[33]

In addition, Goebbels added to the ideological brew by seeking to change the perception of the war from one of conquest of Lebensraum to one of defense of European civilization against the onslaught of the Jewish-Bolshevik hordes. For many observers both inside and outside

Germany, this depiction acquired a greater plausibility as the Wehrmacht was forced onto the defensive and the "Red danger" crept ever closer to Central Europe. In this new formulation, Germany was now the "protective power" working to mobilize "all the strength of the European continent against Jewish-Bolshevism," a task that, if necessary, required the utmost ruthlessness. This barely concealed threat applied not only to the occupied areas but also to the Wehrmacht itself, whose members were now exposed to the harshest punishments. Increasingly in the last year and a half of the war, the men would be kept fighting, if necessary, through fear and terror. Any hint of a failure of will—from defeatist utterances to self-mutilation to desertion—now fell under the vague category of *Wehrkraftzersetzung* (undermining the conduct of the war), the penalty for which often proved swift execution. Military courts-martial were used to impose discipline and the will to fight by showing Landsers the consequences if they flagged: some thirty thousand soldiers were sentenced to death, with perhaps twenty thousand of those executed, most in the last year or so of the war, as against forty-eight executed in all the German armed forces during World War I. If National Socialist ideas failed to inspire a will to resist, then Nazi terror would be used instead. For the average soldier, the war had become, in the most concrete sense, a battle for survival.[34]

With the Germans driven back across the Dnieper, the Red Army had attained the original goal of its summer offensive but now moved to exploit the fruits of its victory. Drawing on the local population for replacements—some eighty thousand men were drafted from the liberated areas and thrown into the battle—and concerned that, if given time, the Germans would take advantage of the river line to stalemate the war, the Soviets bounced the river in a number of places and established bridgeheads on the west bank as launching pads for future operations. Although the Dnieper, with its broad channel, high bluffs on the western side, and swampy eastern bank, afforded the strongest natural defensive line in western Russia, Hitler's stubborn insistence on holding out east of the river had deprived the Germans of most of its advantages. Not only had their strength been sapped, but work on constructing defenses along the river had also lagged. Many Landsers, encouraged by the talk of an Ostwall, were dismayed to find on crossing the river that little had been built and they were left in the open. "We had expected," wrote one, "to find the Ostwall behind the Dnieper. Not even trenches were there."[35]

This shock to the morale of the exhausted German forces was

compounded by the awareness of the vast mismatch in strength between the opposing sides. Although on paper Manstein had sixty divisions at his disposal, in reality most had the strength only of a regiment and some not even of a *Kampfgruppe* (battle group). In early October, Army Group South had only about one thousand combat troops per division, fewer than three hundred operational tanks and assault guns, and not quite six hundred aircraft for itself and Army Group A to its south. Manstein himself admitted gloomily at the end of October that the combat strength of his troops, exhausted by ceaseless battle for months, had "sunk so low . . . that as a result of our insufficient manpower in the front lines the enemy can punch through anywhere he assembles sufficient forces." Instead of organizing a defense along the river line, however, he had to try, with inadequate forces, to eliminate or contain the numerous Soviet bridgeheads, even as the enemy sought to exploit its vast numerical preponderance by launching several attacks simultaneously along the front.[36]

Of these bridgeheads, the ones ultimately most dangerous were north of Kiev at Liutezh and Chernobyl. The Red Army had originally hoped, in a daring blow using massed armor and airborne troops, to burst out of the Bukrin bridgehead to the south of the Ukrainian capital in late September and seize the city in a sweeping move to the west and north. Although this had resulted in a fiasco, Vatutin skillfully moved his troops, under cover of effective camouflage measures, to the northern bridgeheads. Following a massive artillery barrage, Soviet forces on 3 November assaulted the thin German defenses at Liutezh, at the same time breaking out of the bridgehead near Chernobyl. Within two days, the Fourth Panzer Army front had been shattered, and, lacking reserves of any kind, it was helpless to slow the enemy advance. By the sixth, Kiev had fallen, and Soviet forces were pushing westward almost unhindered. Troops of the First Ukrainian Front, storming out of the Chernobyl bridgehead, raced toward the city of Korosten at the border of Army Groups Center and South, having blasted a sixty-mile-wide gap between the two army groups just south of the Pripet Marshes, a no-man's-land that the Germans could cover only with reconnaissance troops and patrols. Although the giant swamps of the Pripet offered the Second Army to the north some flank protection, it was primarily controlled by partisan bands, which left the danger that the Soviets might be able to roll up the soft underbelly of the Second Army from the south. Fortunately for the Germans, the various Soviet, Ukrainian, and Polish partisans operating in the Pripet fought each other as much as the German occupier, so an immediate threat failed to materialize, but the situation remained unstable.[37]

More pressing was the danger from Red Army troops driving out of Liutezh on the key railroad junction of Fastov, thirty miles southwest of Kiev, which controlled the lines supplying Army Group South's central sector. Its fall on the seventh raised the possibility that the army group might be enveloped, especially since the southern wing of the front had been under assault since early October. With his efforts to repair the situation on the northern end of his sector frustrated by Hitler's insistence on defending the great bend of the Dnieper to the south, Manstein flew to Führer Headquarters on the ninth to demand its evacuation, a move that would shorten the front considerably and free units for use in the north. To Manstein, there seemed little operational point to holding on to the Dnieper bend, especially since Zaporozhye and Dnepropetrovsk had already been lost in mid-October. In addition, Soviet troops had shattered the front of the Sixth Army (Army Group A) at Melitopol on 23 October and reached the Black Sea in early November, trapping the Seventeenth Army in the Crimea. As always, however, Hitler insisted that the manganese ore mines near Nikopol could not be given up without great harm to the armaments effort, nor could the Crimea be abandoned since it would provide the Soviets airfields from which to attack the vital Rumanian oil fields. Ironically, the Führer's intransigence had been reinforced late in October by Manstein himself. In expectation of receiving five fresh panzer divisions from the west, the OKW having decided that the danger of an Allied invasion had passed, he proposed an attack, reminiscent of his Kharkov success, to cut off the exposed Soviet forces. By now, however, the urgent danger in the north had pushed aside all thoughts of such an operation, but neither the field marshal nor Gehlen, who warned of a "collapse of the eastern front," proved able to change Hitler's mind. It was, he said, a risk that would have to be taken, although he did allow Manstein to use some of the newly arrived panzer divisions in the area of the Fourth Panzer Army.[38]

One of these was the newly raised Twenty-fifth Panzer Division, just arrived from France after a series of misadventures that had seen it originally sent to the right flank of the army group before being hurried north, with the result that its equipment was scattered over hundreds of miles. Although not trained for fighting on the eastern front, and lacking much of its heavy weapons—it was, as one author noted ironically, a panzer division without panzers—it was the only unit available to slow the Soviet advance at Fastov. Against Guderian's vehement objections, the Twenty-fifth Panzer, with as much strength as it could muster, was thrown on the seventh into a counterattack at Fastov in an attempt to regain the rail juncture. By the time its full complement of armored vehicles arrived two days later, it had already suffered such losses that it was unable to retake the city, an outcome that sent Hitler into a rage. More importantly, in throwing into battle a unit clearly unready for combat, the German leadership had departed from its key principle. In contrast to the Soviets, who had squandered many newly formed divisions by throwing them prematurely into combat, the Germans had allowed units to train behind the front to gain experience before being sent into battle. Still, despite being sacrificed, the Twenty-fifth Panzer had performed a vital task: it had slowed the Soviet advance at Fastov and gave Manstein time to organize a counterattack.[39]

Launched on 15 November, the counterstrike was carried out by General Hermann Balck's Forty-eighth Panzer Corps, which had assembled almost three hundred armored vehicles. Typically at this stage, since the Germans had not yet completely abandoned the idea of regaining the initiative, it aimed at not just pinching off the Soviet advance but ultimately recapturing Kiev. By the twenty-third, Balck's forces had retaken both Brusilov and Zhitomir, while, to the north, German troops had beaten off an enemy attack at Korosten, regaining the city on the twenty-seventh. Manstein now planned a strike directly east toward Kiev, but several days of steady rain turned the roads into muddy quagmires, forcing a halt to the operation. After the ground had frozen, the Germans renewed their assault on 6 December, with the two hundred armored vehicles of the Forty-eighth Panzer Corps assailing nine Soviet armies, among them two full tank armies and a tank corps. Amazingly, in view of the overwhelming enemy superiority, Balck's men achieved a few local victories, recapturing Radomsyl on the sixteenth, and generally spreading anxiety and consternation in the Soviet rear. Still, these local triumphs only confirmed the larger German dilemma. Although they proved time and again tactically superior to the Soviets, the Germans could not convert these local victories into an operational breakthrough because at the crucial moment they lacked the necessary strength. Thus, although between August and December in all operations against Army Group South alone the Soviets suffered the staggering total of 417,323 permanent losses, as against 287,000 German dead on the *entire* eastern front, they were now so numerically superior that they could strike in all areas simultaneously, straining German resources to the breaking point. While, in many sectors, the Germans could not keep a front line completely manned, Manstein estimated that, with the forces available to it, the Red Army could at any time launch a full-scale winter offensive that would leave Army Group South helpless to resist.[40]

Constant enemy pressure and the inability to concentrate meager resources meant that Army Group Center faced the same wearing-away process as its counterpart to the south. Although forced to transfer units to both its hard-pressed neighbors, Army Group Center was still the strongest German force on the eastern front. With the Schwerpunkt of the Soviet offensive clearly in the south, it had been able to withdraw in good order to the Panther position as well as maintain a large slice of land some 190 miles long and 30–40 miles wide east of the Dnieper. Stretching from Loyev (just north of Chernobyl) in the south to east of Orsha in the north, this extended bridgehead was seen by both sides as an opportunity. For Hitler, it represented a launching pad for a future offensive back into Ukraine, while the Soviets saw it as an ideal place from which to destroy much of Army Group Center and liberate Belorussia. Consequently, in the autumn of 1943, they conceived the ambitious plan of launching a pincer attack from Vitebsk in the north and Gomel in the south that would converge on Minsk, trapping sizable German forces in a huge pocket. Although Kluge had throughout October alerted Hitler to the danger from the army group's exposed position, the Führer had brushed aside his warnings. Then, on the twenty-eighth, Kluge suffered serious injuries in an automobile accident and was replaced by Generalfeldmarschall Ernst Busch, who, although regarded as a capable commander, had little tactical frontline experience and, thus, tended to defer to Hitler's judgment.[41]

With little more than two hundred armored vehicles and 450,000 combat troops to defend a line that had swelled to six hundred miles against an enemy force of 1.6 million men and almost twelve hundred tanks and assault guns as well as an estimated 150,000 extremely active partisans operating in his rear, Busch faced a daunting task. Throughout November and December, Soviet forces hammered persistently at Army Group Center on both flanks, but, despite pushing German forces back across the Dnieper in the southern sector, they proved unable to capture the key city of Bobruisk. In the north, the Red Army had even less to show for its battering efforts. Dismissive of losses, the Soviets time and again threw waves of troops against the German defenses. "A Russian infantry attack was a terrifying spectacle," acknowledged one German officer. "They tramped up in long gray lines emitting wild screams so that the defenders had to have nerves of steel." "The Russians didn't think much," said another. "They were usually being driven by their officers." A Red Army attack, with waves of men and tanks abreast, awed even the most hardened German soldiers. "You couldn't believe the way they kept coming—their infantry simply charging . . . , running and shouting. Sometimes our infantry seemed paralyzed by the spectacle.

One thought, 'How can we ever stop such people?'" Still, despite surrounding Vitebsk, the gateway to the Baltic, and pounding away at German defenses well into February 1944, the Soviets nonetheless failed to take the city. Nor, in the center of the front at Orsha, in similar mass attacks on the key highway, or Rollbahn, leading to Minsk that lasted until the end of March 1944, was the enemy able to convert his massive numerical and material superiority into any sort of breakthrough.[42]

For all the extraordinary bravery, or stoicism, of the average Russian soldier, the Soviets paid an enormous price for this persistent attempt to break through German defenses. In total, the battles at Gomel, Vitebsk, and Orsha cost the Soviets nearly a million casualties, a quarter of whom died, yet only in the south along the edge of the Pripet Marshes had they made any serious inroads. On 19 March, Soviet forces surrounded the road junction of Kovel, at the southwest end of the 240-mile-long swamp, the loss of which would expose Army Group Center to encirclement from the south. Even here, however, after Hitler had declared Kovel a "fortified city" that had to be held at all cost, some four thousand surrounded defenders, supplied from the air until a relief column punched through at the end of the month, managed to stabilize the situation until the spring rasputitsa ended all operations. In a mid-April 1944 report to Stalin, the Red Army command admitted the utter failure of these winter operations, ironically ascribing their lack of success to material deficiencies. Hitler, however, drew another, and equally unrealistic, lesson, albeit one with more serious long-term consequences. The meager gains bought at excessive cost confirmed the Führer in his low opinion of Soviet operational capabilities as well as furthering his belief that the enemy must be approaching the limit of his strength. As a result, he thought, a bit more determination and will, holding on to other key cities as "fortified places," would stem the Red tide. Rather than recognize the exposed and dangerous position in which Army Group Center had been left by the winter battles, Hitler was more convinced than ever of the value of a static, stubborn, unyielding defense.[43]

On the extreme left flank of the front, Army Group North of necessity had to follow Hitler's preference for static defense. Since it had been in a relatively stable situation through 1942 and the first half of 1943, no formation had been more burdened by unit transfers than Field Marshal Küchler's army group. In July 1943, it possessed barely 360,000 front troops, with a mere forty tanks and assault guns, a figure that was reduced on 15 September to only seven serviceable tanks. Luftflotte 1 was in an even more dire condition: on 20 July, it disposed of a mere six fighter aircraft to maintain the siege of Leningrad and cover up to five hundred miles of front. With a serious deficiency in motor vehicles and towing machines, Army Group North typified, in an extreme form, what had happened to the entire Ostheer: it had effectively been demotorized and reduced to the status of a World War I outfit, dependent on horses for whatever mobility it possessed. Unable any longer to outmaneuver the enemy, German units had little choice but to resist as long as possible in prepared positions since any retreat threatened to turn into a rout.[44]

Compounding its difficulties, the withdrawal of Army Group Center to the Panther line in the autumn had not only left its neighbor to the north in an exposed position but also forced it to extend its line fifty miles to the south to encompass the important road and rail centers of Nevel and Novosokolniki. By late September, all indications pointed to an enemy offensive in the area of the boundary line between the two army groups. That partisan-infested area, crisscrossed with forests, lakes, swamps, and notoriously poor roads, had long been one of the weakest points on the eastern front; at the time, the Germans had only about twelve hundred men to defend an eleven-mile sector. When the Soviet attack came early on 6 October, it caught the defenders by surprise, largely because they had lost track of Russian troop movements owing to poor weather over the previous days. Before the Germans could react, Red Army forces had stormed into Nevel, seized the city, and punched a hole in the German line at the boundary between the two army groups. Although his forces were badly outmanned, Hitler nonetheless responded in typical fashion: he ordered the flanks of the break-in held and counterattacks to close the gap between the army groups. In addition, and in a gratuitous bit of condescension, he pointed out to his generals that, as was their habit, the Soviets had attacked at unit boundaries, implying that they were both ignorant of this fact and unwilling to cooperate to stop it. This rebuke was the more offensive since German commanders had long been aware of this unimaginative Soviet tactic but were unable effectively to combat it. Nor could much comfort be found in the fact that the Soviets succeeded less from their own skill and more because of the condition of the German forces. With their front lines undermanned and stretched thin, and with few reserves, German commanders were of necessity forced to wait to see which direction the Soviets would turn after a breakthrough before reacting. In this case, Hitler's insistence on holding the flanks proved decisive, for, despite continual attacks until the end of the year, the Soviets failed, at very high cost, to exploit their initial breakthrough.[45]

By now, the crippling German deficiencies in manpower had become apparent to all, except perhaps the Führer. In September, for the first time in the war, army strength on the eastern front (not including Luftwaffe field units or the Waffen-SS) had fallen below 2.5 million, with permanent losses since the invasion of the Soviet Union totaling almost a million men. Moreover, it was proving difficult to dredge up new recruits, while the quality of many of the replacements at the front, as Kluge unsuccessfully tried to convince Hitler in October, was such that they could not withstand a determined enemy attack. The quality of many German infantry units had dropped so alarmingly, in fact, that in October Guderian, in his capacity as inspector-general of the army, proposed creating mobile tank reserves to backstop the infantry. His idea foundered as always on Hitler's resistance to sacrificing any ground to free troops. That the situation was near catastrophic was shown by Army Group North, which, in the last six months of 1943 alone, lost 40 percent of its front divisions to other sectors of the front and now had to make do with a motley collection of understrength infantry units and Luftwaffe field divisions of dubious value, with no panzer or Panzergrenadier divisions of its own. Nor could the report of Foreign Armies East in late March 1944 provide much comfort. The Soviets, Gehlen's unit calculated, had lost 1.2 million men (killed and taken prisoner) just in the last four months of 1943, as against 243,743 Germans, but the frontline and reserve strength of the Red Army had grown to 5.5 million troops. In addition, annual Soviet drafts produced three times more recruits than the Germans were able to, while the Soviet Union had gained (and Germany lost) some 600,000 men in the recovered territories. Finally, in an ominous sign of the growing interconnection of the various strategic fronts, Gehlen estimated that Germany had to divert at least 30 percent, and usually more, of its total strength to OKW theaters, while the Soviet Union diverted only 7 percent to its Far East sector.[46]

Even as Army Group North accelerated preparations of its portion of the Panther line, running behind natural obstacles such as the Narva River, Lake Peipus, and Lake Pskov, Küchler was under no illusions. Like Manstein to the south, he was precariously holding one sector, around Leningrad, primarily for prestige reasons and another, near Nevel, to stave off possible disaster but unlikely in the event of a Soviet offensive to be able to hold either. Hitler, however, believed that the Soviets had lost so many men fighting in Ukraine that an attack in the north was unlikely until spring. Unable to secure Hitler's permission to retire in good order behind the Panther line, Küchler could only wait uneasily for the blow to fall. By mid-January, even as he was forced to transfer two of his best divisions to Army Group South, Küchler faced an enemy force numbering 1.25 million men and sixteen hundred tanks with a front strength of barely 250,000 men. The blow, when it fell on 14 January, was designed by the Soviets to exploit this vast superiority with simultaneous assaults against the Eighteenth Army at Leningrad and Novgorod. Much to the surprise of the Germans, the Stavka's aim was not merely to liberate Leningrad but to drive to the borders of the Baltic states. Despite their vast inferiority, the Germans were able to resist the enemy onslaught until the seventeenth, when Soviet forces achieved a breakthrough in the north between Krasnoe Selo and Pushkin.[47]

On the eighteenth, with the front west of Leningrad collapsing and the Soviets beginning to encircle Novgorod, Army Group North faced a life-and-death crisis. Hitler, as usual, refused to authorize a withdrawal, but, with virtually no reserves to stabilize the situation, Küchler on his own authority ordered a retreat. By the nineteenth, Novgorod had been surrounded, and the Führer reluctantly allowed German troops to break out; the next day, the city fell to the Soviets. Under unrelenting pressure, German troops continued to fall back, with the result that, by 26 January, the Red Army was able to seize the main rail line to Moscow, effectively ending the siege of Leningrad after almost nine hundred days and the loss of between 1.6 and 2 million lives (an amount four to five times greater than all American deaths in World War II). The next day, with Küchler and the other army group and army commanders attending a National Socialist leadership conference at Königsberg, at which Hitler exhorted them on faith as the key to victory, the Soviets celebrated the capture of Leningrad with a powerful artillery salute.[48]

Given the danger that Russian partisans might cut off his ability to withdraw to the Panther line, Küchler had already on 20 January requested permission to retire immediately to this position, a request Hitler rejected with a tirade against his generals. Army Group North, in particular, Hitler claimed, had grown flabby. "I am against all withdrawals," he stressed. "We will have crises wherever we are. There is no guarantee we will not be broken through on the Panther line. . . . [The Russian] must bleed himself white on the way. The battle must be fought as far as possible from the German border." The Führer also mustered his customary economic and strategic arguments in favor of holding fast. The Baltic coast, he emphasized, had to be held in order to guarantee vital iron ore deliveries from Sweden as well as to ensure control of the Baltic Sea for development and trials of new U-boats. By 27 January, however, with the Eighteenth Army having lost fifty-two thousand men, with its effective infantry strength down to seventeen thousand men, and faced with encirclement, even Hitler could no longer ignore the obvious. On 29 January, with the Eighteenth Army now splintered into three parts, Küchler again on his own authority ordered it to retreat in order to prevent its complete destruction. Although Hitler had little choice but to accept this decision, he nonetheless summoned Küchler to his HQ, where he summarily fired the field marshal on the thirty-first, replacing him with Model.[49]

Although regarded as a defensive specialist and brilliant improviser, Model faced a situation that taxed even his legendary energy and toughness. His first moves, in fact, were more psychological than tactical: decreeing not a single step back without his approval and forbidding any reference to the Panther line on the ground that it induced a withdrawal psychosis. More concretely, Model profited from the fact that Hitler tended to give new appointees, particularly his favorites, a bit more leeway as well as from a rather dilatory Soviet advance. Taking full advantage of a new brainchild of the Führer's that allowed withdrawals as long as counterstrikes were planned to regain the lost ground, Model initiated controlled retreats to the Panther line to parry Soviet advances. That he ever intended to thrust was doubtful, for the field marshal was under no illusions about the reality of the situation. Still, the fact that the Germans were able to build a stable front had less to do with Model's formidable skills than the Soviet failure to take advantage of the superior mobility accorded them by extensive American Lend-Lease deliveries of trucks and motor vehicles. Instead of bold encirclement operations, Soviet commanders now preferred methodical frontal assaults that ground the Germans down but failed to annihilate them. As a result, Model's forces not only succeeded in retiring to the Panther line in relatively good order, but also, from mid-February, deflected all Soviet attempts to burst through the narrow neck of land between Lake Peipus and the Gulf of Finland. By 1 March, German troops were behind the Panther line and able, despite continued costly Soviet attempts to take Narva and Pskov, to hold their positions.[50]

The liberation of Leningrad after its long ordeal was greeted with understandable joy in the Soviet Union, but this success had been achieved at a very high price. From July 1943 to the end of the year, the Red Army in the north had lost over 260,000 men, among them 67,000 killed and missing. Then, despite a five-to-one manpower advantage and an incredible thirteen-to-one superiority in tanks and assault guns, the fighting between mid-January and 1 March cost the Soviets another 314,000 troops (77,000 dead and missing), with the attempt to breach the Panther line in March and April resulting in the further loss of 200,000 men. From July 1943 through April 1944, then, the Red Army suffered casualties of almost 775,000 men, a figure equivalent to the total strength of Army Group North. Despite inflicting savage losses on the enemy, Hitler's determination to hold out in front of the Panther position rather than allow an orderly withdrawal to a more defensible line had cost German forces dearly as well. From 10 January to 1 March, Army Group North lost almost 100,000 men, of whom 29,000 were dead and missing, casualties that, given the Germans' catastrophic manpower situation, they could not sustain. The apparent German success in stabilizing the front again allowed Hitler to continue in the illusion that his strategy of holding fast at all costs was working. The Führer, however, was no longer all that interested in the fate of Army Group North, for the situation in the south, the Schwerpunkt of Soviet operations, had once again grown critical.[51]

As in the other sectors, the relentless Soviet attacks had reduced the strength of Army Group South to the point that Manstein could not adequately man the entire front. The problem was not just a lack of troops, or the fact that almost all his men were "apathetic . . . [and] completely indifferent whether they were shot dead by their own officers or the Russians," but the very course of the front line itself. On its northern flank, German forces had been pressed back (where a dangerous gap of sixty miles separated Army Groups South and Center), while, in the south, as always, Hitler insisted on clinging to as much of the great bend of the Dnieper as possible (and refused to evacuate the Crimea). Since the Eighth Army still held a front of some twenty-five miles along the Dnieper in the center (which Hitler hoped to use as the launch pad for a new offensive), this meant that Soviet forces at Korosten in the north were already some three hundred miles to the west of the dangerously exposed German troops at Nikopol and, thus, in a position to strike south toward the Carpathian Mountains and Black Sea and completely envelop Army Group South. Manstein was fully aware of this peril and implored Hitler to allow a withdrawal in the Dnieper bend as well as the Crimea in order to free troops to stabilize the northern flank, but the dictator time and again refused this request.[52]

Until now, the Germans had been lucky that Vatutin, the commander of the First Ukrainian Front, had not tried to exploit the gaps in their lines. Their luck ran out on 24 December, when the Soviets launched their strongest offensive to date in the direction of Zhitomir and Berdichev. Despite the pounding the Soviets had taken in reaching the Dnieper and the poor weather conditions that hampered all movement, Vatutin had assembled over 2 million men and two thousand tanks (supplemented by thousands more during the operation) for this assault.

Given their marked superiority, the Soviets splintered German defenses and achieved a breakthrough in a very short period. In some sectors of the front, German forces were so thin that the men could not see their neighbor in the next foxhole, while the elite Grossdeutschland Division reported that in one area sixty-five men had to hold a position of almost one and a half miles. As Manstein also feared, Vatutin aimed to reach the Carpathians and block the line of retreat of the German forces to the south. After the first week, this appeared very likely since Soviet forces had driven sixty miles west, while, on 3 January 1944, they reached the prewar Polish border at Gorodnitsa, northwest of Zhitomir. German forces were now so depleted that, on 4 January, the Thirteenth Corps reported that its divisions had a frontline infantry strength of only 150–300 men and that the entire corps had the infantry strength of only one regiment.[53]

As the gap in the north along the Pripet Marshes between the army groups grew even wider and the situation developed in a very precarious fashion, Manstein saw the only solution in giving up his positions on the lower Dnieper in order to free troops for a counterattack. His plan, similar to the one that had achieved such success a year earlier at Kharkov, was to blunt the enemy advance by striking him in the flanks and destroying a considerable portion of his exposed forces. Manstein's first mention of this idea, in late December, provoked only a furious outburst in Hitler, who claimed that the field marshal had lost his nerve and wanted only to run away. On 4 January, Manstein flew to Hitler's headquarters to make a personal attempt to persuade the Führer to sanction a withdrawal in the south. Although Hitler likely understood the need for thoroughgoing measures, he again refused even to consider, allegedly for economic and political reasons, giving up the Dnieper bend. Moreover, he now invoked the threat of an Allied invasion in the west to resist any transfer of troops to the east, effectively leaving Manstein to his own resources to deal with the situation. Since by 9 January the Soviet breakthrough in the north had reached truly alarming proportions, with advance units within twenty miles of Uman and threatening his former headquarters at Vinnitsa, Manstein did just that, acting decisively to deal with the crisis. Having already ordered the First Panzer Army to disengage at Nikopol and move north, with its positions to be covered by the newly obtained Sixth Army (from Army Group A), he now resolved to conduct the defensive battle in the north by offensive means. Striking into its flanks and rear, his forces were able to destroy a good portion of the Soviet Fortieth Army, on 15 January even managing at Zvenigorodka and Uman to sever its connections to the rear. Only the lack of infantry prevented a complete exploitation of this triumph. To the north, another counterattack launched on the twenty-fourth led, four days later, to the destruction of further enemy forces at Oratov. In all, some seven hundred Soviet tanks had been destroyed or captured, but, to Manstein's great frustration, the lack of German strength meant that these operations served only to avert catastrophe, not as a springboard for a new offensive.[54]

This basic dilemma was illustrated with great clarity in the center of his front where, on the twenty-fourth, despite the German success in stemming the enemy breakthrough just to the north, Soviet forces launched an attack aimed at cutting off the German salient on the Dnieper at its base. By the twenty-eighth, enemy troops had closed the encirclement, ironically at Zvenigorodka, trapping two German corps, some fifty-six thousand men plus five thousand Soviet Hiwi's, in a pocket roughly forty miles wide and 150 miles in circumference. In all, six weak divisions had been surrounded, the strongest of which was the Fifth SS Viking Division. Manstein's concern now was whether the Soviets would strike deeply into the German rear, as the Wehrmacht had done in 1941, or content themselves with destroying German troops in the Kessel. Perhaps mindful of their ongoing difficulties just to the north as well as Manstein's habit of pulling off painful surprises, the Soviets chose the latter option. In opting for caution, the Red Army leadership seems also to have vastly overestimated German strength in the pocket, claiming that over 130,000 men and 230 armored vehicles were trapped when, in reality, the Germans had less than half that number of men and only twenty-six operational tanks and fourteen assault guns. The weather might also have played a role in the Soviet decision since the unusually warm winter and frequent downpours of rain had turned all roads into muddy quagmires, ensuring that the Germans could not react swiftly, but also slowing Russian advances.[55]

Hitler reacted to this development in typical fashion. Not only did he refuse to allow a breakout, declaring the Cherkassy-Korsun pocket a "fortress on the Dnieper" that had to be held at all cost; he also ordered a wide-ranging operation that went far beyond the relief of the troops in the pocket. Instead, he hoped first, in an attack from the south, to encircle the encirclers and then to exploit the momentum of this presumed success with a further attack in the direction of Kiev to trap enemy forces west of the Dnieper, thus reversing, with this one bold stroke, his fortunes in the east. Manstein protested against this "utopian" plan from the lost world of 1941 but himself conceived a relief operation that was too clever and ambitious. While the Forty-seventh Panzer Corps of the

Eighth Army would spearhead a relief assault from the southeast to make contact with the Kessel, the Third Panzer Corps of the First Panzer Army had the task of driving north through Medvin before turning east to the pocket, thus encircling a portion of the enemy force to the south. Because of Soviet pressure elsewhere that tied down German units earmarked for the relief attack, when it began on 1 February the Forty-seventh Panzer Corps could spare only two units, the Eleventh and Thirteenth Panzer Divisions, which between them could muster only thirty-six operational AFVs. In the following days, the Third and Fourteenth Panzer Divisions, with a mere twenty-two AFVs, joined the assault but made little progress against enemy resistance and the unpredictable weather, with its bouts of freezing, thawing, rain, and snow that turned the countryside into a vast mud bog. The hopes placed in the powerful Twenty-fourth Panzer Division, which had been sent north from Nikopol, also came to naught, for en route it had been ordered by Hitler back to its old positions because of a Soviet attack on the lower Dnieper. Because of the miserable weather and mud, however, it arrived back in the Nikopol region too late to participate in the battle there, with the result that one of the strongest units in Army Group South had been of no use anywhere.[56]

Similarly, the main relief force belonging to the Third Panzer Corps, the heavy Panzer Regiment Bäke, with thirty-four Tiger and forty-six Panther tanks, also found itself helpless in the face of the unseasonably warm weather. On the night of 1–2 February, warm air and rain left a mucky morass that caused the heavy tanks to sink in the mud, consuming enormous quantities of fuel as they tried to churn forward. Even as civilians were commandeered as porters to move fuel and supplies forward, low-flying Ju-52s dropped gas canisters to the tanks below. To add further misery, in the following nights the temperatures again plunged below freezing, with the result that the entombed tanks now had to be hacked out of the frozen ground. The infantry also struggled forward through knee-deep mud, in soaked uniforms, with little food or water, tired, dirty, and hungry. By 4 February, when the attack finally commenced, only the Sixteenth and Seventeenth Panzer Divisions as well as a portion of Panzer Regiment Bäke, with eighty-five total AFVs, were available. Although it achieved an initial breakthrough, the attack bogged down over the next few days as a result of mud and furious Soviet counterattacks. Although the Germans destroyed a large number of enemy tanks, the Russians achieved their goal of delaying the attack.[57]

By now, Manstein realized that his overly ambitious plan had failed and, thus, resolved on a straightforward relief operation from the southwest over Lisjanka. The units for this, however, could not be assembled before 11 February, and, in the meantime, the forces within the pocket, which were never particularly strong to begin with, had been progressively weakened by steady Soviet attacks. Despite the example of Stalingrad, Hitler still clung to the belief that pockets could be supplied from the air, but, given the weather conditions and the enemy defenses, this had never been likely. The Kessel needed 150 tons of supplies daily but received an average of only half that. Unable at times to use the nonasphalted runway at Korsun, the Luftwaffe resorted to dropping supplies, with many lost to the enemy. Having wasted seven days on a fruitless attempt to mitigate defeat, Manstein also recognized that it was now pointless to try to defend the Kessel and, thus, prepared plans for a breakout of the trapped troops.[58]

By 15 February, German troops had fought their way into Lisjanka, slowed as much by the weather as the enemy, but because of a lack of fuel could not take Hill 239, a key enemy position barely more than a mile from the pocket. Ironically, Stalin's impatience at Zhukov's failure to reduce the Kessel quickly enough now offered the Germans an opportunity for escape. Angry that Zhukov had not properly planned joint action between Vatutin and Konev, on 12 February Stalin had given overall command of the encirclement to Konev. This resulted not only in a distinct humiliation for Zhukov but also a redisposition of Soviet forces that left a gap precisely at Lisjanka. Manstein now ordered the remaining forty-six thousand Germans in the pocket to break out on the night of 16–17 February. Commencing at 11:00 P.M. without an artillery barrage, the attack achieved initial surprise, but the first troops out had to pass by Hill 239, which was still in Russian hands. A bloodbath ensued, with many Germans machine-gunned to death or trampled into the ground by Soviet tanks.[59]

The second wave followed ten minutes later, then, at a slower pace, the tanks, assault guns, prime movers, and horse-drawn wagons. As they piled up against the ridges flanking Hill 239 or simply got stuck in the mud, a huge traffic jam ensued that slowed the breakout. Further compounding the confusion, General Stemmermann, the commander in the pocket, was killed at 4:00 A.M. on the seventeenth. All semblance of order now disappeared as the Germans desperately sought to break out while the Russians, finally recognizing what was up, brought them under withering artillery, mortar, and tank attack. Because of the heavy fire from Hill 239, the fleeing Germans passed to its south, which led them to the swampy bottomland and icy cold waters of the Gniloy Tikich River, swollen to more than fifty feet by the recent rain. Even as Germans on the opposite shore watched, many of their comrades perished in the attempt to swim to safety. By midmorning of the seventeenth, however, Bäke's tanks, now supplied with fuel, seized Hill 239, and later units had a relatively undramatic escape from the pocket.[60]

By the eighteenth, with the last units extracted, an estimated thirty-six thousand men had been brought out, which, combined with the over four thousand wounded flown out earlier, meant that some forty thousand troops had been rescued, a figure that Manstein regarded with some satisfaction (although Hitler grumbled at the loss of equipment). The psychological state of those saved, however, was shocking. The relatively good physical condition of those coming out of the pocket surprised the troops of the heavy tank regiment, themselves in constant combat and without a hot meal for a week, but the latter were appalled that those rescued refused to stay and help their lagging comrades. On the seventeenth, fearing for their "inner substance," Manstein decided to send all the survivors back to Poland to rest and recuperate. This was to be no "Stalingrad on the Dnieper," but the Germans nonetheless suffered sizable losses of AFVs: 156 tanks and assault guns, with most disabled by mines and unable to be towed to safety. Similarly, Panzer Regiment Bäke lost twenty-three Panthers and seven Tigers, although only four of the former and one of the latter to enemy fire. Although Stalin celebrated a great triumph and claimed much higher German losses than there were in actuality, the Red Army had again lost disproportionate numbers of men and equipment, with over 80,000 casualties, of whom over 24,000 were killed or missing, and 728 tanks and assault guns destroyed. By contrast, total German casualties numbered less than 20,000, of whom roughly 14,000 could be counted permanent losses. Though heartened by their ability to rescue the majority of those trapped, the German commanders nevertheless faced the sobering realization that this should not have happened in the first place and that the Soviets were now in a position to fight an encirclement battle in addition to keeping pressure on in other areas of the front.[61]

This was shown both by the enemy thrust toward Kovel at the southwestern edge of the Pripet Marshes and by a drive westward from Yampol at the boundary of the Fourth and First Panzer Armies. If successful, this latter thrust would not only shatter the northern wing of Army Group South but also cut the vital rail line running from Lvov to Odessa, thus opening the way through the Carpathians to Hungary and, most worrisome, the oil fields of Rumania. The continuous fighting over the previous months had left the Fourth Panzer Army in an extraordinarily critical situation. On 5 March 1944, after losing the units on its right flank to the First Panzer Army, it had a strength well below 100,000 men, with only thirty AFVs. Convinced that the Russians had to stop attacking eventually, Hitler refused any shortening of the line in order to gather sufficient forces to contest effectively the decisive points on the front. Contrary to the Führer's expectations, however, the Soviets steadily pressed their advantage. The attack from Yampol on 4 March by the First Ukrainian Front had the immediate consequence of ripping a gap between the two panzer armies, although Manstein's determined effort to hold the flanks kept the damage somewhat limited. Nonetheless, by the twenty-third, yet another German force had been encircled in a Kessel, this time at Tarnopol.[62]

Although the force trapped at Tarnopol was much smaller than that at Cherkassy-Korsun, the episode illustrates clearly the direction of Hitler's thinking. On 8 March, in Führer Order No. 11, he declared a new policy of *festen Plätze* (fortified places), the object of which was to deny the enemy key cities and junctions, tie down his forces, and blunt the momentum of his offensive, but which in reality merely preordained encirclements. As at Kovel, on 10 March, Tarnopol was declared a "festen Platz that was to be held to the last man" even though it had no fortifications or airfield, not to mention insufficient troops and supplies to defend against an aggressive Soviet attack. Although the city was not surrounded until the twenty-third, the Germans made few preparations for its supply. Not until the twenty-fifth was a relief attack mounted to bring a convoy of supplies into the besieged city, and even this quickly degenerated into a farce. Despite the fact that the supply trucks never arrived from Lvov and the roughly forty-six hundred men inside the city had not been given permission to break out, the battle group was, nonetheless, ordered to launch its attack. It encountered heavily mined roads, fierce antitank defenses, flank attacks from Soviet tanks, and aerial assaults that forced the Germans to give up the attempt. Since Tarnopol had no airfield, the Luftwaffe tried supplying the pocket by air drops, with the result that most of the supplies fell into enemy hands. The next relief attempt was not made until 11 April, when the Ninth SS Panzer set out in a driving rain and deep mud. Hitler at first refused to allow the besieged men to break out, then relented the next day. By this time, however, the Kessel had been reduced to a few thousand yards, with the German defenders fighting desperately from room to room under massive Soviet artillery fire. Although the remaining troops, some fifteen hundred, attempted a breakout on the fifteenth, it was too late: only fifty-five men were able to make it successfully out of the pocket.[63]

Despite the human tragedy at Tarnopol, a larger drama was playing out at the same time just to the south, where the Soviet breakthrough at Yampol had left the First Panzer Army in a potentially disastrous position, threatened with encirclement and destruction. Even as elements of the Fourth Panzer Army were trapped at Tarnopol, the main Soviet thrust was directed against its neighbor to the south. Here, both the First and the Second Ukrainian Fronts aimed at nothing less than a double envelopment of the most powerful formation in Army Group South that, if successful, would shatter the entire southern wing of the eastern front. The Stavka had assembled overwhelming power to strike the decisive blow: 1.5 million men, over two thousand AFVs, and more than one thousand combat aircraft against a force a fraction of this size. Although Hube's army had a preponderance of the armored strength of Army Group South, he could muster only ninety-six battle tanks and sixty-four assault guns to bolster his 211,000 troops. Nor could this smaller force respond more nimbly to an enemy attack, for the demotorization of the army meant that horses had to fill the role of trucks, effectively limiting its mobility.[64]

Since the Eighth Army to the south was still reeling from the ordeal at Cherkassy-Korsun and had only 152,000 men and virtually no tanks, it could not be expected to provide its neighbor any help in an emergency. In any case, Konev's offensive pushed it back through Uman to the Bug River, effectively eliminating the Eighth Army as an anchor for the First Panzer Army's right wing. The chronic German lack of strength had by now reached alarming proportions, with the result that, even though a large proportion of the enemy infantry was composed of so-called booty Ukrainians, poorly trained recruits scooped up as the Red Army advanced westward, the sheer weight of numbers was too much for the overstrained German divisions. Manstein complained, to no avail, that, although his army group had lost over 405,000 men between July 1943 and January 1944, it had received barely more than half that number in replacements and that even these were primarily young, hastily trained boys rushed to the front. Given the growing reality of a multifront war, however, there was little Manstein could do but chafe as his replacements went increasingly to Western Europe while the Red Army was steadily bolstered with Lend-Lease deliveries from its Western allies. With the hand he was dealt, then, Manstein had little chance to prevent the enemy from encircling areas of its choosing.[65]

The powerful Soviet attack on 4 March thus succeeded in opening a gap between the beleaguered First and Fourth Panzer Armies that, despite their frantic efforts, could merely be contained, not closed. The dam finally broke on the twenty-first, when the three tank armies of Zhukov's First Ukrainian Front burst through the left flank of the First Panzer Army and began racing to the south, pushing the remnants of the German line in front of them. By the twenty-fourth, they had crossed the Dniester into Rumania and five days later reached Cernovicy (Chernovtsy) on the Prut. In the meantime, the Soviet Fourth Tank Army turned eastward and, on the twenty-seventh, met spearheads of the Thirty-eighth Army at Kamenets-Podolsky, thus closing the pincers around the First Panzer Army at Kamenets-Podolsky. Soviet losses had been noticeably high—the Third Guards Tank Army lost 70 percent of its tanks, while the Fourth Tank Army had only sixty remaining—but, despite their skill at shooting up enemy tanks, the Germans could not prevent their own encirclement. On the last day of the month, the situation grew even grimmer as units from both the First and the Second Ukrainian Fronts, the latter having shattered the Eighth Army's defenses, joined at Chotin. The First Panzer Army and elements of the Fourth Panzer Army (Group Mauss, consisting of the Seventh Panzer Division, the First SS Leibstandarte Adolf Hitler, and the Sixty-eighth Infantry Division) were now enveloped both north and south of the Dniester. Worse, within this double envelopment, Hube's forces were initially split into at least three separate pockets. In all, the Soviets had bagged 220,000 troops, lacking artillery, munitions, and fuel, and possessing fewer than one hundred AFVs. In preparation for a breakout, Hube directed his troops to begin destroying nonessential vehicles and requisitioning every *panje* wagon they could seize. As always, however, Hitler's initial instinct ran in a different direction: he was determined to hold fast and, despite the lessons of Stalingrad and Cherkassy-Korsun, supply the Kessel from the air.[66]

Manstein, realizing a catastrophe that would eclipse even Stalingrad was facing his army group, resolved on decisive action. Already on the twenty-third, even before the First Panzer Army had been fully encircled, he had demanded permission to order a breakout. In addition, he proposed that powerful forces be transferred from the west to plug the gap between the First and the Fourth Panzer Armies. At noon the next day, he went a step further, effectively presenting Hitler with an ultimatum: unless instructed otherwise, he would give the order to break out at 3:00 P.M. The answer from Führer Headquarters was both cryptic and cynical. Manstein received permission to allow the First Panzer Army to fight its way westward but was told that it was also to hold its present position. How to do this, given its lack of strength, was left unclear.[67]

On the twenty-fifth, Manstein was summoned to meet Hitler at Berchtesgaden, although before he left the field marshal gave orders to prepare plans for a breakout. That afternoon at the Berghof, Hitler and Manstein engaged in a stormy discussion. Challenging Hitler directly, the field marshal insisted that the First Panzer Army had to break out immediately and demanded that he be given fresh troops to open a path from the west. Hitler brusquely rejected any idea of retreat while ridiculing notions of operational maneuver as merely a ruse for withdrawal. Manstein, he said, had squandered all the troops he had been given and wanted always to go back but never hold anywhere. For his part, Manstein then openly confronted the Führer with a litany of his failed decisions over the previous weeks, which caused a furious Hitler abruptly to break off the discussion. Disgusted, Manstein demanded that Hitler's adjutant, Schmundt, tell the Führer that he saw no purpose to continuing to lead the army group if Hitler did not approve his demands. Much to his surprise, however, when discussions resumed at the evening conference, not only was Manstein treated with outward friendliness by Hitler, but he was also given permission for a breakout. More astonishing, the Führer also agreed that the Second SS Panzer Corps was to be transferred immediately from France, along with two infantry divisions from Hungary. This latter decision must have been especially painful for Hitler since it not only flew in the face of Führer Directive No. 51 to give priority to the west but also jeopardized this strategy just when the Anglo-American invasion appeared imminent. Manstein, apparently, had triumphed across the board, but at a personal price that would soon be apparent.[68]

The field marshal now hurried back to his headquarters to prepare an operation that would not only save the First Panzer Army but also deal his old adversary, Zhukov, one final surprise. Believing that the fate of the First Panzer Army had already been decided, the Stavka on 22 March had changed its operational plans, ordering the bulk of the Second Ukrainian Front to turn southeast in order to destroy Army Group A north of the Black Sea. At the same time, Zhukov, assuming that German forces would attempt to break out to the south, had placed the bulk of his forces in that direction. Manstein, however, realized that any breakout to the south would have to cross a double line of enemy forces and, even if successful, would result in the First Panzer Army being pushed to the south against the Carpathians, thus opening a gigantic breach between itself and the Fourth Panzer Army. Instead, the field marshal proposed a breakout to the west that would be the shortest route to the German front, cut across enemy supply lines, and, perhaps most importantly, take the Russians completely by surprise. Against Hube's vehement opposition, but armed with intelligence information that confirmed his suspicions about enemy dispositions, Manstein ordered the breakout to the west to begin on 28 March. As the operation began that morning in a blinding snowstorm that provided cover, it soon became apparent that the Germans had achieved complete surprise. Not only were enemy positions quickly overrun, but the next day Zhukov also continued dispatching units to the south, evidently unaware of Manstein's intention. Not until 1 April did he recognize his mistake, but by then it was too late. On the second, as he belatedly tried to turn his units around and send them north, his frustration showed in a futile attempt to persuade the escaping Germans to surrender by threatening all who did not with death. That his offer was rejected was no surprise. The true shock that day, the announcement that Manstein was relinquishing his command, was the result of a decision hundreds of miles to the west.[69]

On the thirtieth, Manstein, along with Kleist, the commander of Army Group A, who had also requested permission for his forces to pull back from the Black Sea to the Bug, had once more been summoned to the Berghof. Having on a number of occasions since January openly challenged Hitler's military leadership in front of too many people, the field marshal had few doubts as to what was likely to transpire. Hitler had been fuming since the twenty-third, stung by Manstein's criticisms, and resentful that concessions had been wrung from him. On his arrival, Manstein was told by Zeitzler that Goering, Himmler, and Keitel had been conspiring against him and that Zeitzler's own offer to resign had been rejected. That evening, having indicated his desire to go in another direction, the Führer relieved Manstein and Kleist of their commands, replacing them with Model and Schörner, both tough generals and favorites of Hitler's known for their tenacity and defensive prowess. They were not desk-bound leaders, what Goebbels scornfully termed "hemorrhoid generals," but men who led from the front. Just as importantly, both were politically loyal. The time of *operations*, which he contemptuously regarded as a euphemism for retreat, Hitler clearly indicated, had come to an end. It was now time for rigorous measures to be taken and for the National Socialist fighting spirit to be instilled in the troops. More than just a change in operational styles was evident, for Hitler had never lost his aversion to the old military aristocracy, of whom Manstein and Kleist were prominent representatives. By contrast, Schörner, a convinced Nazi since the early 1930s, and Model, "a man with a National Socialist heart," both had middle-class roots and were attuned to Nazi ideals. They, at least, could be trusted to do the Führer's will, thus overcoming the crisis in confidence between Hitler and his army group commanders. The dismissal of Manstein and Kleist thus illustrated Hitler's continuing makeover of the army into a National Socialist instrument.[70]

Since Model's arrival at Army Group South headquarters in Lvov was delayed by a snowstorm, the actual handover of power did not take place until 2 April. By then, Zhukov had responded with furious assaults in a futile attempt to stop the "wandering pocket" from moving westward toward German lines. His action, however, was too late. On the third, the Germans had thrown back the Soviet attacks, and, on the night of the fourth, ammunition and gasoline had been flown into the pocket, fortifying Hube's forces. The next morning, the Ninth and Tenth SS Panzer Divisions of the Second SS Panzer Corps, which had been hurriedly dispatched from France, launched a powerful attack, supported by the two infantry divisions sent from Hungary, that resulted, the next day, in a linkup with the Sixth Panzer Division, the spearhead of the First Panzer Army. Not only was the enemy encirclement broken, but the First Panzer Army had also been able to bring out virtually all its tanks, artillery, heavy equipment, and wounded. Just as surprising, despite the hard fighting, its losses were not particularly high, with fewer than six thousand reported dead or missing. More importantly, it remained intact as an operational fighting formation. Indeed, in contrast with the units that emerged from the Cherkassy-Korsun pocket, the men of the First Panzer Army were sent immediately after their rescue back into the attack.[71]

Although Hitler had issued an operational order that same 2 April hopefully declaring that the Russian offensive was spent and that the front would soon be stabilized, the reality was different as fighting continued through April into early May. Hitler's determination to hold the Crimea had also yielded to reality. On 10 April, Odessa, the great port on the Black Sea vital to supplying the Crimea, had fallen, with the entire peninsula lost by early May. Although furious at events in the Crimea and threatening courts-martial of the "defeatist" generals involved, Hitler was, nevertheless, forced, in another painful humiliation, to authorize the evacuation of Sevastopol by sea on the night of 8–9 May. The brilliant triumphs of two years earlier were now nothing but a distant memory. By the time the Soviet offensive against Army Group South— the longest and bloodiest of the war, lasting from late December 1943 to early May 1944—had come to an end, the Germans had been pushed back, in places, some six hundred miles, with the physical and materiel strength of the troops exhausted. Soviet success, however, had been bought at an astounding price. Over half the 2,230,000 Soviet troops thrown into the offensive, some 1,192,900, had been lost as casualties, of whom 288,600 were dead or missing. The actual toll was almost certainly higher, however, since, as it moved through Ukraine, the Red Army typically pressed men of the liberated areas into immediate service. Hastily

trained, and regarded as little more than cannon fodder, these unfortunate men died in great numbers without being reported. Soviet materiel
losses were also extraordinarily heavy, with 4,666 AFVs and 676 aircraft
lost. By contrast, German losses were relatively light, with "only" 250,956
men reported as casualties (of whom 41,907 were reported dead and
51,161 missing). Given the virtually complete lack of German reserves,
however, these losses were crippling, a situation obvious to all but the
Führer, who even now, with the eastern front finally restored to some
semblance of stability, was again planning new offensives after the repelling of the Allied invasion of France.[72]

For the Germans, the grim test of an all-out two-front war had been
inevitable since their failure at Stalingrad, a threat that increasingly
influenced all major decisions. Indeed, the second front existed before
it became a reality, for the very threat of an assault somewhere along the
broad coast of Fortress Europe had compelled the Germans to split their
forces, perhaps more severely than necessary, and divide their command
to await an invasion that seemingly never came. The strain had taken
its toll within the higher levels of the military and political command.
Hitler increasingly demanded absolute loyalty from his generals, while
a mood of resignation and nervous exhaustion had set in at the OKH.
Speer thought that a shakeup in the command structure was necessary
to revitalize the military leadership, while Guderian, convinced that, if
used properly, his tanks could still turn the situation around, characterized Zeitzler and the OKH as a bunch of defeatists. By the spring of 1944,
the tensions between the OKH and the OKW over the division of the
armed forces had boiled over. "Fifty-three percent of the Army is fighting in Russia for the existence of the German people," claimed one bitter witticism making the rounds at the OKH, "and the other forty-seven
percent is sitting in Western Europe waiting for an invasion that doesn't
come." Even more subversive, with its comparison to 1918, was the suggestion of decisive resources squandered, that "Germany had lost World
War I because of the Navy in being and will lose this one because of the
Army in being." The sniping between the OKH and OKW reached such
levels, in fact, that Hitler ordered Jodl to do a strategic survey to justify
the dispositions based on the overall German situation.[73]

The assessment, when completed, generally supported the OKW's
position, noting that, of the 341 operational units of the army and
Waffen-SS, only 131 (or just 38 percent) were deployed outside the east
or the home front. Of these, just forty-one divisions had the arms and
equipment suitable for employment on the eastern front, but thirty-two
of them were already engaged in fighting (in Italy, in Finland, or against

the partisans) or were defending the most-threatened coastal areas (Normandy). With specific reference to infantry and armored divisions, the distribution was even more favorable to the Ostfront, with only 46 of 162 of the former (28 percent) and 11 of 34 of the latter (32 percent) not detailed to the east. Moreover, Jodl warned, an Allied landing in the west that was not immediately defeated would, because of the lack of available reserves, result in the rapid loss of the war.[74]

Although these observations were true enough, they certainly must have been of scant comfort to those on the eastern front who, since Stalingrad, had been fighting a noticeably lopsided battle of men and materiel. A mere recitation of numbers of divisions did little to convey the reality facing the fought-out, understrength units of the Ostheer, whose thinning ranks led to a growing disparity with their Soviet counterparts. By late May 1944, German strength stood at nearly 2,243,000 men, while the Red Army numbered almost 6,100,000, meaning that the Soviet surplus of 3,857,000 troops was 1.7 times greater than the total number of Germans. Despite the threat of a second front, in the spring of 1944 the eastern front remained the most important European theater of war. While the Soviets deployed 383 large units in the east (not including reserves), the Western allies had a total of only 120 divisions, over 70 percent of which were either in England (54), in Iceland (2), or in Africa and the Middle East (30) and, thus, not involved in active fighting. Only the introduction of the Panther and Tiger tanks, with their superior striking power, had allowed the Germans to stabilize the front, although their impact was not as great as had been hoped since only about 30 percent were operational at any one time.[75]

Still, with the apparent stabilization of the southern sector of the eastern front, ramshackle though it was, German leaders could breathe a bit more easily. Their forces in the center and north appeared to be holding fast, while the Red Army, at the closest, was almost six hundred miles from Berlin. Moreover, the Soviets themselves gave no indication of further imminent action, evidently contenting themselves with consolidating their gains and preparing their next step. As a result, despite the near disaster of the previous months, in the spring of 1944 the Ostfront lay in the shadow of anticipated events in the west. The invasion would come, Hitler expected, in May or June, but the atmosphere at the Berghof betrayed a deceptive calm, indeed, at times almost a strange euphoria. Hitler seemed fully confident that the invasion would be repulsed and anticipated with eagerness a mass assault on London with his new V-1 pilotless flying bombs, an onslaught that he believed would finish the English plutocracy. Even Rommel had, evidently, overcome his early doubts and professed his assurances. Not a few of Hitler's military advisers asserted that, with the defeat of the invasion, the war would be won, while Goebbels talked confidently of a "second Dunkirk." Even the German public, perhaps influenced by the propaganda minister's latest efforts, invested great expectations in the impending invasion, seeing in it, not merely the resolution of a period of tension and uncertainty, but the possibility for a "quick decision of the war."[76]

For Hitler, as well, a defeat of the invasion was the great chance, the last opportunity to achieve a decisive turning point in the war. Germany, he believed (given the example of World War I), had no hope if it remained on the defensive. In order to win time and break the "unnatural alliance" of his enemies, itself an uneasy association of capitalists and Communists, Germany needed to break out of this "unfruitful defensive" and regain the initiative. This, above all, was a matter of fanatic will. Germany, Hitler asserted, needed to achieve a great victory in order to demonstrate to its enemies that they could not win the war. Just as the iron will of Stalin had saved Russia from collapse in the autumn of 1941, he argued, so now his will would transform the bleak situation. It was, he thought, reminiscent of the period of struggle in the 1920s, when a few determined individuals with a powerful belief in an idea created a movement with its own revolutionary dynamic that accomplished the seemingly impossible. Just as the street agitator had swept to power and achieved undreamed-of triumphs, so now, in the spring of 1944, a few key victories would tip the balance and unleash an unstoppable momentum. The Germans had lost World War I, Hitler believed, because the imperial leadership had given up too soon, a mistake he would not repeat. Always willing to stake everything on an all-or-nothing gamble, he conjured visions of a new "miracle of 1940," of a decisive triumph in the west that would free Germany from the nightmare of a two-front war.[77]

To dismiss Hitler's vision as irrational or unrealistic would miss the mark. Typically, it was a curious mixture of clear-sighted realism and gross self-delusion, of a cogent understanding of Germany's predicament and little sense of its limitations. In truth, at least for a flickering moment, the prospects for victory in the west, after all, appeared not unfavorable. Industrial output was rising, which meant that enough tanks and weapons were being produced to equip new divisions for the west and replace some of the losses in the east. Synthetic oil production had peaked, with stocks of aviation fuel at their highest since 1941. Under Speer's guidance, fighter plane production rose spectacularly, with the result that the Luftwaffe strength in January 1944 of 5,585 planes was over 1,600 more than the year before. Moreover, in the autumn and winter of 1943–1944, the American strategic bombing campaign had been suspended as a result of unacceptable losses. Under Rommel's energetic guidance, defensive preparations in the west along the Normandy coast had also accelerated. Hitler had high hopes for the technologically advanced V weapons as well as a new type of submarine that would enable the American supply line to Great Britain to be cut. In addition, Soviet manpower reserves were not inexhaustible, and the May pause seemed to indicate that the Red Army had passed its culmination point. Finally, the Allied invasion of France was a complicated operation that required months of preparation. If defeated, as Jodl noted, it could not simply be repeated any time soon, and a failure, Hitler anticipated, would result in a severe political crisis in Great Britain and provide Germany an opportunity again to seize the initiative.[78]

These hopes, however, proved illusory. As far back as the autumn of 1943, Hitler had planned to stabilize the eastern front in order to transfer troops west to defeat the Allied invasion of France. Then, once that had been accomplished, he would transfer units back to the east in order to reconquer the vital Ukraine. With Führer Directive No. 51 of November 1943, he had even attempted to enact the first part of this scenario, which was, perhaps, the only strategic option he had left. The Soviets, however, had refused to cooperate and play their assigned role. Instead of sitting passively through the winter, the Red Army had launched a series of continuous offensives that had drained German resources and brought the Ostheer to the breaking point. Although the Second SS Panzer Corps, reluctantly dispatched from France back to the east, had finally brought a halt to the Soviet offensive, its absence in June was to play a key role in the success of the Normandy landing, a circumstance that Hitler complained of bitterly after the fact. Just as crucially, the provision of long-range fighter support allowed a resumption of the American strategic bombing campaign, with devastating consequences. As Allied bombers targeted oil production and synthetic fuel facilities, aircraft engine plants, and key rail yards, any hope the Nazis had of winning the aerial war over Germany was crushed. By mid-May, Speer later conceded, "a new era in the air war" had begun, one that meant "the end of German armaments production." The technological war had been decided; new miracle weapons could no longer save Germany.[79]

In any case, Hitler himself bore considerable responsibility for the failure of his strategy. In his unwillingness to sacrifice land for time, to allow his armies in the east to retreat to more defensible positions and preserve manpower, he had lost the former and gained none of the latter. Worse, in anticipating the decisive blow in the west, he had stripped the Ostheer of its reserves, leaving it exposed and vulnerable to Soviet attack. It would, its commanders realized, have to bear the brunt of the Red storm alone while hoping for a quick decision in the west that would free forces to be sent back to the Ostfront. Manstein's feat in extricating the First Panzer Army and stabilizing the eastern front had averted catastrophe, but the bleak reality of a multifront war now awaited. Within two months, all Hitler's remaining illusions would be shattered and Germany plunged into the abyss. His strategy of striking in the west and holding in the east would fail for the simple reason that the Ostheer was too weak to hold the line. From June 1944 to the end of the war, however, some 3 million Germans would lose their lives, while Germany would suffer its worst devastation since the Thirty Years' War. Hitler's determination not to preside over another November 1918 would, in fact, result in the very thing he had warned was the goal of the Jewish conspiracy: the extinction of Germany.

9

Disintegration

The end of the prolonged fighting into the spring of 1944 had left the eastern front dangerously skewed from the German perspective. South of the Pripet Marshes, Soviet advances in Ukraine had pushed a huge bulge far to the west, only 150 miles from Warsaw. North of the great swamp, however, Army Group Center's success at holding off the Red Army in the winter fighting meant that German troops not only occupied most of Belorussia but also still held a bridgehead east of the Dnieper. The front line now ran roughly where it was in mid-July 1941, at the end of the first German leap into Russia. German possession of this so-called Belorussian balcony posed both grave risks and, to Hitler, strategic possibilities. The danger was obvious to anyone who looked at a map: a breakthrough at Kovel, at the southwestern edge of the Pripet, would allow the Soviets two great opportunities. Red Army forces could be turned to the southwest, with the goal of striking deep into Hungary and Rumania, knocking these German allies out of the war, and encircling and destroying Army Group South. If, however, they pushed to the northwest through Warsaw and on to Danzig, both Army Groups Center and North might be bagged in a giant pocket, the heart of the German position in the east ripped apart, and the way to Berlin, only 320 miles to the west, completely open. In a single action, the OKH feared, the Soviets would strike the death blow to the German war effort.[1]

Hitler was not unaware of the dangers, but he preferred to focus on the opportunity afforded by the German position. In effect, he modeled his behavior on that of his rival dictator, Stalin, who in the summer of 1942, in a similarly dangerous position, had issued his famous "Not one step back" order and insisted on holding bridgeheads across the Don, with the result that a decisive Soviet counterattack had reversed the situation at Stalingrad and allowed the Red Army to sweep to the west. Now, in the summer of 1944, Hitler counted on pulling off a similar feat that would restore the initiative to Germany. Believing that the prolonged, costly Soviet winter offensive in Ukraine had finally bled the Red Army dry, much as the Wehrmacht had been ground down by persistent Soviet resistance at Stalingrad, Hitler hoped to blunt the anticipated Russian offensive, then launch the game-changing German response. Human memory, of course, can be dangerously selective, and, although Hitler correctly remembered the success of the Soviet counterstrike in the autumn of 1942, he ignored the key contextual background that allowed that achievement. The Soviets' triumph had depended on German weakness, failures of leadership, and distraction by events elsewhere as well as a good bit of aid from their Western allies. In 1944, as two years earlier, the balance of all these factors again favored Stalin, not Hitler.

From the OKH's viewpoint, both options available to the enemy had much to recommend them since, if executed properly, either could lead to a decisive, war-ending victory for the Soviets. Here, perhaps, German analysts were guilty of a bit of hubris since they thought that the Soviets would act as they would in a similar situation—to seek to win the war in one bold, decisive blow. OKH staffers originally believed that the Soviets would push the so-called Balkan solution since Ukraine had been the focal point of enemy action for the past year, the bulk of Red Army tank units remained in the south, and Stalin was known to have a desire to get his forces into the Balkans before his Western allies could get a foot in the door. In addition, Southeastern Europe and the Dardanelles had been the traditional focal point of Russian expansion, while the Germans feared that the loss of Rumanian oil would cause a quick end to the war. Much, then, supported the notion of a push to the southwest. By spring 1944, however, many in German intelligence had begun to favor the Baltic solution, not only because of reported enemy troop movements, but also because it was the sort of operation that appealed to German sensibilities. If the Soviets broke out at Kovel and raced to the northwest, they could, in a single bold stroke reminiscent of the brilliant German victory in France four years earlier, end the war by trapping Army Groups Center and North against the Baltic Sea. Not only were distances short and the eastern Polish countryside ideal for mobile warfare, but the exposed Soviet left flank would also be partly covered by the Vistula River. The irony, that spring, was that, while the OKW hoped to prepare a second Dunkirk for the Western allies along the Channel coast, the OKH feared its own Dunkirk along the Baltic.[2]

Anticipating a bold Soviet stroke whichever way they decided to turn, neither the OKH nor Foreign Armies East initially paid much attention to the possibility of a frontal offensive against the Belorussian balcony. Indeed, much spoke against it; an attacker here would have to fight through the endless forests and swamps of Belorussia just to reach the Vistula, almost five hundred miles to the west. In addition, an offensive north of the Pripet struck the Germans as implausible since, even if operationally successful, it would not likely be decisive in a strategic, war-winning sense. Moreover, the OKH misinterpreted the ability of Army Group Center to maintain its front through the winter as indicative of German strength and Soviet weakness. Instead, it resulted from a combination of factors that would be absent in the summer. The Germans had fended off Soviet attacks by using nimble, flexible defensive tactics reminiscent of World War I, in which defenses in depth were prepared so that, when faced with an attack, German forces could withdraw to rear positions, allowing the enemy to punch into air. Then, at the proper moment, counterattacks would snap the Germans back to their approximate original positions. In the summer, however, Hitler would insist on an inflexible, static defense of forward positions that would deny the use of such tactics. More to the point, German troops, dispersed thinly among scattered strongpoints that often could not maintain contact with each other, had neither the front strength nor the reserves necessary to contain enemy breakthroughs. In addition, a good bit of German defensive success in the center had been the result, as Evan Mawdsley put it, of the Stavka reinforcing success and starving failure. In the winter of 1943-1944, Soviet armies in other sectors, especially in Ukraine, had performed much better and, thus, had been given priority in men and equipment. Red Army forces in the center, achieving fewer results, had simply not been reinforced. With the focal point of the Soviet summer offensive in the center, however, this would no longer be the case.[3]

Ironically, however, despite the earlier Soviet willingness to gamble on large, war-winning offensives, and just as the Germans had begun to credit the Soviets with the ability to execute such operations, Stalin himself had decided that such grandiose schemes were beyond Soviet capabilities. Rather than summon its courage, then, in early spring 1944, the Stavka rejected both the Balkan and the Baltic solutions in favor of a third option: use the overwhelming Soviet preponderance in strength to launch a series of staggered offensives, starting from north to south, that would force the Germans to fight everywhere at once and, thus, be unable to concentrate their scarce resources. The initial blow would fall on the Finnish army in Karelia, to be followed in succession by attacks in Belorussia and in northern and southern Ukraine. In effect, there would not be a single Schwerpunkt, although the attack against Army Group

Center would form the main effort. Here, the Soviets hoped to pull off a complicated plan that envisaged, in rapid pincer movements, a quick initial encirclement of Vitebsk and Bobruisk, the German anchor positions at the northern and southern ends of the salient, even as mobile units moved quickly west in a deep envelopment centered on Minsk. Even then, Soviet forces were not to stop but to thrust beyond Minsk on either side, with forces on the right flank hoping to trap as much of Army Group North as possible, while the southern thrust, aided by units shoving through Kovel, would seize Brest-Litovsk before converging on Warsaw. This was not a typical Soviet mass attack across a broad front but one based on the German model that concentrated overwhelming force in key sectors to achieve a breakthrough, then aimed to exploit it through rapid movement to encircle and destroy the enemy defenders. Stalin, suspicious of overly complicated maneuver schemes, initially opposed the idea but was, ultimately, persuaded to accept it. An ambitious plan, although not the war-winning Baltic solution feared by the Germans, it proposed in one leap the liberation of Belorussia and a sweep to the Vistula.[4]

Given the serious German weaknesses and lack of mobility on the Ostfront, the key to Hitler's strategy of holding on in the east and striking in the west was to identify the Soviet Schwerpunkt correctly. Since the Ostheer had neither the mobility nor the operational reserve to pinch off a Soviet breakthrough and, thus, prevent it from turning into a catastrophe, all depended on blunting the Soviet attack at the outset and successfully defending German frontline positions. Since no reinforcements could be expected from the west until the defeat of the Western allies' invasion, the only chance for successful static operations was to identify correctly the Schwerpunkt of the enemy offensive and prepare adequate defenses and forces to counter it. Despite differences in opinion as to the ultimate direction of the enemy summer offensive, the OKH and Foreign Armies East could agree on at least one thing: regardless of whether the Soviets headed for the Balkans or the Baltic, the focal point of their attack would be Kovel. This assessment played into the hands of Field Marshal Model, the aggressive and predatory commander of Army Group North Ukraine, whose units defended the Kovel area, and who now saw a chance to strengthen his forces at the expense of his passive colleague to the north, Ernst Busch. Not surprisingly, on 20 May, Hitler yielded to Model's urging and ordered the powerful Fifty-sixth Panzer Corps transferred to Army Group North Ukraine. At one blow, Army Group Center thus lost 88 percent of its tanks, 50 percent of its tank destroyers, and 33 percent of its heavy artillery.[5]

While on paper what remained of Army Group Center still seemed a formidable force, in reality it was little more than a house of cards. Its four armies (the Third Panzer to the north at Vitebsk, the Fourth in the center defending Orsha and Mogilev, the Ninth to the south in front of Bobruisk, and the Second protecting the far right flank) theoretically possessed forty-seven divisions, but many of them were still in the process of being created or restructured, while others were simply burned out. Numerous security units were not even at the front but engaged in the rear fighting the partisans, who now numbered around 150,000. In reality, then, the army group possessed about thirty-four functional divisions, of which only twenty-nine were directly at the front. Of these, there existed a vast discrepancy between their nominal and their actual strength. On paper, these units numbered some 486,000 men, although only a bit over 336,000 if the Second Army, which was not initially involved in the attack in the Belorussian salient, is removed. Of these, roughly 166,000 were frontline combat troops who faced some 1.25 million Red Army soldiers massed for the first phase of the attack, giving the enemy a seven-and-a-half-to-one superiority in manpower. In total, the Soviets had assembled over 2.5 million men for the entire operation, a figure that swamped corresponding German totals.[6]

Just as serious was the almost complete lack of tanks; the great bulk of the Ostheer's panzers were in southern sectors of the front, while most new production had been sent to the west. The term *Third Panzer Army* was a complete misnomer, for example, since it had no actual battle tanks and only seventy-six assault guns. In fact, at the beginning of June, only a single large tank unit existed on the entire northern half of the eastern front (the Twelfth Panzer Division), and it belonged to Army Group North. Even with the addition of the Twentieth Panzer Division, which was dispatched from Army Group North Ukraine to Army Group Center just before the start of the offensive, the three armies facing the Soviet onslaught possessed only 118 battle tanks and 377 assault guns, as against an enemy force of 2,715 battle tanks and 1,355 assault guns—and these figures were for the first phase alone. For the second phase, the Soviets had a force of 1,126 tanks and 622 assault guns. The inferiority of German artillery proved just as marked (2,589 barrels against 24,383), but it was the discrepancy in aerial strength that made a mockery of Hitler's notion of static defense. Throughout the eastern campaign, the Luftwaffe had often intervened at critical moments to overcome army weaknesses and provide the margin of victory. Given the demotorization of the Ostheer and its almost complete lack of mobility (as noted above, the Third Panzer Army had no battle tanks but did have sixty thousand horses), the Luftwaffe would again have to play a vital role if a defensive front was to be maintained. On the eve of the battle, however, Luftflotte 6 had only 602 operational aircraft, of which little more than a third were fighters or ground attack aircraft. Even these were limited in their activity because of chronic shortages of fuel and spare parts. As with ground forces, the Red Air Force enjoyed a staggering numerical advantage, with over four thousand fighters/ground attack planes. Across the board, then, the Soviets possessed a crushing material superiority—at the initial point of attack upwards of ten to one—that meant that they could achieve a breakthrough at any point they chose to mass forces. Amazingly, in the summer of 1944, they had mobilized a force roughly similar in size to that of the German invasion force three years earlier, but on a front a third the size; Bagration, in effect, was on a larger scale than Barbarossa. Since the Germans had only a fraction of the force available to the Red Army in 1941, this meant that Army Group Center, although perhaps capable of local resistance, would be unable to mount any mobile or operational defense. Nor, given the virtually complete absence of operational reserves, could it hope to launch a decisive counterattack to pinch off any enemy breakthrough. Moreover, it could not even envision a shortening of the front to escape the looming danger, given Hitler's absolute prohibition of tactical withdrawals and aversion to construction of river defense lines.[7]

Just at the time the Soviets were preparing a crushing offensive in the center, then, the Germans were playing into their hands by stripping the already outnumbered forces available to Army Group Center and sending them to Model's command. Traditional accounts emphasize a failure of German intelligence, but this was not really the entire story. In May and June, increased intelligence gathering, especially by individual armies, but also by Foreign Armies East, picked up urgent indications that the main blow might come north of Pripet and be directed at Busch's forces. Army Group Center headquarters, however, took these new estimates less seriously than did its counterparts at the front, nor could the changing assessment from Foreign Armies East, which warned of a series of Soviet attacks and increasing danger in Belorussia, alter the perceptions at the OKH and Army Group Center. They, and Hitler, continued to focus on Kovel as the likely Schwerpunkt.[8]

In any case, even had this information been embraced, it was too late; Army Group Center was far too weak to avert defeat, although, with more prescience, it might have avoided catastrophe. Moreover, Hitler's insistence on static defense and Busch's obsequiousness and blind faith both exacerbated the fundamental problem of German inferiority in strength. With his fortified places order of 8 March 1944, Hitler had seemingly fallen victim to a Verdun mentality reminiscent of World War I and put exaggerated faith in the ability of strongpoints to stem "the Red flood." Despite the sacrifice of some fortress troops at Kovel, Tarnopol, and Kamenets-Podolsky in March and April, the slowing of enemy momentum seemed to confirm his formula, thus reinforcing his determination not to yield—this despite the fact that the Soviet offensive ground to a halt largely because it simply ran out of steam and because of faulty command decisions, not because of the fortified places doctrine. Further compounding the problem was the Führer's insistence on designating so many cities as fortified places despite the fact that, in view of the extreme shortages of manpower and building materials, there existed no hope of ever actually making them strongpoints, nor would they likely ever be relieved if they were besieged by the enemy. In effect, since troops in areas designated as fortified places could be withdrawn only with his express approval, all his order did was to ensure that large numbers of men would be trapped in indefensible places. In a clear lose-lose situation, not only would the fortified places prove too weak to hinder Soviet momentum, especially since their advance forces had been told simply to bypass these areas, much as the Germans had done in 1941, but also the overstretched German defense would be denied the use of those forces trapped in the static positions to plug the holes in the front created by the Soviet attack.[9]

Nor could the commander of Army Group Center be expected to use his own judgment to save his men since any hope that the blindly loyal and obsequious Busch would challenge Hitler evaporated on 20 May. At a conference at Führer Headquarters, the field marshal had, in view of the growing evidence of a Soviet buildup, feebly attempted to make Hitler aware of the looming danger to Army Group Center. The Führer, however, flew into a rage, cutting Busch to the core with his acid remark that he had not known that he "belonged to those generals who were always looking to the rear." Any inclination Busch might have had to confront Hitler vanished as he now endeavored to prove his absolute loyalty, going so far as to call a conference of his own army commanders on the twenty-fourth for the sole purpose of impressing on them the Führer's determination to hold the line at all costs. More damaging, he also informed them that they should curtail construction on rear lines of defense and concentrate only on holding the main battle line. Even though there had been some desultory preparation of defense lines based on various river systems (the so-called Bear, Tiger, and Beaver positions), both Busch and Hitler obstructed construction so consistently that there were virtually no prepared, fortified posts at these positions, so any hope of orderly withdrawals to defensible positions in the face of Soviet pressure was an illusion. Still, even though Hitler's meddling was certainly counterproductive, it was as much a symptom of the problem as its cause. The Germans simply had too few resources and were too over-stretched to have any really effective options left.[10]

When reports of Soviet attacks northwest and southeast of Vitebsk arrived in the morning hours of 22 June, the timing of the Soviet action, at least, came as no surprise to the Germans. It was, after all, the third anniversary of Operation Barbarossa, although, ironically, the one thing the Germans got right was purely by chance. The attack had originally been scheduled for the nineteenth but was postponed for three days by transportation problems. Even then, the staggered nature of the Soviet offensives meant that it took some time for the OKH to realize the enor-mity of what was transpiring. A diversionary offensive in the north in Karelia had begun on the tenth, while on the night of 19–20 June par-tisans had launched a coordinated attack against railroad bridges and transportation junctions in the rear of Army Group Center in an effort to paralyze German supply and troop movements. Even the assault at Vitebsk on the twenty-second, although accompanied by heavy air and artillery bombardments, initially seemed more of a probing attack than a full-fledged offensive. Even so, from the outset, the defenders at Vitebsk faced an untenable situation: they were already surrounded on three sides, so the Soviets merely had to pull the noose shut. Despite the Germans having exacted a stiff price from the attackers, by the twenty-fourth the Soviets had torn through the Third Panzer Army defenses and threatened to encircle German units in Vitebsk. Little could be done to help them, however, since on the twenty-third the enemy had extended the offensive to the Fourth Army in the middle at Orsha and Mogilev, while the next day Rokossovsky's forces in the south, having painstak-ingly constructed wooden causeways through the swamps, burst out to take units of the Ninth Army completely by surprise. Still expecting the Soviet Schwerpunkt to fall against Kovel, however, both the OKH and Busch were reluctant to transfer units from Army Group North Ukraine or the Second Army to blunt enemy momentum.[11]

Just as worrisome, whatever slim chance a static defense had at repuls-ing the Soviets had been shattered since, in contrast to their usual blud-geoning frontal assaults, the Russians had, instead, followed German principles in their attack. Using tightly concentrated infantry, artillery, and air attacks, they had focused on punching holes in a few key sec-tors, through which tank units burst and, without worrying about their flank, drove deep to the west in large encirclement movements. Since the Red Air Force had absolute air superiority—on 22 June, Army Group Center could muster only sixty-one operational fighters, the rest having been transferred to Normandy or to protect German industrial areas—and because Hitler had forbidden any flexible defense, German artillery had been stationed directly on the front, an easy target for destruction. The crisis point had, in fact, already been reached on the twenty-fourth as events spun out of control and the German command floundered about. Even though the Soviets had torn a twenty-five-mile-wide hole in the Third Panzer Army's front and threatened to trap the five divisions of the Fifty-third Army Corps in Vitebsk, Hitler, having declared the city a fortified place, initially refused to authorize a withdrawal but then, following appeals by Reinhardt, Zeitzler, and even Busch, in a strange compromise designed clearly to spare himself the embarrassment of admitting an error, directed that the city be held, but with only one of the five divisions. Even this nonsensical concession came too late, for, as the German leaders bickered, the Soviets snapped the trap shut at Vitebsk, dooming some thirty thousand troops. By the twenty-eighth, with the hole in his front grown to sixty miles and the retreat of his units having degenerated into a wild flight for safety, Reinhardt effectively gave up any effort at overall control, instead ordering the remnants of his shattered army merely to fight a delaying action westward, thus hindering as much as possible enemy breakthroughs.[12]

On the army group's right flank, the Ninth Army was the last to be attacked, on 24 June, but its situation descended into catastrophe almost immediately, partly because of the overwhelming Soviet superiority, and partly because of Rokossovsky's brilliant direction of the battle, especially the surprise effect of tank forces bursting out of the swamps. Already on the first day the Soviets blasted a twenty-mile-wide hole in the front, while, as to the north, German commanders faced the realization that they had no operational reserve to plug the gap. As on the left flank, here, too, the top German leadership worked at cross-purposes, leading to enormous confusion and dissipation of effort. On the twenty-fourth, for example, the Twentieth Panzer Division, which had been dispatched from Army Group North Ukraine just before the attack, was sent to seal off enemy penetrations on the Ninth Army's northern wing. With alarming reports of Soviet breakthroughs on the southern flank flooding in, however, Busch ordered it to break off its attack and move sixty miles south to counter the Soviet threat there. By the time it attacked at noon on the twenty-fifth, however, it was too late; its forty tanks could hardly slow, let alone stop, the enemy breakthrough. Despite the fact that, over the next few days, it destroyed some 213 enemy tanks near Bobruisk, this was a meaningless tactical success in view of the overwhelming Soviet superiority. Even in the best of circumstances, the Twentieth Panzer's forty panzers could hardly be expected to halt Rokossovsky's nine hundred tanks, let alone when it was forced to move hither and yon.[13]

If Busch's misdirection of the Twentieth Panzer was not bad enough, Hitler's intervention on the twenty-seventh produced total chaos. Although Bobruisk had also been proclaimed a fortified place, at 9:00 A.M. on the twenty-seventh the Ninth Army received permission to allow the Thirty-fifth Army Corps and the Forty-first Panzer Corps to break out from the threatening encirclement. Fifteen minutes later, however, at Hitler's behest, a counterorder followed from army group headquarters withdrawing permission to retreat. Chaos and tumult ensued, with some units choosing to defend the city, some fleeing, and some that had begun a withdrawal attempting to return to the city. Not until 4:00 P.M. did the Ninth Army receive a new order, but it hardly clarified the situation. As at Vitebsk, all but one of the surrounded units received permission to break out, but, as in the north, by then it was too late: some seventy thousand German troops, leaderless, confused, and panicky, milled about in the pocket awaiting orders. Having declared Bobruisk a fortified place, Hitler was too proud to admit his mistake. Officers at Ninth Army headquarters condemned this sequence of events as "operational nonsense" and "madness," but perhaps the most poignant statement was made by the commander of the 134th Infantry Division, who in his despair committed suicide.[14]

In the center, the Soviet attack on the Fourth Army had originally been intended to hold it in place long enough to allow the encirclement operation to develop. As on the flanks, Russian preponderance in strength proved so great—in places, a single German battalion confronted two Soviet divisions—that the enemy almost immediately achieved deep penetrations. The most serious occurred at Orsha along the main Moscow-Minsk Rollbahn. Facing the collapse of his center, even the normally compliant Busch on the evening of the twenty-fourth unsuccessfully requested permission from Hitler for a general withdrawal. The next day, in a typically halfhearted fashion, Busch ordered some units to retreat, which merely left the rest in an exposed and untenable position. General Kurt von Tippelskirch, the acting commander of the Fourth Army (Heinrici was on leave), took matters in his own hands and ordered all units in the Dnieper bridgehead to withdraw. Busch became enraged when he heard of this action and directed the units to retake their old positions. Tippelskirch, however, parried Busch's unrealistic order and, temporarily at least, saved some troops from immediate destruction by directing "all front units that had not been attacked to remain in their positions until attacked and forced back by the enemy." By this time, even Busch had succumbed to reality. On the twenty-sixth, he flew to Berchtesgaden to try to convince Hitler of the brewing disaster. The Führer, however, simply restated his determination to hold Orsha and Mogilev, an order that had long been outrun by events. By this time, Soviet forces not only had crossed the Dnieper but were racing toward the Berezina, which they reached on the twenty-seventh, effectively blocking the line of the Fourth Army's retreat. Even as German units now began to struggle westward through the enormous forests and swamps of Belorussia, harassed all the way by partisans and enemy air attacks, Soviet armored units raced westward, in a mirror image of 1941, to close the pincers at Minsk.[15]

On the twenty-eighth, as it dawned on the OKH that the Soviet goal was the encirclement of Army Group Center, even Hitler seemed finally to recognize the enormity of the catastrophe, sacking the hapless Busch, and replacing him with Model. What the latter, although eminently qualified, was to do in the face of a front shattered along a 360-mile width and with Soviet forces already 100 miles to the west, was another matter. That same day, Hitler had drawn another meaningless line on the map and demanded that it be held at all costs. In addition, he ordered that "no yard of ground be given up without a fight" and that the retreating forces—the Ninth Army, smashed to bits; the largely encircled Fourth Army; and the Third Panzer Army, with only one corps left of its original three—should withdraw as slowly as possible to the halt line. Not satisfied with this foray into an illusory world of German strength and Soviet weakness, the Führer also demanded that the Russian spearheads be cut off and the situation reversed in a series of "rapid, hard counterstrikes."[16]

Even as on the twenty-ninth Russian planes pounded the key bridge across the Berezina at Berezino in an attempt to block the Fourth Army's main line of retreat, the OKH made ready two units, the Fifth and Twelfth Panzer Divisions, for Hitler's counterattack. On the thirtieth, the Twelfth Panzer, dispatched from Army Group North, launched a relief attack in the direction of Bobruisk with its forty-four Panzer IIIs and IVs, achieving some success through sheer audacity and surprise. Striking from Marina Gorka, it managed on 1 July to drive a small corridor through Soviet lines and link up with a force attacking out of the Bobruisk pocket, through which perhaps thirty-five thousand of the trapped Germans managed to escape before enemy forces pinched off the corridor. In the meantime, the Fifth Panzer, with a force of fifty-five Pz IVs and seventy Pz Vs (Panthers), supplemented by a heavy tank battalion of twenty Pz VIs (Tigers), had detrained at Borisov, north of Berezino and astride the main Moscow-Minsk highway. Its task was nothing less than to close the sixty-mile gap between the Third Panzer Army and the Fourth Army, in the process destroying Soviet units already to the west. Although it managed in a few days of hard fighting to destroy almost three hundred enemy tanks, its tactical successes did little to alter the balance of forces since on this front alone the Soviets had begun the battle with over eighteen hundred tanks. At best, the operation served only to delay the Russian advance for a few hours since enemy tank commanders quickly learned not to engage the Germans, simply bypassing the defenders by finding alternate routes to the west.[17]

As the Fifth and Twelfth Panzer Divisions fought desperately to stabilize the situation, scenes of gruesome horror played out at Berezino, where, just as in 1812, hordes of men, vehicles, and equipment were ensnared in a chaotic picture of destruction, panic, and despair. Pounded from the air, men desperately pushed across the river in the hope of reaching safety at Minsk, sixty miles to the west. The Russians, however, were bound to win any race to that city. On 2 July, advance Soviet units bypassed Minsk on the north and, the next day, aided by forces arriving from the south, seized the city against virtually no resistance. As the Fourth Army struggled westward, then, it found itself cut up into three smaller pockets within the larger encirclement based on Minsk. The liquidation of these pockets, however, was much more costly and time-consuming than the Soviets had expected. Driven by extreme fear at the prospect of being taken prisoner, large numbers of Landsers, so-called *Ruckkämpfer* (rear fighters, i.e., those fighting to get back), struggled mightily against huge obstacles to fight their way back to German lines that had been formed to the west of Minsk. Normally in small groups, but sometimes as individuals, these Ruckkämpfer, confronted by dense forests and disease-ridden swamps, with no food, and hunted relentlessly by partisans bent on revenge, trekked back in a strange odyssey of courage and determination.[18]

Despite these strange heroics, however—and Ruckkämpfer continued to straggle in through the end of October—in the period from 22 June to 10 July the Soviets had shattered Army Group Center. In roughly three weeks, some 250,000 Germans had been lost and twenty-eight divisions destroyed or so weakened that they were no longer fit for combat. Soviet losses, too, had been surprisingly high, with the most recent estimates from Russian sources citing a figure of over 440,000 casualties between

22 June and the end of July, of whom almost 100,000 were killed. Still, when Model assumed command of Army Group Center, "one could not have imagined a greater crisis," as Hitler admitted a month later. Not only had the army group been ripped to shreds, but both Hitler and the OKH had received reports in the first half of July of disturbing signs of dissolution among the troops, many of whom simply fled in disorder to the west. Model, tough, energetic, talented at improvisation, and seemingly without nerves, recognized the gravity of the situation: not only did the army group face destruction, but the enemy also aimed to keep moving beyond Minsk. In early July, he sought to slow the Soviet advance with delaying actions at Molodechno and Baranovichi, but the grim fact was that over a third of the front could not be manned. In view of the shocking disparity in strength and his inability to form a linear defense, Model now made a daring decision. Since his forces were too weak for defense, he decided to make a virtue of necessity and slow the enemy advance through a series of swift, mobile counterattacks, a sort of hit-and-run defense. As with other such actions, it was tactically successful—in roughly a month, the Fifth Panzer Division, for example, destroyed almost five hundred enemy tanks and assault guns—but could not solve the larger problem.[19]

To effect a real change in the dire German situation, at about the same time Zeitzler proposed, and Model supported, a much more daring plan, in effect a replay of Manstein's backhand blow of 1943 that would have units from Army Group North strike south into the exposed Soviet flanks. Since the necessary forces for the attack could be assembled only through a withdrawal of Army Group North behind the line of the Dvina, thus abandoning Estonia and Latvia, which Hitler categorically refused to do, yet another in a long series of leadership crises was touched off. In one of the most turbulent scenes of the war, Zeitzler confronted Hitler on 30 June at the Berghof, where he told him point-blank that he had twice been forced to make fateful decisions against his convictions (Stalingrad and the Crimea) but that it would not happen a third time. Zeitzler also declared the war lost militarily and offered his resignation, after which he simply disappeared from the Berghof and suffered a nervous breakdown. Hitler, already contemptuous of what he saw as the defeatism of the General Staff, never spoke to Zeitzler again. He did not, in fact, even bother to replace him until 21 July, the day after the attempt on his life, when Guderian, who had proved his loyalty during the coup attempt and, in any case, had long made no secret of his contempt for the leadership of the Ostheer, was appointed to the position. Although the Führer's comments in the days before he departed the Berghof for the last time on 14 July left some of his intimates under the impression that he had no illusions about the outcome of the war, they made it equally clear that he would not capitulate. There would be no repeat of 1918; his strength of will—or obstinate refusal to face reality—remained intact.[20]

In the meantime, despite their losses, the Soviets pressed on past Minsk to the west, on 8 July encircling Vilnius, the Lithuanian capital, which fell on the thirteenth, although the Germans managed to extract most of the four thousand defenders of yet another of Hitler's fortified places. The next day, as the Germans had long expected, Soviet forces under Konev burst out of Kovel and, by the eighteenth, had linked up with armored spearheads from Rokossovsky's units on the Bug River thirty miles west of Lvov. This time, however, Soviet success proved less directly threatening since Army Group Center had already been pushed out of its exposed position to the north. In addition, much to the OKH's relief, enemy forces pushed straight west toward the Vistula rather than turn northwest to Warsaw. Within a week, Brest-Litovsk, the scene of such hard fighting in 1941 and the cornerstone of Army Group Center's defense in the south, was surrounded, falling to the hard-charging Soviets on the twenty-sixth, as over the next few days did Lvov, Lublin, and Kaunas. In celebration of the destruction of Army Group Center, Stalin had already on the seventeenth paraded over fifty-five thousand haggard German prisoners through the streets of Moscow, an action, ironically, that had allowed many of them to survive, but perhaps even he had been astounded at the extent of Russian success. On 27 July, Soviet forces, as the Germans had long feared, finally turned north toward Warsaw. By 1 August, Russian spearheads had reached Praga, a suburb of Warsaw east of the Vistula and, more threateningly, breached the river and established a bridgehead on the west bank at Magnuszew, fifty miles to the south. Further, unable to close the gap with its southern neighbor, and forbidden to retreat—Hitler wanted to hold on to the Baltic coast to give Doenitz time to develop new submarines—Army Group North found itself cut off in the Baltic. North and east of the Vistula at Warsaw, the Germans seemingly had no organized forces to oppose the enemy advance.[21]

By now, however, logistic and supply problems as well as the considerable decimation of enemy tank forces combined to slow the momentum of the Soviet attack. Still, the Russians showed every intention of taking Warsaw, a vital German transportation and supply center, on the run and advancing down the Vistula to cut off German forces to the east. Model, however, capable and energetic in a crisis as always, had one last surprise. The continual shortening of the front caused by the Russian push west allowed him to shift the Fourth and Nineteenth Panzer Divisions, along with the SS Panzer Division Viking and the newly arrived Panzer Division Hermann Goering, into position for a counterstrike. With a total of 223 battle tanks (109 Pz IVs and 114 Pz Vs) as well as a handful of assault guns and tank destroyers, this was a surprisingly strong German force at this stage of the Russian offensive, although, in numbers, it was again dwarfed by the 810 armored vehicles of the Soviet Second Tank Army. Model's operational plan envisioned a pincer attack by the Nineteenth Panzer from the west and SS Viking from the east on Okuniew, just twelve miles east of Warsaw, in order to cut off the Soviet Third Tank Corps, which had advanced far to the north. This would be followed by a concentric attack of all four German tank divisions on the encircled corps with the aim of destroying it.[22]

In their rush toward Warsaw and the north, the Soviets had neglected elementary precautions, such as basic reconnaissance, intelligence gathering, flank protection, and the provision of supply lines, so, when it came on 1 August, Model's attack took the enemy completely by surprise. Over the next four days, in fighting so savage that the noise of battle could be heard in Warsaw, itself now the scene of bitter street fighting, the Germans largely crushed the Third Tank Corps and dealt a sharp blow to the other formations of the Soviet Second Tank Army. Its units suffered such severe losses—on 5 August it had only 263 of its original 810 tanks and assault guns left—that it had to be pulled off the line. Still, Model proved unable completely to destroy the enemy, for, on the fourth and fifth, first the Nineteenth Panzer and then the Hermann Goering Panzer Division had to be withdrawn from the battle and sent to contest the Soviet bridgehead across the Vistula at Magnuszew. Although overshadowed in historical literature by other important events at the same time (the Warsaw Uprising of the Polish Home Army and, the day before, the American breakout from the Cotentin Peninsula at Avranches), this tank battle in front of Warsaw was, perhaps, the key operational turning point on the eastern front in 1944. It allowed the Germans finally to stabilize a defensive line, avoid the encirclement of their remaining forces to the east, and prevent the Soviets from overrunning East Prussia.[23]

The battle also sheds some light on the controversy surrounding Stalin's response to the Warsaw Uprising. Despite later denials, the Russians almost certainly meant to take Warsaw on the run as their forces swept north and west along the Vistula. Model's counterattack, however, had the unintended effect of dooming the Polish uprising, for, after weeks of unbroken fighting, the Soviets had outrun their supply capabilities and passed the culmination point of the offensive. The Poles, hoping to liberate their capital just before the Russians arrived, had assumed, at most, a few days' combat against the German occupiers, followed by the entry of the Red Army into the city. Instead, the uprising lasted sixty-three agonizing days, during which the Soviets at first were unable and then unwilling to help the besieged Poles, even as the Germans destroyed their capital around them.[24]

Despite the success at Warsaw, however, from the German point of view the situation could hardly have been worse. To further compound the grim news in the east, American forces had at the end of July broken out from the Cotentin Peninsula and, after repelling a senseless German counterattack at Mortain, destroyed large numbers of the enemy at Falaise, followed by a swift advance across France. Having recklessly reduced German strength in the east in order to strike a decisive blow in the west, Hitler had now suffered fatal blows in both areas. Even with American forces poised to race across France, the Führer now reversed himself and declared the eastern front once again to be the area of vital concern. As with most of his decisions in the summer of 1944, it came too late. Still, the Germans could take some comfort in the fact that they had managed finally to build a stable front and that, even though the Soviet offensive had been a spectacular operational success, it had not, at the end of the day, knocked them from the war. Hitler, grasping at the thinnest of straws, even posed the question at the end of July as to whether the situation was all that bad. Amazingly, since his desire for Lebensraum had been a prime reason for the invasion of the Soviet Union, the Führer could now state, "If the territory that we now possess can be held, that is an area that will enable us to live, and we don't have this giant rear area."[25]

The blow to Army Group Center, however, had been as spectacular as it had been swift. In a bit more than two months, it had lost almost 400,000 men killed, wounded, and missing, making Operation Bagration a far worse disaster for the Wehrmacht than the comparable one at Stalingrad or even that of Verdun in the previous war. Indeed, only the Battle of the Somme in 1916 had exacted a greater toll. Again, some slight comfort could be found in the fact that the Red Army had paid a very high price for its brilliant success: total casualties of almost 800,000 men, along with almost 3,000 armored vehicles destroyed, while auxiliary operations in the Lvov area had cost another 300,000 casualties and 1,269 armored vehicles. The Germans, however, could not have found much comfort in the reasons behind the enemy success. First, and perhaps foremost, the Soviet quantitative advantage in manpower and materiel had become so great as to produce a qualitative effect. The Soviet edge in manpower remained enormous; despite the losses of Bagration, the strength of the Red Army steadily rose, while that of the Ostheer shrank. In addition, the Soviets' war production, supplemented by Lend-Lease deliveries, swamped that of the Germans. In 1944 alone, for example, the Soviets *lost* 23,000 tanks and assault guns, while the Germans *produced* only 22,000. During the entire war, in fact, the Soviets lost the astounding total (their figures) of 96,500 tanks and assault guns, 106,400 aircraft, and 317,5000 mortars and artillery pieces. Even as his mobilization effort struggled to keep pace with Germany's enemies in equipment, Speer could not generate the resource most desperately needed—trained soldiers. In his analysis of this operation, Niklas Zetterling has noted the astonishing fact that the Germans' "casualty inflicting capability" was 5.4 times greater than that of their adversary yet they still suffered a crushing defeat.[26]

The reason for this lay in the second key factor, the new operational mobility of the Soviets, which allowed them to strike rapidly and deeply into the German rear. More than anything, the Russians could thank Lend-Lease for this decisive advantage, for, during the war, their Western allies delivered over 450,000 trucks and jeeps to the Red Army. Without these vehicles, Bagration simply could not have been executed to its full extent since the Soviets would have had no way to supply or maintain the momentum of the offensive. Indeed, David Glantz has estimated that, without deliveries of these vehicles, the Red Army in its various offensives between 1943 and 1945 would have achieved only shallow penetrations and not meaningful operational breakthroughs, for, without this key element of mobility, the Germans would have been afforded time to build new defensive lines in the rear. The dominant image in the summer of 1944 on the eastern front was one of plodding German columns of men marching on foot accompanied by horse-drawn wagons being overtaken and harassed by Red infantry riding on tanks, trucks, or jeeps. In terms of aid from their Western allies, the Soviets also benefited enormously from the success of the Normandy invasion. Hitler, after all, had stripped the Ostfront of men and equipment in the expectation that a triumph in the west would lead to a decisive change in the east. Instead, the lack of men, equipment, and reserves in Russia all but ensured the success of Bagration.[27]

This overwhelming disparity in strength, in turn, highlighted the third key factor, German mistakes in intelligence assessment and leadership. In this case, deficiencies in intelligence gathering were, perhaps, not as significant as the failure to form an accurate picture from the information obtained. Again, it was not so much that their original assessment of the danger point was wrong as that the Germans credited the Soviets with more boldness than they should have. Then, in the face of the reality of the Soviet attack, they stubbornly clung to this misassessment until it was too late. This accentuated the larger problem of overall leadership, Hitler's unwillingness to withdraw to more defensible positions in order to shorten the front and create an operational reserve in the east. The problem here was not only his stand-fast mania but also the inversion of character between Stalin and himself. At the outset, Hitler had been the gambler and innovator, willing to listen to his generals' advice, while Stalin had been mistrustful of his generals, micromanaged battles, and insisted on not yielding any ground. Having survived his early mistakes, however, Stalin had come to listen to and rely on key advisers such as Vasilevsky and Zhukov. Hitler, on the other hand, became not only inflexible tactically and operationally but, especially after the 20 July assassination attempt, also both contemptuous and distrustful of his generals. The result, ironically, was that Soviet methods in 1944 resembled those of the Germans in 1941. While it had taken the Red Army three years to learn the lesson of mobile warfare and it still suffered far more disproportionate losses, it had now developed the effective use of combined weapons. The Germans, however, under the weight of Hitler's operational mistakes, reacted to the enemy blitzkrieg much as the Soviets had in 1941. As with that earlier German blitzkrieg, despite spectacular operational victories, it ultimately failed to end the war in one blow. For that, the Germans could thank Stalin and the Stavka, who not only passed on the initial chance to strike boldly out of Kovel to the northwest but also compounded their error by refusing, in the face of the evidence of spectacular success, to accede to Zhukov's request on 8 July to alter the plan of attack and strike toward Warsaw. Instead, Stalin stuck to the original idea of a general offensive along the entire front. Perhaps, as Karl-Heinz Frieser has suggested, he remembered all too clearly the disaster, and his role in it, that resulted from another sudden lunge to Warsaw, this time in 1920 during the Russian Civil War. Perhaps, as well, he simply could not believe the spectacle of the German debacle unfolding in front of him.[28]

In retrospect, the most noteworthy aspect of the summer of 1944 was not the heartening (from the Allied point of view) sight of the German debacle but the fact that, despite the savage blows of Normandy, Bagration, the escalating bomber war, and the failed attempt to assassinate Hitler, the regime not only survived but also somehow managed to hold off its demise for another eight months. After all, in just June, July, and August alone, on all fronts the Wehrmacht lost a total of 750,000 men killed (590,000 on the eastern front), or roughly a third of the total number who had died from September 1939 to May 1944 (2.23 million). At the same time, the Western allies dropped ten times more tonnage of bombs on Germany in 1944 than they had in the war to date, and would top the 1944 figure by a third in just over four months in 1945, yet proved unable to break the German war economy. Amazingly, despite the battering the German armaments industry took, its output did not peak until the late summer of 1944. Bagration, as well as the other blows, certainly accelerated the German descent into the abyss, but it was not a decisive, war-winning operation.[29]

The key question, then, is why, despite their overwhelming advantages, the Allies proved incapable of knocking Germany from the war in the summer of 1944. Part of the answer certainly lies in the failures of Allied strategy and decisionmaking. In the east, Stalin and the Stavka shrank from a truly bold initiative that might have dealt the Ostheer a mortal blow, while, in both east and west, a preference for broad frontal advances allowed the Wehrmacht to wriggle free from its death trap. The Allied drives also slowed as a natural consequence of logistic, supply, and manpower problems as the offensives simply reached their culmination point. In addition, the German military leadership showed an uncanny ability time and again to cobble sufficient troops together for well-placed counterattacks that succeeded in knocking the enemy off stride. Finally, the dogged persistence and remarkable fighting skill of the average Landser also played a role.

Just as importantly, however, not only did the institutional pillars of the regime (the Wehrmacht, the SS, the party, and the ministries) remain intact, but the myriad catastrophes of the summer of 1944 unleashed a flurry of activity as the Nazi leadership made one last effort at implementing total war. No one in the inner circle promoted or benefited more from this than Joseph Goebbels, who, of course, had long been obsessed with the need to reorganize the German economy and German society. As early as the winter crisis of 1941–1942, he had warned about the deleterious impact of the continuation of peacetime activities and, instead, sought to harden the public for the demands ahead through a propaganda campaign of "realistic optimism." Again in the winter crisis of the following year, supported this time by Albert Speer, he had railed against the luxuries and excesses of the elite while demanding the extensive mobilization of German society. Young men should be released by the armaments industries for service in the army, he insisted, with their places taken by women. At the same time, production of unnecessary consumer goods should be halted and the bureaucratic ranks combed for men suitable for military service, both of which would free further manpower for the front. He also expected this "war socialism" to generate a huge wave of energy from the body of the Volksgemeinschaft that would result in a national rising against the existential threat from the east. None of this, of course, eventuated as the political infighting among top Nazis ensured that little of lasting consequence would be done.[30]

The summer crisis of 1944, however, presented another opportunity for action. Already on 2 July, Goebbels had published a leading article in *Das Reich*, one intended to begin the psychological mobilization of the masses, in which he answered the question posed in the title, "Are we conducting a total war?" by suggesting, "obviously not total, or at least not total enough." He stressed again his recurrent theme that, in view of the material superiority of the enemy, Germany had to make the most rational and efficient use of its resources. A few days later, he found an ally in his initiative as Albert Speer, in conversations with Hitler between the sixth and the eighth, urged that Goebbels be placed in charge of mobilizing the home front while Himmler be given an expanded role in supervising the Wehrmacht. In a 12 July memorandum to Hitler, Speer explicitly adopted Goebbels's program, setting out a list of "revolutionary measures" for boosting armaments production—closing unnecessary businesses, drafting women into the labor force, combing administrative offices for personnel—that were virtually identical to the propaganda minister's. Speer followed this memorandum with another on the twentieth, the day of the attempted coup, in which he further bolstered his proposals with a favorite Goebbels argument. There was, complained the armaments minister, "an absolute disparity between the numbers of productive [workers] required for the defense of the homeland and those unproductive ones needed to maintain living standards and the bureaucracy." By this time, Goebbels had joined the debate directly. In a memorandum of 18 July to the Führer urging the ruthless mobilization of the German people for total war, he stressed that Germany could still win the war simply by not losing it; that is, given the superiority of its opponents, Germany's only chance for victory lay in a rupture in the enemy coalition. That breach would surely come, Goebbels asserted, but it was questionable, without a full reorganization of the economy, whether Germany would have enough punch left to take advantage of this crisis when it happened.[31]

Given his steadfast loyalty and actions on 20 July, it was hardly a surprise when Hitler named Goebbels plenipotentiary for the total war effort on 25 July, seemingly making him, as Goebbels bragged, dictator over the home front. Since in June Hitler had rejected just such a move to total war and had assured Goebbels that the crisis would be surmounted "in the usual way," his action now amounted to an admission that his regime faced an unprecedented existential threat. As always in the Third Reich, however, this new burst of dynamism worked largely at cross-purposes. Not only did the Gauleiter continue to resist full implementation of total war measures, being particularly opposed to plant closings and limitations on consumer goods, but Goebbels and Speer, although having linked their efforts at procuring Hitler's approval for total war, also had conflicting conceptions of its goal. While Goebbels aimed at a levee en masse, an ideological activation of the Volksgemeinschaft that would throw hundreds of thousands of fanatics at the enemy, Speer envisioned the use of the newly available personnel in armaments factories. Typically, Hitler resolved the dispute by attempting to satisfy both squabbling parties. He allowed Goebbels to undertake an extreme austerity drive within Germany and Speer to make good the lost armaments workers with an increased employment of women and foreign workers.[32]

For both, however, the reality was that they were scraping the bottom of the barrel. Although Goebbels succeeded in instituting a sixty-hour workweek, pruning personnel from the cultural sphere (where theaters, orchestras, and newspapers were shut down), closing many firms producing goods unnecessary for the war effort, and weeding staff from administrative offices, the results proved disappointing. Since a large proportion of the men sifted from the economy and bureaucracies were too old for military service, Goebbels increasingly forced younger men out of exempt occupations—work thought essential for the war effort, including skilled work—and replaced them with older, less-fit, less-qualified workers, with predictable results. The net addition of women to the workforce also proved disappointing, with only about a quarter of a million added. As before, the war economy continued to depend on the widespread employment of foreign labor; by August 1944, roughly every third worker in the German economy was either a foreign worker or a prisoner of war (with a much higher percentage in agriculture and some specific armaments sectors). Despite improvements in working and living conditions, these laborers remained far less productive than their German counterparts, which proved a further hindrance to maximizing output. Although Goebbels's efforts between August and December 1944 freed around a million men to be sent to the front, most of the replacements were either very young or overaged, poorly trained, physically or mentally unfit (hundreds of thousands were rejected by the army as unsuitable for service), and unable to stand the strains of front service. As a result, German casualties in that same period exceeded 1.2 million men.[33]

In yet other ways, as well, the Germans were losing the competition between production and destruction. With the intensification of the Allied bomber war over Germany, efforts were under way to speed production of aircraft and the much-trumpeted wonder weapons. Faced with the imminent extinction of the Luftwaffe in early 1944, Speer joined forces with the Reich Air Ministry to form a *Jägerstab* (fighter staff) to streamline and accelerate fighter production. Aided by the brutally efficient Karl Otto Sauer and Hans Kammler, the Jägerstab enjoyed a priority in armaments production that allowed it to achieve extraordinary gains. Between February and July, aircraft production more than doubled, from 2,015 to 4,219, an armaments "miracle" that was achieved through a combination of material rewards, a longer workweek, the production of only a few models, and the application of coercive violence and the most severe discipline, especially to foreign workers. Himmler's SS also took advantage of the demand for labor by supplying ever-larger numbers of concentration camp prisoners to the aircraft and engine factories; by August in some plants over a third of the workers had been "subcontracted" by the SS. Moreover, the need for labor resulted in the last remaining taboo being broken as Eichmann began furnishing Jewish labor from Hungary, particularly to Kammler's underground rocket factories at Mittelbau-Dora.[34]

Despite these efforts, however, the Jägerstab failed to narrow the gap between German and Allied production. Although Germany produced 39,807 aircraft in 1944, Allied production of 163,000 dwarfed this total, the United States alone churning out over 96,000 aircraft. Similarly, the Allies enjoyed almost a 2.5-to-1 advantage in the production of armored vehicles and artillery pieces. As Adam Tooze has stressed, despite their achievements, the Germans could not overcome the crushing logic of economics: in 1941, the combined GDP of Great Britain, the United States, and the Soviet Union exceeded that of Germany by 4.36 to 1, a disparity the Germans could never surmount. Speer's efforts in 1943 and early 1944 to make better use of Germany's "foreign capacity," especially in France and Belgium, certainly paid dividends, and, without its occupied territories, Germany could likely not have continued in the war beyond 1943, but, in spite of their value, they still could not offset the overwhelming material superiority of Germany's enemies. More to the point, the loss of key raw materials and productive facilities beginning in early 1944, especially Ukrainian ore and Rumanian oil, wrote the death warrant of the German economy. This was accentuated by the disruption produced, after the elimination of the distractions of the Normandy invasion, by the unprecedented intensity of the Allied bombing campaign. From June to October, the British and Americans dropped a greater tonnage of bombs on Germany than in the entire war to that point—and over the next six months equaled that effort. This massive destruction clearly contributed to a growing dislocation of German production as factories were obliterated, machinery buried in mountains of rubble, bridges destroyed, transportation of key parts and materials cut off, synthetic fuel plants crippled, power stations closed, and (not least) the lives of workers disrupted. Although the bombing campaign could not of itself bring the war economy to a standstill, it severely hindered its ability to produce even more material and imposed a time limit on German survival.[35]

Nor was the crisis merely one of production as German society was also eroding. By midsummer, economic officials worried that the nation would soon face an inflation just as severe as the one that had shaken the structure of the Weimar democracy in 1923. With the value of money eroding, economic actors large and small showed increasing disinclination to comply with the regime's directives. Although black marketeering in the occupied areas—Germany's flea market, as Götz Aly put it—had been not just sanctioned but encouraged, with the contraction of the Nazi Empire it became more difficult to acquire many staple consumer items. This proved especially the case with regard to food products since the two regions most important to Germany, Ukraine and France, had been lost to its exploitation by the late summer. Nor were the retreating troops able to loot and transfer sizable quantities of grains and foodstuffs back to the Reich. Moreover, rising demands from the Wehrmacht, which until now had been fed primarily from local supplies in the occupied territories, aggravated the loss of foodstuffs from these areas. In addition, by the autumn and winter, even before the mass postwar treks, millions of Germans had been uprooted, either as evacuees or as refugees, and were largely dependent on state welfare. Now completely reliant on domestic German agricultural production to supply larger numbers of people, Nazi officials were forced in the autumn drastically to reduce rations. Stepped-up Allied bombing of the transportation network, however, meant not only that distribution became more difficult but also that some food supplies never reached their destinations. Faced with a lack of consumer goods and increasing food shortages in stores, average Germans, as in World War I, turned increasingly to the black market—and, as in that earlier war, engaged in criminal activities in order to survive. The regime reacted with growing coercion and violence, but, sensitive as the Nazi leaders were to the example of the previous war, they remained reluctant to impose the full burdens of total war on the Volksgemeinschaft. Instead, they clung stubbornly to the promise made at the beginning of the war not to lower the living standard below a certain basic level. As compensation for scarce food items, the regime introduced ersatz products that supplied essential vitamins and protein and, as always, shifted the burden of shortages onto foreign forced laborers, who suffered the most from lower rations and the increasingly chaotic distribution system.[36]

Despite the Nazis' best efforts, however, the shortage of consumer goods, reduction of rations, longer working hours, and devastating effects of aerial bombardment contributed to a significant decrease in the real standard of living of the German population. By now, in the fifth year of war, with little chance of victory or even of averting total disaster, a noticeable drop in morale set in as the public viewed the massive defeats at the front with "increasing concern." Most alarming was the speed of the Russian advance, which produced an enormous "shock effect" since it not only threatened East Prussia with invasion but also undermined cherished notions of German superiority. Although public reaction to the bomb plot seemed to boost Hitler's popularity temporarily, the effect did not last long. By late summer, SD reports admitted that "part of the population would have welcomed the success of the assassination attempt" in hope of a quick end to the war. Although Goebbels made effective use of the "reactionary clique" of "aristocratic German officers" involved in the anti-Hitler conspiracy to whip up populist anger and general sympathy for the introduction of total war among the working class, he could do little to alter the perception of impending defeat. Whether from a sense of resigned betrayal—that Germany had always been defeated through treachery—or as a result of disillusionment with the military leadership, the public voiced increasing worry and skepticism about the outcome of the war. More pointedly, many blamed the Führer directly for Germany's impending destruction, the SD office in Stuttgart in November noting the not infrequent comment that Hitler had been sent by Providence as the executor of a divine will to destroy the German people.[37]

Although the inflated claims made about the miracle weapons again raised hopes for a way out, the late September decree proclaiming the call-up of young boys and elderly men for the Volkssturm (People's

Storm) was greeted with general dismay. When not ridiculed—grave diggers, went one popular witticism, were said to be searching for recruits for the Volkssturm—the draft was seen as militarily futile, as confirmation of Germany's defeat. Since these men were obviously unsuited for combat, the call-up was not only deeply unpopular but also regarded as nothing less than an execution. Reports indicated the obvious reluctance with which these men arrived at the front as well as the absence of any ideological enthusiasm. The results were predictable; poorly trained and ill equipped, some 175,000 died in the senseless attempt to halt professional armies through a popular uprising. Although Goebbels proclaimed that a "people's war like this one requires heavy sacrifices," those who were to be the victims responded with little of the desired fanatic spirit. Similarly, Himmler promised the enemy in threatening tones that the conquest of German farms and cities would cost "streams of their blood," but his avowal that it was proper for the younger generation to die in order to save the nation failed to produce an echo in the people. As a consequence, from the autumn of 1944, increasingly draconian edicts were issued by Hitler and Himmler threatening death to those who failed adequately to resist the enemy. With this threat carried out with shocking frequency in the last months of the war, the Nazi regime ensured that World War II would end with a bang, not a whimper.[38]

At the beginning of August, the German counterattack in front of Warsaw had succeeded finally in halting the momentum of the Soviet offensive, but not before the enemy had established bridgeheads across the Vistula and in places reached the East Prussian border. The bridgeheads over the Vistula south of Warsaw proved of most immediate concern. The OKH feared that any Soviet breakout could be exploited in a potentially decisive manner by either a turn north to encircle Warsaw or a drive straight west in order to seize the vital economic and industrial resources of Silesia, thus effectively crippling the German war economy. Already, as we have seen, the Germans had been forced to send units from the key tank battle at Warsaw to the south to prevent any Soviet exploitation of the bridgeheads and stabilize the situation. By mid-August, however, the Russians shifted the Schwerpunkt of their attacks to the key area just north of Warsaw where the Vistula, Narew, and Bug Rivers converged. If they could force their way across these rivers, the path to Danzig lay open, with the possibility of trapping German forces in the Baltic and East Prussia. The Soviets opened a new offensive on 18 August and over the next two months continued a series of attacks along the Bug and Narew Rivers designed to achieve a decisive breakthrough. Although the weight of these blows forced the Germans back, and despite the fact that they managed to create a few bridgeheads across the Narew, the Soviets proved unable to break the German defense line. Having achieved rather small tactical gains at a stiff cost in men and equipment, the Russians finally broke off attacks at the end of October.[39]

At the same time as the Soviets began winding down their efforts near Warsaw, a new crisis erupted to the north in East Prussia. Although the Red Army had reached the German border at Schirwindt in mid-August, furious German counterattacks had thrown them back. In mid-October, however, the Soviets launched a frontal assault on Fourth Army positions with the intention, after breaking through, of sending one force streaming toward Königsberg and another to seize Danzig. If they succeeded, they would not only cut off Army Group North in the Baltic but also open the way to Germany proper. The assault began on 16 October with a three- to four-hour artillery and air bombardment of an intensity not previously experienced on the eastern front. By the eighteenth, Russian forces had again crossed the East Prussian border on a broad front and in places were advancing unhindered far to the west. On the twenty-first, they seized an intact bridge across the Angerapp at Nemmersdorf and also threatened to take the key railroad center of Gumbinnen even as German tanks were being unloaded from freight cars. With the roads full of refugees fleeing west in panic, concern rose at Führer Headquarters, less than fifty miles away in Rastenburg and within easy striking distance of enemy tank columns. Hitler, however, worried about the impact on the troops if he evacuated, refused to leave Wolf's Lair, although some staff and files were sent away. Once again, the Germans averted disaster through a bold counterthrust. That same day, German panzer forces battled Soviet tank units near Gumbinnen, while others assaulted the base of the enemy breakthrough at Großwaltersdorf, managing the next day to cut off advance units of the Soviet Second Guards Tank Corps and the Eleventh Guards Army. Despite their numerical superiority, both Russian commanders and soldiers seemed stunned by the sudden turnabout in their situation. Lacking firm leadership, many men simply threw away their weapons and equipment and fled in panic eastward.[40]

This initial foray into East Prussia had been fought with savage intensity and resulted in unusually heavy losses for an operation that lasted less than two weeks. German sources claimed to have destroyed almost one thousand enemy tanks and assault guns, while the Russians admitted to a casualty total of nearly 80,000 men of the 377,000 involved in the attack. Noteworthy, too, were the horrifying scenes that greeted German troops as they retook Gumbinnen and Nemmersdorf. In an explosion of violence, Soviet troops had exacted a first, bloody revenge on German civilians, with scores of women raped and murdered, often in the most gruesome fashion, stores plundered, and houses burned. Having suffered a whole range of German atrocities for three dreadful years, and having seen firsthand the awesome destruction of the scorched-earth retreat, Soviet soldiers engaged in an orgy of revenge that, although perhaps understandable, was, nonetheless, deplorable. Goebbels, of course, immediately seized on Nemmersdorf, that "place of horror," as an example of what all Germans could expect. In a theme that would continue until the end of the war, he made clear that Soviet actions left Germans only one choice—fanatic, suicidal resistance—since they were going to be the victims of enemy cruelties in any case. Controversy still exists as to whether Stalin encouraged such action or whether Soviet commanders simply lost control of their troops, but one thing was clear: the atrocities at Nemmersdorf generally sent a chill through the German people and strengthened their will to resist. Although the SD reported a few examples of Germans drawing comparisons between the actions of their own government and soldiers against the Jews and what had now happened on German territory, the overwhelming majority simply feared that the Russians would do to them what they themselves had already suffered at German hands.[41]

At the same time that the reality of war was being brought home to the German civilian population of East Prussia, an even more costly military drama was playing out in the Baltic as the Soviets now targeted Army Group North. Heretofore largely spared the full fury of the enemy summer offensive, the army group had, nonetheless, seen its strength dwindle as it had been forced to deliver more and more units to the defense of other sectors, even as its southern front expanded because of the disaster befalling Army Group South. By midsummer, it, too, faced a debilitating enemy superiority of up to eight to one across the board, yet Hitler forbade any withdrawal to shorter, more defensible lines. In this case, the Führer's decision reflected less his typical hold-fast mentality than the key significance of certain political, economic, and strategic considerations. Always sensitive to the vital importance of Finnish nickel and Swedish iron ore to the German war effort, Hitler was determined to hold the Baltic as a guarantee of the continued deliveries of these ores. At the same time, he clung to the hope that new weapons technologies, both rockets and submarines, could produce a dramatic change in Germany's fortunes. In the case of the latter weapon, the German navy was in the process of developing and testing two markedly superior types of

U-boats that offered a glimmer of hope that the Battle of the Atlantic could yet be won. To complete sea testing, however, Hitler believed it was essential to hold on to the eastern Baltic coast, although his military (and even naval) advisers regarded this as a luxury Germany could not afford.[42]

By early July, Army Group North found its position increasingly jeopardized by the collapse of its neighbor to the south. With Soviet forces racing west through the "Baltic hole," a twenty-five-mile-wide gap between Army Groups North and Center, the commander of the former army group, General Georg Lindemann, not only had to defend more front with fewer troops but also faced the prospect that the advancing enemy might cut off his forces entirely. Lindemann, of course, reacted to the threat with the rational request that Hitler allow him to withdraw his forces to safety. Just as predictably, Hitler not only refused to give up territory but also ordered Lindemann to launch a counterattack with his nonexistent reserves. The latter responded by renewing his demand to be allowed to evacuate his troops in order to escape encirclement as well as halting the senseless counterattack. These actions left Hitler no choice, and, on 4 July, he replaced Lindemann with General Johannes Friessner, who, although initially determined to carry out Hitler's orders energetically, soon discovered the correctness of his predecessor's prescription. By mid-July, both Friessner and Model pleaded with Hitler to allow a withdrawal of Army Group North, which, as the most intact and battleworthy force on the eastern front, could be used to build the operational reserve so desperately needed to stabilize the front. These divisions, having been spared the brunt of battle in 1942 and 1943, had a level of primary group cohesion and combat effectiveness rare in German units at this point in the war and, thus, would have been invaluable as a backstop. Their fighting ability was on ample display in these weeks of summer fighting when, despite its overwhelming superiority in strength, the Red Army had been unable to achieve an operational breakthrough, instead being forced at high cost to push Friessner's units back. Despite his dogged defensive success—in one month, his troops, mostly in close combat with the lethal handheld *Panzerfaust*, destroyed almost eight hundred enemy armored vehicles—Friessner met the same fate as Lindemann. On 23 July, he was relieved of his command, although formally he exchanged positions with the commander of Army Group South Ukraine, General Ferdinand Schörner. The latter, although given unusual command authority by Hitler, had no answer to the problems of the "poor man's war" that the Germans were now fighting, and he too demanded withdrawal to sensible positions, which the Führer ignored.

By the end of the month, the Soviets finally reached the Baltic coast just west of Riga, effectively trapping Army Group North. Although a tenuous connection to Army Group Center was reopened on 20 August, the position of Army Group North remained highly precarious.[43]

After a temporary respite in order to prepare its forces, the Red Army on 14 September resumed its hammer blows against Army Group North. With any attempt to hold its exposed position untenable, Hitler finally relented two days later, following an impassioned appeal by Schörner, and approved the evacuation of Estonia, which commenced on the eighteenth. Still, he insisted on maintaining a bridgehead around Riga as well as holding on to Courland. Since Finland agreed to an armistice and left the war on 19 September, Hitler's decision seemed to be based on his desire to continue testing the new-type U-boats. In any case, the Soviets continued their pounding attacks along the northern front, their forces increasingly augmented by units transferred from Finland, and, on 10 October, once again reached the Baltic coast. Although the Red Army paid a high price, suffering over 280,000 casualties and losing over five hundred armored vehicles, it had once more trapped Army Group North, with 250,000 troops and over five hundred armored vehicles, this time for good. Over the course of the next weeks and months, neither rational arguments (these tough, battle-hardened units could better be used as an operational reserve to defend Germany than sitting in Courland) nor emotional appeals (since most of the troops were from the eastern provinces, they would fight more fiercely than a bunch of untrained boys and elderly men in the Volkssturm) altered Hitler's determination to hold on to Courland. Nor, despite a series of battles until the end of the war that cost the Red Army a ridiculously high number of casualties, were the Soviets able to take it.[44]

Of all Hitler's controversial decisions in 1944, none has seemed to demonstrate so well his irrational stand-fast mentality as the decision voluntarily to entomb German troops and tanks sorely needed to defend the Reich in a backwater place such as Courland. As an illustration of his irrationality, however, it might be better to seek explanations on the strategic rather than the tactical level, with the key to the Courland puzzle lying in the Ardennes rather than the Baltic. As is generally known, Hitler hoped with the Ardennes offensive in December 1944 (originally scheduled for late November) to achieve a sudden turnaround in the war through an operation remarkably similar to Sickle Cut of May 1940. In this latest version, Great Britain was to play the role of France, with the United States, emulating the English, expected temporarily to withdraw from European affairs. Having dealt a savage blow to his Western enemies, and at the same time perhaps finally splitting the unnatural coalition arrayed against him, Hitler could then mass his remaining forces in the east to repel the Soviet invaders. In effect, he was clinging to the strategy outlined in November 1943 for the coming year: seek a turn-around in the war by striking in the west and holding on in the east. His forces had failed to achieve the desired results in both areas, but, Hitler believed, one last opportunity beckoned. For this plan to work, however, Courland had to be held as a springboard for a new offensive deep into the Soviet rear, while at the same time the new-model U-boats could be unleashed in the Atlantic. Although this interpretation is clearly a flight of fantasy, much speaks in support of it, not least the timing of Hitler's final decisions to hold Courland and launch the Ardennes offensive, made within two days of each other in late October. Just as importantly, such a scheme fit his all-or-nothing mentality, his conviction, as Speer noted, that the war could be won only through offensive action. The Führer yearned to throw off the "eternal defense" into which Germany had been forced and again seize the initiative, but, when his "Blitzkrieg without gasoline," as Karl-Heinz Frieser termed the Ardennes offensive, failed, he was left with the bankruptcy of his strategy. Only now, in early 1945, did he permit some units to be evacuated from Courland and sent back to Germany, although, even here, he could not quite fully abandon the illusion of a miracle that would again turn the war in his favor.[45]

Even as the OKH struggled to build a stable front line out of the ruins of Army Group Center, it faced another disaster in the south in the area of Army Group South Ukraine, itself a mixed German-Rumanian conglomeration. The winter/spring campaign of 1943–1944 had left it in tatters, but under General Schörner's energetic leadership the army group had managed to reestablish its structure, order, and discipline. Nor did it hurt that its front remained quiet as the dramatic events played out to the north. It held seemingly strong forward positions with the formidable obstacle of the Carpathian Mountains at its rear but faced the inescapable German dilemma—in order to cobble together forces to stem the Red tide in the north, Guderian had stripped Army Group South Ukraine of six of its eight panzer divisions and six infantry divisions, leaving it little in the way of a mobile reserve. It was also hampered by a tenuous logistic situation, with its Rumanian allies often diverting supply trains for their own use, while its other nominal ally, the Hungarians, seemed more intent on fighting the Rumanians and Slovaks than the Russians. For political reasons, in order for the Ruma-nians to hold on to Bessarabia (Moldova) and protect the cities of Iassy and Kishinev as well as to guard the Ploesti oil fields, the Germans were compelled to defend an extensive front that bulged eastward from the Carpathians and then along the Dniester to the Black Sea. Although the wise military move would have been to shorten this line and pull back to more defensible positions, this proved impossible, both because Hitler would not have approved such a move and because of the tenuous political situation of Marshal Antonescu, the Rumanian leader. Still, on paper, it seemed a strong force, with approximately 500,000 German troops and 170 armored vehicles, along with some 400,000 Rumanians, although the quality of the latter was, as always, maddeningly uneven. Some units could be counted on to fight bravely and fiercely, while others would simply melt away at the first sign of battle. Having witnessed the debacle to the north, German commanders were in little doubt that the next major Soviet blow would come against them.[46]

Nonetheless, the power of the enemy attack and the speed of the Rumanian collapse took the Germans by surprise. Even at this stage of the war, they seem to have underestimated the striking power of the Soviets, not least since they knew that the Stavka, too, had pulled units from the Second and Third Ukrainian Fronts in order to feed the demands of the larger operation to the north. In addition, although the Red Army in this sector disposed of large numbers of troops, a sizable percentage of them had little or no training. These men, primarily Ukrainians who had been swept up to make good manpower losses as the Red Army liberated Ukraine, filled out the ranks, although German analysts were convinced that Soviet infantry divisions did not have quite the striking power as before. This was likely true, but the Red Army made up for this deficiency by relying more on artillery, tanks, and air support, to devastating effect once the attack had begun. Typically, the Russians amassed a huge force of over 1.3 million men with almost nineteen hundred tanks and assault guns for the offensive. As in Belorussia, the Soviets planned to concentrate their forces at key points in order to achieve an operational breakthrough. The original intention seemed to be just to force the Germans to divert troops away from the central front, thus opening the Warsaw-Berlin axis to further attack. Ultimately, however, the Soviets devised an ambitious new plan that aimed to encircle and destroy enemy forces around Iassy and Kishinev, then advance deep into Rumania to seize Bucharest and the Ploesti oil fields.[47]

The attack began on 20 August, but, despite the fall of Iassy the next day and Kishinev on the twenty-fourth, it did not initially proceed as smoothly as the Russians had hoped. While, in many areas, Rumanian troops put up little opposition, German units resisted stoutly. Not atypically in Rumanian history, politics played a key role in determining the outcome of the battle. Prompted by the attack, opposition leaders in Bucharest, who had been seeking a way out of the war for months, launched a coup against the pro-German government of Antonescu on 23 August. Troops loyal to the new government under the young King Michael, who had promptly taken Rumania out of the war, then successfully prevented a German countercoup. This incited Hitler, who had evidently counted too heavily on the anticommunism of Rumanian politicians and, thus, was taken completely by surprise by the political turn of affairs, to order the bombing of Bucharest, an action that only motivated the Rumanians to enter the war on Russia's side (which allowed them the additional benefit of fighting the hated Hungarians as well as recovering Transylvania). Within a few days, Rumanian troops in some sectors thus went from working alongside the Germans to fighting against them. Although German troops responded to the unexpected collapse of their ally with their usual skill and tenacity, by early September Army Group South Ukraine had suffered a fate similar to that of Army Group Center: the Sixth Army had been destroyed (again), the German front in Rumania had completely collapsed, and both Bucharest and the Ploesti oil fields had been lost. Although earlier in the war the loss of the latter would have occasioned German economic collapse, by this stage it proved largely meaningless. Persistent American bombing raids over Ploesti had virtually ended production at its refineries even before the Russians arrived, while the Germans had long since turned to synthetic production to supply most of their fuel needs. Still, at a relatively small cost of 67,000 casualties, the Red Army had again shattered an entire front, destroyed twenty German divisions, and inflicted a loss of more than 200,000 soldiers on the Germans. The renamed Army Group South, with only some 200,000 men left, now embarked on a lengthy retreat across the Carpathians that did not stop until Soviet forces had penetrated Bulgaria and turned west into Hungary.[48]

As the Soviet advance continued into Hungary, however, it ran into more problems from logistics than from German opposition. By the end of September, Russian forces had swept aside the rather light German and Hungarian forces covering the Carpathian passes and had passed into Hungary. The Stavka now directed that German and Hungarian forces be destroyed and Hungary knocked from the war, but this was to prove much more difficult than anticipated. With the loss of the Ploesti oil fields and refineries as well as the extensive damage done by American bombers to the synthetic fuel plants, Hitler put great store in the oil fields southwest of Lake Balaton as well as those on the Hungarian-Austrian border. Still, with German defenses in Hungary rather thin, the Soviets advanced rapidly, seizing Debrecen, about 120 miles east of Budapest, on 20 October. There they stalled, brought to a halt by a concerted German counterattack. The Soviets now tested the Hungarian defenses to the south of Budapest, taking Szeged, little more than a hundred miles southeast of the capital, on 10 November. Once again, however, stiff German resistance, as well as bad weather, stopped the Russian advance. The Red Army kept up steady pressure, however, and by 3 December had reached the shores of Lake Balaton, no more than forty miles southwest of Budapest. The Soviets tried again in a two-pronged attack on 5 December to seize the city, but, despite a successful opening advance, the Germans shifted forces and prevented the capital either from falling or from being encircled.[49]

Having ousted Admiral Horthy, the aged Hungarian leader, from power following his unsuccessful attempt in mid-October to take Hungary out of the war, Hitler was more determined than ever to hold on to Budapest. In early December, he dispatched two panzer divisions and three sixty-tank Tiger battalions for a counterattack. The question, however, was, Where? In the north or in the south? General Friessner, over-matched and destined along with Busch to become the least successful of German eastern front commanders, saw the greatest danger in the south, while Guderian believed that the main danger lurked in the north. In the end, Hitler approved Friessner's dispositions, with the result that the infantry from the panzer divisions was deployed in the north while the unsupported armor was left to defend the line in the south. These odd deployments meant that, if the Soviets beat the Germans to the punch, the latter were in serious trouble. Bad weather and a bout of caution caused the Russians to delay their assault, but, despite repeated urging from Guderian, Friessner hesitated to attack before the ground froze. As a consequence, much as Guderian had feared, the Soviets struck first, launching a massive two-pronged assault both north and south of Budapest on 20 December. By the twenty-seventh, they had encircled the city, but Hitler was determined to hold the Hungarian capital since, in his mind, success in the Ardennes and success in Hungary were linked. In addition, since it lay athwart the main route to Austria and Bohemia and was the main rail hub in the region, the Russians could not simply bypass it, so, for the first time in the war, the Soviets found themselves laying siege to a major city. Budapest, with its civilian population swollen to 2 million, was to be assaulted in savage air and artillery bombardments to force its surrender.[50]

To break the enemy encirclement, the Germans diverted scarce resources from Army Group Center, most importantly, the Fourth SS

Panzer Corps with the Totenkopf and Viking Divisions, a decision that would have dire consequences when the Soviets resumed their offensive on the Vistula in January. These units proved unable to lift the siege, but bitter fighting continued through the end of December and into the new year. Ironically, in assaulting a major urban area whose buildings provided good cover for the enemy and negated their own strength in armor and air power, the Soviets now got a taste of their own medicine. By mid-January 1945, Pest, on the eastern bank of the Danube, had been secured, but fighting still raged for Buda and the citadel on the west bank. Perhaps most damaging to the Germans was Hitler's decision on 16 January to send the Sixth SS Panzer Army, recently withdrawn from the Ardennes, to Hungary instead of Poland. This decision was incomprehensible from a military perspective since the Russians had already begun the Vistula-Oder offensive but might well have betrayed Hitler's vague hope of forcing the Soviets to the negotiating table by achieving at least a partial military success. Both sides suffered heavy casualties, which neither could afford, as the fighting approached that of Stalingrad in ferocity. Not until 12 February did the last remaining Germans seek to break out. They were repulsed by the Soviets in a bloody slaughter, and, the next day, the citadel finally fell. Even now, however, Hitler refused to relent. On 6 March, Sepp Dietrich's Sixth SS Panzer Army launched the last German counteroffensive of the war, Operation Frühlingserwachen (Spring Awakening). It aimed to push the Russians back from the Danube and retake Budapest. The German force of ten panzer divisions was considerable, including the still formidable Adolf Hitler, Das Reich, and Hitlerjugend Divisions. The Soviets resisted bitterly, however, and after ten days of heavy fighting, largely out of fuel and bogged down in mud, Dietrich was forced to break off the effort. As at Kursk in 1943, it had been a waste of valuable German tank forces to no purpose: it did not seriously distract the Soviets and, with the Red Army on the Oder only forty miles from Berlin, had been a senseless use of elite German units. Lacking any reserves, Germany's other eastern armies could only await the inevitable Russian offensive toward Berlin with resigned trepidation.[51]

10

Death Throes

By January 1945, the point had long been passed where a continuation of the war made any sense since Hitler had no hope of achieving Lebensraum or the envisioned racial reordering of Eastern Europe. Certainly, the unconditional surrender doctrine of the Western allies as well as fear of Soviet revenge played a role in stiffening both the regime and the population, weary as most were of the war. Hitler, however, had an additional reason. For him, as for many of his generation, the collapse of imperial Germany in November 1918 had been a searing trauma. Indeed, the burning desire to redeem this humiliation as well as ensure that it never happened again formed the core of his ideology. His unyielding hatred of the Jewish conspiracy, his determination to break the bonds of Jewish plutocracy as evidenced in the emasculation of Germany by the Treaty of Versailles, his vision of an empire in the east that would cement German hegemony in Europe, and his notion of a racially pure Volksgemeinschaft all stemmed from his understanding of the causes of the collapse in 1918. On the very day Germany had invaded Poland in September 1939, he had stressed to the Reichstag that "a November 1918 shall never occur again in Germany," a theme that became an obsession as the war turned against him. At the height of the Stalingrad battle in early November 1942, he had again contrasted his determination with that of the Kaiser's government. "Germany at that time," he stressed, "laid down its arms at quarter to twelve. In principle, I always stop only at five past twelve." Nor, in the intervening two years, had his stance softened, his last proclamation to the Old Fighters at Munich on 12 November 1944 again emphasizing the destructiveness and exterminationist intent of Jewry. This time, however, he also provided a glimpse of how he intended to stage his own and his regime's demise. He would, he vowed, never capitulate and repeat the shame of 1918; he would instead give the world a "praiseworthy example" of struggle against the "Bolshevik monster."[1]

That this fight to the last, to be staged as a Wagnerian spectacle of epic proportions, would result in the "heroic" destruction of Germany as well as its warlord was self-evident to Hitler, if not welcomed by the mass of Germans. Nonetheless, it resulted in the unparalleled destruction of an advanced industrial society. In the last four months of the war, over 1.4 million German soldiers lost their lives (over 1.5 million through December 1945), Allied bombing reduced the medieval splendor of many German cities to little more than heaps of rubble, and hundreds of thousands of civilians (especially women) felt the brunt of Soviet revenge. Huddled in their ruined cellars beneath mounds of stone, much of the German population at the end of the war resembled nothing more than the cave dwellers of old. True to his racial theories, however, and in accordance with notions of total war developed in the 1930s, Hitler was fully prepared to fight this struggle for the naked existence of Germany to the bitter end, even if it meant the complete destruction of his own people.[2]

A number of factors reinforced Hitler's decision to fight on: the spinelessness of his top military advisers, the ideological indoctrination of young Germans, the conviction of those who had committed crimes that they had nothing to lose by fighting on, and Goebbels's propaganda argument that both the Western allies and the Soviets were determined to destroy Germany. It was also, ironically, given a boost by seemingly objective factors: natural obstacles protected Germany in the west and south, while the German navy still controlled the Baltic Sea to the north. In addition, the last burst of Speer's armaments economy had resulted in an upsurge of weapons production, and, although there was no prospect for continued high output, the enormous losses of 1944 had largely been made good, although the Soviets still enjoyed a crushing material superiority. The most serious problems were shortages of ammunition, trucks, and fuel as well as the fact that Hitler would squander much of the tank production in the Ardennes and Hungary, but the quality of the weapons was still outstanding. Moreover, the shortening of the front in the east meant that for the first time in years the Germans had troops available to man defensive lines (even though the strength of the Ostheer was still 700,000 less than a year earlier) and to form at least a limited tactical reserve and that supply of these forces would be easier and quicker. Finally, it could be expected that German troops would fight bitterly to defend their homeland while even the seemingly inexhaustible Soviet reserves of manpower were reaching their limits. With

the German hope of a successful conclusion of the war reduced to splitting the Allied coalition, Hitler's main goal was simply to win time.[3]

To that end, the Vistula front had been prepared according to the
World War I model. In view of the enemy's manpower and material
superiority and their own continued deficiencies, the Germans aimed to
create successive defensive lines to a depth of 120 miles that would slow
an advancing army by forcing it to fight its way through endless defensive positions while at the same time defending against mobile counter-
thrusts. In addition, the backbone of this defense tactically was to be a
series of fortified front positions that, as in the Great War, would allow
the defenders to withdraw from the exposed forward line during an
enemy artillery bombardment, absorb the energy of the attack and slow
its momentum, and then launch tactical counterattacks that would snap
the defenders back to their original positions. The key problem, however, remained that this sort of defense required sufficient manpower
and mobile reserves, neither of which the Germans possessed. Army
Group A, which would bear the brunt of the Soviet winter offensive, at
best numbered 400,000 troops with just over 300 tanks and 600 assault
guns, while Luftflotte 6, covering the areas of both Army Group A and
Army Group Center, on 10 January 1945 had only 300 fighters against
10,500 enemy aircraft, a ratio of thirty-five to one, which actually represented an improvement from June 1944, when the figure was forty to
one. Although reinforced on the eve of the offensive with another 300
fighters and 700 ground attack aircraft, Luftflotte 6 faced the impossible
task of compensating for army weakness on a five-hundred-mile-wide
front. Nor, evidently, had anyone at the OKH pondered the obvious lesson of July 1943 when, during the Kursk offensive, a far smaller German
force had penetrated a much more elaborate Soviet defensive system.
The question of how a much smaller defending force in far less prepared
positions would halt an attack by an overwhelmingly superior enemy
remained unasked. Indeed, Army Group A's own study had already
shown not only that the Russians could break through and reach the
Silesian border in six days, but also that even stopping them on the Oder
was problematic.[4]

Although, in retrospect, an assault west from Warsaw toward Berlin
appeared most favorable for a rapid and relatively bloodless victory, the
planners at the Stavka seem to have arrived at this option only gradually. By late October 1944, the outlines of what became the Vistula-Oder
operation had been hammered out. While Soviet forces would continue
to attack in Hungary to draw off German reserves, preparations would
be made for the main thrust, with the goal nothing less than a daring

dash to Berlin that would end the war. This, however, required a considerable logistic effort to supply the massive forces involved, which, in turn, necessitated a rebuilding of the Polish railroad system. As a result, and much to Stalin's displeasure, the Red Army was forced to go on the defensive to prepare for what was expected to be the last offensive of the war. As finally developed, the Stavka plan envisioned a complicated two-pronged attack. In the north, the Second and Third Belorussian Fronts would assault East Prussia in a virtual replica of the disastrous August 1914 campaign, with the intention of isolating and destroying Army Group Center. The main attack, however, would be directed at the dangerously weak Army Group A on the middle Vistula. To the south, Konev's First Ukrainian Front would launch its assault from the Sandomierz bridgehead and advance toward Breslau. The next day, Zhukov's First Belorussian Front would unleash the main offensive from the Magnuszew bridgehead in the direction of Lodz and Posen. Both aimed through irresistible power and a rapid tempo to destroy the enemy in front of them and then strike into the heart of the Reich, ending the war in about a forty-five-day campaign. As usual, the Soviets assembled an overwhelming force for the winter offensive. Together, the First Belorussian Front under Zhukov, who had been given the honor of commanding the main thrust to Berlin, and the First Ukrainian Front under Konev had over 2.2 million troops, some seven thousand tanks, and five thousand aircraft. At the same time, the Second and Third Belorussian Fronts together possessed 1.67 million men, thirty-five hundred tanks, and fifteen hundred aircraft. In order to force a breakthrough as quickly as possible, at the point of attack in the bridgeheads the Soviets had amassed a numerical superiority of men, tanks, and artillery of ten to one.[5]

Although Guderian at the OKH, Gehlen at Foreign Armies East, and the army group commanders all anticipated the Soviet offensive—and even got the approximate date right—they expected a reprise of Bagration and, thus, had strengthened the German flanks at the expense of the center. Their response was also hindered by Hitler's failure to take intelligence reports of growing enemy strength and activity seriously and, thus, to allow Army Groups A and Center to withdraw to more defensible positions as well as his decision to deploy most of the Wehrmacht's scarce reserves to Hungary. Typically, as late as 9 January, the Führer not only refused to believe intelligence estimates of Soviet strength, claiming that they had to be inflated, but also even rambled on about the folly of giving ground in Russia in the first place. Although Guderian warned him that the Ostfront was like "a house of cards"—"if the front is broken through at one point, all the rest will collapse"—he had no convincing response. His reply that "the Eastern Front must help itself and make do with what it's got" was dismissed derisively by Guderian as an "ostrich strategy." Even on the tactical level, the Führer's obsession with holding ground undermined the planned German defense in depth. At his insistence, the second and main defensive positions had been built within a few thousand meters of the forward lines, which made them vulnerable to Soviet artillery and, thus, negated the whole German strategy. In addition, German commanders down to the company level, under threat of punishment, could leave their positions only if given explicit orders from their divisions, which, in practice, meant approval from Hitler, again undermining the idea of a flexible defense. Finally, in order to prevent their movement from being disrupted by enemy air attack, many German mobile divisions had been deployed far forward. Not only did they have less room to maneuver, then, but they also would quickly get caught up in the main attack, thus limiting their assigned role of pinching off enemy breakthroughs.[6]

When forward units of the First Ukrainian Front launched their attack in the early morning hours of 12 January, their commander, Marshal Ivan Konev, had taken steps to further negate the German defense in depth. Following an intense twenty-five-minute artillery bombardment, his troops in the Sandomierz bridgehead pushed into the first German position and in some cases the second, then halted before the main battle line, which was then subjected to a shelling lasting well over an hour and a half. Only after destroying up to a quarter of the strength of the defending battalions did the Russians storm ahead behind a rolling barrage. The effect was devastating. As Guderian had predicted, the Ostheer proved unable to withstand the enemy onslaught. Within hours, the Soviets had penetrated up to twelve miles through the German defenses. The speed of the enemy advance swept the German mobile reserve in this area, the Sixteenth and Seventeenth Panzer Divisions, almost immediately into the heat of battle, forcing them to fight for their lives rather than launch a counterattack. By the end of the day, Konev's forces had blasted a hole in German defenses over twenty-five miles wide and twelve miles deep. By the end of the second day, the penetration was thirty-six miles wide and twenty-four miles deep, while, on the sixteenth, the Soviets seized the cities of Radom and Czestochowa. Having achieved an operational breakthrough, Konev's troops raced to the west, sweeping aside or surrounding the remnants of the German defenders.[7]

Having achieved immediate success in the first phase of a staggered operation designed to hinder any movement of German forces opposite the main attack in the center, Soviet troops of Cherniakhovsky's Third Belorussian Front launched their offensive on the thirteenth. Striking against the Third Panzer Army of Army Group Center, they aimed to advance from the eastern border of East Prussia in the direction of Königsberg. Although effective German defense turned the attack into a prolonged penetration rather than a breakthrough, Soviet pressure nonetheless forced the German defenders back. Despite this momentary German success, the situation of Army Group Center began quickly to deteriorate, for the next day, 14 January, Rokossovsky's Second Belorussian Front attacked the Second Army out of its Serock and Rozan bridgeheads across the Narew just north of Warsaw. Quickly penetrating German defenses, Rokossovsky unleashed his mobile forces into the German rear. Soviet tank units swiftly overwhelmed the Seventh Panzer Division, the only formidable German mobile reserve in the area, forcing it to fight its way back to the west. Although Guderian that same day was already warning of an "extraordinarily serious situation," Hitler, as well as the army group commanders, seemed to have only belatedly realized the approaching catastrophe. On the thirteenth, the Führer had ordered two infantry divisions transferred from the west but refused to move the Fourth SS Panzer Corps out of Hungary and, incredibly, two days later directed that the Sixth SS Panzer Army be sent from the Ardennes to the east, but to Hungary, not Poland. On the fourteenth, with the situation of Army Group A nearing the critical point and the danger to Upper Silesia acute, Hitler ordered Army Group Center to transfer Panzer Corps Grossdeutschland and its two powerful divisions, Brandenburg and Hermann Goering, to its neighbor to the south, a decision that hurt the former more than it helped the latter. The result was immediately apparent; by 16 January, the Third Panzer Army neared the breaking point, and the Fourth Army faced encirclement, while, on the eighteenth, the Second Army's front snapped. The Soviets seemed well on their way to achieving their goal of isolating East Prussia and finally destroying their old nemesis, Army Group Center.[8]

With the Germans strained to the breaking point in both the north and the south, on the morning of 14 January Zhukov unleashed his First Belorussian Front from the Magnuszew and Pulawy bridgeheads south of Warsaw. Similar to Konev's successful effort to the south, after a twenty-five-minute artillery barrage, Zhukov's forces launched a series of powerful probing attacks on the forward German positions, followed by the main assault. Even though Zhukov planned to engage his mobile forces only on the second and third days of the attack in order to generate momentum, the power of the Soviet onslaught so unhinged the

Ninth Army's defenses that, by the end of the first day, the Russians in the Magnuszew bridgehead had advanced up to seven miles and the gains at Pulawy were even more impressive. The next day, the Soviets shattered a determined counterattack by the Nineteenth and Twenty-fifth Panzer Divisions and achieved an operational breakthrough. While Russian armored units began their drive toward Lodz, eighty miles northwest of Magnuszew, units of the First Polish Army moved north to encircle Warsaw, in combination with forces of the Soviet Forty-seventh Army that had pushed across the Vistula at Modlin, north of the capital. On the sixteenth, Hitler reacted in typical fashion to the brewing disaster, sacking the hapless commander of Army Group A, General Joseph Harpe, and replacing him with the ubiquitous Ferdinand Schörner. At the same time, he issued a completely delusory directive that Army Group A should not only hold a line from east of Krakow to Warsaw and Modlin but also attack and destroy or throw back the enemy all along the line—even though it could expect no reinforcements for two weeks. Despite the Führer's will, however, the next day Polish forces seized Warsaw with virtually no opposition, an action that touched off an explosion in Berlin. Hitler immediately suspected that the OKH had sabotaged his orders, on the eighteenth ordering the arrest of the three senior officers at Operations Branch, and the next day signing an order that effectively directed all commanders down to the division level to get permission from him for any operational movement, whether attack or withdrawal.[9]

The energetic and ruthless Schörner quickly emulated his Führer by getting rid of various commanders and issuing orders that exuded will and confidence, but to no avail. By the end of the day on the eighteenth, having destroyed forward German defenses and routed their counterattacks, Soviet forces were in a headlong dash westward, with some units advancing twenty-five to thirty miles a day. Behind the front, masses of civilian refugees, and not a few stragglers from combat units, fled westward in treks that would become all too familiar. Although the Grossdeutschland Panzer Corps, sent by train from East Prussia with orders to "restore the situation," and the remnants of the Nineteenth and Twenty-fifth Panzer Divisions tried to halt the Soviet advance near Lodz, they did little to slow Soviet momentum. By now, the Russians had steamrollered any opposition in their way and, enjoying complete aerial domination, swarmed toward the German border. The Stavka had itself been surprised by the swiftness of the collapse of Army Group A but reacted immediately and directed both Zhukov and Konev to push on to the Oder. On the nineteenth, Konev's troops overran the Reich border in Silesia and, three days later, reached the Oder south of Breslau.

Not to be outdone, Zhukov's troops seized the industrial city of Lodz on the nineteenth, encircled Posen on the twentieth, took Bromberg (Bydgoszcz) on the twenty-first, and had reached the fortifications on the east Brandenburg border by the twenty-sixth. Four days later, these had been broken through, and, by the end of January, Zhukov's troops had reached the Oder at Küstrin, over 240 miles from their starting point two weeks earlier. Over the first few days of February, they proceeded to establish bridgeheads across the Oder in preparation for what seemed an imminent strike at the Reich capital. Hitler reacted to this disaster, perhaps hoping to conjure something out of nothing, by renaming his army groups: Army Group Center became North, North became Courland, and A became Center. At the same time, a new army group, misleadingly named Vistula, was created under the most improbable of commanders, Heinrich Himmler, with the task of defending western Pomerania and the port city of Stettin.[10]

The Germans' only success in January—itself limited—had been in East Prussia, where, in putting up fanatic resistance for a piece of strategically pointless territory, they had forced Rokossovsky's thrust to diverge to the north and away from support of Zhukov to his south. By the twenty-fourth, however, troops from the Third Belorussian Front had pushed past Gumbinnen and threatened to cut off the Third Panzer Army in Königsberg, while forces from the Second Belorussian Front reached the coast, cutting off Army Group Center. On the afternoon of the twenty-fourth, seeing no point to the further defense of East Prussia, and hoping to save his troops in order to bring them back to Germany proper, the commander of the Fourth Army, General Friedrich Hossbach, told his corps commanders that they were to prepare for a breakout on the twenty-sixth. It was Hossbach who, as Hitler's military adjutant in November 1937, had secretly recorded notes from a top-level conference at which Hitler had outlined his plans for expansion, notes that were soon to be used as evidence of premeditated Nazi aggression at the postwar Nuremberg Trials. Hossbach now earned a different sort of notoriety. Although his plans for a breakout directly contradicted Hitler's orders, on the twenty-sixth, and with the knowledge of the commander of Army Group Center, General Hans Reinhardt, Hossbach nonetheless ordered his troops to attack to the west. Catching the Russians by surprise, units of the Fourth Army managed to push almost twenty miles to the west before furious enemy counterattacks halted their progress. Confronted with this clear violation of his orders, Hitler fell into a rage and ordered both Hossbach and Reinhardt relieved of their commands (although, amazingly, not of their lives). Just three decades after the great triumph at Tannenberg, which had made heroes of Hindenburg and Ludendorff, Hossbach and Reinhardt had earned only the Führer's ire. Reinhardt was replaced by General Lothar Rendulic, an Austrian of Croatian origin who had gained notoriety for his involvement in shooting hostages in Yugoslavia in 1942. An evident clone of Schörner, Rendulic seemingly took pride in having commanders and ordinary soldiers court-martialed and shot for retreating.[11]

None of this brutal activity could disguise the fact that, in three weeks, the Red Army had won perhaps its most spectacular victory of the war. Not only could Stalin go to the Yalta Conference in control of Poland and only a day's march from the German capital, but his Western allies were also still fighting hard battles west of the Reich border. In late January, moreover, both Zhukov and Konev had indicated their readiness, after a few days' rest to bring up supplies, equipment, and fresh troops, to resume the offensive toward Berlin and the industrial regions of Silesia. In urging that the enemy not be given time to prepare defenses that his forces would only have to break through later at high cost, Zhukov reinforced his argument by noting the absence of either a continuous defensive front or any preparations for a concerted counterattack. Viewed from Moscow, the end of the war seemed tantalizingly close.[12]

By mid-February, however, the Soviet offensive had ground to a halt. Although some have seen politics at work in this decision, more tangible factors played the key role. Although Soviet casualties had been relatively light, with only forty-three thousand permanent losses, the Red Army had lost almost thirteen hundred tanks and assault guns, not an insignificant figure even given its material preponderance. In the dash to the Oder, the Soviets had also bypassed numerous pockets of resistance that now had to be eliminated, especially those astride rail and supply lines. None of these posed a major threat, but they did demand troops and time. More to the point, German resistance on the flanks seemed to be stiffening appreciably, although, now that the Soviets could no longer rely on information from partisans, poor intelligence tended to exaggerate the threat. The heavy fighting in East Prussia had not only tied down large Soviet forces but also, in causing Rokossovsky to veer away from Zhukov's right flank, left the latter dangerously vulnerable to counterattack, which through hard experience the Russians had learned was a favorite German tactic. Nor was Zhukov's left flank fully secure. Although his troops had pushed beyond the Oder and secured large bridgeheads south of Breslau, Konev was also feeling increased German pressure on his left flank. Any drive on Berlin, however, would require

Konev to redeploy forces to his right flank in order to support Zhukov. Before such an operation could commence, then, he would have to clean up the situation on his left as well as deal with the problem of Fortress Breslau. In February, therefore, the Stavka halted the drive in the center and turned its attention to clearing up the flanks.[13]

To that end, on 8 February, Konev's forces in the south launched an attack out of bridgeheads across the Oder both north and south of Breslau and, despite stiff German resistance, had completed the encirclement of the fortress city within a week. Still, Breslau, with some 35,000 troops and 116,000 civilians, under the command of the fanatic Nazi Karl Hanke, stubbornly held out in destructive house-to-house fighting until 6 May. By the end of February, Konev's forces had closed up to the Neisse River and linked up with troops of the First Belorussian Front at the Neisse's junction with the Oder. Although this was largely a strategic backwater for the Soviets, the bloody fighting in February did bring the industrial riches of Silesia, a key area of armaments production out of range of Allied bombers, under their control, a reward not lost on a veteran industrializer like Stalin.[14]

Two days after Konev's attack, units of Rokossovsky's Second Belorussian Front struck northeastward into Pomerania to eliminate the Baltic balcony overhanging Soviet forces in Poland. Five days later, the Germans gave proof of the overstated Soviet fears for their flanks, launching one of the sorriest attacks in their military history. Conceived by Guderian as a typical two-pronged thrust into the flanks of an advancing enemy, Operation Sonnenwende (Solstice) was a fiasco from the beginning. Hitler eliminated the planned southern part of the operation by refusing to transfer the Sixth SS Panzer Army from Hungary, while the northern half fell under the operational control of Himmler's Army Group Vistula. Since the Reichsführer-SS had never actually gone anywhere near the front and, in contrast to his eagerness to persecute helpless racial inferiors, had demonstrated a thorough absence of combat spirit, Guderian managed after a two-hour argument to get his deputy, General Walter Wenck, appointed to lead the offensive. The Führer agreed but, typically, took command power away from Himmler without specifically giving it to Wenck. Although Guderian managed the amazing feat at this stage of the war of cobbling together ten divisions for the counterattack, seven of them panzer, the troops involved were poorly equipped, inexperienced, and woefully led. Even the timing of the attack seemed a comedy of errors as one division lurched forward on the fourteenth, taking the Soviets by surprise, while the rest of the attack went off on 15 February. By the eighteenth, Sonnenwende had sputtered to a halt, having gained at most three miles. Ironically, although a complete failure, it evidently made an outsized contribution to the final Soviet decision to delay the attack toward Berlin. Within days, Zhukov had turned forces north to aid Rokossovsky, while Konev had halted his operations on the Neisse. The Vistula-Oder offensive, however, had, in less than two months, taken the Soviets from Warsaw to the gates of Berlin, inflicted irreplaceable losses on the Germans, and cost the enemy the vital Silesian industrial areas. As everyone knew, the next step would be Berlin.[15]

In his last radio addresses in early 1945, Hitler continued to stress the intention of the "Jewish-international world conspiracy" to eradicate the German people as well as to affirm his belief that the indomitable spirit of the Volksgemeinschaft would still prevail. Although the shared sacrifices and ritual mourning that had elevated the dead to fallen heroes had sustained internal unity for a surprisingly long time, in the face of an obviously lost war the image of fighting valiantly to the end for the Volksgemeinschaft inspired fewer people. Increasingly, the members of that national community now largely ignored their Führer. He was, in fact, so little a presence in their daily lives that rumors had persisted for months that he was seriously ill or dead. Nor was he spared criticism, SD reports now regularly indicating that average Germans held him responsible for deliberately provoking war and, thus, for causing the devastation now being rained on Germany. "What an enormous guilt Hitler bears," declared one soldier in late January. The urban inhabitants of the western industrial centers had been paying the price all along, and now the eastern German population would reap the whirlwind of the savage brutality inflicted on the Soviet peoples by Hitler's unconstrained policies of exploitation and mass murder.[16]

As news spread of the rapid Soviet advance, panic-stricken residents of East Prussia, West Prussia, Pomerania, and Silesia filled roads as they fled, often unprepared, into bitter cold. The sight of long columns of civilians trudging westward, pulling what possessions they could save in carts, became common. "The roads are full of refugees, carts, and pedestrians," recalled one eyewitness. "People are gripped by panic when the cry goes up, 'The Russians are close!'" Others told of the chaos and desperation at railway stations as people scrambled to get on the last trains heading west, trampling each other, even throwing people out of boxcars. Still others related tales of distraught mothers gone mad unwilling to believe the babies they carried in their arms were already dead or conveyed horrifying images of towns and villages burned to the ground, of marauding Red Army soldiers looting and pillaging, of the mass rape of women and the shooting of men who came to their aid, of hospitals turned into death houses, of systematic brutality. All too often, these horror stories turned out to be true, as Red soldiers frequently wreaked vengeance for what had been done to their own country and families. One estimate put the number of civilians killed in the eastern provinces in the first months of 1945 at 100,000, while another suggested that as many as 1.4 million women might have been raped (including one of every two women in Berlin). Since many women were raped repeatedly, even a figure as high as this cannot convey the reality of the constant anxiety, lingering uncertainty, and inner turmoil to which women were subjected. Gang rapes were common, as were sexually transmitted diseases, while many unwanted pregnancies resulted in abortions or abandoned babies. The sexual violence went on for weeks and months, long after the war had ended. Women learned to hide, to disguise themselves, or to find a protector (preferably an officer).[17]

Over and above the impact of Soviet propaganda or political indoctrination that encouraged them to view all Germans, whether men, women, or children, as "Fascists," many of the Russian soldiers were motivated, as a veteran of Rokossovsky's armies put it, by "blind feelings of revenge." And who could wonder at this? Tens of thousands of Soviet soldiers were from areas devastated by German occupation, had lost relatives or loved ones to the invaders, or had themselves been wounded by an enemy invader. In addition, the ferocity of the fighting had hardly abated, and, even at this late stage of the war, the Soviets were suffering very high casualties. The anger and rage of average soldiers, their desire to wreak vengeance on the people held responsible, were visible for all to see. "We are taking revenge on the Germans for all the disgraceful things they did to us," wrote one Ivan in a feeling that was representative of his fellows, who believed that they were simply executing a just punishment on the German population, which was now experiencing firsthand the gruesome reality of war. Many Russians indeed regarded their actions as part of the struggle for "people's justice." "You said we should do the same things in Germany as the Germans did to us," wrote a son to his father. "The court has begun already." "Our fellows have not acted any worse in East Prussia than the Germans did in the Smolensk region," a Red soldier noted in his diary in late January 1945. "We hate Germany and the Germans very much. In a house our boys saw a murdered woman and two children. You often see civilians lying dead in the streets too. But the Germans deserve these atrocities that they unleashed. . . . One need only think of Majdanek and the theory of supermen [Übermenschen] to understand why our soldiers are happily doing this." As Soviet soldiers, in their push westward, liberated hundreds of extermination and labor camps and witnessed firsthand the gas chambers, charred corpses, piles of bodies, and pitiful survivors left to die, the deep impression of these atrocities mingled with memories of their own ruined farms and towns to create a powerful anger and thirst for revenge. "Germany must now experience the taste of tears," wrote one observer after witnessing a destroyed village. "Frightful horrors have been committed on this earth. And Hitler is the one who gave rise to them. And the Germans celebrated these horrors. A gruesome punishment for Germany is only just."[18]

Adding to the powerful rage and lust for destruction was the disconcerting realization of most Red soldiers that the standard of living in Germany was immeasurably higher than their own. "The people here live very well," admitted one at the beginning of February, "better than us. . . . So many fine things!" "There is everything," exulted another, then added tellingly, "even things that we have never seen." "We are eating very well, ten times better than the Germans lived in the Ukraine," claimed one Ivan, while a comrade marveled, "I am swimming in riches." The shrill contrast between the unexpectedly high German living standards and their own miserable conditions at home, however, inevitably produced confusion, then anger. If conditions were so good in Germany, wondered many, why had they attacked Russia? And, asked others, why don't we live as well as the enemy? To deflect the latter question, Soviet propagandists quickly adopted an explanation reflected in many of the soldiers' letters and diaries: the Germans lived well at the expense of others, for their riches were plundered from occupied Europe. Although effective as an explanation, this propaganda line also served to intensify the anger and rage of average soldiers, who set about plundering Germany like a horde of locusts. Not only were vast quantities of industrial machinery, railroad equipment, raw materials, and even people (for forced labor) carried off to the Soviet Union at the behest of state authorities, but ordinary soldiers also looted with a disconcerting frenzy as the orgy of revenge assumed a material as well as a personal dimension. The alcohol that seemed so abundant and freely available in Germany served to escalate the murderous rage of the Russians. Food, drink, watches, household items—anything and everything was taken and much sent home, hopelessly clogging the Red Army postal service. What could not be consumed or dispatched was often simply burned.[19]

This lust for destruction also manifested itself in a systematic and persistent campaign of rape and sexual violence, as noted above. Although not the only violent crime committed by Red Army troops as they swept westward, rape was certainly the most prevalent. In some cases, instances of it had sexual overtones, especially in a restrictive, puritanical, male-dominated society many of whose members were troubled by the sight of German women in provocative Western-style dresses, wearing makeup and in high-heeled shoes. German women, in short, seemed to some both decadent and wickedly seductive and were regarded by many as the spoils of war just as much as food and alcohol. The men's actions, after all, had been encouraged, if not explicitly ordered, by Moscow, whether to destroy the German will to resist or to engage in what would today be regarded as ethnic cleansing, since the stories of Soviet atrocities spurred Germans to flee from precisely those areas to be given to Poland after the war. For most, however, rape had little to do with sex. Rather, it neatly meshed desires for revenge and hatred of the enemy's wealth, reinforced the fragile masculinity of men under enormous strain, and cemented their victory over the German antagonist. It was, as Catherine Merridale has noted, no accident that many German women were gang-raped or raped in the presence of husbands or fathers. In this sense, rape represented the ultimate collective triumph of the group, and, although women were the immediate victims, the larger point was intended for German men: they were now the ones without power who could not intervene to alter the fate of their women or, by extension, their nation. Revealingly, German women often recalled later that, when they protested, Russian soldiers invoked the image not of German soldiers raping their wives but of the invaders killing innocent women and children. They had laid waste to Russia and caused an unimaginable degree of death and destruction; now they would be taught a lesson.[20]

The fear of the Red Army was by no means limited to the civilian population. By this point in the war, most Landsers understood the fundamentally criminal nature of the war in the east and feared that they might be held accountable by the Russians. Reports now indicated a growing problem with morale and discipline, especially among rear support units and outfits hastily cobbled together from the remnants of units shattered by enemy action, in which the men had no sense of primary group loyalty. Among these men, there was a reluctance to fight and a quickness to take flight; fear of Russian revenge predominated, a mood that easily dissolved into panic. Cases of desertions and plundering soared, retreats often turned into routs; soldiers (and local party officials) not infrequently commandeered places on the trains meant to carry civilian refugees westward from the threatened eastern provinces. Soldiers displayed signs of resigned indifference, lack of empathy, a loss of any sense of the future, and a preoccupation with the fates of their families. Increasingly, too, Goebbels's propaganda stressing enemy atrocities and raising fears of Asiatic-Bolshevik hordes descending on Germany backfired. For many, it simply reinforced their will to flee, while others regarded it as profoundly hypocritical since, as one man put it, "Weren't our SS men even more cruel. . . ? We have shown the others how to deal with political enemies." Nor did exhortations on ideological lines have much impact. Holding on seemed foolish to many since it promised only death and destruction, especially as Allied planes now rained down bombs on virtually all areas of Germany unimpeded. Hitler's boast in the 1930s, "Give me ten years and you will have airy and sunny homes, you will not recognize your cities," was now invoked with bitterness and derision. Local party efforts to stir up enthusiasm were often greeted with indifference; where *Sieg Heil* or *Heil Hitler* once predominated, there was now only a conspicuous silence.[21]

German soldiers had long fought from a complex mix of motives. The Nazis had been successful to a great extent in mixing traditional aspects of military life (obedience to orders, discipline, fulfillment of duty, camaraderie) with National Socialist notions of the ideal soldier (service to the Volksgemeinschaft, fighting on behalf of an ideal, the soldier as the kernel of a new society, obligations to comrades), so any precise separation of the lines of motivation is difficult. Traditional ideas of fighting to defend family and country mingled with the Nazi racial emphasis on protecting the Fatherland from the allegedly inferior hordes or the threatening Jewish conspiracy bent on destroying Germany ("Wir kämpfen für das Leben unserer Frauen und Kinder!"). In his propaganda, Goebbels appealed to the men's sense of superiority as well as to the simple survival instinct ("Sieg oder Siberian"), while he even sought to use the logic of the hopeless situation in order to continue the fight: a common slogan among men at the end of the war was, "Enjoy the war because the peace is going to be hell." The Nazis sought to reinfuse men with the original spirit of the movement, reminding them of Nazi accomplishments and that the Volksgemeinschaft was a revolutionary social-egalitarian society that had provided real benefits, both material and nonmaterial. As signs of demoralization and indiscipline increased, Nazi authorities tried other measures, such as active political indoctrination through National Socialist leadership officers. These proved not as effective as hoped, given the time demands on the officers and men, the weariness of the endless retreat, and the fact that propaganda was quickly overtaken by events. Most Landsers instead came to rely for support on trusted officers at the platoon and company level, with their willingness to continue the struggle decisive for many ordinary soldiers.[22]

To combat the unmistakable evidence of growing demoralization and disintegration among the troops, the Nazi regime used increasingly radical measures as the terror that until now had been visited on the subject peoples was directed against the Wehrmacht and the civilian population. Flying courts-martial and drumhead tribunals punished with death those suspected of any action or utterance deemed guilty of undermining the war effort or damaging the fighting spirit. Men in buildings flying white surrender flags were to be shot, while individual soldiers were authorized to take command of their squads if their nominal superior officer failed to obey orders to resist. Anyone suspected of being a deserter, even those luckless men whose units had simply been shattered by enemy attacks, was to be dealt with in the harshest manner. Such men were dismissed by General Otto Wöhler, the commander of Army Group South, as "cowards and shirkers and therefore war criminals who deserve no mercy since they left their comrades to bear the hardness of combat alone. . . . [They] are to be condemned by a court-martial and shot. . . . Who refuses to fight from cowardice will die in shame!" Not to be outdone, Guderian ordered that "cowards were to be shot ruthlessly." The consequence of the Nazis' furor directed against their own troops was plain for all to see. At Frankfurt on the Oder, German soldiers wearing signs that proclaimed, "I am a deserter," hung from both sides of the bridge. Landsers in the final phase of the war grew accustomed to the sight of daily executions or comrades hanging from trees and bridges. In all during the war, Wehrmacht courts sentenced some 35,000 Landsers for desertion, of whom 22,750 received the death sentence, which in roughly 15,000 cases was carried out. In addition, up to 10,000 people, mostly civilians, were summarily executed in this final spasm of terror.[23]

Nor, in its death throes, did the regime neglect to deal with its perceived enemies. Even as it crumbled from both sides, it took its revenge on internal opponents. Hundreds of anti-Nazi resisters and those who had plotted Hitler's assassination were now murdered, often in the cruelest fashion. As Gestapo chief Heinrich Müller told one, in that characteristic Nazi obsession with the earlier war, "We won't make the same mistake as in 1918. We won't leave our internal German enemies alive." In addition, throughout Germany in the last weeks of the war, long, meandering columns of emaciated, starving prisoners became a common sight as the Nazis marched survivors of the camps back to Germany to suffer yet further in horribly overcrowded and disease-ridden facilities. Mortality rates were enormous, with those unable to continue the journey simply shot. "It was," remembered one march participant, "as if they were shooting at stray dogs." Although some Germans took pity and offered food to the wretched marchers, many others reacted with hostility and vindictiveness, not infrequently, in a sign of just how deeply Nazi propaganda had taken hold, lashing out at the Jews for their alleged responsibility in starting the war. Throughout Germany, the conquering Allies stumbled on camp after camp overflowing with the unburied dead and the miserable survivors clinging to life.[24]

By this last phase of the war, Hitler's destructive rage was no longer directed at specific groups, however, but now encompassed the entire nation. In his determination to prevent a repetition of November 1918, no price, even self-destruction (his own and Germany's), was too high to pay. Convinced that his enemies were determined to bring about the ruination of Germany in any case, drawing on his own rigid social Darwinism and, perhaps, as well on Stalin's example, Hitler urged a scorched-earth policy that would deny the enemy the ability to profit from German industrial resources. The idea, of course, was ridiculous since the Allies could easily supply themselves from their own resources, but, if applied, it would have had far-reaching consequences for the German people, whose very existence would have been threatened. In yet another dreadful irony, Hitler, who had long warned that the Jewish conspiracy was out to destroy Germany, resolved himself to take measures that would ensure just such a result. Few in Germany were this fanatic, even those of his close associates who wanted to continue the struggle, and certainly not the mass of the German people, who primarily wondered why he did not end the war and stop, as one put it, "the senseless murder." In yet another ironic invocation of 1918, Victor Klemperer recorded the bitter contrast noted by one man in late March: "It can't go on much longer . . . , but how we shall suffer in the meantime! What decent people Hindenburg and Ludendorff were by comparison! When they saw the game was up, they brought it to an end and didn't let us go on being murdered."[25]

Many in Germany were, indeed, already looking to the future after this lost war and seeking to save what could be saved. One of those evidently was the ambitious Albert Speer, who hoped, in combination with Germany's industrialists, to preserve the substance of the nation's economic resources for the post-Hitler future. In September 1944, he had already persuaded Hitler to allow German factories west of the Rhine to be disabled rather than destroyed, on the argument that they would then be available for production once German counterattacks regained the area. There is no doubt that he also acted to spare French industry from destruction and conspired with some military commanders, among them Guderian, Model, and Heinrici, to limit the destruction of factories, power plants, bridges, mines, and other facilities vital to the German economy. This policy of "paralysis of production" rather than complete destruction was not, at least initially, as unambiguously directed at preserving Germany's material substance for the future as Speer, in his self-serving memoirs, has claimed. In the second half of 1944, Speer, along with Goebbels, had been an avid promoter of total war, a ruthless exponent of mobilizing the *Volkskraft* (the power of the people), whose efforts had resulted in the continued expansion of armaments production that allowed resistance to continue. Until the middle of January 1945, in fact, he projected a rather optimistic assessment to Hitler and other top Nazis, insisting that he could maintain armaments output as long as the Wehrmacht could hold the existing economic area and no more skilled workers were drafted into the army. His confidence had certainly influenced Hitler's January decision to launch attacks in Hungary rather than reinforce the Vistula since Speer had convinced the Führer of the importance of Hungarian oil and bauxite deposits.[26]

Speer's epiphany that the war could no longer be won through armaments production seems to have come rather belatedly, only at the end of January with the failure of the Ardennes offensive and the loss of the vital Silesian industrial area. Even now, however, his actions hardly resembled those of a man intent on ensuring a speedy end to the war. He made it clear in late January that he placed military needs above the interests of the east German population, instructing Gauleiter in the east that the armaments industries should continue working to the last possible moment. He also demanded that the Wehrmacht be given absolute priority in all transport matters, dooming large numbers of civilian refugees. Moreover, after personal consultation with army leaders, he arranged an emergency armaments program that aimed to "force out of the arms production . . . anything which could still be forced out of it," especially fuel and munitions, so that the Wehrmacht could continue to wage a hopeless war. This economic strategy of holding out to the last almost certainly contributed to the belated evacuation orders that resulted in such misery. Nor did Speer show much concern for the plight of the refugees, whose suffering he observed firsthand. Instead, he rather cold-bloodedly accepted the reality of large-scale death, remarking, in the unmistakable language of a Nazi racial ideologue, that this was "a tough selection . . . [that] would contain a good kernel of this unique people for the distant future." Although aware that the war could not be won economically, Speer nonetheless seemed intent on preserving as much Reich territory as possible from absolute destruction.[27]

This formed the background to his famous memorandum to Hitler, written on 15 March but not delivered until the eighteenth, that forecast, from an economic point of view, that the war could last only another four to eight weeks and, therefore, urged the Führer not to destroy the industrial and economic infrastructure of the Reich but only to temporarily disable it. If Speer believed that his earlier argument would again prove successful, Hitler's response on the nineteenth quickly dispelled that illusion. If the war was lost, the Führer suggested, then the only thing left to do was to deny the enemy anything of value in Germany. Besides, even if a miracle occurred and lost territory was recaptured, it was foolish to believe that the enemy would not himself engage in a scorched-earth policy and destroy everything. His famous "Nero Order" of 19 March 1945 ("Destructive Measures on Reich Territory"), which ordered the destruction of all military, transport, industrial, and communications installations as well as all material resources, also betrayed the iron logic of his own social Darwinism. "If the war is lost so too is the Volk," he declared, and no special measures need be taken to ensure its survival since "the Volk [would have] shown itself to be the weaker." The future belonged to the victors. Those Germans left alive would be the dregs of the racial stock since the best would have been killed in the war, so there was no use to provide for their future existence, even on the most primitive of levels.[28]

In the end, this order was never carried out, and Speer certainly played a role in persuading many Gauleiter and military leaders not to implement it. Still, his own immediate reaction to what was clearly a rebuke from his Führer was much more equivocal than he later allowed. He had, in fact, prepared a second memorandum, one written on 18 March, that he now promoted. In it, he demanded that "drastic measures to defend the Reich at the Oder and Rhine are to be taken," including the "ruthless" mobilization of all military personnel and Volkssturm units and their immediate transfer to the river defense lines. "By holding out tenaciously on the present front for a few weeks," he concluded, "we can win the enemy's respect and perhaps bring about a favorable end to the war." In this memorandum, Speer, like Hitler, indicated no wish to capitulate but emulated his Führer in wanting to stake everything on another, fully illusory gamble. He showed no reluctance to use young recruits or poorly trained Volkssturm men as little more than cannon fodder, nor did he evidence any understanding that each day the war was prolonged the death toll on the fronts, as well as from Allied carpet bombing, rose. Ironically, far from his "heroic resistance" to the Nero Order, it was precisely his solidarity with the Führer, at one point demanding that it was "our duty to make every effort to increase resistance to the utmost," that finally persuaded Hitler at the end of March to modify his order since it made "no sense" for such a small territory as Germany. Crucially, as well, the collapse in loyalty to the Nazi regime in the last weeks of the war meant that people at the local level would hardly have implemented the destruction in any case, as Goebbels fully realized.[29]

The nonimplementation of the Nero Order was the first clear sign that Hitler's authority had begun to crumble, at least domestically. Self-destructive warfare, however, continued to be waged by the Wehrmacht, whose leaders continued to obey the Führer's commands to fight the war to the last. Neither side in March had, it seemed, a clear idea of how to end the war. Although Stalin and the Stavka certainly attached great importance to seizing Berlin, it was not evident to them that the final battle would necessarily be fought at the German capital. After all, Hitler might choose to move south into an Alpine fortress—the Russians, too, like the Western allies, were receiving disturbing reports—and continue the fight as a guerrilla struggle. Nor, until late March, had Stalin displayed much urgency about taking Berlin. His attitude changed, however, with the sudden acceleration of the American push across the Rhine, encirclement of the Ruhr (where Model's entire Army Group B, some seventeen divisions, was trapped in the last great Kessel of the war), and rapid movement into central Germany. Although in late March Eisenhower, much to Churchill's and Montgomery's displeasure, had notified the Soviet leader that he intended to turn his forces to the south and southeast to prevent an enemy move into an Alpenfestung, Stalin put little trust in his Western allies. In late March, he had openly expressed to Czech leaders his expectation that the Germans and Anglo-Americans would negotiate a separate peace (something that Hitler's close associates urged on him but that he rejected until he could deal from a position of strength, which effectively meant no negotiations), while, in early April, he openly insulted Roosevelt by suggesting in a letter that the Germans in the west had effectively stopped fighting. Eager to seize the great prize, and fully aware of the political importance of controlling Central Europe, Stalin now insisted on concrete plans for an operation across the Oder aimed directly at Berlin.[30]

For the Germans any hope of a military solution bordered on the delusional, yet even now the generals continued to play their assigned role in Hitler's Götterdämmerung. Although no rational person could be in doubt about the final outcome of the battle, the Germans remained determined to exact a high price for their defeat. The OKW had stripped much of the western front in order to assemble some eighty-five divisions and Volkssturm units for the final struggle in the east. Although old men, untrained boys, soldiers recovering from wounds, and those previously classified as physically unfit composed the great majority of the manpower in these units, they were surrounded by a core of hardened veterans that significantly increased their combat power. In addition, Speer's effort to squeeze the last bit out of the German war economy meant that these men were generally well equipped with small arms, including large numbers of the Panzerfaust, the devastating short-range antitank weapon. Moreover, the Germans could still field large numbers of tanks and aircraft, although severe fuel shortages crippled their effectiveness. Of more immediate help was the transfer of large numbers of flak units to the Oder front, where they would employ their powerful eighty-eight-millimeter guns as antitank weapons.[31]

Perhaps most importantly, the German retreat had shortened the lines considerably, which meant that they would now have sufficient manpower to build and at least partially man three successive lines of defense. Indeed, correctly anticipating the main axis of the enemy attack, the Germans had constructed an elaborate defense in depth on the central Oder consisting of three positions stretching some twenty miles to the rear, or halfway to Berlin. Each of these lines, moreover, contained up to three separate belts of trenches, fortified strongpoints, antitank obstacles and ditches, flak gun emplacements, and dense minefields. During the spectacular campaigns of 1944 and early 1945, the Soviets had grown accustomed to piercing relatively lightly manned front positions, then exploiting their superior mobility, not only to shatter the enemy front, but also to prevent any new defense from being established. Now, however, the Red Army no longer had any maneuver room since Berlin was only forty miles away and the Americans not more than a hundred miles to the west. Instead, the Soviets faced the unpleasant task of fighting a series of penetration battles against successive, fully manned, well-equipped positions whose defenders could be expected to put up fierce resistance. Furthermore, the flat Polish countryside that had favored a mobile attacker had now been replaced by terrain much more suitable for defense. The so-called Oderbruch, the floodplain on the western side of the river that stretched up to ten miles in depth, was a low-lying, marshy area crisscrossed by numerous small streams and drainage ditches, largely devoid of trees or any natural cover, containing many towns and villages that could be turned into strongpoints. Not only would it be difficult for infantry or heavy tanks to traverse this region, but also, once across it, the high bluffs, especially the Seelow Heights, afforded superb positions from which the defenders could make effective use of all their weapons. If, then, Hitler retained any glimmer of hope, it rested on a successful defensive battle that would finally exhaust the Russians, although even here General Busse, the commander of the defending Ninth Army, had a clearer perspective. "Even if American and British tanks slammed into our rear," he indicated, his men were to contest every step of the Russians westward in order to do their "soldierly duty" to their people.[32]

Neither side remained passive as the Soviets built their strength for the inevitable assault on Berlin. In order to prevent the Germans from transferring forces to the Oder front, the Soviets remained active in Hungary and Silesia; both served, as well, to distract Hitler's attention from the main threat. To gain better jumping-off points, the Russians also hammered throughout March at expanding and uniting their various bridgeheads across the Oder, while the Germans resisted just as determinedly. The focal point of the March battles soon became the fortress of Küstrin, at the confluence of the Warthe and Oder Rivers. For a variety of reasons, ranging from the historical to the tactical, Hitler was soon obsessed with holding on to the city, which resulted in a wearying, weeks-long contest that the Germans could not win. At his insistence, they even mounted a late March counterattack from Frankfurt/Oder in order to relieve the besieged city. Although it caught the Soviets by surprise and even reached the outskirts of Küstrin, the attack, which could not possibly have altered the balance of forces, rapidly lost momentum, with the only result a waste of scarce German forces. Amazingly, even at this late date, Hitler could not accept the inability of the Wehrmacht to win operational victories or the fact that the enemy now dictated events. Seething with anger, and searching for a scapegoat, the Führer found him in one of his few remaining rational military leaders, Heinz Guderian. Having vigorously defended the actions of the commanders involved in the Küstrin attack, the field marshal now once more felt Hitler's wrath, being given on 28 March six weeks "sick leave." Although Hitler would have preferred no OKH chief of staff or to surround himself with old free-booting Freikorps types, he nonetheless named General Hans Krebs, a young firebrand, acting chief of staff. Küstrin fell on the thirtieth, an action that brought to a close the grinding March battles along the Oder that had cost both sides dearly.[33]

With the preliminaries resolved, the Stavka could now finalize its plans for the Berlin Operation. Painfully aware of history, of examples of Russian armies denied certain victory because of overconfidence and poor preparation, it was determined to make this the last offensive of the war. Following an impressively rapid redeployment of troops, the Soviets were able to assemble a force of 2.5 million men, 6,250 tanks, and 7,500 aircraft in the three fronts participating in the assault. In order to ensure a breakthrough on the first day of the attack, Zhukov not only created special shock groups but also demanded an extensive tactical concentration of forces, with the result that enormously large numbers of men and equipment were crammed into a very narrow front. In this way, he hoped literally to shove his way through German defenses, but, in the event, he managed only to make a mockery of the Schwerpunkt principle, as the first day would show. Although the Soviets estimated enemy forces at 1 million, with almost 800,000 combat troops, this proved a gross exaggeration of their actual firepower since a sizable percentage of the defenders were Volkssturm battalions or hastily assembled units of undertrained boys. At the beginning of April, the Ninth Army, for example, which would bear the brunt of the attack, reported its strength at around 190,000 men, of whom fewer than 100,000 were regarded as combat troops. To its north, the Third Panzer Army fared no better; on 1 April, it had a daily strength of 51,406 men, with only 27,595 front soldiers. Army Group Vistula, facing the First and Second Belorussian Fronts, had fewer than 800 operational tanks and assault guns, while the Luftwaffe could muster perhaps 1,600 operational aircraft, although the chronic shortage of fuel hindered the effectiveness of both tanks and aircraft. To bolster their defenses, the Germans had managed to designate a pitifully few divisions as a reserve, while the leadership of the Hitler Youth had trained 6,000 boys for specially created *Panzernahkampfeinheit* (tank close combat units). Their task, as the name suggested, was to destroy enemy tanks at close range, not an activity designed to ensure a long life. Nonetheless, on 12 April, Hitler announced that he expected a "colossal" victory since nowhere else in Germany was a front so strongly held or well supplied. That the enemy had an even greater concentration of force and that the German supply of munitions was good for only a few days were facts that he ignored.[34]

The Soviet plan of attack envisioned, as the Germans anticipated, several simultaneous blows along a broad front, with Zhukov's First Belorussian Front providing the main thrust directly opposite Berlin. To his north, Rokossovsky's Second Belorussian Front would support Zhukov's right flank, with its primary task being to strike quickly toward the Baltic ports of Stettin and Rostock. To the south, Konev's Third Ukrainian Front was to attack across the Neisse and Spree Rivers, with the main force advancing west and northwest toward the Elbe and the southern outskirts of Berlin, while a secondary attack aimed in the direction of Dresden. Rather pointedly, however, Stalin refused to draw an exact

boundary line between Konev's and Zhukov's army groups, thus inviting each of his ambitious marshals to entertain notions of capturing the
great prize of the war. In operational terms, in order to ensure that this
would finally be the war-ending operation, the Stavka aimed at shattering and destroying German forces east of Berlin, surrounding and seizing the capital quickly, and splitting Germany in two by advancing to the
Elbe no later than two weeks after the beginning of the offensive. This
latter move would, Stalin believed, not only limit any further German
resistance but also have the salutary effect both of impressing his Western allies and of keeping them as far from Berlin as possible.[35]

Early on 14 April, in order to draw as many enemy troops as possible
into the front line and, thus, expose them to artillery bombardment once
the main attack began, Soviet forces began a preliminary assault against
German defenses in the Oderbruch. In some areas, the weight of the
attack was so great that already in this opening phase the Germans had
to dispatch troops from the reserve to maintain the line. The pressure
continued the next day, and, in places, the Soviet attackers wedged their
way three miles into the first line of defense, but the Germans, by now
familiar with this Soviet tactic, refused to allow more of their troops to be
drawn forward. Not until 3:00 A.M. on 16 April did the Russians launch
the main offensive. In the hope of providing some element of surprise,
Zhukov had chosen to attack two hours before sunrise, relying on 143
searchlights to illuminate the battlefield. Neither the extended preliminary assault of the previous two days nor the intense thirty-minute
artillery barrage accomplished the Russians' goals, however, for the
Germans had simply withdrawn much of their strength to the second
and third positions, with the result that the shells fell largely on empty
trenches. Moreover, since dust and smoke filled the predawn air, the
powerful searchlights merely disoriented the attacking troops, who
floundered about while trying desperately to see the enemy positions
behind the dense dust clouds. As waves of concentrated infantry stumbled blindly forward on the narrow fronts, the troops inevitably piled on
top of each other in the withering German fire. By daybreak, the confusion was complete. Nor could tanks come to the aid of the infantry since
the roads quickly became jammed and the shoulders and fields were too
swampy and heavily mined to allow vehicles to advance. Even when the
infantry managed to reach the base of the Seelow Heights, it could go no
further since a canal running in front proved difficult to cross and the
slopes were too steep for the accompanying vehicles. By late morning,
then, the attack had made disappointingly little progress.[36]

Zhukov, anxiously watching the scene from a forward command post, now compounded the problem by making an error more typical of Soviet commanders in 1942–1943 than in the late stage of the war. Impatient, he ordered his armored exploitation force to move forward in an effort to hasten the penetration of German defenses. Not only did this play to the German strength in antitank defenses, but it also caused the attacking units to become hopelessly entangled. Each time they attempted to move forward through the maze of fortified villages, German infantry armed with Panzerfausts swarmed around, destroying vehicles and further blocking the roads, while armored units launched tactical counterattacks. The opening day for the Soviets had, thus, resembled a comic opera more than a well-planned attack by five Russian armies against vastly inferior enemy forces. Despite high losses, they had not been able to penetrate the first German line of defense, let alone achieve any sort of breakthrough. Disappointed, Zhukov telephoned Stalin with the bad news, which the ill-tempered dictator took surprisingly calmly. This was likely because he had already received a report from Konev indicating that his attack had gone off splendidly, information that he gleefully passed on to the chagrined Zhukov. Moreover, given the disappointing lack of progress of the First Belorussian Front, Stalin the next day deliberately provoked a competition between his commanders to see who could be the first to Berlin. In a tense telephone conversation with Zhukov and Konev late on the seventeenth, Stalin erased even the indistinct boundary line between the two army groups, thus encouraging the bitter rivals to intensify their efforts. Although risky in the sense that it increased the danger of Soviet units slamming into and firing on each other by mistake, this move certainly accomplished its practical purpose, which was to speed the advance.[37]

The defensive success of the Ninth Army had exacted a stiff toll, however, as already on the first day of the attack it had been forced to commit its reserves to the battle, even those intended for operational counterattacks. Thus, when the attack resumed the next day, the lack of German strength began to have noticeable consequences. As Soviet forces pushed inexorably forward in a slow, grinding battle, the brittle German front began to crack in numerous sectors. The most intense fighting had now developed around two key cities, Wriezen to the north and Seelow in the center, where all day on the seventeenth the two sides traded attack and counterattack. Although reinforcements were rushed to the front on Berlin city buses and Hitler allowed tactical withdrawals in some areas to furnish yet more troops, the Germans had begun to approach the limits of their strength. For the Soviets, too, the culmination point appeared near, for Zhukov had thrown service troops into the battle and threatened all who refused to advance with the death penalty. The breaking point came on the eighteenth. Zhukov, now feeling Stalin's whip on account of the increased tempo of the American advance in the west, drove his troops forward ruthlessly. By noon, Seelow had fallen and the Ninth Army's front between that city and Wriezen begun to crumble. Still, not until the next day did the Germans give up the struggle for Wriezen, and not until the twentieth did the Soviets manage finally to break through the third and final line of defense. It had taken four days (six if the two-day preliminary attack is included) for the First Belorussian Front to break the resistance of nine understrength divisions and achieve the objectives set for it for the first day. Russian attacks had bogged down so severely that most of the Landsers had managed to extricate themselves and withdraw. Still, even the most determined of defenders were bound sooner or later to run short of men and ammunition, a weakness exploited by Zhukov in his brute force tactics. The operation had not been a thing of beauty, and the Soviets had paid their usual high price—in less than a week, they had lost thirty thousand men and seven hundred tanks—but at last the Oder line had been broken. In the final irony, at the Oder the Soviets finally reached their manpower limits, as Hitler had always anticipated, but by then it was too late.[38]

For all practical purposes, on 20 April, Hitler's fifty-sixth birthday, the battle for Berlin had been decided. Even as long-range artillery from Zhukov's Third Shock Army brought the eastern suburbs under fire, to the south forces from Konev's First Ukrainian Front were rapidly approaching the city, having successfully broken the Neisse-Spree defenses at Cottbus. Although Konev, too, had encountered unexpectedly fierce resistance, his troops, supported by effective artillery fire, had been much more adept than Zhukov's at piercing the German defenses. On the first day, 16 April, they had not only forced the Neisse but also penetrated the first line of German defenses and punched a mile into the second German belt. German counterattacks the next day were beaten back as the Soviet advance reached a depth of ten miles. By the end of the nineteenth, Konev had achieved an operational breakthrough, with his forward tank units now racing some twenty to thirty miles to the northwest, in the direction of Berlin. On that same 20 April, Konev's panzers cut the central nervous system of the German military, seizing the combined command center of the OKW/OKH at Zossen, thus eliminating any effective control over German military operations. They also penetrated into the southern suburbs of the city itself. Konev's success in part stemmed from more favorable ground on which to operate as well as a curious misjudgment by the OKH, which had believed that the main axis of Konev's advance would be to the southwest, in the direction of Dresden and the industrial areas of Saxony and Bohemia, and, thus, had positioned the strongest defenses on the right flank of Army Group Center.[39]

In these days, the only German success was registered in the north, where Rokossovsky's Second Belorussian Front struggled to force its way across the lower Oder south of Stettin. Although the woefully under-strength Third Panzer Army under General Hasso von Manteuffel had been able to limit Russian attempts, begun with the usual probing attacks on 16 April and then widened to full-scale assaults on the eigh-teenth, to secure and expand bridgeheads on the west bank of the river, even these tactical victories were misread in Berlin. Both Hitler and Krebs convinced themselves that they were not the last desperate efforts of a beaten army but signaled the possibility of building a stable defen-sive front east of Berlin. Inexorably, however, Manteuffel's forces were ground down as the advance of Zhukov's units to the south opened a gap that he could not cover and offered the enemy the possibility of a deep breakthrough to the west. By the twenty-fifth, the same day that troops of Zhukov's First Belorussian Front and Konev's First Ukrainian Front closed the ring around Berlin and that American and Russian troops met at Strehla and Torgau on the Elbe, Rokossovsky's units were also poised for their own decisive breakthrough. Perhaps nothing symbolized so well the wreckage of the once-proud Wehrmacht than this union of its enemies, which split Germany in two. Although the official celebra-tion of this epochal event that shifted the balance of power away from Europe for the first time in three centuries took place at Torgau, fifty miles downriver from Dresden, the initial encounter had actually taken place to the north at the small town of Strehla. There, just before noon, advance American and Soviet patrols had met amid the gruesome car-nage of a German refugee trek. The banks of the Elbe were littered with the corpses of dozens of women, children, and old men, victims not of their enemies but of their own troops. Desperate to escape the oncoming Soviets, German soldiers had blown up the makeshift pontoon bridge even as civilians still streamed across. As many as four hundred might have been blown to bits or drowned.[40]

By this time, Hitler's hopes of forming an effective defense of Ber-lin or of drawing the Soviets into a protracted, Stalingrad-like struggle for the city had evaporated. Although some local defensive successes on both the northern and the southern ends of the front, near Stettin and Görlitz, encouraged the delusional thinking so typical in the Führer's bunker in these days, seemingly more realistic hopes had been placed in the possibility of a successful urban struggle. After all, Berlin would easily be the largest city to be conquered by an enemy army in the war, not only in terms of population, but also with regard to physical size. With a population swollen to 4.5 million people, and sprawling over an immense area, the city seemed perfect for prolonged urban warfare. Not only did it have an extensive subway system and underground network of canals that would facilitate troop movements, but many housing blocks, as well as the numerous flak towers that dotted the city, had already been fortified as strongpoints. In addition, British Bomber Command's futile effort to create another Hamburg in Berlin had resulted in much more extensive destruction of residential areas than industrial complexes; the rubble-clogged streets of these neighborhoods had, thus, already been turned into potential strongpoints for urban fighting. Finally, the failure of Zhukov's offensive to trap and destroy German forces east of Berlin meant that the possibility still existed for them to be drawn back into the city. Although Zhukov had in February already ordered that special storm troop units be formed for just such an eventuality, both he and the Stavka understood just how costly such fighting could be. Nor did Stalin relish the prospect of being tied down in protracted urban fighting since, in his paranoid vision, any time won by the enemy gave his Western allies the further chance to do the deal with Hitler that he expected and feared.[41]

Still, none of this came to pass for the simple reason that the Germans no longer possessed the strength to alter their fate. Although Hitler and Krebs in the Führer's bunker continued to issue orders that were completely out of touch with reality and were regarded by their recipients with incredulity, the remnants of the Wehrmacht fought on more like a headless chicken than the formidable force of old. Even as between 21 and 25 April the Russians worked to complete the encirclement of Berlin, Hitler's attempt to form a defense line, and, thus, his refusal to allow the intact units of the Ninth Army to withdraw, resulted in their being cut off from Berlin, isolated, and encircled. By now, too, the Führer's seemingly endless stream of orders for shattered or nonexistent units to launch relief attacks toward Berlin were simply ignored by his field commanders, who thought increasingly in terms of fighting their way to the west to surrender to the Americans rather than the Soviets. By the time the ring had closed around Berlin, on 25 April, the Ninth Army too found itself surrounded. Rather than fight its way north into the city, however, its commander, General Busse, decided instead to seek a breakout with his remaining forces, perhaps 150,000–200,000 men, to the west and the Elbe. Beginning on the night of 25–26 April, and continuing

over the next week, the troops of the Ninth Army fought desperately in
a dense forest—a "dreadful mash of tortured human bodies," according
to the Soviet writer Konstantin Simonov—against fierce Soviet attacks to
make it westward. On 1 May, in a last great effort, some troops and civilian refugees—with their numbers estimated at anywhere from 20,000 to
40,000—managed to reach their goal; 60,000 of their mates had fallen in
the struggle, while roughly 120,000 went into captivity.[42]

The decisive battle for Berlin had been conducted outside the city.
Despite Hitler's hopes and Zhukov's failures, what went on inside the
city, violent and destructive though it was, amounted to not much more
than a contested mop-up operation as the Germans had fewer than fifty
thousand combat troops and perhaps forty thousand Volkssturm and
Hitler Youth in the city. The surreal scenes in the bunker and the Führer's periodic outbreaks of astonishing rage and hatred were little more
than black comedy. By 30 April, Soviet troops, deliberately attacking
along narrow sectors rather than on a broad front, had cut the defending Germans into four parts, then had begun smashing each piece in
systematic fashion, using their storm troops, supported by artillery firing point-blank, to clear the defenders from fortified apartment blocks.
Although especially heavy fighting raged in the subways, by 29 April
they had cleared some three hundred blocks and, against fanatic resistance, reached the Reichstag building in the heart of Berlin. At 1:00 A.M.
the next morning, 30 April, Hitler heard the final news that all attempts
to relieve the city had failed. Shortly after 6:00 A.M., he held a last conference with his military commanders, at which he was informed that
Soviet troops were near the Reich Chancellery and that the area could be
held for no more than another twenty-four hours. Later that afternoon,
accompanied by his new bride, the Führer committed suicide, following
which his body was partially burned in a shell crater just outside the bunker. The next day, 1 May, troops of the First Belorussian and First Ukrainian Fronts joined just south of the Reichstag. Early the next morning, at
6:30 A.M., the commander of the city garrison, General Helmuth Weidling, capitulated with all resistance ended by that evening.[43]

Berlin had gone down, not, as the Führer had hoped, in a Wagnerian burst of glory that would serve as an inspiration for future generations, but in a ragged wave of destruction. Fierce resistance mingled
with plundering; troops fighting desperately in cellars contrasted with
corpses hanging in the streets, the work even at this late date of flying courts-martial. Scenes of horror were commonplace, but the fighting seemed strangely detached, with none of the urgency of Stalingrad.
This was not the rallying point but the death knell of the Wehrmacht.

It had finally been crushed. The Soviet victory, however, had once more been costly. In the three-week Berlin operation (16 April–2 May), the Soviets lost over 360,000 casualties, of whom slightly more than 78,000 were killed, along with 2,000 armored vehicles destroyed. Total German losses are not known with any precision, the Russians claiming over 450,000 killed on the three fronts involved in the Berlin operation alone. This is certainly an exaggeration since the best estimate of German deaths arrives at an April–May total of 376,000 for all areas of fighting, although perhaps 125,000 German civilians died in the battle for Berlin (far more than in the Allied air raids on the city). For those Germans who had survived the fighting, the reality was both absurd and sobering. Hitler was dead, the Third Reich had vanished like a ghost, with hardly anyone taking notice, but the survivors faced "chaos"—"total and impenetrable chaos."[44]

The fall of Berlin did not, however, end the fighting. As German forces struggled on to allow "valuable German people" to reach safety in the west, Stalin seemed ever more consumed by his paranoia that, at this late stage, his Western allies would still betray him and make a deal with the Germans. Moreover, he showed every determination not to be cheated of his hard-won victory and to acquire as much of value as he could. In both these impulses, one can, perhaps, see the seeds of the future Cold War, but, at the time, the more immediate concern was with the Red Army's old nemesis, Army Group Center, which had come so agonizingly close to conquering Moscow. Ironically, although it had been shattered in the summer of 1944, it now formed a relatively intact force of over 600,000 troops guarding Saxony and Bohemia, the last industrial areas controlled by the Reich. Paradoxically as well, its final destruction would come not in Germany but in Czechoslovakia, one of Hitler's first victims. Soviet attacks in March and April against the right wing of the army group had made disappointingly little progress, but, spurred perhaps by General Omar Bradley's offer on 1 May of American assistance in liberating Czechoslovakia and the presence of Patton's U.S. Third Army poised on the border with Bavaria, Stalin now ordered the First, Second, and Fourth Ukrainian Fronts to accelerate their advance.[45]

Even as Zhukov's forces continued mopping-up operations in Berlin, the Soviets scrambled to regroup for the Prague Operation, which, with a combined force of over 2 million men and sixteen hundred tanks, was designed as a rapid thrust directly on the Czech capital. Although the attack was not intended to begin until 7 May, its timing was altered in response to an uprising in Prague on the morning of the fifth as well as reports of local German withdrawals. As Czech resistance fighters engaged in bitter street battles with German troops, they also made an appeal by radio for Allied assistance. With American troops already in Pilsen, just to the west, Stalin spurred Konev to launch his attack as quickly as possible. Konev responded by launching his strike from the north on the sixth. Within two days, his troops had seized Görlitz, Bautzen, and Dresden and, on the ninth, linked up with advancing Second Ukrainian Front forces for the final drive on Prague. On the night of 8–9 May, with the Western allies already having accepted formal German surrender and a further ceremony to be held in Berlin that day, Konev ordered two special tank detachments to race for the city. Over the next few days, from the ninth to the eleventh, Soviet forces ended the fighting in Prague, which had cost the Czechs some three thousand dead and ten thousand wounded, linked up with forces of the U.S. Third Army east of Pilsen, and accepted the surrender of the more than 600,000 German troops remaining in the Czech pocket. Perhaps fittingly, even at the end of this most destructive of wars, this last military operation, at least three days of which had taken place after the formal end of hostilities, had cost the Soviets twelve thousand killed and over forty thousand wounded. The spiral of violence unleashed by Hitler on 22 June 1941 had now run its course, but only after a final three-week campaign, the Berlin Operation, that resulted in another round of appalling Soviet casualties and the nearly complete destruction of the German capital.[46]

Despite the widespread perception in the West that the Normandy invasion was the event that defeated Nazi Germany, the real war had always taken place in the east as any look at relevant statistics indicates. In 1941, three-fourths of all German troops were fighting in the east, and, from December 1941 to November 1942, over 9 million troops on both sides fought in Russia, while in North Africa a relatively small British force contested Rommel's Afrika Korps (which had relatively few German troops in any case). In November 1942, the British defeated Axis forces at El Alamein, inflicting sixty thousand casualties; that same month, the Soviets at Stalingrad surrounded and eventually destroyed four times that number. In July 1943, while over 2 million German troops fought at Kursk and in Ukraine and over 5 million on the entire eastern front, Allied forces invaded Sicily and expelled sixty thousand Germans from the island. Even after the Allied invasion of Italy, in October 1943, 63 percent of total Wehrmacht forces fought in the east, and, until the Allied invasion at Normandy, the Germans largely considered Western Europe as a reserve area. Nor did Normandy do much to change the proportions of troops on the various fronts since, in August 1944, roughly two-thirds of German troops were still engaged in the east.[47]

Casualty figures also reinforce this reality. In March 1945, the Ostheer had lost a total of 6,172,373 dead, missing, wounded, or taken prisoner, or almost exactly double its strength on 22 June 1941. Moreover, from June 1941, in no month of the war did the Germans suffer more deaths in the west than in the east, with December 1944 (the Ardennes Offensive) the only month that came close. Even then, the Germans suffered 85,000 deaths in the east (during a "quiet" period) compared to 74,363 on all other fronts. In the decisive months of June–August 1944, when the Wehrmacht was being torn asunder, the Ostheer lost 589,425 killed compared to 156,726 on all other fronts combined. Total Wehrmacht casualties in World War II have been estimated at over 11,300,000, including, by the most thorough calculation, 5,318,000 military dead. Of these, 2,743,000 (or 51.6 percent) died on the Ostfront through December 1944, while another 1,230,000 (23.1 percent) were killed during the Endkampf, the final months of the war, again with the great majority (at least two-thirds, if not more, or roughly 811,000) fighting the Russians. A total of 3,554,000 Germans (67 percent of total losses) thus died in combat with the Red Army. In addition, of the roughly 459,000 German prisoners of war who died in captivity, the great majority (363,000) perished in Soviet camps. That pushes the number killed by Soviet actions to at least 3,917,000 (74 percent of the total). By contrast, 340,000 German soldiers (6.4 percent) died in the western theater, with another 151,000 (2.8 percent) killed in Italy. Even if we assume that one-third of the deaths during the Endkampf were inflicted in the west (419,000), that means that 910,000 (17 percent) of total German military deaths were attributable to Anglo-American forces. If one adds the 138,000 deaths suffered by the navy, most in the Battle of the Atlantic, along with the remaining 96,000 who died in captivity, that brings the total of military deaths accounted for by the Western allies to approximately 1,048,000 (21.5 percent). Rather more sobering, anywhere from 360,000 to 465,000 civilians died in Allied bombing raids, a number roughly equivalent to the military deaths inflicted by the Western allies in Italy and the western theater. Almost four of every five German military deaths thus came at the hands of the Red Army. Certainly, no one today can visit any cemetery in Germany, and definitely no military cemetery, without being given a stark visual reminder of this reality: row on row of names with the sobering inscription "died in Russia" or "missing in Russia" next to them.[48]

None of this is meant in any way to denigrate the contributions of the Western allies, which were vital to victory. Lend-Lease aid was of pivotal importance to the Soviet Union, not so much in 1941–1942 as in 1943–1944. Without aid from the Western allies, the Soviet economy would have been even more heavily burdened, while the mobility that allowed the Red Army to fight and win large-scale offensives in 1944 would not have existed. Most probably, without Lend-Lease vehicles, the crushing Soviet drives of that year would have stalled at an early stage, having quickly outrun their logistic tail, thus allowing the Germans time to withdraw, avoid encirclements, and prepare new defensive positions. Allied military actions also came at key points and drew off scarce German resources, while the air war over Germany not only contributed to the Soviet ability to achieve air superiority over the Ostfront but also had an enormous impact on restricting and then crippling the German war economy. The Soviets also enjoyed the advantage of essentially fighting on only one front. Without Western aid, Stalin might well have had to fight another year in order to achieve victory, if his system had survived in the first place, or he conceivably would have sought a negotiated way out of the war. Still, the Red Army (and the Soviet civilian population in general) suffered enormous losses. Although the generally accepted post-Communist figure for total Soviet military deaths has hovered around 11.5 million (or 39 percent of those mobilized during the war), with a total of 29 million military casualties, other estimates of total Soviet armed forces dead have ranged as high as 26 million. At the highest end of the estimates, then, ten Ivans were killed for every Landser lost on the Ostfront. There have been equal discrepancies with regard to civilian deaths (which were not all caused by direct German action), with the estimates ranging from 16.9 to 24 million, with a total demographic loss in the Soviet Union during World War II at anywhere from 35 to 43 million. In addition, the Soviet Union was left physically in ruins, with an extraordinary catalog of destruction: seventy thousand villages, seventeen hundred towns, thirty-two thousand factories, forty thousand miles of railroad track, and over a third of Soviet wealth destroyed. While American GDP had grown anywhere from 50 to 72 percent and German between 14 and 23 percent, Soviet GDP between 1940 and 1942 fell by 34 percent, with a total decline between 1940 and 1945 of 18 percent. By any reckoning, the devastation wrought by the Germans in the Soviet Union had been appalling.[49]

If Soviet forces fought on a few days after the official end of the war in order finally to destroy the Nazi beast, the question remains as to why the Germans fought on in such hopeless circumstances. Hitler, of course, had vowed no repetition of November 1918 and had held to his conviction with extraordinary determination, long after prospects for a military victory had vanished. But that begs the question of why he was able to continue fighting, of why his system did not collapse. In part, he profited from the caution of his enemies. The broad front strategy that both pursued in 1944 was militarily and politically cautious. In this fear of taking any risks, both the Soviets and the Anglo-Americans betrayed great respect for the Wehrmacht, which, although battered, was still capable of springing nasty surprises. Terror and the willingness of the Nazi regime to inflict it on its own citizens also played an important role. Average Germans, in contrast to the Soviet population under Stalin's arbitrary and violent rule, had hardly been exposed to systematic terror during the course of the Third Reich, but now, at the end of a lost war, they experienced a noticeable increase in violence and coercion. Despite signs of apathy, war-weariness, and resignation, they nonetheless responded not by revolting (as in 1918) but by continuing the struggle. Certainly, in the east, Soviet atrocities and Goebbels's lurid propaganda played a role in stiffening the backs of people who might otherwise have given it up. The very brutalization of war seemed to play a role as well, as many Landsers, their feelings stunted by the hardships they had suffered, lacked empathy for German civilians as they retreated. Not only did they seem indifferent to the destruction around them, but it was also hard for them to visualize an alternative. Although some acted to defend their homes or allow their compatriots to get to the west and others, especially officers and younger Landsers, resisted from ideological conviction or Nazi indoctrination, most simply sought to escape war with their own lives. Beyond Hitler, the key responsibility for the senseless continuation of war, however, lies with the weak and irresponsible military leadership that failed to act to oppose his obviously destructive plans and orders. In this, they were abetted by people such as Albert Speer and other technocratic and industrial figures who at all costs kept the armaments economy producing the weapons necessary to maintain the fight. Ultimately, then, the Third Reich expired, not with the "magnificent mystery of the dying hero," or as a result of "heroic idealism," but as a sordid act of Hitlerian willed self-destruction in which far too many people who knew better participated.[50]

Conclusion

Its impressive blitzkrieg triumphs over Poland and France obscured the reality that, when the war began in September 1939, Germany had no clear economic, military, or technical superiority over its Western adversaries. The furious rearmament effort of the 1930s had simply allowed the Germans to make up the vast gulf produced by the Treaty of Versailles and the Great Depression of the early 1930s. Further, the war that did result was, from the perspective expressed in *Mein Kampf*, the wrong war. Hitler had originally intended an Anglo-German alliance to confront the Judeo-Bolshevik threat but in 1939 reversed himself and allied with the Soviet Union in an effort to forestall an Anglo-French declaration of war. After the quick destruction of Poland, then, the war that followed was in the wrong place, at the wrong time, and against the wrong enemy. This conjunction of circumstances has led many historians to conclude one of two things: either rapid rearmament generated an overheated economy that threatened a domestic crisis and, thus, pushed Hitler toward war, or he simply gambled that, having failed to oppose earlier territorial grabs and with little leverage now that Germany's pact with the Soviet Union made it blockade-proof, the Western democracies would once again stand aside in the face of aggression. Both interpretations contain a kernel of truth, for Hitler did make a rational assessment of economic and strategic factors before plunging ahead, but both are incomplete. What they lack, as Adam Tooze has suggested, is the racial-ideological dimension.

Hitler, as has long been known, was obsessed with the alleged Jewish world conspiracy and its threat to Germany. The trauma of the war experience, the revolutionary upheavals and destruction that shook Central and Eastern Europe (especially the triumph of Jewish-Bolshevism in Russia), and the sense of threat and opportunity created by the collapse of empires all left an indelible impression on him. His toxic sense of conspiratorial anti-Semitism reinforced his belief that the Jews had somehow fomented and uniquely profited from the upheavals all around.

Further, the threatened German nationalism he had imbibed as a youth in Vienna was further exacerbated by the outcome of the war, when not just the Habsburg Empire but Germany itself seemed on the verge of destruction. Lost territory represented more than just a province or two changing colors on the map; for Hitler and other racial nationalists, it meant not only a truncation of the German racial body but also an opportunity, in the tangle of ethnic groups and lack of clear boundaries in Central Europe, for other nationalities to profit at Germany's expense. Nor was Hitler in any doubt as to who was responsible for this destruction. In February 1945, in one of his last conversations with Martin Bormann, he remarked, "An unfortunate historical accident fated it that my seizure of power should coincide with the moment at which the chosen one of world Jewry, Roosevelt, should have taken the helm in the [United States]. . . . Everything is ruined by the Jew, who has settled upon the United States as his most powerful bastion." At the very end of a lost war, in which his plans for a great continental empire had been foiled in large part by the relentless resistance of the Soviet Union, it was the pivotal role of Roosevelt and the Jews to which Hitler assigned blame for the German defeat.[1]

Hitler's obsession with the power and strategic potential of the United States had, we now know, emerged as long ago as the late 1920s in his unpublished *Second Book*. The perceived threat from the United States to a large extent also determined, from his point of view, the purpose of the war. America, to Hitler, represented more than just an economic or strategic challenge; its liberal, capitalistic, democratic, pluralist vision, behind which lurked the malevolent Jew, posed an existential threat to his own vision of a homogenous racial community unified in a common vision and led by a strong Führer. Germany, after all, had not lost the Great War but been undermined by jealous enemies. Unable to shed his wartime mind-set, Hitler fully subscribed to the *Dolchstoss* (stab in the back) myth, not least because it neatly encapsulated two key ideas: solidarity and betrayal. In this view, the trench experience had forged a unique "community of the front," itself a microcosm of a new, unified society, while the huge popular investment in the war domestically had been undermined by the "internal enemy." The "real Germany," then, had not lost the war but been betrayed by Jewish war profiteers. Although the myth initially obscured the reality of total war, that Germany had lost a drawn-out war of attrition because it lacked manpower, raw materials, and industrial and financial resources, by the late 1920s Hitler had come to appreciate the importance of these material factors. The only logical response to this situation, as sketched first in *Mein*

Kampf and then in the *Second Book,* was to create a new unified society within Germany, then carve out a Lebensraum for the German Volk sufficient to allow it to compete with the United States in the struggle for global preeminence. The only such vast spaces available in Europe lay in the east and could be taken only by force. The mission of conquest, for economic and racial reasons, thus formed the central core of Hitler's ambition. For him, after all, the purpose of a state was nothing less than to secure the existence of the Volk. It also fit well with his fundamentalist social Darwinism: either the German Volk struggled for Lebensraum and assured its existence, or its racial enemies would deny it the means to life and, thus, assure its extinction.[2]

By the summer of 1939, however, Germany's ability to conduct that existential struggle seemed in doubt. Rapid rearmament had, indeed, provoked an economic crisis, although this was not in itself the key reason for war. More importantly, Hitler's actions had prompted accelerated rearmament efforts by Great Britain, France, and the United States as well as a hardening of the global diplomatic constellation against Germany. Not coincidentally, Hitler's famous threat on 30 January 1939 to annihilate the Jews, to which he returned with such obsessiveness in subsequent years, was intended as a precise warning to Roosevelt to stay out of Germany's "legitimate" affairs in Europe. As before 1914, Hitler saw the hand of the Jewish conspiracy in the effort once again to isolate and encircle Germany. Ironically, Stalin's gamble on provoking an intracapitalist war offered Hitler a way out of his dilemma. Faced with an enemy coalition allegedly orchestrated by world Jewry, he needed to strike hard and fast, an opportunity now available because of the pact with Stalin. In the interim, he could fight a war in the west with no threat of a second front and protected against the worst effects of the much-feared British blockade.[3]

The result, although spectacular, also reinforced the economic and racial logic of Hitler's ideological vision. Great Britain, influenced and supplied by the United States, chose to continue the war rather than settle with Germany, while Roosevelt launched a truly enormous rearmament effort in America that would, in a few years, produce a military force that would swamp the Wehrmacht. Moreover, although Germany's conquests in the west contained valuable industrial and human resources, they lacked precisely the things that Germany most needed and the British proceeded to blockade: raw materials, food resources, and, most importantly, coal and oil. Once more, the logic of the situation forced Hitler to turn his eye to the east—only the raw materials, food supplies, and oil of the Soviet Union would allow Germany to organize an integrated continental economy that could compete with America. Nor would further trade agreements with Stalin suffice. Behind Stalin, Hitler believed, lurked another tentacle of the Jewish conspiracy. Economic dependence on the Soviet Union would result in the same fate for Germany as reliance on the Anglo-American global market: extinction. Propelled by a peculiar combination of racial arrogance (the notion of Slavic inferiority), the sense that the borderlands of the former Russian Empire were up for grabs (Germany, after all, had seized them in World War I), and urgency (a belief that time was against Germany), Hitler saw the only solution to the German dilemma in securing the necessary resources by conquest. If Germany acted immediately, a short window of opportunity existed since the American rearmament program would not bear fruit until 1942, while the spectacular victory over France offered the means: a short blitzkrieg campaign. Barbarossa was, thus, planned as a swift operation that would allow Germany access to the vital resources of the Soviet Union even as it continued preparations for the ultimate struggle against America.

Unable, or perhaps unwilling, to concentrate all its resources on Barbarossa, as early as Smolensk in July–August 1941, and certainly no later than Moscow that autumn, Germany found that blitzkrieg had run aground. Not only did it face the prospect of two wars, but Hitler also initiated actions for a third war as well, that against the Jews of the Soviet Union. If the enormous extent of the Nazi project is to be comprehended, it must be understood in its interrelated political, economic, social, cultural, racial, and military contexts, as a grand mission of colonization, economic exploitation, and racial recivilization. Hitler prided himself on being a *Raumpolitiker*, a geopolitician who thought in imperial terms, rather than merely a *Grenzpolitiker*, one concerned only with border revisions. Expansion was, thus, intended not just to rectify the injustices of Versailles but also, as he put it to the Reichstag after the conquest of Poland, to create "a new order of ethnographic conditions . . . , a resettlement of nationalities." This untangling of ethnic groups, predicated on the establishment of a racially cleansed German community at the heart of a larger European empire, formed the context in which his racial ideas should be understood. The first test case for this racial restructuring was Poland, where efforts began almost immediately to repatriate Volksdeutsche from the Baltic states and the Soviet Union to the Wartheland, the part of western Poland to be annexed to Germany. At the same time, room had to be made for the new arrivals, so ethnic Poles and Jews had to be removed. The Poles could simply be dumped in the General Government, but the Jews, as a perceived racial menace, had to be watched and, thus, were concentrated in a few urban ghettos or, as part of another experiment, sent to the Nisko reservation, an inhospitable border area southeast of Lublin. In all these actions, the Nazis learned a number of things: war legitimized harsh measures against enemies; disentangling populations was a messy, often brutal, business; territorial expansion and ethnic untangling offered vast opportunities for ambitious, ruthless underlings; and Jews had no place in the anticipated New Order.[4]

As Nazi planners confronted the prospect of further expansion to the east, they recognized another problem, one that defied easy solution: greater success in territorial conquest would bring with it more racial inferiors and Jews, thus intensifying the demographic dilemma. The solution lay not merely in shoving people around on a limited scale but in a truly ambitious and revolutionary socioeconomic and demographic project. This formed the context for Generalplan Ost, which was nothing less than a utopian vision of transplanting ethnic Germans and related Aryan peoples into the vast expanse of European Russia. While Western Europe's industrial capacity would be integrated into the German economy, Eastern Europe would be the scene of a complete agricultural and demographic restructuring. Urban areas would be greatly reduced, while a neofeudal system of Germanic farms and villages would be established along key transportation routes. The logic of this "settler colonialism" also involved, as it had in North America and Australia, the large-scale removal of the native population from the land: those who could not be incorporated, above all the Jews, but also large parts of the Polish population, were to be expelled across the Ural Mountains into Asia, left to starve, or both. Although efforts were made to implement some pilot schemes, Generalplan Ost largely fell victim to changing developments in the war. In any case, the most grandiose schemes were always intended to take place after a successful conclusion to the war, when Generalplan Ost would be merged within a broad consolidation of all conquered areas in a general settlement plan.[5]

Although Generalplan Ost had been a brainchild of Himmler's and important primarily for showing the direction of the Nazi colonial vision, another aspect of the same impulse that had far more murderous consequences was the hunger policy, the genesis of which lay not in the SS but in Goering's Four-Year Plan, the Reich Ministry for Food, the quartermaster-general's office in the Wehrmacht, and the military economic-armament office. Behind this lay Hitler's imprint, influenced as always by the experience of World War I and revolution. The key to Germany's defeat in the earlier war, the Führer was convinced, was the British blockade, which exposed the key German weakness—lack of economic self-sufficiency, especially in foodstuffs. This problem was accentuated with the upheavals and revolutionary movements of the postwar period, especially in the new Soviet Union, which moved from being primarily a grain-exporting region to being an industrialized society that consumed all its agricultural production. This meant that a reliable food supply for Germany was even more imperiled. In an "age of economic empires," Hitler had argued as far back as November 1937, "the primitive urge to colonization" had to manifest itself. Bolshevism, the "Guidelines of Economic Policy for the Economic Organization East" asserted in May 1941, echoing the Führer, had caused significant economic disturbances and destroyed the natural balance between food-producing and food-consuming areas. The only solution, reintegrating Russia into this balance, "will necessarily lead to both the industry and a large part of the people in the hitherto food-importing areas [of the Soviet Union] dying off." The full ramifications of the scheme would have resulted in murder on a breathtaking scale: Nazi bureaucrats estimated that anywhere from 30 to 45 million inhabitants of the Soviet Union would have perished, with some believing those figures too low by half.[6]

In the event, pragmatism (the need for labor) and the practical realities on the ground (lack of available manpower) limited the eventual impact of the hunger policy. If not the tens of millions of useless eaters envisioned by its originators, a few million Soviet citizens nonetheless perished as a direct result of deliberate starvation. Among them were urban populations such as Kiev, Kharkov, and Leningrad as well as roughly 2 million Soviet prisoners of war. Although Hitler's endless verbal ramblings to his intimates during the euphoric days of midsummer 1941 betrayed a clear sense of the apparent colonial nature of the project, the key point, as Donald Bloxham has stressed, lies outside this historical precedent and in another. In his emphasis on food supply and reversing the racial fragmentation of Eastern Europe, Hitler revealed the influences of a very specific historical, spatial, and economic context. As an Austrian German, Hitler had been influenced by the sense of threatened ethnicity so prevalent among the German population of the Dual Monarchy. He was also acutely aware, as illustrated in *Mein Kampf*, of the flux and openness for exploitation of the borderland areas of the former Habsburg and Romanov Empires. Moreover, as other statements of the 1930s attest, he recognized that various policies of ethnic cleansing, murderous to a greater or lesser extent, had been carried out before, during, and after World War I—and some with the connivance and encouragement of the victorious Western powers. Finally, the constant allusions to

grain supply fit neatly with his fears of a reoccurrence of the food shortages that he believed had crippled and destroyed the imperial German
war effort. The earlier war experience confirmed his Darwinistic vision:
food resources were both vital and scarce and had to be obtained so that
its enemies could not again starve Germany into submission. If Germany was to win, then others had to lose; for the Führer, it was a zero-
sum game. His vision for the east, then, was less a classic colonial one
of naked economic exploitation and more an attempt to restructure and
unify the area racially, then organize it as part of the broader European
struggle against the American challenge.[7]

It was also within this larger context that the fate of the Jews was
determined. The original goal, to remove them from the German area
of influence and control, largely remained intact in 1939–1940, even as
the Jewish problem intensified. Forced emigration had not been effective, efforts to shove Polish Jews across the demarcation line with Russia
had failed, the reservation scheme came to naught, and the Madagascar
Plan collapsed as a result of British persistence in the war. Although a
territorial solution remained official policy, by the time of Barbarossa a
new dynamic was emerging. Security concerns, the identification of Jews
as Communists and potential partisan fighters, and the fear of the internal enemy undermining the war effort all led to the preinvasion decision
to murder the male Jews of the Soviet Union. In its implementation, the
decision also demonstrated the intersection between policy and ambition. In the early summer of 1941, local initiatives often drove policy forward as ambitious and ruthless SS and SD men used the autonomy given
them to drive forward a murderous solution to a problem they knew had
high priority with the Führer. The decision in the summer of 1941 to
expand the murder to include all Soviet Jews and then the further resolution that same autumn to kill all Jews under German control both
illustrated the importance of the military situation: unexpectedly tough
Soviet resistance, high German losses, the traditional fear of partisan
war and internal upheavals fomented by Jews, and the apparently sudden prospect of complete success combined to create an explosive atmosphere. Inspired, perhaps, by the expectation and euphoria of imminent
victory after such a tough struggle, Hitler now definitively decided that
the Jews had no place in the new Nazi imperium. The territorial solution, which itself had assumed high levels of mortality through "natural
causes," gave way to an "exterminationist solution," which envisioned a
much more immediate death, especially for the Jews in those areas designated for German colonization.

The timing, implementation, and attainment of Hitler's far-reaching goals, of course, depended on military triumphs. The success of the Wehrmacht formed the prerequisite for the realization of Hitler's vision. Military victories and setbacks set the ultimate parameters for the extent to which this imperial policy could be pursued: how much of policy was to be put into effect, the extent and success of this implementation, and the compromises that undermined the full impact of Nazi plans. Solving the Jewish problem and creating the racial-utopian Germanic Lebensraum in the east were both central to the Nazi worldview, and, for both, the war-fighting ability of the German armed forces was the essential component. The realization of this fact also raises the question of the extent to which the Wehrmacht knowingly participated in and supported Nazi criminal activities in the Soviet Union. Despite postwar attempts to depict the Wehrmacht leadership as primarily apolitical and technocratic, from the end of World War I it had been a bastion of aggressive nationalism and revisionism, conservative, strongly anti-Bolshevik, and anti-Semitic. Deeply affected by the war experience and the defeat in 1918, the great majority of its members accepted the Dolchstoss myth and, with Hitler, were determined that Jewish-Bolshevism would not again destroy Germany.[8]

Even before the invasion of the Soviet Union, the army leadership raised no objections to the flood of criminal orders emanating from the Führer and the OKW. From Hitler's injunctions to conduct a brutal and merciless war of extermination to cooperating with the RSHA in delineating spheres of responsibilities behind the front to specific measures such as the Commissar Order and the Barbarossa Jurisdiction Decree, the army leadership could be under no illusions as to the purpose and methods of the coming war in the Soviet Union, but it failed to mount any protest. Indeed, during the summer and autumn of 1941, army leaders, both at the front and in the OKH, often explicitly urged their troops, in ideologically charged, anti-Semitic proclamations, to wage war on National Socialist lines and discard notions of humane treatment of the enemy. Further, the army fully cooperated with the murderous Einsatzgruppen units as they carried out their bloody task, offering logistic, intelligence, and communications support, as well as occasionally furnishing manpower for executions. It also willingly handed over commissars and Jews to the Einsatzgruppen for murder. Moreover, millions of Soviet prisoners of war died in camps under its control as part of a deliberate plan of murder and starvation. Army security units used ruthless methods to suppress the partisan war as well as embracing the use of SS and police units in order to pacify and safeguard rear areas. It remorselessly plundered and stripped the areas under its control of foodstuffs in order to feed itself off the land, regardless of the consequences for local civilians. It also exploited native inhabitants for labor and cooperated with the forced roundups, the infamous Menschenjagd conducted by Sauckel's organization that sent people as forced laborers back to Germany. The nexus between economic, colonial, racial, and military imperatives was, perhaps, best illustrated in Polish eastern Galicia, where local authorities began constructing Durchgangstrasse 4, a key transportation corridor into Ukraine that neatly combined immediate military utility with an eventual use, as part of Generalplan Ost, as an axis of settlement for Volksdeutsche. In the meantime, the Autobahn would be constructed by Jewish laborers, some twenty thousand of whom would be worked to death in a process of extermination through labor.[9]

Complicity of the Wehrmacht and the army leadership in Nazi crimes is, of course, not the same as complicity of average soldiers. This raises the further question of how far typical Landsers participated in these criminal activities. This remains a difficult question to answer with any degree of precision or reliability. In terms of the most serious of these atrocities, the murder of the Jews and the Soviet prisoners of war, it is obvious that, without the logistic and administrative cooperation of the Wehrmacht bureaucracy, mass murder on such a large scale would hardly have been possible. Although the institutional complicity is apparent, it also seems clear that relatively few soldiers took an *active* part in the shootings of Jews. In general, average Landsers probably cooperated with SS killers more in the Baltic than in Ukraine, for example, but best estimates are that, overall, not more than twenty to thirty thousand Wehrmacht personnel, out of the millions who served on the Ostfront, were *active* in explicitly aiding the Security Police in the selection, organization, and shooting of Jews and accounted for only around 1 percent of the victims. Much the same could be said with regard to implementation of the Commissar Order or the treatment of Soviet prisoners of war. Without the functional cooperation of the Wehrmacht, these murderous policies could not have been carried out, but relatively few of the active perpetrators were *front troops*.

This same formulation would apply as well to the partisan war, where, until 1943, most of the violence stemmed from rear security units. The worst of the crimes with which the Ostheer was associated—the murder of the Jews, the shooting of political officials, the systematic starvation of prisoners of war, the colonial exploitation of food and raw materials, and participation in forced labor roundups—were largely perpetrated by occupation and security units. If the typical Landser was a combat infantryman, then, his point of contact with the native inhabitants of

the Soviet Union was more likely to be in the form of the requisitioning of food items than in mass murder. Likely the greatest culpability
the average Landser incurred was during the scorched-earth retreat of
the autumn of 1943. Given the freedom to destroy, and often operating
in areas controlled by partisans, many responded in an orgy of destruction. For the rest, however, SS, party, and Wehrmacht officials scrambled to gain control of the spoils. The Ostheer, as Christian Hartmann
noted, was "supposed to conquer the Lebensraum, perhaps even secure
it, but not organize it." By and large, then, the responsibility for the
greatest crimes committed by the Wehrmacht accrued to those in the
rear areas and in leadership positions. Further, the number of those
involved in serious crimes was very small, perhaps only 5 percent of the
entire Ostheer. This relatively tiny number admittedly accounted for
enormous damage, but it would be false to replace the incorrect view of
the "clean" Wehrmacht with an equally erroneous one in which all were
criminals.[10]

Although not *directly* involved in criminal activities, the bulk of Landsers were *indirectly* complicit in that the racial assumptions and norms of
the regime infused all thought and activity in the Third Reich, making
it relatively easy to justify violence and killing. Not only did they tacitly
accept the radical racial and ideological premises of Barbarossa, but their
successes on the battlefield also enabled the regime to carry out its murderous plans. As with the issue of criminal complicity, the question of
why they fought is complex and multifaceted. For many, of course, it was
a straightforward matter of obligation, of being conscripted into the military and sent to fight. Some fought from old-fashioned patriotism and a
misguided belief in the German cause. Still others were nationalists who,
motivated by a strong sense of grievance, hoped to correct what they saw
as the injustices of Versailles, to recover German honor and international
preeminence, or to restore the nation's lost provinces. Many, troubled by
the reality of war and fighting to maintain a sense of self, struggled on out
of a sense of duty, if not to their country, then to their comrades, whom
they were unwilling to abandon in a difficult situation. Pride, honor, and
a willingness to sacrifice themselves if necessary also played a role as the
focal point became the small group of comrades surrounding oneself. In
the last phase of the war, when hundreds of thousands of Germans were
dying every month, hope in miracle weapons, fear of Soviet (and Allied)
revenge, and harsh, terroristic measures on the part of their own regime
sufficed to keep many doing their hard duty as the racial community
became fully militarized in the heat of total war.

Yet others were staunch Nazi supporters who wholeheartedly embraced the anti-Semitism, anti-Bolshevism, and belief in a racial mission in the east promoted by National Socialist ideology. The impetus for mass murder might well have come from the Nazi elite in the SS and the party, but many of those who acted out of conviction understood, in a form of anticipatory obedience, what was expected and required of them and, thus, did not have to be given explicit orders. At the same time, faith in Nazi ideology could induce a more positive emphasis on the new society, the much-heralded Volksgemeinschaft of unity, opportunity, and (not least) material benefits promised by Hitler. The very economic and foreign policy successes of the regime in the 1930s, which led many Germans to support the general thrust of Nazi policy, thus elicited a sense that Hitler really was creating a new society that would redeem the myriad hardships and injustices suffered by Germany in the recent past. Once begun, acceptance of moral compromise became a habit, one not easily changed in the midst of war. Although most Landsers saw themselves as decent fellows, they nonetheless participated in a wantonly cruel war.[11]

Much the same was true of average Germans in the Volksgemeinschaft, who often accepted the logic in the system not so much because they were ardent Nazis as because it rewarded them. Not only did significant numbers of professional and business people benefit from the Aryanization of property and the theft of Jewish wealth, but ethnic Germans, for example, were also the recipients of the property of deported Poles and murdered Jews. Similarly, Germans left homeless and destitute by Allied bombing profited from the receipt of plundered Jewish clothing, household possessions, and apartments. Moreover, Germans as a whole enjoyed a relatively high standard of living during the war, including low taxes, in part because of the theft of food, property, and wealth from the occupied territories. The euthanasia program directed resources at "healthy" elements of the population, while few Germans could fail to notice the prevalence of foreign, forced workers in industry and agriculture, a fact that kept the German economy and food production going during war. Germans not only benefited from the suffering of others but also witnessed it in their daily lives without much moral distress. Indeed, the Nazis' genius seemed to be their ability to combine rational self-interest with a sense that this was just retribution for past inequities in a system that balanced belief in a new society with racism and exploitation to create that New Order.[12]

It is, in fact, disconcerting to realize that so many Germans supported the Nazi regime either from mistaken notions of idealism or from crass materialistic motives, but it is also disturbing that the average Landser fought so long and so well on behalf of such a murderous system. This raises yet another, final, question: Could Germany have won? As with the others, this is a complex issue that involves a number of factors that must be considered. In contrast to the generally accepted view, when Germany began World War II, its armaments economy was relatively unprepared, both organizationally and in terms of raw materials. The quick victories in 1939–1940, moreover, promised more than they delivered. Both at Dunkirk and during the Battle of Britain, the Germans lacked the resources to compel the British to negotiate an end to the war, while, in North Africa and the Mediterranean, they were dependent on weak and unreliable allies. All this revealed German weakness, not strength. Great Britain remained in the war, so blitzkrieg had failed, while Western Europe, for all its value industrially, proved a drain on Germany precisely at its weakest and most vulnerable point: foodstuffs and basic raw materials. Once the British secured American aid, the time pressure on Hitler rose significantly. His pact with Stalin had made Germany blockade-proof, at least temporarily, but that very dependency opened the Reich to blackmail and pressure from the hated Bolshevik enemy. In any case, war had to come with the Soviet Union sooner or later, for the simple fact that Hitler's entire ideology, with the central role of Lebensraum in all its racial and economic manifestations, demanded it. Hitler did not, contrary to what many Western historians argue, blunder into war with the Soviet Union, for that constituted the entire purpose of Nazism and was what differentiated Hitler from the run-of-the-mill German nationalists who simply wanted a revision of the Versailles system. The Führer envisioned instead a complete reordering of Europe, for which the destruction of the Soviet Union was the necessary first step. Having decided to break the Gordian knot through an invasion of the Soviet Union rather than driving Great Britain from the war, itself an implicit admission of German weakness, he found that the tyranny of time again asserted itself. He needed a quick victory in the east before American power could assert itself in the west.

As early as late July 1941, with the unexpectedly fierce Soviet resistance at Smolensk, some in the German leadership worried that the gamble had already failed, but events in early December resulted in the decisive change in the nature of the war. The setback in front of Moscow, the Japanese attack on Pearl Harbor, and the German declaration of war on the United States all combined to transform what had remained an essentially European struggle into a global war of resources, manpower, and industrial prowess that put Germany at a distinct disadvantage. An additional dimension to the conflict was created by Hitler's deliberate intention to wage a war of extermination in the Soviet Union.

In a terrible irony, the failure to knock Great Britain out of the war, combined with the initial successes in the Soviet Union, had as a consequence the transition of the original intention for a territorial solution to the Nazis' self-imposed Jewish problem to an exterminationist one. Even as the Ostheer began to struggle against its Soviet opponent, however, the murderous activities of the Einsatzgruppen coalesced with efforts to implement the hunger policy and Generalplan Ost, with the result being a stunning level of violence directed against the occupied peoples of the Soviet Union. Having unleashed a war of annihilation, Hitler now redoubled his efforts to see it through, characteristically perceiving a short window of opportunity for action. If Germany could defeat the Soviet Union in 1942 or at least render it incapable of further resistance, the vast resources of European Russia would be available for use in a global war of attrition against the Anglo-Americans.

Fleeting, perhaps, as it was, Hitler in 1942 had one last chance to achieve some sort of triumph that might have allowed a stalemated war, at least until the United States developed the atomic bomb. Militarily and economically, then, 1942 was the key year of the war. Hitler, however, in late July squandered whatever slim chances he had for achieving victory militarily in Russia by splitting his already inadequate forces in the vain hope of achieving simultaneously goals that could have been attained only sequentially, if at all. Economically, too, Germany wasted its apparent advantage, finding itself not only being outproduced by the Anglo-Americans, which was perhaps to be expected, but also being overtaken by a truly stupendous effort on the part of the Soviet Union. The Russians ultimately could not sustain this superhuman effort, and, by 1944, the German war economy had pulled even with Soviet production, but by then it was too late, for American output alone swamped the Germans. Unfortunately, 1942 proved decisive in the other war as well: the success of the Ostheer through much of the year provided the opportunity to complete the Final Solution as the Nazis made a concerted effort to kill the Jews in their sphere of influence. The systematic murders of the Einsatzgruppen in the Soviet Union, the often ad hoc killings at the local level in many areas of occupied Europe, and the efforts of Nazi bureaucrats at the RSHA and the Foreign Office to get allies and satellite nations to hand over their Jews merged to produce a crash program of mass murder undertaken under the cover of German military success. By the autumn of 1943, even as the war had turned decisively against the Reich, Himmler could boast that the Jewish problem had largely been solved in the areas under German control and that what remained was primarily a mopping-up operation.[13]

That same year, 1943, witnessed an increasing interaction of the various fronts—eastern, Mediterranean, Atlantic, the skies over Germany—that pressured even further the already strained German resources. With Hitler unable or unwilling to mobilize the German people as ruthlessly as Stalin had in the Soviet Union, the German economy became increasingly dependent on forced labor from the east and slave workers from the concentration camps. By 1944, Hitler's last remaining hope was to defeat the anticipated Anglo-American invasion in the west and then, in a repeat of the scenario of 1940–1941, turn once more to the east. This meant a reversal in the priority of the fronts, with disastrous results. Because of constant, enormous Soviet pressure in the winter of 1943–1944, the Wehrmacht could never transfer sufficiently large forces to the west to ensure the defeat of the Allied invasion, while the Ostheer found itself with insufficient resources to stabilize the front in the east. Like a rubber band stretched too far, German defenses had to break, and they did so spectacularly in the summer of 1944. Even as Anglo-American forces struggled to escape the narrow confines of Normandy, the Soviets launched one of the most successful blitzkrieg operations of the war in Belorussia, a triumph that effectively ended any lingering hopes Hitler might have retained about stalemating the war. Despite the brave talk of miracle weapons and a split in the enemy coalition, the last nine months of the war were more about Hitler's fanatic determination to prevent another November 1918 than any realistic chance to extricate Germany from its fate. The result, however, was not only a radicalization of the Volksgemeinschaft, as Nazi violence and terror now turned inward, but also the large-scale destruction of German cities and infrastructure as well as the death of millions of people. True to his ideology, Hitler refused to abandon the Darwinistic struggle that he held to be the key to history, nor did he waver racially, insisting in his last testament that the Nazi race laws be upheld, and urging the German people to continue the struggle against the Jewish conspiracy.

From the outset, the German invasion of the Soviet Union had been an enormous gamble that depended for success primarily on the Soviets reacting to the shock of initial defeat as the French had, by ceasing resistance. Unlike the blitzkrieg campaign against France, however, Barbarossa had no clear Schwerpunkt, nor was it likely that the bulk of the Red Army could be trapped and destroyed in the first weeks of the conflict. Hitler also grossly underestimated the political and economic strength and resilience of the Stalinist system as well as the resources that would be necessary to win in the Soviet Union. Although Richard Overy has made a very cogent argument that Allied success in World War II depended on the cumulative impact of narrow triumphs in a number of key areas, the fact remains that the Germans always had only a very slight chance of triumphing in any of these sectors. Their early success owed as much to their enemies' weaknesses as to their own strengths, a fact that has tended to obscure the hard reality facing them. In terms of population, available military manpower, and access to key raw materials, Nazi Germany had no clear advantage over Britain and France, let alone when facing a possible coalition of enemies including the United States and the Soviet Union. Hitler was, in fact, a leader with great ambitions to overturn and remake the European political, economic, and social system but whose vehicle of choice was a medium-size European power with few allies of any consequence. This fundamental weakness was revealed as early as 1940. The best chance for Germany to have won the war, if such a possibility existed, was likely a pursuit of the Mediterranean strategy urged on him by naval leaders and some at the OKW. This, however, would have forced Hitler into dependence on weak and unreliable allies (as he well knew), dispersed German strength, and contradicted his own ideology, which stressed the importance of Lebensraum in the east.

The "right" war, for Hitler, was always the one against the Soviet Union, while all the other conflicts were secondary in importance. He meant finally to solve the "German question," the inability or unwillingness of the British and French to accommodate the Reich in the European balance of power, by establishing German hegemony over Europe, then using a German-dominated Europe to meet the rising threat from the United States. Further, resolving the German question raised the possibility of settling the Jewish question. Nazism had always been fueled by a complex mixture of resentment, fear, and idealism: resentment at those who had supposedly undermined Germany in World War I; fear of the alleged Jewish-Bolshevik threat to destroy the German people; and a utopian vision of a harmonious racial community that would redeem past injustices and suffering. For Hitler, the purpose of a state was to promote and guarantee the existence of the Volksgemeinschaft. To do so required war to conquer the resources necessary to sustain the struggle for national life. Acquiring this Lebensraum, however, opened the possibility of ensuring Germany's future, not only economically but also racially.

For Hitler, then, the war represented nothing less than the opportunity to remake and rationalize Central and Eastern Europe ethnically while removing for all time the "destroyer of peoples," the Jews. Ironically, by the end of his war, a conflict that in Europe consumed perhaps 50 million people and left much of the Continent in ruins, its citizens struggling to rebuild their shattered lives, Hitler had largely accomplished the one goal, but at the expense of the other. Central and Eastern Europe had been ethnically cleansed, the intermingled national groups had been disentangled, the Volksdeutsche had been concentrated back in Germany (in the largest, deadliest, and most rapid migration in human history), and the ancient Jewish culture and communities of Europe had been uprooted and destroyed. The German nation, however, on whose behalf Hitler had ostensibly waged this apocalyptic struggle, had ceased to exist as a political entity. Hitler had prophesied that, if Germany failed to prevail against its enemies, it would face a national catastrophe. His actions, and those of his helpers in the Wehrmacht and the war economy, had ensured just such an outcome. In the end, however, its vanquishers worked not to destroy Germany but to integrate its parts into an admittedly divided Europe. In so doing, the German question was solved at last, and the Germany of Hitler—resentful, aggressive, racist, nationalist—was, like him, crushed forever. The legacy of the Third Reich, however—the awareness of what can result from that explosive mixture of hatred, hypernationalism, racism, and authoritarianism—remains as a constant warning to us, challenging our notions of loyalty, honor, morality, and justice.

Acknowledgments

Two important people in my life died during the writing of this book: my mother, who lived through the war as a young wife worried about the well-being of her husband (and my father) away at sea, and my dear friend and extraordinary colleague Professor Christa Hungate, who was born in Germany during the war and, in her own person, although sharing none of the responsibility, nonetheless bore the burden of guilt for the crimes of her countrymen. Although it is not appropriate to dedicate a book on war to either, both were shaped in significant ways by World War II, and, thus, I was affected as well. My wife, Julia, has as always been a source of enormous encouragement, advice, occasional prodding, and, most importantly, steadfast support. She has also once again brought her logical, scientific mind to the creation of the outstanding maps that accompany and are such an important part of the book. I can also add thanks to my daughter, Kelsey, who in a matter of seconds, it seems, has grown from the baby I held on my lap as I composed my first book to a beautiful, talented, bright young woman—one, moreover, with a passion for history. Over the years, I like to think that I have even helped promote her growing interest in European history. I am sure that our innumerable historical discussions over the dinner table drove Julia to distraction, but her questions have also helped focus and clarify my arguments. More importantly, they have reminded me of the sheer joy of learning. The ancient Chinese philosopher Lao Tzu wrote, "Being deeply loved by someone gives you strength, while loving someone gives you courage." This neatly expresses my gratitude to both Julia and Kelsey—our souls touch and protect each other, and I am always conscious of my nearness to them. I carry their hearts in my heart and am never without them. Without them, my wife and daughter, I can truly say that this book would never have become reality. Both of them have enriched my life beyond measure, and to them this book is lovingly dedicated.

Appendix

Supplementary Data

| Table 1: Comparative Sizes of Major Commands ||
German	Soviet
Army groups: 4–5	Fronts: 10–18
Armies: 2–4 in an army group	Armies: 3–9 in a front (average 5–7)
Corps: 2–7 in an army	Corps: an average of 3 in an army
Divisions: 2–7 in a corps	Divisions: 2–3 in a corps
Authorized Strengths	*Authorized Strengths*
Panzer divisions: 14,000–17,000 (103–125 tanks)	Tank corps: 10,500 (189 tanks)
Motorized divisions: 14,000 (48 tanks)	Mechanized corps: 16,000 (186 tanks)
Infantry divisions: 12,700–15,000	Rifle divisions: 9,375 Guards rifle divisions: 10,585
Artillery divisions: 3,380 (113 guns)	Artillery divisions: 6,550 (210 guns)
Source: Ziemke, *Stalingrad to Berlin,* 506.	

Table 2: German Assessment of the Raw Material Situation, November 1941			
	German Sphere	European Russia	Great Britain/ United States
Oil (million tons)	9.7	29.8	257.8
Manganese ore (in 1,000 tons)	56.5	1,200	1,343
Nickel ore (in 1,000 tons)	4.4	2.8	110.5
Tungsten ore (tons)	1,812	. . .	7,072
Copper ore (in 1,000 tons)	157.5	85.5	2,006.1
Bauxite/aluminum (in 1,000 tons)	398.6	78	278.9
Coal (in million tons hard coal)	396	95.3	815.9
Iron ore (in million tons)	31.2	13.3	48.1
Chrome ore (in 1,000 tons)	31.6	85.3	216.2
Rubber (in 1,000 tons)	80	. . .	816

Source: Kroener, Müller, and Umbreit, eds., *Organization and Mobilization of the German Sphere of Power: Wartime Administration, Economy, and Manpower Resources, 1939-1941,* 711.

Table 3: Heavy Industry, Germany–Soviet Union, 1941–1945 (million tons)					
	1941	**1942**	**1943**	**1944**	**1945**
Coal:					
Germany	315.5	317.9	340.4	347.6	. . .
Soviet Union	151.4	75.5	93.1	121.5	149.3
Steel:					
Germany	28.2	28.7	30.6	25.8	. . .
Soviet Union	17.9	8.1	8.5	10.9	12.3
Aluminum:					
Germany	233.6	264.0	250.0	245.3	. . .
Soviet Union	. . .	51.7	62.3	82.7	86.3
Oil:					
Germany	5.7	6.6	7.6	5.5	1.3
Soviet Union	33.0	22.0	18.0	18.2	19.4

Source: Overy, *Russia's War*, 155.

Table 4: Weapons Production, 1940–1945						
	1940	**1941**	**1942**	**1943**	**1944**	**1945**
Aircraft:						
Germany	10,247	11,776	15,409	24,807	39,807	7,540
Soviet Union	10,565	15,735	25,436	34,900	40,300	20,900
Britain	15,049	20,094	23,672	26,263	26,461	12,070
United States	12,804	26,277	47,826	85,998	96,318	49,761
Tanks:[a]						
Germany	2,200	5,200	9,200	17,300	22,100	4,400
Soviet Union	2,794	6,590	24,446	24,089	28,963	15,400
Britain	1,399	4,841	8,611	7,476	5,000	2,100
United States	c. 400	4,052	24,997	29,497	17,565	11,968
Artillery:[b]						
Germany	5,000	7,000	12,000	27,000	41,000	. . .
Soviet Union	. . .	. . .	49,100	48,400	56,100	28,600
Britain	1,900	5,300	6,600	12,200	12,400	. . .
United States	c. 1,800	29,615	72,658	67,544	33,558	19,699

Sources: Overy, *Why the Allies Won,* 331–32, and *Russia's War,* 155.
[a] Includes self-propelled guns for Germany and the Soviet Union.
[b] Includes only medium and heavy caliber artillery (over seventy-five millimeters).

Table 5: German Deaths (Eastern Front), 1941–1945			
Year	**Month**	**Number of Deaths**	**Total**
1941	June	25,000	
	July	63,099	
	August	46,066	
	September	51,033	
	October	41,099	
	November	36,000	
	December	40,198	302,495
1942	January	48,165	
	February	44,099	
	March	44,132	
	April	23,066	
	May	38,099	
	June	29,033	
	July	38,066	
	August	62,165	
	September	45,033	
	October	25,000	
	November	31,198	
	December	78,759	506,815
1943	January	180,310	
	February	68,330	
	March	46,066	
	April	16,000	
	May	19,066	
	June	13,066	
	July	71,231	
	August	19,198	
	September	57,429	
	October	53,264	
	November	67,363	
	December	49,330	700,635
1944	January	70,330	
	February	64,429	
	March	93,660	
	April	73,264	
	May	48,363	
	June	142,079	
	July	169,881	
	August	277,465	
	September	70,561	
	October	92,528	
	November	45,363	
	December	85,023	1,232,946
Total			2,742,891

Source: Overmans, *Deutsche militärische Verluste im Zweiten Weltkrieg*, 278.

Table 6: German and Soviet Deaths, by Year			
Year	**German Deaths[a]**	**Soviet Deaths**	**Ratio**
1941	302,495	2,993,803	1:9.90
1942	506,815	2,993,536	1:5.91
1943	700,635	1,977,127	1:2.82
1944	1,232,946	1,412,335	1:1.15
1945 (January–June)	1,427,398	631,633	2.26:1
1941–1944	2,742,891	9,376,801	1:3.42
Total	4,170,289	10,008,434	1:2.40

Source: Overmans, *Deutsche militärische Verluste im Zweiten Weltkrieg*, 238, 278; Glantz and House, *When Titans Clashed*, 292.
[a] Eastern Front only for 1941–1944; total deaths for 1945.

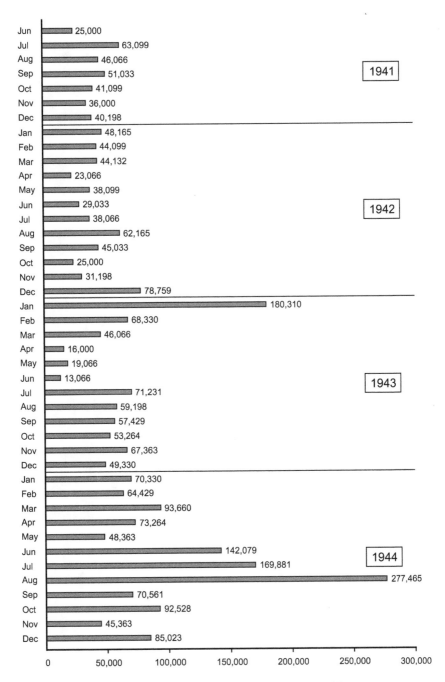

Figure 1. German deaths on the eastern front, 1941–1945.
Source: Overmans, *Deutsche militärische Verluste im Zweiten Weltkrieg,* 238.

Notes

1. Dilemma

1. Shirer, *Berlin Diary*, 21 June 1940, 420-24; Horne, *To Lose a Battle*, 646-47; Kershaw, *Hitler: Nemesis*, 298-99; *TBJG*, 22 June 1940.

2. *TBJG*, 6 June 1940; Hoffmann, *Mit Hitler im Westen;* Hornshøj-Møller, "The Role of 'Produced Reality.'"

3. Albert Speer, *Inside the Third Reich*, 170-72; Kershaw, *Hitler: Nemesis*, 299-300; *TBJG*, 3 July 1940.

4. Mann, "Beim Propheten," 275.

5. Förster, "Hitler's Decision," 30-31; Kershaw, *Fateful Choices*, 56-57; Deist, "The Road to Ideological War," 380-81. For the best extended assessment of Hitler's ideology, see Jäckel, *Hitler's World View.*

6. Hitler, *Mein Kampf*, 284-329; Weinberg, ed., *Hitler's Second Book*, chaps. 1-6; Kershaw, *Hitler: Hubris*, 243-46.

7. Hitler, *Mein Kampf*, 679; Kershaw, *Hitler: Hubris*, 244-45.

8. Jäckel and Kuhn, eds., *Hitler: Sämtliche Aufzeichnungen*, 775; Bloxham, *The Final Solution*, 88; Friedländer, *Nazi Germany and the Jews*, 1:73-113; Herf, *The Jewish Enemy*, 2-3; Kershaw, *Hitler: Hubris*, 244-46.

9. Kershaw, *Hitler: Hubris*, 248-49, and *Fateful Choices*, 56-57; Förster, "Hitler's Decision," 31-32; Hitler, *Mein Kampf*, 610-11; Müller, "Das 'Unternehmen Barbarossa' als wirtschaftlicher Raubkrieg," 174. For an excellent and extended discussion of the concept of Lebensraum, see Liulevicius, *War Land on the Eastern Front*, 247-77.

10. For Hitler's general views on foreign policy, see Hitler, *Mein Kampf*, 607-67; and Weinberg, ed., *Hitler's Second Book*, passim.

11. Tooze, *The Wages of Destruction*, 8-9, 138, 144-45; Hitler, *Mein Kampf*, 654.

12. Weinberg, ed., *Hitler's Second Book*, 15-27, 48-54, 99-118, 160-74; Kershaw, *Hitler: Hubris*, 247-50, and *Fateful Choices*, 56-57; Förster, "Hitler's Decision," 31-32.

13. Kershaw, *Hitler: Hubris*, 249-50; Deist, "The Road to Ideological War," 380-82; Weinberg, ed., *Hitler's Second Book*, chaps. 1-6; Zitelmann, "Zur Begründung des 'Lebensraum' Motivs in Hitlers Weltanschauung"; Vogelsang, "Neue Dokumente zur Geschichte der Reichswehr," 434-36.

14. Schmidt, *Hitler's Interpreter*, 158; Bauer, *Jews for Sale?* 37-38; Jersak, "Blitzkrieg Revisited," 376.

15. Frieser, *The Blitzkrieg Legend*, 10, 13, 17.

16. Hitler, *Mein Kampf*, 126-56, 607-67; Weinberg, ed., *Hitler's Second Book*, 160-74, 228-38; Förster, "Hitler's Decision," 33; Kershaw, *Fateful Choices*, 62; Jersak, "Blitzkrieg Revisited," 570; Ueberschär, "Hitlers Entschluß," 88.

17. Deist, "The Road to Ideological War," 390–91; Treue, "Hitlers Denkschrift"; Noakes and Pridham, eds., *Nazism: A History*, 2:281–87; Overy, *Russia's War*, 34–35.

18. Treue, "Hitlers Denkschrift"; Tooze, *The Wages of Destruction*, 219–22 and chaps. 7–8 generally; Deist, "The Road to Ideological War," 383; Overy, *Russia's War*, 35.

19. Tooze, *The Wages of Destruction*, chaps. 7–9; Deist, "The Road to Ideological War," 374–79, 383; Geyer, "German Strategy in the Age of Machine Warfare," 575, 581. See also Deist, "The Rearmament of the Wehrmacht"; and Volkmann, "The National Socialist Economy in Preparation of War."

20. Jersak, "Blitzkrieg Revisited," 571; Herf, *The Jewish Enemy*, chaps. 1–3.

21. Wildt, ed., *Judenpolitik*, 35–60; Brechtken, *"Madagascar für die Juden,"* 176–85, 193–94; Jansen, *Der Madagaskar-Plan*, 236–39, 284–85; Nicosia, *The Third Reich and the Palestine Question*, 109–44; Jersak, "Blitzkrieg Revisited," 571–72; Kershaw, *Hitler: Nemesis*, 132–35; *TBJG*, 25 July 1938.

22. Tooze, *The Wages of Destruction*, 274–75; Kershaw, *Hitler: Nemesis*, 135–36; Wildt, ed., *Judenpolitik*, 55–57; Barkai, "Schicksalsjahr 1938," 101.

23. Kershaw, *Hitler: Nemesis*, 136–39; *TBJG*, 9, 10 November 1938. See also Graml, *Reichskristallnacht*.

24. Jersak, "Blitzkrieg Revisited," 573; Kershaw, *Hitler: Nemesis*, 150–51 (Goering quote 151).

25. Tooze, *The Wages of Destruction*, 282–83; Herf, *The Jewish Enemy*, 46–49; Kershaw, *Hitler: Nemesis*, 151–52 (*Das schwarze Korps* and Hitler quotes 152).

26. Tooze, *The Wages of Destruction*, 283–84; Jersak, "Blitzkrieg Revisited," 574–75; Kershaw, *Hitler: Nemesis*, 152–53; Domarus, ed., *Hitler: Reden und Proklamationen*, 2:1049, 1057.

27. Domarus, ed., *Hitler: Reden und Proklamationen*, 2:1057–58.

28. Kershaw, *Hitler: Nemesis*, 136–39. See also Fritz, *Frontsoldaten*, 187–218, and "'We are trying . . . to change the face of the world.'"

29. Browning, *The Origins of the Final Solution*, 12–14. See also Sven Lindqvist, *"Exterminate All the Brutes"*; Ehmann, "From Colonial Racism to Nazi Population Policy"; Smith, *Ideological Origins*.

30. Browning, *The Origins of the Final Solution*, 15–16. See also Halder, *War Diary*; Baumgart, "Zur Ansprache Hitlers vor den Führern der Wehrmacht"; "Ansprache des Führers auf dem Berghof am 22. 8. 1939," in Schramm, ed., *Kriegstagebuch*, 1, pt. 2:947–49.

31. Browning, *The Origins of the Final Solution*, 16–24; Groscurth, *Tagebücher*, 202 (9 September 1939), 298 (18 October 1939); Müller, *Das Heer und Hitler*, 667 (doc. 45: Brauchitsch to Army Commanders, 21 September 1939); Kershaw, *Hitler: Nemesis*, 240–44; Mommsen, "Die Realisierung des Utopischen."
For the best assessments of Einsatzgruppen activities in Poland and the army reaction, see Rossino, *Hitler Strikes Poland*, passim. Other important recent works focusing on Poland as the dress rehearsal for later atrocities are Rossino, "Destructive Impulses"; Böhler, *Auftakt zum Vernichtungskrieg*; Westermann, *Hitler's Police Battalions*; and Rutherford, *Prelude to the Final Solution*.

32. Browning, *The Origins of the Final Solution*, 25–28.

33. Ibid., 27–28, 46; *TBJG*, 10 October 1939. See also Aly and Heim, *Architects of Annihilation*, chap. 4.

34. Browning, *The Origins of the Final Solution*, 14; Aly and Heim, *Architects of Annihilation*, 149–59.

35. Browning, *The Origins of the Final Solution*, 36–63; Friedländer, *Nazi Germany and the Jews*, 2:30–37.

36. Browning, *The Origins of the Final Solution*, 36–63; Friedländer, *Nazi Germany and the Jews*, 2:30–37; Goshen, "Eichmann und die Nisko-Aktion"; Moser, "Nisko"; Pohl, *Von der "Judenpolitik" zum Judenmord*, 47–54.

For an extensive collection of documentation concerning Nazi policy in Poland and toward the Jews, see Noakes and Pridham, eds., *Nazism: A History*, vol. 2, chaps. 35, 37. On demographic and academic experts and their role in shaping policy, see Burleigh, *Germany Turns Eastwards;* Aly and Heim, *Vordenker der Vernichtung;* Haar, *Historiker im Nationalsozialismus;* and Rössler and Schleiermacher, eds., *Der "Generalplan Ost."*

37. Friedländer, *Nazi Germany and the Jews*, 2:16–17. For a detailed discussion of Goebbels's project, see Hornshøj-Møller, *"Der ewige Jude,"* and "Der ewige Jude."

38. *TBJG*, 17, 29 October 1939; Hornshøj-Møller, "Der ewige Jude," 66–68; Browning, *The Origins of the Final Solution*, 46; Friedländer, *Nazi Germany and the Jews*, 2:16–24; Kershaw, *Hitler: Nemesis*, 249. Hornshøj-Møller also notes the probable enhanced impact of the ritual slaughter scene on Hitler since he was a confirmed vegetarian.

39. *TBJG*, 2–3, 19 November, 5 December 1939; Hornshøj-Møller, "Der ewige Jude," 66–68; Browning, *The Origins of the Final Solution*, 46; Friedländer, *Nazi Germany and the Jews*, 2:16–24; Kershaw, *Hitler: Nemesis*, 249.

40. Browning, *The Origins of the Final Solution*, 68.

41. Heinrich Himmler, "Reflections on the Treatment of Peoples of Alien Races in the East," doc. NO-1880, Prosecution Exhibit 1314, Nuremberg Trial Documents, reproduced and translated in Bauer, *A History of the Holocaust*, 383–85. Browning (*The Origins of the Final Solution*, 68–70) also translates parts of it.

42. Browning, *The Origins of the Final Solution*, 81–101; Kershaw, *Hitler: Nemesis*, 320–25. For a detailed discussion of the Madagascar Plan, see Brechtken, *"Madagaskar für die Juden";* Jansen, *Der Madagaskar-Plan;* Yahil, "Madagascar," 315–34.

43. *TBJG*, 26 July, 17 August 1940.

44. Halder, *War Diary*, 28 August, 27 September 1939, 37, 62–66; Hitler quoted in Groscurth, *Tagebücher*, 385 (21 October 1939), 414 (23 November 1939); *TBJG*, 14, 17 November, 29 December 1939, 13, 25 January 1940; Frieser, *The Blitzkrieg Legend*, 20, 60–63; Förster, "Hitler's Decision," 19; Ueberschär, "Hitlers Entschluß," 91–92; Tooze, *The Wages of Destruction*, 373.

45. Frieser, *The Blitzkrieg Legend*, 21–54; Tooze, *The Wages of Destruction*, 326–67.

46. Frieser, *The Blitzkrieg Legend*, 55–59; Groscurth, *Tagebücher*, 223; Tooze, *The Wages of Destruction*, 326–67.

47. Frieser, *The Blitzkrieg Legend*, 60–99, 320–53; Murray, *The Change in the European Balance of Power*, 326–32, 361; Reynolds, "1940," 326–27.

48. Tooze, *The Wages of Destruction*, 383–92, 411–20; Müller, "Economic Alliance," 118–36; Aly and Heim, *Architects of Annihilation*, 234–35.

49. Tooze, *The Wages of Destruction*, 383–92, 411–20; Müller, "Economic Alliance," 118–36. See also Harrison, ed., *The Economics of World War II;* Milward, *The New Order and the French Economy;* Overy, Otto, and Houwink ten Cate, eds., *Die "Neuordnung" Europas;* and Müller, "The Mobilization of the German Economy," 564–603, 711.

50. Reynolds, "1940," 328; Tooze, *The Wages of Destruction*, 396–97.

2. Decision

1. *TBJG*, 7 July 1940; Kershaw, *Hitler: Nemesis*, 300–301, and *Fateful Choices*, 65–66.

2. *TBJG*, 9 June 1940 (quote). On America and the Jewish press, see ibid., 16, 23, 26, 28 May, 2, 7, 11–13, 20, 22 June, 6, 18, 23 July, 5 September 1940.

3. Ibid., 30-31 May, 16 (quote) June 1940. On fears of the Soviet Union, see ibid., 17-18, 28, 29 June, 4, 5 (quote), 11, 19, 23 (quote) July 1940. For the rest, see ibid., 11-12 January, 28-29 June, 5-6, 8-9, 20-21 July, 31 August 1940.

4. Ibid., 30, 31 (quote) May, 2 (quote), 3 (quote), 9, 16, 25, 27, 29 (quote) June, 3 (quote) July 1940; Kershaw, *Hitler: Nemesis*, 298, 300.

5. *TBJG*, 7, 9 (quote), 12, 16-17 July 1940.

6. Halder, *War Diary*, 13 July 1940, 227.

7. Kershaw, *Hitler: Nemesis*, 300-303; Halder, *War Diary*, 13 July 1940, 227; Tooze, *The Wages of Destruction*, 397-400; Weinberg, *A World at Arms*, 117-18.

8. Kershaw, *Hitler: Nemesis*, 303-4; Leach, *German Strategy against Russia*, 57; *TBJG*, 20 July 1940; Shirer, *Berlin Diary*, 19 July 1940, 452-57.

9. Kershaw, *Hitler: Nemesis*, 304; Citino, *Death of the Wehrmacht*, 32-34; Shirer, *Berlin Diary*, 20 July 1940, 457; *TBJG*, 21 July 1940.

10. *TBJG*, 14, 17 November, 29 December 1939, 13, 25 January, 21 April 1940; Ueberschär, "Hitlers Entschluß," 91-95; Groscurth, *Tagebücher*, 385 (21 October 1939), 414 (23 November 1939); Below, *Als Hitlers Adjutant*, 217; Halder, *War Diary*, 11 January 1940, 85-86; Speer, *Inside the Third Reich*, 173.

11. Leach, *German Strategy against Russia*, 53-57; Klink, "Military Concept," 228-29; Halder, *War Diary*, 26-27, 30 June, 1, 3 July 1940, 217-21; Koch, "Hitler's 'Programme,'" 896-98.

12. Halder, *War Diary*, 25, 30 June, 3, 11, 13 July 1940, 217-27; Förster, "Hitler's Decision," 18-19; Klink, "Military Concept," 241-51; Koch, "Hitler's 'Programme,'" 897-98.

13. Förster, "Hitler Turns East," 117; Klink, "Military Concept," 240-45; Halder, *War Diary*, 18, 22-23, 25 June, 3-4 July 1940, 209-22; Hitler quoted in Koch, "Hitler's 'Programme,'" 896-97.

14. Halder, *War Diary*, 22 July 1940, 229-33.

15. Ibid.; Förster, "Hitler's Decision," 21-22; Klink, "Military Concept," 251-53; Koch, "Hitler's 'Programme,'" 903-4; Leach, *German Strategy against Russia*, 58; Ueberschär, "Hitlers Entschluß," 96-97.

16. Leach, *German Strategy against Russia*, 60-61, 64; Halder, *War Diary*, 22, 30 July 1940, 232, 240-41; Warlimont, *Inside Hitler's Headquarters*, 112.

17. Ueberschär, "Hitlers Entschluß," 96-97; Förster, "Hitler's Decision," 15, 21-27, and "Hitler Turns East," 118; Kershaw, *Fateful Choices*, 66, 208-20; Tooze, *The Wages of Destruction*, 402-3; Herf, *The Jewish Enemy*, 77-91; Shirer, *Berlin Diary*, 20 July 1940, 457-58.

18. Ueberschär, "Hitlers Entschluß," 97; Förster, "Hitler Turns East," 118; Kershaw, *Fateful Choices*, 69, 78, 232; *TBJG*, 14 March 1941.

19. Gerlach, "German Economic Interests," 213-14; Müller, "Economic Alliance," 118-34; Koch, "Hitler's 'Programme,'" 898-99; Kershaw, *Fateful Choices*, 69.

20. Müller, "Economic Alliance," 118-34; Kershaw, *Fateful Choices*, 69; Tooze, *The Wages of Destruction*, 420.

21. Müller, "Das 'Unternehmen Barbarossa' als wirtschaftlicher Raubkrieg," 177; Koch, "Hitler's 'Programme,'" 899-905; Halder, *War Diary*, 22 May, 25-26 June, 9, 11, 13, 22 July, 26 August, 5 December 1940 (quote), 161, 217-18, 224-25, 232, 251, 294; Tooze, *The Wages of Destruction*, 411-19; Müller, "Economic Alliance," 134-35; Förster, "Hitler's Decision," 23-25. For the Soviet perspective on tensions in the Balkans, see Gorodetsky, *Grand Delusion*, 23-66.

22. Ueberschär, "Hitlers Entschluß," 98; Förster, "Hitler's Decision," 22, 25; Kershaw, *Fateful Choices*, 68-69, and *Hitler: Nemesis*, 307.

23. Halder, *War Diary*, 31 July 1940, 241–46; Förster, "Hitler's Decision," 25–30; Leach, *German Strategy against Russia*, 68–72; Kershaw, *Hitler: Nemesis*, 307–8.

24. Halder, *War Diary*, 31 July 1940, 244–45; Förster, "Hitler's Decision," 25–30; Leach, *German Strategy against Russia*, 69–70; Kershaw, *Hitler: Nemesis*, 307–8.

25. *TBJG*, 9 August 1940; Ueberschär, "Hitlers Entschluß," 100; Förster, "Hitler's Decision," 27–28; Leach, *German Strategy against Russia*, 69–70; Kershaw, *Hitler: Nemesis*, 307–8, and *Fateful Choices*, 69–70.

26. Kershaw, *Fateful Choices*, 70; Förster, "Hitler's Decision," 38; Koch, "Hitler's 'Programme,'" 904–7; Megargee, *Inside Hitler's High Command*, 87–92, and *War of Annihilation*, 20–21; Halder, *War Diary*, 27 August 1940, 252; Schreiber, "Mittelmeerraum," 80–82.

27. Förster, "Hitler's Decision," 40–41.

28. Ibid.; Koch, "Hitler's 'Programme,'" 911–12; Kershaw, *Hitler: Nemesis*, 325–26, and *Fateful Choices*, chaps. 3, 5.

29. Förster, "Hitler's Decision," 40–41; Schreiber, "Mittelmeerraum," 80; Kershaw, *Fateful Choices*, 76–79, and *Hitler: Nemesis*, 326–27. For a detailed discussion of the Mediterranean strategy, see Schreiber, "Political and Military Developments," esp. pt. 2.

30. Schreiber, "Mittelmeerraum," 80–82; Kershaw, *Fateful Choices*, 76–80.

31. Schreiber, "Mittelmeerraum," 82–83; Leach, *German Strategy against Russia*, 72–75; Koch, "Hitler's 'Programme,'" 910; Kershaw, *Hitler: Nemesis*, 327–28, and *Fateful Choices*, 81–82.

32. Kershaw, *Hitler: Nemesis*, 329–30, and *Fateful Choices*, 82–83; Schreiber, "Mittelmeerraum," 83; Halder, *War Diary*, 1 November 1940, 272; Schmidt, *Hitler's Interpreter*, 193–96.

33. Kershaw, *Hitler: Nemesis*, 330–31, and *Fateful Choices*, 82–83; Hillgruber, *Staatsmänner*, 1:142–49; Schmidt, *Hitler's Interpreter*, 198–99; Halder, *War Diary*, 1 November 1940, 272; Weinberg, *A World at Arms*, 206.

34. Below, *Als Hitlers Adjutant*, 249–50; Halder, *War Diary*, 1 November 1940, 272; Bock, *War Diary*, 11 November 1940, 193; Schreiber, "Mittelmeerraum," 84–85, 87; Koch, "Hitler's 'Programme,'" 912; Kershaw, *Hitler: Nemesis*, 331–32, and *Fateful Choices*, 83–84; Engel, *Heeresadjutant bei Hitler*, 4 November 1940, 89–90; Warlimont, *Inside Hitler's Headquarters*, 120. On Gibraltar, see also Goda, "The Riddle of the Rock."

35. Förster, "Hitler's Decision," 42–43; Koch, "Hitler's 'Programme,'" 912; Müller, "Das 'Unternehmen Barbarossa' als wirtschaftlicher Raubkrieg," 177; Kershaw, *Hitler: Nemesis*, 332–33; Gorodetsky, *Grand Delusion*, 67–75.

36. Kershaw, *Hitler: Nemesis*, 332, and *Fateful Choices*, 84; Schreiber, "Mittelmeerraum," 85.

37. Kershaw, *Hitler: Nemesis*, 333–34, and *Fateful Choices*, 84; Förster, "Hitler's Decision," 43–44; Koch, "Hitler's 'Programme,'" 915–19; Read and Fisher, *The Deadly Embrace*, 510–12; Schmidt, *Statist auf diplomatischer Bühne*, 525–27; Weinberg, *A World at Arms*, 201. See also Hillgruber, *Staatsmänner*, 1:166–93; Noakes and Pridham, *Nazism: A History*, 2:801–8; Bezymenskij, "Der Berlin-Besuch von V. M. Molotov"; and Gorodetsky, *Grand Delusion*, 67–75.

38. Kershaw, *Hitler: Nemesis*, 334, and *Fateful Choices*, 84; Förster, "Hitler's Decision," 43–44; Koch, "Hitler's 'Programme,'" 919; Engel, *Heeresadjutant bei Hitler*, 15 November 1940, 91; Schreiber, "Mittelmeerraum," 86; Leach, *German Strategy against Russia*, 77–78, 82; Gorodetsky, *Grand Delusion*, 70, 75–86; Schramm, ed., *Kriegstagebuch*, 15 November 1940, 1, pt. 1:177.

39. Kershaw, *Hitler: Nemesis,* 334–35, and *Fateful Choices,* 84–90; Förster, "Hitler's Decision," 46–48; Halder, *War Diary,* 5 December 1940, 292–98; Schramm, ed., *Kriegstagebuch,* 5, 10 December 1940, 208–9, 1, pt. 1:222; Bock, *War Diary,* 3 December 1940, 2 January 1941, 193–94, 197–98.

40. Kershaw, *Hitler: Nemesis,* 334–35, and *Fateful Choices,* 84–90; Förster, "Hitler's Decision," 28, 46–48; Schreiber, "Mittelmeerraum," 91; Schramm, ed., *Kriegstagebuch,* 9 January 1941, 1, pt. 1:258; Murray, "Betrachtungen," 322–25; Deist, "The Road to Ideological War," 385–92; "Weisung Nr. 21 Fall Barbarossa vom 18. 12. 1940," in Ueberschär and Wette, eds., *"Unternehmen Barbarossa,"* 244–46.

41. Geyer, "German Strategy in the Age of Machine Warfare," 574–93; Murray, "Betrachtungen," 322–25; Deist, "The Road to Ideological War," 385–92; Kershaw, *Hitler: Nemesis,* 342–43; Klink, "Military Concept," 284–85, 320.

42. Engel, *Heeresadjutant bei Hitler,* 18 December 1940, 92; Halder, *War Diary,* 17 February 1941, 320; Leach, *German Strategy against Russia,* 87–123; Klink, "Military Concept," 257–85; Megargee, *War of Annihilation,* 24–32.

43. Leach, *German Strategy against Russia,* 101–3.

44. Ibid., 87–100; Müller, "Das 'Unternehmen Barbarossa' als wirtschaftlicher Raubkrieg," 178–79.

45. Müller, "Das 'Unternehmen Barbarossa' als wirtschaftlicher Raubkrieg," 178–79; Leach, *German Strategy against Russia,* 87–100; Tooze, *The Wages of Destruction,* 432–40, 452–56; Förster, "Hitler's Decision," 48, "Der historische Ort," 632, and "The Dynamics of Volksgemeinschaft," 200–202; Megargee, *War of Annihilation,* 26–28.

46. Frieser, *The Blitzkrieg Legend,* 98–99, 320–49.

47. Schramm, ed., *Kriegstagebuch,* 9 January 1941, 1, pt. 1:257–58; Müller, "Das 'Unternehmen Barbarossa' als wirtschaftlicher Raubkrieg," 179–80.

48. Weinberg, *A World at Arms,* 187–89; Leach, *German Strategy against Russia,* 100–118; Klink, "Military Concept," 257–92; Halder, *War Diary,* 5 December 1940, 297–98; Förster, "Der historische Ort," 631.

49. Leach, *German Strategy against Russia,* 124–32; Klink, "Military Concept," 257–85; Kershaw, *Hitler: Nemesis,* 344–45; Megargee, *War of Annihilation,* 24–32; Tooze, *The Wages of Destruction,* 452–53; Förster, "Der historische Ort," 633; Kroener, "Organisation und Mobilisierung des deutschen Machtbereichs," 846–48, 998.

50. Leach, *German Strategy against Russia,* 133–39; Klink, "Military Concept," 292–97; van Creveld, *Fighting Power,* 43–61; Hartmann, "Verbrecherischer Krieg—verbrecherische Wehrmacht?" 8–9; Tooze, *The Wages of Destruction,* 452–55.

51. Frieser, *The Blitzkrieg Legend,* 29–33; Cooper, *The German Army,* 163; Tooze, *The Wages of Destruction,* 452–55; Kroener, "The 'Frozen Blitzkrieg,'" 146; van Creveld, *Supplying War,* 142–201; DiNardo, *Mechanized Juggernaut?* 35–54.

52. Klink, "Military Concept," 294–97; Halder, *War Diary,* 28 January 1941, 314–15; Schramm, ed., *Kriegstagebuch,* 3 February 1941, 1, pt. 1:299; Müller, "Economic Alliance," 142–70; Kroener, "The 'Frozen Blitzkrieg,'" 142–44.

53. Müller, "Economic Alliance," 142–70; Tooze, *The Wages of Destruction,* 432–40; Kroener, "The 'Frozen Blitzkrieg,'" 142–44; Megargee, *War of Annihilation,* 29.

54. Müller, "Economic Alliance," 150–51; Leach, *German Strategy against Russia,* 140–41; Kershaw, *Hitler: Nemesis,* 344–45; Halder, *War Diary,* 23 December 1940, 28 January 1941, 308–9, 314; Bock, *War Diary,* 1 February 1941, 198.

55. Klink, "Military Concept," 260; Müller, "Economic Alliance," 138–39, 149–50, 172; Tooze, *The Wages of Destruction,* 458–60; Leach, *German Strategy against Russia,* 146–47.

56. Schramm, ed., *Kriegstagebuch*, 3, 11 February 1941, 1, pt. 1:297-301, 316-19; Leach, *German Strategy against Russia*, 143-45; Müller, "Economic Alliance," 150-54; Kershaw, *Hitler: Nemesis*, 345-46; Tooze, *The Wages of Destruction*, 459-60. For an assessment of Thomas's memorandum, see Lübbers, "'Ausnutzung oder Ausschlachtung?'"

57. Browning, *The Origins of the Final Solution*, 213-15; Tooze, *The Wages of Destruction*, 459-60, 476-80; Müller, "Economic Alliance," 150-52, 171, and "Das 'Unternehmen Barbarossa' als wirtschaftlicher Raubkrieg," 181-82; Aly and Heim, *Architects of Annihilation*, 234-42.

Klaus Jochen Arnold and Gert C. Lübbers argue that Backe had received a "special mission" from Hitler in February 1941. See Arnold and Lübbers, "The Meeting of the Staatssekretäre," 616.

58. Müller, "Economic Alliance," 171-77; Tooze, *The Wages of Destruction*, 476-80; Klink, "Military Concept," 294; Arnold and Lübbers, "The Meeting of the Staatssekretäre," 616-18; Aly and Heim, *Architects of Annihilation*, 236-42.

59. Müller, "Economic Alliance," 174-82; Förster, "Operation Barbarossa as a War of Conquest," 481-90; Tooze, *The Wages of Destruction*, 479-80; Browning, *The Origins of the Final Solution*, 234-40; Arnold and Lübbers, "The Meeting of the Staatssekretäre," 619-25; Aly and Heim, *Architects of Annihilation*, 238-39; *TBJG*, 1, 6 May 1941. See also Gerlach, *Kalkulierte Morde*, 46-59, and *Krieg, Ernährung, Völkermord*, 10-84; Aly and Heim, *Vordenker der Vernichtung*, 365-93; Aly, *"Final Solution,"* 172; and Longerich, *Politik der Vernichtung*, 298.

For an argument that the meeting of 2 May 1941 rivaled that at the Wannsee on 20 January 1942 in which plans for the Final Solution were discussed, see Kay, "Germany's Staatssekretäre," and "Revisiting the Meeting of the Staatssekretäre."

Johannes Hürter argues for the term *hunger calculation* rather than *hunger policy*, a point supported by Alex J. Kay, since there was no clear idea among the economic planners as to how this hunger policy was to be implemented. See Hürter, *Hitlers Heerführer*, 491; Kay, *Exploitation, Resettlement, Mass Murder*, 206-7.

60. Müller, "Economic Alliance," 174-82, and "Das 'Unternehmen Barbarossa' als wirtschaftlicher Raubkrieg," 128-83; Förster, "Operation Barbarossa as a War of Conquest," 481-90; Tooze, *The Wages of Destruction*, 479-80; Browning, *The Origins of the Final Solution*, 234-40; Aly and Heim, *Architects of Annihilation*, 242.

Klaus Jochen Arnold emphasizes that, despite the considerable ideological points of agreement between Hitler and the Wehrmacht top brass, responsibility for the implementation of the hunger policy was purposely given to Goering, as head of the Four-Year Plan and Economic Command Staff East, and State Secretary Backe, of the Reich Ministry of Food. See Arnold, *Die Wehrmacht und die Besatzungspolitik*, 74-101, 242-67; and Arnold and Lübbers, "The Meeting of the Staatssekretäre," 613-26. On a number of occasions, Hitler had stressed that the army was not to be "burdened" with administration (Halder, *War Diary*, 5 March 1941, 327), that generals "[were], for the most part, not able to deal with and solve political questions" (*TBJG*, 19 August 1941), and that, with regard to the murder of Jews, "the soldier should not be burdened with these political questions" (3 July 1941, quoted in Arnold and Lübbers, "The Meeting of the Staatssekretäre," 620 n. 42).

61. Goebbels, "Wofür?," quoted in Müller, "Das 'Unternehmen Barbarossa' als wirtschaftlicher Raubkrieg," 174 (see also 184-85); Tooze, *The Wages of Destruction*, 135-61 (quote 141). For a more extreme, and controversial, version of this argument, see Aly, *Hitlers Volksstaat* (translated as *Hitler's Beneficiaries*). For an earlier, less extreme assessment, see also Aly and Heim, *Architects of Annihilation*, passim.

62. Domarus, ed., *Hitler: Reden und Proklamationen*, 2:1663–64; *TBJG*, 1 February 1941. A full-text English translation of Hitler's speech of 30 January as recorded by the Monitoring Service of the British Broadcasting Corporation, courtesy of the Research Project for Totalitarian Communication, New School for Social Research, is available at http://www.ibiblio.org/pha/policy/1941/410130a.html (accessed 29 August 2008).

63. For a comprehensive assessment of *Der ewige Jude*, see Hornshøj-Møller, *"Der ewige Jude,"* 3–39, 179–81, 309–15, "Der ewige Jude," and "The Role of 'Produced Reality.'" See also *TBJG*, 17, 24 October, 1, 8, 28 November, 18 December 1939, 9, 12 January, 6, 27 February, 4, 17 April, 9 May, 9 June, 3, 12, 25 September, 11 October 1940; Aly, *"Final Solution,"* 171–72; Breitman, *The Architect of Genocide*, 146–47; Engel, *Heeresadjutant bei Hitler*, 2 February 1941, 94–95; Kershaw, *Hitler: Nemesis*, 349–51.

64. Aly, *"Final Solution,"* 160–61, 171–74; Longerich, *Politik der Vernichtung*, 287–91; Breitman, *The Architect of Genocide*, 146–47, 151–56; Kershaw, *Hitler: Nemesis*, 349–53; Browning, *The Origins of the Final Solution*, 111–68. Revealingly, Himmler had mentioned to a select group of SS leaders in January 1941 that the Slavic population would have to be reduced by 30 million, roughly the same figure thrown about by army and agricultural planners.

65. Streit, *Keine Kameraden*, 28; Schramm, ed., *Kriegstagebuch*, 3 March 1941, 1, pt. 1:341; Noakes and Pridham, eds., *Nazism: A History*, 2:1087; "Richtlinien auf Sondergebieten zur Weisung Nr. 21 (Fall Barbarossa) vom 13. 3. 1941," in Ueberschär and Wette, eds., *"Unternehmen Barbarossa,"* 246–48; Breitman, *The Architect of Genocide*, 148–49; Browning, *The Origins of the Final Solution*, 215–16; Kershaw, *Hitler: Nemesis*, 353–54.

66. Halder, *War Diary*, 17 March 1941, 339; Aly, *"Final Solution,"* 171–74; Noakes and Pridham, *Nazism: A History*, 2:1088–89; "Befehl des ObdH, Generalfeldmarschall von Brauchitsch, über die Zusammenarbeit mit der Sicherheitspolizei und dem SD für den vorgesehenen Ostkrieg vom 28. 4. 1941," in Ueberschär and Wette, eds., *"Unternehmen Barbarossa,"* 249–50; Förster, "Operation Barbarossa as a War of Conquest," 485; Browning, *The Origins of the Final Solution*, 217–18, 224–34; Kershaw, *Hitler: Nemesis*, 354–55.

67. Halder, *War Diary*, 30 March 1941, 345–46; Förster, "Operation Barbarossa as a War of Conquest," 497–98; Browning, *The Origins of the Final Solution*, 218; Kershaw, *Hitler: Nemesis*, 355–56; Warlimont, *Inside Hitler's Headquarters*, 162.

68. Browning, *The Origins of the Final Solution*, 219–20; "Erlaß über die Ausübung der Kriegsgerichtsbarkeit im Gebiet 'Barbarossa' und über besondere Maßnahmen der Truppe vom 13. 5. 1941, mit Ergänzungen des ObdH vom 24. 5. 1941," in Ueberschär and Wette, eds., *"Unternehmen Barbarossa,"* 251–54.

69. Noakes and Pridham, *Nazism: A History*, 2:1090; "Richtlinien für die Behandlung politischer Kommissare vom 6. 6. 1941," in Ueberschär and Wette, eds., *"Unternehmen Barbarossa,"* 259–60; Browning, *The Origins of the Final Solution*, 220–21; Förster, "Operation Barbarossa as a War of Conquest," 506–20; Streit, *Keine Kameraden*, 44, 59.

70. Kershaw, *Hitler: Nemesis*, 358–59; Streit, *Keine Kameraden*, 50–51; Browning, *The Origins of the Final Solution*, 221–23. On Poland, see Rossino, *Hitler Strikes Poland*; Westermann, *Hitler's Police Battalions*; and Böhler, *Auftakt zum Vernichtungskrieg*.

71. Förster, "Hitler's Decision," 37, and "Operation Barbarossa as a War of Conquest," 519–20; "Befehl des Befehlshabers der Panzergruppe 4, Generaloberst Hoepner, zur bevorstehenden Kampfführung im Osten vom 2. 5. 1941," in

Ueberschär and Wette, eds., *"Unternehmen Barbarossa,"* 251; Browning, *The Origins of the Final Solution,* 222-24; Kershaw, *Hitler: Nemesis,* 358-60.

72. Browning, *The Origins of the Final Solution,* 224-29; Kershaw, *Hitler: Nemesis,* 381-82. On the Einsatzgruppen, see Krausnick and Wilhelm, *Die Truppe des Weltanschauungskrieges;* Ogorreck, *Die Einsatzgruppen und die "Genesis der Endlösung";* Herbert, *Best;* Wildt, *Generation des Unbedingten;* and Browder, *Hitler's Enforcers.*

73. Browning, *The Origins of the Final Solution,* 229-34; Kershaw, *Hitler: Nemesis,* 382. On the Order Police and the Reserve Police battalions, see Westermann, *Hitler's Police Battalions,* "'Friend and Helper,'" "'Ordinary Men' or 'Ideological Soldiers?'" and "Himmler's Uniformed Police on the Eastern Front"; Kwiet, "From the Diary of a Killing Unit"; Mallmann, "Der Einstieg in der Genozid," and "Vom Fussvolk der 'Endlösung'"; Klemp, "Kölner Polizeibataillone in Osteuropa"; Nachtwei, "'Ganz Normale Männer'"; and Browning, *Ordinary Men.*

74. *TBJG,* 1-2, 5-6, 11-12, 24, 26 October, 2, 14 November, 8-9, 11, 13, 19, 20, 22, 24 December 1940, 14, 16-17, 19-20 June 1941; Kershaw, *The "Hitler Myth,"* 158-60.

75. Kershaw, *Hitler: Nemesis,* 382-84; Halder, *War Diary,* 14 June 1941, 405-6; Below, *Als Hitlers Adjutant,* 277-78; Hitler to Goering quoted in Reese, *A Stranger to Myself,* vii.

76. *TBJG,* 16 June 1941; Kershaw, *Hitler: Nemesis,* 387.

77. *TBJG,* 16, 20 June 1941; Kershaw, *Hitler: Nemesis,* 387.

78. *TBJG,* 22 June 1941; Schellenberg, *The Schellenberg Memoirs,* 223; Halder, *War Diary,* 21 June 1941, 408; Domarus and Romane, eds., *The Essential Hitler,* 756-65; Hitler, *Hitler's Secret Conversations,* 59, 94; Leach, *German Strategy against Russia,* 156; Kershaw, *Hitler: Nemesis,* 386-87.

79. Förster, "The Dynamics of Volksgemeinschaft," 192; Tooze, *The Wages of Destruction,* 461-62.

80. Förster, "Der historische Ort," 633-35, and "Hitler's Decision," 35; Engel, *Heeresadjutant bei Hitler,* 18 February 1939, 45.

81. Förster, "Der historische Ort," 634-35; Domarus, ed., *Hitler: Reden und Proklamationen,* 2:1664.

3. Onslaught

1. For a good sense of the atmosphere at the front on the eve of Barbarossa, see Grupe, *Jahrgang 1916,* 149-51; Lubbeck, *At Leningrad's Gates,* 84; Knappe, *Soldat,* 178-80; Schröder, "German Soldiers' Experiences," 309-24, and *Die gestohlenen Jahre;* Wette, "'Es roch nach Ungeheuerlichem,'" 71-73; Fuchs, *Wer spricht von Siegen,* 12; Kuby, *Mein Krieg,* 95-99; Stahlberg, *Bounden Duty,* 160-62; and Hitler's "Aufruf an die Soldaten der Ostfront vom 22. 6. 41," in Ueberschär and Wette, eds., *"Unternehmen Barbarossa,"* 319-23.

2. Leach, *German Strategy against Russia,* 192; DiNardo, *Mechanized Juggernaut?* 40-50; Hoffmann, "Die Sowjetunion bis zum Vorabend des deutschen Angriffs," 88-99; Rotundo, "Stalin and the Outbreak of War in 1941," 280-81; Glantz, *Barbarossa,* 27; Tooze, *The Wages of Destruction,* 452-54; Förster, "The Dynamics of Volksgemeinschaft," 195.

3. Halder, *War Diary,* 22 June 1941, 410-12. Proponents of the idea that Stalin intended a strike against Germany include Suvorov, *Icebreaker;* Topitsch, *Stalin's War;* Raack, "Stalin's Plans for World War II"; and Hoffmann, "The Soviet Union's Offensive Preparations in 1941."

For good historiographic assessments and critiques of this argument, see Uldricks, "The Icebreaker Controversy"; Pietrow-Ennker, *Präventivkrieg?* and "Deutschland im Juni 1941"; Förster, "Die Grosse Täuschung"; Ueberschär, "Das 'Unternehmen Barbarossa' gegen die Sowjetunion"; and Gorodetsky, "Was Stalin Planning to Attack Hitler in June 1941?" "Stalin and Hitler's Attack on the Soviet Union," and "Stalin und Hitlers Angriff auf die Sowjetunion." For a balanced assessment of Stalin's perceptions of the Wehrmacht, see Arlt, "Die Wehrmacht im Kalkül Stalins," 105–11.

4. Rotundo, "Stalin and the Outbreak of War in 1941," 289–96; Gorodetsky, "Stalin and Hitler's Attack on the Soviet Union," 346–50, and *Grand Delusion,* chaps. 8, 12; Churchill, *The Grand Alliance,* 55; Litvinov quoted in Gorodetsky, "Was Stalin Planning to Attack Hitler in June 1941?" 72.

5. Rotundo, "Stalin and the Outbreak of War in 1941," 289–96; Gorodetsky, *Grand Deception,* chap. 6, and "Stalin and Hitler's Attack on the Soviet Union," 346–47, 355–56; Mawdsley, *Thunder in the East,* 32–41; *TBJG,* 16 June 1941.

6. Rotundo, "Stalin and the Outbreak of War in 1941," 284–85, 290–92, 295–96; Uldricks, "The Icebreaker Controversy," 635–36; Mawdsley, *Thunder in the East,* 32–37.

7. Mawdsley, *Thunder in the East,* 32–37; Churchill, *The Hinge of Fate,* 493; Gorodetsky, "Stalin and Hitler's Attack on the Soviet Union," 357–59.

8. Leach, *German Strategy against Russia,* 172; Rotundo, "Stalin and the Outbreak of War in 1941," 280–81; Mawdsley, *Thunder in the East,* 26–31, 42–43, 46–51. Although, as is often supposed, the Soviets had made no special effort in the 1930s to expand industry across the Urals, they had created new factories in the eastern part of European Russia between Moscow and the Urals.

9. Mawdsley, *Thunder in the East,* 44–46. For a good assessment of German intelligence failures, see Thomas, "Foreign Armies East."

10. Mawdsley, *Thunder in the East,* 41–43; Förster, "Hitler's Decision," 48; Leach, *German Strategy against Russia,* chaps. 5–6; Tooze, *The Wages of Destruction,* 456–57; Bock, *War Diary,* 31 January 1941, 196–97.

11. Clausewitz, *On War,* bk. 1, chap. 2.

12. Hayward, "Hitler's Quest for Oil," 99–103; Cooke and Nesbit, *Target, Hitler's Oil,* 16; Reinhardt, *Die Wende vor Moskau,* 117–18.

13. On the problems of horse-drawn transport, see DiNardo, *Mechanized Juggernaut?* 40–50.

14. Förster, "The Dynamics of Volksgemeinschaft," 201; Leach, *German Strategy against Russia,* 234–35. On Soviet military dispositions, see Gorodetsky, *Grand Delusion,* 115–30, 227–45; Mawdsley, *Thunder in the East,* 37–41; and Rotundo, "Stalin and the Outbreak of War in 1941," 286.

15. *TBJG,* 23 June 1941.

16. Glantz, *Barbarossa,* 35; Leach, *German Strategy against Russia,* 192–93; Kershaw, *War without Garlands,* 37, 51–52, 55.

17. Glantz, *Barbarossa,* 37–39; Mawdsley, *Thunder in the East,* 55–59; Overy, *Russia's War,* 73–79. Stalin supposedly commented to Timoshenko and Zhukov, "Lenin founded our state and we've fucked it up," then drove to his dacha at Kuntsevo, where he remained incommunicado until 30 June, when members of the Politburo went to demand he again actively lead the state. Stalin quoted in Radzinskii, *Stalin,* 451–52.

18. Klink, "The Conduct of Operations," 525–26; Megargee, *War of Annihilation,* 46–47; Glantz, *Barbarossa,* 37.

19. Klink, "The Conduct of Operations," 527-32; Megargee, *War of Annihilation*, 47; Guderian, *Panzer Leader*, 158-66; Bock, *War Diary*, 23, 25-26 June 1941, 225-28.

20. Halder, *War Diary*, 22-29 June 1941, 410-32; Leach, *German Strategy against Russia*, 194-95; Bock, *War Diary*, 25 June 1941, 227.

21. Halder, *War Diary*, 22-29 June 1941, 410-32; Bock, *War Diary*, 22-29 June, 2 July 1941, 224-33, 235-36; Kershaw, *War without Garlands*, 76-77, 94; *TBJG*, 28-30 June 1941; Klink, "The Conduct of Operations," 531-32, 536. Soviet figures put the losses at 340,000 men, or half the strength of the Western Front at the outset of the invasion, 4,800 tanks, and 9,400 guns and mortars, figures higher even than the Germans estimated. Mawdsley, *Thunder in the East*, 60.

22. Klink, "The Conduct of Operations," 537-41; Megargee, *War of Annihilation*, 45-46; Glantz, *Barbarossa*, 42-46.

23. Klink, "The Conduct of Operations," 546-69; Megargee, *War of Annihilation*, 47-49; Glantz, *Barbarossa*, 46-53.

24. Glantz, *Barbarossa*, 55; Stolfi, "Barbarossa Revisited," 35-36, and *Hitler's Panzers East*.

25. Halder, *War Diary*, 3 July 1941, 446-47; Ueberschär, "Das Scheitern des Unternehmens 'Barbarossa,'" 146-47.

26. Kroener, "Organisation und Mobilisierung des deutschen Machtbereichs," 567-69; "Sonderakte," in Schramm, ed., *Kriegstagebuch*, 4 July 1941, 1, pt. 2:1020; "Vortragsnotiz über die Besetzung und Sicherung des russischen Raumes und über den Umbau des Heeres nach Abschluß Barbarossa," in ibid., 15 July 1941, 1022-25; "Besprechung Chef OKW mit den Wehrmachtteilen am 16. 8. 41 über Die Auswirkung der Richtlinien des Führers vom 14. 7. 41 sowie die Durchführbarkeit der sich daraus ergebenden neuen Schwerpunkt-Programme," in ibid., 16 August 1941, 1047-54; Ueberschär, "Das Scheitern des Unternehmens 'Barbarossa,'" 149-50; Leach, *German Strategy against Russia*, 219; Reinhardt, *Moscow–the Turning Point*, 26-31, 40-43.

27. Ueberschär, "Das Scheitern des Unternehmens 'Barbarossa,'" 147; Halder, *War Diary*, 8 July 1941, 458; *TBJG*, 9 July 1941; Kershaw, *Hitler: Nemesis*, 400-404; Jochmann, ed., *Monologe im Führerhauptquartier*, 5-6, 11-12, 27 July, 1-2, 8-11, 19-20 August, 17-19, 22-26 September 1941, 38-71; Jürgen Förster, "Securing 'Living Space,'" 1235.

28. Kershaw, *Hitler: Nemesis*, 403-4; Jochmann, *Monologe im Führerhauptquartier*, 23-26 September 1941, 66-71.

29. Kershaw, *Hitler: Nemesis*, 404-5; Jochmann, *Monologe im Führerhauptquartier*, 23-28 September 1941, 65-72; Fritz, *Frontsoldaten*, 187-218, and "'We are trying . . . to change the face of the world.'"

For interpretations that emphasize Hitler's modernity, see Zitelmann, *Hitler;* and Prinz and Zitelmann, eds., *Nationalsozialismus und Modernisierung.* See also Tooze, *The Wages of Destruction*, introduction, chaps. 2, 5; Smelser, "How 'Modern' Were the Nazis?"; Aly and Heim, *Architects of Annihilation*, 1-10; and Aly, *Hitler's Beneficiaries*.

30. Tooze, *The Wages of Destruction*, 462-63; Kershaw, *Fateful Choices*, 448. See also Aly and Heim, *Architects of Annihilation*, passim.

31. Jochmann, *Monologe im Führerhauptquartier*, 13 October 1941, 78; Kershaw, *Hitler: Nemesis*, 434; Tooze, *The Wages of Destruction*, 469-70. For a comparison of Nazi Germany's conduct to that of historical colonial powers, see Zimmerer, "Holocaust und Kolonialismus." For a more critical assessment of this interpretation, see Gerwarth and Malinowski, "Der Holocaust als 'kolonialer Genozid'?" and "Hannah Arendt's Ghosts."

32. Tooze, *The Wages of Destruction*, 466–76; Aly, *"Final Solution,"* 149–60; Aly and Heim, *Architects of Annihilation*, 253–55; Pohl, *Von der "Judenpolitik" zum Judenmord*, 89, 95–97; Schulte, *Zwangsarbeit und Vernichtung*, 248; Madajczyk, "Synchronismus." On Generalplan Ost, see Madajczyk and Biernacki, eds., *Generalplan Ost;* Rössler and Schleiermacher, eds., *Der "Generalplan Ost";* and Wasser, *Himmlers Raumplanung im Osten.*

33. Matthäus, "Operation Barbarossa and the Onset of the Holocaust," 253–56, 268–77, and "Controlled Escalation"; Kershaw, *Fateful Choices*, 452–53; Krausnick, *Hitlers Einsatzgruppen*, 141, 179; Klee, Dressen, and Riess, eds., *"The Good Old Days,"* 28–33. See also Matthäus, *Ausbildungsziel Judenmord?* and Kwiet, "Erziehung zum Mord," "From the Diary of a Killing Unit," and "Rehearsing for Murder."

34. Krausnick, *Hitlers Einsatzgruppen*, 142–43, 151–78; Matthäus, "Operation Barbarossa and the Onset of the Holocaust," 256–59; Boll and Safrian, "Auf dem Weg nach Stalingrad," 263–71; Kershaw, *Fateful Choices*, 454–55, and *Hitler: Nemesis*, 463–64.

35. Klee, Dressen, and Riess, eds., *"The Good Old Days,"* 38–54; Diary of SS-Hauptscharführer Felix Landau, 7 July 1941, in Dollinger, ed., *Kain, wo ist dein Bruder?* 87–88; Matthäus, "Operation Barbarossa and the Onset of the Holocaust," 256, 268–77; Megargee, *War of Annihilation*, 68–69; Kershaw, *Hitler: Nemesis*, 463–64.

36. Streit, "The German Army and the Politics of Genocide," 5–6, and *Keine Kameraden*, 110–12; Boll and Safrian, "Auf dem Weg nach Stalingrad," 263–69; Stahlberg, *Bounden Duty*, 159; Matthäus, "Operation Barbarossa and the Onset of the Holocaust," 260; Krausnick, *Hitlers Einsatzgruppen*, 184, 204–14, 226, 237, 249–51, 278; Longerich, *Politik der Vernichtung*, 405–6; Messerschmidt, "Difficult Atonement," 90–92. While agreeing with the central theme of Wehrmacht cooperation with and participation in these criminal actions, Christian Hartmann nonetheless makes an important distinction between frontline troops and those in the rear: much the greater part of Wehrmacht crimes were committed by security divisions or units behind the front. See Hartmann, *Wehrmacht im Ostkrieg*, 675–98, and "Verbrecherischer Krieg—verbrecherische Wehrmacht?"

37. Matthäus, "Operation Barbarossa and the Onset of the Holocaust," 253–67; Krausnick, *Hitlers Einsatzgruppen*, 180, 189–90.

38. Kershaw, *War without Garlands*, 142–43; Schulte, "Korück 582," and *German Army*, 69–85, 117–49; Matthäus, "Operation Barbarossa and the Onset of the Holocaust," 253–67; Streit, "The German Army and the Politics of Genocide," 8–9, and *Keine Kameraden*, 42–44; Förster, "Securing 'Living Space,'" 1211–16.

39. Förster, "Securing 'Living Space,'" 1189–1234.

40. Matthäus, "Operation Barbarossa and the Onset of the Holocaust," 253–67; Hitler quoted in Hartmann, "Verbrecherischer Krieg—verbrecherische Wehrmacht?" 25. On Soviet atrocities, see De Zayas, *Die Wehrmacht-Untersuchungsstelle*, 273–77, 284; Rass, *"Menschenmaterial,"* 334; and Hoffmann, "The Conduct of the War through Soviet Eyes." It has been estimated that 90–95 percent of German prisoners of war perished in 1941–1942 (De Zayas, *Die Wehrmacht-Untersuchungsstelle*, 277). On the propaganda uses of alleged Soviet atrocities, see generally the entries in *TBJG* for July 1941 (quote from entry of 17 July 1941). Two days earlier, Goebbels had asserted, "Just as every soldier returns from Poland as an anti-Semite, so they will come back from the Soviet Union as an anti-Bolshevik."

41. Prüller, *Diary of a German Soldier*, 5 July 1941, 75; Richardson, ed., *Sieg Heil!* 3 August 1941, 122; Kershaw, *War without Garlands*, 136–38. See also Schulte, *German Army*, 117–49, 211–33.

42. Matthäus, "Operation Barbarossa and the Onset of the Holocaust," 253–67; Förster, "Securing 'Living Space,'" 1189–1234; quote from Manoschek, *"Es gibt nur eines für das Judentum,"* 33. See also Boll and Safrian, "Auf dem Weg nach Stalingrad," 271–72. The letter was eventually displayed in the show windows of various Viennese businesses (ibid., 292 n. 62).

43. Matthäus, "Operation Barbarossa and the Onset of the Holocaust," 253–67; Hartmann, "Verbrecherischer Krieg—verbrecherische Wehrmacht?" 30–31; Förster, "Securing 'Living Space,'" 1189–1234; Pohl, *Nationalsozialistische Judenverfolgung in Ostgalizien*, 45–47; Sandkühler, *"Endlösung" in Galizien*, 114–16; Schulte, *German Army*, 234–39; Diary entries of Robert Neumann, 7 July, 5, 7 October 1941, in Dollinger, ed., *Kain, wo ist dein Bruder?* 88, 100–101.

44. Matthäus, "Operation Barbarossa and the Onset of the Holocaust," 253–67; Förster, "Securing 'Living Space,'" 1189–1234; Streit, "The German Army and the Politics of Genocide," 6–7; Förster, "Hitler Turns East," 130.

On the complexities of the partisan war, see Anderson, "Die 62. Infanterie-Division," and "Germans, Ukrainians and Jews"; Birn, "Two Kinds of Reality?"; Hartmann, "Verbrecherischer Krieg—verbrecherische Wehrmacht?" 19–20, 24–30, 49–57, and *Wehrmacht im Ostkrieg*, 383 (quote).

While the army's criminal culpability as an institution is extensive, and despite the spread of racist ideology through the ranks, it is well to remember that only a strikingly small percentage of Landsers actively participated in the murders of Jews. As Christian Hartmann has argued, soldiers, especially those at the front, primarily focused on daily war tasks and the problem of survival. See Hartmann, "Verbrecherischer Krieg—verbrecherische Wehrmacht?" 17–20, 31–32, 64–74. See also Pohl, "Schauplatz Ukraine," 151, 169–71, and "Die Wehrmacht und der Mord," 50.

45. Matthäus, "Operation Barbarossa and the Onset of the Holocaust," 288–94; Gerlach, *Kalkulierte Morde*, 587–88, 593, 609–13, 628–39; Pohl, "Einsatzgruppe C," 73–74; Boll and Safrian, "Auf dem Weg nach Stalingrad," 275–82; Longerich, *Politik der Vernichtung*, 377–79; Schulte, *German Army*, 224–34.

46. Wette, *Die Wehrmacht*, 115–17; Krausnick, *Hitlers Einsatzgruppen*, 162–69; Klee, Dressen, and Riess, eds., *"The Good Old Days,"* 141–54; Pohl, "Einsatzgruppe C," 71–75; "Auszüge aus verschiedenen 'Ereignismeldungen UdSSR' über die Tätigkeit der Einsatzgruppen A, B, C, und D im Osten vom Juli 1941 bis zum März 1942," in Ueberschär and Wette, eds., *"Unternehmen Barbarossa,"* 314–22. See also Boll and Safrian, "Auf dem Weg nach Stalingrad," 260–96; Rüß, "Wer war verantwortlich für das Massaker?"; and Arnold, "Die Eroberung und Behandlung der Stadt Kiew."

47. Wette, *Die Wehrmacht*, 118–19; Rüß, "Wer war verantwortlich für das Massaker?" 498–506; Arnold, "Die Eroberung und Behandlung der Stadt Kiew," 53; Klee and Dressen, eds., *"Gott mit uns,"* 118, 127.

48. Wette, *Die Wehrmacht*, 119–20; Krausnick, *Hitlers Einsatzgruppen*, 164–65; Rüß, "Wer war verantwortlich für das Massaker?" 493; "Ereignismeldung UdSSR, No. 128, 3 November 1941," in Klee, Dressen, and Riess, eds., *"The Good Old Days,"* 68; Klee and Dressen, eds., *"Gott mit uns,"* 119.

49. Wette, *Die Wehrmacht*, 120–28; "Wer war verantwortlich für das Massaker?" 490–95; Klee, Dressen, and Riess, eds., *"The Good Old Days,"* 63–68; "Ereignismeldung UdSSR, No. 106, 7 October 1941," in Klee and Dressen, eds., *"Gott mit uns,"* 132 (see generally 117–36); Krasnick, *Hitlers Einsatzgruppen*, 237; Messerschmidt, "Difficult Atonement," 92.

50. Förster, "Securing 'Living Space,'" 1217–18, and "Hitler Turns East," 130;

Matthäus, "Operation Barbarossa and the Onset of the Holocaust," 259–64, 277–78;
Krausnick, *Hitlers Einsatzgruppen*, 195–224; Anderson, "Germans, Ukrainians, and
Jews," 339–40; Megargee, *War of Annihilation*, 69–70; Polian, "First Victims of the
Holocaust"; Fleming, *Hitler and the Final Solution*, 73–74; Jochmann, *Monologe im
Führerhauptquartier*, 25 October 1941, 106; Kershaw, *Hitler: Nemesis*, 464, and *Fateful
Choices*, 457; Streit, "The German Army and the Politics of Genocide," 7.

51. *TBJG*, 8 July 1941; Kershaw, *Hitler: Nemesis*, 469–70, and *Fateful Choices*, 434–
36, 455; Förster, "Securing Living Space," 1237.

52. Förster, "Securing 'Living Space,'" 1237; Kershaw, *Fateful Choices*, 434–36;
Friedländer, *Nazi Germany and the Jews*, 1:84–90.

53. "Geheime Absichtserklärungen zur künftigen Ostpolitik: Auszug aus einem
Aktenvermerk von Reichsleiter M. Bormann vom 16. 7. 1941," in Ueberschär and
Wette, eds., *"Unternehmen Barbarossa,"* 330–31; Browning, *The Origins of the Final Solu-
tion*, 309–10; Matthäus, "Operation Barbarossa and the Onset of the Holocaust,"
265–66; Förster, "Securing 'Living Space,'" 1235–36; Ueberschär, "Das Scheitern des
Unternehmens 'Barbarossa,'" 148–49; Kershaw, *Hitler: Nemesis*, 405.

54. Browning, *The Origins of the Final Solution*, 310–11; Kershaw, *Fateful Choices*,
455–56; Matthäus, "Operation Barbarossa and the Onset of the Holocaust," 267;
Förster, "Securing 'Living Space,'" 1237; Kershaw, *Hitler: Nemesis*, 469. See also Cüp-
pers, *Wegbereiter der Shoah;* Förster, "Das andere Gesicht des Krieges," 155–57; Birn,
"Zweierlei Wirklichkeit?"; Büchler, "Himmler's Personal Murder Brigades"; and
Lozowick, "Rollbahn Mord."
Himmler had returned to the Führer Headquarters the day before the meeting
but was perhaps occupied by the news of the capture of Stalin's son.

55. *TBJG*, 9 July 1941; Friedländer, *Nazi Germany and the Jews*, 2:204–5; *Völkischer
Beobachter*, 24 July 1941; Herf, *The Jewish Enemy*, 110–11. See also Benz, "Judenvernichtung"; and Kaufman, *Germany Must Perish!*

56. *TBJG*, 24 July 1941, 3, 13, 19–20, 26, 29 August, 22 October 1941; Friedländer,
Nazi Germany and the Jews, 2:205–7; Herf, *The Jewish Enemy*, 111–15; Benz, "Judenvernichtung," 620–22; Boberach, ed., *Meldungen aus dem Reich*, 31 July 1941.
Top Nazis seem to have come to believe their own propaganda about the Kaufman
book or, more precisely, to have had their irrational, paranoid conspiracy fantasies
confirmed. No longer merely a crank, Kaufman was elevated to a close personal
adviser to Roosevelt and a decisive influence on American policy. Adolf Eichmann,
e.g., suggested in his posthumously published memoirs: "Kaufman intended to
bring about the complete extermination of our people. . . . It is probable that in our
highest leadership circles, the Kaufman plan served as a stimulating factor for [our]
own extermination plans." This sense of a preventive measure fit well the Nazis'
mind-set, which typically justified their own murderous actions as simply a response
to the plans of others or as just retribution for past crimes. See Aschenauer, ed., *Ich,
Adolf Eichmann*, 177–78; Herf, *The Jewish Enemy*, 324 n. 87.

57. Goering's authorization to Heydrich in Noakes and Pridham, eds., *Nazism: A
History*, 2:1104; Browning, *The Origins of the Final Solution*, 315–16; Kershaw, *Fateful
Choices*, 460, and *Hitler: Nemesis*, 470–71; Ueberschär, "Das Scheitern des Unterneh-
mens 'Barbarossa,'" 149.

58. Matthäus, "Operation Barbarossa and the Onset of the Holocaust," 277–85;
Browning, *The Origins of the Final Solution*, 311–17; *TBJG*, 11 August 1941.

59. Browning, *The Origins of the Final Solution*, 311–17; Kershaw, *Fateful Choices*,
456–58, and *Hitler: Nemesis*, 472–74; *TBJG*, 18–19 August 1941.

60. Jersak, "Die Interaktion von Kriegsverlauf und Judenvernichtung," "A Matter of Foreign Policy," and "Decisions to Murder and to Lie," 304–5; Meeting between Hitler and the Spanish ambassador, 12 August 1941, in Hillgruber, *Staatsmänner,* 1:624 (doc. 86); Tooze, *The Wages of Destruction,* 502.

61. *TBJG,* 15–20 August 1941; Browning, *The Origins of the Final Solution,* 318–23; Kershaw, *Fateful Choices,* 407–8, 460–61, and *Hitler: Nemesis,* 960–61 n. 75; Gerlach, "The Wannsee Conference," 777. For a more supportive view of Jersak's thesis, although with some reservations, see Arnold, "Hitlers Wandel im August 1941."

62. For a good English translation of the statistical report of Karl Jäger, see Klee, Dressen, and Riess, eds., *"The Good Old Days,"* 46–58. It is also available on the Internet at "The Jäger Report," *Einsatzgruppen Archives,* http://www.einsatzgruppenarchives .com/jager.html (accessed 2 October 2008).

63. Matthäus, "Operation Barbarossa and the Onset of the Holocaust," 277–85; Browning, *The Origins of the Final Solution,* 311–17, 353; Kershaw, *Fateful Choices,* 456–58.

64. Halder, *War Diary,* 24–25, 27, 29–30 June, 2–3, 5 July 1941, 418–53; Bock, *War Diary,* 23–25, 27–28, 30 June, 1–2 July 1941, 225–35; *TBJG,* 15 July 1941.

65. Quote in Lucas, ed., *War on the Eastern Front,* 31–33.

66. Klink, "Military Conception," 257–85; Leach, *German Strategy against Russia,* 99–118, 193–95, 254–69; Halder, *War Diary,* 29 June 1941, 432; Megargee, *War of Annihilation,* 50–51.

67. Schramm, ed., *Kriegstagebuch,* 4–5, 8 July 1941, 1, pt. 2:1020–21; Halder, *War Diary,* 8 July 1941, 458–59; Leach, *German Strategy against Russia,* 197–98, 216; Klink, "The Conduct of Operations," 569–70; Megargee, *War of Annihilation,* 51–52.

68. Halder, *War Diary,* 8 July, 8 August 1941, 457, 503; Leach, *German Strategy against Russia,* 200–201; Klink, "The Conduct of Operations," 570, 586–87.

69. Leach, *German Strategy against Russia,* 202; Klink, "The Conduct of Operations," 581–88; Citino, *Death of the Wehrmacht,* 41.

70. Hoffmann, "The Conduct of the War through Soviet Eyes," 855–57; Glantz, *Barbarossa,* 71–73; Glantz and House, *When Titans Clashed,* 71–72; Mawdsley, *Thunder in the East,* 48–49.

71. Halder, *War Diary,* 6 July, 2 August 1941, 453–54, 493; Overmans, *Deutsche militärische Verluste,* 277–78; Förster, "The Dynamics of Volksgemeinschaft," 203; Schramm, ed., *Kriegstagebuch,* 5 January 1942, 1, pt. 2:1120–21.

72. Förster, "The Dynamics of Volksgemeinschaft," 202; Halder, *War Diary,* 8 July 1941, 459–60; Reinhardt, *Moscow–the Turning Point,* 40.

73. Halder, *War Diary,* 8 July 1941, 459–60; Reinhardt, *Moscow–the Turning Point,* 40, 61–62; Leach, *German Strategy against Russia,* 203; Müller, "The Failure of the Economic 'Blitzkrieg Strategy,'" 1085, 1127, and "From Economic Alliance to a War of Colonial Exploitation," 219; Förster, "The Dynamics of Volksgemeinschaft," 202–3; Steiger, *Panzertaktik,* 160.

74. Knappe, *Soldat,* 213; Haape, *Moscow Tram Stop,* 52–53, 55; Kershaw, *War without Garlands,* 90–93.

75. Müller, "The Failure of the Economic 'Blitzkrieg Strategy,'" 1118; Leach, *German Strategy against Russia,* 204–5; Förster, "The Dynamics of Volksgemeinschaft," 202; Kershaw, *War without Garlands,* 92–94.

76. Müller, "The Failure of the Economic 'Blitzkrieg Strategy,'" 1107–13; Leach, *German Strategy against Russia,* 205–6; Schüler, "The Eastern Campaign," 205–10.

77. Müller, "The Failure of the Economic 'Blitzkrieg Strategy,'" 1114–26; Leach,

German Strategy against Russia, 205–6, 210–12; Reinhardt, *Moscow—the Turning Point,* 146–47, 157 n. 61; Schüler, "The Eastern Campaign," 210–13. Schüler notes that, in the autumn of 1939, the Reichsbahn had fewer locomotives and less rolling stock than in 1914 (Schüler, "The Eastern Campaign," 206). See also Schüler, *Logistik im Rußlandfeldzug.*

78. Müller, "The Failure of the Economic 'Blitzkrieg Strategy,'" 1117–26; Schüler, "The Eastern Campaign," 212–13.

79. Halder, *War Diary,* 26 July 1941, 487; Leach, *German Strategy against Russia,* 207; Kipp, "The Crisis of Successive Operations," 94–96. The gnawing doubts, worries about the mood in Germany, frustration at the absence of a decisive victory, and a growing sense of crisis can be seen well in Goebbels's diary entries between 18 and 31 July 1941. Quotes from *TBJG,* 24, 31 July 1941.

80. Klink, "The Conduct of Operations," 532–34; Kipp, "The Crisis of Successive Operations," 98–101; Glantz, *Barbarossa,* 77–78; Leach, *German Strategy against Russia,* 198; Halder, *War Diary,* 9, 12 July 1941, 461, 467.

81. Kipp, "The Crisis of Successive Operations," 108–13. Van Creveld (*Supplying War,* 166–71, 175–76) argues that supply problems prevented a successful German advance. For an opposing view, see Stolfi, "Barbarossa Revisited," and *Hitler's Panzers East,* 166–77.

82. Klink, "The Conduct of Operations," 534–36; Hoffmann, "The Conduct of the War through Soviet Eyes," 865–69; Kipp, "The Crisis of Successive Operations," 114–17; Glantz, *Barbarossa,* 77–78; Mawdsley, *Thunder in the East,* 66–69.

83. Klink, "The Conduct of Operations," 534–36; Hoffmann, "The Conduct of the War through Soviet Eyes," 865–69; Kipp, "The Crisis of Successive Operations," 114–17; Glantz, *Barbarossa,* 78–82; Mawdsley, *Thunder in the East,* 66–69; Guderian, *Panzer Leader,* 144; Halder, *War Diary,* 20 July 1941, 480–82; Bock, *War Diary,* 20–21, 23 July 1941, 255, 258, 260.

84. Klink, "The Conduct of Operations," 536–37; Kipp, "The Crisis of Successive Operations," 124–30; Glantz, *Barbarossa,* 82–95; Mawdsley, *Thunder in the East,* 66–69; Bock, *War Diary,* 20–26, 31 July 1941, 255–69; Hoffmann, "The Conduct of the War through Soviet Eyes," 869; Schüler, "The Eastern Campaign," 212–13; Manteuffel, *Die 7. Panzer-Division,* 167–68.

85. Klink, "The Conduct of Operations," 536–37, 574; Kipp, "The Crisis of Successive Operations," 117–19, 130–35; Glantz, *Barbarossa,* 83–84, 219 n. 24; Mawdsley, *Thunder in the East,* 66–69; Bock, *War Diary,* 1, 3, 10, 12, 14 August 1941, 270–81; Halder, *War Diary,* 26 July, 5 August 1941, 485, 497; Bock, *War Diary,* 25 July 1941, 262.

86. Klink, "The Conduct of Operations," 572; Kipp, "The Crisis of Successive Operations," 118; Glantz, *Barbarossa,* 84–85; Megargee, *War of Annihilation,* 55.

87. Klink, "The Conduct of Operations," 572; Kipp, "The Crisis of Successive Operations," 118; Megargee, *War of Annihilation,* 55; "Führerweisungen am 23. Juli 1941," in Schramm, ed., *Kriegstagebuch,* 23 July 1941, 1, pt. 2:1030–31; "Addendum to Directive No. 33," in Glantz, *Barbarossa,* 236–37.

88. Klink, "The Conduct of Operations," 574; Kipp, "The Crisis of Successive Operations," 118; Leach, *German Strategy against Russia,* 207–8; Schramm, ed., *Kriegstagebuch,* 23 July 1941, 1, pt. 2:1033; Bock, *War Diary,* 25, 27–28 July 1941, 262–65; Halder, *War Diary,* 26 July 1941, 485–87.

89. Klink, "The Conduct of Operations," 574–78; Leach, *German Strategy against Russia,* 207–8; Schramm, ed., *Kriegstagebuch,* 25 July 1941, 1, pt. 2:1035–40; Halder, *War Diary,* 26 July 1941, 485–87.

90. Klink, "The Conduct of Operations," 579–80; Leach, *German Strategy against Russia*, 209; Schramm, ed., *Kriegstagebuch*, 28 July 1941, 1, pt. 2:1040; "Directive No. 34," in Glantz, *Barbarossa*, 237; Halder, *War Diary*, 30 July 1941, 490.

91. Klink, "The Conduct of Operations," 579–83; Leach, *German Strategy against Russia*, 209–12; Halder, *War Diary*, 1 August 1941, 491; Bock, *War Diary*, 5 August 1941, 273.

92. Bock, *War Diary*, 2 August 1941, 271; Letters of 10 and 11 August 1941, in Buchbender and Sterz, eds., *Das andere Gesicht des Krieges*, 77–78.

93. Bock, *War Diary*, 7, 12 August 1941, 276, 281.

94. Halder, *War Diary*, 4, 11 August 1941, 496, 505–6.

95. Klink, "The Conduct of Operations," 588–90; Kershaw, *Hitler: Nemesis*, 411; Schramm, ed., *Kriegstagebuch*, 12 August 1941, 1, pt. 2:1044.

96. Klink, "The Conduct of Operations," 590–91; Ueberschär, "Das Scheitern des Unternehmens 'Barbarossa,'" 153; Kershaw, *Hitler: Nemesis*, 411–12; *TBJG*, 19 August 1941.

97. Klink, "The Conduct of Operations," 591–93; Kershaw, *Hitler: Nemesis*, 412–14; "Sonderakte," in Schramm, ed., *Kriegstagebuch*, 20 August 1941, 1, pt. 2:1061; "Operative Gedanken des Führers und Weisungen am 21. August 1941," in ibid., 21 August 1941, 1061–62; "Studie," in ibid., 22 August 1941, 1063–68.

98. Klink, "The Conduct of Operations," 593–94; Wilt, "Hitler's Late Summer Pause," 188; Kershaw, *Hitler: Nemesis*, 414–15; Halder, *War Diary*, 22, 24 August 1941, 514–16; Bock, *War Diary*, 22–24 August 1941, 288–93; Guderian, *Panzer Leader*, 198–202.

99. Klink, "The Conduct of Operations," 593–94; Müller, "The Failure of the Economic 'Blitzkrieg Strategy,'" 1124–41; Schüler, "The Eastern Campaign," 211–13; Leach, *German Strategy against Russia*, 214–15, 218–25, 238–41; Megargee, *War of Annihilation*, 80–81; Kipp, "The Crisis of Successive Operations," 133–34; Glantz, *Barbarossa*, 83–96; Mawdsley, *Thunder in the East*, 71–74.

100. Halder, *War Diary*, 8 August 1941, 500; Ueberschär, "Das Scheitern des Unternehmens 'Barbarossa,'" 154; Megargee, *War of Annihilation*, 81; Klink, "The Conduct of Operations," 593–94; Müller, "The Failure of the Economic 'Blitzkrieg Strategy,'" 1141; Leach, *German Strategy against Russia*, 217, 234–37.

4. Whirlwind

1. *TBJG*, 30 June 1941, 1, 5, 24, 28 July 1941; Kershaw, *Hitler: Nemesis*, 422–23; Steinert, *Hitler's War*, 117–32; Aly and Heim, *Architects of Annihilation*, 237.

2. Kershaw, *Hitler: Nemesis*, 422–23; *TBJG*, 28 June, 14, 17, 31 July, 13, 16, 19 August 1941; Steinert, *Hitler's War*, 122. For the popular mood in general, see *TBJG*, 9–10, 14–17, 20, 23–24, 28–29, 31 July, 7–8, 10–11, 13–16, 25, 28–29 August 1941; and Aly, *Hitler's Beneficiaries*, 131, 169–71.

3. Kershaw, *Hitler: Nemesis*, 424–26, and *Popular Opinion and Political Dissent*, 332–57; Steinert, *Hitler's War*, 122–23.

4. Steinert, *Hitler's War*, 122–24; Kershaw, *Hitler: Nemesis*, 426–28.

5. *TBJG*, 14 August 1941; Browning, *The Origins of the Final Solution*, 184–85. The best book on the rise and impact of eugenics in Germany is Friedlander, *The Origins of Nazi Genocide*, here 15–20. See also Kühl, *The Nazi Connection*, 77–84; Burleigh, *Death and Deliverance;* Burleigh and Wippermann, *The Racial State;* and Mazower, *Dark Continent*, chap. 3.

6. Kershaw, *Hitler: Nemesis*, 252–61; Browning, *The Origins of the Final Solution*, 185–89; Burleigh, *Death and Deliverance*, 97, 111–12; Klee, *"Euthanasie" im NS-Staat*, 46–47, 53, 95–98, 112–15, 192–93; Friedlander, *The Origins of Nazi Genocide*, 39, 43, 62–63. On compulsory sterilization, see Bock, *Zwangssterilisation im Nationalsozialismus*. There are numerous local and regional studies of compulsory sterilization by German historians.

7. Browning, *The Origins of the Final Solution*, 185–93; Kershaw, *Hitler: Nemesis*, 252, 260–61, 429–30; Burleigh and Wippermann, *The Racial State*, 143–48, 153; Klee, *Dokumente zur "Euthanasie,"* 85, and *"Euthanasie" im NS-Staat*, 345–55; Friedlander, *The Origins of Nazi Genocide*, 40–61, 64–110, 106–7, 111–16, 150–63, 270–83.

8. Megargee, *War of Annihilation*, 76, 82; Klink, "The Conduct of Operations," 559–67; Müller, "The Failure of the Economic 'Blitzkrieg Strategy,'" 1117–23; Mawdsley, *Thunder in the East*, 74–77; Glantz, *Barbarossa*, 117–18.

9. Klink, "The Conduct of Operations," 567–68, 594–96; Megargee, *War of Annihilation*, 76–78; Mawdsley, *Thunder in the East*, 77–79.

10. Kershaw, *War without Garlands*, 152; Klink, "The Conduct of Operations," 594–98; Wilt, "Hitler's Late Summer Pause," 189.

11. Klink, "The Conduct of Operations," 599–600; Schramm, ed., *Kriegstagebuch*, 25–31 August, 1–6 September 1941, 1, pt. 2:590–617; Wilt, "Hitler's Late Summer Pause," 189–90; Guderian, *Panzer Leader*, 212; Bock, *War Diary*, 31 August, 2, 4–5 September 1941, 299, 301, 303–5; Kershaw, *War without Garlands*, 155.

12. Klink, "The Conduct of Operations," 600–601; Wilt, "Hitler's Late Summer Pause," 190; Megargee, *War of Annihilation*, 82–83.

13. Mawdsley, *Thunder in the East*, 79–80; Glantz, *Barbarossa*, 126–28.

14. Klink, "The Conduct of Operations," 601–4; Wilt, "Hitler's Late Summer Pause," 190; Stolfi, "The Greatest Encirclement Battle in History"; Kershaw, *War without Garlands*, 156–57; Megargee, *War of Annihilation*, 82–83; Bock, *War Diary*, 15 September 1941, 313.

15. Kershaw, *War without Garlands*, 158–63; Letter of Günter von Scheven, 2 September 1941, in Bähr and Bähr, eds., *Kriegsbriefe*, 112; Letter of 24 September 1941, in Buchbender and Sterz, eds., *Das andere Gesicht des Krieges*, 82; Mawdsley, *Thunder in the East*, 79–80; Glantz, *Barbarossa*, 128–32.

16. Glantz, *Barbarossa*, 132; Mawdsley, *Thunder in the East*, 80–81; Klink, "The Conduct of Operations," 603–4, 604 n. 252. Soviet records corroborate the magnitude of the calamity. On 1 September, the Southwestern Front centered on Kiev numbered approximately 760,000 men (850,000 counting reserves). In the ensuing encirclement, the Soviets admitted to the loss of some 440,000 troops. Overall, the Southwestern Front suffered over 700,000 casualties, with 616,304 killed, wounded, captured, or missing during the Battle for Kiev.

17. Wilt, "Hitler's Late Summer Pause," 190; Reinhardt, *Moscow—the Turning Point*, 60; Megargee, *War of Annihilation*, 83–84; Bock, *War Diary*, 15–16, 19, 21–22 September 1941, 313, 315–16.

18. Klink, "The Conduct of Operations," 631–41; Wilt, "Hitler's Late Summer Pause," 188; Mawdsley, *Thunder in the East*, 83–84; Glantz, *Barbarossa*, 101–6.

19. Halder, *War Diary*, 5 September 1941, 524; Klink, "The Conduct of Operations," 631–41, 644–46; Wilt, "Hitler's Late Summer Pause," 189; Megargee, *War of Annihilation*, 85; Mawdsley, *Thunder in the East*, 84–85; Glantz, *Barbarossa*, 107–13; "Directive No. 35," in ibid., 239–40.

20. Klink, "The Conduct of Operations," 643–47; Wilt, "Hitler's Late Summer

Pause," 189; Megargee, *War of Annihilation*, 85–86; Mawdsley, *Thunder in the East*, 84–85; Glantz, *Barbarossa*, 107–14.

21. Klink, "The Conduct of Operations," 643–47; Wilt, "Hitler's Late Summer Pause," 189; Megargee, *War of Annihilation*, 85–86.

22. Leach, *German Strategy against Russia*, 218–26, 234–41.

23. Van Creveld, *Supplying War*, 145–53; Müller, "The Failure of Economic 'Blitzkrieg Strategy,'" 1125–32; Klink, "The Conduct of Operations," 667–70; Reinhardt, *Moscow–the Turning Point*, 60–69; Schüler, "The Eastern Campaign," 212; Kershaw, *War without Garlands*, 164–67.

24. Van Creveld, *Supplying War*, 153–61; Kershaw, *War without Garlands*, 167; Reinhardt, *Moscow–the Turning Point*, 146–47.

25. Reinhardt, *Moscow–the Turning Point*, 60–69; Müller, "The Failure of the Economic 'Blitzkrieg Strategy,'" 1125–32; Klink, "The Conduct of Operations," 667–70; Schüler, "The Eastern Campaign," 213; Megargee, *War of Annihilation*, 88.

26. Müller, "The Failure of the Economic 'Blitzkrieg Strategy,'" 1127–32; Klink, "The Conduct of Operations," 667–70; Reinhardt, *Moscow–the Turning Point*, 60–69; Schüler, "The Eastern Campaign," 214; Wilt, "Hitler's Late Summer Pause," 189.

27. Müller, "The Failure of the Economic 'Blitzkrieg Strategy,'" 1127–32; Klink, "The Conduct of Operations," 667–70; Reinhardt, *Moscow–the Turning Point*, 60–69; Schüler, "The Eastern Campaign," 213; Halder, *War Diary*, 26, 28–29 August 1941, 517, 519, 521; Schramm, ed., *Kriegstagebuch*, 5 January 1942, 1, pt. 2:1120–21; Overmans, *Deutsche militärische Verluste*, 277–80; Hammer and Nieden, eds., *Sehr selten habe ich geweint*, 235–48; Golovchansky, ed., *"Ich will raus aus diesem Wahnsinn,"* 31–35; Dollinger, ed., *Kain, wo ist dein Bruder?* 107, 110–13; Bähr and Bähr, eds., *Kriegsbriefe*, 71, 209–11; Buchbender and Sterz, eds., *Das andere Gesicht des Krieges*, 81; Boberach, ed., *Meldungen aus dem Reich*, 25 August, 8, 18, 22 September, 23 October 1941; Kershaw, *War without Garlands*, 169–76, 251; Bartov, *The Eastern Front*, 19–20.

28. Reinhardt, *Moscow–the Turning Point*, 57–70; Klink, "The Conduct of Operations," 664–72.

29. Reinhardt, *Moscow–the Turning Point*, 57–70; Klink, "The Conduct of Operations," 664–72; Megargee, *War of Annihilation*, 86–89.

30. Reinhardt, *Moscow–the Turning Point*, 71–78; Hoffmann, "The Conduct of the War through Soviet Eyes," 885–87; Glantz, *Barbarossa*, 141–44.

31. Klink, "The Conduct of Operations," 672–73; Glantz, *Barbarossa*, 144–47; Reinhardt, *Moscow–the Turning Point*, 79; Hoffmann, "The Conduct of the War through Soviet Eyes," 887–92; Ziemke and Bauer, *Moscow to Stalingrad*, 164.

32. Klink, "The Conduct of Operations," 673–74; Reinhardt, *Moscow–the Turning Point*, 80–87; Glantz, *Barbarossa*, 147–48; Glantz and House, *When Titans Clashed*, 80–81; Guderian, *Panzer Leader*, 233, 235.

33. Klink, "The Conduct of Operations," 673–74; Reinhardt, *Moscow–the Turning Point*, 80–87; Halder, *War Diary*, 8 October 1941, 550; Glantz, *Barbarossa*, 149–53.

34. Megargee, *War of Annihilation*, 100–101; Kershaw, *Hitler: Nemesis*, 430–33; *TBJG*, 4 October 1941.

35. Halder, *War Diary*, 4 October 1941, 546; Kershaw, *Hitler: Nemesis*, 433; Megargee, *War of Annihilation*, 102; Klink, "The Conduct of Operations," 675–76; Reinhardt, *Moscow–the Turning Point*, 87–89, 95–96; Bock, *War Diary*, 7 October 1941, 325–26.

36. Reinhardt, *Moscow–the Turning Point*, 99–101; Hoffmann, "The Conduct of the War through Soviet Eyes," 886–93; Glantz and House, *When Titans Clashed*, 82;

Harrison, "'Barbarossa': Die sowjetische Antwort," 458; Magenheimer, *Hitler's War*, 110–11; Henderson, "'Hitler's Biggest Blunder,'" 42.

37. Reinhardt, *Moscow–the Turning Point*, 99–101, 121–22 n. 165; Hoffmann, "The Conduct of the War through Soviet Eyes," 886–93; Kershaw, *War without Garlands*, 194–95; Mawdsley, *Thunder in the East*, 95, 105; Glantz, *Barbarossa*, 153.

38. Klink, "The Conduct of Operations," 676–77; Reinhardt, *Moscow–the Turning Point*, 88–89, 92–93; Fritz, *Frontsoldaten*, 105–7; Ziemke and Bauer, *Moscow to Stalingrad*, 40–41; Kershaw, *War without Garlands*, 186–87.

39. Klink, "The Conduct of Operations," 677; Müller, "The Failure of the Economic 'Blitzkrieg Strategy,'" 1133; Reinhardt, *Moscow–the Turning Point*, 93–94, 149, 152; Haupt, *Heeresgruppe Mitte*, 91–92; Bock, *War Diary*, 20, 24 October 1941, 337, 340.

40. Fritz, *Frontsoldaten*, 109–10; Haupt, *Heeresgruppe Mitte*, 91–92; Bock, *War Diary*, 15 October 1941, 333; Haape, *Moscow Tram Stop*, 140–41, 182; Diary entry of Harald Henry, 18 October 1941, in Bähr and Bähr, eds., *Kriegsbriefe*, 81–82; Kershaw, *War without Garlands*, 188–91.

41. Diary entry of Harald Henry, 20 October 1941, in Bähr and Bähr, eds., *Kriegsbriefe*, 83; Letter of 25 October 1941, in Buchbender and Sterz, eds., *Das andere Gesicht des Krieges*, 85; Kershaw, *War without Garlands*, 188–91; Reinhardt, *Moscow–the Turning Point*, 120 n. 149; Boberach, ed., *Meldungen aus dem Reich*, 30 October, 3, 6, 10 November 1941; Bock, *War Diary*, 25 October 1941, 340.

42. Klink, "The Conduct of Operations," 678–79; Glantz, *Barbarossa*, 153–55, 157–58; Reinhardt, *Moscow–the Turning Point*, 91–92, 148–49, 179 n. 29; Paul, *Erfrorener Sieg*, 122; Kershaw, *War without Garlands*, 166–67.

43. Klink, "The Conduct of Operations," 678–79, 685; Reinhardt, *Moscow–the Turning Point*, 91–92; Glantz, *Barbarossa*, 153–55, 157–58; Kershaw, *War without Garlands*, 182–85; Bock, *War Diary*, 13 October 1941, 331.

44. Klink, "The Conduct of Operations," 678–81; Reinhardt, *Moscow–the Turning Point*, 93–95; Glantz, *Barbarossa*, 158; Megargee, *War of Annihilation*, 103–4; Bock, *War Diary*, 25 October 1941, 340.

45. Klink, "The Conduct of Operations," 680–84; Reinhardt, *Moscow–the Turning Point*, 94–99; Bock, *War Diary*, 29, 31 October, 1 November 1941, 345–48.

46. Klink, "The Conduct of Operations," 607–8; Megargee, *War of Annihilation*, 105.

47. Klink, "The Conduct of Operations," 609–12; Megargee, *War of Annihilation*, 106–7.

48. Klink, "The Conduct of Operations," 613–19; Megargee, *War of Annihilation*, 107–8; Halder, *War Diary*, 7 November 1941, 554.

49. Klink, "The Conduct of Operations," 619–26; Megargee, *War of Annihilation*, 112–13; Halder, *War Diary*, 29 November 1941, 567–70.

50. Klink, "The Conduct of Operations," 619–26; Megargee, *War of Annihilation*, 112–13; Kershaw, *Hitler: Nemesis*, 441; Ziemke and Bauer, *Moscow to Stalingrad*, 55–57; Halder, *War Diary*, 30 November, 1, 3 December 1941, 571, 573–76.

51. Reinhardt, *Moscow–the Turning Point*, 128–34.

52. Ibid., 135–37, 154 n. 18, 263–67, 273 n. 26; Herbert, "Labour and Extermination," 165–67; Ciano, *The Ciano Diaries*, 25 November 1941, 411; Aly and Heim, *Architects of Annihilation*, 248–50.

53. Hoffmann, "The Conduct of the War through Soviet Eyes," 849–52; Klink, "The Conduct of Operations," 686 n. 523; Tooze, *The Wages of Destruction*, 482–83; Streit, "Sowjetische Kriegsgefangene," 747–49, "Die Behandlung der sowjetischen

Kriegsgefangen," "Die Behandlung der verwundeten sowjetischen Kriegsgefangenen," and *Keine Kameraden*, 162–64; Streim, *Sowjetische Gefangene*, 313–15, and "Das Völkerrecht."

54. Letter of 26 August 1941, in Moltke, *Letters to Freya*, 155–56; Müller, "The Failure of the Economic 'Blitzkrieg Strategy,'" 1147, 1172–73; Berkhoff, "'Russian' Prisoners of War"; Herbert, "Labour and Extermination," 152 n. 18; Reinhardt, *Moscow–the Turning Point*, 263–67; Hartmann, "Verbrecherischer Krieg—verbrecherische Wehrmacht?" 11–12, 21–25.

Christian Gerlach argues that the high mortality rates suffered by Soviet prisoners of war during the transport phase were not simply due to neglect but part of a systematic strategy of annihilation. See Gerlach, *Kalkulierte Morde*, 843–45.

Christian Hartmann disputes the notion of a deliberate plan to murder Soviet prisoners of war but does admit that the autumn 1941 order to deny food to those incapable of working had devastating consequences. By his reckoning, some 2 million Soviet prisoners of war died in the winter of 1941–1942. See Hartmann, *Wehrmacht im Ostkrieg*, 531, 566–67, 592.

55. Streit, "Sowjetische Kriegsgefangene," 748–50, "Die Behandlung der sowjetischen Kriegsgefangen," "The German Army and the Politics of Genocide," 9–10, and *Keine Kameraden*, 106–8, 136; Gerlach, *Kalkulierte Morde*, 774–76, and "Verbrechen deutscher Fronttruppen in Weißrußland," 92–94; Diary entry of Gustav Vetter, 26 December 1941, in Dollinger, ed., *Kain, wo ist dein Bruder?* 114; Konrad Jarausch, Letters of 23, 25 October, 1, 14 November, 1941, 10 January 1942, in Jarausch, ed., *Reluctant Accomplice*, 307–9, 311, 314, 324, 361.

56. Streit, "Sowjetische Kriegsgefangene," 748–50, "Die Behandlung der sowjetischen Kriegsgefangen," "The German Army and the Politics of Genocide," 9–10, *Keine Kameraden,* 136, and "Die Behandlung der verwundeten sowjetischen Kriegsgefangenen"; MacKenzie, "Treatment of Prisoners of War"; Schulte, "Korück 582," 327–30, and *German Army*, 180–210; *TBJG*, 27 August 1941; Müller, "The Failure of the Economic 'Blitzkrieg Strategy,'" 1147–48; Hartmann, *Wehrmacht im Ostkrieg*, 592. For Bock's reaction, see Bock, *War Diary*, 20 October 1941, 337.

57. Streit, "Sowjetische Kriegsgefangene," 748–49, *Keine Kameraden,* 87–105, and "Die Behandlung der verwundeten sowjetischen Kriegsgefangenen"; MacKenzie, "Treatment of Prisoners of War," 504–12; Förster, "Operation Barbarossa as a War of Conquest," 520; Müller, "The Failure of the Economic 'Blitzkrieg Strategy,'" 1177; Berkhoff, "'Russian' Prisoners of War," 4–5.

Considerable controversy surrounds the number of Soviet troops who died in German captivity as well as both the extent of Wehrmacht cooperation in the killings of commissars and the total number shot. In the former debate, Christian Streit and Hans-Adolf Jacobsen argue for a figure of 5.7 million prisoners, of whom 3.3 million died, while Alfred Streim puts the numbers at 5.3 and 2.5 million, respectively. Joachim Hoffmann, on the basis of Soviet records, asserts a figure of 5,245,882 prisoners, with some 2 million dead by the spring of 1942.

In terms of deaths by direct shootings, Streit has claimed that at least 580,000–600,000 Soviet prisoners of war fell victim to the shooting squads or army killers, a number that is certainly too high (as he essentially concedes in the third edition of his book). By contrast, Alfred Streim puts the actual number executed as at least 140,000 while stressing that the number could be considerably higher since no exact figures are available for Ukraine. Hoffmann and Christian Gerlach, on the other hand, put the number shot by the Einsatzgruppen at perhaps less than 30,000, while

Reinhard Otto claims 38,000 men were shot up to the end of July 1942. See Streit, *Keine Kameraden,* 10, 105; Jacobsen, "Kommissarbefehl und Massenexekutionen sowjetischer Kriegsgefangener," 197, 279; Streim, *Die Behandlung sowjetischer Kriegsgefangener,* 244; Hoffmann, "The Conduct of the War through Soviet Eyes," 852 n. 71; Gerlach, *Kalkulierte Morde,* 839; and Otto, *Wehrmacht,* 63–65, 263–68. See also Hartmann, "Massensterben oder Massenvernichtung?" and "Verbrecherischer Krieg—verbrecherische Wehrmacht?" 49. For Bock's objections to the use of these "special detachments," see Bock, *War Diary,* 9 November 1941, 353.

58. Reinhardt, *Moscow—the Turning Point,* 140-61, 267–68; Schuler, "Eastern Campaign as Transportation and Supply Problem," 216; Tooze, *The Wages of Destruction,* 493-99.

59. Reinhardt, *Moscow—the Turning Point,* 140-61, 270-72; Schuler, "Eastern Campaign as Transportation and Supply Problem," 216; Hayward, "Hitler's Quest for Oil," 101-7; Tooze, *The Wages of Destruction,* 493-99.

60. *TBJG,* 9 July 1941; Streit, "The German Army and the Politics of Genocide," 9; Müller, "The Failure of the Economic 'Blitzkrieg Strategy,'" 1141-45, 1149; Aly and Heim, *Architects of Annihilation,* 244.

61. Streit, "The German Army and the Politics of Genocide," 9; Müller, "The Failure of the Economic 'Blitzkrieg Strategy,'" 1145-49, and "Menschenjagd," 93; Tooze, *The Wages of Destruction,* 481-82; Herbert, "Extermination Policy," 31-34; Hartmann, "Verbrecherischer Krieg—verbrecherische Wehrmacht?" 36-42; Gerlach, *Kalkulierte Mord,* 265-318, and "German Economic Interests," 215-17; Kershaw, *Hitler: Nemesis,* 471.

62. Tooze, *The Wages of Destruction,* 480-84; Müller, "The Failure of the Economic 'Blitzkrieg Strategy,'" 1161-66, and "Das 'Unternehmen Barbarossa' als wirtschaftlicher Raubkrieg," 185-88; Hartmann, "Verbrecherischer Krieg—verbrecherische Wehrmacht?" 42; "Schreiben des Rüstungsinspekteurs Ukraine, General Leutnant Hans Leykauf, an den Chef des Wehrwirtschafts- und Rüstungsamtes im OKW, General d. Inf. Thomas, vom 2. 12. 1941," in Ueberschär and Wette, eds., *"Unternehmen Barbarossa,"* 338-39.

For examples of efforts by local commanders to ameliorate local civilian hunger, see Hürter, "Die Wehrmacht vor Leningrad," 404-6. For an example of an order to release food supplies from army rear areas to the civilian population, see "Schreiben des Generalquartiermeisters Wagner an den Wirtschaftsführungsstab vom 3.8.1942," in Hamburger Institut für Sozialforschung, ed., *Verbrechen der Wehrmacht,* 305.

63. Müller, "The Failure of the Economic 'Blitzkrieg Strategy,'" 1163-72; Tooze, *The Wages of Destruction,* 483-85; Schulte, *German Army,* 86-116; *TBJG,* 19 August 1941.

64. Müller, "The Failure of the Economic 'Blitzkrieg Strategy,'" 1163-72; Tooze, *The Wages of Destruction,* 483-85; Schulte, *German Army,* 86-116; *TBJG,* 19 August 1941; "Die Ernäherung der Front und der Heimat. Richtlinien für die Behandlung in Frontzeitungen (Nicht zum wörtlichen Abdruck bestimmt)," OKH, 1 November 1941, in Reinhardt, *Moscow—the Turning Point,* 124 n. 187, 269-70.

65. Herbert, "Extermination Policy," 37-41; Matthäus, "Operation Barbarossa and the Onset of the Holocaust," 297-300, and "Ausbildungsziel Judenmord?" 692; Rosenberg quoted in Gerlach, *Kalkulierte Morde,* 581; Browning, *The Origins of the Final Solution,* 320-21, and *Ordinary Men,* 179.

66. Matthäus, "Operation Barbarossa and the Onset of the Holocaust," 286-87; Browning, *The Origins of the Final Solution,* 320-25, and "Nazi Ghettoization

Policy in Poland"; Gerlach, "The Wannsee Conference," 760, 763; Kershaw, *Fateful Choices*, 460-61; Herbert, "Extermination Policy," 34, 37-38, and "Labour and Extermination."

For an early argument of the connection between the murder of the Jews and economic considerations, see Aly and Heim, "The Economics of the Final Solution." For suggestions of a link between the murder of the Jews and the Nazi desire to reduce the Eastern European population for food-related reasons, see Aly and Heim, *Architects of Annihilation*, 250-52; Aly, *"Final Solution,"* 214-42; Kettenacker, "Hitler's Final Solution and its Rationalization"; Gerlach, *Krieg, Ernährung, Völkermord*, 13-30, 167-257, and "German Economic Interests"; Dieckmann, "The Killing of the Lithuanian Jews," 253-66; Herbert, "Extermination Policy," 31-34.

67. Browning, *The Origins of the Final Solution*, 323-25; Kershaw, *Hitler: Nemesis*, 476-81. See also Witte, "Two Decisions."

68. Browning, *The Origins of the Final Solution*, 325-27; Gerlach, "The Wannsee Conference," 763-64; Kershaw, *Fateful Choices*, 462-63.

69. Browning, *The Origins of the Final Solution*, 328-30, 333-34; Kershaw, *Fateful Choices*, 462-63; Matthäus, "Operation Barbarossa and the Onset of the Holocaust," 304-5; Müller, "The Failure of the Economic 'Blitzkrieg Strategy,'" 1137.

70. Browning, *The Origins of the Final Solution*, 392-98; Matthäus, "Operation Barbarossa and the Onset of the Holocaust," 304-5; Gerlach, "The Wannsee Conference," 766-71.

71. Browning, *The Origins of the Final Solution*, 328-30, 353-54, 396-98; Matthäus, "Operation Barbarossa and the Onset of the Holocaust," 356; Gerlach, "The Wannsee Conference," 769-71; Müller, "The Failure of the Economic 'Blitzkrieg Strategy,'" 1137.

72. Browning, *The Origins of the Final Solution*, 354-58, 365-68; Gerlach, "The Wannsee Conference," 762-63; Kershaw, *Hitler: Nemesis*, 483-87; van Pelt and Dwork, *Auschwitz*, 279-83, 292-93; Allen, "'The Devil in the Details,'" 199-201; Pressac, "Machinery of Mass Murder," 198-201.

73. Browning, *The Origins of the Final Solution*, 362-69.

74. Ibid., 366-73, 416-23; Jochmann, *Monologe im Führerhauptquartier*, 17, 21, 25 October 1941, 90-91, 96-99, 106; Gerlach, "Failure of Plans," 60-64, and *Kalkulierte Morde*, 650-53; Aly, *"Final Solution,"* 223-25.

75. Kershaw, *Fateful Choices*, 464-66, and *Hitler: Nemesis*, 487-91; Browning, *The Origins of the Final Solution*, 416-19; Jochmann, *Monologe im Führerhauptquartier*, 5 November, 2 December 1941, 125-26, 130-31, 148; Domarus, ed., *Hitler: Reden und Proklamationen*, 2:1772-73, 1781; *TBJG*, 13 December 1941.

Christian Gerlach sees Hitler's 12 December speech as marking the fundamental shift from a policy of locally driven murder campaigns, justified on the basis of specific situations, to a centrally ordered policy of genocide. This is an overstatement of the significance of the speech from the point of view of decisionmaking, but, certainly, it had a clarifying effect on the party leadership. See Gerlach, "The Wannsee Conference."

76. Kershaw, *Fateful Choices*, 465-67, and *Hitler: Nemesis*, 490-94; Gerlach, "The Wannsee Conference," 780-86; Browning, *The Origins of the Final Solution*, 372-73, 398-415, 540 n. 120; Longerich, *Politik der Vernichtung*, 440, 448, 456, 466-82, 514-15.

77. Gerlach, "The Wannsee Conference," 780-81, 790, 793-800; Kershaw, *Fateful Choices*, 465-67, and *Hitler: Nemesis*, 490-94; Browning, *The Origins of the Final Solution*, 408-15.

78. Gerlach, "The Wannsee Conference," 780–81, 790, 793–800; Kershaw, *Fateful Choices*, 465–67, and *Hitler: Nemesis*, 490–94; Browning, *The Origins of the Final Solution*, 408–15; Longerich, *Politik der Vernichtung*, 440, 448, 456, 466–82, 514–15; Sandkühler, "Anti-Jewish Policy," 115, 118–19; Kaienburg, "Jüdische Arbeitslager," 19–20. Tooze (*The Wages of Destruction*, 476, 751 n. 46) maintains that, at Wannsee, Heydrich clung to the idea of working Jews to death on road construction and not killing them through gassing or shooting. See also Roseman, *The Villa, the Lake, the Meeting*.

The only heated debate at Wannsee concerned the issue of Mischlinge. Heydrich wanted to deport (i.e., exterminate) half Jews but treat quarter Jews as Germans. Jews in mixed marriages would be assessed on a case-by-case basis. Wilhelm Stuckart of the Interior Ministry favored compulsory sterilization of half Jews, while Otto Hofmann of the Race and Resettlement Main Office proposed giving them a choice between sterilization and deportation. These issues were never resolved, although they continued to be debated over the next two years. See Browning, *The Origins of the Final Solution*, 412–13; and Gerlach, "The Wannsee Conference," 801–3.

79. Kershaw, *Hitler: Nemesis*, 494; Gerlach, "The Wannsee Conference," 806–12; Domarus, ed., *Hitler: Reden und Proklamationen*, 2:1829. On the German invasion as a program of planned murder, see Müller, "Economic Alliance," 150–54, 170–87; and Gerlach, *Kalkulierte Morde*, and *Krieg, Ernährung, Völkermord*.

80. "Beurteilung der Kampfkraft des Ostheeres," in Schramm, ed., *Kriegstagebuch*, 6 November 1941, 1, pt. 2:1074–75; Halder, *War Diary*, 19 November 1941, 558; Klink, "The Conduct of Operations," 684–89; Reinhardt, *Moscow–the Turning Point*, 170–90.

81. Bock, *War Diary*, 11, 20–21 November 1941, 354, 365–66; Halder, *War Diary*, 11 November 1941, 555; Ziemke and Bauer, *Moscow to Stalingrad*, 43.

82. Klink, "The Conduct of Operations," 689–90; Reinhardt, *Moscow–the Turning Point*, 191–94; Ziemke and Bauer, *Moscow to Stalingrad*, 43–46; Megargee, *War of Annihilation*, 109–10.

83. Klink, "The Conduct of Operations," 691–92; Reinhardt, *Moscow–the Turning Point*, 173–83; Ziemke and Bauer, *Moscow to Stalingrad*, 43; Bock, *War Diary*, 18 November 1941, 362; Halder, *War Diary*, 22 November 1941, 561–62.

84. Reinhardt, *Moscow–the Turning Point*, 173–83; Halder, *War Diary*, 18 November 1941; Boberach, *Meldungen aus dem Reich*, 6 November 1941; Steinert, *Hitler's War*, 131–32; *Das Reich*, 8 November 1941.

85. Reinhardt, *Moscow–the Turning Point*, 199–201, 203 n. 19; Klink, "The Conduct of Operations," 692–93; Bock, *War Diary*, 11, 16–17 November 1941, 355, 359, 361. Halder was informed on 30 November that the Ostheer had a shortage of 340,000 men but that only thirty-three thousand replacements existed in Germany. See Halder, *War Diary*, 30 November 1941, 571–72.

86. Müller, "The Failure of the Economic 'Blitzkrieg Strategy,'" 1130–41; Schüler, "The Eastern Campaign," 216–19; van Creveld, *Supplying War*, 173; Reinhardt, *Moscow–the Turning Point*, 199–204; Kershaw, *War without Garlands*, 197–98; Halder, *War Diary*, 11, 30 November 1941, 556, 571–72.

87. Reinhardt, *Moscow–the Turning Point*, 205–8; Hoffmann, "The Conduct of the War through Soviet Eyes," 894–96; Ziemke and Bauer, *Moscow to Stalingrad*, 47–49; Bock, *War Diary*, 18 November 1941, 362; Mawdsley, *Thunder in the East*, 111–17; Glantz, *Barbarossa*, 165–69.

88. Reinhardt, *Moscow–the Turning Point*, 214–16; Klink, "The Conduct of Operations," 693; Ziemke and Bauer, *Moscow to Stalingrad*, 49–54; Megargee, *War of Annihilation*, 113; Kershaw, *War without Garlands*, 198.

89. Reinhardt, *Moscow–the Turning Point*, 216-17; Klink, "The Conduct of Operations," 693-96; Guderian, *Panzer Leader*, 251-52; Bock, *War Diary*, 21, 23 November 1941, 365-66, 368.

90. Kershaw, *War without Garlands*, 198-203.

91. Fritz, *Frontsoldaten*, 110-16, 120-21; Kershaw, *War without Garlands*, 198-203, 208-10; Müller, "The Failure of the Economic 'Blitzkrieg Strategy,'" 1135-38; Schüler, "The Eastern Campaign," 216-19; Prüller, *Diary of a German Soldier*, 19 December 1941, 129; Henry, letter of 1 December 1941, in Bähr and Bähr, eds., *Kriegsbriefe*, 86; Deck, *Der Weg der 1000 Toten*, 105; Hansmann, *Vorüber, nicht vorbei*, 15.

92. Halder, *War Diary*, 19, 24 November 1941, 558, 564; Engel, *Heeresadjutant bei Hitler*, 25 November 1941, 116; Kershaw, *Hitler: Nemesis*, 438-41; Ueberschär, "Das Scheitern des Unternehmens 'Barbarossa,'" 160-61; Reinhardt, *Moscow–the Turning Point*, 254-55, 262; Rohland, *Bewegte Zeiten*, 77-78; Seidler, *Fritz Todt*, 356-57; Tooze, *The Wages of Destruction*, 507-8; *TBJG*, 30 November 1941.

93. Halder, *War Diary*, 23 November 1941, 562-64; Reinhardt, *Moscow–the Turning Point*, 224-26; Klink, "The Conduct of Operations," 696-99.

94. Reinhardt, *Moscow–the Turning Point*, 220-22; Klink, "The Conduct of Operations," 700-701; Manteuffel, *Die 7. Panzer-Division*, 225-27, 231-36, 240-41; Bock, *War Diary*, 28 November 1941, 372; Kershaw, *War without Garlands*, 206-7, 210-11.

95. Ziemke and Bauer, *Moscow to Stalingrad*, 53-54; Kershaw, *War without Garlands*, 207-8, 212; Reinhardt, *Moscow–the Turning Point*, 220-23; Klink, "The Conduct of Operations," 700-701; Strauss, *Friedens und Kriegserlebnisse einer Generation*, 99; Bock, *War Diary*, 29 November 1941, 373.

96. Bock, *War Diary*, 1 December 1941, 375-76; Reinhardt, *Moscow–the Turning Point*, 221-24, 227-28, 236 n. 95, 240 n. 147, 243; Klink, "The Conduct of Operations," 700-702.

97. Reinhardt, *Moscow–the Turning Point*, 221-24, 227-28, 236 n. 95, 240 n. 147, 243-45; Ueberschär, "Das Scheitern des Unternehmens 'Barbarossa,'" 161; Klink, "The Conduct of Operations," 700-702; Fritz, *Frontsoldaten*, 191.

98. Schramm, ed., *Kriegstagebuch*, 21 December 1940, 1, pt. 2:996 (doc. 45); Hosenfeld, *"Ich versuche jeden zu retten,"* 561; *TBJG*, 8 December 1941; Görlitz, ed., *Generalfeldmarschall Keitel*, 285; Syring, "Hitlers Kriegserklärung," 690; Kershaw, *Hitler: Nemesis*, 442, and *Fateful Choices*, 382-83, 418.

99. Kershaw, *Fateful Choices*, 386-96; Syring, "Hitlers Kriegserklärung," 684-85; Gassert, *Amerika im Dritten Reich*, 34-36, 87-103; Below, *Als Hitlers Adjutant*, 200.

100. Kershaw, *Fateful Choices*, 397-411; Syring, "Hitlers Kriegserklärung," 686-87; Reinhardt, *Moscow–the Turning Point*, 257-59.

101. Kershaw, *Fateful Choices*, 412-16, and *Hitler: Nemesis*, 442-44; Syring, "Hitlers Kriegserklärung," 688-89.

102. *TBJG*, 8 December 1941; Haffner, *Von Bismarck zu Hitler*, 293; Waite, *The Psychopathic God*, 409; Junker, *Kampf um die Weltmacht*, 32; Syring, "Hitlers Kriegserklärung," 683; Kershaw, *Fateful Choices*, 416-23; Reinhardt, *Moscow–the Turning Point*, 257-59.

103. Syring, "Hitlers Kriegserklärung," 691-92; Kershaw, *Fateful Choices*, 423-30.

104. Kershaw, *Fateful Choices*, 422-23, and *Hitler: Nemesis*, 444-49, 491-92; Domarus, ed., *Hitler: Reden und Proklamationen*, 2:1794-2111; *TBJG*, 12-14 December 1941; Gerlach, "The Wannsee Conference," 787; Broszat, "Hitler und die Genesis der 'Endlösung,'" 759.

105. Kershaw, *Fateful Choices*, 423-24, and *Hitler: Nemesis*, 456-57; Jochmann,

Monologe im Führerhauptquartier, 7 January 1942, 184; Overy, *Why the Allies Won,* 15; Churchill's speech to the Lord Mayor's Luncheon, Mansion House, "The End of the Beginning," 10 November 1942 ("Now this is not the end. It is not even the beginning of the end. But it is, perhaps, the end of the beginning"), Churchill Center and Museum at the Churchill War Rooms, London, http://www.winstonchurchill .org/learn/speeches/quotations (accessed 6 September 2010); Reinhardt, *Moscow– the Turning Point,* 260 n. 16, 375–76. According to Jodl, Hitler was fully aware that, from early 1942 on, victory could no longer be attained and the war was lost. See Schramm, ed., *Kriegstagebuch,* 15 May 1945, 4, pt. 2:1503; Reinhardt, *Moscow,* 376–77, n. 3.

5. Reckoning

1. Reinhardt, *Moscow–the Turning Point,* 291; Megargee, *War of Annihilation,* 130; Bock, *War Diary,* 3, 5, 7 December 1941, 378–79, 381, 383–84; Klink, "Military Concept," 701–2; Glantz, *Barbarossa,* 185–89; Kershaw, *War without Garlands,* 223.

2. Reinhardt, *Moscow–the Turning Point,* 279–83; Hoffmann, "The Conduct of the War through Soviet Eyes," 896–99; Ziemke and Bauer, *Moscow to Stalingrad,* 59–67; Glantz, *Barbarossa,* 187–88. Discrepancies in the number of forces on each side abound, with figures for Germany around 1.7 million men and for the Soviets about 1.1 million. However, the German figures include all personnel in Army Group Center, which had a very large rear echelon, while those for the Soviets contain only the forces assigned to the counterattack. Nor do the Soviet figures include some 800,000 troops held by the Stavka in reserve, a number likely equal to the actual combat strength of the frontline German divisions. For a discussion of the relative strengths of each, see Ziemke and Bauer, *Moscow to Stalingrad,* 66–67.

3. Mawdsley, *Thunder in the East,* 118–20; Reinhardt, *Moscow–the Turning Point,* 280–81; Hoffmann, "The Conduct of the War through Soviet Eyes," 898–99; Megargee, *War of Annihilation,* 130–31; Ziemke and Bauer, *Moscow to Stalingrad,* 66; Glantz, *Barbarossa,* 185–89.

4. Ziemke and Bauer, *Moscow to Stalingrad,* 65, 76; Reinhardt, *Moscow–the Turning Point,* 291–93; Hoffmann, "The Conduct of the War through Soviet Eyes," 899–900; Glantz, *Barbarossa,* 189–204; Megargee, *War of Annihilation,* 131–32.

5. Klink, "The Conduct of Operations," 702–8; Reinhardt, *Moscow–the Turning Point,* 292–93, 299–302; Ziemke and Bauer, *Moscow to Stalingrad,* 69–76; "Weisung für die Aufgabe des Ostheeres im Winter 1941/42," in Schramm, ed., *Kriegstagebuch,* 8 December 1941, 1, pt. 2:1078–79.

6. Klink, "The Conduct of Operations," 702–8; Reinhardt, *Moscow–the Turning Point,* 292–93, 299–302; Ziemke and Bauer, *Moscow to Stalingrad,* 69–76; Bock, *War Diary,* 8, 10 December 1941.

7. Reinhardt, *Moscow–the Turning Point,* 293–94, 301; Schüler, "The Eastern Campaign," 219–20; Dollinger, ed., *Kain, wo ist dein Bruder?* 111; Buchbender and Sterz, eds., *Das andere Gesicht des Krieges,* 7 December 1941, 90; Ziemke and Bauer, *Moscow to Stalingrad,* 77; Kershaw, *War without Garlands,* 227–32; Letter of Harald Henry, 21 December 1941, in Bähr and Bähr, eds., *Kriegsbriefe,* 90.

8. Reinhardt, *Moscow–the Turning Point,* 295–301; Ziemke and Bauer, *Moscow to Stalingrad,* 75–81; Megargee, *War of Annihilation,* 131–32; Bock, *War Diary,* 10–11, 13 December 1941, 387–91; Klink, "The Conduct of Operations," 708–13.

9. Reinhardt, *Moscow–the Turning Point,* 295–301; Ziemke and Bauer, *Moscow to*

Stalingrad, 75–81; Megargee, *War of Annihilation*, 131–32; Bock, *War Diary*, 10–11, 13 December 1941, 387–91; Klink, "The Conduct of Operations," 708–13.

10. Reinhardt, *Moscow–the Turning Point*, 302–6; Klink, "The Conduct of Operations," 709–13; Ziemke and Bauer, *Moscow to Stalingrad*, 78–80; Bock, *War Diary*, 16 December 1941, 395.

11. Reinhardt, *Moscow–the Turning Point*, 306–7; Klink, "The Conduct of Operations," 714–15, 723–24; Ziemke and Bauer, *Moscow to Stalingrad*, 80–83; Bock, *War Diary*, 16–18 December 1941, 394–98.

12. Reinhardt, *Moscow–the Turning Point*, 306–8; Klink, "The Conduct of Operations," 715–16; Ziemke and Bauer, *Moscow to Stalingrad*, 82–83; Bock, *War Diary*, 10 December 1941, 387.

13. Halder, *War Diary*, 7, 20 December 1941, 582, 593; Bock, *War Diary*, 13, 16–19 December 1941, 392, 394–99; Ziemke and Bauer, *Moscow to Stalingrad*, 85–87; Reinhardt, *Moscow–the Turning Point*, 311; Klink, "The Conduct of Operations," 716–20; Kershaw, *Hitler: Nemesis*, 451–54; Hartmann, "Verbrecherischer Krieg—verbrecherische Wehrmacht?" 59–60; "Fernschreiben des Wehrmachtsführungsstabs vom 21.12.1941," in Schramm, ed., *Kriegstagebuch*, 21 December 1941, 1, pt. 2:1085.

14. Ziemke and Bauer, *Moscow to Stalingrad*, 85–87; Reinhardt, *Moscow–the Turning Point*, 311; Klink, "The Conduct of Operations," 716–20; Kershaw, *Hitler: Nemesis*, 454–55; Guderian, *Panzer Leader*, 264–68.

15. Ziemke and Bauer, *Moscow to Stalingrad*, 88–90; Mawdsley, *Thunder in the East*, 121–22.

16. Ziemke and Bauer, *Moscow to Stalingrad*, 90–92; Reinhardt, *Moscow–the Turning Point*, 310, 331 n. 67.

17. Reinhardt, *Moscow–the Turning Point*, 311–14; Klink, "The Conduct of Operations," 720–22; Ziemke and Bauer, *Moscow to Stalingrad*, 94–100; Guderian, *Panzer Leader*, 270.

18. Reinhardt, *Moscow–the Turning Point*, 314–16; Klink, "The Conduct of Operations," 722–23; Ziemke and Bauer, *Moscow to Stalingrad*, 100–104.

19. Ziemke and Bauer, *Moscow to Stalingrad*, 118–20; Reinhardt, *Moscow–the Turning Point*, 317–23; Klink, "The Conduct of Operations," 725–26; Halder, *War Diary*, 2–3, 5 January 1942, 597–99.

20. Ziemke and Bauer, *Moscow to Stalingrad*, 120–34; Reinhardt, *Moscow–the Turning Point*, 322–24; Klink, "The Conduct of Operations," 726–28. On 1 January, both the Third and the Fourth Panzergruppen were made armies.

21. Ziemke and Bauer, *Moscow to Stalingrad*, 120–34; Reinhardt, *Moscow–the Turning Point*, 322–24; Klink, "The Conduct of Operations," 726–28.

22. Ziemke and Bauer, *Moscow to Stalingrad*, 134–42; Reinhardt, *Moscow–the Turning Point*, 346–48; Hoffmann, "The Conduct of the War through Soviet Eyes," 919–28.

23. Reinhardt, *Moscow–the Turning Point*, 349–50; Klink, "The Conduct of Operations," 728–29; "Führerbefehl an die H.Gr.Mitte vom 15. Januar 1942 zum Rückzug auf die 'Winterstellung,'" in Schramm, ed., *Kriegstagebuch*, 2, pt. 4:1268–69.

24. Ziemke and Bauer, *Moscow to Stalingrad*, 143–72; Reinhardt, *Moscow–the Turning Point*, 350–55; Klink, "The Conduct of Operations," 728–34.

25. Ziemke and Bauer, *Moscow to Stalingrad*, 172–77; Mawdsley, *Thunder in the East*, 123–24.

26. Ziemke and Bauer, *Moscow to Stalingrad*, 172–77; Mawdsley, *Thunder in the East*, 123–24.

27. Mawdsley, *Thunder in the East*, 125–26; Ziemke and Bauer, *Moscow to Stalingrad*, 173–98; Klink, "The Conduct of Operations," 734–51.

28. Mawdsley, *Thunder in the East*, 126–27, 129–36; Ziemke and Bauer, *Moscow to Stalingrad*, 194–98, 257–60; Müller, "The Failure of the Economic 'Blitzkrieg Strategy,'" 1141–72.

29. Mawdsley, *Thunder in the East*, 119, 127–29, 146–48.

30. Ibid., 123–24; Reinhardt, *Moscow–the Turning Point*, 317, 365–67, 381–82; Overmans, *Deutsche militärische Verluste*, 277–78. Monthly German deaths on the Eastern Front in late 1941/early 1942 were 40,198 in December, 48,165 in January, 44,099 in February, 44,132 in March, and 23,066 in April, compared to an average monthly loss from June to November 1941 of 43,716.

31. Reinhardt, *Moscow–the Turning Point*, 367–70, 372 n. 19, 373 n. 35; Müller, "The Failure of the Economic 'Blitzkrieg Strategy,'" 1180–82.

32. Reinhardt, *Moscow–the Turning Point*, 367–70, 372 n. 19, 373 n. 35; Schüler, "The Eastern Campaign," 220–21; Müller, "The Failure of the Economic 'Blitzkrieg Strategy,'" 1182–87. On the importance of Lend-Lease for the Soviets, see Sokolov and Glantz, "The Role of Lend-Lease."

33. Reinhardt, *Moscow–the Turning Point*, 375–78; Schramm, ed., *Kriegstagebuch*, 15 May 1945, 4, pt. 2:1503; Schramm, *Hitler*, 161; *TBJG*, 15 February, 20 March 1942; Kershaw, *Hitler: Nemesis*, 455–57, 500–501, 504–6.

34. Fritzsche, *Life and Death in the Third Reich*, 4–5; Jochmann, ed., *Monologe im Führerhauptquartier*, 25 January 1942, 228–29; *TBJG*, 14 February 1942.

35. Friedländer, *Nazi Germany and the Jews*, 2:333–37; *TBJG*, 27 March 1942; Klemperer, *I Will Bear Witness*, 28 April 1942, 45.

36. Hilberg, *The Destruction of the European Jews*, 1:386–90; Jäger's report of 9 February 1942, in Friedlander and Milton, eds., *Archives of the Holocaust*, 22:177 (doc. 82).

37. Gerlach, "The Wannsee Conference," 800–802; Browning, *The Origins of the Final Solution*, 414–15.

38. Gerlach, "The Wannsee Conference," 803–4, and *Krieg, Ernährung, Völkermord*, 181–210; Browning, *The Origins of the Final Solution*, 416–21; *TBJG*, 27 April, 24, 30 May 1942; Kershaw, *Hitler: Nemesis*, 510, 516, 520–23.

39. Tooze, *The Wages of Destruction*, 513–16; Overy, *War and Economy in the Third Reich*, 261, 303–11; Reinhardt, *Moscow–the Turning Point*, 398–99; Mazower, *Hitler's Empire*, 294–95.

40. Tooze, *The Wages of Destruction*, 513–16; Overy, *War and Economy in the Third Reich*, 261, 303–11; Reinhardt, *Moscow–the Turning Point*, 398–99; Mazower, *Hitler's Empire*, 294–95; Herbert, *Hitler's Foreign Workers*, 35, 100–111.

41. Tooze, *The Wages of Destruction*, 516–18; Reinhardt, *Moscow–the Turning Point*, 499; Mazower, *Hitler's Empire*, 298–307; Streit, "Sowjetische Kriegsgefangene," 755–57; Müller, "Die Zwangsrekrutierung von 'Ostarbeitern,'" 773–78. See also Herbert, *Hitler's Foreign Workers*, 146–62, and "Labour and Extermination"; Spoerer, *Zwangsarbeit;* Homze, *Foreign Labor in Nazi Germany;* Kroener, "The Manpower Resources of the Third Reich," 1090–93.

42. Tooze, *The Wages of Destruction*, 518–23; Herbert, *Hitler's Foreign Workers*, 143–50; Müller, "Menschenjagd," 92–103, and "Die Rekrutierung sowjetischer Zwangsarbeiter für die deutsche Kriegswirtschaft," 234–50 (here 236); Spoerer, *Zwangsarbeit*, 222–23; Keller and Otto, "Das Massensterben der sowjetischen Kriegsgefangenene"; Spoerer, *Zwangsarbeit*, 131, 229.

43. Tooze, *The Wages of Destruction*, 524–37; Gerlach, "German Economic

Interests," 218–29; Herbert, "Labour and Extermination," 165–80, 182, 192–93, and *Hitler's Foreign Workers*, 137–252; Longerich, *Politik der Vernichtung*, 476; Pohl, *Von der "Judenpolitik" zum Judenmord*, 110–29; Spoerer, *Zwangsarbeit*, 227–28; Browning, *Ordinary Men*, xv. See also Allen, *The Business of Genocide*, 1–77; Kaienburg, *Die Wirtschaft der SS*, 114–38, 434–35; Schulte, *Zwangsarbeit und Vernichtung*, 103–25, 392–94; Aly and Heim, *Architects of Annihilation*, 174–214.

44. Overy, *War and Economy in the Third Reich*, 261, 274–91; Tooze, *The Wages of Destruction*, 538–40.

45. Tooze, *The Wages of Destruction*, 540–44; Herbert, *Hitler's Foreign Workers*, 189; Corni and Gies, *Brot, Butter, Kanonen*, 562–64; *TBJG*, 10 February 1942, 16–20 March 1942; Steinert, *Hitler's War*, 156–57; Boberach, ed., *Meldungen aus dem Reich*, 2, 19, 22–23, 26, 30 March, 2, 9, 13 April 1942; Kershaw, *Hitler: Nemesis*, 506–7, 510–11; Friedländer, *Nazi Germany and the Jews*, 2:336. Speer claimed that Hitler continually worried about the possibility of a revolt by a disaffected population, along the lines of November 1918. See Speer, *Inside the Third Reich*, 214.

46. Tooze, *The Wages of Destruction*, 540–44; Gerlach, *Krieg, Ernährung, Völkermord*, 182–237, 245–57, and "German Economic Interests"; Aly, *Hitler's Beneficiaries*, 169–70. See also Aly and Heim, *Architects of Annihilation*, 215–52.

47. Tooze, *The Wages of Destruction*, 545–48; Gerlach, *Krieg, Ernährung, Völkermord*, 175, 192–97, 210–37, 245–57; Müller, "Das 'Unternehmen Barbarossa' als wirtschaftlicher Raubkrieg," 190, and "The Failure of the Economic 'Blitzkrieg Strategy,'" 1186–87; Aly and Heim, *Architects of Annihilation*, 242–48; Aly, *Hitler's Beneficiaries*, 170–73; Mazower, *Hitler's Empire*, 284–86.

48. Tooze, *The Wages of Destruction*, 547–48; Mazower, *Hitler's Empire*, 284–87.

49. Reinhardt, *Moscow–the Turning Point*, 386–87, 401–2; Müller, "The Mobilization of the German Economy," 652–721, 758–73.

50. Reinhardt, *Moscow–the Turning Point*, 388–90; Müller, "The Mobilization of the German Economy," 754–73; Tooze, *The Wages of Destruction*, 349–53, 508–9, 560; Overy, *War and Economy in the Third Reich*, 343–56.

51. Reinhardt, *Moscow–the Turning Point*, 390, 395; Müller, "The Mobilization of the German Economy," 773–74; Kershaw, *Hitler: Nemesis*, 502–3.

52. Overy, *War and Economy in the Third Reich*, 356–57; Reinhardt, *Moscow–the Turning Point*, 396–97; Müller, "The Mobilization of the German Economy," 773–86, and "Albert Speer und die deutsche Rüstungspolitik," 281–98; Tooze, *The Wages of Destruction*, 558–64; Buchheim, "Unternehmen in Deutschland," 369–71.

53. Overy, *War and Economy in the Third Reich*, 358–64, 370–71; Reinhardt, *Moscow–the Turning Point*, 397; Tooze, *The Wages of Destruction*, 562–63, 566–67, 576–77; Müller, "The Mobilization of the German Economy," 773–86.

54. Tooze, *The Wages of Destruction*, 553–56, 566–77; Boberach, ed., *Meldungen aus dem Reich*, 23 April 1942; SD Reports of 14, 28 May 1942, in Tooze, *The Wages of Destruction*, 554; *TBJG*, 9 May 1942.

55. Tooze, *The Wages of Destruction*, 588–89; Harrison, ed., *The Economics of World War II*, 15–16; Harrison, *Soviet Planning in Peace and War*, "Resource Mobilization for World War II," and "The Volume of Soviet Munitions Output"; Overy, *Russia's War*, 154–56, 161–67, 223–34, and *Why the Allies Won*, 180–90; Sokolov and Glantz, "The Role of Lend-Lease." On the Soviet home front, see Barber and Harrison, *The Soviet Home Front*.

56. *TBJG*, 20 March 1942; Kershaw, *Hitler: Nemesis*, 494–95.

57. *TBJG*, 20 March 1942; Reinhardt, *Moscow–the Turning Point*, 423–24; Wegner,

"Vom Lebensraum zum Todesraum," 17–18, and "The War against the Soviet Union," 843–44, 858, 861; Hayward, *Stopped at Stalingrad*, 22; Halder, *War Diary*, 28 March 1942, 612.

58. *TBJG*, 20 March 1942; Reinhardt, *Moscow–the Turning Point*, 423–24; Wegner, "Vom Lebensraum zum Todesraum," 17–18, and "The War against the Soviet Union," 843–44, 858, 861; Halder, *War Diary*, 28 March 1942, 612; Citino, *Death of the Wehrmacht*, 157–65; Hayward, *Stopped at Stalingrad*, 23–25; Glantz, *To the Gates of Stalingrad*, 12–15.

59. Wegner, "Vom Lebensraum zum Todesraum," 18, and "The War against the Soviet Union," 1207–8; Halder, *War Diary*, 28 March, 12 June 1942, 612, 623; *TBJG*, 21 March 1942; Citino, *Death of the Wehrmacht*, 50–51.

60. Wegner, "The War against the Soviet Union," 848–49, 860–62, 869, 1210, "Vom Lebensraum zum Todesraum," 20–21, and "Hitlers zweiter Feldzug," 653, 655, 658; Tooze, *The Wages of Destruction*, 586–87; Reinhardt, *Moscow–the Turning Point*, 403, 425; Speer, *Inside the Third Reich*, 215; Kroener, "The Manpower Resources of the Third Reich," 1100–1112.

61. Wegner, "The War against the Soviet Union," 848–49, 860–62, 869, 1207, "Vom Lebensraum zum Todesraum," 20–21, and "Hitlers zweiter Feldzug," 653, 655, 658; Halder, *War Diary*, 12 June 1942, 623; Tooze, *The Wages of Destruction*, 586–87; Reinhardt, *Moscow–the Turning Point*, 403, 425; Speer, *Inside the Third Reich*, 215; Kroener, "The Manpower Resources of the Third Reich," 1100–1112; Goebbels, "Wofur?"

62. Hayward, "Hitler's Quest for Oil," 108–9, and *Stopped at Stalingrad*, 18–22; *TBJG*, 24 May 1942; Jochmann, *Monologe im Führerhauptquartier*, 5 August 1942, 328–29; Tooze, *The Wages of Destruction*, 586; Wegner, "The War against the Soviet Union," 850–58, 869, "Vom Lebensraum zum Todesraum," 18–19, and "Hitlers zweiter Feldzug," 654–55. As early as 1928, Hitler claimed that Russian oil deposits had the same importance in the twentieth century as iron and coal deposits had in previous centuries. See Hitler, *Second Book*, 157.

63. Hayward, "Hitler's Quest for Oil," 108–9; Tooze, *The Wages of Destruction*, 586; Wegner, "The War against the Soviet Union," 858, 869, "Vom Lebensraum zum Todesraum," 18–19, and "Hitlers zweiter Feldzug," 654–55; *TBJG*, 24 May 1942; Kershaw, *Hitler: Nemesis*, 514–17. According to Goebbels, Hitler once again explicitly mentioned the liquidation of the Jews as a further consequence of the war (*TBJG*, 24 May 1942).

64. Tooze, *The Wages of Destruction*, 557–58; Reinhardt, *Moscow–the Turning Point*, 423–24; Wegner, "The War against the Soviet Union," 843–44, 858, 861, 1208, "Hitlers zweiter Feldzug," 655–56, and "The Road to Defeat," 116–17. As late as 23 November 1942—ironically, the day the ring around Stalingrad was closed—Himmler proclaimed in a speech that the east would be "colonies today, settlement area tomorrow, and Reich the day after tomorrow." Quoted in Wegner, "Hitlers zweiter Feldzug," 656.

65. Wegner, "The War against the Soviet Union," 863–69, 872, 904–27, and "Vom Lebensraum zum Todesraum," 22–24; Halder, *War Diary*, 21 April 1942, 613–14; Citino, *Death of the Wehrmacht*, 152–53.

66. Wegner, "The War against the Soviet Union," 871–82, 895, and "Vom Lebensraum zum Todesraum," 22; Warlimont, *Inside Hitler's Headquarters*, 239–40; Citino, *Death of the Wehrmacht*, 152–53; Glantz, *To the Gates of Stalingrad*, 15–16. On the demodernization of the Wehrmacht, see Bartov, *Hitler's Army*, chap. 1.

67. Wegner, "The War against the Soviet Union," 871–82, and "Vom Lebensraum

zum Todesraum," 22. See also Mierzejewski, "A Public Enterprise in the Service of Mass Murder."

68. *TBJG*, 23, 26 April 1942; Wegner, "The War against the Soviet Union," 882–903, "Vom Lebensraum zum Todesraum," 23–24, and "Hitlers zweiter Feldzug," 658–59; Kershaw, *Hitler: Nemesis*, 509. By 1 May 1942, the Soviet armed forces were back up to an overall strength of roughly 11 million soldiers, with about 5.6 million in the field army. See Glantz, *To the Gates of Stalingrad*, 46–47.

69. Wegner, "The War against the Soviet Union," 882–903; Thomas, "Foreign Armies East," 280–82; Reinhardt, *Moscow–the Turning Point*, 421–26; Müller, "The Mobilization of the German Economy," 722–24, 751–52; Tooze, *The Wages of Destruction*, 558, 587–89; Harrison, *Soviet Planning in Peace and War*, 63–65, 81–82; Hayward, "Hitler's Quest for Oil," 117–21; *TBJG*, 26 April 1942; Kershaw, *Hitler: Nemesis*, 509. See also Harrison, "The Volume of Soviet Munitions Output," and "Resource Mobilization for World War II"; Sokolov and Glantz, "The Role of Lend-Lease," 567–86; and Glantz, *To the Gates of Stalingrad*, 46–50. For a later reassessment of Soviet strength, see Halder, *War Diary*, 3 August 1942, 651–52.

70. Wegner, "The War against the Soviet Union," 902.

6. All or Nothing

1. Hayward, *Stopped at Stalingrad*, 3–4, 7–9, 27–31; Wegner, "The War against the Soviet Union," 929–30; Jochmann, ed., *Monologe im Führerhauptquartier*, 5–6 July, 17 October 1941, 39, 91; Dallin, *German Rule in Russia*, 253–66; Citino, *Death of the Wehrmacht*, 52.

2. Hayward, *Stopped at Stalingrad*, 31–66, and "Von Richthofen's 'Giant Fire-Magic,'" 98–99; Citino, *Death of the Wehrmacht*, 52–70; Glantz, "Forgotten Battles of the German-Soviet War: Pt. 6," 121–70, and "Prelude to German Operation Blau," 171–78. See also Manstein, *Lost Victories*, 204–59.

3. Hayward, *Stopped at Stalingrad*, 67–78, and "Von Richthofen's 'Giant Fire-Magic,'" 99–102; Ziemke and Bauer, *Moscow to Stalingrad*, 262–63; Citino, *Death of the Wehrmacht*, 70–71.

4. Hayward, *Stopped at Stalingrad*, 67–78, and "Von Richthofen's 'Giant Fire-Magic,'" 99–107; Citino, *Death of the Wehrmacht*, 70–71; Ziemke and Bauer, *Moscow to Stalingrad*, 263–64 (Manstein quote 264); Wegner, "The War against the Soviet Union," 930–31. A Fliegerkorps normally had between 350 and 600 aircraft. See Hayward, "Von Richthofen's 'Giant Fire-Magic,'" 121–22 n. 21.

5. Ziemke and Bauer, *Moscow to Stalingrad*, 264–66; Hayward, *Stopped at Stalingrad*, 70–78, and "Von Richthofen's 'Giant Fire-Magic,'" 107–8; Bock, *War Diary*, 28 April, 5 May 1942, 467, 469–70; Citino, *Death of the Wehrmacht*, 70–71. The bustard is a black game bird that inhabits the Crimea in great numbers but is largely harmless—perhaps a snide reference to the Germans' Soviet opponents.

6. Ziemke and Bauer, *Moscow to Stalingrad*, 266–67; Hayward, *Stopped at Stalingrad*, 78–81, and "Von Richthofen's 'Giant Fire-Magic,'" 112–15; Citino, *Death of the Wehrmacht*, 73–75; Glantz, *To the Gates of Stalingrad*, 72–77. Colonel Grodeck, in fact, was severely wounded in one of the friendly fire incidents and would die of his wounds a few days later. Citino, *Death of the Wehrmacht*, 75.

7. Ziemke and Bauer, *Moscow to Stalingrad*, 267–69; Hayward, *Stopped at Stalingrad*, 81–86, and "Von Richthofen's 'Giant Fire-Magic,'" 115–21; Citino, *Death of the Wehrmacht*, 75–77; Glantz, "Prelude to German Operation Blau," 178; Wegner, "The

War against the Soviet Union," 932–34. Some Soviet troops reaching the far shore seemed to have been fired on by their own troops, while prisoners reported rumors of a Stalin order demanding that they fight on from the cover of the numerous caves on the peninsula (Ziemke and Bauer, *Moscow to Stalingrad*, 269).

8. Weinberg, *A World at Arms*, 411; Citino, *Death of the Wehrmacht*, 77–79; Hayward, *Stopped at Stalingrad*, 86–91; Ziemke and Bauer, *Moscow to Stalingrad*, 309–10; Glantz, *To the Gates of Stalingrad*, 85–87; Wegner, "The War against the Soviet Union," 935–37.

9. Citino, *Death of the Wehrmacht*, 77–79; Hayward, *Stopped at Stalingrad*, 86–91; Ziemke and Bauer, *Moscow to Stalingrad*, 309–10; Glantz, *To the Gates of Stalingrad*, 87–88; Wegner, "The War against the Soviet Union," 935–37.

10. Ziemke and Bauer, *Moscow to Stalingrad*, 310–12; Wegner, "The War against the Soviet Union," 937–38; Hayward, *Stopped at Stalingrad*, 95–102; Citino, *Death of the Wehrmacht*, 79–80; Glantz, *To the Gates of Stalingrad*, 88–90.

11. Ziemke and Bauer, *Moscow to Stalingrad*, 319–21; Wegner, "The War against the Soviet Union," 938–39; Hayward, *Stopped at Stalingrad*, 102–13; Citino, *Death of the Wehrmacht*, 80–81.

12. Ziemke and Bauer, *Moscow to Stalingrad*, 321; Wegner, "The War against the Soviet Union," 939–41; Hayward, *Stopped at Stalingrad*, 115–19; Citino, *Death of the Wehrmacht*, 81–84; Weinberg, *A World at Arms*, 413.

13. Citino, *Death of the Wehrmacht*, 85–93; Wegner, "The War against the Soviet Union," 942–45; Hayward, *Stopped at Stalingrad*, 120–21; Ziemke and Bauer, *Moscow to Stalingrad*, 272–73; Bock, *War Diary*, 25, 30 April 1942, 465–66, 468.

14. Glantz, *To the Gates of Stalingrad*, 37–45; Knjazkov, "Die sowjetische Strategie," 39–46; Citino, *Death of the Wehrmacht*, 89–91; Wegner, "The War against the Soviet Union," 947; Ziemke and Bauer, *Moscow to Stalingrad*, 269–72.

15. Erickson, *The Road to Stalingrad*, 344; Bock, *War Diary*, 5 May 1942, 469–70; Glantz, *To the Gates of Stalingrad*, 33–37, 45, 77–79; Glantz and House, *When Titans Clashed*, 99–101, 111–14; Citino, *Death of the Wehrmacht*, 90–91, 94–97. David Thomas, on the other hand, asserts that Foreign Armies East interpreted Soviet intentions at Kharkov as being defensive in nature. See Thomas, "Foreign Armies East," 281–82.

16. Glantz, *To the Gates of Stalingrad*, 77–82; Glantz and House, *When Titans Clashed*, 114–15; Citino, *Death of the Wehrmacht*, 95–100; Ziemke and Bauer, *Moscow to Stalingrad*, 273–76; Wegner, "The War against the Soviet Union," 947–48; Hayward, *Stopped at Stalingrad*, 121–23; Bock, *War Diary*, 12 May 1942, 475.

17. Glantz, *To the Gates of Stalingrad*, 77–82; Glantz and House, *When Titans Clashed*, 114–15; Citino, *Death of the Wehrmacht*, 95–102; Ziemke and Bauer, *Moscow to Stalingrad*, 273–76; Wegner, "The War against the Soviet Union," 947–48; Hayward, *Stopped at Stalingrad*, 121–23.

18. Bock, *War Diary*, 16 May 1942, 479–80; Citino, *Death of the Wehrmacht*, 102–4; Glantz, *To the Gates of Stalingrad*, 81–82; Ziemke and Bauer, *Moscow to Stalingrad*, 278–79; Wegner, "The War against the Soviet Union," 948–49; Hayward, *Stopped at Stalingrad*, 123–25.

19. Citino, *Death of the Wehrmacht*, 104–6; Glantz, *To the Gates of Stalingrad*, 82–83; Ziemke and Bauer, *Moscow to Stalingrad*, 278–82; Wegner, "The War against the Soviet Union," 948–49; Hayward, *Stopped at Stalingrad*, 123–25.

20. Bock, *War Diary*, 26 May 1942, 488; Citino, *Death of the Wehrmacht*, 107–15; Glantz, *To the Gates of Stalingrad*, 82–85; Ziemke and Bauer, *Moscow to Stalingrad*, 279–82; Wegner, "The War against the Soviet Union," 949–50; Hayward, *Stopped at*

Stalingrad, 125–26. Evan Mawdsley puts permanent Soviet losses (i.e., killed, missing, and taken prisoner) at 170,000. See Mawdsley, *Thunder in the East,* 119.

21. Hayward, "The German Use of Air Power at Kharkov"; Wegner, "The War against the Soviet Union," 950–51; Glantz, *To the Gates of Stalingrad,* 90–98.

22. Wegner, "The War against the Soviet Union," 951–54; Glantz, *To the Gates of Stalingrad,* 98–102; Bock, *War Diary,* 31 January, 14, 17–19, 22, 24 June 1942, 416, 498–500, 502–4.

23. Müller, *Hitlers Ostkrieg,* 105; Benz, "Der Generalplan Ost," 45–50; Mazower, *Hitler's Empire,* 180–84, 286; Tooze, *The Wages of Destruction,* 469–73; Kershaw, *Hitler: Nemesis,* 434, 516–17; *TBJG,* 24, 30 May 1942. See also Pringle, *The Master Plan;* Hutton, *Race and the Third Reich;* Heinemann, *"Rasse, Siedlung, deutsches Blut";* Ehrenreich, *The Nazi Ancestral Proof,* and "Otmar von Verschuer"; and Bloxham, *The Final Solution,* 1–32, 170–211.

24. Aly and Heim, *Architects of Annihilation,* 130–85; Mazower, *Hitler's Empire,* 189–98, 216; Benz, "Der Generalplan Ost," 45–50; Müller, *Hitlers Ostkrieg,* 11–82; "Reflections on the Treatment of Peoples of Alien Races in the East," Memorandum by Himmler given to Hitler on 25 May 1940, Document NO-1880, Prosecution Exhibit 1314, Nuremberg Trial Documents, in Bauer, *A History of the Holocaust,* 353–54.

25. Heiber, "Der Generalplan Ost"; Roth, "'Generalplan Ost'—'Gesamtplan Ost'"; Madajczyk, "Synchronismus," 844–45; Benz, "Der Generalplan Ost," 49–51; Mazower, *Hitler's Empire,* 204–7, 210; Bloxham, *Final Solution,* 22–23. See also the relevant documents in Madajczyk and Biernacki, eds., *Generalplan Ost.*

26. Aly, *"Final Solution,"* 218–21; Aly and Heim, *Architects of Annihilation,* 263–64; Mazower, *Hitler's Empire,* 207–11, 217–19; Madajczyk, "Synchronismus," 845–47; Benz, "Der Generalplan Ost," 52–53; Erhard Wetzel, "Stellungnahme und Gedanken zum Generalplan Ost des Reichsführer SS," 27 April 1942, in Heiber, "Generalplan Ost," 300, 308, 313; Schubert, "Die Bereitstellung von Menschen für die Eindeutschung neuer Siedlungsräume im Osten."

27. Mazower, *Hitler's Empire,* 210–11; Madajczyk, "Synchronismus," 847–48, 852–53; Müller, *Hitlers Ostkrieg,* 108; Benz, "Der Generalplan Ost," 52–53; Speer, *Spandau,* 47–50; Tooze, *The Wages of Destruction,* 526.

28. Mazower, *Hitler's Empire,* 205–6, 285–86, 384–87; Tooze, *The Wages of Destruction,* 467–68, 525–28, 540–48; Herbert, "Labour and Extermination," 175; Browning, "A Final Hitler Decision?" On the forced labor roundups, see also Müller, "Die Zwangsrekrutierung von 'Ostarbeitern,'" 772–83, and "Menschenjagd"; Streit, "Sowjetische Kriegsgefangene"; and Eikel, "'Weil die Menschen fehlen.'"

29. Aly and Heim, *Architects of Annihilation,* 275–76; Mazower, *Hitler's Empire,* 211–12; Madajczyk, "Synchronismus," 849–50; Müller, *Hitlers Ostkrieg,* 106.

30. Aly and Heim, *Architects of Annihilation,* 276–77; Mazower, *Hitler's Empire,* 213–14; Madajczyk, "Synchronismus," 849–50; Tooze, *The Wages of Destruction,* 468–69.

31. Aly and Heim, *Architects of Annihilation,* 276–78; Mazower, *Hitler's Empire,* 213–14; Madajczyk, "Synchronismus," 849–50; Herbert, "Labour and Extermination," 179; Wasser, "Die 'Germanisierung' im Distrikt Lublin." The culmination of this exchange came on 27 February 1943 in the "factory operation," when 1,689 of the 2,757 Berlin Jews rounded up were killed immediately after being sent to Auschwitz. See Krausnick, "The Persecution of the Jews," 359.

32. Aly and Heim, *Architects of Annihilation,* 276–78; Mazower, *Hitler's Empire,* 214–16; Tooze, *The Wages of Destruction,* 468; Madajczyk, "Synchronismus," 849–50; Wasser, "Die 'Germanisierung' im Distrikt Lublin."

33. Himmler, speech of 16 September 1942, in Madajczyk and Biernacki, eds., *Generalplan Ost*, 172; Himmler, speech of 23 November 1942, in Wegner, *Hitlers politische Soldaten*, 48; Mazower, *Hitler's Empire*, 219–20; Madajczyk, "Synchronismus," 850–52; Müller, *Hitlers Ostkrieg*, 110; Gerlach, *Krieg, Ernährung, Völkermord*, 210–37.

34. Tooze, *The Wages of Destruction*, 528–31; Mazower, *Hitler's Empire*, 307–9; Herbert, "Labour and Extermination," 177–79; Schulte, *Zwangsarbeit und Vernichtung*, 103–25, 335–60, 392–94; Allen, *The Business of Genocide*, 19–56, 112–27; Kaienburg, *Die Wirtschaft der SS*, 114–38.

35. Tooze, *The Wages of Destruction*, 523, 526–27, 531–33; Mazower, *Hitler's Empire*, 310–18; Herbert, "Labour and Extermination," 180–82; Schulte, *Zwangsarbeit und Vernichtung*, 208–32; Allen, *The Business of Genocide*, 133–201; Overy, *Why the Allies Won*, 180–207.

36. Schramm, ed., *Kriegstagebuch*, 27 May 1942, 2, pt. 3:386–87; Wegner, "The War against the Soviet Union," 958; Citino, *Death of the Wehrmacht*, 160–63; Glantz, *To the Gates of Stalingrad*, 13–16.

37. Citino, *Death of the Wehrmacht*, 155–59; Warlimont, *Inside Hitler's Headquarters*, 231; Glantz, *To the Gates of Stalingrad*, 532 n. 1; Ziemke and Bauer, *Moscow to Stalingrad*, 288–90; Halder, *War Diary*, 28 March, 20 June 1942, 612, 625.

38. Wegner, "The War against the Soviet Union," 958; Citino, *Death of the Wehrmacht*, 164; Glantz, *To the Gates of Stalingrad*, 102–3; Ziemke and Bauer, *Moscow to Stalingrad*, 330–31; Jukes, *Hitler's Stalingrad Decisions*, 31–33; Bock, *War Diary*, 20 June 1942, 501.

39. Glantz, *To the Gates of Stalingrad*, 102–3; Ziemke and Bauer, *Moscow to Stalingrad*, 330–31; Bock, *War Diary*, 25, 27 June 1942, 505, 507; Halder, *War Diary*, 24 June 1942, 627–28; Wegner, "The War against the Soviet Union," 958–59; Citino, *Death of the Wehrmacht*, 164–65.

40. Glantz, *To the Gates of Stalingrad*, 37, 103–4; Knjazkov, "Die sowjetische Strategie," 42–47; Wegner, "The War against the Soviet Union," 957, 959–63; Ziemke and Bauer, *Moscow to Stalingrad*, 328–30, 332.

41. Wegner, "The War against the Soviet Union," 966–68; Citino, *Death of the Wehrmacht*, 165–67; Glantz, *To the Gates of Stalingrad*, 122–46; Ziemke and Bauer, *Moscow to Stalingrad*, 333–37; Bock, *War Diary*, 28–30 June, 1–4 July 1942, 508–15; Halder, *War Diary*, 28, 29 June, 1, 3, 6 July 1942, 629–32, 635.

42. Bock, *War Diary*, 28, 30 June, 1–3 July 1942, 508–13; Halder, *War Diary*, 30 June, 1, 3 July 1942, 630–32; Hayward, *Stopped at Stalingrad*, 137–39; Citino, *Death of the Wehrmacht*, 167–71; Glantz, *To the Gates of Stalingrad*, 156–57; Ziemke and Bauer, *Moscow to Stalingrad*, 337–39; Wegner, "The War against the Soviet Union," 968–69.

43. Bock, *War Diary*, 4–7 July 1942, 514–20; Halder, *War Diary*, 5–6 July 1942, 633–36; Hayward, *Stopped at Stalingrad*, 139–40; Citino, *Death of the Wehrmacht*, 172–74; Glantz, *To the Gates of Stalingrad*, 149–63, and "Forgotten Battles of the German-Soviet War: Pt. 7"; Ziemke and Bauer, *Moscow to Stalingrad*, 339–44; Wegner, "The War against the Soviet Union," 970–71.

44. Wegner, "The War against the Soviet Union," 971–73; Citino, *Death of the Wehrmacht*, 172–74; Glantz, *To the Gates of Stalingrad*, 149–63; Ziemke and Bauer, *Moscow to Stalingrad*, 339–44; Bock, *War Diary*, 7–8 July 1942, 520.

45. Wegner, "The War against the Soviet Union," 973–77; Citino, *Death of the Wehrmacht*, 174–75; Glantz, *To the Gates of Stalingrad*, 171–205; Ziemke and Bauer, *Moscow to Stalingrad*, 344–47; Bock, *War Diary*, 13 July 1942, 525–26.

46. Bock, *War Diary*, 13, 15 July 1942, 526; Halder, *War Diary*, 13 July 1942, 639–40; Wegner, "The War against the Soviet Union," 977–78; Citino, *Death of the*

Wehrmacht, 176–80; Glantz, *To the Gates of Stalingrad*, 190–95; Ziemke and Bauer, *Moscow to Stalingrad*, 347–51.

47. Wegner, "The War against the Soviet Union," 988–89; Glantz, *To the Gates of Stalingrad*, 195–96; Jukes, *Hitler's Stalingrad Decisions*, 39; Halder, *War Diary*, 6 July 1942, 635; "Führerbefehl vom 9. Juli 1942 betr. Verlegung von Waffen-SS Verbänden in den Bereich des OB West," in Schramm, ed., *Kriegstagebuch*, 9 July 1942, 2, pt. 4:1280–81.

48. Wegner, "The War against the Soviet Union," 978–79, 989; Glantz, *To the Gates of Stalingrad*, 195–96; Manstein, *Lost Victories*, 260–61; Halder, *War Diary*, 18 July 1942, 642–43; "Richtlinien des Führers vom 17. Juli 1942 für die Fortführung der Operation der Heeresgruppen A und B," in Schramm, ed., *Kriegstagebuch*, 18 July 1942, 2, pt. 4:1284.

49. Glantz, *To the Gates of Stalingrad*, 195–205, 217–69; Ziemke and Bauer, *Moscow to Stalingrad*, 349–58; Wegner, "The War against the Soviet Union," 978–81, 983–84; Mawdsley, *Thunder in the East*, 150; Citino, *Death of the Wehrmacht*, 176–82; Bock, *War Diary*, 13 July 1942, 525–26.

50. Halder, *War Diary*, 16, 18–19, 21, 23 July 1942, 641–46; Hartmann, *Halder*, 325–26; Roberts, *Victory at Stalingrad*, 60; Below, *Als Hitlers Adjutant*, 313; Wegner, "The War against the Soviet Union," 982–84, 986, and "Vom Lebensraum zum Todesraum," 19, 21; Glantz, *To the Gates of Stalingrad*, 185–90, 205.

51. Wegner, "The War against the Soviet Union," 984–85; Glantz, *To the Gates of Stalingrad*, 205–8; Ziemke and Bauer, *Moscow to Stalingrad*, 358–60; Citino, *Death of the Wehrmacht*, 223–27; Hayward, *Stopped at Stalingrad*, 148–49.

52. Halder, *War Diary*, 23 July 1942, 646; Wegner, "The War against the Soviet Union," 984–87; Glantz, *To the Gates of Stalingrad*, 209–13; Ziemke and Bauer, *Moscow to Stalingrad*, 358–60; Citino, *Death of the Wehrmacht*, 224–27; Hayward, *Stopped at Stalingrad*, 148–49, 183–84.

53. Wegner, "The War against the Soviet Union," 984–85; Glantz, *To the Gates of Stalingrad*, 209–13; Ziemke and Bauer, *Moscow to Stalingrad*, 358–60; Citino, *Death of the Wehrmacht*, 224–27; Hayward, *Stopped at Stalingrad*, 148–49.

54. Wegner, "The War against the Soviet Union," 1022; Citino, *Death of the Wehrmacht*, 224–27; Glantz, *To the Gates of Stalingrad*, 396–400.

55. Wegner, "The War against the Soviet Union," 1022–23; Harrison, *Soviet Planning in Peace and War*, 79–81.

56. Wegner, "The War against the Soviet Union," 1023–25; Glantz, *To the Gates of Stalingrad*, 261–65, 273; Ziemke and Bauer, *Moscow to Stalingrad*, 361–62; Roberts, *Victory at Stalingrad*, 65–74.

57. Werth, *The Year of Stalingrad*, 133, 170–71, and *Russia at War*, 384–88; Beevor, *Stalingrad*, 125; Roberts, *Victory at Stalingrad*, 68–71.

58. Wegner, "The War against the Soviet Union," 1025–26; Citino, *Death of the Wehrmacht*, 228–29; Glantz, *To the Gates of Stalingrad*, 400–409, 416–31; Ziemke and Bauer, *Moscow to Stalingrad*, 367–71; Halder, *War Diary*, 30 July 1942, 649.

59. Wegner, "The War against the Soviet Union," 1026–28; Citino, *Death of the Wehrmacht*, 233–34; Glantz, *To the Gates of Stalingrad*, 270–71, 410–16; Ziemke and Bauer, *Moscow to Stalingrad*, 362–65; Hayward, *Stopped at Stalingrad*, 155–56; Halder, *War Diary*, 30 July, 9 August 1942, 649, 655.

60. Schramm, ed., *Kriegstagebuch*, 12 August 1942, 2, pt. 3:573; Halder, *War Diary*, 12–13 August 1942, 656; Wegner, "The War against the Soviet Union," 1029–31, 1038–41; Citino, *Death of the Wehrmacht*, 231–32; Glantz, *To the Gates of Stalingrad*,

419–24; Ziemke and Bauer, *Moscow to Stalingrad*, 370–72; Hayward, *Stopped at Stalingrad*, 159–60.

61. Glantz, *To the Gates of Stalingrad*, 396–97, 431–32, 436–37; Wegner, "The War against the Soviet Union," 1034–36; Citino, *Death of the Wehrmacht*, 236–37; Jukes, *Hitler's Stalingrad Decisions*, 52–54; Ziemke and Bauer, *Moscow to Stalingrad*, 374–75; Hayward, *Stopped at Stalingrad*, 164–66.

62. Ziemke and Bauer, *Moscow to Stalingrad*, 373–74; Glantz, *To the Gates of Stalingrad*, 424–31; Wegner, "The War against the Soviet Union," 1032–34; Engel, *Heeresadjutant bei Hitler*, 15–16 August 1942, 123–24.

63. Glantz, *To the Gates of Stalingrad*, 438–53; Wegner, "The War against the Soviet Union," 1032–34; Hayward, *Stopped at Stalingrad*, 168–70.

64. Wegner, "The War against the Soviet Union," 1036–38; Citino, *Death of the Wehrmacht*, 237–38; Hayward, *Stopped at Stalingrad*, 170–71; Schramm, ed., *Kriegstagebuch*, 29, 30, 31 August, 3 September 1942, 2, pt. 3:654, 658, 662–63, 674.

65. Schramm, ed., *Kriegstagebuch*, 8 September 1942, 2, pt. 3:695–98; Wegner, "The War against the Soviet Union," 1048–49; Megargee, *Inside Hitler's High Command*, 179–89; Citino, *Death of the Wehrmacht*, 238–39; Hayward, *Stopped at Stalingrad*, 166, 170–71; Kershaw, *Hitler: Nemesis*, 527, 530; Beevor, *Stalingrad*, 79–80; *TBJG*, 20 August 1942; Halder, *War Diary*, 22 August 1942, 660; Below, *Als Hitlers Adjutant*, 313; Speer, *Inside the Third Reich*, 239–40.

66. Wegner, "The War against the Soviet Union," 1048–50; Halder, *War Diary*, 9 September 1942, 669; Schramm, ed., *Kriegstagebuch*, 9 September 1942, 2, pt. 1:705–7; Megargee, *Inside Hitler's High Command*, 179–80; Below, *Als Hitlers Adjutant*, 315; Warlimont, *Inside Hitler's Headquarters*, 254–56; Hartmann, *Halder*, 333; Ziemke and Bauer, *Moscow to Stalingrad*, 377–78.

67. Engel, *Heeresadjutant bei Hitler*, 4, 24 September 1942, 124–25, 128; Warlimont, *Inside Hitler's Headquarters*, 256–60; Below, *Als Hitlers Adjutant*, 315–16; Halder, *War Diary*, 24 September 1942, 670; Hartmann, *Halder*, 328–31, 337–39; Megargee, *Inside Hitler's High Command*, 180–84; Kershaw, *Hitler: Nemesis*, 531–34; Wegner, "The War against the Soviet Union," 1050–52; Ziemke and Bauer, *Moscow to Stalingrad*, 449–50.

68. Wegner, "The War against the Soviet Union," 1053–59; Glantz, *To the Gates of Stalingrad*, 473–86.

69. Wegner, "The War against the Soviet Union," 1053–59; Hayward, *Stopped at Stalingrad*, 212; "Führerbefehl vom 8. September 1942 über 'grundsätzliche Aufgaben der Verteidigung,'" in Schramm, ed., *Kriegstagebuch*, 8 September 1942, 2, pt. 4:1292–97; "Führerbefehl vom 13. September 1942 betr. Ablösung abgekämpfter Divisionen aus dem Osten," in ibid., 13 September 1942, 1298–99; "Operationsbefehl Nr. 1 vom 14. Oktober 1942 betr. weitere Kampfführung im Osten," in ibid., 14 October 1942, 1301–4; Engel, *Heeresadjutant bei Hitler*, 27 August, 8, 18 September 1942, 125, 127–28 (on 27 August, Hitler had said that he would like to "trample" on his uniform).

70. Glantz, *To the Gates of Stalingrad*, 432–37; Citino, *Death of the Wehrmacht*, 239–40; Ziemke and Bauer, *Moscow to Stalingrad*, 374–75, 379–81.

71. Citino, *Death of the Wehrmacht*, 239–43; Glantz, *To the Gates of Stalingrad*, 432–37; Ziemke and Bauer, *Moscow to Stalingrad*, 374–75, 379–81, 453–54; Hayward, *Stopped at Stalingrad*, 172–82; Wegner, "The War against the Soviet Union," 1042–43, 1047–48. Destruction of the Maikop and Grozny oil fields would not strike a decisive blow to Soviet oil production as even German experts estimated it would reduce it by only 15 percent (Wegner, "The War against the Soviet Union," 1048 n. 115).

72. Beevor, *Stalingrad*, 75–77, 87–88.

73. Wegner, "The War against the Soviet Union," 1060–65; Citino, *Death of the Wehrmacht*, 244–45; Glantz, *To the Gates of Stalingrad*, 217–48, 265–67; Ziemke and Bauer, *Moscow to Stalingrad*, 382–83; Beevor, *Stalingrad*, 92–95; Halder, *War Diary*, 25, 27–28, 30 July 1942, 646–49.

74. Engel, *Heeresadjutant bei Hitler*, 29 July 1942, 123; Wegner, "The War against the Soviet Union," 1060–65; Citino, *Death of the Wehrmacht*, 244–45; Glantz, *To the Gates of Stalingrad*, 272–73; Ziemke and Bauer, *Moscow to Stalingrad*, 382–83; Roberts, *Victory at Stalingrad*, 64.

75. Wegner, "The War against the Soviet Union," 1064–65; Glantz, *To the Gates of Stalingrad*, 290–303; Citino, *Death of the Wehrmacht*, 246–47; Ziemke and Bauer, *Moscow to Stalingrad*, 382–83.

76. Wegner, "The War against the Soviet Union," 1065–66; Glantz, *To the Gates of Stalingrad*, 297–303, 308–19; Citino, *Death of the Wehrmacht*, 247.

77. Wegner, "The War against the Soviet Union," 1066; Glantz, *To the Gates of Stalingrad*, 321–26; Doerr, *Der Feldzug nach Stalingrad*, 127–29; Hayward, *Stopped at Stalingrad*, 185.

78. Wegner, "The War against the Soviet Union," 1066–67; Glantz, *To the Gates of Stalingrad*, 329–38; Beevor, *Stalingrad*, 110. More ominously, as early as 16 August, OKW had received reports of substantial quantities of tanks and armored equipment from America arriving at Stalingrad. See Schramm, ed., *Kriegstagebuch*, 16 August 1942, 2, pt. 3:597.

79. Glantz, *To the Gates of Stalingrad*, 339–64; Wegner, "The War against the Soviet Union," 1068–69; Beevor, *Stalingrad*, 102–19; Roberts, *Victory at Stalingrad*, 77–78; Citino, *Death of the Wehrmacht*, 247–48; Hayward, *Stopped at Stalingrad*, 188–89. Estimates of the number of people killed in the German bombing of Stalingrad run as high as forty thousand, although a more conservative estimate of twenty-five thousand is probably more accurate. For a very useful summary of the literature on both the air attack on Stalingrad and the fighting in the city itself, see Citino, *Death of the Wehrmacht*, 367–71 nn. 89 and 91.

80. Glantz, *To the Gates of Stalingrad*, 339–64; Wegner, "The War against the Soviet Union," 1068–69; Roberts, *Victory at Stalingrad*, 77–78; Hayward, *Stopped at Stalingrad*, 188–89; Citino, *Death of the Wehrmacht*, 247–48; Ziemke and Bauer, *Moscow to Stalingrad*, 387; Schramm, ed., *Kriegstagebuch*, 26 August 1942, 2, pt. 3:642; Halder, *War Diary*, 25–28 August 1942, 661–63.

81. Wegner, "The War against the Soviet Union," 1069–70; Glantz, *To the Gates of Stalingrad*, 277–90.

82. Glantz, *To the Gates of Stalingrad*, 364–81; Wegner, "The War against the Soviet Union," 1070–71; Citino, *Death of the Wehrmacht*, 248.

83. Glantz, *To the Gates of Stalingrad*, 383–93; Wegner, "The War against the Soviet Union," 1072–76; Halder, *War Diary*, 29 August 1942, 663; Schramm, ed., *Kriegstagebuch*, 27 August 1942, 2, pt. 3:646–47.

84. Wegner, "The War against the Soviet Union," 1077–79; Hayward, *Stopped at Stalingrad*, 192; Schramm, ed., *Kriegstagebuch*, 2 September 1942, 2, pt. 3:649–70.

85. Roberts, *Victory at Stalingrad*, 79–81; Citino, *Death of the Wehrmacht*, 249–50.

86. Wegner, "The War against the Soviet Union," 1081–83; Zhukov, *Memoirs*, 378–79; Citino, *Death of the Wehrmacht*, 250. For a compilation of documents from the Soviet side, see Glantz, "The Struggle for Stalingrad City: Pt. 1."

87. Wegner, "The War against the Soviet Union," 1083; Zhukov, *Memoirs*, 382–83.

88. Wegner, "The War against the Soviet Union," 1083–86; Hayward, *Stopped at Stalingrad*, 216; Schramm, ed., *Kriegstagebuch*, 16 August, 9 September 1942, 2, pt. 3:597–98, 703, 705; Beevor, *Stalingrad*, 129.

89. Roberts, *Victory at Stalingrad*, 82–83; Beevor, *Stalingrad*, 146–49; Citino, *Death of the Wehrmacht*, 250–51; Glantz and House, *When Titans Clashed*, 122–23; Wegner, "The War against the Soviet Union," 1086; Doerr, *Der Feldzug nach Stalingrad*, 52.

90. Beevor, *Stalingrad*, 149–51; Citino, *Death of the Wehrmacht*, 252; Roberts, *Victory at Stalingrad*, 86.

91. Roberts, *Victory at Stalingrad*, 83–84; Beevor, *Stalingrad*, 129–37; Citino, *Death of the Wehrmacht*, 251; Wegner, "The War against the Soviet Union," 1086; Chuikov, *Stalingrad*, 205.

92. Hayward, *Stopped at Stalingrad*, 193–96.

93. Beevor, *Stalingrad*, 139–41; Roberts, *Victory at Stalingrad*, 84, 101–2; Ziemke and Bauer, *Moscow to Stalingrad*, 396; Hayward, *Stopped at Stalingrad*, 200–201; Wegner, "The War against the Soviet Union," 1086–87; Halder, *War Diary*, 20 September 1941, 670.

94. Beevor, *Stalingrad*, 160–65; Roberts, *Victory at Stalingrad*, 84; Ziemke and Bauer, *Moscow to Stalingrad*, 396–97; Hayward, *Stopped at Stalingrad*, 196–204; Wegner, "The War against the Soviet Union," 1089; Citino, *Death of the Wehrmacht*, 252.

95. Wegner, "The War against the Soviet Union," 1096–97; Below, *Als Hitlers Adjutant*, 318; Boberach, ed., *Meldungen aus dem Reich*, 31 August, 3, 8, 10, 28 September 1942; Steinert, *Hitler's War*, 166–69; *TBJG*, 28–29 September 1942.

96. Domarus, ed., *Hitler: Reden und Proklamationen*, 2:1913–24; Kershaw, *Hitler: Nemesis*, 535–36; Hayward, *Stopped at Stalingrad*, 201.

97. *TBJG*, 2 October 1942; Kershaw, *Hitler: Nemesis*, 536–37; Wegner, "The War against the Soviet Union," 1089–95, and "Vom Lebensraum zum Todesraum," 33–34; Kehrig, *Stalingrad*, 74–80; Hayward, *Stopped at Stalingrad*, 206; Engel, *Heeresadjutant bei Hitler*, 2–3, 22 October 1942, 129–32; Müller, "'Was wir an Hunger ausstehen müssen,'" 134.

98. Wegner, "The War against the Soviet Union," 1096–97, and "Vom Lebensraum zum Todesraum," 34–35; Kershaw, *Hitler: Nemesis*, 537–38, and *The "Hitler Myth,"* 190; Jochmann, *Monologe im Führerhauptquartier*, 6 September 1942, 392; Engel, *Heeresadjutant bei Hitler*, 2, 10 October 1942, 129–30; Beevor, *Stalingrad*, 187; Groscurth, *Tagebücher*, 528.

99. Hayward, *Stopped at Stalingrad*, 205–7; Ziemke and Bauer, *Moscow to Stalingrad*, 397; Beevor, *Stalingrad*, 188–91.

100. Beevor, *Stalingrad*, 192–97, 208–12; Chuikov, *Stalingrad*, 248; Wegner, "The War against the Soviet Union," 1097–98; Hayward, *Stopped at Stalingrad*, 206, 210–15; Kehrig, *Stalingrad*, 37–45; Roberts, *Victory at Stalingrad*, 102.

101. Hayward, *Stopped at Stalingrad*, 206; Wegner, "The War against the Soviet Union," 1098–99; Beevor, *Stalingrad*, 211–12.

102. Wegner, "The War against the Soviet Union," 1098–99; Beevor, *Stalingrad*, 212; Kershaw, *Hitler: Nemesis*, 538–39; Below, *Als Hitlers Adjutant*, 321–22; Engel, *Heeresadjutant bei Hitler*, 8 November 1942, 134.

103. *TBJG*, 9 November 1942; Domarus, ed., *Hitler: Reden und Proklamationen*, 2:1935–38; Kershaw, *Hitler: Nemesis*, 539–40, and *The "Hitler Myth,"* 186–89; Beevor, *Stalingrad*, 213–14; Hayward, *Stopped at Stalingrad*, 215–16; Steinert, *Hitler's War*, 166–70.

104. Citino, *Death of the Wehrmacht*, 253; Wegner, "The War against the Soviet

Union," 1099–1100; Beevor, *Stalingrad*, 214–19; Roberts, *Victory at Stalingrad*, 84–85. For a good sense of how suddenly the weather turned cold at night, see the relevant letters in Spratte, ed., *Stalingrad*.

105. "Führerbefehl vom 17. November 1942 betr. Fortführung der Eroberung Stalingrads durch die 6. Armee," in Schramm, ed., *Kriegstagebuch*, 17 November 1942, 2, pt. 4:1307; Citino, *Death of the Wehrmacht*, 253, 306; Wegner, "The War against the Soviet Union," 1099–1100; Beevor, *Stalingrad*, 214–19.

7. Total War

1. Zhukov, *Greatest Battles*, 139–42; Erickson, *The Road to Stalingrad*, 389; Glantz and House, *When Titans Clashed*, 130–32; Mawdsley, *Thunder in the East*, 174–76; Chorkov, "Die sowjetische Gegenoffensive bei Stalingrad," 55–58; Beevor, *Stalingrad*, 220–21; Hayward, *Stopped at Stalingrad*, 222–24; Wegner, "The War against the Soviet Union," 107–10.

2. Roberts, *Victory at Stalingrad*, 110–12; Glantz and House, *When Titans Clashed*, 130–32, 136–39; Ziemke and Bauer, *Moscow to Stalingrad*, 445–47. For Operation Mars, see Glantz, *Zhukov's Greatest Defeat*.

3. Roberts, *Victory at Stalingrad*, 118; Wegner, "The War against the Soviet Union," 1101–2; Glantz, *Soviet Military Deception in the Second World War*, 113–17; Hayward, *Stopped at Stalingrad*, 223–24.

4. Roberts, *Victory at Stalingrad*, 114–18; Service, *A History of Twentieth Century Russia*, 278; Harrison, "The USSR and Total War," and "Resource Mobilization for World War II"; Mawdsley, *Thunder in the East*, 186–203; Beevor, *Stalingrad*, 223–25; Sokolov and Glantz, "The Role of Lend-Lease."

5. Wegner, "The War against the Soviet Union," 1117–22; Kehrig, *Stalingrad*, 102–5, 112–13, and "Die 6. Armee im Kessel von Stalingrad," 76–80; Schramm, ed., *Kriegstagebuch*, 16, 27 August, 9 September 1942, 2, pt. 3:597, 646, 703; ibid., 26, 27 October 1942, 2, pt. 4:865, 868.

6. Wegner, "The War against the Soviet Union," 1117–22; Kehrig, *Stalingrad*, 102–5, 112–13, and "Die 6. Armee im Kessel von Stalingrad," 76–80; Schramm, ed., *Kriegstagebuch*, 2, 4 November 1942, 2, pt. 4:889, 902.

7. Wegner, "The War against the Soviet Union," 1118, 1121; Kershaw, *Hitler: Nemesis*, 541–43; Below, *Als Hitlers Adjutant*, 322–23.

8. Roberts, *Victory at Stalingrad*, 118–19; Wegner, "The War against the Soviet Union," 1103–5, 1111, 1123; Beevor, *Stalingrad*, 226–27; Hayward, *Stopped at Stalingrad*, 224–25.

9. Wegner, "The War against the Soviet Union," 1123; Kehrig, "Die 6. Armee im Kessel von Stalingrad," 80–81, and *Stalingrad*, 131–34; Beevor, *Stalingrad*, 231, 239–44; Hayward, *Stopped at Stalingrad*, 227–28.

10. Wegner, "The War against the Soviet Union," 1123–24; Kehrig, "Die 6. Armee im Kessel von Stalingrad," 80–81, and *Stalingrad*, 136; Beevor, *Stalingrad*, 245–48; Hayward, *Stopped at Stalingrad*, 228; Ziemke and Bauer, *Moscow to Stalingrad*, 468–70.

11. Wegner, "The War against the Soviet Union," 1124–25; Kehrig, "Die 6. Armee im Kessel von Stalingrad," 81, and *Stalingrad*, 145–54; Beevor, *Stalingrad*, 248–53; Hayward, *Stopped at Stalingrad*, 230–31; Ziemke and Bauer, *Moscow to Stalingrad*, 470–72.

12. Wegner, "The War against the Soviet Union," 1125–27; Kehrig, "Die 6. Armee im Kessel von Stalingrad," 82–83, and *Stalingrad*, 160, 163, 170–72; Beevor, *Stalingrad*, 253–56; "Lagebericht OKH," in Schramm, ed., *Kriegstagebuch*, 21 November 1942,

2, pt. 4:1001–2; Ziemke and Bauer, *Moscow to Stalingrad*, 473–74; Hayward, *Stopped at Stalingrad*, 231.

13. Kehrig, "Die 6. Armee im Kessel von Stalingrad," 83–84, and *Stalingrad*, 173–75; Beevor, *Stalingrad*, 256–65; Wegner, "The War against the Soviet Union," 1128–29; Fischer, "Über den Entschluss zur luftversorgung Stalingrads," 51–53; Ziemke and Bauer, *Moscow to Stalingrad*, 472.

14. Wegner, "The War against the Soviet Union," 1131–32; Hayward, *Stopped at Stalingrad*, 233–46. For the most complete account of the decision for the airlift, see Fischer, "Über den Entschluss zur luftversorgung Stalingrads," 7–68.

15. Hayward, *Stopped at Stalingrad*, 233–46; Wegner, "The War against the Soviet Union," 1132–33; Kehrig, "Die 6. Armee im Kessel von Stalingrad," 85–87; Beevor, *Stalingrad*, 266–74.

16. Wegner, "The War against the Soviet Union," 1133–39; Manstein, *Lost Victories*, 294–97, 303; Stahlberg, *Bounden Duty*, 215; Kehrig, "Die 6. Armee im Kessel von Stalingrad," 87–89, and *Stalingrad*, 237–38, 253.

17. Wegner, "The War against the Soviet Union," 1137–40, 1148; Hayward, *Stopped at Stalingrad*, 243, 259–60; Kehrig, "Die 6. Armee im Kessel von Stalingrad," 89–92; Beevor, *Stalingrad*, 276–77; Roberts, *Victory at Stalingrad*, 125. Kehrig claims that the talks between Manstein and Richthofen took place on 26 November, but both Wegner and Hayward (who relies on Richthofen's diary) place the discussion on the twenty-seventh.

18. Wegner, "The War against the Soviet Union," 1140–41; Kehrig, "Die 6. Armee im Kessel von Stalingrad," 92–93, and *Stalingrad*, 308, 313–15; Beevor, *Stalingrad*, 293–96.

19. Wegner, "The War against the Soviet Union," 1143–45, 1153; Kehrig, "Die 6. Armee im Kessel von Stalingrad," 93–94, 100, and *Stalingrad*, 324–30; Beevor, *Stalingrad*, 296–97.

20. Wegner, "The War against the Soviet Union," 1145–48; Kehrig, "Die 6. Armee im Kessel von Stalingrad," 95–99, and *Stalingrad*, 354–69; Beevor, *Stalingrad*, 297–99.

21. Wegner, "The War against the Soviet Union," 1153–58; Kehrig, "Die 6. Armee im Kessel von Stalingrad," 99–102, and *Stalingrad*, 408–10; Beevor, *Stalingrad*, 293, 299–310; Roberts, *Victory at Stalingrad*, 127.

22. Wegner, "The War against the Soviet Union," 1153–58; Kehrig, "Die 6. Armee im Kessel von Stalingrad," 99–102, and *Stalingrad*, 408–10; Beevor, *Stalingrad*, 293, 299–310; Zeitzler, "Stalingrad," 155; Hayward, *Stopped at Stalingrad*, 275–76.

23. Müller, "'Was wir an Hunger ausstehen müssen,'" 131–33.

24. Ibid., 133–34; Wegner, "The War against the Soviet Union," 1090–95.

25. Müller, "'Was wir an Hunger ausstehen müssen,'" 134–38; Wegner, "The War against the Soviet Union," 1151–53, 1158–59.
It was not unusual, however, for many of those supplies to be worthless: candy, contraceptives, herbs and spices, unusable engineering equipment, and propaganda leaflets. In all, between 24 November 1942 and 2 February 1943, the Luftwaffe delivered an average of 117.6 tons of supplies daily and evacuated some thirty thousand wounded soldiers, at a cost of almost five hundred aircraft (including a third of the Luftwaffe's total complement of Ju-52 transports). For a detailed account of the effort to supply Stalingrad by air, see Hayward, *Stopped at Stalingrad*, 247–310.

26. Müller, "'Was wir an Hunger ausstehen müssen,'" 138–45; Below, *Als Hitlers Adjutant*, 325; Letter from Panzer soldier, 19 December 1942, in Dollinger, ed., *Kain, wo ist dein Bruder?* 169; Letter from corporal, 31 January 1942, cited in Sauer,

ed., *Stalingrad–Feldpost,* 32; Wegner, "The War against the Soviet Union," 1158–60; Beevor, *Stalingrad,* 311–30, 338–47; Hayward, *Stopped at Stalingrad,* 286–92.

27. Wegner, "The War against the Soviet Union," 1161–62; Roberts, *Victory at Stalingrad,* 131; Beevor, *Stalingrad,* 352–64; Kehrig, "Die 6. Armee im Kessel von Stalingrad," 105–7; Hayward, *Stopped at Stalingrad,* 290–96.

28. Wegner, "The War against the Soviet Union," 1162–69; Beevor, *Stalingrad,* 364–80; Kehrig, "Die 6. Armee im Kessel von Stalingrad," 107–9; Ziemke and Bauer, *Moscow to Stalingrad,* 499–500. For a good fictional account of the battle and the final agony based on interviews with survivors, see Plievier, *Stalingrad.*

29. Beevor, *Stalingrad,* 380–83, 387–96; Ziemke and Bauer, *Moscow to Stalingrad,* 501–2; Wegner, "The War against the Soviet Union," 1163–65; Roberts, *Victory at Stalingrad,* 133–34; Kershaw, *Hitler: Nemesis,* 549–51; Hayward, *Stopped at Stalingrad,* 308–10.

30. Beevor, *Stalingrad,* 281, 398, 413–15, 439–40; Overmans, "Das andere Gesicht des Krieges," 442, and *Deutsche militärische Verluste,* 277–78; Ziemke and Bauer, *Moscow to Stalingrad,* 501; Roberts, *Victory at Stalingrad,* 134–36; Mawdsley, *Thunder in the East,* 150; Glantz and House, *When Titans Clashed,* 142; Erickson, "Soviet War Losses," 264. Total German and Axis (Rumanian, Hungarian, and Italian) casualties resulting from the Stalingrad campaign were probably in the vicinity of 1.25 million, while the comparable Soviet figures are estimated to be over 1.11 million.

31. Wegner, "The War against the Soviet Union," 1169–72; Beevor, *Stalingrad,* 404–5; Roberts, *Victory at Stalingrad,* 136.

32. Wegner, "The War against the Soviet Union," 1171–81; Ziemke, *Stalingrad to Berlin,* 81–88.

33. Frieser, "Schlagen aus der Nachhand," 101–2; Wegner, "The War against the Soviet Union," 1181–84; Roberts, *Victory at Stalingrad,* 139; Erickson, *The Road to Berlin,* 45.

34. Frieser, "Schlagen aus der Nachhand," 104–6; Wegner, "The War against the Soviet Union," 1184–89; Ziemke, *Stalingrad to Berlin,* 90–96; Erickson, *The Road to Berlin,* 45–53. For Manstein's assessment of the winter operations, see Manstein, *Lost Victories,* 368–442.

35. Wegner, "The War against the Soviet Union," 1190–91; Ziemke, *Stalingrad to Berlin,* 96–97; Erickson, *The Road to Berlin,* 453–55.

36. Frieser, "Schlagen aus der Nachhand," 107; Wegner, "The War against the Soviet Union," 1192–93, and "Von Stalingrad nach Kursk," 6, 51–60; Roberts, *Victory at Stalingrad,* 139–40, 183–87.

37. Weinberg, *A World at Arms,* 609–11, and "Zur Frage eines Sonderfriedens im Osten"; Fleischhauer, *Die Chance des Sonderfriedens,* 81–82, 285–86, and passim; Magenheimer, *Hitler's War,* 192–96. See also Koch, "The Specter of a Separate Peace," 531–49.

38. Boberach, ed., *Meldungen aus dem Reich,* 31 August, 3 September, 9 November 1942, 28 January, 1, 8, 11, 15, 22 February, 8 March, 5, 12 April 1943; "Stimmungsumschwung in der deutschen Bevölkerung," in Wette and Ueberschär, eds., *Stalingrad,* 61–66; Kershaw, *The "Hitler Myth,"* 192; Steinert, "Stalingrad," 174–76, and *Hitler's War,* 184–86; Wegner, "The War against the Soviet Union," 1212–13, and "Die Aporie des Krieges," 211.

39. Wegner, "The War against the Soviet Union," 1213–15, and "Von Stalingrad nach Kursk," 3–8, 35–36; Roberts, *Victory at Stalingrad,* 189–94.

40. Kershaw, *Hitler: Nemesis,* 561–62; Evans, *The Third Reich at War,* 423–25;

Moltmann, "Goebbels' Speech on Total War, February 18, 1943," 319–22; Boelcke, *"Wollt ihr den totalen Krieg?"* 445–46; Herf, *The Jewish Enemy*, 192–95; Fritzsche, *Life and Death in the Third Reich*, 283–84.

41. Steinert, *Hitler's War*, 188–89; Boberach, ed., *Meldungen*, 22 February 1943; Kroener, "'Nun, Volk, steh auf . . .!'" 152–62; Evans, *The Third Reich at War*, 424; Boelcke, *"Wollt ihr den totalen Krieg?"* 414.

42. Wegner, "Von Stalingrad nach Kursk," 14–15; Kroener, "'Nun, Volk, steh auf . . .!'" 152–62.

43. Kroener, "'Nun, Volk, steh auf . . .!'" 164–66.

44. Kershaw, *Hitler: Nemesis*, 562–64, 566–72; Wegner, "Von Stalingrad nach Kursk," 15–16; Speer, *Inside the Third Reich*, 258; *TBJG*, 2 March 1943.

45. Wegner, "Von Stalingrad nach Kursk," 19–21; Tooze, *The Wages of Destruction*, 593–95.

46. Overy, *Why the Allies Won*, 114–22, 331–32; Tooze, *The Wages of Destruction*, 596–98, 600, 688 table A6; Speer, *Inside the Third Reich*, 280–87; Evans, *The Third Reich at War*, 441–42; Blank, "Kriegsalltag," 366–70; Boog, "The Strategic Air War," 22–29; *TBJG*, 7 March 1943.

47. Evans, *The Third Reich at War*, 442–50; Tooze, *The Wages of Destruction*, 601–5; Boog, "The Strategic Air War," 43–51; Middlebrook, *The Battle of Hamburg*, 252–327; Friedrich, *The Fire*, 165–68, 329–30; Boberach, ed., *Meldungen aus dem Reich*, 19 August 1943; Steinert, *Hitler's War*, 202–4, 213–15, 228–33; Kershaw, *The "Hitler Myth,"* 202–3; Speer, *Inside the Third Reich*, 283–84.

48. Overy, *War and Economy in the Third Reich*, 303–11; Stibbe, *Women in the Third Reich*, 91–96; Evans, *The Third Reich at War*, 358–61.

49. Herbert, "Labour and Extermination," 179–81, and *Hitler's Foreign Workers*, 189, 265–68; Müller, "Die Zwangsrekrutierung von 'Ostarbeitern,'" 100–101; Fings, "Slaves for the 'Home Front,'" 233–57, 265–71; Mazower, *Hitler's Empire*, 300–303; Evans, *The Third Reich at War*, 351–57, 361–63, 370–71; Tooze, *The Wages of Destruction*, 517–19.

50. Shepherd, "Hawks, Doves and 'Tote Zonen,'" 349–52, "'Wehrmacht' Security Regiments," 492–98, and "The Continuum of Brutality," 49–59; Wegner, "The War against the Soviet Union," 1005–10.
On the partisan war generally, see Mulligan, "Reckoning the Cost of People's War"; Klinkhammer, "Der Partisanenkrieg der Wehrmacht"; Richter, "Die Wehrmacht und der Partisanenkrieg"; Chiari, "Die Büchse der Pandora"; Umbreit, "Das unbewältigte Problem"; Anderson, "Germans, Ukrainians and Jews," "Incident at Baranivka," and "Die 62. Infanterie-Division"; Schulte, *German Army;* Shepherd, *War in the Wild East;* Slepyan, *Stalin's Guerrillas;* and Musial, *Sowjetische Partisanen.*

51. Wegner, "The War against the Soviet Union," 1011–13, 1017; Gerlach, *Kalkulierte Morde*, 946–73; Mulligan, "Reckoning the Cost of People's War," 45–47; Shepherd, "Hawks, Doves and 'Tote Zonen,'" 352–53, "'Wehrmacht' Security Regiments," 498–520, and "The Continuum of Brutality," 59–81; Schramm, ed., *Kriegstagebuch*, 14 August 1942, 2, pt. 3:587–89.

52. Shepherd, "Hawks, Doves and 'Tote Zonen,'" 353–54, 362–64, and "'Wehrmacht' Security Regiments," 494–96; Richter, "Die Wehrmacht und der Partisanenkrieg," 855–57; Gerlach, *Kalkulierte Morde*, 975–1036.

53. Evans, *The Third Reich at War*, 363–69; Mazower, *Hitler's Empire*, 307–16; Tooze, *The Wages of Destruction*, 445–46, 531–33; Herbert, "Labour and Extermination," 181–89; Hayes, *Industry and Ideology*, 361–65, 439–67.

54. Evans, *The Third Reich at War*, 363–69, 663–65; Mazower, *Hitler's Empire*, 307–16; Tooze, *The Wages of Destruction*, 531–33, 627–31; Herbert, "Labour and Extermination," 181–89; Wachsmann, *Hitler's Prisons*, 394–95; Speer, *Inside the Third Reich*, 372–74; Neufeld, *The Rocket and the Reich*, 197–238.

55. Tooze, *The Wages of Destruction*, 605–11; Sereny, *Albert Speer*, 420–21.

56. Evans, *The Third Reich at War*, 371–72; Mazower, *Hitler's Empire*, 317–18; Speer, *Inside the Third Reich*, 323–45; Wegner, "Defensive ohne Strategie," 197; Overmans, *Deutsche militärische Verluste*, 238.

57. Wegner, "Von Stalingrad nach Kursk," 33, and "Defensive ohne Strategie," 198–99.

58. Wegner, "Von Stalingrad nach Kursk," 11–14, 19–28, 65, 74, "Defensive ohne Strategie," 199–200, and "Das Ende der Strategie," 212–19.

59. Wegner, "Von Stalingrad nach Kursk," 28–41, "Defensive ohne Strategie," 202–5, and "Das Ende der Strategie," 221–26.

60. Wegner, "Von Stalingrad nach Kursk," 61–66, and "Defensive ohne Strategie," 200–201; Frieser, "Schlagen aus der Nachhand," 107–10; Töppel, "Die Schlacht bei Kursk," 375; Mulligan, "Spies, Ciphers, and 'Zitadelle.'"

61. Wegner, "Von Stalingrad nach Kursk," 62, 68–69, and "Defensive ohne Strategie," 200–201; *TBJG*, 25 June, 5 July 1943; Töppel, "Die Schlacht bei Kursk," 372–73.

62. Wegner, "Von Stalingrad nach Kursk," 68–70; Töppel, "Die Schlacht bei Kursk," 376–78; Klink, *Das Gesetz des Handelns*, 60; "Operationsbefehl Nr. 6," in Schramm, ed., *Kriegstagebuch*, 15 April 1943, 3, pt. 6:1425–27.

63. Wegner, "Von Stalingrad nach Kursk," 70–76; Töppel, "Die Schlacht bei Kursk," 376–78.

64. Wegner, "Von Stalingrad nach Kursk," 70–76; Töppel, "Die Schlacht bei Kursk," 376–78; Frieser, "Schlagen aus der Nachhand," 111–13; Guderian, *Panzer Leader*, 306–7. As early as 2 March, Goebbels declared in his diary that the difficult relations between Hitler and his generals were the result of the fact that they no longer believed in him.

65. Guderian, *Panzer Leader*, 307–10; Wegner, "Von Stalingrad nach Kursk," 76–77, and "Defensive ohne Strategie," 201; Töppel, "Die Schlacht bei Kursk," 378; *TBJG*, 7 May 1943; Klink, *Das Gesetz des Handelns*, 163–64; Schramm, ed., *Kriegstagebuch*, 5 July 1943, 3, pt. 6:749; Frieser, "Die Schlacht im Kursker Bogen," 139–40.

66. Töppel, "Die Schlacht bei Kursk," 378–81; Klink, *Das Gesetz des Handelns*, 165–66; Wegner, "Von Stalingrad nach Kursk," 72–73, 77–79.

67. Guderian, *Panzer Leader*, 308–11; Wegner, "Von Stalingrad nach Kursk," 77–79; Schramm, ed., *Kriegstagebuch*, 5 July 1943, 3, pt. 6:750; *TBJG*, 25 June 1943; Warlimont, *Inside Hitler's Headquarters*, 333–34; Kershaw, *Hitler: Nemesis*, 591; Manstein, *Lost Victories*, 447.

68. Frieser, "Die Schlacht im Kursker Bogen," 82–103.

69. Ibid.; Ziemke, *Stalingrad to Berlin*, 133–35. See, as well, the statistical assessment in Zetterling and Frankson, *Kursk 1943*, 58–67, in which the total number of Tigers taking part in the offensive is put at 146. Zetterling and Frankson concur with the figure of 200 Panthers, most under the control of the Grossdeutschland Division; thus, the Second SS Panzer Corps had no Panthers. The overwhelming majority of German AFVs, over 85 percent of the total, were Panzer IIIs and IVs and the Sturmgeschütz (assault gun) III.

70. Frieser, "Die Schlacht im Kursker Bogen," 82–103.

71. Ibid., 104–16.

72. Ibid., 98, 106–8; Glantz and House, *The Battle of Kursk*, 64.

73. Frieser, "Die Schlacht im Kursker Bogen," 108–9; Glantz and House, *The Battle of Kursk*, 93; Ziemke, *Stalingrad to Berlin*, 135–36.

74. Frieser, "Die Schlacht im Kursker Bogen," 109–11; Glantz and House, *The Battle of Kursk*, 115–17; Ziemke, *Stalingrad to Berlin*, 136.

75. Frieser, "Die Schlacht im Kursker Bogen," 111–12; Ziemke, *Stalingrad to Berlin*, 136–37.

76. Frieser, "Die Schlacht im Kursker Bogen," 87, 93, 100, 112–14; Guderian, *Panzer Leader*, 310–11. See also Sydnor, *Soldiers of Destruction*, 281–90.

77. Frieser, "Die Schlacht im Kursker Bogen," 114–16; Glantz and House, *The Battle of Kursk*, 102–3, and *When Titans Clashed*, 165–66.

78. Frieser, "Die Schlacht im Kursker Bogen," 117–19; Glantz and House, *The Battle of Kursk*, 147, 152, 336; Manstein, *Lost Victories*, 448.

79. Frieser, "Die Schlacht im Kursker Bogen," 119–20, and "Schlagen aus der Nachhand," 124–25; Töppel, "Die Schlacht bei Kursk," 381–82.

80. Frieser, "Die Schlacht im Kursker Bogen," 120–22, 132–33, and "Schlagen aus der Nachhand," 120–22; Töppel, "Die Schlacht bei Kursk," 381–82. Even the careful calculations of historians such as Frieser and Töppel have resulted in some confusion. In his earlier work ("Schlagen aus der Nachhand"), Frieser suggests that the Second SS Panzer Corps had 273 operational tanks on 12 July, while, in his later work ("Die Schlacht im Kursker Bogen," "Der Rückschlag des Pendels," and "Der Zusammenbruch im Osten"), taking into account tanks in maintenance, he has corrected the figure to 211 operational tanks. Töppel, meanwhile, claims 236 operational tanks while agreeing with Frieser's total of 58 assault guns and 43 tank destroyers. See, as well, Zetterling and Frankson, *Kursk 1943*, 102–10.

81. Frieser, "Die Schlacht im Kursker Bogen," 123–25, 134, and "Schlagen aus der Nachhand," 125–26; Töppel, "Die Schlacht bei Kursk," 383.

82. Frieser, "Die Schlacht im Kursker Bogen," 125–27; Töppel, "Die Schlacht bei Kursk," 383.

83. Frieser, "Die Schlacht im Kursker Bogen," 121, 129–39; Töppel, "Die Schlacht bei Kursk," 384–87, 393–95; Zetterling and Frankson, *Kursk 1943*, 134. The elite Grossdeutschland Division possessed the great majority of Army Group South's Panthers.

84. Frieser, "Die Schlacht im Kursker Bogen," 139–42; Wegner, "Das Ende der Strategie," 226, and "Defensive ohne Strategie," 201; Töppel, "Die Schlacht bei Kursk," 387–89; Manstein, *Lost Victories*, 448–49.

85. Frieser, "Die Schlacht im Kursker Bogen," 142–47, and "Schlage aus der Nachhand," 132; Töppel, "Die Schlacht bei Kursk," 387–92.

86. *TBJG*, 19 July 1943; Frieser, "Die Schlacht im Kursker Bogen," 148–72; Magenheimer, *Hitler's War*, 192; Töppel, "Die Schlacht bei Kursk," 393–97; Glantz and House, *The Battle of Kursk*, 135, 274; Sokolov, "The Battle for Kursk," 278 (on the entire Eastern Front the Germans lost 71,231 men killed in July). See also Sokolov, "The Cost of War"; and Zetterling and Frankson, *Kursk 1943*, 111–31, 145–52. As Frieser notes, in all of World War II, the Germans produced 25,000 battle tanks, exclusive of assault guns and tank destroyers, while the Allies churned out more than 200,000 ("Die Schlacht im Kursker Bogen," 171).

87. Frieser, "Die Schlacht im Kursker Bogen," 158–72; Zetterling and Frankson, "Eastern Front Battles," 190–92, and *Kursk 1943*, 132–44.

88. Frieser, "Die Schlacht im Kursker Bogen," 173–85.

89. Ibid., 185–86; Wegner, "Die Aporie des Krieges," 219–20; Glantz and House, *The Battle of Kursk*, 232; Ziemke, *Stalingrad to Berlin*, 138–39.

90. Frieser, "Die Schlacht im Kursker Bogen," 187–90; Schramm, ed., *Kriegstagebuch*, 4 August 1943, 3, pt. 6:891; Slepyan, *Stalin's Guerrillas*, 91–101; Erickson, *The Road to Berlin*, 114–15; Ziemke, *Stalingrad to Berlin*, 141; Glantz and House, *The Battle of Kursk*, 237, 273; Mawdsley, *Thunder in the East*, 250, 268–69; Sokolov, "The Battle for Kursk," 82–83 (where some 860,000 Soviet casualties are claimed).

91. Frieser, "Die Schlacht im Kursker Bogen," 190–93; Ziemke, *Stalingrad to Berlin*, 143–51; Schramm, ed., *Kriegstagebuch*, 5–8 August 1943, 3, pt. 6:895, 904–5, 910–11, 915; Glantz and House, *The Battle of Kursk*, 225–26, 241, 247.

92. Frieser, "Die Schlacht im Kursker Bogen," 193–96; Schramm, ed., *Kriegstagebuch*, 18, 20, 22, 24 August 1943, 3, pt. 6:963, 975–76, 986, 996–97; Glantz and House, *The Battle of Kursk*, 251, 426.

93. Frieser, "Die Schlacht im Kursker Bogen," 197–98; Manstein, *Lost Victories*, 454–58.

94. Frieser, "Die Schlacht im Kursker Bogen," 199–204; Mawdsley, *Thunder in the East*, 250; Sokolov, "The Battle for Kursk," 81–84; Zetterling and Frankson, *Kursk 1943*, 116–17, 129; Glantz and House, *The Battle of Kursk*, 252, 425. On the Eastern Front as a whole in July and August, the Red Army lost almost ninety-three hundred tanks to slightly more than thirteen hundred for the Wehrmacht.

95. Frieser, "Die Schlacht im Kursker Bogen," 200, 204–8; Töppel, "Die Schlacht bei Kursk," 397; Guderian, *Panzer Leader*, 312; Warlimont, *Inside Hitler's Headquarters*, 334; Sokolov, "The Battle for Kursk," 88, and "The Cost of War," 187.

8. Scorched Earth

1. Wegner, "Die Aporie des Krieges," 211–12, and "Hitler und die Choreographie des Untergangs," 493–94.

2. Boberach, ed., *Meldungen aus dem Reich*, 30 May 1943; Wegner, "Die Aporie des Krieges," 212–14.

3. Wegner, "Die Aporie des Krieges," 212–14, and "Hitler und die Choreographie des Untergangs," 495–98; *TBJG*, 2 March 1943; Browning, *Ordinary Men*, xv.

4. Wegner, "Die Aporie des Krieges," 214, and "Hitler und die Choreographie des Untergangs," 506–7; Friedländer, *Nazi Germany and the Jews*, 2:473–75; *TBJG*, 17–18 April 1943; Kershaw, *Hitler: Nemesis*, 583; Herf, *The Jewish Enemy*, 192–213.

5. Friedländer, *Nazi Germany and the Jews*, 2:473–77; *TBJG*, 8, 10, 13 May 1943; Kershaw, *Hitler: Nemesis*, 582–84, 588–89; Herf, *The Jewish Enemy*, 213–15.

6. Kershaw, *Hitler: Nemesis*, 604–6; *TBJG*, 7 October 1943; Noakes and Pridham, eds., *Nazism: A Documentary Reader*, 3:1199–1200; Breitman, *The Architect of Genocide*, 242–43. For the full text of Himmler's 4 October speech, see "Himmler's Summation, October 4, 1943," in Dawidowicz, ed., *A Holocaust Reader*, 130–40. Both the German and the English text of the specific references to the Jews, as well as an audio recording of Himmler's 4 October speech, are available at http://www.holocaust-history.org/himmler-poznan (accessed 19 January 2010).

7. Kershaw, *Hitler: Nemesis*, 626–28; *TBJG*, 18 April 1944; Friedländer, *Nazi Germany and the Jews*, 2:613–15, 617–19; Evans, *The Third Reich at War*, 616–17.

8. Kershaw, *Hitler: Nemesis*, 601, 626–28; *TBJG*, 10, 23 September 1943, 18 April 1944; Friedländer, *Nazi Germany and the Jews*, 2:613–15, 617–19; Evans, *The Third Reich at War*, 617–18; Wegner, "Hitler und die Choreographie des Untergangs," 506–8.

9. Tooze, *The Wages of Destruction*, 625, 627–28.

On the aerial war over Germany, see Boog, "The Strategic Air War," 15–256.

10. Wegner, "Die Aporie des Krieges," 214–18; Friedrich, *The Fire*, 9–10, 16–17, 128–29, 144, 366; *TBJG*, 25, 29 July, 2, 6 August, 8, 10, 12–13, 21, 23 September, 1, 20 December 1943; Blank, "Wartime Daily Life."

11. Rass, *"Menschenmaterial,"* 367–71; Wegner, "Die Aporie des Krieges," 262–64.

12. Tooze, *The Wages of Destruction*, 629–31; Herbert, "Labour and Extermination," 188–92; Heinrich Himmler, "Speech to High-Ranking Wehrmacht Officers" ("Rede vor den Teilnehmern des politisch-weltanschaulichen Lehrgangs") at the SS Ordenburg Sonthofen, 24 May 1944, NARA, RG 242, T-175, roll 94, frames 4648–56; Typed Copy, with Himmler's Handwritten Corrections, NARA, RG 242, T-175, roll 94, frame 4647; Typed Copy, with Himmler's Handwritten Corrections, NARA, RG 242, T-175, roll 145, frames 3270–93; Final Copy for the SS Archive, NARA, RG 242, T-175, roll 94, frames 4609–46; Incomplete Audio Recording, NARA, Tape 242-11; Mazower, *Hitler's Empire*, 309–16; Fings, "Slaves for the 'Home Front,'" 233–74.

13. Glantz and House, *When Titans Clashed*, 175.

14. Frieser, "Der Rückschlag des Pendels," 277, 360–62; Wegner, "Die Aporie des Krieges," 218–20, and "Hitler und die Choreographie des Untergangs," 496–506; Ziemke, *Stalingrad to Berlin*, 153–54.

15. Wegner, "Die Aporie des Krieges," 218–20, 246–50, and "Hitler und die Choreographie des Untergangs," 496–506; Frieser, "Der Rückschlag des Pendels," 361–62; Ziemke, *Stalingrad to Berlin*, 216–17.

16. Frieser, "Der Rückschlag des Pendels," 277; Wegner, "Die Aporie des Krieges," 222–25, 246–56; Ziemke, *Stalingrad to Berlin*, 163–65, 211–16; Messerschmidt, "Die Wehrmacht," 224, 228, 232–33.

17. Kershaw, *Hitler: Nemesis*, 603, 617–19; *TBJG*, 21 July 1943, 4 March 1944; Frieser, "Der Rückschlag des Pendels," 361–62; Ziemke, *Stalingrad to Berlin*, 163–65; Wegner, "Die Aporie des Krieges," 222–23.

18. Frieser, "Der Rückschlag des Pendels," 361–62; Ziemke, *Stalingrad to Berlin*, 163–65; Wegner, "Die Aporie des Krieges," 221–22; Manstein, *Lost Victories*, 458–69.

19. Frieser, "Der Rückschlag des Pendels," 297–301; Ziemke, *Stalingrad to Berlin*, 158–60; Mawdsley, *Thunder in the East*, 274.

20. Frieser, "Der Rückschlag des Pendels," 301–5; Ziemke, *Stalingrad to Berlin*, 167–68.

21. Frieser, "Der Rückschlag des Pendels," 344–57.

22. Ibid., 357–58; Ziemke, *Stalingrad to Berlin*, 160–62, 166.

23. Frieser, "Der Rückschlag des Pendels," 357–59; Ziemke, *Stalingrad to Berlin*, 166–67; Mawdsley, *Thunder in the East*, 274.

24. Ziemke, *Stalingrad to Berlin*, 168–69, 172; Frieser, "Der Rückschlag des Pendels," 362–63.

25. Ziemke, *Stalingrad to Berlin*, 171; Wegner, "Die Aporie des Krieges," 256–57; Rass, *"Menschenmaterial,"* 378–85.

26. Letters of Erwin Kolbenhoff, 10 August, 24 September 1943, and Albert Pretzel, 21 September 1943, in Latzel, *Deutsche Soldaten*, 155; Letter of Helmut Pabst, 10 September 1943, in Bähr and Bähr, eds., *Kriegsbriefe*, 259–60; Fritz, *Frontsoldaten*, 149–50; Letters of Hans-Jochen Bauer, 17 September 1943, and Hans Olte, 10 October 1943, in Latzel, *Deutsche Soldaten*, 74, 144; Wegner, "Die Aporie des Krieges," 258–59.

27. Wegner, "Die Aporie des Krieges," 259–60; Ziemke, *Stalingrad to Berlin*, 171–72; Evans, *The Third Reich at War*, 491–92.

28. Wegner, "Die Aporie des Krieges," 261–63; Rass, *"Menschenmaterial,"* 365–71, 379–83.

29. Wegner, "Die Aporie des Krieges," 258-61, 264-69; Rass, *"Menschenmaterial,"* 375, 384-85; Gerlach, "Verbrechen deutscher Fronttruppen in Weißrußland," 101-8. See also the letters of 17 September and 12 October 1943 by Hans-Jochen Bauer in Latzel, *Deutsche Soldaten,* 144.

30. Evans, *The Third Reich at War,* 492, 499; Letters of O'Gefr. A. G., 1 March 1942, Uffz. A. N., 15, 29 May 1943, and Uffz. O. D., 16 August 1944, in Manoschek, *"Es gibt nur eines für das Judentum,"* 52, 69, 74; Wegner, "Die Aporie des Krieges," 230-31. See also Müller, "Nationalismus in der deutschen Kriegsgesellschaft," 9-92.

31. Rass, *"Menschenmaterial,"* 63-204, esp. 192-204, and "Social Profile," 694-705; Evans, *The Third Reich at War,* 496-97. On the importance of primary group loyalty, see Shils and Janowitz, "Cohesion and Disintegration in the Wehrmacht."

32. Rass, *"Menschenmaterial,"* 63-204, esp. 88-134, and "Social Profile," 716-21; Fritz, *Frontsoldaten,* 187-218, and "'We are trying . . . to change the face of the world'"; Kühne, "Gruppenkohäsion und Kameradschaftsmythos in der Wehrmacht"; Evans, *The Third Reich at War,* 498-501. For a discussion of camaraderie, see Fritz, *Frontsoldaten,* 156-86. On a dissenting view of primary group stability, see Bartov, *Hitler's Army.*

33. Wegner, "Die Aporie des Krieges," 228-29; Förster, "Ideological Warfare in Germany," 582-647; Evans, *The Third Reich at War,* 498-99; Fritz, *Frontsoldaten,* 199-202.

34. Wegner, "Die Aporie des Krieges," 234-39; Evans, *The Third Reich at War,* 501-3; Fritz, *Frontsoldaten,* 91-97, 239-40, 251 n. 44, 252 n. 49, and *Endkampf,* 116-18; Messerschmidt and Wüllner, *Die Wehrmachtjustiz im Dienste des Nationalsozialismus,* 50, 63-89, 102-3, 132-68, 305-14.

35. Ziemke, *Stalingrad to Berlin,* 172-74; Frieser, "Der Rückschlag des Pendels," 364.

36. Ziemke, *Stalingrad to Berlin,* 172-74; Frieser, "Der Rückschlag des Pendels," 367-70.

37. Ziemke, *Stalingrad to Berlin,* 184-85; Mawdsley, *Thunder in the East,* 277-78; Frieser, "Der Rückschlag des Pendels," 334-35, 364-67, 370-73.

38. Frieser, "Der Rückschlag des Pendels," 373-74, 379-83; Ziemke, *Stalingrad to Berlin,* 174-81, 185.

39. Frieser, "Der Rückschlag des Pendels," 374-75; Ziemke, *Stalingrad to Berlin,* 186-87; Guderian, *Panzer Leader,* 316-22.

40. Frieser, "Der Rückschlag des Pendels," 375-78, 385; Ziemke, *Stalingrad to Berlin,* 187-89; Mawdsley, *Thunder in the East,* 274; Overmans, *Deutsche militärische Verluste,* 278.

41. Frieser, "Der Rückschlag des Pendels," 305-8; Ziemke, *Stalingrad to Berlin,* 189-92.

42. Frieser, "Der Rückschlag des Pendels," 308-31; Ziemke, *Stalingrad to Berlin,* 192-96, 205-7, 303-9; Hastings, *Armageddon,* 112-13.

43. Frieser, "Der Rückschlag des Pendels," 331-38, 420-22; Ziemke, *Stalingrad to Berlin,* 207. Not until 5 April was the siege of Kovel finally broken.

44. Frieser, "Der Rückschlag des Pendels," 278-79; Ziemke, *Stalingrad to Berlin,* 197. On the demotorization of the Wehrmacht, see Bartov, *Hitler's Army,* 12-28.

45. Ziemke, *Stalingrad to Berlin,* 198-205; Frieser, "Der Rückschlag des Pendels," 283-84.

46. Ziemke, *Stalingrad to Berlin,* 213-16, 248-49; Frieser, "Der Rückschlag des Pendels," 284-85.

47. Ziemke, *Stalingrad to Berlin*, 249–51; Frieser, "Der Rückschlag des Pendels," 284–88.

48. Ziemke, *Stalingrad to Berlin*, 251–57; Frieser, "Der Rückschlag des Pendels," 288–89.

49. Frieser, "Der Rückschlag des Pendels," 289–91; Ziemke, *Stalingrad to Berlin*, 255–58.

50. Ziemke, *Stalingrad to Berlin*, 257–65; Frieser, "Der Rückschlag des Pendels," 291–93.

51. Frieser, "Der Rückschlag des Pendels," 282, 284–85, 290, 294–95; Glantz and House, *When Titans Clashed*, 297–98; Mawdsley, *Thunder in the East*, 274.

52. Frieser, "Der Rückschlag des Pendels," 385–86.

53. Ibid., 387–90; Ziemke, *Stalingrad to Berlin*, 218–22; Manstein, *Lost Victories*, 493–96.

54. Frieser, "Der Rückschlag des Pendels," 390–93; Ziemke, *Stalingrad to Berlin*, 222–26; Manstein, *Lost Victories*, 496–509.

55. Frieser, "Der Rückschlag des Pendels," 393–97; Ziemke, *Stalingrad to Berlin*, 226–28; Glantz and House, *When Titans Clashed*, 186–87; Mawdsley, *Thunder in the East*, 277.

56. Frieser, "Der Rückschlag des Pendels," 397–400; Ziemke, *Stalingrad to Berlin*, 228–31; Buchner, *Ostfront*, 16–18; Manstein, *Lost Victories*, 514–16. For the best, most comprehensive treatment of the battle of Cherkassy-Korsun in English, see Nash, *Hell's Gate*, and "No Stalingrad."

57. Frieser, "Der Rückschlag des Pendels," 400–402; Ziemke, *Stalingrad to Berlin*, 228–29; Buchner, *Ostfront*, 16–18; Manstein, *Lost Victories*, 516.

58. Frieser, "Der Rückschlag des Pendels," 402–3, 405; Ziemke, *Stalingrad to Berlin*, 231–32; Manstein, *Lost Victories*, 516.

59. Frieser, "Der Rückschlag des Pendels," 403–4, 406–8; Ziemke, *Stalingrad to Berlin*, 232–33; Glantz and House, *When Titans Clashed*, 187–88; Mawdsley, *Thunder in the East*, 278–79; Nash, "No Stalingrad," 126.

60. Frieser, "Der Rückschlag des Pendels," 408–16; Ziemke, *Stalingrad to Berlin*, 234–37; Buchner, *Ostfront*, 35–37, 39–40; Nash, "No Stalingrad," 129–31.

61. Frieser, "Der Rückschlag des Pendels," 416–19; Ziemke, *Stalingrad to Berlin*, 237–38; Manstein, *Lost Victories*, 217; Nash, "No Stalingrad," 73, 149–50.

62. Frieser, "Der Rückschlag des Pendels," 335–37, 419–24; Ziemke, *Stalingrad to Berlin*, 244–47, 272–78; Manstein, *Lost Victories*, 520–23.

63. Frieser, "Der Rückschlag des Pendels," 424–31; Ziemke, *Stalingrad to Berlin*, 277, 279–80, 288–89. Ziemke claims that only fifty-three men made it out of the pocket.

64. Frieser, "Der Rückschlag des Pendels," 432–34; Ziemke, *Stalingrad to Berlin*, 273–76.

65. Frieser, "Der Rückschlag des Pendels," 432–34; Ziemke, *Stalingrad to Berlin*, 277–79.

66. Frieser, "Der Rückschlag des Pendels," 434–38; Ziemke, *Stalingrad to Berlin*, 276–80.

67. Manstein, *Lost Victories*, 530–38; Frieser, "Der Rückschlag des Pendels," 438–39.

68. Manstein, *Lost Victories*, 538–43; Frieser, "Der Rückschlag des Pendels," 439–40; Ziemke, *Stalingrad to Berlin*, 280; Kershaw, *Hitler: Nemesis*, 629–30.

69. Manstein, *Lost Victories*, 538–40, 542–44; Frieser, "Der Rückschlag des Pendels," 436, 440–44; Ziemke, *Stalingrad to Berlin*, 280–82.

70. Manstein, *Lost Victories*, 544–48; Frieser, "Der Rückschlag des Pendels," 442–44,

448-49; Wegner, "Die Aporie des Krieges," 221-25, and "Die Kriegführung des 'als ob,'" 1171-73; *TBJG*, 31 March, 1, 5, 23 April, 18 May 1944; Ziemke, *Stalingrad to Berlin*, 281-82, 286; Kershaw, *Hitler: Nemesis*, 616-19, 629-30. At the same time, the names of the army groups were altered, to Army Group North Ukraine and Army Group South Ukraine, a change meant less to reflect reality, since Ukraine had already been lost, than to stiffen the morale of the troops by implying that these areas would be retaken.

71. Manstein, *Lost Victories*, 546-48; Frieser, "Der Rückschlag des Pendels," 444-45; Ziemke, *Stalingrad to Berlin*, 282, 286, 288-91.

72. Klaus Schönherr, "Der Rückzug der Heeresgruppe A," 451-90; Frieser, "Der Rückschlag des Pendels," 445-47; Ziemke, *Stalingrad to Berlin*, 291-95; *TBJG*, 18 April 1944; Kershaw, *Hitler: Nemesis*, 630-31.

73. Ziemke, *Stalingrad to Berlin*, 309-11; Wegner, "Die Kriegführung des 'als ob,'" 1165, 1171-73.

74. Ziemke, *Stalingrad to Berlin*, 310; Wegner, "Die Kriegführung des 'als ob,'" 1165-66; Frieser, "Der Zusammenbruch im Osten," 499-500.

75. Ziemke, *Stalingrad to Berlin*, 310-12; Wegner, "Die Kriegführung des 'als ob,'" 1166-70. Wegner, using estimates from Foreign Armies East, notes that, on 1 July 1944, the Red Army disposed of 5,730,000 men on the Eastern Front, which meant that it had a surplus of troops (3,495,000) 1.5 times greater than the total number of German troops (2,235,000).

76. Wegner, "Die Kriegführung des 'als ob,'" 1177-78; Frieser, "Der Zusammenbruch im Osten," 493-97; Kershaw, *Hitler: Nemesis*, 637-40; Steinert, *Hitler's War*, 234-35, 240-41.

77. Frieser, "Der Zusammenbruch im Osten," 493-96.

78. Ziemke, *Stalingrad to Berlin*, 311-12; Wegner, "Die Kriegführung des 'als ob,'" 1177-78; Frieser, "Der Zusammenbruch im Osten," 495, 498; Kershaw, *Hitler: Nemesis*, 632-40; *TBJG*, 6 June 1944; Tooze, *The Wages of Destruction*, 626-34; Weinberg, *A World at Arms*, 656-66, and "German Plans for Victory."

79. Ziemke, *Stalingrad to Berlin*, 311-12; Wegner, "Die Kriegführung des 'als ob,'" 1174-75, 1177-79; Kershaw, *Hitler: Nemesis*, 631, 633; Speer, *Inside the Third Reich*, 346; Frieser, "Der Rückschlag des Pendels," 449-50, and "Der Zusammenbruch im Osten," 498-501.

9. Disintegration

1. Frieser, "Der Zusammenbruch im Osten," 501-5.

2. Ibid., 501-5; Ziemke, *Stalingrad to Berlin*, 313-14; Glantz and House, *When Titans Clashed*, 195-96.

3. Frieser, "Der Zusammenbruch im Osten," 501-5; Ziemke, *Stalingrad to Berlin*, 313-14; Baker, "Explaining Defeat," 139-40; Mawdsley, *Thunder in the East*, 298-99.

4. Frieser, "Der Zusammenbruch im Osten," 505-7, 536-37; Ziemke, *Stalingrad to Berlin*, 316-18; Baker, "Explaining Defeat," 133; Glantz and Orenstein, eds., *Belorussia 1944*, 7; Glantz and House, *When Titans Clashed*, 196-99.

5. Frieser, "Der Zusammenbruch im Osten," 504-5; Ziemke, *Stalingrad to Berlin*, 313-14; Baker, "Explaining Defeat," 140-41.

6. Frieser, "Der Zusammenbruch im Osten," 526-30; Ziemke, *Stalingrad to Berlin*, 315; Baker, "Explaining Defeat," 136-37; Niepold, *Battle for White Russia*, 56-64; Glantz and House, *When Titans Clashed*, 198.

7. Frieser, "Der Zusammenbruch im Osten," 530-35, 593; Ziemke, *Stalingrad*

to Berlin, 315; Baker, "Explaining Defeat," 136–38; Niepold, Battle for White Russia, 33–34, 44; Glantz and Orenstein, eds., Belorussia 1944, 41–42, 47–48, 55–64; Glantz and House, When Titans Clashed, 201–2.

8. Frieser, "Der Zusammenbruch im Osten," 507–15; Ziemke, Stalingrad to Berlin, 315–16.

9. Frieser, "Der Zusammenbruch im Osten," 518–25; Baker, "Explaining Defeat," 140–42.

10. Frieser, "Der Zusammenbruch im Osten," 517–18; Ziemke, Stalingrad to Berlin, 314–16; Baker, "Explaining Defeat," 134–35.

11. Frieser, "Der Zusammenbruch im Osten," 537–39; Ziemke, Stalingrad to Berlin, 319–20; Glantz and House, When Titans Clashed, 201–5; Mawdsley, Thunder in the East, 299–300.

12. Frieser, "Der Zusammenbruch im Osten," 539–43; Ziemke, Stalingrad to Berlin, 320–21; Niepold, Battle for White Russia, 110, 146–47.

13. Frieser, "Der Zusammenbruch im Osten," 545–46; Ziemke, Stalingrad to Berlin, 320–21.

14. Frieser, "Der Zusammenbruch im Osten," 546–48; Ziemke, Stalingrad to Berlin, 321–22.

15. Frieser, "Der Zusammenbruch im Osten," 543–45; Ziemke, Stalingrad to Berlin, 321, 323; Glantz and House, When Titans Clashed, 206–7.

16. Frieser, "Der Zusammenbruch im Osten," 548–49; Ziemke, Stalingrad to Berlin, 324–25.

17. Frieser, "Der Zusammenbruch im Osten," 550–52; Ziemke, Stalingrad to Berlin, 324–25; Glantz and House, When Titans Clashed, 207.

18. Frieser, "Der Zusammenbruch im Osten," 552–57; Ziemke, Stalingrad to Berlin, 324–25; Glantz and House, When Titans Clashed, 207–8.

19. Frieser, "Der Zusammenbruch im Osten," 556–60; Messerschmidt, "Die Wehrmacht," 236; Ziemke, Stalingrad to Berlin, 325–28, 336–39.

20. Frieser, "Der Zusammenbruch im Osten," 556–63; Ziemke, Stalingrad to Berlin, 335–36; Below, Als Hitlers Adjutant, 378–80; Kershaw, Hitler: Nemesis, 649–51.

21. Frieser, "Der Zusammenbruch im Osten," 563–72; Ziemke, Stalingrad to Berlin, 337–39.

22. Frieser, "Der Zusammenbruch im Osten," 565, 570–82.

23. Ibid., 582–87; Ziemke, Stalingrad to Berlin, 341–42.

24. Frieser, "Der Zusammenbruch im Osten," 585–87; Ziemke, Stalingrad to Berlin, 340–42. For a recent account of the Warsaw Uprising, one that criticizes Stalin for deliberately allowing the Poles to be crushed, see Davies, Rising '44.

25. Messerschmidt, "Die Wehrmacht," 237–38.

26. Frieser, "Der Zusammenbruch im Osten," 592–94, 601; Wegner, "Im Schatten der 'Zweiten Front'?" 129–30; Overy, Why the Allies Won, 332; Glantz and House, When Titans Clashed, 215; Zetterling, "Loss Rates on the Eastern Front," 900–902.

27. Frieser, "Der Zusammenbruch im Osten," 594–95; Hubert Van Tuyll, "D-Day in the East," 222–24; Glantz and House, When Titans Clashed, 150; Mawdsley, Thunder in the East, 306.

28. Frieser, "Der Zusammenbruch im Osten," 586–87, 596–603; Glantz and House, When Titans Clashed, 214–15; Mawdsley, Thunder in the East, 307–8.

29. Overmans, Deutsche militärische Verluste, 238, 278; Boog, "The Strategic Air War," 293, and "Die strategische Bomberoffensive"; Tooze, The Wages of Destruction, 649; Blank, "Wartime Daily Life," 475–76.

30. Kershaw, Hitler: Nemesis, 705; Longerich, "Joseph Goebbels," 287–96.

31. "Führen wir einen totalen Krieg?" *Das Reich*, 2 July 1944; Longerich, "Joseph Goebbels," 297-99; Beyer, "Pläne der faschistischen Führung zum totalen Krieg"; Speer, *Inside the Third Reich*, 396-97.

32. Kershaw, *Hitler: Nemesis*, 707-8, 711-13; *TBJG*, 22 June 1944, 23-25 July 1944; Hancock, *National Socialist Leadership*, 127-38; Speer, *Inside the Third Reich*, 398-407; Tooze, *The Wages of Destruction*, 637-38; Müller, "Der Zusammenbruch des Wirtschaftslebens," 75.

33. Kershaw, *Hitler: Nemesis*, 712-15; Hancock, *National Socialist Leadership*, 152-58, and "Employment in Wartime"; Herbert, *Fremdarbeiter*, 270-73, and *Hitler's Foreign Workers*, 359-64; Müller, "Der Zusammenbruch des Wirtschaftslebens," 53, 69-71; Kunz, "Die Wehrmacht," 13-17, 25-27.

34. Müller, "Der Zusammenbruch des Wirtschaftslebens," 53, 74-84; Tooze, *The Wages of Destruction*, 627-39; Allen, *The Business of Genocide*, 232-39; Herbert, "Labour and Extermination," 187-91. For a good short discussion of the various miracle weapons, see Evans, *The Third Reich at War*, 660-75.

35. Tooze, *The Wages of Destruction*, 627-39, 648-51; Boog, "The Strategic Air War in Europe," 118; Müller, "Albert Speer und die deutsche Rüstungspolitik," 432; Blank, "Wartime Daily Life," 462-64; Mierzejewski, *The Collapse of the German War Economy*, 103-76; Overy, *Why the Allies Won*, 127-32, 331-32.

36. Tooze, *The Wages of Destruction*, 642-48; Aly, *Hitler's Beneficiaries*, 110-17, 132-34; Müller, "Der Zusammenbruch des Wirtschaftslebens," 60-62, and "Albert Speer und die deutsche Rüstungspolitik," 476-77, 492-93.

37. Steinert, *Hitler's War*, 262, 264-73; Kershaw, *Hitler: Nemesis*, 698-705; Evans, *The Third Reich at War*, 702-4; Blank, "Wartime Daily Life," 458-74.

38. Steinert, *Hitler's War*, 273-86; Evans, *The Third Reich at War*, 675-78; Mammach, *Der Volkssturm*, 150; Seidler, *Deutscher Volkssturm*, 374; Kunz, "Die Wehrmacht," 14-16, 26-27; Müller and Ueberschär, eds., *Kriegsende 1945*, 154-72; Fritz, "'This is the way wars end,'" and *Endkampf*, 115-58. For the best account of the Volkssturm in English, see Yelton, *Hitler's Volkssturm*.

39. Frieser, "Der Zusammenbruch im Osten," 604-12.

40. Ibid., 612-19; Kershaw, *Hitler: Nemesis*, 738; *TBJG*, 23-24 October 1944.

41. Frieser, "Der Zusammenbruch im Osten," 619-22; Glantz, "The Failures of Historiography," 803-5; Evans, *The Third Reich at War*, 562; Steinert, *Hitler's War*, 287-90; Zeidler, "Die Rote Armee auf deutschem Boden."

42. Frieser, "Der Zusammenbruch im Osten," 623-28.

43. Ibid., 629-35, 666-67; Glantz and House, *When Titans Clashed*, 226-27.

44. Frieser, "Der Zusammenbruch im Osten," 635-64, 670; Glantz and House, *When Titans Clashed*, 228-29; Ziemke, *Stalingrad to Berlin*, 403-9.

45. Frieser, "Der Zusammenbruch im Osten," 668-78; Kershaw, *Hitler: Nemesis*, 747. See also Grier, *Hitler, Dönitz, and the Baltic Sea*, esp. chap. 7.

46. Glantz and House, *When Titans Clashed*, 216-17; Mawdsley, *Thunder in the East*, 338-41; Schönherr, "Die Rückzugskämpfe in Rumänien und Siebenbürgen," 731-43; Ziemke, *Stalingrad to Berlin*, 346-50.

47. Glantz and House, *When Titans Clashed*, 217-18; Mawdsley, *Thunder in the East*, 341-42; Schönherr, "Die Rückzugskämpfe in Rumänien und Siebenbürgen," 743-46; Ziemke, *Stalingrad to Berlin*, 349-50.

48. Glantz and House, *When Titans Clashed*, 218-21; Mawdsley, *Thunder in the East*, 342-43; Schönherr, "Die Rückzugskämpfe in Rumänien und Siebenbürgen," 746-815; Ziemke, *Stalingrad to Berlin*, 350-56.

49. Glantz and House, *When Titans Clashed*, 221–23; Mawdsley, *Thunder in the East*, 347–48; Ungvary, "Kriegsschauplatz Ungarn," 849–83; Ziemke, *Stalingrad to Berlin*, 359–64.

50. Glantz and House, *When Titans Clashed*, 224–25; Mawdsley, *Thunder in the East*, 348–49; Ungvary, "Kriegsschauplatz Ungarn," 883–902; Ziemke, *Stalingrad to Berlin*, 378–86.

51. Glantz and House, *When Titans Clashed*, 233–36; Mawdsley, *Thunder in the East*, 347–48; Ungvary, "Kriegsschauplatz Ungarn," 902–43; Ziemke, *Stalingrad to Berlin*, 359–64.

A possible explanation for Hitler's obsession with counterattacking in Hungary might be found in a remark to Goebbels at the beginning of March: "The preconditions for entering discussions [for a separate peace] with one side or the other is that we have a military success. Stalin must first be dealt a blow [*muß erst Federn lassen*] before he will have anything to do with us" (*TBJG*, 5 March 1945; Lakowski, "Der Zusammenbruch der deutschen Verteidigung," 524).

10. Death Throes

1. Lakowski, "Der Zusammenbruch der deutschen Verteidigung," 491–93; Domarus, ed., *Hitler: Reden und Proklamationen*, 1:1312–17, 2:1935, 2162–67; Kershaw, *Hitler: Nemesis*, 740, 753–55; Wegner, "Hitler und die Choreographie des Untergangs," and "Die Choreographie des Untergangs," 1192–1209; Mawdsley, *Thunder in the East*, 362.

2. Overmans, *Deutsche militärische Verluste*, 238.

3. Lakowski, "Der Zusammenbruch der deutschen Verteidigung," 494–97; Ziemke, *Stalingrad to Berlin*, 410–14.

4. Lakowski, "Der Zusammenbruch der deutschen Verteidigung," 495–506; Glantz and House, *When Titans Clashed*, 236; Mawdsley, *Thunder in the East*, 335; Ziemke, *Stalingrad to Berlin*, 418.

5. Lakowski, "Der Zusammenbruch der deutschen Verteidigung," 510–15; Glantz and House, *When Titans Clashed*, 236–41; Mawdsley, *Thunder in the East*, 333–36; Ziemke, *Stalingrad to Berlin*, 417–20.

6. Lakowski, "Der Zusammenbruch der deutschen Verteidigung," 496, 502–6; Kershaw, *Hitler: Nemesis*, 756–57; Guderian, *Panzer Leader*, 383–88; Glantz and House, *When Titans Clashed*, 241–42; Ziemke, *Stalingrad to Berlin*, 417–18.

7. Lakowski, "Der Zusammenbruch der deutschen Verteidigung," 516–18; Glantz and House, *When Titans Clashed*, 242–44; Ziemke, *Stalingrad to Berlin*, 420–22; Le Tissier, *Zhukov at the Oder*, 29–41.

8. Lakowski, "Der Zusammenbruch der deutschen Verteidigung," 518–19, 531–37; Glantz and House, *When Titans Clashed*, 247–48; Ziemke, *Stalingrad to Berlin*, 422, 428–29; Le Tissier, *Zhukov at the Oder*, 29–41.

9. Lakowski, "Der Zusammenbruch der deutschen Verteidigung," 520–23; Glantz and House, *When Titans Clashed*, 244–45; Ziemke, *Stalingrad to Berlin*, 421–22; Guderian, *Panzer Leader*, 392–94; Le Tissier, *Zhukov at the Oder*, 29–41.

10. Lakowski, "Der Zusammenbruch der deutschen Verteidigung," 523–26; Glantz and House, *When Titans Clashed*, 245–47; Ziemke, *Stalingrad to Berlin*, 423–27.

11. Lakowski, "Der Zusammenbruch der deutschen Verteidigung," 537–50; Glantz and House, *When Titans Clashed*, 248; Mawdsley, *Thunder in the East*, 376–78; Ziemke, *Stalingrad to Berlin*, 429–33.

12. Glantz and House, *When Titans Clashed*, 249–50; Mawdsley, *Thunder in the*

East, 367–70; Lakowski, "Der Zusammenbruch der deutschen Verteidigung," 527–31; Ziemke, *Stalingrad to Berlin,* 439–44.

13. Glantz and House, *When Titans Clashed,* 249–50; Mawdsley, *Thunder in the East,* 367–70; Lakowski, "Der Zusammenbruch der deutschen Verteidigung," 527–31; Ziemke, *Stalingrad to Berlin,* 439–44.

Stalin also seemed to have been reminded by Zhukov of the Soviet experience in 1920 in front of Warsaw when, in its haste to break through and spread the Bolshevik Revolution to Germany, the Red Army under Tukachevsky (and with Stalin serving as political commissar) left its flanks exposed. The overextended forces were routed in a counterattack by Marshal Pilsudki and driven back in disorder. Stalin was also aware, as was Hitler, of the disaster that had befallen czarist forces in front of Berlin in 1760. Zhukov, *Memoirs,* 571–76.

14. Lakowski, "Der Zusammenbruch der deutschen Verteidigung," 568–88; Glantz and House, *When Titans Clashed,* 250–51; Mawdsley, *Thunder in the East,* 378–81; Ziemke, *Stalingrad to Berlin,* 439–44.

15. Ziemke, *Stalingrad to Berlin,* 444–48; Guderian, *Panzer Leader,* 412–15; Lakowski, "Der Zusammenbruch der deutschen Verteidigung," 550–68; Glantz and House, *When Titans Clashed,* 251–52, 254–55; Mawdsley, *Thunder in the East,* 370–74.

16. Kershaw, *Hitler: Nemesis,* 741, 746, 751–52, 762; Domarus, ed., *Hitler: Reden und Proklamationen,* 2:2180–84; Echternkamp, "At War, Abroad and at Home," 75–78; Diary entry of 28 January 1945, in Breloer, ed., *Mein Tagebuch,* 359–60; *TBJG,* 2 December 1944; Steinert, *Hitler's War,* 288, 294–95, 298–300, 304.

17. Kershaw, *Hitler: Nemesis,* 762–63; Zeidler, "Die Rote Armee auf deutschem Boden," 714–17; Overy, *Russia's War,* 260; Evans, *The Third Reich at War,* 710–11; Merridale, *Ivan's War,* 312–20; Naimark, *The Russians in Germany,* 69–83; Lehndorff, *Ostpreußisches Tagebuch,* 18–25; Kardorff, *Berliner Aufzeichnungen,* 228–29, 231; Andreas-Friedrich, *Battleground Berlin,* 1–19, 36–37, 54–57, 60–61, 83–84; Johr, "Die Ereignisse in Zahlen," 47–48, 58–59; Grossmann, "A Question of Silence"; *A Woman in Berlin,* passim.

18. Zeidler, "Die Rote Armee auf deutschem Boden," 705–9, 719–23, and *Kriegsende im Osten,* 105–34; Overy, *Russia's War,* 260; Evans, *The Third Reich at War,* 707–8; Merridale, *Ivan's War,* 300–306.

19. Zeidler, "Die Rote Armee auf deutschem Boden," 681, 710–12, 721–22, and *Kriegsende im Osten,* 135–67; Evans, *The Third Reich at War,* 708–10; Merridale, *Ivan's War,* 320–26; Andreas-Friedrich, *Battleground Berlin,* 17.

20. Merridale, *Ivan's War,* 312–20; Grossmann, "A Question of Silence," 46, 51; Naimark, *The Russians in Germany,* 69–83, 108, 133; Evans, *The Third Reich at War,* 710–12; Zeidler, "Die Rote Armee auf deutschem Boden," 715–16.

21. Kunz, "Die Wehrmacht," 28–29, 34; Longerich, *"Davon haben wir nichts gewußt!"* 325; Bajohr and Pohl, *Der Holocaust als offenes Geheimnis,* 65–67; Echternkamp, *Kriegsschauplatz Deutschland,* 86; Kershaw, *Hitler: Nemesis,* 759, 763–66, and *The "Hitler Myth,"* 220–25; Evans, *The Third Reich at War,* 683–86; Steinert, *Hitler's War,* 281, 285, 287–88, 293–95, 298–300, 308.

22. Kunz, "Die Wehrmacht," 29–33; Echternkamp, "The War, Abroad and at Home," 49–60; Förster, "Ideological Warfare in Germany," 648–69; Fritz, *Frontsoldaten,* 187–218, and "'We are trying . . . to change the face of the world.'"

23. Kunz, "Die Wehrmacht," 33–41; Fritz, *Endkampf,* 115–58; Messerschmidt and Wüllner, *Die Wehrmachtjustiz im Dienste des Nationalsozialismus,* 87, 91, 130–33, 143; Kershaw, *Hitler: Nemesis,* 763–64; Evans, *The Third Reich at War,* 686–87; Müller and

Ueberschär, eds., *Kriegsende 1945*, 161–64, 166, 169–73; Paul, "'Diese Erschiessungen haben mich innerlich gar nicht mehr berührt.'"

24. Kershaw, *Hitler: Nemesis*, 766–68; Evans, *The Third Reich at War*, 686–90; Blatman, "Die Todesmärsche," 1063–92; Krakowski, "Death Marches"; Bauer, "The Death Marches"; Goldhagen, *Hitler's Willing Executioners*, 327–71.

25. Kershaw, *Hitler: Nemesis*, 784; Evans, *The Third Reich at War*, 714–15; Klemperer, *I Will Bear Witness*, 437, 453.

26. Kershaw, *Hitler: Nemesis*, 784; Evans, *The Third Reich at War*, 714–15; Schwendemann and McEwan, "'Drastic Measures,'" 599–600, 602, 611–12; Müller, "Der Zusammenbruch des Wirtschaftslebens," 74–84.

27. Schwendemann and McEwan, "'Drastic Measures,'" 599–603, 612; Müller, "Der Zusammenbruch des Wirtschaftslebens," 74–84, 106–19.

28. Schwendemann and McEwan, "'Drastic Measures,'" 603, 607–8; Müller, "Der Zusammenbruch des Wirtschaftslebens," 85–86; Kershaw, *Hitler: Nemesis*, 785–86; Evans, *The Third Reich at War*, 716–17.

29. Schwendemann and McEwan, "'Drastic Measures,'" 605–7, 609–14; Müller, "Der Zusammenbruch des Wirtschaftslebens," 87–106; Kershaw, *Hitler: Nemesis*, 785–86; Evans, *The Third Reich at War*, 717–18; *TBJG*, 28 March 1945.

30. Mawdsley, *Thunder in the East*, 386–89; Fritz, *Endkampf*, 3–6, 10–22; Kershaw, *Hitler: Nemesis*, 771, 789; *TBJG*, 28 January 1945; Lakowski, "Der Zusammenbruch der deutschen Verteidigung," 625–26; Ziemke, *Stalingrad to Berlin*, 467–69.

31. Glantz and House, *When Titans Clashed*, 256–57; Lakowski, "Der Zusammenbruch der deutschen Verteidigung," 608–9, 616–18.

32. Lakowski, "Der Zusammenbruch der deutschen Verteidigung," 610–23; Glantz and House, *When Titans Clashed*, 257–59; Ziemke, *Stalingrad to Berlin*, 461–64; Le Tissier, *Zhukov at the Oder*, 107–36.

33. Lakowski, "Der Zusammenbruch der deutschen Verteidigung," 588–607; Glantz and House, *When Titans Clashed*, 257–58; Ziemke, *Stalingrad to Berlin*, 463–64; Guderian, *Panzer Leader*, 427–29; Le Tissier, *Zhukov at the Oder*, 43–98.

34. Lakowski, "Der Zusammenbruch der deutschen Verteidigung," 608–18, 621, 629, 631; Frieser, "Die Schlacht um die Seelower Höhen," 141; Glantz and House, *When Titans Clashed*, 258–59; Mawdsley, *Thunder in the East*, 389–90; Ziemke, *Stalingrad to Berlin*, 470–71, 473.

35. Lakowski, "Der Zusammenbruch der deutschen Verteidigung," 619–31; Glantz and House, *When Titans Clashed*, 258–61; Mawdsley, *Thunder in the East*, 389–90; Ziemke, *Stalingrad to Berlin*, 470–71.

36. Lakowski, "Der Zusammenbruch der deutschen Verteidigung," 631–34; Glantz and House, *When Titans Clashed*, 263; Ziemke, *Stalingrad to Berlin*, 473–74; Le Tissier, *Zhukov at the Oder*, 157–90.

37. Glantz and House, *When Titans Clashed*, 265–66; Lakowski, "Der Zusammenbruch der deutschen Verteidigung," 633–36; Ziemke, *Stalingrad to Berlin*, 474; Le Tissier, *Zhukov at the Oder*, 157–90; Beevor, *The Fall of Berlin*, 216–33.

38. Lakowski, "Der Zusammenbruch der deutschen Verteidigung," 636–42; Glantz and House, *When Titans Clashed*, 265; Ziemke, *Stalingrad to Berlin*, 474–76; Le Tissier, *Zhukov at the Oder*, 39, 191–240; Mawdsley, *Thunder in the East*, 391; Beevor, *The Fall of Berlin*, 234–48.

39. Lakowski, "Der Zusammenbruch der deutschen Verteidigung," 643–49; Glantz and House, *When Titans Clashed*, 265–66; Ziemke, *Stalingrad to Berlin*, 475–76; Beevor, *The Fall of Berlin*, 249–60.

40. Lakowski, "Der Zusammenbruch der deutschen Verteidigung," 649–56; Glantz and House, *When Titans Clashed*, 266–68; Tooze, *The Wages of Destruction*, 656.

41. Lakowski, "Der Zusammenbruch der deutschen Verteidigung," 656–59.

42. Lakowski, "Der Zusammenbruch der deutschen Verteidigung," 660–71; Ziemke, *Stalingrad to Berlin*, 480–88; Le Tissier, *Zhukov at the Oder*, 141–50; Beevor, *The Fall of Berlin*, 280–338.

43. Lakowski, "Der Zusammenbruch der deutschen Verteidigung," 671–73; Ziemke, *Stalingrad to Berlin*, 488–94; Glantz and House, *When Titans Clashed*, 269–72; Beevor, *The Fall of Berlin*, 339–405.

44. Lakowski, "Der Zusammenbruch der deutschen Verteidigung," 671–73; Ziemke, *Stalingrad to Berlin*, 488–94; Glantz and House, *When Titans Clashed*, 269–72; Mawdsley, *Thunder in the East*, 392–93; Overmans, *Deutsche militärische Verluste*, 238; Wegner, "Die Choreographie des Untergangs," 1192–1209; Andreas-Friedrich, *Battleground Berlin*, 13–14.

45. Glantz and House, *When Titans Clashed*, 272–76; Lakowski, "Der Zusammenbruch der deutschen Verteidigung," 673–74; Ziemke, *Stalingrad to Berlin*, 498.

46. Glantz and House, *When Titans Clashed*, 273–75, 300; Lakowski, "Der Zusammenbruch der deutschen Verteidigung," 674–75.

47. Glantz and House, *When Titans Clashed*, 283–84.

48. Hartmann, "Verbrecherischer Krieg—verbrecherische Wehrmacht?" 17; Overmanns, *Deutsche militärische Verluste*, 238, 265, 278, 288, 333–36; Glantz and House, *When Titans Clashed*, 307; Blank, "Wartime Daily Life," 474–76.

49. Glantz and House, *When Titans Clashed*, 284–86, 292; Sokolov and Glantz, "The Role of Lend-Lease"; Erickson, "Soviet War Losses," 256–58, 262–66; Sokolov, "The Cost of War," 156–71; Korol and Glantz, "The Price of Victory"; Overy, *Russia's War*, 288, 291–92; Mawdsley, *Thunder in the East*, 403–6; Ziemke, *Stalingrad to Berlin*, 500–504; Keegan, ed., *Times Atlas*, 203; Harrison, "The Economics of World War II: An Overview," 10.

50. Müller, "Das deutsche Reich und das Jahr 1945," 699–720; Wegner, "Hitler und die Choreographie des Untergangs," 511–18.

Conclusion

1. Tooze, *The Wages of Destruction*, 657–58.

2. Ibid., 658; Fritzsche, *Germans into Nazis*, chaps. 1–2; Bloxham, *The Final Solution*, 135–36.

3. Tooze, *The Wages of Destruction*, 662–64.

4. Bloxham, *The Final Solution*, 170–79.

5. Ibid., 180–83.

6. Ibid., 181–85.

7. Ibid., 92–110, 170–71, 182–85.

8. Ibid., 158–59; Messerschmidt, "'Harte Sühne am Judentum'"; Wette, *The Wehrmacht*, chaps. 1–2; Wegner, "'Hitlers Krieg'?"; Gerlach, "Die Verantwortung der Wehrmachtführung."

9. For a nuanced assessment of the role of the Wehrmacht in Russia, see Hartmann, "Verbrecherischer Krieg—verbrecherische Wehrmacht?"; Hürter, "Konservative Akteure oder totale Krieger?"; Angrick, "Das Beispiel Charkow," 117–24; Kunz, "Das Beispiel Charkow"; Eichholtz, "Der Krieg gegen die Sowjetunion"; Chiari, "Zwischen Hoffnung und Hunger."

On the road construction projects in Galicia, see Sandkühler, *"Endlösung" in Galizien,* 146–59; Kaienburg, "Jüdischer Arbeit."

10. Hartmann, "Verbrecherischer Krieg—verbrecherische Wehrmacht?" 30–46, 52–54 66–68, 71–73, and "Wie verbrecherisch war die Wehrmacht?"; Pohl, "Die Wehrmacht und der Mord," 50, "Schauplatz Ukraine," 151, 169–71, and "Die Kooperation zwischen Heer, SS und Polizei"; Rass, *"Menschenmaterial,"* 331–402, and "Verbrecherische Kriegführung an der Front"; Jureit, "Motive—Mentalitäten—Handlungsspielräume." See also Hartmann, *Wehrmacht im Ostkrieg;* and Pohl, *Die Herrschaft der Wehrmacht.*

11. For a good discussion of anticipatory obedience, see Lower, "'Anticipatory Obedience.'" See also Fritz, *Frontsoldaten,* 187–218, and "'We are trying . . . to change the face of the world.'"

12. Aly, *Hitler's Beneficiaries;* Bloxham, *The Final Solution,* 262–63.

13. Bloxham, *The Final Solution,* 243–44.

Bibliography

Allen, Michael Thad. *The Business of Genocide: The SS, Slave Labor, and the Concentration Camps.* Chapel Hill: University of North Carolina Press, 2002.
———. "'The devil in the details': The Gas Chambers of Birkenau, October 1941." *Holocaust and Genocide Studies* 16, no. 2 (2002): 189-216.
Aly, Götz. *Hitler's Beneficiaries: Plunder, Racial War, and the Nazi Welfare State.* Translated by Jefferson Chase. New York: Metropolitan, 2007.
———. *Hitlers Volksstaat: Raub, Rassenkrieg und nationaler Sozializmus.* Frankfurt: S. Fischer, 2005.
———. *"Final Solution": Nazi Population Policy and the Murder of the European Jews.* Translated by Belinda Cooper and Allison Brown. New York: Oxford University Press, 1999.
———. *"Endlösung": Völkerverschiebung und der Mord an den europäischen Juden.* Frankfurt: S. Fischer, 1995.
Aly, Götz, and Susanne Heim. *Architects of Annihilation: Auschwitz and the Logic of Destruction.* Translated by A. G. Blunden. Princeton, NJ: Princeton University Press, 2002.
———. "Deutsche Herrschaft 'im Osten': Bevölkerungspolitik und Völkermord." In *Erobern und Vernichten: Der Krieg gegen die Sowjetunion, 1941-1945,* ed. Peter Jahn and Reinhard Rürup, 84-105. Berlin: Argon, 1991.
———. *Vordenker der Vernichtung: Auschwitz und die deutschen Pläne für eine neue europäische Ordnung.* Hamburg: Hoffmann & Campe, 1991.
———. "The Economics of the Final Solution: A Case Study from the General Government." *Simon Wiesenthal Center Annual* 5 (1988): 3-48.
Ancel, Jean. "The German-Romanian Relationship and the Final Solution." *Holocaust and Genocide Studies* 19, no. 2 (2005): 252-75.
Anderson, Truman O. "Germans, Ukrainians and Jews: Ethnic Politics in Heeresgebiet Süd, June-December 1941." *War in History* 7, no. 3 (2000): 325-51.
———. "A Hungarian Vernichtungskrieg? Hungarian Troops and the Soviet Partisan War in Ukraine, 1942." *Militärgeschichtliche Mitteilungen* 58, no. 2 (1999): 345-66.
———. "Incident at Baranivka: German Reprisals and the Soviet Partisan Movement in Ukraine, October-December 1941." *Journal of Modern History* 71, no. 3 (1999): 585-623.
———. "Die 62. Infanterie-Division: Repressalien im Heeresgebiet Süd, Oktober bis Dezember 1941." In *Vernichtungskrieg: Verbrechen der Wehrmacht, 1941-1944,* ed. Hannes Heer and Klaus Naumann, 297-314. Hamburg: Hamburger Edition, 1995.
Andreas-Friedrich, Ruth. *Battleground Berlin: Diaries, 1945-1948.* Translated by Anna Boerresen. New York: Paragon, 1990.

Angrick, Andrej. "Das Beispiel Charkow: Massenmord unter deutscher Besatzung." In *Verbrechen der Wehrmacht: Bilanz einer Debatte,* ed. Christian Hartmann, Johannes Hürter, and Ulrike Jureit, 117–24. Munich: Beck, 2005.

Angrick, Andrej, and Peter Klein. *Die "Endlösung" in Riga: Ausbeutung und Vernichtung, 1941-1944.* Darmstadt: Wissenschaftliche Buchgesellschaft, 2005.

Arad, Yitzhak. "The Holocaust of Soviet Jewry in the Occupied Territories of the Soviet Union." *Yad Vashem Studies* 21 (1991): 1–47.

Arlt, Kurt. "Die Wehrmacht im Kalkül Stalins." In *Die Wehrmacht: Mythos und Realität,* ed. Rolf-Dieter Müller and Hans-Erich Volkmann, 105–22. Munich: Oldenbourg, 1999.

Armstrong, Richard N. "Prokhorovka: The Great Tank Battle." *Military Review* 73, no. 7 (1993): 64–67.

Arnold, Klaus Jochen. *Die Wehrmacht und die Besatzungspolitik in den besetzten Gebieten der Sowjetunion: Kriegführung und Radikalisierung im "Unternehmen Barbarossa."* Berlin: Duncker & Humblot, 2005.

———. "Hitlers Wandel im August 1941: Ein Kommentar zu den Thesen Tobias Jersaks." *Zeitschrift für Geschichtswissenschaft* 48, no. 3 (2000): 239–50.

———. "Die Eroberung und Behandlung der Stadt Kiew durch die Wehrmacht im September 1941: Zur Radikalisierung der Besatzungspolitik." *Militärgeschichtliche Mitteilungen* 58, no. 1 (1999): 23–63.

Arnold, Klaus Jochen, and Gert C. Lübbers. "The Meeting of the Staatssekretäre on 2 May 1941 and the Wehrmacht: A Document Up for Discussion." *Journal of Contemporary History* 42, no. 4 (2007): 613–26.

Aschenauer, Rudolf, ed. *Ich, Adolf Eichmann: Ein historischer Zeugenbericht.* Leoni am Starnberger See: Druffel, 1980.

Bähr, Walter, and Hans Walter Bähr, eds. *Kriegsbriefe gefallener Studenten, 1939-1945.* Tübingen: Wunderlich, 1952.

Bajohr, Frank. *"Aryanisation" in Hamburg: The Economic Exclusion of Jews and the Confiscation of Their Property in Nazi Germany.* New York: Berghahn, 2002.

———. "The 'Folk Community' and the Persecution of the Jews: German Society under National Socialist Dictatorship, 1933–1945." *Holocaust and Genocide Studies* 20, no. 2 (2006): 183–206.

———. "Arisierung als gesellschaftlicher Prozess: Verhalten, Strategien und Handlungsspielräume jüdischer Eigentümer und 'arischer' Erwerber." *Jahrbuch zur Geschichte und Wirkung des Holocaust* 4 (2000): 15–30.

———. "Verfolgung aus gesellschaftsgeschichtlicher Perspektive: Die Wirtschaftliche Existenzvernichtung der Juden und die deutsche Gesellschaft." *Geschichte und Gesellschaft* 26, no. 4 (2000): 629–52.

Bajohr, Frank, and Dieter Pohl. *Der Holocaust als offenes Geheimnis: Die Deutschen, die NS-Führung und die Alliierten.* Munich: Beck, 2006.

Bajohr, Frank, and William Templer. "The Beneficiaries of 'Aryanization': Hamburg as a Case Study." *Yad Vashem Studies* 26 (1998): 173–201.

Bajohr, Frank, and Michael Wildt, eds. *Volksgemeinschaft: Neue Forschungen zur Gesellschaft des Nationalsozialismus.* Frankfurt: Fischer Taschenbuch, 2009.

Baker, Lee. "Explaining Defeat: A Reappraisal of 'Operation Bagration,' 1944." *Journal of Slavic Military Studies* 21, no. 1 (January 2008): 129–45.

Bankier, David. *Probing the Depths of German Antisemitism: German Society and the Persecution of the Jews, 1933-1941.* New York: Berghahn, 2000.

———. "The Germans and the Holocaust: What Did They Know?" *Yad Vashem Studies* 20 (1990): 69–98.

——. "Hitler and the Policy-Making Process on the Jewish Question." *Holocaust and Genocide Studies* 3, no. 1 (1988): 1–20.

Baranova, Olga. "Nationalism, Anti-Bolshevism or the Will to Survive? Collaboration in Belarus under the Nazi Occupation of 1941–1944." *European Review of History* 15, no. 2 (2008): 113–28.

Barber, John, and Mark Harrison. *The Soviet Home Front, 1941-1945: A Social and Economic History of the USSR in World War II.* New York: Longman, 1991.

Barkai, Avraham. "Schicksalsjahr 1938." In *Der Judenpogrom 1938: Von der "Reichskristallnacht" zum Völkermord,* ed. Walter H. Pehle, 94–117. Frankfurt: Fischer Taschenbuch, 1988.

Bartov, Omer. *Germany's War and the Holocaust: Disputed Histories.* Ithaca, NY: Cornell University Press, 2003.

——. "Germany's Unforgettable War: The Twisted Road from Berlin to Moscow and Back." *Diplomatic History* 25, no. 3 (2001): 405–23.

——. "Defining Enemies, Making Victims: Germans, Jews, and the Holocaust." *American Historical Review* 103, no. 3 (1998): 771–816.

——. "German Soldiers and the Holocaust: Historiography, Research and Implications." *History and Memory* 9, nos. 1–2 (1997): 162–88.

——. *Murder in Our Midst: The Holocaust, Industrial Killing, and Representation.* New York: Oxford University Press, 1996.

——. "An Idiot's Tale: Memories and Histories of the Holocaust." *Journal of Modern History* 67, no. 1 (1995): 55–82.

——. "War, Memory and Repression: Alexander Kluge and the Politics of Representation in Postwar Germany." *Tel Aviver Jahrbuch für deutsche Geschichte* 23 (1994): 413–32.

——. "The Conduct of War: Soldiers and the Barbarization of Warfare." *Journal of Modern History* 64 (1992): S32–S45.

——. "The Myths of the Wehrmacht." *History Today* 42 (April 1992): 30–36.

——. *Hitler's Army: Soldiers, Nazis, and War in the Third Reich.* New York: Oxford University Press, 1991.

——. "Brutalität und Mentalität: Zum Verhalten deutscher Soldaten an der 'Ostfront.'" In *Erobern und Vernichten: Der Krieg gegen die Sowjetunion, 1941-1945,* ed. Peter Jahn and Reinhard Rürup, 183–99. Berlin: Argon, 1991.

——. "The Missing Years: German Workers, German Soldiers." *German History* 8, no. 1 (1990): 46–65.

——. "Daily Life and Motivation in War: The Wehrmacht in the Soviet Union." *Journal of Strategic Studies* 12, no. 2 (1989): 200–214.

——. *The Eastern Front, 1941-45: German Troops and the Barbarisation of Warfare.* New York: St. Martin's, 1986.

——. "Indoctrination and Motivation in the Wehrmacht: The Importance of the Unquantifiable." *Journal of Strategic Studies* 9, no. 1 (1986): 16–34.

——. "The Barbarisation of Warfare: German Officers and Men on the Eastern Front, 1941–1945." *Jahrbuch des Instituts für deutsche Geschichte* 13 (1984): 305–39.

Bauer, Yehuda. *Rethinking the Holocaust.* New Haven, CT: Yale University Press, 2001.

——. *Jews for Sale? Nazi-Jewish Negotiations, 1933-45.* New Haven, CT: Yale University Press, 1994.

——. "Who Was Responsible and When? Some Well-Known Documents Revisited." *Holocaust and Genocide Studies* 6, no. 2 (1991): 129–49.

——. "The Death Marches, January–May 1945." In *The Nazi Holocaust: Historical*

Articles on the Destruction of the European Jews (9 vols.), ed. Michael R. Marrus, 9:491–511. Westport, CT: Greenwood, 1989.

———. "The Death-Marches, January–May 1945." *Modern Judaism* 3, no. 1 (1983): 1–21.

———. *A History of the Holocaust.* New York: Franklin Watts, 1982.

———. "Genocide: Was It the Nazis' Original Plan?" *Annals of the American Academy of Political and Social Science,* no. 450 (1980): 35–45.

———. "'Onkel Saly'—die Verhandlungen des Saly Mayer zur Rettung der Juden, 1944/45." *Vierteljahrshefte für Zeitgeschichte* 25, no. 2 (1977): 188–219.

Baumgart, Winfried. "Zur Ansprache Hitlers vor den Führern der Wehrmacht am 22. August 1939." *Vierteljahrshefte für Zeitgeschichte* 16, no. 2 (1968): 120–49.

Beevor, Antony. *The Fall of Berlin, 1945.* New York: Viking, 2002.

———. "Stalingrad." *MHQ: Quarterly Journal of Military History* 11, no. 1 (1998): 6–17.

———. *Stalingrad, the Fateful Siege: 1942-1943.* London: Penguin, 1998.

Bellamy, Chris. *Absolute War: Soviet Russia in the Second World War.* New York: Knopf, 2007.

Below, Nicolaus von. *At Hitler's Side: The Memoirs of Hitler's Luftwaffe Adjutant, 1937-1945.* Translated by Geoffrey Brooks. London: Greenhill, 2001.

———. *Als Hitlers Adjutant, 1937-45.* Mainz: Hase & Koehler, 1980.

Benz, Wolfgang. "Der Judenmord im Bewusstsein der Deutschen." *Bohemia* 34, no. 2 (1993): 305–13.

———. "Der Generalplan Ost: Zur Germanisierungspolitik des NS-Regimes in den besetzten Ostgebieten, 1939-1945." In *Die Vertreibung der Deutschen aus dem Osten: Ursachen, Ereignisse, Folgen,* ed. Wolfgang Benz, 45–57. Frankfurt: Fischer Taschenbuch, 1985.

———. *Die Vertreibung der Deutschen aus dem Osten: Ursachen, Ereignisse, Folgen.* Frankfurt: Fischer Taschenbuch, 1985.

———. "Judenvernichtung aus Notwehr? Die Legenden um Theodore N. Kaufman." *Vierteljahrshefte für Zeitgeschichte* 29, no. 4 (1981): 615–30.

Berkhoff, Karel C. "The Mass Murder of Soviet Prisoners of War and the Holocaust: How Were They Related?" *Kritika: Explorations in Russian and Eurasian History* 6, no. 4 (2005): 789–96.

———. *Harvest of Despair: Life and Death in Ukraine under Nazi Rule.* Cambridge, MA: Harvard University Press, 2004.

———. "The 'Russian' Prisoners of War in Nazi-Ruled Ukraine as Victims of Genocidal Massacre." *Holocaust and Genocide Studies* 15, no. 1 (2001): 1–32.

Bernig, Jörg. *Eingekesselt: Die Schlacht um Stalingrad im deutschsprachigen Roman nach 1945.* New York: Peter Lang, 1997.

Bessel, Richard. "Murder amidst Collapse: Explaining the Violence of the Last Months of the Third Reich." In *Years of Persecution, Years of Extermination: Saul Friedländer and the Future of Holocaust Studies,* ed. Christian Wiese and Paul Betts, 255–68. London: Continuum, 2010.

———. "The Shadow of Death in Germany at the End of the Second World War." In *Between Mass Death and Individual Loss: The Place of the Dead in Twentieth-Century Germany,* ed. Alon Confino, Paul Betts, and Dirk Schumann, 51–68. New York: Berghahn, 2008.

———. "The War to End All Wars: The Shock of Violence in 1945 and Its Aftermath in Germany." In *No Man's Land of Violence: Extreme Wars in the Twentieth Century,* ed. Alf Lüdtke and Bernd Weisbrod, 71–99. Göttingen: Wallstein, 2006.

Beyer, Wilhelm Raimund. *Stalingrad: Unten, Wo das Leben Konkret War.* Frankfurt am Main: Athenäum, 1987.

Beyer, Wolfgang. "Pläne der faschistischen Führung zum totalen Krieg im Sommer 1944." *Zeitschrift für Geschichtswissenschaft* 17 (1969): 1312–39.

Bezymenskij, Lev. "Der Berlin-Besuch von V. M. Molotov im November 1940 im Lichte neuer Dokumente aus sowjetischen Geheimarchiven." *Militärgeschichtliche Mitteilungen* 57, no. 1 (1998): 199–215.

Biddle, Tami Davis. "Bombing by the Square Yard: Sir Arthur Harris at War, 1942–1945." *International History Review* 21, no. 3 (1999): 626–64.

Bidermann, Gottlob Herbert. *In Deadly Combat: A German Soldier's Memoir of the Eastern Front.* Edited and translated by Derek S. Zumbro. Lawrence: University Press of Kansas, 2000.

Birn, Ruth Bettina. "Two Kinds of Reality? Case Studies on Anti-Partisan Warfare." In *From Peace to War: Germany, Soviet Russia, and the World, 1939-1941,* ed. Bernd Wegner, 277–91. Providence, RI: Berghahn, 1997.

———. "Zweierlei Wirklichkeit? Fallbeispiele zur Partisanenbekämpfung im Osten." In *Zwei Wege nach Moskau: Vom Hitler-Stalin-Pakt zum "Unternehmen Barbarossa,"* ed. Bernd Wegner, 275–90. Munich: Piper, 1991.

Black, Peter R. "Rehearsal for 'Reinhard'? Odilo Globocnik and the Lublin 'Selbstschutz.'" *Central European History* 25, no. 2 (1992): 204–26.

Blank, Ralf. "Wartime Daily Life and the Air War on the Home Front." In *German Wartime Society, 1939-1945: Politicization, Disintegration, and the Struggle for Survival* (vol. 9/1 of *Germany and the Second World War*), ed. Jörg Echternkamp, trans. Derry Cook-Radmore, 371–476. Oxford: Clarendon, 2008.

———. "Kriegsalltag und Luftkrieg an der 'Heimatfront.'" In *Die deutsche Kriegsgesellschaft, 1939 bis 1945: Politisierung, Vernichtung, Überleben* (vol. 9/1 of *Das deutsche Reich und der Zweite Weltkrieg*), ed. Jörg Echternkamp, 357–461. Munich: Deutsche Verlags-Anstalt, 2004.

Blatman, Daniel. "Die Todesmärsche." In *Die nationalsozialistischen Konzentrationslager: Entwicklung und Struktur* (2 vols.), ed. Ulrich Herbert, Karin Orth, and Christoph Dieckmann, 2:1063–92. Göttingen: Wallstein, 1998.

Bloxham, Donald. *The Final Solution: A Genocide.* Oxford: Oxford University Press, 2009.

———. "Organized Mass Murder: Structure, Participation, and Motivation in Comparative Perspective." *Holocaust and Genocide Studies* 22, no. 2 (2008): 203–45.

Boberach, Heinz. "Stimmungsumschwung in der deutschen Bevölkerung." In *Stalingrad: Mythos und Wirklichkeit einer Schlacht,* ed. Wolfram Wette and Gerd R. Ueberschär, 61–66. Frankfurt: Fischer Taschenbuch, 1992.

———, ed. *Meldungen aus dem Reich: Auswahl aus den geheimen Lageberichten des Sicherheitsdienstes der SS, 1939-1944.* Neuwied: Luchterhand, 1965.

Bock, Fedor von. *Generalfeldmarschall Fedor von Bock: The War Diary, 1939-1945.* Edited by Klaus Gerbet. Translated by David Johnston. Atglen, PA: Schiffer, 1996.

Bock, Gisela. *Zwangssterilisation im Nationalsozialismus: Studien zur Rassenpolitik und Frauenpolitik.* Opladen: Westdeutscher, 1986.

Boelcke, Willi. *"Wollt ihr den totalen Krieg?" Die geheimen Goebbels-Konferenzen, 1939-1943.* Stuttgart: Deutsche Verlags-Anstalt, 1967.

Böhler, Jochen. *Auftakt zum Vernichtungskrieg: Die Wehrmacht in Polen, 1939.* Frankfurt: Fischer Taschenbuch, 2006.

Boll, Bernd, and Hans Safrian. "Auf dem Weg nach Stalingrad: Die 6. Armee, 1941/42." In *Vernichtungskrieg: Verbrechen der Wehrmacht, 1941-1944,* ed. Hannes Heer and Klaus Naumann, 260–96. Hamburg: Hamburger Edition, 1995.

Boog, Horst. "Die strategische Bomberoffensive der Alliierten gegen Deutschland und die Reichsluftverteidigung in der Schlußphase des Krieges." In *Der Zusammenbruch des deutschen Reiches, 1945: Die militärische Niederwerfung der Wehrmacht* (vol. 10/1 of *Das deutsche Reich und der Zweite Weltkrieg*), ed. Rolf-Dieter Müller, 777–884. Munich: Deutsche Verlags-Anstalt, 2008.

——. "The Strategic Air War in Europe and Air Defense of the Reich." In *The Strategic Air War in Europe and the War in the West and East Asia, 1943-1944/5* (vol. 7 of *Germany and the Second World War*), ed. Horst Boog, Gerhard Krebs, and Detlef Vogel, trans. by Derry Cook-Radmore, 7–458. Oxford: Clarendon, 2006.

——, ed. *The Global War: Widening of the Conflict into a World War and the Shift of the Initiative, 1941-1943.* Translated by Ewald Osers. Vol. 6 of *Germany and the Second World War.* Oxford: Clarendon, 2001.

——. "German Air Intelligence in the Second World War." *Intelligence and National Security* 5, no. 2 (1990): 350–424.

——, ed. *Der globale Krieg: Die Ausweitung zum Weltkrieg und der Wechsel der Initiative, 1941-1943.* Vol. 6 of *Das deutsche Reich und der Zweite Weltkrieg.* Stuttgart: Deutsche Verlags-Anstalt, 1990.

——. "Luftwaffe and Logistics in the Second World War." *Aerospace Historian* 35, no. 2 (1988): 103–10.

——, et al., eds. *Der Angriff auf die Sowjetunion.* Vol. 4 of *Das deutsche Reich und der Zweite Weltkrieg.* Stuttgart: Deutsche Verlags-Anstalt, 1983.

——. "The Luftwaffe and Technology." *Aerospace Historian* 30, no. 3 (1983): 200–206.

Boog, Horst, Jürgen Förster, Joachim Hoffmann, Ernst Klink, Rolf-Dieter Müller, and Gerd R. Ueberschär, eds. *The Attack on the Soviet Union.* Translated by Dean S. McMurrey, Ewald Osers, and Louise Willmot. Vol. 4 of *Germany and the Second World War.* Oxford: Clarendon, 1998.

Boog, Horst, Gerhard Krebs, and Detlef Vogel, eds. *The Strategic Air War in Europe and the War in the West and East Asia, 1943-1944/5.* Translated by Derry Cook-Radmore. Vol. 7 of *Germany and the Second World War.* Oxford: Clarendon, 2006.

——, eds. *Das deutsche Reich in der Defensive: Strategischer Luftkrieg in Europa, Krieg im Westen und in Ostasien, 1943-1944/45.* Vol. 7 of *Das deutsche Reich und der Zweite Weltkrieg.* Stuttgart: Deutsche Verlags-Anstalt, 2001.

Brand, Dieter. "Vor 60 Jahren: Prochorowka: Aspekte der Operation Zitadelle; Juli 1943 im Abschnitt der Heeresgruppe Süd." *Österreichische militärische Zeitschrift* 41, no. 5 (2003): 587–98.

Brechtken, Magnus. *"Madagaskar für die Juden": Antisemitische Idee und politische Praxis, 1885-1945.* Munich: Oldenbourg, 1997.

Breitman, Richard. *Official Secrets: What the Nazis Planned, What the British and Americans Knew.* New York: Farrar Straus Giroux, 1998.

——. "A Deal with the Nazi Dictatorship? Himmler's Alleged Peace Emissaries in Autumn 1943." *Journal of Contemporary History* 30, no. 3 (1995): 411–30.

——. "American Inaction during the Holocaust." *Dimensions* 8, no. 2 (1994): 3–8.

——. "Plans for the Final Solution in Early 1941." *German Studies Review* 17, no. 3 (1994): 483–93.

——. "American Rescue Activities in Sweden." *Holocaust and Genocide Studies* 7, no. 2 (1993): 202–15.

——. *The Architect of Genocide: Himmler and the Final Solution.* New York: Knopf, 1991.

——. "Himmler and the 'Terrible Secret' among the Executioners." *Journal of Contemporary History* 26, nos. 3-4 (1991): 431–51.

———. "Himmler's Police Auxiliaries in the Occupied Soviet Territories." *Simon Wiesenthal Center Annual* 7 (1990): 23–39.

———. "Hitler and Genghis Khan." *Journal of Contemporary History* 25, nos. 2–3 (1990): 337–51.

———. "A Nazi Crusade?" *Simon Wiesenthal Center Annual* 7 (1990): 187–99.

———. "In Search of a National Identity: New Interpretations of the Holocaust." *Dimensions* 3, no. 1 (1987): 9–13.

———. "The Allied War Effort and the Jews, 1942–1943." *Journal of Contemporary History* 20, no. 1 (1985): 135–56.

———. "Auschwitz and the Archives." *Central European History* 18, nos. 3–4 (1985): 365–83.

———. "Documentation about the Holocaust: Emigration." *Simon Wiesenthal Center Annual* 1 (1984): 241–48.

Breitman, Richard, and Shlomo Aronson. "The End of the 'Final Solution'? Nazi Plans to Ransom Jews in 1944." *Central European History* 25, no. 2 (1992): 177–203.

———. "Dokumentation: Eine Unbekannte Himmler-Rede vom Januar 1943." *Vierteljahrshefte für Zeitgeschichte* 38, no. 2 (1990): 337–48.

Breitman, Richard, and Alan M. Kraut. *American Refugee Policy and European Jewry, 1933-1945*. Bloomington: Indiana University Press, 1988.

Breloer, Heinrich, ed. *Mein Tagebuch: Geschichten vom Überleben, 1939-1947*. Cologne: Verlagsgesellschaft Schulfernsehen, 1984.

Broszat, Martin. "Hitler and the Genesis of the 'Final Solution': An Assessment of David Irving's Theses." In *The "Final Solution": Historical Articles on the Destruction of the European Jews* (9 vols.), ed. Michael R. Marrus, 1, pt. 3:115–67. Westport, CT: Meckler, 1989.

———. "Hitler und die Genesis der 'Endlösung': Aus Anlass der Thesen von David Irving." *Vierteljahrshefte für Zeitgeschichte* 25, no. 4 (1977): 739–75.

Broszat, Martin, Klaus-Dietmar Henke, and Hans Woller, eds. *Von Stalingrad zur Währungsreform: Zur Sozialgeschichte des Umbruchs in Deutschland*. Quellen und Darstellungen zur Zeitgeschichte, vol. 26. Munich: Oldenbourg, 1988.

Browder, George C. "Perpetrator Character and Motivation: An Emerging Consensus?" *Holocaust and Genocide Studies* 17, no. 3 (2003): 480–97.

———. *Hitler's Enforcers: The Gestapo and the SS Security Service in the Nazi Revolution*. New York: Oxford University Press, 1996.

———. *Foundations of the Nazi Police State: The Formation of Sipo and SD*. Lexington: University Press of Kentucky, 1990.

Brown, Paul B. "The Senior Leadership Cadre of the Geheime Feldpolizei, 1939–1945." *Holocaust and Genocide Studies* 17, no. 2 (2003): 278–304.

Browning, Christopher R. *The Origins of the Final Solution: The Evolution of Nazi Jewish Policy, September 1939-March 1942*. Lincoln: University of Nebraska Press, 2004.

———. *Nazi Policy, Jewish Workers, German Killers*. New York: Cambridge University Press, 2000.

———. "A Final Hitler Decision for the 'Final Solution'? The Riegner Telegram Reconsidered." *Holocaust and Genocide Studies* 10, no. 1 (1996): 3–10.

———. "Völkermord aus der Sicht der NS-Ethnokraten: G. Alys neueste Forschungen zur Entstehungsgeschichte der 'Endlosung.'" *Neue politische Literatur* 41, no. 1 (1996): 7–10.

———. "The Euphoria of Victory and the Final Solution: Summer–Fall 1941." *German Studies Review* 17, no. 3 (1994): 473–81.

——. *Ordinary Men: Reserve Police Battalion 101 and the Final Solution in Poland.* New York: HarperCollins, 1992.

——. *The Path to Genocide: Essays on Launching the Final Solution.* New York: Cambridge University Press, 1992.

——. "A Reply to Martin Broszat regarding the Origins of the Final Solution." In *The "Final Solution": Historical Articles on the Destruction of the European Jews* (9 vols.), ed. Michael R. Marrus, 1, pt. 3:168-87. Westport, CT: Meckler, 1989.

——. "The Decision concerning the Final Solution." In *The "Final Solution": Historical Articles on the Destruction of the European Jews* (9 vols.), ed. Michael R. Marrus, 1, pt. 3:188-216. Westport, CT: Meckler, 1989.

——. "Genocide and Public Health: German Doctors and Polish Jews, 1939-41." *Holocaust and Genocide Studies* 3, no. 1 (1988): 21-36.

——. "Nazi Ghettoization Policy in Poland: 1939-41." *Central European History* 19, no. 4 (1987): 343-68.

——. "Nazi Resettlement Policy and the Search for a Solution to the Jewish Question, 1939-41." *German Studies Review* 9, no. 3 (1986): 497-519.

——. "Zur Genesis der 'Endlosung': Eine Antwort an Martin Broszat." *Vierteljahrshefte für Zeitgeschichte* 29, no. 1 (1981): 97-109.

——. *The Final Solution and the German Foreign Office.* New York: Holmes & Meier, 1979.

——. "Referat Deutschland, Jewish Policy and the German Foreign Office (1933-1940)." *Yad Vashem Studies* 12 (1977): 37-74.

Buchbender, Ortwin, and Reinhold Sterz, eds. *Das andere Gesicht des Krieges: Deutsche Feldpostbriefe, 1939-1945.* Munich: Beck, 1982.

Buchheim, Christoph. "Das NS-Regime und die Überwindung der Weltwirtschaftskrise in Deutschland." *Vierteljahrshefte für Zeitgeschichte* 56, no. 3 (2008): 381-414.

——. "Unternehmen in Deutschland und NS-Regime, 1933-1945: Versuch einer Synthese." *Historische Zeitschrift* 282, no. 2 (2006): 351-90.

——. "Die Vielen Rechenfehler in der Abrechnung Götz Alys mit den Deutschen unter dem NS-Regime." *Sozial.Geschichte: Zeitschrift für historische Analyse des 20. und 21. Jahrhunderts* 20, no. 3 (2005): 67-76.

——. "Dokumentation: Die besetzten Länder im Dienste der deutschen Kriegswirtschaft während des Zweiten Weltkriegs: Ein Bericht der Forschungstelle für Wehrwirtschaft." *Vierteljahrshefte für Zeitgeschichte* 34, no. 1 (1986): 117-45.

Buchheim, Christoph, and Jonas Scherner. "The Role of Private Property in the Nazi Economy: The Case of Industry." *Journal of Economic History* 66, no. 2 (2006): 390-416.

Büchler, Yehoshua. "'Unworthy Behavior': The Case of SS Officer Max Taubner." *Holocaust and Genocide Studies* 17, no. 3 (2003): 409-29.

——. "The Deportation of Slovakian Jews to the Lublin District of Poland in 1942." *Holocaust and Genocide Studies* 6, no. 2 (1991): 151-66.

——. "Kommandostab Reichsführer-SS: Himmler's Personal Murder Brigades in 1941." *Holocaust and Genocide Studies* 1, no. 1 (1986): 11-25.

Buchner, Alex. *Ostfront 1944: The German Defensive Battles on the Russian Front, 1944.* Translated by David Johnston. West Chester, PA: Schiffer, 1991.

Burleigh, Michael. "A Political Economy of the Final Solution? Reflections on Modernity, Historians and the Holocaust." *Patterns of Prejudice* 30, no. 2 (1996): 29-41.

——. "Between Enthusiasm, Compliance and Protest: The Churches, Eugenics and the Nazi 'Euthanasia' Programme." *Contemporary European History* 3, no. 3 (1994): 253–63.

———. *Death and Deliverance: "Euthanasia" in Germany, c. 1900-1945.* Cambridge: Cambridge University Press, 1994.

———. "Nazis and 'Euthanasia.'" *Modern History Review* 6, no. 1 (1994): 31–33.

———. "Racism as Social Policy: The Nazi 'Euthanasia' Programme, 1939–45." *Ethnic and Racial Studies* 14, no. 4 (1991): 453–73.

———. *Germany Turns Eastwards: A Study of "Ostforschung" in the Third Reich.* Cambridge: Cambridge University Press, 1988.

Burleigh, Michael, and Wolfgang Wippermann. *The Racial State: Germany, 1933-1945.* Cambridge: Cambridge University Press, 1991.

Bussmann, Walter. "Kursk-Orel-Dnjepr: Erlebnisse und Erfahrungen im Stab des XXXXVI. Panzerkorps während des 'Unternehmens Zitadelle.'" *Vierteljahrshefte für Zeitgeschichte* 41, no. 4 (1993): 503–18.

Caplan, Jane, and Hannes Heer. "The Difficulty of Ending a War: Reactions to the Exhibition 'War of Extermination: Crimes of the Wehrmacht, 1941 to 1944.'" *History Workshop Journal,* no. 46 (1998): 187–203.

Chiari, Bernhard. "Zwischen Hoffnung und Hunger: Die sowjetische Zivilbevölkerung unter deutscher Besatzung." In *Verbrechen der Wehrmacht: Bilanz einer Debatte,* ed. Christian Hartmann, Johannes Hürter, and Ulrike Jureit, 145–54. Munich: Beck, 2005.

———. "Die Büchse der Pandora: Ein Dorf in Weißrußland, 1939 bis 1944." In *Die Wehrmacht: Mythos und Realität,* ed. Rolf-Dieter Müller and Hans-Erich Volkmann, 879–900. Munich: Oldenbourg, 1999.

———. *Alltag Hinter der Front: Besatzung, Kollaboration und Widerstand in Weissrussland, 1941-1944.* Dusseldorf: Droste, 1998.

———. "Mythos und Alltag: Voraussetzungen und Probleme eines west-östlichen Dialogs zur Historiographie des Zweiten Weltkriegs." *Militärgeschichtliche Mitteilungen* 54, no. 2 (1995): 535–63.

Chickering, Roger, Stig Förster, and Bernd Greiner, eds. *A World at Total War: Global Conflict and the Politics of Destruction, 1937-1945.* New York: Cambridge University Press, 2005.

Chorkov, Anatolij G. "Die sowjetische Gegenoffensive bei Stalingrad." In *Stalingrad: Ereignis–Wirkung–Symbol,* ed. Jürgen Förster, 55–74. Munich: Piper, 1992.

Chuikov, V. I. *The Battle for Stalingrad.* New York: Holt, Rinehart & Winston, 1964.

Churchill, Winston S. *The Grand Alliance.* Vol. 3 of *The Second World War.* Boston: Houghton Mifflin, 1950.

———. *The Hinge of Fate.* Vol. 4 of *The Second World War.* Boston: Houghton Mifflin, 1950.

Ciano, Galeazzo. *The Ciano Diaries, 1939-1943: The Complete, Unabridged Diaries of Count Galeazzo Ciano, Italian Minister for Foreign Affairs, 1936-1943.* New York: Doubleday, 1946.

Cimbala, Stephen J. "Intelligence, C3 and the Initial Period of War." *Journal of Soviet Military Studies* 4, no. 3 (1991): 397–447.

Citino, Robert M. *Death of the Wehrmacht: The German Campaigns of 1942.* Lawrence: University Press of Kansas, 2007.

Clausewitz, Carl von. *On War.* Translated by O. J. Matthijs Jolles. New York: Modern Library, 1943.

Connelly, Mark. "The British People, the Press and the Strategic Air Campaign against Germany, 1939–45." *Contemporary British History* 16, no. 2 (2002): 39–58.

Cooke, Ronald, and Roy Nesbit. *Target, Hitler's Oil: Allied Attacks on German Oil Supplies, 1939-1945.* London: Kimber, 1985.

Cooper, Matthew. *The German Army, 1933-1945.* Lanham, MD: Rowman & Littlefield, 1997.

Corni, Gustavo, and Horst Gies. *Brot, Butter, Kanonen: Die Ernährungswirtschaft in Deutschland unter der Diktatur Hitlers.* Berlin: Akademie, 1997.

Cüppers, Martin. *Wegbereiter der Shoah: Die Waffen-SS, der Kommandostab Reichsführer-SS und die Judenvernichtung, 1939-1945.* Darmstadt: Wissenschaftliche Buchgesellschaft, 2005.

Dallin, Alexander. "Hitler and Russia." *Canadian Slavonic Papers* 16, no. 3 (1974): 460-65.

——. *German Rule in Russia, 1941-1945: A Study of Occupation Policies.* London: Macmillan, 1957.

Davies, Norman. *Rising '44: The Battle for Warsaw.* New York: Viking, 2004.

Dawidowicz, Lucy, ed. *A Holocaust Reader.* West Orange, NJ: Behrman, 1976.

De Zayas, Alfred. *Die Wehrmacht-Untersuchungsstelle: Deutsche Ermittlungen über Allierte Völkerrechtsverletzungen im Zweiten Weltkrieg.* Munich: Universitas, 1980.

Deck, Josef. *Der Weg der 1000 Toten.* Karlsruhe: Badenia, 1978.

Deichmann, Hans, and Peter Hayes. "Standort Auschwitz: Eine Kontroverse über die Entscheidungsgründe für den Bau des I. G. Farben-Werks in Auschwitz." *1999: Zeitschrift für Sozialgeschichte des 20. und 21. Jahrhunderts* 11, no. 1 (1996): 79-101.

Deist, Wilhelm. "The Road to Ideological War: Germany, 1918–1945." In *The Making of Strategy: Rulers, States, and War,* ed. Williamson Murray, MacGregor Knox, and Alvin H. Bernstein, 352–92. Cambridge: Cambridge University Press, 1994.

——. "The Rearmament of the Wehrmacht." In *The Build-Up of German Aggression* (vol. 1 of *Germany and the Second World War*), ed. Wilhelm Deist, trans. P. S. Falla, Dean S. McMurry, and Ewald Osers, 373–540. Oxford: Clarendon, 1990.

Dieckmann, Christoph. "The War and the Killing of the Lithuanian Jews." In *National Socialist Extermination Policies: Contemporary German Perspectives and Controversies,* ed. Ulrich Herbert, 240–75. New York: Berghahn, 2000.

DiNardo, R. L. *Germany and the Axis Powers from Coalition to Collapse.* Lawrence: University Press of Kansas, 2005.

——. *Mechanized Juggernaut or Military Anachronism? Horses and the German Army of World War II.* Westport, CT: Greenwood, 1991.

Diner, Dan. "Rationalisierung und Methode: Zu einem neuen Erklärungsversuch der 'Endlösung.'" *Vierteljahrshefte für Zeitgeschichte* 40, no. 3 (1992): 359–82.

Doerr, Hans. *Der Feldzug nach Stalingrad: Versuch eines Operativen Überblick.* Darmstadt: E. S. Mittler, 1955.

Dollinger, Hans, ed. *Kain, wo ist dein Bruder? Was der Mensch im Zweiten Weltkrieg erleiden musste, Dokumentiert in Tagebüchern und Briefen.* Frankfurt: Fischer Taschenbuch, 1991.

Domarus, Max, ed. *Hitler: Reden und Proklamationen, 1932-1945.* 2 vols. Neustadt a.d. Aisch: Schmidt, 1963.

Domarus, Max, and Patrick Romane, eds. *The Essential Hitler: Speeches and Commentary.* Wauconda, IL: Bolchazy-Carducci, 2007.

Dunn, Walter S. *Soviet Blitzkrieg: The Battle for White Russia, 1944.* London: Lynne Rienner, 2000.

Ebert, Jens. *Feldpostbriefe aus Stalingrad.* Göttingen: Wallstein, 2003.

Echternkamp, Jörg. "At War, Abroad and at Home: The Essential Features of

German Society in the Second World War." In *German Wartime Society, 1939-1945: Politicization, Disintegration, and the Struggle for Survival* (vol. 9/1 of *Germany and the Second World War*), ed. Jörg Echternkamp, trans. Derry Cook-Radmore, 1-101. Oxford: Clarendon, 2008.

——, ed. *German Wartime Society, 1939-1945: Politicization, Disintegration, and the Struggle for Survival.* Translated by Derry Cook-Radmore. Vol. 9/1 of *Germany and the Second World War.* Oxford: Clarendon, 2008.

——. *Kriegsschauplatz Deutschland, 1945: Leben in Angst, Hoffnung auf Frieden: Feldpost aus der Heimat und von der Front.* Paderborn: Schöningh, 2006.

——, ed. *Die deutsche Kriegsgesellschaft, 1939 bis 1945: Politisierung, Vernichtung, Überleben.* Vol. 9/1 of *Das deutsche Reich und der Zweite Weltkrieg.* Munich: Deutsche Verlags-Anstalt, 2004.

——. "Wut auf die Wehrmacht? Vom Bild der deutschen Soldaten in der unmittelbaren Nachkriegszeit." In *Die Wehrmacht: Mythos und Realität,* ed. Rolf-Dieter Müller and Hans-Erich Volkmann, 1058-80. Munich: Oldenbourg, 1999.

Echternkamp, Jörg, and Ralf Blank, eds. *Die deutsche Kriegsgesellschaft, 1939 bis 1945: Ausbeutung, Deutungen, Ausgrenzung.* Vol. 9/2 of *Das deutsche Reich und der Zweite Weltkrieg.* Munich: Deutsche Verlags-Anstalt, 2005.

Ehmann, Annegret. "From Colonial Racism to Nazi Population Policy: The Role of the So-Called Mischlinge." In *The Holocaust in History: The Known, the Unknown, the Disputed, and the Reexamined,* ed. Michael Berenbaum and Abraham J. Peck, 115-33. Bloomington: Indiana University Press, 1998.

Ehrenreich, Eric. "Otmar von Verschuer and the 'Scientific' Legitimization of Nazi Anti-Jewish Policy." *Holocaust and Genocide Studies* 21, no. 1 (2007): 55-72.

——. *The Nazi Ancestral Proof: Genealogy, Racial Science, and the Final Solution.* Bloomington: Indiana University Press, 2007.

Eichholtz, Dietrich. *Krieg um Öl: Ein Erdölimperium als deutsches Kriegsziel, 1938-1943.* Leipzig: Leipziger Universitätsverlag, 2006.

——. "Der Krieg gegen die Sowjetunion als Wirtschaftsexpansion und Raubkrieg." In *Verbrechen der Wehrmacht: Bilanz einer Debatte,* ed. Christian Hartmann, Johannes Hürter, and Ulrike Jureit, 125-35. Munich: Beck, 2005.

——. "Der Anfang vom Ende: Die Fogen der Invasion für die deutsche Kriegführungsfähigkeit." In *Invasion 1944,* ed. Hans Umbreit, 95-115. Hamburg: E. S. Mittler, 1998.

Eikel, Markus. "'Weil die Menschen fehlen': Die deutschen Zwangsarbeitsrekrutierungen und -deportationen in den besetzten Gebieten der Ukraine, 1941-1944." *Vierteljahrshefte für Zeitgeschichte* 53, no. 5 (2005): 405-34.

Einsiedel, Heinrich Graf von. *The Onslaught: The German Drive to Stalingrad.* New York: Norton, 1985.

Engel, Gerhard. *Heeresadjutant bei Hitler, 1938-1943.* Edited by Hildegard von Kotze. Stuttgart: Deutsche Verlags-Anstalt, 1974.

Erickson, John. "Barbarossa June 1941: Who Attacked Whom?" *History Today* 51 (July 2001): 11-17.

——. "Soviet War Losses: Calculations and Controversies." In *Barbarossa: The Axis and the Allies,* ed. John Erickson and David Dilks, 255-77. Edinburgh: Edinburgh University Press, 1994.

——. "New Thinking about the Eastern Front in World War II." *Journal of Military History* 56, no. 2 (1992): 283-92.

——. "Stalin Revisited." *RUSI Journal* (Royal United Services Institute for Defence Studies) 136, no. 1 (1991): 69-72.

——. "Liberation, Soviet Style, 1944–45." *History Today* 34 (July 1984): 36–41.

——. *The Road to Berlin: Continuing the History of Stalin's War with Germany*. Boulder, CO: Westview, 1984.

——. *The Road to Stalingrad*. New York: Harper & Row, 1975.

——. "The Soviet Response to Surprise Attack: Three Directives, 22 June 1941." *Soviet Studies* 23, no. 4 (1972): 519–53.

Erickson, John, and David Dilks, eds. *Barbarossa: The Axis and the Allies*. Edinburgh: Edinburgh University Press, 1994.

Evans, Richard. *The Third Reich at War*. New York: Penguin, 2009.

Farrell, Brian P. "Yes, Prime Minister: Barbarossa, Whipcord, and the Basis of British Grand Strategy, Autumn 1941." *Journal of Military History* 57, no. 4 (1993): 599–625.

Fings, Karola. "Slaves for the 'Home Front': War Society and Concentration Camps." In *German Wartime Society, 1939-1945: Politicization, Disintegration, and the Struggle for Survival* (vol. 9/1 of *Germany and the Second World War*), ed. Jörg Echternkamp, trans. Derry Cook-Radmore, 207–85. Oxford: Clarendon, 2008.

Fischer, Johannes. "Über den Entschluss zur luftversorgung Stalingrads: Ein Beitrag zur militärischen Führung im Dritten Reich." *Militärgeschichtliche Mitteilungen* 2, no. 2 (1969): 7–68.

Fleischhauer, Ingeborg. *Die Chance des Sonderfriedens: Deutsch-sowjetische Geheimgespräche, 1941-1945*. Berlin: Siedler, 1986.

——. "'Unternehmen Barbarossa' und die Zwangsumsiedlung der Deutschen in der UdSSR." *Vierteljahrshefte für Zeitgeschichte* 30, no. 2 (1982): 299–321.

Fleming, Gerald. *Hitler and the Final Solution*. Berkeley and Los Angeles: University of California Press, 1984.

Foerster, Roland G., ed. *Seelower Höhen, 1945*. Hamburg: E. S. Mittler, 1998.

——, ed. *Gezeitenwechsel im Zweiten Weltkrieg? Die Schlachten von Char'kov und Kursk in operativer Anlage, Verlauf und politischer Bedeutung*. Hamburg: E. S. Mittler, 1996.

Förster, Jürgen. "Ideological Warfare in Germany, 1919-1945." In *German Wartime Society, 1939-1945: Politicization, Disintegration, and the Struggle for Survival* (vol. 9/1 of *Germany and the Second World War*), ed. Jörg Echternkamp, trans. Derry Cook-Radmore, 485–669. Oxford: Clarendon, 2008.

——. "Ludendorff and Hitler in Perspective: The Battle for the German Soldier's Mind, 1917-1944." *War in History* 10, no. 3 (2003): 321–34.

——. "Die Grosse Täuschung—der 'Fall Barbarossa' als Präventivschlag." *Tel Aviver Jahrbuch für deutsche Geschichte* 30 (2002): 466–70.

——. "Wehrmacht, Krieg und Holocaust." In *Die Wehrmacht: Mythos und Realität*, ed. Rolf-Dieter Müller and Hans-Erich Volkmann, 948–63. Munich: Oldenbourg, 1999.

——. "Hitler's Decision in Favour of War against the Soviet Union." In *The Attack on the Soviet Union* (vol. 4 of *Germany and the Second World War*), ed. Horst Boog et al., trans. Dean S. McMurrey, Ewald Osers, and Louise Willmot, 13–51. Oxford: Clarendon, 1998.

——. "Operation Barbarossa as a War of Conquest and Annihilation." In *The Attack on the Soviet Union* (vol. 4 of *Germany and the Second World War*), ed. Horst Boog et al., trans. Dean S. McMurrey, Ewald Osers, and Louise Willmot, 481–521. Oxford: Clarendon, 1998.

——. "Securing 'Living-Space.'" In *The Attack on the Soviet Union* (vol. 4 of *Germany and the Second World War*), ed. Horst Boog et al., trans. Dean S. McMurrey, Ewald Osers, and Louise Willmot, 1189–1244. Oxford: Clarendon, 1998.

——. "Hitler Turns East—German War Policy in 1940 and 1941." In *From Peace to War: Germany, Soviet Russia, and the World, 1939-1941,* ed. Bernd Wegner, 115-33. Providence, RI: Berghahn, 1997.

——. "The Russo-German Conflict as Part of the Second World War." *Contemporary European History* 6, no. 1 (1997): 145-48.

——. "Das Verhältnis von Wehrmacht und Nationalsozialismus im Entscheidungs-jahr 1933." *German Studies Review* 18, no. 3 (1995): 471-80.

——. "The Relation between Operation Barbarossa as an Ideological War of Exter-mination and the Final Solution." In *The Final Solution: Origins and Implementa-tion,* ed. David Cesarani, 137-47. London: Routledge, 1994.

——. "Das andere Gesicht des Krieges: Das 'Unternehmen Barbarossa' als Erober-ungs- und Vernichtungskrieg." In *"Unternehmen Barbarossa": Zum historischen Ort der deutsch-sowjetischen Beziehungen vom 1933 bis Herbst 1941,* ed. Roland G. Foers-ter, 151-62. Munich: Oldenbourg, 1993.

——. "Barbarossa Revisited: Strategy and Ideology in the East." *Jewish Social Studies, 1988* 50, nos. 1-2 (1992): 21-36.

——, ed. *Stalingrad: Ereignis—Wirkung—Symbol.* Munich: Piper, 1992.

——. "Der historische Ort ses Unternehmens Barbarossa." In *Der Zweite Weltkrieg: Analysen, Grundzüge, Forschungsbilanz,* ed. Wolfgang Michalka, 626-40. Munich: Piper, 1989.

——. "The Dynamics of Volksgemeinschaft: The Effectiveness of the German Mili-tary in the Second World War." In *Military Effectiveness* (3 vols.), ed. Allan R. Mil-lett and Williamson Murray, 3:180-220. London: Unwin Hyman, 1988.

——. "The German Army and the Ideological War against the Soviet Union." In *The Policies of Genocide: Jews and Soviet Prisoners of War in Nazi Germany,* ed. Gerhard Hirschfeld, 15-29. London: Allen & Unwin, 1986.

——. "The Wehrmacht and the War of Extermination against the Soviet Union." *Yad Vashem Studies* 14 (1981): 7-34.

——. "Hitler's War Aims against the Soviet Union and the German Military Lead-ers." *Militarhistorisk Tidskrift* 1 (1979): 83-93.

Förster, Jürgen, and Evan Mawdsley. "Hitler and Stalin in Perspective: Secret Speeches on the Eve of Barbarossa." *War in History* 11, no. 1 (2004): 61-103.

Frei, Norbert, Sybille Steinbacher, and Bernd Wegner, eds. *Ausbeutung, Vernichtung, Öffentlichkeit: Neue Studien zur nationalsozialistischen Lagerpolitik.* Munich: K. G. Saur, 2000.

Friedlander, Henry. *The Origins of Nazi Genocide: From Euthanasia to the Final Solution.* Chapel Hill: University of North Carolina Press, 1995.

——. "The Deportation of the German Jews—Post-War German Trials of Nazi War Criminals." *Leo Baeck Institute Year Book* 29 (1984): 201-28.

——. "Step by Step: The Expansion of Murder, 1939-1941." *German Studies Review* 17, no. 3 (1994): 495-507.

Friedlander, Henry, and Sybil Milton, eds. *Archives of the Holocaust: An International Collection of Selected Documents.* 22 vols. New York: Garland, 1989.

——, eds. *The Holocaust: Ideology, Bureaucracy, and Genocide: The San Jose Papers.* New York: Kraus, 1981.

Friedländer, Saul. *Nazi Germany and the Jews.* Vol. 1, *The Years of Persecution, 1933-1939.* Vol. 2, *The Years of Extermination, 1939-1945.* New York: Harper Collins, 1997-2007.

Friedrich, Jörg. *The Fire: The Bombing of Germany, 1940-1945.* Translated by Allison Brown. New York: Columbia University Press, 2006.

Frieser, Karl-Heinz, ed. *Die Ostfront, 1943/44: Der Krieg im Osten und an den Neben-fronten.* Vol. 8 of *Das deutsche Reich und der Zweite Weltkrieg.* Munich: Deutsche Verlags-Anstalt, 2007.

———. "Die Schlacht im Kursker Bogen." In *Die Ostfront, 1943/44: Der Krieg im Osten und an den Nebenfronten* (vol. 8 of *Das deutsche Reich und der Zweite Weltkrieg*), ed. Karl-Heinz Frieser, 83–208. Munich: Deutsche Verlags-Anstalt, 2007.

———. "Der Rückschlag des Pendels: Das Zurückweichen der Ostfront von Sommer 1943 bis Sommer 1944." In *Die Ostfront, 1943/44: Der Krieg im Osten und an den Nebenfronten* (vol. 8 of *Das deutsche Reich und der Zweite Weltkrieg*), ed. Karl-Heinz Frieser, 177–450. Munich: Deutsche Verlags-Anstalt, 2007.

———. "Der Zusammenbruch im Osten: Die Rückzugskämpfe seit Sommer 1944." In *Die Ostfront, 1943/44: Der Krieg im Osten und an den Nebenfronten* (vol. 8 of *Das deutsche Reich und der Zweite Weltkrieg*), ed. Karl-Heinz Frieser, 493–678. Munich: Deutsche Verlags-Anstalt, 2007.

———. *The Blitzkrieg Legend: The 1940 Campaign in the West.* Translated by John T. Greenwood. Annapolis, MD: Naval Institute Press, 2005.

———. "Die deutschen Blitzkriege: Operativer Triumph—strategische Tragödie." In *Die Wehrmacht: Mythos und Realität*, ed. Rolf-Dieter Müller and Hans-Erich Volk-mann, 182–96. Munich: Oldenbourg, 1999.

———. "Die Schlacht um die Seelower Höhen im April 1945." In *Seelower Höhen, 1945*, ed. Roland G. Foerster, 128–43. Hamburg: E. S. Mittler, 1998.

———. "Schlagen aus der Nachhand—Schlagen aus der Vorhand: Die Schlachten von Charkow und Kursk 1943." In *Gezeitenwechsel im Zweiten Weltkrieg? Die Schlachten von Char'kov und Kursk im Frühjahr und Sommer 1943 in operativer Anlage, Verlauf und politischer Bedeutung*, ed. Roland G. Foerster, 101–35. Hamburg: E. S. Mit-tler, 1996.

Fritz, Stephen G. *Endkampf: Soldiers, Civilians, and the Death of the Third Reich.* Lex-ington: University Press of Kentucky, 2004.

———. "'This is the way wars end, with a bang not a whimper': Middle Franconia in April 1945." *War and Society* 18, no. 2 (2000): 121–53.

———. "'We are trying . . . to change the face of the world': Ideology and Motivation in the Wehrmacht on the Eastern Front: The View from Below." *Journal of Mili-tary History* 60, no. 4 (1996): 683–710.

———. *Frontsoldaten: The German Soldier in World War II.* Lexington: University Press of Kentucky, 1995.

———. "Reflections on Antecedents of the Holocaust." *History Teacher* 23, no. 2 (1990): 161–79.

Fritzsche, Peter. *Life and Death in the Third Reich.* Cambridge, MA: Belknap Press of Harvard University Press, 2008.

———. *Germans into Nazis.* Cambridge, MA: Harvard University Press, 1999.

Fröhlich, Elke, ed. *Die Tagebücher von Joseph Goebbels: Sämtliche Fragmente.* 15 vols. Munich: K. G. Saur, 1987.

———. "Simmung und Verhalten der Bevölkerung unter den Bedingungen des Krieges." In *Bayern in der NS-Zeit* (6 vols.), ed. Martin Broszat, Elke Fröhlich, and Falk Wiesemann, 1, pt. 7:571–689. Munich: Oldenbourg, 1977.

Fuchs, Helmut. *Wer spricht von Siegen: Der Bericht über unfreiwillige Jahre in Rußland.* Munich: Knaus, 1987.

Fugate, Bryan I. *Operation Barbarossa: Strategy and Tactics on the Eastern Front.* Novato, CA: Presidio, 1984.

Fulbrook, Mary. "Hitler's Willing Robbers: The Deadly Sin of Greed, and Guilt by Extension." *Neue politische Literatur* 50, no. 2 (2005): 203–10.

Gassert, Philipp. *Amerika im Dritten Reich: Ideologie, Propaganda und Volksmeinung, 1933-1945.* Stuttgart: F. Steiner, 1997.

Gerlach, Christian. "Die Verantwortung der Wehrmachtführung: Vergleichende Betrachtungen am Beispiel der sowjetische Kriegsgefangenen." In *Verbrechen der Wehrmacht: Bilanz einer Debatte,* ed. Christian Hartmann, Johannes Hürter, and Ulrike Jureit, 40–49. Munich: Beck, 2005.

——. "Network of Terror: The Nazi Concentration Camps." *Yad Vashem Studies* 29 (2001): 423–32.

——. "German Economic Interests, Occupation Policy, and the Murder of the Jews in Belorussia, 1941–1943." In *National Socialist Extermination Policies: Contemporary German Perspectives and Controversies,* ed. Ulrich Herbert, 210–39. New York: Berghahn, 2000.

——. *Kalkulierte Morde: Die deutsche Wirtschafts- und Vernichtungspolitik in Weissrussland, 1941 bis 1944.* Hamburg: Hamburger Edition, 1999.

——. "Verbrechen deutscher Fronttruppen in Weißrußland, 1941–1944: Eine Annäherung." In *Wehrmacht und Vernichtungspolitik: Militär im nationalsozialistischen System,* ed. Karl Heinrich Pohl, 89–114. Göttingen: Vandenhoeck & Ruprecht, 1999.

——. *Krieg, Ernährung, Völkermord: Forschungen zur deutschen Vernichtungspolitik im Zweiten Weltkrieg.* Hamburg: Hamburger Edition, 1998.

——. "The Wannsee Conference, the Fate of German Jews, and Hitler's Decision in Principle to Exterminate All European Jews." *Journal of Modern History* 70, no. 4 (1998): 759–812.

——. "Failure of Plans for an SS Extermination Camp in Mogilev, Belorussia." *Holocaust and Genocide Studies* 11, no. 1 (1997): 60–78.

——. "Die Wannsee-Konferenz, das Schicksal der deutschen Juden und Hitlers politische Grundsatzentscheidung, alle Juden Europas zu Ermorden." *Werkstatt-Geschichte,* no. 18 (1997): 7–44.

Gerwarth, Robert. "The Central European Counter-Revolution: Paramilitary Violence in Germany, Austria and Hungary after the Great War." *Past and Present* 200, no. 1 (2008): 175–209.

Gerwarth, Robert, and Stephan Malinowski. "Hannah Arendt's Ghosts: Reflections on the Disputable Path from Windhoek to Auschwitz." *Central European History* 42, no. 2 (2009): 279–300.

——. "Der Holocaust als 'kolonialer Genozid?' Europäische Kolonialgewalt und nationalsozialistischer Vernichtungskrieg." *Geschichte und Gesellschaft* 33, no. 3 (2007): 439–66.

Geyer, Michael. "Endkampf, 1918 and 1945: German Nationalism, Annihilation, and Self-Destruction." In *No Man's Land of Violence: Extreme Wars in the Twentieth Century,* ed. Alf Lüdtke and Bernd Weisbrod, 37–67. Göttingen: Wallstein, 2006.

——. "German Strategy in the Age of Machine Warfare, 1914–1945." In *Makers of Modern Strategy,* ed. Peter Paret, 527–97. Princeton, NJ: Princeton University Press, 1986.

Gibbons, Robert. "Opposition gegen 'Barbarossa' im Herbst 1940: Eine Denkschrift aus der deutschen Botschaft in Moskau." *Vierteljahrshefte für Zeitgeschichte* 23, no. 3 (1975): 332–40.

Glantz, David M. *To the Gates of Stalingrad: Soviet-German Combat Operations, April-August 1942.* Lawrence: University Press of Kansas, 2009.

——. "The Struggle for Stalingrad City: Opposing Orders of Battle, Combat Orders and Reports, and Operational Maps: Pt. 1, The Fight for Stalingrad's Suburbs, Center City, and Factory Villages, 3 September–13 October 1942." *Journal of Slavic Military Studies* 21, no. 1 (2008): 146–238.

——. "The Struggle for Stalingrad City: Opposing Orders of Battle, Combat Orders and Reports, and Operational and Tactical Maps: Pt. 2, The Fight for Stalingrad's Factory District, 14 October–18 November 1942." *Journal of Slavic Military Studies* 21, no. 2 (2008): 377–471.

——. "Prelude to German Operation Blau: Military Operations on Germany's Eastern Front, April–June 1942." *Journal of Slavic Military Studies* 20, no. 2 (2007): 171–234.

——. "The Red Army's Lublin-Brest Offensive and Advance on Warsaw (18 July–30 September 1944): An Overview and Documentary Survey." *Journal of Slavic Military Studies* 19, no. 2 (2006): 401–41.

——. *Colossus Reborn: The Red Army at War, 1941–1943.* Lawrence: University Press of Kansas, 2005.

——. "The Red Army's Donbas Offensive (February–March 1943) Revisited: A Documentary Essay." *Journal of Slavic Military Studies* 18, no. 3 (2005): 369–503.

——. *The Battle for Leningrad, 1941–1944.* Lawrence: University Press of Kansas, 2002.

——. *Barbarossa: Hitler's Invasion of Russia.* Stroud: Tempus, 2001.

——. "Forgotten Battles of the German-Soviet War (1941–1945): Pt. 7, The Summer Campaign (12 May–18 November 1942): Voronezh, July 1942." *Journal of Slavic Military Studies* 14, no. 3 (2001): 150–220.

——. "Forgotten Battles of the German-Soviet War (1941–45): Pt. 6, The Winter Campaign (5 December 1941–April 1942): The Crimean Counteroffensive and Reflections." *Journal of Slavic Military Studies* 14, no. 1 (2001): 121–70.

——. "Forgotten Battles of the German-Soviet War (1941–45): Pt. 3, The Winter Campaign (5 December 1941–April 1942): The Moscow Counteroffensive." *Journal of Slavic Military Studies* 13, no. 2 (2000): 139–85.

——. "Forgotten Battles of the German-Soviet War (1941–45): Pt. 4, The Winter Campaign (5 December 1941–April 1942): The Demiansk Counteroffensive." *Journal of Slavic Military Studies* 13, no. 3 (2000): 145–64.

——. "Forgotten Battles of the German-Soviet War (1941–45): Pt. 5, The Winter Campaign (5 December 1941–April 1942): The Leningrad Counteroffensive." *Journal of Slavic Military Studies* 13, no. 4 (2000): 127–92.

——. "Forgotten Battles of the German-Soviet War (1941–45): Pt. 1." *Journal of Slavic Military Studies* 12, no. 4 (1999): 149–97.

——. *Zhukov's Greatest Defeat: The Red Army's Epic Disaster in Operation Mars, 1942.* Lawrence: University Press of Kansas, 1999.

——. *Stumbling Colossus: The Red Army on the Eve of World War.* Lawrence: University Press of Kansas, 1998.

——. "Counterpoint to Stalingrad, Operation 'Mars' (November–December 1942): Marshal Zhukov's Greatest Defeat." *Journal of Slavic Military Studies* 10, no. 4 (1997): 104–55.

——. "Soviet Military Strategy during the Second Period of War (November 1942–December 1943): A Reappraisal." *Journal of Military History* 60, no. 1 (1996): 115–50.

——. "The Failures of Historiography: Forgotten Battles of the German-Soviet War (1941–1945)." *Journal of Slavic Military Studies* 8, no. 4 (1995): 768–808.

——. "Prelude to Kursk: Soviet Strategic Operations, February–March 1943." *Journal of Slavic Military Studies* 8, no. 1 (1995): 1–35.

——. "Soviet Operational Intelligence in the Kursk Operation, July 1943." *Intelligence and National Security* 5, no. 1 (1990): 5–49.

——. *Soviet Military Deception in the Second World War.* London: Frank Cass, 1989.

Glantz, David M., and Jonathan M. House. *The Battle of Kursk.* Lawrence: University Press of Kansas, 1999.

——. *When Titans Clashed: How the Red Army Stopped Hitler.* Lawrence: University Press of Kansas, 1995.

Glantz, David M., and Harold S. Orenstein, eds. *Belorussia 1944: The Soviet General Staff Study.* Translated by David M. Glantz and Harold S. Orenstein. London: Frank Cass, 2001.

——. "Combat Operations of Briansk and Voronezh Front Forces in Summer 1942 on the Voronezh Axis." *Journal of Slavic Military Studies* 6, no. 2 (1993): 300–340.

Goda, Norman J. W. "Black Marks: Hitler's Bribery of His Senior Officers during World War II." *Journal of Modern History* 72, no. 2 (2000): 413–52.

——. "Franco's Bid for Empire: Spain, Germany, and the Western Mediterranean in World War II." *Mediterranean Historical Review* 13, nos. 1–2 (1998): 168–94.

——. *Tomorrow the World: Hitler, Northwest Africa, and the Path toward America.* College Station: Texas A&M University Press, 1998.

——. "The Riddle of the Rock: A Reassessment of German Motives for the Capture of Gibraltar in the Second World War." *Journal of Contemporary History* 28, no. 2 (1993): 297–314.

Goebbels, Joseph. "Wofur?" *Das Reich,* 31 May 1942.

——. "Führen wir einen totalen krieg?" *Das Reich,* 2 July 1944.

Goldhagen, Daniel Jonah. *Hitler's Willing Executioners: Ordinary Germans and the Holocaust.* New York: Knopf, 1996.

Golovchansky, Anatoly, ed. *"Ich will raus aus diesem wahnsinn": Deutsche Briefe von der Ostfront, 1941-1945: Aus sowjetischen Archiven.* Wuppertal: P. Hammer, 1991.

Görlitz, Walter, ed. *Generalfeldmarschall Keitel: Verbrecher oder Offizier? Erinnerungen, Briefe, Dokumente des Chefs OKW.* Göttingen: Musterschmidt, 1961.

Gorodetsky, Gabriel. *Grand Delusion: Stalin and the German Invasion of Russia.* New Haven, CT: Yale University Press, 1999.

——. "Stalin and Hitler's Attack on the Soviet Union." In *From Peace to War: Germany, Soviet Russia, and the World, 1939-1941,* ed. Bernd Wegner, 343–59. Providence, RI: Berghahn, 1997.

——. "Russian 'Appeasement' of Germany: Spring 1941." *Tel Aviver Jahrbuch für deutsche Geschichte* 24 (1995): 257–82.

——. "The Impact of the Ribbentrop-Molotov Pact on the Course of Soviet Foreign Policy." *Cahiers du monde russe et sovietique* 31, no. 1 (1990): 27–41.

——. "Stalin und Hitlers Angriff auf die Sowjetunion: Eine Auseinandersetzung mit der Legende vom deutschen Präventivschlag." *Vierteljahrshefte für Zeitgeschichte* 37, no. 4 (1989): 645–72.

——. "Churchill's Warning to Stalin: A Reappraisal." *Historical Journal* 29, no. 4 (1986): 979–90.

——. "The Hess Affair and Anglo-Soviet Relations on the Eve of 'Barbarossa.'" *English Historical Review* 101, no. 399 (1986): 405–20.

——. "Was Stalin Planning to Attack Hitler in June 1941?" *RUSI Journal* (Royal United Services Institute for Defence Studies) 131, no. 2 (1986): 69–72.

——. *Stafford Cripps' Mission to Moscow, 1940-42*. New York: Cambridge University Press, 1985.

Goshen, Seev. "Eichmann und die Nisko-Aktion im Oktober 1939: Eine Fallstudie zur NS-Judenpolitik in der letzten Epoche vor der 'Endlösung.'" *Vierteljahrshefte für Zeitgeschichte* 29, no. 1 (1981): 74-96.

Graml, Hermann. *Reichskristallnacht: Antisemitismus und Judenverfolgung im Dritten Reich*. Munich: Deutscher Taschenbuch, 1988.

Grier, Howard D. *Hitler, Dönitz, and the Baltic Sea: The Third Reich's Last Hope, 1944-1945*. Annapolis, MD: Naval Institute Press, 2007.

Groehler, Olaf. "Ziele und Vernunft: Hitler und die deutschen Militärs." *Soviet and Post-Soviet Review* 18, nos. 1-3 (1991): 59-77.

Groscurth, Helmut. *Tagebücher eines Abwehroffiziers, 1938-1940*. Edited by Helmut Krausnick and Harold C. Deutsch. Stuttgart: Deutsche Verlags-Anstalt, 1970.

Grossmann, Atina. "A Question of Silence: The Rape of German Women by Occupation Soldiers." *October* 72 (1995): 43-63.

Gruchmann, Lothar. "Die 'verpassten strategischen Chancen' der Achsenmächte im Mittelmeerraum, 1940/41." *Vierteljahrshefte für Zeitgeschichte* 18, no. 4 (1970): 456-75.

Grupe, Friedrich. *Jahrgang 1916: Die Fahne war Mehr als der Tod*. Munich: Universitas, 1989.

Guderian, Heinz. *Panzer Leader*. Translated by Constantine Fitzgibbon. New York: Dutton, 1952.

Haape, Heinrich. *Moscow Tram Stop: A Doctor's Experiences with the German Spearhead in Russia*. London: Collins, 1957.

Haar, Ingo. *Historiker im Nationalsozialismus: Deutsche Geschichtswissenschaft und der "Volkstumkampf" im Osten*. Göttingen: Vandenhoeck & Ruprecht, 2002.

Haase, Norbert. "Justizterror in der Wehrmacht am Ende des Zweiten Weltkrieges." In *Terror nach Innen: Verbrechen am Ende des Zweiten Weltkrieges*, ed. Cord Arendes, Edgar Wolfrum, and Jörg Zedler, 80-100. Göttingen: Wallstein, 2006.

Haberer, Erich. "Die Einsatzgruppen in der besetzten Sowjetunion, 1941/42: Die Tätigkeits- und Lageberichte des Chefs der Sicherheitspolizei und des SD." *Shofar: An Interdisciplinary Journal of Jewish Studies* 19, no. 4 (2001): 149-51.

Haffner, Sebastian. *Von Bismarck zu Hitler: Ein Rückblick*. Munich: Kindler, 1987.

Halder, Franz. *The Halder War Diary, 1939-1942*. Edited and translated by Charles Burdick and Hans Adolf Jacobsen. Novato, CA: Presidio, 1988.

Hamburger Institut für Sozialforschung, ed. *Verbrechen der Wehrmacht: Dimensionen des Vernichtungskrieges, 1941-1944: Ausstellungskatalog*. Hamburg: Hamburger Institut für Sozialforschung, 2002.

Hammer, Ingrid, and Susanne zur Nieden, eds. *Sehr selten habe ich geweint: Briefe und Tagebücher aus dem Zweiten Weltkrieg von Menschen aus Berlin*. Zurich: Schweizer, 1992.

Hammermann, Gabriele. "Die Todesmärsche aus den Konzentrationslagern, 1944/1945." In *Terror nach Innen: Verbrechen am Ende des Zweiten Weltkrieges*, ed. Cord Arendes, Edgar Wolfrum, and Jörg Zedler, 122-48. Göttingen: Wallstein, 2006.

Hancock, Eleanor. "Employment in Wartime: The Experience of German Women during the Second World War." *War and Society* 12, no. 2 (October 1994): 43-68.

——. *The National Socialist Leadership and Total War, 1941-5*. New York: St. Martin's, 1991.

Hansen, Randall. *Fire and Fury: The Allied Bombing of Germany, 1942-1945*. New York: New American Library, 2008.

Hansmann, Claus. *Vorüber, nicht vorbei: Russische Impressionen, 1941-1943*. Frankfurt: Ullstein, 1989.

Harrison, Mark. "The USSR and Total War: Why Didn't the Soviet Economy Collapse in 1942?" In *A World at Total War: Global Conflict and the Politics of Destruction, 1937-1945*, ed. Roger Chickering and Stig Förster, 137-56. Cambridge: Cambridge University Press, 2005.

————. *Soviet Planning in Peace and War*. Cambridge: Cambridge University Press, 2002.

————, ed. *The Economics of World War II: Six Great Powers in International Comparison*. New York: Cambridge University Press, 1998.

————. "The Economics of World War II: An Overview." In *The Economics of World War II: Six Great Powers in International Comparison*, ed. Mark Harrison, 1-42. New York: Cambridge University Press, 1998.

————. "'Barbarossa': The Soviet Response, 1941." In *From Peace to War: Germany, Soviet Russia, and the World, 1939-1941*, ed. Bernd Wegner, 431-48. Providence, RI: Berghahn, 1997.

————. "'Barbarossa': Die sowjetische Antwort, 1941." In *Zwei Wege nach Moskau: Vom Hitler-Stalin-Pakt zum "Unternehmen Barbarossa,"* ed. Bernd Wegner, 443-63. Munich: Piper, 1991.

————. "The Volume of Soviet Munitions Output, 1937-1945: A Reevaluation." *Journal of Economic History* 50, no. 3 (1990): 569-89.

————. "Resource Mobilization for World War II: The U.S.A., U.K., U.S.S.R. and Germany, 1938-1945." *Economic History Review* 41, no. 2 (1988): 171-92.

Hartmann, Christian. *Wehrmacht im Ostkrieg: Front und militärisches Hinterland, 1941-42*. Munich: Oldenbourg, 2009.

————. "Wie Verbrecherisch war die Wehrmacht? Zur Beteiligung von Wehrmachtsangehörigen an Kriegs- und NS-Verbrechen." In *Verbrechen der Wehrmacht: Bilanz einer Debatte*, ed. Christian Hartmann, Johannes Hürter, and Ulrike Jureit, 69-79. Munich: Beck, 2005.

————. "Verbrecherischer Krieg—verbrecherische Wehrmacht? Überlegungen zur Struktur des deutschen Ostheeres, 1941-1944." *Vierteljahrshefte für Zeitgeschichte* 52, no. 1 (2004): 1-75.

————. "Massensterben oder Massenvernichtung? Sowjetische Kriegsgefangene im 'Unternehmen Barbarossa': Aus dem Tagebuch eines deutschen Lagerkommandanten." *Vierteljahrshefte für Zeitgeschichte* 49, no. 1 (2001): 97-158.

————. *Halder: Generalstabschef Hitlers, 1938-1942*. Paderborn: Schöningh, 1991.

Hartmann, Christian, Johannes Hürter, and Ulrike Jureit, eds. *Verbrechen der Wehrmacht: Bilanz einer Debatte*. Munich: Beck, 2005.

Hartmann, Christian, Johannes Hürter, Dieter Pohl, and Andreas Toppe. "Wehrmacht in der nationalsozialistischen Diktatur: Ein Forschungsprojekt des Instituts für Zeitgeschichte Munchen." *Zeitgeschichte* 30, no. 4 (2003): 192-206.

Hastings, Max. *Armageddon: The Battle for Germany, 1944-45*. New York: Vintage, 2005.

Haupt, Werner. *Die Schlachten der Heeresgruppe Mitte, 1941-1944*. Dorheim: Podzun-Pallas, 1983.

Hayes, Peter. "Industrie und Ideologie: Die IG Farben in der Zeit des Nationalsozialismus." *Zeitschrift für Unternehmensgeschichte* 32, no. 2 (1987): 124-36.

——. *Industry and Ideology: IG Farben in the Nazi Era.* Cambridge: Cambridge University Press, 1987.

Hayward, Joel. "Too Little, Too Late: An Analysis of Hitler's Failure in August 1942 to Damage Soviet Oil Production." *Journal of Military History* 64, no. 3 (2000): 769-94.

——. "A Case Study in Early Joint Warfare: An Analysis of the Wehrmacht's Crimean Campaign of 1942." *Journal of Strategic Studies* 22, no. 4 (1999): 103-30.

——. *Stopped at Stalingrad: The Luftwaffe and Hitler's Defeat in the East, 1942-1943.* Lawrence: University Press of Kansas, 1998.

——. "The German Use of Air Power at Kharkov, May 1942." *Air Power History* 44, no. 2 (1997): 18-29.

——. "Von Richthofen's 'Giant Fire-Magic': The 'Luftwaffe's' Contribution to the Battle of Kerch, 1942." *Journal of Slavic Military Studies* 10, no. 2 (1997): 97-124.

——. "Hitler's Quest for Oil: The Impact of Economic Considerations on Military Strategy, 1941-42." *Journal of Strategic Studies* 18, no. 4 (1995): 94-135.

Heer, Hannes. "Vom Verschwinden der Täter: Die Auseinandersetzungen um die Ausstellung 'Vernichtungskrieg: Verbrechen der Wehrmacht 1941 bis 1944.'" *Zeitschrift für Geschichtswissenschaft* 50, no. 10 (2002): 869-98.

——. "Ein Übung in den Holocaust: Lemberg, Juni/Juli 1941." *Zeitschrift für Geschichtswissenschaft* 49, no. 5 (2001): 409-27.

——. "Am Anfang haben wir es aus Überzeugung, später dann aus Pflicht getan." *BIOS* 11, no. 1 (1998): 42-68.

——. "Killing Fields: The Wehrmacht and the Holocaust in Belorussia, 1941-1942." *Holocaust and Genocide Studies* 11, no. 1 (1997): 79-101.

Heer, Hannes, and Klaus Naumann, eds. *War of Extermination: The German Military in World War II, 1941-1944.* New York: Berghahn, 1999.

——. *Vernichtungskrieg: Verbrechen der Wehrmacht, 1941-1944.* Hamburg: Hamburger Edition, 1995.

Heiber, Helmut. "Der Generalplan Ost: Dokumentation." *Vierteljahrshefte für Zeitgeschichte* 6, no. 3 (1958): 280-326.

Heiber, Helmut, and David M. Glantz. *Hitler and His Generals: Military Conferences, 1942-1945: The First Complete Stenographic Record of the Military Situation Conferences, from Stalingrad to Berlin.* New York: Enigma, 2003.

Heim, Susanne, and Götz Aly. "The Holocaust and Population Policy: Remarks on the Decision on the 'Final Solution.'" *Yad Vashem Studies* 24 (1994): 45-70.

Heinemann, Isabel. *"Rasse, Siedlung, deutsches Blut": Das Rasse- und Siedlungshauptamt der SS und die rassenpolitische Neuordnung Europas.* Göttingen: Wallstein, 2003.

——. "'Another Type of Perpetrator': The SS Racial Experts and Forced Population Movements in the Occupied Regions." *Holocaust and Genocide Studies* 15, no. 3 (2001): 387-411.

Henderson, Nicholas. "'Hitler's Biggest Blunder.'" *History Today* 43 (April 1993): 35-44.

Herbert, Ulrich. "Extermination Policy: New Answers and Questions about the History of the 'Holocaust' in German Historiography." In *National Socialist Extermination Policies: Contemporary German Perspectives and Controversies,* ed. Ulrich Herbert, 1-52. New York: Berghahn, 2000.

——, ed. *National Socialist Extermination Policies: Contemporary German Perspectives and Controversies.* New York: Berghahn, 2000.

——. *Fremdarbeiter: Politik und Praxis des "Ausländer-Einsatzes" in der Kriegswirtschaft des Dritten Reiches*. Bonn: J. H. W. Dietz, 1999.

——. *Nationalsozialistische Vernichtungspolitik, 1939-1945: Neue Forschungen und Kontroversen*. Frankfurt: Fischer Taschenbuch, 1998.

——. *Hitler's Foreign Workers: Enforced Foreign Labor in Germany under the Third Reich*. Translated by William Templer. New York: Cambridge University Press, 1997.

——. *Best: Biographische Studien über Radikalismus, Weltanschauung und Vernunft, 1903-1989*. Bonn: J. H. W. Dietz, 1996.

——. "Immigration, Integration, Foreignness: Foreign Workers in Germany since the Turn of the Century." *International Labor and Working-Class History*, no. 48 (1995): 91-93.

——. "Zwischen Beschaulichkeit und Massenmord: Die Kriegswende 1943 aus der Perspektive des Alltags." *Neue politische Literatur* 40, no. 2 (1995): 185-89.

——. "Racism and Rational Calculation: The Role of 'Utilitarian' Strategies of Legitimation in the National Socialist 'Weltanschauung.'" *Yad Vashem Studies* 24 (1994): 131-45.

——. "Labour and Extermination: Economic Interest and the Primacy of Weltanschauung in National Socialism." *Past and Present*, no. 138 (1993): 144-95.

——, ed. *Europa und der "Reichseinsatz": Ausländische Zivilarbeiter, Kriegsgefangene und KZ-Häftlinge in Deutschland, 1938-1945*. Essen: Klartext, 1991.

——. "Zwangsarbeit in Deutschland: Sowjetische Zivilarbeiter und Kriegsgefangene, 1941-1945." In *Erobern und Vernichten: Der Krieg gegen die Sowjetunion, 1941-1945*, ed. Peter Jahn and Reinhard Rürup, 106-30. Berlin: Argon, 1991.

——. *A History of Foreign Labor in Germany, 1880-1980: Seasonal Workers/Forced Laborers/Guest Workers*. Translated by William Templer. Ann Arbor: University of Michigan Press, 1990.

——. "Arbeiterschaft im 'Dritten Reich': Zwischenbilanz und offene Fragen." *Geschichte und Gesellschaft* 15, no. 3 (1989): 320-60.

——. "Good Times, Bad Times." *History Today* 36 (February 1986): 42-48.

Herbert, Ulrich, and Bill Templer. "Forced Laborers in the Third Reich: An Overview." *International Labor and Working-Class History*, no. 58 (2000): 192-218.

Herf, Jeffrey. *The Jewish Enemy: Nazi Propaganda during World War II and the Holocaust*. Cambridge, MA: Belknap Press of Harvard University Press, 2006.

——. "The 'Jewish War': Goebbels and the Antisemitic Campaigns of the Nazi Propaganda Ministry." *Holocaust and Genocide Studies* 19, no. 1 (2005): 51-80.

——. "The Nazi Extermination Camps and the Ally to the East: Could the Red Army and Air Force Have Stopped or Slowed the Final Solution?" *Kritika: Explorations in Russian and Eurasian History* 4, no. 4 (2003): 913-30.

Herman, John. "Soviet Peace Efforts on the Eve of World War Two: A Review of the Soviet Documents." *Journal of Contemporary History* 15, no. 3 (1980): 577-602.

Heusler, Andreas. "Die Eskalation des Terrors: Gewalt gegen ausländische Zwangsarbeiter in der Endphase des Zweiten Weltkrieges." In *Terror nach Innen: Verbrechen am Ende des Zweiten Weltkrieges*, ed. Cord Arendes, Edgar Wolfrum, and Jörg Zedler, 172-82. Göttingen: Wallstein, 2006.

Hilberg, Raul. *The Destruction of the European Jews*. 3 vols. 3rd ed. New Haven, CT: Yale University Press, 2003.

Hildebrand, Klaus. "Dimension des Völkermords: Zu einer Neuerscheinung des Instituts für Zeitgeschichte." *Geschichte in Wissenschaft und Unterricht* 42, no. 11 (1991): 710-13.

——. "Hitler's War Aims." *Journal of Modern History* 48, no. 3 (1976): 522-30.

Hillgruber, Andreas. "The German Military Leaders' View of Russia Prior to the Attack on the Soviet Union." In *From Peace to War: Germany, Soviet Russia, and the World, 1939-1941,* ed. Bernd Wegner, 169-85. Providence, RI: Berghahn, 1997.

——. "Das Rußland-Bild der führenden deutschen Militärs vor Beginn des Angriffs auf die Sowjetunion." In *Zwei Wege nach Moskau: Vom Hitler-Stalin-Pakt zum "Unternehmen Barbarossa,"* ed. Bernd Wegner, 167-84. Munich: Piper, 1991.

——. "War in the East and the Extermination of the Jews." In *The "Final Solution": Historical Articles on the Destruction of the European Jews* (9 vols.), ed. Michael R. Marrus, 1, pt. 3:85-114. Westport, CT: Meckler, 1989.

——. "The Extermination of the European Jews in Its Historical Context—a Recapitulation." *Yad Vashem Studies* 17 (1986): 1-15.

——. "Der Ostkrieg und die Judenvernichtung." In *"Unternehmen Barbarossa": Der deutsche Überfall auf die Sowjetunion, 1941; Berichte, Analysen, Dokumente,* ed. Gerd R. Ueberschär and Wolfram Wette, 219-36. Paderborn: Schöningh, 1984.

——. "Noch Einmal: Hitlers Wendung gegen die Sowjetunion 1940." *Geschichte in Wissenschaft und Unterricht* 33, no. 4 (1982): 214-26.

——. "Der Hitler-Stalin-Pakt und die Entfesselung des Zweiten Weltkrieges: Situationsanalyse und Machtkalkül der Beiden Paktpartner." *Historische Zeitschrift* 230, no. 2 (1980): 339-61.

——. "Die ideologisch-dogmatische Grundlage der nationalsozialistischen Politik der Ausrottung der Juden in den besetzten Gebieten der Sowjetunion und ihre Durchfuhrung, 1941-1944." *German Studies Review* 2, no. 3 (1979): 263-96.

——. "England in Hitlers aussenpolitischer Konzeption." *Historische Zeitschrift* 218, no. 1 (1974): 65-84.

——. "England's Place in Hitler's Plans for World Domination." *Journal of Contemporary History* 9, no. 1 (1974): 5-22.

——. "Grundzüge der nationalsozialistischen Aussenpolitik, 1933-45." *Saeculum* 24, no. 4 (1973): 328-45.

——. "Die 'Endlösung' und das deutsche Ostimperium als Kernstück des rassenideologischen Programms des Nationalsozialismus." *Vierteljahrshefte für Zeitgeschichte* 20, no. 2 (1972): 133-53.

——. "Japan und der Fall 'Barbarossa.'" *Wehrwissenschaftliche Rundschau* 18, no. 6 (1968): 312-36.

——. *Staatsmänner und Diplomaten bei Hitler: Vertrauliche Aufzeichnungen über Unterredungen mit Vertretern des Auslandes.* Vol. 1. Frankfurt: Bernard & Graefe, 1967-1970.

Hinsley, H. F. "British Intelligence and Barbarossa." In *Barbarossa: The Axis and the Allies,* ed. John Erickson and David Dilks, 43-75. Edinburgh: Edinburgh University Press, 1994.

Hirschfeld, Gerhard, and Tobias Jersak. *Karrieren im Nationalsozialismus: Funktionseliten zwischen Mitwirkung und Distanz.* Frankfurt: Campus, 2004.

Hitler, Adolf. *Mein Kampf.* Translated by Ralph Mannheim. Boston: Houghton Mifflin, 1971.

——. *Hitler's Secret Conversations, 1941-1944.* Translated by Norman Cameron and R. H. Stevens. New York: Farrar, Straus & Young, 1953.

Hoffmann, Heinrich. *Mit Hitler im Westen.* Berlin: Zeitgeschichte Verlag, 1940.

Hoffmann, Joachim. "The Conduct of the War through Soviet Eyes." In *The Attack on the Soviet Union* (vol. 4 of *Germany and the Second World War*), ed. Horst Boog et al., trans. Dean S. McMurrey, Ewald Osers, and Louise Willmot, 833–940. Oxford: Clarendon, 1998.

———. "The Soviet Union's Offensive Preparations in 1941." In *From Peace to War: Germany, Soviet Russia, and the World, 1939-1941,* ed. Bernd Wegner, 361–80. Providence, RI: Berghahn, 1997.

———. *Stalins Vernichtungskrieg, 1941-1945.* Munich: Verlag für Wehrwissenschaften, 1995.

———. "Die Sowjetunion bis zum Vorabend des deutschen Angriffs." In *Der Angriff auf die Sowjetunion* (vol. 4 of *Das deutsche Reich und der Zweite Weltkrieg*), ed. Horst Boog et al., 69–140. Frankfurt: Fischer Taschenbuch, 1991.

———. "Die Kriegsführung aus der Sicht der Sowjetunion." In *Der Angriff auf die Sowjetunion* (vol. 4 of *Das deutsche Reich und der Zweite Weltkrieg*), ed. Horst Boog et al., 848–964. Frankfurt: Fischer Taschenbuch, 1991.

———. *Kaukasien, 1942-3: Das deutsche Heer und die Orientvölker der Sowjetunion.* Freiburg: Rombach, 1991.

———. *Die Geschichte der Wlassow-Armee.* Freiburg i. Br.: Rombach, 1984.

Homze, Edward. *Foreign Labor in Nazi Germany.* Princeton, NJ: Princeton University Press, 1967.

Horne, Alistair. *To Lose a Battle: France, 1940.* Harmondsworth: Penguin, 1969.

Hornshøj-Møller, Stig. *"Der ewige Jude": Quellenkritische Analyse eines antisemitischen Propagandafilms.* Göttingen: Institut für den wissenschaftlichen Film, 1995.

———. "Der Ewige Jude: Legitimation und Auslöser eines Völkermordes." In *Unser Jahrhundert in Film und Fernsehen,* ed. Karl Friedrich Reimers, Christiane Hackl, and Brigitte Scherer, 59–98. Munich: Ölschläger, 1995.

———. "The Role of 'Produced Reality' in the Decision-Making Process Which Led to the Holocaust." Paper presented at the conference "Genocide and the Modern World," sponsored by the Association of Genocide Scholars, Montreal, 11–13 June 1997.

Hornshøj-Møller, Stig, and David Culbert. "'Der Ewige Jude' (1940): Joseph Goebbels' Unequaled Monument to Anti-Semitism." *Historical Journal of Film, Radio and Television* 12, no. 1 (1992): 41–67.

Hosenfeld, Wilm. *"Ich versuche jeden zu retten": Das Leben eines deutschen Offiziers in Briefen und Tagebüchern.* Edited by Thomas Vogel. Munich: Deutsche Verlags-Anstalt, 2004.

Housden, Martyn. "Hans Frank: Empire Builder in the East, 1939-41." *European History Quarterly* 24, no. 3 (1994): 367–93.

Humpert, David M. "Viktor Suvorov and Operation Barbarossa: Tukhachevskii Revisited." *Journal of Slavic Military Studies* 18, no. 1 (2005): 59–74.

Hürter, Johannes. *Hitlers Heerführer: Die deutschen Oberbefehlshaber im Krieg gegen die Sowjetunion, 1941/42.* Munich: Oldenbourg, 2006.

———. "Konservative Akteure oder totale Krieger? Zum Transformationsprozess einer militärische Elite." In *Verbrechen der Wehrmacht: Bilanz einer Debatte,* ed. Christian Hartmann, Johannes Hürter, and Ulrike Jureit, 50–59. Munich: Beck, 2005.

———. "Auf dem Weg zur Militäropposition: Tresckow, Gersdorff, der Vernichtungskrieg und der Judenmord: Neue Dokumente über das Verhältnis der Heeresgruppe Mitte zur Einsatzgruppe B im Jahr 1941." *Vierteljahrshefte für Zeitgeschichte* 52, no. 3 (2004): 527–62.

———. "Die Wehrmacht vor Leningrad: Krieg und Besatzungspolitik der 18. Armee im Herbst und Winter 1941–1942." *Vierteljahrshefte für Zeitgeschichte* 49, no. 3 (2001): 377–440.

———. "Es Herrschen Sitten und Gebräuche, Genauso Wie im 30-Jährigen Krieg." *Vierteljahrshefte für Zeitgeschichte* 48, no. 2 (2000): 329–403.

Hürter, Johannes, Jürgen Zarusky, and Vasilii Semenovich Grossman, eds. *Besatzung, Kollaboration, Holocaust: Neue Studien zur Verfolgung und Ermordung der europäischen Juden.* Munich: Oldenbourg, 2008.

Hutton, Christopher. *Race and the Third Reich: Linguistics, Racial Anthropology and Genetics in the Dialectic of Volk.* Cambridge: Cambridge University Press, 2005.

Jäckel, Eberhard. *Hitler's World View: A Blueprint for Power.* Translated by Herbert Arnold. Cambridge, MA: Harvard University Press, 1972.

Jäckel, Eberhard, and Axel Kuhn, eds. *Hitler: Sämtliche Aufzeichnungen.* Stuttgart: Deutsche Verlags-Anstalt, 1980.

Jacobsen, Hans-Adolf. "Kommissarbefehl und Massenexekutionen sowjetischer Kriegsgefangener." In *Konzentrationslager, Kommissarbefehl, Judenferfolgung* (vol. 2 of *Anatomie des SS-Staates*), ed. Hans Buchheim, Martin Broszat, Hans-Adolf Jacobsen, and Helmut Krausnick, 163–283. Freiburg: Walter, 1965.

Jahn, Peter. "'Russenfurcht' und Antibolschewismus: Zur Entstehung und Wirkung von Feindbildern." In *Erobern und Vernichten: Der Krieg gegen die Sowjetunion, 1941-1945,* ed. Peter Jahn and Reinhard Rürup, 47–64. Berlin: Argon, 1991.

Jahn, Peter, and Reinhard Rürup, eds. *Erobern und Vernichten: Der Krieg gegen die Sowjetunion, 1941-1945.* Berlin: Argon, 1991.

Jansen, Hans. *Der Madagaskar-Plan: Die beabsichtigte Deportation der europäischen Juden nach Madagaskar.* Munich: Herbig, 1997.

Jarausch, Konrad, ed. *Reluctant Accomplice: A Wehrmacht Soldier's Letters from the Eastern Front.* Princeton, NJ: Princeton University Press, 2011.

Jarausch, Konrad, Klaus Jochen Arnold, and Hans-Jochen Vogel. *"Das Stille Sterben . . .": Feldpostbriefe aus Polen und Russland, 1939-1942.* Paderborn: Schöningh, 2008.

Jersak, Tobias. "Decisions to Murder and to Lie: German War Society and the Holocaust." In *German Wartime Society, 1939-1945: Politicization, Disintegration, and the Struggle for Survival* (vol. 9/1 of *Germany and the Second World War*), ed. Jörg Echternkamp, trans. Derry Cook-Radmore, 287–368. Oxford: Clarendon, 2008.

———. "Blitzkrieg Revisited: A New Look at Nazi War and Extermination Planning." *Historical Journal* 43, no. 2 (2000): 565–82.

———. "Die Interaktion von Kriegsverlauf und Judenvernichtung: Ein Blick auf Hitlers Strategie im Spätsommer 1941." *Historische Zeitschrift* 268, no. 2 (1999): 311–74.

———. "A Matter of Foreign Policy: 'Final Solution' and 'Final Victory' in Nazi Germany." *German History* 21, no. 3 (2003): 369–91.

Jick, Leon A. "Method in Madness: An Examination of the Motivations for Nazi Mass Murder." *Modern Judaism* 18, no. 2 (1998): 153–72.

Jochmann, Werner, ed. *Adolf Hitler: Monologe im Führerhauptquartier, 1941-1944: Die Aufzeichnungen Heinrich Heims.* Hamburg: Knaus, 1980.

Johr, Barbara. "Die Ereignisse in Zahlen." In *Befreier und Befreite: Krieg, Vergewaltigung, Kinder,* ed. Helke Sander and Barbara Johr, 46–72. Munich: A. Kunstmann, 1992.

Jukes, Geoffrey. *Hitler's Stalingrad Decisions.* Berkeley and Los Angeles: University of California Press, 1985.

Junker, Detlef. *Kampf um die Weltmacht: Die USA und das Dritte Reich, 1933-1945.* Dusseldorf: Schwann-Bagel, 1988.

Jureit, Ulrike. "Motive—Mentalitäten—Handlungsspielräume: Theoretische Anmerkungen zu Handlungsoptionen von Soldaten." In *Verbrechen der Wehrmacht: Bilanz einer Debatte,* ed. Christian Hartmann, Johannes Hürter, and Ulrike Jureit, 163-70. Munich: Beck, 2005.

Kagan, Frederick. "The Evacuation of Soviet Industry in the Wake of 'Barbarossa': A Key to the Soviet Victory." *Journal of Slavic Military Studies* 8, no. 2 (1995): 387-414.

Kaienburg, Hermann. *Die Wirtschaft der SS.* Berlin: Metropol, 2003.

———. "Jüdische Arbeitslager an der 'Strasse der SS.'" *1999: Zeitschrift für Sozialgeschichte des 20. und 21. Jahrhunderts* 11, no. 1 (1996): 13-39.

Kaiser, Wolf, ed. *Täter im Vernichtungskrieg: Der Überfall auf die Sowjetunion und der Völkermord an den Juden.* Berlin: Propyläen, 2002.

Kardorff, Ursula von. *Berliner Aufzeichnungen: Aus den Jahren 1942-1945.* 2nd ed. Munich: Deutscher Taschenbuch, 1982.

Kárný, Miroslav. "'Vernichtung durch Arbeit' in Leitmeritz: Die SS-Führungsstäbe in der deutschen Kriegswirtschaft." *1999: Zeitschrift für Sozialgeschichte des 20. und 21. Jahrhunderts* 8, no. 4 (1993): 37-61.

Kaufman, Theodore N. *Germany Must Perish!* New York: Argyle, 1941.

Kay, Alex J. "Revisiting the Meeting of the Staatssekretäre on 2 May 1941: A Response to Klaus Jochen Arnold and Gert C. Lübbers." *Journal of Contemporary History* 43, no. 1 (2008): 93-103.

———. *Exploitation, Resettlement, Mass Murder: Political and Economic Planning for German Occupation Policy in the Soviet Union, 1940-1941.* New York: Berghahn, 2006.

———. "Germany's Staatssekretäre, Mass Starvation and the Meeting of 2 May 1941." *Journal of Contemporary History* 41, no. 4 (2006): 685-700.

Keegan, John. "Berlin." *MHQ: Quarterly Journal of Military History* 2, no. 2 (1990): 72-83.

———. *The Times Atlas of the Second World War.* New York: Harper & Row, 1989.

Kehrig, Manfred. "Die 6. Armee im Kessel von Stalingrad." In *Stalingrad: Ereignis—Wirkung—Symbol,* ed. Jürgen Förster, 76-110. Munich: Piper, 1992.

———. *Stalingrad: Analyse und Dokumentation einer Schlacht.* Stuttgart: Deutsche Verlags-Anstalt, 1974.

Keller, Rolf, and Reinhard Otto. "Das Massensterben der sowjetischen Kriegsgefangenen und die Wehrmachtbürokratie: Unterlagen zur Registrierung der sowjetischen Kriegsgefangenen 1941-1945 in deutschen und russischen Institutionen." *Militärgeschichtliche Mitteilungen* 57, no. 1 (1998): 149-80.

Keller, Sven. "Verbrechen in der Endphase des Zweiten Weltkrieges: Überlegungen zu Abgrenzung, Methodik und Quellenkritik." In *Terror nach Innen: Verbrechen am Ende des Zweiten Weltkrieges,* ed. Cord Arendes, Edgar Wolfrum, and Jörg Zedler, 25-50. Göttingen: Wallstein, 2006.

Kellogg, Michael. *The Russian Roots of Nazism: White Emigrés and the Making of National Socialism, 1917-1945.* New York: Cambridge University Press, 2005.

Kershaw, Ian. *Fateful Choices: Ten Decisions That Changed the World, 1940-1941.* New York: Penguin, 2007.

———. "Hitler's Role in the 'Final Solution.'" *Yad Vashem Studies* 34 (2006): 7-43.

———. "Hitler and the Uniqueness of Nazism." *Journal of Contemporary History* 39, no. 2 (2004): 239-54.

————. *Hitler, 1936-1945: Nemesis.* New York: Norton, 2000.

————. *Hitler, 1889-1936: Hubris.* New York: Norton, 1999.

————. "Ideologue and Propagandist: Hitler in Light of His Speeches, Writings and Orders, 1925-1928." *Yad Vashem Studies* 23 (1993): 321-34.

————. "Improvised Genocide? The Emergence of the 'Final Solution' in the 'Warthegau.'" *Transactions of the Royal Historical Society* 2 (1992): 51-78.

————. *The "Hitler Myth": Image and Reality in the Third Reich.* New York: Oxford University Press, 1987.

————. "German Popular Opinion and the 'Jewish Question,' 1939-1943: Some Further Reflections." In *Die Juden im nationalsozialistischen Deutschland,* ed. Arnold Paucker, 365-86. Tübingen: J. C. B. Mohr, 1986.

————. *Popular Opinion and Political Dissent in the Third Reich: Bavaria, 1933-1945.* Oxford: Oxford University Press, 1983.

————. "The Persecution of the Jews and German Popular Opinion in the Third Reich." *Leo Baeck Institute Year Book* 26 (1981): 261-89.

————. "Antisemitismus und Volksmeinung: Reaktionen auf die Judenverfolgung." In *Bayern in der NS-Zeit* (6 vols.), ed. Martin Broszat, Elke Fröhlich, and Falk Wiesemann, 2, pt. A:281-348. Munich: Oldenbourg, 1979.

Kershaw, Robert J. *War without Garlands: Operation Barbarossa, 1941/42.* Rockville Centre, NY: Sarpedon, 2000.

Kersting, Franz-Werner. "Wehrmacht und Schule im 'Dritten Reich.'" In *Die Wehrmacht: Mythos und Realität,* ed. Rolf-Dieter Müller and Hans-Erich Volkmann, 436-55. Munich: Oldenbourg, 1999.

Kettenacker, Lothar. "Hitler's Final Solution and Its Rationalization." In *The Policies of Genocide: Jews and Soviet Prisoners of War in Nazi Germany,* ed. Gerhard Hirschfeld, 73-96. London: Allen & Unwin, 1986.

King, Curtis S. "Operation Bagration: A Soviet Victory." *Military Review* 74, no. 4 (1994): 89-94.

Kipp, Jacob. "Barbarossa and the Crisis of Successive Operations: The Smolensk Engagements, July 10–August 7, 1941." *Soviet and Post-Soviet Review* 19, no. 1 (1992): 91-136.

Kitterman, David H. "Those Who Said 'No!': Germans Who Refused to Execute Civilians during World War II." *German Studies Review* 11, no. 2 (1988): 241-54.

Klee, Ernst. "Die Ermordung der Unproduktiven: Euthanasie im Dritten Reich und ihre Aufarbeitung im Nachkriegsdeutschland." In *Ende des Dritten Reiches—Ende des Zweiten Weltkriegs: Eine perspektivische Rückschau,* ed. Hans-Erich Volkmann, 341-67. Munich: Piper, 1995.

————. *"Euthanasie" im NS-Staat: Die "Vernichtung Lebensunwerten Lebens."* Frankfurt: Fischer, 1985.

————, ed. *Dokumente zur "Euthanasie."* Frankfurt: Fischer Taschenbuch, 1985.

Klee, Ernst, and Willi Dressen, eds. *"Gott mit uns": Der deutsche Vernichtungskrieg im Osten, 1939-1945.* Frankfurt: Fischer, 1989.

Klee, Ernst, Willi Dressen, and Volker Riess, eds. *"The Good Old Days": The Holocaust as Seen by Its Perpetrators and Bystanders.* Translated by Deborah Burnstone. New York: Free Press, 1991.

Klein, Peter. "Die Erlaubnis zum Grenzenlosen Massenmord—das Schicksal der Berliner Juden und die Rolle der Einsatzgruppen bei dem Versuch, Juden als Partisanen 'Auszurotten.'" In *Die Wehrmacht: Mythos und Realität,* ed. Rolf-Dieter Müller and Hans-Erich Volkmann, 923-47. Munich: Oldenbourg, 1999.

Klein, Peter, and Andrej Angrick, eds. *Die Einsatzgruppen in der besetzten Sowjetunion, 1941/42: Die Tätigkeits- und Lageberichte des Chefs der Sicherheitspolizei und des SD.* Berlin: Edition Hentrich, 1997.

Klemp, Stefan. "Kölner Polizeibataillone in Osteuropa: Die Polizeibataillone 69, 309, 319 und die Polizeireservekompanie Köln." In *Wessen Freund und Wessen Helfer? Die Kölner Polizei im Nationalsozialismus,* ed. Harald Buhlan and Werner Jung, 277–98. Cologne: Emons, 2000.

Klemperer, Victor. *I Will Bear Witness: A Diary of the Nazi Years, 1942-1945.* Translated by Martin Chalmers. New York: Random House, 1999.

Klink, Ernst. "The Military Concept of the War against the Soviet Union." In *The Attack on the Soviet Union* (vol. 4 of *Germany and the Second World War*), ed. Horst Boog, trans. Dean S. McMurrey, Ewald Osers, and Louise Willmot, 225–385. Oxford: Clarendon, 1998.

———. *Das Gesetz des Handelns: Die Operation "Zitadelle," 1943.* Stuttgart: Deutsche Verlags-Anstalt, 1966.

———. "The Conduct of Operations." In *The Attack on the Soviet Union* (vol. 4 of *Germany and the Second World War*), ed. Horst Boog, trans. Dean S. McMurrey, Ewald Osers, and Louise Willmot, 525–763. Oxford: Clarendon, 1998.

Klinkhammer, Lutz. "Der Partisanenkrieg der Wehrmacht, 1941-1944." In *Die Wehrmacht: Mythos und Realität,* ed. Rolf-Dieter Müller and Hans-Erich Volkmann, 815–36. Munich: Oldenbourg, 1999.

Knappe, Siegfried. *Soldat: Reflections of a German Soldier, 1936-1949.* Edited by Ted Brusaw. New York: Orion, 1992.

Knjazkov, Anatolij S. "Die sowjetische Strategie im Jahre 1942." In *Stalingrad: Ereignis–Wirkung–Symbol,* ed. Jürgen Förster, 39–51. Munich: Piper, 1992.

Koch, H. W. "Operation Barbarossa—the Current State of the Debate." *Historical Journal* 31, no. 2 (1988): 377–90.

———. "Hitler's 'Programme' and the Genesis of Operation 'Barbarossa.'" *Historical Journal* 26, no. 4 (1983): 891–920.

———. "The Spectre of a Separate Peace in the East: Russo-German 'Peace Feelers,' 1942-1944." *Journal of Contemporary History* 10, no. 3 (1975): 531–49.

———. "Hitler and the Origins of the Second World War: Second Thoughts on the Status of Some of the Documents." *Historical Journal* 11, no. 1 (1968): 125–43.

Kohlhaas, Elisabeth. "'Aus einem Haus, aus dem eine weiße Fahne Erscheint, sind alle Männlichen Personen zu erschießen': Durchhalteterror und Gewalt gegen Zivilisten am Kriegsende 1945." In *Terror nach Innen: Verbrechen am Ende des Zweiten Weltkrieges,* ed. Cord Arendes, Edgar Wolfrum, and Jörg Zedler, 51–79. Göttingen: Wallstein, 2006.

Korol, V. E., and David M. Glantz. "The Price of Victory: Myths and Reality." *Journal of Slavic Military Studies* 9, no. 2 (1996): 417–26.

Koschorrek, Günter K. *Blood Red Snow: The Memoirs of a German Soldier on the Eastern Front.* Edited by Roger Chesneau. Translated by Olav R. Crone-Aamot. Mechanicsburg, PA: Stackpole, 2002.

Krakowski, Schmuel. "The Death Marches in the Period of the Evacuation of the Camps." In *The Nazi Holocaust: Historical Articles on the Destruction of the European Jews* (9 vols.), ed. Michael R. Marrus, 9:476–90. Westport, CT: Greenwood, 1989.

Krausnick, Helmut. *Hitlers Einsatzgruppen: Die Truppe des Weltanschauungskrieges, 1938-1942.* Frankfurt: Fischer Taschenbuch, 1985.

——. "Kommissarbefehl und 'Gerichtsbarkeitserlass Barbarossa' in neuer Sicht." *Vierteljahrshefte für Zeitgeschichte* 25, no. 4 (1977): 682–738.

——. "The Persecution of the Jews." In *Anatomy of the SS State*, ed. Helmut Krausnick, Hans Buchheim, Martin Broszat, and Hans-Adolf Jacobsen, trans. Richard Barry, Marian Jackson, and Dorothy Long, 1–124. New York: Walker, 1968.

——. "Hitler und die Morde in Polen: Ein Beitrag zum Konflikt zwischen Heer und SS um die Verwaltung der besetzten Gebiete." *Vierteljahrshefte für Zeitgeschichte* 11, no. 2 (1963): 196–209.

——. "Denkschrift Himmlers über die Behandlung der Fremdvölkischen im Osten (Mai 1940)." *Vierteljahrshefte für Zeitgeschichte* 5, no. 1 (1957): 194–98.

Krausnick, Helmut, Hans Buchheim, Martin Broszat, and Hans-Adolf Jacobsen, eds. *Anatomy of the SS State*. Translated by Richard Barry, Marian Jackson, and Dorothy Long. New York: Walker, 1968.

Krausnick, Helmut, and Hans-Heinrich Wilhelm. *Die Truppe des Weltanschauungskrieges: Die Einsatzgruppen der Sicherheitspolizei und des SD, 1938-1942.* Stuttgart: Deutsche Verlags-Anstalt, 1981.

Kreuter, Siegbert. "Das Unternehmen Zitadelle vom 5.–15.7.1943." *Österreichische militärische Zeitschrift* 41, no. 5 (2003): 583–86.

Kroener, Bernhard R. "'Frontochsen' und 'Etappenbullen': Zur Ideologisierung militärischer Organisationsstrukturen im Zweiten Weltkrieg." In *Die Wehrmacht: Mythos und Realität*, ed. Rolf-Dieter Müller and Hans-Erich Volkmann, 371–84. Munich: Oldenbourg, 1999.

——. "The 'Frozen Blitzkrieg': German Strategic Planning against the Soviet Union and the Causes of Its Failure." In *From Peace to War: Germany, Soviet Russia, and the World, 1939-1941*, ed. Bernd Wegner, 135–49. Providence, RI: Berghahn, 1997.

——. "'Nun, Volk, steh auf . . . !' Stalingrad und der 'totale' Krieg, 1942–1943." In *Stalingrad: Ereignis—Wirkung—Symbol*, ed. Jürgen Förster, 151–70. Munich: Piper, 1992.

——. "Organisation und Mobilisierung des deutschen Machtbereichs: Pt. 1, Kriegsverwaltung, Wirtschaft und Personelle Ressourcen 1939–1941." In *Organisation und Mobilisierung des deutschen Machtbereichs: Kriegsverwaltung, Wirtschaft und Personelle Ressourcen 1939-1941* (vol. 5/1 of *Das deutsche Reich und der Zweite Weltkrieg*), ed. Bernhard R. Kroener, Rolf-Dieter Müller, and Hans Umbreit, 349–692. Stuttgart: Deutsche Verlags-Anstalt, 1988.

——. "The Manpower Resources of the Third Reich." In *Organization and Mobilization of the German Sphere of Power: Wartime Administration, Economy, and Manpower Resources, 1939-1941* (vol. 5/1 of *Germany and the Second World War*), ed. Bernhard R. Kroener, Rolf-Dieter Müller, and Hans Umbreit, trans. John Brownjohn, 787–1154. New York: Clarendon, 2000.

Kroener, Bernhard R., Rolf-Dieter Müller, and Hans Umbreit, eds. *Organization and Mobilization of the German Sphere of Power: Wartime Administration, Economy, and Manpower Resources, 1942-1944/5.* Translated by Derry Cook-Radmore, Ewald Osers, and Barry Smerin. Vol. 5/2 of *Germany and the Second World War.* Oxford: Clarendon, 2003.

——, eds. *Organization and Mobilization of the German Sphere of Power: Wartime Administration, Economy, and Manpower Resources, 1939-1941.* Translated by John Brownjohn. Vol. 5/1 of *Germany and the Second World War.* New York: Clarendon, 2000.

——, eds. *Organisation und Mobilisierung des deutschen Machtbereichs: Kriegsverwaltung,*

Wirtschaft und Personelle Ressourcen, 1942-1944/45. Vol. 5/2 of *Das deutsche Reich und der Zweite Weltkrieg*. Stuttgart: Deutsche Verlags-Anstalt, 1999.

——, eds. *Organisation und Mobilisierung des deutschen Machtbereichs: Kriegsverwaltung, Wirtschaft und Personelle Ressourcen 1939-1941*. Vol. 5/1 of *Das deutsche Reich und der Zweite Weltkrieg*. Stuttgart: Deutsche Verlags-Anstalt, 1988.

——. "Auf dem Weg zu einer 'nationalsozialistischen Volksarmee': Die soziale Öffnung des Heeresoffizierkorps im Zweiten Weltkrieg." In *Von Stalingrad zur Währungsreform: Zur Sozialgeschichte des Umbruchs in Deutschland*, ed. Martin Broszat, Klaus-Dietmar Henke, and Hans Woller, 651-82. Munich: Oldenbourg, 1988.

Kuby, Erich. *Mein Krieg: Aufzeichnungen aus 2129 Tagen*. Munich: Nymphenburger, 1975.

Kühl, Stefan. *The Nazi Connection: Eugenics, American Racism, and German National Socialism*. New York: Oxford University Press, 1994.

Kühne, Thomas. "Gruppenkohäsion und Kameradschaftsmythos in der Wehrmacht." In *Die Wehrmacht: Mythos und Realität*, ed. Rolf-Dieter Müller and Hans-Erich Volkmann, 534-49. Munich: Oldenbourg, 1999.

Kunz, Andreas. "Die Wehrmacht, 1944/45: Eine Armee in Untergang." In *Der Zusammenbruch des deutschen Reiches, 1945: Die Folgen des Zweiten Weltkrieges* (vol. 10/2 of *Das deutsche Reich und der Zweite Weltkrieg*), ed. Rolf-Dieter Müller and Jörg Echternkamp, 3-54. Munich: Deutsche Verlags-Anstalt, 2008.

——. *Wehrmacht und Niederlage: Die Bewaffnete Macht in der Endphase der nationalsozialistischen Herrschaft, 1944 bis 1945*. Munich: Oldenbourg, 2005.

——. "Die 'Aktion Leuthen': Das Ende des deutschen Ersatzheeres im Frühjahr 1945." *Zeitschrift für Geschichtswissenschaft* 48, no. 9 (2000): 789-806.

Kunz, Norbert. "Das Beispiel Charkow: Eine Stadtbevölkerung als Opfer der deutschen Hungerstrategie, 1941/42." In *Verbrechen der Wehrmacht: Bilanz einer Debatte*, ed. Christian Hartmann, Johannes Hürter, and Ulrike Jureit, 136-44. Munich: Beck, 2005.

Kwiet, Konrad. "Erziehung zum Mord—Zwei Beispiele zur Kontinuität der deutschen 'Endlösung der Judenfrage.'" In *Geschichte und Emanzipation: Festschrift für Reinhard Rürup*, ed. Michael Grüttner, 435-57. Frankfurt: Campus, 1999.

——. "Rehearsing for Murder: The Beginning of the Final Solution in Lithuania in June 1941." *Holocaust and Genocide Studies* 12, no. 1 (1998): 3-26.

——. "From the Diary of a Killing Unit." In *Why Germany?* ed. John Milfull, 75-90. Oxford: Berg, 1992.

——. "Forced Labour of German Jews in Nazi Germany." *Leo Baeck Institute Year Book* 36 (1991): 389-410.

Lakowski, Richard. "Der Zusammenbruch der deutschen Verteidigung zwischen Ostsee und Karpaten." In *Der Zusammenbruch des deutschen Reiches, 1945: Die militärische Niederwerfung der Wehrmacht* (vol. 10/1 of *Das deutsche Reich und der Zweite Weltkrieg*), ed. Rolf-Dieter Müller et al., 491-679. Munich: Deutsche Verlags-Anstalt, 2008.

Laqueur, Walter, and Richard Breitman. *Breaking the Silence*. New York: Simon & Schuster, 1986.

Latzel, Klaus. "Wehrmachtssoldaten zwischen 'Normalität' und NS-Ideologie, Oder: Was Sucht die Forschung in der Feldpost?" In *Die Wehrmacht: Mythos und Realität*, ed. Rolf-Dieter Müller and Hans-Erich Volkmann, 573-88. Munich: Oldenbourg, 1999.

——. *Deutsche Soldaten–nationalsozialistischer Krieg? Kriegserlebnis, Kriegserfahrung, 1939-1945.* Paderborn: Schöningh, 1998.

Le Tissier, Tony. *Zhukov at the Oder: The Decisive Battle for Berlin.* Westport, CT: Praeger, 1996.

Leach, Barry A. *German Strategy against Russia.* Oxford: Clarendon, 1973.

Lehndorff, Hans Graf von. *Ostpreußisches Tagebuch: Aufzeichnungen eines Arztes aus den Jahren 1945-1947.* Munich: Deutscher Taschenbuch, 1967.

Levine, Alan J. "Was World War II a Near-Run Thing?" *Journal of Strategic Studies* 8, no. 1 (1985): 38-63.

Lieb, Peter. "Täter aus Überzeugung? Oberst Carl von Andrian und die Judenmorde der 707. Infanteriedivision 1941/42." *Vierteljahrshefte für Zeitgeschichte* 50, no. 4 (2002): 523-57.

Liedtke, Gregory. "Furor Teutonicus: German Offensives and Counter-Attacks on the Eastern Front, August 1943 to March 1945." *Journal of Slavic Military Studies* 21, no. 3 (2008): 563-87.

Lindqvist, Sven. *"Exterminate All the Brutes."* New York: New Press, 1996.

Liulevicius, Vejas Gabriel. *War Land on the Eastern Front: Culture, National Identity, and German Occupation in World War I.* New York: Cambridge University Press, 2000.

Lochner, Louis P., ed. *The Goebbels Diaries, 1942-1943.* Translated by Louis P. Lochner. Garden City, NY: Doubleday, 1948.

Longerich, Peter. *"Davon haben wir nichts gewusst!" Die Deutschen und die Judenverfolgung, 1933-1945.* Munich: Siedler, 2006.

——. *The Unwritten Order: Hitler's Role in the Final Solution.* Stroud: Tempus, 2003.

——. "Working towards the Führer." *Yad Vashem Studies* 30 (2002): 405-26.

——. *Politik der Vernichtung: Eine Gesamtdarstellung der nationalsozialistischen Judenverfolgung.* Munich: Piper, 1998.

——. "From Mass Murder to the 'Final Solution': The Shooting of Jewish Civilians during the First Months of the Eastern Campaign within the Context of Nazi Jewish Genocide." In *From Peace to War: Germany, Soviet Russia, and the World, 1939-1941,* ed. Bernd Wegner, 253-91. Providence, RI: Berghahn, 1997.

——. "Dokumentation: Joseph Goebbels und der Totale Krieg: Eine Unbekannte Denkschrift des Propagandaministers vom 18. Juli 1944." *Vierteljahrshefte für Zeitgeschichte* 35, no. 2 (1987): 289-314.

Lower, Wendy. "'Anticipatory Obedience' and the Nazi Implementation of the Holocaust in the Ukraine: A Case Study of Central and Peripheral Forces in the Generalbezirk Zhytomyr, 1941-1944." *Holocaust and Genocide Studies* 16, no. 1 (2002): 1-22.

Lozowick, Yaakov. "Rollbahn Mord: The Early Activities of Einsatzgruppe C." *Holocaust and Genocide Studies* 2, no. 2 (1987): 221-42.

Lubbeck, William. *At Leningrad's Gates: The Story of a Soldier with Army Group North.* Edited by David B. Hurt. Philadelphia: Casemate, 2006.

Lübbers, Gert C. "Die 6. Armee und die Zivilbevölkerung von Stalingrad." *Vierteljahrshefte für Zeitgeschichte* 54, no. 1 (2006): 87-123.

——. "'Ausnutzung oder Ausschlachtung?' Zur Genese der deutschen Wirtschaftsplanungen für das Unternehmen 'Barbarossa.'" In *Krieg und Verbrechen: Situation und Intention: Fallbeispiele,* ed. Timm C. Richter, 173-83. Munich: Meidenbauer, 2006.

Lucas, James, ed. *War on the Eastern Front: The German Soldier in Russia.* New York: Bonanza, 1979.

MacKenzie, S. P. "The Treatment of Prisoners of War in World War II." *Journal of Modern History* 66, no. 3 (1994): 504–12.

Madajczyk, Czeslaw. "Besteht ein Synchronismus zwischen dem 'Generalplan Ost' und der Endlösung der Judenfrage?" In *Der Zweite Weltkrieg: Analysen, Grundzüge, Forschungsbilanz*, ed. Wolfgang Michalka, 844–57. Munich: Piper, 1989.

Madajczyk, Czeslaw, and Stanislaw Biernacki, eds. *Vom Generalplan Ost zum Generalsiedlungsplan.* Munich: Saur, 1994.

Madej, Victor, and Shelby Stanton. "The Smolensk Campaign, 11 July–5 August 1941." *Strategy and Tactics* 57, no. 1 (1976): 4–19.

Magenheimer, Heinz. *Hitler's War: German Military Strategy, 1940–1945.* Translated by Helmut Bögler. London: Arms & Armour, 1998.

——. "Zum deutsch-sowjetischen Krieg, 1941: Neue Quellen und Erkenntnisse." *Österreichische militärische Zeitschrift* 32, no. 1 (1994): 51–60.

Maier, Klaus A., ed. *Germany's Initial Conquests in Europe.* Translated by Dean S. McMurry, Ewald Osers, and P. S. Falla. Vol. 2 of *Germany and the Second World War.* Oxford: Clarendon, 1991.

——, ed. *Die Errichtung der Hegemonie auf dem europäischen Kontinent.* Vol. 2 of *Das deutsche Reich und der Zweite Weltkrieg.* Stuttgart: Deutsche Verlags-Anstalt, 1979.

Mallmann, Klaus-Michael. "Menschenjagd und Massenmord: Das neue Instrument der Einsatzgruppen und -kommandos, 1938–1945." In *Die Gestapo im Zweiten Weltkrieg: "Heimatfront" und besetztes Europa*, ed. Gerhard Paul and Klaus-Michael Mallmann, 291–316. Darmstadt: Primus, 2000.

——. "'Aufgeräumt und Abgebrannt': Sicherheitspolizei und 'Bandenkampf' in der besetzten Sowjetunion." In *Die Gestapo im Zweiten Weltkrieg: "Heimatfront" und besetztes Europa*, ed. Gerhard Paul and Klaus-Michael Mallmann, 501–20. Darmstadt: Primus, 2000.

——. "Der Einstieg in den Genozid: Das Lübecker Polizeibataillon 307 und das Massaker in Brest-Litovsk Anfang Juli 1941." *Archiv für Polizeigeschichte* 10 (1999): 82–88.

——. "Vom Fussvolk der 'Endlösung': Ordnungspolizei, Ostkrieg und Judenmord." *Tel Aviver Jahrbuch für deutsche Geschichte* 26 (1997): 355–91.

Mallmann, Klaus-Michael, Volker Riess, and Wolfram Pyta, eds. *Deutscher Osten, 1939–1945: Der Weltanschauungskrieg in Photos und Texten.* Darmstadt: Wissenschaftliche Buchgesellschaft, 2003.

Mammach, Klaus. *Der Volkssturm: Bestandteil des totalen Kriegseinsatz der deutschen Bevölkerung, 1944/45.* Berlin: Akademie, 1981.

Mann, Thomas. "Beim Propheten." In *Werke*, vol. 1, *Die Erzählungen*, 275–81. Frankfurt: Fischer, 1967.

Manoschek, Walter. "Vernichtungskrieg: Verbrechen der Wehrmacht, 1941 bis 1944: Innenansichten einer Ausstellung." *Zeitgeschichte* 29, no. 2 (2002): 64–75.

——. *"Es gibt nur eines für das Judentum": Vernichtung: Das Judenbild in deutschen Soldatenbriefen, 1939–1944.* Hamburg: Hamburger Edition, 1995.

——. *"Serbien ist Judenfrei": Militärische Besatzungspolitik und Judenvernichtung in Serbien, 1941/42.* Munich: Oldenbourg, 1993.

Manstein, Erich von. *Lost Victories.* Translated by Anthony G. Powell. Chicago: Regnery, 1958.

Manteuffel, Hasso von. *Die 7. Panzer-Division im Zweiten Weltkrieg: Einsatz und Kampf der "Gespenster-Division," 1939–1945.* Friedberg: Podzun, 1986.

Maslov, A. A., and David M. Glantz. "How Were Soviet Blocking Detachments Employed?" *Journal of Slavic Military Studies* 9, no. 2 (1996): 427–35.

Mastny, Vojtech. "Stalin and the Prospects of a Separate Peace in World War II." *American Historical Review* 77, no. 5 (1972): 1365-88.

Matthäus, Jürgen. "Controlled Escalation: Himmler's Men in the Summer of 1941 and the Holocaust in the Occupied Soviet Territories." *Holocaust and Genocide Studies* 21, no. 2 (2007): 218-42.

———. "Operation Barbarossa and the Onset of the Holocaust, June–December 1941." In *The Origins of the Final Solution: The Evolution of Nazi Jewish Policy, September 1939-March 1942*, by Christopher R. Browning and Jürgen Matthäus, 244-308. Lincoln: University of Nebraska Press, 2004.

———. *Ausbildungsziel Judenmord? "Weltanschauliche Erziehung" von SS, Polizei und Waffen-SS im Rahmen der "Endlösung."* Frankfurt: Fischer Taschenbuch, 2003.

———. "Ausbildungsziel Judenmord? Zum Stellenwert der 'Weltanschaulichen Erziehung' von SS und Polizei im Rahmen der 'Endlösung.'" *Zeitschrift für Geschichtswissenschaft* 47, no. 8 (1999): 677-99.

———. "Jenseits der Grenze: Die Ersten Massenerschiessungen von Juden in Litauen (Juni–August 1941)." *Zeitschrift für Geschichtswissenschaft* 44, no. 2 (1996): 101-18.

———. "Perspektiven der NS-Forschung: Neuerscheinungen zu 'Euthanasie' und 'Endlösung.'" *Zeitschrift für Geschichtswissenschaft* 44, no. 11 (1996): 991-1005.

———. "What about the 'Ordinary Men'? The German Order Police and the Holocaust in the Occupied Soviet Union." *Holocaust and Genocide Studies* 10, no. 2 (1996): 134-50.

Mawdsley, Evan. *Thunder in the East: The Nazi-Soviet War, 1941-1945.* London: Hodder Arnold, 2005.

Mazower, Mark. *Hitler's Empire: How the Nazis Ruled Europe.* New York: Penguin, 2008.

———. *Dark Continent: Europe's Twentieth Century.* New York: Knopf, 1999.

Megargee, Geoffrey P. *War of Annihilation: Combat and Genocide on the Eastern Front, 1941.* Lanham, MD: Rowman & Littlefield, 2006.

———. *Inside Hitler's High Command.* Lawrence: University Press of Kansas, 2000.

Merridale, Catherine. *Ivan's War: Life and Death in the Red Army, 1939-1945.* New York: Picador, 2006.

———. "Culture, Ideology and Combat in the Red Army, 1939-45." *Journal of Contemporary History* 41, no. 2 (2006): 305-24.

Messerschmidt, Manfred. "Ideologie und Befehlsgehorsam im Vernichtungskrieg." *Zeitschrift für Geschichtswissenschaft* 49, no. 10 (2001): 905-26.

———. "Das Bild der Wehrmacht in Deutschland seit 1945." *Revue d'Allemagne et des pays de langue allemande* 30, no. 2 (1998): 117-25.

———. "The Difficult Atonement toward Judaism: Command Structure and Knowledge in the German Military." In *The German Public and the Persecution of the Jews, 1933-1945: "No One Participated, No One Knew,"* ed. Jörg Wollenberg, trans. Rado Pribic, 83-95. Atlantic Highlands, NJ: Humanities, 1996.

———. "Die Wehrmacht: Vom Realitätsverlust zum Selbstbetrug." In *Ende des Dritten Reiches—Ende des Zweiten Weltkriegs: Eine perspektivische Rückschau,* ed. Hans-Erich Volkmann, 223-57. Munich: Piper, 1995.

———. "June 1941 Seen through German Memoirs and Diaries." *Soviet Union* 18, nos. 1-3 (1991): 205-19.

———. "'Harte Sühne am Judentum': Befehlswege und Wissen in der deutschen Wehrmacht." In *"Niemand war dabei und keiner hat's gewußt": Die deutsche Öffentlichkeit und die Judenverfolgung, 1933-1945,* ed. Jörg Wollenberg, 113-28. Munich: Piper, 1989.

———. "Die Wehrmacht in der Endphase: Realität und Perzeption." *Aus Politik und Zeitgeschichte* 32–33 (4 August 1989): 33–46.

———. "Der Kampf der Wehrmacht im Osten als Traditionsproblem." In *"Unternehmen Barbarossa": Der deutsche Überfall auf die Sowjetunion, 1941; Berichte, Analysen, Dokumente,* ed. Gerd R. Ueberschär and Wolfram Wette, 253–63. Paderborn: Schöningh, 1984.

———. "The Wehrmacht and the Volksgemeinschaft." *Journal of Contemporary History* 18, no. 4 (1983): 719–44.

Messerschmidt, Manfred, and Fritz Wüllner. *Die Wehrmachtjustiz im Dienste des Nationalsozialismus: Zerstörung einer Legende.* Baden-Baden: Nomos, 1987.

Michalka, Wolfgang, ed. *Der Zweite Weltkrieg: Analysen, Grundzüge, Forschungsbilanz.* Munich: Piper, 1989.

———. *Nationalsozialistische Aussenpolitik.* Darmstadt: Wissenschaftliche Buchgesellschaft, 1978.

Middlebrook, Martin. *The Battle of Hamburg: Allied Bomber Forces against a German City in 1943.* London: Allen Lane, 1980.

Mierzejewski, Alfred C. "A Public Enterprise in the Service of Mass Murder: The Deutsche Reichsbahn and the Holocaust." *Holocaust and Genocide Studies* 15, no. 1 (2001): 33–46.

———. *The Collapse of the German War Economy, 1944-1945: Allied Air Power and the German National Railway.* Chapel Hill: University of North Carolina Press, 1988.

———. "When Did Albert Speer Give Up?" *Historical Journal* 31, no. 2 (1988): 391–97.

———. "The Deutsche Reichsbahn and Germany's Supply of Coal, 1939–45." *Journal of Transport History* 8, no. 2 (1987): 111–25.

Millett, Allan R., and Williamson Murray. "Lessons of War." *National Interest,* no. 14 (1988): 83–95.

———, eds. *Military Effectiveness.* 3 vols. Boston: Allen & Unwin, 1988.

Milward, Alan. *The New Order and the French Economy.* Oxford: Oxford University Press, 1984.

Mitcham, Samuel W., Jr. *Crumbling Empire: The German Defeat in the East, 1944.* Westport, CT: Praeger, 2001.

Moltke, Helmuth James von. *Letters to Freya, 1939-1945.* Translated by Beate Ruhm von Oppen. New York: Vintage, 1990.

Moltmann, Günter. "Goebbels' Speech on Total War, February 18, 1943." In *Republic to Reich,* ed. Hajo Holborn, trans. Ralph Mannheim, 298–342. New York: Vintage, 1973.

Mommsen, Hans. "Die Realisierung des Utopischen: Die 'Endlösung der Judenfrage' im 'Dritten Reich.'" *Geschichte und Gesellschaft* 9, no. 3 (1993): 381–420.

Moritz, Erhardt, and Werner Stang. "Unternehmen Barbarossa: Zum historischen Ort der deutsch-sowjetischen Beziehungen von 1933 bis 1942." *Zeitschrift für Geschichtswissenschaft* 40, no. 3 (1992): 287–88.

Moser, Jonny. "Nisko: The First Experiment in Deportation." *Simon Wiesenthal Center Annual* 2 (1985): 1–30.

Müller, Klaus-Jürgen. "The Brutalisation of Warfare, Nazi Crimes and the Wehrmacht." In *Barbarossa: The Axis and the Allies,* ed. John Erickson and David Dilks, 229–37. Edinburgh: Edinburgh University Press, 1994.

———. *Das Heer und Hitler: Armee und nationalsozialistische Regime, 1933-1940.* Stuttgart: Deutsche Verlags-Anstalt, 1969.

Müller, Rolf-Dieter. "'Das deutsche Reich und der Zweite Weltkrieg': Konzeption und Erfahrungen eines Wissenschaftlichen Grossprojektes." *Zeitschrift für Geschichtswissenschaft* 56, no. 4 (2008): 301–26.

——. "Der Zusammenbruch des Wirtschaftslebens und die Anfänge des Wiederaufbaus." In *Der Zusammenbruch des deutschen Reiches, 1945: Die Folgen des Zweiten Weltkrieges* (vol. 10/2 of *Das deutsche Reich und der Zweite Weltkrieg*), ed. Rolf-Dieter Müller and Jörg Echternkamp, 55–198. Munich: Deutsche Verlags-Anstalt, 2008.

——. "Das deutsche Reich und das Jahr 1945: Eine Bilanz." In *Der Zusammenbruch des deutschen Reiches, 1945: Die Folgen des Zweiten Weltkrieges* (vol. 10/2 of *Das deutsche Reich und der Zweite Weltkrieg*), ed. Rolf-Dieter Müller and Jörg Echternkamp, 699–732. Munich: Deutsche Verlags-Anstalt, 2008.

——. *An der Seite der Wehrmacht: Hitlers ausländische Helfer beim "Kreuzzug gegen den Bolschewismus," 1941-1945.* Berlin: Christoph Links, 2007.

——. "The Mobilization of the German Economy for Hitler's War Aims." In *Organization and Mobilization of the German Sphere of Power: Wartime Administration, Economy, and Manpower Resources, 1939-1941* (vol. 5/1 of *Germany and the Second World War*), ed. Bernhard R. Kroener, Rolf-Dieter Müller, and Hans Umbreit, trans. John Brownjohn, 405–786. New York: Clarendon, 2000.

——. "Speers Rüstungspolitik im totalen Krieg: Zum Beitrag der Modernen Militärgeschichte im Diskurs mit der Sozial- und Wirtschaftsgeschichte." *Militärgeschichtliche Mitteilungen* 59, no. 2 (2000): 343–85.

——. "Die Wehrmacht—historische Last und Verantwortung: Die Historiographie im Spannungsfeld von Wissenschaft und Vergangenheitsbewältigung." In *Die Wehrmacht: Mythos und Realität*, ed. Rolf-Dieter Müller and Hans-Erich Volkmann, 3–35. Munich: Oldenbourg, 1999.

——. "Hans Kehrl: Ein Parteibuch-Industrieller im 'Dritten Reich'?" *Jahrbuch für Wirtschaftsgeschichte*, no. 2 (1999): 195–213.

——. "Albert Speer und die deutsche Rüstungspolitik im totalen Krieg." In *Organisation und Mobilisierung des deutschen Machtbereichs: Kriegsverwaltung, Wirtschaft und Personelle Ressourcen, 1942-1944/45* (vol. 5/2 of *Das deutsche Reich und der Zweite Weltkrieg*), ed. Bernhard R. Kroener, Rolf-Dieter Müller, and Hans Umbreit, 275–776. Stuttgart: Deutsche Verlags-Anstalt, 1999.

——. "From Economic Alliance to a War of Colonial Exploitation." In *The Attack on the Soviet Union* (vol. 4 of *Germany and the Second World War*), ed. Horst Boog, trans. Dean S. McMurrey, Ewald Osers, and Louise Willmot, 118–224. Oxford: Clarendon, 1998.

——. "The Failure of the Economic 'Blitzkrieg Strategy.'" In *The Attack on the Soviet Union* (vol. 4 of *Germany and the Second World War*), ed. Horst Boog, trans. Dean S. McMurrey, Ewald Osers, and Louise Willmot, 1081–1188. Oxford: Clarendon, 1998.

——. "Menschenjagd: Die Rekrutierung von Zwangsarbeitern in der besetzten Sowjetunion." In *Vernichtungskrieg: Verbrechen der Wehrmacht, 1941-1944*, ed. Hannes Heer and Klaus Naumann, 92–103. Hamburg: Hamburger Edition, 1995.

——. "'Was wir an Hunger ausstehen müssen, könnt ihr Eurch gar nicht denken': Eine Armee Verhungert." In *Stalingrad: Mythos und Wirklichkeit einer Schlacht*, ed. Wolfram Wette and Gerd R. Ueberschär, 131–45. Frankfurt: Fischer Taschenbuch, 1993.

——. "Die Rekrutierung sowjetischer Zwangsarbeiter für die deutsche Kriegswirtschaft." In *Europa und der "Reichseinsatz": Ausländische Zivilarbeiter,*

Kriegsgefangene und KZ-Häftlinge in Deutschland, 1938-1945, ed. Ulrich Herbert, 234-50. Essen: Klartext, 1991.

———. *Hitlers Ostkrieg und die deutsche Siedlungspolitik: Die Zusammenarbeit von Wehrmacht, Wirtschaft und SS.* Frankfurt: Fischer Taschenbuch, 1991.

———. "Die Mobilisierung der Wirtschaft für den Krieg—eine Aufgabe der Armee? Wehrmacht und Wirtschaft, 1933-1942." In *Der Zweite Weltkrieg: Analysen, Grundzüge, Forschungsbilanz,* ed. Wolfgang Michalka, 349-62. Munich: Piper, 1989.

———. "Die Zwangsrekrutierung von 'Ostarbeitern,' 1941-1944." In *Der Zweite Weltkrieg: Analysen, Grundzüge, Forschungsbilanz,* ed. Wolfgang Michalka, 772-82. Munich: Piper, 1989.

———. "Das 'Unternehmen Barbarossa' als wirtschaftlicher Raubkrieg." In *"Unternehmen Barbarossa": Der deutsche Überfall auf die Sowjetunion, 1941; Berichte, Analysen, Dokumente,* ed. Gerd R. Ueberschär and Wolfram Wette, 173-94. Paderborn: Schöningh, 1984.

———. "Industrielle Interessenpolitik im Rahmen des 'Generalplans Ost.'" *Militärgeschichtliche Mitteilungen* 1, no. 1 (1981): 101-41.

Müller, Rolf-Dieter, Horst Boog, and Jörg Echternkamp, eds. *Der Zusammenbruch des deutschen Reiches, 1945: Die militärische Niederwerfung der Wehrmacht.* Vol. 10/1 of *Das deutsche Reich und der Zweite Weltkrieg.* Munich: Deutsche Verlags-Anstalt, 2008.

Müller, Rolf-Dieter, and Jörg Echternkamp, eds. *Der Zusammenbruch des deutschen Reiches, 1945: Die Folgen des Zweiten Weltkrieges.* Vol. 10/2 of *Das deutsche Reich und der Zweite Weltkrieg.* Munich: Deutsche Verlags-Anstalt, 2008.

Müller, Rolf-Dieter, and Gerd R. Ueberschär. *Hitlers Krieg im Osten, 1941-1945: Ein Forschungsbericht.* Darmstadt: Wissenschaftliche Buchgesellschaft, 2000.

———. *Hitler's War in the East, 1941-1945: A Critical Assessment.* Providence, RI: Berghahn, 1997.

———, eds. *Kriegsende 1945: Die Zerstörung des deutschen Reiches.* Frankfurt: Fischer Taschenbuch, 1994.

Müller, Rolf-Dieter, and Hans-Erich Volkmann. *Die Wehrmacht: Mythos und Realität.* Munich: Oldenbourg, 1999.

Müller, Sven Oliver. "Nationalismus in der deutschen Kriegsgesellschaft, 1939-1945." In *Die deutsche Kriegsgesellschaft, 1939 bis 1945: Ausbeutung, Deutungen, Ausgrenzung* (vol. 9/2 of *Das deutsche Reich und der Zweite Weltkrieg*), ed. Jörg Echternkamp and Ralf Blank, 9-92. Munich: Deutsche Verlags-Anstalt, 2005.

Mulligan, Timothy. "Spies, Ciphers, and 'Zitadelle': Intelligence and the Battle of Kursk." *Journal of Contemporary History* 22, no. 1 (1987): 235-60.

———. "Reckoning the Cost of People's War: The German Experience in the Central USSR." *Russian History* 9, no. 1 (1982): 27-48.

Murphy, David E. *What Stalin Knew: The Enigma of Barbarossa.* New Haven, CT: Yale University Press, 2005.

Murray, Williamson. "Betrachtungen zur deutschen Strategie im Zweiten Weltkrieg." In *Die Wehrmacht: Mythos und Realität,* ed. Rolf-Dieter Müller and Hans-Erich Volkmann, 307-30. Munich: Oldenbourg, 1999.

———. "Did Strategic Bombing Work?" *MHQ: Quarterly Journal of Military History* 8, no. 3 (1996): 28-41.

———. "Barbarossa." *MHQ: Quarterly Journal of Military History* 4, no. 3 (1992): 8-17.

———. "Clausewitz: Some Thoughts on What the Germans Got Right." *Journal of Strategic Studies* 9, no. 2 (1986): 267-86.

———. *The Change in the European Balance of Power, 1938-1939: The Path to Ruin.* Princeton, NJ: Princeton University Press, 1984.

———. "Attrition and the Luftwaffe." *Air University Review* 34, no. 3 (1983): 66–77.

———. "Force Strategy, Blitzkrieg Strategy and the Economic Difficulties: Nazi Grand Strategy in the 1930s." *RUSI Journal* (Royal United Services Institute for Defence Studies) 128, no. 1 (1983): 39–43.

———. "The Strategy of the 'Phoney War': A Re-Evaluation." *Military Affairs* 45, no. 1 (1981): 13–17.

Murray, Williamson, MacGregor Knox, and Alvin Bernstein, eds. *The Making of Strategy: Rulers, States, and War.* New York: Cambridge University Press, 1994.

Musial, Bogdan. *Sowjetische Partisanen, 1941-1944: Mythos und Wirklichkeit.* Paderborn: Schöningh, 2009.

———. "The Origins of 'Operation Reinhard': The Decision-Making Process for the Mass Murder of the Jews in the 'Generalgouvernement.'" *Yad Vashem Studies* 28 (2000): 113–53.

Nachtwei, Winfried. "'Ganz Normale Männer': Die Verwicklung von Polizeibataillonen aus dem Rheinland und Westfalen in den nationalsozialistischen Vernichtungskrieg." In *Villa Ten Hompel: Sitz der Ordnungspolizei im Dritten Reich,* ed. Alfons Kenkmann, 54–77. Munster: Agenda, 1996.

Naimark, Norman. *The Russians in Germany.* Cambridge, MA: Belknap Press of Harvard University Press, 1995.

Nash, Douglas E. *Hell's Gate: The Battle of the Cherkassy Pocket, January to February 1944.* Southbury, CT: RZM Imports, 2002.

———. "No Stalingrad on the Dnieper: The Korsun-Shevchenkovsky Operation, January to February 1944." Master's thesis, Army Command and General Staff College, 1995.

Nedelmann, Birgitta. "Kommentar zu Hannes Heer 'Am Anfang haben wir es aus Überzeugung, später dann aus Pflicht getan.'" *BIOS* 11, no. 1 (1998): 69–75.

Neitzel, Sönke. "Des Forschens noch Wert? Anmerkungen zur Operationsgeschichte der Waffen-SS." *Militärgeschichtliche Zeitschrift* 61, no. 2 (2002): 403–29.

Neufeld, Michael. *The Rocket and the Reich: Peenemünde and the Coming of the Ballistic Missile Era.* New York: Free Press, 1995.

Nicosia, Francis R. *The Third Reich and the Palestine Question.* London: I. B. Tauris, 1985.

Nieden, Susanne zur. "Chronistinnen des Krieges: Frauentagebücher im Zweiten Weltkrieg." In *Ende des Dritten Reiches—Ende des Zweiten Weltkriegs: Eine perspektivische Rückschau,* ed. Hans-Erich Volkmann, 835–60. Munich: Piper, 1995.

Niepold, Gerd. *Battle for White Russia: The Destruction of Army Group Centre, June 1944.* Translated by Richard Simpkin. London: Brassey's, 1987.

Noakes, Jeremy, and Geoffrey Pridham, eds. *Nazism, 1919-1945: A Documentary Reader.* 4 vols. 1974. Reprint. Exeter: University of Exeter Press, 1995.

———, eds. *Nazism: A History in Documents and Eyewitness Accounts, 1919-1945.* 2 vols. New York: Schocken, 1988.

Ogorreck, Ralf. *Die Einsatzgruppen und die "Genesis der Endlösung."* Berlin: Metropol, 1996.

Orenstein, Harold S. "The Battle of Kursk (Continued): Tank Forces in Defence of the Kursk Bridgehead." *Journal of Slavic Military Studies* 7, no. 1 (1994): 82–118.

———. "The Defensive Battle for the Kursk Bridgehead, 5-15 July 1943." *Journal of Slavic Military Studies* 6, no. 4 (1993): 656–700.

Orenstein, Harold S., and David M. Glantz. "The Kharkov Operation, May 1942." *Journal of Soviet Military Studies* 5, no. 4 (1992): 611–86.

Osterloh, Jörg. "'Hier handelt es sich um die Vernichtung einer Weltanschauung . . .': Die Wehrmacht und die Behandlung der sowjetischen Gefangenen in Deutschland." In *Die Wehrmacht: Mythos und Realität*, ed. Rolf-Dieter Müller and Hans-Erich Volkmann, 783–802. Munich: Oldenbourg, 1999.

Otto, Reinhard. "Die Zusammenarbeit von Wehrmacht und Stapo bei der 'Aussonderung' sowjetischer Kriegsgefangener im Reich." In *Die Wehrmacht: Mythos und Realität*, ed. Rolf-Dieter Müller and Hans-Erich Volkmann, 754–82. Munich: Oldenbourg, 1999.

———. *Wehrmacht, Gestapo und sowjetische Kriegsgefangene im deutschen Reichsgebiet, 1941/42.* Munich: Oldenbourg, 1998.

Overmans, Rüdiger. "Das Schicksal der deutschen Kriegsgefangenen des Zweiten Weltkrieges." In *Der Zusammenbruch des deutschen Reiches, 1945: Die Folgen des Zweiten Weltkrieges* (vol. 10/2 of *Das deutsche Reich und der Zweite Weltkrieg*), ed. Rolf-Dieter Müller and Jörg Echternkamp, 379–507. Munich: Deutsche Verlags-Anstalt, 2008.

———. *Deutsche militärische Verluste im Zweiten Weltkrieg.* Munich: Oldenbourg, 1999.

———. "Das andere Gesicht des Krieges: Leben und Sterben der 6. Armee." In *Stalingrad: Ereignis–Wirkung–Symbol*, ed. Jürgen Förster, 419–55. Munich: Piper, 1992.

———. "Die Toten des Zweiten Weltkriegs in Deutschland: Bilanz der Forschung unter besonderer Berücksichtung der Wehrmacht- und Vertreibungsverluste." In *Der Zweite Weltkrieg: Analysen, Grundzüge, Forschungsbilanz*, ed. Wolfgang Michalka, 858–73. Munich: Piper, 1989.

Overy, Richard. *Russia's War: A History of the Soviet War Effort, 1941–1945.* New York: Penguin, 1997.

———. *Why the Allies Won.* New York: Norton, 1995.

———. "Rationalization and the 'Production Miracle' in Germany during the Second World War." In *Ende des Dritten Reiches–Ende des Zweiten Weltkriegs: Eine perspektivische Rückschau*, ed. Hans-Erich Volkmann, 457–87. Munich: Piper, 1995.

———. *War and Economy in the Third Reich.* Oxford: Clarendon, 1994.

Overy, Richard, Gerhard Otto, and Johannes Houwink ten Cate, eds. *Die "Neuordnung" Europas: NS-Wirtschaftspolitik in den besetzten Gebieten.* Berlin: Metropol, 1997.

Paul, Gerhard. "'Diese Erschiessungen haben mich innerlich gar nicht mehr berührt': Die Kriegsendphasenverbrechen der Gestapo, 1944–1945." In *Die Gestapo im Zweiten Weltkrieg: "Heimatfront" und besetztes Europa*, ed. Gerhard Paul and Klaus-Michael Mallmann, 543–68. Darmstadt: Primus, 2000.

Paul, Gerhard, and Klaus-Michael Mallmann, eds. *Die Gestapo im Zweiten Weltkrieg: "Heimatfront" und besetztes Europa.* Darmstadt: Primus, 2000.

Paul, Wolfgang. *Erfrorener Sieg: Die Schlacht um Moskau, 1941/1942.* Esslingen: Bechtle, 1975.

Perz, Bertrand, and Thomas Sandkühler. "Auschwitz und die 'Aktion Reinhard,' 1942–45: Judenmord und Raubpraxis in Neuer Sicht." *Zeitgeschichte* 26, no. 5 (1999): 283–316.

Phayer, Michael. "'Helping the Jews Is Not an Easy Thing to Do': Vatican Holocaust Policy: Continuity or Change?" *Holocaust and Genocide Studies* 21, no. 3 (2008): 421–53.

Pietrow-Ennker, Bianka. *Präventivkrieg? Der deutsche Angriff auf die Sowjetunion.* Frankfurt: Fischer Taschenbuch, 2000.

———. "Stalinistische Aussenpolitik, 1939–1941: Ein Beitrag zur Vorgeschichte des deutschen Angriffs auf die Sowjetunion am 22. Juni 1941." *Beiträge zur Geschichte der Arbeiterbewegung* 33, no. 6 (1991): 811–17.

———. "Das Feinbild im Wandel: Die Sowjetunion in den nationalsozialistischen Wochenschauen, 1935–1941." *Geschichte in Wissenschaft und Unterricht* 41, no. 6 (1990): 337–51.

———. "Deutschland im Juni 1941—ein Opfer sowjetischer Aggression? Zur Kontroverse über die Präventivkriegsthese." In *Der Zweite Weltkrieg: Analysen, Grundzüge, Forschungsbilanz,* ed. Wolfgang Michalka, 586–607. Munich: Piper, 1989.

———. "Die Sowjetunion in der Propaganda des Dritten Reiches: Das Beispiel der Wochenschau." *Militärgeschichtliche Mitteilungen* 46, no. 2 (1989): 79–120.

Pleshakov, Constantine. *Stalin's Folly: The Tragic First Ten Days of World War II on the Eastern Front.* Boston: Houghton Mifflin, 2005.

Plievier, Theodor. *Stalingrad.* Translated by Richard Winston and Clara Winston. New York: Carroll & Graf, 1984.

Pohl, Dieter. *Die Herrschaft der Wehrmacht: Deutsche Militärbesatzung und einheimische Bevölkerung in der Sowjetunion, 1941-1944.* Munich: Oldenbourg, 2008.

———. "Die Einsatzgruppe C, 1941/42." In *Die Einsatzgruppen in der besetzten Sowjetunion, 1941/42: Die Tätigkeits- und Lageberichte des Chefs der Sicherheitspolizei und des SD,* ed. Peter Klein and Andrej Angrick, 71–87. Berlin: Edition Hentrich, 1997.

———. "Die Kooperation zwischen Heer, SS und Polizei in den besetzten sowjetischen Gebieten." In *Verbrechen der Wehrmacht: Bilanz einer Debatte,* ed. Christian Hartmann, Johannes Hürter, and Ulrike Jureit, 107–16. Munich: Beck, 2005.

———. "Die Wehrmacht und der Mord an den Juden in den besetzten sowjetischen Gebieten." In *Täter im Vernichtungskrieg: Der Überfall auf die Sowjetunion und der Völkermord an den Juden,* ed. Wolf Kaiser, 39–53. Berlin: Propyläen, 2002.

———. "Schauplatz Ukraine: Der Massenmord an den Juden in Militärverwaltungsgebiet und im Reichskommissariat, 1941–1943." In *Ausbeutung, Vernichtung, Öffentlichkeit: Neue Studien zur nationalsozialistischen Lagerpolitik,* ed. Norbert Frei, Sybille Steinbacher, and Bernd Wegner, 135–73. Munich: K. G. Saur, 2000.

———. "Schlachtfeld zweier totalitarer Diktaturen: Die Ukraine im Zweiten Weltkrieg." *Österreichische Osthefte* 42, nos. 3–4 (2000): 339–62.

———. "Hans Krüger and the Murder of the Jews in the Stanislawow Region (Galicia)." *Yad Vashem Studies* 26 (1998): 239–64.

———. "Die Holocaust-Forschung und Goldhagens Thesen." *Vierteljahrshefte für Zeitgeschichte* 45, no. 1 (1997): 1–48.

———. *Nationalsozialistische Judenverfolgung in Ostgalizien, 1941-1944: Organisation und Durchführung eines Staatlichen Massenverbrechens.* Munich: Oldenbourg, 1996.

———. "Grossraumplanung und NS-Volkermord." *Historisches Jahrbuch* 114, no. 1 (1994): 175–82.

———. "Rückblick auf das 'Unternehmen Barbarossa.'" *Jahrbücher für Geschichte Osteuropas* 42, no. 1 (1994): 77–94.

———. *Von der "Judenpolitik" zum Judenmord: Der Distrikt Lublin des Generalgouvernements, 1934-1944.* Frankfurt: Peter Lang, 1993.

———. "Nationalsozialistischer Judenmord als Problem von osteuropäischer Geschichte und Osteuropa-Geschichtsschreibung." *Jahrbücher für Geschichte Osteuropas* 40, no. 1 (1992): 96–119.

———. "Polen und Juden unter deutscher Besatzung, 1939–1945: Zu einigen Neuerscheinungen." *Jahrbücher für Geschichte Osteuropas* 38, no. 2 (1990): 255–60.

——. *Die Ermordung der europäischen Juden: Eine umfassende Dokumentation des Holocaust, 1941-1945.* Munich: Piper, 1989.

Pohl, Dieter, and Peter Witte. "The Number of Victims of Belzec Extermination Camp: A Faulty Reassessment." *East European Jewish Affairs* 31, no. 1 (2001): 15-22.

Pohl, Karl Heinrich, ed. *Wehrmacht und Vernichtungspolitik: Militär im nationalsozialistischen System.* Göttingen: Vandenhoeck & Ruprecht, 1999.

Polian, Pavel. "First Victims of the Holocaust: Soviet-Jewish Prisoners of War in German Captivity." *Kritika: Explorations in Russian and Eurasian History* 6, no. 4 (2005): 763-87.

Post, Walter. *Unternehmen Barbarossa: Deutsche und sowjetische Angriffspläne, 1940/41.* Hamburg: E. S. Mittler, 1996.

Pressac, Jean-Claude. "The Machinery of Mass Murder at Auschwitz." In *Anatomy of the Auschwitz Death Camp,* ed. Yisrael Gutman and Michael Berenbaum, 183-245. Bloomington: Indiana University Press, 1998.

Pringle, Heather. *The Master Plan: Himmler's Scholars and the Holocaust.* New York: Hyperion, 2006.

Prinz, Michael, and Rainer Zitelmann, eds. *Nationalsozialismus und Modernisierung.* Darmstadt: Wissenschaftliche Buchgesellschaft, 1991.

Proctor, Robert N. "Nazi Health and Social Policy." *Simon Wiesenthal Center Annual* 7 (1990): 145-67.

Pronko, Valentin. "Die sowjetische Strategie im Jahre 1943." In *Stalingrad: Ereignis–Wirkung–Symbol,* ed. Jürgen Förster, 313-26. Munich: Piper, 1992.

Prüller, Wilhelm. *Diary of a German Soldier.* Translated by H. C. Robbins Landon. New York: Coward-McCann, 1963.

Prusin, Alexander Victor. "A Community of Violence: The SiPo/SD and Its Role in the Nazi Terror System in Generalbezirk Kiew." *Holocaust and Genocide Studies* 21, no. 1 (2007): 1-30.

Quinkert, Babette. *Propaganda und Terror in Weißrußland, 1941-1944: Die deutsche "geistige" Kriegsführung gegen Zivilbevölkerung und Partisanen.* Paderborn: Schöningh, 2008.

Raack, R. C. "Stalin's Role in the Coming of World War II." *World Affairs* 158, no. 4 (1996): 198-211.

——. *Stalin's Drive to the West, 1938-1945: The Origins of the Cold War.* Stanford, CA: Stanford University Press, 1995.

——. "Stalin's Plans for World War Two Told by a High Comintern Source." *Historical Journal* 38, no. 4 (1995): 1031-36.

——. "Stalin Plans His Post-War Germany." *Journal of Contemporary History* 28, no. 1 (1993): 53-73.

——. "Clearing Up the History of World War II." *Society for Historians of American Foreign Relations Newsletter* 23, no. 1 (1991): 27-40.

——. "Stalin's Plans for World War II." *Journal of Contemporary History* 26, no. 2 (1991): 215-27.

Radzinskii, Edvard. *Stalin: The First In-Depth Biography Based on Explosive New Documents from Russia's Secret Archives.* New York: Doubleday, 1996.

Rass, Christoph. "The Social Profile of the German Army's Combat Units, 1939-1945." In *German Wartime Society, 1939-1945: Politicization, Disintegration, and the Struggle for Survival* (vol. 9/1 of *Germany and the Second World War*), ed. Jörg Echternkamp, trans. Derry Cook-Radmore, 671-770. Oxford: Clarendon, 2008.

——. "Verbrecherische Kriegführung an der Front: Eine Infanteriedivision und Ihre Soldaten." In *Verbrechen der Wehrmacht: Bilanz einer Debatte*, ed. Christian Hartmann, Johannes Hürter, and Ulrike Jureit, 80–90. Munich: Beck, 2005.

——. *"Menschenmaterial": Deutsche Soldaten an der Ostfront: Innenansichten einer Infanteriedivision, 1939-1945.* Paderborn: Schöningh, 2003.

Ratley, Lonnie O., III. "A Lesson of History: The Luftwaffe and Barbarossa." *Air University Review* 34, no. 3 (1983): 50–65.

Read, Anthony, and David Fisher. *The Deadly Embrace: Hitler, Stalin, and the Nazi-Soviet Pact, 1939-1941.* New York: Norton, 1988.

Reese, Willy Peter. *A Stranger to Myself: The Inhumanity of War: Russia, 1941-1944.* Edited by Stefan Schmitz. Translated by Michael Hofmann. New York: Farrar Straus Giroux, 2005.

Rein, Leonid. "Local Collaboration in the Execution of the 'Final Solution' in Nazi-Occupied Belorussia." *Holocaust and Genocide Studies* 20, no. 3 (2006): 381–409.

Reinhardt, Klaus. *Moscow—the Turning Point: The Failure of Hitler's Strategy in the Winter of 1941-42.* Translated by Karl B. Keenan. Oxford: Berg, 1992.

——. *Die Wende vor Moskau: Das Scheitern der Strategie Hitlers im Winter 1941/42.* Stuttgart: Deutsche Verlags-Anstalt, 1972.

Reynolds, David. "The Origins of the Two 'World Wars': Historical Discourse and International Politics." *Journal of Contemporary History* 38, no. 1 (2003): 29–44.

——. "1940: Fulcrum of the Twentieth Century." *International Affairs* 66, no. 2 (1990): 325–50.

Richardson, Horst Fuchs, ed. *Sieg Heil! War Letters of Tank Gunner Karl Fuchs, 1937-1941.* Hamden, CT: Archon, 1987.

Richter, Timm C. *Krieg und Verbrechen: Situation und Intention: Fallbeispiele.* Munich: Meidenbauer, 2006.

——. "Die Wehrmacht und der Partisanenkrieg in den besetzten Gebieten der Sowjetunion." In *Die Wehrmacht: Mythos und Realität*, ed. Rolf-Dieter Müller and Hans-Erich Volkmann, 837–57. Munich: Oldenbourg, 1999.

Ritchie, David James. "Russo-German War Plans, 1941: The Genesis of Barbarossa." *Strategy and Tactics*, no. 108 (1986): 42–56.

Roberts, Geoffrey. *Victory at Stalingrad: The Battle That Changed History.* Harlow: Longman, 2002.

Rohland, Walter. *Bewegte Zeiten: Erinnerungen eines Eisenhüttenmannes.* Stuttgart: Seewald, 1978.

Röhr, Werner. *Europa unterm Hakenkreuz: Die Okkupationspolitik des deutschen Faschismus.* Vol. 8, *Analysen, Quellen, Register.* Berlin: Hüthig, 1996.

Roseman, Mark. *The Villa, the Lake, the Meeting: Wannsee and the Final Solution.* London: Allen Lane/Penguin, 2002.

——. "Review Article: Recent Writing on the Holocaust." *Journal of Contemporary History* 36, no. 2 (2001): 361–72.

Rossino, Alexander B. *Hitler Strikes Poland: Blitzkrieg, Ideology, and Atrocity.* Lawrence: University Press of Kansas, 2003.

——. "Polish 'Neighbours' and German Invaders: Anti-Jewish Violence in the Bialystok District during the Opening Weeks of Operation Barbarossa." *Polin: Studies in Polish Jewry* 16 (2003): 431–52.

——. "Destructive Impulses: German Soldiers and the Conquest of Poland." *Holocaust and Genocide Studies* 7, no. 3 (1997): 351–65.

Rössler, Mechtild, and Sabine Schleiermacher, eds. *Der "Generalplan Ost": Hauptlinien der nationalsozialistischen Planungs- und Vernichtungspolitik.* Berlin: Akademie, 1993.

Roth, Karl Heinz. "'Generalplan Ost'–'Gesamtplan Ost': Forschungsstand, Quellenprobleme, Neue Ergebnisse." In *Der "Generalplan Ost": Hauptlinien der nationalsozialistischen Planungs- und Vernichtungspolitik,* ed. Mechthild Rössler and Sabine Schleiermacher, 25-45. Berlin: Akademie, 1993.

Rotundo, Louis. *Battle for Stalingrad: The 1943 Soviet General Staff Study.* Elmsford, NY: Pergamon/Brassey's International Defense, 1989.

——. "Stalin and the Outbreak of War in 1941." *Journal of Contemporary History* 24, no. 2 (1989): 277-99.

——. "The Road to Stalingrad Revisited." *RUSI Journal* (Royal United Services Institute for Defence Studies) 132, no. 2 (1987): 57-65.

——. "War Plans and the 1941 Kremlin Wargames." *Journal of Strategic Studies* 10, no. 1 (1987): 84-97.

——. "The Creation of Soviet Reserves and the 1941 Campaign." *Military Affairs* 50, no. 1 (1986): 21-28.

Rüß, Hartmut. "Wer war verantwortlich für das Massaker von Babij Jar?" *Militärgeschichtliche Mitteilungen* 57, no. 2 (1998): 483-508.

Rutherford, Jeff. "Life and Death in the Demiansk Pocket: The 123rd Infantry Division in Combat and Occupation." *Central European History* 41, no. 3 (2008): 347-80.

Rutherford, Phillip. *Prelude to the Final Solution: The Nazi Program for Deporting Ethnic Poles, 1939-1941.* Lawrence: University Press of Kansas, 2007.

Rzheshevski, O. A., and David M. Glantz. "The Race for Berlin." *Journal of Slavic Military Studies* 8, no. 3 (1995): 566-79.

Salewski, Michael. "Die Abwehr der Invasion als Schlüssel zum 'Endsieg?'" In *Die Wehrmacht: Mythos und Realität,* ed. Rolf-Dieter Müller and Hans-Erich Volkmann, 210-23. Munich: Oldenbourg, 1999.

Sanden, Erika. *Das Kriegsgefangenenlager Langwasser als Forschungsobjekt.* Nuremberg: Pädagogisches Institut, 1986.

Sandkühler, Thomas. "Anti-Jewish Policy and the Murder of the Jews in the District of Galicia." In *National Socialist Extermination Policies: Contemporary German Perspectives and Controversies,* ed. Ulrich Herbert, 104-27. New York: Berghahn, 2000.

——. *"Endlösung" in Galizien: Der Judenmord in Ostpolen und die Rettungsinitiativen von Berthold Beitz, 1941-1944.* Bonn: J. H. W. Dietz, 1996.

Sauer, Bernhard. "Freikorps und Antisemitismus in der Frühzeit der Weimarer Republik." *Zeitschrift für Geschichtswissenschaft* 56, no. 1 (2008): 5-29.

——. "Vom 'Mythos eines ewigen Soldatentums': Der Feldzug deutscher Freikorps im Baltikum im Jahre 1919." *Zeitschrift für Geschichtswissenschaft* 43, no. 10 (1995): 869-902.

Sauer, Erich, ed. *Stalingrad–Feldpost, 1942-43.* Fuldatal: A. Knauf, 1988.

Scheel, Klaus. "Flugblätter der Roten Armee zur Berliner Operation 1945 (mit Dokumenten)." *Jahrbuch für Geschichte* 35 (1987): 389-425.

Schellenberg, Walter. *The Schellenberg Memoirs.* Edited and translated by Louis Hagen. London: A. Deutsch, 1956.

Scherner, Jonas. "Bericht zur deutschen Wirtschaftslage, 1943/44: Eine Bilanz des Reichsministeriums für Rüstung und Kriegsproduktion über die Entwicklung der deutschen Kriegswirtschaft bis Sommer 1944." *Vierteljahrshefte für Zeitgeschichte* 55, no. 3 (2007): 499-546.

——. "Das Verhältnis zwischen NS-Regime und Industrieunternehmen—Zwang oder Kooperation?" *Zeitschrift für Unternehmensgeschichte* 51, no. 2 (2006): 166–90.

Scherner, Jonas, and Jochen Streb. "Das Ende eines Mythos? Albert Speer und das sogenannte Rüstungswunder." *Vierteljahrschrift für Sozial und Wirtschaftsgeschichte* 93, no. 2 (2006): 172–96.

Schilling, Rene. "Die 'Helden der Wehrmacht'—Konstruktion und Rezeption." In *Die Wehrmacht: Mythos und Realität*, ed. Rolf-Dieter Müller and Hans-Erich Volkmann, 550–72. Munich: Oldenbourg, 1999.

Schlie, Ulrich. *Kein Friede mit Deutschland: Die geheimen Gespräche im Zweiten Weltkrieg, 1939-1941*. Munich: Langen Müller, 1994.

Schmidt, Paul-Otto. *Hitler's Interpreter*. Edited and translated by R. H. C. Sneed. New York: Macmillan, 1951.

——. *Statist auf diplomatischer Bühne, 1923-1945: Erlebnisse des Chefdolmetschers im Auswärtigen Amt mit den Staatsmännern Europas: Von Stresemann und Briand bis Hitler, Chamberlain und Molotow*. Bonn: Athenäum, 1949.

Schmidt, Rainer F. "Eine verfehlte Strategie für alle Fälle: Stalins Taktik und Kalkül im Vorfeld des Unternehmens 'Barbarossa.'" *Geschichte in Wissenschaft und Unterricht* 45, no. 6 (1994): 368–79.

Schönherr, Klaus. "Der Rückzug der Heeresgruppe A über die Krim bis Rumanien." In *Die Ostfront, 1943/44: Der Krieg im Osten und an den Nebenfronten* (vol. 8 of *Das deutsche Reich und der Zweite Weltkrieg*), ed. Karl-Heinz Frieser, 451–90. Munich: Deutsche Verlags-Anstalt, 2007.

——. "Die Rückzugskämpfe in Rumänien und Siebenbürgen im Sommer/Herbst 1944." In *Die Ostfront, 1943/44: Der Krieg im Osten und an den Nebenfronten* (vol. 8 of *Das deutsche Reich und der Zweite Weltkrieg*), ed. Karl-Heinz Frieser, 731–848. Munich: Deutsche Verlags-Anstalt, 2007.

Schörken, Rolf. "'Schülersoldaten'—Prägung einer Generation." In *Die Wehrmacht: Mythos und Realität*, ed. Rolf-Dieter Müller and Hans-Erich Volkmann, 456–73. Munich: Oldenbourg, 1999.

Schramm, Percy Ernst. *Hitler: The Man and the Military Leader*. Translated by Donald S. Detwiler. Chicago: Quadrangle, 1971.

——, ed. *Kriegstagebuch des Oberkommandos der Wehrmacht, 1940-1945*. 8 vols. 1961–1965. Reprint. Munich: Bernard & Graefe, 1982.

Schreiber, Gerhard. "Political and Military Developments in the Mediterranean Area, 1939-1940." In *The Mediterranean, South-East Europe, and North Africa, 1939-1941: From Italy's Declaration of Non-Belligerence to the Entry of the United States into the War* (vol. 3 of *Germany and the Second World War*), ed. Gerhard Schreiber, Bernd Stegemann, and Detlef Vogel, trans. Dean S. McMurry, Ewald Osers, and Louise Willmot, 5–301. New York: Oxford University Press, 1995.

——. "Hitler's Strategic Deliberations in Connection with the Attack on the Soviet Union." In *The Mediterranean, South-East Europe, and North Africa, 1939-1941: From Italy's Declaration of Non-Belligerence to the Entry of the United States into the War* (vol. 3 of *Germany and the Second World War*), ed. Gerhard Schreiber, Bernd Stegemann, and Detlef Vogel, trans. Dean S. McMurry, Ewald Osers, and Louise Willmot, 573–640. New York: Oxford University Press, 1995.

——. "Italien im machtpolitischen Kalkül der deutschen Marineführung, 1919 bis 1945." *Quellen und Forschungen aus italienischen Archiven und Bibliotheken* 62 (1982): 229–69.

——. "Der Mittelmeerraum in Hitlers Strategie 1940." *Militärgeschichtliche Mitteilungen* 39, no. 2 (1980): 69–99.

Schreiber, Gerhard, Bernd Stegemann, and Detlef Vogel, eds. *The Mediterranean, South-East Europe, and North Africa, 1939-1941: From Italy's Declaration of Non-Belligerence to the Entry of the United States into the War.* Translated by Dean S. McMurry, Ewald Osers, and Louise Willmot. Vol. 3 of *Germany and the Second World War.* New York: Oxford University Press, 1995.

——, eds. *Der Mittelmeerraum und Südosteuropa: Von der "Non Belligeranza" Italiens bis zum Kriegseintritt der Vereinigten Staaten.* Vol. 3 of *Das deutsche Reich und der Zweite Weltkrieg.* Stuttgart: Deutsche Verlags-Anstalt, 1984.

Schröder, Hans Joachim. "German Soldiers' Experiences during the Initial Phase of the Russian Campaign." In *From Peace to War: Germany, Soviet Russia, and the World, 1939-1941,* ed. Bernd Wegner, 309-59. Providence, RI: Berghahn, 1997.

——. *Die gestohlenen Jahre: Erzählgeschichten und Geschichtserzählung im Interview: Der Zweite Weltkrieg aus der Sicht ehemaliger Mannschaftssoldaten.* Tübingen: Niemeyer, 1992.

Schroder, Klaus. "Die Gedanken des Oberbefehlshabers der Kriegsmarine zum Kampf gegen England im Atlantik und im Mittelmeer, 1939-1940." *Marine-Rundschau* 67, no. 5 (1970): 257-72.

Schroeder, Christa. *Er War Mein Chef: Aus dem Nachlaß der Sekretärin von Adolf Hitler.* Edited by Anton Joachimsthaler. Munich: Langen Müller, 1985.

Schubert, Helmut. "Die Bereitstellung von Menschen für die Eindeutschung neuer Siedlungsräume im Osten." In *Vom Generalplan Ost zum Generalsiedlungsplan,* ed. Czeslaw Madajczyk and Stanislaw Biernacki, 138-50. Munich: Saur, 1994.

Schüler, Klaus. "The Eastern Campaign as a Transportation and Supply Problem." In *From Peace to War: Germany, Soviet Russia, and the World, 1939-1941,* ed. Bernd Wegner, 205-22. Providence, RI: Berghahn, 1997.

——. *Logistik im Rußlandfeldzug: Die Rolle der Eisenbahn bei Planung, Vorbereitung und Durchführung des deutschen Angriffs auf die Sowjetunion bis zur Krise vor Moskau im Winter 1941/42.* Frankfurt: Peter Lang, 1987.

Schulte, Jan Erik. *Zwangsarbeit und Vernichtung: Das Wirtschaftsimperium der SS: Oswald Pohl und das SS-Wirtschafts-Verwaltungshauptamt, 1933-1945.* Paderborn: Schöningh, 2001.

Schulte, Theo J. "Korück 582." In *Vernichtungskrieg: Verbrechen der Wehrmacht, 1941-1944,* ed. Hannes Heer and Klaus Naumann, 323-42. Hamburg: Hamburger Edition, 1995.

——. *The German Army and Nazi Policies in Occupied Russia.* Oxford: Berg, 1989.

Schustereit, Hartmut. "Planung und Aufbau der Wirtschaftsorganisation Ost vor dem Russlandfeldzug-Unternehmen 'Barbarossa' 1940/41." *Vierteljahrschrift für Sozial und Wirtschaftsgeschichte* 70, no. 1 (1983): 50-70.

Schwartz, Michael. "Ethnische 'Säuberung' als Kriegsfolge." In *Der Zusammenbruch des deutschen Reiches, 1945: Die Folgen des Zweiten Weltkrieges* (vol. 10/2 of *Das deutsche Reich und der Zweite Weltkrieg*), ed. Rolf-Dieter Müller and Jörg Echternkamp, 506-656. Munich: Deutsche Verlags-Anstalt, 2008.

Schwarz, Eberhard. "Zwischen Stalingrad und Kursk: Die Stabilisierung der Ostfront im Februar/März 1943." In *Stalingrad: Ereignis—Wirkung—Symbol,* ed. Jürgen Förster, 113-29. Munich: Piper, 1992.

Schwendemann, Heinrich. "Die deutsche Zusammenbruch im Osten, 1944/45." In *Kriegsende 1945: Verbrechen, Katastrophen, Befreiungen in Nationaler und Internationaler Perspektive,* Bernd-A. Rusinek, 125-50. Göttingen: Wallstein, 2004.

——. "Strategie der Selbstvernichtung: Die Wehrmachtführung im 'Endkampf' um das 'Dritte Reich.'" In *Die Wehrmacht: Mythos und Realität,* ed. Rolf-Dieter Müller and Hans-Erich Volkmann, 224-44. Munich: Oldenbourg, 1999.

Schwendemann, Heinrich, and Helen F. McEwan. "'Drastic Measures to Defend the Reich at the Oder and the Rhine': A Forgotten Memorandum of Albert Speer of 18 March 1945." *Journal of Contemporary History* 38, no. 4 (2003): 597-614.

Seidler, Franz W., ed. *Verbrechen an der Wehrmacht: Kriegsgreuel der Roten Armee, 1941/42.* 3rd ed. Selent: Pour le Merite, 1998.

———. *Deutscher Volkssturm: Das letzte Aufgebot, 1944/45.* Munich: Herbig, 1989.

———. *Fritz Todt: Baumeister des Dritten Reiches.* Munich: Herbig, 1986.

———. "Das nationalsozialistische Kraftfahrerkorps und die Organisation Todt im Zweiten Weltkrieg." *Vierteljahrshefte für Zeitgeschichte* 32, no. 4 (1984): 625-36.

———. "Die Fahnenflucht in der deutschen Wehrmacht während des Zweiten Weltkrieges." *Militärgeschichtliche Zeitschrift* 2, no. 2 (1977): 23-42.

———. "Zur Führung der Osttruppen in der deutschen Wehrmacht im Zweiten Weltkrieg." *Europäische Sicherheit: Politik–Streitkräfte–Wirtschaft–Technik* 20, no. 12 (1970): 683-702.

Sella, Amnon. "'Barbarossa': Surprise Attack and Communication." *Journal of Contemporary History* 13, no. 3 (1978): 555-83.

Seraphim, Hans-Gunther, and Andreas Hillgruber. "Hitlers Entschluss zum Angriff auf Russland: Eine Entgegnung." *Vierteljahrshefte für Zeitgeschichte* 2, no. 3 (1954): 240-54.

Sereny, Gitta. *Albert Speer: His Battle with Truth.* New York: Knopf, 1995.

Service, Robert. *A History of Twentieth Century Russia.* London: Penguin, 1997.

Shepherd, Ben. "Partisan and Anti-Partisan Warfare in German-Occupied Europe, 1939-1945: Views from Above and Lessons for the Present." *Journal of Strategic Studies* 31, no. 5 (2008): 675-93.

———. *War in the Wild East: The German Army and Soviet Partisans.* Cambridge, MA: Harvard University Press, 2004.

———. "The Continuum of Brutality: 'Wehrmacht' Security Divisions in Central Russia, 1942." *German History* 21, no. 1 (2003): 49-81.

———. "'Wehrmacht' Security Regiments in the Soviet Partisan War, 1943." *European History Quarterly* 33, no. 4 (2003): 493-529.

———. "Hawks, Doves and 'Tote Zonen': A Wehrmacht Security Division in Central Russia, 1943." *Journal of Contemporary History* 37, no. 3 (2002): 349-69.

Shils, Edward, and Morris Janowitz. "Cohesion and Disintegration in the Wehrmacht in World War II." *Public Opinion Quarterly* 12 (1948): 280-315.

Shirer, William L. *Berlin Diary: The Journal of a Foreign Correspondent, 1934-1941.* New York: Knopf, 1941.

Slepyan, Kenneth. *Stalin's Guerrillas: Soviet Partisans in World War II.* Lawrence: University Press of Kansas, 2006.

Smelser, Ronald. "How 'Modern' Were the Nazis? DAF Social Planning and the Modernization Question." *German Studies Review* 13, no. 2 (1990): 285-302.

Smelser, Ronald, and Edward J. Davies II. *The Myth of the Eastern Front: The Nazi-Soviet War in American Popular Culture.* New York: Cambridge University Press, 2008.

Smith, Woodruff D. *The Ideological Origins of Nazi Imperialism.* New York: Oxford University Press, 1986.

Sokolov, Boris V. "The Cost of War: Human Losses for the USSR and Germany, 1939-1945." *Journal of Slavic Military Studies* 9, no. 1 (1996): 152-93.

——. "The Battle for Kursk, Orel, and Char'kov." In *Gezeitenwechsel im Zweiten Weltkrieg? Die Schlachten von Char'kov und Kursk im Frühjahr und Sommer 1943 in operativer Anlage, Verlauf und politischer Bedeutung*, ed. Roland G. Foerster, 79–86. Hamburg: E. S. Mittler, 1996.

Sokolov, Boris V., and David M. Glantz. "The Role of Lend-Lease in Soviet Military Efforts, 1941–1945." *Journal of Slavic Military Studies* 7, no. 3 (1994): 567–86.

Speer, Albert. *Spandau: The Secret Diaries.* Translated by Richard Winston and Clara Winston. London: Collins, 1976.

——. *Inside the Third Reich: Memoirs.* Translated by Richard Winston and Clara Winston. New York: Macmillan, 1970.

Spoerer, Mark. *Zwangsarbeit unter dem Hakenkreuz: Ausländische Zivilarbeiter, Kriegsgefangene und Häftlinge im deutschen Reich und im besetzten Europa, 1939-1945.* Stuttgart: Deutsche Verlags-Anstalt, 2001.

Spratte, Wido, ed. *Stalingrad: Feldpostbriefe des Oberleutnants Harald Bleker.* Osnabrück: Wenner, 2000.

Staerck, Christopher. "Dresden: A Good Intelligence Decision?" *Modern History Review* 10, no. 4 (1999): 13–15.

Stahlberg, Alexander. *Bounden Duty: The Memoirs of a German Officer, 1932-45.* Translated by Patricia Crampton. London: Brassey's, 1990.

Stargardt, Nicholas. "Speaking in Public about the Murder of the Jews: What Did the Holocaust Mean to Germans?" In *Years of Persecution, Years of Extermination: Saul Friedländer and the Future of Holocaust Studies*, ed. Christian Wiese and Paul Betts, 133–56. London: Continuum, 2010.

Starkov, Oleg. "Militärischer Geheimnisverrat am Vorabend von 1941 'Barbarossa.'" *Österreichische militärische Zeitschrift* 29, no. 4 (1991): 327–30.

Stegemann, Bernd. "Geschichte und Politik: Zur Diskussion über den deutschen Angriff auf die Sowjetunion, 1941." *Beiträge zur Konfliktforschung* 17, no. 1 (1987): 73–97.

——. "Der Entschluss zum Unternehmen Barbarossa: Strategie oder Ideologie?" *Geschichte in Wissenschaft und Unterricht* 33, no. 4 (1982): 205–13.

——. "Hitlers Ziele im Ersten Kriegsjahr, 1939/40: Ein Beitrag zur Quellenkritik." *Militärgeschichtliche Mitteilungen* 27, no. 1 (1980): 73–105.

——. "Politik und Kriegführung in der Ersten Phase der deutschen Initiative." In *Die Errichtung der Hegemonie auf dem europäischen Kontinent* (vol. 2 of *Das deutsche Reich und der Zweite Weltkrieg*), ed. Klaus A. Meier. Stuttgart: Deutsche Verlags-Anstalt, 1979.

Steiger, Rudolf. *Panzertaktik im Spiegel deutscher Kriegstagebücher, 1939-1941.* Freiburg: Rombach, 1973.

Steinbach, Peter. "Widerstand und Wehrmacht." In *Die Wehrmacht: Mythos und Realität*, ed. Rolf-Dieter Müller and Hans-Erich Volkmann, 1150–70. Munich: Oldenbourg, 1999.

Steinert, Marlis. "Stalingrad und die deutsche Gesellschaft." In *Stalingrad: Ereignis–Wirkung–Symbol*, ed. Jürgen Förster, 171–85. Munich: Piper, 1992.

——. *Hitler's War and the Germans: Public Mood and Attitude during the Second World War.* Translated by Thomas E. J. de Witt. Athens: Ohio University Press, 1977.

Stibbe, Matthew. *Women in the Third Reich.* London: Arnold, 2003.

Stolfi, R. H. S. "The Greatest Encirclement Battle in History." *RUSI Journal* (Royal United Services Institute for Defence Studies), 141, no. 6 (1996): 64–72.

——. *Hitler's Panzers East: World War II Reinterpreted.* Norman: University of Oklahoma Press, 1991.

———. "Barbarossa Revisited: A Critical Reappraisal of the Opening Stages of the Russo-German Campaign (June–December 1941)." *Journal of Modern History* 54, no. 1 (1982): 27–46.

Strauss, F. J. *Friedens und Kriegserlebnisse einer Generation–Pz. Abt. 38 (SF) 2. (Wiener) Panzerdivision.* Neckargemünd: Kurt Vowinckel, 1977.

Streim, Alfred. "Das Völkerrecht und die sowjetischen Kriegsgefangenen." In *Zwei Wege nach Moskau: Vom Hitler-Stalin-Pakt zum "Unternehmen Barbarossa,"* ed. Bernd Wegner, 291–308. Munich: Piper, 1991.

———. *Sowjetische Gefangene in Hitlers Vernichtungskrieg: Berichte und Dokumente, 1941-1945.* Heidelberg: Müller, 1982.

———. *Die Behandlung sowjetischer Kriegsgefangener im "Fall Barbarossa": Eine Dokumentation unter Berücksichtigung der Unterlagen deutscher Strafverfolgungsbehörden und der Materialien der Zentralen Stelle der Landesjustizverwaltungen zur Aufklärung von NS-Verbrechen.* Heidelberg: Müller, 1981.

Streit, Christian. "Die Behandlung der verwundeten sowjetischen Kriegsgefangenen." In *Vernichtungskrieg: Verbrechen der Wehrmacht, 1941-1944,* ed. Hannes Heer and Klaus Naumann, 78–91. Hamburg: Hamburger Edition, 1995.

———. *Keine Kameraden: Die Wehrmacht und die sowjetischen Kriegsgefangenen, 1941-1945.* Bonn: J. H. W. Dietz, 1991.

———. "Ostkrieg, Antibolschewismus und 'Endlösung.'" *Geschichte und Gesellschaft* 17, no. 2 (1991): 242–55.

———. "Partisans—Resistance—Prisoners of War." *Soviet Union* 18, nos. 1–3 (1991): 259–76.

———. "Sowjetische Kriegsgefangene—Massendeportationen—Zwangsarbeiter." In *Der Zweite Weltkrieg: Analysen, Grundzüge, Forschungsbilanz,* ed. Wolfgang Michalka, 747–60. Munich: Piper, 1989.

———. "The German Army and the Politics of Genocide." In *The Policies of Genocide: Jews and Soviet Prisoners of War in Nazi Germany,* ed. Gerhard Hirschfeld, 1–14. London: Allen & Unwin, 1986.

———. "Die Behandlung der sowjetischen Kriegsgefangen." In *"Unternehmen Barbarossa": Der deutsche Überfall auf die Sowjetunion, 1941; Berichte, Analysen, Dokumente,* ed. Gerd R. Ueberschär and Wolfram Wette, 197–209. Paderborn: Schöningh, 1984.

Suvorov, Viktor. *Icebreaker: Who Started the Second World War?* Translated by Thomas B. Beattie. London: Hamish Hamilton, 1990.

Sydnor, Charles W., Jr. *Soldiers of Destruction: The SS Death's Head Division, 1933-1945.* Princeton, NJ: Princeton University Press, 1977.

Syring, Enrico. "Hitlers Kriegserklärung an Amerika vom 11. Dezember 1941." In *Der Zweite Weltkrieg: Analysen, Grundzüge, Forschungsbilanz,* ed. Wolfgang Michalka, 683–96. Munich: Piper, 1989.

Tams, Karl-Hermann. "Als Kompaniechef in Seelow im April 1945." *Militärgeschichte* 29, no. 6 (1990): 565–75.

TBJG. See Fröhlich, ed., *Die Tagebücher Joseph Goebbels.*

Thamer, Hans-Ulrich. "Die Erosion einer Säule: Wehrmacht und NSDAP." In *Die Wehrmacht: Mythos und Realität,* ed. Rolf-Dieter Müller and Hans-Erich Volkmann, 420–35. Munich: Oldenbourg, 1999.

Thomas, David. "Foreign Armies East and German Military Intelligence in Russia, 1941–45." *Journal of Contemporary History* 22, no. 2 (1987): 261–301.

Tooze, Adam. "Hitler's Gamble?" *History Today* 56 (November 2006): 22–28.

——. *The Wages of Destruction: The Making and Breaking of the Nazi Economy.* New York: Viking, 2006.

——. "No Room for Miracles: German Industrial Output in World War II Reassessed." *Geschichte und Gesellschaft* 31, no. 3 (2005): 439–64.

——. "'Punktuelle Modernisierung': Die Akkumulation von Werkzeugmaschinen im 'Dritten Reich.'" *Jahrbuch für Wirtschaftsgeschichte*, no. 1 (2003): 79–98.

Topitsch, Ernst. *Stalin's War: A Radical New Theory of the Origins of the Second World War.* Translated by A. Taylor and B. E. Taylor. New York: St. Martin's, 1987.

Töppel, Roman. "Legendenbildung in der Geschichtsschreibung—die Schlacht bei Kursk." *Militärgeschichtliche Zeitschrift* 61, no. 2 (2002): 369–401.

Treue, Wilhelm. "Hitlers Denkschrift zum Vierjahresplan, 1936." *Vierteljahrshefte für Zeitgeschichte* 3, no. 2 (1955): 184–210.

Tyaglyy, Mikhail I. "The Role of Antisemitic Doctrine in German Propaganda in the Crimea, 1941–1944." *Holocaust and Genocide Studies* 18, no. 3 (2004): 421–59.

Ueberschär, Gerd R. "Das 'Unternehmen Barbarossa' gegen die Sowjetunion—ein Präventivkrieg? Zur Wiederbelebung der Alten Rechtfertigungsversuche des deutschen Überfalls auf die UdSSR 1941." In *Wahrheit und "Auschwitzlüge": Zur Bekämpfung "revisionistischer" Propaganda,* ed. Brigitte Bailer-Galanda, Wolfgang Benz, and Wolfgang Neugebauer, 163–82. Vienna: Deuticke, 1995.

——. *Der 20. Juli 1944: Bewertung und Rezeption des deutschen Widerstandes gegen das NS-Regime.* Cologne: Bund, 1994.

——. "Hitler's Decision to Attack the Soviet Union in Recent German Historiography." *Soviet Union* 18, nos. 1–3 (1991): 297–315.

——. "General Halder and the Resistance to Hitler in the German High Command, 1938–40." *European History Quarterly* 18, no. 3 (1988): 321–47.

——. "Zur Wiederbelebung der 'Präventivkriegsthese': Die Neuen Rechtfertigungsversuche des deutschen Überfalls auf die UdSSR 1941 im Dienste 'psychopolitischer Aspekte' und 'psychologischer Kriegführung.'" *Geschichtsdidaktik* 12, no. 4 (1987): 331–42.

——. "Hitlers Entschluß zum 'Lebensraum' Krieg im Osten: Programmatisches Ziel oder militärstrategisches Kalkül?" In *"Unternehmen Barbarossa": Der deutsche Überfall auf die Sowjetunion, 1941; Berichte, Analysen, Dokumente,* ed. Gerd R. Ueberschär and Wolfram Wette, 83–110. Paderborn: Schöningh, 1984.

——. "Das Scheitern des Unternehmen 'Barbarossa': Der deutsch-sowjetische Krieg vom Überfall bis zur Wende vor Moskau im Winter 1941–42." In *"Unternehmen Barbarossa": Der deutsche Überfall auf die Sowjetunion, 1941; Berichte, Analysen, Dokumente,* ed. Gerd R. Ueberschär and Wolfram Wette, 141–72. Paderborn: Schöningh, 1984.

——. "Ausgewählte Dokumente zum 'Unternehmen Barbarossa.'" In *"Unternehmen Barbarossa": Der deutsche Überfall auf die Sowjetunion, 1941; Berichte, Analysen, Dokumente,* ed. Gerd R. Ueberschär and Wolfram Wette, 295–402. Paderborn: Schöningh, 1984.

Ueberschär, Gerd R., and Lev Bezymenskij. *Der deutsche Angriff auf die Sowjetunion, 1941: Die Kontroverse um die Präventivkriegsthese.* Darmstadt: Primus, 1998.

Ueberschär, Gerd R., and Wolfram Wette, eds. *"Unternehmen Barbarossa": Der deutsche Überfall auf die Sowjetunion, 1941; Berichte, Analysen, Dokumente.* Paderborn: Schöningh, 1984.

Uldricks, Teddy J. "The Icebreaker Controversy: Did Stalin Plan to Attack Hitler?" *Slavic Review* 58, no. 3 (1999): 626–43.

——. "Stalin and Nazi Germany." *Slavic Review* 36, no. 4 (1978): 599–603.

Umbreit, Hans. "Die Verantwortlichkeit der Wehrmacht als Okkupationsarmee." In *Die Wehrmacht: Mythos und Realität*, ed. Rolf-Dieter Müller and Hans-Erich Volkmann, 743–53. Munich: Oldenbourg, 1999.

——, ed. *Invasion 1944*. Hamburg: E. S. Mittler, 1998.

——. "Das Unbewältigte Problem: Der Partisankrieg im Rücken der Ostfront." In *Stalingrad: Ereignis–Wirkung–Symbol*, ed. Jürgen Förster, 130–50. Munich: Piper, 1992.

Ungvary, Krisztian. "Kriegsschauplatz Ungarn." In *Die Ostfront, 1943/44: Der Krieg im Osten und an den Nebenfronten* (vol. 8 of *Das deutsche Reich und der Zweite Weltkrieg*), ed. Karl-Heinz Frieser, 849–958. Munich: Deutsche Verlags-Anstalt, 2007.

van Creveld, Martin. "Die deutsche Wehrmacht: Eine militärische Beurteilung." In *Die Wehrmacht: Mythos und Realität*, ed. Rolf-Dieter Müller and Hans-Erich Volkmann, 331–45. Munich: Oldenbourg, 1999.

——. *Fighting Power: German and US Army Performance, 1939-1945*. Westport, CT: Greenwood, 1982.

——. *Supplying War: Logistics from Wallenstein to Patton*. Cambridge: Cambridge University Press, 1977.

——. "In the Shadow of Barbarossa: Germany and Albania, January–March 1941." *Journal of Contemporary History* 7, nos. 3–4 (1972): 221–30.

van Pelt, Robert Jan, and Deborah Dwork. *Auschwitz: 1270 to the Present*. New York: Norton, 1996.

Van Tuyll, Hubert P. "D-Day in the East: American Aid and Soviet Victory, 1944." *Journal of the Georgia Association of Historians* 15 (December 1994): 220–34.

Vogel, Detlef. "Germany's Balkan Policy in the Autumn of 1940 and the Spring of 1941." In *The Mediterranean, South-East Europe, and North Africa, 1939-1941: From Italy's Declaration of Non-Belligerence to the Entry of the United States into the War* (vol. 3 of *Germany and the Second World War*), ed. Gerhard Schreiber, Bernd Stegemann, and Detlef Vogel, trans. Dean S. McMurry, Ewald Osers, and Louise Willmot, 449–555. New York: Oxford University Press, 1995.

Vogelsang, Thilo. "Neue Dokumente zur Geschichte der Reichswehr, 1930–1933." *Vierteljahrshefte für Zeitgeschichte* 2, no. 4 (1954): 397–436.

Vogt, Martin. "Selbstbespiegelung in Erwartung des Sieges." In *Der Zweite Weltkrieg: Analysen, Grundzüge, Forschungsbilanz*, ed. Wolfgang Michalka, 641–51. Munich: Piper, 1989.

Volkmann, Hans-Erich. "Historiker im Banne der Vergangenheit: Volksgeschichte und Kulturbodenforschung zwischen Versailles und Kalten Krieg: Versuch eines thematischen Aufrisses." *Zeitschrift für Geschichtswissenschaft* 49, no. 1 (2001): 5–12.

——. "Zur Verantwortlichkeit der Wehrmacht." In *Die Wehrmacht: Mythos und Realität*, ed. Rolf-Dieter Müller and Hans-Erich Volkmann, 195–222. Munich: Oldenbourg, 1999.

——, ed. *Ende des Dritten Reiches—Ende des Zweiten Weltkriegs: Eine perspektivische Rückschau*. Munich: Piper, 1995.

——. "The National Socialist Economy in Preparation for War." In *The Build-Up of German Aggression* (vol. 1 of *Germany and the Second World War*), ed. Wilhelm Deist, trans. P. S. Falla, Dean S. McMurry, and Ewald Osers, 157–372. Oxford: Clarendon, 1990.

——. "Landwirtschaft und Ernährung in Hitlers Europa, 1939–45." *Militärgeschichtliche Zeitschrift* 35, no. 1 (1984): 9–74.

——. "Zur Ansiedlung der Deutschbalten im 'Warthegau.'" *Zeitschrift für Ostforschung* 30, no. 4 (1981): 527–58.

Volkogonov, Dmitri. "The German Attack, the Soviet Response, Sunday, 22 June 1941." In *Barbarossa: The Axis and the Allies,* ed. John Erickson and David Dilks, 76–94. Edinburgh: Edinburgh University Press, 1994.

Vollnhals, Clemens, ed. *Wehrmacht, Verbrechen, Widerstand: Vier Beiträge zum nationalsozialistischen Weltanschauungskrieg.* Dresden: Hannah-Arendt-Institut für Totalitarismusforschung e. V. an der Technischen Universität, 2003.

Wachsmann, Nikolaus. *Hitler's Prisons: Legal Terror in Nazi Germany.* New Haven, CT: Yale University Press, 2004.

Waddington, Geoffrey T. "Ribbentrop and the Soviet Union, 1937–1941." In *Barbarossa: The Axis and the Allies,* ed. John Erickson and David Dilks, 7–32. Edinburgh: Edinburgh University Press, 1994.

Waite, Robert G. L. *The Psychopathic God: Adolf Hitler.* New York: Basic, 1977.

Warlimont, Walter. *Inside Hitler's Headquarters, 1939-1941.* Translated by R. H. Barry. New York: Praeger, 1964.

Wasser, Bruno. "Die 'Germanisierung' im Distrikt Lublin als Generalprobe und erst Realisierungsphase der GPO." In *Der "Generalplan Ost": Hauptlinien der nationalsozialistischen Planungs- und Vernichtungspolitik,* ed. Mechthild Rössler and Sabine Schleiermacher, 271–94. Berlin: Akademie, 1993.

——. *Himmlers Raumplanung im Osten: Der Generalplan Ost in Polen, 1940-1944.* Basel: Birkhäuser, 1993.

Wegner, Bernd. "Von Stalingrad nach Kursk." In *Die Ostfront, 1943/44: Der Krieg im Osten und an den Nebenfronten* (vol. 8 of *Das deutsche Reich und der Zweite Weltkrieg*), ed. Karl-Heinz Frieser, 3–79. Munich: Deutsche Verlags-Anstalt, 2007.

——. "Die Aporie des Krieges." In *Die Ostfront, 1943/44: Der Krieg im Osten und an den Nebenfronten* (vol. 8 of *Das deutsche Reich und der Zweite Weltkrieg*), ed. Karl-Heinz Frieser, 211–74. Munich: Deutsche Verlags-Anstalt, 2007.

——. "Die Kriegführung des 'als ob': Deutschlands strategische Lage seit Frühjahr 1944." In *Die Ostfront, 1943/44: Der Krieg im Osten und an den Nebenfronten* (vol. 8 of *Das deutsche Reich und der Zweite Weltkrieg*), ed. Karl-Heinz Frieser, 1165–91. Munich: Deutsche Verlags-Anstalt, 2007.

——. "Die Choreographie des Untergangs." In *Die Ostfront, 1943/44: Der Krieg im Osten und an den Nebenfronten* (vol. 8 of *Das deutsche Reich und der Zweite Weltkrieg*), ed. Karl-Heinz Frieser, 1192–1209. Munich: Deutsche Verlags-Anstalt, 2007.

——. "'Hitlers Krieg'? Zur Entscheidung, Planung und Umsetzung des 'Unternehmen Barbarossa.'" In *Verbrechen der Wehrmacht: Bilanz einer Debatte,* ed. Christian Hartmann, Johannes Hürter, and Ulrike Jureit, 29–39. Munich: Beck, 2005.

——. "The War against the Soviet Union, 1942-1943." In *The Global War: Widening of the Conflict into a World War and the Shift of the Initiative, 1941-1943* (vol. 6 of *Germany and the Second World War*), ed. Horst Boog, trans. Ewald Osers, 843–1215. Oxford: Clarendon, 2001.

——. "Hitler, der Zweite Weltkrieg und die Choreographie des Untergangs." *Geschichte und Gesellschaft* 26, no. 3 (2000): 493–518.

——. "Defensive ohne Strategie: Die Wehrmacht und das Jahr 1943." In *Die Wehrmacht: Mythos und Realität,* ed. Rolf-Dieter Müller and Hans-Erich Volkmann, 197–209. Munich: Oldenbourg, 1999.

——. "Im Schatten der 'Zweiten Front'? Anmerkungen zum deutschen Zusammenbruch im Osten im Sommer 1944." In *Invasion 1944*, ed. Hans Umbreit, 117–32. Hamburg: E. S. Mittler, 1998.

——, ed. *From Peace to War: Germany, Soviet Russia, and the World, 1939-1941*. Providence, RI: Berghahn, 1997.

——. "Das Ende der Strategie: Deutschlands politische und militärische Lage nach Stalingrad." In *Gezeitenwechsel im Zweiten Weltkrieg? Die Schlachten von Char'kov und Kursk im Frühjahr und Sommer 1943 in operativer Anlage, Verlauf und politischer Bedeutung*, ed. Roland G. Foerster, 211–28. Hamburg: E. S. Mittler, 1996.

——. "Vom Lebensraum zum Todesraum: Deutschlands Kriegführung zwischen Moskau und Stalingrad." In *Stalingrad: Ereignis–Wirkung–Symbol*, ed. Jürgen Förster, 17–38. Munich: Piper, 1992.

——, ed. *Zwei Wege nach Moskau: Vom Hitler-Stalin-Pakt zum "Unternehmen Barbarossa."* Munich: Piper, 1991.

——. "The Road to Defeat: The German Campaigns in Russia, 1941-43." *Journal of Strategic Studies* 13, no. 1 (1990): 105–27.

——. "Hitlers zweiter Feldzug gegen die Sowjetunion: Strategische Grundlagen und historische Bedeutung." In *Der Zweite Weltkrieg: Analysen, Grundzüge, Forschungsbilanz*, ed. Wolfgang Michalka, 652–66. Munich: Piper, 1989.

——. *Hitlers politische Soldaten: Die Waffen-SS, 1933-1945; Studien zu Leitbild, Struktur und Funktion einer nationalsozialistischen Elite*. Paderborn: Schöningh, 1982.

Wehner, Gü. "Die Letzten Tage des Krieges: Schulaufsätze von 1946." *Beiträge zur Geschichte der Arbeiterbewegung* 33, no. 5 (1991): 390–98.

Weinberg, Gerhard L. "Aspects of World War II German Intelligence." *Journal of Intelligence History* 4, no. 1 (2004): 1–6.

——. "Die Wehrmacht und Verbrechen im Zweiten Weltkrieg." *Zeitgeschichte* 30, no. 4 (2003): 207–10.

——, ed. *Hitler's Second Book: The Unpublished Sequel to Mein Kampf by Adolf Hitler.* Translated by Krista Smith. New York: Enigma, 2003.

——. "Unexplored Questions about the German Military during World War II." *Journal of Military History* 62, no. 2 (1998): 371–80.

——. "Zur Frage eines Sonderfriedens im Osten." In *Gezeitenwechsel im Zweiten Weltkrieg? Die Schlachten von Char'kov und Kursk im Frühjahr und Sommer 1943 in operativer Anlage, Verlauf und politischer Bedeutung*, ed. Roland G. Foerster, 173–83. Hamburg: E. S. Mittler, 1996.

——. "22 June 1941: The German View." *War in History* 3, no. 2 (1996): 225–33.

——. "Germany's War for World Conquest and the Extermination of the Jews." *Holocaust and Genocide Studies* 10, no. 2 (1996): 119–33.

——. *Germany, Hitler, and World War II: Essays in Modern German and World History*. New York: Cambridge University Press, 1995.

——. "Who Won World War II and How?" *Journal of Mississippi History* 57, no. 4 (1995): 275–87.

——. *A World at Arms: A Global History of World War II*. Cambridge: Cambridge University Press, 1994.

——. "Comments on the Papers by Friedlander, Breitman, and Browning." *German Studies Review* 17, no. 3 (1994): 509–12.

——. "German Plans for Victory, 1944-45." *Central European History* 26, no. 2 (1993): 215–28.

——. "Some Thoughts on World War II." *Journal of Military History* 56, no. 4 (1992): 659–68.

———. "Why Hitler Declared War on the United States." *MHQ: Quarterly Journal of Military History* 4, no. 3 (1992): 18–23.

———. "German Diplomacy towards the Soviet Union." *Soviet Union* 18, nos. 1–3 (1991): 317–33.

———. "What Can German History Tell Us about the German Question?" *Proceedings of the South Carolina Historical Association*, 1991, 1–8.

———. "Hitler's Memorandum on the Four-Year Plan: A Note." *German Studies Review* 11, no. 1 (1988): 133–35.

———. *World in the Balance: Behind the Scenes of World War II*. Hanover, NH: University Press of New England, 1981.

———. "Adolf Hitler und der NS-Führungsoffizier (NSFO)." *Vierteljahrshefte für Zeitgeschichte* 12, no. 4 (1964): 442–56.

———. "Hitler's Image of the United States." *American Historical Review* 69, no. 4 (1964): 1006–21.

Weinzierl, Erika. "Nationalsozialistische Besatzungspolitik in Europa: Einige Bemerkungen zur Rolle von Österreichern." *Zeitschrift für Geschichtswissenschaft* 44, no. 7 (1996): 593–607.

Werth, Alexander. *Russia at War, 1941-1945*. New York: Avon, 1964.

———. *The Year of Stalingrad*. London: Hamish Hamilton, 1946.

Westermann, Edward B. *Hitler's Police Battalions: Enforcing Racial War in the East*. Lawrence: University Press of Kansas, 2005.

———. "Hitting the Mark, but Missing the Target: Luftwaffe Deception Operations, 1939-1945." *War in History* 10, no. 2 (2003): 206–21.

———. "'Ordinary Men' or 'Ideological Soldiers?' Police Battalion 310 in Russia, 1942." *German Studies Review* 21, no. 1 (1998): 41–68.

———. "Himmler's Uniformed Police on the Eastern Front: The Reich's Secret Soldiers, 1941-1942." *War in History* 3, no. 3 (1996): 309–29.

———. "'Friend and Helper': German Uniformed Police Operations in Poland and the General Government, 1939-1941." *Journal of Military History* 58, no. 4 (1994): 643–61.

Wette, Wolfram. *The Wehrmacht: History, Myth, Reality*. Translated by Deborah Lucas Schneider. Cambridge, MA: Harvard University Press, 2007.

———. *Die Wehrmacht: Feindbilder, Vernichtungskrieg, Legenden*. Frankfurt: Fischer Taschenbuch, 2005.

———. "'Es roch nach Ungeheuerlichem': Zeitzeugenbericht eines Panzerschützen über die Stimmung in einer Einheit des deutschen Ostheeres am Vorabend des Überfalls auf die Sowjetunion, 1942." *1999: Zeitschrift für Sozialgeschichte des 20. und 21. Jahrhunderts* 4, no. 4 (1989): 62–73.

———. "Das Massensterben als 'Heldenepos': Stalingrad in der NS-Propaganda." In *Stalingrad: Mythos und Wirklichkeit einer Schlacht*, ed. Wolfram Wette and Gerd R. Ueberschär, 43–60. Frankfurt: Fischer Taschenbuch, 1992.

———. "'Unsere Stimmung ist auf dem Nullpunkt angekommen.' Berichte von Feldpostprüfstellen über die 'Kessel-Post.'" In *Stalingrad: Mythos und Wirklichkeit einer Schlacht*, ed. Wolfram Wettle and Gerd R. Ueberschär, 90–101. Frankfurt: Fischer Taschenbuch, 1992.

———. "Die propagandistische Begleitmusik zum deutschen Überfall auf die Sowjetunion am 22. Juni 1941." In *"Unternehmen Barbarossa": Der deutsche Überfall auf die Sowjetunion, 1941; Berichte, Analysen, Dokumente*, ed. Gerd R. Ueberschär and Wolfram Wette, 111–28. Paderborn: Schöningh, 1984.

Wette, Wolfram, Ricarda Bremer, and Detlef Vogel, eds. *Das Letzte Halbe Jahr: Stimmungsberichte der Wehrmachtpropaganda, 1944/45.* Essen: Klartext, 2001.

Wette, Wolfram, and Gerd R. Ueberschär, eds. *Stalingrad: Mythos und Wirklichkeit einer Schlacht.* Frankfurt: Fischer Taschenbuch, 1992.

Wettstein, Adrian. "Operation 'Barbarossa' und Stadtkampf." *Militärgeschichtliche Zeitschrift* 66, no. 1 (2007): 21–44.

Wieder, Joachim, and Heinrich Graf von Einsiedel, eds. *Stalingrad: Memories and Reassessments.* Translated by Helmut Bogler. London: Arms & Armour, 1993.

Wildt, Michael. "The Spirit of the Reich Security Main Office (RSHA)." *Totalitarian Movements and Political Religions* 6, no. 3 (2005): 333–49.

———. *Nachrichtendienst, politische Elite, Mordeinheit: Der Sicherheitsdienst des Reichsführers SS.* Hamburg: Hamburger Edition, 2003.

———. *Generation des Unbedingten: Das Führungskorps des Reichssicherheitshauptamtes.* Hamburg: Hamburger Edition, 2002.

———, ed. *Die Judenpolitik des SD, 1935 bis 1938: Eine Dokumentation.* Munich: Oldenbourg, 1995.

Wilhelm, Hans-Heinrich. *Rassenpolitik und Kriegsführung: Sicherheitspolizei und Wehrmacht in Polen und in der Sowjetunion, 1939-1942.* Passau: Richard Rothe, 1991.

Wilt, Alan F. "Hitler's Late Summer Pause in 1941." *Military Affairs* 48, no. 4 (1981): 187–91.

Witte, Peter. "A New Document on the Deportation and Murder of Jews during 'Einsatz Reinhardt,' 1942." *Holocaust and Genocide Studies* 15, no. 3 (2001): 468–86.

———. "Two Decisions concerning the 'Final Solution to the Jewish Question': Deportations to Lodz and Mass Murder in Chelmno." *Holocaust and Genocide Studies* 9, no. 3 (1995): 318–45.

Wollenberg, Jörg, ed. *"Niemand war dabei und keiner hat's gewußt": Die deutsche Öffentlichkeit und die Judenverfolgung, 1933-1945.* Munich: Piper, 1989.

———, ed. *The German Public and the Persecution of Jews, 1933-1945: "No One Participated, No One Knew."* Translated by Rado Pribic. Atlantic Highlands, NJ: Humanities, 1996.

A Woman in Berlin: Eight Weeks in the Conquered City: A Diary. Translated by Philip Boehm. New York: Picador, 2000.

Yahil, Leni. "Madagascar—Phantom of a Solution for the Jewish Question." In *Jews and Non-Jews in Eastern Europe,* ed. George Mosse and Bela Vago, 315–34. New York: Wiley, 1974.

Yelton, David K. *Hitler's Volkssturm: The Nazi Militia and the Fall of Germany, 1944-1945.* Lawrence: University Press of Kansas, 2002.

Zeidler, Manfred. "Die Rote Armee auf deutschem Boden." In *Der Zusammenbruch des deutschen Reiches, 1945: Die militärische Niederwerfung der Wehrmacht* (vol. 10/1 of *Das deutsche Reich und der Zweite Weltkrieg*), ed. Rolf-Dieter Müller et al., 681–775. Munich: Deutsche Verlags-Anstalt, 2008.

———. *Kriegsende im Osten: Die Rote Armee und die Besetzung Deutschlands östlich von Oder und Neiße, 1944/45.* Munich: Oldenbourg, 1996.

Zeitzler, Kurt. "Stalingrad." In *The Fatal Decisions,* ed. Seymour Freidin, William Richardson, and Werner Kreipe, trans. Constantine Fitzgibbon, 132–96. New York: W. Sloan, 1956.

Zellhuber, Andreas. *"Unsere Verwaltung treibt einer Katastrophe zu . . .": Das Reichsministerium für die besetzten Ostgebiete und die deutsche Besatzungsherrschaft in der Sowjetunion, 1941-1945.* Munich: Ernst Vögel, 2006.

Zetterling, Niklas. "Loss Rates on the Eastern Front during World War II." *Journal of Slavic Military Studies* 9, no. 4 (1996): 895–906.

Zetterling, Niklas, and Anders Frankson. *Kursk 1943: A Statistical Analysis.* London: Frank Cass, 2000.

———. "Analyzing World War II Eastern Front Battles." *Journal of Slavic Military Studies* 11, no. 1 (1998): 176–203.

Zhukov, Georgii. *The Memoirs of Marshal Zhukov.* New York: Delacorte, 1971.

———. *Marshal Zhukov's Greatest Battles.* New York: Harper & Row, 1969.

Ziemke, Earl. *Stalingrad to Berlin: The German Defeat in the East.* Washington, DC: Office of the Chief of Military History, U.S. Army, 1968.

Ziemke, Earl, and Magna E. Bauer. *Moscow to Stalingrad: Decision in the East.* Washington, DC: Center of Military History, U.S. Army, 1987.

Zimmerer, Jürgen. "The Birth of the 'Ostland' out of the Spirit of Colonialism: A Postcolonial Perspective on the Nazi Policy of Conquest and Extermination." *Patterns of Prejudice* 39, no. 2 (2005): 197–219.

———. "Holocaust und Kolonialismus: Beitrag zu einer Archäologie des Genozidalen Gedankens." *Zeitschrift für Geschichtswissenschaft* 51, no. 12 (2003): 1098–1119.

Zitelmann, Rainer. *Hitler: Selbstverständnis eines Revolutionärs.* Hamburg: Berg, 1987.

———. "Zur Begründung des 'Lebensraum' Motivs in Hitlers Weltanschauung." In *Der Zweite Weltkrieg: Analysen, Grundzüge, Forschungsbilanz,* ed. Wolfgang Michalka, 551–67. Munich: Piper, 1989.

Index

Abganerovo, 288
Abganerovo Station, 288
Afrika Korps, 469
aircraft industry (German), 329, 363–64, 426
air fleets (German). *See* Luftflotte
air force (German). *See* Luftwaffe
air force (Soviet). *See* Red Air Force
Air Ministry, Reich, 426
Aksai (Aksay) River, 288
Aktion Reinhard, 361
Alagir, 282
Algeria, 46
allies, German, xxiv, 46, 48, 51, 71, 83, 234, 298, 306, 405, 434, 484, 486–87
allies, Western, 216, 234, 268, 325, 330–31, 359, 362–63, 394, 400, 406, 408, 421, 423, 426, 439–40, 447, 455, 458, 462, 466, 468–71, 542n86
  losses, 470
Alpenfestung, 458
Alsace-Lorraine, 256
Angerapp River, 430
Anti-Comintern Pact, 45
anti-Semitism (Germany). See *ewige Jude, Der;* Final Solution; German army; Germany; Goebbels; Hitler; Jews; Kristallnacht; National Socialism; pogroms
Antonescu, Marshal Ion, 109, 435–36
appeasement, 10, 78–79
Archangel, 55, 238
Ardennes, 27, 433–34, 437–38, 440, 444, 456, 470
Ardon River, 282
Armed Forces High Command. *See* Oberkommando der Wehrmacht (OKW)
Armies (German)
  First Panzer, 143–44, 163–65, 266–68, 276, 278, 282, 355, 370–71, 388, 390, 392–96, 398, 403, 414
  Second, 143, 145, 161, 184–85, 187, 201, 203, 208, 210, 264, 266, 369, 371, 378, 409, 412, 444
  Second Panzer, 117, 126, 142–44, 145, 149, 151, 153–54, 156, 158–62, 184, 186, 187, 191, 200–201, 203, 207–8, 210–11, 216, 345–46, 353
  Third Panzer, 126, 146, 152–56, 162, 184, 186–87, 191, 200, 202–3, 211, 409, 412–13, 415–16, 444, 446, 461, 465
  Fourth, 156, 161–62, 184–85, 187, 192, 200, 208–12, 354, 409, 412, 414–16, 430, 444, 446
  Fourth Panzer, 88, 142, 147, 152–55, 156, 162, 184, 186, 191, 192, 200, 203, 209, 211, 264, 267, 276, 284, 286, 288–89, 292, 309, 314, 323, 339, 346, 351, 355, 370, 378–79, 392, 394–96, 525n20
  Sixth, 97, 102, 104, 126, 129, 141, 163–64, 185, 248, 250, 261, 264–65, 267, 269, 271–72, 283–84, 286, 288–92, 295, 297, 301, 303–4, 306–20, 322, 325, 355, 370, 379, 388, 436
  Sixth SS Panzer, 438, 444, 448
  Eighth, 284, 356, 370, 387, 390, 394–95
  Ninth, 161, 167–68, 184–86, 203, 208–11, 215, 339–40, 343–46, 350,

Armies (German) *(cont.)*
353, 409, 412–15, 445, 460–61,
463–64, 466–67
Eleventh, 163, 241, 247, 268, 276
Seventeenth, 143, 161–64, 248, 276, 379
Eighteenth, 69, 211, 385
Replacement, 116, 151–52, 189, 204
Armies (Italian)
Eighth, 284, 289, 292, 315
Armies (Polish)
First, 445
Armies (Soviet)
First Shock, 191
First Tank, 285
Second Shock, 211, 213
Second Tank, 419
Second Guards Tank, 430
Third Guards Tank, 395
Fourth Shock, 211
Fourth Tank, 395
Fifth Guards, 348
Fifth Guards Tank, 348–49, 357
Sixth Guards, 356
Seventh Guards, 348
Eleventh Guards, 430
Twenty-seventh, 356
Twenty-eighth, 250
Twenty-ninth, 211
Thirty-third, 211
Thirty-eighth, 250, 395
Fortieth, 388
Forty-seventh, 445
Sixty-second, 285, 291, 293–94
Sixty-fourth, 291
armor strength (German). *See*
German army: tanks
armor strength (Soviet). *See* Red
Army: tanks
Army Detachment Kempf, 346–48, 355
army (German). *See* German army
army (Soviet). *See* Red Army
Army Groups (German)
A, 27, 261, 266, 271–72, 275–77,
280, 283–84, 303–4, 315–16, 319,
322, 378–79, 388, 396–97, 441–42,
444–45
B, 261, 271–72, 275–76, 284, 289,
303, 306, 308–9, 312, 458
Center, 53, 86–87, 89, 97, 113, 117,

120, 123–26, 128–29, 131–33,
141–42, 146–47, 149, 151–52, 155,
160–61, 172, 183–86, 192, 200, 202–
4, 206–7, 209–11, 214–16, 218–19,
236, 304–5, 324, 339, 344, 346,
350–51, 354, 365, 368, 372–73, 378,
381–83, 387, 405–13, 415–18, 420,
432–34, 437, 441–42, 444, 446,
465, 468, 524n2
Courland, 446
Don, 309, 312, 315–16, 321–22
North, 53, 88, 97, 113, 120, 126, 128,
146–47, 156, 205, 211, 213, 216, 236,
365, 382–85, 387, 405–6, 408–9,
415, 417–18, 430–33, 446
North Ukraine, 408–9, 412–13
South, 53, 89, 117, 120, 123, 125,
129, 141, 143, 163–65, 184–85, 203,
216, 226, 233, 236, 243, 249, 261,
265–66, 323, 339, 345, 347, 350–51,
355–56, 365, 371–73, 378, 380,
384, 387, 390, 392, 394, 398, 405,
431, 436, 454
South Ukraine, 432, 434, 436
Vistula, 446, 448, 461
Army Groups (Soviet). *See* Fronts
Army High Command. *See*
Oberkommando des Heeres (OKH)
Aryanization, 483
Asia, 17, 22, 45, 64, 68, 70, 97, 186,
255, 375, 453, 477
Astrakhan, 55, 271, 275, 277
Atlantic, Battle of the, xxiv, 46, 194, 196,
233, 268, 339, 432, 434, 470, 486
Atlantic Charter, 109–10, 131
atomic bomb, 232, 485
Auftragstaktik (mission oriented
tactics), 102, 229, 352
Auschwitz, 177–78, 181, 220, 223,
226, 254, 257–58, 260, 317, 362.
See also concentration camps;
extermination camps
Austria, 12, 14, 106, 436–37, 447, 478
Avranches, 419
Azov, Sea of, 323, 365, 370

Babi Yar, 102–3
Backe, Herbert, 60–62, 171, 224–26,
505n57, 505n60

Bach-Zelewski, Erich von dem
    (SS-Obergruppenführer), 333
Bagration, Operation, xv, 405–10,
    420–23, 442
Bakhmut River, 165
Baku, 106, 271–72, 279, 282
Balaton, Lake, 436–37
Balck, Hermann (General), 380
Balkans, 32, 36–38, 43, 46, 48–50, 71,
    84, 204, 336–37, 341, 362, 406,
    408
Baltic Sea, 55, 77, 113, 128, 146, 365,
    382, 385, 406, 418, 432–33, 440,
    461
Baltic solution, 406–8
Baltic states, 19–20, 32, 36–38, 41–42,
    49–50, 53, 56, 88–89, 93, 106, 120,
    148, 172, 219, 255–56, 385, 408,
    418, 429–31, 433, 448, 476, 481
Bamberg, 300
Baranovichi, 417
Barbarossa, Operation, xv, xxiv, 72–76
    aim of, 50–52, 66–67, 75–76
    Barbarossa Jurisdiction Decree (13
        May 1941), 68–69, 480
    Commissar Order, xv, 68–69, 94,
        480–81, 519n57
    crisis of confidence, 125–34
    decision for, 35–44, 48–52
    Directive No. 21 (Barbarossa
        Directive), 51, 66
    Directive No. 33, 125–28
    Directive No. 34, 128–29
    economic objectives of, 40–42,
        60–61, 82–83
    and Einsatzgruppen, 66, 70–71,
        94–96, 101–4
    escalating problems, 58–60, 81–82,
        87–88, 112–18
    failure of, 191–93
    "Guidelines for Special Areas"
        (Einsatzgruppen), 66
    Hitler's intervention in military
        matters, 125–28
    invasion launched, 77–78, 86–91
    and Kiev pocket, 141–46
    and Leningrad, 146–47
    logistic problems, 56–57, 118–20,
        149–51, 158–59, 185–86, 215–16
    morale of troops, 89, 109, 111–12,
        121, 130, 152, 155, 159, 162–64,
        182, 188–90, 192–93, 201–2
    operational plan, 82–85
    and operations in the Balkans, 71–72
    and operations in Ukraine, 140–46,
        163–65
    and Operation Typhoon, 152–57,
        160–63, 182–93
    and partisan war, 86–87, 98, 101–2,
        104, 106, 108, 111, 149, 160, 174,
        180, 193, 198
    planning for, 52–60
    popular German reaction, 121, 135–
        36, 184, 229–30
    Soviet counterattack (Moscow),
        199–205, 210–15; and German
        response, 205–12, 215–17
    Soviet resistance, 85–88, 111–12,
        114–15, 122–25, 156–58
    Stalin's reaction, 78–81
    Supplement to Directive No. 33,
        126–28
    Supplement to Directive No. 34, 131
    as war of extermination, 66–71,
        75–76, 91–111, 166–73, 217–26
    See also Typhoon
Barrikady gun factory, 290, 296,
    298–99
Barvenkovo, 248, 250–51
Basargino Station, 288
battle group. See Kampfgruppe
Bautzen, 469
Bavaria, 137, 468
Beck, Ludwig (General), 36
Belaja Kalitva, 317
Belaya Tserkov, 102
Belgorod, 323–24, 351, 353, 355
Belorussia (White Russia), 37–38, 86,
    89, 93, 95, 102, 106, 140, 172, 176,
    178, 254, 256, 333, 381, 405, 407–
    10, 415, 435, 486
Below, Nicolaus von (Captain), 296
Belzec, 178, 181, 220, 226, 253, 361
Berchtesgaden, 309, 395, 415,
Berdichev, 387
Berezina River, 415
Berezino, 415–16
Berezovka, 219

Berghof, xv, 18, 33, 42, 307, 396–97, 400, 417–18. *See also* Obersalzberg
Berlin
  Allied bombing raids on, 363, 466
  Battle of, 438, 441–42, 447, 449, 458–69
  deportation of Jews, 14, 24, 109, 175–76, 258–59, 531n31
  food situation, 136
  Hitler's triumphal return (1940), 31
  Red Army atrocities in, 450
  signs of war weariness in, 325
  Sportpalast, 63, 155, 181, 296, 298, 326
Bessarabia, 32, 49, 434
Bialystok, 86–88, 94–95, 97
Birkenau, 177, 220, 257. *See also* concentration camps
black market, 136, 171, 224, 427–28
Black Sea, 77, 141, 241, 245, 271–72, 277–78, 355, 379, 387, 396–98, 435
Black Sea Fleet (Soviet), 241, 245
Blau, Operation, xv, 230–39, 241, 246, 248, 252–53, 261–67, 269–70, 291, 338
blitzkrieg, xv, xxiii, 9, 26–29, 52–55, 57, 74, 82, 87, 110, 125, 129, 160, 171, 214, 231–32, 293, 324, 346, 422, 434, 473, 476, 484, 486
Blobel, Paul, 102–3
blocking units (Red Army), 143, 273
Blomberg, Werner von (General), 11
BMW, 260
Bobruisk, 381, 408–9, 414–15
Bock, Fedor von (Field Marshal)
  dismissal of (July 1942), 267
  dismissal of (December 1941), 205–6
  doubts about Operation Barbarossa, 51, 59, 82
  Operation Barbarossa, 86–87, 111, 113, 123–25, 127, 129, 131–33, 140, 142–44, 146
  Operation Blau, 243, 248–51, 253, 261, 263, 265–67, 269
  Operation Typhoon, 145, 151–56, 159–62, 170, 182–85, 187–88, 191–92
  protests "Jew trains," 176
  Soviet counterattack (Moscow), 199–200, 202–7

Bohemia, 437, 465, 468
Bolshaya (bridgehead), 307–8
Bolshevism
  German determination to eradicate, 42, 66–68, 73, 97–98, 101, 121, 170–73, 175
  "Jewish," xxi–xxii, 5, 7–11, 26, 35, 42, 66, 68, 70, 74, 78, 94, 101, 110, 135, 360, 375, 377, 473, 480, 487
  in Hitler's worldview, xxi, 5, 7–11, 17, 26, 35–36, 42, 44, 66–67, 72–73, 75, 78, 91, 94, 110, 235, 360, 366, 440, 473, 478, 480, 484
  in Nazi ideology, 68, 254, 478, 480, 487
  in Nazi propaganda, 99, 107, 135, 137, 236, 320–22, 327, 376–77, 453, 512n56
"booty" Ukrainians, 373, 377, 384, 394, 398–99, 435
Borisov, 416
Bormann, Martin, 105, 178, 328–29, 474
Bouhler, Philipp, 138–39, 180
Brack, Viktor, 138, 180
Bradley, Omar (General), 468
Brandenburg, 446
Brandt, Karl, 139
Brauchitsch, Walter von (Field Marshal), 19, 27, 38–39, 42–43, 50, 66, 69, 75, 101, 124, 127, 131–32, 148, 164, 190, 201
  dismissal of, 205–6
Braun, Eva, 467
Breker, Arno, 3
Brenner Pass, 47
Breslau, 442, 445, 447–48
Brest-Litovsk, 39, 86, 408, 418
brigades, German
  First SS, 70, 106, 203
  Grodeck, 244
Britain, xxii
  Battle of, 33–34, 38–39, 41–43, 46–49, 484–85
  Bomber Command, 330, 466
  bombing campaign, 50, 72, 83, 109, 136–37, 427
  and "destroyers for bases" deal, 40, 45

Dunkirk evacuation, 484
and eugenics movement, 138
and German invasion of Poland, 8,
25
and German plans for invasion of
USSR, 42, 58, 75
Germany and, xxiii, 2, 6-7, 24,
28-29, 41, 44, 51-52, 60, 71, 83,
469, 475, 477, 479
Hitler and, 3, 6, 8-10, 12-14, 16,
32-33, 36-38, 40, 43, 63-64, 71,
75, 91, 156, 194, 217, 268, 296, 400,
402, 433, 475
Hitler's "peace offer," 25, 33-35, 37,
45, 326, 363, 484
Joint Intelligence Subcommittee,
336
and Lend-Lease, 40
and Mers-el-Kebir, 33
Soviet Union and, xxii, 144, 165,
276, 341
U.S. and, 39-40, 45, 71, 110, 194, 484
warnings to Stalin, 80
British Empire, 2, 8, 29, 34
German plans for attack on, 43, 50,
233
Japan and, 34, 42-43, 45, 51, 71-72,
194, 217, 233
Bromberg (Bydgoszcz), 446
Brusilov, 380
Bryansk, 153-55, 156, 157, 160, 211,
219, 232, 346, 348, 369
Budenny, Semen (Marshal), 145
Bucharest, 435-36
Budapest, xv, 362, 437-38
Bug River, 86, 141, 394, 397, 418, 429
Bukovina, 32, 49
Bukrin (bridgehead), 378
Busch, Ernst (Field Marshal), 381,
408, 410-15, 437
Busse, Theodor (General), 460, 466
Bustard Hunt, Operation
(Trappenjagd), xvii, 243, 529n5

Carpathian Mountains, 140, 387-88,
392, 396, 434-36
Caspian Sea, 55, 233, 272
casualties, German. See German
army: casualties

casualties, Soviet. See Red Army:
casualties
Catholic Church, 136-38
Caucasus
in German planning, 53, 59, 130,
132, 162-64, 182, 190, 231-32, 234,
239, 241, 313, 316, 336, 342
oil in, 53, 59, 83-84, 89, 91, 126, 129,
132, 145, 165, 182, 235, 238, 277,
280, 326
operations in, 245, 261-62, 268, 270-
72, 274-79, 281-84, 291, 296, 301,
306, 322, 324
and Soviet planning, 84, 200, 269,
304, 315
Chamberlain, Neville, 10
Chelmno, 178, 219-20, 226, 253
Cernovicy (Chernovtsy), 395
Cherkassy, 141, 389-95, 398
Cherniakhovsky, Ivan Danilovich
(General), 444
Chernigov, 365, 368-69
Chernobyl, 369, 371, 378, 381
Chir River, 307, 314
Chotin, 395
Chuikov, Vasilii Ivanovich (General),
288, 293-94, 296, 298, 301, 304
Churchill, Winston, 32-34, 37-38, 46,
79-80, 110, 131, 157, 174, 197, 328,
458
Ciano, Count Galeazzo, 32, 166, 190
Citadel, Operation (Zitadelle)
consequence of, 357
delays, 340-42
doubts about, 339-42
losses, 352-53
operations, 344-53
plans for, 338-39, 341, 343
strength of opposing forces, 343-44
See also Kursk, Battle of
Clausewitz, Carl von, 82-83
climate. See weather
coal, 28, 150, 169, 226, 229, 297, 322,
366, 475, 492-93
collaborators (with Germans), 97
Cologne, 144
colonies, 17, 46, 48, 170, 259
colonization, 7, 92-93, 173, 241, 254-
57, 476-79

Commissar Order (6 June 1941), xv, 68–69, 94, 480–81, 519n57
Communist Party (Soviet), 94, 156–57
Compiegne, 2
concentration camps
  Auschwitz, 178–79, 181, 220, 223, 226, 254, 257–58, 260, 317, 362
  Dachau, 260
  death marches, 454–55
  destruction through labor, 94–95, 180, 223, 260–61, 334, 481
  euthanasia in, 139
  forced labor in, 93–94, 221–22, 259–61, 332, 334–36, 364, 428, 481, 486
  Mauthausen, 260
  Mittelbau-Dora, 335, 426
  Oranienburg, 260
  Ravensbrück, 260
  Sachsenhausen, 260
  See also extermination camps; forced labor
continental bloc, 44–48, 51
Corps (German)
  Second SS Panzer, 323, 347–51, 396, 398, 402, 541n69, 542n80
  Third Panzer, 251, 275, 282, 355–56, 390
  Fourth SS Panzer, 444
  Fifth, 275
  Eighth Air, 242
  Eleventh, 285, 317
  Thirteenth, 388
  Fourteenth Armored, 298
  Fourteenth Panzer, 285–87, 289, 309
  Twentieth, 209
  Twenty-fourth, 142
  Twenty-fourth Motorized, 154
  Twenty-fourth Panzer, 211, 285, 351, 355–56
  Twenty-ninth, 370
  Thirtieth, 246
  Thirty-fifth, 414
  Thirty-ninth Motorized, 147
  Fortieth Panzer, 275
  Forty-first Panzer, 414
  Forty-third, 208
  Forty-fourth, 275
  Forty-seventh Motorized, 154
  Forty-seventh Panzer, 389–90

Forty-eighth, 294
Forty-eighth Panzer, 288, 291, 306–8, 280
Fifty-first, 288, 294, 298, 301, 312
Fifty-second, 275, 293
Fifty-third, 413
Fifty-fourth, 246
Fifty-sixth Panzer, 408
Fifty-seventh Panzer, 275, 314
Grossdeutschland Panzer, 444–45
Corps (Italian)
  Alpine, 277
Corps (Rumanian)
  Sixth, 288
Corps (Soviet)
  Third Tank, 419
  Twenty-first Tank, 251
  Twenty-third Tank, 251
  Twenty-sixth Tank, 310
  Twenty-ninth Tank, 349
Cotentin peninsula, 419–20
Cottbus, 464
Courland, 433–34, 446
Crete, 71
Crimea, 91, 105, 132, 163–64, 210, 241–47, 253, 255, 379, 387, 398
Czechoslovakia, 12, 14, 468–69
Czestochowa, 443

Dachau, 260. See also concentration camps
Daimler-Benz, 260
Dakar, 46
Dannecker, Theodor, 65
Danube River, 438
Danzig, 405, 429–30
Das Reich. See Divisions (German)
Das Reich (journal), 234, 424
D-Day. See Normandy
death penalty, soldiers, 331, 464
Debrecen, 437
Demyansk, 146, 213–14, 311
Desna River, 142, 154, 365
destroyers for bases, 40, 45
diet. See food supplies
Dietrich, Josef "Sepp" (SS-General), 438
Dietrich, Otto, 156, 296
Divisions (German)
  Brandenburg, 444

Das Reich (2nd SS), 191, 268, 324, 348, 350, 355, 438
Grossdeutschland, 266, 268, 277, 324, 355, 388, 444, 541n69, 542n83
Hermann Goering Panzer, 419, 444
Leibstandarte Adolf Hitler (First SS), 268, 324, 348-51, 395
Luftwaffe field, 306, 369, 384
Panzergrenadier (motorized infantry), 355, 367, 384
Totenkopf (Third SS), 324, 355, 438
Viking (Fifth SS), xvii, 269, 351, 355, 389, 419, 438
Second Panzer, 191
Third Panzer, 142, 355
Fourth Panzer, 142, 155, 160, 208
Fifth Panzer, 191, 346, 353, 415-17
Sixth Panzer, 160, 192, 202, 306, 356, 398
Seventh Panzer, 191, 202, 355, 395, 444
Eighth Panzer, 353
Ninth SS Panzer, 393, 398
Tenth Motorized, 142
Tenth Panzer, 191
Tenth Panzergrenadier, 355
Tenth SS Panzer, 398
Eleventh Panzer, 191, 390
Twelfth Panzer, 146-47, 346, 409, 415-16
Thirteenth Panzer, 269, 282, 390
Fourteenth Panzer, 298, 306, 308, 390
Sixteenth Motorized, 277
Sixteenth Panzer, 286, 308, 390, 443
Seventeenth Panzer, 315, 351, 390, 443
Eighteenth Motorized, 146-47
Eighteenth Panzer, 117
Nineteenth Panzer, 419, 445
Twentieth Motorized, 146-47
Twentieth Panzer, 409, 413, 414
Twenty-second Panzer, 242, 244, 277, 292, 306, 308
Twenty-third Panzer, 263, 282, 314-15, 351
Twenty-fourth Panzer, 266, 289, 308, 390

Twenty-fifth Panzer, 379-80, 445
Twenty-ninth Motorized Infantry, 309
Thirty-ninth Infantry, 357
Fiftieth Infantry, 247
Sixty-second Infantry, 100
Sixty-eighth Infantry, 395
134th Infantry, 414
168th Infantry, 356
253rd Infantry, 375
221st Security, 203
454th Security, 250
Divisions (Hungarian)
108th Light Infantry, 250
Divisions (Rumanian)
First Armored, 306
Divisions (Soviet)
Thirteenth Guards Rifle, 294, 303
Dnieper, Battle of, 369
Dnieper bend, 379, 387-88
Dnieper line, 114, 117, 120, 143
Dnieper River, 52, 56-57, 81-82, 86, 88-90, 120, 122, 124, 126, 128, 140-41, 143, 149-50, 154, 365, 368-74, 377, 379, 381, 387-92, 405, 414-15
Dniester River, 52, 395, 435
Dnepropetrovsk, 141, 163, 370, 379
Doenitz, Karl (Admiral), 418
Doerr, Hans (General), 293
Don-Chir bridgehead, 314
Donets Basin (industrial area), 126, 141, 145, 163, 165, 270, 273, 322, 324, 338-39, 351, 366-67, 369
Donets River, 248-49, 251, 267, 347, 353, 370
Don River, 162, 163-65, 185, 232, 261, 264-65, 267-69, 271-72, 275, 283-86, 288-89, 292, 296, 303-4, 306-10, 312, 314-17, 319, 321-22, 324, 405
Dora (artillery piece), 245
Dora camp. *See* concentration camps; Mittelbau-Dora
Dresden, 461, 465, 469
Drohobycz, 96
Dubno, 89
Dunkirk, 244, 328, 401, 406, 484
Durchgangstrasse 4, 481

Dvina-Dnieper line, 56–57, 81–82
Dvina River, 52, 88, 90, 417
Dzerzhinsky tractor works, 290, 295

Eagle's Nest, 10
East Prussia, 88, 94, 104, 311, 419,
    428–31, 442, 444–47, 449–50
East Prussian operation, 430, 442,
    444, 446–47
Edelweiss, Operation, xv, 272, 276
Edward, Duke of Windsor, 38
Egypt, 233
Eichmann, Adolf, 21, 65, 108, 171, 178,
    255, 426, 512n56
Einsatzgruppen (SS), xv, 18–19, 66,
    69–70, 76, 94–98, 100–102, 104,
    108, 171, 177, 219–20, 332, 360,
    480, 485
  A, 94–95, 97, 110–11, 219
  B, 95, 97, 219
  C, 95, 98, 102
  D, 219
  Poland, 500n31
  Soviet Union, 95, 104, 171, 219, 485
Einsatzkommando (SS), xv, 95, 110,
    176, 219
Eisenhower, Dwight D. (General), 458
El Alamein, 281, 299, 307, 469
Elbe River, 461–62, 465–66
Elbrus, Mount, 279
Elista, 275, 277
Engel, Gerhard (Major), 48, 50, 189,
    278, 284
English Channel, 127
Eremenko, A. I. (Marshal), 154, 287
Estonia, 32, 88, 146, 417, 433
ethnic Germans. *See* Volksdeutsche
eugenics, 138, 515n5
Eurasian continental bloc, 44–45
euthanasia, 137–40, 177–80, 483
ewige Jude, Der (The eternal Jew; film),
    22, 64, 506n63
extermination camps, 177–78, 180,
    219, 237, 260, 361–62, 451
  Auschwitz, 177–78, 181, 220, 223,
    226, 254, 257–58, 260, 317, 362
  Belzec, 177–78, 181, 220, 226, 253, 361
  Chelmno, 177–79, 220, 226, 253
  Maidanek (Majdanek), 258, 450

Sobibor, 177, 181, 253, 361
Treblinka, 181, 226, 254, 257, 361
See also Auschwitz; Belzec;
    Chelmno; Maidanek; Sobibor;
    Treblinka

"factory operation" (February 1943),
    531n31
Falaise, 420
Far East, 43, 183, 186, 193, 200, 384
Fastov, 379–80
Final Solution
  centrality to war, xx–xxi, xxiv, 20,
    23, 485
  death marches, 454–55
  decision for, 104–11, 173–82, 521n75
  destruction through labor, 94–95,
    180, 223, 260–61, 334, 481
  Einsatzgruppen and (*see*
    Einsatzgruppen)
  euthanasia and, 139–40
  evolution of, 13–25, 63–71, 94–104
  gas chambers, 139, 178, 181, 220,
    226, 258, 362, 451
  gas vans, 111, 219–20
  Generalplan Ost and (*see*
    Generalplan Ost)
  Heydrich and, 13,18–19, 24, 65–67,
    70, 94–96, 104, 108, 110, 174–81,
    219, 225, 522n78
  Himmler and, 19, 23–24, 65–66, 95,
    101, 104–6, 111, 175–76, 178–80,
    197, 217–19, 225, 254–55, 257, 335–
    36, 361, 364, 485, 512n54
  in Hungary, 361–62
  hunger Policy and (*see* Germany:
    hunger policy)
  implementation of, 150, 173–82, 217–
    20, 225–26, 253–54, 257, 361–63,
    485, 522n78
  numbers killed, 226, 257, 361
  public knowledge of, 334–35,
    452–53
  Speer and, 219, 260, 334–36
  territorial solution, 16, 24, 65, 67,
    479, 485
  See also Auschwitz; extermination
    camps; racial policies; forced
    labor; SS; Wannsee Conference

Finland, 44, 49–50, 79, 399, 433
  nickel, 431
  Winter War, 36
First World War. *See* World War I
Five Year Plans (Soviet), 81
flak, 246, 298, 310, 328, 459, 466
Flanders, 3, 206
Fliegerkorps, 242, 529n4
forced labor, 93, 166, 180, 258–60,
    327, 334, 372, 481, 486
  in aircraft industry, 334–36, 426
  deaths, 222, 336
  destruction through labor, 94–95,
    180, 223, 260–61, 334, 481
  food, 224, 226
  Jews, 95, 101, 171, 173, 180, 222–23,
    226, 257–58, 362–64, 426, 481
  labor camps, 93, 259–61, 334–35,
    364, 451
  numbers of, 222–23, 332, 425
  Ostarbeiter (eastern workers), 174,
    221–24, 259–60, 332, 486
  round-ups, 221–22, 259–60, 317, 327–
    28, 332, 334, 364, 371–74, 481
  and Sauckel, 220–23
  Soviet prisoners of war, 166, 174
  treatment of, 222, 332, 334–35, 364,
    425, 428
Foreign Armies East, 238, 249, 253,
    276, 337, 341, 384, 406, 408, 410,
    442, 530n15, 547n75
foreign policy (German), 7, 10–13, 483
Forster, Albert, 19
"fortified places," 382, 393, 411, 418
Four-Year Plan (German), 11, 166, 477,
    505n60
France, xxiii, 184
  armistice with Germany (1940), 1,
    29, 36–37
  blitzkrieg in, xxiii, 2, 23–24, 26–28, 44,
    46, 53–54, 56–57, 78, 81–82, 87, 90,
    111, 115–16, 127, 129, 135, 148, 151,
    160, 186, 263, 406, 473, 476, 486
  deportation of Jews from, 174, 178
  economic importance of, 28, 221,
    226, 426–27, 455
  Hitler's peace offer, 25
  Hitler's view of, 14, 33, 47–48, 133,
    194, 337, 366, 399, 402, 420, 433

Madagascar Plan, 24
  and Mussolini, 46
Franco, Francisco, 3, 46–48, 51
Frank, Hans, 19, 21, 65, 73, 180, 258–59
Frankfurt (Oder), 454, 460
Frederick II, "the Great"(king of
    Prussia), 206
Fredericus, Operation, xv, 248, 250–
    51, 253
Freikorps, xv, 460
Fricke, Kurt (Rear Admiral), 42
Friessner, Johannes (General), 432,
    437
Fromm, Friedrich (General), 58, 189,
    204, 233
Fronts (Soviet)
  Belorussian: First, 442, 444, 448,
    461, 463–65, 467; Second, 442,
    444, 446, 448, 461, 465; Third,
    442, 444, 446
  Bryansk, 211, 346, 348
  Central, 345
  Don, 306, 319
  Kalinin, 211, 214
  Leningrad, 142
  Southern, 269
  Southwest, 141
  Stalingrad, 269, 287, 307
  Steppe, 348
  Ukrainian: First, 378, 387, 393–95,
    442–43, 464–65, 467–68; Second,
    394–96, 435, 468–69; Third, 435,
    461; Fourth, 468
  Volkhov, 213
  Voronezh, 347
  West, 211, 214, 346
Frühlingserwachen, xv, 438. *See also*
    Spring Awakening, Operation
Führer's bunker, 465–67
Führer Headquarters, 23, 104, 109,
    132, 135, 193, 206, 230, 238, 262,
    275, 279, 298, 368, 371, 379, 395,
    411, 430
Führer Orders, 125, 156, 281, 310,
    365–66, 393, 396, 402
Funk, Walter, 41

Galen, Clemens August Graf von
    (Bishop of Münster), 137–39

Galicia, 89, 96, 106, 180, 220, 255, 481

Garsden, 94

Gauleiter, xv, 137, 174, 196, 220, 225, 296, 327, 335, 360-61, 425, 456-57

Gavrilovka, 288

Gehlen, Reinhard (Colonel), 337, 341-42, 379, 384, 442

General Government (Poland), 21, 65, 73, 180, 218-19, 225-26, 256-57, 259, 476

Generalplan Ost (General Plan East), xv, 93, 236, 253-54, 256-57, 259-60, 317, 334, 477, 481, 485

General Staff (German), 33, 53, 59, 84, 113, 270, 280, 417

General Staff (Soviet), 339

Geneva Convention, 167

Georgian Military Road, 282

German army

  ammunition shortages, 57-58, 120, 149-50, 169, 188, 190, 207-8, 216, 229, 236, 251, 262, 276-77, 283-85, 297, 299, 318-19, 329-30, 363, 440, 464

  anti-Bolshevism in, 36-37, 42, 67-70, 97-98, 101-2, 320, 374-75, 440, 453, 483, 510n40

  anti-Semitism in, 66-67, 69-70, 96-104, 374-75, 480-82, 511n44

  atrocities in occupied territories, 96-104, 170-72, 333-34, 372-74, 510n36, 510n40, 511n44

  breakdown in discipline, 69, 202-4, 373-74, 377, 434, 452-54

  casualties, 90, 116, 151-52, 162, 185, 192-93, 214-15, 236, 247, 321, 333, 352, 355-57, 367, 369, 380, 384, 387, 392, 395, 399, 416, 420-21, 426, 433, 436, 468-70, 539n30

  combat effectiveness, 56, 115-18, 121, 123, 125, 146, 150-52, 162, 182, 187-88, 192-93, 236, 271-72, 293, 295, 297, 301, 369-70, 375-76, 378, 380, 429, 432, 454, 459

  and Commissar Order, xv, 68-69, 94, 480-81, 519n57

  courts-martial, 377, 398, 447, 454, 467

  defeatism, 27-28, 230, 331, 334, 368, 417

  demotorization of, 26, 57, 383, 394, 409

  French campaign, xxiii, 2, 23-24, 26-28, 44, 46, 53-54, 56-57, 78, 81-82, 87, 90, 111, 115-16, 127, 129, 135, 148, 151, 160, 186, 263, 406, 473, 476, 486

  fuel shortages, 32, 38, 41, 56-58, 83-84, 119-20, 141-42, 145-46, 149-50, 154, 158, 162, 163-64, 169-70, 185-89, 190, 201-2, 205, 207, 209, 216, 233, 237, 251, 253, 262, 266-69, 271-72, 275-76, 278, 281-85, 288, 297, 308-13, 315, 318-20, 390-91, 395, 398, 401-2, 410, 427, 434, 436, 438, 440, 456, 459, 461

  horses in, 26, 54, 57, 78, 83, 119, 158-59, 161-62, 164, 216, 237, 277, 297, 317-18, 343, 369, 383, 391, 394, 410, 421

  and influence of Nazi ideology, 67-70, 96-98, 374-76, 480-82

  and killing of Jews, 96-104, 510n36, 511n44

  logistic problems, 26, 52-57, 59, 60-61, 83-84, 88-89, 117-20, 122-29, 133, 140-42, 145-46, 149-52, 154-55, 157-64, 169-70, 172, 174, 176, 182-83, 185-86, 188-90, 191-93, 199, 202-3, 205, 209-13, 216, 226, 231-32, 237, 239, 252-53, 261-62, 270, 272, 277-78, 282-84, 290-91, 297, 309-13, 317-18, 333, 339-40, 354, 366, 369, 393, 395, 427, 440, 514n81

  and Mediterranean strategy, 39, 43-51, 233

  morale, 89, 109, 111-12, 121, 130, 151-52, 155, 159, 162-64, 182, 188-90, 192-93, 201-3, 262, 283, 293, 295, 297, 299, 319-20, 359, 370-71, 376-77, 399, 452, 546-47n70

  motivation of soldiers, 374-77, 480-83

  motor vehicles in, 26, 149, 169, 216, 272, 383

  and Operation Barbarossa (*see* Barbarossa)

and Operation Blau (*see* Blau)

and opposition to Hitler by senior officers, 27, 422, 428

and opposition to war by senior officers, 26-27, 39, 58-59, 82

and partisan war, 81, 86, 94, 98, 101-2, 104, 106, 108, 111, 149, 160, 174, 180, 193, 198, 212, 259, 282, 297, 317, 332-34, 340, 353-54, 374, 378, 381, 383, 385, 400, 409, 412, 415-16, 447, 479-82

plunder, 61-62, 94, 120, 172, 224-25, 310, 317, 333, 373-74, 467, 480-81

Polish campaign, 18-20

rearmament, xxiii, 10-13, 473, 475

replacements, 116-17, 126, 151-52, 160, 185, 190, 193, 202, 205, 208-9, 215, 276, 352, 367, 375, 384, 394, 426, 522n85

scorched earth policy (Russia), 369, 372-74

tanks, 27, 53, 114-16, 199, 201, 205; fear of German models, 345, 346-47, 352; losses of, 117, 141-42, 147, 149-51, 155, 160, 187, 190, 215, 237, 346, 350, 352, 356-57, 392, 408, 433, 440, 543n94; numbers of, 77, 116-18, 125, 141-42, 147, 150-52, 160, 169, 187, 190, 202, 215-16, 230, 237, 272, 283, 285-86, 289, 304, 306-8, 314-15, 319, 329-30, 340, 343, 345, 346, 348, 350, 353, 355-57, 370, 378, 380-82, 389-90, 394, 409, 413, 416, 419, 426, 435, 437, 441, 461, 542n80, 542n86; superiority of Panthers and Tigers, 345-47, 352-53, 400 (*see also* Germany: tank production)

troop strength, xxiii, 37-38, 53, 77-78, 87, 114, 116-17, 121, 125-26, 151-52, 182, 187, 190-93, 209, 215-16, 236, 262, 272, 292, 295, 299, 301, 309, 340, 355, 365, 367, 370, 378, 384, 387, 394, 399-400, 404, 409, 461, 470, 524n2, 547n75

trucks, 56-57, 59, 119, 114, 149, 158-60, 185, 209, 216, 237, 271-72, 297, 310, 339, 393-94, 440

use of forced labor, 364, 369, 372-73

and Vistula-Oder campaign (1945), 440-49

and winter campaign (1941-1942) (*see* Barbarossa)

and winter campaign (1942-1943), 322-25

and winter campaign (1943-1944), 368-99

See also Armies; Army Groups; Corps; Divisions; Ostheer; Wehrmacht

German navy, 34, 37-38, 57, 90, 226, 229, 330, 399, 431, 440, 470

German-Soviet peace feelers, 300, 363

Germany

agricultural policy, 40-41, 59-62, 170-72, 221, 224, 255, 258, 427, 477-78, 483, 506n64

Allied bombing of, 50, 83, 136-38, 174, 197, 330-32, 335, 339, 361-63, 366, 402, 422-23, 426-28, 436, 440, 453, 457, 466, 470, 483

anti-American propaganda, 15, 40, 64, 107-8, 110, 474

anti-Bolshevik propaganda (*see* Bolshevism)

anti-Jewish actions in, 13-15, 21-22, 64, 110, 174, 218

armaments industry: aircraft production, 238, 329-31, 363-64, 402, 426-27; ammunition production, 58, 229, 236, 329-30, 440; armaments production, 37, 57-58, 90, 169, 215-17, 229-31, 260-61, 289-90, 329-31, 335, 338, 363-64, 402, 424, 426, 440, 448, 456; collapse of, 426-27, 455-58; effect of Allied bombing, 330-31; productivity, 227-30, 332; propaganda about, 230; raw materials shortages, xxii-xxiii, 11-13, 26, 28, 39-42, 49, 55, 58, 60-63, 71, 83, 133, 166, 169, 223, 226-30, 234, 338, 427, 475, 481, 484, 487; tank production, 91, 117, 151, 190, 215, 229, 236, 238, 305, 322, 328-30, 340, 367, 401, 440, 542n86; total war mobilization, 227-30, 326-30, 423-27, 456-57

Germany *(cont.)*
  (see also Speer, Albert; tank
    production [German])
  black market activities, 136, 171, 224,
    427–28
  deportation of Jews, 14, 21, 64–65,
    108, 110, 173–78, 180, 219–20, 257,
    259, 362, 522n78
  food: rationing, 72, 135–36, 149,
    220, 223, 226, 427–28; supply,
    xxii–xxiii, 12–13, 28, 32, 40–41,
    49, 55, 58–62, 64, 69, 71–73, 92,
    135–36, 149, 167, 170–71, 217, 221,
    223–26, 257, 316, 366, 427–28, 475,
    477–84
  foreign labor in *(see* forced labor)
  Four-Year Plan *(see* Goering)
  hunger policy *(see* hunger policy)
  labor: compulsory, 328, 424–
    25; foreign *(see* forced labor);
    Ostarbeiter *(see* forced labor);
    roundups *(see* forced labor);
    shortages, xxiii, 58, 166, 174, 204,
    215, 217, 220–24, 227–29, 257,
    328, 331, 334, 363–64, 424, 426;
    slave *(see* forced labor); use of
    concentration camp prisoners *(see*
    forced labor); women, 166, 221–
    22, 328, 331–32, 424–25
  Labor Service *(Reichsarbeitsdienst;*
    RAD), 376
  morale, xxiii, 72, 109, 121, 135–37,
    155, 167, 224, 230, 296–97, 325,
    328–31, 359, 363, 427–29
  occupation policy of, 18–25, 28,
    40–42, 60–68, 91–94, 105–6,
    170–74, 221–26, 332–34, 372–74,
    426–27, 483, 485
  popular support for Hitler, 2,
    10, 31–32, 72, 135–37, 325, 428,
    483–84
  and total war, 326–30, 423–27, 440,
    456–57
  war economy, 41–42, 55, 58–61, 83,
    166, 216, 220, 226–27, 232, 258–59,
    261, 327, 330, 332, 423, 425, 427–
    29, 459, 471, 485, 488
  women, rape of by Soviet soldiers,
    431, 449–52

Germany Must Perish (Theodore
  Kaufman), 107
Gestapo, xv, 94, 137, 178, 330, 454
Geyr von Schweppenburg, Leo
  (General), 142, 154
ghettos, 21–22, 64–65, 94, 100, 174–76,
  218, 220, 223 257, 318, 361–62, 477
Gibraltar, 45, 48, 51
Globocnik, Odilo, 257–59
Gniloy Tikich River, 391
Goebbels, Joseph, 31–33, 63
  and anti-Bolshevism, 44, 99, 217,
    322, 376, 431, 453
  anti-Semitism of, 2, 14–15, 20–24,
    36, 40, 64, 73, 99, 107–9, 174, 179,
    218, 220, 360–61, 376
  on Atlantic Charter, 110
  and Battle of Stalingrad, 322
  and bombing raids on German
    cities, 137, 363
  and Churches, 137–38
  and declaration of war on U.S., 194–95
  and *Der ewige Jude,* 22–23, 64
  and Final Solution, 109–10, 172, 174–
    75, 179, 218, 220, 360–62, 528n63
  and food supply, 136, 170, 224, 428
  and Hitler, 2, 22, 31, 33, 35–36, 44,
    64, 73–74, 131, 155, 172, 175, 179,
    190, 217–18, 220, 230–31, 238, 279,
    296, 300, 329, 341–42, 360–62
  and Madagascar Plan, 24
  and peace offers to Stalin, 363,
    550n51
  and popular mood in Germany, 63,
    72, 108–9, 135–37, 155, 230, 363,
    401, 428–29, 514n79
  as Propaganda Minister, 21–24, 40,
    63–64, 99, 107–8, 135, 184, 230,
    234, 247, 322, 327, 360, 363, 376,
    401, 423–24, 428–29, 431, 440,
    453, 472, 510n40
  as Reich Plenipotentiary for Total
    War, 425–26
  "total war" initiatives, 230, 232, 326–
    29, 423–26, 456, 458
  Total War speech, February 1943,
    326–27
  urges Hitler to address nation, 155,
    296, 300

and war against the Soviet Union,
63, 72-73, 77, 79, 85, 88, 99, 105,
111, 121, 131, 155, 170, 184, 190,
217, 238, 247, 279, 296, 300, 322,
338, 341-42, 351-52, 367, 376,
397
Goering, Hermann (Reichsmarschall)
and anti-Bolshevism, 66
and anti-Jewish policy, 15, 18, 24, 66,
105, 108
colonial thinking of, 18, 105, 169, 477
declining influence of, 227-28, 397
doubts about war, 9, 31, 34, 56, 72
economic exploitation of the Soviet
Union, 166, 169-72, 225-26
and Final Solution, 66, 108
and food supplies, 136, 170, 172, 223-6
Four-Year Plan, 11-12, 166, 477
and Hitler, 34, 72, 105
and hunger policy, 62, 505n60
and Luftwaffe, 132, 243-44, 312, 318
and Stalingrad, 312, 318, 320
and total war, 227-28, 328-29
Golubinsky, 309
Gomel, 123, 381-82
Gonchara, 289
Gorky, 182, 186
Görlitz, 465, 469
Gorodnitsa, 388
Gothengau, 255
GPU (Soviet Secret Police), 67, 69
Great Britain. See Britain
Greece, 47, 49, 71
Greiser, Arthur, 19, 175
Grimm, Hans, 6
Groscurth, Helmuth (Lieutenant-
Colonel), 18-19, 298
Grossdeutschland. See Divisions
(German)
Großraumwirtschaft (greater German
economic sphere), 41, 62
Großwaltersdorf, 430
Grozny, 83, 235, 271-72, 275, 277, 279,
281-82
Grynszpan, Herschel, 14
Guderian, Heinz (General)
and Barbarossa, 86, 117, 122-23,
125-26, 132-33, 141-45, 149, 153-
55, 187-88, 190, 200, 202-8

as Chief of Staff (OKH), 417, 434,
437, 442-44, 448, 454-55, 460
criticism of Hitler, 206, 443
criticism of OKH, 399, 417
dismissal, 208, 460
doubts about Citadel (Kursk), 340,
342, 346
and French campaign, 27-28
as Inspector General for Armor,
340, 367, 379, 384
"Guidelines of Economic Policy
for the Economic Organization
East," 478
Gulf of Finland, 146, 386
Gumbinnen, 430-31, 446
Gumrak, 289, 320
Gzhatsk, 211

Habsburg Empire, 474, 478
Hagen position, 354-55
Hague Convention, 167
Halder, Franz (General)
and anti-Bolshevism, 37
and Barbarossa, 36-39, 42-44,
50-52, 55-59, 67, 78, 82, 84, 87,
89-90, 111-14, 121-23, 126, 131,
141-43, 146-48, 164, 171, 182
and Blau, 232-34, 248-50, 253, 265-
67, 269-71, 275-76, 281, 283
concerns about arms production,
116-17
concerns about manpower situation,
114-16, 142, 151-52, 234, 236, 522n85
concerns about progress in the
USSR, 125-26, 130, 133
dismissal, 280
and encirclement operations, 87,
89, 111-13, 121-22, 127, 141, 152-
53, 155
and French campaign, 27
and German strategic confusion,
44-45, 233
and Hitler, 18, 27, 52, 55-56, 67, 74,
84, 87, 112-13, 121, 126-28, 131-34,
142, 152-53, 189-90, 206, 263, 267,
270-71, 275, 280, 292
and invasion of Britain, 33, 37
and Soviet counteroffensive
(December 1941), 201-11

Halder, Franz (General) *(cont.)*
  and Stalingrad, 269, 275, 283–85,
    289, 292
  suggests demotorization of the
    army, 26, 57
  and Typhoon, 147–48, 152–53, 155–
    56, 182–87, 190–91
Hamburg
  bombing of, 330, 363, 466
  deportation of Jews from, 174
Hanke, Karl, 448
Harpe, Joseph (General), 445
Harvest Festival, Operation
    (Erntefest), 361–62
Harz Mountains, 335
Haushofer, Karl, 6
Hausser, Paul (SS-General), 324, 349
Heim, Ferdinand (General), 307–8
Heinkel, 260
Heinrici, Gotthard (General), 215,
    414, 455
Hendaye, 47
Hess, Rudolf, 79, 254
Hewel, Walther, 23
Heydrich, Reinhard
  and deportation of Jews, 110, 174–78
  and Einsatzgruppen, 70, 94–96, 104,
    219
  and ethnic cleansing in Poland, 18–19
  and Final Solution, 65–66, 108, 110,
    174–81, 219, 225
  and forced laborers, 180, 522n78
  and Himmler, 74, 175–76, 178
  and Hitler, 104, 174–75, 178
  and Madagascar Plan, 13, 24
  and Reich Commissariat for the
    Strengthening of the German
    People (RKFDV), 93, 254, 256
  and RSHA (Reich Security Main
    Office), 24, 65, 480, 485
  and Security Service (SD), 13
  at Wannsee Conference, 181
  and Wehrmacht cooperation, 66–67,
    70, 96
Himmler, Heinrich (Reichsführer-SS)
  and Army Group Vistula, 446,
    448–49
  and colonial thinking, 62, 93, 477,
    528n64

  and deportation of Jews, 21, 65, 175,
    176, 178, 219–20, 257, 362
  and Final Solution, 66, 95, 101, 104,
    106–7, 111, 175–80, 197, 218–19,
    225, 257, 335–36, 361–62, 364,
    485, 512n54
  and forced labor, 260, 334–35, 364,
    426
  and Generalplan Ost, 62, 65, 93,
    253–61, 477, 528n64
  and Hitler, 19, 74, 104, 178–80, 197,
    218, 361, 364, 397
  and Madagascar Plan, 23–25
  and partisan war, 104, 106, 108, 111,
    180, 258–59, 332–34
  population transfer programs,
    19–25, 65, 92, 257–59 (*see also*
    Generalplan Ost)
  Posen speech (October 1943),
    335–36
  and racial policy, 19, 21, 62, 65, 225,
    254–61, 506n64
  "Reflections on the Treatment of
    Peoples of Alien Races in the
    East," (May 1940), 23–24, 254–55
  and Reich Commissariat for the
    Strengthening of the German
    People (RKFDV), 93, 254, 256
  and Speer, 333–36, 424
  and SS economic empire, 65, 259–
    61, 334–35, 364, 426
  and Volkssturm, 428–29
  and Zamosc, 258–59
Hitler, Adolf
  and Antonescu, 109, 435–36
  armistice with France, 1–3
  assassination attempt, 422, 428,
    454
  and Anti-Comintern Pact, 45
  anti-communism of (*see* Bolshevism)
  and Atlantic Charter, 109–10, 131
  and Bagration (*see* Bagration)
  and Balkans (*see* Balkans)
  and Barbarossa (*see* Barbarossa)
  and Blau (*see* Blau)
  and Britain, 3, 6, 8–10, 12–14, 16,
    32–33, 36–38, 40, 43, 63–64, 71,
    75, 91, 156, 194, 217, 268, 296, 400,
    402, 433, 475

and the British blockades: 1914–
1918, xxiii, 6, 8, 12, 28, 35, 41, 60,
62, 69, 91, 473, 475, 478; 1939–
1945, 60, 71, 83
and the Cherkassy pocket (see
Cherkassy)
and Churchill, 32–34, 37–38, 46,
110, 131, 174, 328
and Citadel (see Citadel)
colonial thinking of, xxii, 6–8,
17–18, 33, 45–48, 62, 92–93, 105–6,
173, 241, 254–59, 476–81
and Caucasus operations (see
Caucasus)
and the Crimea (see Crimea)
declares war on the U.S., 193–98
and defense of Berlin (see Berlin)
determination to invade the USSR
(see Barbarossa)
directives (see Führer Directives;
Operational Orders)
economic ideas, 6–8
and eugenics, 138
and euthanasia, 137–40, 177–78, 180,
483
and Final Solution (see Final
Solution)
and Finland (see Finland)
and food supply (see Germany: food
supply)
and forced labor (see forced labor)
and fortified places, 382, 393, 411, 418
and Four-Year Plan (see Four-Year Plan)
and France (see France)
and Franco, 46–48, 51
and German Navy (see German navy)
and Germany's "India," xxii, 91,
105, 175, 196
and Greece (see Greece)
and Halder, 18, 27, 52, 55–56, 67, 74,
84, 87, 112–13, 121, 126–28, 131–34,
142, 152–53, 189–90, 206, 263, 267,
270–71, 275, 280, 292
hopes for split in Allied coalition,
360, 424, 434, 441, 486
and Horthy, 362, 437
and Hungary (see Hungary)
and the hunger policy (see hunger
policy)

ideology (worldview) (see
Bolshevism; Lebensraum)
and invasion of Britain, 33–35,
38–39, 43
and Italy, 38, 45–49, 58, 234, 337,
341, 350–51, 354
and Japan, 34, 42–43, 45, 51, 71–72,
91, 179, 193–97, 217, 235
and Japanese attack on Pearl
Harbor, 179, 193–97, 484
and Jews: anti-Semitism, xxi, 4–6,
13–17, 21–22, 105, 108, 155, 178–80,
181, 196–97, 217–18, 220, 231, 254,
257, 360, 362, 476–77, 479, 485,
488; belief in Jewish conspiracy,
xxiii, 2, 5–7, 11–12, 15, 20–21, 26,
31–32, 35, 40, 42, 64–66, 74–75,
78, 94, 105, 107, 110, 136, 155,
179–80, 181, 194, 196–97, 217–18,
254, 300, 328, 360–63, 439–40,
449, 453, 455, 473–76, 480, 486–
87, 512n56, 528n63; prophesies
against, 15–17, 64, 73, 104, 109,
173, 179, 181, 218, 281, 296, 300,
360, 475; sanctions deportation
of from Germany, 109–10, 150,
173–76
leadership style, 22, 25, 107, 329,
422
and Lebensraum (see Lebensraum)
and Leningrad operations (see
Leningrad)
and Madagascar Plan (see
Madagascar Plan)
and Mediterranean strategy (see
Mediterranean strategy)
Mein Kampf, 4–5, 7, 15, 105, 179, 473,
478
as military commander, 422
and Moscow offensive (Typhoon)
(see Typhoon)
and Mussolini, 36, 46–49, 72, 232
and Nazi-Soviet Non-Aggression
Pact, 9, 19, 32, 36, 45
"Nero Order" (March 1945), 457–58
and Normandy invasion (see
Normandy)
and North Africa (see North Africa)
obsession with November 1918, xxiv,

Hitler, Adolf (*cont.*)
   1–2, 4–5, 16, 28, 40–41, 60, 64,
     68–69, 135–36, 179, 197, 223, 230,
     325, 331, 336, 359–60, 363, 399,
     403, 418, 439, 454–55, 471–72,
     480, 486, 527n45
   occupation policy (*see* Germany:
     occupation policy)
   and partisan war (*see* German army)
   peace offer to Britain, 25, 33–35, 37,
     40, 45, 326, 363, 484
   peace offer to Stalin, 131, 195, 300,
     363, 550n51
   and Petain, 47–48
   physical deterioration of, 131, 217,
     230–31
   and Poland, 9–10, 18–26, 60, 65–66,
     73, 139
   political testament, 105, 486
   and possible Anglo-American
     landings (*see* second front)
   and Reichel incident, 263–64
   and relations with his generals, 18,
     27, 31, 39, 55–56, 59–60, 67, 74,
     84, 87, 113, 121, 126–28, 131–34,
     141, 152, 189, 206, 208–9, 263–67,
     270–71, 280, 292, 312, 320–21, 323,
     340, 350–51, 367–68, 376, 384,
     388, 395–97, 399, 417, 422, 443,
     445, 541n64
   and Roosevelt, 15, 32, 40, 45, 107,
     110, 174, 194, 196–97, 458, 474–75,
     512n56
   scorched earth policy (*see* German
     army)
   Second Book, 4, 194, 474–75
   and second front (*see* second front)
   social Darwinism of, 4, 7–8, 12, 17, 19,
     70, 91, 138, 455, 457, 475, 479, 486
   and Spain (*see* Spain)
   speeches, 6, 16, 32–34, 63–65,
     155–56, 179, 181, 193, 196–97, 218,
     296–98, 300, 307, 360, 439, 476,
     521n75
   and "stab-in-the-back" myth, 69,
     474, 480
   and Stalin, 32, 38, 66, 75, 78, 90–91,
     110, 131, 155, 231, 300, 475–76, 484
   and Stalingrad (*see* Stalingrad)

   suicide, 467
   and summer campaign, 1943 (*see*
     Citadel)
   and tank production (*see* Germany:
     tank production)
   and United States (*see* United States:
     Hitler's calculations)
   and total war economy (*see*
     Germany: total war)
   tours World War I battlefields, 2–3
   and Treaty of Versailles, 2, 4, 10, 12,
     18, 57, 194, 439, 473, 476, 482, 484
   view of Soviet Union, xxi–xxii,
     3, 11, 35, 40–44, 49–50, 55–56,
     59–60, 62, 65, 69–70, 72, 82–83,
     170, 181–82, 235, 268, 473, 475–76,
     478, 484, 487 (*see also* Bolshevism;
     Lebensraum)
   Volksgemeinschaft conception, xvii,
     13, 17, 92, 136, 224, 328, 363, 376,
     424–25, 428, 439, 449, 453, 483,
     486–87
   war as essence of human activity, 91
   and winter campaign, 1941–1942 (*see*
     German army)
   and winter campaign, 1942–1943
     (*see* German army)
   and winter campaign, 1943–1944
     (*see* German army)
   and women in workforce (*see*
     Germany: labor)
   and World War I (*see* World War I)
Hitler Youth, 376, 461, 467
Hiwis (Hilfswillige; Russian
   auxiliaries), xv, 321
Hoepner, Erich (General), 69, 88, 97,
   128, 154, 209
Hoeppner, Rolf-Heinz, 255
Hofmann, Otto, 522n78
Holland, 86
horses, 26, 54, 57, 78, 83, 119, 158–59,
   161–62, 164, 172, 216, 224, 237,
   249, 252, 277, 297, 317–19, 343,
   369, 383, 391, 394, 410, 421
Horthy, Admiral Miklos, 362, 437
Hossbach, Friedrich (General),
   446–47
Hoth, Herman (General), 98
   and Blau, 284, 286, 288

commander, Fourth Panzer Army,
264–65, 276, 292, 323–24, 339,
346, 355
commander, Seventeenth Army, 161
and Stalingrad, 288–89, 291–92,
294, 314–16
and Third Panzer Group, 86, 122–
23, 125–26, 154
Hube, Hans (General), 286–87, 319,
394–96, 398
Hungarian army, 236, 250, 266, 289,
436–37
Hungary, 234, 392, 405, 436, 440–42,
460
deportation of Jews, 223, 362
fighting in, 392, 405, 436–38, 440–
42, 444, 448, 456, 460, 550n51
forces fighting in the Soviet Union,
539n30
German occupation, 362, 437–38,
456, 550n51
Jewish labor sent to Germany, 364,
426
hunger policy, 61–63, 76, 113, 166–67,
170–72, 224–25, 317, 477–78, 485,
505n60

Iassy, 434–35
I. G. Farben, 260
Ilmen, Lake, 128
India, 48–49, 81, 91, 233
Indian Ocean, 46
inflation, 12, 427
Ingermanland, 255
intelligence (German), 54, 131, 200,
207, 211, 340, 348, 362, 396, 406,
410, 421, 442, 480
intelligence (Soviet), 80, 154, 201, 341,
343, 349, 419, 447
Iran. See Persia
Iraq, 271
Italian army, 39, 43, 46, 71, 236, 284,
289, 292, 315–16, 341
Italy, xxii, 38, 45–49, 58, 234, 337, 341,
350–51, 354, 368, 399, 469–70
Ivanov, 182
Izyum, 164, 244, 247–53, 267, 370

Jägerstab (fighter staff), 426–27. See
also aircraft industry (German);
Reich Air Ministry
Jakovlevo, 347
Japan, xxii
Anti-Comintern Pact, 45
attack on Pearl Harbor, 179, 193,
194–96, 197, 484
Hitler places hopes in, 42–43, 51, 71,
91, 193, 194–96, 197, 217, 233, 235
Hitler's attitude toward, 34, 217
Hitler seeks an anti-Soviet alliance
with, 72
jeeps, 286, 421
Jeschonnek, Hans (General), 311, 331,
340
"Jewish conspiracy," xxiii, 5, 7, 10,
13, 15–17, 20, 32, 40, 105, 107,
110, 328, 335, 403, 439, 453, 455,
475–76, 486
"Jewish question," xxi, 5, 15–16, 20,
22–23, 35, 60, 64–66, 92, 94, 98,
108, 111, 173, 174, 178, 180–81, 220,
360, 362, 487
Jews
and Aktion Reinhard, 361
atrocities against, in the Baltic
states, 94–96, 98, 176, 178, 220
blamed for world wars (see
Bolshevism; Hitler; World War I)
confiscation of property
("Aryanization"), 175, 483
death camps (see extermination
camps; Final Solution)
deportation of (see Final Solution;
Germany)
destruction of synagogues, 15,
94–95
and Einsatzgruppen killings (see
Einsatzgruppen; Final Solution)
emigration, 13–14, 20, 23–24, 93,
108, 178, 181, 479
evolution of Final Solution (see
Final Solution)
expulsion, 13, 20, 64, 93, 108, 178,
181
extermination of (see Final Solution)
food rations, 171–72
forced labor (see forced labor)
ghettos, 21–22, 64–65, 94, 100,

Jews (*cont.*)
174–77, 218, 220, 223 257, 318, 361–62, 477
Hitler's prophesies against (*see* Hitler)
in Hungary, 362, 364, 426
Madagascar Plan, 13, 24, 65, 92, 108, 479
Nazi demonization of (*see* Bolshevism; *ewige Jude, Der*; Germany; Goebbels; Hitler)
"Night of Broken Glass" (*see* Kristallnacht)
and Operation Harvest Festival, 361–62
Ostjuden (eastern Jews), 20, 22, 176
reservations in Poland, 21, 139, 477, 479
territorial solution, 16, 24, 65, 67, 479, 485
See also Einsatzgruppen; extermination camps; Final Solution; ghettos; Hitler
Jodl, Alfred (General), 33, 39, 42, 45, 48, 51, 66, 128, 133, 156, 193, 199, 216, 275–76, 279–80, 312, 342, 375, 399–400, 402, 524n105
Ju-52 transport planes, 284, 311, 390, 538n25
Jupiter, Operation, 304

Kalach, 285–86, 288, 306–10, 314
Kalinin, 156, 161, 204, 211
Kalmyk Steppe, 275, 277
Kaluga, 156
Kamenets-Podolsky, 395, 411
Kammler, Hans, 335, 426
Kampfgruppe (battle group), xvi, 191, 378, 393
Kamyshin, 282
Karelia, 146, 407, 412
Karpovka, 306, 314
Katyn Forest, 360
Katyusha rocket launchers, 293, 309
Kaufman, Theodore, 107–8, 512n56
Kaufmann, Karl, 174
Kaunas, 94–95, 98, 176, 418
Kazakhstan, 115

Keitel, Wilhelm (Field Marshal), 27, 31, 39, 42, 48, 59, 68, 101, 105, 235, 268, 280, 329, 376, 397
Kempf, Werner (General), 356
Kerch, 242, 244–45, 247
Kerch peninsula, 241–42, 244–45
Kerch strait, 244, 268, 272, 278
Kesselring, Albert (Field Marshal), 280
Kharkov, 126, 145, 163–64, 172, 244–45, 247–53, 261–62, 317, 323–24, 338–39, 353, 355–56, 379, 388, 478
Khersones, 247
Kholm, 154, 213
Khrushchev, Nikita S., 145, 251, 348
Kiev, 52, 89, 102, 104, 122, 126, 128–29, 140–41, 143–46, 148, 153, 154, 155, 172, 174, 317, 369, 371–72, 378–80, 389, 478
Kiev pocket, 145–46, 148, 163, 174, 516n16
Kishinev, 434–35
Kleist, Ewald von (General), 164–65, 248, 250–53, 266–67, 275–76, 278, 282, 397
Klemperer, Victor, 218, 455
Kletskaya (bridgehead), 307–8
Klin, 186, 191, 201, 204
Kluge, Günther von (Field Marshal), 86, 161, 162, 184, 187, 192
and Citadel, 342, 344, 346
and Guderian, 207–8
and Hitler, 208–9, 340, 350–51, 367–68, 381, 384
and retreat to Dnieper, 368–69, 381
and Soviet counteroffensive, December 1941, 207–9
Koch, Erich, 225
Koch, Robert, 105
Konev, Ivan (Marshal), 214, 348, 391, 394, 418, 442–45, 447–49, 461–65, 469
Königsberg, 385, 430, 444, 446
Konstantinovka, 267, 370
Korosten, 378, 380, 387
Korsun, 389, 391, 393–95, 398
Kotelnikovo, 314
Kovel, 382, 392–93, 405–6, 408, 410–12, 418, 422

Kozlov, D. T. (General), 243
Krakow, 445
Krassnaya Polyana, 191
Krasnodar, 275, 277–78
Krasnoe Selo, 385
Krasnograd, 249
Krasny Oktyabr (Red October)
    metallurgical works, 290, 295
Krebs, Hans (General), 460, 465–66
Kremenchug, 141, 143
Kremenskaya, 285
Kremlin, 191
Kristallnacht (Night of Broken Glass,
    November 1938), 15, 21
Krivaya River, 307
Kronstadt, 79
Krosigk, Graf Lutz Schwerin von, 59
Krueger, Friedrich (Higher SS and
    Police Leader), 257
Kuban, 272, 274–75, 277–78
Kube, Wilhelm, 176
Küchler, Georg von (Field Marshal),
    69, 382, 384–86
Kuporosnye, 291
Kursk, 156, 187, 203, 264, 323
    Battle of, 338–48, 350–53, 357, 366,
        438, 441, 469, 541n69, 542n80,
        542n83, 542n86, 543n94
    See also Citadel, Operation
Küstrin, 446, 460
Kutuzov, Operation, 353
Kvaternik, Sladko (Marshal), 108

Ladoga, Lake, 146, 162
Lammers, Hans, 105, 329
Latvia, 32, 176, 367, 417. See also Courland
Laval, Pierre, 47
Lazur chemical works, 290, 295, 301
Lebensraum (living space), xvi, xxi–
    xxii, 4, 6–8, 10–12, 16–20, 22, 23,
    25, 28–29, 35, 39–42, 44, 52, 55,
    60, 63, 65, 70–71, 73, 75, 82, 91,
    94, 104, 139, 197, 233, 235–36, 241,
    316–17, 322, 376, 420, 439, 475,
    480, 482, 484, 487, 499n9
Leeb, Wilhelm Ritter von (Field
    Marshal), 88, 97–98, 146–47
Leibstandarte-SS Adolf Hitler. See
    Divisions (German)

Leipzig, 70
Lend-Lease, 40, 64, 182, 194, 216, 230,
    238, 286, 305, 324, 343, 367, 370,
    386, 394, 421, 471
Leningrad, 56, 59, 79, 88, 91, 113, 120,
    126, 128–29, 132, 142, 144, 146–47,
    151, 152, 153, 156, 172, 174, 210,
    213–14, 255, 268, 276, 303, 336,
    382, 384–86, 478
"lightning war." See blitzkrieg
Lindemann, Georg (General), 432
Lisichansk, 267
Lisjanka, 391
List, Wilhelm (Field Marshal), 261,
    269, 276–80, 288
Lithuania, 20, 32, 86, 94–96, 176, 257
Little Saturn, Operation, 315
Litvinov, Maxim, 79
Liutezh, 378–79
living space. See Lebensraum
living standards (Germany), 7, 296,
    336, 424, 451
living standards (USSR), 451
Livny, 203, 208
Lloyd George, David, 38
Lodz, 22, 175–76, 178, 220, 442, 445–46
logistics, German. See German army:
    logistics
logistics, Soviet. See Red Army:
    logistics
Lokhvitsa, 144
London, 10, 33, 156, 268, 400
losses, German. See German army:
    casualties
losses, Soviet. See Red Army:
    casualties
Loyev, 381
Lublin, 21, 23, 89, 177, 218, 220, 257,
    361, 418, 477
Ludendorff, Erich (General), 359,
    447, 455
Luftflotte, xvi
    1, 382
    2, 184
    6, 410, 441
Luftwaffe
    armaments production, 37, 90, 226,
        229, 329–30, 363–64, 401–2, 426
    (see also Germany)

Luftwaffe (cont.)
and Bagration, 409–10
and Barbarossa, 56, 85, 127, 154, 164, 169, 188, 213
and Blau, 244, 251–52, 285–86
bombing of Baku oil fields, 282–83
and Citadel, 344, 352
and Crimea (1942), 242–44, 246
failure of, 243–44, 331, 366
field divisions, 306, 369, 384
fighter production (see Germany)
and French campaign, 54
fuel shortages (see Germany)
and Goering, 132, 243–44, 312, 318
and Hitler, 37
and invasion of Britain, 33, 38
losses, 169, 352, 357, 399
numbers, 78, 85, 343, 355, 369, 378, 382, 394, 410, 441, 452, 461
and Stalingrad, 287, 306, 310–14, 318, 320–21, 538n25
and winter campaign (1943–1944), 366, 391, 393
See also Fliegerkorps; Luftflotte
Lutze, Viktor, 361
Lvov, 89, 392–93, 398, 418, 420

Mackensen, Eberhard von (General), 252
Madagascar Plan, 13, 24, 65, 92, 108, 479
Maginot Line, 54
Magnuszew, 418–19, 442, 444–45
Maidanek, 258, 450. See also extermination camps
Maikop, 83, 164, 182, 235, 268, 271–72, 275–78, 534n71
malnutrition, 94, 166, 167–68. See also hunger policy
Mamayev Kurgan, 290, 294–95
Mann, Thomas, 3
Manstein, Erich von (Field Marshal)
anti-Semitism of, 98
Army Group Don, 309, 312, 316, 322
"back-hand blow" strategy, 338, 417
Barbarossa, 88, 128,
Cherkassy pocket, 389–92

Citadel, 339–40, 342, 350–51
Crimea, 164, 241–47
defensive battles in Ukraine (1943–1944), 323–25, 338–40, 346–47, 350–51, 355–56, 367–68, 378–80, 387–97, 403
dismissal of, 397
and Donets, 322, 338, 367–68
Eleventh Army, 163, 241, 247, 268, 276
and Hitler, 312, 323, 340, 342, 350–51, 356, 367–68, 379, 388, 395–97
Kharkov, 323–24, 338–39, 356
relief attack on Stalingrad, 312–16
retreat to Dnieper, 368, 371, 378
and "Sickle-cut," 27, 54, 56, 323
Manteuffel, Hasso von (General), 465
Manych River, 275
Marcks, Erich (General), 52
Marina Gorka, 415
Marne, Battle of, 183, 190, 192
Mars, Operation, xvi, 304
Mauthausen, 260. See also concentration camps
Mediterranean Sea, xxiv, 39, 43, 45, 184, 307, 311, 341–42, 350–51, 484, 486
Mediterranean strategy, 45–51, 71, 233, 487
Medyn, 210–11
Mekhlis, L. Z., 243
Melitopol, 365, 379
Mers-el-Kebir, 33
Meyer, Konrad, 93, 253, 255–56
Michael I (king of Rumania), 436
Middle East, 39, 46, 117, 233, 272, 279, 336, 400
Mikhailov, 203
Milch, Erhard (Field Marshal), 222, 229, 319
Millerovo, 261, 267, 269
Minsk, 86–88, 97, 100, 111, 122, 127, 130, 140, 158, 167, 176, 220, 381–82, 408, 414–18
Mississippi River, 93
Mittelbau-Dora, 426. See also concentration camps
Mius River, 163, 165, 322, 353, 370
Model, Walther (Field Marshal), 455

Army Group B, 458
Army Group Center, 415, 417–19
Army Group North, 386
Army Group North Ukraine, 408, 410
Army Group South, 397–98
Bagration, 408, 410, 415, 417–19, 432
Citadel, 339–40, 344–47, 353–55
and Hitler, 344, 354, 386, 397, 408, 417, 432
Ninth Army, 211, 339, 344, 355
Orel salient, 345–46, 353–54
retreat to Panther position, 386
and sabotage of Hitler's "Nero Order," 455–56
Mogilev, 123, 178, 219, 409, 412, 415
Molodechno, 417
Molotov, Vyacheslav, 48–50, 80, 268
Monowitz, 260
Montoire, 47
morale (German), xxiii, 89, 109, 121, 136, 152, 155, 159–60, 164, 166–67, 182, 188–90, 192–93, 202, 224, 230, 248, 262, 283, 293, 295–97, 319, 328, 330–31, 359, 363, 376–77, 428, 452
morale (Soviet), 273, 322
Moltke, Helmuth James von, 167
Morocco, 46, 178
Morozovsk, 267
Mortain, 420
Moscow. See Barbarossa; Red Army: Moscow; Stalin: counterattack at Moscow; Stalin: defense of Moscow; Typhoon
Moscow-Volga canal, 182, 184, 191, 201
Moskva (Moscow) River, 182
Mozdok, 282
Mozhaisk, 153, 161
Mozhaisk Line, 156
Mtsensk, 155, 160, 161
mud, 81, 89, 118–19, 143, 146, 149, 151, 152, 153, 157–59, 163–64, 185, 199, 213, 238, 380, 389–91, 393, 438
Müller, Heinrich, 178, 454
Munich, 2, 4, 14, 144, 218, 300, 340
Conference, 14
Hitler's annual address, 179, 299, 307, 439

Murmansk, 238
Mussolini, Benito, 36, 46–49, 72, 232
Myshkova River, 315–16

Napoléon, 3, 54, 73, 77, 205, 216, 231, 327
Narew River, 429–30, 444
Nasyr line, 242, 244
National Socialist Leadership officers, 453
National Socialist People's Welfare Organization (NSV), xvi, 137, 363
Nazi-Soviet Non-Aggression Pact, 9, 19, 25, 32, 36, 45, 50
Nebe, Arthur, 97
Neisse River, 448–49, 461, 464
Neman River, 86
Nemmersdorf, 430–31
"Nero Order" (March 1945), 457–58
neutrality, 32, 241
Neva River, 146
Nevel, 383–84
"New Order," 12, 22, 105, 257, 414, 476–77, 483
New York, 15
Nezhin, 371
Night of Broken Glass (November 1938). See Kristallnacht
Nikopol, 371, 379, 387–88, 390
Nisko, 21, 477,
NKVD, 157, 269
Normandy, 337, 367, 400, 402, 413, 421–22, 427, 469, 486
North Africa, 39, 44, 71, 197, 247, 281, 299–301, 307, 313, 325, 336, 341, 469, 484
North Sea, 79
Norway, 268, 337
"Not one step back" decree (Stalin Order No. 227), 273
Novgorod, 142, 146, 385
Novorossiysk, 278
Novosokolniki, 383
Nuremberg, 446
nutrition, 166–67, 171–73, 297. See also malnutrition

Oberkommando der Wehrmacht (OKW), xvi

Oberkommando der Wehrmacht *(cont.)*
assessments of German strength,
116, 182, 237, 384, 399
attitude toward communism, 66, 68,
97, 168–69
attitude toward Jews, 66, 68, 97,
168–69
and Barbarossa, 58, 66, 116, 125–26,
128, 132–33, 143, 162–63
and Battle of Moscow, 151, 162–63
and Citadel, 339, 342, 350,
and defense of Berlin, 458–59, 464
and France, 27, 406
and Hitler, 132, 162–63, 264, 280,
342, 350
logistics, 150–51, 169
and Mediterranean strategy, 45, 487
and Nazi ideology, 68, 168, 376, 480
and occupation policy, 66, 68, 97
Operations Branch, 445
and raw materials, 58, 169
rivalry with OKH, 264, 342, 366–
68, 399–400
and Soviet prisoner policy, 168–69
and Stalingrad, 276, 280
strategy, 162–63, 336–37, 379, 399–
400, 406, 458–59
Oberkommando des Heeres (OKH),
xvi
assessments of German strength,
114–16, 142, 151–52, 169, 209, 234,
236, 262, 353, 367, 522n85
and Bagration, 405–12, 415, 418, 429
and Barbarossa, 52–54, 84, 112–13,
121, 123, 125, 128, 148, 151, 156,
158, 163–65
and Battle for Moscow, 162, 183–84,
187–88, 192, 199
and Blau, 231, 233, 263, 267, 269–70,
275
and Citadel, 342–43, 351
cooperation with Einsatzgruppen,
101
and defense of Berlin, 460, 464
and Hitler, 27, 112–13, 121, 128, 148,
206, 209, 245, 262–64, 275, 280,
312, 368, 399, 445, 460
and hunger policy, 172–73
logistics, 158, 162, 169–70

Military Geography Branch, 59
and Nazi ideology, 480
and retreat to Dnieper, 353, 368–69
rivalry with OKW, 342, 366–68,
399–400
and Soviet counterattack (Moscow),
201–2, 209
and Soviet winter offensive (1944–
1945), 434
and Stalingrad, 284, 306, 315–16
and Vistula-Oder offensive, 441–42,
445
and Zossen, 464
Obersalzberg, 10. *See also* Berghof
Oder River, 438, 441, 445–48, 457–60,
464–65
Odessa, 141, 144, 163, 219, 392, 398
oil
Caucasus, 53, 59, 83, 89, 91, 106,
126, 129, 132, 165, 182, 190, 231,
238, 262–63, 268, 271–77, 279–80,
282–83, 296, 300–301, 313, 322,
326
Hungarian, 436, 456
importance of, xxii–xxiii, 28, 41,
46–47, 49, 53, 55, 60–62, 91, 127,
133, 141, 165, 169, 226, 234–36,
239, 264, 270–71, 322, 326, 402,
406, 427, 475, 528n62, 534n71
Middle Eastern, 46, 233
Rumanian, 37, 39, 47, 49, 83–84, 132,
169, 241, 245, 379, 392, 406, 427,
434–36
shortages, 53, 82–84, 141–42, 169,
402, 475 (*see also* German army)
synthetic, 401–2, 436
Oka River, 208
OKH. *See* Oberkommando des
Heeres
Okuniew, 419
OKW. *See* Oberkommando der
Wehrmacht
Olkovatka, 345
Operational Directives (German), 44,
68, 94, 111–12, 141–42, 148, 152,
156, 162–63, 165, 172, 206, 279–
80, 310, 333, 367, 445
No. 2, 316
No. 5, 338

No. 6, 339
No. 16, 34
No. 18, 49
No. 21, 51, 66
No. 32, 90
No. 33, 125-28
No. 34, 128, 131
No. 35, 147
No. 41, 231-32, 262-63
No. 45, 271, 284
No. 51, 366-67, 396, 402
See also Führer Orders
Oranienburg, 260. *See also*
  concentration camps
Oratov, 389
Order Police, 70-71, 173
Ordzhonikidze, 282
Orel, 154-55, 203, 338, 340, 343, 345-
  46, 348, 350-51, 353-56, 372
Orsha, 100, 123, 182, 381-82, 409, 412,
  414-15
Ossetian Military Road, 282
Ostarbeiter. *See* forced labor
Ostbahn, 340
Ostheer (Eastern Army), xvi, 56, 60,
  94, 116, 121, 149-51, 159-61, 164,
  182, 185, 187, 192-93, 197, 204,
  209, 215-16, 218, 221, 226, 235-39,
  262, 292, 317, 324, 328-29, 336-37,
  343, 367, 383, 400, 402-3, 408-9,
  417, 421, 423, 440, 443, 470,
  481-82, 485-86, 522n85. *See also*
  German army
Ostwall, 364-66, 377

Pacific Ocean, 42, 194-95, 197
Palestine, 13
panje wagons, xvi, 119, 162, 213, 395
Panther position, xvi, 366, 368, 371,
  381, 387
Panther tank. *See* German army: tanks
Panzer Armies. *See* Armies (German)
Panzerfaust, xvi, 432, 459, 463
Paris, 3, 14, 29, 82, 133, 183
partisans (Soviet), 81, 86, 98, 101-2,
  104, 108, 111, 149, 160, 180, 198,
  212, 297, 333, 340, 354, 378, 381,
  385, 400, 409, 412, 415-16, 447,
  482

Patton, George S. (General), 468
Paulus, Friedrich (Field Marshal)
  and Barbarossa, 53, 128
  and Blau, 250, 265
  on breakout from Stalingrad, 311-
  12, 315
  and Hitler, 280, 320-21
  and Stalingrad, 272, 277, 283-89,
  292-99, 301, 304, 308-12, 315,
  319-21
  and surrender, 319-21
Pearl Harbor, 179, 193, 484
Peipus, Lake, 128, 384, 386
Persia, 238, 271-72
Persian Gulf, 48-49
Petain, Henri-Philippe, 47-48
Phony War (Sitzkrieg), 27, 71
Piatigorsk, 275
Pilsen, 469
Pitomnik, 289, 320
Ploesti, 434-36
pogroms, 15, 94-95. *See also*
  Kristallnacht
Pohl, Oswald, 260
Poland
  Final Solution in, 95-96, 176-77,
  180-81, 219, 223, 225-26, 237, 254,
  257, 361
  forced labor, 221, 223
  General Government, 65, 73,
  225-26
  German anti-Jewish actions in,
  20-24, 65-66, 69, 73, 92, 94-96,
  176-77
  German invasion, 9-10, 25-26, 439,
  473
  German racial policy in, 18-21,
  23-24, 60, 92, 139, 254, 256, 476
  Home Army, 419
  Jews in, 259, 479
  Soviet actions in, 26, 36, 447-48,
  452
  as staging area for Barbarossa, 36,
  89, 150
  See also Auschwitz; Bagration; Final
  Solution; forced labor; ghettos;
  Vistula-Oder operation; Warsaw
Poltava, 249, 265
Pomerania, 446, 448-49

Ponyri, 345

Posen, 171, 255, 335, 361, 442, 446

Praga (Warsaw), 418

Prague, 175, 468–69

Pripet, 410

Pripet Marshes, 52, 56, 89, 106, 123, 125–26, 129, 140–41, 378, 382, 388, 392, 405, 407

prisoners of war (German), 68, 98, 470, 510n40

prisoners of war (Soviet), 99, 104, 166–68, 170, 172, 174, 198, 215, 220, 222, 260, 317, 332, 478, 480–81, 519n54, 519n57

Prokhorovka, 347–50

Proletarskaya, 275

propaganda, German. *See* Bolshevism: in Nazi propaganda; Germany; Goebbels; Jews

propaganda, Soviet, 273–75, 322, 450

Protectorate (Bohemia and Moravia), 175

Prussia. *See* East Prussia; West Prussia

Prut River, 52, 395

Psel River, 347, 351

Pskov, 386

Pskov, Lake, 384

public opinion (German), 135

Pulawy, 444–45

purges (Red Army), 44, 78–79

Pushkin, 385

Putsch, Beer Hall, 14, 179, 299, 307

quartermaster-general, 66, 128, 156, 168, 170–71, 183, 189, 477

Race and Resettlement Main Office, 522n78

racial policy (German). *See* Bolshevism: "Jewish"; colonization; Commissar Order; Einsatzgruppen; Final Solution; forced labor; Generalplan Ost; German army; Germany; hunger policy

Radom, 443

Radomsyl, 380

Raeder, Erich (Admiral), 33, 42–43, 45–46, 50

RAF Bomber Command. *See* Britain: Bomber Command

railroads, 52, 57, 88, 119, 133, 150, 156, 192, 199, 237, 288, 366, 370, 373, 379, 412, 430, 442, 451, 471. *See also* Ostbahn; Reichsbahn

rape, 431, 449–52

rasputitsa, xvi, 158, 161, 212, 214, 217, 324–25, 339, 382

Rastenburg (East Prussia), 104, 228, 430

Ratzel, Friedrich, 6

Rauff, Walter, 177

Ravensbrück, 260. *See also* concentration camps

raw materials, xxii–xxiii, 11–13, 26, 28, 39–42, 46–47, 49, 55, 58, 60–61, 63, 71, 73, 79, 83, 89, 133, 165–66, 169, 223, 226–30, 234, 273, 338, 362, 427, 451, 474–75, 481, 484, 487

rearmament (German), xxiii, 10–13, 473, 475

Red Air Force, 90, 153, 161, 344, 352, 410, 413

Red Army

  advance into East Prussia, 430–31

  atrocities against Germans, 430–31, 440, 449–52

  and Bagration, 405–20

  and Barbarossa, 52–53, 56, 78, 80–81, 85–86, 88–89, 112–14, 120–21, 126, 130, 133, 140–41

  and Berlin offensive, 459–69, 551n13,

  and Blau, 234, 253, 264–69, 273–75

  casualties, xxi–xxii, 88–89, 114, 125, 166–67, 214, 239, 247, 251, 269, 304–5, 320, 322, 337, 352, 354, 356–57, 369, 380, 382, 384, 386, 392, 398, 416–17, 420, 430, 433, 436, 447, 468–69, 471, 509n21, 516n16, 530n20, 539n30, 543n90

  in Caucasus, 272–73, 276–78, 281–83

  and Crimea, 241–47

  deep battle, concept of, 79, 210, 249, 303–4, 341

  German assessment of, 26, 36, 44, 52–53, 79, 81, 85, 112, 114, 120–22,

148, 237–38, 262–63, 275, 305, 337, 402, 406
and Kharkov, 248–52, 323–24, 353, 355–56
and Kiev pocket, 141–45
and Kursk, 341–53
logistics, 122, 186, 252, 421–22, 471
and Moscow: counterattack at, 199–204, 207–14; defense of, 152–63, 182–85, 186–92
prisoners of war (*see* prisoners of war [Soviet])
replacements, 145, 210, 373, 377
and Stalingrad, 269, 283–99, 303–10, 315–16, 319–22
and summer offensive (1943), 353–57
tanks: fear of Soviet models, 114–15, 155, 188, 204, 207, 310; losses of, 88–90, 125, 214, 252, 305, 319–20, 149, 245, 252, 305, 349–52, 354, 356–57, 369, 371, 389, 392, 399, 414, 416–17, 420–21, 430, 433, 447, 468, 509n21, 543n94; numbers of, 78, 81, 114, 200, 230, 272, 283, 304, 319, 343, 348, 353, 355, 369, 381, 384, 386–87, 409, 419, 421, 435, 442, 461, 468, 535n78; superiority of, 114–15, 155, 159, 204, 207 (*see also* tank production [Soviet])
troop strength, 78, 114, 117, 125, 151–52, 153, 183–84, 199–200, 207, 212, 307, 367, 369, 381, 384, 400, 409–10, 421, 435, 442, 460–61, 524n2, 547n75
use of blocking units, 143, 273
trucks, 370, 386, 421
and winter offensive (1943–1944), 365, 369–73, 377–95, 402
and winter offensive (1944–1945), 432–38
Vistula-Oder offensive (January 1945), 441–49
and Warsaw Uprising, 419–20,
See also Armies; Corps; Divisions; Fronts
Red October Steel Works. *See* Krasny Oktyabr
refugees, 16, 287, 427, 430, 445, 449, 452, 456, 465, 467

regiments (German)
Panzer Regiment Bäke, 390, 392
Police Regiment South, 103
Reich Air Ministry, 426–27
Reich Chancellery, 8, 31, 72, 137, 329, 467
Reich Commissariat for the Strengthening of the German People (RKFDV), 93, 254, 256
Reichel, Joachim (Major), 263
Reichenau, Walter (Field Marshal), 27, 97–98, 102, 141, 164–65
Reich Labor Service (RAD), 376
Reich Ministry for Armaments and Munitions, 228–29
Reich Ministry for Food, 224, 477, 505n60
Reichsbahn, 120, 150, 170, 220. *See also* railroads
Reich Security Main Office (RSHA), xvi, 24, 65, 168, 177, 480, 485
Criminal Technical Institute, 177
Reichskommissariat Ostland, 180
Reichstag, 32–34, 64, 109, 178, 196, 218, 224, 439, 467, 476
Reinhardt, Hans (General), 88, 161, 413, 446–47
Rendulic, Lothar (General), 447
reparations, 12, 47
Replacement Army (German). *See* Armies (German): Replacement
Reserve Police Battalions, 70
resettlement, 20–21, 65, 83, 92–93, 106, 108, 139, 177, 181, 254, 257–59, 476
Rhine River, 455, 457–58
Ribbentrop, Joachim von, 9, 24, 36, 45, 48–49, 195, 299, 363
Richthofen, Wolfram von (General), 242–44, 250, 287, 294–95, 299, 311–13, 315
Riga, 88, 176, 178, 220, 433
Ring, Operation, xvi, 319
roads, 54, 56–57, 89, 118–19, 142, 150, 154, 161, 203, 208–9, 219, 245, 255, 261, 282, 310, 382–83. *See also* Rollbahn
rockets (German), 335, 431
rockets (Soviet), 309. *See also* Katyusha rocket launchers

Rohland, Walter, 189–90
Röhm Purge (1934), 69
Rokossovsky, Konstantin (Marshal), 345, 444, 447, 449
Roland, Operation, 351
Rollbahn, xvi, 158, 382, 414
Rommel, Erwin (Field Marshal), 247, 281, 299, 307, 400, 402, 469
Romny, 143–44
Roosevelt, Franklin D., 15, 32, 39–40, 45, 64, 107, 110, 157, 174, 194, 196–97, 458, 474–75
Roques, Franz von (General), 98
Rosenberg, Alfred, 62, 105, 173, 174, 180, 219, 256
Roslavl, 210–12
Rostock, 461
Rostov, 164–65, 200, 267, 269–72, 283, 292, 303–4, 306, 315, 322
Rotkopf ammunition, 207
Rotmistrov, Pavel (General), 348–50
Rovno, 89
Rozan bridgehead, 444
rubber, 58, 63, 119, 169, 486
Ruhr, 137, 230, 330–31, 337, 458
Rumania
  changes sides in war, 436
  fighting in, 89, 141, 395, 405, 435
  forces fighting in the Soviet Union: assessment of, 306–7, 309, 314, 367, 434–36; in Barbarossa, 89, 141; in Blau, 236, 276; in the Crimea, 242, 245, 278; morale in, 307; at Stalingrad, 288–89, 292, 306–9, 314–15, 321, 539n30
  and Germany, 44, 234, 236, 306, 362, 435
  German military intervention in, 49
  oil, 37, 39, 41, 47, 49, 83–84, 132, 169, 241, 245, 272, 277, 379, 392, 406, 427
  relations with Hungary, 49, 436
  Soviet pressure on, 32, 36, 41, 49–50
  surrender, 436
Rundstedt, Gerd von (Field Marshal), 89, 140–41, 143, 145, 164–65, 170
Russia. *See* Soviet Union
Rybinsk, 182
Rynok, 286

Rzhev, 161, 167–68, 210–11, 213–14, 303–4

Sachsenhausen, 260. *See also* concentration camps
Salsk, 275
Sandomierz, 442–43
Sapun Heights, 246
Saratov, 282
Saturn, Operation, xvi, 304, 316
Sauckel, Fritz, 178, 220–23, 226, 257, 259, 327–28, 332, 481
Sauer, Karl Otto, 426
Saxony, 465, 468
Schirwindt, 430
Schlieffen Plan, 74
Schmidt, Paul, 8–9
Schmidt, Rudolf (General), 147, 208, 313
Schmundt, Rudolf (General), 36, 203–4, 281, 396
Schörner, Ferdinand (General), 397, 432–34, 445, 447
Schubert, Helmut, 256
Schwerin von Krosigk, Lutz. *See* Krosigk, Lutz Schwerin von
Schwerpunkt, xvii, 28, 53, 56, 84, 125, 243, 252, 276, 344, 381, 387, 407–8, 410, 412, 429, 461, 486
scorched-earth policy (German), 206, 372, 374, 455, 457
SD (Sicherheitsdienst [Security Service]), xvii, 13, 70, 103, 107–9, 135–36, 171, 178, 325, 331, 359, 428, 431, 449, 479
SD2 fragmentation bombs (devil's eggs), 243–44
Sea Lion, Operation, 38
Sea of Azov, 323, 365, 370
second front, 234–35, 268, 277, 299, 325, 337–39, 342, 366, 399–400, 475
security troops (German), 333
security troops (Soviet), 269
Seelow, 463–64
Seelow Heights, 459, 462
Sejm River, 144, 154
Serafimovich, 285
Serock bridgehead, 444

Sevastopol, 164, 241, 245–47, 264, 268, 291, 398
Severnaya Bay, 246
Seydlitz-Kurzbach, Walter von (General), 213, 301, 312
Shaposhnikov, Boris (Marshal), 248–49
Shirer, William L., 1, 34, 40
Shlisselburg, 146
shortages. See German army: logistic problems; Red Army: logistics
Siberia, 62, 108, 115, 162, 174, 186, 200, 256, 327
Sicily, 350–52, 469
Sickle Cut, Operation (Sichelschnitt), 27–28, 54, 433
Siemens, 260
Silesia, 38–39, 260, 429, 441, 444–45, 447–49, 456, 460
Simonov, Konstantin, 274, 467
Sinelnikovo, 370
slave labor (German). See forced labor
Slavs
    Nazi racial policy toward, 62, 93, 178, 225, 256, 259, 506n64
    viewed as subhuman, 7, 18, 44, 69–70, 91, 106, 170, 254, 476
    See also forced labor; Generalplan Ost; hunger policy; Lebensraum
Slovenia, 256
Slutsk, 86
Smolensk, 86–88, 113, 120–30, 133, 140, 149, 152, 200, 207, 219, 326, 360, 368–69, 450, 476, 484
Sobibor, 177, 181, 253, 361. See also concentration camps
social Darwinism. See Hitler
Sodenstern, George von (General), 143, 184
Somme, Battle of, 420
Sonnenwende, Operation, 448
Soviet Union
    armaments production, 12, 41, 59, 81–82, 115
    civilians: evacuated by Germans, 369, 372–74 (see also forced labor); German use of forced labor (see forced labor); Soviet use of to build fortifications, 157, 186

climate (see mud; rasputitsa; weather)
economic importance to Germany, 40–41, 58–62, 82–83, 127
foreign policy of (see Stalin)
German atrocities in (see Einsatzgruppen; Final Solution; Generalplan Ost; German army; Germany: occupation policy; hunger policy; Jews)
German invasion of (see Barbarossa)
German racial policies in (see Final Solution; Generalplan Ost; Germany: occupation policy; hunger policy; Lebensraum)
German treatment of civilians (see Generalplan Ost; Germany: occupation policy; hunger policy)
German transportation difficulties in (see German army: logistics; mud; rasputitsa; weather)
Hitler's plans for "living space" (see Generalplan Ost; Lebensraum)
Hitler's views of (see Bolshevism; Hitler)
and hunger policy (see hunger policy)
impact of war on, xxii, 94, 214, 230, 238, 305, 333–34, 369–71, 471, 481
and Lend-Lease, 184, 230, 305, 471, 535n78
manganese mines, 371, 379
NKVD (secret police), 157, 269
Non-Aggression Pact with Germany, 9, 19, 25, 32, 36, 45, 50
oil in (see oil)
partisan war (see German army; partisans)
prisoners of war (see Red Army: prisoners of war)
relocation of industry, 115
and resettlement of Volga Germans, 174
Russian nationalism, 273–75
and Soviet patriotism, 273–75
State Defense Committee, 156–57
tank production, 90, 115, 189–90, 230, 238, 305, 367
use of Germans as forced labor, 451
and Western allies (see Stalin)
See also Red Army; Stalin; Stavka

Spain, 38, 44, 46–48
Speer, Albert
  and aircraft industry, 334–35, 401–2,
    426
  and Allied bombing of Germany,
    330–31, 363, 402
  and armaments production, 228–30,
    239, 260, 328, 366, 401–2, 421,
    426–27, 440, 459, 472
  and cooperation with Himmler, 331,
    334–35
  and establishment of "rings," 229
  and Final Solution, 219
  and forced labor, 334–36
  and Hitler, 3, 228, 268, 279, 399,
    424, 434, 527n45
  physical breakdown, 336
  plans for preservation of post-war
    economy, 455–56
  at Posen (October 1943), 335
  and rationalization of war economy,
    228–30, 239, 260, 328
  and scorched earth (Germany),
    456–57
  and self-responsibility concept, 229
  succeeds Todt, 228
  and total war mobilization, 328–30,
    334–36, 423–26
  and war, 233
  Zentrale Planung, 229
Spree River, 461, 464
Spring Awakening, Operation, 438
SS (Schutzstaffel)
  Central Resettlement Office, 255
  clashes with Hans Frank, 19, 21, 65,
    73, 180, 258–59
  Economic and Administrative Main
    Office (WVHA), 260–61
  economic empire, 65, 259–61, 334–
    35, 364, 426
  Waffen-SS, 103, 384, 399 (*see also*
    Armies; Corps; Divisions)
  See also Einsatzgruppen; Final
    Solution; Generalplan Ost;
    Heydrich; Himmler; hunger
    policy
"Stab in the back" myth (*Dolchstoss*),
  69, 474, 480, 487
Stahlecker, Franz Walter, 94, 97, 111

Stalin, Joseph
  and Bagration, 406–8, 418
  and Barbarossa, 84–86, 89, 124, 140,
    508n17
  and battle for Kiev, 140–45
  and Berlin offensive, 458, 460–66,
    468–69
  and Blau, 264–66, 273, 276
  and counterattack at Moscow, 200,
    207, 210–12, 214
  and defense of Moscow, 148, 156–
    58, 186–87, 200
  deportation of Volga Germans, 174
  fear of Allied-German separate
    peace, 458, 466, 468
  foreign policy, 29, 32, 37–38, 40–41,
    45, 48–49, 73, 475
  and the Hess affair, 79
  and Hitler, 32, 38, 66, 75, 78, 90–91,
    110, 131, 155–56, 231, 300, 475–76,
    484
  and Lend-Lease, 184, 230, 305, 471,
    535n78
  and mobilization of USSR, xxiii,
    12, 23, 54, 75, 81, 115, 148, 230–31,
    336, 357, 401, 455, 472, 486, 508n8
  and offensive (spring 1942,
    Kharkov), 248–52
  and offensive (summer 1943), 348,
    356–57
  and offensive (winter 1942–1943),
    323–24
  and offensive (autumn-winter 1943–
    1944), 369–70, 382, 391–92
  and Operation Jupiter, 304
  and Operation Little Saturn, 315–16
  and Operation Mars, 304
  and Operation Saturn, xvi, 304, 316
  and Operation Uranus, xvii, 292,
    303–4, 306
  and Order No. 227 ("Not one step
    back"), 273, 281, 405
  and Order No. 270 (1941), 141
  and partisan war, 98, 332
  pre-invasion strategy, 78–80
  and purge of Red Army, 44, 367
  and the Reichel affair, 264
  and separate peace with Germany,
    131, 157, 184, 300, 325

and Stalingrad, 287–91, 303
and Stavka, 264, 324, 423, 458, 460
  (see also Stavka)
as Supreme Commander, 75, 84,
  89, 124, 140, 210, 212, 214–15, 244,
  247–49, 264, 276, 323–25, 348,
  356, 370, 406–8, 422–23, 431, 462
and Vistula-Oder operation, 441–
  42, 447–48, 551n13
and Warsaw Uprising (1944), 419–
  20, 551n13
and Western allies, xxii, xxiv, 110,
  157, 406, 458, 462, 468–69, 471
Stalingrad
  battle for, 289–301
  encirclement of Sixth Army, 304–10,
    316–18
  German air attack on, 287, 535n79
  German army moves toward, 271–
    72, 277, 283–89
  German airlift for, 213, 311–12, 318
    538n25
  in German calculations, 164, 182,
    213, 261, 267–69, 271, 275–76
  and German relief attack, 313–16
  and Hitler, 276, 281, 284, 290, 296–
    98, 300–301, 313, 405–6, 439
  last days, 320–22
  losses at, 116, 321–22, 337, 539n30
  significance of, 197, 232, 259, 275–
    76, 284, 290, 298, 322, 325–26,
    328, 336, 399, 469
  Soviet counteroffensive, 303–10
  Soviet defense of, 290–92, 293–94,
    301, 535n78
Stalino, 279
Stavka (Soviet Supreme High
    Command), 122–24, 144, 154–55,
    186, 207, 213–14, 248, 264, 288–89,
    304, 324, 354, 385, 394, 396, 407,
    422–23, 435–36, 441–42, 445,
    448, 458, 460, 462, 466, 524n2
steel, 26, 169, 229, 289, 322, 330, 338,
    366
Stemmermann, Wilhelm (General), 391
Stettin, 144, 446, 461, 465
Stockholm, 300
strategic bombing. See Germany:
    Allied bombing of

Strecker, Karl (General), 321
Strehla, 465
Stuckart, Wilhlem, 522n78
Stukas, xvii, 222, 243–44, 291, 294,
    298–99
submarines, 38, 402, 418, 431
Sudeten crisis, 14
Sudetenland, 14
Sukhinichi, 208, 210–13
Sukhumi, 278–79
Sultanovka line, 242, 244
Sumy, 143
supply. See German army: logistic
    problems; Red Army: logistics
Sweden, 298, 385
  iron ore, 385, 431
Szeged, 437

Taganrog, 163, 165
Taifun, xvii, 145. See also Typhoon,
    Operation
Tallinn, 146
Taman peninsula, 278
tank losses
  German (see German army)
  Soviet (see Red Army)
tank production
  German (see Germany: tank
    production)
  Soviet (see Soviet Union: tank
    production)
Tarnopol, 393–94, 411
Terek River, 272, 275–77, 282
Thomas, Georg (General), 9
  and armaments production, 227
  and Hunger Policy, 61
  and invasion of Soviet Union, 58–61,
    66, 83, 165, 233, 235, 239
  and Speer, 233
Thuringia, 220
Tikhvin, 200
Tiger tanks. See German army: tanks
Tilsit, 94
Timoshenko, Semyon (Marshal), 80,
    123–24, 144, 234, 244, 249–51,
    508n17
Tim River, 208
Tinguta Station, 288
Tippelskirch, Kurt von (General), 414

Tobruk, 247
Todt, Fritz, 11, 178, 189–90, 227–28
Topf Company, 178
Torgau, 465
Toropets, 211, 213
"total war" initiative. *See* Germany: and total war
tractor factory (Stalingrad). *See* Krasny Oktyabr
Transnistria, 219
Trappenjagd (Operation Bustard Hunt). *See* Bustard Hunt, Operation
Treaty of Versailles. *See* World War I
Treblinka, 181, 226, 254, 257, 361. *See also* extermination camps
Tripartite Pact, 45, 48–50
troop strength, German. *See* German army: troop strength
troop strength, Soviet. *See* Red Army: troop strength
trucks. *See* German army: trucks; Red Army: trucks
Tsaritsa River, 290, 294
Tuapse, 277–78
Tula, 155, 156, 162, 184, 186–87, 190, 200, 203
Tundutovo Station, 288
Tunisia, 46
Turkey, 46, 241, 298
Turkish Wall, 242
Typhoon, Operation, 145, 150, 152–54, 175, 185–87, 200, 207, 211, 214

U-boats, German, 196, 233, 359, 385, 432–34
Ukraine
  fighting in, 53, 56, 59, 84, 89, 115, 140–46, 148, 153, 323, 369–72, 377–81, 384, 387–99, 405–8, 434–35, 469
  importance of, 37, 129, 132–33, 224–25, 255–56, 259, 402, 427 (*see also* Lebensraum)
  murder of Jews in, 95, 97, 102, 254–56, 259, 481, 511n44
  resources of, 55, 59, 61, 73, 89, 113, 140, 148, 172, 224–25, 366, 427
  and scorched earth policy, 371–74

Ulianovo, 354
Uman, 141, 388, 394
United States
  aid for Britain, 40, 45, 47, 51, 484
  and aerial bombardment of Germany, 330–31, 363, 402, 427, 436
  and casualties inflicted on Wehrmacht, 470–71
  "destroyers for bases" deal, 40, 45
  economic power, xxii–xxiii, 2, 10, 12, 29, 39–41, 44, 165, 325, 330, 335, 337, 359, 426–27, 471, 475, 485, 487
  and entry into the war, 179, 193–97, 484
  in Hitler's calculations, xxiii, 6–8, 12, 15–17, 34–40, 42–46, 51–52, 58, 64, 71, 73, 75, 83, 90–91, 109–10, 174, 179, 193–97, 217, 226, 234–35, 253, 268, 271, 299, 326, 342, 350, 366, 368, 396, 419–20, 433, 474–76, 479, 484–87
  influence on Lebensraum, 91, 93, 254, 477, 479
  intelligence assessment of German situation, 324, 359–60
  and "Jewish conspiracy," 15–17, 31–32, 107–8, 110, 180, 194, 474–75, 512n56
  and Lend-Lease, 40, 47, 64, 194 (*see also* Lend-Lease)
  Lend-Lease assistance to the Soviet Union, 165, 184, 191, 230, 238, 286, 305, 386, 471, 535n78
  linkup with Soviets at the Elbe, 465
  in Stalin's calculations, 157, 325, 458–59, 464, 468–69
Ural Mountains, 65, 93, 477
Uranus, Operation, xvii, 292, 304
USSR. *See* Soviet Union

Vasilevsky, A. M. (Marshal), 248–49, 251, 264, 292, 303, 316, 349, 422
Vatutin, N. F. (General), 347–48, 378, 387–88, 391
Verdun, Battle of, 192, 293, 298, 300, 322, 325, 345, 411, 420
Verkhne-Chirsky, 314

Versailles, Treaty of. *See* World War I
Vertyachiy, 286
Vichy France, 46, 48
Vienna, 14, 175, 277, 325, 474
Vilnius (Vilna), 86, 418
Vinnitsa, 279, 291–92, 367, 388
Vistula-Oder operation, 438, 441, 449
Vistula River, 406–8, 418–19, 429, 438, 441–42, 445–46, 448, 456
Vitebsk, 122, 381–82, 408–9, 412–14
Vlasov, A. A. (General), 211, 213
Volchansk, 249, 252–53
Volga Germans, 174
Volga River, 81, 93, 156, 162, 184, 186, 200, 213, 232, 238, 268–71, 275, 281, 284–87, 289–91, 293–94, 296, 299, 300–301, 303, 322
Volkhov River, 205, 211, 213
Volksdeutsche (ethnic Germans), xvii, 18, 20, 21, 254–55, 257–59, 476, 481, 488
Volksgemeinschaft (national community), xvii, 13, 17, 92, 136, 224, 328, 363, 376, 424–25, 428, 439, 449, 453, 483, 486–87
Volkssturm (German national militia), xvii, 428–29, 433, 457, 459, 461, 467
Vologda, 182
Voronezh, 162, 185, 187, 232, 261, 264–67, 270, 283, 313, 323
Voroshilovgrad, 182
V-2 rockets, 335
Vyazma, 152–57, 160, 199, 211, 214, 232

Waffen-SS, xvii, 103, 384, 399
Wagner, Adolf (Gauleiter of Bavaria), 137
Wagner, Eduard (General), 66, 156, 168, 169, 189
Walther, Gebhardt von, 59
Wannsee Conference, 180–81, 219, 236, 505n59, 522n78
War Economy and Armaments Office, 59, 83, 165
Warlimont, Walter (General), 67, 280, 341
Warsaw, 22, 272, 405, 408, 418, 441, 449

fighting for, 418–20, 422, 429–30, 444–45
ghetto, 257, 318, 361
Uprising, 419, 548n24
Warthegau, 175, 220,
Wartheland, 20, 177, 476
Warthe River, 460
Washington, 40, 268
weather, 27, 39, 73, 116, 118–19, 126, 129, 142, 144, 150, 155, 157–59, 162, 163, 168, 170, 183, 185, 219, 261, 297, 308, 310, 312, 318, 383, 387, 389–91, 437
Wehrkraftzersetzung (undermining the war effort), xvii, 377, 454
Wehrmacht. *See* German army; German navy; Luftwaffe; Oberkommando der Wehrmacht
Weichs, Maximilian von (General), 284, 292, 298, 308, 312
Weidling, Helmuth (General), 467
Weimar Republic, 254, 427
Weizsäcker, Ernst von, 36, 50
Wenck, Walter (General), 448
Werwolf complex (Vinnitsa), 279
West Prussia, 20, 255, 449
Wetzel, Erhard, 256
White Russia, 37–38. *See also* Belorussia
Wietersheim, Gustav von (General), 287
Wilhelm, Operation, 252–53
Winter Relief, 296
Winter Storm, Operation (Wintergewitter), xvii, 313, 315
Winter War, 36
Wirth, Christian, 177
Wöhler, Otto (General), 356, 454
Wolf's Lair (Wolfsschanze), xvii, 263, 311, 430
wonder weapons, 426
"working toward the Führer," 22, 107
World War I, 1–2, 6, 37, 124, 138, 238, 337, 377, 383
American entry into, 194
Battle of the Marne, 183, 190, 192
Battle of Verdun, 192, 293, 298, 300, 322, 325, 345, 411, 420
blockade, 7, 12, 69

World War I (*cont.*)
   collapse of German home front, 328
   exchange of populations, 478–79
   food shortages, 60–61, 224–25, 428
   German encirclement in, 234
   German surrender, 12
   hunger, 12, 69, 171, 317
   influence on German generals, 9,
      26, 29, 81, 98, 125, 399, 480
   influence on Hitler, xxiii, 4–9, 12,
      16–17, 63, 104–5, 170–71, 178–79,
      194, 206, 208–9, 218, 234, 254,
      280, 317, 328, 401, 411, 476–78
   reparations, 12
   "stab in the back" myth, 69, 474,
      480, 487
   Treaty of Versailles, 2, 4, 10, 12, 18,
      57, 194, 439, 473, 476, 482, 484
   trench war, 206, 293, 343, 407, 441
Wotan position, 366
Wriezen, 463–64

Yakhroma, 191
Yalta Conference, 447
Yampol, 392–94
Yaroslavl, 182
Yelnya, 133, 141
Yugoslavia, 71, 447
Yukhnov, 154, 210–12

Zamosc, 257–59
Zaporozhye, 141, 163, 323, 368, 371,
   379
Zeitzler, Kurt (General)
   appointed Chief of Staff, OKH, 280
   attempts to resign, 397
   and Bagration, 413, 417
   and Citadel, 340, 342, 351, 366
   dismissed, 417
   and Hitler, 366, 397, 399
   and Stalingrad, 305, 307–8, 312–13,
      316, 319
Zentrale Planung, 229
Zety, 288
Zhitomir, 141, 380, 387–88
Zhukov, Georgi (Marshal)
   and Berlin Operation, 461–68,
      551n13
   and Cherkassy pocket, 391

   and counteroffensive (Moscow),
      200–201, 206–7, 210, 214
   and defense of Leningrad, 142
   and defense of Moscow, 156–57, 161,
      186–87
   and defense of Stalingrad, 290–92,
      303–4, 316
   and Kursk, 347
   and Operation Little Saturn, 316
   and Operation Mars, 304
   and Operation Uranus, 292
   and preemptive strike against
      Germany, 80
   and Stalin, 80, 142, 143, 200, 207,
      210, 214, 248, 290–92, 316, 391,
      422, 462–63, 508n17, 551n13
   and Stavka, 207, 248
   and summer campaign, 1942, 248
   and summer offensive, 1944, 422
   and Vistula-Oder offensive, 442,
      444–449
   and winter offensive, 1943–1944,
      394–98
Zossen, 464
Zubtsov, 211
Zvenigorodka, 388–89
Zyklon-B, 177
Zymlyanskaya, 267

Printed in the USA
CPSIA information can be obtained
at www.ICGtesting.com
LVHW011512051023
759672LV00003B/3/J

9 780813 134161